TORT LAW

LONGMAN LAW SERIES

GENERAL EDITORS
PROFESSOR I.H. DENNIS, *University College London*
PROFESSOR J.A. USHER, *University of Edinburgh*

PUBLISHED TITLES

ERIC BARENDT AND LESLEY HITCHENS, *Media Law: Cases and Materials*
ANDREW CHOO, *Evidence: Text and Materials*
R. HALSON, *Contract Law*
JONATHAN HERRING, *Family Law*
NICHOLAS J. McBRIDE AND RODERICK BAGSHAW, *Tort Law*
BEN PETTET, *Company Law*
ROGER J. SMITH, *Property Law*
ROGER J. SMITH, *Property Law: Cases and Materials*
MAURICE SUNKIN AND ANDREW LE SUEUR, *Public Law*
MARTIN WASIK, THOMAS GIBBONS AND MIKE REDMAYNE, *Criminal Justice: Text and Materials*
WILLIAM WILSON, *Criminal Law: Doctrine and Theory*

Visit the *Tort Law*, second edition Companion Website at
www.pearsoned.co.uk/mcbride
to find regular updates on recent developments in
Tort Law, plus expanded case notes on cases featured
in the book

TORT LAW

SECOND EDITION

NICHOLAS J McBRIDE
Fellow of Pembroke College, Cambridge

and

RODERICK BAGSHAW
Fellow of Magdalen College, Oxford

PEARSON
Longman

Harlow, England • London • New York • Boston • San Francisco • Toronto
Sydney • Tokyo • Singapore • Hong Kong • Seoul • Taipei • New Delhi
Cape Town • Madrid • Mexico City • Amsterdam • Munich • Paris • Milan

Pearson Education Limited
Edinburgh Gate
Harlow
Essex CM20 2JE
England
and Associated Companies throughout the world

Visit us on the World Wide Web at:
www.pearsoned.co.uk

First published 2001
Second edition published 2005

ISBN 0 273 68678 X

British Library Cataloguing-in-Publication Data
A catalogue record for this book is available from the British Library

Library of Congress Cataloging-in-Publication Data
McBride, Nicholas J.
  Tort law / Nicholas J. McBride and Roderick Bagshaw.—2nd ed.
    p. cm.—(Longman law series)
  Includes index.
  ISBN 0-273-68678-X (alk. paper)
  1. Torts—England. I. Bagshaw, Roderick, II. Title. III. Series.

KD1949.M38 2005
346.4203—dc22   2004057847

10 9 8 7 6 5 4 3 2 1
08 07 06 05

Typeset in 10/12pt Plantin by 3
Printed and bound by Henry Ling Ltd, The Dorchester Press, Dorset, UK

The Publisher's policy is to use paper manufactured from sustainable forests.

Dedicated to the memory of

JANE VAULKS
19 June 1976 – 16 October 2003

The Lord bless you and keep you
The Lord make his face shine upon you
and be gracious to you
The Lord turn his face toward you
and give you peace
(Numbers 6:24–26)

Supporting resources

Visit www.pearsoned.co.uk/mcbride to find valuable online resources

For students and instructors
- Updates on recent developments in Tort Law
- Expanded case notes on cases featured in the book

For more information please contact your local Pearson Education sales representative or visit **www.pearsoned.co.uk/mcbride**

CONTENTS

vii

PART III. REMEDIES

PART IV. ALTERNATIVE SOURCES OF COMPENSATION

ACKNOWLEDGMENTS

Nick McBride and Roderick Bagshaw write: Thanks are owed first of all to Michelle Gallagher, the acquisitions editor of the Law & Criminology section at Pearson Education. She commissioned us to write this second edition and was a constant source of encouragement and enthusiasm. Thanks are also owed to everyone else at Pearson Education who helped out with the production of this book, especially: Michelle's deputy, Lissa Matthews; Melanie Beard, who so ably runs and updates the McBride and Bagshaw tort law website; Aylene Rogers, our editor; and Barbara Massam, our proofreader. We would both like to acknowledge the great support we have each received from our respective colleges. We would also like to thank our students for the enthusiastic reception they gave the first edition – which was encouraging, and spurred us on to produce something even better next time around.

Roderick Bagshaw writes: In the previous edition I thanked my wife, Liz, for her assistance. She deserves even more this time for all the ways in which she supports me. In particular, we are now lucky enough to have a son, Corin, and Liz has shouldered a disproportionate share of domestic duties to allow me to work on the book. Many, many thanks and much love. Thanking a co-author may seem unusual, but I must also thank Nick. There would be no tort textbook with my name on the cover, let alone one as good as this is, without his intelligence, diligence and commitment. I find it impossible to imagine a better person to work with.

Nick McBride writes: In the previous edition of this book, I thanked my then girlfriend Jane Vaulks for all the support and reassurance she had provided me. Sadly, Jane died on 16 October 2003 – nine months before we were due to get married. I would not have been able to get through the harrowing months following Jane's death – and this book could not have been completed – without the help and comfort provided me by a large number of people. I would like to thank in particular: my family and relatives (especially my mother and my brother, Ben); Sarah Shelton; Maria Shelton and her husband, Mark; my two little friends, Mikayla and Helayna Shelton; Bridget Callaghan and her husband, Craig; the Master, Fellows and staff of Pembroke College, Cambridge (especially Trevor Allan, Frances Kentish and the Revd Brian Watchorn); my students, both past and present (especially Cressida, Anna, Emily, Leigh, Liz, Rob, Andrew, Duncan, Caroline and Suzanne); Jane's family and friends (especially Carrie, Katy, Sam and Siobhan, as well as Sarah); Isabel Haskey; and, of course, Rod Bagshaw and his wife, Liz. I have also benefited immensely from reading Vassula Ryden's astounding series of notebooks – by an almost infinite distance, the most valuable and important books I have ever had the privilege to read. I owe all of these people an enormous debt. But in each case the debt pales in comparison with the debt I will always owe Jane, for all the love she gave me in the years we were together and all the lessons she taught me both in her life and in her death. With her, nothing seemed impossible. Without her, everything is a hundred times harder than it was before.

PREFACE

In the first edition of this book, we tried to restore some order to a subject that was fast in danger of becoming an intellectual shambles.[1] In this edition we have set our sights a bit higher, and attempted to produce the best student textbook on English tort law ever written.[2] To this end, a number of improvements have been made on the first edition:

(1) *Style.* The text has been completely rewritten so as to make this book as clear, as readable, as lively and as succinct as any book of this kind can hope to be. For example, in the first edition, we used the letters 'D' to refer to someone who commits a tort, and 'V' to refer to the victim of a tort. On reflection, we thought this usage seriously impaired the enjoyment of reading this textbook, and have abandoned it in this edition. Instead, in stating general rules of tort law we have used the letters 'A', 'B' and 'C' whenever we have needed to refer to an individual;[3] and in describing concrete situations giving rise to tort liability, we have used proper names (such as 'Sarah' or 'Paul') throughout.

(2) *References.* The self-confessed defects of the first edition – not enough references to cases decided outside the United Kingdom or academic writing on tort law – have been completely repaired. This edition refers to almost four times as many non-UK cases as the first edition. The exhaustive bibliography at the end of this book testifies to the wealth of academic writing on tort law that is referred to in this edition.[4]

---

[1] Of course, there are some academics who insist that as a subject tort law *is* an intellectual shambles and cannot be anything else. (Curiously enough, most of them seem to hail from Cambridge: see Weir 2001, ix ('Tort is what is in the tort books, and the only thing holding it together is the binding'); Hedley 2002, 8 ('. . . "tort" up to a point consists of odds and ends . . . [and is] ramshackle [in] nature'); Howarth & O'Sullivan 2000, 1 ('[it is] particularly difficult to present a rational or logical classification of [tort law]'). But not all: see Oliphant 2002, 3: 'the scope of tort law is determined by convention, not . . . principle.') We disagree. The American Law Institute ('ALI') – which periodically produces Restatements of various areas of American law as a guide for courts across the United States – also seems to have given up on the idea that tort law forms a coherent whole. In producing a third series of Restatements, the ALI did not commission a general *Restatement of Tort Law* – something which, as we hope to show in this book, would have been quite easy and straightforward to write – but has for the time being merely commissioned a *Restatement of the Law on Liability for Physical Harm: General Principles.*

[2] While this book is primarily intended for students studying tort law – whether as part of a two or three year degree in Law or on the BVC or LPC – and students taking advanced courses in the law of obligations at undergraduate or graduate level, we feel sure that academics, practitioners and judges will find much of interest in these pages.

[3] It should be noted that the letters 'A', 'B' and 'C' are *not* used consistently to describe a particular type of individual – for example, someone who commits a tort or the victim of a tort. So, for example, the reader should *not* assume that in stating some general rule of tort law, the letter 'A' *always* describes someone who has committed a tort.

[4] *Important note.* We have, for the most part, used the Harvard system of citation in referring to books and articles in this edition. (Five textbooks on tort law are referred to using abbreviations: see the bibliography for details.) To explain: in the main text we refer to a particular book or article by referring to the author and the date of publication. A reader interested in finding out

(3) *New material*. Two new chapters have been added to this edition: a chapter on torts concerned with invasions of privacy, and a chapter on loss compensation schemes. At the same time, we have discussed various key issues in much greater depth and detail than was the case in the first edition. These issues include: the nature of a tort and the scope of tort law; the rationale and justifiability of the 'compensation rule' in tort law; the scope of the various principles which determine when one person will owe another a duty of care; the impact of Article 6 of the European Convention of Human Rights on a tortfeasor's ability to raise a defence to a claim for damages that has been made against him; the application of the 'wrong kind of loss' limit on what losses suffered by the victim of a tort are actionable; the rationale and application of the law on vicarious liability; the availability of restitutionary damages in tort cases; and the question of when a product will count as being 'defective' under the Consumer Protection Act 1987.

Despite these changes, we have not had any reason to revise or rethink any of the major ideas that underpinned the first edition.[5] Indeed, and gratifyingly, there are signs that many of these ideas are entering the academic mainstream, at least among thoughtful scholars.

For example, the admirable work of Professors John Goldberg and Benjamin Zipursky in the United States – building on the work of Professors Ernest Weinrib[6] and Jules Coleman[7] – has served to re-emphasise the importance of the notion of 'duty' in understanding tort law generally and the tort of negligence in particular.[8] We, of course, take the same view; and we do so in opposition to many tort academics in the United Kingdom who are violently hostile to the idea that tort liability arises, and can only arise, out of the breach of a legal duty owed to another.[9] But our sense is that – thanks to contributions

---

more about that book or article should turn to the bibliography where full details of the book or article in question are given. So, for example, Atiyah 1996 refers (turning to the bibliography and looking at the entries for 'Atiyah') to a paper called 'Personal injuries in the twenty-first century: thinking the unthinkable', which appears in Birks 1996b, at pages 1–46. Turning to the entries for 'Birks', we discover that Birks 1996b refers to a book edited by PBH Birks, entitled *Wrongs and Remedies in the 21st Century*, and published by Clarendon Press, Oxford.

[5] It is, we think, a mark of how well those ideas have stood up that, of all the cases decided in the four years since the publication of the first edition of this book, we have been surprised by the outcome of only *one* – *Lister* v *Hesley Hall Ltd* [2002] 1 AC 215. The outcome of all the other major cases decided in the last four years – in particular, the decisions in *A* v *National Blood Authority* [2001] 3 All ER 289, *B (a child)* v *McDonald's Restaurants Ltd* [2002] EWHC 490, *Gorringe* v *Calderdale MBC* [2004] UKHL 15, *Kane* v *New Forest DC* [2002] 1 WLR 312, *Kuddus* v *Chief Constable of Leicestershire Constabulary* [2002] 2 AC 122, *Loutchansky* v *Times Newspapers Ltd* [2002] QB 321, *Merrett* v *Babb* [2001] QB 1174 and *Transco plc* v *Stockport Metropolitan Borough Council* [2003] 3 WLR 1467 – would have come as no surprise to the attentive reader of the first edition of this book.

[6] See Weinrib 1995.

[7] See Coleman 1993, 2001.

[8] See, in particular, Goldberg & Zipurksy 2001 and Zipursky 1998a; also Goldberg 2000, 2002, 2003a; Goldberg & Zipursky 1998; Zipursky 1998b, 2002.

[9] It is hard to know the reason for this hostility. It might arise out of a more basic hostility to the idea that we owe each other duties not to hit each other or duties not to defame each other unjustly or duties not to interfere with other people's property or any of the other duties that would have to exist for views such as ours as to the basis of tort liability to be correct. If this bit of psychoanalysis is right then, of course, tort academics would not be the only people in our

such as those made by Goldberg and Zipursky – the balance of debate is swinging our way, and in ten years' time, the position we have taken on the relevance of 'duty' to tort law will be widely accepted to be correct.

Again, many academics seem to be moving towards, or to have taken up, positions that we adopted in the first edition of this book. Three examples can be given. First, Professor Stephen Waddams has recently suggested that we should seriously consider the possibility that liabilities arising under the rule in *Rylands* v *Fletcher* or under the Consumer Protection Act 1987 should be 'classified as falling outside tort law'.[10] We, of course, had already made this move in the first edition of this book: the rule in *Rylands* v *Fletcher* and the Consumer Protection Act 1987 are not treated in this book as part of tort law, but rather as 'alternative sources of compensation'.[11]

Secondly, Professor Jane Stapleton has recently made it clear that she does not think that the rules on remoteness of damage form part of the law on causation – which is how they have traditionally been regarded. Such rules, she says, are better treated as part of the law on 'scope of liability for consequences'.[12] Again, this move had already made in the first edition of this book, which – in dealing with the law on the availability of compensatory damages – clearly distinguished between the law on causation, which determines whether a loss was caused by a defendant's tort, and the law on actionability, which takes the losses that were caused by a defendant's tort and determines which of them are actionable. The law on remoteness of damage was treated as part of the law on actionability, not the law on causation.

Thirdly, Professor James Edelman's recent monograph on *Gain-Based Damages* distinguishes between two forms of gain-based damages. First, there are damages that are designed to strip a wrongdoer of a profit that he has made by his committing his wrong. Secondly, there are damages that are designed to make a wrongdoer give back to the victim of his wrong the value of any benefit that he has obtained from the victim of his wrong by committing that wrong.[13] Again, we can fairly claim to have been there first: Edelman's distinction mirrors the distinction that we made in the first edition between type one restitutionary damages and type two restitutionary damages.

Two points of style remain to be made:

(1) *Plaintiff/claimant.* Since 1999, a person who sues someone else in an English court has been known as a 'claimant', rather than a 'plaintiff'. In the first edition of this book, we continued to use the term 'plaintiff' to describe someone who sues someone else. However, in this edition we have switched to the modern usage. Overseas readers of this book who live in jurisdictions where 'claimants' are still described as 'plaintiffs' will simply have to make a mental

---

society who are hostile to the idea that we owe each other such elementary duties: children, vandals and football hooligans feel the same way.
[10] Waddams 2003, at 106, referring to Davies 2000, at 410 n. 10, and Smith 1916.
[11] Our reasons for doing this are explained below, at pp. 31–3.
[12] See Stapleton 2003, at 389.
[13] See Edelman 2002b, at 65–87.

bleep whenever they come across the word 'claimant' and substitute the word 'plaintiff'.

(2) *Footnotes*. This edition is, inevitably, much more heavily footnoted than the first edition. Some footnotes are more important than others – most, for example, will only be of interest to students writing a dissertation or a thesis, or professionals engaged in legal research. The most important footnotes are marked '*Important note*' and should be read by everyone who uses this book.

The law as stated in this book was up-to-date as of 1 October 2004. More recent developments in the law of tort are dealt with on the McBride and Bagshaw website, of which more on the next page.

Nick McBride
Roderick Bagshaw
1st October 2004

THE McBRIDE AND BAGSHAW TORT LAW WEBSITE

The McBride and Bagshaw tort law website can be accessed at http://www.pearsoned.co.uk/mcbride. The website is free to access and requires no password. It provides the following features:

Casenotes

The casenotes on the McBride and Bagshaw website summarise and comment on tort law cases decided since the publication of the first edition of this textbook – including many cases discussed in this edition. The casenotes are divided into *Recent Cases* and *Archived Cases* (each in turn are subdivided into alphabetical groups, A–D, E–H, I–O, P–S, and T–Z). Click on *Recent Cases* to access casenotes on cases that have been decided since 1 August 2004, such as the decision of the House of Lords in *Gregg* v *Scott*. Click on *Archived Cases* to access casenotes on cases that have been decided before 1 August 2004. The *Recent Cases* section will be updated at least twice a year.

Recent statutes

This section provides summaries and comments on statutory reforms to tort law that have taken place since the publication of the first edition of this textbook. This section will be updated whenever an important statute affecting English tort law is enacted.

Tort law research resource

This section is divided into two. *Bibliography* allows people to access the bibliography at the back of this book. *Recent articles and papers* provides brief summaries of articles and papers on tort law that have appeared since 1 August 2004 and that have caught our eye. This section will be updated once a year.

Reading list

Click on this section to access a model tort law reading list. This will be updated once a year.

Problem questions

Students often find it very difficult to answer tort law problem questions properly. This section is designed to help them out. It provides students with tips on answering tort law problem questions, and model answers to nine typical tort law problem questions.

Sample chapters

This section allows those who have not already bought this book to access Chapters 2 (An Overview of Tort Law) and 35 (Vicarious Liability) of this book.

TABLE OF CASES

Pages where a case is discussed in detail are <u>underlined</u>

xv

TABLES OF STATUTES, STATUTORY INSTRUMENTS AND CONVENTIONS

STATUTES

STATUTORY INSTRUMENTS

CONVENTIONS

PART I

THE PROVINCE OF TORT LAW

1

WHAT IS A TORT?

A tort is a form of civil wrong.[1] So in order to understand what a tort is, one must first understand what a civil wrong is.

THE NATURE OF A CIVIL WRONG[2]

Someone will commit a civil wrong if he or she breaches a legal duty owed to another. This needs some explanation.

Legal duty

Someone will have a legal duty to act in a particular way if he is required by law to act in that way.[3] How can we tell what the law requires us to do? Well, we look to *statutes* enacted by Parliament and *cases* decided by the courts to tell us what the law requires us to do.

Under our legal system, A will have a legal duty to do *x* if: (*a*) a statute that was enacted by Parliament and not subsequently repealed says that A has a legal duty to do *x*; *or* (*b*) previous decisions of the courts that have not been subsequently overruled and are not likely to be overruled explicitly or implicitly say that A has a legal duty to do *x*.

If A has a legal duty to do *x* because (*a*) is true then we say that A has a *statutory duty* to do *x*. If A has a legal duty to do *x* because (*b*) is true then we say that A has a *judge-made duty* to do *x*. In order to make this book easier to read, we will from now on refer to legal duties simply as 'duties'.

Duty owed to another

Duties may be divided up into duties that are owed to other people and duties that are owed to no one in particular. A given duty is owed to someone else if it was imposed for the benefit of that someone else. A given duty is owed to no

---

[1] The word 'tort' derives from the Latin *tortus* which means 'twisted, crooked, contorted, distorted' (Lewis & Short, *Latin Dictionary*).

[2] See Birks 1995.

[3] Cf. M&D, 19: ' "Duty" means a prohibition of a certain kind of behaviour in a given kind of situation.' This is right. However, M&D goes on to say on the same page that if the law says 'you ought not to injure a person by a careless act, [this] means that the law recognises that there *could* be liability [if you injure that person carelessly]'. This is wrong. The fact that someone will incur some kind of liability if he does *x* does not necessarily mean that he is prohibited from doing *x*. Someone who drives into central London will incur a liability to pay a congestion charge: but he is of course not prohibited from driving into central London.

one in particular if it was not imposed for the benefit of a particular individual but was imposed for the benefit of the community as a whole or for the benefit of some section of the community.

So, for example, under s 6 of the Police Act 1996 '[every] police authority . . . shall secure the maintenance of an efficient and effective police force for its area'. That duty is not owed to anyone in particular: it is imposed on each police authority for the benefit of the community served by that police authority. In contrast, if you take two given individuals, A and B, A will have a duty under the Protection from Harassment Act 1997 not to 'pursue a course of conduct – (a) which amounts to harassment of [B]; and (b) which he knows or ought to know amounts to harassment of [B]'. This duty of A's is owed to B – it is imposed on A for the benefit of a particular individual: B. As has already been said, someone will commit a *civil wrong* if he breaches a duty owed to another. Someone who breaches a duty owed to no one in particular may be said to have committed a *public wrong*.

One of the marks of a duty that is owed to another is that it may be waived by that other.[4] A duty which is owed to no one in particular cannot be waived by a particular individual. This follows as a matter of logic from what has already been said as to the nature of duties owed to others and duties owed to no one in particular. Suppose, for example, that John has a duty to do x and that duty is owed to Mary. Given that John's duty to do x was imposed on him for Mary's benefit, there does not seem much point in the law's requiring John to do x if Mary makes it clear that she is happy for John not to do x – unless, of course, Mary is in no position to form rational wishes as to how she wants to be treated by others because she is, for example, too immature or not in her right mind or ill-informed. So, as John's duty to do x is owed to Mary, Mary may release John from that duty so long, of course, as she is in her right mind, aware of the full implications of what she is doing and mature enough to decide for herself whether or not she wants John to do x. And, obviously, if Mary does release John from that duty, John will do no wrong to Mary if he does not do x. A Latin tag expresses this point – *volenti non fit injuria*: no wrong will be done to the willing.

On the other hand, suppose that Gary has a duty to do x and that duty is owed to no one in particular because it was imposed on Gary for the benefit of the whole community. In such a case, no particular individual will have the power to release Gary from this duty – as the duty in question was imposed on Gary for the benefit of the whole community, Gary can only be released from that duty if the whole community, acting through its representatives, indicates that it wishes Gary to be released from that duty.

There is an important exception to the rule that a duty that is owed to another may be waived by that other. This is the case where A owes B a duty which requires him to stop B doing something that she knows is dangerous. So suppose

---

[4] This might account for why – if A has a duty to do x which was imposed on him for B's benefit – we say that A's duty to do x is *owed* to B. As B may waive A's duty to do x, we mentally associate A's duty to do x with a debt *owed* to B; the idea being that just as B may waive a debt that is owed to her, so she can waive A's duty to do x.

that Beth wants to sniff some glue – she knows that sniffing glue is dangerous but she is willing to take the risk in order to experience the temporary high that results from sniffing glue. Accordingly, she attempts to buy some glue from Paul's shop. Suppose further that Paul has a duty not to sell Beth any glue because it is obvious that she wants to buy it for the purposes of sniffing it. The law will have imposed this duty on Paul in a paternalistic attempt to save Beth from herself – so Paul's duty is imposed on him for Beth's benefit and will therefore be owed to Beth. Beth will not be able to waive this duty, though she would obviously like to do so. The law's intentions in imposing a duty on Paul not to sell glue to Beth would be frustrated if Beth were free to waive that duty. Beth would inevitably waive the duty and Paul would then be free to sell her the glue, which is not what the law wants.

So if A owes B a duty to stop B doing something that she knows is dangerous, then B will not be able to waive that duty of A's. It is quite unusual for one person to owe another this kind of duty: if B wants to do something that she knows is dangerous, the law will generally allow her to get on with it and will not impose duties on other people to stop her doing what she wants to do. However, it has become increasingly common for someone who has knowingly put herself in harm's way and suffered some kind of loss as a result to try and sue for compensation for that loss on the ground that someone else owed her a duty to stop her endangering herself. The courts have generally been hostile to such claims, only allowing that such a duty might have been owed in cases where the person who put herself in harm's way was incapable of thinking rationally because she was too immature or because she was not in her right mind.[5]

So it has been accepted that if a prisoner is a clear suicide risk, the prison authorities will owe him a duty to take steps to stop him committing suicide.[6] It has also been held that a petrol station manager will owe a child a duty not to sell him petrol if it is obvious that he wants to buy the petrol to get high by sniffing it.[7] And it has been accepted that a school will owe a child on a school skiing trip a duty to take reasonable steps to stop him skiing off-piste – and this is so even if the child is aware of the risks involved in skiing off-piste.[8] In contrast, a claim that the police owed a criminal a duty to stop him jumping out of a high window in an attempt to escape police custody was rejected by two judges out of three in the Court of Appeal.[9] Similarly, in *Tomlinson* v *Congleton BC*[10] the House of

---

[5] See *Tomlinson* v *Congleton BC* [2004] 1 AC 46, at [46] (per Lord Hoffmann): 'A duty to protect . . . self-inflicted harm exists only in cases where there is . . . some lack of capacity, such as the inability of children to recognise danger . . . or the despair of prisoners which may lead them to inflict injury on themselves . . .'

[6] *Reeves* v *Commissioner of Police of the Metropolis* [2000] AC 360.

[7] *E (a child)* v *Souls Garages Ltd*, The Times, 23 January 2001.

[8] *Chittock* v *Woodbridge School* [2002] ELR 735 (although no breach of the duty was established in this case).

[9] *Vellino* v *Chief Constable of Greater Manchester Police* [2002] 1 WLR 218 (the House of Lords refused leave to appeal: [2002] 1 WLR 1552).

[10] [2004] 1 AC 46. The claimant in that case disregarded notices warning him that it was dangerous to swim in a lake controlled by the defendant council. The claimant suffered an injury as a result of diving into the lake and sued the defendant council for compensation, claiming that it had owed him a duty to stop him swimming in the lake. His claim was rejected (though the Court of Appeal had ruled 2:1 in his favour).

Lords unanimously *rejected* an argument that if a council knows or ought to know that some adults are knowingly endangering themselves on council property – by, for example, swimming in a lake or climbing trees on land controlled by the council – the council will owe those adults a duty to stop them endangering themselves. It may also be noted that in Australia it has been held that a casino will not owe an inveterate gambler a duty not to allow him to lose his money at its tables.[11]

THE NATURE OF A TORT

A tort is only *a form* of civil wrong – not all civil wrongs amount to torts. In order to understand when someone who commits a civil wrong will commit a tort, it is convenient to distinguish between cases where someone commits a civil wrong by breaching a judge-made duty owed to another and cases where someone commits a civil wrong by breaching a statutory duty owed to another.

Judge-made duties

Someone will commit a tort in breaching a judge-made duty owed to another if, and only if, the judge-made duty in question was *a non-contractual, common law duty owed to another to do something other than pay money to another*. This needs a bit of explanation.

The idea of a common law duty
Judge-made duties are commonly divided up into *common law duties* and *equitable duties*. The distinction goes back to the time when in England there were two distinct types of courts: Courts of Law (or Common Law) and Courts of Equity. The Courts of Equity acted as a corrective to the Courts of Law, granting remedies that were unavailable in the Courts of Law when it would be just and equitable to do so or setting aside remedies that were granted in the Courts of Law when it would be just and equitable to do so. This cut both ways. A claimant seeking a legal remedy for some grievance of his who had had no luck in the Courts of Law could try and see if the more generous Courts of Equity would help him. A defendant who had lost in a Court of Law and had a remedy granted against him could ask a Court of Equity to see if they would grant an order requiring his adversary not to take advantage of that remedy.

Of course, this is all history now. By the end of the nineteenth century, the two sets of courts were 'fused' with the result that all cases were heard by one set of courts. However, at the time when there was still a distinction between Courts of Law and Courts of Equity, a duty which someone had because the decisions of the Courts of Law said that he had that duty was known as a *common law duty* and a duty which someone had solely because the decisions of the Courts of Equity said that he had that duty was called an *equitable duty*.

---

[11] *Reynolds v Katoomba RSL All Services Club Ltd* [2001] NSWCA 234 (discussed, Cane 2001b). For an account of the (similarly negative) position of American law in this area, see Wolfe 1995.

So, for example, suppose that before the Courts of Law and the Courts of Equity were fused, Tom was given a parcel of land – Blackacre – to hold 'on trust' for Sarah. Suppose further that Tom asked a lawyer what duties he had in managing Blackacre. The lawyer would have told Tom that he had a common law duty to ensure that he did not use Blackacre in a way that unreasonably interfered with his neighbours' use and enjoyment of their land – that is, he would have told Tom that according to the decisions of the Courts of Law he had a duty not to use Blackacre in a way that unreasonably interfered with his neighbours' use and enjoyment of their land. The lawyer would also have told Tom that he had an equitable duty to manage Blackacre in Sarah's best interests – that is, he would have told Tom that according to the decisions of the Courts of Equity (but not the Courts of Law) he had a duty to manage Blackacre in Sarah's best interests.

Nowadays, despite the fusion of the Courts of Law and Courts of Equity, we continue to divide up our judge-made duties according to whether they are common law duties or equitable duties. Those judge-made duties that were called equitable duties pre-fusion are still called equitable duties today. Likewise, those judge-made duties that were called common law duties pre-fusion are still called common law duties today. So if someone holds a piece of land on trust for someone else we still say nowadays that the owner of that land has a common law duty not to use it in a way that unreasonably interferes with his neighbours' use and enjoyment of their land and an equitable duty to manage the land in the best interests of whoever he holds it on trust for. What about a judge-made duty that came into existence after the fusion of the Courts of Law and Courts of Equity? Do we call that duty a common law duty or an equitable duty? How do we decide what to call it? The answer is: we tend to look at the form of the judge-made duty in question. If it is similar in content to a lot of other judge-made duties that we currently classify as being common law duties then we will tend to classify this duty as being a common law duty as well. Similarly, if it is similar in content to a lot of other judge-made duties that we currently classify as being equitable duties, we will tend to say that the duty at hand is an equitable duty as well. It is mainly a matter of impression.

It should be clear from what has just been said that the distinction between common law duties and equitable duties is completely arbitrary. It comes down to historical accident whether we classify a particular judge-made duty as being a common law duty or an equitable duty. The law should therefore treat someone who breaches a common law duty and someone who breaches an equitable duty in exactly the same way. Sensibly, the law is starting to do so.[12] The result is that, increasingly, only writers of textbooks on tort law have any interest in answering the question – has this individual breached a common law duty or an equitable duty? More often, the answer to that question has little

---

[12] See *United Scientific Holdings v Burnley Borough Council* [1978] AC 904, 924G–925B; *Tinsley v Milligan* [1994] 1 AC 340, 371A–C; *Target Holdings v Redferns* [1996] AC 421, 432F–H; *Bristol and West BS v Mothew* [1998] Ch 1, 17; Burrows 2002b. However, differences in the treatment of breaches of equitable and common law duties remain. A description of the more important ones may be found in Davies 1993; see also Meagher, Heydon and Leeming 2002, 831–41.

significance to the law and therefore to legal practitioners. Only writers of text-books on tort law need concern themselves with this question because, by definition, someone who merely breaches an equitable duty has not committed a tort and is therefore of no interest to someone writing a textbook on tort law.[13] This limitation on the concept of a tort has one useful side effect. If the concept of a tort embraced some or all breaches of equitable duties then a book on the English law of tort – dealing as it does with questions such as: In what situations will someone commit a tort? and What remedies will be made available if someone has committed a tort? – would become unmanageably large to write or read.

Contractual and non-contractual common law duties

Common law duties can be divided up into *contractual duties* and *non-contractual duties*. If A has a common law duty to do *x*, that duty will be contractual in nature if it arose because he or she entered into a valid contract with someone else. On the other hand, A's duty to do *x* will be non-contractual in nature if it arose for some other reason. Someone who breaches a contractual common law duty owed to another commits a *breach of contract*. Someone who breaches a non-contractual common law duty owed to another will commit a *tort* – so long as the duty in question was not a duty to pay money to another.

Suppose Alan has entered into a valid contract with Lara. In such a case, Alan will owe Lara a common law duty to do what Lara reasonably believed Alan was undertaking to do when he entered into that contract.[14] This duty of Alan's is contractual in nature: it has arisen because Alan entered into a valid contract with Lara. So if Alan breaches this duty, he will commit a breach of contract. Suppose, on the other hand, Alan is driving down the road in his car. In such a case, Alan will owe other users of the road a common law duty to take care not to drive the car dangerously. This duty of Alan's is non-contractual in nature. It has not arisen because Alan has entered into a valid contract with someone. Rather, it has arisen for some other reason – the fact that it is reasonably foreseeable that other users of the road will be exposed to an unreasonable risk of being harmed if Alan drives the car dangerously. If Alan breaches this duty he will commit a tort.

---

[13] *Important note*. Edelman 2002a offers two arguments in favour of the view that we should say that the breach of an equitable duty owed to another (in other words, an equitable wrong) is a tort. His first argument is that a tort involves the breach of a duty owed to another – and therefore the concept of a tort encompasses equitable wrongs (which also involve the breach of a duty owed to another). This argument does not stand up: we would not say that rape is murder because both involve committing a crime. His second argument is that the law responds to an equitable wrong in exactly the same way as it does to someone's committing a tort. Again, this argument does not stand up. We would not say that rape is murder even if the law responded to a rape in exactly the same way as it does to someone's committing a murder. The latest (18th) edition of *Clerk and Lindsell on Torts* includes chapters on breach of fiduciary duty and breach of confidence (both equitable wrongs) but this is not because the editors of that book think that these equitable wrongs are torts (they expressly say that they are not: C&L, 8), but because some tort cases raise issues of breach of fiduciary duty and breach of confidence and it therefore makes sense for pragmatic reasons to deal with those topics in a book on tort law.

[14] *Smith* v *Hughes* (1871) LR 6 QB 597; *McCutcheon* v *David MacBrayne Ltd* [1964] 1 WLR 125, 128; *The Hannah Blumenthal* [1983] 1 AC 854, 915H–916A.

It is important to note that contractual duties and non-contractual duties can overlap. Suppose, for example, that Karen pays Ian, a mini-cab driver, to take her to the airport. Once Karen is in Ian's cab, it is reasonably foreseeable that Karen will be exposed to an unreasonable risk of being injured if Ian drives the cab in a dangerous fashion. As a result, Ian will owe Karen a common law duty to take care not to drive the cab in a dangerous fashion.[15] This duty will be non-contractual in nature. It does not arise because Ian and Karen have entered into a valid contract with each other. Rather, it arises because of the impact that Ian's driving the cab in a dangerous fashion may have on Karen's health. But when Karen gets into Ian's mini-cab, Ian and Karen will enter into a valid contract with each other and Karen will believe – and it will be reasonable for her to believe – that Ian is undertaking in that contract not only to take Karen to the airport but also to take care not to drive the cab in a dangerous fashion. As a result, when Karen gets into Ian's cab, Ian will owe Karen a *contractual* duty to take care not to drive the cab in a dangerous fashion. The upshot of all this is that when Karen gets into Ian's cab, Ian will owe Karen a contractual duty *and* a non-contractual common law duty to take care not to drive the cab in a dangerous fashion. So if Ian does, through lack of care, drive the cab in a dangerous fashion, he will commit both a breach of contract *and* a tort.

It is of considerable importance to the law to establish whether a person's conduct in a given case amounts to: (*a*) a breach of contract; *or* (*b*) a tort; *or* (*c*) a breach of contract *and* a tort. This is because the law treats people who break contracts very differently from the way it treats people who commit torts:

(1) *Exemplary damages.*[16] The law does not allow exemplary damages – damages awarded in order to punish someone for the way he has behaved – to be awarded against someone who commits a breach of contract;[17] but it does, in some cases, allow exemplary damages to be awarded against someone who commits a tort.[18]

(2) *Limitation.* The limitation period for obtaining a remedy against someone who commits a breach of contract runs from the moment the breach occurs;[19] the limitation period for obtaining a remedy against someone who commits a tort generally runs from the moment the victim of that tort suffers 'damage' as a result of that tort being committed.[20]

(3) *Remoteness.* Suppose Carl breaches a contract made with Nita and Nita suffers some kind of loss as a result. In this case, Nita will only be able to sue Carl for compensation for that loss if Carl knew or ought to have known, *at the time he entered into the contract* with Nita, that Nita was likely to suffer that

---

[15] See below, p. 67.
[16] Another, and in many ways preferable, term for exemplary damages is 'punitive damages'.
[17] *Addis* v *Gramophone Co. Ltd* [1909] AC 488; *Perera* v *Vandiyar* [1953] 1 WLR 672; *Kenny* v *Preen* [1963] 1 QB 499. McBride 1995 criticises the law's refusal to allow exemplary damages to be awarded against someone who has deliberately committed a breach of contract.
[18] See below, pp. 673–85.
[19] Limitation Act 1980, s 5.
[20] See below, pp. 518–9.

loss if he breached the contract in question. On the other hand, if Carl has committed a tort X in relation to Nita and Nita has suffered some kind of loss as a result, Nita will usually be able to sue Carl for compensation for that loss if it was reasonably foreseeable, *at the time Carl committed tort X*, that Nita would suffer that kind of loss as a result – and Nita may be able to recover compensation for that loss even if it was *not* reasonably foreseeable, at the time Carl committed tort X, that she would suffer that kind of loss as a result.[21]

Non-contractual common law duties to pay money to another

The breach of a non-contractual common law duty owed to another to pay money to someone else will *not* amount to a tort.

So, for example, suppose Eric has paid Dawn £500 by mistake. And let's suppose – as will usually be the case – that Dawn has a common law duty to pay the money back. This duty will be non-contractual in nature: Dawn won't have an duty to pay the money back because she contractually agreed to do so; she'll have a duty to pay the money back because she would be unjustly enriched if she kept it. Dawn will usually have a duty to pay the money back. But if Dawn fails to give the money back, she will not commit a tort.

Again, suppose that Wendy carelessly runs down Vijay in the street and Vijay sues her for damages, seeking to obtain compensation for the injuries he has suffered as a result of being run down. Suppose further that Vijay wins his case and judgment is entered against Wendy. In this case Wendy will owe Vijay a common law duty – obviously non-contractual in nature – to pay him the damages that she has been ordered to pay by the court. If she breaches this duty and does not pay up, she will not commit a tort.

Let's call a duty to do something other than pay money to another, a 'specific' duty; and a duty to pay money to another, a 'non-specific duty'. So the breach of a specific non-contractual common law duty owed to another will amount to a tort, while the breach of a non-specific non-contractual common law duty owed to another will not.

Statutory duties

When, if ever, will the breach of a statutory duty owed to another amount to a tort?

For example, if A is a public authority and B is any given member of the public, A will, broadly speaking, owe B a statutory duty under s 6 of the Human Rights Act 1998 not to violate any of B's 'human rights' as set out in the European Convention on Human Rights and the various Protocols to that Convention.[22] If A breaches this duty, will A commit a tort? Again: if Mary visits Fred in his house, Fred will usually owe Mary a duty under the

---

[21] See below, pp. 557–60.

[22] The official title of the Convention referred to here is 'The European Convention for the Protection of Human Rights and Fundamental Freedoms'. However, in this book we will simply refer to this Convention as 'the European Convention on Human Rights' (ECHR for short).

Occupiers' Liability Act 1957 to take reasonable steps to see that she will be reasonably safe while she is in his house.[23] If Fred breaches this duty, will he commit a tort?

Most lawyers would say 'no' to the first question[24] but 'yes' to the second. But why? The most elegant answer, we feel, is that *the breach of a statutory duty owed to another will amount to a tort if the law will respond to the breach of that duty in the same way as it would respond to the breach of a specific non-contractual common law duty owed to another.* In other words, the breach of a statutory duty owed to another will amount to a tort if the rules that determine what remedies will be available when a specific non-contractual common law duty owed to another is breached will also apply to determine what remedies will be available when that statutory duty is breached. To save words, let's call these rules, *the tort remedy rules.*

So, the most important tort remedy rule says this: if A breaches a specific non-contractual, common law duty owed to B, B will be entitled – unless A has some kind of defence – to recover *compensatory damages* from A sufficient to compensate her for the actionable losses that A's breach has caused her to suffer. The same rule does *not* apply if A, a public authority, violates one of B's human rights in breach of the statutory duty that it owes B not to do so under s 6 of the Human Rights Act 1998. Section 8(1) of the 1998 Act merely provides that in 'relation to any act ... of a public authority which the court finds is (or would be) unlawful, it may grant such relief or remedy, or make such order, within its powers as it considers just and appropriate'. Section 8(3) goes on to say that:

> [no] award of damages is to be made unless, taking account of all the circumstances of the case, including – (a) any other relief or remedy granted, or order made, in relation to the act in question . . ., and (b) the consequences of any decision ... in respect of that act, the court is satisfied that the award is necessary to afford just satisfaction to the person in whose favour it is made.

Finally, s 8(4) provides that in 'determining ... whether to award damages . . . the court must take into account the principles applied by the European Court of Human Rights in relation to the award of compensation under [the European Convention on Human Rights]'. Given these provisions, we cannot say that a public authority will commit a tort if it breaches the statutory duty it owes an individual under s 6 of the Human Rights Act 1998 not to violate his 'human rights' under the European Convention on Human Rights – the law's response to such a breach will not be governed by the same rules as the law's response to the breach of a non-contractual common law duty owed to another.

In contrast, it is well-established that the tort remedy rules *will* apply to determine what remedies will be available when an occupier of land breaches the duty he owes one of his visitors under the Occupiers' Liability Act 1957 to ensure that that visitor is reasonably safe for the purposes for which he or she

---

[23] Occupiers' Liability Act 1957, s 2(2).

[24] However, Stanton 2003 argues (at 3) that 'it seems almost certain' that a breach of duty under the 1998 Act 'will be regarded as a tort'.

is on the occupier's land. So if Mary visits Fred's house and Fred breaches the duty he owes her under the 1957 Act to take reasonable steps to ensure that she is reasonably safe while she is in his house, Mary will be entitled to sue Fred, unless Fred has some kind of defence, for compensatory damages sufficient to compensate her for the actionable losses that Fred's breach caused her to suffer – just as she would be if Fred breached a specific non-contractual common law duty owed to Mary. In other words, the breach of an occupier's statutory duty under the Occupiers' Liability Act 1957 will be actionable in the same way as the breach of a non-contractual common law duty owed to another. Given this, we may say that an occupier who breaches this duty will commit a tort.

To take another example, under s 94(1) of the Employment Rights Act 1996 an employer will owe each of his employees a statutory duty not to dismiss that employee unfairly. If an employer breaches this duty will he commit a tort? The answer is 'no'.[25] The tort remedy rules will *not* apply to determine what remedies will be available when an employer breaches his statutory duty under the 1996 Act not to dismiss one of his employees unfairly. The rules which *do* apply to determine what remedies will be available when an employer dismisses one of his employees unfairly are set out in ss 111–132 of the 1996 Act and, while they are similar to the tort remedy rules, they are not the same.

It is, of course, for Parliament to determine what remedies will be available if a particular statutory duty owed to another is breached. Suppose we take a particular statutory duty owed to another and ask: will the tort remedy rules apply to determine what remedies will be available if that duty is breached? The answer will depend on what Parliament intended when it created the duty in question. If Parliament intended that the tort remedy rules should apply, then they will – and breach of the duty in question will amount to a tort. If Parliament intended that the tort remedy rules should not apply, then they will not – and breach of the duty in question will not amount to a tort.

Parliament sometimes makes it clear when it creates a statutory duty owed to another that it intends that the tort remedy rules should apply to determine what remedies will be available if that duty is breached. So, for example, when Parliament enacted the Sex Discrimination Act 1975 it created a raft of statutory duties owed to others not to discriminate against them on grounds of their sex. At the same time, it made it clear that the tort remedy rules should apply to determine what remedies will be available if one of those statutory duties is breached. Under s 66 of the 1975 Act, '[a] claim by any person . . . that another person . . . has committed an act of discrimination against [him or her] which is unlawful [under the Act] . . . may be made the subject of civil proceedings in like manner as any other claim in tort'.

Parliament will also sometimes make it clear when it creates a statutory duty owed to another that it does *not* intend that the tort remedy rules should apply to determine what remedies will be available if that duty is breached. As we have seen, this is the case with the Human Rights Act 1998 and the duty not to dismiss an employee unfairly under s 94(1) of the Employment Rights Act

---

[25] Stanton 2003, 4.

1996. Again, in s 2 of the Health and Safety at Work Act 1974, Parliament stipulated that an employer will owe each of his employees a 'duty . . . to ensure, so far as is reasonably practicable, the health, safety and welfare at work of [that employee]' while making clear at the same time that '[nothing in this Act] shall be construed . . . as conferring a right of action in any civil proceedings in respect of any failure to comply with [the] duty imposed by [s] 2'.[26]

More often that not, though, when Parliament creates a statutory duty owed to another, it will not make it clear one way or the other whether it intends that the tort remedy rules should apply to determine what remedies will be available if that duty is breached. In such a case, it has to be *inferred* what Parliament's intention on this matter is.

Summary

A tort is a form of civil wrong – a breach of a legal duty owed to another. However, not all civil wrongs amount to torts. A will commit a tort if, and only if, the duty that he breached was: (*a*) a specific non-contractual common law duty; or (*b*) a statutory duty *and* the law's response to that breach will be governed by the same rules that govern the law's response to the breach of a specific non-contractual, common law duty owed to another.[27] If A breaches any other kind of duty owed to another, he will not commit a tort. (See Diagram 1, overleaf.)

Is there a convenient term that we can use to describe a duty owed to another, breach of which will amount to a tort? Andrew Burrows uses the term 'tortious obligation' to describe this kind of duty.[28] The use of the word 'obligation' is unexceptionable – 'obligation' is just a fancy word for a duty that is owed to someone else. But 'tortious'? To say that a duty which is owed to someone else is a 'tortious obligation' is, literally, to say that it is a wrongful obligation – which is nonsense. But we have been unable to come up with anything better and so from now on we will use the term 'tortious' to describe any duty owed to another, the breach of which will amount to a tort.

So: someone will commit a tort if he breaches a tortious duty owed to another – and a duty owed to another will be tortious if: (*a*) that duty is a specific non-contractual common law duty; *or* (*b*) that duty is a statutory duty *and* the law will respond to the breach of that duty in the same way as it does to the breach of a specific non-contractual common law duty owed to another.

---

[26] Health and Safety at Work 1974, s 47(1)(a).

[27] Cf. the definition of a tort offered by Judge Toulmin QC in *R v Secretary of State for Transport, ex p Factortame Ltd (No. 7)* [2001] 1 WLR 942, at [150]: 'I define a tort as a breach of a non-contractual duty which gives rise to a private law right to the party injured to recover compensatory damages at common law from the party causing the injury.' This definition suffers from a couple of difficulties that make it inferior to our definition: (*a*) it does not make it clear that a breach of duty will only amount to a tort if the duty breached is owed to another; (*b*) it is possible for someone to commit a tort without being held liable to pay anyone else compensatory damages.

[28] Burrows 1994, 3; also Waddams 2003, 44.

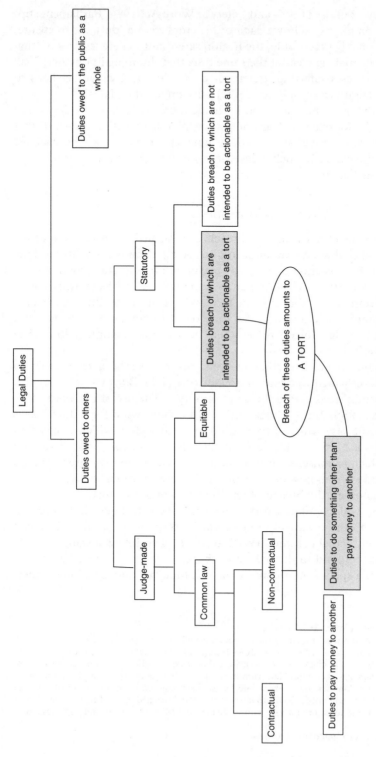

Diagram 1. What is a Tort?

2

AN OVERVIEW OF TORT LAW

WHAT IS TORT LAW?

Tort law is, literally, the law relating to torts and tortfeasors (that is, people who commit torts). But this is too broad a characterisation of what tort law is. For instance, tort law does not tell us when a tortfeasor may be criminally punished for what he has done – the criminal law tells us that, not tort law.[1] So it would be more accurate to say that tort law tells us: (*a*) in what situations someone will commit a tort – that is, breach a tortious duty owed to another; *and* (*b*) what remedies people will be able to obtain if someone has committed a tort or is committing a tort. Someone who studies tort law, then, is solely concerned to find out the answers to two questions. First, in what situations will someone commit a tort? Secondly, what remedies will people be able to obtain if someone has committed a tort or is committing a tort? In this chapter we will briefly answer these two questions before answering them in much more detail in Parts II and III of this book.

IN WHAT SITUATIONS WILL SOMEONE COMMIT A TORT?

The answer to this question depends, of necessity, on how the law stands on the issue of when one person will owe another a tortious duty: A will not have committed a tort by doing *x* in situation S unless he owed someone else a tortious duty not to do *x* in situation S. So, for example, suppose that Ruth – a child – fell into a deep pond and while she was drowning Eric saw her plight but did nothing to assist her. Did Eric commit a tort in this situation? It depends on whether Eric owed Ruth a tortious duty to try to save her from

---

[1] Sometimes someone who commits a tort will at the same time commit a crime and become liable to suffer criminal punishment for what he has done. This will be the case, for example, if A beats B up: A's conduct will amount both to a tort and to a crime. Someone who commits a tort innocently or unknowingly will, as a general rule, not commit a crime in so acting – the law generally requires the perpetrator of a crime not only to act wrongfully (that is, to commit an *actus reus*) but also to do so with a guilty mind (a *mens rea*). That is not to say that someone who knowingly commits a tort will necessarily commit a crime in so acting. For example, if a hiker deliberately takes a short cut across another's land when he has no right to do so, he will commit a tort but no crime. However, trespassing on another person's property will sometimes amount to a crime: see Theft Act 1968, s 9 (definition of the offence of burglary); Criminal Justice and Public Order Act 1994, s 68 (definition of the offence of aggravated trespass); Sexual Offences Act 2003, s 63 (definition of offence of trespass with intent to commit a sexual offence).

drowning. In fact, if you come across a stranger in danger, you will *not* owe him or her any kind of duty to do your best to rescue him or her. So in the situation we are considering, Eric will not have committed any kind of wrong – let alone a tort – in acting as he did.

So, in what situations *will* someone commit a tort? A typical – though by no means complete – list of the situations in which someone will commit a tort might run as follows. Someone, A, will commit a tort if: (*a*) he breaches a tortious duty of care owed to another; *or* (*b*) he directly applies force to another's person when he has no lawful justification or excuse for doing so; *or* (*c*) he tells damaging lies about someone else when he has no lawful justification or excuse for doing so; *or* (*d*) he unreasonably interferes with another's use and enjoyment of land; *or* (*e*) he induces someone else to break a contract when he has no lawful justification or excuse for doing so; *or* (*f*) he intentionally interferes with someone else's business using unlawful means to do so; *or* (*g*) he knowingly or recklessly tells lies to someone else in order to induce that person to act in some way; *or* (*h*) he maliciously brings a criminal prosecution against someone else when he has no reasonable cause to do so; or (*i*) he breaches a tortious statutory duty owed to another. In Part II, we will present a far more detailed and expansive list of the situations in which someone will commit a tort but this rudimentary list will serve for the moment. Four points may be made about it.

(1) *The naming of torts.* Lawyers like to give names to the different ways in which a tort may be committed. So lawyers say that someone will commit 'the tort of negligence' if he breaches a tortious duty of care owed to another; 'the tort of battery' if he directly applies force to another's person when he has no lawful justification or excuse for doing so; 'the tort of private nuisance' if he unreasonably interferes with another's use and enjoyment of land; 'the tort of inducing a breach of contract' if he induces someone else to break a contract when he has no lawful justification or excuse for doing so; 'the tort of intimidation' if he intentionally interferes with another's business by unlawfully intimidating that business's employees or customers; 'the tort of deceit' or 'the tort of fraud' if he knowingly or recklessly tells lies to someone else to induce that person to act in some way; 'the tort of malicious prosecution' if he maliciously brings a criminal prosecution against someone else when he has no reasonable cause to do so; and 'the tort of breach of statutory duty' if he breaches a tortious statutory duty owed to another.

Lawyers like to give names to the different ways in which a tort may be committed because it is convenient to do so. Suppose, for example, that a lawyer wants to argue: 'A committed a tort because he directly applied force to another's person when he had no lawful justification or excuse for doing so.' This is very long-winded. However, the fact that lawyers have given the above names to the different ways in which a tort may be committed means that our lawyer can put his argument in a much shorter form. He can say: 'A committed the tort of battery.' Again, suppose a writer of a textbook on tort law wants to say: 'Aggravated damages[2] may

---

[2] Damages designed to assuage the victim of a tort's sense of outrage at the way he or she has been treated.

be awarded against someone who commits a tort by directly applying force to another's person when he has no lawful justification or excuse for doing so; but they may not be awarded against someone who commits a tort by breaching a tortious duty of care owed to another.' This is *very* long-winded. Conveniently, the fact that lawyers have given the above names to the different ways in which a tort may be committed allows our writer to make this point more succinctly. He or she can simply say: 'Aggravated damages may be awarded against someone who commits the tort of battery; but they may not be awarded against someone who commits the tort of negligence.'

It may also be noted at this juncture that lawyers also like to give names to *groups* of torts. This is usually for reasons of either history or convenience or just to make a point about a certain group of torts. So, for example, lawyers often group together the torts of battery, assault and false imprisonment, and dub all these torts, 'torts involving a trespass to the person'. This is for reasons of history: these torts, which are all committed by interfering with another's person, were traditionally remedied by obtaining a writ of *trespass*.[3] Again, section 1 of the Torts (Interference with Goods) Act 1977 uses the term 'wrongful interference with goods' to describe the torts of conversion, trespass to goods and other torts which result in 'damage to goods or to an interest in goods'. This is, of course, for reasons of convenience: the 1977 Act was designed to reform the law on what remedies would be available when someone's goods were damaged or misappropriated through someone else's committing a tort, and so – for the purpose of setting out what those remedies would be – the Act needed to invent a catch-all term to describe all the torts that could form the basis of an action where someone else's goods were damaged or misappropriated. Finally, the torts dealt with in Chapters 19–24 of this book (such as the torts of inducing a breach of contract, conspiracy, intentional interference with trade by unlawful means, deceit and passing off) are often grouped together by lawyers and given the collective name of the 'economic torts'. The name makes two points about these torts: (*a*) they are usually committed by causing another to suffer economic loss; *and* (*b*) someone who

[3] A writ was an order, requiring the courts to hear someone's case. The writ of trespass was not available to every victim of a tort who wanted to obtain a remedy for that tort's having been committed. The victim of a tort would often have to obtain an alternative writ, called the writ of trespass *on the case*, to have his case heard. But in order to obtain such a writ, he had to prove that he had suffered some kind of loss. So torts that were *not* covered by the writ of trespass were only actionable on proof of damage. By contrast, a victim of a tort who could obtain a writ of trespass, ordering the courts to hear his case, did not have to prove that he had suffered any kind of loss as a result of that tort being committed. So torts which were covered by the writ of trespass were actionable *per se* – that is, actionable even if the claimant had not suffered any loss as a result of that tort's having been committed. (See, generally, Ibbetson 1999.) Even though we no longer require people to obtain or issue writs in order to sue other people in tort, it remains the case to this day that torts that were traditionally remedied through the award of a writ of trespass are usually actionable *per se* and torts that were traditionally remedied through the writ of trespass on the case are usually only actionable on proof of damage. Having said that, 'the old distinction between actions for trespass and actions on the case does not provide a clearcut solution in every case [where the question of whether a tort is actionable *per se* arises]': *Watkins* v *Secretary of State for the Home Department* [2004] EWCA Civ 966. For a complete account of which torts are actionable *per se* and which are not, see below, Chapter 36.

has suffered a form of pure economic loss[4] will only usually be allowed to sue for compensation for that loss if he has been a victim of one of these torts.

(2) *Tort and duty*. The above list of situations where someone will commit a tort helps to conceal or obscure the fact that committing a tort involves breaching a tortious duty owed to another. Only the presence of items (*a*) and (*i*) on the list helps to remind us that committing a tort involves breaching a tortious duty owed to another. So, for example, the list says that A will commit a tort – the tort of battery – if he directly applies force to B's person when he has no lawful justification or excuse for doing so. It does not make clear that the reason *why* A will commit a tort if he does this is that A will owe B a non-contractual, common law duty not to act in this way. This is left unsaid or suppressed – and as a result can often be forgotten or overlooked.[5]

So, for example, Tony Weir says that 'liability for deceit or trespass is so self-evident that we do not consider it as resulting from a breach of duty'.[6] But it does.[7] If A hit B when he had no lawful justification or excuse for doing so, the reason we hold A liable to compensate B for the resulting injuries suffered by B is that A acted *wrongfully* in hitting B – A owed her a duty not to beat her up and he breached that duty. Of course, if B wants to sue A for damages, all she has to do is show that A hit her and that A had no lawful justification or excuse for doing so. She does not have to show *in addition* that A owed her a duty not to hit her. But that does not mean – as Weir suggests it does – that A's liability is not based on the fact that he breached a duty owed to B in acting as he did. The reason that B does not have to show that A owed her a duty not to hit her is that it is *self-evident* that A owed B a duty not to hit her if he had no lawful justification or excuse for doing so. The only issue is whether A breached that duty in acting as he did – that is, the only issue is whether A hit B when he had no lawful justification or excuse for doing so.

It might be argued that the House of Lords' decision in *Stubbings* v *Webb*[8] establishes that the view taken here is incorrect. In that case, the claimant sued the defendant in August 1987, claiming that between 1959 and 1971 the defendant had sexually abused her, thereby committing the tort of battery. Unfortunately, the law says that actions in tort have to be brought within six years of the time when the tort complained of first caused the claimant to suffer some kind of harm. As the defendant's last sexual assault on the claimant took place in 1971, the limitation period for suing the defendant in tort ran out for

---

[4] 'Pure' economic loss is economic loss not consequent on someone's person or property being harmed. So, for example, a gambler who loses a bet suffers a form of pure economic loss.

[5] But not, curiously enough, by *restitution* lawyers, who readily acknowledge that committing a tort involves breaching a duty owed to another: see, for example, Burrows 1983; 1998, 9–10; Edelman 2002a. This is almost entirely due to the salutary influence of Professor Peter Birks, who was – until his recent and most untimely death – the world's foremost restitution lawyer: see Birks 1983, 1995, 1997a, 2000b.

[6] Weir 2001, 30; quoted with approval by Lord Rodger of Earlsferry in *Standard Chartered Bank* v *Pakistan Shipping Corpn (Nos. 2 and 4)* [2003] 1 AC 959, at [41].

[7] Winfield 1931, 32: 'Tortious liability arises from the breach of a duty . . .'; also M&D, 19: '[E]very tort [involves] the breach of some legal duty . . .'

[8] [1993] AC 498.

the claimant in 1977. The claimant sought to get round this point by taking advantage of the Limitation Act 1980, s 11 which provides that:

(1) This section applies to any action for damages for negligence, nuisance or breach of duty ... where the damages claimed by the [claimant] for the negligence, nuisance or breach of duty consist of or include damages in respect of personal injuries ...

(4) ... [the limitation period applicable to this kind of action] is three years from – (a) the date on which the cause of action accrued; or (b) the date of knowledge (if later) of the person injured.

The claimant argued that her action arose out of a 'breach of duty' and that she only acquired knowledge of the fact that the defendant's sexual assaults on her had caused her to suffer some kind of personal injury in September 1984, when she started undergoing therapy and realised her mental problems were due to the fact that she had been sexually assaulted by the defendant. So, the claimant argued, she had had until September 1987 (three years from when she first acquired knowledge of the effect the defendant's sexual assaults had had on her) to bring proceedings against the defendant. She had therefore issued proceedings against the defendant just in time by suing him in August 1987.

The House of Lords rejected this argument, holding that the claimant's action against the defendant for sexually assaulting her did not arise out of a 'breach of duty' and that s 11 of the 1980 Act did not therefore apply to the claimant's claim. The claimant's action was therefore dismissed on the ground that proceedings against the defendant had been issued too late.[9] Lord Griffiths remarked, somewhat cryptically, 'If I invite a lady to my house one would naturally think of a duty to take care that the house is safe but would one really be thinking of a duty not to rape her?'[10] But it is quite clear from Lord Griffiths's decision in *Stubbings* v *Webb* – with which the other Law Lords agreed – that he ruled against the claimant because he thought that the *phrase* 'breach of duty' in s 11 of the 1980 Act was not *intended* to cover such torts as battery. Lord Griffiths did *not* mean to *deny* that if A beats B up and B later sues A for damages, A's liability to pay B damages arises out of the fact that A acted wrongfully in beating B up.[11]

(3) *Negligence and duty.* A lot of academics are so hostile to the idea that liabilities in tort arise out of the breach of a duty owed to another that they even deny that liability in *negligence* arises out of the breach of a duty of care owed to another. Let us call such academics, *duty-sceptics.*[12] According to the duty-sceptics, when the courts say that A will owe B a duty of care in a given situation, all they mean to say by that is that A will be held liable to pay damages

---

[9] A subsequent claim that the claimant's rights to a fair trial under Article 6 of the European Convention on Human Rights had been violated because the law on limitation of actions prevented her making out her claim against the defendant was dismissed by the European Court of Human Rights: *Stubbings* v *United Kingdom* [1997] 1 FLR 105.

[10] [1993] AC 498, 508.

[11] To the same effect, Edelman 2002a, n. 55.

[12] The intellectual origins of duty-scepticism among tort academics are well explored in Goldberg 2002, 2003a.

to B if he carelessly harms B in that situation.[13] So – on this view – if A is held liable in negligence to pay damages to B, he is not held liable because he breached a duty of care owed to B by acting in the way he did (for no such duty existed); rather, he is held liable because he carelessly harmed B in a situation where someone who carelessly causes another harm will be held liable for that harm.[14] This view of duties of care in negligence is simply wrong and should be rejected by all right-thinking students. It cannot survive the devastating criticisms that have been made of it, both by one of us writing elsewhere[15] and by Professors Goldberg and Zipursky.[16] We need waste no more time on it here.

(4) *The birth and death of torts.* The list of situations in which someone will commit a tort is never fixed. This is because the law on when one person will owe another a tortious duty is constantly evolving in response to changes in social attitudes and values.

For example, it used to be the case that if a man was married, other men would normally owe him: (*a*) a tortious statutory duty not to commit adultery with his wife;[17] (*b*) a non-contractual common law duty not to encourage his wife to leave him; (*c*) if his wife left him, a non-contractual common law duty not to harbour his wife.[18] So someone would normally commit a tort if he committed adultery with a man's wife or encouraged a man's wife to leave him or harboured a man's wife when she left him. As McCardie J frankly admitted in *Butterworth* v *Butterworth and Englefield*, the reason for this was that '[a] wife was in substance regarded by the common law as the property of her husband'[19] – so interfering with a man's wife was regarded as being akin to interfering with his property. Now that society has rejected the idea that a man's wife is his property, the idea that other men will owe a married man a duty not to interfere with his marriage has also been rejected. Nowadays, someone who

---

[13] *Important note.* See, for example, Cane 1999a, 58: 'To say that a person owes a duty of care in a particular situation means (*and means only*) that the person will be liable for causing damage by negligence in that situation' (emphasis added). See, to identical effect, Weir 1998b, 242–3; M. Jones 2002, 41; Hedley 2002, 28; M&D, 77 (note the glaring inconsistency between the statements on this page and the statement in M&D, at 19, that '[E]very tort [involves] the breach of some legal duty . . .'). Two thoughts occur on reading statements such as these. (1) It is striking how often academics who think like this go on to complain that the law of negligence is 'incoherent' or 'in a mess': see, for example, Hepple 1997; Ibbetson 2003, 475. They never seem to consider the possibility that the law of negligence is not *actually* incoherent or in a mess; and that it only seems that way to them because they refuse to take seriously the notion that liability in negligence arises out of the breach of a duty of care owed to another. (2) It is as well that tort textbooks and articles do not enjoy a wide circulation outside legal circles. For example, would we really *want* doctors and nurses to think that the common law does not actually require them to treat their patients with a reasonable degree of care and skill; that the *only* thing the common law requires them to do is to pay their patients damages if they fail to treat them properly?

[14] So, according to the duty-sceptics, liability in negligence is not wrong-based but *fault-based.* Thus Howarth & O'Sullivan 2000, 2: 'Negligence is liability for *fault*' (emphasis in original). To similar effect, see Cane 1999a, 7; Giliker & Beckwith 2000, 3; Burrows 1998, 123.

[15] See McBride 2004.

[16] See Goldberg 2000; Zipursky 1998b; Goldberg & Zipursky 1998, 2001.

[17] Matrimonial Causes Act 1857, s 33.

[18] *Winsmore* v *Greenbank* (1745) Willes 577, 125 ER 1330.

[19] [1920] P 126, 130.

interferes with a man's marriage will not commit a tort[20] – or, indeed, any other kind of legal wrong.

Again, as we have seen, the law says at the moment that if you come across a stranger who is in danger of being killed or injured, you will not owe him a duty to rescue him. In taking this position, the law reflects the liberal values currently prevalent in society – in particular, the idea that a man should be legally free to do what he likes, however wicked or immoral, so long as his doing what he likes does not actually *cause* anyone else to suffer any harm. However, it is conceivable that our society will come to value the promotion of collective welfare more than the preservation of individual liberty. Should that happen, Parliament may well change the law and enact a statute which provides that: (*a*) if someone comes across a stranger who is in danger of being killed or injured, he will have a duty to rescue that stranger if he can do so without endangering himself; and (*b*) the tort remedy rules will apply to determine what remedies will be available if someone breaches this duty. If Parliament does change the law in this way, then someone *will* commit a tort if he or she comes across a stranger in danger of suffering some kind of harm and does nothing to assist that stranger when he or she could easily have rescued him.

(5) *The number of torts.* The list set out above of the situations in which someone will commit a tort lists nine different torts. There are in fact *at least* 25 different kinds of torts – a complete list of the torts recognised in English law might in fact comprise about 40 different torts.[21] Why are there so many torts? Well, there are as many torts in English law as there are different kinds of tortious duties that we owe each other – so the more tortious duties that we owe each other, the more torts there will be. So, if you take two given individuals, A and B, there are at least 25 different kinds of tortious duties that A will owe B and, correspondingly, at least 25 different kinds of tort that A can commit.

But are these different kinds of duties all that different? Might they just be facets or instances of one or two or three 'master duties'? If they are then the various 'different' torts recognised in English law are just facets or instances of one or two or three 'master torts'.[22] Sir Percy Winfield, a very great tort lawyer, thought that all the various torts recognised in English law were all just facets or instances of *one* 'master tort' – the tort of causing someone else harm when

---

[20] Section 4 of the Law Reform (Miscellaneous Provisions) Act 1970 provides that 'no person shall be entitled to ... claim ... damages from any other person on the ground of adultery with the wife of the first-mentioned person'. Section 5 of the 1970 Act provides that '[no] person shall be liable in tort...(a) to any other person on the ground only of his having induced the wife ... of that other person to leave or remain apart from [that person]; ... (c) to any other person for harbouring the wife ... of [that person] ...'. Section 2 of the Administration of Justice Act 1982 provides that '[no] person shall be liable in tort ... to a husband on the ground only if having deprived him of the services or society of his wife ...'. The last remaining traces of the idea that a man's wife is his property were removed from the law by the House of Lords in *R* v *R* [1992] 1 AC 599, ruling that a man is not allowed to have sexual intercourse with his wife without her consent.

[21] Rudden 1991–1992 provides us with a list of over 70 torts which have been recognised at one time or another in the common law jurisdictions. But it is doubtful whether some of the listed 'torts' are actually torts – for example, 'homicide' or 'products liability'.

[22] Cf. Sugarman 2002, criticising the common law (at 378) for having 'too many torts'.

one has no lawful justification or excuse for doing so.[23] However, the established authorities seem to indicate that there is no such 'master tort' recognised in English law: there are plenty of occasions when someone will be allowed to harm someone else even if he has no lawful justification or excuse for doing so.[24]

Others have sought to argue, in private conversation with the authors, that the various tortious duties that one person will owe another in English can essentially be reduced to about three – and that, correspondingly, the various torts recognised in English law can be reduced to about three. On this view, if you take two given individuals, A and B, A will owe B: (*a*) a tortious duty to ensure that he does not intentionally cause B harm when he has no lawful justification or excuse for doing so; (*b*) a tortious duty to take care that he does not cause B to suffer some kind of serious harm such as damage to B's person or property; (*c*) a tortious duty to ensure that B does not suffer any serious harm which A has exposed B to an unusual risk of suffering. All the existing torts recognised in English law essentially involve the breach of one or other of these three duties.

So all the existing torts recognised in English can therefore be seen as facets or instances of one or other of three 'master torts' – the first, a tort of intention, is committed by intentionally and unjustifiably causing someone else to suffer some kind of harm (however trivial); the second, a tort of negligence, is committed by carelessly causing someone else to suffer some form of serious harm; the third, a tort of strict liability, is committed by exposing someone else to an unusual risk of suffering some kind of harm and then failing to ensure that that risk does not materialise.

This view of English law is too crude to be sustainable. For example, what about the case where A commits a tort by carelessly *failing to save* B from suffering some kind of harm? A must in this case have breached a tortious duty owed to B – but it is not a duty which fits within the scheme of duties set out above. So there are not just three tortious duties that one person will owe another but at least four. And what about the case where A commits a tort by carelessly causing B to suffer some kind of harm which is not that serious – such as pure economic loss? Again, A must have breached a tortious duty owed to B in this situation – but it is again not a duty which fits within the scheme of duties set out above. So the number of tortious duties that one person will owe another will not be four but must be at least five. And with similar arguments, we could easily show that the number of tortious duties that one person will owe another is in fact at least 25 – which is the figure we started off with.

So suggestions that the various torts recognised in English law are just facets or instances of a small number of 'master torts' seem wide of the mark.[25] In fact there is an irreducibly large number of torts recognised in English law – and this

---

[23] Winfield 1927; 1931, 32–9.

[24] For examples, see below pp. 409, 413. See also Goodhart 1938; Williams 1939–1941.

[25] Which is not to say that there are not *some* torts which can be seen as facets or instances of a wider tort. See, for example, Chapter 20, below, where we argue that a number of different nominate torts are instances of the 'master tort' of using unlawful means to cause another loss.

is merely a reflection of the complexity and diversity of the tortious duties that we owe each other under English law.

WHAT REMEDIES WILL BE AVAILABLE WHEN SOMEONE COMMITS A TORT?

Let us now turn to the second question dealt with by the law of tort – what remedies will people be able to obtain if someone has committed or is committing a tort? There are in fact a wide variety of remedies that may be obtained, depending on the circumstances.

Compensatory damages

Basic principles

Suppose Carl has committed a tort in relation to Lara.[26] In such a case, Lara will usually be entitled to sue Carl for *compensatory damages* sufficient to compensate her for the *actionable* losses that Carl's tort has *caused* her to suffer.[27]

However, Lara may be barred from suing Carl for anything by way of compensatory damages.[28] If she is, we say that Carl has a *defence* to Lara's claim for compensatory damages. For example, if Lara provoked Carl into committing his tort by committing some serious criminal offence, Carl may be able to raise a defence of *illegality* to Lara's claim for compensatory damages. Again, if Lara delays too long before suing Carl for damages – usually, more than six years from the date she first suffered harm as a result of Carl's tort – Carl will be able to raise a *limitation* defence to Lara's claim for damages.[29]

Even if, in the situation we are considering, Lara is not barred from suing Carl for compensatory damages, the amount of compensatory damages payable by Carl to Lara *may* be reduced below the level necessary to compensate Lara for the actionable losses that his tort has caused her to suffer.[30] This may happen, for example, if Lara was partly to blame for the fact that she suffered those losses – in which case we say that the damages payable to Lara will be reduced on the grounds that she was *contributorily negligent*. Similarly, the damages payable to Lara may be reduced if Lara received some kind of benefit as a result of Carl's committing his tort.

Third parties: I

Suppose again that Carl has committed a tort in relation to Lara. Suppose further that Vijay, a third party, has suffered a loss as a result of Carl's tort. In

---

[26] *Important note.* This is just a shorthand way of saying 'Suppose Carl has committed a tort by breaching a tortious duty owed to Lara.' Another shorthand way of saying the same thing is to say 'Suppose Carl has committed a tort and Lara was the victim of that tort.'

[27] It should be noted that Lara will usually also be entitled to sue Carl for damages in respect of the actionable losses that Carl's tort *may* cause her to suffer in the future: see below, pp. 588, 591–3. This point will be disregarded in what follows.

[28] See below, pp. 496–518.

[29] See below, pp. 513–20.

[30] See below, pp. 600–15.

such a case, as a general rule, Vijay will *not* be entitled to sue Carl for compensation for the loss that he has suffered as a result of Carl's tort.

A very famous American case illustrates the point best. In *Palsgraf* v *Long Island Railroad Co.*,[31] a young man – let's call him John – attempted to get onto a train as the train started to move off. He was carrying a package at the time. A railwayman who was nearby – let's call him Tom – attempted to help John onto the train but in doing so carelessly knocked the package carried by John to the ground. Unfortunately the package contained fireworks and when the package hit the ground, the fireworks exploded. Helen Palsgraf was standing some way away, but the shock of the explosion caused some scales which she was standing beside to fall over and hit her. She sued for compensation for the injuries she suffered when the scales hit her.

The issue in the *Palsgraf* case boiled down to whether Helen Palsgraf was entitled to sue Tom for compensation for her injuries. It was held that she was not so entitled. Tom *had* committed a tort in acting as he did. He had owed *John* a non-contractual common law duty to take care not to knock John's package to the ground because it was reasonably foreseeable that doing so would damage the contents of the package; and Tom had breached that duty. So Tom, in acting as he did, committed a tort in relation to John and Helen Palsgraf suffered loss as a result. But this did not entitle her to sue Tom for compensation for that loss: in order to do that, she had to show that Tom had committed a tort *in relation to her* in acting as he did. In other words, she had to show that Tom had owed *her* a non-contractual common law duty to take care not to knock John's package to the ground. But this she could not do: as it was not foreseeable that she would be injured if the package was knocked to the ground (on the face of it, the package looked perfectly innocuous), there was no reason why Tom should have owed *her* a duty to take care not to knock John's package to the ground.

There are two important exceptions to the general rule that if A commits a tort in relation to B and C suffers loss as a result, C will *not* be entitled to sue A for compensation for that loss.

(1) *Fatal torts.* Suppose Gary has committed a tort in relation to Karen and Karen has died as a result. In such a case, Karen's husband (if any) or parents (if Karen was a minor and unmarried at the time she died) will normally be entitled to sue Gary for damages designed to compensate them for their bereavement.[32] Karen's dependants (if any) will also normally be entitled to sue Gary for compensation for the loss of financial support that they have suffered as a result of Karen's death.[33] Neither group of people will be entitled to sue Gary for such damages if Karen would not have been entitled to sue Gary for compensation for her injuries had she survived Gary's tort and merely been injured by it.

---

[31] 248 NY 339, 162 NE 99 (1928).
[32] See below, p. 627–8.
[33] See below, pp. 623–7.

(2) *Subrogation.* Suppose Nita has negligently crashed into Fred's car and that Fred's car was insured with Easimind against its being damaged. In this case, Fred has two ways of recovering compensation for the damage done to his car: he could sue Nita or make a claim on his insurance policy with Easimind. Suppose he chooses to make a claim on his insurance policy. If he does this, then Easimind will be entitled to bring an action against Nita in Fred's name and sue her for compensation for the damage that she did to Fred's car. (In lawyer's language, Easimind will be *subrogated* to Fred's rights to sue Nita. Lawyers sometimes make the same point in a more colourful way by saying that Easimind will be allowed to 'stand in Fred's shoes' and sue Nita in Fred's name.) In this way, they will recoup the money they had to pay out to Fred for the damage done to his car.

At first sight, this is unsatisfactory. Easimind will have been well paid in the form of insurance premiums to take the risk that it would have to compensate Fred if his car was damaged. So when Easimind compensates Fred for the damage done to his car, why should Easimind be allowed to turn round and, using the law on subrogation, recover that money from Nita? It might be argued that if Easmind were not subrogated to Fred's rights to sue Nita, then Fred would be entitled to claim compensation for the damage done to his car from his insurance company *and* then sue Nita in his own right for compensation for the damage done to his car.[34] Fred would as a result be doubly compensated for the damage done to his car and would therefore enjoy an undeserved windfall.[35] But this problem could be addressed by making Fred hand over to Easimind any damages he recovered from Nita.[36] And if Fred has no intention of suing Nita – and there is therefore no prospect of Fred enjoying an undeserved windfall – why do we, on this explanation, still allow Easimind to be subrogated to Fred's right to sue Nita?[37]

In *Banque Financière de la Cité* v *Parc (Battersea) Ltd*,[38] Lord Hoffmann explained that Easimind will be subrogated to Fred's rights to sue Nita because there will have been a term in Easimind's contract of insurance with Fred, stipulating that if Easimind compensated Fred for damage done to his car, Easmind would be subrogated to any rights Fred had to sue for compensation for that damage. So, in subrogating Easimind to Fred's rights to sue Nita, the law is simply giving effect to the contract between Fred and Easimind.[39] However, this does not seem convincing:[40] Easimind will be subrogated to Fred's rights to sue Nita even if Fred's contract of insurance with Easimind was

---

[34] For reasons that will be explained below at pp. 604–5, the compensation payable by Nita to Fred will not be reduced to take account of the fact that he has already been compensated by Easimind for the damage done to his car.

[35] See Burrows 2002a, 109–12; Degeling 2003, 180–3, 191–230.

[36] In fact, this *is* what will happen if Fred – having been compensated for the damage done to his car by Easimind – subsequently recovers compensation for that damage from Nita. Easimind will have a charge over the damages recovered from Nita: *Lord Napier and Ettrick* v *Hunter* [1993] AC 713.

[37] See Cane 1996, 436–7.

[38] [1999] 1 AC 221.

[39] Ibid., at 231.

[40] See Burrows 2002a, 108–9; Rotherham 2002, 138.

silent on this issue.[41] Probably the best explanation as to why Easimind will be subrogated to Fred's rights to sue Nita in this situation is that the public interest demands that people who commit torts should suffer some kind of loss as a result – so as to deter people from committing torts. So Easimind is allowed to sue Nita in Fred's name for compensation for the damage she did to Fred's car because if it were not allowed to do this, Nita would be able to escape any kind of sanction for negligently damaging Fred's car.[42]

Third parties: II

Suppose that Ian has committed a tort and Ruth has suffered some kind of loss as a result. As a general rule, Ruth will not be entitled to sue anyone but Ian for compensation for the loss that she suffered as a result of Ian's tort.[43] However, there is one very important exception to this rule: if Ian was employed by Dawn when he committed his tort and there was a 'close and direct connection' between Ian's tort and what he was employed to do, then Dawn may be held *vicariously liable* in respect of Ian's tort. What this means is that Dawn will be treated in law as though she committed Ian's tort along with him. The result is that if Ruth is entitled to sue Ian for compensation for the loss she has suffered as a result of his tort, she will also be entitled to sue Dawn for such compensation.

Contribution[44]

Suppose Paul, an eight-year-old boy, was regularly beaten up at school by Alan, the school bully. Beth, the school's headmistress, was aware that Paul was

---

[41] *Important note.* This will *not* be the case if Nita negligently *injured* Fred and Fred claimed compensation for his injuries under a personal injury insurance policy with Easimind. In this situation, Easimind will *only* be subrogated to Fred's rights to sue Nita for compensation for his injuries if Fred's contract of insurance with Easimind provided this should happen. Furthermore, Fred will – unless his contract of insurance with Easimind provides otherwise – be free both to make a claim on his insurance contract with Easimind *and* sue Nita for damages in respect of his injuries: see *Dalby* v *India and London Life Assurance Co.* (1854) 15 CB 365, 139 ER 465; *Bradburn* v *Great Western Railway Co.* (1874) LR 10 Ex 1. It is thought that allowing Fred to do this will not confer an undeserved windfall on him – 'it is difficult to assert that he [would] be overcompensated [if he were allowed to make a claim against Easimind and Nita] given that no precise market value can be placed upon his pain and suffering and loss of amenity': Lewis 1999, 29.

[42] For criticisms of this explanation, see Lewis 1999, 44–6. It must be admitted that this explanation does not completely convince in the case we are considering. Even if Nita is held liable in this case, she will not ultimately have to foot the bill for the damage that she has done to Fred's car. When she crashed into Fred's car, she will almost certainly have been carrying liability insurance (otherwise known as 'third party' insurance – to be distinguished from 'first party' insurance where someone insures his person or property against the risk of it being damaged). So if she is held liable in this case, her liability insurer will pay the bill. However, it could be argued that even in this case Nita will face some kind of sanction for committing her tort – her liability insurance premiums will go up; and this is something that would not have happened had Fred's insurer not been subrogated to Fred's rights to sue Nita.

[43] It should be noted that if Ian is held liable to pay Ruth something by way of damages, Ian may be entitled to shift the cost of paying Ruth off onto a third party. This will be the case if Ian has insured against the possibility of being held liable to Ruth; in such a case, Ian will be able to require his liability insurer to indemnify him against the cost of compensating Ruth for the loss that she suffered as a result of his tort.

[44] No detailed account of the law on contribution will be given in this book. For such an account, the reader is advised to consult a standard textbook on the law of restitution.

being bullied but took no action to deal with the problem. In this case, Paul will of course be able to sue Alan in tort for compensation for the injuries he suffered when he was beaten up by Alan. But Paul will also be able to sue *Beth* for compensation for the injuries he suffered. The reason is that Beth owed Paul a non-contractual common law duty to take reasonable steps to stop him being bullied at school; she breached that duty by doing nothing to protect Paul from being beaten up by Alan; and Paul would not have been beaten up had Beth discharged the duty she owed Paul and intervened to stop Alan beating him up.

So suppose that Paul sues Beth for compensation for the injuries that he suffered as a result of being beaten up by Alan and that Paul succeeds in obtaining such compensation from Beth. In this situation, Beth will then be entitled to bring what is called a claim in contribution against Alan. In other words, she'll be able to sue Alan for a proportion of the compensatory damages that she has had to pay out to Paul. This is the result of s 1(1) of the Civil Liability (Contribution) Act 1978, which provides that: '... any person liable in respect of any damage suffered by another person may recover contribution from any other person liable in respect of the same damage.' How much will Beth be able to recover from Alan? Section 2(1) provides that 'the amount of the contribution recoverable from any person shall be such as may be found by the court to be just and equitable having regard to the extent of that person's responsibility for the damage in question'.

What happens if Paul sues Alan, and not Beth, for compensation for the injuries that he suffered? The same analysis applies: Alan, having compensated Paul, will then be entitled to bring a claim in contribution against Beth and thereby recoup from Beth at least some of the damages that he has had to pay out to Paul. This seems less than satisfactory. Why should Alan be allowed to shift some of the cost of compensating Paul onto Beth's shoulders? After all, it was Alan who was primarily responsible for Paul's being injured in this case. However, it is clear that Alan will be able to make a claim in contribution against Beth in this case, though presumably he would not be allowed to sue Beth for very much.[45]

What happens if Paul waives any rights he might have to sue Beth for compensation before he sues Alan for such compensation? If Alan pays up, can he then bring a claim in contribution against Beth? One would have thought not: when Paul sued Alan for compensation, Paul – having waived his rights against Beth – could not *at that time* have also sued Beth for such compensation. But in fact this makes no difference: Alan will be able to make a claim in contribution against Beth even if, at the time Paul sued Alan, Paul no longer had any rights to sue Beth. This is because s 1(3) of the 1978 Act provides that: '[a] person shall be liable to make contribution by virtue of subsection (1) above notwithstanding that he has ceased to be liable in respect of the damage in question since the time when the damage occurred, unless he has ceased to be liable by virtue of the expiry of a period of limitation ... which extinguished the right on which the claim against him in respect of the damage was based.'

---

[45] *K* v *P* [1993] Ch 140.

Nominal damages

Suppose Gary has committed a tort in relation to Nita but Nita has suffered no loss as a result of Gary's tort. In this case, Nita may still be entitled to sue Gary for a nominal sum in damages known as *nominal damages*.[46] Nita will only be entitled to sue Gary for such damages if the kind of tort committed by Gary is actionable *per se* – that is, actionable at the instance of the victim of that tort even though he or she has not suffered any loss as a result of that tort being committed.

Aggravated damages

Suppose Wendy has committed a tort in relation to Fred and Wendy acted in an arrogant and high-handed way in committing that tort. In such a case, Fred may be entitled to sue Wendy for *aggravated damages* – that is, damages designed to assuage Fred's feelings of outrage at the way in which he has been treated by Wendy.[47]

Exemplary damages

Suppose Carl has committed a tort in relation to Helen. Let's call the tort committed by Carl, *tort X*. In such a case, Helen may be entitled to sue Carl for *exemplary damages* – that is, damages designed to punish Carl for committing tort X. The English courts have placed very strict limits on when the victim of a tort may sue the person who committed that tort for exemplary damages.[48]

In the case we are considering, if Helen wants to sue Carl for exemplary damages, she will have to show first of all that Carl deserves to be punished for committing tort X. So Helen will have to show that Carl deliberately committed tort X or that his conduct in committing tort X was so outrageous that it is worthy of punishment.

Helen will have to show next that if she is not allowed to sue Carl for exemplary damages, Carl will be insufficiently punished for committing tort X. So if Carl has already been criminally punished for committing tort X, it is unlikely Helen will be allowed to sue Carl for exemplary damages; similarly, if Carl's committing tort X has resulted in him losing his job. Again, if Helen suffered a great deal of loss as a result of Carl's tort and is therefore entitled to sue him for a hefty sum by way of compensatory damages, Helen might be barred from suing Carl for exemplary damages on the ground that if she merely sues him for compensatory damages, he will be sufficiently punished for his conduct in committing tort X.

Finally, Helen will have to show that her case is the sort of case in which exemplary damages can be awarded. To do this she will have to show: (*a*) that Carl is a servant of the government and in committing tort X, Carl acted in an

---

[46] See below, pp. 663–5.
[47] See below, pp. 666–72.
[48] See below, pp. 673–8.

oppressive, arbitrary or unconstitutional manner; *or* (*b*) that Carl deliberately committed tort X because he thought he would gain more by committing tort X than he would have to pay Helen in compensatory damages; *or* (c) Helen is authorised by statute to sue Carl for exemplary damages in this sort of case.

Restitutionary damages

Suppose Vijay has committed a tort in relation to Karen. Again, let's call the tort committed by Vijay, *tort X*. Suppose further that Vijay obtained some kind of benefit as a result of committing tort X. In such a case, Karen may be entitled to sue Vijay for what we will call *type one restitutionary damages* – damages designed to make Vijay hand over to Karen the value of the benefit he obtained by committing tort X.[49] Alternatively, Karen may be entitled to sue Vijay for what we will call *type two restitutionary damages* – damages designed to make Vijay pay Karen a reasonable sum for the benefit he obtained by committing tort X.[50]

Type one restitutionary damages

If Vijay committed a tort in relation to Karen by *selling* Karen's property without her authority then Karen will be entitled to sue Vijay for type one restitutionary damages – in other words, she will be entitled to sue Vijay for damages equal to the value of the money Vijay made by selling Karen's property. So, for example, in *Oughton* v *Seppings*[51] the defendant was a sheriff who sold the claimant's pony. The defendant committed a tort in selling the claimant's pony and the claimant was held entitled to sue the defendant for damages equal to the value of the money the defendant received in return for the claimant's pony.

There are other occasions when the victim of a tort will be entitled to sue the tortfeasor for type one restitutionary damages. For instance, if Vijay has committed a tort in relation to Karen by infringing Karen's patent, Karen will be entitled to sue Vijay under s 61(1)(d) of the Patents Act 1977 for damages equivalent to the value of the profits made by Vijay in infringing her patent – but only so long as when Vijay infringed the patent he knew, or ought to have known, of the existence of the patent.

Type two restitutionary damages

If Vijay has committed a tort in relation to Karen by *using* Karen's property then Karen will be entitled to sue Vijay for type two restitutionary damages – damages equal to the sum a reasonable man would have paid Karen to use Karen's property in the way Vijay did.

So, for example, in *Strand Electric Engineering Co. Ltd* v *Brisford Entertainments*[52] a theatre group vacated a theatre and left behind some electric

---

[49] See below, pp. 686, 687–9.
[50] See below, pp. 686, 690–1.
[51] (1830) 1 B & Ad 241, 109 ER 776.
[52] [1952] 2 QB 246.

switch boards which they had hired from the claimants. The defendants took over the theatre. At the end of the switch boards' period of hire, the claimants demanded the switch boards back but the defendants refused to hand them over; instead, the defendants used the switch boards themselves. In so using the switch boards, the defendants committed a tort and it was held that the claimants were entitled to sue the defendants for damages equivalent to the sum a reasonable man would have paid the claimants to use their switch boards in the way the defendants did.

Injunction

Suppose Mary is about to commit a tort or is engaged in a course of conduct which involves her in committing a tort. In such a case the victim of the tort that Mary is committing or about to commit may be able to obtain an injunction requiring Mary not to commit that tort.[53] For example, if Mary commits a tort in relation to Tom by using her land in such a way that Tom's use and enjoyment of his land is unreasonably interfered with, Tom will – as a general rule – be able to obtain an injunction requiring Mary not to use her land in that way. The issuing of an injunction is a very effective way of preventing someone from committing a tort. This is because someone who breaches an injunction may be found to be in contempt of court and may be sent to prison as a result.

Specific restitution of goods

If John is in possession of Ruth's goods and he commits a tort by refusing to give them up, Ruth may be able to obtain an order from the courts requiring John to hand over her goods.[54]

BEYOND TORT LAW

We have already seen that tort law contains a number of rules and doctrines which specify when one person will be allowed to sue another for compensation for some kind of loss that he or she has suffered. If B has suffered some kind of loss and is entitled to sue A for compensation for that loss under these rules and doctrines lawyers usually say that B is entitled to sue A *in tort* for compensation for that loss or, alternatively, that A is liable *in tort* to compensate B for the loss that she has suffered.

But even if B is not entitled to sue A in tort for compensation for the loss that she has suffered, she may still be entitled to sue A for such compensation under some other area of law. If B is entitled to sue A for compensation under some other area of law, let's say that she's entitled to bring a *non-tortious* claim for compensation against A. There are a number of situations where someone will

---

[53] See below, pp. 708–17.
[54] See below, pp. 721–2.

be entitled to bring a non-tortious claim for compensation against someone else.

Appropriation

Suppose the State lawfully appropriates B's land. In such a case, B will not be able to sue the State in tort for compensation for the loss of her land. The State could not have committed a tort in taking B's land as it was allowed to do so. But B will still be entitled to bring a non-tortious claim against the State to be compensated for the loss of her land.[55]

The rule in *Rylands* v *Fletcher*

Suppose Fred keeps a tank of oil on his land. He regularly has the tank checked for leaks but, in between inspections, the tank – against all expectations – develops a leak during a particularly hot summer and some of the oil in the tank leaks onto land owned by Mary, Fred's neighbour, and damages Mary's roses. In this situation, Mary may be entitled to sue Fred for compensation for the damage done to her roses under what's called 'the rule in *Rylands* v *Fletcher*'. According to this rule, 'the person who, for his own purposes, brings on his land, and collects and keeps there anything likely to do mischief if it escapes, must keep it at his peril, and, if he does not do so, he is prima facie answerable for all the damage which is the natural consequence of its escape'.[56]

Let us assume that Mary *is* entitled to sue Fred for compensation for damage done to her roses under the rule in *Rylands* v *Fletcher*. There are some academics who will explain this result in the following terms: 'There is nothing mysterious about why Mary is entitled to sue Fred in this situation: she is entitled to sue him *in tort* for compensation for the damage done to her roses. Fred owed Mary a non-contractual common law duty to *ensure* that his oil did not leak onto Mary's land. So when Fred's oil did leak onto Mary's land, he committed a tort in relation to her and became liable to compensate her in tort for the loss suffered by her as a result of the leak – namely, the damage done to Mary's roses.'[57]

However, the better view is that Fred did *not* commit any kind of tort in this situation – at best, Fred owed Mary a non-contractual common law duty *to take care* that his oil did not leak onto her land, and he did not breach that duty. So Fred is held liable to compensate Mary for the damage done to her roses not because he committed a tort in allowing oil to leak onto Mary's land but

---

[55] The State's liability to compensate B arises out of the fact that its appropriating B's property will not be lawful unless it compensates B. For an interesting philosophical discussion of when it will, and when it will not, be legitimate for the State to appropriate B's property and compensate her for the loss of that property, see Goodin 1989.

[56] *Rylands* v *Fletcher* (1866) LR 1 Ex 265, 279 per Blackburn J. For a full account of the rule, see below, pp. 739–50.

[57] See Burrows 1983, 226, n. 23; Birks 1995, 41–2; Gardner 2002, 112; Ripstein 2002, 657; W&J, 63.

because it simply seems fair that he should.[58] As Carleton Kemp Allen explained:

> It is often said that in respect of peculiarly dangerous things, there is a 'duty' irrespective of negligence or wilful aggression, to 'insure' neighbours and others against damage. This use of the term 'duty' is unfortunate ... There is of course a duty of careful management of any material thing, whether it belong to the family of 'Rylands v Fletcher objects' or not; but it is difficult to see that there is any 'duty' to prevent a dangerous thing escaping through causes which have nothing to do with the maintainer's fault ... The true situation seems to be that he who maintains for his own advantage a peculiarly dangerous thing in proximity to others, necessarily imposes upon those others a risk of injury ... greater than is to be reasonably expected in the ordinary circumstances of social life, and it is therefore just and expedient that he himself should bear the risk of making good any damage to others which results from the maintenance of the object. This is certainly a liability; but it is a confusion of ideas to [say that it arises out of the breach of] a duty.[59]

If this is correct, then – in the situation we are considering – Mary is not entitled to sue Fred *in tort* for the damage done to her roses; no such claim is available to her as Fred did not commit a tort in relation to Mary in this situation. Rather, Mary is entitled to bring a *non-tortious* claim for compensation against Fred for the damage done to her roses.[60]

[58] *Important note.* In *Transco plc v Stockport Metropolitan Borough Council* [2003] 3 WLR 1467, the House of Lords showed itself to be deeply confused as to the basis of liability under the rule in *Rylands v Fletcher*. On the one hand, their Lordships made it clear that they thought that liability under that rule arose under the law on private nuisance (ibid., at [9], per Lord Bingham; at [52] per Lord Hobhouse; at [92], per Lord Walker) and therefore (as someone who creates, authorises, adopts or continues a private nuisance clearly commits a tort) that liability under the rule in *Rylands v Fletcher* is a form of tort liability. On the other hand, when their Lordships sought to justify the existence of the rule, they did *not* do so on the basis that a defendant who was held liable under it to pay damages to a claimant is held liable because he will have committed some kind of legal wrong in relation to the claimant (which would be the case if the defendant's liability was genuinely a form of tort liability) but on the basis that if a defendant has exposed a claimant's land to a risk of being harmed by using his land in a non-natural way, then it is only fair that, if that risk materialises, the defendant should be held liable to compensate the claimant: ibid., at [6] (per Lord Bingham) and [29] (per Lord Hoffmann).

[59] Allen 1931, 193–4. See also Holmes 1873, 653; Wright 1961, 86; Restatement Torts 2d (1965) §4 Comment b; Cane 1998, 165; Waddams 1998, 124–5.

[60] *Important note.* Having said that, it is not as yet widely acknowledged that you can have a non-tortious claim for compensation for some loss that you have suffered. As a result, academics are liable for the foreseeable future to regard claims for compensation under the rule in *Rylands v Fletcher* as arising 'in tort'. Likewise claims for compensation in public nuisance or under the Consumer Protection Act 1987, which are dealt with below, are likely for the foreseeable future to be classified, incorrectly, by the academic community as arising 'in tort'. (It took about 350 years for it to be widely acknowledged that claims to recover money paid over by a mistake or claims to be paid a reasonable sum for work done at another's request did not arise 'in contract' – as *Slade's Case* (1602) 4 Co Rep 92a seemed to suggest – but rather arose 'in restitution'. It is, of course, to be hoped that we will not have to wait a similar period of time for it to be recognised that one can have a non-tortious claim for compensation for loss that one has suffered.) This means that if, in an exam, you are asked to consider what 'claims in tort' are available to the parties in a particular problem situation, you should interpret the term 'claims in tort' very loosely, as not only covering claims in tort *stricto sensu* but also non-tortious claims for compensation. Another consequence of the fact that the existence of non-tortious claims for compensation is not yet widely acknowledged is that the procedural rules (such as the laws on limitation of actions and the rules on conflicts of law) which govern when claims can be brought

The Consumer Protection Act 1987

Suppose Dawn manufactures a microwave oven, taking the utmost care to use the highest quality components in manufacturing the oven. Suppose further that Paul eventually acquires the oven and one of its components fails, with the result that the oven blows up and Paul is injured. In this case, Paul will be entitled to sue Dawn for compensation under the Consumer Protection Act 1987. No one could seriously say in this situation that Dawn, in manufacturing the microwave oven, committed a tort in relation to Paul.[61] At best, Dawn owed Paul a non-contractual common law duty to take care to see that the microwave oven would not be unreasonably dangerous to use – and she did not breach that duty. So Paul's right to sue Dawn for compensation for his injuries will be non-tortious in nature.

Public nuisance

Suppose Gary creates a public nuisance and Wendy suffers some kind of special loss as a result – that is, loss over and above that suffered by the rest of the community as a result of Gary's actions. In such a case, Wendy will be entitled to bring a non-tortious claim against Gary for compensation for the loss that she has suffered.

Why can't we analyse Wendy's right to sue Gary in this case as arising in tort? The reason is that someone who creates a public nuisance will not commit a tort. To explain: someone will create a public nuisance if he unlawfully interferes with a *public* good – a good which, when it exists, may be enjoyed by everyone. So an example of a public good is a highway. If a highway exists then everyone may use it. So if A unlawfully interferes with a highway – either by unreasonably obstructing it or by unreasonably endangering other people who use the highway – then he creates a public nuisance. It follows from this that someone who creates a public nuisance commits a *public wrong* – not a civil wrong. The duty not to create a public nuisance is not imposed on someone for the benefit of any particular individual but for the benefit of the community as

---

and in what courts do not cover non-tortious claims for compensation. Such procedural rules only cover claims 'in contract', claims 'in tort' and (now) claims 'in restitution'. Until these procedural rules are updated to take account of the possibility that one can have a non-tortious claim for compensation, one should apply the procedural rules that govern claims 'in tort' to non-tortious claims for compensation. (The alternative – which is to say that there are *no* procedural rules governing non-tortious claims for compensation so that, for example, there is no period of limitation on when a non-tortious claim for compensation may be brought – is unthinkable.)

[61] The Act itself seems to acknowledge that someone who is held liable under it will not necessarily have committed a tort. Section 6(1) of the 1987 Act provides that 'Any damage for which a person is liable under [the Act] shall be *deemed* to have been caused . . . by that person's wrongful act, neglect or default' (emphasis added). This provision would not be necessary if, in the situation we are considering, Dawn's liability under the 1987 Act to compensate Paul for his injuries arose out of the fact that she had *actually* committed a tort in manufacturing the microwave oven that injured Paul. Surprisingly, Stanton 2003 argues (at 7) that claims brought under the 1987 Act 'may be stated to be for breach of statutory duty.' This is just wrong: the Act does *not* impose a statutory duty on various individuals and then specify what should happen when that duty is breached. All it does is require certain individuals in certain circumstances to pay compensation to other individuals.

a whole. And as the creation of a public nuisance does not amount to a civil wrong, it cannot amount to a tort.

The Human Rights Act 1998

Suppose a public authority breaches the statutory duty it owes Eric under s 6 of the Human Rights Act 1998 not to violate his human rights, as set out in the European Convention on Human Rights. We have already seen that such a breach will not of and in itself amount to a tort.[62] So if Eric is entitled to sue the public authority in question for compensation for violating his human rights, that claim will be non-tortious in nature.

Strictly speaking, a book on tort law need not concern itself with the issue of when one person will be entitled to bring a non-tortious claim for compensation against another. If it merely sets out the situations in which someone will commit a tort and explains what remedies will be available when someone commits a tort it will have done what it purports to do: provide the reader with a comprehensive guide to the current state of tort law in this country.

Yet, in Part IV of this book, we have chosen to set out – under the heading 'Alternative Sources of Compensation' – a number of situations in which one person will be entitled to bring a non-tortious claim for compensation against someone else. We have chosen to do this for the same reason that textbooks on contract law detail the circumstances in which someone will be entitled to bring a non-contractual claim to be paid for work that he has done for someone else.

Someone who wants to be paid for work he has done for someone else will want to know of *all* his possible avenues of redress – so a contract lawyer who only knows when someone will be entitled to bring a *contractual* claim to be paid for work he has done for someone else will not be of much help to him. A good contract lawyer will be in a position to advise someone who wants to be paid for work he has done of *all* his possible avenues of redress – he will not only be able to advise his client as to whether he can bring a *contractual* claim to be paid for the work he has done but he will also be in a position to advise his client as to whether he can bring a *non-contractual* claim to be paid for doing that work.

Similarly, someone who wants to be compensated for a loss that he has suffered will want to be advised of *all* his possible avenues of redress. So he will not want to be advised by a lawyer who can only tell him whether he is entitled to sue someone *in tort* for the compensation he wants. He will want to be advised by a lawyer who is also in a position to tell him whether he will be able to bring a non-tortious claim so as to be compensated for the loss he has suffered. So a good tort lawyer will not only be familiar with the situations in which someone who wants to be compensated for a loss that he has suffered will be able to bring a claim in tort for such compensation – he will also be familiar with the situations in which someone who wants to be compensated for a

---

[62] See above, pp. 11–12.

loss that he has suffered will be able to bring a non-tortious claim for such compensation. As the object of a tort textbook is to produce good tort lawyers, this textbook would be deficient if it did not make reference to at least some of the situations in which someone will be entitled to bring a non-tortious claim to be compensated for a loss that he has suffered. Thus the necessity for Part IV of this book.

3

TORT LAW AND ITS CRITICS

Perhaps the most pernicious myth about tort law which has been popularised by tort lawyers over the past 30 or 40 years goes as follows: The function of tort law is to determine when someone who has suffered loss at another's hands may sue that other to recover compensation for that loss.

An early statement of this view of tort law may be found in Cecil Wright's article 'Introduction to the law of torts'.[1] In that article, Wright observed:

> Arising out of the various and ever-increasing clashes of the activities of persons living in a common society, carrying on business in competition with fellow members of that society, owning property which may in any of a thousand ways affect the persons or property of others – in short, doing all the things that constitute modern living – there must of necessity be losses, or injuries of many kinds sustained as a result of the activities of others. *The purpose of the law of torts is to adjust these losses and to afford compensation for injuries sustained by one person as a result of the conduct of another.*[2]

In fact, this is incorrect. The function of tort law is *not* to determine whether or not someone who has suffered loss at another's hands will be entitled to recover compensation for that loss.

Tort law can be split up into two parts, corresponding to Parts II and III of this book. Each part serves a different function. The function of the first part – which we can call the *duty-imposing* part – is to help determine what specific duties we owe each other.[3] The function of the second part – which we can call the *remedial* part – is to help determine what remedies will be available when one of these duties is breached. In other words, the function of the remedial part of tort law is to determine what remedies will be available when someone commits a tort. So if A has caused B to suffer some kind of loss but he has done so *without committing a tort*, the law of tort takes *no view* – one way or the other – as to whether B should be entitled to sue A for compensation for the loss she has suffered at A's hands. The question of whether or not B should be entitled to sue A for compensation for the loss she has suffered at A's hands *has nothing to do* with either the duty-imposing part of tort law or the remedial part of tort law. The duty-imposing part of tort law is not engaged because that part of tort law is concerned to help determine what *specific* duties we owe to each other and the question here is whether the law should impose a duty on A to pay *money* to B.[4] The remedial part of tort law is not engaged here because that part

---

[1] Wright 1944, 238.
[2] Ibid. (emphasis added).
[3] This function is of course not performed exclusively by tort law: contract law and the criminal law also help to determine what specific duties we owe to each other.

36

of tort law is purely concerned to determine what remedies will be available when someone commits a tort – and no tort has been committed here.

All this must seem very strange to those who learned their tort law in the 1960s, 1970s and 1980s. Sadly, Cecil Wright's view of the function of tort law has won almost universal acceptance in such quarters.[5] For example, *Prosser and Keeton on the Law of Torts* – the classic American textbook on tort law – tells us that '[the] law of torts . . . is concerned with the allocation of losses arising out of human activities; and since these cover a wide scope, so does this branch of the law'.[6] It then goes on to quote with approval the above passage from Wright's article. The late John Fleming agreed with the view taken by the editors of *Prosser and Keeton*. In the ninth edition of his *The Law of Torts*, he wrote, 'The law of torts is . . . concerned with the allocation of losses incident to man's activities in modern society.'[7] Once again, Wright's article was quoted with approval. Closer to home, the 16th edition of *Winfield and Jolowicz on Tort* observes that 'tort [law] is concerned with the allocation and prevention of losses, which are bound to occur in our society . . . It is the business of the law of tort to determine when the law will and when it will not grant redress for damage suffered . . .'[8] Paula Giliker and Gillian Beckwith take the same view: 'Tort law determines who bears the loss which results from the defendant's actions.'[9] As do David Howarth and Janet O'Sullivan: 'The primary task of tort law is to define the circumstances in which a person whose interests have been harmed by another may seek compensation.'[10] As do the comparative lawyers Walter van Gerven, Jeremy Lever and Pierre Larouche: 'Tort law . . . consists of a body of rules determining the circumstances, and conditions, under which harm suffered by a victim will be borne by another person, most frequently, the perpetrator of a harm . . . Tort law is therefore about [the] (re-)distribution of losses . . .'[11] As does the legal philosopher Jules Coleman: 'Tort law is about messes. A mess has been made, and the only question before the court is, who is to clean it up?'[12] Unsurprisingly, this view of tort law has become popular among judges – if only because judges read law books and tend to believe what they read in them. So, for example, Lord Bingham remarked in the case of *Fairchild* v *Glenhaven Funeral Services Ltd* that, 'The overall object of tort law is

---

[4] It will be recalled that a specific duty is a duty to do something *other* than pay money to someone else: see above, p. 10.

[5] There are some honourable exceptions: see Weir 2004, 1: '. . . the prime function of the area of social regulation we call "tort" is to determine when one person must pay another compensation for harm *wrongfully* caused' (emphasis in original); GS&Z, 38: 'Tort law . . . provides injured parties with redress from those who have wronged . . . them'; also Oliphant 2002, at 26.

[6] Keeton 1984, 6.

[7] Fleming 1998, 5.

[8] W&J, 1, 3. See also M. Jones 2002, 1.

[9] Giliker & Beckwith 2000, 1.

[10] Howarth & O'Sullivan 2000, 1.

[11] Van Gerven, Lever & Larouche 2000, 13. See also Zweigert & Kötz 1998, 597: '. . . it is the function of the law of tort to determine when the victim ought to be able to shift on to the shoulders of another the harm to which he has been exposed.'

[12] Coleman 1998, 302.

to define cases in which the law may justly hold one party liable to compensate another.'[13]

Why is this misconception about the function of tort law so pernicious? The reason is that its widespread popularity has given rise to an equally widespread perception that tort law is in dire need of reform. The point can be illustrated by reference to the case of *Roe v Minister of Health*.[14] In that case, two patients went into hospital for minor surgery and came out permanently paralysed. In both cases, the hospital surgeon had injected the patient's spine with nupercaine to anaesthetise him and in both cases paralysis had resulted because the nupercaine was contaminated. The nupercaine was contaminated because before it was injected into the patients' spines it was stored in ampoules which were placed in phenol, a disinfectant. The ampoules had, unknown to everyone, tiny invisible cracks in them through which the phenol had percolated, contaminating the nupercaine. The patients in *Roe* sued the hospital in tort, seeking to obtain compensation for the losses they had suffered as a result of their paralysis. Their claims failed.

Now – if one thinks that the function of tort law is to determine when someone who has suffered loss at another's hands may sue that other for compensation for that loss, one would be entitled to think that tort law let down the patients in this case. There is a good case for saying that the patients in *Roe* *should* have been allowed to sue the hospital for compensation for the losses suffered by them. The hospital caused the claimants to suffer those losses and was in a much better position to bear those losses than the claimants. If the hospital had been ordered to compensate the claimants for the losses suffered by them, it would have passed on the costs of meeting the judgment against it to its insurers (who would have undertaken to meet the costs of any liabilities incurred by the hospital). The hospital's insurers would, in turn, have passed on the costs of indemnifying the hospital against its liabilities to the claimants in *Roe* to its customers in the form of fractionally higher premiums.

So – if the patients in *Roe* had been allowed to sue the hospital for compensation for the losses suffered by them as a result of their being paralysed, the two patients in *Roe* would not have had to shoulder the costs of the accident in *Roe*. Instead, hundreds of thousands of people – the hospital's insurers' customers – would have borne those costs instead. Would it have been better if the costs of the accident in *Roe* had been borne by the two patients in *Roe* or by the hundreds of thousands of people who were the customers of the hospital's insurers in *Roe*? To ask the question is to answer it: it would of course have been better if the costs of the accident in *Roe* had been borne by the customers of the hospital's insurers. So it would have been better if the two patients in *Roe* had been allowed to sue the hospital in *Roe* for compensation for the losses suffered by them as a result of their being paralysed. It follows that if you think that the function of tort law is to determine when someone who has suffered loss at another's hands will be entitled to sue another for compensation for that

---

[13] [2003] 1 AC 32 at [9].
[14] [1954] 2 QB 66.

loss, you will think that tort law failed the patients in the *Roe* case – it did not allow them to sue the hospital for compensation when it should have.

But the truth is more complicated. The reason why the patients' claims in *Roe* failed was that the patients could not establish that the hospital had committed a *civil wrong* in the way it treated the patients. True, the duty-imposing part of tort law imposed on the hospital a duty to treat the patients with a reasonable degree of care and skill; but the hospital fully discharged that duty. The patients were treated in accordance with best medical practice. No one could have foreseen that treating the patients in the way they were treated would expose them to a risk of paralysis. Of course, if the duty-imposing part of tort law had imposed on the hospital a duty to *ensure* that the patients did not suffer any kind of long-term harm as a result of being treated by the hospital, then the patients would have been allowed to sue the hospital in tort for compensation for their injuries. Each of the patients would have been able to argue, 'The hospital committed a civil wrong in relation to me in treating me the way it did – it owed me a duty to *ensure* that I did not suffer any kind of long-term harm as a result of being treated by the hospital, and it breached that duty.' So if any part of tort law was to 'blame' for the fact that the patients in *Roe* were not allowed to sue for compensation for their injuries, it was the duty-imposing part, which failed to impose on the hospital a duty to ensure that the patients in *Roe* did not suffer any long-term harm as a result of being treated in the hospital.

But was the duty-imposing part of tort law at fault for not imposing such a duty on the hospital? Would it be reasonable for the law to say that a hospital owes each of its patients a duty to *ensure* that that patient does not suffer any kind of long-term harm as a result of its treatment of that patient? Again, to ask the question is to answer it: of course it would not be reasonable for the law to impose such a duty on a hospital.[15] The most a hospital can reasonably be expected to do for its patients is to treat them with a reasonable degree of care and skill – and, as we have already seen, the duty-imposing part of tort law *does* impose a duty on hospitals to do exactly that. Unfortunately for the patients in *Roe*, they simply could not establish that *that* duty had been breached. So *tort law* did *not* let down the patients in *Roe*. The duty-imposing part of tort law would have acted in a wholly unreasonable fashion had it imposed on the hos-

---

[15] Though see Gardner 2002 for a different view. Generally, the law will only impose on you a duty to *ensure* that *x* happens if you have promised in a *contract* to ensure that *x* will happen. If you do this, it is entirely reasonable for the law to impose on you a duty to ensure that *x* will happen – if you did not want to be subject to such an onerous duty, you should not have made the contract in the first place. The fact that only a contract can usually give rise to a duty to *ensure* that *x* happens led Stapleton 1997 to argue that the crucial difference between liability in contract and liability in tort is that all a claimant can sue for in tort are damages designed to put her in the position she would have been in had the defendant treated her reasonably (the 'normal expectancies' measure of damages), while a claimant can sue in contract to be put in the position that the other party to the contract contractually guaranteed to put her in (the 'entitled result' measure of damages) – whether or not it was reasonable to expect to be put in that position. This is to confuse an *accidental* feature of liability in tort and contract with an *essential* feature. For some trenchant criticisms of Stapleton's views, see Friedmann 1997 and Smith 1997.

pital in *Roe* the kind of duty that would have allowed the patients in *Roe* to sue the hospital *in tort* for compensation for their injuries. The only duty that it was reasonable for the duty-imposing part of tort law to impose on the hospital was amply discharged by the hospital, thus making it impossible for the claimants to establish that the hospital had done anything *wrong* in the way it treated the claimants.

So it would have been quite wrong to allow the patients in *Roe* to sue the hospital *in tort* for compensation for the injuries they suffered. Of course, it may be they should have been allowed to bring some other kind of claim against the hospital – what we have called a claim for 'compensation without wrong-doing'.[16] So it may be that *the law as a whole* could be blamed for failing to provide the claimants with a means of obtaining compensation for their injuries; but *tort law* was blameless in this regard.

All of which is not to say that tort law is not in need of reform – it is merely to point out that critiques of tort law which attack tort law on the ground that it sometimes does not afford a remedy to someone who has suffered loss at another's hands when, in justice, that person ought to be allowed to obtain such a remedy rest on a false premise. They wrongly assume that the function of tort law is to determine when someone who has suffered a loss at another's hands will be entitled to sue that other for compensation for that loss.[17] Criticising tort law on this ground is akin to criticising this book on the basis that it does not do a very good job of teaching people how to keep their motor-bikes in good repair. As it is not the function of this book to teach people the art of motorcycle maintenance, the criticism is completely inappropriate. Given that the function of tort law is to help determine what specific duties we owe each other and to determine what remedies will be available when one of those duties is breached, tort law can only be judged according to how well or badly it does *that* job. A case for saying that tort law is in need of reform can only be made out by showing that the duty-imposing part of tort law operates in an oppressive, arbitrary or unduly permissive fashion in helping to determine what specific duties we owe each other; or by showing that the rules laid down by the remedial part of tort law that determine what remedies will be available when someone commits a tort are inadequate or unjust or irrational or undesirable.

---

[16] See above, pp. 37–8. In fact, Kennedy 2001 recommended (at chapter 26, para 35) that patients who are injured in hospital should be able to recover compensation for their injuries without having to show that their injuries were due to anyone's acting negligently or doing anything else legally wrong. However, this proposal has been rejected on grounds of cost: Donaldson 2003, 15.

[17] For examples of such critiques of tort law see Abel 1994, 102–5; Cane 1999a; Conaghan & Mansell 1999. For a critique of such critiques, which takes the same view of tort law as that taken here, see Goldberg 2002, 1519: 'we ... need to ask less ... of tort. In particular, we ... have to wean ourselves from the habit of treating tort as a means of devising *ad hoc* solutions to per-ceived social ills. By this I do not mean to say that tort ought not to address contemporary problems – it does and it should. Rather, I am suggesting that we must recapture the idea that tort cases are concerned with the focused task of identifying and remedying instances in which an actor has wronged another, as opposed to providing localized compensation or insurance schemes, regulating antisocial conduct for the good of society, or the like. Relatedly, we ... have to recapture a sense of tort as a body of law, rather than as an occasion for doing whatever seems right or practical at the time.' See, to the same effect, Klar 1998; also Morgan 2004, 394–400.

Is tort law in need of reform? Almost certainly. We tend not, in this book, to go in for criticisms of the duty-imposing part of tort law, but a number of obvious criticisms can be made of the rules laid down by the remedial part of tort law that govern what remedies will be available when someone commits a tort; those criticisms are set out in Part III of this book.[18] One rule that is often the subject of criticism is the *compensation rule* – that is, the rule that says that if A commits a tort in relation to B, B will normally be entitled to sue A for compensation for the losses suffered by her as a result of A's tort. Many people think that the law should not give effect to this rule. For example, the legal philosopher John Finnis argues that 'our law is simplistic, unbalanced, and to some extent unjust and unjustifiable in maintaining a quasi-universal rule of full compensation for [the] . . . losses caused by [A's] breach of [a] duty [that he owes] to [B], however minor that breach and whatever the relative resources of [A] and [B]'.[19] Is this criticism justified?

This is a very large question which we can perhaps reduce to manageable proportions by considering a homely analogy. Suppose that Wendy is thinking of going to Hawaii on holiday; the holiday will cost £2,500. She asks you whether, all things considered, she should go. In advising her, you would probably ask her three questions. First, why do you want to go to Hawaii – what will you get out of it? Suppose she says she'd like to go because she's heard it's a good place to get a good tan and eat good seafood. Once you know that, you would then ask her: Is there a cheaper way of getting a good tan and eating good seafood? If there is – say going to Marseille on holiday is just as good in these respects and would only cost £1,000 – then you would advise her not to go to Hawaii, and to go to Marseille instead. If there isn't, you would then ask Wendy: Is getting a good tan and eating good seafood so important that it's worth spending £2,500 of your hard-earned money on it? If it isn't, then you would advise her not to go to Hawaii. But if it is, then you would conclude that she should go to Hawaii.

We can adopt the same procedure here to determine whether the law is justified in giving effect to the compensation rule. We begin by asking: Why does the law give effect to the compensation rule – what end or goal is it trying to achieve in giving effect to this rule? Once we have identified what this end or goal is – call it the *compensation goal* – we can then ask: Is giving effect to the compensation rule the most cost-effective way of achieving the compensation goal? Is there in fact a cheaper way of giving effect to the compensation goal? If there is, then we would conclude that Finnis is right: the law should not give effect to the compensation rule. But if there is not, we would then ask: Is achieving the compensation goal so important that the costs involved in giving effect to the compensation rule represent an acceptable price to pay to achieve that goal? If the answer is 'no', then we would again conclude that the law should not give effect to the compensation rule. But if the answer is 'yes', then

---

[18] See, for example, pp. 529, 561–3, 607, 651–3, 679–81, below.
[19] Finnis 2002, 656.

we would conclude that the law should give effect to the compensation rule and criticisms of the rule such as Finnis's are misguided.

So – let's start with the first question. Why does the law give effect to the compensation rule? To help us out on this question, we can assemble a panel of tort scholars to discuss this issue. Call the members of the panel, John, Paul, Mary, Eric, Beth and Ruth. Their discussion as to the justifiability or otherwise of the compensation rule might go as follows:

John: It's very simple. The law holds tortfeasors liable to pay compensatory damages to the victims of their torts in order to *deter* people from breaching the tortious duties that they owe each other. If you know you are going to be held liable to pay damages if you breach a tortious duty owed to another, then you are less likely to breach that duty.[20]

Paul: That's too simplistic. I admit that *punitive* damages – damages designed to punish someone for committing a tort – are awarded to deter people from committing torts; but it seems strange to say that the law gives effect to the compensation rule for the same reason. If the law's only concern were to deter people from committing torts, it is hard to see why it would seek to do so by giving effect to the compensation rule. Why would it not simply hold a tortfeasor liable to pay a sum to the victim of his tort graduated according to the tortfeasor's means and his degree of fault in committing his tort? Indeed, why would the law hold the tortfeasor liable to pay damages to the *victim of his tort*? Why would it not hold him liable to pay damages to the State instead? And if awards of compensatory damages are made in order to deter people from committing torts, why is it that it is usually only the *victims* of torts who can claim such damages? Why does the law not say that *anyone* who has suffered loss as a result of a tort's being committed is allowed to sue for damages in respect of that loss? Furthermore, if the law gives effect to the compensation rule in order to deter people from committing torts, why does the law allow people to take out liability insurance to protect themselves against the consequences of being held liable to pay other people damages in tort under the compensation rule?

Mary: I agree – it is completely implausible to say that the law gives effect to the compensation rule in order to deter people from committing torts. My own view is that the law gives effect to the compensation rule because justice demands that if A commits a tort in relation to B, A should compensate B for the losses that she has suffered as a result of A's tort.

Paul: But I always thought justice related to the distribution of goods among a community: justice demands that they be distributed fairly among the members of the community.[21] So what's justice got to do with the question of whether people should be held liable for the harm caused by their torts?

Mary: What you're talking about is one form of justice – distributive justice. But once all the goods have been shared out fairly, you've got to have some way of preventing people interfering with the distribution and taking more than their fair share. So if A takes goods which properly belong to B, justice demands that A be made to give the goods back. We call this form of justice, corrective justice. It's a kind of handmaiden to distributive justice – it ensures that fair distributions of goods aren't wrongfully disturbed.[22] So if A commits a tort and deprives B of a good that B was entitled to, the

---

[20] See Cane 2002, 34–5, 60–2.
[21] See Aristotle, *Nicomachean Ethics*, V.3.
[22] See Gordley 1995.

law holds A liable to compensate B for the loss of that good in order to restore the just distribution of goods that obtained before A committed his tort.

Paul: but the law holds A liable whether or not the good which B was deprived of was fairly distributed to her in the first place. And aren't there some goods, such as body parts, which *can't* be distributed but which *are* routinely the subject of tort actions – as when someone sues someone else for negligently breaking her leg or causing her brain damage? How can one say that *those* kinds of tort actions are concerned to restore a 'just distribution of goods'?

Eric: I agree. The problem with Mary's explanation is that her conception of corrective justice is far too narrow. In fact, corrective justice has nothing whatsoever to do with distributive justice: it stands on its own two feet. Corrective justice demands that if A wrongs B, A should put B back in the position she would have been in had A not wronged her. Once you realise that, it's easy to see that the law gives effect to the compensation rule because corrective justice demands that if A breaches a duty owed to B, A should be held liable to compensate B for the losses that she has suffered as a result of his breach, thereby putting her in the position she would have been in had the breach not occurred.[23]

Paul: Okay – but I don't see that really gets us very far in understanding why the law gives effect to the compensation rule. The law may give effect to the compensation rule because corrective justice demands that those who wrong others put those others in the position they would have been in had the wrong not occurred.[24] But why does the law give effect to the demands of corrective justice? And you can't say, 'Because corrective justice demands that it does' because that gets us nowhere.

Beth: Exactly. I wonder if what we're missing at the moment is some sort of 'psychological' explanation of the compensation rule. It may be that the reason why the law gives effect to the compensation rule goes as follows. If A wrongs B, B is liable to feel extremely aggrieved and resentful towards A. If the law doesn't do anything to assuage that feeling, B may try and 'get her own back' on A, and a feud will develop between A and B – which is bad for everyone. So the law requires A to pay compensatory damages to B in an attempt to pacify B and preserve the social order.[25]

Paul: That seems to me a good explanation of why the law will sometimes award *aggravated* damages to the victim of a tort, but not necessarily a good explanation of why the law will routinely award *compensatory* damages to the victim of a tort – after all some torts can be committed quite innocently and it's hard to see why, where a tort has been committed without any fault on the part of the tortfeasor, the victim of the tort should feel at all aggrieved or resentful towards the tortfeasor. Even a dog can distinguish between someone's carelessly tripping over him and someone's deliberately kicking him.

Ruth: I think there's something to Beth's explanation, but my explanation is slightly different. If A wrongs B, B has a natural right to take action against A to force him to make up for his wrong. However, the law can't tolerate the disturbance to the social order that this would involve. So it forbids B from taking direct action against A and instead provides B with a peaceful means of getting A to make up for his wrong by

---

[23] See Weinrib 1995; Coleman 1993; 2001.

[24] Though see Zipursky 2003, pointing out that in a case where A has committed a tort in relation to B, the law – in giving effect to the compensation rule – does not actually *require* A to put B in the position she would have been in had A's tort not been committed; it merely gives B a *power* to sue A for damages that will have the effect of putting her in the position she would have been in had A's tort not been committed. See also Goldberg 2003b, 577.

[25] See Kelly 1967; Kelley 1990; Goldberg 2003c, 1341–2; Sherwin 2003.

allowing B to sue A for compensation for the losses that she has suffered as a result of A's wrong. So the law gives effect to the compensation rule in order to provide the victim of a wrong with a peaceful means of obtaining redress from the person who committed that wrong.[26]

Paul: But it's not at all clear that if you wrong me I have a 'natural right' to force you to make up for your wrong[27] – after all, if it were, we would hardly be having this discussion, would we?

My own view is that a modified form of Beth's explanation provides us with a good explanation of why the law gives effect to the compensation rule. If A wrongs B, B won't necessarily feel aggrieved or resentful towards A for wronging her. But if A's wrong has resulted in B suffering some *uncompensated losses*, B *will* feel very resentful and aggrieved if A does not then offer to compensate her for those losses. The reason is quite complicated but it goes as follows. The duty A breached when he wronged B was imposed on A for B's benefit. In other words, it was imposed on A because B was – in the eyes of the law – important: someone worth going out of your way for.

Now – if A genuinely regrets having breached the duty he owed B, he will want to undo the effects of his breach. In other words, he will want to compensate B for any uncompensated losses that she has suffered as a result of A's breach. So if A does not offer to compensate B for those losses, he will signal to B that he does not regret his breach. But if he does not regret his breach, that must mean he does not think he should have been subject to the duty that he breached. In other words, if he does not regret his breach, he must not think that B is as important as the law thinks B is. So if A does not offer to compensate B for the uncompensated losses she has suffered as a result of A's breach, he will signal to B that he thinks that she is a person of little worth, certainly not worth the bother that the law demanded he take over her. Such a message is liable to make B very aggrieved and resentful.

So every time someone commits a tort and the victim of the tort suffers uncompensated losses as a result, a potential flashpoint is created in the relationship between the victim of the tort and the tortfeasor. Either the tortfeasor can offer to compensate the victim of the tort for the uncompensated losses that she has suffered as a result of his tort – in which case, all is well and good. Or the tortfeasor can refuse to do any such thing – in which case, the victim of the tort will feel very aggrieved and resentful towards the tortfeasor and attempt to get her own back, with deleterious consequences for the social order. In order to prevent this flashpoint arising, the law does not give the tortfeasor the opportunity to refuse to compensate the victim of his tort for the uncompensated losses that she has suffered as a result of his tort. Instead, it requires him to compensate her for those losses. So I agree with Beth that ultimately the law gives effect to the compensation rule in order to help preserve the social order – but I take a somewhat different view as to why someone's committing a tort has the potential to destabilise society.[28]

Our view is that Paul's explanation of why the law gives effect to the compensation rule is the best on offer at the moment.[29] If Paul's account of what the

---

[26] See Zipursky 1998a; 2002, 639–44.

[27] See Finnis 2002, 656.

[28] For an earlier attempt to present such an explanation as to why the law gives effect to the compensation rule, see McBride 2000.

[29] A couple of criticisms of it could be made. First, Paul's explanation seems inconsistent with the fact that if A commits a tort in relation to B and B dies as a result, B's estate will be allowed to sue A for compensation in respect of any actionable losses suffered by B as a result of A's tort before B died: Law Reform (Miscellaneous Provisions) Act 1934, s 1(1). If B is dead, then there is no potential flashpoint

law is trying to achieve in giving effect to the compensation rule is correct, we can then move on to ask – is there a cheaper way of preventing dangerous feuds arising between someone who commits a tort and the victim of a tort?

In order to answer this question, we must first have some idea of how much it costs us as a society to give effect to the compensation rule. Let's call this, the *social cost* of giving effect to the compensation rule. In calculating the social cost of giving effect to the compensation rule, we must not disregard the *incidental benefits* that we obtain by giving effect to the compensation rule. For example, while it cannot be said that the *purpose* of giving effect to the compensation rule is to deter people from committing torts, it cannot be denied that the existence of the compensation rule may *in fact* deter people from breaching the duties they owe other people. Incidental benefits like these help to keep down the social cost of giving effect to the compensation rule and must be taken into account in calculating that cost. So – in order to determine the social cost of giving effect to the compensation rule, we must first add up the costs involved in giving effect to the compensation rule and then make a deduction to take account of the value of the incidental benefits obtained by giving effect to the compensation rule.

The table below sets out in the left hand column the costs involved in giving effect to the compensation rule and in the right hand column the incidental benefits obtained by giving effect to the compensation rule. So the social cost of giving

COSTS INVOLVED IN GIVING EFFECT TO THE COMPENSATION RULE	INCIDENTAL BENEFITS[30]
(1) Costs of running courts to hear tort cases (2) Costs of employing lawyers to argue tort cases (3) Costs of recovering damages from a defendant against whom an award has been made in a tort case (4) Costs of taking out liability insurance to protect oneself against the possibility of being sued for damages in tort (5) Costs arising out of damages awards being made against defendants in tort cases (bankruptcies etc) (6) Costs arising out of defendants taking unnecessary precautions to avoid the slightest possibility that they might be sued in tort	(1) Relief to public purse from having cost of treating and maintaining victims of accidents borne by defendants and their liability insurers rather than by the State (through the NHS and social security payments) (2) Benefits arising out of damages awards being made to the victims of torts (minimisation of disruption caused to their life by tort being committed etc.) (3) Benefits arising out of fact that people may be deterred by existence of the compensation rule from committing torts

Table 1. Calculating the social cost of giving effect to the compensation rule

---

in the relationship between A and B that needs to be eliminated. However, the rule used to be that B's estate could *not* sue in this situation – which tends to strengthen Paul's explanation. Secondly, Paul's explanation does not explain why, if A commits a tort and damages B's property as a result, A will be held liable for the damage done to B's property even if B has already obtained full compensation for the damage done from her insurance company (see above, pp. 25–6). Paul's explanation, admittedly, does not account for why A is held liable in this case. It may be that A is held liable here so as to help ensure that people like A will be deterred from breaching the tortious duties they owe others (ibid.).

[30] For a lively and always interesting account of the incidental benefits of giving effect to the compensation rule – which does not, however, come anywhere close to dealing with the actual *purpose* of giving effect to the compensation rule – see Koenig & Rustad 2001.

effect to the compensation rule equals the sum of the costs set out in the left hand column *minus* the sum of the incidental benefits set out in the right hand column.

It may be that the social cost of giving effect to the compensation rule will actually be a *negative* figure. In this case, the compensation rule 'pays for itself' – the incidental benefits obtained by giving effect to the compensation rule are so substantial that they outweigh the costs involved in giving effect to the compensation rule. If this is the case, then we should not abolish the compensation rule, anymore than someone who wants to go on holiday to Hawaii should turn down an offer to pay her to go on holiday to Hawaii. However, it is likely that the social cost of giving effect to the compensation rule will turn out to be a *positive* figure; in other words, the total costs involved in giving effect to the compensation rule will outweigh the incidental benefits obtained by giving effect to the compensation rule. If this is the case, then the compensation rule should be abolished if we can show that there is a cheaper way of preventing dangerous feuds arising between the victims of torts and tortfeasors.

One obvious alternative strategy would be to set up a *victims' loss compensation scheme,* under which victims of torts will be able to obtain compensation from the State for the losses suffered by them as a result of those torts being committed. If such a scheme existed, then if A committed a tort in relation to B, B would not suffer any uncompensated losses as a result of A's tort, and there would therefore be no need for A to do anything to 'undo' his tort – and so A would not have the opportunity to refuse to 'undo' his tort and thereby insult B. But would setting up such a loss compensation scheme represent a cheaper way of preventing tensions arising between victims of torts and tortfeasors than the current system, under which the law attempts to prevent those tensions arising by giving effect to the compensation rule?

In order to answer this question, we would need to calculate the social cost of giving effect to a victims' loss compensation scheme. This cost would be calculated in exactly the same way as we would calculate the cost of giving effect to the compensation rule: we add up the costs involved in giving effect to a victims' loss compensation scheme and subtract the incidental benefits involved in giving effect to such a scheme. Going back to Table 1, while costs (3)–(6) in the left-hand column would *not* be incurred under a victims' loss compensation scheme, costs (1)–(2) would be; and added to these would be the costs of raising the money needed to fund and run such a scheme. Turning to the right hand column in Table 1, while incidental benefit (2) would also be obtained under a victims' loss compensation scheme, benefits (1) and (3) would not be obtained. So – it turns out – the social cost of running a victims' loss compensation scheme will be smaller than the social cost of giving effect to the compensation rule *if* the sum of costs (3)–(6) in Table 1 *minus* the sum of benefits (1) and (3) in Table 1 *exceeds* the cost of raising the money required to fund and run a victims' loss compensation scheme. It is beyond the scope of this book to make such a calculation – but it is unlikely that the social cost of running a victims' loss compensation scheme will be smaller than the social cost of giving effect to the compensation rule.

If this is the case, how about a *no-fault loss compensation scheme?* Under such a scheme, *anyone* who suffered a loss would be entitled to claim compensation for that loss. There would be three major differences between this kind of compensation scheme and a victims' loss compensation scheme, all arising out of the fact that an applicant for compensation under a no fault compensation scheme would not need to show that he was the victim of a tort to qualify for compensation. First, the courts and lawyers would play a minimal role in the running of a no-fault loss compensation scheme. Secondly, the amount paid out in compensation under a no-fault loss compensation scheme would dwarf the amount paid out in compensation under a victims' loss compensation scheme. Thirdly, people generally would obtain a lot more protection against having their lives disrupted through the 'slings and arrows of outrageous fortune' than they would under a victims' loss compensation scheme – a lot more people would qualify for protection under a no-fault loss compensation scheme than would be the case under a victims' loss compensation scheme.

A no-fault compensation scheme would be just as efficacious as the compensation rule in preventing dangerous feuds arising between victims of torts and tortfeasors – but would the social cost of running such a compensation scheme be less than the social cost involved in giving effect to the compensation rule? To find out the answer to this, one must first add up costs (1)–(6) in Table 1 and then subtract the value of benefit (3) in Table 1. Let's say the resulting figure is £x. One must then find out how much it would cost to fund and run a no-fault loss compensation scheme and subtract from that the value of the benefits that will arise out of making compensation payments to those who would not qualify for compensation under the compensation rule. Let's say the resulting figure is £y. If £x is more than £y, then the social cost of running a no-fault loss compensation scheme will be *less* than the social cost of giving effect to the compensation rule, and the compensation rule should be abolished in favour of a no-fault loss compensation scheme. Again, it is beyond the scope of this book to make that kind of calculation – but it seems likely that £x will not be more than £y.

There is a third alternative that *may* provide a more cost-effective way of eliminating the tensions that arise when someone commits a tort in relation to someone else. That is to have a *mixed system* under which certain categories of people who have suffered loss are compensated for those losses under no-fault loss compensation schemes, while the compensation rule is given effect to in cases where the victim of a tort has suffered loss that is not covered by one of these no-fault compensation schemes. This is, for example, the system they have in New Zealand where those who suffer personal injuries in accidents are compensated under a no-fault compensation scheme, while victims of torts who suffer other kinds of losses are left free to claim compensation for those losses under the compensation rule.[31] Calculating the social cost involved in administering a mixed system such as this would be extremely difficult, but it is certainly very possible that the social cost of running such a mixed system

---

[31] The New Zealand Accident Compensation Scheme is described in more detail below, at pp. 791–2.

would be smaller than the social cost of giving full effect to the compensation rule. So it may be that the current state of affairs – under which the law gives full effect to the compensation rule when the victim of a tort suffers loss as a result of that tort being committed – cannot be justified. It may be that the law's aims in giving effect to the compensation rule could be more cheaply achieved if we switched to a mixed system, under which certain categories of people who suffer loss are protected under no-fault compensation schemes while the compensation rule is given effect to in cases where victims of torts suffered losses which are not covered by those schemes.

But equally it may be the case that giving full effect to the compensation rule is actually the cheapest way of eliminating the tensions that would otherwise arise when a tort has been committed. If this is the case, then our inquiry into the justifiability of the law's giving effect to the compensation rule can move on to the third stage – that of asking, 'Are the benefits of eliminating the tensions that would otherwise arise when a tort has been committed outweighed by the social cost of giving effect to the compensation rule?' To put the same question another way, 'If the compensation rule were abolished tomorrow, there might be a rise in revenge attacks on tortfeasors by the victims of their torts but is the social cost involved in giving effect to the compensation rule a price worth paying to ensure that these attacks do not occur?'[32] Again, it is beyond the scope of this book to answer this question – our purpose here is simply to identify the questions that have to be asked before we can come to a final verdict on the justifiability of the law's giving effect to the compensation rule.

However, it should also be noted that this discussion is, at the moment, of purely academic interest. Whether the law is justified or not in giving effect to the compensation rule, it looks like the compensation rule is here to stay. It is so deeply entrenched in our law that only an Act of Parliament could remove it and there is no sign that Parliament is interested in abolishing the compensation rule or narrowing its ambit. Indeed, as Tony Weir has pointed out, almost all legislative interventions in tort law over the past century have been designed to remove various limits that the courts had previously placed on the ambit of the compensation rule.[33]

[32] This is assuming of course that the compensation rule does not 'pay for itself' and that there is a social cost attached to giving effect to the compensation rule.
[33] Weir 2001, 3.

PART II

TORTS

NEGLIGENCE

DEFINITIONS

A will commit the tort of negligence in relation to B if he breaches a duty of care owed to B.[1] The term 'duty of care', it should be noted, is ambiguous. We use the term 'duty of care' to describe at least three different kinds of duty that one person might owe another.

First, we say A owes B a 'duty of care' if A owes B a duty to take care not to act in some way.[2] Secondly, we say A owes B a 'duty of care' if A owes B a duty to perform some task with a certain degree of care and skill. Thirdly, we say that A owes B a 'duty of care' if A owes B a duty to take reasonable steps to ensure that some end or goal is achieved. Breach of any of these kinds of duty – being a breach of a 'duty of care' – amounts to negligence.

So a driver of a car owes other users of the road a duty of care – he owes them a duty to take care not to drive dangerously. If he breaches that duty he will

---

[1] *Important note.* From now on, we will be using the term 'a duty of care' as shorthand for 'a *tortious* duty of care'. So when we say that A will commit the tort of negligence in relation to B if he breaches a duty of care owed to B, we are merely saying in shorter form that A will commit the tort of negligence if he breaches a *tortious* duty of care owed to B. Of course, someone will not commit the *tort* of negligence if he breaches a *non-tortious* duty of care owed to another. So, for example, if A holds property on trust for B, A will owe B a duty to invest the trust property with reasonable skill and care. This duty of care will be non-tortious in nature as it is an equitable duty. So if A breaches this duty of care he will not commit the tort of negligence. Again, we have already seen that if A is B's employer, A will owe B a duty under s 2 of the Health and Safety at Work Act 1974 to take reasonable steps to ensure that B's health, safety and welfare at work is secured (see above, p. 13). This duty of care will be non-tortious in nature – s 47 of the 1974 Act makes it clear that breach of this statutory duty will not be actionable in the same way as the breach of a tortious duty owed to another. So if A is B's employer and he breaches the duty of care he owes him under s 2 of the 1974 Act, he will not commit the tort of negligence. Another example of a non-tortious duty of care is provided by the Human Rights Act 1998. The decision of the European Court of Human Rights in *Osman* v *United Kingdom* [1999] FLR 193 indicates that if the police *know* that C, a criminal on the loose, is *very likely* to kill B if he is not arrested, the police will violate B's right to life under Art 2 of the European Convention on Human Rights if they do not take reasonable steps to apprehend C. If this is right then, in the situation just described, the police will owe B a duty under the Human Rights Act 1998 to take reasonable steps to arrest C. This duty of care will be non-tortious in nature: a public authority which breaches a duty owed to another under the 1998 Act will not commit a tort (see above, pp. 10–11). So if, in the situation just described, the police breach the duty of care they owe B and fail to take reasonable steps to apprehend B, they will not commit the tort of negligence. (For a discussion of what the legal position will be if a public authority breaches a duty owed to another under the 1998 Act, see below, pp. 729–38.)

[2] If A owes B a duty to take care not to do x but x is the sort of thing that can only be done deliberately if it is done at all, we usually simply say that A owes B a duty not to do x – but the duty A owes B will still be a duty of care and breach of the duty will still amount to negligence. So, for example, suppose A is playing golf and is waiting to tee off at a particular hole. Suppose further that he knows that B is on the fairway in front of him. In such a case, A will owe B a duty to take care not to drive his ball down the fairway (see below, p. 67). But as A's driving his ball down the fairway is the sort of thing that can only be done deliberately if it is done at all, we can simply say that, in the situation we are considering, A will owe B a duty not to drive his golf ball down the fairway.

commit the tort of negligence. Likewise, a doctor owes a patient of his a duty of care – he owes her a duty to treat her with a certain degree of care and skill; the sort of care and skill that a professional doctor would exercise in treating a patient. If he breaches that duty he will commit the tort of negligence. Similarly, an occupier of land will owe his visitors a duty of care – he will owe them a duty to take reasonable steps to ensure that they will be reasonably safe for the purposes for which they are on his land. If he breaches that duty he will commit the tort of negligence.

DUTY OF CARE

Let's now look at how we establish whether someone owed another some kind of duty of care in a particular situation. Suppose, for example, that Carl is a drug addict with no prospects; as a result, he is estranged from his wealthy parents. He blames his parents for his current condition, claiming that a lot of his problems are attributable to his parents' decision to send him to boarding school when he was young. Had his parents kept him at home, he claims, he would have been much happier, done much better at school, and not fallen into the state he is in now. Carl wants to sue his parents in negligence, claiming that they owed him, and breached, a duty to raise him with a reasonable degree of care and skill and that his life would have gone much better had his parents not breached that duty of care.[3] How do we *test* for whether Carl's parents owed Carl such a duty of care?

[3] *Important note.* Of course, Carl could frame his case more narrowly and simply claim that his parents owed him a duty not to send him to boarding school, leaving to one side the issue of whether his parents owed him a more general duty to raise him with a reasonable degree of care and skill. If you have occasion to consider whether a claimant can sue a defendant in negligence we would recommend that you characterise the duty of care that the defendant might have owed the claimant and breached in quite narrow terms. So if *you* were considering Carl's case and attempting to determine whether or not he could sue his parents, we would recommend that you concentrate on the issue of whether Carl's parents owed him a duty not to send him to boarding school and ignore the wider issue of whether Carl's parents owed him a more general duty to raise him with a reasonable degree of skill and care. Why is this? Well, characterising the duty of care that Carl's parents might have owed Carl in very narrow terms makes it much easier to determine whether or not Carl's parents actually owed Carl a duty of care and, if they did, to determine whether or not they breached that duty of care. However, for the purposes of illustrating how one determines whether one person owed another a duty of care, *we* will focus on the issue of whether Carl's parents owed him a duty to raise him with a reasonable degree of care and skill. As an illustration of the point being made here, suppose that Nita threw a snowball at Ian and it hit him in the face. Ian was injured as a result because a small stone had got caught up in the snowball when it was being made and the stone scratched Ian's face when the snowball hit him. Can Ian sue Nita in negligence? One *could* approach this issue by asking: (*a*) Did Nita owe Ian a duty to take care not to injure him? and (*b*) If so, did Nita breach this duty? But this would be inadvisable – the duty of care that Nita is supposed to have owed Ian and breached has been characterised at such a general level that it is hard to determine whether or not Nita did owe Ian such a duty and even if one can tell this, establishing a breach of the duty will involve a lot of work as well. Far better to ask: (*a*) Did Nita owe Ian a duty to take care not to throw a snowball at him which contained a small stone? and (*b*) If so, did Nita breach this duty? These questions are far easier to handle. As we will see, Nita *will* have owed Ian a duty to take care not to throw a snowball at him which contained a small stone: see below, p. 67. But whether or not Nita breached the duty will depend on the particular circumstances of the case. Note that even if Nita *did* take care to ensure that the snowball she threw at Ian was stone-free, that is not the end of the case. One should go on to ask: (*a*) Did Nita owe Ian a duty not to throw a snowball

Two tests

One would have thought, on the basis of what has already been said, that one simply looks to the decided cases and in-force statutes to see if they establish, explicitly or implicitly, that Carl's parents owed him a duty to raise him with a reasonable degree of care and skill. And that is right – that is one test we can use to establish whether Carl's parents owed him such a duty of care. Let's call this test the *established categories test*.

At the same time, the cases suggest another test that we can use to determine whether Carl's parents owed him a duty to raise him with a reasonable degree of care and skill. They clearly establish that Carl's parents will have owed him such a duty of care if:

> (1) it was *reasonably foreseeable* that Carl would suffer some kind of harm if his parents did not raise him with a reasonable degree of care and skill; *and* (2) there was a relationship of *proximity* between Carl and his parents; *and* (3) it would be *fair, just and reasonable* to find that Carl's parents owed him a duty to raise him with a reasonable degree of care and skill.

Let's call this test for determining whether Carl's parents owed him a duty of care, the *Caparo test* – so named because it was in the case of *Caparo Industries plc* v *Dickman* that this test for determining whether or not someone owed another some kind of duty of care was first promulgated.[4]

So we have *two* tests that we can use to determine whether Carl's parents owed him a duty of care – the established categories test and the *Caparo* test.[5]

---

at him? (notice that we don't need to say 'a duty *to take care* not to throw a snowball at him' as throwing a snowball at someone can only be done deliberately if at all) and (*b*) If so, did Nita breach that duty? The difficult issue here is whether Nita owed Ian a duty not to throw a snowball at him – obviously, if she did owe him such a duty, then she breached it. This will depend on whether it was reasonably foreseeable that Ian would suffer some kind of physical injury if Nita threw a snowball at him: see below, pp. 70–6.

[4] [1990] 2 AC 605.

[5] *Important note*. If one looks at recent decisions which deal with the issue of when one person will owe another a duty of care, each decision seems to use the *Caparo* test to determine whether a duty of care was owed in the situation dealt with by the decision. This fact leads unwary students (and a surprising number of academics) to conclude that the *Caparo* test is the *only* test that we can use to determine whether or not one person owed another a duty of care of some kind in a given situation. This is wrong. There is a very simple reason why, for example, the Court of Appeal in *Kent* v *Griffiths* [2001] QB 36 used the *Caparo* test to determine whether the London Ambulance Service (LAS) owed the claimant a duty to take reasonable steps to get her to hospital when she suffered an asthma attack. If it had been well established that the LAS owed the claimant such a duty of care, the case would never have gone to court in the first place on the issue of whether the LAS owed the claimant such a duty of care. It was only because it was *not* well established that a duty of care was owed in *Kent* v *Griffiths* that the Court of Appeal was asked to determine whether the LAS owed the claimant a duty to take reasonable steps to get her to hospital when she suffered an asthma attack. And, naturally, as it was not well established that a duty of care was owed in *Kent* v *Griffiths*, the Court of Appeal used the *Caparo* test to determine whether the LAS owed the claimant a duty of care of the kind it was claimed it did. And this is true of all the recent cases which deal with the issue of when one person will owe another a duty of care – in each case, had it been well established that a duty of care was owed, the case would never have gone to court on the issue of whether a duty of care was owed; and because it was not well established that a duty of care was owed in each of these cases, the courts deciding these cases fell into using the *Caparo* test to determine whether or not a duty of care was owed.

We use these tests to determine whether Carl's parents owed him a duty of care in the following way. We first see whether the established categories test indicates that Carl's parents owed him a duty of care – in other words, we look at the decided cases and in-force statutes to see if they establish, explicitly or implicitly, that Carl's parents owed him a duty to raise him with a reasonable degree of care and skill. If the established categories test *does* indicate that Carl's parents owed him such a duty of care, that is the end of the matter – we conclude that Carl's parents *did* owe him a duty to raise him with a reasonable degree of care and skill.

If, on the other hand, the decided cases and in-force statutes do *not* establish that Carl's parents owed him a duty to raise him with a reasonable degree of care and skill, we then apply the *Caparo* test and see if, under that test, Carl's parents owed him such a duty of care. If the *Caparo* test *does* indicate that Carl's parents owed Carl such a duty of care, then, again, we will conclude that Carl's parents *did* owe him a duty to raise him with a reasonable degree of care and skill. If the *Caparo* test does *not* indicate that Carl's parents owed him such a duty of care, then we will conclude that Carl's parents did *not* owe him a duty to raise him with a reasonable degree of care and skill; and, accordingly, Carl's claim against his parents will fail.

Let's now apply these tests to determine whether Carl's parents owed him a duty of care in the situation we are considering. Starting with the established categories test, the decided cases and in-force statutes do *not* establish that Carl's parents owed him a duty to raise him with a reasonable degree of care and skill. So we have to turn to the *Caparo* test to see if Carl's parents owed him a duty to raise him with a reasonable degree of care and skill. Was it reasonably foreseeable that Carl would suffer some kind of harm if his parents did not raise him with a reasonable degree of care and skill? Clearly, yes. Was there a relationship of proximity between Carl and his parents? Well, as we will see, the concept of proximity is a very mysterious one. Despite this, it is hard to see how it could be said that there was not a 'proximate relationship' between Carl and his parents: it is hard to imagine relationships much more 'proximate' than the one between a child and his parents. Finally, would it be 'fair, just and reasonable' to find that Carl's parents owed him a duty to raise him with a reasonable degree of care and skill? It is difficult to say.

Carl's lawyer could argue:

> Of course it would be fair, just and reasonable to find that Carl's parents owed him a duty to raise him with a reasonable degree of care and skill. When he was young, Carl's parents possessed a huge amount of power over him. It was up to them to determine where he lived, who he was allowed to see, what books he read – and how he was educated. It would be intolerable if the law left this degree of power that parents possess over their children unsupervised and unchecked. Given this, it would be appropriate to find that Carl's parents owed him a duty to raise him with a reasonable degree of care and skill; power attracts reponsibility. After all, we already find that parents owe their children a duty to take reasonable steps to see that they do not come to any *physical* harm; is it not just as important that the law require parents do their best to see that their children do not come to any *moral* harm?

On the other hand, the lawyer for Carl's parents could argue:

> It is nonsense to suggest that it would be fair, just and reasonable to find that Carl's parents owed him a duty to raise him with a reasonable degree of care and skill.
>
> First of all, finding that such a duty was owed by Carl's parents to Carl will do more harm than good. Some parents may be encouraged by a judgment in favour of Carl to take their responsibilities to their children more seriously. But at the same time, a judgment in favour of Carl here will only serve to encourage children to make all sorts of frivolous and time-wasting claims against their parents, to the general detriment of family life in this country.
>
> Secondly, there is no need to find that parents owe their children a duty to raise them with a reasonable degree of care and skill. In serious cases of neglect, the social services possess adequate powers to intervene in the interests of the child. So finding a duty here will just add another layer of regulation to an already well-regulated area of social life.
>
> Thirdly, if we find that parents owe their children a duty to raise them with a reasonable degree of care and skill, we will be involving the courts in all sorts of difficulties that they are not well suited to resolving. As a result, the courts will be brought into disrepute. Take this case here. If Carl wins on the 'duty' point, he will still have to show 'breach' – but how are the courts meant to decide what raising a child with a 'reasonable degree of care and skill' involves?[6] The courts should not be involved in setting down standards for parents as to how they should raise their children. And even if Carl wins on 'breach', he still has to show that the breach caused him loss. He will have to show that had his parents not decided to send him off to boarding school, his life would have gone a lot better than it did. But how can the courts determine whether or not this is true? The issue is completely speculative.

One has to exercise one's judgment to determine which set of arguments are more convincing.[7] So the *Caparo* test for determining whether one person owed another a duty of care is not easy to apply – one cannot apply it mechanically. But the established categories test is not easy to apply either. Let's now look at this test in a bit more detail.

Applying the established categories test

An initial problem

Suppose that we want to find out whether A owed B a duty of care in some situation. In applying the established categories test to see whether such a duty of

---

[6] This argument proved influential in convincing the Supreme Court of Canada to rule that a mother could not be held to owe a duty of care to her unborn baby: *Dobson* v *Dobson* [1999] 2 SCR 753, at [54].

[7] While the parents' lawyer may seem to have the better of the argument so far, Carl's lawyer could counter by arguing that: (*a*) the courts possess more than adequate powers to strike out frivolous or time-wasting claims; (*b*) the social services have never been able to guarantee the welfare of all children in need and so the law does need to do more in this area to protect the interests of children; (*c*) it is for Carl to prove his case on 'breach' and 'causation of loss' – if he cannot, then he loses; if he can, then the courts' acknowledgement of the fact that 'breach' and 'loss' have been established cannot bring them into disrepute. However, at the time of writing, the courts seem to be of the view that it would *not* be 'fair, just and reasonable' to find that Carl's parents owed him a duty of care in bringing him up: see *Barrett* v *Enfield LBC* [1998] QB 367, 377 (per Lord Woolf MR); [2001] 2 AC 550, 587 (per Lord Hutton).

care was owed, we ask – Do the decided cases or in-force statutes explicitly or implicitly establish that A owed B a duty of care? But when we try to answer this question, we immediately run into a very large problem. If you take any given 'duty case' (that is, a case in which it has been held that one person owed another a duty of care), it is often very difficult to tell what that case establishes.[8]

Take, for example, the case of *Costello* v *Chief Constable of the Northumbria Police*.[9] In that case, the claimant was a woman police officer. She took a prisoner down to the cells at a police station. One Sergeant Hall accompanied her, just in case the prisoner attempted to attack the claimant. When they reached the cell area, Hall saw that there was a police inspector, an Inspector Bell, in attendance there. Thinking that Bell would intervene if there was any trouble, Hall went back upstairs. The prisoner then attacked the claimant and Bell did nothing to assist the claimant. The claimant sued the defendant chief constable for compensation, claiming that Bell breached a duty of care owed to the claimant when he failed to go to the claimant's assistance and that the defendant was vicariously liable in respect of Bell's negligence. The claimant won at first instance and the defendant appealed, claiming that Bell had not owed the claimant a duty to take reasonable steps to save her from being attacked. The Court of Appeal found for the claimant. They held that Bell *had* owed the claimant a duty to take reasonable steps to save her from being attacked.

Now – what does this case establish? To answer that question, we need to know *why* the court found that Bell owed the claimant a duty of care. If the court found that Bell owed the claimant a duty of care because facts XYZ were established, then the decision in *Costello* indicates that one person will owe another a duty of care in a situation where facts XYZ hold true. However, the judgments in *Costello* do not make it clear *why* the court found that Bell owed the claimant a duty of care. May LJ handed down the only substantial judgment. He indicated that Bell owed the claimant a duty to take reasonable steps to save her from being attacked because he 'assumed a responsibility' to the claimant.[10] But the phrase 'assumed a responsibility' is so vague that the bare statement 'Bell owed the claimant a duty of care because he assumed a responsibility to her' tells us hardly anything about *why* Bell owed the claimant a duty of care.

So, if we want to know why the court found that Bell owed the claimant a duty of care in this case, we are going to have to make an educated guess. Suppose we reassemble the panel of legal scholars that we met in Chapter 3 to help us with this question. The discussion between them as to why Bell owed the claimant a duty of care in *Costello* might well go as follows:

John: I can't see a problem with this case. Bell clearly owed the claimant a duty of care in *Costello* because he was a policeman and as such he had a responsibility to stop the criminal assault to which the claimant was subjected.

---

[8] See, in addition to the text below, Stone 1946's discussion (at 187–8) of what the House of Lords' decision in *Donoghue* v *Stevenson* [1932] AC 562 established.

[9] [1999] 1 All ER 550.

[10] Ibid., 564.

Paul: No – that's too wide. Why would the court have placed such emphasis on what Bell *did* in finding that he owed the claimant a duty of care, if he owed her that duty of care simply because he was a policeman? The truth is, Bell owed the claimant a duty of care because he indicated to the claimant that she could rely on him to save her if she were attacked and she, in turn, probably relied on him by dropping her guard a bit.

Mary: I agree with Paul that John's interpretation of the case is too wide, but Paul's explanation is just fantasy – there is no evidence in the case that the claimant dropped her guard or was even aware of Bell's presence in the room. The truth is, Bell owed the claimant a duty of care because they were both police officers, and police officers have a responsibility to go to each other's assistance if they are attacked. Otherwise, police officers will not be sure that they can depend on each other in going into dangerous situations and the efficacy of police operations will be substantially impaired.

Eric: I agree with Mary that Paul's explanation is untenable; but I think Mary and John are making a mistake in thinking that Bell's status as a policeman was crucial to the finding of a duty of care here. The reason why Bell owed the claimant a duty of care here goes as follows. When the claimant walked down to the cells, Hall was ready to intervene if the claimant was attacked. But then Bell encouraged Hall to go back upstairs, thus depriving the claimant of her 'bodyguard'. As a result, Bell had a duty to go to the claimant's assistance if she was attacked.

Beth: I agree with Eric that Mary and John are placing too much weight on Bell's status as a policeman. But the trouble with Eric's explanation is that Bell didn't really encourage Hall to go back upstairs; he merely *allowed* Hall to go back upstairs. I think we have to acknowledge that the real reason Bell was held to owe the claimant a duty of care here is that he was in a position to help her; the court, in finding a duty of care here, was simply giving effect to the moral principle that if you are in a position to help someone in need, you should.

Ruth: You're all wrong. The mistake you're all making is to focus on one or two elements in the factual matrix presented by the *Costello* case and say – *that's* the reason why the court found that a duty of care was owed in this case. So John focuses on the fact that Bell was a policeman and a criminal assault took place. Paul focuses on the fact of a possible understanding that existed between Bell and the claimant. Mary focuses on the fact that Bell and the claimant were both police officers. Eric focuses on the fact that had it not been for Bell's actions (or, as Beth points out, non-actions), Hall would have gone to the claimant's assistance. And Beth focuses on the fact that Bell was in a position to save the claimant. In truth, *all* these facts probably played a part in the court's decision in *Costello* to find that Bell owed the claimant a duty of care. Had any one of these facts not been present, then the decision may well have been different.

All these explanations of why the court in *Costello* found that a duty of care was owed in that case give rise to different accounts as to what the decision in *Costello* establishes. If you take John's view, *Costello* establishes that if B is being beaten up and A, a policeman, comes on the scene, A will owe B a duty to take reasonable steps to rescue her. If you take Paul's view, *Costello* establishes that if A indicates to B that he can be safely relied upon to go to her assistance if needs be, and B does so rely on A, A will owe B a duty to take reasonable steps to go to B's assistance if B needs such assistance. If you take Mary's view, *Costello* establishes that if A and B are both police officers, and B is in some kind of danger, and A is in a position to help – A will owe B a duty to go to B's assistance. If you take Eric's view, *Costello* establishes that if B is in some kind of danger and A discourages a third party from going to B's assistance, then A will owe B a duty to take reasonable steps to rescue B. If you take Beth's view, *Costello* establishes that if B is in some kind of danger and A is in a position to help B, then A will owe B a duty to go to her assistance. Finally, if you take Ruth's view, *Costello* simply establishes that in the factual situation presented in *Costello*, a duty of care will be owed.

So – just one 'duty case' like *Costello* can give rise to (at least) six different accounts as to what that case establishes.[11] And this is what makes it difficult to apply the established categories test. Suppose you want to find out whether A owed B a duty of care in a given case. And suppose the available in-force statutes have nothing to say on the matter. So you ask: Do the decided cases establish, explicitly or implicitly, that A owed B a duty of care? As our panel's discussion of the *Costello* case reveals, there are many decided 'duty cases' where there is no settled understanding as to what they establish.[12] You will have to decide for yourself what is established by those cases. You may adopt a very narrow interpretation of what those cases say. If you do, you will probably find that the decided cases do *not* establish that A owed B a duty of care and you will have to use the *Caparo* test to determine whether or not A owed B such a duty. But you may adopt a more imaginative interpretation of what those cases establish – in which case, you may well find that the decided cases *do* establish that A owed B a duty of care.

In Chapters 4 to 7 of this book, we present our understanding of what the available 'duty cases' establish. In our view, our reading of the cases is the best available. However, as should already be clear, other readings of many of the cases we mention are available. For instance, a scholar like Ruth – who takes a very crabbed, conservative view of what the duty cases establish – may well think our account pushes the cases too far: that we read too much into the cases. We disagree – but would invite the reader to decide. He or she, having read our account of what the available 'duty cases' have to say, should seek out those cases, read them and see whether he or she agrees with our account of what those cases establish.

Duty situations

So what do the decided cases and in-force statutes say on the issue of when one person will owe another a duty of care? We will deal with this issue in Chapters 4 to 7 but it may be helpful if we summarise the main conclusions of those chapters here. The decided cases, as translated by us, and in-force statutes seem to establish that:

---

[11] This is not to say that all these accounts are equally valid. Paul's explanation of the *Costello* case does seem far-fetched and John and Beth's explanations do seem to run counter to the tenor of May LJ's judgment in *Costello*.

[12] This is not, however, true of *all* 'duty cases'. Sometimes a court deciding a 'duty case' will be very precise as to why exactly it is finding that a duty of care was owed in that case. Similarly, sometimes a later court will provide an authoritative statement as to how an earlier 'duty case' should be understood.

(1) *The physical danger principle*. A will *normally* owe B a duty to take care not to do *x* if it is reasonably foreseeable that someone like B will suffer some kind of physical injury if A does *x*.

(2) *Psychiatric illness*. If A's doing *x* was responsible for B's developing a psychiatric illness and it was reasonably foreseeable that someone like B would develop such a psychiatric illness if A did *x*, A *may* have owed B a duty to take care not to do *x*, depending on how B's illness was triggered.

(3) *The property harm principle*. If property was harmed as a result of A's doing *x* and B had a sufficient interest in that property when it was harmed and it was foreseeable that that kind of property would suffer some kind of harm if A did *x*, A will *normally* have owed B a duty to take care not to do *x*.

(4) *The creation of danger principle*. If it is reasonably foreseeable that A's actions have put B in danger of suffering some kind of harm to her person or property, A will owe B a duty to take reasonable steps to ensure that B will not suffer the kind of harm in question.

(5) *The interference principle*. If B is in danger of suffering some kind of harm to her person or property and A has dissuaded a third party, T, from taking steps to ensure that B will not suffer that kind of harm, A will owe B a duty to take reasonable steps to ensure that B will not suffer the kind of harm in question.

(6) *The control principle*. If A has taken control of a person or animal, T, and T is very likely to do harm to B's person or property if T is not restrained from doing so, A will usually owe B a duty to take reasonable steps to restrain T from harming B.

(7) *The basic principle in Hedley Byrne*. If A has taken on the job of advising B on a particular matter and has indicated to B that she can safely rely on his advice on that matter, A will owe B a duty to take care that he does not give B incorrect advice on the matter in question.

(8) *The extended principle in Hedley Byrne*. If A has indicated to B that B can safely rely on him to perform a particular task with a certain degree of care and skill and B has so relied on A, A will owe B a duty to perform that task with that degree of care and skill.

(9) *The dependency principle*. If A has taken on a task, knowing that if he fails to perform that task properly B's future well-being will be, or is likely to be, severely impaired, A will owe B a duty to perform that task with a reasonable degree of care and skill.

(10) *The principle in White v Jones*. If a third party, T, wants to confer a benefit on B and A undertook to assist T to confer that benefit on B but then, due to something A did, T was prevented from conferring that benefit on B, A will have owed B a duty to take care not to act in the way he did.

(11) *Bailment*. If A holds B's goods on a bailment, A will *normally* owe B a duty to take reasonable steps to see that those goods are not destroyed or damaged.

(12) *Occupiers and visitors*. If A occupies premises which B enters as A's visitor, A will *normally* owe B a duty to take reasonable steps to ensure that B will be reasonably safe in using those premises for the purposes for which she has entered them.

(13) *Occupiers and trespassers*. If B has entered A's premises as a trespasser *and* those premises have a dangerous feature *and* A knows or ought to know of the existence of that dangerous feature *and* A knows or ought to know that a trespasser might come into the vicinity of that dangerous feature *and* A could reasonably be expected to offer B some protection against this dangerous feature, then A will owe B a duty to take reasonable steps to ensure that B is not killed or injured as a result of A's premises having this dangerous feature.

(14) *Occupiers and neighbours*. If a fire starts on land occupied by A and it is reasonably foreseeable that the fire will spread onto land owned by B if it is not put out, A will owe B a duty to take reasonable steps to put out the fire.

(15) *Employers*. If A employs B, A will normally owe B a duty to take reasonable steps to ensure that A does not suffer some kind of personal injury in working for him; and that B's working conditions are not such that it is reasonably foreseeable that he will suffer a psychiatric illness as a result of working for A.

(16) *Carriers*. If A takes B somewhere in a vehicle, A will owe B a duty to take reasonable steps to ensure that B is not killed or injured while she is in the vehicle.

(17) *Parents*. If A is B's parent and B is a child, A will owe B a duty to take reasonable steps to ensure that B does not come to any physical harm.

(18) *Teachers*. If A is B's teacher, A will owe B a duty to take reasonable steps to see that B does not come to any physical harm at school; and if B has special needs, A will owe B a duty to take reasonable steps to see that B receives a decent education consistent with those needs.

Brief reflection on this list of *duty situations* reveals that the decided cases and in-force statutes that deal with the issue of when one person will owe another a duty of care seem to reflect, and give limited effect to, certain moral precepts, namely: (*a*) take care not to cause other people to suffer serious harm;[13] (*b*) don't let others down – live up to the expectations that you have encouraged other people to have of you;[14] (*c*) *noblesse oblige* – that is, the possession of power over other people carries with it certain responsibilities;[15] as does the occupation of certain privileged statuses in society.[16]

---

[13] See situations (1)–(5), (9).
[14] See situations (7)–(8), and – to some extent – situations (11), (12) and (16).
[15] See situations (6), (17)–(18).
[16] See situations (12)–(15).

Applying the *Caparo* test

In Chapter 8, we will explain how to apply the *Caparo* test for determining whether one person owed another a duty of care of some kind in a given situation. As has already been said, it is only necessary to apply the *Caparo* test to determine whether A owed B a duty of care of some kind in a given situation if the decided cases and in-force statutes do not establish that A owed B such a duty of care. For example, the decided cases and in-force statutes establish that *in certain situations* A will owe B a duty to take positive steps to rescue B or B's property from some danger that B or B's property is in. But these situations are few and far between. Given this, in cases where it is claimed that a defendant owed a claimant a duty to rescue the claimant from some danger she was in, one will generally have to use the *Caparo* test to determine whether this claim is correct; as a general rule, the decided cases and in-force statutes will not establish that the defendant owed the claimant the duty of care in question.

So, in recent years, the courts have used the *Caparo* test to determine whether: police investigating a break-in at a clothing store owed the owner of the store a duty to take reasonable steps to investigate the break-in thoroughly; a commanding officer owed a soldier under his command a duty to take reasonable steps to ensure that that soldier did not become hopelessly drunk; a health authority owed a mentally ill man who had been released into the community a duty to take reasonable steps to treat him properly; the police owed a boy and his family a duty to take reasonable steps to apprehend one of his teachers after the teacher developed a crush on the boy and made threats to the boy and his family; a local authority owed a child who was at risk of being sexually abused in his home a duty to take reasonable steps to save him from being abused; a fire brigade which was summoned to put out a fire at a commercial property owed the owners of the property a duty to take reasonable steps to put out the fire; a highway authority owed users of a stretch of road a duty to take reasonable steps to eliminate a dangerously high bank beside the road which prevented oncoming traffic from seeing the users of that road; the police owed a social worker a duty to take reasonable steps to give her appropriate counselling after employing her to attend and supervise police interviews with a suspected mass murderer.

In most of these cases the courts, having applied the *Caparo* test, concluded that no duty was owed. (What (im)moral precept would the courts have given effect to if they had concluded that a duty *was* owed in these cases? Perhaps – *from each according to his abilities, to each according to his needs*.) In Chapter 8 we will attempt to set out some of the considerations that the courts take into account in applying the *Caparo* test to determine whether, in a given situation, one person owed another a duty of care of some kind.

BREACH OF DUTY

Let us now turn to the issue of when someone who owed another a duty of care of some kind will be found to have breached that duty. Not much need be said on this issue at this stage. However, it is worth emphasising at this point that there is no uniform formula for determining in a given case whether someone breached a duty of care owed to someone else. Whether or not the courts will hold that a defendant breached a duty of care that he owed to a claimant will depend on a variety of considerations.

Sometimes the courts will presume that the defendant breached the duty of care that he owed the claimant unless the defendant can show that he did not breach the duty in question; more often the burden of proof will be on the claimant. Sometimes the courts will hold that a defendant breached a duty of care that he owed the claimant because of something a third party did; more often they will just focus on the defendant's actions to determine whether or not he breached that duty of care. Sometimes the courts will take into account a defendant's personal circumstances in determining whether or not he breached a duty of care that he owed a claimant; sometimes they will not. No hard and fast rules can be set up – what considerations the courts will take into account depends a lot on who the defendant is and what the nature of the duty of care that he owed the claimant was.

FURTHER POINTS

Three further points about the law on when someone will commit the tort of negligence may be made at this stage.

Negligence and intention

Sir Percy Winfield once suggested that someone would commit the tort of negligence if, and only if, he 'breach[ed] a legal duty to take care by an *inadvertent* act or omission'.[17] This seems wrong.[18] Suppose Beth drives down a street at 80 miles an hour and as a result runs over Tom. Tom attempts to sue Beth in negligence for compensation. Could Beth really rebut Tom's claim that Beth committed the tort of negligence in driving as she did by arguing that while she admittedly owed Tom a duty to take care not to drive dangerously, she did not commit the tort of negligence in relation to Tom in driving as she did because she *deliberately* drove down the road at 80 miles an hour? The answer is 'no'. If Beth, in driving at 80 miles an hour down the street, breached the duty of care that she owed Tom not to drive dangerously, she will have committed the tort of negligence in relation to Tom – it will not matter whether she drove down the street at 80 miles an hour deliberately or inadvertently. Extrapolating from this, A will commit the tort of negligence in relation to B if he breaches a duty of care owed to B – and this is so even if A's breach is deliberate.

Perhaps acknowledging this point, Winfield later suggested that someone would commit the tort of negligence if: (*a*) he breached a duty of care owed to

---

[17] Winfield 1926, 184 (emphasis added).

[18] It is also inconsistent with the House of Lords' ruling in *Wainwright* v *Home Office* [2003] 3 WLR 1137 that if A *deliberately* lies to B, telling her that her husband had been injured when he has not, and B is made physically sick as a result of hearing this, then B will be able to sue A for damages in negligence. See below, p 68, n. 14.

another *and* (*b*) when he breached that duty he did not intend to harm that other.[19] Again, there does not seem any reason for this limitation on the scope of the tort of negligence. Suppose, for example, that Gary's mother-in-law, Lara, visited him in his house. While she was in Gary's house, she put her foot through a rotten floorboard on Gary's staircase which Gary had neglected to replace and as a result twisted her ankle. Now suppose that Lara sues Gary in negligence, claiming that her injury happened as a result of Gary's breach of the duty of care that he owed her to take reasonable steps to see that she would be reasonably safe while she was on his premises. Could Gary really defeat Lara's claim by arguing that he did not commit the tort of negligence in relation to her when he failed to replace the rotten floorboard on his staircase because 'When I found out that the floorboard was rotten and liable to give way, I deliberately left it untouched in the hope that when Lara came visiting she would put her foot through it?' Surely not[20] – the fact that Gary breached the duty of care he owed Lara as his visitor with the intention of harming her would not stop any court from concluding that Gary committed the tort of negligence in relation to Lara in this case.

Negligence and carelessness

'Negligence' is *not* to be equated with 'carelessness'. A number of different aspects of the law show that it would be an error to equate 'negligence' with 'carelessness'.

First, in the example we have just been considering, Gary's conduct in failing to replace his rotten floorboard in the hope that Lara would put her foot through it and injure herself amounts to 'negligence' – but we would hardly describe it as 'careless'.

Secondly, conduct we would characterise as 'careless' sometimes does not amount to 'negligence' because it does not involve the breach of a duty of care owed to someone else. For example, if the police carelessly fail to arrest a criminal who goes on to steal property from Paul's shop, the conduct of the police, while careless, is not 'negligent' – the police, in acting as they did, did not breach any duty of care owed to Paul.

Thirdly, a given defendant will sometimes be held to have committed the tort of negligence although *he* was not 'careless' in any way. So, for example, suppose an employer brought in a contractor to check the electrical appliances in his factory to ensure that none of the employer's workers were in danger of being electrocuted. Suppose the contractor failed to do a good job of checking the appliances and as a result failed to spot a defect in an appliance which later caused one of the employer's workers to suffer an electric shock. In such a case,

---

[19] Winfield 1934, 41.

[20] Cf. *New South Wales* v *Lepore* [2003] HCA 4, at [162] (per McHugh J): '[a claimant] may, if he or she chooses, sue in negligence for the intentional infliction of harm'; also *Blake* v *Galloway* [2004] EWCA Civ 814, at [17] (per Dyson LJ): 'If the defendant . . . [had] deliberately aimed the piece of bark at the claimant's head, then [the claimant might have been able to sue the defendant in negligence].'

the employer will be held to have breached the duty he owed the electrocuted worker to take reasonable steps to see that that worker would be reasonably safe in working for him – and this is so even if the employer took the greatest pains to ensure that the contractor was competent to check the electrical appliances in the employer's factory and did all he could to supervise the contractor to ensure that he did a good job.[21]

Negligence and damage

It is often said that 'damage is the gist of negligence' – that is, A will not commit the tort of negligence in relation to B by acting in some way unless B suffers some kind of harm as a result of A's actions. It seems to us that those who hold this view mix up two separate questions. First, when will someone commit the tort of negligence? Secondly, when will the victim of negligence be entitled to obtain a remedy in respect of that negligence?

Negligence is one of those torts (like slander, in most of its forms) where the courts will only give a remedy to the victim of that tort if he has actually suffered some harm as a result of that tort being committed. So if A has breached a duty of care owed to B, B will only be entitled to obtain a remedy in respect of A's conduct if she has suffered some kind of harm as a result of A's breach. But whether or not she is entitled to obtain a remedy against A in respect of A's conduct has no bearing on whether or not A committed a tort in relation to her in acting as he did. We would say that when A breached the duty of care he owed B he committed the tort of negligence in relation to B – the issue of whether A's breach resulted in B suffering some kind of harm is only relevant to the question of whether B will be entitled to obtain a remedy in respect of A's breach.[22]

---

[21] See below, pp. 228–9.

[22] Goldberg & Zipursky 2002 take a different view, arguing that the reason why negligence is only actionable on proof of loss is that if A owes B a duty of care of some description, A will not usually breach that duty if he is merely careless – A will only breach that duty if his carelessness results in B's suffering some kind of harm. See ibid., at 1652: 'The duty of care owed in most cases of actionable negligence is a duty to take care to avoid causing an ultimate harm . . . not a duty to take care to avoid [exposing someone to a] heightened risk [of suffering harm]. It is a duty to take care not to injure, rather than a duty to take care not to engage in . . . conduct that risks causing an ultimate injury . . .' We disagree. It seems to us that there are at least two problems with this view. (1) It seems likely that the fact that negligence is only actionable on proof of loss has more to do with historical accident (see above, p 17, n. 3) than a point of principle about the nature of the duties of care we owe each other. (2) Goldberg & Zipursky concede that not all of the duties of care that we owe each other conform to their analysis – but why then should we accept that any of the duties of care that we owe each other conform to their analysis? They cannot argue that their analysis should be accepted because that accounts for why negligence is only actionable on proof of loss, because then their argument becomes circular. In effect, they would be arguing that the reason why negligence is only actionable on proof of loss is that most of the duties of care we owe each other are only breached when loss is suffered; and the proof that most of the duties of care we owe each other are only breached when loss is suffered is that negligence is only actionable on proof of loss.

4

ESTABLISHED DUTY SITUATIONS I: THE
LEGACY OF *DONOGHUE* V *STEVENSON*

In this chapter we will begin to set out what the decided cases and in-force
statutes have to say on the issue of when one person will owe another a duty of
care. We start with probably the most famous case in English law dealing with
that issue: *Donoghue* v *Stevenson*.[1]

THE DECISION IN *DONOGHUE* V *STEVENSON*

In *Donoghue* v *Stevenson*, a friend of the claimant bought her a 'ginger beer float'
– a concoction made up of ice cream and ginger beer – at a café. The proprietor of the café opened a bottle of ginger beer and poured some of it over ice
cream to make the float. There was some ginger beer left in the bottle and he
handed that over to the claimant's friend. The claimant ate some of the float.
Her friend then poured the rest of the ginger beer into a glass for her to drink.
The decomposing remains of a snail floated out into the glass. Unsurprisingly,
the claimant fell very ill. Now: the offending bottle of ginger beer had been
bottled by the defendant and it was thought that the snail had managed to get
into the offending bottle before it was filled with ginger beer and sealed in the
defendant's factory. So the claimant sued the defendant in negligence, seeking
to recover compensation for the illness she had suffered. The following question went to the House of Lords: Did the defendant owe the claimant a duty to
take care that he did not bottle his ginger beer using bottles that contained
noxious items such as snails? If he did not, then the claimant's claim in negligence was doomed to fail.

The House of Lords, by a bare majority, held that – other things being equal
– the defendant *did* owe such a duty to the claimant. Why? Lord Atkin, delivering the leading judgment on the side of the majority, thought that the decided
cases established that the following *neighbour principle* was part of English law
and that under this principle, the defendant owed a duty of care to the
claimant:

> . . . in English law there must be, and is, some general conception of relations giving
> rise to a duty of care, of which the particular cases found in the books are but
> instances. The liability for negligence, whether you style it such or treat it as in other
> systems as a species of 'culpa', is no doubt based upon a general public sentiment of
> moral wrongdoing for which the offender must pay. But acts or omissions which any

---

[1] [1932] AC 562.

moral code would censure cannot in a practical world be treated so as to give a right to every person injured by them to demand relief. In this way rules of law arise which limit the range of complainants and the extent of their remedy. The rule that you are to love your neighbour becomes in law, you must not injure your neighbour; and the lawyer's question, Who is my neighbour? receives a restricted reply. *You must take reasonable care to avoid acts or omissions which you can reasonably foresee would be likely to injure your neighbour. Who, then, in law is my neighbour? The answer seems to be – persons who are so closely and directly affected by my act that I ought reasonably to have them in contemplation as being so affected when I am directing my mind to the acts or omissions which are called in question.*[2]

As it was reasonably foreseeable that someone like the claimant would be injured if the defendant bottled his ginger beer with bottles containing noxious items such as snails, the defendant had owed the claimant a duty to take care that he did not bottle his ginger beer using such bottles. It would have been different, Lord Atkin held, if sellers of the ginger beer bottled by the defendant could have been expected to detect whether or not the ginger beer contained any noxious items or objects before allowing the general public to purchase it.[3] In such a case, it would *not* have been reasonably foreseeable that someone like the claimant – a consumer of the defendant's ginger beer – would be injured if the defendant used bottles that contained noxious items or objects such as snails to bottle his ginger beer. In such a case, it could have been expected that those charged with the task of selling the defendant's bottles of ginger beer would have intercepted any bottles which *did* contain noxious items such as snails before those bottles ever reached the lips of the general public.

Lord Atkin's neighbour principle is far too widely drawn to be acceptable as a statement as to when one person will owe another a duty of care under English law.[4] Under the neighbour principle no distinction is drawn – in determining whether a given defendant owed a given claimant a duty of care – between cases where the defendant has made the claimant worse off and cases where the defendant has failed to make the claimant better off. But English law does make a big distinction between these two kinds of case: as we will see, it is far harder to establish a duty of care in the latter kind of case (an *omissions* case) than the former (a case involving a *positive act*). Moreover, under the neighbour principle, foreseeability of harm is the sole criterion to be taken into account in judging whether a given defendant owed a given claimant a duty of care. However, this is simply not the case in English law – even if it is foreseeable that a claimant will suffer some kind of harm as a result of a defendant's doing x, the defendant will not necessarily owe the claimant a duty to take care not to do x.

THE PHYSICAL DANGER PRINCIPLE

Donoghue v *Stevenson* is regarded as important nowadays because of Lord Atkin's judgment and its attempt to come up with a general statement as to

[2] Ibid., 580 (emphasis added).
[3] Ibid., 582.
[4] See Smith & Burns 1983a, 1983b.

when one person will owe another a duty of care.[5] However, the decision of the House of Lords in *Donoghue* v *Stevenson* was also important because it helped to establish that the following principle – a far narrower principle than Lord Atkin's neighbour principle – is part of English law. This principle – we can call it the *physical danger principle* – goes as follows: If it is reasonably foreseeable that someone like B will suffer some kind of physical injury if A does *x*, then A will normally owe B a duty to take care not to do *x*. *Donoghue* v *Stevenson* itself provides an example of this principle at work. In that case, it was reasonably foreseeable that someone like the claimant – a consumer of the defendant's ginger beer – would be physically injured if the defendant bottled his ginger beer using bottles that contained noxious items such as snails. Accordingly, the defendant owed the claimant a duty to take care not to bottle his ginger beer using bottles which contained noxious items such as snails.

There are plenty of cases – in addition to *Donoghue* v *Stevenson* – which seem to support the idea that the physical danger principle is part of English law. They variously hold that:

(1) If A sells goods to B, A will normally owe B a duty to take care not to sell him goods that are unsafe to use or consume in the way they are intended to be used or consumed.

(2) If A is out driving, A will owe other users of the road a duty to take care not to drive dangerously; similarly, if A is parking his car, A will owe other users of the road a duty to take care not to park the car in a dangerous fashion.[6]

(3) If A and B are playing football and A attempts to tackle B, A will owe B a duty to take care not to execute the tackle in an unnecessarily dangerous manner.[7]

(4) If A is in possession of a dangerous chattel – such as a loaded firearm, a poison, or an explosive[8] – and B is incapable of handling that chattel properly, A will normally owe B and anyone else who might be harmed by the chattel's improper use a duty not to entrust it to B's care.[9]

---

[5] For an earlier attempt see the judgment of Brett MR (subsequently Lord Esher) in *Heaven* v *Pender* (1883) 11 QBD 503, 510. The attentive reader may have already gathered that we are deeply sceptical as to whether any such general statement can be made without lapsing into unintelligible language. There seems to be no justification for Lord Atkin's statement that '. . . in English law there must be, and is, some general conception of relations giving rise to a duty of care, of which the particular cases found in the books are but instances'. The better view, we would submit, is that there are many *different* kinds of situations and relationships in which one person will owe another a duty of care; to think that all these different situations and relationships have something in common which accounts for why they give rise to a duty of care is folly and can only lead to confusion. See, to the same effect, Tettenborn 2000a.

[6] *Maitland* v *Raisbeck* [1944] KB 689; *Parish* v *Judd* [1960] 1 WLR 867.

[7] *Condon* v *Basi* [1985] 1 WLR 866.

[8] *Dominion Natural Gas Co.* v *Collins* [1909] AC 640, 646.

[9] *Dixon* v *Bell* (1816) 5 M & S 198, 199, 105 ER 1023, 1024; *Bamfield* v *Goole & Sheffield Transport Co.* [1910] 2 KB 94; *Oliver* v *Saddler & Co.* [1929] AC 584, 599; *Burfitt* v *A & E Killie* [1939] 2 KB 743; *Donaldson* v *McNiven* [1952] 2 All ER 691; *Beckett* v *Newalls Insulation Co. Ltd* [1953] 1 WLR 8; *Philco Radio* v *Spurling* [1949] 2 All ER 882; *Newton* v *Edgerley* [1959] 1 WLR 1031; *Gorely* v *Codd* [1967] 1 WLR 19.

(5) If A owns a car and B – who is obviously drunk – asks A for the key to his car, intending to go for a drive in it, A will owe users of the highway a duty not to give B the keys to his car.[10]

(6) If A, a highway authority, places signs alongside a highway, A will owe each driver on that highway a duty to take care not to position those signs in such a way that that driver will be unreasonably endangered.[11]

(7) If A is building a house, A will normally owe any future occupants of that house a duty to take care not to build the house in such a way that it will become unreasonably dangerous to live in.[12]

(8) If it is reasonably foreseeable that C will be put in danger if A sets a building on fire, and that someone like B will attempt to rescue C if this happens, thereby putting himself in danger, A will owe B a duty to take care not to set that building on fire.[13]

(9) If B is married to C, A will owe B a duty to take care that he does not misinform her that C has been killed or injured if it is reasonably foreseeable that she will be made physically sick by this news.[14]

---

[10] *P Perl (Exporters) Ltd* v *Camden LBC* [1984] QB 342, 359.

[11] *Levine* v *Morris* [1970] 1 WLR 71.

[12] *Dutton* v *Bognor Regis United Building Co. Ltd* [1972] 1 QB 373, overruling *Bottomley* v *Bannister* [1932] KB 458 and *Otto* v *Bolton & Norris* [1936] 2 KB 46. The decision in *Dutton* was subsequently affirmed by the House of Lords in *Anns* v *Merton LBC* [1978] AC 728. The House of Lords has now disapproved both *Dutton* and *Anns*: *D & F Estates* v *Church Commissioners* [1989] AC 177; *Murphy* v *Brentwood DC* [1991] 1 AC 398. The better view of those decisions, we submit, is that they did *not* disapprove of the view taken in *Dutton* and *Anns* that if A builds a house he will owe B, a subsequent occupier of that house, a duty to take care to ensure that he does not build that house in such a way that it will become dangerous to live in. In *D & F Estates* and *Murphy* the House of Lords disapproved the view taken in *Dutton* and *Anns* that if (1) A builds a house and in doing so breaches the duty he owes B, a subsequent occupier of that house, to take care not to build the house in such a way that it will become dangerous to live in and (2) as a result, B is put to expense making the house safe to live in then, other things being equal, (3) B will be entitled to sue A in negligence so as to be reimbursed for the expense she was put to. For an explanation as to why B will not be entitled to sue A in negligence in this situation, see below, pp. 566–8. The fact that B will not be entitled to sue A *in negligence* to recover the money she spent on repairing her house does not, of course, mean that B will not be entitled to sue A *at all* to recover that money. She may have an action under the Defective Premises Act 1972 (on which, see below, pp. 485–7, 568). For an interesting argument that she would be entitled to bring a claim in restitution against A to recover the expense incurred by her in making her house safe to live in, see Moran 1997.

[13] *Ogwo* v *Taylor* [1988] AC 431. More difficult is the situation where A owes C a duty to save him from harm, A breaches that duty, and B attempts to save C instead, thereby endangering himself. One cannot use the physical danger principle here to establish that A owed *B* a duty to rescue C because A is merely guilty of an omission here and it is not clear why the fact that A owed *C* a duty to rescue her should mean that he also owed *B* a duty to rescue C. That A *will* have owed B a duty to rescue C in this situation is established by the decision of the Court of Appeal in *Baker* v *T E Hopkins* [1959] 1 WLR 966, though the Supreme Court of Canada took a different view in *Horsley* v *McClaren, The Ogopogo* [1971] 2 Lloyd's Rep 410.

[14] *Wilkinson* v *Downton* [1897] 2 QB 57, as reinterpreted by *Wainwright* v *Home Office* [2003] 3 WLR 1137. In *Wilkinson* v *Downton*, the defendant played a joke on the claimant by telling her that her husband had met with a serious accident and that both his legs had been broken. In fact, as the defendant well knew, this was not true. The claimant was so upset to receive this news that she was physically sick. The claimant subsequently sued the defendant for compensation. At the time the case was decided, there existed a rule (which was subsequently abolished in *Dulieu* v *White & Sons* [1901] 2 KB 669, discussed below, p. 586) that you could not sue a defendant in negligence for compensa-

(10) If A is labelling bottles of medicine, he will owe B a duty to take care that he does not mislabel those bottles of medicine if it is reasonably foreseeable that someone like B will suffer some kind of physical injury if those bottles are mislabelled.[15]

(11) If B's mother asks A, a local authority, whether T would make a suitable child-minder for B, A will owe B a duty not to tell B's mother that T would make a suitable child-minder for B if A knows, or ought to know, that such advice will be acted on and that T has violent tendencies that mean that B will in fact be in danger of being killed or injured if she is looked after by T.[16]

(12) If B wants to adopt a child through A, an adoption agency, A will normally owe B a duty not to place with her a child which A knows or ought to know suffers from a personality disorder which means that the child is very likely to injure B if he is placed with B.[17]

(13) If A is asked to certify that an aircraft is ready to fly, he will owe those who are due to fly on the aircraft a duty not to say that the aircraft is ready to fly if he knows or ought to know that the aircraft is not fit to fly.[18]

Decisions like these – along with the decision in *Donoghue* v *Stevenson* – seem to show that the physical danger principle is well established in English law. This principle, it should be noted, is narrower than Lord Atkin's neighbour principle in two respects.

First of all, the principle only covers *positive acts*, not *omissions*. If Fred and Lara are standing at the edge of a cliff then Lara will obviously owe Fred a duty to take care not to push him over the cliff edge under the physical danger principle because it is reasonably foreseeable that Fred will suffer some kind of physical injury if Lara pushes him over the edge. If, on the other hand, Fred is blind and is unknowingly walking towards a cliff edge, Lara – who is standing nearby – will *not* owe Fred a duty to shout out a warning to him under the physical danger principle.[19] True, it is reasonably foreseeable that Fred will suffer some kind of physical injury if Lara does not shout out a warning to him but her not shouting out a warning amounts to a failure to act, not an act – and,

---

tion for some physical injury that you had suffered if the defendant had caused you to suffer that physical injury by making you distressed or upset. Wright J, who decided *Wilkinson* v *Downton*, got round this rule by holding that the claimant was not confined to suing the defendant in negligence but could sue the defendant on the ground that he had committed a quite different tort in relation to her, which was subsequently dubbed 'the tort in *Wilkinson* v *Downton*'. The House of Lords has now ruled in *Wainwright* v *Home Office* that post-*Dulieu* there is no need to maintain the fiction that there is such a thing as 'the tort in *Wilkinson* v *Downton*' ([2003] 3 WLR 1137, at [36]–[47] (per Lord Hoffmann)) and that all *Wilkinson* v *Downton*-type claims should be brought in negligence. So, for example, in *Janvier* v *Sweeney* [1919] 2 QB 316, the claimant was made physically sick as a result of being threatened by the defendants. She was allowed to sue the defendants for compensation, arguing that they had committed the tort in *Wilkinson* v *Downton* by threatening her. Post-*Wainwright*, were the same facts to occur today, the claimant would simply sue the defendants in negligence, claiming that they owed her a duty under the physical danger principle not to threaten her.

[15] *Caparo Industries plc* v *Dickman* [1990] 2 AC 605, 636C.
[16] *T* v *Surrey County Council* [1994] 4 All ER 577.
[17] *A* v *Essex County Council* [2003] 1 FLR 615.
[18] *Perrett* v *Collins* [1998] 2 Lloyd's Rep 255 (discussed, Witting 2000a).
[19] *Yuen Kun Yeu* v *Att-Gen of Hong Kong* [1988] AC 175, 192.

as we have already observed, the physical danger principle only applies to positive acts, not omissions.[20]

Secondly, the principle only applies in cases where it is foreseeable that B will suffer some kind of *physical injury* as a result of A's doing x – where the term 'physical injury' covers death or lesser harms that any normal person would regard as forms of 'physical injury', such as wounds or bruises.[21] It should be noted that the term 'physical injury' does *not* cover any form of *psychiatric illness*.[22] So if it is reasonably foreseeable that B will suffer some kind of psychiatric illness if A does x, one cannot invoke the physical danger principle to say that A will owe B a duty to take care not to do x – and this is so even though many forms of psychiatric illness have a physiological origin.[23]

Interpretation

Let's now look at the physical danger principle in more detail. Suppose that Wendy has suffered some kind of loss as a result of Alan's doing x and we want to use the physical danger principle to establish that Alan owed Wendy a duty to take care not to do x. To do this, we will have to show that at the *time* Alan did x, a reasonable person in Alan's *position* would have realised that there was a *real risk* that *someone like* Wendy would suffer some kind of physical injury if the defendant did x.[24] The four italicised terms in the previous sentence all require some attention.

[20] *Important note.* In *Haseldine* v *Daw* [1941] 2 KB 343, A employed an engineer, B, to mend a lift on his premises. B failed to do the job properly, with the result that C was injured the next day when he used the lift and it fell to the bottom of the lift shaft. It was held that: (1) B had owed C a duty to mend the lift with a reasonable degree of care and skill; (2) B had breached that duty; and (3) B was therefore liable to compensate C for his injuries. Finding (1) cannot be supported by reference to the physical danger principle, as the principle does not apply to omissions (here, the failure to repair the lift properly). However, we *can* use the physical danger principle to justify the result in *Haseldine*. It was reasonably foreseeable that if B told A that the lift was fit to use when it was not, someone like C would be physically injured as result. So B owed C a duty to take care not to tell A that the lift was fit to use when it was not under the physical danger principle. B breached this duty and C was injured as a result. So B was rightly held liable in negligence to compensate C for his injuries.

[21] It also seems to cover getting pregnant, which not many people would regard as a form of physical injury: see *Walkin* v *South Manchester HA* [1995] 1 WLR 1543; *Richardson* v *LRC Products* [2000] Lloyd's Rep Med 280; *Parkinson* v *St James and Seacroft NHS Hospital* [2002] QB 266; though the House of Lords was more equivocal in *McFarlane* v *Tayside Health Board* [2000] 2 AC 59, with Lords Steyn (at 81G) and Millett (107G) saying that pregnancy is a form of physical injury, Lord Slynn saying that it is not (at 74C–D), and Lords Hope (at 86C, 86H–87A) and Clyde (at 102F–H) saying that pregnancy is *analogous* to a physical injury. If pregnancy is a form of physical injury, then if John has sexual intercourse with Mary using contraception which he knows or ought to know is unreliable and Mary gets pregnant as a result and carries the child to term, will she be entitled to sue him for damages on the basis that he owed her, and breached, a duty to take care that he did not use unreliable contraception in having sex with her?

[22] Though the courts in other contexts do sometimes treat a psychiatric illness as though it were a form of physical injury: see *Page* v *Smith* [1996] AC 155, discussed below at pp. 561–2.

[23] For example, it is well established that most forms of depression are caused by chemical imbalances in the brain.

[24] *Important note.* This is subject to one very important qualification. Suppose that A does x and as a result a third party, T, physically injures B. Suppose further that B wants to invoke the physical danger principle to establish that A owed her a duty to take care not to do x. In this sort of *three-party case* the courts will *only* find that it was reasonably foreseeable that B would suffer some form of physical injury if A did x if a reasonable person in A's position would have realised that it was *very likely* (*Lamb* v *Camden LBC* [1981] QB 625, 642 (per Oliver LJ)) or

Someone like

It is not necessary to show – to invoke the physical danger principle in the above case – that at the time Alan did *x* a reasonable person in Alan's position would have thought 'If Alan does *x*, there's a real risk that *Wendy* will suffer some kind of physical injury.' It is enough if a reasonable person in Alan's position would have thought 'If Alan does *x*, there's a real risk that this kind of person will suffer some kind of physical injury' and Wendy turned out to be that kind of person. Two cases make the point.

In *Farrugia* v *Great Western Railway Co.*,[25] the defendant company loaded one of their lorries with a container that was too large for the lorry in question. The container was knocked off the lorry when it passed under a bridge and injured the claimant, who was running behind the lorry in order to hitch a ride on it. Let's say the name of the claimant was 'John Farrugia'.[26] The Court of Appeal held that the defendant company had owed the claimant a duty to take care that it did not overload its lorry. Of course, at the time the defendant company loaded its lorry, a reasonable person in the defendant company's position would not have been able to say, 'If this lorry is overloaded, there's a real risk that John Farrugia will be injured' because before the accident, a reasonable person in the defendant company's position would never have heard of John Farrugia. But at the time the defendant company loaded the lorry, a reasonable person in the defendant company's position would have realised, 'If this lorry is overloaded, there's a real risk that a pedestrian walking near the lorry when it's on the road will suffer some kind of physical injury.' As things turned out, this description fitted the claimant – he was a pedestrian walking near the lorry when it was on the road – so it was reasonably foreseeable at the time the defendant company loaded its lorry that if it overloaded the lorry *someone like* the claimant would suffer some kind of physical injury. This was enough to establish that the defendant company owed the claimant a duty to take care not to overload its lorry under the physical danger principle.

In *Haley* v *London Electricity Board*,[27] the defendants, acting under a statutory power, dug a trench in the pavement. While they worked, they left a long handled hammer (called a punner) leaning against some railings at one end of the trench in order to help ensure that pedestrians would not unwittingly fall into the trench. They did not take any steps to fence off the trench. The claimant, a blind man called John Haley who was walking along the pavement, missed the punner with his stick, tripped over it and fell into the trench. The

---

probable (*Smith* v *Littlewoods Organisation Ltd* [1987] AC 241, 258 (per Lord Mackay)) that T would injure someone like B if A did *x*. This is a higher standard than requiring B to show that a reasonable person in A's position would have realised that there was a *real risk* that T would physically injure B if A did *x*. So if Alan tells Eric that Wendy, Eric's wife, has been having an affair, and Eric is so angered by this news that he beats Wendy up, Wendy will probably *not* be able to establish that Alan owed her a duty not to tell Eric of her affair under the physical danger principle. While there was a real risk that Eric would beat Wendy up on being told that she was having an affair, it could not be said that it was very likely or probable that Eric would beat Wendy up.

[25] [1947] 2 All ER 565.

[26] The report does not make it clear what the claimant's first name was.

[27] [1965] AC 778.

House of Lords held that the defendants had owed the claimant a duty not to dig the trench and then leave it unfenced. At the time the defendants dug the trench, a reasonable person in the position of the defendants would not have realised, 'If the defendants dig a trench on this street and then leave it unfenced, there's a real risk that John Haley will suffer some kind of physical injury' because a reasonable person in the position of the defendants would never have heard of John Haley before his unfortunate accident. But a reasonable person in the position of the defendants would have realised, 'If the defendants dig a trench and then leave it unfenced, there's a real risk that a blind man will fall into the trench and suffer some form of physical injury.' So, at the time the defendants dug the trench, it was reasonably foreseeable that *someone like* John Haley – a blind man – would be injured if the defendants dug the trench and then did nothing to fence it off. This was enough to establish that the defendants owed John Haley a duty not to dig the trench and then leave it unfenced.

Real risk

What if the trench dug by the defendants in *Haley* had not been on a public street but in a video arcade? Would a reasonable person in the position of the defendants have thought, 'If the defendants dig a trench here and leave it unfenced, there's a real risk that a blind man will fall into the trench and suffer some form of physical injury'?

Of course not – the possibility that a blind man might come into the vicinity of the trench would simply not have occurred to him, given the fact that the trench was being dug in a video arcade, a place which only sighted people would be interested in visiting. And if someone had suggested to him that a blind man might come near the trench, he would have dismissed the possibility as 'far-fetched or fantastic'.[28] So if a blind man did chance to approach the trench and fall into it, he would not be able to establish that it was reasonably foreseeable that someone like him would be injured if the defendants dug the trench and left it unfenced. He would not therefore be able to invoke the physical danger principle to establish that the defendants owed him a duty not to dig the trench and leave it unfenced.

It was different in *Haley* because the trench in *Haley* was on a public street and the House of Lords – much impressed by statistics offered by counsel as to the number of blind people in the country – did not think that a reasonable person in the position of the defendants would have dismissed the suggestion that a blind man might come into the vicinity of the trench and fall into it as being 'far-fetched or fantastic'. So in *Haley* a reasonable person in the defendants' position would have realised that there was a real risk that a blind man would be injured if the defendants dug their trench and then left it unfenced.

---

[28] *Overseas Tankship (UK) Ltd* v *The Miller Steamship Co. Pty Ltd, The Wagon Mound (No. 2)* [1967] 1 AC 617, 642 per Lord Reid.

Position

Going back to the case of Alan and Wendy: in judging whether it was reasonably foreseeable at the time Alan did x that Wendy would suffer some kind of physical injury if Alan did x, we ask whether a reasonable person in Alan's *position* would have realised at the time Alan did x that there was a real risk that someone like Wendy would suffer some form of physical injury if Alan did x. In order to decide what a reasonable person in Alan's position would have realised at the time Alan did x, we must first give him or her some attributes – an age, a certain level of knowledge, possibly a gender. The fact that we are asking what a reasonable person in Alan's position would have realised means that he or she should share some of Alan's attributes – but which? If Alan was particularly stupid or thoughtless, we would *not* give that attribute to our imaginary reasonable person and ask whether a particularly stupid or thoughtless person would have realised at the time Alan did x that there was a real risk that Wendy would suffer some kind of physical injury if Alan did x.[29] So which of Alan's attributes do we give our reasonable person?

(1) *Knowledge*. In judging what a reasonable person in Alan's position would have realised at the time Alan did x, we give this reasonable person all the knowledge Alan had at the time Alan did x. So suppose Alan and Wendy were both in a laboratory and Alan had two beakers on his desk, each containing a different kind of chemical. Due to his researches and experiments, Alan knew that these two chemicals were liable to explode if they were mixed together – but nobody else in the world knew this at the time. Alan carelessly managed to knock the beakers over, the chemicals mixed, there was an explosion and Wendy was injured. There will be no problem establishing that Alan owed Wendy a duty to take care not to knock the beakers over when they were in the laboratory together – at that time, a reasonable person who knew what Alan knew would have realised that there was a real risk that Wendy would suffer some form of physical injury if Alan knocked the beakers over.

(2) *Age*. In judging what a reasonable person in Alan's position would have realised at the time Alan did x, we ask what a reasonable person of Alan's age would have realised. This follows from the decision of the Court of Appeal in *Mullin* v *Richards*.[30]

In that case, two 15-year-old school children – Teresa Mullin and Heidi Richards – were playfully fencing with plastic rulers when one of the rulers snapped and a fragment of plastic from the snapped ruler entered Mullin's right eye, blinding her in that eye. Mullin sued Richards in negligence, seeking to obtain compensation for the loss of her eye. Mullin claimed that, at the time they were fencing with the rulers, Richards owed Mullin a duty not to carry on the fencing match. Mullin further argued that Richards owed her such a duty because, at the time they were playing around, it was reasonably foreseeable

---

[29] *Vaughan* v *Menlove* (1837) 3 Bing NC 468, 132 ER 490.
[30] [1998] 1 WLR 1304.

that Mullin would be injured if Richards carried on fencing with Mullin. This argument was rejected in the Court of Appeal on the ground that at the time they were fencing, a *reasonable 15-year-old* would not have realised that there was a real risk that Mullin would be injured if Richards and Mullin carried on their fencing match – at the time Mullin and Richards were playing around, it simply would not have occurred to a 15-year-old, however reasonable, that the rulers used by Mullin and Richards in their fencing match would shatter. (Though presumably it would be different if the fencing match had been a particularly violent one.)

(3) *Mental age?* What if John and Paul, two 40-year-old men with a mental age of 15, started fencing playfully with some plastic rulers with the result that one of the rulers shattered and John's eye was damaged? Suppose John sued Paul, arguing that Paul owed him a duty not to carry on with the fencing match because a reasonable person in Paul's position would have realised that there was a real risk that John would be injured if Paul carried on his fencing match with John.

In judging what a reasonable person in Paul's position would have realised, do we ask – Would a reasonable person with a mental age of 15 have realised that there was a real risk that John would be injured if Paul carried on his fencing match with John? In which case, the answer seems to be 'no' and John's claim against Paul will fail, just as Mullin's claim against Richards failed in *Mullin* v *Richards*. Or do we ask – Would a reasonable person aged 40 have realised that there was a real risk that John would be injured if Paul carried on his fencing match with John? In which the case the answer may well be 'yes' and John's claim against Paul will succeed.

The consensus of academic opinion seems to be that in the above case the courts would disregard Paul's low mental age and ask whether a reasonable person of Paul's physical age (40) would have realised that there was a real risk that John would be injured if Paul carried on the fencing match.[31] To take any other line would open up the door to stupid and thoughtless defendants claiming that, like one's mental age, their stupidity or thoughtlessness is an inherited condition which should be taken into account in judging what a reasonable person in their position would have realised.[32]

(4) *Gender?* There is some evidence to suggest that, to some extent, men and women reason differently,[33] which creates the possibility that in judging what a reasonable person in a given defendant's position would have realised, it might be necessary to assign a gender to the reasonable person and ask whether a reasonable person with that gender would have realised that there was a real risk that the claimant would suffer some kind of physical injury if the defendant did what the defendant did. Presumably, if such a case were to arise, the reasonable person would be given the same gender as the defendant.

---

[31] See Moran 2003, 18–26.
[32] For criticism of this argument, see ibid., 28–31; also Mullender 2000.
[33] The classic work is Gilligan 1982.

However, the effect of doing this could be to discriminate unfairly against women. If it is accepted that women, as a whole, are more caring and empathetic than men and therefore more likely to appreciate the consequences of their actions, then it follows the courts will be more likely to find that it was reasonably foreseeable that a claimant would be injured as a result of the defendant's actions – and therefore find that the defendant owed the claimant a duty to take care not to act in the way the defendant did – if the defendant is female.[34] Given this, it might be more satisfactory to determine whether it was reasonably foreseeable that the claimant would be injured as a result of the defendant's actions by asking, *in all cases*, whether a reasonable *male* in the defendant's position would have realised that there was a real risk that the claimant would suffer some kind of physical injury if the defendant did what the defendant did.

Time

In *Roe* v *Minister of Health*,[35] it will be recalled, each of the claimants went into hospital for an operation. In both cases, their spines were injected with nupercaine at the start of the operation to anaesthetise them. Unfortunately, the nupercaine in question had been stored in ampoules which had, in turn, been stored in phenol, a disinfectant. Some of this phenol passed through tiny invisible cracks in the ampoules and contaminated the nupercaine which was injected into the claimants' spines. As a result, the claimants were permanently paralysed. Before the nupercaine was injected into the claimants' spines the ampoules had been inspected for cracks but none were visible and as a result the claimants' doctors thought that it was safe to inject the claimants' spines with the nupercaine; at the time, nobody realised that it was possible that ampoules of nupercaine might suffer from invisible cracks as a result of which the nupercaine contained in those ampoules might become contaminated.

It follows that, once the claimants' doctors had inspected the ampoules of nupercaine for visible cracks and found that there were none, the doctors did *not* owe the claimants a duty not to inject their spines with nupercaine under the physical danger principle. *At that time* (when the injections were administered), a reasonable person in the position of the claimants' doctors would not have thought that there was a real risk that the claimants would suffer some form of physical injury if their spines were injected with nupercaine. Of course, thanks to the experience of people like the claimants in *Roe* we now know better – we now know that if you inject someone's spine with nupercaine which comes from an ampoule which has no visible cracks, there is still a real risk that that nupercaine is contaminated and that that someone will suffer some form of physical injury as a result of being injected with that nupercaine. However, the crucial thing in *Roe* was that at the time the claimants were operated on, nobody realised this – as a result, it was not possible to argue that the claimants' doctors in *Roe* had owed the claimants a duty not to inject their spines with nupercaine under the physical danger principle.

---

[34] See Moran 2003, 92–130, 150–4.
[35] [1954] 2 QB 66.

Similarly, in *Abouzaid* v *Mothercare (UK) Ltd*[36] the claimant was a 12-year-old boy who attempted to attach a sleeping bag to a pushchair. The sleeping bag was attached to the pushchair by passing two elasticated straps attached to either side of the sleeping bag around the back of the pushchair and buckling them together using a metal buckle attached to the end of one of the straps. Unfortunately, when the claimant attempted to buckle the straps together, they slipped from his grasp and the strap with the metal buckle at the end recoiled, hitting the claimant in his left eye. (Presumably the claimant was standing in front of or beside the pushchair when he let go of the straps; had he been standing behind the pushchair, the straps would have recoiled away from him when he let go of them.) The claimant's left eye was blinded as a result and he sued the defendants, who sold the sleeping bag through their stores, for compensation.

His claim in negligence was dismissed: he could not establish that the defendants had owed him a duty not to market the sleeping bag.[37] The reason was that *at the time the defendants marketed the sleeping bag* a reasonable person in the position of the defendants would not have realised that there was a real risk that people like the claimant might suffer some form of physical injury as a result of the sleeping bag being designed the way it was. Before the claimant was injured, there was no reason for anyone to think that someone using the sleeping bag could suffer this kind of accident – presumably because everyone assumed that anyone attaching the sleeping bag to a pushchair would do so by standing behind the pushchair and pulling the straps attached to the sleeping bag towards them; not by standing beside or in front of the pushchair and pulling the straps away from them. Of course we now know better and, as a result, it may well be that stores nowadays owe their customers (and their customers' children) a duty not to market sleeping bags designed in the same way as the sleeping bag in the *Abouzaid* case.

Exceptions

If it is reasonably foreseeable that someone like B will suffer some kind of physical injury if A does *x*, A will *normally* owe B a duty to take care not to do *x*. It's not true to say that A will *always* owe B such a duty – there are a number of exceptional situations where such a duty will not be owed. They are as follows.

Reasonable conduct

Even if it is reasonably foreseeable that B will suffer some kind of physical injury if A does *x*, A will not owe B a duty to take care not to do *x* if – all things considered – it would be *reasonable* for A to do *x*.

There is an understandable temptation to think that if there is a real risk that B will suffer some kind of physical injury if A does *x*, it will always be unrea-

---

[36] The Times, 20 February 2001.
[37] The claimant was, however, allowed to sue for compensation under the Consumer Protection Act 1987: see below, p. 767.

sonable for A to do x. However, a moment's reflection will reveal that this cannot be true. Suppose, for example, that Gary and Vijay are playing football. Now there is a real risk that Vijay will suffer some kind of physical injury if Gary tackles Vijay – the possibility that Vijay will suffer such an injury cannot be dismissed as 'far-fetched or fantastic'. But no one would suggest that it would be unreasonable of Gary to tackle Vijay. Similarly, if you give a friend a lift down to the shops in your car, there is a real risk that your friend will suffer some kind of physical injury as a result: even if you take the utmost care in driving, there is always a possibility that you will have an accident while driving and that your friend will be injured as a result. But, again, no one would suggest that in driving your friend down to shops, you are acting unreasonably.

Let's now look at some cases to see how this idea – that A will not owe B a duty to take care not to do x if, all things considered, it would be reasonable for A to do x – works in practice.

In *Bolton* v *Stone*,[38] the claimant, who was standing outside the defendants' cricket ground, was hit by a cricket ball that had been hit for six and cleared the seven-foot-high fence around the defendants' cricket ground. The claimant sued the defendants in negligence but the House of Lords dismissed her claim. Why? The claimant argued that at the time of her accident a reasonable person in the defendants' position would have realised that there was a real risk that someone like her – a pedestrian walking outside the ground – would suffer some form of physical injury if the defendants played cricket at their ground. It was conceded that this was true. It was not unknown for cricket balls to be hit out of the defendants' ground – in the previous 28 years, a cricket ball had been hit out of the ground six times – so, at the time of the claimant's accident the suggestion that 'If the defendants play cricket on their ground, someone outside the ground may be hit on the head and suffer some form of physical injury' could not have been dismissed as 'far-fetched or fantastic'.

So why did the House of Lords not find that the defendants owed the claimant a duty not to play cricket on their ground or, alternatively, that the defendants owed the claimant a duty not to play cricket on their ground without increasing the height of the fence around their ground to such an extent that it would be virtually impossible for someone to hit a cricket ball out of the ground? The reason was that while there was a real risk that someone like the claimant would suffer some form of physical injury as a result of the defendants' playing cricket on their ground, that risk was extremely small[39] and eliminating it would have put the defendants to a great deal of trouble – they would have had either to stop playing cricket on their ground or to increase the size of the fence around their ground.

Given this, the defendants acted quite reasonably in ignoring the risk and carrying on playing cricket without doing anything to increase the size of the fence around the ground. So it could not be argued either that the defendants owed the claimant a duty not to play cricket on their ground (because it was reasonable for the defendants to play cricket on their ground) or that the

---

[38] [1951] AC 850.

[39] In *Overseas Tankship (UK) Ltd* v *The Miller Steamship Co. Pty Ltd, The Wagon Mound (No. 2)* [1967] 1 AC 617, 642 Lord Reid estimated that the risk of someone being hit by a ball hit out of the defendants' ground was such that it would only happen once every thousand years or so.

defendants owed the claimant a duty not to play cricket on their ground without increasing the size of the fence around the ground (because, again, it was reasonable for the defendants to play cricket on their ground without doing anything about the size of the fence around their ground).

The situation was arguably very different in *Miller* v *Jackson*.[40] In that case, a housing estate had been built next to a cricket ground which was owned by the defendants. About eight or nine times a season, a cricket ball would be hit out of the defendants' ground and would fall into the housing estate. The defendants tried a number of different schemes to stop this happening – they raised the fence around the ground as high as they could and instructed cricket players using the ground to try and hit balls for four, not six – but none of them worked completely. The only way of stopping balls being hit into the housing estate next to the ground completely was to stop using the ground as a cricket ground. And that is what the claimants – who owned one of the houses on the estate – demanded that the defendants do. They argued the defendants owed them a duty not to play cricket on their ground because it was reasonably foreseeable that people like them – people living on the housing estate – would suffer some kind of physical injury if the defendants continued to play cricket on their ground.

There was no doubt that this was true. So the crucial issue in *Miller* v *Jackson* was whether the defendants could bring themselves within the exception discussed here: could they show that, all things considered, it was reasonable for them to carry on playing cricket on their ground, despite the dangers involved for the inhabitants of the nearby housing estate? Of the three members of the Court of Appeal who had to deal with this issue, Lord Denning MR thought that it *was* reasonable for the defendants to carry on playing cricket.[41] The defendants provided a useful amenity in maintaining their ground as a place to play cricket and, besides, the ground had been used as a cricket ground long before the housing estate had been built up and it was hard to see why the defendants should have to stop playing cricket just because some developer had been selfish enough to build an estate on the defendants' doorstep. So Lord Denning took the view that the defendants did *not* owe the claimants a duty not to play cricket on their ground.[42]

Geoffrey Lane LJ took the opposite line. He held that, unlike the case in *Bolton* v *Stone*, the dangers to which people like the claimants were exposed as a result of the defendants' playing cricket on their ground were so serious that it could not be said that it was reasonable for the defendants to carry on playing cricket. So he took the view that the defendants' case did not fall within the exception discussed here. The defendants, then, owed the claimants a duty not

[40] [1977] QB 966.
[41] Ibid., 980.
[42] Confusingly, Lord Denning held that if a ball was hit out of the defendants' ground and hit one of the claimants, the defendants *would* be liable to pay damages to the affected claimant: ibid., 981–2. How can this be if the defendants did no wrong in playing cricket on their ground? It may be that the defendants' liability could be explained away as an example of compensation without wrongdoing (on which, see above, pp. 30–1). A classic example of compensation without wrongdoing is, of course, liability under the rule in *Rylands* v *Fletcher* (on which, see above, pp. 31–2 and below, pp. 739–50) but it was assumed in *Bolton* v *Stone* that the rule does not apply to the case where someone is hit on the head by a cricket ball escaping from a cricket ground: [1951] AC 850, 857, 867.

to play cricket on their ground. The judge went on to hold that the claimants should be awarded an injunction, forbidding the defendants from playing cricket on their ground, albeit postponed for a year to give the defendants time to find another ground on which to play cricket.

Cumming-Bruce LJ's judgment is probably the most difficult to understand. He agreed with Geoffrey Lane LJ that the defendants owed the claimants a duty in negligence not to play cricket on their ground but he refused to award an injunction against the defendants requiring them not to play cricket on their ground. He thought that the public interest demanded that the defendants be allowed to continue playing cricket on their ground and so an injunction should be refused in this case.[43] But if the public interest in the defendants being allowed to continue to play cricket on their ground was so weighty, it was surely reasonable for the defendants to carry on playing cricket on their ground – so how could the defendants have owed the claimants a duty in negligence not to play cricket on their ground?

At any rate, the end result was that the defendants in *Miller* v *Jackson* were allowed to continue playing cricket on their ground and merely had to pay damages to the claimants.

In *Ward* v *London County Council*,[44] the defendant was driving a fire engine to a fire. He ran a stop-light at a light-controlled crossing and, in doing so, collided with the car which was proceeding over the crossing with the lights in its favour. The car was being driven by the claimant at the time. Charles J held the defendant liable to the claimant, holding that the defendant had owed the claimant a duty not to run the stop-light: a reasonable person in the defendant's position would have realised at the time the defendant approached the stop-light that there was a real risk that someone like the claimant would be injured if the defendant ran the stop-light.

Why didn't the defendant come within the exception to the physical danger principle discussed here? Why wasn't it reasonable for the defendant to run the stop-light? Two reasons can be given. First, it is doubtful whether the defendant gained anything by running the stop-light – the delay involved in observing the stop-light could only have amounted to a few seconds, not enough to make any difference to the defendant's ability to fight the fire to which he was driving. Secondly, even if the defendant's running the stop-light had made some difference to his ability to put out the fire to which he was driving, life is more important than property and it was not reasonable for the defendant to endanger people like the claimant by running a stop-light in order to save someone else's property from being damaged.

In a case where we are attempting to see whether the defendant owed a claimant a duty to take care not to do *x* under the physical danger principle, it can often be difficult to tell whether or not the defendant acted reasonably in doing *x*. One often has to make difficult value judgements – one has to weigh

---

[43] It has been held subsequently that the courts are not allowed to take considerations of the 'public interest' into account in deciding whether or not to award an injunction against an admitted wrongdoer: see below, pp. 716–17.

[44] [1938] 1 All ER 341.

the social benefit of the defendant's being allowed to do *x* against the dangers to which the defendant's doing *x* exposed other people and decide which is more important. To assist them in making these value judgements, the courts will often consult community and professional opinion as to what sort of risk-creating conduct is reasonable.

So, for example, suppose that a claimant was hit by a defendant driving down the road at 30 mph: the claimant walked out into the road and the defendant's speed was such that he was unable to avoid hitting her. The claimant sues the defendant, contending that under the physical danger principle he owed her a duty not to drive down the road at 30 mph: at the time, a reasonable person in the defendant's position would have realised that there was a real risk that someone like the claimant would be injured if he drove down the road at 30 mph. The defendant admits this but counters that he acted reasonably in driving down the road at that speed, seeking to bring himself within the exception to the physical danger principle discussed here. If the road was clear and visibility was good it is unlikely that the courts will disagree: it is generally accepted that it is reasonable for a driver to drive down a road at 30 mph if the road is clear and visibility is good.[45]

Again, suppose a surgeon operated on a patient using a general anaesthetic. When the operation finished, the patient failed to come round and slipped into a coma. Did the surgeon owe the patient a duty not to give her a general anaesthetic under the physical danger principle? Obviously, when the operation took place, it was reasonably foreseeable that the patient might suffer some kind of physical injury if she was given a general anaesthetic – there is always a risk that a patient who is operated on under a general anaesthetic will not come round once the operation is concluded. But the surgeon may attempt to argue that the physical danger principle does not apply here because he acted reasonably in giving the patient a general anaesthetic.

In assessing whether it was reasonable for the surgeon to do this, the courts will consult expert medical opinion – if there is a body of medical opinion which says that operating on the patient using a general anaesthetic was a reasonable thing to do, the courts will *normally* find that the surgeon did not owe the patient a duty not to give her a general anaesthetic – and this is so *even if* there is another body of opinion which thinks that giving her a general anaesthetic was an unreasonable thing to do: normally the courts will be unwilling to take sides in medical disputes between different camps of responsible doctors.[46] However, the courts will only *consult* expert medical opinion on this matter – if there is a body of opinion which says that it was reasonable for the surgeon to operate using a general anaesthetic, the courts may still depart from that opinion and rule that it was unreasonable for the surgeon to give the patient a general anaesthetic if there is good reason to think that the contrary medical opinion is corrupt or illogical or anachronistic.[47]

---

[45] *Moore* v *Poyner* [1975] RTR 127. If, on the other hand, the defendant had been driving in excess of the speed limit when he hit the claimant, the claimant should not have much difficulty establishing that the defendant owed her a duty to take care not to drive at the speed he was driving: see, on this, *Grealis* v *Opuni* [2003] EWCA Civ 177.

[46] *Bolam* v *Friern Hospital Management Committee* [1957] 1 WLR 582.

[47] *Bolitho* v *City and Hackney Health Authority* [1998] AC 232.

Volenti non fit injuria

Of course, the surgeon in the above case would not normally have to show that it was reasonable for him to give the patient a general anaesthetic to defeat the claim that he owed her a duty not to give her a general anaesthetic under the physical danger principle. He could simply say – 'She agreed to my giving her a general anaesthetic – so the maxim *volenti non fit injuria* applies here.'

This will usually be a good answer to the claim against him: if it was reasonably foreseeable that B would suffer some kind of physical injury as a result of A's doing *x*, A will not have owed B a duty to take care not to do *x* under the physical danger principle if B agreed that A could do *x*. This assumes of course that B's consent was not vitiated – that is, that B was sane and understood what A's doing *x* involved, that B was not acting under pressure in agreeing that A could do *x*, and that B was old enough to decide for herself whether or not she wanted A to do *x*. If B's consent was vitiated, then the maxim that *volenti non fit injuria* will not apply.

So, for example, suppose two grown adults of sound mind, Carl and Nita, decide to re-enact William Tell's famous exploit of hitting an apple perched on a child's head with an arrow fired from a crossbow. Carl takes the part of William Tell; Nita takes the part of the child. In such a case, Carl will not owe Nita a duty not to fire the arrow at the apple on her head under the physical danger principle – even though there is clearly a risk that Nita will suffer some kind of physical injury if Carl fires the arrow. Similarly, if a customer asks a tattooist to inscribe a tattoo on his arm, the tattooist will not owe the customer a duty not to tattoo him – even though there is clearly a risk that the customer will suffer some kind of physical injury as a result of having his arm tattooed. The customer's consent to being tattooed releases the tattooist from the duty he might otherwise owe the customer not to tattoo him.[48]

In *Johnstone* v *Bloomsbury Health Authority*,[49] the claimant was employed by the defendant health authority. Under the terms of his contract of employment the claimant was required to work 40 hours a week and the health authority had the power to require the claimant to work an additional 48 hours a week 'overtime'. Did this mean that the health authority was free to require the claimant to work 88 hours a week even if it was reasonably foreseeable that the claimant's health would suffer if he was asked to work such hours? The Court of Appeal said 'no': in agreeing that the defendant health authority *could* call on him to work up to 88 hours a week, the claimant did not agree that the defendant health authority could call on him to work such hours if it was reasonably foreseeable that doing so would make him ill.

But what if the claimant *had* agreed that the defendant health authority could call on him to work up to 88 hours a week – even if it was reasonably foreseeable that doing so would make him ill? Two members of the Court of Appeal (Leggatt LJ and Browne-Wilkinson V-C) seemed to think that, in such a case, the defendant health authority would have been free to require the claimant to work up to 88 hours a week – even if it were reasonably foreseeable that the claimant's health would suffer if he were asked to work such hours. But this is

---

[48] Of course, the tattooist will still owe the customer other duties, such as a duty to tattoo the customer with a professional degree of care and skill: see below, pp. 127–9.

[49] [1992] QB 333.

only true, we submit, if the claimant *willingly* agreed that the defendant health authority could call on him to work up to 88 hours a week even if it were reasonably foreseeable that doing so would make him unwell. It is very doubtful whether any doctor would *willingly* agree to this. It is far more likely that he would agree simply because the only alternative to doing so would be to leave his profession. As Stuart-Smith LJ pointed out, 'Any doctor who wishes to practice has to serve at least one year as a house officer in a hospital; the national health service (NHS) is effectively a monopoly employer.'[50] For this reason, Stuart-Smith LJ thought that if a doctor expressly agrees to work up to 88 hours even if it is reasonably foreseeable that making him work such hours will make him unwell, his employer will still not be free to require him to work up to 88 hours a week if it is reasonably foreseeable that the doctor's health will break down if he is made to work such hours.

The Road Traffic Act 1988, s 149 has made one important inroad on the principle of *volenti non fit injuria*. Under s 149(3) of the 1988 Act, if A takes B for a ride in a motor vehicle and B has willingly agreed that A can drive the vehicle dangerously, A will still owe B a duty to take care that he does not drive the vehicle in a dangerous manner. As s 149(3) provides: '[t]he fact that [B] has willingly accepted as his the risk of negligence on the part of [A] shall not be treated as negativing any [liability that A would otherwise incur to B].'

So, in *Pitts* v *Hunt*[51] the claimant and defendant went for a ride on the defendant's motorbike. They were both very drunk and the claimant encouraged the defendant to drive the bike in a more and more dangerous fashion. Eventually, as a result of the defendant's reckless driving, the bike was involved in an accident and the claimant was injured. The claimant sued the defendant so as to be compensated for the injuries suffered by him. It was argued that the defendant did not owe the claimant a duty to take care not to drive the motorbike in a dangerous fashion because the claimant had agreed that the defendant could drive the bike in such a way. This argument was dismissed: the claimant's agreement was of no effect under s 148(3) of the Road Traffic Act 1972 (the predecessor of s 149(3) of the Road Traffic Act 1988) and did not release the defendant from the duty that he owed the claimant under the physical danger principle to take care that he did not drive the bike in a dangerous manner.

Public policy

In *Mulcahy* v *Ministry of Defence*,[52] the claimant was a soldier serving with a British Army artillery unit during the Gulf War. While his unit was deployed in Saudi Arabia firing a howitzer into Iraq, his gun commander ordered him to fetch some water from in front of the howitzer. While the claimant was in front of the gun, the gun commander fired the gun. As a result the claimant's hearing was severely affected. The claimant sued the Ministry of Defence for damages, claiming that the gun commander had been negligent in firing the gun and that

[50] Ibid., 344–5.
[51] [1991] 2 QB 24.
[52] [1996] QB 732.

the Ministry of Defence was vicariously liable in respect of the gun commander's negligence.

In order to make out his claim, the claimant had to show that the gun commander owed him a duty to take care not to fire the gun while he was in front of it. Now – the claimant had a good case for arguing that the gun commander owed him such a duty of care under the physical danger principle: a reasonable person in the gun commander's position would have appreciated that there was a real risk that the claimant would suffer some form of physical injury if the commander fired the gun while the claimant was in front of it. Moreover, neither of the exceptions to the physical danger principle that we have already looked at applied here. It was not reasonable for the gun commander to fire the gun while the claimant was in front of it. And the claimant certainly did not agree that the gun commander could fire the gun while he was in front of it.

Despite this, the Court of Appeal refused to find that the gun commander had owed the claimant a duty of care. Why was this? The Court of Appeal's reasoning went something like this:

> We simply cannot allow the physical danger principle to apply to military officers operating in battle conditions. If we do, then officers will become unduly cautious in making decisions on the battlefield. An officer who is thinking about making some order which will put his men in danger of being killed or injured will think twice about making the order. He'll worry that if he gives the order and some of his men are killed and injured as a result, he could be sued by those men or their families – that those men or their families will argue that he owed his men a duty not to issue the order because it was reasonably foreseeable that some of his men would be killed or injured if he gave that order and the order was an unreasonable one to give. Of course, the officer will be confident that he would win any such litigation – he would be confident that he could show that any orders he gave were reasonable under the circumstances. But that's hardly relevant – being sued is an evil in itself which any rational person will try their best to avoid. So if we allow the physical danger principle to apply to officers acting in the heat of battle, we will only encourage them to become extremely cautious and timid in making decisions on the battlefield – only ordering their men forward, for example, when it is absolutely clear that it is safe to do so. Such an attitude is hardly conducive to winning wars. It would be better then not to apply the physical danger principle at all to military officers acting in the heat of battle – which means that we should rule in this case that the gun commander did not owe the claimant a duty to take care not to fire the gun while the claimant was in front of it.

So the Court of Appeal refused to find that the gun commander owed the claimant a duty of care in *Mulcahy*, not because there was no grounds for finding that such a duty of care was owed, but because they thought that it was in the public interest to find that no such duty of care was owed.

In so doing, it should be noted, the Court of Appeal effectively gave the gun commander an *immunity* from being sued in negligence – and, in so far as *Mulcahy* is a precedent which applies to all cases where a soldier is injured in battle as a result of something done by his superiors, the decision granted all military officers an *immunity* from being sued in negligence by soldiers injured in battle as a result of their actions. What do we mean when we say that the gun commander in *Mulcahy* was given an immunity from being sued in negligence?

A defendant will enjoy an immunity from being sued in negligence if a claimant would *normally* be entitled to sue the defendant in negligence but in fact she is prevented from doing so by some special legal rule.[53] This was the case in *Mulcahy*. The claimant would normally have been entitled to sue the gun commander in negligence for compensation for his loss of hearing – normally, he would have been able to invoke the physical danger principle to show that the gun commander owed him a duty to take care not to fire the gun while the claimant was in front of it; he would have been able to show that the gun commander breached that duty; that his loss of hearing was attributable to that breach of duty; and so on. But the normal rules did not apply in *Mulcahy* – the Court of Appeal created a special exception to those rules, holding that the physical danger principle did not apply to cases such as the claimant's, thereby ensuring that the claimant could not sue the gun commander in negligence.

Contrast this with the case where Alan, a blind man, unwittingly walks over the edge of a cliff and is severely injured. Wendy watched Alan approach the cliff edge but did not bother to call out a warning to him. On discovering this, Alan sues Wendy in negligence for compensation for his injuries. His case is dismissed on the ground that Wendy did not owe Alan a duty to warn him that he was in danger of walking over a cliff-edge. In this case, it would be wrong to say that Wendy enjoys an immunity from being sued in negligence. She does not: it is impossible to say that Alan would *normally* be entitled to sue Wendy in negligence for compensation for his injuries. No special exception has been created to the basic rules governing when someone can sue someone else in negligence to protect Wendy from being sued here – Alan cannot sue Wendy here because according to those very rules he has no case against her.

It is important that one gets clear in one's head when it can be said that someone enjoys an immunity from being sued in negligence because it is becoming increasingly clear that if a claimant is prevented from suing a defendant because the defendant enjoys an immunity from being sued by the claimant, the claimant *may* be able to claim that his rights under Article 6(1) of the European Convention on Human Rights have been violated.

To explain: Article 6(1) provides that, 'In the determination of his civil rights and obligations . . . everyone is entitled to a fair and public hearing within a reasonable time by an independent and impartial tribunal established by law.' This provision has been held to imply the existence of a right of *access to the civil courts.* The classic situation which is covered by this right is the situation where A has an *arguable* case against B but is prevented for some reason from taking B to court or making his case out against B once in court. So, for example, in *Golder* v *United Kingdom* [54] a prisoner wanted to sue the governor of his prison for libel – his claim was that the governor had libelled him by putting him in solitary confinement for some infraction of the prison rules that he did not actually commit. However, the prisoner was denied access to a solicitor and was as

---

[53] This definition is in fact not wholly satisfactory (a more complicated definition of when someone will enjoy an immunity from being sued will be advanced below, at p. 522) but it will serve for present purposes.

[54] (1975) 1 EHRR 524.

a result prevented from taking the governor to court. It was held that his Article 6(1) rights had been violated.

What is of interest to us here is that the case law emanating from the European Court of Human Rights seems to suggest that Article 6(1) does not just cover this kind of situation but also the situation where A has *no* case against B because B enjoys an *immunity* from being sued by A.[55] In such a case, the Court has held, A will be able to claim that his Article 6(1) rights have been violated *if* giving B an immunity from being sued by A serves no legitimate purpose or giving B such an immunity serves a legitimate purpose but in a disproportionate way. It follows from this that the courts in future will have to be cautious about granting defendants immunities from being sued in negligence, as they did in *Mulcahy* – they will have to be careful that they only grant a class of people an immunity from being sued in negligence if doing so would serve a legitimate purpose and sacrificing the interests of those who might want to sue that class is an acceptable price to pay to achieve that purpose.[56] And all existing immunities, such as the immunity granted to military officers in *Mulcahy*, will have to be looked at again to ensure that their existence does not violate the Article 6(1) rights of potential claimants; if an existing immunity serves no legitimate purpose or serves a legitimate purpose but in a disproportionate way, it will have to be abolished.[57]

It seems likely that the immunity enjoyed by military officers from being sued in negligence for their actions on the battlefield will survive this process of scrutiny: the immunity serves a useful purpose and the test of whether an immunity is a 'proportionate' one seems a very relaxed one, if recent cases decided by the European Court of Human Rights are anything to go by. Of course, none of this has any relevance to the case where Alan wants to sue Wendy in negligence for the injuries sustained by him as a result of his walking off the edge of a cliff. As he has no case against Wendy, not because she has an immunity from being sued in negligence, but because he simply has no case, dismissing his claim cannot possibly violate his Article 6(1) rights.[58]

---

[55] See below, p. 522. It must be admitted, though, that the English courts have been unwilling to follow the example of the European Court of Human Rights and hold that Article 6(1) covers cases where someone enjoys an immunity from being sued. See, for example, the Court of Appeal's observation in *Matthews* v *Ministry of Defence* [2002] 1 WLR 2621, at [50] that it 'would be wrong to suggest that article 6(1) could be engaged by a provision of the substantive law of a member state which provides that certain groups will be under no liability in circumstances where others would be under such liability'. When *Matthews* was appealed to the House of Lords, their Lordships took a similarly restrictive view of the scope of Article 6(1): [2003] 1 AC 1163. The House of Lords' decision in *Matthews* is discussed in detail below: pp. 523–4.

[56] The courts are, of course, required not to violate claimants' Article 6(1) rights under the Human Rights Act 1998 (on which, see below, pp. 729–38).

[57] This has already happened with the immunity that barristers enjoyed from being sued in negligence by their clients: *Arthur J S Hall & Co. (a firm)* v *Simons* [2002] 1 AC 615.

[58] *Important note.* At one stage, the European Court of Human Rights (ECHR) seemed to think that a defendant enjoyed an immunity from being sued in negligence *whenever* a claimant was prevented from suing her on the ground that she did not owe the claimant a duty of care: *Osman* v *United Kingdom* [1999] FLR 193. It seemed to follow that *in any case* where A was prevented from suing B in negligence because B did not owe her a duty of care, A could claim that her Article 6(1) rights had been violated (whether they had been or not would depend on whether denying A's claim served a legitimate purpose and sacrificing A's interests was an acceptable price to pay to serve that purpose). The *Osman* case concerned the decision of the Court of

Beyond the physical danger principle

As we have already said, the decision of the House of Lords in *Donoghue* v *Stevenson* helped to entrench what we have called the physical danger principle in English law. But the decision in *Donoghue* v *Stevenson* had wider ramifications. The decision – and in particular Lord Atkin's neighbour principle – emboldened the courts to start finding that defendants owed claimants duties of care based only on the fact that it was reasonably foreseeable that the claimant would suffer some kind of harm as a result of the defendant's acting in the way he did.

Of course, there were limits as to how far the courts were willing to go in doing this. They never accepted, for example, that foreseeability of harm was a sufficient ground to impose a duty on a defendant to perform some positive act. And they never accepted that a defendant would owe a claimant a duty to take care not to act in a particular way if the only harm that it was foreseeable that the claimant would suffer as a result of the defendant's acting in that way was comparatively trivial, such as distress or anxiety or pure economic loss.[59] However, the courts have shown themselves willing to give at least partial effect to Lord Atkin's neighbour principle in two kinds of cases.[60]

Appeal in *Osman* v *Ferguson* [1993] 4 All ER 344. In that case, the police were sued in negligence for failing to arrest a deputy headmaster before he attacked and killed the father of a boy with whom the deputy headmaster was obsessed. The claim was dismissed on the ground that the police had not owed the father a duty of care. The EHCR held that the Court of Appeal had violated the claimants' Article 6(1) rights in so ruling: the Court of Appeal had, in dismissing the claim, conferred an immunity from being sued in negligence on the police and they acted in a disproportionate way in conferring that immunity on the police. But, of course, the decision in *Osman* v *Ferguson* did *not* confer an immunity from being sued in negligence on the police – no sensible person could say that, 'One would normally expect the police to have been held liable in negligence for failing to arrest the deputy headmaster, but the Court of Appeal in *Osman* created a special exception for the police in this case to protect them from being sued.' Given this, it is hard to see how the Court of Appeal in *Osman* violated the claimants' Article 6(1) rights by throwing out their claim in negligence against the police. Subsequently, the ECHR has recanted and confessed that its decision in *Osman* was based on a misunderstanding of the English law of negligence: *Z* v *United Kingdom* [2001] 2 FLR 612 at [100]. The *Z* case concerned the decision of the House of Lords in *X* v *Bedfordshire CC* [1995] 2 AC 633. In that case the claimants sued the social services in negligence for failing to protect them from being abused as children. The House of Lords dismissed the claims on the ground that the social services had not owed the claimants a duty of care. The ECHR held that the House of Lords threw out the claimants' claim *not* because they wanted to give the social services an immunity from being sued in negligence but because, according to the well-established principles governing the law of negligence in England, the claimants simply had no case: [2001] 2 FLR 612 at [100]. So, the ECHR held, it was impossible to argue that the House of Lords had violated the claimants' Article 6(1) rights in throwing out their claims.

[59] 'Pure economic loss' is economic loss suffered by a claimant which is not a result of the claimant's person or property being damaged.

[60] *Important note.* There is a third type of case where the courts may be willing to give effect to Lord Atkin's neighbour principle, and that is where A's actions are liable to have the effect of causing B to lose her *freedom*. See, for example, *Clarke* v *Chief Constable of Northamptonshire*, The Times, 14 June 1999 where the Court of Appeal ruled that the police will owe a prisoner a duty to take care not to misrecord the date on which he was taken into custody if the foreseeable effect of doing so would be to cause the prisoner to be detained for longer than he ought to be detained. Also *Al-Kandari* v *J R Brown & Co.* [1988] QB 665, where the Court of Appeal ruled that if C has a proven record of attempting to kidnap B's children and A currently holds C's passport so as to prevent him attempting to leave the country with B's children, A will owe B's children a duty to take care that he does not do anything which would result in C getting his passport back.

First, cases where a claimant has suffered a psychiatric illness[61] as a result of a defendant's doing x. (Let's call these *psychiatric illness cases*.) If the claimant can show that it was reasonably foreseeable at the time the defendant acted that someone like him would suffer a psychiatric illness as a result of the defendant's doing x, the courts may well find that the defendant owed the claimant a duty to take care not to do x – though, for reasons we will explore below, whether they will or not will often depend on how the claimant's psychiatric illness was triggered.

Secondly, cases where a defendant did x and an item of property P has been harmed as a result. (Let's call these cases *harm to property cases*.) If a claimant can show that it was reasonably foreseeable at the time the defendant acted that an item of property like P would be harmed if the defendant did x and the claimant had a sufficient interest in P at the time it was harmed, the courts will normally find that the defendant owed the claimant a duty to take care not to do x.

In the rest of this chapter we will look at when exactly the courts will find that a defendant owed a claimant a duty of care in these two kinds of cases. We will start with psychiatric illness cases.

PSYCHIATRIC ILLNESS CASES

We are concerned here with the situation where B has developed a psychiatric illness as a result of A's doing x; and B wants to sue A in negligence for compensation for that illness. To make out her claim, she will have to show that A owed her a duty to take care not to do x. When will B be able to do this?

Sometimes, she will be able to use the physical danger principle to establish that A owed her a duty to take care not to do x. This will be the case, for example, if A ran into B's car while she was in it and she was so frightened by the experience that she subsequently developed a psychiatric illness. In this case, B will be able to invoke the physical danger principle to establish that A owed her a duty to take care not to run into her car.[62] A similar analysis will

---

[61] A mental condition will only amount to a psychiatric illness if it is recognised by the psychiatric profession as being such. On the distinction between psychiatric illnesses and lesser forms of mental distress, see *Reilly* v *Merseyside RHA* [1996] 6 Med LR 246 (apprehension, fear, discomfort and shortness of breath arising out of being trapped in a lift do not amount to a psychiatric illness) and *Group B Plaintiffs* v *Medical Research Council* [2000] Lloyd's Rep Med 161 (sleeplessness arising out of being told that one might contract the CJD virus in future is capable of amounting to a psychiatric illness).

[62] Note that in order to establish that A owed her a duty to take care not to run into her car, B will *not* have to show that it was reasonably foreseeable that she would suffer a psychiatric illness as a result of A's running into her car. In order to invoke the physical danger principle here, she merely has to show that it was reasonably foreseeable that she would be physically injured as a result of A's running into her car: *Page* v *Smith* [1996] AC 155. If, in crashing into B's car, A breached the duty of care he owed B under the physical danger principle to take care not to crash into her car, the usual rule is that B will only be able to recover for the reasonably foreseeable losses suffered by her as a result of the crash. However, *Page* v *Smith* created a special exception for people in B's position – it says that B will be able to claim for compensation for the psychiatric illness that she suffered as a result of A's negligence even if it was not a reasonably foreseeable consequence of A's negligence: the fact that it was reasonably foreseeable that B would suffer some kind of physical injury as a result of A's negligence will be enough to make B's psychiatric illness actionable. There is little to be said in favour of this concession to claimants and the courts have subsequently shown themselves eager to confine *Page* v *Smith* to its own facts: see below, at pp. 561–2.

apply in the case where – as happened in the case of *Group B Plaintiffs* v *Medical Research Council*[63] – A injects B with some hormone which may be contaminated with a deadly virus and B, on learning this, develops a psychiatric illness as a result of worrying about whether the hormone which was injected into her was contaminated or not. Provided that A knew or ought to have know that the hormone was potentially contaminated, B will be able to invoke the physical danger principle to establish that A owed her a duty not to inject her with the hormone.

But there are many cases where B has suffered a psychiatric illness as a result of A's doing *x* where B will *not* be able to invoke the physical danger principle to establish that A owed her a duty to take care not to do *x*. Let's call these *non-physical danger psychiatric illness cases*. Here are five such cases:

(1) *Psychiatric illness arising out of someone else's being killed or injured.* A does something which results in C being killed or injured. B suffers a psychiatric illness as a result.

(2) *Psychiatric illness arising out of someone else's being maltreated.* A maltreats C – without killing or injuring C – and B suffers a psychiatric illness as a result.

(3) *Pyschiatric illness arising out of being given bad news.* A tells B some bad news – for example, that her daughter is dead. B suffers a psychiatric illness as a result.

(4) *Psychiatric illness arising out of being treated in a distressing or humiliating way.* A treats B in a distressing or humiliating way – such as making her undress in front of complete strangers. B suffers a psychiatric illness as a result.

(5) *Psychiatric illness arising out of being subjected to a stressful experience.* A makes B do some work which is extremely stressful. B suffers a psychiatric illness as a result.

B will not be able to invoke the physical danger principle in any of these cases to establish that A owed her a duty of care not to act in the way he did. But the courts may still find that A owed B a duty of care not to act in the way he did. In order to establish that A owed B such a duty of care, the *first* thing that has to be shown – in line with Lord Atkin's neighbour principle – is that it was *reasonably foreseeable* that someone like B would suffer a psychiatric illness as a result of A's acting in the way he did. But even if this is shown, that does not necessarily mean that A owed B a duty of care not to act in the way he did. The courts may require *something more* to be established before they will find that A owed B a duty of care not to act in the way he did. Let's now flesh this out by looking at each of the above non-physical danger psychiatric illness cases in detail and seeing what will have to be established before the courts will find that a duty of care was owed in those cases.

---

[63] [2000] Lloyd's Rep Med 161 (discussed, O'Sullivan 1999).

Psychiatric illness arising out of someone else's being killed or injured

Let's suppose that A has caused an accident *x* to occur in which various people were killed or injured.[64] Suppose further that B was not physically involved in the accident, but she still developed a psychiatric illness as a result of witnessing, or thinking about or hearing about the accident.[65] As we have already observed, if B wants to establish that A owed her a duty of care not to act as he did, the first thing she will have to show is that it was reasonably foreseeable that she would suffer a psychiatric illness as a result of A's causing that accident to occur.[66]

The requirement of reasonable foreseeability

It seems that B will only be able to satisfy this requirement of reasonable foreseeability in four situations.

(1) *Close and loving relationship.* Suppose that Carl accidentally ran Ian's fiancee, Dawn, down in his car and she was killed. Ian is so grief-stricken by the news of Dawn's death that he develops a psychiatric illness. Clearly in this case it will have been reasonably foreseeable that someone like Ian – someone who was in a close and loving relationship with Dawn – would develop a psychiatric illness if Carl ran Dawn down.

(2) *Rescue.* Continuing with the above case, suppose that Lara ran to Dawn's aid once she had been run over. She saw Dawn's injuries close up, heard Dawn's last words and Dawn died in her arms. Lara is so affected by this experience that she develops post-traumatic stress disorder, a form of psychiatric illness. Again, it will have been reasonably foreseeable that someone like Lara – who attempted to rescue Dawn after she was run down and witnessed at close quarters Dawn's condition having been run down – would develop a psychiatric illness if Carl ran Dawn down.

---

[64] The principles laid out here are not just confined to accident cases, but will also apply in a case where, for example, A *deliberately* killed or injured C and B developed a psychiatric illness as a result: see *W* v *Essex CC* [2001] 2 AC 592 (discussed below, at n. 72 and at p. 100, below).

[65] If B was involved in the accident, she would probably be able to invoke the physical danger principle to establish that A owed her a duty of care not to act as he did: see above, pp. 87–8.

[66] For a case where the claimant could not satisfy this requirement, see *Bourhill* v *Young* [1943] AC 92. In that case, a motorcyclist who was driving at an excessive speed drove into a motorcar and was killed. The claimant was fifty feet from the accident when it happened. She heard, but did not witness, the crash and developed a psychiatric illness as a result of the shock of hearing the crash. The claimant sued the motorcyclist's estate for compensation, claiming that the motorcyclist had owed her, and breached, a duty to take care not to run into the motorcar. The claimant's claim for compensation was dismissed by the House of Lords on the ground that the motorcylist had not owed the claimant such a duty of care. It was simply not reasonably foreseeable that someone like the claimant – who was fifty feet away from the accident when it happened, who did not witness the accident occur, and who was unrelated to anyone involved in the accident – would develop a psychiatric illness if the motorcyclist ran into the motorcar. Of course, the claimant heard the crash occur, but the noise of the crash was not so horrific that someone of reasonable fortitude or 'phlegm' who heard it could have been expected to develop a psychiatric illness as a result – so the fact that the claimant heard the crash occur did not help her show that it was reasonably foreseeable that someone like her would develop a psychiatric illness if the motorcyclist ran into the motorcar.

(3) *Feelings of responsibility.* Suppose that Dawn had been walking to the shops when she was run down. She had asked an acquaintance of hers, Gary, to give her a lift to the shops in his car, but he had turned her down, saying he was too busy. When Gary heard the news of what had happened to Dawn, he was horrified and felt that he was, in part, responsible for Dawn's death. Overwhelmed by his feelings of guilt, Gary eventually developed a psychiatric illness. Again, it is clearly arguable in this case that it was reasonably foreseeable that someone like Gary – who felt responsible for Dawn's death – would develop a psychiatric illness if Carl ran over Dawn.

(4) *Witnessing an acutely horrific accident occur.* Suppose that Ruth saw Carl knock Dawn down. She did not know Dawn at all, she did not attempt to assist Dawn after she was knocked down and she did not feel at all responsible for Dawn's being run down. However, the impact of what she saw was such that she still developed a psychiatric illness. Here, Ruth will find it difficult to establish that it was reasonably foreseeable that someone like her – a mere bystander who saw Dawn being run down – would develop a psychiatric illness if Carl ran Dawn down. A bystander of reasonable fortitude or 'phlegm' could be expected to cope a little better with the experience of seeing a complete stranger being run down. But it is possible to conceive of accidents which are so acutely horrifying that a mere bystander witnessing the accident occur *could* be expected to develop a psychiatric illness as a result. In argument before the House of Lords in the case of *Alcock* v *Chief Constable of South Yorkshire Police*,[67] the example was given 'of a petrol tanker careering out of control into a school in session and bursting into flames'.[68] It does seem reasonably foreseeable that a passer-by witnessing this happen would develop a psychiatric illness as a result.

So – if A has caused an accident *x* to occur in which various people were killed and injured and B, who was not physically involved in the accident, developed a psychiatric illness as a result of witnessing, hearing about or thinking about the accident, B will *only* be able to establish that it was reasonably foreseeable that she would develop a psychiatric illness as a result of A's causing accident *x* to occur if: (*a*) B was in a close and loving relationship with someone killed or injured in accident *x*; *or* (*b*) B attempted to rescue people who were killed or injured in accident *x*; *or* (*c*) B felt responsible for accident *x*'s occurring; *or* (*d*) B witnessed accident *x* occur and the accident was so acutely horrifying that anyone of reasonable fortitude or 'phlegm' witnessing it occur could have been expected to develop a psychiatric illness as a result.

But, of course, it is important to remember that even if B falls into one of these categories that does not necessarily mean that it *was* reasonably foreseeable that someone like B would develop a psychiatric illness as a result of A's causing accident *x* to occur. The reasonable foreseeability requirement might still not be satisfied. Two examples where this requirement will not be satisfied can be given.

[67] [1992] 1 AC 310.
[68] Ibid., 403.

First, Paul accidentally knocks Karen to the ground. Karen bruises her knee as a result. Sarah, Karen's mother, sees the bruise and develops a psychiatric illness as a result. Clearly it was not reasonably foreseeable that someone like Sarah would develop a psychiatric illness as a result of Paul's brusing Karen's knee. This is so even though Sarah was in a close and loving relationship with Karen.

Secondly, John accidentally runs Wendy down in his car. Fred sees the accident occur and calls an ambulance on his mobile 'phone, but otherwise does nothing to assist Wendy. He is subsequently so affected by the experience that he develops a psychiatric illness. Clearly it was not reasonably foreseeable that someone like Fred – someone who witnessed Wendy being run down and called an ambulance for her – would develop a psychiatric illness if John ran Wendy down. This is so even though, technically, one could say that Fred 'rescued' Wendy in the aftermath of the accident.

Reasonable foreseeability is not enough

The courts have not been willing to give *complete* effect to Lord Atkin's neighbour principle in this area. Even if B can show, in the situation we are considering, that it was reasonably foreseeable that she would develop a psychiatric illness as a result of A's causing accident *x* to occur, that will *not* be enough to establish that A owed B a duty of care not to act as he did. Something more will always be required to be shown before a duty of care will be found. What that 'something more' will be will depend on *how* B's psychiatric illness was triggered. Before we look at some of these cases that deal with this issue, let us sum up what they say:

(1) *Close and loving relationship*. Let's suppose that B developed her psychiatric illness because she was in a 'close and loving relationship' with C, who was killed or injured in accident *x*. In this sort of case, A will *only* have owed B a duty of care not to act as he did *if B's psychiatric illness was triggered by her witnessing accident x occur or its immediate aftermath*.

So, for example, suppose that C was so badly injured in accident *x* that B had to give up her job and look after C on a full-time basis. Suppose further that the strain of looking after C got too much for B and as a result she developed a psychiatric illness. In this sort of case, B will *not* be able to establish that A owed her a duty of care not to act as he did.[69] Even though it was perfectly foreseeable that she would develop a psychiatric illness as a result of A's causing accident *x* to occur, B's illness was not triggered by her witnessing accident *x* or its immediate aftermath.

This rule, it should be noted, gives rise to two points of difficulty. First of all, suppose that A caused an accident to occur in which B's son was badly injured. He was taken to hospital for treatment. B arrived at the hospital shorty afterwards and witnessed her son die. B subsequently developed a psychiatric illness. Before the courts will find that A owed B a duty to take care not to cause the

---

[69] Ibid., 400 (per Lord Ackner).

accident in question, they will need to be satisfied that B's illness occurred because of what she saw when she saw her son in hospital in the immediate aftermath of the accident and that B's illness was not simply an abnormal reaction to the fact that her son died. So it must be shown that B's seeing her son in hospital amounted to a 'horrifying event, which violently agitated [her] mind'.[70]

Secondly, suppose that A caused an accident to occur in which B's son was injured. Her son was taken to hospital and B came to the hospital some time later and developed a psychiatric illness as a result of what she saw and heard when she went to the hospital. Will B be able to claim that she witnessed the *immediate aftermath* of the accident when she went to the hospital? Obviously it will depend on how much time elapsed between the time the accident occurred and the time B went to the hospital. An hour's delay would not prevent B claiming that she witnessed the immediate aftermath of the accident[71] but a day's delay probably would.[72]

(2) *Rescue.* If B developed her psychiatric illness because she attempted to rescue some of the victims of accident *x*, A will only have owed her a duty to take care not to cause accident *x* if B put herself in physical danger in attempting to rescue the victims of the accident or she thought she was in danger when she attempted to rescue the victims of the accident.

(3) *Feelings of responsibility.* If B developed her psychiatric illness because she felt responsible for the fact that accident *x* occurred, A will only have owed

---

[70] Ibid., 401. For criticisms of this requirement, see Teff 1996. This requirement was not satisfied in *Sion* v *Hampstead HA* [1994] 5 Med LR 170 where the claimant's son was involved in a motorcycle accident caused by the defendant that caused him to go into a coma and die after 14 days. The claimant attended his son's bedside all that time and developed a psychiatric illness after his son died. It was held that the claimant's psychiatric illness was not triggered by his seeing his son in the aftermath of the accident – as he saw nothing particularly horrifying or shocking in the aftermath of the accident that could have triggered a psychiatric illness. The claimant's psychiatric illness simply amounted to an abnormal reaction to the loss of his son.

[71] *McLoughlin* v *O'Brian* [1983] 1 AC 410.

[72] *Alcock* v *Chief Constable of South Yorkshire Police* [1992] 1 AC 310. But regard must be had to the decision of the House of Lords in *W* v *Essex CC* [2001] 2 AC 592. In that case – an example of a trauma case which did not involve an accident – the defendants were a local authority who placed a 15-year-old boy with the claimants, two parents who acted as foster carers and who had four children of their own, then aged between 8 and 12. The 15-year-old boy – as the defendants well knew – had a history of sexual abuse. While he was fostered with the claimants, the 15-year-old boy sexually abused all of the claimants' children. When the claimants discovered this *four weeks later*, they each developed forms of psychiatric illness. The claimants sued the defendants in negligence, claiming that the defendants had owed them a duty not to foster the boy with them. The defendants applied to have the claims struck out, arguing that they had not owed the claimants such a duty. (It should be noted that the defendants almost certainly owed such a duty to the claimants' *children* under the physical danger principle.) The House of Lords refused to strike out the claims, holding that the claimants had an arguable case against the defendants. Foreseeability was clearly made out: the claimants were in a close and loving relationship with their children. But could they show that their psychiatric illness was triggered by their seeing that their children had been abused *in the immediate aftermath of that abuse*? Lord Slynn, giving the only judgment, held that it was arguable that this requirement was made out despite the long gap between the children's being abused and the claimants' finding out about it: 'it seems to me that the concept of "the immediate aftermath" of the incident has to be assessed in the particular factual situation. I am not convinced here that in a situation like the present the parents must come across the abuser or the abused "immediately" after the sexual incident has terminated': ibid., 601.

her a duty to take care not to cause accident *x* if B witnessed accident *x* occur.

(4) *Witnessing an acutely horrifying accident occur.* If B developed her psychiatric illness merely because she witnessed accident *x* occur as a mere bystander, the decided cases seem to have taken the view that A will simply not have owed B a duty to take care not to cause accident *x* to occur. This is so even if accident *x* was so acutely horrific that anyone witnessing it as a mere bystander could have been expected to develop a psychiatric illness as a result.

Let's now look at some of the cases from which the above propositions of law are drawn.[73]

(1) *Alcock* v *Chief Constable of the South Yorkshire Police.*[74] This case arose out of the Hillsborough disaster where 95 football fans were crushed to death and hundreds more were injured at the Leppings Lane end of Hillsborough Football Stadium in Sheffield before an FA Cup semi-final between Liverpool and Nottingham Forest. The immediate cause of the disaster was the decision of the police to open an outer gate to the Leppings Lane end of the Hillsborough Stadium without cutting off access to spectator pens 3 and 4 at that end which were already full. Football fans rushed through the opened gate into pens 3 and 4 with the result that those at the front of those pens were crushed. The claimants in *Alcock* were relatives of the dead who had developed psychiatric illnesses – forms of post-traumatic stress disorder – in the aftermath of the disaster. None of the claimants whose cases were decided by the House of Lords in *Alcock* succeeded in their claims for compensation; none of them could establish that the police owed them a duty to take care not to cause the accident at Hillsborough.[75]

Most of the claimants in *Alcock* failed to establish that the police owed them a duty of care because they could not show that it was reasonably foreseeable that they would develop a psychiatric illness as a result of the accident at Hillsborough occurring. The only way they could show that it was reasonably foreseeable that they would develop a psychiatric illness as a result of the Hillsborough tragedy occurring was by showing that they were in a close and loving relationship with someone killed or injured at Hillsborough. But the House of Lords held that most of the *Alcock* claimants were *not* in a close and loving relationship with anyone killed or injured at Hillsborough. For example, Brian Harrison suffered post-traumatic stress disorder when he lost his two

---

[73] For a good, critical survey of the law in this area, see Butler 2002.

[74] [1992] 1 AC 310.

[75] One claimant succeeded in his claim for compensation at first instance: William Pemberton, who went by coach with his son to the match. His son had a ticket to watch the match; Pemberton stayed on in the coach, intending to watch the match on the coach's television. Pemberton watched the disaster unfold on the television and then searched for his son. His son had in fact died in the disaster and Pemberton identified his body at around midnight. No appeal was made against the first instance judge's decision that the police had owed Pemberton a duty to take care not to cause the accident at Hillsborough: ibid., 339, 348, 351, 365.

brothers at Hillsborough. His claim that the police owed him a duty to take care not to cause the accident at Hillsborough failed because there was nothing in the evidence before the House of Lords to suggest that he enjoyed a sufficiently close and loving relationship with his brothers as to make it reasonably foresee-able that he would develop a psychiatric illness as a result of their being killed and the House of Lords was not prepared to presume that Brian Harrison enjoyed such a relationship with his brothers.

It was different in the case of Mr and Mrs Copoc, who lost their son at Hillsborough and subsequently suffered post-traumatic stress disorder. In their case, the House of Lords *was* prepared to presume – in the absence of any evidence going the other way – that they enjoyed such a close and loving relationship with their son that it was reasonably foreseeable that they would develop a psychiatric illness in the aftermath of the Hillsborough dis-aster. Their claims that the police owed them a duty to take care not to cause the accident at Hillsborough failed because they could not establish that their psychiatric illnesses were triggered by their witnessing the Hillsborough disaster unfold or its immediate aftermath. They *did* see live pictures of the Hillsborough disaster unfolding on television but the fact that broadcasting guidelines forbade the transmission of live pictures showing scenes of recognisable human suffering led the House of Lords to think that what the Copocs saw on television could not have accounted for their subsequently developing post-traumatic stress disorder. The pictures they saw were insufficiently shocking – they gave rise to anxiety, but nothing more. Nor could the Copocs establish that they developed their psychiatric illnesses as a result of witnessing the *immediate* aftermath of the Hillsborough tragedy. Only one of the Copocs – Mr Copoc – travelled to Sheffield after the disaster and he only saw his son's body the next day, long after the disaster had occurred. The real reason why the Copocs suffered post-traumatic stress disorder in the aftermath of the Hillsborough disaster was because of what they *imagined* their son had gone through – not because of what they *saw*.

The House of Lords was only prepared to presume that one other *Alcock* claimant enjoyed a close and loving relationship with someone killed or injured in the Hillsborough tragedy. This was Alexandra Penk. She lost her fiancé, Carl Rimmer, at Hillsborough and subsequently suffered post-traumatic stress dis-order.[76] But again, Ms Penk's claim that the police owed her a duty to take care not to cause the accident at Hillsborough to occur failed because she could not establish that her psychiatric illness was triggered by her witnessing the Hillsborough tragedy unfold or its immediate aftermath. All Ms Penk saw were

---

[76] Would the House of Lords have been prepared to presume that she was in a close and loving relationship with Carl Rimmer had they actually been married at the time of the Hillsborough tragedy? One would have thought so, but see Lord Keith's remarks in *Alcock*: '[the] kinds of relationship which may involve close ties of love and affection ... may be present in family relationships or those of close friendship and may be stronger in the case of engaged couples than in that of persons who have been married to each other for many years': [1992] 1 AC 310, 397.

live pictures of the tragedy unfolding – and they were insufficiently shocking for her post-traumatic stress disorder to be attributed to her witnessing them.

So – the House of Lords' decision in *Alcock* principally established two things. First, if B developed a psychiatric illness because she was in a close and loving relationship with someone killed or injured in an accident *x* that was caused by A, A will only have owed B a duty to take care not to cause accident *x* if B's pyschiatric illness was triggered by her witnessing the accident occur or its immediate aftermath.

Secondly, if a third party, T, was involved in an accident *x* that was caused by A, and B wishes to show that she was in a close and loving relationship with T for the purpose of establishing that A owed her a duty to take care not to cause accident *x* to occur, the courts will only presume that B was in such a close and loving relationship with T – in the absence of any evidence going the other way – if T was B's child, parent, fiancé or (presumably) spouse. If T was none of these things, then the courts will find that B did *not* have a close and loving relationship with T unless she can supply the courts with evidence tending to indicate that she did enjoy such a relationship with T.

Can either the first or second aspects of the House of Lords' decision in *Alcock* be supported?

We can understand the rationale behind the first aspect of the House of Lords' decision in *Alcock* by considering its effect in the following case. Fred participates in a live television show in which members of the public undertake various dangerous challenges. Fred's challenge is to undergo a bungee jump. Because Tom, a technician on the show, failed properly to attach Fred to the bungee rope, Fred fell to his death when he undertook the jump. Fred's fiancée, Beth, went with Fred to watch him undertake the bungee jump and saw him fall to his death. She was so traumatised by what she saw that she developed post-traumatic stress disorder as a result. Fred's mother, Mary, saw Fred fall to his death because she watched Fred undertake the bungee jump at home on television. The shock of witnessing Fred's death resulted in her developing post-traumatic stress disorder. Fred's father, Eric, did not see Fred make his jump but he went to the mortuary two days after the accident to identify Fred's remains. He was so traumatised by what he saw that he subsequently suffered post-traumatic stress disorder. Ruth, Fred's daughter by his fiancée, did not see Fred make his jump. She suffered post-traumatic stress disorder when she was told that Fred had died and how he had died.

The decision in *Alcock* means that although it was reasonably foreseeable that Beth, Mary, Eric and Ruth would each develop some kind of psychiatric illness as a result of the occurrence of the accident involving Fred, Tom will only have owed Beth and Mary a duty to take care not to cause that accident to occur. No duty will have been owed to Eric because his post-traumatic stress disorder was not triggered as a result of his witnessing the *immediate* aftermath of Fred's death. No duty will have been owed to Ruth because her post-traumatic stress disorder arose because of how she reacted to the *news* of Fred's death, not because she *witnessed* Fred's death or its immediate aftermath.

Now: why do the courts artificially restrict the range of people to whom Tom owed a duty to take care not to cause the accident involving Fred in this way?

Why will they say that Tom owed a duty of care in the situation we are considering to Beth and Mary but not to Eric or Ruth? It is hard to resist the impression that courts artificially restrict the range of people to whom Tom owed a duty of care so as to ensure that if Tom did carelessly cause Fred to fall to his death, he will not be held liable to compensate Beth *and* Mary *and* Eric *and* Ruth for the post-traumatic stress disorders that they each developed when Fred died. If Tom did carelessly cause Fred to fall to his death and was held liable to *that* extent, his liability would be out of all proportion to his fault. So, in the case just described, the courts will deny that Fred owed Eric and Ruth a duty to take care not to cause the accident that killed Fred as a rough-and-ready way of preventing Tom's liability in the event that he carelessly caused Fred to fall to his death getting out of all proportion to his fault. The way in which the courts limit Tom's liability is, admittedly, unprincipled – there is, for example, no real distinction between the situations of Fred's two parents, Mary and Eric, here and thus no reason why Mary should be allowed to recover from Tom if he carelessly caused Fred to fall to his death while Eric should not – but the desire to limit Tom's liability in the case just described is an intelligible one.

Less defensible is the second aspect of the House of Lords' ruling in *Alcock*. Suppose John caused an accident in which Nita's cousin was killed. Nita witnessed the accident and developed a psychiatric illness as a result. As a result of the second aspect of the House of Lords' ruling in *Alcock*, Nita will not be able to establish that John owed her a duty to take care not to cause the accident in which her cousin was killed unless she can come up with evidence that indicates that she was in a close and loving relationship with her cousin – and if Nita does advance evidence indicating that she was in a close and loving relationship with her cousin, John will be entitled to question the reliability of that evidence and, more broadly, cast doubt on whether Nita and her cousin were that close. It is obvious that both Nita and John will find this whole process immensely embarrassing, distasteful and unseemly. Moreover, the courts will have to undertake the grotesque and disreputable task of sifting the evidence presented by Nita and John to determine how close Nita actually was to her cousin. It is hardly likely that the courts will come out of this process with their dignity intact. Given this, it might be better if the House of Lords had held in *Alcock* that certain relationships will be conclusively presumed to have been close and loving relationships[77] and that all other relationships will be conclusively presumed not to have been close and loving relationships.

(2) *The rescue cases.* In *Chadwick v British Transport Commission*,[78] two trains crashed into each other at Lewisham. The defendants were responsible. The accident occurred about 200 yards from Henry Chadwick's home. He went to

---

[77] The Law Commission has proposed that if T was killed or injured in an accident caused by A and B developed a psychiatric illness as a result, the courts should conclusively presume that B was in a close and loving relationship with T if: (1) T and B were married at the time of the accident; (2) B was T's parent; (3) B was T's child; (4) T was B's brother or sister; (5) T and B had been living together as lovers for at least two years at the time of the accident. See Law Com. No. 249, *Liability for Psychiatric Illness* (1998).

[78] [1967] 1 WLR 912.

help the survivors of the accident and spent about nine hours crawling through the wreckage, administering injections to passengers who were injured and helping them to extricate themselves from the wreckage. As a result of what he saw and heard at the scene of the accident, Chadwick became psycho-neurotic and had to spend six months in a mental hospital. Chadwick sued the defendants in negligence for compensation for his illness, claiming that the defendants had owed him, and breached, a duty to take care not to cause the Lewisham train crash. The court agreed on the basis that it was reasonably foreseeable that someone like Chadwick – someone who did what he did and saw what he saw in rescuing the victims of the Lewisham train crash – would develop a psychiatric illness in the aftermath of the Lewisham train crash. So *Chadwick* established that if A caused an accident *x* to occur and B developed a psychiatric illness as a result of what he saw and heard in helping and rescuing the victims of the accident and it was to be expected that B would develop such a psychiatric illness, then A will have owed B a duty to take care not to cause accident *x* to occur.

However, the decision in *Chadwick* was recently qualified by the House of Lords' decision in *White* v *Chief Constable of South Yorkshire Police*.[79] Again, the case arose out of the Hillsborough tragedy. This time the claimants were police officers who suffered post-traumatic stress disorder as a result of what they saw and heard when helping out in the aftermath of the Hillsborough disaster. Two of the claimants helped carry the dead, two of the claimants tried unsuccessfully to resuscitate injured spectators in the stadium and one of the claimants assisted at a mortuary to which the dead were taken. The claimants attempted to obtain compensation for their post-traumatic stress disorders, claiming that the senior police officers who were in charge of the policing of the Hillsborough semi-final had owed *them* a duty to take care not to cause the accident at Hillsborough. The House of Lords held that no such duty of care had been owed. In order to establish that the officers who were in charge at Hillsborough had owed them a duty to take care not to cause the accident at Hillsborough it was not enough for the claimant police officers to show that their post-traumatic stress disorders had arisen because of what they saw and heard in rescuing the victims of the Hillsborough disaster – they had also to show that they had put themselves in danger in rescuing the victims of the Hillsborough disaster or had thought they were in danger when they rescued the victims of the Hillsborough disaster. As neither of these things were true of the claimants in *White*, the officers who were in charge at Hillsborough had *not* owed the claimants a duty to take care not to cause the accident at Hillsborough.

Why did the House of Lords qualify the effect of the decision in *Chadwick* in this way? It is hard to avoid the impression that the House of Lords decided *White* the way they did because they thought that the law would be brought into disrepute if the claimant police officers in *White* were allowed to claim

---

[79] [1999] 2 AC 455. The case is otherwise known as *Frost* v *Chief Constable of South Yorkshire Police*.

compensation for the post-traumatic stress disorders that they suffered in the aftermath of Hillsborough when the relatives in *Alcock* had not been allowed to claim compensation for the post-traumatic stress disorders that they suffered in the aftermath of the Hillsborough disaster. Indeed, both Lord Steyn and Lord Hoffmann explicitly acknowledged as much in their judgments in *White*.[80] The easiest way of ensuring that the claimants in *White* would not be able to claim compensation for the post-traumatic stress disorders that they suffered in the aftermath of Hillsborough was, of course, to deny that the officers who were in charge at Hillsborough had owed those police officers a duty to take care not to cause the Hillsborough accident to occur and the House of Lords seized on the fact that the claimants in *White* were never in any physical danger and never thought they were in any physical danger as a 'reason' for finding that the officers who were in charge at Hillsborough had not owed the claimants in *White* such a duty.

In deciding *White* the way they did, the House of Lords did not overrule the decision in *Chadwick* that the defendants in that case *did* owe Chadwick a duty to take care not to cause the Lewisham train crash. This is because there was some evidence in Chadwick's case that he had put himself in danger of being killed or injured when he assisted in the aftermath of the Lewisham train crash. However, the decision in *White* does have an unfortunate implication, best highlighted by an 'extreme' case posited by Lord Goff, who dissented in *White*:

> Suppose there was a terrible train crash and that there were two Chadwick brothers living nearby, both of them ... distinguished by their courage and humanity. Mr A Chadwick worked on the front half of the train, and Mr B Chadwick on the rear half. It so happened that, although there was some physical danger present in the front half of the train, there was none in the rear. Both worked for 12 hours or so bringing aid and comfort to the victims. Both suffered [post traumatic stress disorder] in consequence of the general horror of the situation.[81]

According to the decision in *White*, in this case, before the train crash, the defendants responsible for the train crash only owed Mr A Chadwick a duty to take care not to bring about the train crash. No duty was owed to Mr B Chadwick by the defendants before the train crash to take care not to bring about the train crash. Thus, as Lord Goff pointed out, if it were proved that the defendants carelessly brought about the train crash 'Mr A would recover but Mr B would not. To make things worse, the same conclusion must follow even if Mr A was unaware of the existence of physical danger in his half of the train. This is surely unacceptable.'[82] One can only agree.

White is a good example of the maxim that hard cases make bad law. The House of Lords in *White* found itself in a situation where it would have been politically unacceptable to allow the claimant police officers to recover compensation for the post-traumatic stress disorders suffered by them in the aftermath of the Hillsborough tragedy. But in order to dismiss the claimants' claims in

[80] Ibid., pp. 499H (per Lord Steyn), 510E–F (per Lord Hoffmann).
[81] Ibid., 487G–H.
[82] Ibid.

White the House of Lords introduced an arbitrary and unjustifiable rule into English law – that if A has caused an accident *x* to occur and B has developed a psychiatric illness as a result of what she saw and heard in rescuing the victims of that accident, A will only have owed B a duty to take care not to cause accident *x* to occur if B either put herself in danger in rescuing those victims or thought that she was in danger in rescuing those victims.[83]

(3) *The responsibility cases.* In *Dooley* v *Cammell Laird & Co. Ltd*,[84] the claimant was a crane driver. The claimant was in his crane and was lowering a sling-load of materials into a hold when the rope which attached the sling-load to his crane snapped. The sling-load of materials fell into the hold where several of the claimant's colleagues were working. Fortunately, no one was injured. However, the claimant, sitting high up in his crane, did not know that and, thinking he was responsible for the accident that had occurred, developed a psychiatric illness at the thought of what he had done. In fact the accident was the fault of the defendants – the claimant's employers who had failed to check that the rope was strong enough for lifting purposes and the firm that had manufactured the rope – and the claimant sued the defendants, seeking compensation for the psychiatric illness that he had developed. The claimant's claim was allowed. It was held that the defendants had owed the claimant a duty to take care not to cause the accident that had occurred on the ground that because the claimant thought he was responsible for the accident that occurred it was reasonably foreseeable that the claimant would develop a psychiatric illness as a result of that accident's occurring. So the decision in *Dooley* established that if A caused an accident to occur and B developed a psychiatric illness as a result because he mistakenly thought he was responsible for the fact that that accident had occurred, then A will have owed B a duty to take care not to cause that accident to occur.

However, just as the decision in *Chadwick* was recently substantially qualified by the decision of the House of Lords in *White*, so the decision in *Dooley* has recently been substantially qualified by the decision of the Court of Appeal in *Hunter* v *British Coal Corp.*[85] In that case, the claimant was employed by the defendants to work at their coal mine. He was driving a vehicle along a track when he became aware of a water hydrant protruding into the track. The claimant tried to manoeuvre the vehicle round the hydrant but the track was too narrow and the claimant managed to strike the hydrant, causing water to flow from it. The claimant stopped his vehicle and got out and tried to stop the

---

[83] The House of Lords might have dismissed the claimants' claims in *White* on the ground that they could not be allowed to seek compensation for harms that they voluntarily took the risk of suffering 'on the job'. (This is known as the 'fireman's rule' in some American states.) However, the House of Lords had previously ruled in *Ogwo* v *Taylor* [1988] AC 431 that a claimant's claim to be compensated for harm suffered by him could not be dismissed on the ground that he had voluntarily taken on the risk of suffering that kind of harm as part of his job and the House of Lords in *White* showed no inclination to overrule *Ogwo*. See below p. 504.

[84] [1951] 1 Lloyd's Rep 271.

[85] [1999] QB 140.

flow of water from the hydrant with the assistance of a fellow employee, one Tommy Carter. The claimant ran off, looking for a water hose that he could use to channel the flow of water from the hydrant, while Carter continued to attempt to shut the hydrant off. When the claimant was 30 metres away from the hydrant, it burst and Carter was killed in the explosion. The claimant only learned that Carter had died on his way back to the scene of the accident. Feeling responsible for Carter's death, the claimant developed a deep depression. In fact, the defendants were responsible for the accident that occurred: it was their fault the track down which the claimant had been driving had been too narrow with the result that the claimant's vehicle struck the hydrant with tragic consequences.

The claimant sued the defendants, seeking compensation for the depression that he had suffered in the aftermath of Carter's death. The Court of Appeal turned down the claimant's claim. They held that the defendants had not owed the claimant a duty to take care not to cause the accident that caused Carter's death. The claimant had to have witnessed the accident for such a duty to have been owed to the claimant. Not much can be said by way of justification or explanation of the Court of Appeal's decision. The Court of Appeal may have been motivated to decide *Hunter* that way because it was concerned that if it held that a duty of care was owed to the claimant in *Hunter* then it would follow that A, a motorist who ran down a child, would have to be found to have owed a duty to take care not to run down the child to anyone who developed a psychiatric illness because they felt responsible for the child's death whether they were on the scene of the accident when it occurred or not. If this were the law then a potentially large number of claims could be made against A (or, more accurately, his insurance company) and A's liability would grow out of all proportion to his fault in running down the child in question.

However, it should be noted that *Hunter* may not contain the last word on the issue of what has to be established before a duty of care will be found in this sort of case. In *W* v *Essex CC*,[86] the claimant foster parents each developed a psychiatric illness when a boy who had been placed with them sexually abused their children. They sued the local authority who had placed the boy with them in negligence. The House of Lords refused to strike out the claimants' claims, holding that it was arguable that the local authority had owed them a duty not to place the boy with them. The House of Lords thought that a duty of care might have been owed to the claimants in this case because they *felt responsible* for what had happened to their children.[87] If so, then the decision in *W* casts doubt on whether *Hunter* was correctly decided as, of course, the claimants were not present when their children were sexually abused.

(4) *The horrific accident cases.* Let us now consider what the authorities have to say about the following situation. A caused an accident *x* to occur in which a number of people were killed or injured. B developed a psychiatric illness as a result of witnessing this accident occur. B had no connection with anyone

---

[86] [2001] 2 AC 592.
[87] Ibid., 601.

involved in the accident but it was still reasonably foreseeable that she would develop this psychiatric illness because the accident was so horrific that someone of reasonable fortitude or 'phlegm' who witnessed the accident occur could have been expected to develop a psychiatric illness as a result. Will A have owed B a duty to take care not to cause accident *x* to occur?

Lord Ackner in *Alcock* thought that the answer may well be 'yes'.[88] Lord Oliver of Aylmerton agreed: 'I would not exclude the possibility ... of a successful claim, given circumstances of such horror as would be likely to traumatise even the most phlegmatic spectator, by a mere bystander'.[89] Lord Keith took the same view.[90] However, since then, both the Court of Appeal, in *McFarlane* v *E E Caledonia Ltd*,[91] and the House of Lords, in *White* v *Chief Constable of South Yorkshire*,[92] have held that the House of Lords decided in *Alcock* that someone who suffers a psychiatric illness simply as a result of witnessing an accident occur will only be able to sue in negligence for compensation for that illness if he or she was in a sufficiently 'close and loving relationship' with someone involved in the accident. On this reading of *Alcock*, the decision of the House of Lords in that case establishes that in the situation we are considering, B will *not* be able to argue that A owed her a duty to take care not to cause accident *x* to occur: she was not in a sufficiently 'close and loving relationship' with anyone involved in the accident.

However, this reading of *Alcock* is simply wrong and completely inconsistent with the *dicta* from *Alcock* cited above. In fact, this reading of *Alcock* gets *Alcock* backwards. *Alcock* did *not* say that a mere bystander who develops a psychiatric illness as a result of witnessing an accident occur will only be able to sue in negligence for compensation for her illness if she was in a 'close and loving relationship' with someone involved in the accident. What *Alcock* said was that someone who develops a psychiatric illness because she was in a 'close and loving relationship' with someone who was involved in the accident will only be able to sue in negligence for compensation for her illness if her illness was triggered by her witnessing the accident or the immediate aftermath.

So the courts have tended to assume since *Alcock* that in the situation we are considering, A will *not* have owed B a duty to take care not to cause accident *x* to occur even though there is nothing in *Alcock* that compels that conclusion

---

[88] [1992] 1 AC 310, 403: 'while it may be very difficult to envisage a case of a stranger, who is not actively and foreseeably involved in a disaster or its aftermath, other than in the role of a rescuer, suffering shock-induced psychiatric injury by the mere observation of apprehended or actual injury of a third person in circumstances that could be considered reasonably foreseeable, I see no reason in principle why he should not, if in the circumstances, a reasonably strong-nerved person would have been so shocked. In the course of argument your Lordships were given, by way of an example, that of a petrol tanker careering out of control into a school in session and bursting into flames. I would not be prepared to rule out a potential claim by a passer-by so shocked by the scene as to suffer psychiatric illness.'

[89] Ibid., 416.

[90] Ibid., 397.

[91] [1994] 2 All ER 1, at 14.

[92] [1999] 2 AC 455, 462E–H (per Lord Griffiths), 472F (per Lord Goff), 496H–497B (per Lord Steyn), 502D–H (per Lord Hoffmann). Lord Browne-Wilkinson, the other judge in *White*, agreed with the judgments of Lords Steyn and Hoffmann: 462B–C.

and indeed there are some *dicta* in *Alcock* that suggest that in the right circumstances A may well have owed B such a duty of care. The point, we would suggest, remains open to argument, though there may be valid reasons for denying the possibility of a duty of care being owed in this kind of situation.[93]

Self-harm: an exception to the rule?

In *Greatorex* v *Greatorex*,[94] C's son, S, was out driving in a friend's car when he crashed it and was injured as a result. C – acting in his capacity as a fire officer – attended the scene of the car crash and saw S unconscious, injured and trapped in the car. As a result of seeing this C developed a psychiatric illness. C then sued S for damages in respect of his psychiatric illness. (This was not as heartless as it seems. While S was not covered by liability insurance in driving his friend's car, the Motor Insurers' Bureau would have covered any judgment entered against S.) C argued that S owed him a duty to take care not to cause the car crash in which S was injured and that S's breach of this duty of care caused C to develop his psychiatric illness. Now, on the basis of what has already been said, one would expect the court to have ruled that S *did* owe C a duty to take care not to cause the car crash in which S was injured. C was in a close and loving relationship with S and developed his psychiatric illness as a result of attending the immediate aftermath of the accident in which S was injured. However, Cazalet J ruled that S had *not* owed C a duty to take care not to cause the car crash in which he was injured. Cazalet J gave two reasons why he thought it would be wrong to rule that S had owed C such a duty of care.

First of all, he thought that S's 'right of self-determination' would have been unacceptably limited if he had owed C a duty to take care not to crash the car he was driving.[95] It is not clear that this is correct. If someone *wants* to kill himself, there is a case for saying that he will *not* owe those members of his family who might be affected by his death a duty not to kill himself – the existence of such a duty would, it is true, completely take away his 'right of self-determination'.[96] But S was not trying to kill himself when he crashed his friend's car. Given this, it is not clear why his 'right to self-determination' would have been infringed if he had owed C a duty to take care that he did not crash his friend's car.

Cazalet J's second reason for denying that S owed C a duty of care in this case was that to allow that a duty of care will be owed in cases such as these is

---

[93] For example, the Court of Appeal in *McFarlane* argued that it would be undesirable to allow that a duty of care might be owed to a mere bystander who had suffered a psychiatric illness as a result of witnessing a horrific accident occur: given that people's responses to horrific accidents are invariably subjective it would be difficult to determine whether or not the bystander's psychiatric illness was reasonably foreseeable: [1994] 2 All ER 1, at 14.

[94] [2000] 1 WLR 1970.

[95] Ibid., 1984.

[96] The physical danger principle will still bind the would-be suicide – so he will owe other people a duty not to commit suicide in such a way that, it can reasonably be foreseen, will result in their suffering some kind of physical injury. So someone who wants to commit suicide will have a duty not to do it by taking a plane flight and blowing it up in mid-flight. Similarly, he will have a duty not to commit suicide by throwing himself off the top of a skyscraper if it is reasonably foreseeable that people walking around the base of the skyscraper will suffer some kind of physical injury if he does so.

to 'open up the possibility of a particularly undesirable type of litigation between the family, involving questions of relative fault as between its members'. He continued:

> To take an example, A, while drunk, seriously injures himself. B his wife [develops a psychiatric illness as a result of seeing A injure himself]. What if A raises, by way of a defence, the fact that he had drunk too much because B had unjustifiably threatened to leave him for another man or had fabricated an allegation of child sexual abuse against him? Should the law of tort concern itself with this issue? In a case where A's self-harm is deliberate, the possibility that B's claim may be met by a defence of contributory negligence, alleging that B's behaviour caused A to harm himself, is an alarming one.[97]

Once again, this is not wholly convincing. Suppose, to take Cazalet J's example, A – in his drunken state – carelessly set fire to the family home and B only escaped the fire after she had been severely burned. In this case, the law will not prevent B from suing A in negligence in respect of her burns – even though allowing her to bring such an action will give rise to the same sort of difficulties as Cazalet J thought would arise if, in his example, B were allowed to sue A in negligence in respect of her psychiatric illness.

Primary and secondary victims

Suppose Alan has caused an accident *x* to occur and Lara has developed a psychiatric illness as a result. Judges and academics usually say that whether or not Alan owed Lara a duty to take care not to cause accident *x* to occur will depend on whether Lara was a 'primary' or 'secondary' victim of accident *x*. If Lara was a 'primary' victim of accident *x* then one set of rules will apply to determine whether Alan owed her a duty to take care not to cause accident *x* to occur. If Lara was a 'secondary' victim of accident *x* then a different set of rules will apply. We have eschewed such language in discussing what has to be shown to establish that Alan owed Lara a duty to take care not to cause accident *x*. This is for two reasons.

First of all, the courts cannot seem to agree on when Lara will have been a 'primary' victim of accident *x* and when she will have been a 'secondary' victim of accident *x*. The distinction between 'primary' and 'secondary' victims of an accident was first introduced into English law in the *Alcock* case by Lord Oliver of Aylmerton. Lord Oliver said that Lara will have been a 'primary' victim of accident *x* if she 'was involved, either mediately or immediately, as a participant'[98] in accident *x* and held that she would be so involved if she was 'physically involved in [accident *x*], either through the direct threat of bodily injury to [herself as a result of the occurrence of accident *x*] or in coming to the aid of others injured or threatened [as a result of the occurrence of accident *x*]'[99] or if the occurrence of accident *x* 'put [her] in the position of being, or of thinking that [s]he is about to be or has been the involuntary cause of another's death or injury and [Lara's psychiatric illness] stemmed from the shock to [her] of the consciousness of this supposed fact'.[100]

[97] Ibid., 1985.
[98] [1992] 1 AC 310, 407.
[99] Ibid., 408.
[100] Ibid., 408.

On the other hand, Lara will have been a 'secondary' victim of accident x if she 'was no more than the passive and unwilling witness of injury caused to others'.[101]

So, on Lord Oliver's view, the claimants in *Page* v *Smith*, *Chadwick* v *British Railways Board* and *Dooley* v *Cammell Laird & Co. Ltd* were all 'primary victims' while the claimants in *Alcock* were 'secondary victims'. However, in *Page* v *Smith*,[102] Lord Lloyd proposed that in the case we are considering – where B developed a psychiatric illness as a result of A's causing accident x to occur – B will only have been a 'primary victim' of accident x if it was foreseeable that someone like B would suffer some kind of physical injury if accident x occurred.[103] On this view, the claimants in *Page* v *Smith* and *Chadwick* v *British Railways Board* were 'primary victims' while the claimants in *Dooley* v *Cammell Laird & Co. Ltd* and *Alcock* were 'secondary victims'. Lord Steyn endorsed Lord Lloyd's view of when someone will be a 'primary victim' of an accident in *White* v *Chief Constable of South Yorkshire*.[104] However, in the recent case of *W* v *Essex County Council*, Lord Slynn remarked that 'the categorisation of those claiming to be included as primary or secondary victims to be included as primary or secondary victims is not as I read the cases finally closed. It is a concept still to be developed in different factual situations'[105] and seemed to endorse Lord Oliver's view in *Alcock* that the claimant in *Dooley* v *Cammell Laird & Co. Ltd* was properly to be classified as being a 'primary victim' of the accident in that case.[106]

Given this confusion over the meanings of the terms 'primary victim' and 'secondary victim' it seemed to us better to dispense with these terms in discussing this area of the law: a clear understanding of the law can only be achieved if the law is stated in clear terms.[107] Our second reason for ignoring the fashionable distinction between 'primary' and 'secondary' victims is that the distinction is completely unnecessary. One can perfectly well discuss this

---

[101] Ibid., 407.

[102] [1996] AC 155.

[103] Lord Goff has questioned whether Lord Lloyd could possibly have meant to say this: see *White* v *Chief Constable of South Yorkshire* [1999] 2 AC 455, 478B–480D. However, Lord Goff assumed in White that a 'secondary victim' of an accident who developed a psychiatric illness as a result of the occurrence of that accident could only recover in respect of his illness if there was a close tie of love and affection between him and someone involved in the accident and he witnessed the accident occur or its immediate aftermath: ibid., 472F. (Note that this understanding of the law is flat contrary to what was said in the *Alcock* case: see above, p. 101.) If this is right and one takes Lord Lloyd's view that someone is only a primary victim of an accident if it was foreseeable that the occurrence of that accident would put him in danger of suffering some kind of accident, then that would mean *Dooley* v *Cammell Laird & Co. Ltd* [1951] Lloyd's Rep 271 was wrongly decided. Hence Lord Goff's incredulity at Lord Lloyd's restrictive definition of when someone will be a 'primary victim' of an accident. But if one dispenses with Lord Goff's assumption as to when a 'secondary victim' of an accident will be entitled to recover in respect of a psychiatric illness that he has suffered as a result of the occurrence of that accident, then Lord Lloyd's view becomes unexceptionable.

[104] [1999] 2 AC 455, 496H–B. Subject, presumably, to the qualification that someone will count as having been a 'primary victim' of an accident if he *believed* (incorrectly) that the occurrence of that accident put him in danger of suffering some kind of harm.

[105] [2001] 2 AC 592, 601.

[106] Ibid., 601.

[107] Cf. Teff 1998, 113–14: '. . . preoccupation with a victim's "primary" or "secondary" status only adds a further layer of obfuscation, distracting attention from the central issue . . . The primary/secondary divide . . . is . . . a recipe for more litigation and further confusion.'

area of the law without making use of this distinction at all – as we have attempted to do above.[108]

Psychiatric illness arising out of someone else's being maltreated

We are concerned here with the situation where A has maltreated C – without killing or injuring him – and B has as a result developed a psychiatric illness. Authority on when B will be able in this kind of situation to establish that A owed her a duty of care not to act in the way he did is currently thin on the ground.[109] Presumably, in order to determine whether A owed B a duty of care in this kind of case, the courts would apply by analogy the principles set out above that determine when a duty of care will have been owed in the case where A killed or injured C and B suffered a psychiatric illness as a result. So for example, suppose Eric threatened to kill Wendy's girlfriend, Karen, and Wendy developed a psychiatric illness as a result. And suppose Wendy wanted to sue Eric for damages, arguing that he owed her a duty not to act as he did. Wendy would certainly first have to show that it was reasonably foreseeable that she would develop a psychiatric illness as a result of Eric's threats. If she sought to establish reasonable foreseeability on the basis that she was in a 'close and loving relationship' with Karen, she would presumably then have to show that her psychiatric illness was triggered as a result of her witnessing Eric threatening Karen or the immediate aftermath of Eric's threats.[110]

Psychiatric illness arising as a result of being given bad news

We are concerned here with the situation where A has given B some bad news and B has developed a psychiatric illness as a result. Say, for example, that A told B her daughter was dead and B developed a psychiatric illness as a result.

---

[108] *Important note*. Regrettably, the courts seem to be going in the opposite direction from that advocated in the text and have started to regard the distinction between 'primary' and 'secondary' victims as of crucial importance for the purpose of whether a duty of care was owed in *any* case where someone has suffered a psychiatric illness as a result of someone else's actions. See, for example, *Hatton* v *Sutherland* [2002] 2 All ER 1, at [19]–[22]. That case concerned the question of whether an employer owed an employee a duty not to make her do stressful work without giving her any assistance or counselling. It beggars belief that the courts think that the (vague) distinction between 'primary' and 'secondary' victims can be applied outside the context of a situation where a defendant's actions have result in someone's being killed or injured and a third party has suffered a psychiatric illness as a result. In *that* sort of context, one *might* distinguish between the person who was killed or injured (a 'primary' victim of the defendant's actions) and the psychiatric-illness-suffering third party (a 'secondary' victim of the defendant's actions). But in a case where A has made B do particularly stressful work which has resulted in B's suffering a psychiatric illness, it makes absolutely no sense whatsoever to ask whether B is a 'primary' or 'secondary' victim of A's actions.

[109] Recent examples: *Duddin* v *Home Office* [2004] EWCA Civ 181 (claimant prisoner claimed to have developed a psychiatric illness as a result of a prisoner officer's making inappropriate remarks of a sexual nature to the claimant's wife; claim dismissed because no foreseeability of psychiatric illness established); *A* v *Leeds Teaching Hospital NHS Trust* [2004] EWHC 644 (claimant parents whose babies had died claimed to have developed psychiatric illnesses as a result of the defendant hospital's retaining body parts belonging to their babies without the claimants' consent; issue of whether the hospital owed the claimants a duty of care not to act in the way they did disposed of by holding that in the immediate aftermath of the babies' deaths, the claimants were the hospital's patients).

[110] This is consistent with the approach adopted by the Court of Appeal in *Duddin* v *Home Office* [2004] EWCA Civ 181.

She now wants to sue A in negligence for compensation, arguing that he owed her a duty of care not to act as he did.[111] Four different variations on this situation need to be distinguished.

(1) *B's daughter was dead and A acted responsibly in telling B this news.* In this case, B will not be able to establish that A owed her a duty of care not to act as he did: A acted perfectly reasonably and no one can be held to owe another a duty of care not to act reasonably.[112]

(2) *B's daughter was dead but A acted insensitively in telling B this news in the way he did.* The question of whether A will have owed B a duty in this situation to take care that he did not act insensitively in breaking the news to her of her daughter's death has not finally been decided. The issue came up in *AB* v *Tameside & Glossop HA,*[113] where a number of claimants claimed to have developed psychiatric illnesses because the defendant health authority had acted insensitively in telling them *by letter* (rather than face to face) that they might have been treated by a nurse who was HIV+. However, it was held that under the circumstances the defendant health authority had acted reasonably and that it could not therefore be argued that the defendant health authority had owed the claimants a duty of care not to act as it did. What the position would have been had the defendant health authority been held to have acted insensitively was never therefore decided. It may be that in the case we are considering, the courts would simply give effect to Lord Atkin's neighbour principle in this case and hold that A did owe B a duty to take care not to be insensitive in the way he broke the news to her of her daughter's death if it was reasonably foreseeable that A's being insensitive would cause B to develop a psychiatric illness.[114]

(3) *B's daughter was not dead, but A had good reason to think that she was and acted responsibly in telling B that her daughter was dead.* In this case, B will *not* be able to establish that A owed her a duty of care not to act as he did because A acted reasonably under the circumstances.

(4) *B's daughter was not dead and A had no good reason for thinking that she was.* In this case, A could not argue that he acted reasonably in telling B that her daughter was dead. Could B then argue that A owed her a duty of care not to act as he did? It seems to be the case that so long as it was reasonably foreseeable that B would develop a psychiatric illness as a result of A's misinforming her as to the

---

[111] If B's daughter was killed as a result of C's actions, then whether or not B can sue C in negligence for compensation for her psychiatric illness, arguing that C owed her a duty to take care not to act as he did, will depend on the principles set out above, at pp. 91–2.

[112] See above, pp. 76–80.

[113] (1997) 35 BMLR 79 (noted, Dziobon & Tettenborn 1997).

[114] But even if the existence of a duty of care were allowed in this case, it would still have to be shown that A breached that duty of care and, more importantly, that A's breach triggered B's psychiatric illness; in other words, that B suffered her psychiatric illness because A was insensitive and not because her daughter had died.

[115] This might be hard to establish in the case where B was told by A that her daughter was dead but was told two minutes later that in fact her daughter was alive and well. One would expect B to feel overwhelming relief in this situation, and not to suffer a psychiatric illness. But see, on this, the case of *Farrell* v *Avon Health Authority* [2001] Lloyd's Rep Med 458, where a claimant who developed post-traumatic stress disorder after being told incorrectly that his newly born

fate of her daughter,[115] then the courts will find that A *did* owe B a duty of care not to act as he did.[116] So in this sort of case, the courts will give full effect to Lord Atkin's neighbour principle, and so long as A's conduct was unreasonable and it was reasonably foreseeable that B would suffer a psychiatric illness as a result of A's conduct, they will find that A owed B a duty of care not to act as he did.[117]

Psychiatric illness arising as a result of being subjected to a distressing or humiliating experience

In *Wainwright* v *Home Office*,[118] a man named Patrick O'Neill was arrested and taken into custody on a charge of murder. His mother and his brother went to visit him in prison. When they arrived at the prison they were strip-searched to check that they were not carrying any drugs that they could hand over to O'Neill. The strip-search was conducted by ordering the mother and the brother to undress, though the prison guards did touch the brother in the course of the strip-search. The mother was very distressed by the whole experience. The consequences of the strip-search for the brother were more serious: it was found that the strip-search had caused to him suffer a psychiatric illness.

The mother and the brother sued the prison authorities for damages. The mother could not sue the prison authorities in negligence because it is well established that you cannot normally sue in negligence for damages for pure distress.[119] And the brother did not need to rely on the law of negligence to sue the prison authorities: he could argue that the prison guards committed the tort of battery[120] in touching him, and sue them for damages on the basis that his psychiatric illness was triggered by their committing that tort. The interesting question for our purposes is whether the brother *could* have sued the prison authorities in negligence for compensation for his psychiatric illness, by arguing that they owed him a duty of care not to subject him to the distressing and humiliating experience of being strip-searched. Let's assume for the purposes

---

son was dead was allowed to sue for compensation even though he was told five minutes later that there had been a mistake and his son was alive and well.

[116] *Allin* v *City & Hackney HA* [1996] 7 Med LR 167.

[117] The decision of the House of Lords in *Wainwright* v *Home Office* [2003] 3 WLR 1137 supports this point. That decision makes it clear that were the facts of *Wilkinson* v *Downton* [1897] 2 QB 57 (discussed above, n. 14) to occur today – that is, were a claimant to be made physically sick as a result of a defendant's lying to her and telling her that her husband had been injured when he had not been – the claimant would be allowed to sue the defendant in negligence. The House of Lords' decision also makes it pretty clear that the same would be true if the claimant merely suffered a *psychiatric illness* as a result of the defendant's lies – she would be allowed to sue the defendant in negligence for compensation for her illness.

[118] [2003] 3 WLR 1137.

[119] See below, p. 569. Instead, the mother sought to sue the prison authorities on the basis: (1) that the common law recognises a tort of invasion of privacy and the prison authorities committed that tort when they ordered her to undress; and (2) that the prison authorities committed the tort in *Wilkinson* v *Downton* by ordering her to undress. The House of Lords dismissed the mother's claim, holding that: (1) the common law does not recognise a tort of invasion of privacy (see below, p. 309); and (2) that the tort in *Wilkinson* v *Downton* should be subsumed within the tort of negligence and that therefore a claim cannot be brought under *Wilkinson* v *Downton* where a claim in negligence would not be available (see above, n. 14).

[120] Discussed below, pp. 244–55.

of discussing this question that: (1) it was reasonably foreseeable that strip-searching the brother would result in his suffering a psychiatric illness (thus bringing *Wainwright* within the scope of Lord Atkin's neighbour principle); and (2) the prison authorities acted unreasonably in strip-searching the brother.

Given these two assumptions, could the brother have argued that the prison authorities owed him a duty of care not to order him to undress? The House of Lords' decision in *Wainwright* is frustratingly unclear on the issue.[121] In favour of the answer 'yes' is Lord Hoffmann's treatment in *Wainwright* of the case of *Janvier* v *Sweeney*.[122] In that case, the claimant was made physically sick as a result of the defendants' threatening her. She sued the defendants for damages and was allowed to recover on the ground that the defendants had committed a tort in relation to her in threatening her – the tort in *Wilkinson* v *Downton*. Lord Hoffmann made it clear that he thought: (1) that the claimant in *Janvier* v *Sweeney* could have sued the defendants in negligence; and (2) that the claimant would have been entitled to succeed against the defendants even if she had merely suffered a psychiatric illness as a result of their threats.[123]

But if this is right, and the claimant in *Janvier* could have argued that the defendants in that case owed her a duty of care not to threaten her, then the claimant in *Wainwright* could equally well have argued that the defendants in that case owed him a duty of care not to order him to undress. However, there is a *dictum* in *Wainwright* which goes against this and indicates that the brother could not have sued the prison authorities in negligence, arguing that they owed him a duty of care not to order him to undress. In his judgment, Lord Scott observed, 'I agree with the Court of Appeal [in *Wainwright*], and with your Lordships, that if there had been no touching, as there was not in [the mother's] case, no tort would have been committed.'[124] If this is right then if no one had touched the brother, the brother would not have been able to sue the prison authorities in negligence or anything else – and this is so even if the whole experience of being strip-searched caused the brother to suffer a psychiatric illness.

Our own view, for what it is worth, is that Lord Scott was wrong and that the brother in *Wainwright* could have sued the prison authorities in negligence had he chosen to do so.[125] To take any other position would mean that a claimant (such as the claimant in *Janvier* v *Sweeney*) who suffered a psychiatric illness as a result of being subjected to intolerable threats by someone else would have no

---

[121] This is perhaps understandable given the way *Wainwright* was argued.

[122] [1919] 2 KB 316.

[123] [2003] 3 WLR 1137, at [40]: 'By the time of *Janvier* v *Sweeney* . . . the law was able comfortably to [deal with this kind of case] in the law of *nervous shock caused by negligence*' (emphasis added).

[124] Ibid., at [60].

[125] In support of this it may be observed that Lord Scott seemed completely to forget that the brother in *Wainwright* suffered a psychiatric illness: see ibid., at [57]: 'The essence of the complaint of each claimant is that he or she was subjected to conduct by the prison officers . . . that was calculated to, and did, cause humiliation and distress' (this was of course *not* the essence of the brother's complaint); and at [58]: '. . . there is an important difference between the case of [the brother] and that of [the mother]. In the course of, and as part of, the strip-search . . . one of the prison officers [touched the brother] . . .' (the other important difference, unnoted by Lord Scott, is of course that the brother suffered a psychiatric illness and the mother did not).

remedy.[126] The House of Lords cannot have intended its ruling in *Wainwright* v *Home Office* to have that effect.

Psychiatric illness arising as a result of being made to do stressful work

We are concerned here with the situation where A makes B do some work which is very stressful and B develops a psychiatric illness as a result. Provided that it was reasonably foreseeable that B would develop a psychiatric illness if she was made to do that work without being given any assistance or any counselling before or after doing the work, B will usually be able to establish that A owed her a duty not to make her do that work without giving her some such assistance or counselling.[127]

So in *Walker* v *Northumberland County Council*,[128] the claimant was employed by the defendant local authority as an area social services officer from 1970 to 1987. He was responsible for managing teams of social services fieldworkers in an area which had a high proportion of child care problems. In 1986 the claimant had a nervous breakdown as a result of the stress his job was putting on him. When he came back to work he discovered that there was a considerable backlog of work waiting for him to clear up and within six months he had another nervous breakdown which led to his stopping work permanently. When he was dismissed by the defendant local authority on grounds of permanent ill health, the claimant sued the defendant local authority in negligence so as to be compensated for the loss of income resulting from his second, irremediable, nervous breakdown. The claimant argued that when he came back to work the defendant local authority had owed him a duty not to insist that he carry on performing all his duties without giving him some sort of assistance and that his second nervous breakdown had occurred because the defendant had breached this duty. The court agreed that the defendant local authority had owed the claimant such a duty on the ground that when the claimant came back to work after his first breakdown it had been reasonably foreseeable that he would suffer a second breakdown if the local authority insisted that he perform his duties without giving him any kind of assistance.

However, it was crucial to the outcome of the case that the claimant in *Walker* had *already* suffered a nervous breakdown. It was that first breakdown

---

[126] Unless, of course, the threats amounted to a course of conduct (in which case, a claim would be available under the Protection from Harassment Act 1997, discussed below, pp. 307–8) or were made by an employer to an employee (in which case, the employee could bring a claim in contract against the employer for breach of his implied duty to maintain a relationship of 'trust and confidence' between him and the employee: *Eastwood* v *Magnox Electric plc* [2004] UKHL 35). The claimant would of course not be able to sue post-*Wainwright* under the tort in *Wilkinson* v *Downton* because the House of Lords has ruled that that tort should be subsumed within the law of negligence.

[127] Though note the worries expressed by Lord Rodger of Earlsferry in *Barber* v *Somerset County Council* [2004] 1 WLR 1089, at [34], as to whether such a duty could be owed where it contradicted the terms of the employee's contract of employment.

[128] [1995] 1 All ER 737.

that made his second breakdown reasonably foreseeable. The decision of the Court of Appeal in *Hatton* v *Sutherland*[129] makes it clear that an employee who suffers a nervous breakdown as a result of being made to do particularly stressful work without any assistance or counselling will find it *very* difficult to show that her breakdown was reasonably foreseeable if nothing was done or nothing happened before her breakdown to alert her employers to the fact that she was having difficulty coping with the amount or type of work that she had to do. In that case, the Court of Appeal was hostile to the idea that the mere nature of an employee's work may be enough to make it reasonably foreseeable that she will develop a psychiatric illness if she is made to do that work without any kind of assistance or counselling.[130] The court went on to observe that, '*Unless he knows of some particular problem or vulnerability, an employer is entitled to assume that his employee is up to the normal pressures of the job.*'[131]

HARM TO PROPERTY CASES
The property harm principle

The other type of case where Lord Atkin's neighbour principle has been applied to find that a defendant owed a claimant a duty of care is the case where A has done *x* and an item of property has suffered some kind of harm as a result. The basic principle that applies here is that A will normally have owed B a duty to take care not to do *x* if: (*a*) at the time the property was harmed as a result of A's doing *x*, B had a sufficient interest in that property; *and* (*b*) it was reasonably foreseeable at the time A did *x* that his doing *x* would result in that type of property being harmed. Let's call this principle the *property harm principle*. A couple of examples can be given from the cases of this principle at work.

In *Spartan Steel & Alloys Ltd* v *Martin & Co. (Contractors) Ltd*,[132] the defendants – contractors who were employed to dig up a road – damaged an electric power cable that supplied power to the claimants' factory. The claimants were producers of stainless steel and were, at the time of the power cut, melting some metal in their furnaces to turn it into stainless steel ingots. The power cut caused the metal in the furnaces to be damaged. The claimants sued the defendants in negligence for compensation for damage done to the 'melts' that they were processing at the time of the power cut. The Court of Appeal allowed the claimants to recover, holding that the defendants had owed the claimants, and breached, a duty to take care not to damage any electric power cables running under the road on which they were working. The defendants had owed the

---

[129] [2002] 2 All ER 1.

[130] Ibid., at [12] and at [24].

[131] Ibid., at [29] (emphasis in original). In *Barber* v *Somerset County Council* [2004] 1 WLR 1089, the House of Lords expressed broad agreement with this statement: ibid., at [5] (per Lord Scott: '[The Court of Appeal's decision in *Hatton* succeeds] in succinctly and accurately expressing the principles that ought to be applied') and, more tepidly, at [64] (per Lord Walker: '[The Court of Appeal's decision in *Hatton* provides] useful practical guidance, but it must be read as that, and not as having anything like statutory force').

[132] [1973] 1 QB 27. See also *SCM (United Kingdom) Ltd* v *W & J Whittall & Son Ltd* [1971] 1 QB 337.

claimants such a duty under the property harm principle: it was reasonably foreseeable at the time the defendants were working that if they damaged any electric power cables running under the road, the supply of electricity to nearby factories such as the claimants' would be interrupted and property being used or processed in those factories would be damaged as a result.[133]

In *Capital & Counties plc* v *Hampshire CC*,[134] the claimants were tenants of a modern commercial building called 'The Crescent'. The Crescent caught on fire and the fire brigade was called to deal with the fire. Although the seat of the fire had not been located, the fire officer ordered that the building's sprinkler system be turned off. As a result, the fire spread rapidly and destroyed The Crescent. The claimants sued for compensation, claiming that the fire officer had owed them a duty not to switch off the sprinkler system. The Court of Appeal agreed that such a duty had been owed. The fire officer owed the claimants this duty under the property harm principle: it had been reasonably foreseeable at the time the fire officer attended the fire at The Crescent that The Crescent would burn down if its sprinkler system was turned off.

Let's now look at some of the key terms employed in the property harm principle in more detail.

What sort of harm?

What sort of harm to property has to have been done before this rule can be invoked? Two points can be made in response to this question.

(a) Destruction and damage

If A's doing *x* results in an item of property being destroyed or damaged,[135] then A's doing *x* will obviously have harmed the property for the purposes of the property harm principle. However, there are two very important qualifications to this.

(1) *Creating an item of property with a defect in it.* Suppose A creates an item of property which has a defect in it. The defect eventually results in the item of property being destroyed or damaged. In this sort of case, it cannot be said that A did anything to harm the item of property in question. A did not make the item of property in question worse in any way; he merely failed to make it better.

So, for example, suppose that Acme Products Ltd employed Megamix

---

[133] The claimants were, however, *not* allowed to sue for damages in respect of the money they would have made had they been allowed to continue working during the time their power was cut off. For an explanation of this aspect of the *Spartan Steel* case, see below, pp. 568–9.

[134] [1997] QB 1004.

[135] *Important note.* Property will be 'damaged' if it is *physically changed in a way that makes it less useful or valuable*: *Hunter* v *Canary Wharf* [1997] AC 655, 676 (per Pill LJ). So in the *Hunter* case, the Court of Appeal held that the deposit of *excessive* dust on a carpet could constitute property damage for the purposes of negligence – but that the mere fact that it would cost money to remove a contaminant did not mean that there had been property damage. And in *Blue Circle Industries* v *Ministry of Defence* [1999] Ch 289, the Court of Appeal was willing to hold that the intermingling of plutonium with soil so that *it could not be removed* amounted to a form of property damage. See Weston 1999 for a very useful discussion of when someone who has lost computer data can argue that their property has been damaged.

Construction Ltd to build a warehouse for them. Megamix gave Concreto Ltd the job of laying the floor of the warehouse. Unfortunately, Concreto used the wrong kind of concrete in laying the floor of the warehouse and, as a result, four years later the floor began to crack up. Acme attempts to sue Concreto in negligence for compensation for the fact that the floor of their warehouse has begun to crack up, claiming that Concreto owed them a duty to take care not to use the wrong kind of concrete in laying the floor. Now – it is well established, in England at least, that Acme's claim will fail. In the absence of any 'special relationship' between Acme and Concreto – which, let us suppose, did not exist here[136] – the courts will find that Concreto did *not* owe Acme a duty to take care not to use the wrong kind of concrete in laying the floor.[137]

Why can't Acme use the property harm principle here to establish that Concreto owed them a duty of care in this case? Why can't they argue: (*a*) the floor belonged to us when it was harmed as a result of Concreto's using the wrong kind of concrete to lay the floor; *and* (*b*) it was reasonably foreseeable at the time Concreto laid the floor that the floor would suffer some harm in the future if they used the wrong kind of concrete in laying it? The reason why they can't use this argument is that (*a*) will not be true. The fact is, the floor was *never* harmed as a result of Concreto's using the wrong kind of concrete to lay the floor. Concreto's actions did not make the floor worse; Concreto merely failed to make it better.

(2) *Inflicting a defect on a previously sound item of property.* Suppose that there exists some sound item of property and A does something to make it defective. Suppose further that that defect destroys or damages that item of property at some time in the future. In this sort of case, A will be held to have harmed the item of property in question *when he made it defective, not* when the defect in the property destroyed or damaged the item of property.

So suppose that B puts a vase up for auction. The vase is displayed for inspection to potential bidders the day before the auction, along with all the other auction items. A looks at the vase but he puts the vase back on its stand a little roughly and as a result a small crack develops in the base of the vase. No one else notices the crack and at the auction C successfully bids for the vase. She takes the vase home. However, over time, the crack spreads and eventually the vase shatters. It is well established that in this sort of situation, C will *not* be entitled to sue A in negligence for compensation for the loss of her vase. She will not be able to establish that A owed her a duty to take care not to handle the vase roughly when inspecting it.[138]

But why can't she use the property harm principle here to establish that A owed her such a duty of care? Why can't she say: (a) the vase belonged to me when it was harmed as a result of A's rough handling of it; *and* (b) it was

---

[136] Such a 'special relationship' did exist in *Junior Books Ltd* v *Veitchi Co. Ltd* [1983] 1 AC 520, discussed below, pp. 130–1.

[137] *Murphy* v *Brentwood DC* [1991] 1 AC 398; *Dept of the Environment* v *Thomas Bates & Son Ltd* [1991] 1 AC 499.

[138] *The Aliakmon* [1986] AC 785, discussed below, p. 116.

reasonably foreseeable at the time A inspected the vase that it would be harmed if he handled it roughly? The reason she can't say this is that (a) will not be true. The vase was not harmed as a result of A's rough handling when it shattered but when A's rough handling caused it to develop a crack – and the vase belonged to B at that time, not C.

So an item of property which is *already* defective will suffer no *further* harm if the defect subsequently destroys or damages that item of property. It follows that if B acquires an item of property that was already defective and the defect destroys or damages that item of property, B will not be able to claim that the item of property in question was harmed when it was in her hands. So she will not be able to use the property harm principle to establish that whoever was responsible for the property being defective owed her a duty to take care not to act as they did.

While this rule is easy to state, it is not easy to apply. That is because it can be difficult to tell – in a given case where B has acquired an item of property which has subsequently been damaged or destroyed – whether that item of property was damaged or destroyed by a defect which was present in that property before B acquired it (in which case B will not be able to claim that the item of property in question was harmed while it was in her hands) or whether that item of property was basically sound when B acquired it and it was damaged or destroyed by an outside source (in which case B can claim that she had an interest in the property when it was harmed).

For example, suppose Paul buys a plastic bottle of lemonade from the supermarket, takes it home and places it in his fridge. The bottle of lemonade was produced by XYZ Ltd. Unfortunately, due to some fault in the manufacture of the plastic bottle, the bottle does not cope well with the cold of Paul's fridge and eventually shatters, spilling lemonade all over the place. Paul wants to sue XYZ in negligence, claiming that they owed him, and breached, a duty to take care not to bottle the lemonade using a plastic bottle that was liable to shatter in the cold.

Now – what has happened here? Did Paul, in buying the bottle of lemonade, acquire *one* item of property – a bottle of lemonade – which suffered from a defect? If so, he cannot claim that the bottle of lemonade was harmed when it burst in Paul's fridge. As it was always defective, XYZ did not ever do anything to harm the bottle of lemonade; they merely failed to make it better than it was. It follows that Paul will not be able to use the property harm principle to establish that XYZ owed him a duty to take care not to bottle the bottle of lemonade using a plastic bottle that was liable to shatter in the cold: XYZ did nothing to harm his bottle of lemonade.

But, on the other hand, could it be argued that Paul, in buying the bottle of lemonade, acquired *two* items of property – a plastic bottle, which was defective, and some lemonade, which was basically sound but was harmed when it spilled all over Paul's fridge and kitchen floor? If this analysis is correct, Paul could use the property harm principle to establish that XYZ owed him a duty to take care not to bottle the lemonade in a plastic bottle that was liable to shatter in the cold. He could argue: (*a*) I had an interest in the lemonade when it was harmed as a result of XYZ bottling it in a plastic bottle that was liable to shatter in the cold; *and* (*b*) it was reasonably foreseeable at the time XYZ bottled the lemonade that the lemonade would be harmed if XYZ bottled it using a plastic bottle that was liable to shatter in the cold.

So which is it to be? Did Paul acquire one item of property here or two? It is very difficult to say.[139] In *Aswan Engineering v Lupdine Ltd*,[140] Lloyd LJ (with whom Fox LJ agreed) took the 'provisional view'[141] that in this sort of case Paul would be able to argue that the lemonade and the bottle were two separate items of property and that Paul could therefore invoke the property harm principle to establish that XYZ owed him a duty to take care not to bottle the lemonade in a bottle which was liable to shatter when cold.

The problem also crops up – to take some other examples offered by Lloyd LJ in the *Aswan* case – where a claimant's car is damaged because one of its tyres (which was supplied with the car) bursts and where a bottle of wine acquired by the claimant becomes undrinkable because its cork is defective. In both these cases we have to determine whether what has happened is that *an* item of property (a car complete with tyres, a bottle of wine) has been damaged because it suffered from a defect which affected the property long before it was acquired by the claimant or whether it would be more accurate to say that a sound item of property belonging to the claimant (a car minus one of its tyres, wine) has been damaged by a separate item of property (a tyre, a cork) which suffered from a defect. Lloyd LJ's provisional view was that the latter analysis is correct in both cases. If this is right, the claimant will be able to argue that the manufacturer of the car/bottle of wine owed him a duty to take care not to fit/plug the car/bottle of wine with a defective tyre/cork.[142]

---

[139] Nolan 2002 suggests (at 803, referring to Tettenborn 2000b) that if a component part of a chattel can be removed without damaging the other parts of the chattel, the component and the rest of the chattel should be regarded as being two separate items of property. But it is not clear how this test would apply in this case. On the one hand, Nolan clearly thinks the test indicates that the plastic bottle and the lemonade are separate items of property. On the other hand, if the plastic bottle were separated from the lemonade, surely the lemonade would spill and be spoiled?

[140] [1987] 1 WLR 1. In that case, the claimants ordered some waterproofing compound from L. L, in turn, ordered some pails from the defendants to store the compound in when shipping it to the claimants. Having obtained the pails from the defendants, L filled them with compound and L shipped them to the claimants in Kuwait, where they were left in the blazing sun. Eventually the heat caused the plastic pails to collapse and the compound was lost. The claimants sued the defendants in negligence, claiming that the defendants had owed them a duty not to supply L with the pails that they did because it was reasonably foreseeable that doing so would result in the compound sold by L to the claimants being lost. Lloyd and Fox LJJ dismissed the claim on the ground that as the defendants had no idea the pails would be shipped to Kuwait, it was not reasonably foreseeable that the compound sold by L to the claimants would be lost if it was shipped to the claimants in the pails that the defendants supplied to L. Nicholls LJ dismissed the claim on the ground that the manufacturer of a container will not owe a duty of care in manufacturing the container to anyone who loses his or her property as a result of the container being insufficiently sturdy.

[141] Ibid., 21.

[142] For another case raising this kind of problem, see *Bellefield Computer Services Ltd* v *E Turner & Sons Ltd* [2000] BLR 97, noted Duncan Wallace 2000. A wall separating a storage area within a building from the rest of the building was badly constructed with the result that when a fire broke out in the storage area, it spread to the rest of the building; held that this was a case of one item of property – a building divided up into different areas by a wall – being damaged because it suffered from a

(b) Loss

If a claimant's property has not actually been destroyed or damaged but merely lost, will it count as being harmed under the property harm principle? To get an easy case out of the way, if A's doing *x* has resulted in B's property being sunk at sea, B will have no problem establishing that A owed him a duty to take care not to do *x* under the property harm principle – so long, of course, as it was foreseeable that A's doing *x* would have the kind of effect it did.

But what about the case where A's doing *x* has resulted in B's property being stolen? Suppose, for example, that Gary and Fred are both in prison; Fred has been sentenced to five years in prison for a number of burglary offences. Gary happens to tell Fred one day that his aunt, Beth, has an extremely precious stamp collection but she does not bother to keep it in a safe or take any security precautions to ensure her house is not broken into. As soon as Fred is released, he tracks Beth down and steals her stamp collection. Can Beth sue Gary, arguing that he owed her a duty not to tell Fred about her stamp collection? It was, after all, reasonably foreseeable – here, very likely or probable[143] – that if he told Fred about her stamp collection, he would attempt to steal it from her. There is no authority on the issue but there seems little reason why, if the property harm principle applies to cases where property has been destroyed or damaged, it should not also extend to cases where property has been stolen. If it does, then Beth will probably be able to argue that Gary owed her a duty not to tell Fred about her stamp collection.

What sort of property?

The property harm principle applies, of course, in cases where *tangible* property – land, buildings, moveables – has been harmed. But what about *intangible* property? It seems the property harm principle will also apply to cases where intangible property has been destroyed as a result of a defendant's actions, though such cases will necessarily be very rare, as intangible property – not taking a physical form – is very hard to destroy. However, one such case presented itself in *Ministry of Housing v Sharp*.[144]

In that case, the claimants had a charge on land owed by N. P proposed to buy the land from N and searched the land charges register to see who had an interest in the land. The defendant informed P that the register was clear – there were no encumbrances on the land. This meant that when P purchased the land from N – as it subsequently did – it took the land free from any encumbrances. The claimants therefore lost their charge over N's land when it was purchased by P. The claimants sued the defendant in negligence for

---

defect rather than a case of a sound item of property – the area of the building outside the storage area – being damaged because another item of property – the wall separating the storage area from the rest of the building – was defective. It might be different in the case where the electric wiring in a building is defective with the result that the building burns down: *Murphy* v *Brentwood DC* [1991] 1 AC 398, at 470, per Lord Keith. Also in the case where a defective boiler or 'electrical installation' in a house malfunctions and causes the house to burn down: ibid., at 478, per Lord Bridge. See also the discussion in *Payne* v *John Setchell Ltd* [2002] PNLR 146, at [26]–[41] (Humphrey Lloyd QC).
[143] See above, p 70, n. 24.
[144] [1970] 2 QB 223.

compensation for the loss of their charge. The Court of Appeal allowed the claimants to sue, holding that the defendant had owed the claimants a duty to take care that he did not tell P that the register was clear of charges when it was not. It could be argued that the duty of care arose under the property harm principle. That is, it could be argued the defendant owed the claimant a duty to take care that he did not tell P that the register was clear of charges when it was not because it was reasonably foreseeable that if he did this any charges over the land owned by N would be destroyed.

What sort of interest?

If property has been harmed as a result of A's doing x and it was reasonably foreseeable at the time A did x that his doing x would have that sort of effect, B will only be able to invoke the property harm principle to establish that A owed her a duty to take care not to do x if she had a sufficient interest in the property that was harmed at the time it was harmed. What sort of interest will suffice?

This question was dealt with by the House of Lords in *The Aliakmon*.[145] The answer is B will have had a sufficient interest in the property that was harmed if, at the time the property was harmed, she had a *legal interest* in the property or *possession* of the property. But if she merely had an *equitable interest* in the property at the time it was harmed, then that will not be enough.[146]

In *The Aliakmon*, Leigh & Sillavan Ltd agreed to buy a quantity of steel coils from Kinso-Mataichi Corp. The steel coils were to be shipped to Leigh & Sillavan Ltd on *The Aliakmon,* a ship owned by the defendants. Because there were some doubts as to Leigh & Sillavan's ability to pay for the coils, Leigh & Sillavan would become liable to pay for the coils as soon as they were shipped but the coils would remain the property of Kinso-Mataichi until they were paid for. When the coils were placed aboard *The Aliakmon,* the defendant stowed them badly with the result that when Leigh & Sillavan received the coils, they were badly damaged. However, Leigh & Sillavan still had to pay for the coils because they had agreed with Kinso-Mataichi that they would pay full price for the coils on delivery, whatever their condition.

Leigh & Sillavan sued the defendants for compensation for the fact that the coils they had received and paid for were badly damaged as a result of the defendants' bad stowage. The defendants had had a duty to take care not to stow the coils badly under the basic rule discussed here – it had been reasonably foreseeable at the time the coils were shipped that they would be damaged if they were stowed badly. But was that duty owed to Leigh & Sillavan? Only if they had a sufficient interest in the steel coils at the time they were damaged – that is, during their voyage aboard *The Aliakmon.* The House of Lords held that they did not. Leigh & Sillavan did not legally own the coils at the time they were being transported and neither did they have possession of the coils. At most they had an equitable interest in the coils, but that was not enough.

---

[145] [1986] AC 785.
[146] Ibid., 812A–813B.

Exceptions

The exceptions to the physical danger principle that have already been discussed will also apply to the property harm principle. So if A does *x* and as a result B's property is harmed, B will not be able to argue that A owed her a duty to take care not to do *x* if it was reasonable for A to do *x*, all things considered. So suppose A is on a mountain and he gets caught in a life-threatening snowstorm. In the blizzard, he comes across a locked and empty cabin, which belongs to B. In an attempt to save his life, A breaks a window of the cabin to gain access. As it is reasonable for A to do so, B will not be able subsequently to sue A for compensation for the loss of her window on the basis that A owed her, and breached, a duty not to break the window.[147] She might, however, be able to argue that A owed her, and breached, a duty to take care not to get caught on the mountain in inclement weather – because it was reasonably foreseeable that if he did so, he would be forced to break into her cabin to save his life.

Similarly, the *volenti* exception equally applies to the property harm principle and the courts have shown themselves willing to set aside the property harm principle where public policy demands. This was the case in *The Nicholas H*.[148] In that case, the eponymous ship, which was carrying the claimant's cargo, developed a crack in its hull while it was travelling from South America to Italy. The ship anchored off Puerto Rico and was inspected by the defendant classification society. The defendants told the shipowners that they would be willing to pass *The Nicholas H* as seaworthy – and thus allow it to continue on its way – if the shipowners temporarily repaired its hull and then repaired it properly as soon as possible after it discharged its cargo. The temporary repairs were done and *The Nicholas H* went on its way. However, it sank a week later when the temporary repairs failed. The claimant's cargo, which was worth $6,200,000, was lost. The claimant could only recover $500,000 from the shipowner by way of compensation for the loss of his cargo due to a limitation clause in the contract between the claimant and the shipowner.

The claimant sued the defendants for the balance of his loss, claiming that they had been negligent in allowing *The Nicholas H* to proceed on its way. The House of Lords dismissed the claim, holding that the defendants had not owed the claimant a duty to take care not to approve the ship as seaworthy when it was not. This was so even though it had been perfectly foreseeable that the claimant's cargo would be destroyed if the defendants approved the *Nicholas H* as seaworthy when it was not. So why did the House of Lords not give effect to the basic rule discussed here?[149] The reason was that the House of Lords

---

[147] But even if A did not act wrongfully in breaking the window, he will probably still have to compensate B for the damage done to her window: an example of compensation without wrongdoing (on which, see above pp. 30–1). See, for example, the American case of *Vincent* v *Lake Erie Transportation Co.*, 124 NW 221 (1910), discussed below at pp. 354, 696.

[148] [1996] AC 211.

[149] Lord Lloyd, dissenting, thought that the property harm principle should have been applied in the *Nicholas H* and a duty of care found: 'All that is required is a straightforward application of *Donoghue* v *Stevenson*' (ibid., 230). It seems likely that had anyone on board the *Nicholas H* been drowned when it sank, the House of Lords would not have hesitated to give full effect to the physical danger principle set out above and found that the defendants owed the people on board the *Nicholas H* a duty to take care not to approve the ship as being seaworthy when it was not – on the basis that it was

117

thought it would be contrary to the public interest to rule that a classification society will owe the owners of cargo aboard a ship a duty to take care not to say that a ship is seaworthy when it is not. Lord Steyn, giving the leading judgment, gave two reasons why so ruling would be contrary to the public interest.

First, classification societies act in the general public interest in certifying whether or not ships are seaworthy – their doing so helps to save lives, ships and cargo at sea. If classification societies could be sued in negligence when their surveyors carelessly passed as seaworthy ships that were not seaworthy, then they would not – Lord Steyn thought – be able to carry out their functions as efficiently. They would be exposed to a wide number of claims; their surveyors would be overly inclined to label ships as unseaworthy if there was any doubt on the matter; classification societies' staff and resources would be tied up in dealing with claims made against them instead of being used for the main task of classifying ships.[150]

Secondly, Lord Steyn thought that if classification societies could be sued in negligence when their surveyors carelessly passed as seaworthy ships that were not seaworthy, then they would, before passing a ship as seaworthy, demand that the shipowner agree to indemnify them against any negligence liability they might incur as a result of passing the ship as seaworthy. So, in the end, any liabilities incurred by the classification societies in negligence would be passed on to shipowners – thus bypassing the limitations of liability that shipowners insert into their contracts of carriage with cargo owners. Shipowners would no longer be able to predict for insurance purposes the extent of the liabilities they would incur if their ships sank and merchant shipping would as a result be disrupted.

One further exception to the property harm principle is worthy of note. In *Stephens v Anglian Water Authority*,[151] the claimant, the owner of a cottage, complained that part of her land had collapsed because the defendant had extracted so much water from under his land that the water under her land had drained away. The claimant sued the defendant for compensation, arguing that the defendant had owed her a duty not to extract as much water from under his land as he had. The Court of Appeal rejected the claim, holding that the defendant had not owed the claimant a duty of care in extracting water from under his land.[152]

Why didn't the Court of Appeal apply the property harm principle in this case? It was after all perfectly foreseeable that the claimant's land would collapse if the defendant extracted as much water from under his land as he did. The reason was simply that, under English law, an owner of land is free to extract as much water as he likes from under his land – regardless of what effect his extracting that water has on his neighbours.[153] It would have been different if the defendant had extracted so many *minerals* from under his land that min-

---

reasonably foreseeable when the *Nicholas H* was in dock that those on board on the *Nicholas H* would suffer some kind of physical injury if the defendants approved it as being seaworthy when it was not.

[150] For much the same reason, it has been held that the Civil Aviation Authority will not owe the owner of an aircraft a duty to take care that it does not certify the aircraft as being fit to fly when it is not: *Philcox v Civil Aviation Authority*, The Times, 8 June 1995.

[151] [1987] 1 WLR 1381.

[152] The House of Lords refused leave to appeal: [1988] 1 WLR 476.

[153] *Bradford Corporation v Pickles* [1895] AC 587, discussed below pp. 370, 413.

erals shifted out from under the claimant's land with the result that the claimant's land collapsed. A landowner is *not* free under English law to extract as many minerals from under his land as he likes regardless of the consequences that his doing so might have on his neighbours. So, if the defendant in *Stephens* had caused the claimant's land to collapse by extracting an excessive quantity of minerals from under his land, the defendant probably would have owed the claimant a duty not to act in the way he did under the property harm principle.[154]

THE LIMITS OF *DONOGHUE* V *STEVENSON*

As we have already observed, the courts have always refused to give full effect to Lord Atkin's neighbour principle. They have not accepted that A will have a positive duty to act if it is reasonably foreseeable that B will suffer some kind of harm if A does nothing. However, they have been prepared to accept that in certain limited situations one person will owe another a duty to act. We will look at these situations in Chapters 6 and 7.

The courts have also refused to accept that A will necessarily owe B a duty to take care not to do *x* if it is reasonably foreseeable that A's doing *x* will result in B suffering some kind of pure economic loss.[155] So in the great case of *Hedley Byrne & Co. Ltd* v *Heller & Partners Ltd*[156] – where the claimants suffered financial loss as a result of relying on the misleading advice of the defendant bankers as to the creditworthiness of one of the bankers' customers – the claimants could not rely on Lord Atkin's neighbour principle to help them establish that the defendants owed them a duty to take care not to mislead them as to that customer's creditworthiness. But they still came within an ace of establishing that such a duty of care was owed to them. In the next chapter we will look at what that case established as to when one person will owe another a duty of care.

---

[154] *Lotus* v *British Soda Ltd* [1972] Ch 123.
[155] To see why, see below, pp. 208–11.
[156] [1964] AC 465.

5

ESTABLISHED DUTY SITUATIONS II: THE PRINCIPLE IN *HEDLEY BYRNE* AND ASSOCIATED PRINCIPLES

THE PRINCIPLE IN *HEDLEY BYRNE*

The basic principle

In *Hedley Byrne & Co. Ltd* v *Heller & Partners Ltd*,[1] Hedley Byrne, a firm of advertising agents, wanted to find out whether a company called Easipower Ltd was creditworthy or not before they placed some advertising orders on Easipower's behalf. Hedley Byrne were personally liable for the cost of these advertising orders and were therefore understandably concerned to know whether they could recoup the cost of placing those orders from Easipower. Hedley Byrne's bankers approached Heller & Partners, Easipower's bankers, for a reference as to Easipower's creditworthiness. Heller gave Easipower a favourable reference, on the strength of which Hedley Byrne placed a number of advertising orders on Easipower's behalf. Soon afterwards, Easipower went into liquidation and Hedley Byrne were unable to recover from Easipower the money they had laid out on Easipower's behalf in placing those advertising orders.

Hedley Byrne sued Heller, claiming that Heller had owed them a duty to take care that it did not mislead them as to Easipower's creditworthiness and that Heller breached that duty when it supplied them with a positive reference as to Easipower's creditworthiness. The House of Lords dismissed Hedley Byrne's claim on the ground that Heller's advice to Hedley Byrne as to Easipower's creditworthiness had been given 'without responsibility'.[2] But the House of Lords made clear that had Heller not done this, it *would* have owed Hedley Byrne a duty to take care not to mislead them as to Easipower's creditworthiness. But why would Heller have owed Hedley Byrne a duty of care? Their Lordships came up with a number of different explanations. Lord Reid: Heller would have 'accepted a responsibility' for the accuracy of their advice or would have 'accepted a relationship' with Hedley Byrne which required them to take care in advising Hedley Byrne.[3] Lord Morris: Heller would have 'assumed a responsibility' to tender Hedley Byrne 'deliberate advice'.[4] Lord Morris (with

[1] [1964] AC 465.
[2] Ibid., 492, 504, 511, 532–3, 539–40.
[3] Ibid., 486.
[4] Ibid., 494.

the agreement of Lord Hodson): Heller would have known or ought to have known that their advice would be relied upon by Hedley Byrne.[5] Lord Hodson: there would have existed a 'sufficiently close'[6] or 'special'[7] relationship between Heller and Hedley Byrne which would have given rise to a duty of care owed by Heller to Hedley Byrne. Lord Devlin: there would have existed a 'special relationship' between Heller and Hedley Byrne that was 'equivalent to contract'; in other words, Heller would have 'assumed a responsibility' towards Hedley Byrne in circumstances where, if Heller had been paid by Hedley Byrne to assume that responsibility, there would have existed a contract between Hedley Byrne and Heller.[8] Lord Pearce: there would have existed a 'special relationship' between Heller and Hedley Byrne which gave rise to an 'assumption that care as well as honesty' was demanded when Heller advised Hedley Byrne.[9]

Given the vagueness and variety of these statements it is understandable that there has been a great deal of debate as to when exactly one person will owe another a duty of care under the decision in *Hedley Byrne*. Subsequent case law establishes that Lords Morris and Hodson's view that if A knows or ought to know that B will rely on some advice of his, A will owe B a duty of care in rendering that advice is too wide to be acceptable.[10] Something more is required before A will be found to have owed B a duty of care. But what is that 'something more'? The speeches of Lords Reid, Devlin and Morris in *Hedley Byrne* suggest that it needs to be shown that A 'assumed a responsibility' towards B for the quality of his advice. But when will A be held to have done this? There are essentially two schools of thought on this issue.

The first is that the concept of an 'assumption of responsibility' is essentially meaningless – so the courts will be free to find that A 'assumed a responsibility' towards B for the quality of his advice whenever they want to find that A owed B a duty of care in giving that advice. This was the line taken by Lord Griffiths in the case of *Smith* v *Eric S Bush*: 'I do not think . . . assumption of responsibility is a helpful or realistic test of liability [under *Hedley Byrne*] . . . The phrase "assumption of responsibility" can only have any real meaning if it is understood as referring to the circumstances in which the law will deem the maker of the statement to have assumed responsibility to the person who acts upon the advice.'[11]

The second is that the concept of an 'assumption of responsibility' is meaningful – in other words, it is only possible to say truthfully that someone has 'assumed a responsibility' to another in *certain definable circumstances*. Of course, the courts may have in the past found that a defendant 'assumed a

[5] Ibid., 503, 514.
[6] Ibid., 509.
[7] Ibid., 511.
[8] Ibid., 528–9, 530.
[9] Ibid., 539.
[10] See, in particular, the decision of the House of Lords in *Williams* v *Natural Life Health Foods Ltd* [1998] 1 WLR 830, discussed below at pp. 124–5.
[11] [1990] 1 AC 831, 862. See also the judgment of Lord Roskill in *Caparo Industries plc* v *Dickman* [1990] 2 AC 605 at 629; Stapleton 1998, 64–5; Barker 1993.

responsibility' to a claimant outside those circumstances, but in those cases the courts were guilty of abusing the concept – in those cases the courts wanted to find that the defendant owed the claimant a duty of care for such-and-such a reason and they simply *said* that the defendant 'assumed a responsibility' to the claimant in order to provide themselves with some legal justification for their finding that the defendant owed the claimant a duty of care.[12] Lord Steyn took this view in *Williams* v *Natural Life Health Foods Ltd*: 'There was, and is, no better rationalisation for [this] head of tort liability than assumption of responsibility ... There is nothing fictional about this species of liability in tort.'[13]

We prefer the second view, not least because it seems that Lords Reid, Devlin and Morris must have had *something* in mind when they talked of a defendant owing a claimant a duty of care if he 'assumed a responsibility' to her. We would go further and say that if A takes on the job of advising B on a particular matter, A will 'assume a responsibility' to B for the quality of his advice if and only if *he indicates to B that she can safely rely on his advice*. If this is right then we can say that the House of Lords' decision in *Hedley Byrne* estab-lishes that: If A takes on the job of advising B on a particular matter and he indicates to B that B can safely rely on that advice, then A will owe B a duty to take care that he does not give B any incorrect advice on that matter. Let us call this the *basic principle* in *Hedley Byrne*.[14] Let's now look at a number of cases to see this principle in action.

(1) *Hedley Byrne*. In *Hedley Byrne* itself, Heller did not owe Hedley Byrne a duty of care in advising Hedley Byrne as to Easipower's creditworthiness under this basic principle because it did not indicate to Hedley Byrne that its advice could be safely relied on: it gave its advice 'without responsibility'.

(2) *Chaudhry* v *Prabhakar*.[15] It was different in *Chaudhry*. In that case, Chaudhry asked Prabhakar to find her a car in good condition. Prabhakar advised her to buy a Golf car that was on sale for £4,500. Chaudhry bought the car on the strength of Prabhakar's advice that the car was in good condition; Prabhakar discouraged her from getting a qualified mechanic to look at the car before buying it. The car subsequently proved to be unroadworthy. Chaudhry

---

[12] See Lord Goff's judgment in *White* v *Jones* [1995] 2 AC 207 for a particularly transparent example of this happening. This is also what may have happened in the case of *Costello* v *Chief Constable of Northumbria Police* [1999] 1 All ER 550, discussed above at pp. 56–7 and below at p. 157.

[13] [1998] 1 WLR 830, 837. See also the judgment of Lord Browne-Wilkinson in *White* v *Jones* [1995] 2 AC 207, at 273–4.

[14] It is worth noting that this basic principle cannot explain the House of Lords' finding in *Smith* v *Eric S Bush* [1990] 1 AC 831 that a duty of care was owed in that case: see below, p. 142, n. 71. It is hardly surprising, then, that Lord Griffiths should have poured scorn in that case on the idea that an assumption of responsibility was a prerequisite to a duty of care being owed under *Hedley Byrne*: had he found that an assumption of responsibility *was* required, he would not have been able to rely on the decision of the House of Lords in *Hedley Byrne* as authority for the view that a duty of care was owed in *Smith* v *Eric S Bush*. For an explanation of the decision in *Smith* v *Eric S Bush*, see below, pp. 142–4.

[15] [1989] 1 WLR 29.

sued Prabhakar in negligence. She argued that Prabhakar had owed her a duty to take care that he did not mislead her as to the condition of the Golf car and that if he had taken such care he would have told her that the car was unroadworthy and she would not have bought it. The Court of Appeal allowed Chaudhry's claim. By discouraging Chaudhry from getting a qualified mechanic to look at the car, Prabhakar had indicated to her that his advice that the car was in good condition could be safely relied on. As a result, Prabhakar had owed Chaudhry a duty to take care that he did not mislead her as to the condition of the Golf car under the basic principle in *Hedley Byrne*.

In *Chaudhry* v *Prabhakar*, Prabhakar *explicitly* indicated to Chaudhry that she could safely rely on his advice. However, it is also possible *implicitly* to indicate to someone that your advice on a particular matter can be safely relied on. For example, suppose that: (1) Mary asks John for his advice on a particular matter; (2) John knows that Mary will rely on whatever advice he gives her on that matter unless she is discouraged from doing so; (3) Mary knows that John knows this; (4) John goes on to gives Mary some advice on the matter she is asking about without discouraging Mary from relying on that advice – by, for example, telling Mary that the advice is unreliable or given 'without responsibility'.

In such a case, Mary will think – and will be entitled to think – 'John knew that I would rely on his advice unless I was discouraged from doing so. Given that he knew this, he surely would have discouraged me from relying on his advice if his advice could not be safely relied on. But he did not do this – he gave me his advice and did nothing to discourage me from relying on it. Surely, then, his advice can be safely relied on.' So, in the case just described, by giving Mary advice in the way he did, John at one and the same time took on the job of advising Mary on the matter Mary asked about *and* he implicitly indicated to Mary that Mary could safely rely on his advice. So, in advising Mary, John will have owed Mary a duty of care under the basic principle in *Hedley Byrne*.[16]

What is the position if Mary asks John for his advice on a particular matter on a *social occasion*? In such a case, given the informality of the occasion, John will *not* expect that Mary will rely on whatever advice he gives Mary; and Mary will know that this is the case. So – even if John gives Mary some advice on the matter Mary is inquiring about and does not discourage Mary from relying on that advice, Mary will *not* be entitled to think that John, by acting in this way, implicitly indicated to Mary that his advice could be safely relied on. So if Mary asks John for his advice on a particular matter on a social occasion and John

---

[16] See Lord Reid's judgment in *Hedley Byrne & Co. Ltd* v *Heller & Partners Ltd* [1964] AC 465, at 486: 'A reasonable man, knowing that he was being trusted or that his skill or judgment were being relied on, would, I think, have three courses open to him. He could keep silent or decline to give the information or advice sought: or he could give an answer with a clear qualification that he accepted no responsibility for it or that it was given without that reflection or inquiry which a careful answer would require: or he could simply answer without any such qualification. If he chooses to adopt the last course he must, I think, be held to have accepted some responsibility for his answer being given carefully, or to have accepted a relationship with the inquirer which requires him to exercise such care as the circumstances require.'

gives Mary some advice on that matter without discouraging Mary from relying on that advice, John will *not* owe Mary a duty of care in giving her that advice under the basic principle in *Hedley Byrne* unless, of course, he *explicitly* indicates to Mary that Mary can safely rely on his advice.[17]

(3) *Williams* v *Natural Life Health Foods Ltd.*[18] Natural Life Health Food Shops Ltd was a company which provided the following service. People who were interested in opening a health food shop could approach Natural Life for an assessment as to how successful the health food shop was likely to be. If, on the basis of that assessment, they were still interested in opening the shop, Natural Life would, for a fee, allow them to open their shop using the Natural Life Health Foods trade name and would advise them as to how to run their shop. The claimants approached Natural Life because they were interested in opening a health food shop in Rugby. The managing director of Natural Life, Richard Mistlin, prepared some reports which predicted that the health food shop the claimants were proposing to open would enjoy a healthy turnover. Even though he prepared the reports, Mistlin never actually had any dealings with the claimants – they dealt with another employee of the company, Ron Padwick. On the strength of Mistlin's reports, the claimants opened a health food shop in Rugby under the Natural Life trade name. However, the shop enjoyed less success than Mistlin's reports indicated it would and the claimants, after trading at a loss for 18 months, were finally forced to close the shop.

The claimants sued Natural Life in negligence. Unfortunately, Natural Life was not worth suing; it was wound up a couple of years after the claimants commenced proceedings against Natural Life. Mistlin, on the other hand, did have substantial assets – so the claimants then tried to sue him in negligence. They argued that he had owed them, and breached, a duty to take care that he did not mislead them as to how successful that Rugby health food shop was likely to be; and that had he not breached this duty, he would have told them that the Rugby health food shop was unlikely to be a success and they would never have invested their money in it.

The House of Lords rejected the claimants' claim. Lord Steyn, giving the only judgment, ruled that Mistlin had not owed the claimants a duty of care in

---

[17] See *Hedley Byrne & Co. Ltd* v *Heller & Partners Ltd* [1964] AC 465, 482–3 per Lord Reid; *Howard Marine & Dredging Co.* v *A Ogden (Excavations) Ltd* [1978] QB 574, 592–3 per Lord Denning MR. The same will be true if John rang Mary out of the blue for her advice without making it clear that he was going to be relying on her advice: *Tidman* v *Reading Borough Council* [1994] Times LR 592; *Fashion Brokers Ltd* v *Clarke Hayes* [2000] PNLR 473. Or if the circumstances of John's inquiry were generally such as not to put Mary on warning that John was going to rely on her advice: see *James McNaughton Paper Group Ltd* v *Hicks Anderson & Co* [1991] 2 QB 113 (held, no liability for an off-the-cuff statement made by accountant as to profitability of a company in the course of negotiations to take over the company). A different result would have been reached if it had been made clear to the accountant that his statement would be relied upon: *Galoo* v *Bright Grahame Murray* [1994] 1 WLR 1360; *Law Society* v *KPMG Peat Marwick* [2000] 1 WLR 1921. Puzzlingly, it has been held that a solicitor working for someone selling a house will *not* owe the purchaser of the house a duty of care in answering the purchaser's inquiries even if it is made abundantly clear to him that those answers will be relied upon by the purchaser: *Gran Gelato Ltd* v *Richcliff (Group) Ltd* [1992] Ch 560 (Nicholls V-C). For criticisms of the decision in *Gran Gelato*, see Reed 1996, 69–73; also Bernstein 1998, 642–4.

[18] [1998] 1 WLR 830 (discussed, Armour 1999).

preparing his reports as to how profitable the Rugby health food shop was likely to be under the basic principle in *Hedley Byrne*. While Mistlin *did* take on the job of preparing the reports given to the claimants on the potential profitability of the Rugby health food shop, the lack of contact between Mistlin and the claimants meant that *Mistlin* did not at any point indicate to the claimants that they could safely rely on his advice. In contrast, Natural Life – a separate person from Mistlin – *did* indicate to the claimants that they could safely rely on the advice Natural Life gave them as to how profitable the Rugby health food shop was likely to be. So Natural Life *did* owe the claimants a duty under the basic principle in *Hedley Byrne* to take care that that they did not supply the claimants with any incorrect advice as to how profitable the Rugby health food shop was likely to be. However, as has already been observed, this was of little comfort to the claimants as Natural Life was not worth suing.

(4) *Welton* v *North Cornwall District Council.*[19] In this case, the claimants owned a guest house which constituted food premises for the purpose of the Food Act 1984 and the Food Safety Act 1990. The claimants were visited by one E, a health inspector. E said that the claimants' kitchen was not up to scratch. He could have closed the claimants' kitchen down – effectively putting their guest house out of business – but instead took it upon himself to advise the claimants as to what they needed to do to their kitchen to bring it up to a satisfactory standard. Acting on this advice, the claimants made numerous alterations to their kitchen, 90 per cent of which – they subsequently discovered – were completely unnecessary. The claimants sued, claiming that when E had taken on the job of advising them as to what they needed to do to their kitchen to bring it up to scratch, he had owed them a duty to take care that he did not give them any incorrect advice and that they had suffered loss as a result of E's breaching this duty. The Court of Appeal allowed the claimants' claim, holding that E *had* owed the claimants a duty to take care not to give them any incorrect advice under the basic principle in *Hedley Byrne*. This was right: E took on the job of advising the claimants as to what they had to do to bring their kitchen up to scratch and plainly indicated to them that they could safely rely on his advice.

(5) *Mutual Life and Citizens' Assurance Co. Ltd* v *Evatt.*[20] We have left this case until last because it was either wrongly decided or it establishes an exception to the basic principle in *Hedley Byrne* set out above. In this case, Evatt, the claimant, was a policy holder in Mutual Life, the defendant company. Mutual Life and Palmer (Consolidated) Ltd were both subsidiaries of a third company, MLC Ltd. Evatt asked Mutual Life to advise him on whether it was safe to invest in Palmer. Mutual Life advised him that Palmer was a sound and stable company, knowing that giving Evatt such advice would encourage him to invest in Palmer. As it happened, Evatt *was* encouraged by this advice to retain his existing investments in Palmer and to make further investments.

---

[19] [1997] 1 WLR 570.
[20] [1971] AC 793.

Evatt subsequently lost a lot of money when Palmer proved not to be as stable and as safe to invest in as Mutual Life had made out.

Evatt sued Mutual Life in negligence, claiming that they had owed him, and breached, a duty to take care not to mislead him as to how sound Palmer was as a company and that had Mutual Life not breached this duty they would have told him that Palmer was not sound and he would as a result not have put any further money into Palmer and would have liquidated his existing investments in Palmer. By a bare majority, the Privy Council[21] held that the facts alleged in Evatt's statement of claim did not establish that Mutual Life owed Evatt a duty to take care that it did not mislead him as to the soundness of Palmer. This was so even though the facts alleged in Evatt's statement of claim made it clear that, in advising Evatt as it did, Mutual Life took on the job of advising Evatt as to whether it was safe to invest in Palmer *and* that Mutual Life – on the reasoning advanced above[22] – implicitly indicated to Evatt that he could safely rely on their advice as to whether it was safe to invest in Palmer.

Lord Diplock, giving the leading judgment, held that Evatt's failure to allege that Mutual Life held itself out as possessing any *special expertise* to judge whether or not it was safe to invest in Palmer meant that it was not possible to say, on the facts alleged by Evatt in his statement of claim, that Mutual Life owed Evatt a duty to take care that it did not mislead him as to the soundness of Palmer when it advised him as to whether or not it was safe to invest in Palmer. Clearly, then, the majority in *Mutual Life v Evatt* took the view that if A took on the job of advising B on a particular matter and indicated to B that she could safely rely on his advice on that matter, A will only have owed B a duty to take care he did not give B any incorrect advice on that matter *if* A, in taking on the job of advising B, claimed or gave the impression that he possessed some special expertise on the matter in question.

Of course, decisions of the Privy Council are not binding on English courts and the decision in *Mutual Life v Evatt* has met with a cool reception in England.[23] Certainly, there is nothing in the decision in *Hedley Byrne* that warranted the Privy Council reaching the conclusion it did in *Mutual Life v Evatt*. Indeed, the two dissents in *Mutual Life v Evatt* came from Lords Reid and Morris – both of whom also sat in *Hedley Byrne*. Moreover, the majority decision in *Mutual Life v Evatt* rested on the claim that A could not take care that he did not give B any incorrect advice on a particular matter unless he possessed some special expertise on that matter. It would therefore be unreasonable to impose on A a duty to take care to ensure that he did not give B any incorrect advice on a particular matter if he did not possess – or did not hold himself out as possessing – any special expertise on that matter. However, this is not true. A *can* take care

---

[21] The case was on appeal from the High Court of Australia.

[22] See above, p. 123.

[23] See *Esso Petroleum Co. Ltd v Mardon* [1976] QB 801; *Howard Marine & Dredging Co. v A Ogden (Excavations) Ltd* [1978] QB 574; *Spring v Guardian Assurance plc* [1995] 2 AC 296, 320F–H, per Lord Goff; *Commissioner of Police of the Metropolis v Lennon* [2004] 2 All ER 266.

to ensure that he does not give B any incorrect advice on whether or not a particular car is in good condition even if he has no expert knowledge about cars. 'Taking care' in his case will involve looking out for any *obvious* defects or problems with the car. Similarly, in *Mutual Life* v *Evatt*, even though Mutual Life – being an insurance company – had no expert knowledge on investment decisions, it was still open to it to take steps – to take care – to ensure that it did not give Evatt the wrong impression as to Palmer's soundness. It could, for example, have contacted responsible people in its head company, MLC, to take their views.

So whether *Mutual Life* v *Evatt* is good law in England is open to doubt. However, this is not to say that when A takes on the job of advising B on a particular matter A's expertise in that matter will not be relevant to whether or not A will owe B a duty to take care that he does not give B any incorrect advice on that matter. For example, suppose Vijay and Lara are both first-year students at university. Vijay is a law student and Lara is a medical student. Vijay asks Lara to advise him on whether he needs an operation on his knee. Lara looks at the knee and says that it seems fine. In such a case, Lara, in advising Vijay, will not expect Vijay to rely on her advice – even if Vijay is not discouraged from doing so. This is because Lara is aware that her relative lack of expertise in medical matters is known to Vijay. So it is hard to say that when Lara advises Vijay, she – by failing to discourage Vijay from relying on her advice – implicitly indicates to Vijay that it is safe to rely on that advice.

The situation was quite different in *Mutual Life* v *Evatt*. It was clear to Mutual Life – and Evatt knew it was clear to Mutual Life – that Evatt would rely on Mutual Life's advice as to whether or not it was safe to invest in Palmer unless he was discouraged from doing so. Even though Evatt appreciated that Mutual Life had no expertise in advising on investment decisions, the close association between Mutual Life and Palmer meant that Evatt would treat any advice coming from Mutual Life as to whether or not it was safe to invest in Palmer as though it came from someone with a special expertise in investment decisions. And Mutual Life appreciated that Evatt would treat their advice in this way. So when Mutual Life advised Evatt that it was safe to invest in Palmer without doing anything to discourage him from relying on that advice, Mutual Life implicitly indicated to Evatt that he could safely rely on their advice.

The extended principle

It is now well acknowledged that *Hedley Byrne* is not *just* authority in favour of the proposition that someone who takes on the task of advising another on a particular matter will, in certain circumstances, owe that other a duty of care in giving that advice. Certain *dicta* in *Hedley Byrne* suggest that if A has indicated to B[24] that B can safely rely on him to perform a particular task with a certain degree of care and skill, and B has so relied on A, A will owe B a duty to perform that task with that degree of care and skill.[25]

---

[24] By 'B' we mean either B or B's agent, acting on B's behalf.

[25] Lord Morris: '... it should now be regarded as settled that if someone possessed of a special skill undertakes, quite irrespective of contract, to apply that skill for the assistance of another person who relies upon such skill, a duty of care will arise' ([1964] AC 465, at 502–3); Lord Hodson:

Many cases, decided before and after *Hedley Byrne,* seem to support this suggestion. Most of them deal with the following kind of situation: (1) Paul is a professional – that is, he holds himself out as being able to perform a particular task T with a high degree of care and skill – a 'professional' degree of care and skill; (2) as a result, Karen is led to believe that Paul can be safely relied on to perform task T with a 'professional' degree of care and skill; (3) Karen asks Paul to perform task T for her; (4) Paul knows that Karen's request is made in the belief that Paul can be safely relied on to perform task T with a 'professional' degree of care and skill and Karen knows that Paul knows this; (5) Paul agrees to perform task T for Karen.

In such a case, Karen will think – and she will be entitled to think – 'Paul knew that I was only requesting him to perform task T in the belief that he could be safely relied on to perform task T for me with a "professional" degree of care and skill. Given that he knew this, he surely would not have agreed to perform task T for me if he could not be safely relied on to perform task T with a "professional" degree of care and skill. But he did not do this – he agreed to perform task T for me. Surely, then, Paul *can* be safely relied on to perform task T for me with a "professional" degree of care and skill.' In the case just described, then, Paul – by agreeing to perform task T for Karen – will have implicitly indicated to Karen that Karen can safely rely on him to perform task T with a 'professional' degree of care and skill. And Karen will have relied on Paul to perform that task with a 'professional' degree of care and skill by not asking anyone else to perform task T for her.

A lot of cases hold that, in this kind of situation, Paul will owe Karen a duty to perform task T with a 'professional' degree of care and skill. These cases therefore seem to support the suggestion that if A indicates to B that B can safely rely on him to perform a particular task with a certain degree of care and skill and B does so rely on A, then A will owe B a duty to perform that task with that degree of care and skill. These cases variously hold that:

(1) a doctor will owe his patient a duty to treat his patient with the care and skill that a reasonably competent doctor would exercise in treating a patient;[26] similarly,

(2) a dentist will owe his patient a duty to treat that patient with the care and skill that a reasonably competent dentist would exercise in treating a patient;[27]

'... those who hold themselves out as possessing a special skill are under a duty to exercise it with reasonable care' (ibid., at 505); Lord Devlin: 'If a defendant says to a [claimant]: "Let me do this for you; do not waste your money in employing a professional, I will do it for nothing and you can rely on me," I do not think he could escape liability . . .' (ibid., at 531); Lord Pearce: '. . . if persons holding themselves out in a calling or situation or profession take on a task within that calling or situation or profession, they have a duty of skill and care' (ibid., at 538).

[26] *Gladwell* v *Steggal* (1839) 5 Bing NC 733, 132 ER 1283; *Pippin* v *Sherrard* (1822) 11 Price 400, 147 ER 512; *Barnett* v *Chelsea & Kensington Hospital Management Committee* [1969] 1 QB 428. The concept of a doctor–patient relationship was stretched *very* far by Gage J in *A* v *Leeds Teaching Hospital NHS Trust* [2004] EWHC 644, holding that the parents of a baby that had died in hospital enjoyed a doctor–patient relationship with the baby's doctor, so that the doctor owed the parents a duty to act towards them with reasonable skill and care – particularly in relation to explaining to them what the baby's post-mortem would involve and whether any of the baby's organs would be retained.

[27] *Edwards* v *Mallan* [1908] 1 KB 1002; *Fish* v *Kapur* [1948] 2 All ER 176.

(3) a vet who treats an animal at the owner's request will owe that owner a duty to treat that animal with the care and skill that a reasonably competent vet would exercise in treating that animal;[28]

(4) a solicitor who handles a case or transaction on behalf of a client will owe that client a duty to handle that case or transaction with the care and skill that a reasonably competent solicitor would exercise in handling that case or transaction;[29] similarly,

(5) a barrister who handles a client's case in court will owe that client a duty to conduct that case in court with the care and skill that a reasonably competent barrister would exercise in conducting that case;[30]

(6) a surveyor will owe a client of his who has asked him to value a house or piece of land that he is thinking of purchasing a duty to survey that house or land with the care and skill that a reasonably competent surveyor would exercise in surveying a house or a piece of land;

(7) an architect will owe a client who has commissioned him to design a building a duty to design that building with the care and skill that a reasonably competent architect would exercise in designing a building; moreover,

(8) an architect who has been commissioned by a client to supervise the construction of a building will normally owe that client a duty to supervise the construction work with the care and skill that a reasonably competent architect would exercise in supervising that sort of work; likewise,

(9) an engineer who has been engaged to undertake some building work by a client will owe that client a duty to execute that work with the care and skill that a reasonably competent engineer would exercise in doing that sort of work;[31]

(10) an accountant will owe a client who has commissioned him to draw up a set of accounts a duty to draw up those accounts with the care and skill that a reasonably competent accountant would exercise in drawing up a set of accounts;

(11) the referee of a game will owe the participants in the game a duty to referee the game with a reasonable degree of care and skill.[32]

It should be emphasised that if A – implicitly or explicitly – indicates to B that he can be safely relied on to perform a particular task T with a certain degree of care and skill and B did so rely on him, he will not owe B a duty to perform that task T with any *more* care and skill than he indicated he could be safely relied on to exercise in performing task T.[33]

---

[28] *Chute Farms v Curtis*, The Times, 10 October 1961.
[29] *Nocton v Lord Ashburton* [1914] AC 465; *Midland Bank v Hett, Stubbs and Kemp* [1979] Ch 383.
[30] *Arthur J S Hall v Simons* [2002] 1 AC 615.
[31] *Congregational Union v Harriss and Harriss* [1988] 1 All ER 15; *Ketteman v Hansel Properties* [1987] AC 189.
[32] *Vowles v Evans* [2003] 1 WLR 1607 (noted, Elvin 2003a).
[33] Ibid., at [28], holding that it is arguable that someone who volunteers to referee a game as a

So – in *Philips* v *William Whiteley Ltd*,[34] the claimant asked the defendants, a firm of jewellers, to pierce her ears. The claimant suffered some ill effects from the operation and sought to recover compensation for those ill effects by suing the defendants in negligence. The court dismissed the claimant's claim: it held that the defendants had owed the claimant a duty to pierce her ears with the skill and care that a reasonably competent jeweller would exercise in piercing someone's ears and that the defendants had not breached that duty. The claimant's claim that the defendants had owed the claimant a more stringent duty of care – a duty to pierce her ears with the skill and care that a reasonably competent surgeon would exercise in piercing someone's ears – was dismissed: the defendants had never indicated to the claimant that they could be safely relied on to pierce her ears with the skill and care that a surgeon would exercise in piercing someone's ears.

Similarly, in *Wilsher* v *Essex Area Health Authority*,[35] the Court of Appeal held that if A treats B, a hospital patient, A will owe B a duty to treat B with the skill and care that a reasonably competent person *in A's post* would exercise in treating that patient. It would be unreasonable to take A as indicating that he will exercise any higher degree of care and skill in treating B. So a junior house officer who treats a patient will owe that patient a duty to treat that patient with the skill and care that a reasonably competent junior house officer would exercise in treating a patient; a level of skill and care which would, presumably, be lower than the level of skill and care that a reasonably competent consultant would exercise in treating a patient.[36]

It is worth noting at greater length two cases that seem to lend some support to the suggestion that if A indicates to B that B can safely rely on him to perform a particular task with a certain degree of care and skill and B does so rely on A, then A will owe B a duty to perform that task with that degree of care and skill.

(1) *Junior Books Ltd* v *Veitchi Co. Ltd*.[37] Junior Books Ltd engaged Ogilvie Builders Ltd to build a factory for them. The work of laying the floor was contracted out to Veitchi Co. Ltd, on the instructions of Junior Books' architect. Veitchi laid the floor of Junior Books' factory but did a poor job of it. Two years after the floor was laid, it began to crack up and needed to be completely replaced. Junior Books sued Veitchi in negligence so as to recover the cost of relaying the floor of their factory. In order to make out their claim, they had to establish that Veitchi, in laying the floor, owed Junior Books a duty to lay the floor with a certain degree of care and skill. The House of Lords held that Veitchi did owe Junior Books such a duty. The decision caused some consternation at the time; it was hard to see what principle underlay the House of Lords' decision and therefore how widely it applied. However – whatever the

---

replacement for a referee who has not turned up will not be expected to referee the game with as much skill and care as someone who has been trained to act as a referee: 'the volunteer cannot reasonably be expected to show the skill of one who holds himself out [to be a] referee, or perhaps even to be fully conversant with the [l]aws of the [g]ame.'

[34] [1938] 1 All ER 566. See also *Shakoor* v *Situ* [2001] 1 WLR 410.

[35] [1987] 1 QB 730, reversed on other grounds by the House of Lords: [1988] 1 AC 1074.

[36] Of course, one way in which a reasonably competent junior house officer might act negligently would be in failing to seek assistance from a more qualified physician when it ought to have been clear to a reasonably competent junior house officer that such assistance was necessary.

[37] [1983] 1 AC 520.

views were of the Law Lords who decided the case at the time – the decision is nowadays justified on the basis that Veitchi indicated, in negotiations with Junior Books' architect, that it could be safely relied on to lay the floor of Junior Books' factory with a certain degree of care and skill and Junior Books did so rely on Veitchi to take such care by causing Veitchi to be nominated as subcontractors by their architect.[38] Viewed in this way, the decision in *Junior Books* was an outgrowth of the *dicta* in *Hedley Byrne* referred to above.[39]

(2) *Henderson v Merrett Syndicates Ltd.*[40] In this case, the claimants were Lloyd's names who were members of syndicates managed by the defendants. Each syndicate was made up of a number of Lloyd's names. A syndicate's managing agent performed a number of functions. First, he would decide which risks should be insured by the syndicate. Secondly, in the case of risks which were insured by the syndicate, he would decide whether or not those risks should be re-insured with someone else. Thirdly, he would decide how to deal with claims against the syndicate – whether to settle those claims, and if so on what terms, and so on. Losses suffered by a syndicate were to be borne by the names who were members of that syndicate. A name's potential liability was unlimited – the greater the losses suffered by a syndicate of which he or she was a member, the greater would be his or her liability, without limit. The claimants suffered spectacular losses because (they claimed) the defendant managing agents had failed to run the affairs of their syndicates with the sort of care and skill that the claimants had expected them to when they joined those syndicates.

Each Lloyd's name, when he entered Lloyd's, signed an 'underwriting agency agreement' with an underwriting agent, whose job it was to place him with a syndicate. If the underwriting agent placed the name in a syndicate which he himself managed, the name was known as a 'direct name'. In such a

---

[38] In contrast, in *Simaan v Pilkington Glass Ltd (No. 2)* [1988] QB 758, the claimant contractors were appointed to construct a building in Abu Dhabi (the 'Al-Oteiba building', named after the sheikh who commissioned it). One of the main features of the building was to be a curtain wall, made out of green panels. The job of building the curtain wall was subcontracted to a company named Feal and the claimants instructed Feal to use glass panels manufactured by the defendants in constructing the building. The glass panels proved not to be suitable and the sheikh who commissioned the building refused to pay the claimants the full price due under their contract with the sheikh. The claimants sought to recover their loss from the defendants by suing them in negligence but it was held that the defendants had not owed the claimants a duty to construct the glass panels with reasonable care and skill. The crucial distinction between this case and *Junior Books* is that the defendants did not indicate to the claimants that they could be safely relied upon to do a good job of constructing the glass panels and the defendants had not so relied on them. In fact, the only reason why the claimants instructed Feal to use the defendants' glass panels in constructing the curtain wall was that the building's *architect* wanted the defendants' panels to be used.

[39] A view taken by Lord Oliver of Aylmerton (*D & F Estates v Church Commissioners* [1989] 1 AC 177, 215D: 'the decision of this House in *Junior Books* . . . rests . . . upon the *Hedley Byrne* doctrine of reliance') and Lord Keith of Kinkel (*Murphy v Brentwood DC* [1991] 1 AC 398, 466G–H: 'The case would accordingly fall within the principle of *Hedley Byrne* . . . I regard *Junior Books* . . . as being an application of that principle'). See also, to the same effect, Perry 1992, 302–8. However, others have found it difficult to see how *Junior Books* can be explained on this basis: see *Payne v John Setchell Ltd* [2002] PNLR 146, at [24] and references contained therein.

[40] [1995] 2 AC 145.

case, the underwriting agency agreement between the underwriting agent and the name created a contractual relationship between the name and the under-writing agent *qua* managing agent of the member's syndicate. It was conceded that there was an implied term in the contract between a direct name and his underwriting agent *qua* managing agent that the latter would administer the affairs of the name's syndicate with a certain degree of care and skill.[41] If the underwriting agent placed the name in a syndicate which he did not manage himself, the name was known as an 'indirect name'. In such a case, there was no contractual relationship between the name and the managing agent of the name's syndicate.

The claimants in *Henderson* v *Merrett Syndicates Ltd* comprised a mixture of direct and indirect names. Obviously – assuming that the defendants did fail to take care to administer the affairs of their syndicates properly – the claimants who were direct names had an action in *contract* against the managing agents of their syndicates to recover compensation for the money they lost due to those agents' mismanagement. However, they wished to sue their managing agents in *negligence* to take advantage of the fact that the limitation periods for bringing actions in negligence expire later than the limitation periods for bringing actions for breach of contract. Of course, the claimants who were indirect names could not bring a claim in contract against the managing agents of their syndicates – even assuming that they could prove those managing agents did fail to take care to administer the affairs of their syndicates properly – and so could only seek redress against the managing agents of their syndicates by bringing an action in negligence against those agents. So each claimant in *Henderson* v *Merrett Syndicates Ltd* sought to establish – for the purpose of making out a claim in negligence against the managing agent of his syndicate – that the managing agent of his syndicate owed him a duty to administer the affairs of the syndi-cate with a certain degree of care and skill.[42] The House of Lords was of the opinion that every claimant in *Henderson* v *Merrett Syndicates Ltd* could estab-lish that the managing agent of his syndicate owed him such a duty.

In the case of claimants who were *direct* names, this is easily explained by ref-erence to the principle of law examined here: that if A indicates to B that he can be safely relied on to perform a particular task with a certain degree of care and skill and B does so rely on A, A will owe B a duty to perform that task with that degree of care and skill. When a name became a member of a syndicate which was managed by the name's underwriting agent – thereby becoming a direct name – the agent contracted with the name that he would run the affairs of the name's syndicate with a certain degree of care and skill and thereby indicated to the name that the name could safely rely on him to run the affairs of the syn-dicate with that degree of care and skill. The direct name would, in turn, rely on his underwriting agent to run the affairs of his syndicate with that degree of

---

[41] Ibid., 176.

[42] It is worth re-emphasising at this juncture that the word 'duty' is used here to refer to a *non-con-tractual*, non-equitable duty. It was obviously true that – in the case of a claimant who was a direct name – the managing agent of his syndicate (who was also his underwriting agent) owed him a *contractual* duty to take care to administer the affairs of the syndicate properly.

care and skill by agreeing to join the underwriting agent's syndicate and by staying on as a member of that syndicate while the underwriting agent administered its affairs.

In the case of the claimants who were *indirect* names, we can again explain the House of Lords' ruling by reference to the principle of law examined here. Before an indirect name became a member of a syndicate managed by a particular managing agent, the managing agent would expressly or impliedly indicate to the name, through the name's underwriting agent, that he could be safely relied on to manage the affairs of his syndicate with a certain degree of care and skill. The indirect name would in turn rely on the managing agent to run the affairs of his syndicate with that degree of care and skill by agreeing to join the managing agent's syndicate and by staying on as a member of the syndicate while the managing agent administered its affairs.

So the ruling of the House of Lords in *Henderson* v *Merrett Syndicates Ltd* that the claimant names could establish that the managing agents of their syndicates owed them a duty to administer the affairs of those syndicates with a certain degree of care and skill can be explained by reference to the principle of law examined here. Seen in this way, the decision in *Henderson* v *Merrett Syndicates Ltd* was, like the decision in *Junior Books*, an outgrowth of the *dicta* in *Hedley Byrne* that were referred to above – and that is, indeed, how the Law Lords who decided *Henderson* v *Merrett Syndicates Ltd* viewed their decision.

If it is the law (and it is)[43] that A will owe B a duty to perform a task with a certain degree of care and skill if he has indicated to B that he can be safely relied on to perform that task with that degree of care and skill and B has so relied on A, then it must be the law – by extension – that if A has indicated to B that he can be safely relied on to take reasonable steps to achieve some goal or end and B has so relied on A, A will owe B a duty to take reasonable steps to achieve that goal or end. There are a couple of cases that seem to indicate that this is true.

In *Welsh* v *Chief Constable of Merseyside Police*,[44] the claimant appeared before a magistrates' court charged with two offences of theft. He was remanded on bail to appear again on 19 August 1987. On 7 August the claimant was due to appear before the Crown Court to be sentenced for committing various criminal offences. Before his case was called, the claimant indicated to the Crown Prosecution Service (CPS) that he did commit the two theft offences for which he was due to appear before the magistrates on 19 August and he wanted the Crown Court to take into account those two offences in sentencing him. The Crown Court took those offences into account and the claimant – believing that the CPS would tell the magistrates that the Crown Court had already dealt with the two theft offences which they were due to try him for – failed to turn up to his hearing before the magistrates on 19 August. The

---

[43] Whittaker 1997 wishes it were not so, arguing that the extended principle in *Hedley Byrne* undermines the law of contract, which also makes 'assumptions of responsibility' binding, but only if they are made in a deed or if consideration is provided for them.

[44] [1993] 1 All ER 692.

magistrates, knowing nothing of the Crown Court hearing, issued a warrant for the claimant's arrest. The claimant was arrested under the warrant and held in custody for two days until the true facts came to light.

The claimant sued the CPS, claiming that they had owed him a duty to take reasonable steps to alert the magistrates to the fact that he had already been sentenced in the Crown Court for committing the two theft offences for which he was due to be tried in the magistrates' court. Tudor Evans J refused to strike out the claimant's claim, holding that it was strongly arguable that the CPS had owed him such a duty of care. It could be argued that the CPS indicated to the claimant that he could safely rely on them to take reasonable steps to inform the magistrates of what had happened in the Crown Court and that the claimant had relied on the CPS to take such steps by not turning up to his hearing on the 19 August.[45]

In *Swinney* v *Chief Constable of Northumbria Police*,[46] the claimant passed on to the police information which indicated that T was involved in the killing of a police officer. The claimant gave the police this information in confidence and made it clear that she did not want T to find out that she had informed on him to the police. As the claimant gave her information to the police, it was written down on a document which named the claimant as the source of the information. This document was then left in an unattended police car which was broken into by criminals. The document was stolen and passed on to T. T then threatened the claimant with violence and arson and the claimant developed a psychiatric illness as a result. The claimant sued the police, arguing that the police had owed her, and breached, a duty to take reasonable steps to see that T would not find out that she had informed on him. The police sought to have the claimant's claim struck out on the ground that they had not owed her a duty of care. However, the Court of Appeal refused to strike out the claim: it thought it was strongly arguable that the police had owed the claimant a duty to take reasonable steps to ensure that T would not find out that she had informed on him. The reason why the Court of Appeal thought it was strongly arguable that the police had owed the claimant such a duty of care was that the police had indicated to her that they could be safely relied on to take reasonable steps to ensure that T would not find out that she had informed on him and the claimant did so rely on the police by giving them her information about T.[47]

To sum up this section then, the cases seem to establish that: (*a*) if A indicates to B that he can be safely relied on to perform some task with a certain

---

[45] It is quite clear that if the CPS had *not* indicated to the claimant that they could be safely relied on to take reasonable steps to inform the magistrates of his conviction, they would not have owed him a duty to take any steps to inform the magistrates of his conviction: *Elguzouli-Daf* v *Commissioner of the Police of the Metropolis* [1995] QB 335.

[46] [1997] QB 464.

[47] When the case went to trial, the judge (Jackson J) found that the police had indeed owed the claimant a duty to take reasonable steps to see that T did not find out that she had informed on him. However, the claimant's claim was dismissed on the ground that the police had not breached that duty of care. See *Swinney* v *Chief Constable of Northumbria Police (No. 2)*, The Times, 25 May 1999.

degree of care and skill and B does so rely on A, then A will owe B a duty to perform that task with that degree of care and skill; *and (b)* if A indicates to B that he can be safely relied on to take reasonable steps to achieve some goal or end and B does so rely on A, then A will owe B a duty to take reasonable steps to achieve that goal or end. Let's call this the *extended principle* in *Hedley Byrne*, to contrast it with the basic principle, which only applies to cases where A takes on the task of advising B on some matter. The extended principle applies to all kinds of tasks, not just the giving of advice.

The *SAAMCO* principle

The '*SAAMCO* principle' was introduced into our law in the case of *South Australia Asset Management Corp* v *York Montague Ltd*[48] – hence, *SAAMCO*. The principle affects how much A can sue B for by way of damages if A breaches a duty of care owed to B under either the basic or extended principle in *Hedley Byrne*. Strictly speaking, then, we should not talk of it here. A discussion of the *SAAMCO* principle properly belongs in Part III of this book, which deals with what remedies will be available when someone commits a tort. However, it seems convenient for teaching purposes to mention it here rather than postponing discussion of the principle for a few hundred pages.

The *SAAMCO* principle has been described as being 'easier to formulate than to apply'.[49] This is not true: the *SAAMCO* principle is *both* extremely difficult to formulate *and* extremely difficult to apply.[50] The basic idea behind it seems to go like this.[51] Suppose B got A to perform some task for her or to give her some advice on a particular matter. Suppose further that A owed B a duty of care in performing that task or giving that advice and A breached that duty of care with the result that B suffered some kind of evil or failed to obtain some kind of good. The *SAAMCO* principle says that B will not be entitled to sue A in negligence for compensation for the fact that she suffered that evil or failed to obtained that good unless *B got A to perform the task or give her the advice in question in order to avoid that evil or obtain that good.*

In the *South Australia* case, Lord Hoffmann – the originator of the *SAAMCO* principle – gave an example of a situation where the principle would bite: 'A mountaineer about to undertake a difficult climb is concerned about the fitness of his knee. He goes to a doctor who negligently makes a superficial examination and pronounces the knee fit. The climber goes on the expedition, which

---

[48] [1997] AC 191 (noted, O'Sullivan 1997). The case is otherwise known as *Banque Bruxelles Lambert SA* v *Eagle Star Insurance Co. Ltd.*

[49] *Nykredit plc* v *Edward Erdman Ltd* [1997] 1 WLR 1627, 1631 per Lord Nicholls.

[50] A couple of cases illustrate the difficulties that the courts have experienced in applying the *SAAMCO* principle. See *Platform Home Loans* v *Oyston Shipways Ltd* [2000] 2 AC 190 (discussed below, pp. 612–13), where the House of Lords reversed a unanimous Court of Appeal's application of the *SAAMCO* principle, but not without dissent from one Law Lord (Lord Cooke); also *Aneco Reinsurance Underwriting Ltd* v *Johnson & Higgins Ltd* [2001] UKHL 51 where neither the House of Lords nor the Court of Appeal below could reach a unanimous decision as to how the *SAAMCO* principle applied in that case.

[51] For more detailed treatments of the SAAMCO principle and how it operates, see Dugdale 2000; Evans 2001; Peel 2003a and Butler 2003.

he would not have undertaken if the doctor had told him the true state of his knee. He suffers an injury which is an entirely foreseeable consequence of mountaineering but has nothing to do with his knee.'[52] In this case, the doctor will have breached a duty of care owed to the climber under either the basic or the extended principle in *Hedley Byrne* and the climber has suffered injury as a result. But the climber will not be entitled to sue the doctor for compensation for that injury under the *SAAMCO* principle because he asked the doctor to advise him on the fitness of his knee in order to avoid suffering an injury as a result of his knee giving way – he did not ask the doctor to advise him on the fitness of his knee in order to avoid the kind of injury that he ended up suffering: that is, a non-knee-related injury.

The *South Australia* case was concerned with the following kind of situation. C applies to B for a loan of £200,000 and offers certain properties – call them 'security properties' – as security for the loan. B gets A to value them and A values the properties as being worth £220,000. In fact, A failed to value the security properties with a professional degree of care and skill, thereby breaching the duty of care he owed B in valuing the properties. The security properties were in fact only worth £180,000. B – thinking that the security properties are actually worth £220,000 – loans C the £200,000 requested. Come the time for repayment, C defaults on the loan. B then seeks to get his money back by selling the security properties but – due to a fall in the market – the properties are now only worth £110,000. So B makes a net loss of £90,000 on the loan – the difference between the value of the loan and what he has managed to claw back by selling the security properties.

B discovers that A was negligent in valuing the security properties and he sues A for compensation for the £90,000 he lost on the loan to C. B argues that if A had not been negligent, A would have told B that the security properties were only worth £180,000 and so B would not have loaned C anything – C would have been unable to offer him sufficient security for the loan. It follows that had A not been negligent, B would not have lost £90,000. However, B will only be able to sue A for *£40,000* in damages under the *SAAMCO* principle. Why is this? The reason is that B got A to advise him as to the value of the security properties in order to ensure that he did not suffer a loss *as a result of lending money to C on inadequate security.*

Now – how much of the loss suffered by B here is suffered *because he lent money to C on inadequate security*? Well, the fact that B was willing to lend C £200,000 on security that was valued at £220,000 shows that he thought that security worth that much was adequate security for his loan. Had B lent C £200,000 on security worth that much, that security would have been worth £150,000 when the time came for C to repay. (We assume here that the security would have declined in value by £70,000 as a result of a fall in the market, just like the security properties that C actually offered to B as security for B's loan to him.) So had B lent money to C on adequate security, he would still have lost £50,000 on his loan to C. It follows that of the £90,000 loss suffered by B in this case, only £40,000 of that loss was suffered by him as a result of his lending money to C on inadequate security. So, under the *SAAMCO*

---

[52] [1997] AC 191, 213.

principle, B will only be able to sue A for compensation for that £40,000 loss – B got A to value the security properties in order to help ensure that he did not suffer any loss as a result of lending money to C on inadequate security and, as things have turned out, B has lost £40,000, but no more than £40,000, as a result of lending money to C on inadequate security.[53]

A pre-*SAAMCO* case which can, in its result, be seen as giving effect to the *SAAMCO* principle is *Caparo Industries plc* v *Dickman*.[54] In that case, Caparo Industries plc were a company which held shares in Fidelity plc. Touche Ross, the defendants, audited Fidelity's accounts before they were circulated to Fidelity's shareholders. Touche Ross stated that the company's accounts gave a 'true and fair' representation of the company's financial position. This was not correct and Touche Ross should have known it. The accounts showed that Fidelity enjoyed a pre-tax profit of £1.3m. The true position was that Fidelity had suffered a loss of over £400,000. Caparo launched a takeover bid for Fidelity, relying on the fact that Touche Ross had given the company's accounts their seal of approval. The takeover bid was successful but when Caparo took a closer look at the books it discovered that it had paid too much for Fidelity.

Caparo sued Touche Ross in negligence, arguing that Touche had owed them, as one of Fidelity's shareholders, a duty of care in auditing the accounts and that Touche had breached that duty of care and that, had they not breached that duty, Touche would have uncovered the truth about Fidelity's financial position and as a result Caparo would not have taken over Fidelity or Caparo would have paid a much smaller price for Fidelity. Caparo's claim for compensation was dismissed. It was conceded that Touche had owed Caparo a duty of care in auditing Fidelity's accounts – but Touche had only owed Caparo that duty in their capacity as shareholders. The loss that Caparo

[53] It would have been different if the fall in the property market had been more modest: say the security properties were actually worth £170,000 when C defaulted, having been originally worth £180,000. In that case, B's loss on the loan would have come to £30,000 and the loss he would have suffered had he lent C £200,000 on adequate security (that is, security worth £220,000) would have been £0 – the security properties would have declined in value from £220,000 to £210,000 but that would still have afforded enough security to allow B to get back all his money that he loaned C. So *all* of the £30,000 loss suffered by B in this scenario would have been attributable to the fact that he loaned C money on inadequate security and A would therefore be liable to compensate B *fully* for the loss suffered by him as a result of A's negligence.

[54] [1990] 2 AC 605. Another pre-*SAAMCO* case which can be seen as giving effect to the *SAAMCO* principle is *Stevens* v *Bermondsey & Southwark Group Hospital Management Committee* (1963) 107 Sol J 478. The defendant's negligent diagnosis of the extent of the injuries suffered by the claimant as a result of a third party's negligence caused the claimant to settle his claim for damages against the third party for £125, when he would have been entitled to sue for much more. The claimant sued the defendant for the extra amount he would have demanded from the third party had the defendant not been negligent. Held that the claimant could not recover – the claimant had employed the defendant to diagnose his injuries in order to help him get better; not in order to help him determine how much he should sue the third party for compensation. See also *Reeman* v *Department of Transport* [1997] 2 Lloyd's Rep 648, where the claimant bought a boat which had been certified as being seaworthy by the defendant. In fact, the boat was not seaworthy and was, as a result, practically valueless. The claimant's action for damages was dismissed: the defendant had been employed to determine whether or not it would be safe for people to travel on the boat, not to ensure that the claimant did not make a bad bargain in buying a boat.

suffered as a result of Touche's negligence was suffered by Caparo in a quite different capacity – in their capacity as corporate raiders. Given this, Caparo could not sue Touche for compensation for the loss, by analogy to the rule that if A commits a tort in relation to B and C suffers some kind of loss as a result, C will not normally be entitled to sue A for compensation for that loss. Touche committed a tort in relation to Caparo *qua* shareholders in auditing Fidelity's accounts but it was Caparo *qua* corporate raiders who suffered a loss as a result.

Nowadays, Caparo's claim for compensation could be dismissed by reference to the *SAAMCO* principle – Caparo's loss in this case arose out of the fact that it bid too much for Fidelity when it took it over, but the purpose of getting Touche Ross to audit Fidelity's accounts was *not* to help ensure that Caparo did not bid too much for Fidelity on taking it over. Touche were employed to audit Fidelity's accounts in order to help Caparo and the other shareholders in Fidelity decide whether to reward or punish Fidelity's board of directors for their performance over the previous financial year.[55]

Two common misconceptions about *Hedley Byrne*

Before concluding our discussion of the principle in *Hedley Byrne* we should briefly pause to note and dismiss two common misconceptions about *Hedley Byrne*.[56] Both arise out of the twin facts that: (1) in *Hedley Byrne* the claimants suffered a form of pure economic loss;[57] and (2) it was in *Hedley Byrne* that the House of Lords first countenanced the possibility that a claimant might be entitled to sue a defendant in negligence for compensation for some form of pure economic loss that she had suffered as a result of the defendant's actions.

The first misconception is that *Hedley Byrne* is only ever relevant in establishing that a duty of care was owed in a case where a claimant has suffered a form of pure economic loss as a result of a defendant's actions. On this view, in cases where a claimant has suffered some other kind of harm – such as per-

---

[55] The *Caparo* case was distinguished in *Morgan Crucible Co. plc* v *Hill Samuel & Co. Ltd* [1991] Ch 295 where, it was claimed, the defendant representatives of a company made various representations to the claimants, who were thinking of taking over the company, as to the financial health of the company with the object of persuading the claimants to increase their bid for the company. The claimants subsequently discovered that they had bid too much for the company and sued for compensation. It was held that if these facts were made out, the claimants had an arguable claim against the defendants.

[56] A third possible misconception which some students might entertain is that a duty to take care not to mislead others can only exist in a *Hedley Byrne*-type case. (This misconception may be encouraged by the discussion in W&J, at 381f, of 'liability for negligent misstatement'; also McGregor 2003, 1507: 'For long English law resisted giving a remedy for negligent misrepresentation . . . Not until *Hedley Byrne* . . . was it held that negligent misrepresentation [could] constitute an actionable wrong.') This is obviously incorrect. In the right circumstances, the physical danger principle can operate to impose a duty to take care on someone not to mislead someone else. For example, if a blind man asks you if it is safe to cross the road, you will owe him a duty under the physical danger principle to take care that you do not tell him that it is safe to cross the road when it is not (it being reasonably foreseeable that if you do so he will suffer some kind of physical injury as a result). See *Haseldine* v *Daw* [1941] 2 KB 343 (discussed above, p. 70, n. 20) for an example of a decision which could be explained on the basis that the defendant breached a duty to take care not to mislead someone else which arose under the physical danger principle.

[57] That is, economic loss not consequent on the claimants' having suffered damage to their persons or their property.

sonal injury or psychiatric illness – as a result of a defendant's actions or non-actions, the decision in *Hedley Byrne* will be irrelevant to the inquiry as to whether or not the defendant owed the claimant a duty of care. This is non-sense: there is no sign that the Law Lords in *Hedley Byrne* meant their remarks as to when one person will owe another a duty of care to be confined to cases where a defendant has caused another to suffer a form of pure economic loss.[58]

The second misconception is that if a claimant has suffered a form of pure economic loss as a result of a defendant's actions, the claimant will *only* be able to establish that the defendant owed her a duty of care not to act as he did if the House of Lords' decision in *Hedley Byrne* covers her case;[59] so if it does not, then the defendant will not have owed the claimant a duty of care.[60] This is, again, nonsense: there is no reason to think that the Law Lords in *Hedley Byrne* were seeking to lay down for all time an exhaustive set of rules as to when a duty of care will be owed in a pure economic loss case. Unfortunately, this misconception is quite widespread and has given rise to the further misconception that *any* pure economic loss case in the law reports in which the courts found that a duty of care was owed is a '*Hedley Byrne* case'.[61]

Anyone labouring under this further misconception will find it quite

---

[58] For examples of *personal injury* cases where a claimant will be able to invoke *Hedley Byrne* to estab-lish that a defendant owed her a duty of care, see any medical negligence case that involves a failure to treat a patient with reasonable skill and care. For an example of a *property damage* case where the claimant was allowed to invoke *Hedley Byrne* to establish that the defendant owed her a duty of care see the Canadian case of *Densmore* v *Whitehorse* [1986] 5 WWR 708 (discussed, Bagshaw 1999). In that case, a fire started in the claimant's house. The claimant rang the fire department and was told a fire engine would be on its way; but none was actually sent and the claimant's house and its contents were destroyed. Held, that the fire department had owed the claimant a duty to take care not to mislead the claimant as to whether a fire engine would be sent under the basic principle in *Hedley Byrne* as it was made clear to them when she rang them that if they told her a fire engine was on its way she would not take any steps herself to save the contents of her house. See also *Stansbie* v *Troman* [1948] 2 KB 48 (discussed below, at pp. 552–3) and *Bailey* v *HSS Alarms Ltd*, The Times, 20 June 2000 (failure to protect business from being burgled). A *psychi-atric illness* case where *Hedley Byrne* could have been used to establish that the defendant owed the claimant a duty of care is *McLoughlin* v *Grovers* [2002] QB 1312, where the claimant developed a psychiatric illness as a result of being wrongfully convicted of robbery and causing grievous bodily harm; he sued his solicitors for compensation for his illness claiming that he would not have been convicted had they conducted his case with reasonable skill and care; held, that the claimant had an arguable claim against the defendants and his claim should not be struck out.

[59] See, for example, Murphy 2003, at 243: 'Outside the . . . *Hedley Byrne* principle, it seems that no duty to protect others from economic loss will arise, however predictable that loss may be . . .'; M. Jones 2002, at 141: 'unless a case can be brought under the umbrella of *Hedley Byrne* . . . there is generally no liability in respect of pure economic loss caused by a negligent act'; Howarth 2002, at 568: 'The rule that pure economic loss is not recoverable in negligence is subject to one . . . exception. Pure economic loss is recoverable if the defendant has assumed responsibility for the claimant's economic well-being.'

[60] For an example of this misconception at work, see the Court of Appeal's decision in *Phelps* v *Hillingdon LBC* [1999] 1 WLR 500, where the claimant sued for compensation for the harm done to her prospects as a result of the defendant's failure to diagnose her as being dyslexic while she was at school. As this was regarded in the Court of Appeal as being a pure economic loss case, it was conceded on all sides that the defendant could *only* have owed the claimant a duty of care in treating her if the decision in *Hedley Byrne* applied to the claimant's case: ibid., 513–14. It was found that it did not as the defendant had not 'assumed a responsibility' to the claimant. The claimant in *Phelps* appealed to the House of Lords, and their Lordships found that a duty of care *was* owed to the claimant: [2001] 2 AC 619. For an explanation of the House of Lords' decision in *Phelps*, see below: p. 147.

[61] One of the authors of this book has not been immune to this misconception in the past: see McBride & Hughes 1995. This second misconception seems to have originated in a misreading

impossible to come up with an intelligible account as to when one person will owe another a duty of care under *Hedley Byrne*. The reason is that while *most* of the pure economic loss cases in the law reports in which the courts have found that a duty of care was owed *are Hedley Byrne* cases, *not all of them are* – some of those cases rest on quite different principles, which we will explore below. So there is no *single* principle underlying all of the pure economic loss cases in the law reports in which the courts have found that a duty of care was owed and any attempt to discover such a principle will be doomed to failure.

THE DEPENDENCY PRINCIPLE

The following cases are often seen as being *Hedley Byrne* cases because, for the most part, they involve a claimant being allowed to sue a defendant in negligence for some pure economic loss that she has suffered. But it is in fact impossible to see the duties of care in these cases as arising under either the basic or extended principle in *Hedley Byrne*. The better view is that these duties of care arise under a quite different principle, which we will call the *dependency principle*. The dependency principle goes like this: If A has taken on a particular task, knowing that B's future well-being is almost completely dependent on his performing that task properly, then A will normally owe B a duty to perform that task with a reasonable degree of care and skill. While no English court or judge has ever explicitly said that A will owe B a duty of care in this kind of situation,[62] the dependency principle provides a satisfying explanation as to why the courts found that a duty of care was owed in the following cases.

(1) *The manslaughter cases.*[63] These cases are concerned with the following kind of situation. B is – whether through addiction or illness or old age – unable to look after herself. A takes on the job of looking after B but A so neglects B that B eventually dies while in his care. A is charged with manslaughter. Because A did not cause B's death through a positive act, before A can be convicted of manslaughter it needs to be shown that A owed B a duty to look after her with a reasonable degree of care and skill and that B would not have died had A discharged that duty. Invariably, in this sort of case, the courts *will* find that A owed B a duty of care. It is hard to see the duty of care that A will owe B in this kind of situation as being based on anything other than the dependency principle: A will owe B a duty to look after her with a reasonable degree of care and skill because he has taken on the job of looking after her knowing that her

---

of some of the speeches in the House of Lords in *Murphy* v *Brentwood DC* [1991] AC 398. Lord Bridge, for instance, stated (at 475) that 'purely economic [losses are] . . . not recoverable in tort in the absence of a special relationship of proximity . . .' and some have misread this as meaning that 'purely economic losses are not recoverable in tort in the absence of a special relationship of the kind involved in *Hedley Byrne*-type cases'.

[62] Though see Lord Phillips MR's statement in *Watson* v *British Board of Boxing Control Ltd* [2001] QB 1134 at [49]: 'It seems to me that the authorities support a principle that where A places himself in a relationship with B in which B's physical safety becomes dependent upon the acts or omissions of A, A's conduct can suffice to impose on A, a duty to exercise reasonable care for B's safety.'

future well-being (indeed, her continued existence in this case) is almost completely dependent on his looking after her properly.

(2) *Cases concerning the treatment of an unconscious person.* There are *dicta* in the cases which suggest that a doctor who takes on the job of treating an unconscious person will owe that person a duty to treat her with a reasonable degree of care and skill.[64] The decision in *Barrett v Ministry of Defence*[65] seems to suggest that these *dicta* are correct. In that case a serviceman on a military base got drunk, passed out and eventually died from inhaling his own vomit. It was held that the authorities at the base had not owed the serviceman a duty to take reasonable steps to stop him getting drunk.[66] However, when he passed out the authorities took charge of him, took him to his cabin and generally tried to look after him. The Court of Appeal held that *at that stage* the authorities owed the serviceman a duty to look after him with a reasonable degree of care and skill.[67]

It is impossible to see the duty of care arising in this kind of case as arising under the extended principle in *Hedley Byrne*. If A takes on the job of looking after B – who is unconscious and in desperate need of attention – A will have no means of indicating to B that she can safely rely on him to look after her with a reasonable degree of care and skill and, indeed, B will not rely on A to look after her with such a degree of care and skill.[68] A better explanation of why a duty of care is owed in these cases is that the duty arises under the dependency

---

[63] *R v Instan* [1893] 1 QB 450; *R v Bonnyman* (1942) 28 Cr App Rep 131; *R v Stone and Dobinson* [1977] QB 354.

[64] *Banbury v Bank of Montreal* [1918] AC 626, 689, per Lord Atkinson: 'It is well established that if a doctor proceeded to treat a patient gratuitously, even in a case where the patient was insensible at the time and incapable of employing him, the doctor would be bound to exercise all the professional skill and knowledge he possessed, or professed to possess, and would be guilty of gross negligence if he omitted to do so'; *Hedley Byrne & Co. Ltd v Heller & Partners* [1964] AC 465, 495, per Lord Morris: 'A medical man may unexpectedly come across an unconscious man, who is a complete stranger to him, and who is in urgent need of skilled attention: if the medical man, following the fine traditions of his profession, proceeds to treat the unconscious man he must exercise reasonable skill and care in doing so.' See also GS&Z, 100. See, however, the Canadian case of *Horsley v MacLaren, The Ogopogo* [1970] 1 Lloyd's Rep 257, 263: 'even if a person embarks upon a rescue and does not carry it through, he is not under any liability to the person to whose aid he had come so long as discontinuance of his efforts did not leave the other in a worse condition than when he took charge' (per Schroeder JA, in the Ontario Court of Appeal). The case was appealed to the Supreme Court of Canada, but the Supreme Court found it unncessary to deal with the issue raised by Schroeder JA's *dictum*: [1971] 2 Lloyd's Rep 410.

[65] [1995] 1 WLR 1217.

[66] For a discussion of this point, see below, p. 206.

[67] [1995] 1 WLR 1217, 1223. It was further held that the authorities breached this duty of care by failing to check up on him frequently enough and that this breach contributed to the serviceman's death. The serviceman's widow was therefore entitled to sue the authorities under the Fatal Accidents Act 1976, though the damages payable were reduced by two-thirds to take account of the fact that the serviceman was partly to blame for his own death: ibid., 1225–6.

[68] *Important note.* The reader should note that the word 'rely' here does *not* mean 'depend' – it means 'do something that one would otherwise not have done'. As B is unconscious, she is not in a position to do anything, let alone do something that she would not otherwise have done had A not assured her that she could rely on him.

principle – when A takes on the job of treating B, he will know that B's future well-being is almost completely dependent on A's looking after B properly.

If this is right, then this suggests that if B has been involved in a car accident and is unconscious, a passing doctor who undertakes to treat B's injuries will *not* owe her a duty to treat her injuries with a reasonable degree of care and skill if those injuries are not obviously life-threatening.[69] If B merely has a broken leg, it is not possible to say that her future well-being is *almost completely* dependent on the doctor's treating her properly. In principle, this is correct. However, given the difficulty of defining when someone's condition was life-threatening and when it was not, the courts may well choose to say – in the interests of legal certainty – that *whenever* a doctor treats an unconscious patient he will owe her a duty to treat her with a reasonable degree of care and skill, whatever her condition. The result is that the courts will sometimes give effect to the dependency principle by finding that a duty of care was owed in situations where the dependency principle will not, strictly speaking, apply. But there is nothing surprising or unjust about this: the courts cannot *just* give effect to the dependency principle – they have to do so in a way which will not make the law intolerably uncertain. And the only way of doing this is to rule that a doctor who treats an unconscious patient will *always* owe that patient a duty to treat her with a reasonable degree of care and skill, whatever her condition.

(3) *The survey cases.*[70] These cases are concerned with the following kind of situation. B – who was not particularly well off – wanted to buy a house. She managed to find a fairly cheap house at the bottom end of the property market and applied to C, a building society or a local authority, for a loan to help her buy the house. C appointed A – a surveyor – to survey the house for them to check that the house would provide them with adequate security for the loan. A surveyed the house and reported back that it was worth at least as much as the loan for which B was applying. Unfortunately, A failed to survey the house properly and failed to spot some defects in the house which meant that it was worth much less than B was proposing to pay for it. B was too poor to afford her own survey, but was reassured that the house was in good condition when C approved the loan to her – after all, she thought, if C's surveyor had spotted any problems with the house, C would hardly have agreed to loan her the money she needed to buy it. So B went ahead and purchased the house with the assistance of the loan from C. She then discovered that the house was worth much less than she agreed to pay for it.

It is now well established that in this sort of situation, A will have owed B a duty to survey the house with a reasonable degree of care and skill. It is impossible to explain this result by reference to the extended principle in *Hedley Byrne* because the existence of the duty of care owed by A to B does not depend on

---

[69] *Capital & Counties Plc* v *Hampshire CC* [1997] QB 1004, 1035 (per Stuart-Smith LJ): 'If [a passing doctor] volunteers his assistance [to help the victim of a traffic accident], his only duty as a matter of law is [to take care] not to make the victim's condition worse.' The doctor's duty to take care not to make the victim's injuries worse arises under the physical danger principle, set out above, pp. 66–7.

[70] *Smith* v *Eric S Bush, Harris* v *Wyre Forest District Council* [1990] 1 AC 831; *Merrett* v *Babb* [2001] QB 1174.

A's having had any contact with B.[71] So why will A have owed B a duty of care in this situation? Again the dependency principle seems to provide a good explanation of why A owed B a duty of care. When A took on the job of surveying the house he knew – from the fact that the house was at the bottom end of the property market – that B, the prospective purchaser, was not particularly well off. This means he knew two further things.

First of all, he knew that it was likely that B would not commission her own survey of the house – so he knew that if he said the house afforded sufficient security for C's loan to B and C made a loan to B, B would probably buy the house without more ado. She would think that if C had agreed to lend B the money she wanted to buy the house, C's surveyor must have said the house was in good condition and would think there was little reason for her to incur the extra – and, to her, grievous – expense of getting another survey of the house done. Secondly, when A took on the job of valuing the house, he knew that if B bought the house and it turned out to be worth much less than she paid for it, B would not be able easily to bear this loss. Already badly off, her buying the house would make her much worse off and bring her to the brink of destitution.

So when A took on the job of surveying the house, he knew – simply from the fact that the house was at the low end of the property market – that if he said the house was in good condition, B would certainly buy the house as a result and that if it turned out not to be in good condition, B would suffer a huge financial loss which she could ill afford to bear. So when A took on the job of surveying the house, he knew that B's future well-being was almost completely dependent on

[71] *Important note.* This has been made crystal clear by the decision of the Court of Appeal in *Merrett* v *Babb*, above. In that case, the claimant, Merrett, lost a lot of money purchasing a defective house with the assistance of a loan from a building society. The building society asked a firm of surveyors to value the house for them and an employee of the firm, Babb, valued the house as being worth at least as much as Merrett was wanting to borrow to buy the house. Before Merrett had a chance to sue the firm of surveyors in negligence, they went out of business. So instead she sued Babb – who had substantial assets – claiming that *he* personally had owed her a duty to survey the house with a reasonable degree of care and skill. By the time *Merrett* was decided, the decision of the House of Lords in *Williams* v *Natural Life Health Foods Ltd* [1998] 1 WLR 830 had made it clear that the existence of contact between the defendant and claimant was essential for a duty of care to arise between the defendant and claimant under *Hedley Byrne*. (See also, on this point, *Mills* v *Winchester Diocesan Board of Finance* [1989] Ch 428, *Mariola Marine Corp.* v *Lloyd's Register of Shipping* [1990] 1 Lloyd's Rep 547 and *A & J Fabrication (Batley) Ltd* v *Grant Thornton (a firm)* [1999] PNLR 811.) However, there had been absolutely no contact between Merrett and Babb at the time Babb surveyed the house that Merrett ended up purchasing; indeed, she was not even aware of his identity at that time. Despite this, the Court of Appeal still found that Babb *had* owed Merrett a duty of care in valuing the house and the House of Lords refused leave to appeal: [2001] 1 WLR 1859. So the duty of care in *Merrett* v *Babb* and the other survey cases *cannot* be explained by reference to the extended principle in *Hedley Byrne*. (Mullis & Oliphant 2003 attempt (at 75) to explain the survey cases on the basis that 'each involved a direct assumption of responsibility by the valuer to the house purchaser …'. However, that explanation – always implausible – cannot survive the decision in *Merrett* v *Babb*.) Of course, those who have fallen into the trap of thinking that *all* pure economic loss cases where a defendant has been held to have owed a claimant a duty of care are *Hedley Byrne* cases cannot but think that there is some conflict between the decisions in *Williams* v *Natural Life* and *Merrett* v *Babb*. There is, of course, no conflict: the *Williams* case was concerned with when one person will owe another a duty of care under *Hedley Byrne*; the duty of care in *Merrett* v *Babb* arose under a completely different principle.

his surveying the house properly. As a result, he owed B a duty to survey the house with a reasonable degree of care and skill under the dependency principle.[72]

If this is right, then, in a case where B wants to buy a house with the assistance of a loan from C and C appoints A to survey the house to check that it will provide adequate security for the loan, A will only owe B a duty to survey the house with a reasonable degree of care and skill if A *knows* that B is going to rely on his survey and not commission her own survey of the house. It is only in that situation that A will know that B's future well-being is dependent on his surveying the house properly. If A expects B to get her own survey of the house done then, in A's mind, nothing much will depend on A's survey. A will think that it will not matter if he fails to spot some defect in the house which affects its value in a big way; B's surveyor will probably see it instead and warn B against buying the house.

It *does* seem to be the case that A will *only* owe B a duty of care in surveying the house if he *knows* that B is not going to commission her own survey of the house.[73] Given this, it is highly unlikely that A will owe B such a duty if B is purchasing a house at the top end of the property market. A will expect B in such a case to commission her own survey of the house: if she is rich enough to buy a house at that end of the property market, she will be rich enough to afford her own survey. Similarly, if a company wants to buy a set of offices and it applies to a bank for a loan and the bank appoints a surveyor to value the offices, it is highly unlikely that the surveyor will owe the company a duty of care in surveying the offices; the surveyor will expect the company to commission its own survey of the offices.[74]

(4) *The reference cases.* In *Spring* v *Guardian Assurance plc*,[75] Spring was employed as a sales director and office manager by Corinium Ltd. Corinium sold life assurance policies on behalf of Guardian Assurance, the defendants. When Corinium was taken over by the defendants, Spring was dismissed. Spring attempted to go into business on his own selling life assurance policies for Scottish Amicable. When he approached Scottish Amicable, that company asked the defendants to supply them with a reference for Spring. Scottish Amicable was obliged to do this under the rules of the Life Assurance and Unit Trust Regulatory Organisation (Lautro), of which Scottish Amicable was a member. The defendants supplied

---

[72] Cf. Hoffmann J's explanation of *Smith* v *Eric S Bush* in *Morgan Crucible Co. plc* v *Hill Samuel & Co. Ltd* [1991] Ch 295, at 302. Stapleton 1991 seems to think (at 277–83) that it is hard to understand why A will have owed B a duty of care here when a builder of a house will *not* owe a subsequent purchaser of the house a duty to build that house with a reasonable degree of care and skill. In fact, as Stapleton 1995 seems to recognise (at 335–7) there is no contradiction here. The reason why a builder will not owe a subsequent purchaser of a house a duty to build that house with a reasonable degree of care and skill is that there will usually exist no relationship of severe dependency between the builder and the subsequent purchaser. The subsequent purchaser of a house can protect herself against the risk that the house will turn out to be no good by having the house surveyed or by taking out insurance.

[73] See *Smith* v *Eric S Bush, Harris* v *Wyre Forest District Council* [1990] 1 AC 831, 844 (per Lord Templeman), 865 (per Lord Griffiths), 871–2 (per Lord Jauncey); also *Caparo Industries plc* v *Dickman* [1990] 2 AC 605, 638–9 (per Lord Oliver); 661 (per Lord Jauncey).

[74] See *Omega Trust* v *Wright, Son & Pepper* [1997] PNLR 424; *Barex Brothers* v *Morris* [1999] PNLR 344.

[75] [1995] 2 AC 296.

Scottish Amicable with a reference for Spring that stated, among other things, that Spring was 'a man of little or no integrity and could not be regarded as honest'. Unsurprisingly, Scottish Amicable declined to allow Spring to sell life assurance policies on its behalf. The same thing happened when Spring approached two other life assurance companies and for the same reason.

Spring sued the defendants in negligence, arguing that the defendants had owed him, and breached, a duty to use reasonable skill and care in supplying his prospective employers with references about him. The House of Lords found that the defendants had owed Spring such a duty of care. Why was this? It is impossible to explain this result on the basis that the defendants owed Spring such a duty under the extended principle in *Hedley Byrne*.[76] The defendants never indicated to Spring that he could safely rely on them to use reasonable skill and care in preparing references about him for prospective employers; and even if they did Spring never did anything in the expectation that they would act in that way. It would have been different if Spring had asked the defendants if he could give his prospective employers their name as a possible source of references and the defendants had agreed that he could. The defendants, by agreeing to supply Spring with a reference, would have implicitly indicated to him that he could safely rely on them to supply his prospective employers with references that were prepared with a reasonable degree of care and skill and Spring would have so relied on them by telling his prospective employers that they could ask the defendants for a reference about him. But this was not the case here. In *Spring*, the references supplied by the defendants were asked for, and supplied, over Spring's head.

So if this cannot be seen as being a *Hedley Byrne* case, why did the defendants owe Spring a duty of care in supplying his prospective employers with references for him? There are two possible explanations: one narrow, one wide. The narrow explanation of the case is that the defendants owed Spring such a duty of care because they were his *employers* and as such they had some responsibility not to endanger his future employment prospects unnecessarily, in the same way as, when Spring was employed by them, they had a responsibility not to unnecessarily endanger his person.[77]

The wide explanation sees the duty of care in *Spring* as arising under the dependency principle. When Spring's potential employers asked the defendants for a reference about him, the defendants knew that they held Spring's future career in their hands. If they supplied him with a bad reference, they would effectively terminate his career in the insurance industry and force him into a lengthy process of retraining to do something else. So they knew that Spring's future well-being was almost completely dependent on their doing their job as referees properly; as such they owed Spring a duty to do that job with a reasonable degree of care and skill.[78]

---

[76] Admittedly, Lord Goff thought that this *was* a *Hedley Byrne* case (ibid., at 316) and Lord Lowry agreed with him (at 325). However, none of the other Law Lords agreed.

[77] Ibid., 342 (per Lord Woolf); see also Cooke 1998, 47–51.

[78] Cf. Lord Lowry's reference in *Spring* to: 'the probability, often amounting to a certainty, of damage to the individual [resulting from a bad reference] which in some cases will be serious and may indeed be irreparable. The entire future prosperity and happiness of someone who is the subject of a damaging reference which is given carelessly but in perfectly good faith may be irretrievably blighted' (ibid., 326).

The Court of Appeal adopted the narrow explanation of *Spring* in *Kapfunde v Abbey National plc.*[79] In that case, the claimant applied for a job with the Abbey National. The Abbey National asked the defendant doctor to advise them as to the state of the claimant's health. Having inspected the claimant, the defendant advised that she was likely to have a higher than average level of absence from work. The claimant was turned down for the job as a result. She sued the defendant in negligence but the Court of Appeal dismissed her claim on the ground that the defendant doctor had not owed the claimant a duty of care in assessing her. It was held that the duty of care in *Spring* arose out of the fact that the claimant was once the defendant's employee and therefore the House of Lords' decision in *Spring* was of no assistance to the claimant here – there having been no pre-existing relationship of any kind, let alone an employment relationship, between the defendant and the claimant in *Kapfunde.*[80]

However, this narrow explanation of the decision in *Spring* seems untenable given that Spring was *never actually an employee* of the defendants in *Spring*. In fact, there was *never any kind of contractual relationship between Spring and the defendants.*[81] Moreover, their Lordships thought it unnecessary to inquire into the nature of the relationship between Spring and the defendants to determine whether or not the defendants owed Spring a duty of care.[82] Given this, the better view of the decision in *Spring* is that the duty of care in that case arose under the dependency principle and that a duty of care may be owed by a defendant who supplies a reference about a claimant to a prospective employer even if there is no pre-existing relationship between the defendant and the claimant.

If this is right then if B applies for a job with C and A supplies C with a reference about B, A will owe B a duty to prepare the reference with a reasonable degree of care and skill – whatever the nature of the relationship between A and B. Of course such a rule goes well beyond what the dependency principle would demand: if B is applying for a job and A is asked to supply a reference, it is hardly the case that B's future well-being will be almost *entirely* dependent on A's writing the reference properly. If B does not get the job, she can always apply for another one. However, the interests of legal certainty demand that if the courts impose a duty of care in a *Spring* situation – where there was a very severe degree of dependency (Spring simply could not get a job anywhere in the insurance industry without the defendants' support) – they should also impose a duty of care whenever someone supplies a prospective employer with a reference about a prospective employee. The law would be intolerably uncertain if the law discriminated at all between different kinds of reference cases.

---

[79] [1999] ICR 1.

[80] In so ruling the Court of Appeal disapproved the first instance judgment in *Baker* v *Kaye* [1997] IRLR 219, holding that a doctor conducting a medical on a prospective employee for his prospective employers owed the prospective employee a duty to conduct the medical with a reasonable degree of care and skill. Why? Because when the doctor takes on the job of conducting the medical, he knows that whether or not the employee gets the job is 'wholly dependent on his assessment': ibid., 225.

[81] [1995] 2 AC 296, 315 (per Lord Goff).

[82] Ibid., 321 (per Lord Goff), 337 (per Lord Slynn), 340–1 (per Lord Woolf).

(5) *Phelps* v *Hillingdon London Borough Council.*[83] In this case, the claimant suffered from dyslexia and as a result suffered severe learning difficulties at school. At the time her dyslexia was undiagnosed. In an attempt to find out what was wrong, the claimant was sent at age 11 to an educational psychologist to be tested. The psychologist failed to notice that the claimant was dyslexic; she reported that the claimant suffered from no specific weaknesses and suggested that the source of the claimant's learning difficulties was a lack of confidence. She recommended that action be taken to boost the claimant's confidence in her abilities. With her dyslexia undiagnosed, the claimant continued to experience learning difficulties and left school at age 16 with no GCSEs.

Shortly after the claimant left school her parents paid for her to be tested again and this time around the claimant's dyslexia was diagnosed. The claimant sued the defendants, the psychologist's employers, claiming that the psychologist had owed her, and breached, a duty to test her with a reasonable degree of care and skill and that the defendants were vicariously liable in respect of the psychologist's negligence. The House of Lords held that the educational psychologist had indeed owed the claimant a duty to test her with a reasonable degree of skill and care.

It is pretty clear that the House of Lords' finding that such a duty of care was owed was based on the dependency principle: when the educational psychologist took on the job of testing the claimant, she knew that the claimant's future well-being was almost entirely dependent on her testing the claimant properly – she knew that if she misdiagnosed the source of the claimant's problems, the claimant would receive a completely inappropriate education and, as a result, her subsequent career prospects would look distinctly bleak. As Lord Slynn observed in *Phelps*: '[The psychologist] knew . . . of the fact that her advice would be followed and of the importance of her assessment and advice to [the claimant's] future.'[84] Lord Nicholls also thought that this fact played a vital role in establishing that the psychologist owed the claimant a duty to test her with reasonable care and skill: '. . . [the claimant] was very dependent on [the psychologist's] assessment. [The claimant] was in a singularly vulnerable position . . . This seems to me to be, on its face, an example *par excellence* of a situation [where a duty of care will be owed].'[85]

(6) *The child abuse cases.* Suppose that A is a child and the social services are told that A is being abused at home. Suppose further that the social services investigate these allegations. It has now been held that in this case, the social services will owe A a duty to investigate the allegations that she is being abused with a reasonable degree of care and skill.[86] The dependency principle provides

---

[83] [2001] 2 AC 619.

[84] Ibid., 655.

[85] Ibid., 666.

[86] *D* v *East Berkshire Community NHS Trust* [2004] QB 558. The position in New Zealand is the same: see *Attorney-General* v *Prince* [1998] 1 NZLR 262 (NZCA) and *B* v *Attorney-General* [2003] 4 All ER 833 (PC). In *X* v *Bedfordshire CC* [1995] 2 AC 633, the House of Lords refused to find that the social services would owe A such a duty of care, fearing that such a finding would induce the social services to become excessively cautious in investigating and acting on allegations of child abuse: ibid., at 650. However, it has since become clear that if the social services take a child into care who is not at risk of being abused, or fail to take a child into care when he is being abused, the child may be able to sue

a good explanation as to why the social services will owe A such a duty of care. When the social services take on the job of investigating the allegations that A is being abused, they will know that if they perform that job badly – and either take A into care when there is no need to, or leave A in the family home when she is being abused there – then A's future well-being will be radically impaired. So when the social services take on the task of investigating the allegations that A is being abused, they will know that A's future well-being is almost completely dependent on their performing their job properly.[87]

THE PRINCIPLE IN *WHITE* V *JONES*

In *White* v *Jones*,[88] B quarrelled with his two daughters over his deceased wife's will. As a result, he made a will in which he left them nothing. Three months later – in June 1986 – he was reconciled with his daughters and resolved to make a new will under which his two daughters would receive £9,000 each. On 17 July 1986 he instructed the defendant solicitors to draw up a new will in those terms. By 14 September 1986, when B died, the defendant solicitors had still not got around to drawing up B's new will, so the daughters received nothing from B's estate. They sued the defendant solicitors in negligence, arguing that the defendants had owed them a duty to draw up B's new will with a reasonable degree of care and skill; that the defendants had breached that duty in taking so long over drawing up the will; and that had the defendants not breached that duty, they would have inherited £9,000 each from B's estate.

None of the principles of law examined so far in this chapter were of any assistance to the claimants in their attempt to argue that the defendants owed them a duty of care in drawing up B's will. The defendants of course owed *B* such a duty of care under the extended principle in *Hedley Byrne*: they had indicated to B that they could be safely relied on to draw up the will with a reasonable degree of care and skill and B had so relied on them by getting them, rather than anyone else, to draw up the will. But the defendants never indicated to the *claimants* that they could be relied on and indeed the claimants did not

---

the social services under the Human Rights Act 1998 (in the first case, for violating his rights to privacy and family life under Article 8 of the ECHR; in the second case, for violating his rights to be free of cruel and degrading treatment under Article 3 of the ECHR): see *TP and KM* v *United Kingdom* [2001] 2 FLR 549 and *Z* v *United Kingdom* [2001] 2 FLR 612. Given this, the Court of Appeal in the *D* case thought there was little point in continuing to rule in *X*-type cases that no duty of care would be owed by the social services to a child whose case they were investigating: such a ruling would attempt to preserve for the social services an immunity from being sued that no longer existed.

[87] The same could be said of A's parents: when the social services take on the job of investigating the allegations that A is being abused, they will know that if they do that job badly and conclude that A is being abused when she is not, then the future well-being of A's parents will be radically impaired. A will almost certainly be taken away from them; they will probably be subjected to criminal prosecution; and possibly suffer vilification from the wider community. However, in *D* v *East Berkshire Community NHS Trust*, the Court of Appeal refused to hold that the social services would owe a duty of care to A's parents in the situation we are considering: [2004] QB 558, at [86]. See also, to the same effect, *B* v *Attorney General* [2003] 4 All ER 833. For an explanation of this point, see below, p. 212.

[88] [1995] 2 AC 207 (criticised, Weir 1995; also Klar 1998, 317–19).

rely on the defendants to draw up the will with a reasonable degree of skill and care; the claimants, for example, did not both go out and buy new cars in the expectation that they would receive £9,000 each under B's will. There was in fact no contact between the defendants and the claimants. So the extended principle in *Hedley Byrne* did not apply here. Nor was the dependency principle of any assistance to the claimants – it could not be said that when the solicitors took on the job of drawing up B's new will, they knew that the claimants' future well-being was almost *entirely* dependent on their drawing up the will properly. It would have been nice for the claimants to receive £9,000 each under B's will but it would hardly have been devastating for them *not* to receive such a comparatively small sum.[89]

Despite all this, the House of Lords still held by a bare majority that the defendants *had* owed the claimants a duty to draw up B's will with a reasonable degree of care and skill. It was for a time thought that the decision was to be confined to its own facts – that is, to the case where A undertook to draw up a will for B, A failed to draw up the will properly and as a result C failed to receive an inheritance from B's estate. However, this view is no longer tenable. For example, in *Gorham* v *British Telecommunications plc*,[90] *White* v *Jones* was seen as authority for the proposition that a pensions adviser will not only owe the advisee a duty to advise him with a reasonable degree of care and skill; such a duty will also be owed to the advisee's family.[91] So how far does *White* v *Jones* go? To answer that question we need to know what principle or principles underlay their Lordships' finding that a duty of care was owed to the claimants in *White* v *Jones*. A number of alternatives suggest themselves:

(1) *The extended dependency principle.* In his judgment in *White* v *Jones*, Lord Browne-Wilkinson justified his finding that the defendants owed the claimants a duty of care in drawing up B's will in the following terms:

[89] A subtle argument that might be made in favour of thinking that the dependency principle *does* apply here goes as follows: 'Had the claimants been left *a house* under the will, then the dependency principle *would* have applied to impose a duty of care on the solicitors to draw up the will with a reasonable degree of care and skill: the solicitors would have known *in that case* that if they performed the job of drawing up the will badly, the future well-being of the claimants would have been radically impaired. Now – the law would become intolerably uncertain if it said that a solicitor will owe a duty of care in drawing up a will to those who are due to inherit a "large" legacy under the will, but not to those who are due to inherit a "small" legacy. So the only practicable way the law can give effect to the dependency principle in a *White* v *Jones* situation is to say that if A is instructed to draw up a will under which B is due to inherit a legacy, A will owe B a duty to draw up that will with a reasonable degree of care and skill, whatever the size of the legacy B is due to receive under the will.' The problem with this argument is that it rests on an unjustified premise: even if the claimants in *White* v *Jones* had been due to receive a house under their father's will, it is hard to see why the claimants' future well-being would have been radically *impaired* had the solicitors done a bad job of drawing up that will. They would merely have missed out on a large bonus.

[90] [2001] 1 WLR 2129.

[91] See also *Goodwill* v *British Pregnancy Advisory Service* [1996] 1 WLR 1397 (held by the Court of Appeal that if A wants to be sterilised so as to avoid getting his wife B pregnant, and C undertakes the operation, C may owe B a duty of care under *White* v *Jones* to carry out the operation properly) and *Dean* v *Allin & Watts* [2001] 2 Lloyd's Rep 249 (held by the Court of Appeal that if A wants to borrow money from B and appoints C, a solicitor, to act for him and ensure that the loan is secured, the solicitor will owe B a duty of care under *White* v *Jones* to ensure that the loan of money from B to A is secured).

The solicitor who accepts instructions to draw up a will knows that the future econ-omic welfare of the intended beneficiary is dependent on his careful execution of the task. It is true that the intended beneficiary (being ignorant of the instructions) may not rely on the particular solicitor's actions. But ... liability is not dependent upon actual reliance by the [claimant] on the defendant's actions but on the fact that, as the [defendant] is well aware, the [claimant]'s economic well-being is dependent upon the proper discharge by the [defendant] of his duty.[92]

Lord Browne-Wilkinson seems to be saying here that if A takes on a task, knowing that B's future economic well-being will be impaired if he fails to perform that task properly, A will owe B a duty to perform that task with a reasonable degree of care and skill. However, this is far too wide: it is not the law, and never has been the law, that A will owe B a duty of care in such a situation.[93] At a minimum, it would have to be shown that A knew when he took on the task in question that B's future economic well-being would be *severely* impaired if he failed to perform the task properly. Anything less than that – and the facts of *White* v *Jones* fell well short of that – will not be enough to warrant A's owing B a duty of care.[94]

(2) *The practical justice principle.* Lord Goff, in his judgment in *White* v *Jones*, said that 'practical justice' demanded that their Lordships find that the defendants owed the claimants a duty of care. Otherwise, 'the only person who might have a valid claim (i.e. the testator and his estate) [would] have suffered no loss, and the only person who has suffered a loss (i.e. the disappointed beneficiary) [would have] no claim'.[95] But this is only a problem if you accept that the defendants in *White* v *Jones* ought to have been held liable to *someone* for what they did. If the defendants ought to have been held liable to someone for what they did then it would indeed have been unjust for the defendants to escape liability for what they did because of the accident that the one party with a valid claim against the defen-dants suffered no loss.

So Lord Goff clearly thought that the defendants in *White* v *Jones* should have been held liable to someone for what they did. But why? There seems to be only one

---

[92] [1995] 2 AC 207, 275.
[93] See Weir 2004, 80. For an alternative view, see Stapleton 2002a, 551–6 and references con-tained therein, suggesting that if A is 'vulnerable' to suffering harm at B's hands, that is a sufficient reason for the law to find that B will owe A a duty to take care not to harm B. To the same effect, see also McBride & Hughes 1995; Murphy 1996, 52–3; Witting 2000b, 631–4. A very strong High Court of Australia authority that seems to take this view is *Perre* v *Apand Pty Ltd* (1999) 198 CLR 180 (noted, Davis 2000). In that case, Sparnon – a farmer in South Australia – grew some potatoes on his land using seed supplied by the defendants. The potato crop turned out to be diseased because the seed supplied by the defendants was diseased. Legislation in Western Australia prohibited the importation of potatoes grown within 20 km of an infected crop for 5 years after the crop was discovered to be infected. This meant that the claimant – whose farm was 20 km away from Sparnon's – was not allowed to sell *his* potatoes in Western Australia for 5 years. The farmer sued the defendants in negligence and it was held that the defendants *had* owed the claimant a duty to take care not to supply Sparnon with dis-eased seed. Particular emphasis was laid on the fact that the defendants knew when they supplied the seed to Sparnon that if it was diseased people like the claimant would be shut out of the Western Australia potato market and that there was nothing the claimant could do to protect himself against the effect of the defendants' supplying diseased seed to Sparnon.
[94] For an explanation why not, see below, pp. 208–11.
[95] [1995] 2 AC 207, 259.

possible answer and it runs as follows. The defendant solicitors were professionals who acted unprofessionally. It can hardly be disputed that professionals who act unprofessionally deserve to have some kind of punishment or sanction inflicted on them – it is one of the main tasks of professional bodies such as the Law Society or the General Medical Council to punish those of its members who fail to live up to professional standards in their dealings with the public. The defendant solicitors in *White* v *Jones* therefore deserved to be punished for what they did – to be held liable to someone for what they did. On this analysis, then, Lord Goff was in favour of finding that the defendants owed the claimants a duty of care in *White* v *Jones* because if no such duty were found the defendant solicitors would have been allowed to act unprofessionally without incurring any punishment or sanction in response.[96]

However, this analysis of the principle underlying the decision in *White* v *Jones* – if one can call it a principle – is weakened by the fact that the Court of Appeal has since made it clear that a solicitor who has failed to draw up a will properly will have owed the beneficiaries under that will a duty of care in drawing it up *even if* the deceased's estate is entitled to sue the solicitor for substantial damages for failing to draw up the will properly.[97]

(3) *The unhelpful assistance principle.* Probably the best analysis of the principle underlying the decision in *White* v *Jones* goes as follows. If A wanted to confer a benefit on B, and C undertook to assist A in conferring that benefit on B, but due to C's doing *x*, A was *prevented* from conferring that benefit on B, C will be found to have owed B a duty to take care not to do *x*.[98] The merit of this formulation is that it seems to fit all the available case law on when someone will and will not owe another a duty of care under *White* v *Jones*.

First of all, the formulation obviously fits the facts of *White* v *Jones* itself. In that case, B wanted to give each of his daughters £9,000 in his will. The defendants in that case undertook to assist B to confer that benefit on his daughters but due to their delay in drawing up B's will, B was prevented from conferring that benefit on his daughters. As a result, the defendants were held to have owed the daughters a duty to take care that they did not delay in drawing up the will.

Secondly, this formulation explains why a duty of care was owed under *White* v *Jones* in the *Gorham* case. In that case, G, a married man with two young children, wanted to set up a pension which would provide some financial security for his wife and children should he predecease them. He went to Standard Life for some advice and they failed to advise him properly. They advised him to take out a

---

[96] Of course, the defendant solicitors were still liable to be disciplined by their professional body, the Law Society. Lord Mustill, in dissent, thought it inappropriate for the claimant daughters to be given a remedy against the defendant solicitors in order to ensure that the defendants' unprofessional conduct did not go unpunished: 'The purpose of the courts when recognising tortious acts and their consequences is to compensate claimants who suffer actionable breaches of duty, not to act as second-line disciplinary tribunals imposing punishment in the shape of damages' (ibid., 278). See, to the same effect, Klar 1998, 316–17.

[97] *Carr-Glynn* v *Frearsons* [1999] Ch 326.

[98] Lord Mustill thought that some such principle had to underlie the decision in *White* v *Jones* and on that basis condemned the majority decision as going 'far beyond anything so far contemplated by the law of negligence': [1995] 2 AC 207, at 291.

Standard Life pension when in fact G's wife and children would have been far better off had G joined the occupational pension scheme run by his employer, British Telecom. When G died, G's wife and children sued Standard Life claiming that Standard Life had owed them, and breached, a duty to take care that they did not give G bad pensions advice. The Court of Appeal held that Standard Life had owed G's wife and children such a duty of care under *White* v *Jones*. Rightly so, if we accept the analysis of the principle underlying *White* v *Jones* advanced here. G wanted to provide his wife and children with as much financial security as possible after he died. Standard Life undertook to assist him in doing that but they in fact prevented him from doing that by giving him bad pensions advice. So – on the analysis of *White* v *Jones* advanced here – Standard Life owed G's wife and children a duty to take care that they did not give G bad pensions advice.

Thirdly, this formulation of the principle underlying *White* v *Jones* helps to explain why no duty of care will be owed under *White* v *Jones* in the following case.[99] A wants to transfer some land – Blackacre – to B. C undertakes to do the conveyancing but on his first attempt he fails to convey Blackacre properly. Before he makes a second attempt, A tells him that she has changed her mind: she no longer wants to give Blackacre to B. It seems to be generally acknowledged that B will not be entitled to sue C in negligence here. B will not be able to argue that when C attempted to convey Blackacre to him, C owed him a duty to take care not to botch the conveyance.[100] The reason why *White* v *Jones* will not apply here – on the analysis advanced here – is that C's failure to convey Blackacre to B at the first attempt did not *prevent* A from conveying Blackacre to B. But it might be different if A never changed her mind about conveying Blackacre to B but she died before C could make a second attempt at conveying Blackacre to B. In such a case, C's failure to convey Blackacre to B at the first attempt *will* have had the effect of preventing A from conveying Blackacre to B. So on the analysis of *White* v *Jones* advanced here, in this case, C may well have owed B a duty under *White* v *Jones* to take care that he did not fail to convey Blackacre the first time he tried to do so.

---

[99] It also explains why no duty of care was owed under *White* v *Jones* to the claimant in *Goodwill* v *British Pregnancy Advisory Service* [1996] 1 WLR 1397, who became pregnant after having sex with M, who was supposed to have been sterilised by the defendants. Held, no duty of care was owed to the claimant by the defendants when they operated on M because it was hardly realistic to say that, in being sterilised, M was attempting to confer a benefit on women such as the claimant (the benefit of not getting pregnant): ibid., 1403. It might have been different though if the claimant had been M's wife – in such a case, it would have been possible to argue that M wanted to confer a benefit on the claimant in being sterilised. So if the claimant had been M's wife, it might have been possible to argue that the defendants owed the claimant a duty under *White* v *Jones* to take care that they did not botch M's operation: ibid.

[100] [1995] 2 AC 207, 262, per Lord Goff. See also *Hemmens* v *Wilson Browne* [1995] Ch 223 (held: no duty owed by firm of solicitors to claimant in drawing up deed under which claimant would have had the right to call on A at any time to pay her £110,000); *Wells* v *First National Commercial Bank* [1998] PNLR 552 (held: bank which agrees to refinance company and, as part of the deal, agrees to pay off some of the company's debts will not owe the debtors a duty to pay off those debts); and *Briscoe* v *Lubrizol* [2000] ICR 694 (held: underwriters of company's health insurance scheme owe no duty of care to employee claiming under that scheme when they assess whether his claim is genuine or not; even if they turn down his claim when it is genuine, that will not prevent the employee obtaining what he is entitled to under the scheme).

6

ESTABLISHED DUTY SITUATIONS III: SITUATIONS GIVING RISE TO A DUTY TO ACT

In the previous chapter we looked at the principle in *Hedley Byrne* and some associated principles under which it is established that one person will owe another a duty of care. It is clear that one person will often be held to have owed another a duty to perform some positive act under these principles.

For example, if Gary agrees to work for Ruth as her bodyguard, he will owe Ruth a duty under the extended principle in *Hedley Byrne* to take reasonable steps to ensure her safety while he is on duty. So if Ruth is attacked while Gary is on duty, Gary will have a duty to take reasonable steps to fend off the attack. Again, if Beth asks Fred to draw up a will for her under which Sarah will inherit £1,000, and Fred dallies for too long over drawing up the will with the result that Beth dies before the will is drawn up, Fred will be held to have owed Sarah a duty to draw up Beth's will with reasonable skill and care under the principle in *White* v *Jones*.

However, there are many other situations where it is well established that one person will owe another a duty to perform some positive act. The next two chapters are devoted to setting out these situations. In Chapter 7, we will set out a number of situations where it is established that A will owe B a duty to perform some positive act because A occupies some special status or position – such as that of being an occupier of land, or a landlord, or a teacher. This chapter, by way of contrast, is concerned with situations where A will owe B a duty to perform some positive act *not* because A occupies some special status or position, but simply by virtue of the situation in which A and B find themselves.

THE CREATION OF DANGER PRINCIPLE

A number of cases seem to establish that if it is reasonably foreseeable that A's doing *x* has had the effect of putting B in danger of suffering some kind of serious harm, A will owe B a duty to take reasonable steps to ensure that B does not suffer that kind of harm.[1] So, to take an example from the American case law

---

[1] See: *Ellis* v *Home Office* [1953] 2 All ER 149 (held: if A and B are imprisoned in the same jail and it is foreseeable that A will attack B if given the chance, the prison authorities will owe B a duty to take reasonable steps to see that A does not attack B as they have, by confining B to the same jail as A, put him in danger of being attacked by A); *E Hobbs (Farms) Ltd* v *Baxenden Chemicals* [1992] 1 Lloyd's Rep 54 (manufacturer of foam insulation installed in claimant's farm buildings held to have owed claimant a duty to warn him that the foam was combustible: 'a manufacturer's duty of care does not end when the goods are sold. A manufacturer who realises that omitting to warn past customers about

giving effect to this principle,[2] if Carl is driving along the road one night and he happens to hit and kill a large animal on the road he will owe other users of the road a duty to take reasonable steps to see that they do not crash into the obstacle he has created. While what we can call the *creation of danger principle* is easy enough to understand, it is unclear how far it goes. The following issues arise:

(1) *What sort of harm?* Clearly if A has created a danger that B will suffer some kind of physical injury, then A will have a duty to take reasonable steps to eliminate that risk. But what if A has just created a danger that B's property will be destroyed or damaged? Will he owe B a duty to take reasonable steps to eliminate that danger? For example, suppose Carl takes Beth's dog for a walk and he happens to throw the dog's favourite ball into a pond. The dog plunges into the pond to fetch it but it becomes clear to Carl that the dog cannot swim and is in danger of drowning. Will Carl owe Beth a duty to take reasonable steps to save her dog from drowning? One would have thought so.[3] However, it should be noted that the formulation of the creation of danger principle in the American Restatement 2d of Torts has it applying only to cases where someone creates a danger that someone else will suffer a *physical injury*.[4]

(2) *Three party cases.* Suppose that John told Eric that he saw Eric's wife, Beth, at a nightclub the previous night. Eric was visibly maddened by this news: Beth had

---

something which might result in injury to them must take reasonable steps to attempt to warn them, however lacking in negligence he may have been at the time the goods were sold'; ibid., 65); *Watson v British Board of Boxing Control* [2001] 1 QB 1134 (defendants, who were – at a very general level – involved in the putting on of a boxing fight, thereby creating a danger that the boxers would suffer brain damage as a result, held to have owed the boxers a duty to take reasonable steps to see that they did not suffer such brain damage; which duty was breached by their failing to provide ring-side medical facilities to treat boxers who were knocked out in the ring); *Kane v New Forest DC* [2002] 1 WLR 312 (defendant planning authority, which approved creation of right of way passing over main road at 'blindspot' for car drivers driving along main road, held to have owed users of the right of way a duty to take reasonable steps to see that they were not run over in crossing over the main road).

[2] *Hardy v Brooks*, 118 SE 2d 492 (1961).

[3] *Important note.* The clearest authority in favour of the idea that the creation of danger principle applies in the case where someone has created a danger of someone else's property being damaged is a criminal law case: *R v Miller* [1983] 2 AC 161. The defendant fell asleep in someone else's house. In so doing he dropped a lit cigarette onto the mattress on which he was lying. Soon after, the defendant woke up and realised that the mattress was on fire, but did nothing to deal with the problem. Instead he simply moved to another room. The fire subsequently spread to the rest of the house. The defendant was charged with the offence of arson, which is committed by intentionally or recklessly causing property to be destroyed or damaged by fire: Criminal Damage Act 1971, s 1. The defendant's act of dropping his cigarette could not give rise to criminal liability because while that caused the house to be burned down, he had not acted intentionally or recklessly in dropping the cigarette. While the defendant *had* acted recklessly when he woke up and failed to take steps to save the house from burning down, that failure could only be said to have *caused* the house to burn down if the defendant had had a *duty* to take such steps. The House of Lords held that the defendant *did* have such a duty. This was because the defendant had – albeit unwittingly – *created* the danger that the house would burn down; as a result, he had a duty, when he became aware of the danger, to take reasonable steps to deal with that danger. Accordingly, their Lordships held that the defendant had committed the offence of arson.

[4] §321: '[Someone who] does an act and subsequently realizes or should realize that it has created an unreasonable risk of causing physical injury to another ... is under a duty to exercise reasonable care to prevent the risk from taking effect ... even though at the time of the act [he had] no reason to believe that it [would] involve such a risk' (American Law Institute, 1965). See GS&Z, 99–100.

told him she was going out to play bingo. He subsequently went home and beat Beth up. Beth now wants to sue John for damages. Beth will not be able to invoke the physical danger principle to establish that John owed her a duty not to tell Eric that he had seen her at a nightclub: it was not reasonably foreseeable that Eric would beat her up on being told this news.[5]

But will Beth be able to invoke the creation of danger principle to establish that John owed her a duty to warn her that he had told Eric that he had seen her at a nightclub and to tell her to get out of her house until Eric had had a chance to calm down? It is hard to see why she should not be allowed to – so long, of course, as she can establish that Eric's reaction to John's news made it reasonably foreseeable that he would attack Beth as a result of John's disclosure. Whether or not the requirement is satisfied here will of course depend on how extreme Eric's reaction was to John's news: whether he uttered any threats against Beth, and so on.[6] But if it was reasonably foreseeable that Eric would attack Beth as a result of John's disclosure, there seems no reason why John should not be held to have owed Beth a duty to take reasonable steps to see that she was not attacked by Eric – by, for example, warning her that Eric was angry with her and that she should keep out of his way.

(3) *Self-harm.* If A's doing x has created a foreseeable danger that B will do something to harm himself, will A owe B a duty to take reasonable steps to stop B harming himself? The question has arisen in two contexts.

First of all, consider the case where the police or prison authorities have locked B up and it is reasonably foreseeable that their doing so has created a risk that B will attempt to kill himself. In this sort of case, it is well established that the police or prison authorities in question will owe B a duty to take reasonable steps to prevent him killing himself. This is so whether B is mentally ill[7] or completely sane.[8] It should be emphasised that it has to be reasonably foreseeable that B is a suicide risk before any duty will be owed to him to save

---

[5] It should be remembered that the test for reasonable foreseeability in these sorts of three party cases, where A does x and as a result C harms B, will only be satisfied if it was *very likely* or *probable* that C would harm B as a result of A's doing x: see above, p. 70, n. 24. This test is obviously not satisfied here.

[6] This requirement was not satisfied in *Topp* v *London Country Bus (South West) Ltd* [1993] 1 WLR 976. In that case, the defendants caused a minibus belonging to them to be left outside a pub, unlocked and with the keys in the ignition. Nine hours later an unidentified third party got into the bus, drove it down the road and knocked down and killed the claimant's wife. Held: the defendants did *not* owe the claimant's wife a duty to pick the bus up before anyone drove off with it. A reasonable person in the position of the defendants would *not* have thought that it was very likely or probable that someone would get in the minibus and drive off in it in a dangerous manner. It was not therefore reasonably foreseeable that leaving the minibus outside the pub, unlocked and with the keys in the ignition, would put people like the claimant's wife in danger of being killed or injured. So the creation of danger principle did not apply to impose on the defendants a duty to pick the bus up before anyone else drove off in it. The result may have been different had the defendants known that the pub outside which the bus was left was frequented by people who were 'particularly likely to steal vehicles and engage in joy-riding': ibid., 978.

[7] *Kirkham* v *Chief Constable of the Greater Manchester Police* [1990] 2 QB 283; *Knight* v *Home Office* [1990] 3 All ER 237.

[8] *Reeves* v *Commissioner of the Police of the Metropolis* [2000] AC 360 (where the point was conceded without argument).

him from himself – and the mere fact that he has been locked up will not be enough to make it foreseeable that he will attempt to kill himself.[9]

Secondly, what is the position if A has served B a large amount of alcohol and B now proposes to drive himself home – and it is clear, from B's drunken state, that B will almost certainly crash his car and injure himself if he attempts to do any such thing? It seems clear enough that A will owe other users of the road a duty to take steps to stop B driving home under the creation of danger principle – A having helped to create the danger here that when B drives home he will injure other people.[10] But will A owe *B* such a duty of care? There is no English authority on the issue; the available Canadian authorities indicate that the answer is 'yes', [11] while the High Court of Australia has recently ruled that the answer is 'no'.[12]

(4) *Reasonable steps.* If A has created a foreseeable danger that B will suffer some kind of serious harm, with the result that he owes B a duty to take reasonable steps to ensure that B does not suffer that kind of harm, what will A actually be required to do? The question has received little attention in England, from either the courts or tort academics,[13] but it is possible to speculate a little.

Leaving aside for the moment cases where A has created a danger that B will harm himself, if the danger that A has exposed B to is one which B could avoid at no cost to himself if he were aware of it, then all A will be required to do is warn B of the danger. If the danger is one which B cannot easily avoid at no cost to himself, then A may be required to do more than just warn B of the danger. It is likely that A's duty in this case will be 'measured'[14] – so what A will be required to do will depend on how wealthy A is and how responsible A was for creating the danger to which B is exposed.

If A has created a danger that B will do something to harm himself, presumably a warning to B that he is in danger of harming himself will not be enough to discharge the duty A will owe B to take reasonable steps to see that he does not harm himself. A will have to do something more. Again his duty will be 'measured' but it seems unlikely that A will be required to do anything that would involve A violating B's 'rights'. So A will not be required to lay hands on B or take his property away from him in order to ensure that B does not harm himself if B has a 'right' that A not lay his hands on him or take his property away.[15]

---

[9] *Orange v Chief Constable of West Yorkshire Police* [2002] QB 347.

[10] See the Canadian cases of *Stewart v Pettie* [1995] 1 SCR 131 and *Prevost v Vetter* (2002) 100 BCLR (3d) 44.

[11] *Jordan House Ltd v Menow* [1974] SCR 239; *Crocker v Sundance Northwest Resorts Ltd* [1988] 1 SCR 1186. See, generally, Dalphond 2002; also Solomon & Payne 1996 and Orr 1995.

[12] *Cole v South Tweed Heads Rugby League Football Club Ltd* [2004] HCA 29.

[13] For an American examination of the issue, see Matula 1996; also GS&Z, 926–52, 984–98.

[14] On the concept of a 'measured' duty of care, see below, p. 376.

[15] If B is put into custody, the officers in charge of B *will* be permitted to remove his belt and shoelaces to prevent him committing suicide. As doing these things will not violate B's 'rights', a failure to do these things may amount to negligence if it is reasonably foreseeable that B will attempt to commit suicide in custody.

THE INTERFERENCE PRINCIPLE

A couple of cases seem to establish that *if* : (1) A knows or ought to know that B is in danger of suffering some kind of serious harm H, *and* (2) A knows or ought to know that: *either* (i) he has done something that has had the effect of dissuading someone else from taking steps to save B from suffering harm H; *or* (ii) he has done something positive[16] that has had the effect of preventing someone else from taking steps to save B from suffering harm H, *then* (3) A will owe B a duty to take reasonable steps *himself* to see that B does not suffer harm H. We can call this *the interference principle* as the duty of care A will owe B in this situation arises out of the fact that he has interfered with someone else's taking steps to save B from suffering harm.

We have already set out the facts of *Costello* v *Chief Constable of Northumbria Police*.[17] To recap: the claimant was a woman police officer who was attacked by a prisoner when she took the prisoner down to the cells in a police station. Another officer, H, accompanied the claimant in taking the prisoner down to the cells in order to help her out if there was any trouble. However, when H saw B – a police inspector – standing by the cells, H went back upstairs, assuming that B would assist the claimant if she was attacked by the prisoner. When the claimant was attacked, B – contrary to expectation – stood by and did nothing. The Court of Appeal found that B had owed the claimant a duty to take reasonable steps to save her from being attacked. While it is not clear why the court came to that conclusion, it can be inferred that they decided B owed the claimant a duty to take reasonable steps to save her from being attacked because, as B well knew, the claimant was in danger of being attacked by the prisoner and B dissuaded H from taking steps to ensure that the claimant would not be attacked by the prisoner.

In *Kent* v *Griffiths*,[18] the claimant suffered an asthma attack. Her doctor came to see her and decided that she had to be taken to hospital. She rang the London Ambulance Service – the LAS – and they told her they would send an ambulance along to take the claimant to hospital. No ambulance had arrived 13 minutes later so the claimant's husband rang the LAS to be told that the ambulance would be another seven or eight minutes. The ambulance still had not arrived 29 minutes after the original call so the claimant's doctor rang the LAS and was told the ambulance would be there in a couple of minutes. The ambulance finally arrived 34 minutes after the original call. The claimant arrived in

---

[16] So a mere *failure to assist* that has the effect of stopping a third party from saving someone else from harm will not engage the principle discussed here. Suppose, for example, that Beth is a diabetic child who is starting to go into a hypoglycaemic state due to lack of sugar. Beth's mother, Nita, rushes into a chocolate shop run by Fred and asks Fred for some chocolate that she can give to Beth. Fred refuses to give her any chocolate as Nita has forgotten her purse and cannot pay for it. Without any chocolate, Beth's condition rapidly worsens and she faints, smashing her head open on the pavement. Beth will not be able to establish that Fred owed her a duty to take reasonable steps to alleviate her condition under the principle discussed here: Fred did not do something *positive* to prevent Nita from helping Beth; Fred merely *failed to assist* Nita to help Beth.

[17] [1999] 1 All ER 550, discussed above, pp. 56–7.

[18] [2001] QB 36.

hospital 46 minutes after the original call and she promptly suffered a respiratory arrest which resulted in her suffering a miscarriage, a change of personality and serious memory impairment. At first instance, Turner J held that the LAS had owed the claimant, and breached, a duty to take her to hospital as quickly as was reasonably possible and that had the LAS not breached that duty, the claimant would have reached hospital 32 minutes after the original call and would have received the treatment she needed to prevent her suffering a respiratory arrest. Accordingly, Turner J held the LAS liable to compensate the claimant for her arrest and the injuries that she had suffered as a result. The LAS appealed, claiming that it had not owed the claimant a duty of care. The Court of Appeal dismissed the appeal. Again, it is not clear why the court came to the conclusion that the LAS owed the claimant a duty to get her to hospital as quickly as was reasonably possible. However, it can be inferred that they reached this conclusion by the following chain of reasoning:[19] (1) when the claimant suffered her asthma attack she was in danger of suffering a respiratory arrest; (2) the claimant's doctor and husband could have taken the claimant to hospital themselves in order to ensure that she did not suffer a respiratory arrest; however, (3) they were dissuaded from doing so by the LAS's repeated assurances that an ambulance was on the way to pick the claimant up;[20] as a result, (4) the LAS owed the claimant a duty to take reasonable steps to ensure that the claimant did not suffer a respiratory arrest – in other words, the LAS owed the claimant a duty to take her to hospital as quickly as was reasonably possible.

If the interference principle is part of English law, a number of issues arise as to how it applies.

(1) *The problem of identity.* The interference principle only applies where A dissuades or prevents *someone else* from attempting to save B from some serious harm that B is in danger of suffering. The interference principle will not of course apply where A dissuades or prevents *himself* from attempting to save B. But it can be difficult to determine in a given case whether a defendant prevented someone else from attempting to save the claimant or whether the defendant merely prevented himself from attempting to save the claimant.

The issue came up in *OLL Ltd* v *Secretary of State for Transport.*[21] In that case, a party of eight children and one teacher got into severe difficulty on a canoeing trip in the sea off Lyme Regis. The coastguard was mobilised but bungled the rescue operation, directing a lifeboat and a Royal Navy helicopter to search for the party in the wrong area. As a result, all the members of the party suffered severe hypothermia and four of the children died. It was claimed in the subsequent litigation that the coastguard had owed the members of the party a duty to take reasonable steps to rescue them. It was arguable that the interference

---

[19] An alternative explanation is that the LAS owed the claimant a duty of care under the dependency principle set out above (p. 140): when the LAS took on the job of getting the claimant to hospital, it knew that if it failed to do that job properly, her future well-being would be severely impaired.

[20] Ibid., at [17]: 'But for the acceptance of the 999 call the [claimant] would have been driven to the hospital and would have arrived prior to her "arrest".'

[21] [1997] 3 All ER 897 (discussed, Bagshaw 1999).

principle applied here: it could have been argued that the coastguard prevented the lifeboat crew and the Royal Navy from rescuing the stricken party and as a result the coastguard owed the party a duty to take reasonable steps to rescue them. However, May J refused to find that a duty of care was owed by the coastguard here, holding that it would be 'artificial'[22] to distinguish between the coastguard and other rescue organisations that were attempting to save the teacher and children at sea. This was a case of one person getting in his own way in attempting to rescue the canoeing party; not a case of one person getting in another's way in attempting to rescue the party.

(2) *Hypothetical third parties.* For the interference principle to apply, it seems it does not have to be shown that an *identifiable* third party was actually prevented or dissuaded from saving the claimant by the defendant; it merely has to be shown that it was very likely that *someone* would have tried to assist the claimant had the defendant not acted in the way he did.[23] The point is made by the American case of *Zelenko v Gimbel Bros.*[24] Mary Zelenko was taken ill in the defendant's store. The defendant took on the job of looking after her but failed to do anything for her for six hours. It could not be shown that any particular individual had been dissuaded or prevented from looking after Zelenko as a result of the defendant's taking charge of her. However, the court was satisfied that it was 'beyond doubt [that if the defendant had left Zelenko alone] some bystander ... would have summoned an ambulance'[25] and as a result found that the defendant had owed Zelenko a duty to take reasonable steps to treat her illness.

(3) *The position of people who are employed to rescue others.* Suppose that Alan is employed to work as a lifeguard on a beach. Lara visits the beach and goes for a swim. However, she soon gets cramp and struggles to keep her head above water. Alan sees Lara's predicament but does nothing to assist her. Eventually, Lara drowns. Can we say that Alan owed Lara a duty to take reasonable steps to rescue her? The answer is obviously 'yes' if there were other people on the

---

[22] Ibid., 907.

[23] *Important note.* This requirement was not satisfied in *Sutradhar v Natural Environment Research Council* [2004] EWCA Civ 175. In that case, the defendants carried out a survey of the water supply in north-eastern Bangladesh and issued a report – which was seen by the Bangladeshi government – saying that the water in that area was safe to drink. In fact, it contained arsenic. The claimants subsequently suffered arsenic poisoning from drinking the local water. They sued the defendants, arguing that the defendants had owed them a duty of care in carrying out the survey. While there is no doubt that the Bangladeshi government would have taken action *had it been told that the water was unsafe to drink*, there was no evidence that had the defendants *not* issued their report, the Bangladeshi government or anyone else would have conducted a survey of the water supply in north-eastern Bangladesh, detected the presence of arsenic in the water and taken steps to protect people like the claimants from drinking the local water. It could not therefore be said that the defendants' report had the effect of dissuading the Bangladeshi government or anyone else from taking steps to ensure that people like the claimants did not drink poisoned water. The interference principle did not therefore apply in this case; and, in our view, the Court of Appeal was correct to hold that the defendants did *not* owe the claimants a duty of care in carrying out their survey. (For further discussion of this point, see below, pp. 197–201.)

[24] 287 NYS 134 (1935).

[25] Ibid., 135.

beach who saw that Lara was in trouble but did not go to her assistance because they thought Alan would rescue her – the interference principle would apply.

But suppose that, with the exception of Alan, the beach was deserted and so no one was discouraged from rescuing Lara as a result of Alan's presence. At first sight, it seems that it is not possible to argue that Alan owed Lara a duty to take reasonable steps to rescue her under the interference principle. But is this too quick? After all, when Alan was employed to work as a lifeguard on the beach, there must have been other people who applied for the job. Can we not say that Alan – by successfully applying for the job of lifeguard – has prevented these other people from rescuing Lara and as a result, Alan owes Lara a duty to take reasonable steps to rescue Lara himself?

To apply the interference principle here would probably be a step too far – certainly, the available English authorities indicate that Alan would *not* owe Lara a duty to take reasonable steps to rescue her in this situation.[26] First of all, Alan has not really *prevented* any of the other applicants for his job from rescuing Lara in this situation – if they had wanted to work on the beach saving people for free, Alan would, presumably, have been grateful for the assistance. Alan has merely prevented the other applicants from earning the money that was on offer for working as a lifeguard on the beach; which is not the same thing. Secondly, if we want to hold that Alan owed Lara a duty here under the interference principle, we must be able to say who would have been given Alan's job had Alan not been available to take it and we must be able to show that that someone would have been in a position to rescue Lara when she started to struggle, that he would have had the inclination to rescue Lara at that time, and that he would have been able to rescue her before she drowned. It is unlikely that any of these things could be determined with any degree of certainty. So, in the interests of legal certainty and ensuring that the courts' time is not wasted on fruitless inquiries, it would be better if the interference principle were held not to extend to this kind of situation.

(4) *Prevention of self-help*. While the interference principle, as we have presented it above, only applies in cases where A dissuades or prevents a *third party* from going to B's assistance, there is no reason why the interference principle should not extend to cases where A dissuades or prevents B from saving herself from

---

[26] *Alexandrou* v *Oxford* [1993] 4 All ER 328 (policemen investigating possible break-in at shop will *not* owe shopkeeper a duty to carry out their investigations with reasonable skill and care); *Capital & Counties plc* v *Hampshire County Council* [1997] QB 1004 (firemen summoned to fight fire that has broken out on claimant's property will *not* owe claimant a duty to take reasonable steps to put the fire out expeditiously). On the other hand, see *Lowns* v *Woods* (1996) 36 NSWLR 344 (noted, Haberfield 1998; see also Williams 2001). The case concerned an 11-year-old boy who suffered from epilepsy. One day he suffered an epileptic fit and his sister was sent to fetch a doctor. She went to the local surgery and asked the doctor there – who was not the boy's doctor – to come and look at her brother. He refused, insisting that the boy should be brought to the surgery. As a result of the doctor's refusal to go and see the boy, there was a delay in treating his epileptic fit, with the result that the boy became quadriplegic. Held: the doctor had owed the boy a duty to take reasonable steps to treat him. There are also some *dicta* in in the case of *Barnett* v *Chelsea & Kensington Hospital Management Committee* [1969] 1 QB 428 which indicate that if A turns up to a casualty department seeking treatment, the doctor on call at the time will almost always owe A a duty to treat him: ibid., at 437.

suffering some kind of harm. So, for example, it is well-established that if Vijay is in prison and falls sick, the prison authorities will owe Vijay a duty to take reasonable steps to treat him.[27] The reason for this is that Vijay will be prevented, because he is in prison, from taking steps himself to obtain treatment for his illness.

Again, in *Mercer v South Eastern & Chatham Railway Companies' Managing Committee*[28] the claimant was hit by a passing train as he crossed a railway line. The gate to the path over the railway line was usually locked by the defendant when a train was due to come by, but the defendant had on this occasion left the gate unlocked and this had led the claimant to believe that it was safe to cross the railway line. It was held that the defendant had owed the claimant a duty to take reasonable steps to ensure that he locked the gate to the path over the railway line when a train was due to come by. The result can be justified by reference to the extension of the interference principle discussed here. The defendant's practice of locking the gate had had the effect of dissuading pedestrians from taking steps themselves to ensure that they were not run down by a passing train as they crossed the railway line: if the gate was unlocked they blithely assumed that it was safe to cross and crossed the railway line without a second thought. Given this, the defendant owed people like the claimant a duty to take reasonable steps to see that they were not run down by a passing train as they crossed the railway line. This, in turn, meant that he owed a duty to people like the claimant to take reasonable steps to ensure that he locked the gate when a train was due to go by.

THE CONTROL PRINCIPLE

It seems to be well established that if A is in control of a dangerous *substance* or *animal*, and it is reasonably foreseeable that someone like B will be harmed by that substance or animal if A allows it to escape his control, then A will owe B a duty to take reasonable steps to keep that thing or that animal under his control.[29] What is controversial is whether this principle – which we can call the *control principle* – extends to cases where A is in control of a *human being* and it is foreseeable that someone like B will be harmed if that human being escapes A's control. Whether or not A will owe B a duty to take reasonable steps to prevent the human being escaping his control seems to depend on what sort of human being it is.

(1) *Children.* It seems to be accepted that if A is in control of a child and it is reasonably foreseeable that someone like B will be injured if that child is allowed to escape A's control, A *will* owe B a duty to take reasonable steps to keep the child in question under his control.

---

[27] *Brooks v Home Office* [1999] 2 FLR 33.
[28] [1922] 2 KB 549.
[29] If the substance or animal escapes A's control without any negligence on his part and B is harmed as a result, B may still be entitled to sue A for compensation under either the rule in *Rylands v Fletcher* or the Animals Act 1971: see below, Chapter 44.

For example, in *Carmarthenshire County Council v Lewis*[30] a four-year-old boy attending nursery school wandered off the school premises and onto the road running alongside the nursery school. The claimant's husband, who was driving along the road, swerved to avoid the boy and crashed into a tree and died. The claimant sued, claiming that the defendant county council – which owned the school – and the teachers at the school had owed her husband, and breached, a duty to take reasonable steps to keep control of the children at the school. The House of Lords agreed that the defendant county council and the teachers at the school had owed the claimant's husband such a duty of care. The defendant county council and the teachers at the school were jointly in control of the children at the school and it was, of course, eminently foreseeable that children at the school would wander into the road outside the school and cause accidents if the defendant county council and the teachers at the school did not keep control of them. It followed that the defendant county council and the teachers at the school owed people driving past the school – including the claimant's husband – a duty to take reasonable steps to keep control of the children at the school.

(2) *Adults*. The position is more restrictive where A is in control of an adult – call him T – and it is reasonably foreseeable T will harm someone like B if he is allowed to escape A's control. In such a case, it seems that A will only owe B a duty to take reasonable steps to see that T does not escape his control if B is *especially* at risk of being harmed by T if T is allowed to escape A's control. Let's call this requirement that must be satisfied before the control principle will apply to impose a duty on someone who is in control of a dangerous adult, the *special danger* requirement.

So, for example, Lord Morris suggested in the case of *Dorset Yacht Co. Ltd v Home Office* that 'If a person who is in lawful custody has made a threat, accepted as seriously intended, that, if he can escape, he will injure X . . . a duty [will be] owed to X to take reasonable care to prevent escape.'[31] In such a case, the special danger requirement will be satisfied: if the prisoner in question is allowed to escape, X will be at greater danger of being attacked by the prisoner than the rest of the population. If, on the other hand, A – a well-known psychopath – is in prison and the prison authorities allow A to escape and A goes on to attack and injure B, a random stranger, the special danger requirement will not be satisfied and the prison authorities will not be held to have owed B a duty to take reasonable steps to prevent A escaping.[32] While it was reasonably foreseeable that someone like B would be injured if A was allowed to escape custody – it was very likely or probable that A would attack a random member of the population if he were allowed to escape – B was at no greater danger of being attacked by A if A escaped custody than anyone else.

The special danger requirement was satisfied in the *Dorset Yacht* case itself. In that case, seven Borstal boys were on a training exercise on Brownsea Island in

---

[30] [1955] AC 549.
[31] [1970] AC 1004, at 1039.
[32] See *Palmer v Tees Health Authority* [1999] Lloyd's Rep Med 351 (boy killed by psychopath in care of defendant medical authorities: held, the defendants did not owe the boy or the boy's mother a duty of care to control the psychopath).

Poole Harbour. They were under the supervision of three officers. One night the Borstal boys escaped, taking advantage of the fact that all three officers had, contrary to instructions, gone to bed. They boarded one of the vessels in the harbour and set sail in it but it collided with the claimant's yacht. They then boarded the claimant's yacht and did further damage to it. The claimant sued the Home Office for compensation, arguing that the officers had owed him a duty to take reasonable steps not to let the Borstal boys escape. The House of Lords found that such a duty had been owed to the claimant. There was no problem showing that it was reasonably foreseeable that someone like the claimant would suffer harm if the Borstal boys were allowed to escape the officers' control. This is because it was reasonably foreseeable – very likely or probable – that if the Borstal boys were allowed to escape the officers' control, they would commandeer one of the boats in the harbour in an attempt to get off the island and make good their escape, and in so doing would damage the boat. It followed that it was reasonably foreseeable that someone like the claimant – someone who owned a boat in the harbour – would suffer harm if the Borstal boys were allowed to escape their officers' control.

The special danger requirement was satisfied here because people like the claimant – people who owned boats in the harbour – were at greater risk of suffering harm as a result of the Borstal boys' escape than other members of the population such as shopkeepers or owners of bikes on the island. Their boats would be especially valuable to the Borstal boys were the Borstal boys allowed to escape – so their boats were especially likely to be targeted by the Borstal boys on escape as compared with other items of property such as groceries or bikes. It follows that the result of the case would have been different had the Borstal boys, on escaping, robbed a shop on the island.[33] No duty would have been owed to the shopkeeper to take reasonable steps to prevent the Borstal boys escaping as there would have been no special risk that the shopkeeper's wares would be targeted by the Borstal boys on escape.

The special danger requirement was not satisfied in *K* v *Secretary of State for the Home Dept.*[34] In that case, M, a Kenyan citizen, was imprisoned for sexual assault and then for burglary. He was detained, awaiting deportation, but was released on order of the Home Secretary. M subsequently raped the claimant. The claimant sued the Home Secretary in negligence, claiming that he had owed her a duty not to release M. The Home Secretary applied to have the action struck out. For the purposes of hearing the striking out claim, it was assumed against the Home Secretary that he had acted unreasonably in ordering M to be released and that it was reasonably foreseeable that if M was released, he would attack someone like the claimant. It made no difference: the Court of Appeal still refused to find that the Home Secretary had owed the claimant a duty not to release M. The special danger requirement was not satisfied here. The claimant was at no greater risk of being attacked by M on release than the rest of the population or the rest of the female population.

Why does the special danger requirement have to be satisfied before we will find that someone who is in control of a dangerous adult will owe someone else a duty to take reasonable steps to prevent that adult escaping his control? Laws LJ, who

---

[33] [1970] AC 1004, 1070 (per Lord Diplock).
[34] [2002] EWCA Civ 1983.

delivered the leading judgment in the *K* case, expressed himself fearful that if he found that the Home Secretary had owed the claimant a duty not to release M, then he would have to find that the Home Secretary owed such a duty to *anyone* who was harmed by M after he was released. The Home Secretary's liability as a result of his decision to release M would become open-ended and potentially get out of all proportion to his fault in deciding to release M.[35] But this is not particularly convincing: the courts seem quite happy not to place any limits on the application of the control principle in cases where people are in charge of dangerous substances, animals or children even though applying the control principle in an unqualified way in those cases can result in people incurring open-ended liabilities.

A better explanation as to why the courts might be unhappy at the thought of applying the control principle without limit to cases where someone is in control of a dangerous adult goes as follows.[36] Suppose that A was in control of a dangerous adult, T, and T escaped A's control and harmed B. It seems undeniable that if anyone should be made to bear the costs of compensating B for the harm she has suffered in this situation, it should be T, not A.[37] Now – if we find that A owed B a duty here to take reasonable steps to control T, B may simply look to A to compensate her for the harm that she has suffered. Of course, if A *is* held liable to compensate B, it will always be open to A to bring contribution proceedings against T. But this is an inefficient way of making T shoulder the burden of compensating B for the harm she has suffered – we first of all make A compensate B and then allow A to shift the cost of compensating B onto T by making a claim in contribution against T. And it is by no means guaranteed that T will be made to shoulder the *whole* of the cost of compensating B for the harm she has suffered in the contribution proceedings – it may be that a court will decide that it would be 'just and equitable' for T and A to split the cost of compensating B for the harm she has suffered on a 50:50 basis.[38] Given this, it would be better to cut A out of the picture entirely and declare that A did *not* owe B a duty to take reasonable steps to control T. That way, B will have no choice but to sue T directly for compensation for the harm she has suffered. T will be made to shoulder the cost of compensating B for the harm that she has suffered in the most direct and efficient manner possible.[39]

However, this explanation goes too far – it suggests that the control principle should not be applied *at all* in cases where someone is in control of a dangerous adult. It does not explain why the courts are willing to apply the control principle to cases where someone is in control of a dangerous adult – but only if the special danger requirement is satisfied. The rationale for this requirement therefore remains something of a mystery.

---

[35] Ibid., at [17].

[36] See, generally, Stapleton 1995, 313–14.

[37] This is especially so given that A, in this situation, will invariably be some kind of public body or public servant – so making A liable to compensate B for the harm she has suffered here will merely divert public resources away from where they are needed and into private hands: see Weir 1989.

[38] This is assuming T is solvent, which may well not be the case. If T is not, then A will have to bear the entire cost of compensating B.

[39] And, of course, as B could not have sued A for compensation for her injuries, T will not be able to make a claim for contribution against A, thereby shifting some of the cost of compensating B onto A's shoulders.

7

ESTABLISHED DUTY SITUATIONS IV: STATUSES GIVING RISE TO A DUTY TO ACT

There are a variety of cases where it is established that someone will have a duty to take reasonable steps to act in some way simply by virtue of the fact that he or she occupies some special status or position. In this chapter we will look at what these special statuses and positions are and the duties of care to which they give rise.

OCCUPIERS OF PREMISES

An occupier of premises – a term which we will use here to cover not only an area of land but buildings or parts of buildings as well – will normally owe a whole host of duties of care to other people by virtue of the fact that he is an occupier. Before we look at the duties of care that will be owed by an occupier of premises, we should first of all clarify what is involved in being an occupier of premises.

Who is an occupier?

When will it be true that a certain set of premises are 'occupied' by A? In *Wheat v E Lacon & Co. Ltd*, Lord Denning suggested: 'wherever a person has a sufficient degree of control over premises that he ought to realise that any failure on his part to use care may result in injury to a person coming lawfully there, then he is an "occupier"... In order to be an occupier it is not necessary for a person to have entire control over the premises. He need not have exclusive occupation. Two or more people may be "occupiers".'[1]

Given this test, it is clear that if, at a given time, a house is legally owned by A and A – or no one[2] – lives in it then, at that time, that house is occupied by A. Moreover, if, at a given time, a house is legally owned by A but A does not live in it because he has leased the house to B then, at that time, that house is occupied by B but not by A: B, as lessee, will have control over the premises, not A. What about the intermediate situation where, at a given time, a house is legally owned by A but A does not

---

[1] [1966] AC 552, 577.

[2] Cf. *Harris* v *Birkenhead Corporation* [1976] 1 WLR 279 (a house which was abandoned on being compulsorily purchased by the defendant local authority was occupied by the defendant local authority even though it never took possession of the house).

live in it because he is allowing B to live in it without, however, having formally leased the house to B? Is the house, at that time, occupied by A? Probably – the fact that A does not live in the house at that time because he is allowing B to stay in it as a licensee does not mean that A no longer has a sufficient degree of control over the house.

In *Wheat* v *E Lacon & Co. Ltd* itself, the defendants owned a pub which was run by a manager. The defendants allowed the manager to use the first floor of the pub as his private accommodation. A guest of the manager fell down some stairs on the first floor of the pub and was killed. It was held that at the time of the accident the first floor of the pub was occupied by the defendants and that the defendants therefore owed the deceased a duty to take care to see that he was reasonably safe for the purposes for which he was on the first floor. In *Ribee* v *Norrie*,[3] the defendant owned a hostel which contained a number of bedrooms which various people would rent from him. A fire started in the sitting room of the hostel which was set aside for the communal use of those using the hostel. The fire damaged a house adjoining the hostel. Whether the defendant was liable for the fire damage turned on whether he occupied the sitting room where the fire started. The court held that he did – he exercised a sufficient degree of control over the sitting room. As Ward LJ remarked, 'he had full power to regulate how that part of the hostel was to be used or not used as the case may be'.[4]

What about the case where A owns a house and he has engaged B to do some work on it? No doubt in such a case when B starts work the house will still be occupied by A – but what about B? It depends on how much *de facto* control over the house B exercises over it once he starts work on it. So if the work involves a major operation where no one is allowed to enter the house without B's say-so then there seems little doubt that the house will also be occupied by B once B starts work on it.

Having clarified when someone will be regarded as 'occupying' a certain set of premises, we can now turn to describe the duties of care that an occupier of premises will normally owe other people. We will begin with the duties of care that an occupier of premises will normally owe his 'visitors'.

Visitors

The 'common duty of care'
Section 2 of the Occupiers' Liability Act 1957 provides that if B enters premises occupied by A as A's 'visitor' – a term which we will shortly define – A will *normally* owe B a duty 'to take such care as is reasonable in all the circumstances of the case to see that [B] will be reasonably safe in using the premises for the purpose for which he is invited or permitted by [A] to be there'.[5] This duty is referred to by the Act as the 'common duty of care'.

---

[3] (2001) 33 HLR 777.

[4] Ibid., at [20].

[5] *Important note*. A will also owe B a duty to take reasonable steps to see that any property B brings with him onto A's premises is reasonably safe; and this is so whether or not the property in question actually belongs to B: s 1(3)(b). There is a question whether A is merely required by this duty to take reasonable steps to see that B's property is not destroyed or damaged or whether he is *also* required to take reasonable steps to see that B's property is not *stolen*. On this issue, see *AMF International Ltd* v *Magnet Bowling Ltd* [1968] 1 WLR 1028, at 1050 (per Mocatta J).

There is a question whether the duty so owed by A to B is a duty to take reasonable steps to see that B is not injured by reason of the *state of the premises* occupied by A or whether the duty is, more broadly, a duty to take care to see that B is not injured by reason of the state of those premises *or* by reason of *things done* on those premises. Section 1(1) of the 1957 Act seems to indicate that the latter view is correct. It provides that the 1957 Act will 'regulate the duty which an occupier of premises owes to his visitors in respect of dangers due to the state of the premises *or to things done or omitted to be done on them*'.[6] However, the Court of Appeal has now ruled in *Fairchild* v *Glenhaven Funeral Services Ltd* that the former view is correct.[7]

Who is a 'visitor'?

Not everyone who enters a given set of premises enters those premises as the occupier's 'visitor'. If B enters a set of premises occupied by A, B will enter those premises as A's 'visitor' *if*: (a) B was invited or permitted to enter those premises by A; *or* (b) B was invited or permitted to enter those premises by someone who had the ostensible authority to issue such an invitation or permission on A's behalf.[8]

In a case where B entered premises occupied by A, there is generally no difficulty about establishing whether or not A invited B to enter those premises.[9] It is more difficult to establish, in a case where B entered premises occupied by A without A's invitation, whether or not A *permitted* B to enter those premises. For example, in *Lowery* v *Walker*[10] members of the public had for about 35 years taken a short cut across the defendant's field to get to a railway station. In all that time, the defendant never started legal proceedings to try and get people to stop crossing his field. The House of Lords found that by acting in this way the defendant impliedly permitted members of the public to cross his land and, therefore, when they entered his land they did so as visitors and were owed a duty of care by the defendant. In contrast, in *Edwards* v *Railway Executive*[11] the House of Lords found that the defendant railway company did not permit children to enter onto its land for the purpose of tobogganing down an embankment on its land even though children had been accustomed to entering the defendant's land for precisely that purpose for many years. In coming to its finding, the House of Lords emphasised that the defendant company had done its best to stop children from coming onto its land to play – it put a fence around its land and whenever it discovered that children had breached a hole in it the defendant company sought to repair the fence.

---

[6] Emphasis added.
[7] [2002] 1 WLR 1052, at [109]–[133]. The point was not raised when the case was appealed to the House of Lords.
[8] For a discussion of the concept of 'ostensible authority' in this context, see *Ferguson* v *Welsh* [1987] 1 WLR 1553, 1563, per Lord Goff.
[9] Though see the extraordinary facts of *R* v *Collins* [1973] QB 100, where the defendant climbed up to the window of a young lady's bedroom and she invited him in for sex, in the mistaken belief that he was her boyfriend.
[10] [1911] AC 10.
[11] [1952] AC 737.

A may invite or permit B to enter one set of premises occupied by him but not another set of premises occupied by him. In such a case, if B enters the latter set of premises, she will not enter those premises as a visitor and A will not owe her a duty under the 1957 Act to see that B is reasonably safe while she is on that latter set of premises. So, for example, if Wendy stays the night in a hotel managed by Alan and during the middle of the night Wendy breaks into the kitchens to make a sandwich for herself, Wendy will not enter the kitchens as a visitor and Alan will not owe Wendy a duty under the 1957 Act to take care to see that Wendy is not harmed in using the kitchens. By permitting Wendy to enter and use the hotel, Alan does not permit Wendy to enter and use the hotel's kitchens.

Exceptions to the rule

If B enters premises occupied by A as A's visitor, A will not *always* owe B a duty to take reasonable steps to see that B is reasonably safe in using those premises for the purpose for which she is invited or permitted or allowed to enter those premises. There are two cases in particular where A will not owe B such a duty.

(1) *Exclusion of duty*. Under s 2(1) of the 1957 Act, A is free to 'restrict, modify or exclude' this duty owed to B 'by agreement [with B] or otherwise'.

So in *White* v *Blackmore*,[12] W attended a motor race with his family. At the entrance to the field where the races were held was a notice which said: 'Warning to the public, Motor Racing is dangerous ... [it is] a condition of admission that all persons having any connection with the promotion and/or organisation and/or conduct of the meeting, including ... the drivers of the vehicles ... are absolved of all liabilities arising out of accidents causing damage or personal injury (whether fatal or otherwise) howsoever caused to spectators or ticketholders.' W was killed while watching one of the motor races. The Court of Appeal held that, on the day of the races, the chairman of the motor club that was holding the race and the racing organiser did not owe W any duty under the 1957 Act to take care to see that he was reasonably safe in watching the races. The notice was effective to exclude the duty that would otherwise have been owed to W under the 1957 Act as all reasonable steps had been taken to draw its existence to W's attention.

However, an important limit on the ability of *businesses* that occupy premises to exclude the duties of care they would otherwise owe their visitors has been created by the Unfair Contract Terms Act 1977. Section 2(1) of the Act provides that, 'a person cannot by reference to any contract term or notice given to persons generally or to particular persons exclude or restrict his [business][13]

---

[12] [1972] 2 QB 651.

[13] Under s 1(3) of the 1977 Act, s 2 applies 'only to business liability, that is liability for breach of obligations or duties arising – (a) from things done or to be done by a person in the course of a business . . .; or (b) from the occupation of premises used for business purposes of the occupier'. Section 1(3) also makes it clear that the 'liability of an occupier of premises for breach of an obligation or duty towards a person obtaining access to the premises for recreational or educational purposes ... is not a business liability of the occupier unless granting that person such access for the purposes concerned falls within the business purposes of the occupier'.

liability for death or personal injury resulting from negligence'.[14] Section 13 of the 1977 Act provides that, 'to the extent that [s 2 of the Act] prevents the exclusion or restriction of any liability it also prevents . . . (to the same extent) [the exclusion or restriction] of liability by reference to terms or notices which exclude [an] obligation or duty'.

So suppose that B visited A's business premises. Suppose further that she was injured on the premises and that she wants to sue A for damages. Suppose further that when B visited A's premises, he notified her that he was taking no responsibility for her safety. Now – the result of the above provisions in the 1977 Act is that, in deciding whether or not B is entitled to sue A for damages, the courts will *disregard* the notice that A gave B and decide the case on the basis that B was *not* notified that A was not assuming any responsibility for her safety. So they will find that A owed B a duty under the 1957 Act to take reasonable steps to see that she would be reasonably safe while she was on his premises. And if B can show that A breached that duty and that she was injured as a result, then B will be entitled to compensation from A. It may be, then, that *White* v *Blackmore* would be decided differently today were the same facts to occur. The courts would disregard the notice given by motor race organisers and hold that they owed W a duty to take reasonable steps to see that he would be reasonably safe in watching the races. So – if W's dependants wanted to bring a fatal accidents claim against the organisers, all they would have to show is that the organisers failed to take reasonable steps to see that W would be safe watching the races, and that W was killed as a result.

(2) Assumption of risk. If B willingly takes the risk that she will be harmed in a particular way when she enters premises occupied by A, A will *not* owe B a duty to take reasonable steps to ensure that B is not harmed in that way while she is on those premises. The maxim *volenti non fit injuria* will apply.

This is the result of s 2(5) of the 1957 Act which provides that the 1957 Act 'does not impose on an occupier any obligation to a visitor in respect of risks willingly accepted as his by the visitor . . . '. So – in *Simms* v *Leigh Rugby Football Club*,[15] the defendant rugby club's ground had a concrete barrier running around the pitch, seven feet from the touchline, in order to keep the spectators from going onto the pitch. It was held that S, a rugby player who played on the defendant rugby club's ground, took the risk that he would be injured by being thrown against this concrete barrier when he stepped onto the pitch – the existence and location of the barrier being permitted under the byelaws of the game, as laid down by the Rugby Football League. So the defendant rugby club did not owe S a duty to take care to ensure that he was not injured by being thrown against the concrete barrier around the pitch.

It is clear that when B enters premises occupied by A in the *knowledge* that she might be harmed in a particular way as a result, B will not be held to have willingly taken the risk that she would be harmed in that way if she had no

---

[14] A business is allowed to exclude or restrict its liability in negligence for harm that has been done to property or pure economic loss, but only if it would be reasonable to do so: s 2(2).
[15] [1969] 2 All ER 923.

choice but to enter A's premises.[16] For example, in *Burnett* v *British Waterways Board*,[17] B was employed to work on a barge which was being towed into the defendant's lock when the rope towing the barge snapped and hit B. It was held that B did not take the risk that he would be injured in this way when the barge was being towed into the defendant's lock – even if at the time of the accident he knew he might be injured in this way as a result of the barge's being towed into the defendant's lock. This is because B had no choice but to stay on the barge as it was towed into the defendant's lock.

Trespassers

The basic rule

If B goes onto premises occupied by A, not as a visitor, but as a trespasser, then A may owe B a duty of care under the Occupiers' Liability Act 1984. This duty will require A to take reasonable steps to ensure that B is not killed or injured[18] by reason of a danger arising 'due to the state of the premises or to things done or omitted to be done on them' *if*: (1) A is, or ought to be, aware of the existence of the danger; *and* (2) A knows or ought to know that B is in, or may come into, the vicinity of the danger; *and* (3) A can reasonably be expected to offer B some protection against that danger.[19] Three points need to be made about this provision.

(1) *State of the premises.* The 1984 Act is plainly designed *only* to cover cases where B trespassed on A's premises and she was killed or injured because those premises had a dangerous *feature*. In such a case, A may have owed B a duty under the 1984 Act to take reasonable steps to see that she would not be killed or injured by that feature and may therefore be liable for B's being killed or injured. If, on the other hand, B trespassed on A's premises and was killed or injured on those premises but *not* because those premises had a dangerous feature, her case will fall outside the scope of the 1984 Act.

For example, in *Revill* v *Newbery*[20] Revill attempted to break into a shed on Newbery's allotment so as to steal some valuable items that Newbery kept there. Newbery – who had been subject to the repeated attentions of vandals and thieves in the area – was sleeping in the shed to protect his property. On hearing Revill's attempts to break in, Newbery took a shotgun, loaded it, poked

---

[16] Cf. Occupiers' Liability Act 1957, s 2(4)(a): 'where damage is caused to a visitor by a danger of which he had been warned by the occupier, the warning is not to be treated without more as absolving the occupier from liability, unless in all the circumstances it was enough to enable the visitor to be reasonably safe'.

[17] [1973] 1 WLR 700.

[18] Section 1(9). So A will *not* owe B a duty under the 1984 Act to take reasonable steps to see that any property that B has in his possession when he goes onto A's premises is not destroyed or damaged.

[19] The quoted words come from s 1(1)(a) of the 1984 Act. The conditions for A's owing B under the Act may be found in s 1(3) of the 1984 Act. Section 1(4) of the 1984 Act specifies what duty A will owe B if the conditions specified in s 1(3) are fulfilled.

[20] [1996] QB 567.

the barrel through a hole in the door and fired the gun in order to scare Revill away. Revill was shot in the arm and sued Newbery. The Court of Appeal did not think that Revill could bring a claim against Newbery under the 1984 Act. It is submitted that this was correct. Revill was not injured because Newbery's premises had a dangerous *feature*; he was injured because Newbery shot him. It would have been different if Newbery had laid down man traps around his shed to deter thieves and one of these man traps had caught Revill. In such a case, Revill *would* have been injured as a result of Newbery's premises having a dangerous feature (the presence of the man traps) and he might therefore have been able to bring a claim against Newbery under the 1984 Act, claiming that Newbery owed him a duty under the 1984 Act to take reasonable steps to see that he would not be killed or injured as a result of the presence of the man traps.

Similarly, in *Tomlinson* v *Congleton BC*[21] the claimant was injured when he went swimming in a lake on the defendant council's land. He had no permission to go swimming in the lake and so was trespassing on the council's land when he went into the lake. The claimant sued the council for compensation under the 1984 Act but his claim was dismissed: he could not show that he had been injured because the council's land had a dangerous feature. As Lord Hoffmann observed of the lake in the *Tomlinson* case, 'There was nothing special about [the lake]; there were no hidden dangers. It was shallow in some places and deep in others, but that is the nature of lakes. Nor was the council doing or permitting anything to be done which created a danger to persons who came to the lake. No power boats or jet skis threatened the safety of either lawful windsurfers or unlawful swimmers.'[22]

Could the claimant have argued that the lake *itself* was a dangerous feature of the land on which it was located and that he had therefore been injured because the council's land had a dangerous feature? Not on the facts of *Tomlinson*, where the claimant was a mature adult: the mere existence of the lake did not pose any kind of danger to *him*.[23] However, it would have been different if the claimant in *Tomlinson* had been a small child who fell into the lake and was injured. In such a case, it would have been quite easy to argue that in relation to the *child*, the lake *itself* counted as a dangerous feature of the land on which it was located and that as a result the council owed the child a duty to take reasonable steps to protect him from that danger.[24]

(2) *The conditions for a duty to arise under the Act.* Suppose that B trespassed on land occupied by A. Suppose further that there was some quicksand on A's land and that B fell into the quicksand and died. A will only have owed B a duty

---

[21] [2004] 1 AC 46.

[22] Ibid., at [26].

[23] See *Donoghue* v *Folkestone Properties Ltd* [2003] QB 1008, at [36]: 'An expanse of water, be it a lake, pond, river or the sea, does not normally pose any danger to a person on land.'

[24] If the child had been allowed to come onto the council's land then said duty would have been owed under the Occupiers' Liability Act 1957; if he had not been, then the duty would have been owed under the 1984 Act (assuming of course that all the other conditions required for a duty to have been owed under the 1984 Act were satisfied in this case).

to take reasonable steps to see that she would not fall into the quicksand if: (1) A knew or ought to have known of the existence of the quicksand; (2) *at the time B trespassed on A's premises*, A knew or ought to have known that someone like B might go into the vicinity of the quicksand; and (3) A could reasonably have been expected to do something to ensure that someone like B would not fall into the quicksand.

The italicised words do not appear in the 1984 Act but it follows from the decision of the Court of Appeal in *Donoghue v Folkestone Properties Ltd*[25] that they should be read into the Act. In that case, the claimant dived into the defendant council's harbour in the middle of winter. He hit his head on a submerged gridbed and was severely injured. He sued the council for compensation claiming that it had owed him a duty under the 1984 Act to take reasonable steps to see that he did not injure himself on the submerged gridbed.[26] The claimant's claim was dismissed on the ground that at the time the claimant dived into the harbour – the *middle of winter* – the defendants had no reason to think that anyone would try to dive into the harbour. So they had no reason to think at the relevant time that anyone would go anywhere near the submerged gridbed. It would have been different if the diver had executed his dive in the middle of *summer*. At *that* time of year it would have been reasonably foreseeable that trespassers *would* go near the submerged gridbed (by jumping into the harbour at a spot over the gridbed) and so the council in *Donoghue* would have come under a duty to provide trespassers with some protection against that danger by, for example, posting up warning signs telling people not to jump into the harbour.

(3) *The boundary between the 1984 Act and the 1957 Act.* Suppose that Sarah held a dinner party at her house. She told her guests, including Paul, that they could go anywhere they liked in the house, but not into the kitchen. Paul – suspecting that Sarah had prohibited her guests from going into the kitchen to prevent them discovering that she had not actually cooked the dinner herself but was instead serving takeaway food – walked into the kitchen and promptly slipped on the floor and suffered a severe spinal injury. Sarah had in fact told everyone not to go into the kitchen because she had had to clean up some food that she had spilled on the floor and as a result the floor was extremely slippery.

Paul now wants to sue Sarah in negligence for compensation for his injury. The only way his claim can succeed is if he can establish that Sarah owed him a duty to take reasonable steps to stop him going into the kitchen and that she breached that duty by, for example, not locking the kitchen door.[27] Now – which Occupiers' Liability Act will apply here to determine whether Sarah owed Paul such a duty? The argument for thinking that we must look to the 1957 Act is that we want to know whether Sarah owed Paul a duty to take rea-

---

[25] [2003] QB 1008.

[26] The claimant brought his claim under the 1984 Act because he was trespasser when he dived into the harbour.

[27] Paul will not be able to argue that *once he was in the kitchen,* Sarah owed him a duty to take reasonable steps to stop him falling over and injuring himself because once Paul was in the kitchen, Sarah could not reasonably have been expected to do anything to save him from falling over.

sonable steps to *stop* him going into her kitchen. That duty must have been owed to Paul *before* he went into Sarah's kitchen and *at that stage* Paul enjoyed the status of being a 'visitor' on Sarah's premises.[28] So we should look to the 1957 Act – which 'regulate[s] the duty which an occupier of premises owes to his visitors' – to determine whether Sarah owed Paul a duty to take reasonable steps to stop him going into her kitchen.

The logic of this argument seems impeccable, but a majority of the House of Lords ruled in *Tomlinson* v *Congleton BC*[29] that we should in fact look at the *1984* Act to determine whether Sarah owed Paul a duty to take reasonable steps to stop him going into her kitchen.[30] On this view, the 1984 Act not only determines when you have a duty to protect a *trespasser* on your land from some danger arising on your premises but also when you have a duty to take reasonable steps to stop a *visitor* of yours from entering a dangerous area of your land which she is not permitted to enter.

Exceptions to the rule

Suppose B trespasses onto premises occupied by A. Suppose further that those premises have some dangerous feature. Even if conditions (1) – (3), above, are fulfilled, A will not necessarily owe B a duty to take reasonable steps to ensure that B is not killed or injured by that feature. For example, if B has voluntarily taken the risk that he will be killed or injured by that feature, then A will *not* owe B a duty to take reasonable steps to save him from being killed or injured.[31] The maxim *volenti non fit injuria* will apply.

So – in *Ratcliff* v *McConnell*,[32] R was a student who suffered serious injuries when he dived into his college's swimming pool at the shallow end. The pool was locked up for the winter and so when R used the swimming pool he did not do so as a visitor. R sued the college's governors, seeking to recover compensation for his injuries. He claimed that the governors owed him a duty under the 1984 Act to take reasonable steps to ensure that he would not be killed or injured if he dived into the swimming pool. The Court of Appeal dismissed R's claim, holding that when he dived into the swimming pool he willingly took the risk that he would be killed or injured as a result. He knew when he made his dive that there was a risk that the swimming pool would be too shallow to dive in but he nevertheless went ahead with his dive. Similarly, in *Titchener* v *British Railways Board*[33] it was held that someone who walks across a railway line

---

[28] Of course, as soon as he entered the kitchen, he became a trespasser: see above, p. 168.

[29] [2004] 1 AC 46.

[30] Applying the Act, the question of whether Sarah did owe Paul such a duty under the 1984 Act will largely turn on whether Sarah knew or ought to have known that despite her prohibition someone like Paul would attempt to enter the kitchen. If this condition is satisfied, then the courts may well find that Sarah owed Paul a duty to take reasonable steps to stop him going into the kitchen.

[31] Section 1(6): 'No duty is owed ... to any person in respect of risks willingly accepted as his by that person ...'

[32] [1999] 1 WLR 670.

[33] [1983] 1 WLR 1427 (decided under the Occupiers' Liability (Scotland) Act 1960).

knowing that trains run along that line willingly takes the risk that he will be run down and killed or injured by a passing train.

What is the position if B trespasses on premises occupied by A and A has posted up notices outside the premises saying 'No responsibility accepted for the safety of trespassers'? Seemingly, those notices will be of no effect. A will still owe B a duty of care under the 1984 Act if there is some dangerous feature on the premises and conditions (1) – (3), above, apply. There is nothing in the 1984 Act to indicate that the duties of care arising under that Act may be excluded in the same way as the duties of care arising under the 1957 Act can be. However, this creates a paradox. Someone who occupies premises not used for business purposes can 'by agreement or otherwise' ensure that he owes his visitors *no* duty to take reasonable steps to ensure that they will not be harmed by some dangerous feature on the premises – but he may at the same time owe people who trespass onto the premises a duty, which cannot be excluded, to take reasonable steps to ensure that they will not be killed or injured by that feature. In such a case, the occupier's visitors will be worse off than people who trespass on his premises. It is not certain that this was intended by the legislature when it enacted the 1984 Act but only new legislation can remove the problem.

Persons entering premises by right

Now let's look at the position where B goes onto premises owned or occupied by A not because she has been invited or permitted to go onto those premises but because she has a *legal right* to do so. Obviously, B will be neither a 'visitor' nor a trespasser in this situation. So what duties of care will A owe her? The position is very complicated.

The *normal rule* is that B will be treated as though she were one of A's visitors. So A will normally owe her a duty under the Occupiers' Liability Act 1957 to take reasonable steps to see that she will be reasonably safe while she is on A's premises. This is the result of s 2(6) of the Occupiers' Liability Act 1957, which provides that, 'persons who enter premises for any purpose in the exercise of a right conferred by law are to be treated as permitted by the occupier to be there for that purpose, whether they in fact have his permission or not'. So a policewoman who lawfully goes onto A's premises to conduct a search will be protected under the 1957 Act: A will owe her a duty to take reasonable steps to see that she is reasonably safe while she is on his premises.

However, the normal rule does *not* apply where there is a *right of way* over A's land and B uses that right of way to cross A's land.[34] This may be because it would be unduly burdensome to inflict on A a duty to take care to see that people using the right of way over his land are reasonably safe in using that right

---

[34] The Occupiers' Liability Act 1957, s 1(4) provides that the normal rule will not apply where B crosses A's land using a private right of way or a right of way arising under – (i) an access agreement; or (ii) an order granted under the National Parks and Access to the Countryside Act 1949; or (iii) under the Countryside and Rights of Way Act 2000. The House of Lords ruled in *McGeown v Northern Ireland Housing Executive* [1995] 1 AC 233 that the normal rule will not apply where a highway crosses A's land and B uses it to pass over A's land.

of way.[35] Whether or not A will owe B a duty of care in such a case, and what sort of duty A will owe B, will depend on what *sort* of right of way it is that B is using to cross A's land.

(1) *Where the right of way is a private right of way or arises under an access agreement or under the National Parks and Access to Countryside Act 1949.* In such a case, B will be protected by the Occupiers' Liability Act 1984.[36] So if some dangerous feature exists on the right of way (such as a pot-hole) *and* A knows or ought to know about it *and* A knows or ought to know that someone like B is likely to come into the vicinity of that dangerous feature *and* that dangerous feature is one which A could reasonably be expected to do something about, then A will owe B a duty to take reasonable steps to see that she is not killed or injured by that feature.

(2) *Where the right of way arises under s 2(1) of the Countryside and Rights of Way Act 2000.* In such a case, B will again be protected under the Occupiers' Liability Act 1984.[37] However, ss 1(6A) and 1(6C) of the 1984 Act place an important limit on the duty that A would normally owe B under the Act. They provide that A will *not* owe B a duty to protect her against '(a) a risk resulting from the existence of any natural feature of the landscape, or any river, stream, ditch or pond whether or not a natural feature, or (b) a risk [that she will suffer injury] when passing over, under or through any wall, fence or gate, except by proper use of the gate or of a stile' unless he has intentionally or recklessly exposed her to such a risk.

(3) *Where the right of way amounts to a public highway.* In such a case, B will not be protected under the 1984 Act.[38] The only duties of care that A will owe B in such a case will arise under the common law. In such a case, A will of course owe B a duty of care under the *physical danger principle* to take care not to do something which will reasonably foreseeably have the effect of injuring B. A may also owe B a duty to act to save B from some harm in using the highway if 'common humanity' would demand that he so act.[39]

---

[35] Cf. Lord Keith of Kinkel's remarks in *McGeown*: 'Rights of way pass over many different types of terrain, and it would place an impossible burden upon landowners if they had not only to submit to the passage over them of anyone who might choose to exercise them but also were under a duty to maintain them in safe condition' (ibid., 243).

[36] This is the result of the combined effect of s 1(4) of the 1957 Act and s 1(1) of the 1984 Act.

[37] See n. 34, above.

[38] Occupiers' Liability Act 1984, s 1(7). However, if the public right of way is maintainable at public expense, the highway authority in charge of the right of way will owe B a duty to 'maintain' it: Highways Act 1980, s 41. If B is injured because the right of way in question is not in a good condition, the relevant highway authority will have a defence to any action B might make against it for damages if it can show that it took 'such care as in all the circumstances was reasonably required to secure that the part of the [right of way] to which the action relates was not dangerous for traffic': s 58. See below, p. 485.

[39] *Herrington* v *British Railways Board* [1972] AC 877. The case was concerned with the question of when an occupier of land will owe a *trespasser* on the land a duty to save that trespasser from harm and was superseded in large part by the 1984 Act. However, if before the Act occupiers of land owed trespassers on the land a duty of 'common humanity' then there seems no reason why occupiers of land should not owe the same duty in this day and age to people crossing their land via a public highway.

175

Neighbours

Suppose that A occupies a set of premises and a dangerous situation arises on those premises that threatens to damage neighbouring land belonging to B. In such a situation, if A is aware of the danger to B's land that has arisen on his land, or ought to be aware of the danger, A will owe B a duty to take reasonable steps to eliminate the danger.

So in *Goldman* v *Hargrave*,[40] lightning struck a redgum tree on the defendant's land and set it on fire. The defendant cut down the tree but then did not do enough to put out the fire. The fire spread onto the claimant's land, causing much damage. The claimant successfully sued the defendant in negligence for compensation for the damage done to his land.[41] The Privy Council held that the defendant had owed the claimant a duty to take reasonable steps to put out the fire on his land, and that the defendant had breached that duty.[42] Decisions of the Privy Council are, of course, not binding on the English courts but the House of Lords has indicated that the decision in *Goldman* v *Hargrave* was correct.[43]

It is more uncertain whether A will owe a duty to his neighbour B to take reasonable steps to prevent his premises *becoming* a source of danger to B's land. The question was raised in *Smith* v *Littlewoods*.[44] The defendants purchased a

---

[40] [1967] 1 AC 645.

[41] *Important note.* The claimant could have alternatively sued the defendant in *private nuisance* for compensation for the damage done to his land (see below, pp. 374–7) and, indeed, it is customary nowadays for claims for damage done to land as a result of dangerous situations arising on neighbouring land to be brought in private nuisance rather than negligence (see, for example, *Leakey* v *National Trust for Places of Historic Interest or Natural Beauty* [1980] QB 485 and *Holbeck Hall Hotel Ltd* v *Scarborough BC* [2000] QB 836). It is submitted that it makes no difference whether the claims in these sorts of cases are framed in either private nuisance or negligence (see *Leakey*, at 514–15 (per May LJ); also *Smith* v *Littlewoods* [1987] AC 241, at 274 (per Lord Goff)). This is because if a fire spontaneously starts on A's land, A will only owe people who own or have an interest in neighbouring land a duty to take reasonable steps to put out the fire and that duty will be imposed on A in order to help ensure that that neighbouring land is not damaged. So suppose that a fire started on A's land and A failed to take reasonable steps to put out the fire, with the result that it spread onto neighbouring land belonging to B. B was badly burned in the fire and C, a lodger staying on B's land with B's permission, had to move out because the fire damage done to B's land was so extensive. It is doubtful whether B could sue A in private nuisance for his injuries (see below, pp. 383, 570) and C would not be able to sue A in private nuisance for the inconvenience he has been put to because he did not have an interest in B's land when it was damaged (see below, pp. 381–2). It is submitted that neither party will be better off bringing a claim in negligence against A. B's claim for compensation for his burns will be dismissed because even though A owed him, and breached, a duty to take reasonable steps to put out the fire, the physical injuries suffered by B as a result of the fire spreading do not count as the 'right of kind of loss' – the kind of loss which the duty breached by A was imposed on him in order to avoid. (For an explanation of the 'right kind of loss' limit on the damages recoverable in a tort case, see below, pp. 566–70.) Any claim C might bring against A in negligence for the inconvenience he was put to as a result of A's allowing the fire to spread onto B's land will be dismissed on the ground that as C did not have an interest in B's land, A did not owe *C* a duty to take reasonable steps to put out the fire.

[42] Had the fire been intentionally or carelessly started by the defendant, the claimant would have been entitled to sue the defendant for compensation for the damage done to his land without having to prove that the defendant was at all careless in allowing the fire to spread: see below, pp. 750–2.

[43] *Stovin* v *Wise* [1996] AC 923, 930G–H (per Lord Nicholls), 944D–H (per Lord Hoffmann).

[44] [1987] AC 241.

cinema: they intended to knock it down and redevelop the land. For a few months the cinema was left unattended and unlocked. Vandals broke into the cinema and set it on fire. The fire spread to and damaged the claimants' premises. The claimants sued the defendants: they argued that the defendants had owed them a duty to take reasonable steps to keep the cinema secure, so as to prevent the cinema becoming a source of danger to their premises. The House of Lords dismissed the claimants' claim on the ground that it had not been reasonably foreseeable that the claimants' premises would be harmed if the defendants' cinema was not kept secure.[45]

In the course of deciding the case, Lords Brandon and Griffiths indicated that in the situation we are considering, A *will* owe B a duty to take reasonable steps to prevent his premises *becoming* a source of danger to B's land.[46] In contrast, Lord Goff thought that an occupier of land will *not* owe his neighbours a duty to take proactive steps to prevent his land *becoming* a source of danger to his neighbours' land: he will only owe his neighbours a duty of care in a *Goldman* v *Hargrave*-type situation where a danger *has* arisen on his land and he knows or ought to know of its existence.[47] Lord Mackay steered a middle path between these two extremes. He thought that if A occupies some premises and it is reasonably foreseeable that if those premises are not kept secure, vandals will break into A's premises and start a fire which is liable to spread to B's land, then A *will* owe B a duty to take reasonable steps to keep his premises secure, thereby preventing them becoming a source of danger to B's land.[48] But Lord Mackay thought things would be different in the case where it is reasonably foreseeable that if A's premises are not kept secure, thieves will break into A's premises and use those premises to gain access to B's land and steal property from B.[49] While he did not go so far as to say that *no* duty of care would be owed in this situation,[50] he plainly thought this case more difficult than the 'fire' case just discussed. Puzzlingly, the fifth judge to decide *Smith* v *Littlewoods* – Lord Keith of Kinkel – expressed agreement with the judgments of Lord Mackay *and* Lord Goff, despite the clear differences between them.

So *Smith* v *Littlewoods* did not finally resolve the issue of whether an occupier of premises will owe his neighbours a duty to take reasonable steps to prevent his property becoming a source of danger to his neighbours' land. The most that can be said

---

[45] Ibid., at 250 (per Lord Brandon), 251 (per Lord Griffiths), 258–9 (per Lord Mackay).

[46] Ibid., at 250: '[the defendants] owed to the [claimants] a duty to exercise reasonable care to ensure that the cinema ... did not become ... a source of danger to neighbouring buildings owned or occupied by the claimants' (per Lord Brandon); 'the duty of care owed [by the defendants] was a duty to take reasonable care that the condition of the premises they occupied was not a source of danger to neighbouring property' (per Lord Griffiths).

[47] Ibid., at 272–4, 277–9.

[48] Ibid., at 258.

[49] Ibid., at 268.

[50] He did think that if A came back home to find a thief boring a hole through one of his walls to gain access to B's house, then A would owe B a duty to take reasonable steps to stop the thief gaining access to B's house in this way: ibid, at 265. However, this result can easily be justified by reference to *Goldman* v *Hargrave*. In the case considered here a danger *will* have arisen on A's land which A knows about and therefore A will owe those of his neighbours who will be affected by that danger a duty to take reasonable steps to deal with it.

in light of the decisions in that case is that there was a clear majority in favour of the proposition that such an occupier *will* owe his neighbours a duty to take reasonable steps to keep his premises secure *if* it is reasonably foreseeable that if he does not, vandals will break in and start a fire which is liable to spread to his neighbours' land.

Passers-by

Suppose A occupies premises that adjoin a highway. Suppose further that there is some fixture attached to those premises – such as a sign or a tree – which is liable to fall into the highway if it falls into disrepair. In such a case, A will owe people using the highway next to his premises a duty to take reasonable steps to see that the fixture in question does not fall into the highway and injure them.[51] So if the fixture in question is in an obviously dangerous condition, A will have a duty to take reasonable steps to repair the fixture or take it down.[52] And even if the fixture in question looks perfectly sound, A will have a duty from time to time to have an expert look at it to see that it does not suffer from any latent defects which mean that it is a danger to passers-by.[53]

OTHER OCCUPIERS

The regime of duties of care created by the 1957 and 1984 Acts also applies to occupiers of fixed or moveable structures[54] such as boats[55] or taxis or ladders.[56]

LANDLORDS

Section 4 of the Defective Premises Act 1972 provides that *if*: (1) A lets premises to someone else; *and* (2) A knows or ought to know the premises suffer

---

[51] If the fixture does fall into a state of disrepair and as a result falls into the highway, anyone injured as a result may be entitled to bring a claim in *public nuisance* for compensation for their injuries. See below, pp. 783–4, for a discussion of the availability of such a claim.

[52] *Tarry* v *Ashton* (1876) 1 QBD 314. The duty is non-delegable in nature. That is, if A employs someone else to repair the fixture, and that person fails to take reasonable steps to repair it properly, then A will be held to have breached his duty to take reasonable steps to repair the fixture: ibid. For a discussion of non-delegable duties of care, see below, pp. 227–33.

[53] *Caminer* v *Northern and London Investment Trust* [1951] AC 88 (held: occupiers not liable in negligence for injuries caused as a result of an elm tree falling into a road from their premises because the tree was apparently healthy; and, while the occupiers had failed to get anyone in to inspect the tree, even if they had, no action would have been taken to repair the tree or take it down because inspection by an expert would not have revealed that there was a problem with the tree).

[54] Occupiers' Liability Act 1957, s 1(3)(a); Occupiers' Liability Act 1984, s 1(2).

[55] In *Horsley* v *MacLaren, The Ogopogo* [1971] 2 Lloyd's Rep 410, the Supreme Court of Canada ruled that if A invites B onto his boat and B falls overboard, A will owe B a duty to take reasonable steps to rescue him. Such a conclusion could not be reached under the Occupiers' Liability Act 1957. Under the 1957 Act, A's only duty would be to take reasonable steps to see that B was not injured as a result of the condition of the boat. Perhaps the Supreme Court's conclusion could be justified under the 'creation of danger principle', discussed above, pp. 153–6.

[56] If A gives B a ladder to stand on, can the ladder be said to be 'occupied' by A at the time B stands on it? The court thought not in *Wheeler* v *Copas* [1981] 3 All ER 405, holding that a bricklayer who was injured when a ladder given him by the defendant farmer collapsed had no claim against the farmer under the 1957 Act.

from a defect;[57] *and* (3) under the contract of tenancy A would have an obligation to repair that defect were he aware of it;[58] *then* (4) A will *normally* owe 'all persons[59] who might reasonably be expected to be affected by defects in the state of the premises a duty to take such care as is reasonable in all the circumstances to see that they are reasonably safe from personal injury or from damage caused to their property by [that] defect'.[60]

By s 4(4) of the 1972 Act, if A lets premises to someone else and under the contract of tenancy he reserves the right to re-enter the premises to effect certain repairs to the premises, A is to be regarded for the purposes of s 4 of the 1972 Act as having an obligation under the contract of tenancy to effect those repairs to the premises. However, A cannot be treated by virtue of s 4(4) as having had an obligation under the contract of tenancy to repair a given defect in the premises if the responsibility for repairing that defect was clearly placed on the tenant under the contract of tenancy.

In *McAuley* v *Bristol City Council*,[61] M was a council tenant who fell from an unstable step in her garden and injured her ankle. She sued the council, arguing that she had sustained her injury because the council owed her, and breached, a duty to take care to see that she would not be injured by the unstable step in her garden. The council had not undertaken under the contract of tenancy to repair the unstable step in the garden.[62] However, the Court of Appeal *implied* a term in the tenancy agreement that the council had the power to enter the claimant's garden to inspect and repair any defective structures in the garden. This allowed the Court of Appeal to treat the council, for the purposes of applying s 4 of the 1972 Act, as though it *was* obliged under the contract of tenancy to repair the unstable step in the claimant's garden – and therefore to find that the council did owe the claimant a duty to take care to see that she would not be injured by that step.

It would have been different if *either* the council had expressly provided in the contract of tenancy that the responsibility for repairing defective structures in the claimant's garden fell on the claimant (in which case the council could not have been treated by virtue of s 4(4) of the 1972 Act as having had an obligation under the contract of tenancy to repair the unstable step in the claimant's garden) *or* the council had expressly provided in the contract of tenancy that it had no right to repair defective structures in the claimant's garden (in which case it would have been impossible for the Court of Appeal to have implied a term into the contract of tenancy that the council had the

---

[57] Section 4(2). The Court of Appeal has made it clear that it need not be shown, for the purposes of this requirement, that A had actual knowledge of the existence of the defect or of facts which indicated that the defect existed: it is enough to show that a reasonable man in A's position would have discovered the existence of the defect. See *Sykes* v *Harry* [2001] QB 1014 (leave to appeal refused by the House of Lords: [2002] 1 WLR 2286).

[58] Section 4(3).

[59] Including the tenant(s) of the let premises: *McAuley* v *Bristol City Council* [1992] 1 QB 134; *Sykes* v *Harry* [2001] QB 1014, at [21].

[60] Section 4(1).

[61] [1992] 1 QB 134.

[62] So no claim for breach of contract was available to the claimant.

right to enter the claimant's garden to inspect and repair any defective structures there). However, the council did neither of these things.

EMPLOYERS

It has long been well established that if A employs B, A will *normally* owe B a duty to take reasonable steps to see that she is not killed or physically injured in working for him. So A will *normally* owe B a duty to take reasonable steps to ensure: (1) that B's fellow employees are competent and are therefore not likely to act in ways which would unreasonably endanger B's health and safety; (2) that B's place of work is reasonably safe to enter and work in; (3) that B and B's fellow employees will do their work in a way that will not unreasonably endanger B's health and safety; and (4) that B is provided with the necessary plant and equipment to enable him to do his work without unreasonably endangering his health and safety and that that plant and equipment is reasonably safe to use.

This duty will rarely be displaced on the grounds that *volenti non fit injuria*. For example, the mere fact that B goes to work every day knowing that her workplace is not a reasonably safe place to work in does not establish that she is willing to work for A in a place of work that is not reasonably safe for her to work in.[63] In such a case – where B's only alternative to turning up for work is to quit her job and seek alternative employment on an uncertain job market – it cannot be said that B *willingly* chooses to work for A in a dangerous workplace when she continues to turn up for work in the knowledge that her workplace is not a reasonably safe place to work in.[64] Similarly, if A warned B before employing her that her future place of work would not be reasonably safe to work in and B agreed to work for A on that basis, B cannot be said to have *willingly* chosen to work for A in a dangerous workplace if her only reason for agreeing to work for A in the knowledge that doing so would involve an unreasonable risk of her being killed or injured was that she needed a job. So, in the case just described, A, having employed B, will – despite his warning to B – still owe B a duty to take reasonable steps to ensure that B's workplace is reasonably safe for her to work in.

How far does the duty that A will owe B to take reasonable steps to see that she will not be killed or injured working for him go? For example, suppose that A employs B to do a particular kind of work and it becomes clear that B is very likely to suffer injury if she is made to carry on doing that kind of work. No doubt in such a case it would be good practice for A to reassign B to some other kind of work which is less dangerous. But what if there is no other work available? Will A owe B a duty to dismiss her? For a long time, the courts took the view that A could not owe B such a duty.[65] However, in *Coxall v Goodyear GB*

[63] *McCafferty v Metropolitan Police District Receiver* [1977] 1 WLR 1073.
[64] *Smith v Baker* [1891] AC 325.
[65] See *Withers v Perry Chain Co. Ltd* [1961] 1 WLR 1314, at 1317 (per Sellers LJ): 'I cannot believe that the common law requires employers to refuse to employ a person who is willing to work for them simply because they think that it is not in the person's best interests to do the work. That would be imposing a restriction on the freedom of the individual which I think is foreign to the whole spirit of the common law of our country.'

Ltd[66] Simon Brown LJ took the view that if the risk that B will be injured if she carries on working for A is serious enough, then A may well owe B a duty to dismiss her.[67]

So far we have discussed the duty an employer will owe his employee to see that she is not *killed or injured* while working for him. Will he also owe her a duty to take reasonable steps to see that she will not suffer *other kinds of harm*? The decision of the House of Lords in *White v Chief Constable of South Yorkshire*[68] seems to establish that an employer will not owe his employees a *general* duty to take reasonable steps to see that they do not suffer any kind of *psychiatric illness* in working for him. However, we have already seen that it is well established that if it is reasonably foreseeable that an employee will suffer a nervous breakdown if she is made to do a certain kind of work without any kind of assistance or counselling, then the employer will owe his employee a duty to take reasonable steps to see that she gets that assistance or counselling.[69] Furthermore, the House of Lords has held that it is strongly arguable that if A employs B and A knows or ought to know that B is being harassed to such an extent by her fellow employees that there is a danger she will suffer a breakdown, A will owe B a duty to take reasonable steps to stop the harassment.[70]

Turning to harms to property and economic harms, it seems that an employer will not owe an employee a duty to take reasonable steps to see that her property is not harmed while she is working for him;[71] neither will he owe her a duty to take reasonable steps to see that she does not suffer some kind of pure economic loss in working for him.[72]

BAILEES

If A holds B's goods on a bailment for B,[73] A will *normally* owe B a duty to take

---

[66] [2003] 1 WLR 536.

[67] Ibid., at [29]. In *Barber v Somerset County Council* [2004] UKHL 13, Lord Rodger of Earlsferry took much the same view, acknowledging that in cases where an employee would be exposed to a substantial risk of injury if he carried on working, his employer might owe him a duty to sack him: ibid., at [30].

[68] [1999] 2 AC 455.

[69] See above, pp. 109–10.

[70] *Waters v Commissioner of Police of the Metropolis* [2000] 1 WLR 1607 (held that it was strongly arguable that this principle applied in the case where the defendant commissioner occupied a status analogous to an employer in relation to the claimant policewoman, who suffered a breakdown as a result of being subjected to severe harassment from her fellow police officers for reporting that she had been raped by a fellow police officer).

[71] *Deyong v Shenburn* [1946] KB 227 (no duty to prevent theft of clothes from dressing room). However, if an employee's property is destroyed or damaged while she is working in her employer's factory, she may be able to bring a claim in negligence against her employer under the Occupiers' Liability Act 1957. See above, n. 5.

[72] *Reid v Rush & Tompkins Group plc* [1990] 1 WLR 212 (no duty to advise employee of advisability of taking out insurance when working for defendant abroad).

[73] It is possible for A to hold *someone else's* goods on a bailment for B. This will be the case where C delivers goods to B to look after them, and B then hands those goods over to A to look after them. In this case – what is called a 'sub-bailment' – A will hold C's goods on a bailment for B and will owe B a duty to take reasonable steps to see that they are not harmed. (Whether A will *also* hold C's goods on a bailment for *C* – and therefore owe *C* a duty to take reasonable steps to see that they are not harmed – will depend on whether A was aware that the goods in question were not B's when they were handed over to him: *The Pioneer Container* [1994] 2 AC 324, 342 (per Lord Goff); *Marcq v Christie's* [2003] 3 WLR 980, at [49]–[50].) If he breaches this duty

reasonable steps to ensure that those goods are not harmed.[74] (In such a case, A is said to be a 'bailee' of B's goods and B is said to be a 'bailor'.) A will hold B's goods on a bailment for B if he is *voluntarily in possession*[75] of those goods.[76] So if B drops a wallet in the street, and A picks it up, he will hold it on a bailment for B.[77] If, on the other hand, B sends some unsolicited goods to A through the post, A will not hold those goods on a bailment for B because he will not have voluntarily taken possession of those goods.[78]

If A holds B's goods on a bailment for B, he will not necessarily owe B a duty to take reasonable steps to ensure that those goods are not harmed. For example, if B asks A to look after his watch and A makes it clear at the time he accepts the watch that he does not want to be responsible for its safety, then A will not owe B a duty to take reasonable steps to ensure that the watch is not harmed: *volenti non fit injuria*. What is the position if B handed over some goods to C to look after them, and then C asked A to look after those goods – and A took possession of the goods, but only on condition that he would not be responsible for their safety? The first point to be made is that A will not have held the goods in question on a bailment for B unless he was aware at the time he accepted them that they were not C's.[79] If A was aware that the goods were not C's at the time he accepted them, then he will have held the goods on a bailment for B and will have owed B a duty to take reasonable steps to ensure that they were not harmed – *unless* B authorised C to sub-bail his goods on terms similar to those that C agreed with A.[80] If B did not give such authorisation, then A's agreement with C that he would not be responsible for the safety of B's goods will have no effect on B.

CARRIERS

As we have seen,[81] if A gives B a lift in his car, A will normally owe B a duty under the Occupiers' Liability Act 1957 to take reasonable steps to ensure that the condition of his car is such that B will be reasonably safe in taking a lift in

---

and C's goods are lost as a result, he can be sued by B for the value of the goods, even if B has not actually suffered any loss as a result of C's goods being lost: *The Sanix Ace* [1987] 1 Lloyd's Rep 465. However, B will hold any damages so recovered on trust for C.

[74] By 'harmed' here, we mean destroyed, damaged or stolen.

[75] For an account of when someone will be held to be in 'possession' of goods, see below, pp. 334–6.

[76] There is an exception where C hands goods over to A to look after them and then sells the goods to B while they are still in A's possession. In such a case, A will only hold those goods on a bailment for B if he attorns to B (that is, if he acknowledges that he holds those goods on a bailment for B): Palmer 2000, 359, 398.

[77] Similarly if A steals B's wallet: ibid., 359; though see Bell 1998, 470.

[78] In such a situation, A will still owe B a duty under the 'property harm principle' (above, pp. 110–19) to take care not to damage the goods in question. A will, however, be free to treat the goods as his own to dispose of if he remains in possession of them six months after first receiving them or 30 days after he notified B that they were unsolicited and invited B to arrange to pick them up: Unsolicited Goods and Services Act 1971.

[79] See above, n. 73.

[80] *Morris v C W Martin Ltd* [1966] 1 QB 716, 729 (per Lord Denning MR); *The Pioneer Container* [1994] 2 AC 324.

[81] See above, p. 178.

his car. But A will, in any case, owe B a more general duty to take reasonable steps to ensure that B will not be killed or injured in taking a lift in his car.

For example, in *Jebson* v *Ministry of Defence*[82] the claimant was a soldier who went to Portsmouth with some fellow soldiers for a night out. Anticipating that the claimant and his companions would be in no condition to get back to their barracks after their night out, the defendants – the claimant's employer – sent a lorry to take them back home. The claimant – who was considerably worse for wear after his night out – attempted to climb onto the roof of the lorry as it took him back to barracks. Unfortunately for the claimant, he failed in his attempt and fell off the lorry and into the road, suffering various injuries in the process. He claimed that the defendants had owed him a duty to take reasonable steps to ensure that he would not suffer any kind of injury in travelling in their lorry and that they had breached that duty in failing to have someone in the back of the lorry to supervise him and his companions and to make sure that they did not – in their drunken state – try to climb out of the lorry while it was travelling along. The Court of Appeal allowed the claimant's claim.

PARENTS

It seems to be well established that a parent will owe his or her children a duty to take reasonable steps to ensure that they do not come to any harm.[83]

The point is for the most part academic. Suppose a child, Beth, suffered some kind of injury because of her father's carelessness. Beth will, generally speaking, have no incentive to sue her father for damages as suing him for such damages will usually only deprive him of money that he needs to raise Beth. However, the point made here becomes of great importance in the case where Eric, a car driver, carelessly runs down and injures Wendy, a child. If Mary, Wendy's mother, carelessly allowed Wendy to run into the road, Eric – on being sued for damages by Wendy – will be able to make a claim for contribution against Mary, arguing that Mary is just as liable as he is to compensate Wendy for her injuries. The end result is that Wendy will not be fully compensated for her injuries as, in practice, the claim in contribution against Mary will have to be satisfied out of the proceeds of Wendy's claim against Eric.

Section 2 of the Congenital Disabilities (Civil Liability) Act 1976 establishes that if Ruth is pregnant and is driving a car, Ruth will be 'under the same duty to take care for the safety of her unborn child as the law imposes on her with respect to the safety of other people'. So Ruth will owe her unborn child a duty to take care not to drive dangerously. It may be asked why this is. Why will Ruth owe her unborn child a duty of care *while she is driving* but not in other situations? For example, why will Ruth not owe her unborn child a duty to take care not to drink alcohol or smoke or fall down the stairs? The answer is that it would be pointless to hold that Ruth owes her unborn child a duty to take care not to do these things. Suppose, for example, that Ruth drinks heavily while she is

---

[82] [2000] 1 WLR 2055.
[83] *Surtees* v *Kingston-upon-Thames Borough Council* [1991] 2 FLR 559.

pregnant and as a result her baby when it is born suffers from certain disabilities. And suppose we conceded that while the baby was in Ruth's womb, Ruth owed the baby a duty not to drink heavily. This concession would allow Ruth's baby to sue Ruth for compensation for the fact that he was born disabled – but why would he? He would only deprive Ruth of money that she needs to raise him.

It is different if Ruth drives her car while she is pregnant in such a dangerous manner that she ends up crashing the car, with the result that her baby is born disabled. In such a case, Ruth will have liability insurance that will cover her if she is held liable to compensate her baby for the fact that he has been born disabled as a result of her dangerous driving. So saying that in this case Ruth owed her unborn baby a duty to take care not to drive dangerously will serve a useful purpose. Ruth's baby will be able to sue her for the fact that he has been born disabled – but the damages payable will not come out of Ruth's pocket; rather they will come out of the pocket of Ruth's liability insurer.

TEACHERS

It seems well established that a teacher will owe the students in his charge a duty to take reasonable steps to see that those students do not come to any harm while on the school premises.[84] As Lord Clyde observed in the recent case of *Phelps v Hillingdon London Borough Council*: '[there] is no question that a teacher owes a duty of care for the physical safety of a child attending school under the charge of that teacher. The teacher has a duty to take reasonable care that the child does not come to any harm through any danger which may arise during the course of the child's attendance at the school.'[85]

It also seems to be accepted that if a student has 'special needs' or suffers from learning difficulties, his teachers will owe him a duty to take reasonable steps to ensure that that student is not disadvantaged as a result of the fact that he suffers from those special needs or learning difficulties. So in *X v Bedfordshire County Council*, Lord Browne-Wilkinson held – with the agreement of the other Law Lords deciding the case – that if 'it comes to the attention of [a] headmaster that a pupil is under-performing, he does owe a duty to take such steps as a reasonable teacher would consider appropriate to try to deal with such under-performance'.[86] In the *Phelps* case the House of Lords refused to strike out a number of claims which were premised on the basis that the teachers of a student who suffers from special needs or learning difficulties will owe him a duty to take reasonable steps to ensure that that student is not disadvantaged from the fact that he suffers from those special needs or learning difficulties.

---

[84] The duty does not extend to seeing that the child does not come to any harm off the school premises: *Bradford-Smart v West Sussex County Council* [2002] EWCA Civ 7 (discussed, Elvin 2003b).

[85] [2001] 2 AC 619, 670. See also *Van Oppen v Clerk to the Bedford Charity Trustees* [1990] 1 WLR 235, at 250 (per Balcombe LJ). The same is true of educational authorities: see *New South Wales v Lepore* [2003] HCA 4.

[86] [1995] 2 AC 633, 766.

The House of Lords held it was arguable that the teacher of a student who suffers from special needs or learning difficulties would owe him such a duty of care. Lord Nicholls – with the agreement of Lord Jauncey of Tullichettle – went further and held that 'a teacher [will] owe a duty of care to a child with learning difficulties . . . A teacher must exercise due skill and care to respond appropriately to the manifest problems of such a child, including informing the head-teacher or others about the child's problems and carrying out any instructions he is given.'[87]

The cases do not go so far as to say that the teachers of a *normal* student will owe him a duty to teach him with reasonable skill and care. Lord Nicholls held that the teachers of a normal student would owe him such a duty of care in *Phelps*[88] but only one of the other six Law Lords who decided *Phelps* indicated that he agreed with Lord Nicholls on this point. It follows that a normal student who wishes to establish that one of his teachers owed him a duty to teach him with reasonable skill and care will have to use the *Caparo* test for determining whether one person owed another a duty of care to establish that such a duty of care was owed to him. It is to this test for determining whether one person owed another a duty of care that we will now turn.

---

[87] [2001] 2 AC 619, 667.
[88] Ibid.

8

THE *CAPARO* TEST

ANTECEDENTS OF THE TEST

Suppose that John constantly truanted from school and as a result, he left school with no qualifications and few prospects. He now wants to sue the school authorities in negligence for compensation, claiming that they failed to take reasonable steps to stop him truanting, and that had they done so, he would have done much better at school than he did and would now therefore have much better prospects than he does. The very first thing he will have to establish, of course, is that the authorities owed him a duty to take reasonable steps to stop him truanting from school. Now – there are no in-force statutes or decided cases that establish that such a duty of care was owed to John. But that fact is not necessarily fatal to his claim. It has long been acknowledged, as Lord Wilberforce observed in *Anns* v *Merton LBC*, that 'in order to establish that a duty of care arises in a particular situation, it is not necessary to bring the facts of that situation within those of previous situations in which a duty of care has been held to exist'.[1]

Lord Wilberforce went on to suggest a *two-stage test* that could be used to determine whether a duty of care was owed in a 'novel' case such as the one we are discussing – that is, a case where the decided cases and in-force statutes have not already established that a duty of care was owed. Taking as an example the case we have been considering – according to the *Anns* two-stage test, one would determine whether the school authorities owed John a duty to take reasonable steps to see that he did not truant from school in the following way. First, one would ask: Was it *reasonably foreseeable* that John would suffer some kind of harm if the authorities did not take reasonable steps to see that he did not truant from school? If the answer is 'no' then no duty of care was owed in the case we are considering. If the answer is 'yes', one then asks: Are there any reasons of *public policy* why we should *not* say that the school authorities owed John a duty to take reasonable steps to see that he did not truant from school? This time, if the answer is 'yes' then the authorities did *not* owe John a duty of care. But if the answer is 'no' then, under the *Anns* two-stage test for determining whether a duty of care was owed in a 'novel' case, the school authorities *did* owe John a duty to take reasonable steps to see that he did not truant from school.

While the *Anns* two-stage test for determining whether a duty of care was owed in a 'novel' case proved initially popular with the courts, it has now been

---

[1] [1978] AC 728, 751G–752B.

disowned, largely thanks to the efforts of Lord Keith of Kinkel.[2] This was for two reasons. First, the two-stage test made the law on when one person will owe another a duty of care too uncertain. Secondly, the courts were too ready to find that the second stage of the two-stage test was satisfied in a given case. As a result there was a danger that the courts would find that one person owed another a duty of care in a given situation using the *Anns* two-stage test even though it was contrary to the public interest for them to find that such a duty of care was owed. In response to these concerns, the courts suggested a number of modifications that could be made to the *Anns* two-stage test for determining whether a duty of care was owed in a 'novel' case. Finally, in *Caparo Industries plc* v *Dickman*, the House of Lords adopted a new, *three-stage*, test for determining whether one person owed another a duty of care in a 'novel' case.[3] This test has been used ever since by courts in England to determine whether one person owed another a duty of care in a 'novel' case.[4]

APPLYING THE TEST

How the test works

To see how the *Caparo* test for determining whether a duty of care was owed in a 'novel' case works, let us go back to the situation we have been considering. According to this test, we determine whether the school authorities owed John a duty to take reasonable steps to see that he did not truant from school in the following way.

First, we ask: Was it *reasonably foreseeable* that John would suffer some kind of harm if the authorities did not take reasonable steps to see that he did not truant from school? If the answer is 'yes' we then ask: Was there are a relationship of *proximity* between John and the school authorities at the time John was truanting from school? If the answer is 'yes' we then ask: Would it be *fair, just and reasonable* to find that the school authorities owed John a duty to take reasonable steps to see that he did not truant from school? If the answer is 'yes' then the school authorities did indeed owe John a duty to take reasonable steps to see that he did not truant from school. If, on the other hand, the answer to *any* of these three questions is 'no' then the school authorities did *not* owe John any such duty of care.

---

[2] Lord Keith criticised the *Anns* two-stage test in: *Peabody Donation Fund* v *Sir Lindsay Parkinson & Co. Ltd* [1985] AC 210, 240F–241C; *Yuen Kun Yeu* v *Att-Gen for Hong Kong* [1988] AC 175, 190H–194F; *Rowling* v *Takaro Properties Ltd* [1988] AC 473, 501E–F; and *Hill* v *Chief Constable of West Yorkshire* [1989] AC 53, 60C.

[3] [1990] 2 AC 605, 617H–618B (per Lord Bridge of Harwich).

[4] The *Anns* test still enjoys some popularity in other common law jurisdictions: see, for example, the Supreme Court of Canada's decision in *Cooper* v *Hobart* [2001] 3 SCR 537 (noted, Neyers 2002). However, the version of the *Anns* test employed in *Cooper* v *Hobart* is so attenuated that it looks very much like the *Caparo* test.

The redundancy of 'proximity'

It is doubtful whether the second stage of the *Caparo* three-stage test for determining whether someone owed another a duty of care in a 'novel' case serves
any useful purpose. To see why consider the case we have been discussing in
this chapter – the case where John wants to sue the school authorities in negligence for failing to take reasonable steps to stop him truanting from school.
Now: under the *Caparo* test, the authorities will only have owed John a duty to
take reasonable steps to see that he did not truant from school if there was a
relationship of 'proximity' between them. However, it is hard to imagine that
any court would deny that there was a relationship of 'proximity' between John
and the school authorities *if* it was reasonably foreseeable that John would
suffer some kind of harm if the authorities did not take reasonable steps to see
that he did not truant from school *and* it would be 'fair, just and reasonable' to
find that the authorities owed John a duty to take reasonable steps to see that
he did not truant from school. In other words, it is hard to imagine that any
court would deny that the *second* stage of the three-stage *Caparo* test for determining whether the school authorities owed John a duty of care has been
satisfied if the *first and third* stages of that three-stage test have been satisfied.

This impression is strengthened when one looks at the cases in which the
courts have denied that one person owed another a duty of care under the
Caparo test on the ground that there was no relationship of 'proximity' between
the two parties. In all these cases, as Lord Oliver of Aylmerton observed in
Caparo Industries plc v *Dickman* itself, the finding that there was no relationship
of proximity between the defendant and the claimant 'can most rationally be
attributed to the court's view that it would not be fair and reasonable to hold
the defendant responsible'.[5] So it seems that the second stage of the *Caparo*
three-stage test for determining whether one person owed another a duty of
care in a 'novel' case is redundant: the second stage of the three-stage test will
always be satisfied if the first and third stages of the three-stage test are satisfied.[6] If this is right, then the *Caparo* test for determining whether one person
owed another a duty of care in a 'novel' case *in substance* really amounts to a
two-stage test. If we want to apply the *Caparo* test to determine whether the
school authorities owed John a duty to take reasonable steps to see that he did
not truant from school, all we *really* have to do is ask: (*a*) Was it reasonably
foreseeable that John would suffer some kind of harm if the authorities did not
take reasonable steps to see that he did not truant from school; *and* (*b*) Would
it be 'fair, just and reasonable' to find that the authorities owed John a duty to
take reasonable steps to see that he did not truant from school? If the answer

---

[5] [1990] 2 AC 605, 633C–D.
[6] Indeed, in some cases, the second stage of the three-stage test will be satisfied if only the *first*
stage of the three-stage test is satisfied. See, for example, Mann LJ's observation in *The Nicholas
H* [1994] 1 WLR 1071, at 1085–6, that he was 'content to assume that the foreseeability of
damage to the [claimants'] cargo [if the defendants failed to take care that they did not certify
the ship carrying the claimants' cargo was seaworthy when it was not] was sufficient to constitute "a relationship of proximity" between them and the [defendants]'.

to both questions is 'yes' then the authorities *will* have owed John a duty of care under the *Caparo* test.[7]

Two approaches to applying the *Caparo* test

We can now distinguish two different approaches employed by the judges in applying the *Caparo* test: the *incremental approach* and the *activist approach*.

The incremental approach

The incremental approach to applying the *Caparo* test is extremely popular among judges nowadays.[8] We can illustrate how it works by referring again to the hypothetical example we have been considering all along in this chapter. Suppose that Judge Little had to decide John's case and his preferred method of applying the *Caparo* test is to use the incremental approach. Judge Little would begin by seeing whether it was reasonably foreseeable that John would suffer some kind of harm if the authorities did not take reasonable steps to see that he did not truant from school. This condition is obviously satisfied in this case. Judge Little would then see whether the *existing case law* indicates that it *might* be 'fair, just and reasonable' to find that the authorities owed John a duty of care in this case. For example, someone who wanted to argue that the existing case law indicates that it might be 'fair, just and reasonable' to find that the authorities owed John a duty to take reasonable steps to stop him committing suicide might well argue as follows:

> The law already thinks that it is 'fair, just and reasonable' to find that prison authorities owe suicide risks in their custody a duty to take reasonable steps to stop them committing suicide. Given this, it may well be 'fair, just and reasonable' to find that a duty of care was owed here – there are many similarities between the case here and the case where a suicide risk is in custody. The school authorities in this case had the power to stop John truanting, just like the prison authorities have the power to stop a suicide risk in custody from committing suicide. John – being young and immature – could hardly be trusted to know what to do in his best interests, just like someone who has been traumatised by the experience of being taken into custody. Finally, the harm that John did to himself by truanting from school, while not as serious as the harm involved in killing oneself, was still extremely serious; indeed, it is not going too far to say that persistent truanting from school amounts to a form of suicide, in that a

---

[7] Compare: suppose there exists a rule that X will be true if A, B and C are true. If B will always be true if A and C are true, then if we want to know whether X is true all we have to do is ask: (*a*) Is A true? and (*b*) Is C true? If the answer to both questions is 'yes' then X will be true.

[8] The incremental approach originates in Brennan J's judgment in the Australian case of *Sutherland Shire Council* v *Heyman* (1985) 127 CLR 424, where he criticised (at 481) the *Anns* two-stage test, saying that, 'It is preferable, in my view, that the law should develop novel categories of negligence incrementally and by analogy with established categories, rather than by a massive extension of a prima facie duty of care restrained only by indefinable "considerations which ought to negative, or to reduce or limit the scope of the duty or the class of the person to whom it is owed".' This *dictum* was referred to with approval by Lord Bridge in *Caparo Industries plc* v *Dickman* [1990] 2 AC 605, at 618 and since then the 'incremental' approach to applying the *Caparo* test has been widely adopted by judges in England. See Stanton 1997 for a detailed account of the 'incremental approach' to finding a duty of care as employed by English judges.

persistent truant is killing off the kind of person he or she could have been had he or she attended school.

Judge Little would have to determine whether John's case was *sufficiently close to* – a mere *incremental* step away from – the suicide in custody cases to indicate that it *might* be 'fair, just and reasonable' to find that the school authorities owed John a duty of care here or whether, despite the similarities between John's case and the suicide in custody cases, the differences between them were so large that the suicide in custody cases do *not* indicate that it *might* be 'fair, just and reasonable' to find that the school authorities owed John a duty of care here. If – contrary to the argument set out above – Judge Little found that there were significant differences between John's case and the suicide in custody cases[9] then he would conclude that no duty of care was owed in John's case. If, on the other hand, he concluded that John's case was sufficiently close to the suicide in custody cases he would then move on to the final stage of the incremental approach, which is to ask if there is any reason why it would *not* be 'fair, just and reasonable' to find that the authorities owed John a duty of care. If there is, then again Judge Little would conclude that the authorities did *not* owe John a duty of care in the situation we are considering. But if there is not, he would conclude that they *did* owe John a duty of care.

The activist approach

The crucial feature of the incremental approach to applying the *Caparo* test is that one can only find that a duty of care was owed in a 'novel' case if the *existing* case law suggests that it might be 'fair, just and reasonable' to do so. So a judge like Judge Little, who employs the incremental approach to determine whether a duty of care was owed in a 'novel' case, will often be *forced* to find that *no* duty of care was owed because there is nothing in the existing case law that suggests that it might be 'fair, just and reasonable' to find that a duty of care was owed.

Another judge – let's call him Judge Large – might therefore criticise Judge Little for adopting an incremental approach to applying the *Caparo* test. He might say,

> We shouldn't be so hidebound by the existing precedents. If, on balance, it would be a good idea to find that a duty of care was owed in a particular case, then we should say that such a duty of care was owed – irrespective of whether there is anything in the existing case law which suggests that it might be 'fair, just and reasonable' to find that such a duty of care was owed. It strikes me that we would do an injustice if we refused to find that a duty of care was owed in a particular situation merely because

---

[9] For example, someone who wanted to argue that there were significant differences between the suicide in custody cases and John's case could argue that: 'The reason why it is fair, just and reasonable for the police and prison authorities to owe a duty to prisoners in their custody to take reasonable steps to stop them committing suicide is that they have *created a risk* that those prisoners will commit suicide. There is nothing like this here – the school authorities in John's case did not create a risk that he would truant from school. So one cannot infer from the suicide in custody cases that it might be "fair, just and reasonable" to find that the school authorities owed John a duty to take reasonable steps to stop him truanting from school.'

our predecessors never had occasion to consider whether a duty of care was owed in that situation, or any analogous situation.[10]

Judge Large will therefore prefer a different approach to applying the *Caparo* test, which we can dub the *activist approach*.[11]

Going back to the example we have been considering, Judge Large would determine whether the *Caparo* test was satisfied in John's case in the following way. He would first see whether it was reasonably foreseeable that John would suffer some kind of harm if the authorities did not take reasonable steps to see that he did not truant from school. If it was (and it was), then he would *presume* that it *would* be 'fair, just and reasonable' to find that the authorities owed John a duty to take reasonable steps to see that he did not truant from school unless he could see some reason why it would not be. So if he could not find any reason why it would *not* be 'fair, just and reasonable' to find that the authorities owed John a duty of care, he would conclude that the *Caparo* test is satisfied and find that the authorities owed John a duty to take reasonable steps to stop him truanting. But if he can see some reason why it would *not* be 'fair, just and reasonable' to find that the authorities owed John such a duty of care, he would conclude that the *Caparo* test is *not* satisfied and find that the authorities did *not* owe John a duty of care.[12]

The place of proximity under each approach

We have already observed that the second stage in the three-stage *Caparo* test – that is, the requirement that there must have been a relationship of 'proximity' between the claimant and the defendant – is redundant. However, this is not to say that the courts make no reference to the notion of the proximity in applying the *Caparo* test. Suppose, for example, that the courts have to determine whether or not A owed B a duty to take care not to do *x* and the case is a 'novel' one – it has not already been established that A owed B such a duty of care. Suppose further that it is accepted that it was reasonably foreseeable that B would suffer some kind of harm if A did *x*.

---

[10] Judge Little might reply, 'Of course we should aim to do justice in individual cases, but *one* judge *acting alone* is rarely a *good* judge of where justice lies in an individual case. It is better that our sense of justice should be guided by the many thousands of judgments that have accumulated over the years – if there is *no* support in those judgments for the proposition that it would be "fair, just and reasonable" to find a duty of care was owed in an individual case, I would hesitate long and hard before finding that it would, nonetheless, still be "fair, just and reasonable" to find a duty of care was owed. Moreover, we should not just aim to do justice in individual cases – we should also ensure that the law is sufficiently certain and predictable to allow people to know where they stand. The only way we can do this – in approaching the issue of whether or not a duty of care was owed in a 'novel' case – is to adopt the incremental approach to the issue of whether a duty of care was owed in such a case.' For a defence of the incremental approach along these lines, see McHugh J's decision in *Perre v Apand Pty Ltd* (1999) 198 CLR 180, at [80]–[81], [88]–[92].

[11] 'Activist' because this approach to applying the *Caparo* test is liable to be adopted by judicial activists such as Judge Large, who are impatient of the existing precedents and are unafraid to remould the law to fit their vision of what it should say.

[12] The alert reader will spot that the activist approach to applying the *Caparo* test is just a rehashed version of the *Anns* two-stage approach to finding whether or not a duty of care was owed in a 'novel' case.

If the courts adopt the incremental approach to determine whether or not A owed B a duty to take care not to do *x*, their next step will be to see whether the existing case law suggests that it might be 'fair, just and reasonable' to find that A owed B such a duty of care. If it does not, then the courts will usually conclude that A did not owe B such a duty of care because there was no relationship of 'proximity' between them. If, on the other hand, the existing case law does suggest that it might be 'fair, just and reasonable' to find that A owed B a duty to take care not to do *x*, the courts will find that there *was* a relationship of 'proximity' between the parties, and then go on to determine whether there is any reason why it would *not* be 'fair, just and reasonable' to find that A owed B such a duty of care.

What if a judge adopts the activist approach to determine whether or not A owed B a duty to take care not to do *x*? Foreseeability of harm having been established, an activist judge will go on to see whether there is any reason why it would not be 'fair, just and reasonable' to find that A owed B such a duty of care. If he cannot find one, he will say that the second and third stages of the *Caparo* three-stage test have been satisfied and conclude that A owed B a duty of care. But if there is a reason why it would not be 'fair, just and reasonable' to find that A owed B a duty of care, he will find that the *Caparo* three-stage test has been failed. If A and B are strangers and our activist judge *would* have been willing to find that A owed B a duty of care had they been in a *special relationship*, then he might well say that the *Caparo* three-stage test has not been satisfied in *this* case because there was no 'proximity' between A and B.[13] But he will otherwise simply say that the *Caparo* three-stage test is not satisfied in this case because it would not be 'fair, just and reasonable' to find that A owed B a duty to take care not to do *x*.[14]

Fair, just and reasonable

Whichever approach one takes in applying the *Caparo* test, a duty of care will not be found in a 'novel' case if it would not be 'fair, just and reasonable' to find that such a duty of care was owed. When will it *not* be 'fair, just and reasonable' to find that one person owed another a duty of care?[15] The easiest way for a novice to approach this question is to consider a number of situations – some made up, some drawn from the case law – where the courts will *refuse* to find that one person owed another a duty of care even though it was reasonably foreseeable that a lack of care on the first person's part would result in the second person suffering some kind of harm. If you can understand why the

---

[13] So in the case of the wicked stranger (discussed below, at pp. 197–201) or the sleepy lorry driver (discussed below, at pp. 208–11), a judicial activist might well rationalise his finding that no duty of care was owed by saying that there was no 'proximity' between the parties. However, the *real* reason for his finding that no duty of care was owed will be that it would not be 'fair, just and reasonable' to find that a duty of care was owed.

[14] He might also observe that given that the third stage of the *Caparo* three-stage test is not satisfied, it does not really matter whether or not there was a relationship of 'proximity' between A and B – and thereby evade entirely the difficult issue of when such a relationship will exist.

[15] On this issue, see, generally, Stapleton 1998, 73–83.

courts will refuse to find that a duty of care was owed *in these situations*, you will gain a better understanding as to when *generally* it will not be 'fair, just and reasonable' to find that one person owed another a duty of care.

The successful inventor

Suppose that John made a tidy living manufacturing mousetraps. Unfortunately, this came to an end when Fred invented and marketed a mousetrap – the 'Mousehunter' – that was better than John's: all John's customers flocked to buy the 'Mousehunter' and John went out of business. John now wants to sue Fred in negligence, claiming that Fred owed him a duty not to market the 'Mousehunter'. John will of course lose his case. Even though it was reasonably foreseeable that someone like John would go out of business if Fred marketed the 'Mousehunter', it would *not* be 'fair, just and reasonable' to find that Fred owed John a duty not to market the 'Mousehunter' because it was perfectly reasonable – and, indeed, desirable – for Fred to put the 'Mousehunter' onto the market. So the lesson we can draw from this example is that it will not be 'fair, just and reasonable' to find that A owed B a duty to take care not to do *x* if it was reasonable or desirable for A to do *x*.[16]

The improvident testator

Suppose that Tom, a multi-millionaire, was diagnosed as having only three months to live. He put all his affairs in order, drawing up a will which provided that Lara was to inherit 'My country mansion, Xanadu, and all its contents'. Shortly before he died, Tom decided on a whim to make a statement about the vanity of personal possessions by setting fire to Xanadu. The mansion and all its contents were completely destroyed. As a result, when Tom died, Lara inherited nothing. Had Tom not done what he did, Lara would have inherited property worth £5,000,000.

Could Lara sue Tom's estate, claiming that he owed her a duty not to do what he did? Of course not – and this is so even though it was reasonably foreseeable that Lara would be made worse off if Tom did what he did. Why would it not be 'fair, just and reasonable' to find that Tom owed Lara a duty of care in this case? The reason is that even though it was not reasonable for Tom to do what he did, Tom had a perfect right to do what he did. Before he died, he could do what he liked with his property – so long, of course, as he did not endanger anyone else or breach any binding undertakings that he had made to anyone else. So – it will not be 'fair, just and reasonable' to find that A owed B a duty to take care not to do *x* if A had a perfect right to do *x*.[17]

---

[16] For the same reason, if B applies for a job with C and A, B's former employer, is asked to supply C with a reference for B, A will *not* owe B a duty to take care that he does not supply C with a reference that is *fair and accurate* – and this is so even if a fair and accurate reference would be so damaging to B as to extinguish B's chances of getting a job from C: *Lawton v BOC Transhield* [1987] 2 All ER 608. The reason for this is that it would be reasonable – and indeed desirable – for A to supply C with a reference that is fair and accurate. The *only* duty A will owe B in this situation is a duty to take care that he does not supply C with a reference that is *unfairly* damaging about B: see above, pp. 144–5.

[17] Similarly, if A commits suicide by shooting himself and B, A's mother, comes across A's body in the immediate aftermath of his shooting himself and develops a psychiatric illness as a result, B will not be able to sue A's estate, claiming that A owed her a duty not to shoot himself: see *Greatorex v Greatorex* [2000] 1 WLR 1970 (discussed above, pp. 102–3). The reason why no

The dilatory highway authority

In *Stovin* v *Wise*,[18] Stovin was knocked off his motorcycle and severely injured when Wise ran into him in her car. At the time of the accident, Stovin was riding along Station Road in Wymondham. Wise was attempting to turn right into Station Road from Cemetery Road. Cemetery Road joined Station Road at an acute angle and between the two roads, at the point where they met, was a raised bank with a high fence on top of it. The existence of this bank, which was owned by British Rail, meant that drivers like Wise who attempted to join Station Road from Cemetery Road, could not directly see whether anything was coming along Station Road until they had nosed out into the road; before then they could only tell whether anything was coming along by listening for the sound of traffic and – at night – looking for the light cast by approaching headlights. Wise did not keep a proper lookout when turning into Station Road and the accident with Stovin was the consequence. Wise was therefore held liable in negligence to compensate Stovin for his injuries.

However, Wise attempted[19] to recoup some of the money she had to pay to Stovin by bringing a claim in contribution against Norfolk City Council. The council had had the power under s 79 of the Highways Act 1980[20] to order British Rail to remove the bank between Station Road and Cemetery Road but had not exercised that power, despite concerns about the number of accidents that the presence of the bank caused at that junction. Wise argued that the council were also liable in negligence to compensate Stovin for his injuries and that the council should therefore shoulder some of the burden of compensating Stovin for those injuries. Obviously, to make out her claim, Wise had to show that the council owed Stovin a duty to take reasonable steps to get the bank between Station Road and Cemetery Road removed. And this is where her claim fell down. By a bare majority, the House of Lords refused to find that the council had owed Stovin such a duty of care – even though it was reasonably foreseeable that people like Stovin would be injured if the bank between Station Road and Cemetery Road were not removed. There were a couple of reasons why it would not have been 'fair, just and reasonable' to find that the council owed Stovin a duty of care in this case. The major one went as follows.

Section 79(1) of the Highways Act 1980 *did* give the council the power to eliminate the danger posed by the existence of the bank at the junction between Station Road and Cemetery Road. But, having granted the council that power,

---

duty of care will have been owed here was that A was perfectly entitled to shoot himself, so long as he did not physically endanger anyone else in doing so. For another situation where a duty of care will be denied on the ground that the defendant was perfectly entitled to act as he did, see *Stephens* v *Anglian Water Authority* [1987] 1 WLR 1381 (discussed above, pp. 118–19).

[18] [1996] AC 923.

[19] Actually, it was Wise's liability insurers who attempted to recoup the money from Norfolk County Council – it was they who had to cover Wise's liability to pay Stovin damages.

[20] Section 79(1) of the Highways Act 1980 provides: 'When the highway authority ... deem it necessary for the prevention of danger arising from obstruction to the view of persons using the highway to impose restrictions with respect to any land at ... any junction of the highway with a road ... the authority *may* ... serve a notice ... on the owner or occupier of the land, directing him to alter any wall ... so as to cause it to conform with any requirements specified in the notice' (emphasis added). Section 79(17) of the same Act defines 'wall' as including any 'bank'.

s 79(1) of the 1980 Act also gave the council a *discretion* as to whether or not to use it. Parliament therefore intended that the council should be free to decide whether or not to eliminate the danger posed by the existence of the bank at the junction between Station Road and Cemetery Road. This freedom was not unlimited: Parliament did not intend that the council should be free to refuse to do anything about the bank if it would have been utterly irrational to do so.[21] But if it would *not* have been utterly irrational to leave the bank as it was, Parliament intended that the council should be *free* to decide whether or not to have the bank removed. And if Parliament intended that the council should be free to decide whether or not to have the bank removed, then the courts – which, under our constitution, are subordinate to Parliament – could *not* find that the council owed a duty to people like Stovin to take reasonable steps to have the bank removed.[22]

[21] *Important note.* Had the council not done anything about the danger when it would have been utterly irrational not to do so, it would have – in the terminology used by administrative lawyers – acted *ultra vires* (beyond the bounds of) its powers to eliminate dangers affecting the road. A further point of terminology: an utterly irrational decision – that is, one which no rational person could have made – is said by administrative lawyers to be '*Wednesbury* unreasonable', after the case in which the Court of Appeal first ruled that a public authority which was vested with a discretion would act outside its powers if it exercised that discretion in a way which 'was so absurd that no sensible person could ever dream that it lay within the powers of the authority': *Associated Picture Houses Ltd* v *Wednesbury Corp.* [1948] 1 KB 223, 229 (per Lord Greene MR, giving the example of dismissing a teacher because she had red hair).

[22] *Important note.* This assumes, of course, that Parliament intended that the only limit on the council's discretion as to what to do about dangers affecting users of the road was that it should not exercise its discretion in a *Wednesbury* unreasonable way. Let's say that if this was what Parliament intended, it intended to grant the council a *virtually unfettered* discretion as to what to do about dangers affecting users of the road. It was common ground among the judges in the House of Lords in *Stovin* v *Wise* that Parliament *did* intend to grant the council in *Stovin* v *Wise* such a discretion – but it should be noted that public bodies do *not* have a virtually unfettered discretion as to how and when to exercise *all* the powers granted them by Parliament. For example, suppose that Parliament gave a council the power to take children in its area into care and that it intended that that power should be used *whenever* it was reasonable to think that a child was in danger. In such a case, the council would have *no effective* discretion as to when to use its power to take children into care. It follows that it will not be necessary – for the purposes of showing that the council acted *ultra vires* its powers in failing to take a child into care – to show that the council acted in a *Wednesbury* unreasonable way in failing to take the child into care: a mere finding that it failed to act when it was reasonable to think a child was in danger would be sufficient. And if the council failed to take a child into care when it was in danger, no *constitutional* objection could be made to the courts' finding that the council owed the child a duty to take it into care. The reason is that Parliament did not intend that the council should have been free to refuse to take that child into care. To take another example, Parliament may also have intended, in giving the council the power to take children into care, that the council should have a *limited* discretion as to how to look after any children that it did take into care. For example, it may have intended that the council should be free to choose what arrangements to make for the upkeep of the children in its care *so long as those arrangements would meet with the approval of a professional child care expert.* Again, if this is the case, it would not be necessary – for the purposes of showing that the council acted *ultra vires* its powers in making arrangements for the upkeep of the children in its care – to show that the council acted in a *Wednesbury* unreasonable way in bringing up the children in its care in the way it did. All that would need to be shown is that the public body kept the children in its care in conditions that would be criticised by a professional child care expert. And, again, if the council raised one of the children in its care in conditions that would be criticised by a professional child care expert, no *constitutional* objection could be made to the courts' finding that the council owed the child a duty not to raise him in those conditions. The reason for this is, again, that Parliament did not intend that the council should be free to raise the child in such conditions.

So – the council could not possibly have had a duty to take reasonable steps to eliminate the danger posed by the existence of the bank *if it would not have been utterly irrational of the council to leave the bank as it was*. Lord Hoffmann, giving the leading judgment in the House of Lords, found that it would *not* have been unreasonable or irrational for the council not to have done anything about the bank: it could not, therefore, be argued that the council owed Stovin, or anyone else, a duty to take reasonable steps to eliminate the danger posed by the existence of the bank.[23]

The lesson we can drawn from all this is that it will not be 'fair, just and reasonable' to find that A owed B a duty to take care not to do *x* if it would be constitutionally improper to find that A owed B such a duty – and this will be the case if Parliament intended that A should be free to do *x*.[24] However, it is

---

[23] In *Gorringe* v *Calderdale MBC* [2004] 1 WLR 1057, the House of Lords unanimously held that *Stovin* v *Wise* had been correctly decided. However, in reaching this conclusion their Lordships did not place much emphasis on the fact that the council was authorised by Parliament to decide for itself whether or not to do anything about the danger at the junction between Cemetery Road and Station Road. Instead, it preferred to justify the decision in *Stovin* v *Wise* on the ground that the mere fact that a public authority has a power (or a public law duty) to deal with a problem cannot justify its being subjected to a common law duty to take reasonable steps to deal with that problem: ibid., at [32] (per Lord Hoffmann). For an explanation of why it would not be 'fair, just and reasonable' to impose such a duty of care in such a situation see below, pp. 203–5 ('the incompetent local authority').

[24] *Important note.* There are some confusing *dicta* in the case law which seem to contradict the position taken in the text: see, for example, *Barrett* v *Enfield London Borough Council* [2001] 2 AC 550, at 583 (per Lord Hutton); *Phelps* v *Hillingdon London Borough Council* [2001] 2 AC 619, at 653 (per Lord Slynn); and *Gorringe* v *Calderdale Metropolitan Borough Council* [2004] 1 WLR 1057, at [4]–[5] (per Lord Steyn, quoting with approval Craig 2003, at 898). Lord Slynn's *dictum* in *Phelps* is representative: '[T]he fact that acts which are claimed to be negligent are carried out *within the ambit of a statutory discretion* is not in itself a reason why it should be held that no claim for negligence can be brought in respect of them. It is only where what is done has involved the weighing of competing public interests or has been dictated by considerations on which Parliament could not have intended that the courts would substitute their views for the views of ministers or officials that the courts will hold that the issue is non-justiciable on the ground that the decision was made in the exercise of a statutory discretion' (emphasis added). If this is right then – contrary to what was held in *Stovin* v *Wise* – a public body *could* be held liable in negligence for acting in a particular way *even if it was authorised by Parliament to act in that way*. This cannot be right. Let us put aside for a second the fact it would be constitutionally improper for the courts to find that a public body owed someone a duty not to do *x* when that body had been authorised by Parliament to do *x*. Adopting Lord Slynn's view might also give rise to the following paradoxical result. Suppose that Parliament gave a public body the power to do *x* and also gave it a discretion as to whether or not to do *x*. (It does not matter for our present purposes whether the discretion was virtually unfettered or limited.) Suppose further that the public body did *x* and its doing *x* was within the ambit of the statutory discretion that Parliament granted it – in other words, Parliament intended that the public body should have been free to do *x* in the situation in which it found itself. Suppose further that A suffered some kind of loss as a result of the public body's doing *x*. Because the public body did not exceed its powers in doing *x*, nobody could have brought a claim for judicial review to stop the public body doing *x*. But on Lord Slynn's view, this does *not* necessarily mean that A could *not* sue the public body in negligence for compensation for the loss he suffered as a result of the public body's doing *x*. But if A *were* allowed to sue, this would produce a very strange result – in effect the law would have allowed the public body to harm A but would then allow A to sue the public body in negligence for damages for the harm suffered by him. This would not be so puzzling if A's claim was an example of what we have called 'compensation without wrongdoing' (see above, pp. 30–1) but an action for negligence is *not* an action for 'compensation without wrongdoing'. Of course, none of this is meant to question the correctness of the House of Lords' decisions in cases such as *Barrett* and *Phelps* that it was *arguable* in those cases that a claim in negligence could be made against the defendant public bodies. It *was* arguable in both those cases that the defendant public bodies exceeded their powers in acting as they did (in *Barrett*'s case, by bringing up the claimant

---

important not to misapply this lesson. Suppose that a council was authorised under an Act of Parliament to install traffic lights wherever it saw fit within a certain area. The council installed a set of traffic lights at a T-junction outside Wendy's house. Unfortunately, the noise made by the traffic lights kept her up at nights. Moreover, the traffic lights were defective. As a result, one day Eric and Vijay approached the T-junction at right angles to each other and were both given a green signal (for 'Go') by the traffic lights at the junction. They therefore both crossed the junction at the same time and crashed into each other.

Now – in this situation, Wendy will have no chance of establishing that the council owed her a duty not to install the set of traffic lights at the T-junction outside her house.[25] We can presume that: (*a*) Parliament intended to confer a virtually unfettered discretion[26] on the council as to when and how it would use its power to install traffic lights; and (*b*) it was not utterly irrational for the council to install a set of traffic lights at the T-junction outside Wendy's house. Given this, Parliament intended that the council should be free to decide whether or not to install traffic lights at that T-junction, and it would therefore be constitutionally improper for the courts to find that the council actually had a duty not to install the traffic lights there. However, Eric and Vijay should have no problem in establishing that the council owed *them* a duty to take care not to install a *defective* set of traffic lights at the T-junction outside her house.[27] While Parliament intended that the council should be free to decide whether or not to install traffic lights at that T-junction, it never intended that the council should be free to install a defective set of traffic lights at that T-junction.[28]

The wicked stranger

Suppose that Sarah was walking behind an obviously blind man, Carl, when she realised that he was walking towards an open, unprotected, manhole. She could have easily called out a warning to Carl and told him what was ahead, but she chose not to do so. As a result, Carl continued on his way, fell into the manhole and was severely injured. The courts have traditionally taken the stance that in the absence of some kind of special relationship between Sarah

---

in a way which disrupted his education and his ability to form attachments to other people; in the *Phelps* case, by failing to make adequate provision for the special educational needs of the claimants) and so it was arguable that no constitutional objection could have been made to the courts' finding that a duty of care was owed by the defendant public bodies in both those cases.

[25] It should be assumed for the purposes of this example that the noise created by the traffic lights was a necessary by-product of their operation; that is, they had to make the noise they did. So it would not be open to Wendy to argue in this case that the council owed her a duty to take care not to install unduly noisy traffic lights – she would have to argue that the council owed her a duty not to install the traffic lights at all.

[26] It will be recalled (see n. 22, above) that a public body will enjoy a virtually unfettered discretion to do *x* if the only limit Parliament intended to place on its exercise was that it should not be exercised in a *Wednesbury* unreasonable way.

[27] To do this, they could invoke the 'physical danger principle' set out above, at pp. 66–7: it was reasonably foreseeable that people like Eric and Vijay's persons and property would be harmed if the council installed a defective set of traffic lights at the T-junction.

[28] For a more lengthy statement of this obvious point, see Lord Slynn's judgment in *Barrett* v *Enfield Borough Council* [2001] 2 AC 550, at 570–1.

and Carl, Sarah will not have owed Carl a duty to call out a warning to him – and this is so even though it was eminently foreseeable that if she did not call out a warning, Carl would fall into the manhole and suffer severe, and possibly fatal, injuries.

Why have the courts taken the view that it would not be 'fair, just and reasonable' to find that Sarah owed Carl a duty of care in this situation? Three reasons can be given. Undoubtedly, the most important is that the courts are concerned to preserve individual liberties.[29] To find that Sarah owed Carl a duty here to save him from harm when she did nothing to invite that duty on herself[30] would be to subject her to a form of 'forced labour'.[31] While Carl was walking towards the manhole, Sarah would not be allowed to pursue her own ends but would instead be forced to serve Carl's interests. In other words, she would be forced to act as Carl's servant.

The second reason why the courts have traditionally taken the view that it would not be 'fair, just and reasonable' to find that Sarah owed Carl a duty of care in the situation we are considering is that the law has to leave people some room to do the right thing *of their own free will*. The conservative commentator Dinesh D'Souza explains why:

> [Suppose] that I am walking down the street, eating a sandwich, when I am approached by a hungry man [who] wants to share my sandwich. Now if I give him the sandwich, I have done a good deed, and I feel good about it. The hungry man is grateful, and even if he cannot repay me for my kindness, possibly he will try to help someone else when he has the chance. So this is a transaction that benefits the giver as well as the receiver. But see what happens [if the law *requires* me to give the hungry man my sandwich]. The government takes my sandwich from me by force. Consequently, I am a reluctant giver. The government then bestows my sandwich upon the hungry man. Instead of showing me gratitude, however, the man feels entitled to this benefit. In other words, the involvement of the [law] has utterly stripped the transaction of its moral value, even though the result is exactly the same.[32]

The third reason why the courts have traditionally been unwilling to find that Sarah owed Carl a duty of care in the situation we are considering is the chronic

---

[29] For another case where a duty of care was denied out of a concern to preserve individual liberties, see *Greatorex* v *Greatorex* [2000] 1 WLR 1970 (denying that the claimant's son owed the claimant a duty to take care not to harm himself because to do so would 'create a significant ... limitation on a person's freedom of action': ibid., at 1985 (per Cazalet J)).

[30] *Important note.* It should be noted that in all the situations where it is established that A will have a duty to take steps to save B from harm, A can be said to have brought the duty on himself – either by 'assuming a responsibility' to B (above, pp. 120–40); or by putting B in danger of suffering the harm in question (pp. 153–6); or by dissuading others from saving B from the harm in question (pp. 157–61); or by taking on the job of saving B from that harm (pp. 140–8); or by taking control of some thing or person which may cause B to suffer the harm in question (pp. 161–4); or by occupying land (pp. 165–78); or by becoming B's landlord (pp. 178–80); or by becoming B's employer (pp. 180–1); or by becoming a bailee of B's property (pp. 181–2); or by carrying B in his car (pp. 182–3); or by looking after B (pp. 183–5).

[31] Nozick 1974, 169.

[32] D'Souza 2002, 81-2. See also Weir 2001, 1: 'The understandable urge to bring legal standards up to those of delicate morality should be resisted, or there would be no room for generosity or for people to go beyond the call of legal duty.'

uncertainty in the law that such a finding would create. For if we find that Sarah owed Carl a duty of care in this situation, where do we stop? As Richard Epstein points out, 'Once one decides that ... an individual is required under some circumstances to act at his own cost for the exclusive benefit of another, then it is very hard to set out in a principled manner the limits of social interference with individual liberty.'[33] He asks, for example: If we admit that someone crossing a bridge has a duty to throw a rope to someone drowning in the waters below, would someone who is asked to donate a very small amount of money to charity to help save a life have a legal duty to make that donation? If a patient needed a life-saving operation which only one surgeon in the world could perform, would that surgeon come under a legal duty to travel to the patient's bedside and perform that operation – assuming of course that someone could be found who would be willing to cover his travel expenses?[34] It is hard to see whether or not a 'duty to rescue' would exist in these cases. This is unsurprising: as Epstein observes, as soon as one allows that there is a duty to rescue in cases such as Sarah's case or the case of the drowning man, 'it becomes impossible to tell where liberty ends and obligation begins'.[35]

Despite this, the rule that says that Sarah did not owe Carl a duty to warn him that he was about to fall into a manhole has come under heavy criticism. Three principal arguments are advanced in favour of the suggestion that the law should recognise a duty to rescue in cases such as Sarah's. It is said, first of all, that society as a whole would be better off if the law recognised that there was a duty to rescue in cases such as Sarah's.[36] It is far from clear that this is the case. It is likely that finding a duty to rescue in cases such as Sarah's would generate a huge amount of expensive litigation in order to probe the scope of this duty to rescue. Moreover, it is not clear that imposing a legal duty to rescue in cases such as Sarah's would result in *more* people being saved from harm; it is in fact entirely conceivable that were a duty to rescue to be imposed in cases such as Sarah's, *fewer* people would be rescued from danger by other people.

For example, suppose that Beth comes across Ian drowning in a pond in a public park. Assume that the law says that 'If A can easily rescue B from suffering some kind of physical harm, then A will owe B a duty to do so'. In this situation, Beth might well think, 'If I walk away, and this lad drowns, I may be held liable – but only if someone finds out that I failed to save him from drowning. That's not very likely: I'm on my own at the moment and if I'm caught, I can always pretend that I thought he was splashing about in the pond for fun. On the other hand, if I attempt to rescue him, and for some reason fail to do so, everyone will know from my wet clothes and

---

[33] Epstein 1973, 198.

[34] Ibid., 198–9.

[35] Ibid., 199. The same point is made – with reference to the French law in this area (where a duty to rescue is recognised) – in Tomlinson 2000. For a different view, see Weinrib 1980, 268–79. Weinrib argues that a duty to rescue between strangers should be limited to cases where the potential rescuer could not, or could not easily, *charge* the person in danger for rescuing him, and that if the duty to rescue were limited in this way, its scope would become easy enough to mark out. However, this assumes that the law on when someone can charge someone else for rescuing him from danger is relatively clear; but it is not.

[36] Ames 1908, 112.

so on that I was in a position to rescue him and I will probably end up being sued for failing to rescue him. My best option is therefore to walk away and not get involved.' So Beth may well end up leaving Ian to his fate – when had the law *not* said that there is a duty to rescue in 'easy rescue' cases, Beth might well have tried to save Ian, safe in the knowledge that if she failed, she could not be sued.[37]

It is argued, secondly, that the law should encourage people to act morally – and imposing a duty to rescue in cases such as Sarah's would be one way of doing that.[38] An immediate objection to this is that it is doubtful whether someone can be said to act *morally* if they rescue someone solely because they are required to do so by law. This point is not, however, conclusive. The law *can* encourage people to act morally by forcing them to do the right thing over and over again, thereby habituating them to do the right thing. The idea is that people – once they are habituated to do the right thing – will then learn to *enjoy* doing the right thing and thereby start to act morally. That is, they will start to do the right thing because it's the right thing to do.[39] However, it is doubtful whether imposing a duty to rescue in cases such as Sarah's would have the effect of habituating people to rescue others in peril: the number of times a given person would incur such a duty would be far too infrequent for such a person to make a habit of rescuing other people in peril and thereby get into a position where he could start to enjoy rescuing other people and do it for its own sake.

A third argument in favour of recognising a duty to rescue in cases such as Sarah's is that not to do so puts good people at a disadvantage.[40] In the absence of a duty to rescue in cases such as Sarah's, the only people who will incur the risks and inconvenience involved in rescuing other people from peril will be good people – wicked people will simply have no incentive to save other people from danger. The argument is an attractive one, but suffers from a fatal flaw. To see why this is so, we need to distinguish between two kinds of rescue cases. The first is an 'easy rescue' case – where A can save B from suffering some kind of harm at no, or little, inconvenience to himself. The second is a 'hard rescue' case – where A can save B from suffering some kind of harm, but he can only do so by incurring a substantial risk or a great deal of inconvenience. Now – if the law does not recognise a duty to rescue in 'easy rescue' cases, then the only people who will carry out rescues in such cases will, of course, be good people – but they will *not* be put at a disadvantage as a result because, by definition, 'easy rescue' cases are ones where someone can save someone else from harm at no, or very little, cost to himself. It is only if the law does not recognise a duty to rescue in

---

[37] To accommodate this objection, most states in the United States have enacted 'Good Samaritan laws', which typically provide that 'Any person who, in good faith, renders emergency medical care or assistance to an injured person at the scene of an accident or other emergency without the expectation of receiving or intending to receive compensation from such injured person for such service, shall not be liable in civil damages for any act or omission, not constituting gross negligence, in the course of such care or assistance.' See GS&Z, 100–1.

[38] See Tunc 1966, 43; and Rudzinski 1966, 122. It is of course assumed that Sarah has a moral obligation to save Carl: the point is discussed in Menlowe 1993.

[39] The idea goes back to Aristotle: see his *Nicomachean Ethics*, x. 9. 1179^b–1180^a.

[40] See Honoré 1966, 239.

'hard rescue' cases that good people will be put at a disadvantage.[41] So this third argument can only justify the existence of a duty to rescue in 'hard rescue' cases, not 'easy rescue' cases – and unfortunately, the only cases where people suggest there should be a duty to rescue are 'easy rescue' cases, such as Sarah's case.

So – while finding that a duty to rescue was owed in cases such as Sarah's might do some good, it is doubtful whether that good would be substantial enough to outweigh the harm that would be done by recognising the existence of such a duty to rescue.[42] Given this, it is doubtful whether it would be 'fair, just and reasonable' to find that a duty to rescue was owed in cases such as Sarah's.

The indifferent policeman

Suppose that Karen was attacked in the street by Alan. Suppose further that Paul, a policeman, saw this happen but did nothing to stop Alan attacking Karen. Under English law, Karen would not be able to sue Paul in negligence for failing to rescue her: she would not be able to establish that Paul owed her[43] a duty to take reasonable steps to save her from being attacked by Alan.[44]

That may not actually matter much to her: she would almost certainly be able to sue Paul under the Human Rights Act 1998[45] on the ground that his failure to stop Alan attacking her violated her rights under Article 3 of the European Convention on Human Rights not to be subjected to 'inhuman or degrading treatment'.[46] However, for our present purposes, it is highly relevant

---

[41] Is even this true? The absence of a duty to rescue in 'hard rescue' cases means that a good person who rescues someone else from danger in a 'hard rescue' case gets a lot of credit and recognition, which credit and recognition would disappear were a duty to rescue to be imposed in 'hard rescue' cases.

[42] There is also an issue as to how far one can justify interfering with individual liberties on the ground that doing so is for the 'common good'. We would not, after all, allow surgeons to extract a terminally ill 80-year-old's heart and lungs against his will on the grounds that a young patient needs them and transplanting them into the young patient would do more good than harm.

[43] *Important note.* Of course, Paul owed a duty to the public at large to prevent the attack and so committed a *public wrong* in doing nothing to assist Karen. (The concept of a public wrong is explained above, p. 4.) As a result Paul could be subjected to criminal proceedings for failing to assist Karen. However, those who suffer loss as a result of the commission of a public wrong are rarely allowed to sue for compensation for that loss. In order to sue Paul, Karen would have to show that Paul committed a wrong *in relation to her* in failing to stop Alan attacking her, and she will be unable to do this.

[44] See *Osman* v *Ferguson* [1993] 4 All ER 344 (if A is very likely to be attacked by a criminal who is currently on the run, the police will not owe A a duty to catch the criminal before he attacks A); *Ancell* v *McDermott* [1993] 4 All ER 355 (a policeman who comes across a dangerous oil slick in the middle of a road will not owe a duty to oncoming motorists to warn them of the danger). It should be noted that English law is very much out on its own in taking this stance: other common law jurisdictions might well find that Paul *did* owe Karen a duty to take reasonable steps to save her from being attacked by Alan. See, for example, *O'Rourke* v *Schacht* [1976] 1 SCR 53 (held, a policeman who becomes aware that there is an unprotected hole in the middle of the road will owe a duty to oncoming motorists to warn them of the danger).

[45] See Chapter 43, below, for an account of when someone will be entitled to sue someone else under the 1998 Act.

[46] You might think that the only way a policeman could violate Karen's rights under Article 3 of the European Convention on Human Rights (ECHR) was by *his* treating her in an inhuman or degrading way. However, the European Court of Human Rights takes a much wider view of the scope of people's rights under Article 3 of the ECHR. It has held that a public authority *may* violate someone's rights under Article 3 if it *fails* to take reasonable steps to prevent that person being subjected to inhuman or degrading treatment *by someone else*: see, for example, *A* v *United Kingdom* (1999) 27 EHRR 611 and *Z* v *United Kingdom* [2001] 2 FLR 612. A similarly wide view is taken of the other rights set out in the ECHR. For example, the police will violate A's right to life under

to inquire why exactly the courts in England have taken the view that it would *not* be 'fair, just or reasonable' to find that Paul owed Karen a duty of care in this situation.

Intelligent discussion of this issue has long been impeded by the habit academics have of saying that Paul enjoys an *immunity* from being sued in negligence here.[47] Such language suggests that the courts give Paul *special treatment* when they refuse to find that Paul owed Karen a duty to take reasonable steps to stop Alan attacking her.[48] Anyone who thinks in these terms will find it *very* difficult to understand why it would *not* be 'fair, just and reasonable' to find that Paul owed Karen a duty of care in this situation – it is, after all, very difficult to see why someone like Paul should be given special treatment by the courts.

However, it is clear that Paul is *not* being given any kind of special treatment here. Had a normal, private citizen failed to stop Alan attacking Karen, the courts would *not* find that *he* owed Karen a duty to take reasonable steps to stop Alan attacking her.[49] So in finding that *Paul* did not owe Karen a duty of care, the courts are treating Paul in the same way it would a normal, private citizen.[50] Those who would like the courts to hold that Paul owed Karen a duty of care in the situation we are considering are therefore really calling for the courts to treat Paul *more harshly* than they would a normal, private citizen who failed to stop Alan attacking Karen.[51]

Clearly, the courts think that it would not be 'fair, just and reasonable' to do this.[52] Why is this? Well – the *only* difference between Paul and a normal, private citizen who failed to save Karen from being attacked by Alan is that Paul was

---

Article 1 of the ECHR if they know that A is in danger of being killed by B and they fail to take reasonable steps to save A from being killed by B: *Osman* v *United Kingdom* [1999] FLR 193.

[47] See, for example, Lunney & Oliphant 2003, 127; Jones 2002, 74; Howarth 2002, 586; Wright J 2001, 83; Giliker 2000, 373; Markesinis 1999, 96; Hoyano 1999, passim; Monti 1999, 758.

[48] Cf. Hedley 2002, at 65, saying that the police are treated 'with special generosity by the courts'.

[49] This follows from the discussion of Sarah's case, above pp. 197–201.

[50] See Weir 2004, 17. Contra, M&D, 156: 'as a matter of policy [public bodies] are treated differently from private citizens and corporations for the purposes of the duty of care in negligence' (this is simply *not* true); Bell 2002, at xviii, remarking that the fact that 'The public-private divide is less sharp than it once was . . . [makes stark the] incongruity of [the law's applying] different rules for compensation between public and private sectors . . .' (but English law does *not* apply one set of rules to the private sector and one set to the public sector: it applies the same rules across the board); Howarth & O'Sullivan 2000, at 91, asking 'Should public authorities be in a special position with regard to negligence actions?' (suggesting that they are, when in fact they are not); and Bowman & Bailey 1984 and Bailey & Bowman 2000, arguing that public bodies are unnecessarily given special protection by the law of negligence – that the 'policy concerns' underlying this special treatment can be easily accommodated within the normal rules governing liability in negligence (but public bodies enjoy no such special treatment at the moment).

[51] See Feldthusen 1997, 24–9.

[52] See, in addition to the authorities cited at n. 44, above, *Hill* v *Chief Constable of West Yorkshire* [1989] AC 53 (police will *not* owe potential victims of criminal on the loose a duty to take reasonable steps to arrest the criminal); *Alexandrou* v *Oxford* [1993] 4 All ER 328 (police investigating a possible break-in at a shop will *not* owe the shopkeeper a duty to stop thieves taking goods out of the shop); and *Capital and Counties plc* v *Hampshire CC* [1997] QB 1004 (firemen summoned to fight a fire on someone's premises will *not* owe that someone a duty to get to the fire or, once there, a duty to fight the fire with a reasonable degree of care and skill).

employed to save people like Karen. It is hard to see why this should make a great difference to Paul's position vis-à-vis *Karen*.[53] Paul's employer might have good reason to complain about Paul's failure to save Karen – he paid Paul to save people like Karen and Paul failed to do this. However, Karen has no similar grounds for complaint.[54] *From her point of view* there is no moral difference between Paul and a normal, private citizen who might have failed to save her from being attacked by Alan. Given this, it would *not* be 'fair, just and reasonable' to find that Paul owed Karen a duty to save her from being attacked by Alan.[55]

The incompetent local authority

In *East Suffolk Rivers Catchment Board* v *Kent*,[56] the claimant's lands were flooded when a neighbouring river burst through a sea wall. The defendant river authority took on the job of repairing the sea wall but spent an excessively long time repairing the wall with the result that the claimant's land remained flooded for far longer than necessary. The claimant sued the defendant river authority, seeking to recover compensation for the extra damage done to his land due to its remaining flooded longer than necessary. The House of Lords dismissed the claimant's claim: they held that the defendant river authority had *not* owed the claimant a duty to repair the sea wall with a reasonable degree of care and skill.[57]

---

[53] The fact that Paul was being paid by his employers to save people like Karen from being attacked will, of couse, have had a big effect on Paul's *overall* legal position: Paul will have owed a duty to his employers to save Karen from being attacked and would therefore be liable to be disciplined for failing to assist Karen (as well as possibly facing criminal proceedings: see above, n. 43). Gray & Edelman 1998 argue that because Paul *took on the job* of saving people like Karen, he *should* be held to owe people like Karen a duty to take reasonable steps to save them from harm. But why? Why should Spiderman be subject to duties that he would not be subject to were he to put away his costume and remain plain old Peter Parker?

[54] It might be objected that Karen is a taxpayer and that therefore she *can* complain that she has not received the service from Paul that she (indirectly) paid him for. This is an attractive argument but it is not clear that those who would like people like Paul to be subject to a duty to rescue would want to say that such duties should only be owed to adult taxpayers.

[55] *Important note.* This is a *principled* argument for refusing to find that Paul owed Karen a duty of care in this situation. However, could a *pragmatic* argument not be made in favour of finding that a duty of care was owed here? Namely – 'It would be in the public interest to find that Paul owed Karen a duty of care here. Doing so would encourage people like Paul to do their jobs properly because they would know that they could be sued if they did not do their jobs properly and someone was harmed as a result.' While we would agree with one commentator that 'fraud, laziness, ineptitude and money-grabbing are the hallmark of Britain's public sector' (Leo McKinstry, 'Idle, greedy and up on a pedestal' *Sunday Telegraph*, 2nd May 2004), it is not clear that finding that a duty of care was owed in this kind of case would bring about any improvement in the dismal performance of public bodies in the UK. As Weir 1989 points out, expanding the scope of public bodies' liability in negligence only serves to starve them of the money they need to perform their services, as more and more of their funding is diverted into paying for litigation and making compensation payments to claimants.

[56] [1941] AC 74.

[57] Note that it again makes no sense here to say that the defendant river authority enjoyed an 'immunity' from being sued in negligence. The facts of the *East Suffolk* case were not such that the defendant river authority would normally be held to have owed the claimant a duty of care: it was not the defendant river authority's fault that the sea wall collapsed; they did not interfere with someone else's mending the sea wall; and the defendant river authority did not indicate to the claimant that he could safely rely on them to repair the sea wall with a reasonable degree of care and skill.

Why did the House of Lords think that it would not have been 'fair, just and reasonable' to find that the defendant river authority owed the claimant a duty of care here? Well – had the defendant river authority done *nothing*, the House of Lords thought that the claimant could not have asserted that they owed him a duty to take reasonable steps to mend the sea wall.[58] Given this, it would be paradoxical to find that once the defendants decided to do something about the sea wall, they owed the claimant a duty to mend the sea wall with a reasonable degree of care and skill. To make such a finding would make the defendants worse off than they would have been had they remained blithely indifferent to the claimant's plight and done nothing for him.[59]

This argument, though sound,[60] is incomplete – it still has to be shown why, if the defendant river authority had done *nothing*, it would not have been 'fair, just and reasonable' to find that the defendants owed the claimant a duty to take reasonable steps to repair the sea wall. One of the reasons for this has already been mentioned – it would have been constitutionally improper to find that the defendants owed the claimant a duty to take reasonable steps to mend the sea wall.[61] Parliament intended that the defendants should have a discretion as to how it would use its resources and the courts would have illegitimately interfered with this discretion had they found that the defendants owed the claimant a duty to take reasonable steps to repair the sea wall beside his land.

However, even if this constitutional objection could not have been made – say it would have been utterly irrational for the defendants not to have done something for the claimant here – another, deeper, reason can be given as to why it would not have been 'fair, just or reasonable' to find that the defendants in *East Suffolk* owed the claimant a duty to take reasonable steps to mend the sea wall beside his land. Suppose that the defendant river authority in *East Suffolk* had *not existed* at the time the claimant's land was flooded. If this were true, the claimant could not have contended that the *State* owed him a duty to take reasonable steps to mend the sea wall beside the claimant's land. For one thing, to make such a finding would have been constitutionally improper – it would have illegitimately fettered the State's discretion as to how best to make use of the resources available to it. For another, the interests of the claimant in seeing his land drained of water would simply not have been important enough to justify burdening the State with

---

[58] That this is correct has been made crystal clear by the decision of the House of Lords in *Gorringe* v *Calderdale Metropolitan Borough Council* [2004] 1 WLR 1057 (held: highway authority could not be held to have owed motorist a duty to put up warning sign telling her to slow down at a bend merely because it had the power to put up such a sign).

[59] Lord Atkin dissented on the ground that '[It is] established that a public authority whether doing an act which it is its duty to do, or doing an act which it is merely empowered to do, must in doing the act do it without negligence, or as it is put in some of the cases must not do it carelessly or improperly': [1941] AC 74, 90. But the authorities relied on by him as establishing this were all cases where a public body in carrying out some works it was empowered to do *caused some damage to the claimant*, not cases where the public body, having decided to confer a benefit on someone else, failed to confer that benefit on him in an expeditious manner.

[60] Cf. Lord Hoffmann in *Stovin* v *Wise* [1996] AC 923, 949: 'If [a] public authority is under no duty to act, either by virtue of its statutory powers or any other basis, it cannot be held liable because it has acted but has negligently failed to confer a benefit on the [claimant] or to protect him from loss.'

[61] See above, pp. 196–7.

an obligation to co-ordinate the resources and manpower necessary to mend the sea wall beside the claimant's land. So – if the defendant river authority in *East Suffolk* had not existed at the time the claimant's land was flooded, the claimant could not have contended that the State owed him a duty to take reasonable steps to mend the sea wall beside his land. Given this, it would be paradoxical to find that the defendant river authority in *East Suffolk* owed the claimant a duty to take reasonable steps to mend the sea wall beside his land. To make such a finding would render the State – viewed as a whole – worse off than it would have been had it never created the defendant river authority. It would – via the defendant river authority – come under an obligation to help the claimant out that it would never have been subject to had it not created the defendant river authority.[62]

It is for this reason that whenever a public authority fails to confer some benefit on A or protect A from suffering some kind of loss, the courts will invariably find that the *mere* fact that the public authority was in a position to help A *will not be enough* to justify their finding that the public authority owed A a duty to take reasonable steps to help him.[63] To do otherwise would be to make the State worse off than it would have been had it not created that authority in the first place.[64]

---

[62] To put it another way, had a duty of care been found in the *East Suffolk* case, the principle that 'no good deed goes unpunished' would have become part of the law of England: any attempt by the State to do some good would result in its being subjected to legal duties to do that good.

[63] See, for example, *Peabody Donation Fund* v *Sir Lindsay Parkinson & Co. Ltd* [1985] AC 210 (local authority which has powers to ensure that houses owned by claimants are being built in conformity to approved designs will not owe claimants a duty to exercise those powers); *Hill* v *Chief Constable of West Yorkshire* [1989] AC 53 (police authorities do not owe potential victims of criminal on the loose a duty to take reasonable steps to arrest the criminal); *Yuen Kun Yeu* v *Att-Gen for Hong Kong* [1988] AC 175 and *Davis* v *Radcliffe* [1990] 1 WLR 821 (banking authorities do not owe depositors with a bank a duty to take reasonable steps to see that the bank's affairs are properly run); *X* v *Bedfordshire CC* [1995] 2 AC 633 (local authority does not owe duty of care to children who are alleged to be victims of abuse in deciding whether or not to take those children into care); *Stovin* v *Wise* [1996] AC 923 (no duty owed by highway authority to motorists on road to remove line-of-sight obstructions that might endanger them, even when failure to do so would be completely irrational); *Hussain* v *Lancaster City Council* [2000] QB 1 (victims of racial harassment by council tenants are not owed duty by council to take reasonable steps to bring harassment to an end); *Gorringe* v *Calderdale Metropolitan Borough Council* [2004] 1 WLR 1057 (no duty owed by highway authority to warn motorists to slow down at dangerous bends); *Sutradhar* v *Natural Environment Research Council* [2004] EWCA Civ 175 (no duty owed by organisation carrying out hydrochemical survey of water supply in north-eastern Bangladesh to alert Bangladeshi government to presence of arsenic in water that was drunk by the claimants).

[64] *Important note.* A big exception to this was created by the decision of the House of Lords in *Anns* v *Merton LBC* [1978] AC 728, where it was held that a local authority which decided to inspect the foundations of houses being built in its area in order to ensure that they were being safely constructed would owe future occupants of the houses a duty to carry out the inspections with a reasonable degree of care and skill. This aspect of the decision in *Anns* has *never* been overruled though it has been questioned whether it is correct: see *Murphy* v *Brentwood DC* [1991] 1 AC 398, 457H (per Lord Mackay), 463G (per Lord Keith of Kinkel); *Stovin* v *Wise* [1996] AC 923, 948H–951A (per Lord Hoffmann). The only retrenchment that has taken place in relation to *Anns* (other than the abandonment of the two-stage test for determining whether a duty of care is owed in a 'novel' case) is in relation to what can be sued for if the local authority carries out its inspections carelessly with the result that a house is built on inadequate foundations and subsequently becomes dangerous to live in. In *Anns*, it was held that: (1) anyone living in the house could sue for compensation for harm to his or her person or property caused by the house being in a dangerous condition; *and* (2) the owner of the house could sue for compensation in respect of the cost of having the house made safe to live in. (1) may still be good law in England (though it is hard to see how this aspect

The drunken soldier

In *Barrett* v *Ministry of Defence*,[65] a soldier died after he had too much to drink at a party held in his barracks. It was argued that the soldier's commanding officer owed the soldier a duty to take reasonable steps to ensure that he did not drink too much at the party. The Court of Appeal rejected this claim, holding that it would not be 'fair, just and reasonable' to find that the commanding officer had owed the soldier such a duty.[66] Why was this? The court's reasoning seemed to run as follows:

> If we find that a duty of care was owed in *Barrett* then we will have to say – if we are going to be consistent – that whenever official parties are held in an army barracks, the commanding officers of the soldiers attending the party will owe them a duty to take reasonable steps to see that they do not drink too much. But taking this position could be positively harmful to soldiers who attend official army parties – if we take the position set out above, then we could make it *more* likely that soldiers will drink too much at official parties. This is for two reasons.
>
> First, if we take the position set out above then a soldier who attends an official army party will tend not to take steps himself to ensure that he does not drink too much – he will rely instead on his commanding officer to do that. But the commanding officer will not be as well placed as the soldier to judge whether the soldier has drunk too much. Given this, soldiers who rely on their commanding officers to stop them drinking too much are likely to end up drinking far more than soldiers who rely on their own judgment to tell them when they have had too much to drink.
>
> Secondly, if we take the position set out above, a soldier who attends an official party at his barracks will lack an important internal constraint on his drinking too much: the knowledge that if he drinks too much, he will have to bear the consequences of his drinking too much himself. If we take the position set out above, then a soldier who attends an official party at his barracks will have every reason to think, 'Well, if I drink too much and suffer as a result, there's always the chance I can sue the army for compensation for the harm suffered by me as a result of my excessive drinking.' It should be obvious that a soldier who thinks in this way is far more likely to drink too much at an official party than a soldier who knows that if he drinks excessively he will have to bear the consequences of his excessive drinking himself.

As the Court of Appeal observed in *Barrett*, '[It is] fair, just and reasonable for the law to leave a responsible adult to assume responsibility for his own actions in consuming alcoholic drink. No one is better placed to judge the amount that he can safely consume or to exercise control in his own interest as well as the interests of others. To dilute self-responsibility and to blame one adult for another's lack of self-control is neither just nor reasonable . . .'[67]

---

of the decision in *Anns* can survive the House of Lords' recent decision in *Gorringe* v *Calderdale MBC* [2004] 1 WLR 1057); however, (2) is no longer true: see *Murphy* v *Brentwood DC* [1991] 1 AC 398.

[65] [1995] 1 WLR 1217.

[66] However, once the soldier fell into a drunken stupor and the officers in charge undertook to look after him, they owed him a duty to look after him with a reasonable degree of care and skill: ibid., 1223. See above, p. 141.

[67] Ibid., 1224F-G. Of course, it is harder to make out such an argument when a *child* is involved – as a result, the law is more willing to find that people owe *children* duties to take steps to see that they do not do things that are liable to harm them. See, for example, *E (a child)* v *Souls Garages Ltd*, The Times, 23 January 2001 (petrol station manager will owe duty to child not to sell him petrol if it is reasonably foreseeable that the child is buying the petrol to sniff).

The absent-minded neighbour

Suppose that Carl and Nita were neighbours. Carl one day left his house, leaving a ground-floor window open. Tom, a thief, gained access to Carl's house through the window while Carl was away. Tom then went into Carl's back garden, hopped over the fence into Nita's garden and from there gained access to Nita's house. Tom proceeded to steal a substantial quantity of valuables from Nita's house. Could Nita sue Carl in negligence for the loss of these valuables? In *Smith* v *Littlewoods Ltd*,[68] Lord Goff thought that even if it was reasonably foreseeable that someone like Tom would do what he did if Carl left his house with a ground-floor window open,[69] Carl would still *not* have owed Nita a duty to take care that he did not leave his house with a ground-floor window open.[70] Why would it not be 'fair, just and reasonable' to find that Carl owed Nita a duty of care in this case. Two reasons can be given.[71]

First of all, if we find in cases such as Carl's that neighbours owe each other duties of care not to leave their houses without first ensuring that they are lock-fast, then homeowners in crime-ridden areas will be subject to an extremely oppressive duty. Every time a homeowner in a crime-ridden area left his house, he would first have to do a tour of the house to see that it was securely locked up. This would be an intolerable burden to inflict on someone.

Secondly, finding that a duty of care is owed in cases such as Carl's would be oppressive in another way. Suppose that A owes his neighbour B a duty not to leave his house without taking reasonable steps to ensure that it is securely locked up. Suppose further that A breaches this duty – he leaves a lower-floor window open when going to work one day. A thief takes advantage of A's negligence to

---

[68] [1987] AC 241 (discussed above, pp. 176–7).

[69] This would be difficult to establish: it will be recalled (see above, p. 70, n. 24) that the requirement of reasonable foreseeability would only be established if a reasonable person in Carl's position would have realised that it was *very likely* that someone like Tom would do what Tom did if Carl left his house with a ground-floor window open. But there are circumstances where this requirement would be satisfied: say, if Carl's house was in a bad neighbourhood where there had been a lot of break-ins recently.

[70] Ibid., 277–8. Lord Mackay – who gave the other leading judgment in *Smith* v *Littlewoods Ltd* – was more equivocal. He took the view (which Lord Goff did not) that if it was reasonably foreseeable that if A left his premises unlocked, vandals would enter A's premises and start a fire on the premises that would spread to B's premises, then A would have owed B a duty to take care that he did not leave his premises unlocked: ibid., 262. However, he went on to say that cases of theft were distinct from cases of fire: ibid., at 267–8. But it is difficult to know whether that means he agreed with Lord Goff that no duty of care will have been owed in the situation we are considering.

[71] In fact, there are more than just two reasons why it would not be 'fair, just and reasonable' to find that Carl owed Nita a duty here. First, it is not clear what social interest would be served by finding that Carl owed Nita a duty here. The only people who would benefit from such a finding would be Nita's insurers, who would be allowed through the doctrine of subrogation to pass the bill for compensating Nita for the loss of her valuables to Carl. Secondly, finding that Carl owed Nita a duty of care here might discourage Nita from taking measures herself to ensure that someone could not access her house from Carl's back garden. (Though a counter-argument to this is that if it was partly Nita's fault that Tom was allowed to get into her house, the damages payable to her by Carl could be reduced for contributory negligence.) Thirdly, finding that Carl owed Nita a duty of care here would result in both Carl and Tom being held liable for the loss of Nita's valuables when really it should be Tom who should be held primarily responsible for the loss of Nita's valuables. (For another situation where this last argument may militate against someone being held to owe another a duty of care, see above, pp. 162–4.)

gain access to A's house and he moves from there to gain access to B's house. Unknown to A, B has a very valuable collection of vases in his house worth £100,000 and the thief spirits all these vases away. B will be able to sue A in negligence for the loss of his vases. As a result A will find himself being subjected to a huge liability for a trivial act of negligence: that of leaving a window open.

So – the lesson we can draw from this is that it may not be 'fair, just and reasonable' to find that one person owed another a duty of care if to do so would result in people being subjected to an intolerable burden[72] or if to do so would result in people incurring a liability out of all proportion to their fault in breaching that duty.[73]

The sleepy lorry driver

Suppose that Fred was a lorry driver and in order to meet a deadline, he drove his lorry two days and nights continuously without sleeping. Eventually, he fell asleep at the wheel of his lorry and the lorry crashed into an electricity substation, producing a power cut that affected hundreds of businesses in the area. Wendy's factory was affected by the power cut and she estimates that the power cut cost her £10,000 in lost profits. She wants to sue Fred in negligence for compensation in respect of her loss. However, her claim will fail: she will not be able to establish that Fred owed her a duty to take care not to crash his lorry into the sub-station. And this is so even though it was reasonably foreseeable that if he did something like that, someone like Wendy – who ran a business in the area – would suffer economic loss as a result.[74] Why would it not be 'fair, just and reasonable' to find that Fred owed Wendy a duty of care in this situation?[75]

---

[72] Cf. *Orange* v *Chief Constable of West Yorkshire Police* [2002] QB 347, holding that the police would not owe a duty to all prisoners in their custody to take reasonable steps to see that they did not commit suicide because to do so would result in an 'unacceptable level of control and precaution' (ibid., at [42]). See also *McGeown* v *Northern Ireland Housing Executive* [1995] 1 AC 233, holding that the Occupiers' Liability Act 1957 will not apply to impose a duty of care on A to ensure B's safety in the case where B uses a highway to cross A's land because 'Rights of way pass over many different types of terrain, and it would place an impossible burden upon landowners if they not only had to submit to the passage over them of anyone who might choose to exercise the right but also were under a duty to maintain them in a safe condition' (ibid., at 243 (per Lord Keith of Kinkel)).

[73] Cf. our explanation above (at pp. 95–6) of the limits set by the courts on when one person will owe another a duty of care not to do something which foreseeably had the effect of causing that other to suffer a psychiatric illness.

[74] *Spartan Steel & Alloys Ltd* v *Martin & Co. (Contractors) Ltd* [1973] 1 QB 27.

[75] The next few paragraphs set out a *pragmatic* argument for thinking that it would not be 'fair, just and reasonable' to find that Fred owed Wendy a duty of care. For a *principled* argument that it would not be 'fair, just and reasonable' to find that Fred owed Wendy a duty of care, see Benson 1995. His argument basically runs as follows. At the time Fred crashed into the power station, Wendy had *no* proprietary interest in the power station. This means that, as against Fred, Wendy had *no* right to exclude him from crashing into the power station. *Therefore* one cannot find that Fred owed Wendy a duty to take care not to crash into the power station – to find otherwise would give Wendy a right against Fred which only someone with a proprietary interest in the station could have had. There are two problems with this argument. First, the argument rests on the following syllogism: (1) Wendy *would* have had a right to exclude Fred from crashing into the power station had she had a proprietary interest in the power station, therefore (2) the fact that she did *not* have a proprietary interest in the power station means that she *could not* have had a right to exclude Fred from crashing into the power station. However, this is a *non sequitur*: (1) does *not* imply (2). Secondly, if Benson's argument is right, it is hard to explain why, if Fred had *deliberately* crashed into the power station with the *intention* of disrupting Wendy's business, the courts would have no hesitation in finding that Fred committed a tort in relation to Wendy in acting as he did: see below, pp. 417–19.

The basic reason for this lies in the fact that there was no kind of relationship between Fred and Wendy which could ground a duty of care in this case. So the *only* reason for finding that Fred owed Wendy a duty of care in this situation is that it was reasonably foreseeable that she would suffer some kind economic loss if he drove into the sub-station. It follows that if we found that Fred owed Wendy a duty of care in this situation, then we would have to say that A will normally owe B a duty to take care not to do *x* if it is reasonably foreseeable that B will suffer some kind of economic loss as a result of A's doing *x*. But if we said *that*, then a number of unattractive consequences would follow.[76]

First, ordinary people would be subjected to a vastly increased number of duties of care and will suffer a corresponding diminution in their personal liberty – there being countless occasions when it is reasonably foreseeable that acting in some way is likely to result in another suffering economic loss.[77] Secondly, and consequently, the probability that a given individual would at some time in his life be caught up in litigation – an evil in itself – would become extremely high. Thirdly, the amount of litigation that the courts would have to handle would be greatly increased with the result that either taxpayers would have to pay for an increased number of courts to deal with the greater litigation or delays in getting one's case heard in court – already long – would become even longer.

Fourthly, if foreseeability of economic loss was sufficient to ground a duty of care then people might well be exposed to indeterminate liabilities which would be out of all proportion to their fault.[78] For example, if a duty of care was owed by Fred to Wendy here, then Fred would also have to have owed a duty of care to all the other businesses affected by the power cut. As a result, he would incur a huge liability out of all proportion to his fault in falling asleep at the wheel of his lorry. Fifthly, people often have alternative methods of protecting their economic interests than by relying on tort law. For example, in the case we are considering here, Wendy could have guarded against the consequences of a power cut by installing a back-up generator. To find that foreseeability of economic loss is sufficient to ground a duty of care might well discourage people like Wendy from doing what they can to ensure that their finances are not affected by the actions of people like Fred.[79]

Sixthly, the good that would be done by recognising that foreseeability of economic loss is enough to ground a duty of care would not be enough to outweigh these harms. Recognising this might allow a claimant who suffered a form of pure economic loss as a result of a defendant's carelessness to sue that

---

[76] See, generally, Bernstein 1998, 11–22, 146–54, 198–203; also GS&Z, 90–1.

[77] Cf. Goldberg & Zipursky 1998, 1833: 'To add ... [a] general [duty] to take care to avoid causing ... economic injuries [to all the other duties of care we owe others] would be enormously burdensome.'

[78] Cf. Cardozo CJ in *Ultramares Corporation* v *Touche*, 174 NE 441 (1931), holding that auditors should not owe a duty of care to potential investors in a company when auditing the company's accounts, because to do so would 'expose accountants to a liability in an indeterminate amount for an indeterminate time to an indeterminate class' (ibid., at 444).

[79] Cf. Lord Denning MR's remarks in *Spartan Steel & Alloys Ltd* v *Martin & Co. (Contractors) Ltd* [1973] 1 QB 27, at 38, discussed below, pp. 575–6.

defendant for compensation for that loss. However, the economic loss suffered would almost always be comparatively trivial;[80] and in the rare cases where the claimant's loss was large, it would almost certainly be insured against – in which case the only institution to benefit from the recognition of a duty of care would be the claimant's insurance company.

It is for reasons like these that the courts – in England at any rate – have always insisted that it is *not* 'fair, just and reasonable' to find that A owed B a duty of care *merely* because it was reasonably foreseeable that B would suffer some kind of economic loss as a result of A's actions. So if the only argument for finding that A owed B a duty of care is that it was reasonably foreseeable that B would suffer some kind of economic loss as a result of A's actions, a duty of care will *always* be denied.[81] Something more is required before a duty of

---

[80] For an interesting argument that cases of someone's suffering pure economic losses are always more trivial than cases of someone's suffering property damage (because property is more important to our personalities than stocks of wealth), see Witting 2001.

[81] *Important note.* Cases where a duty of care was denied because the only ground for imposing it would have been that it was foreseeable that the defendant would suffer economic loss as a result of the claimant's actions include: *Cattle* v *Stockton Waterworks Co.* (1875) LR 10 QB 453 (no duty of care owed to contractors not to delay them in their work, thereby making their contract to do that work less profitable); *Simpson & Co.* v *Thomson* (1877) 3 App Cas 279 (no duty of care owed to insurer not to damage insured property); *Société Anonyme de Remourquage à Hélice* v *Bennetts* [1911] 1 KB 243 (no duty of care owed by defendants not to sink ship being towed by tug, thereby preventing the tug earning a fee for towing the ship); *Weller & Co.* v *Foot and Mouth Disease Research Institute* [1966] 1 QB 569 (virus causing foot and mouth disease escaped from defendants' premises and caused outbreak of foot and mouth disease in area with the result that claimants' business as cattle auctioneers was temporarily suspended; no duty of care not to release virus owed by defendants to claimants); *Candlewood Navigation Corporation Ltd* v *Mitsui OSK Lines Ltd, The Mineral Transporter* [1986] AC 1 (no duty of care owed to claimants not to damage ship which claimants did not have proprietary interest in but which the claimants had to pay hire for even if the ship was damaged); *Leigh & Sillavan Ltd* v *Aliakmon Shipping Co. Ltd, The Aliakmon* [1986] AC 785 (no duty of care owed to claimant not to damage goods which the claimant had contracted to pay for but which he had not yet acquired ownership or possession of); *Simaan General Contracting Co.* v *Pilkington Glass Ltd (No. 2)* [1988] QB 758 (job of constructing building in Saudi Arabia given to claimant; building was to include a green glass curtain wall and the job of constructing the wall was subcontracted to F; job of constructing the glass that would make up the wall was sub-subcontracted to defendant; defendant's glass panels were not the right shade of green with the result that the fee payable to the main contractor for constructing the building was reduced; held, that defendant had not owed the claimant a duty of care in constructing the panels); *CBS Songs* v *Amstrad Consumer Electronics plc* [1988] AC 1013 (no duty of care owed to claimant recording company whose royalties might be reduced as a result of defendants' marketing tape-to-tape recording machine which would allow illegal copies of cassette tapes to be made); *Van Oppen* v *Clerk to the Bedford Charity Trustees* [1990] 1 WLR 235 (no duty of care owed by school to pupil to arrange insurance on his behalf against his being injured playing rugby at the school); *Pacific Associates* v *Baxter* [1990] 1 QB 993 (no duty of care owed by engineers employed to judge whether contractors should be paid for the work they have done to use reasonable skill and care in making those judgements). It is customary to mention, alongside these cases, cases such as *D & F Estates* v *Church Commissioners* [1989] AC 177 and *Murphy* v *Brentwood DC* [1991] 1 AC 398 (held in both cases, no action maintainable in negligence against builders of a dangerously defective house for the cost of repairing the defects in the building). However, in those cases a duty of care *was* owed (see above, p. 68): the real significance of those cases was that they set a limit on the losses that someone would be liable for if he or she breached that duty of care. Those cases are therefore more appropriately dealt with in Part III of this book, which deals with the remedies that will be available when someone commits a tort. An explanation of the House of Lords' rulings in *D & F Estates* and *Murphy* is set out below, at pp. 566–8.

care will be found such as an 'assumption of responsibility'[82] or a relationship of severe dependency.[83] Merely to say that 'It was reasonably foreseeable that B would suffer some kind of economic loss as a result of A's actions' is *never* enough to justify a finding that A owed B a duty of care.

Situations where a duty of care will be denied in the public interest

We have already seen some examples of situations where the courts will deny that a duty of care was owed because to do so would be harmful to the public interest.[84] Other examples can be given. For instance, a judge deciding a civil case will not owe the parties to the case a duty to decide the case with a reasonable degree of care and skill.[85] The reason for this goes as follows:

> If we say that a judge deciding a civil case owes a duty to the parties in that case to decide the case with a reasonable degree of care and skill, then a judge in a civil case will decide that case with the threat hanging over him that if one of the parties to the case feels aggrieved by his judgment – and one of them always will – he might be sued by the aggrieved party. In order to avoid the threat of litigation, the judge may be tempted to ignore the law in deciding the case and instead attempt to 'split the difference' between the parties to the litigation in order to appease each of them. Or he might be tempted to avoid spelling out the reasons for his decision in too much detail so as to make it as difficult as possible for another court to find that he failed to decide the case with a reasonable degree of care and skill. It is obviously contrary to the public interest for judges to act in this way – but judges would be forced to act in this way if we found that a judge deciding a civil case owed a duty of care to the parties in that case. Given this, it would not be 'fair, just and reasonable' that a judge owes such a duty of care.[86]

There are two different ways in which imposing a duty of care on someone might actually harm the public interest and therefore not be 'fair, just and reasonable'.

(1) *Excessive caution.* First of all, suppose that A has some job which serves the public interest. Suppose further that if the law said that A owed B a duty to do his job with a reasonable degree of care and skill, A would – out of a desire to avoid being sued by B – become *excessively cautious* in doing that job and his ability to do that job *well* would as a result be impaired. If this is the case, then

---

[82] See above, pp. 120–40.

[83] See above, pp. 140–8.

[84] See *Marc Rich & Co. AG* v *Bishop Rock Marine Co.. Ltd, The Nicholas H* [1996] AC 211 (discussed above, pp. 117–18) and *Mulcahy* v *Ministry of Defence* [1996] QB 732 (discussed above, pp. 82–4).

[85] *Rondel* v *Worsley* [1969] 1 AC 191, 270 (per Lord Pearce); *Sirros* v *Moore* [1975] QB 118; *FM (a child)* v *Singer* [2004] EWHC 793.

[86] Notice that on this occasion it *is* correct to say that the judge enjoys an *immunity* from being sued in negligence: one would normally expect the courts to apply the extended principle in *Hedley Byrne* and find that judges deciding civil cases *will* owe a duty to the parties in that case to decide the case with a reasonable degree of care and skill – however, for public interest reasons, the courts will treat judges as a special case and refuse to apply the extended principle in *Hedley Byrne* to them.

it might not be 'fair, just and reasonable' to find that A owes B a duty to do his job with a reasonable degree of care and skill.

This is the reason why an officer will not owe a duty of care to the soldiers under his command in the heat of battle;[87] why a certification society will not owe a duty of care to the owners of cargo aboard a ship that is due to be certificated as fit or unfit to sail;[88] and, as we have just seen, why a judge in a civil or criminal case will not owe a duty of care to the parties to that case.[89] This is also the reason why, if the police suspect A of committing a crime they will not owe A a duty of care in carrying out their investigations into whether or not he committed that crime.[90] If they did owe A such a duty of care, they might become excessively cautious in charging him: they might only charge him when they were absolutely certain that there was no possibility that he might be innocent and therefore no possibility that he would ever have grounds to sue them. This same kind of concern caused the Court of Appeal to rule in *Harris* v *Evans*[91] that a health and safety inspector did *not* owe a duty of care to a claimant whose business was severely disrupted by the health and safety inspector making what turned out to be unjustified demands on the claimant. The Court of Appeal was fearful that if it found that health and safety inspectors owed duties of care to businesses affected by their findings and decisions, inspectors would – out of a desire to avoid being sued – become very cautious about making any decisions or findings that might adversely affect someone's business.[92] Similarly, in *D* v *East Berkshire Community NHS Trust*[93] the Court of Appeal held that if the social services investigate allegations that A is abusing his children, the social services will *not* owe A a duty to carry out their investigations with a reasonable degree of care and skill.[94] The court feared that if the social services owed A such a duty of care, they would become excessively cautious about taking A's children into care, for fear that they might be sued by A if they made a mistake and took the children into care when they were not actually at risk.

In other cases, the courts have been unpersuaded that they should refuse to find that a duty of care was owed because (so it was claimed) finding that such

---

[87] See above, pp. 82–3.

[88] See above, pp. 117–18.

[89] See above, p. 211.

[90] *Calveley* v *Chief Constable of Merseyside Police* [1989] AC 1228.

[91] [1998] 1 WLR 1285.

[92] Ibid., 1298 (per Sir Richard Scott V-C). Even if there had been no public policy objection to finding a duty of care in *Harris* v *Evans*, it is still debatable whether there was sufficient *ground* for finding that a duty of care was owed in that case. There existed no *Hedley Byrne*-type relationship between the claimant and the defendant that could have justified the finding that a duty of care was owed in *Harris* (contra, M&D, 162). A finding that a duty of care was owed could have been justified on the basis of the 'extended dependency principle' (see above, pp. 149–50) – but if one does not, as we do not, accept that that principle is part of English law, it is hard to find a satisfactory rationale for finding that a duty of care was owed in *Harris*. (The mere fact that it was foreseeable that the claimant would suffer economic loss if the defendant failed to do his job properly is, of course, not enough to justify a finding that a duty of care was owed: see above, pp. 208–11.)

[93] [2004] QB 558.

[94] The position is the same in Australia (*Sullivan* v *Moody* (2001) 207 CLR 562, at [62]) and New Zealand (*B* v *Attorney General* [2003] 4 All ER 833).

---

a duty existed would make people working in the public interest excessively cautious in doing their jobs. For example, the courts have never hesitated to find that doctors owe duties of care to their patients in treating them, despite widely-expressed fears that doing so only encourages doctors to practise 'defensive medicine', giving patients excessive tests and treatments in an attempt to demonstrate publicly that everything has been done for the patient and avoid litigation.[95] Similarly, an argument that it would not be 'fair, just and reasonable' to find that firefighters owed owners of a property on fire a duty to take care not to make the fire worse because doing so would encourage firefighters to fight fires 'defensively' was rejected in *Capital & Counties plc v Hampshire CC*.[96] Again, in *Spring v Guardian Assurance*[97] the House of Lords dismissed fears that if they found that an employer will owe an ex-employee a duty to take care that he did not write the ex-employee an unfair reference, employers would become excessively cautious about saying anything negative about ex-employees in writing references for them – even though within the law of defamation references are protected by qualified privilege precisely because it is feared that, if they were not, referees would become unduly cautious about expressing themselves frankly in their references.[98] Finally, it used to be the law that a barrister would not owe a duty to his or her client to conduct that client's case in court with a reasonable degree of care and skill. One of the reasons for this was that it was feared that if barristers owed their clients such a duty of care, a desire to avoid 'the possibility of being sued in negligence would at least subconsciously lead some counsel to undue prolixity which would not only be harmful to [his or her] client but against the public interest in prolonging trials'.[99] However, the House of Lords in *Arthur J S Hall v Simons*[100] was less concerned about this and as a result swept away the no-duty rule in relation to barristers.

(2) *Disruption.* The second way the imposition of a duty of care can harm the public interest is as follows. Suppose that A is an agency that carries out work which is in the public interest. Suppose further that if we found that A owes other people a duty of care in carrying out its work, A would be swamped with litigation and its operations would as a result be severely disrupted – either because meeting the costs of fighting off the litigation will divert resources from A's 'front-line' activities or because conducting the litigation will involve A's employees having to take time off work to make witness statements, appear in

---

[95] American studies estimate the cost of defensive medicine in the United States as being in the tens of *billions* of dollars: see, for example, US Congress Office of Technology Assessment, *Defensive Medicine and Medical Malpractice*, OTA-H-602 (1994); Kessler & McClellan 1996.

[96] [1997] QB 1004, 1043: 'It seems hardly realistic that a fire officer who has to make a split second decision as to the manner in which fire-fighting operations are to be conducted will be looking over his shoulder at the possibility of his employers being made vicariously liable for his negligence' (per Stuart-Smith LJ).

[97] [1995] 2 AC 296.

[98] For an account of the law on qualified privilege, see below, pp. 291–7.

[99] *Rondel v Worsley* [1969] 1 AC 191, 229 (per Lord Reid).

[100] [2002] 1 AC 615 (discussed, Seneviratne 2001).

court and so on. If this is the case, it might not be 'fair, just and reasonable' to find that A owes anyone a duty of care in carrying out its operations.

In *Hill* v *Chief Constable of West Yorkshire*,[101] this was one of the reasons why the House of Lords thought it would not be 'fair, just and reasonable' to find that the police owed potential victims of a criminal on the loose a duty to take reasonable steps to arrest him. Lord Keith – delivering the leading judgment – expressed himself fearful that if the courts found that the police owed such a duty of care to the potential victims of crime, then the police would be swamped with litigation brought by the victims of crime. In many such cases, 'elaborate investigation of the facts might be necessary to ascertain whether or not [the police were negligent]. A great deal of police time, trouble and expense might be expected to have to be put into the preparation of the defence to the action and the attendance of witnesses at the trial. The result would be a significant diversion of police manpower and attention from their most important function, that of the suppression of crime.'[102]

In other cases, this argument for finding that it would not be 'fair, just and reasonable' to find that one person will owe another a duty of care has been less successful. In *Phelps* v *London Borough of Hillingdon*, Lord Nicholls – with the agreement of Lord Jauncey of Tullichettle – suggested that the time had come to recognise that the teacher of a normal student will owe that student a duty to teach him with reasonable skill and care. He acknowledged some would be concerned that taking such a step would adversely affect the public interest:

> The principal objection [to recognising that the teacher of a normal student will owe that student a duty to teach him or her with a reasonable degree of care and skill] is the spectre of a rash of 'gold digging' actions brought on behalf of under-achieving children by discontented parents, perhaps years after the events complained of. If teachers are liable, education authorities will be vicariously liable, since the negligent acts and omissions were committed in the course of the teachers' employment. So, it is said, the limited resources of education authorities and the time of teaching staff will be diverted away from teaching and into defending unmeritorious legal claims. Further, schools will have to prepare and keep full records, lest they be unable to rebut negligence allegations, brought out of the blue years later. For one or more of these reasons [it is argued], the overall standard of education given to children is likely to suffer if a legal duty of care were held to exist.[103]

[101] [1989] AC 53. The claimants were the family of Jacqueline Hill, the last victim of Peter Sutcliffe, the Yorkshire Ripper. They sued the police under the Fatal Accidents Act 1976, claiming that had the police been more careful in conducting its investigation into the Yorkshire Ripper they would have caught him long before he killed Jacqueline Hill. But in order to make out their claim, they had to establish that the police owed people like Jacqueline Hill a duty to take reasonable steps to catch the Yorkshire Ripper.

[102] Ibid., 63. Many academics (see, for example, Hoyano 1999, 912) seem to believe that this was the *only* reason why no duty of care was found in *Hill*. In fact the above passage was inserted into Lord Keith's judgment almost as an after-thought, *after* he had *already* set out his reasons for finding that no duty of care was owed in *Hill*. The *key* reason why no duty of care was owed in *Hill* was that to find that such a duty of care was owed in such a case would subject policemen and women to a duty to which normal, ordinary citizens would not be subject – our reasons for thinking that it would not be 'fair, just and reasonable' to do this are set out above, at pp. 202–3.

[103] [2001] 2 AC 619, 667.

However, Lord Nicholls felt able airily to dismiss these concerns: 'I am not persuaded by these fears.'[104]

Resolving John's case

Now that we have a better understanding of when it will *not* be 'fair, just and reasonable' to find that one person owed another a duty of care, we can address the question of whether John's school really did owe him a duty to take reasonable steps to stop him truanting from school. It was of course reasonably foreseeable that John would suffer harm if the school did not take reasonable steps to stop him truanting, and – if we adopt an incremental approach to applying the *Caparo* test – we can assume that there is enough in the case law to suggest that it *might* be 'fair, just and reasonable' to find that the school owed John a duty of care here.[105] So the decisive question is whether there is any reason why it would *not* be 'fair, just and reasonable' to find that the school owed John a duty of care here.

Three reasons can be given as to why it would not be 'fair, just and reasonable' to find that a duty of care was owed here. First, doing so would encourage people like John to truant from school – people like John would think that if they harmed themselves by truanting from school, they would always be able to sue their school for compensation. Secondly, if the law said that schools owe their students a duty to take reasonable steps to prevent their students truanting from school, the operation of schools would be considerably disrupted – scarce resources would be diverted from teaching those who want to learn and would instead have to be devoted to getting recalcitrant students to go to school. Thirdly, it is not clear that it would be constitutionally proper for the courts to interfere with the allocation of school resources in this way, at least so far as State schools are concerned – Parliament may have intended that the decision as to whether and, if so, how much of the resources available to State schools should be spent on preventing truanting should be left up to local education authorities. And if the courts could not find that a State school had a duty to take reasonable steps to prevent its students truanting, then it could hardly find that such a duty was owed to its students by a privately-run school: to do so would give an unfair advantage to State schools.

So – on balance – it is unlikely that the courts would apply the *Caparo* test in John's case to find that his school owed him a duty to take reasonable steps to prevent him truanting.

---

[104] Ibid.

[105] An incrementalist would, of course, express this by saying that the case law establishes that there was a relationship of 'proximity' between John and the school: see above, pp. 191–2.

9

BREACH OF DUTY

In the last five chapters we have looked at the question: When will one person owe another a duty of care? In this chapter, we are concerned with the question: When will someone who owed another a duty of care be held to have breached that duty? The law in this area is far from straightforward to understand. We will begin by setting out the most basic principles that govern the inquiry into whether or not someone has breached a duty of care owed to another; later on, the picture will become more complex.

BASIC PRINCIPLES

Suppose A owed B a duty of care of some description – say, a duty to take reasonable steps to save B from harm. Obviously, A will be held to have breached that duty of care if A *personally* failed to take reasonable steps to save B from harm. In judging whether or not A was guilty of such a personal failure, the courts will take a number of different considerations into account.

Degree and foreseeability of risk

Suppose A owed B a duty to take reasonable steps to ensure that B would be reasonably safe in doing x, say, visiting A's premises or working for A. If it is claimed that A breached this duty because he personally failed to take reasonable steps to eliminate some risk of harm that B was exposed to in doing x, the courts will, in evaluating this claim, first ask: Did A know or ought he have known of the existence of this risk? If the answer is 'no', he will not have breached the duty of care he owed B.

   If, on the other hand, the answer is 'yes', the courts will then ask: How serious was the risk?[1] If the risk was *non-trivial*, then A will have breached the duty of care he owed B to take reasonable steps to ensure that B would be reasonably safe in doing x if he did not take sufficient measures to eliminate the risk in question; whether the measures, if any, A personally took to eliminate the risk in question were 'sufficient' will depend on how serious the risk was.

   If the risk was *trivial*, the courts will ask: How difficult or costly would it have been to eliminate the risk? If it would have been difficult or costly to eliminate the risk in question, then A will not have breached the duty he owed B to take reasonable steps to ensure that B would be reasonably safe in doing x even

---

[1] The seriousness of a risk is measured by mutiplying the probability that that risk will eventuate by the size of the harm that will be done if that risk eventuates.

216

though he did nothing to eliminate the risk in question. If, on the other hand, it would have been easy for D to eliminate the risk in question then A's failure to eliminate that risk will have put him in breach of the duty he owed B to take reasonable steps to ensure that B would be reasonably safe in doing *x*.

Let us illustrate these propositions by considering a few cases. In *Paris v Stepney Borough Council*,[2] the claimant was employed as a fitter in the defendants' garage. The claimant, who was already blind in one eye, lost the use of the other eye when, in removing a bolt on a rusty vehicle by striking it with a hammer, a chip flew up from the bolt and into his good eye. The claimant sued the defendants, claiming that the defendants breached the duty that they owed him to take reasonable steps to see that he would be reasonably safe in working for them when they failed to provide him with goggles to wear in doing 'bolt work' for them. The House of Lords allowed the claimant's claim. While the probability that the claimant would suffer an eye injury in doing 'bolt work' for the defendants was extremely low, the seriousness of the harm that would be suffered by the claimant if he did suffer an eye injury in doing 'bolt work' for the claimant was very high, given that he only had one good eye and would therefore be completely blinded if he suffered an eye injury in doing 'bolt work' for the defendants. Given this, the risk that the claimant would suffer an eye injury in doing 'bolt work' for the defendants could not be dismissed as trivial and the defendants, in failing to provide the claimant with goggles to wear when doing 'bolt work' for them, failed to take sufficient measures to eliminate that risk, given its seriousness.[3]

In *Hudson v Ridge Manufacturing Co. Ltd*,[4] the claimant was employed by the defendants and was injured when C, one of the claimant's fellow employees, tripped him up. It was held that the defendants were liable to compensate the claimant for his injuries: the claimant's accident had happened, in part, because the defendants had breached the duty they owed the claimant to take reasonable steps to ensure that he would be reasonably safe in working for them. C had for years been in the habit of engaging in this sort of horseplay which exposed his colleagues – including the claimant – to a very high degree of risk of suffering some kind of injury. When the defendants found out about C's behaviour they failed to take reasonable steps to prevent C from acting in this way. They did reprimand C for his behaviour when it occurred but, given the seriousness of the risk that C's behaviour posed for his colleagues, this was not sufficient. The defendants should have done more to deter C from engaging in horseplay when the system of reprimands plainly failed to work to cure his behaviour.

In *Latimer v A E C*,[5] the claimant was employed by the defendants. He was injured when he slipped on an oily cooling mixture which had spread onto the

---

[2] [1951] AC 367.

[3] It might have been different if the claimant had had *two* good eyes when working for the defendants. In such a case, the harm that he would have suffered if he had injured an eye in doing 'bolt work' for the defendants would not have been so serious and as a result the risk of him suffering an eye injury in doing 'bolt work' for the defendants would not have been so serious and might have even qualified as trivial – in which case, the defendants' failure to eliminate it by providing him with goggles that he could wear in doing 'bolt work' might have been excused on cost grounds.

[4] [1957] 2 QB 348.

[5] [1953] AC 643.

floor of the defendants' factory where the claimant worked. The defendants had put down some sawdust to make the floor less slippery but the sawdust did not cover all the areas of the factory floor where the oil had spread. The claimant slipped on one of the untreated areas and sued the defendants, claiming that the defendants had breached the duty they owed him to take reasonable steps to ensure that the factory would be reasonably safe for him to work in. The claimant's claim was dismissed. The presence of the oily cooling mixture on the factory floor did, initially, expose the claimant – and other employees – to a serious risk of being injured in some way. However, by spreading sawdust on the floor, the defendants turned that risk into a trivial one. Once the sawdust was spread, the risk that the claimant would suffer some kind of injury by slipping on the floor became negligible. As it would have been costly and inconvenient for the defendants to take further steps – such as closing the factory down while the floor dried out – to eliminate the remaining risk that the claimant would suffer some kind of injury by slipping on the floor, the defendants did not breach the duty they owed the claimant to take reasonable steps to ensure that he would be reasonably safe in working for them when they failed to eliminate that remaining risk.

Personal circumstances

When will the courts take into account A's personal circumstances – such things as his wealth, health and physical skills – in judging whether A breached a duty of care owed to B? It depends on what kind of duty of care it was that A owed B.[6]

(1) *Negative duties.* If A owed B a duty to take care not to do *x* and A did *x* because he suffered from some kind of personal failing, the courts will find that A breached that duty if he knew or ought to have known that he suffered from that failing; on the other hand, if he did not know and had no reason to know that he suffered from that failing, the courts may well find that A did not breach the duty of care that he owed B.

So – in *Nettleship* v *Weston*,[7] the claimant gave the defendant, a friend's wife, some driving lessons. In the third lesson, he instructed her to turn left at a junction. She began to turn left but then she panicked and failed to straighten the car. The car mounted the pavement and struck a lamp post. As a result, the claimant's kneecap was smashed. The claimant sued the defendant, claiming that she had breached the duty she owed him to take care not to drive dangerously. At first instance, his claim was dismissed on the ground that the defendant had done her best to drive safely: it was her lack of experience that had resulted in her driving as dangerously as she did. The Court of Appeal reversed the decision at first instance. In the Court of Appeal's view, the defendant's lack of experience was not to be taken into account in judging whether

---

[6] See, generally, Kidner 1991, 2–16.
[7] [1971] 2 QB 691.

or not she breached the duty she owed the claimant to take care not to drive dangerously.

In *Nettleship* v *Weston*, the defendant was aware that she was an inexperienced driver. *Mansfield* v *Weetabix Ltd*,[8] on the other hand, was a case where the defendant lorry driver was unaware, and had no reason to be aware, of the personal failing that caused him to drive his lorry into the claimants' shop. The defendant in that case unknowingly suffered from malignant insulinoma – a condition which meant that, if he did not eat properly, his brain would be starved of the quantities of glucose necessary for it to function properly. On the day of the accident, the defendant had set out on a 40 mile journey without eating properly and, as a result, his driving became more and more erratic, culminating in his driving off the road and into the claimants' shop. The claimants sued the defendant, claiming that he had breached the duty he owed them to take care not to drive dangerously. The Court of Appeal dismissed the claim.[9] The defendant's malignant insulinoma meant that he could not have helped driving the way he did and so the defendant did not breach the duty he owed the claimants to take care not to drive dangerously. Of course, it would have been different if the defendant had been aware of his condition and gone out driving without taking care to eat properly. His failure to take reasonable steps to ensure that his driving would not be affected by his condition would have put him in breach of the duty he owed all those on or near the roads used by him – including the claimants – to take care not to drive dangerously.

(2) *Extended Hedley Byrne principle.* If A owed B a duty to perform a task with a certain degree of care and skill under the extended principle in *Hedley Byrne*, the courts will hold that A breached that duty if he failed to perform that task with that degree of care and skill.[10] It will be irrelevant whether or not A was actually capable of performing that task with that degree of care and skill. This seems fair enough: if A was so inexperienced that he could not perform the task in question with the requisite degree of care and skill, he has only himself to blame for the fact that, in the end, he was fixed with a duty that he was incapable of fulfilling. If he was incapable of performing the task in question with the degree of care and skill required, he should never have taken the job on or encouraged B to think that he was capable of doing the job with that degree of care and skill.

(3) *Positive duties that were not voluntarily assumed.* If A owed B a duty to take reasonable steps to see that B did not suffer some kind of harm, and that duty of care was not voluntarily assumed,[11] then the courts will not hold that A

---

[8] [1998] 1 WLR 1263.

[9] In so doing, they disapproved Neill J's judgment in *Roberts* v *Ramsbottom* [1980] 1 All ER 7, which suggested that a driver who drove his car dangerously due to the fact that he suffered some personal failing would be held to have breached the duty he owed others to take care not to drive dangerously if, at the time he was driving, he enjoyed some *limited* control of the car.

[10] See above, pp. 129–30, for a discussion of how much care and skill someone who takes on a task for another will be required to take under the extended principle in *Hedley Byrne*.

[11] Positive duties of care that are not voluntarily assumed are quite rare: the duty of care an occupier owes trespassers on his land and his neighbours would be an example; as is the duty of care that the police and prison authorities owe suicide risks in their custody. The duty of care that A will owe B to rescue B if A has discouraged other people from saving B is *not* an example: by discouraging those other people from rescuing B, A voluntarily assumed the duty of care that he

breached that duty of care if A did his *best* – given his personal circumstances – to see that B did not suffer the harm in question.

So, for example, we have already seen that if a fire starts on land occupied by Eric and threatens to spread onto Wendy's land, Eric will normally owe Wendy a duty to take reasonable steps to put out that fire.[12] In judging whether or not Eric breached this duty, the courts will take into account Eric's personal resources:

> [L]ess must be expected of the infirm than of the able-bodied: the owner of a small property where a hazard arises which threatens a neighbour with substantial interests should not have to do as much as one with larger interests of his own at stake and greater resources to protect them: if the small owner does what he can . . . he may be held to have done his duty: he should not be held liable unless it is clearly proved that he could, and reasonably in his individual circumstances should, have done more.'[13]

The result is that Eric will merely be required to do the best he can, with the resources he has, to put out the fire. If he does that, then he will discharge the duty of care that he owes Wendy. Similarly, we have already seen that if Gary is imprisoned and it is reasonably foreseeable that he is a suicide risk, the prison authorities will owe Gary a duty to take reasonable steps to see that he does not commit suicide.[14] In judging whether the prison authorities breached this duty, the courts will take into account the prison authorities' resources – so the prison authorities will not necessarily be held to have breached the duty of care they owed A to see that he did not commit suicide if they, through lack of resources, were unable to give him the kind of supervision and treatment that he would have received on a psychiatric ward.[15]

Having said that, suppose A owed B a duty to take reasonable steps to eliminate some danger to which B was exposed, and that duty was not voluntarily assumed. Suppose further that A's resources were such that he could have paid for the services of a professional to come in and eliminate the danger in question. If A chose not to do this and instead attempted to deal with the problem himself, then he will be held to have breached the duty of care that he owed B if he failed to use the same degree of care and skill in dealing with that danger as a professional would have used. It will be no defence for A to say that he did the best he could to eliminate the danger given the abilities he had.

So, for example, suppose that there was some dangerous fixture on Ruth's land and Ruth owed Vijay a duty to take reasonable steps to make the fixture

---

owed B. Similarly, in the case where A owes B a positive duty of care under the extended principle in *Hedley Byrne*. The duty of care that an occupier will normally owe his visitors is more difficult to classify – in the case where the occupier chooses to invite a visitor onto his land, there is a case for thinking that the duty of care that he will owe the visitor is voluntarily assumed.

[12] See above, p. 175.

[13] *Goldman* v *Hargrave* [1967] AC 645, 663 (per Lord Wilberforce). If putting the fire out was beyond A, given his resources, he may still be held to have breached the duty of care that he owed B to take reasonable steps to put the fire out if he did not warn B of the danger and invite B to join with him in putting the fire out: see *Holbeck Hall Hotel Ltd* v *Scarborough BC* [2000] QB 836.

[14] See above, pp. 155–6.

[15] *Knight* v *Home Office* [1990] 3 All ER 237.

safe. Suppose further that Ruth could have paid for a professional to mend that fixture, but she chose instead to mend it herself. If Ruth did not mend the fixture with the sort of care and skill that a professional would have shown in mending it, Ruth will be held to have breached the duty of care that she owed Vijay – and this is so even if Ruth did the best she could, given her relative lack of expertise in the matter, to mend the fixture herself.[16] Similarly, if Carl falls sick in prison with the result that the prison authorities owe him a duty to take reasonable steps to treat him, if the prison authorities choose to treat him themselves instead of sending him to a proper hospital, they will be required to treat him with the degree of care and skill that he would have been treated with had he been sent to hospital. If the prison authorities' treatment falls short of that standard, then the prison authorities will breach the duty of care they owe Carl – and this is so even if they did their best to treat Carl properly, given the resources they had.[17]

Professional standards

Suppose A owed B a duty to perform some task with the skill and care that a reasonably competent professional would have exercised in performing that task. Say, for example, that A owed B a duty to perform an operation on her brain with the skill and care that a reasonably competent brain surgeon would have exercised in performing that operation.

As a general rule, in judging whether or not A's performance was up to scratch, the courts will allow themselves to be guided by the opinion of professionals in the field. So if there is a substantial body of opinion within the field of brain surgery that holds that A did nothing wrong in performing the operation on B in the way he did, then the courts will normally find that A discharged the duty of care he owed B in operating on her. If, on the other hand, no one can be found among the community of brain surgeons other than a few cranks and eccentrics to say that A acted properly in operating on B, the courts will normally find that A breached the duty of care he owed B by operating on her in the way he did.

The case of *Maynard* v *West Midlands Regional Health Authority*[18] illustrates the point.[19] In treating the claimant, the defendants subjected the claimant to a diagnostic procedure called a mediastinoscopy which damaged the claimant's vocal cords. The claimant sued the defendants, claiming that they had breached the duty they owed her to treat her with a professional degree of skill

---

[16] *Wells* v *Cooper* [1958] 2 QB 265 (dangerous handle on door).

[17] *Brooks* v *Home Office* [1999] 2 FLR 33 (pregnant prisoner treated in prison rather than being sent to hospital).

[18] [1984] 1 WLR 634.

[19] The general rule traces its origin to the direction of McNair J in *Bolam* v *Friern Hospital Management Committee* [1957] 1 WLR 582, 587: 'A doctor is not guilty of negligence if he has acted in accordance with a practice accepted as proper by a responsible body of medical men skilled in that particular art ... Putting it the other way round, a doctor is not negligent, if he is acting in accordance with such a practice, merely because there is a body of opinion that takes a contrary view.'

and care. The claim failed: the defendants could show that a substantial body of medical opinion would have supported the claimant's being subjected to a mediastinoscopy given her condition.

However, this general rule is subject to an important exception. Returning to the hypothetical example set out above, even if a substantial number of brain surgeons are of the opinion that it was quite proper for A to operate on B in the way he did, the courts will still hold that A breached the duty of care he owed B in operating on her if it was plainly illogical or unreasonable for A to have operated on B in the way he did.[20]

So in *Edward Wong Finance Co. Ltd* v *Johnson Stokes & Master*,[21] the claimants agreed to lend a company $1,355,000 to enable it to purchase a factory in Hong Kong. The loan was to be secured by, among other things, a mortgage of the factory. The defendant firm of solicitors acted for the claimants in the transaction. The factory was already subject to a mortgage which would have to be cleared by the time it was purchased. The defendant firm of solicitors followed the practice – usual in Hong Kong at the time – of forwarding to the sellers the purchase price in return for the sellers' giving them undertakings that they would apply the purchase price to clear the existing mortgage on the factory. The sellers did no such thing and absconded with the purchase money, leaving the claimants with a greatly reduced security for the money they had lent the company to purchase the factory. The claimants sued the defendant firm of solicitors in negligence. They won: it was held that the defendant firm had breached the duty of care it owed the claimants in relation to how it handled the purchase and mortgage of the factory. Given that the defendant firm could easily have secured the claimants' interests by paying off the existing mortgagee rather than relying on the sellers of the factory to do so, the defendant firm could not establish that it handled the purchase and mortgage of the factory with the skill and care that a reasonably competent solicitor would have handled it. The fact that most solicitors in Hong Kong would have acted – and would have thought it proper to act – in the same way as the defendants did was irrelevant.

Common sense

In determining whether or not A breached a duty of care that he owed to B, the courts will always take into account considerations of common sense such as the ones listed below.

Emergencies and other stressful situations
It is common sense that people tend to react sub-optimally in emergencies or in other stressful situations. So if A owed B a duty to take reasonable steps to see that B would be reasonably safe, A should not necessarily be held to have breached that duty of care if he, in an emergency or other stressful situation,

---

[20] *Bolitho* v *City and Hackney Health Authority* [1998] AC 232.
[21] [1984] 1 AC 296. See also *Lloyd's Bank Ltd* v *E B Savory and Co.* [1933] AC 201 and *G & K Landenbau (UK) Ltd* v *Crawley & De Reya* [1978] 1 WLR 266.

failed to do as much as he might have done to ensure that B would be reasonably safe and his failure could reasonably be attributed not to any personal indifference on his part but to the situation in which he found himself.

In *Surtees v Kingston-upon-Thames Borough Council*,[22] it was alleged that a foster mother had breached the duty she owed the claimant, a child in her care, to take reasonable steps to ensure that the claimant did not come to any harm. The case was dismissed: there was no evidence that the foster mother had breached that duty. Sir Nicolas Browne-Wilkinson V-C warned that the courts:

> should be wary in its approach to holding parents in breach of a duty of care owed to their children ... The studied calm of the Royal Courts of Justice, concentrating on one point at a time, is light years away from the circumstances prevailing in the average home. The mother is looking after a fast moving toddler at the same time as cooking a meal, answering the telephone, looking after the other children and doing all the other things that the average mother has to cope with simultaneously, or in quick succession, in the normal household. We should be slow to characterise as negligent the care which ordinary loving mothers are able to give individual children, given the rough-and-tumble of home life.[23]

The House of Lords took a similar line in *Carmarthenshire County Council v Lewis*.[24] In that case, it will be recalled, a four-year-old boy attending nursery school wandered off the school premises and onto the road running alongside the nursery school. The claimant's husband, who was driving a lorry along the road, swerved to avoid the boy, crashed into a tree and died. The claimant claimed – and the House of Lords accepted – that the teachers at the school had owed her husband a duty to take reasonable steps to ensure that children at the school did not wander into the road outside the school.

In determining whether any of the teachers at the school had breached this duty of care, their Lordships focused on the conduct of one Miss Morgan, who was supposed to be supervising the boy and one other child at the time the accident happened. She was supposed to take the pair for a walk and had briefly left them alone in a classroom. Having left them, she was then detained attending to a child who needed to have a bandage put on because he had hurt himself. The four-year-old boy took advantage of her absence to leave the classroom, walk across the playground and wander out into the road. The House of Lords refused to find that Morgan had breached the duty she owed users of the road to take reasonable steps to ensure that children at the nursery did not escape into the road. Lord Tucker noted, '[i]t is very easy after the event to think of several things she might have done which would have avoided the accident that resulted from her absence' but refused to find that she had failed to take reasonable steps not to allow the four-year-old boy to wander off the premises – in the circumstances, faced with the sudden need to bandage up another child's wounds, Morgan's conduct had been quite natural.[25]

---

[22] [1991] 2 FLR 559.

[23] Ibid., 583–4.

[24] [1955] AC 549.

[25] A claim against the council succeeded in the *Carmarthenshire* case: it was held that they also owed people like the claimant's husband a duty to take reasonable steps to see that the children at the

Similarly, in *Wilsher* v *Essex Area Health Authority* Mustill LJ held that, in considering whether or not a doctor or a nurse had failed in his or her duty to treat a patient with the degree of care and skill that a reasonably competent doctor or nurse occupying the same post would exercise in treating a patient, 'full allowance must be made for the fact that certain aspects of the treatment may have [had] to be carried out in what [one may call] "battle conditions". An emergency may overburden the available resources, and, if an individual is forced by circumstances to do too many things at once, the fact that he does one of them incorrectly should not lightly be taken as negligence.'[26]

Games

A similar principle applies in the case of games involving physical contact. If A and B are engaged in playing such a game, it is common sense that each of them is liable in the heat of the moment to do something that involves some kind of error of judgement or lapse, with the result that the other is injured in some way. So if A is guilty of such an error or lapse, he will not automatically be held to have breached the duty of care he owed B in playing their game: it is only if his error or lapse involved a wanton or reckless disregard for B's safety that he will be held to have breached the duty of care he owed B.[27]

Self-help

It is common sense that adults can be expected to act in their own best interests. Given this, if A owes B, an adult, a duty to take reasonable steps to ensure that B is not harmed in some way, A can usually discharge that duty by putting B in a position to save himself from being harmed in that way. And if B is already in a position to save himself from being harmed in that way, A will not breach the duty of care he owes B if he takes no steps to ensure that B will not be harmed in that way.

So suppose Gary visited Dawn in her house. As we have seen, under the Occupiers' Liability Act 1957, Dawn will have owed Gary a duty to take reasonable steps to see that he was reasonably safe in visiting her. In determining whether or not Dawn breached that duty, the courts are enjoined by the Act to take the following considerations into account.

First, s 2(4)(a) of the Act provides that if Gary suffered harm because of a danger which he had been warned of by Dawn then Dawn should not be held to have breached the duty of care she owed Gary if the warning was 'in all the circumstances ... enough to enable [Gary] to be reasonably safe'. If Dawn warned Gary of the danger and the warning was sufficient to enable Gary to

---

school did not escape into the road, and the council breached that duty because they did not take adequate steps to see that the school gates were kept locked.

[26] [1987] 1 QB 730, 749. To the same effect, in relation to soldiers conducting peace-keeping operations, see *Bici* v *Ministry of Defence* [2004] EWHC 786, at [46].

[27] *Wooldridge* v *Sumner* [1963] 2 QB 43 (spectator injured when defendant rode his horse too fast); *Condon* v *Basi* [1985] 1 WLR 866 (footballer injured as a result of foul tackle by defendant); *Caldwell* v *Fitzgerald* [2001] EWCA Civ 1054 (jockey injured in race as a result of actions of two other jockeys); *Blake* v *Galloway* [2004] EWCA Civ 814 (claimant struck in eye by piece of bark thrown at him by defendant in course of good-natured horseplay).

avoid the danger himself then Dawn, by giving the warning, will have discharged the duty she owed Gary to take reasonable steps to ensure that he would not be harmed by the existence of that danger. Dawn could reasonably expect, having equipped Gary with that warning, that Gary would act to save himself from being harmed as a result of the existence of that danger.[28]

Secondly, s 2(3)(b) provides that the courts, in assessing whether Dawn breached the duty of care she owed Gary, must take into account the fact that 'an occupier may expect that a person, in the exercise of his calling, will appreciate and guard against any risks ordinarily incident to it, so far as the occupier leaves him free to do so'. So if Gary visited Dawn's house to mend a defective light fitting and Dawn did not take any steps to ensure that Gary would not be electrocuted in mending the fitting, Dawn will not have breached the duty she owed Gary to see that he would be reasonably safe in visiting her premises – Dawn could reasonably have expected Gary to take steps to ensure that he would not be electrocuted in mending the fitting.

The same principles apply in the employment context. So, in *Qualcast (Wolverhampton) Ltd v Haynes*[29] the claimant spilled some molten metal onto his left foot and was injured as a result. The claimant claimed the accident happened because his employer, the defendant, had breached the duty it owed him to take reasonable steps to ensure that he did not do his work in a way that would unreasonably endanger his health and safety. It was held that the defendant had not breached this duty. The defendant had made available to the claimant a stock of protective spats which were designed to ensure that employees would not suffer any injury if they spilled molten metal on themselves. As the claimant was an experienced worker and knew of the need to wear spats when handling molten metal to protect himself from injury, the defendant, in providing the claimant with such spats, had done all he needed to do to ensure that the defendant would not do his work in a way that would unreasonably endanger his health and safety. It would have been different if the claimant had been inexperienced; in such a case, the defendant – in order to discharge the duty of care he owed the claimant – would have had not only to supply the claimant with protective spats but also to instruct him to put them on when handling molten metal.

In *James v Hepworth & Grandage Ltd*,[30] the claimant – like the claimant in *Qualcast* – spilled molten metal on himself and suffered injury because he was not wearing protective spats. In this case, the claimant's employer, the

---

[28] See *Roles v Nathan* [1963] 1 WLR 1117 (smoke from a boiler which heated the Manchester Assembly Rooms began to fill the boiler room; the claimants' husbands, chimney sweeps, were called in to clean the flues along which the smoke was supposed to travel before reaching a chimney; an expert was called in to inspect the problem and he warned the chimney sweeps not to work in the flues while the boiler was lit as there was a substantial danger that they would suffer carbon monoxide poisoning as a result; the sweeps disregarded the warning and died as a result; held – occupier of the Assembly Rooms did not breach the duty of care he owed the sweeps under the 1957 Act: the warning they had been given was enough to ensure that they would be reasonably safe from suffering carbon monoxide poisoning while working on the flues).

[29] [1959] AC 743.

[30] [1968] 1 QB 94.

defendant, had made available to his employees a stock of protective spats and had posted warnings instructing his employees to wear spats when handling molten metal. The claimant was illiterate and therefore did not understand the warnings and the need to wear spats when handling molten metal. He sued the defendant, claiming that the accident occurred because the defendant had breached the duty it owed him to take reasonable steps to ensure that he did not do his work in a way that would unreasonably endanger his health and safety. The Court of Appeal held that the defendant did not breach this duty: the defendant had no reason to believe that the claimant was illiterate and was therefore entitled to expect that he would heed any warnings it gave him as to what he should wear in performing particular tasks. The defendant therefore discharged the duty of care it owed the claimant by supplying him with protective spats and warning him of the need to use them.

Children

It is common sense that, while adults can be expected to act in their own best interests, children cannot be expected to do the same. Given this, if A owes B, a child, a duty to take reasonable steps to ensure that B is not harmed in some way, A may be required to do more to ensure that B is not harmed in that way than he would if B were an adult. The Occupiers' Liability Act 1957 recognises this. Section 2(3)(a) of the Act provides that if an occupier of premises owes a child visiting those premises a duty under the Act to see that the visitor would be reasonably safe in using those premises for the purpose for which he was there, the courts should take into account – for the purpose of deciding whether or not the occupier breached that duty – the fact that 'an occupier must be prepared for children to be less careful than adults'.

So if Karen's premises contain a staircase which is dangerous to use and Karen posts a notice warning visitors of that fact, Karen's putting up that notice will discharge the duty she owes her adult visitors to take reasonable steps to ensure that they are not harmed as a result of the staircase being dangerous to use (so long as it is not necessary to use the staircase) but might not discharge the common duty of care that she will owe children who visit her premises. Children might be expected to disregard any warning notice and so taking reasonable steps to ensure that they will not be harmed as a result of the staircase being dangerous to use might require Karen to take some further steps to discourage children from using that staircase, such as cordoning it off.

While Karen must – in taking reasonable steps to ensure that child visitors to her premises will not be harmed as a result of using her premises for the purposes for which they are there – be prepared for children to be less careful than adults, if Paul, a child, visits Karen's premises under the supervision of his parents, Karen will be entitled to expect Paul's parents to take reasonable steps to ensure Paul's safety. So if it is reasonable to think that Paul's parents will take steps to ensure that Paul is not harmed as a result of the existence of some danger on Karen's premises, Karen will not breach the duty of care she owes Paul to see that Paul will be reasonably safe in using those premises for the purpose for which he is on those premises if she fails to take any steps *herself* to ensure that Paul is not harmed as a result of the existence of that danger.

So – in *Phipps* v *Rochester Corporation*,[31] a boy and a girl walked across a large open space of grassland which formed part of a building site which was occupied by the defendants. A long trench had been dug across the grassland for the purpose of laying a sewer and the boy fell into it, suffering injury as a result. It was held that the defendants *had* owed the boy a duty to take reasonable steps to see that he would not suffer injury crossing their land but they did not breach that duty when they failed to take any steps to ensure that the boy did not fall into the trench. The defendants could reasonably have expected that the boy's parents would accompany him on his trip across the grassland to ensure that he did not come to any harm or to have ascertained that the grassland had a long trench dug across it and forbidden him to walk in the vicinity of the trench.

BREACH THROUGH OTHERS

Suppose that A owed B some kind of duty of care – say a duty to take reasonable steps to save B from some kind of harm. Now, normally, in judging whether or not A breached that duty of care, we will look to see what *A* did. However, this is not always the case. Sometimes *A* will be held to have breached the duty of care that he owed B because *someone else* failed to take reasonable steps to save B from harm. This will be the case in two situations.

Non-delegable duties of care

The basic idea

Suppose that A owed B a duty to take reasonable steps to save B from suffering some kind of harm. And suppose that A gave C the job of saving B from that harm. And suppose that C failed to take reasonable steps to save B from that harm. Will A be held to have breached the duty of care that he owed B? One's instinctive response would be to say –

> It depends on whether C appeared to be a fit and proper person to whom to give the job of saving B. If he was, then A took reasonable steps to save B by giving the job of saving B to C. If he was not, then A failed to take reasonable steps to save B when he gave the job of saving B to C. He should have done the job himself and not relied on C to do it for him.

And that is the correct answer *if* the duty of care owed to B was what is known as *delegable*. An example of a delegable duty of care is the duty that an occupier owes his visitors to take reasonable steps to see that they will be reasonably safe in visiting his premises.

So, for example, suppose that one of the stairs on the staircase in Mary's house was loose. Mary rang Vijay, a local carpenter, to repair the stair. Vijay came round and after half an hour's work appeared to have solved the problem. However, two days later Sarah came round to visit Mary and suffered a bad fall when she went upstairs and tripped on the defective stair, which suddenly came

---

[31] [1955] 1 QB 450.

loose under her feet. If Vijay seemed like a reputable contractor and seemed to have solved the problem with the stair, it will not be possible to argue that Mary breached the common duty of care she owed Sarah to take reasonable steps to see that Sarah would be reasonably safe in visiting her. She *did* take such steps: she got a reputable contractor in to repair the dangerous stair on her staircase and only let him go when she was satisfied that he had repaired the problem.[32]

But – returning to the general example with which we began our discussion – our instinctive answer will be quite wrong if the duty owed by A to B to take reasonable steps to save B from harm was *non-delegable*. If it was non-delegable then *C's* failure to take reasonable steps to save B from harm will have put *A* in breach of the duty of care that he owed B. It's as if C's lack of care is transferred to A and A is held to have failed to take care to save B from harm. So even if A *personally* took reasonable steps to save B from harm by giving C the job of saving B – which will be the case if C seemed a fit and proper person to whom to give the job of saving B – A will *still* be held to have breached the duty of care that he owed B.

But note that if the duty of care that A owed B was non-delegable, C's failure will only have put A in breach of the duty of care that A owed B *because A gave C the job of saving B*. For example, it is well established that the duty of care that an employer owes his employees to take reasonable steps to see that they are not killed or injured working for him is non-delegable.[33] So if Carl employs Lara to work on a particular machine and he gives Tom the job of maintaining the machine to ensure that it is safe to work on, then if Tom fails to take reasonable steps to see that the machine is in good repair, Tom's carelessness will put Carl in breach of the duty of care that he owes Lara as her employer. But if Fred, a fellow employee, carelessly bumps into Lara while she is working on the machine and she is injured as a result, then Fred's carelessness will not put Carl in breach of the duty of care that he owes Lara. The reason is that Carl never gave Fred the job of seeing that Lara would not be killed or injured while she worked for him.[34]

---

[32] See the Occupiers' Liability Act 1957, s 2(4)(b): 'where any damage is caused to a visitor by a danger due to the faulty execution of any work of construction, maintenance or repair by an independent contractor employed by the occupier, the occupier is not to be treated without more as answerable for the danger if in all the circumstances he had acted reasonably in entrusting the work to an independent contractor and had taken such steps (if any) as he reasonably ought in order to satisfy himself that the contractor was competent and that the work had been properly done.'

[33] See below, p. 229.

[34] See *Davie v New Merton Board Mills Ltd* [1959] AC 604 (employee injured by defective tool unable to sue employer on ground that manufacturer's negligence in manufacturing tool put employer in breach of non-delegable duty of care that he owed employée because employer never gave manufacturer job of ensuring that employees would be safe; note, however, employee would now be able to sue employer under s 1 of the Employers' Liability (Defective Equipment) Act 1969). Also *O'Reilly v National Rail & Tramway Appliances Ltd* [1966] 1 All ER 499 (employee injured as a result of fellow employees' negligence in handling live shell that was in a pile of scrap metal being processed by employees unable to sue employer on ground that employees' negligence put employer in breach of the non-delegable duty of care that he owed employee because employees not given job of ensuring employee's safety).

Examples of non-delegable duties of care

So – how do we tell whether a given duty of care is delegable or non-delegable? There is no general test – either set out in the cases or emerging from the cases – that we can use to determine whether a given a duty of care is delegable or non-delegable.[35] We simply have to look at the cases to see whether the courts have *held* that the duty of care in question is delegable or non-delegable.[36] The following duties of care have been held to be non-delegable:

(1) *Employment.* As has just been observed, the duty of care that an employer owes his employees to take reasonable steps to see that they are not killed or injured in working for him is non-delegable.[37]

(2) *Bailment.* It is well established that the duty a bailee owes a bailor to take reasonable steps to safeguard the bailed property is non-delegable in nature.[38]

An example of the application of this principle is provided by the case of *Morris v C W Martin & Sons Ltd.*[39] In that case, the claimant gave her fur coat to a firm of furriers to be cleaned. They then sent the coat to the defendant cleaners. The defendants were bailees of the coat for the claimant and as such they owed her a duty to take reasonable steps to safeguard the coat. Unfortunately, the defendants gave the job of looking after the coat to one of their employees, who promptly stole it. Lord Denning MR held[40] that the employee's theft of the coat put the defendants in breach of the duty of care that they owed the claimant to safeguard her coat and accordingly held the defendants liable to the claimant for the loss of her coat.[41] The fact that it was the employee *who had been given the job*

---

[35] There are some duties which are, of necessity, non-delegable. For example, if A is under a *strict duty* to *ensure* that outcome *x* does not occur, then if A gives B the job of seeing that that outcome does not occur and B fails to ensure that outcome *x* does not occur, A will have breached his duty: he was under a duty to ensure that outcome *x* did not occur and he failed to do this. A's duty is therefore non-delegable. Strict duties like this are rare in English law and, of course, are not relevant to the current discussion, which is concerned with duties of care.

[36] See *KLB v British Columbia* [2003] 2 SCR 403, at [31] (per McLachlin CJ). So if the duty of care in question has only recently been established and there is no authority on the issue of whether it is delegable or non-delegable, there is simply no way of knowing which it is.

[37] *Wilsons & Clyde Coal Co. Ltd* v *English* [1938] AC 57; *McDermid* v *Nash Dredging & Reclamation Co. Ltd* [1987] 1 AC 906.

[38] *Riverstone Meat Co. Pty Ltd* v *Lancashire Shipping Co. Ltd* [1961] AC 807; *Port Swettenham Authority* v *T W Wu & Co.* [1979] AC 580, 591.

[39] [1966] 1 QB 716.

[40] Ibid., 725, 728.

[41] *Important note.* There is some dispute as to whether the true basis of the defendants' liability in this case was that: (a) the defendants' employee put them in breach of the non-delegable duty that they owed the claimant to safeguard her coat; or (b) the defendants were vicariously liable in respect of the tort committed by their employee (the tort of conversion) when the employee stole the coat. Lord Denning MR's judgment supports view (a). Diplock LJ's judgment in the same case supports view (b). Salmon LJ's judgment straddles both views. In *Lister* v *Hesley Hall Ltd* [2002] 1 AC 215 it was assumed without any debate that *Morris* v *C W Martin* was a vicarious liability case: ibid., at [19] (per Lord Steyn), [46] (per Lord Clyde), [57] (per Lord Hobhouse), [75]–[76] (per Lord Millett). In *Dubai Aluminium Co. Ltd* v *Salaam* [2003] 2 AC 366, Lord Millett once again assumed without debate that *Morris* was a vicarious liability case (at [129]). Lord Nicholls was less dogmatic (at [29]), noting that there was some debate over the basis of liability in *Morris*. However, he thought it unnecessary to express his views on the issue. The High Court of Australia was divided in *New South Wales* v *Lepore* [2003] HCA 4 over the issue of how best to analyse the basis of liability in *Morris*. Gleeson CJ (at [48]) and Kirby P (at [312]) held that *Morris* was a vicarious liability

of looking after the coat who stole it was crucial to the finding that the defendants had breached the duty of care that they owed the claimant. Had it been some other employee who stole the coat, the defendants would not have been held liable unless they, or the employee who was given the job of looking after the coat, were personally at fault for the occurrence of the theft.[42]

(3) *Extended* Hedley Byrne *principle I.* A number of authorities indicate that if A owes B a duty to perform a certain task with a certain degree of care and skill under the extended principle in *Hedley Byrne*, that duty of care will be non-delegable.

So Denning LJ remarked in *Cassidy* v *Ministry of Health* that, 'when hospital authorities undertake to treat a patient, and themselves select and appoint . . . the professional men and women who are to give the treatment, then they are responsible for the negligence of those persons in failing to give proper treatment, no matter whether they are doctors, surgeons, nurses or anyone else'.[43]

Similarly, it was held in *Philips* v *William Whiteley Ltd*[44] that the defendant firm of jewellers in that case owed the claimant a non-delegable duty to pierce her ears with the degree of care and skill that a reasonably competent jeweller would exercise in piercing someone's ears. The defendants had summoned an employee of another firm to perform the operation but, fortunately for the defendants, the employee in question pierced the claimant's ears with the requisite degree of care and skill and did not therefore put the defendants in breach of the duty of care that they owed the claimant.

It may be that the decision in *Lloyd* v *Grace, Smith & Co.*[45] can also be explained on this basis. The claimant in that case consulted a firm of solicitors with a view to increasing the income she received from her investments. Her affairs were entrusted to the care of the firm's managing clerk, who used his position to defraud the claimant of two cottages that she owned. The firm was held liable for the loss suffered by the claimant. The case is often viewed as one where the firm was held vicariously liable in respect of the managing clerk's deceit.[46] However, it is possible to argue that the true basis of the firm's liability in this case was that the firm owed a non-delegable duty to the claimant to

---

case; Kirby P going so far as to deride alternative explanations of the case as 'feeble' (ibid.). However, Gaudron J (at [127]) and McHugh J (at [147], [161]) both viewed the defendants' liability in *Morris* as resting on the fact that their employee had put them in breach of a non-delegable duty of care that they owed the claimant. Tony Weir is in no doubt that the latter analysis is correct, pointing out that the defendants would have been just as liable in *Morris* to the claimant had they given her fur coat to an independent contractor to look after, which he then stole: Weir 2001, 102. (Had that happened, of course, there would have been no possibility of the defendants being held vicariously liable for the tort committed by the contractor in stealing the coat because one cannot ever be held vicariously liable in respect of torts committed by one's independent contractors: see below, p. 636.) This seems to us the clinching argument and establishes that the liability in *Morris* is more satisfactorily viewed as arising out of the fact that the defendants' employee's actions put them in breach of the non-delegable duty of care that they owed the claimant to safeguard her coat.

[42] [1966] 1 QB 716, 740–1, per Salmon LJ.
[43] [1951] 2 KB 343, 362. See also *Gold* v *Essex County Council* [1942] 2 KB 293, at 301–2 (per Lord Greene MR).
[44] [1938] 1 All ER 566.
[45] [1912] AC 716.
[46] *Lister* v *Hesley Hall Ltd* [2002] 1 AC 215, at [19] (per Lord Steyn), [73] (per Lord Millett).

handle her affairs with a reasonable degree of care and skill and that the managing clerk – who was given the job of handling the claimant's affairs – put the firm in breach of that duty of care when, far from handling her affairs with a reasonable degree of care and skill, he defrauded her of her cottages.[47]

(4) *Extended* Hedley Byrne *principle II.* It seems to follow from what has already been said that if A owes B a duty under the extended principle in *Hedley Byrne* to take reasonable steps to achieve some goal or end, then that duty of care will be non-delegable.[48]

So suppose that Mary owned a factory and she employed John to guard it at night, to see that no one broke into it. John will have owed Mary a duty to take reasonable steps to see that the factory was not broken into at night under the extended principle in *Hedley Byrne* – he indicated to Mary that she could safely rely on him to take reasonable steps to see that her factory was not broken into at night and she so relied on him. Furthermore it follows from what has just been said that this duty of care will have been non-delegable in nature. Suppose now that John gave the job of looking after the factory to Fred and Fred allowed a gang of thieves to loot the factory. Fred's failure to take reasonable steps to see that the factory was not broken into will have put John in breach of the non-delegable duty of care that he owed Mary. Mary will as a result be allowed to sue John in negligence for the loss she has suffered as a result of her factory being looted.[49]

(5) *Danger.* It seems that if A owes B a duty to take reasonable steps to elim-

---

[47] See *New South Wales* v *Lepore* [2003] HCA 4, at [127] (per Gaudron J).

[48] This is perhaps the only way of justifying the result in *Rogers* v *Night Riders* [1983] RTR 324. The claimant in that case was injured when she took a trip in a mini-cab and a defective door on the mini-cab flew open. The claimant had summoned the mini-cab by ringing the defendant firm. The firm did not own any mini-cabs or employ any drivers itself – instead it had a list of drivers who were available to pick up customers and it would call drivers on that list when someone wanted a lift somewhere. (The drivers paid a fee for being placed on the list.) The Court of Appeal held that the defendant firm had owed the claimant a duty to take reasonable steps to check that the mini-cabs used by the drivers on its list were reasonably safe; that that duty was non-delegable; that the defendant firm had given the drivers on its list the job of checking their own mini-cabs for faults; that the claimant's driver had been at fault in failing to spot that the door on his mini-cab was defective and that his fault put the defendants in breach of the non-delegable duty of care that they owed the claimant. Accordingly, the claimant was entitled to sue the defendant for damages. It is difficult to know why the defendants owed the claimant a duty of care here. Conceivably, the extended principle in *Hedley Byrne* applied here – it is possible that the defendants implicitly indicated to the claimant that she could safely rely on them to take reasonable steps to see that her mini-cab was safe to travel in and that the claimant did so rely on the defendants. If this is right, then the finding that the duty of care owed by the defendants to the claimant here was non-delegable was unexceptionable.

[49] Cf *Photo Production* v *Securicor* [1980] AC 827. The defendant security company in that case was employed to patrol the claimants' factory at night to see that it was not burned down or broken into during the night. The job of patrolling the factory was given to one of the defendants' security guards who, one night, deliberately started a fire in the factory with the result that the factory burned down. The defendant security company was held *prima facie* liable for the fire damage. (In fact, there was an exclusion clause in the contract between the defendants and the claimants that absolved the defendants of liability.) There are *dicta* in the case which indicate that the source of the defendants' *prima facie* liability in this case was that they were vicariously liable for the tort committed by their employee in starting the fire: at 846 (per Lord Wilberforce) and 852 (per Lord Salmon). However, it is possible to argue that the real source of the defendants' liability in this case was that their employee's lack of care put them in breach of a non-delegable duty of care that they owed the claimants: see *New South Wales* v *Lepore* [2003] HCA 4, at [146]–[148] (per McHugh J).

inate or minimise some serious hazard, then that duty of care is non-delegable.

So if a fixture attached to A's land is in obvious danger of falling into the highway and injuring someone, A will owe people using the highway a non-delegable duty to repair the fixture or take it down.[50] Similarly, if A creates an obstruction in the road which people are liable to run into at night. The duty A will owe users of the road to take reasonable steps to clear the road of the obstruction or warn them of its existence will be non-delegable.[51] Again, if A gets C to do something for him which is *inherently dangerous*[52] for B, then A will owe B a non-delegable duty to take reasonable steps to minimise the danger to which B will be exposed as a result of C's activities.[53]

(6) *Educational authorities.* As we have seen, an educational authority will owe children at a school under its control a duty to take reasonable steps to see that they do not come to any physical harm while they are at school.[54] The High Court of Australia has held in *New South Wales* v *Lepore* that that duty of care is non-delegable in nature[55] and there is no reason to think that an English court would come to any other conclusion if the question arose here.

Intentional misconduct

Suppose that A owed B a non-delegable duty to take reasonable steps to save B from harm. Suppose further that A gave C the job of seeing that B did not come to any harm. And suppose finally that C intentionally harmed B. Can we say that C – by intentionally harming B – put A in breach of the non-delegable duty of care that he owed B?

One would have thought so: C could hardly be said to have taken reasonable steps to save B from harm if he intentionally harmed B. However, three of the seven judges who decided *New South Wales* v *Lepore* argued that in the case just described, C's actions will *not* have put A in breach of the non-delegable duty

---

[50] *Tarry* v *Ashton* (1876) 1 QBD 314. The question of what amounts to a 'serious hazard' is fraught with difficulty. However, it seems that a danger affecting users of the highway will amount to a serious hazard.

[51] *Saper* v *Hungate Builders Ltd* [1972] RTR 380.

[52] This requirement was not satisfied in *Salsbury* v *Woodland* [1970] 1 QB 324, where the claimant was injured as a result of the carelessness of a contractor in cutting down a tree on the defendant's land. The act of cutting down the tree was not inherently dangerous – 'The act . . . if done with ordinary elemental caution by skilled men, presented no hazard to anyone at all' (ibid., at 338, per Widgery LJ).

[53] *Honeywill & Stein Ltd* v *Larkin Brothers* [1934] 1 KB 191 (defendant had a third party set off a magnesium flash in a theatre owned by the claimant, with the result that the theatre burned down; held, the defendant had owed the claimant a duty to take reasonable steps to see that the fire involved in setting off the flash did not spread; that he delegated the job of seeing the fire did not spread to the third party and the third party put the defendant in breach of the non-delegable duty that he owed the claimant by failing to take reasonable steps to see that the fire did not spread).

[54] See above, p. 184.

[55] [2003] HCA 4. Callinan J dissented on this point: see [340].

of care that he owed B.[56] C's actions, they held, will only have put A in breach of the non-delegable duty of care that he owed B if C *carelessly* failed to save B from harm. So, they held, a teacher who commits a sexual assualt on a child at school will *not* put the education authority that is in charge of that school in breach of the non-delegable duty that they owe that child to take reasonable steps to see that that child does not come to any harm while he is at school. Such a teacher would only put the education authority in breach of its non-delegable duty of care if he or she *carelessly* failed to take steps to see that a child in his or her care did not come to any harm by, for example, failing to stop other children assaulting the child.

This is *not* the law in England, though it used to be. As Lord Salmon observed in *Port Swettenham Authority* v *T W Wu & Co.*, it used to be the law[57] that 'a master who was under a duty to guard another's goods was liable if the servant he sent to perform the duty for him performed it so negligently as to enable thieves to steal the goods, but was not liable if that servant joined with the thieves in the very theft'.[58] But, as Lord Salmon went on to say, 'This proposition is clearly contrary to principle and common sense, and to the law . . . [as stated in] *Morris* v *C W Martin and Sons Ltd.*'[59] It is somewhat surprising, then, to see at least some members of the High Court of Australia attempting to revive this rule. But it is highly unlikely that any such attempt will be made here.

Companies and other artificial legal persons

A company is an artificial legal person. As such, as Lord Diplock remarked in *Tesco Supermarkets Ltd* v *Natrass*, 'it is incapable itself of doing any physical act or being in a state of mind'.[60] If a company is to act, then, it can only do so through natural persons – people who are, of course, capable of performing physical actions. This creates a problem when we want to determine whether or not a company breached a duty of care that it owed to someone else.[61] Whose actions should we look at in order to determine whether or not that duty of care was breached? The facts of the *Tesco Supermarkets* case illustrate the problem.

---

[56] Ibid., at [31]–[37] (per Gleeson CJ) and at [264]–[267] (per Gummow and Hayne JJ). McHugh J disagreed: at [161]–[163]. Though it is not entirely clear, it seems that Gaudron J also disagreed, given the fact that she analysed both *Morris* and *Lloyd* v *Grace, Smith* as being cases where the defendants were put in breach of a non-delegable duty of care by the intentional actions of a third party: at [127]. Kirby P preferred to reserve his position on the issue: at [293]. As Callinan J did not think that the education authorities in the *New South Wales* case owed a non-delegable duty of care to the claimants, the issue did not arise for him.

[57] See *Cheshire* v *Bailey* [1905] 1 KB 237.

[58] [1979] AC 580, 591.

[59] Ibid.

[60] [1972] AC 153, 198.

[61] Of course, this issue only comes up if we want to establish whether a company is *personally* liable to compensate a claimant for some loss that he or she has suffered. If it is not personally liable to pay such compensation it may still be *vicariously liable* to pay such compensation if one of its employees caused the claimant to suffer the loss in question by committing the tort and there was a sufficiently close connection between what the employee was employed to do and the tort committed by the employee: see below, pp. 636, 650–1.

In that case, a customer at a Tesco store was charged 3s. 11d. for a packet of washing powder when posters in the window of the store advertised that brand of washing powder as being on special offer at 2s. 11d. per packet. The general manager of the store, one Mr Clement, was at fault for this: he had failed to take reasonable steps to ensure that the store was stocked with some packets with the lower price on them. Tesco was charged with committing an offence under s 11(2) of the Trade Descriptions Act 1968 which provided that 'if any person offering to supply any goods gives ... any indication likely to be taken as an indication that the goods are being offered at a price less than that at which they are in fact being offered he shall, subject to the provisions of this Act, be guilty of an offence'. In their defence, Tesco sought to rely on s 24(1) of the Act which provided that '[i]n any proceedings for an offence under this Act ... it shall be a defence for the person charged to prove – (a) that the commission of the offence was due ... to the act or default of another person and (b) that he took all reasonable precautions and exercised all due diligence to avoid the commission of such an offence by himself or any person under his control'.

Tesco could establish that (a) was true – the offence was committed because of Mr Clement's 'default'. Could it establish that (b) was true – that it took all reasonable care to ensure that its goods were not sold at a price higher than the advertised price? Clearly, *Mr Clement* did not take such care – but did that mean that *Tesco*, Mr Clement's employer, did not take such care? More generally, whose actions should be looked at to determine whether Tesco took reasonable care to ensure that its goods were not sold at a price higher than the advertised price? The House of Lords' answer was that one should look at the actions of those who represented Tesco's 'guiding mind or will' – only if *they* failed to take care to ensure that Tesco's goods were not sold at a price higher than the advertised price would it be proper to say that *Tesco* failed to take care to ensure that its goods were not sold at a price higher than the advertised price. Mr Clement, the House of Lords held, did not 'function as the directing mind or will of the company. He was ... being directed.'[62]

So *Mr Clement's* failure to take care to ensure that Tesco's goods were not sold at a price higher than the advertised price did not mean that *Tesco* failed to take such care. In fact, those who *did* represent Tesco's 'guiding mind or will' – the board of directors of Tesco and those to whom they had delegated the job of running Tesco – *had* taken reasonable care to ensure that Tesco's goods were not sold at a price higher than the advertised price. They had taken steps to instruct their store managers as to how their stores should be run; they had appointed a host of branch inspectors to go round the stores and make sure that the store managers were observing company policy in their running of the stores; and they had employed area inspectors to supervise the work of the branch inspectors. So Tesco – in the person of those who represented Tesco's 'guiding mind or will' – *had* taken reasonable care to ensure that Tesco's goods were not sold at a price higher than the advertised price and therefore had a

[62] [1972] AC 153 180 (per Lord Morris).

defence under s 24(1) of the Trade Descriptions Act 1968 to the charge that they had committed an offence under s 11(2) of that Act.

The principle, endorsed in the *Tesco Supermarkets* case, that we ascertain what a company did at a particular time by looking at the acts of those who represented the 'guiding mind or will' of the company at that time is well established.[63] However, this principle has recently been brought into question at the highest level where it has been suggested that *how* we ascertain what a company did depends very much on the *nature and purpose* of the legal rule which requires us to find out what that company did.

In *Re Supply of Ready Mixed Concrete (No. 2)*,[64] four companies which were engaged in the supply of ready mixed concrete entered into agreements with each other which fixed the prices at which they would supply ready mixed concrete to customers and determined what share each company would enjoy of the market for ready mixed concrete in the area in which the four companies operated. These agreements were unlawful under s 35(1) of the Restrictive Trade Practices Act 1976. The Director General of Fair Trading obtained injunctions against the four companies, requiring them not to enter into or give effect to any such agreements in future.

After the injunctions were obtained, employees of the four companies, without the knowledge of the management of those companies and contrary to their express instructions, started to operate a new agreement to fix prices and allocate work among the four companies. The Director General claimed that the companies had breached the injunctions and were therefore in contempt of court. In defence, the companies claimed that they had not entered into or given effect to any unlawful price fixing and work allocation agreement. The House of Lords dismissed the companies' claim – what the companies' employees did, the companies did. So if the companies' employees entered into and gave effect to an unlawful price fixing and work allocation agreement among themselves, the companies entered into and gave effect to such an agreement among themselves in breach of the injunction against them. This was so even though there was no way the companies' employees could be said to have represented the 'guiding mind or will' of the companies.

---

[63] It traces its origin to the judgment of Viscount Haldane LC in *Lennard's Carrying Co. Ltd* v *Asiatic Petroleum Co. Ltd* [1915] AC 705, 713: 'My Lords, a corporation is an abstraction. It has no mind of its own any more than it has a body of its own; its active and directing will must consequently be sought in the person of somebody who for some purposes may be called an agent, but who is really the directing mind and will of the corporation, the very ego and centre of the personality of the corporation.' Denning LJ found a characteristically colourful way to express the principle in *H L Bolton (Engineering) Co. Ltd* v *T J Graham & Sons Ltd* [1957] 1 QB 159, 172: 'A company may in many ways be likened to a human body. It has a brain and a nerve centre which controls what it does. It also has hands which hold the tools and act in accordance with directions from the centre. Some of the people in the company are mere servants or agents who are nothing more than hands to do the work and cannot be said to represent the mind or will. Others are directors and managers who represent the directing mind or will of the company, and control what it does. The state of mind of these managers is the state of mind of the company and is treated by the law as such. So you will find that in cases where the law requires personal fault as a condition of liability in tort, the fault of the manager will be the personal fault of the company.'

[64] [1995] 1 AC 456.

In a subsequent Privy Council case, *Meridian Global Funds Management Asia Ltd* v *Securities Commission*,[65] Lord Hoffmann – giving the only judgment – endorsed the result in *Re Supply of Ready Mixed Concrete (No. 2)* and sought to reconcile it with the decision in the *Tesco Supermarkets* case by arguing that: if applying a particular legal rule to a company requires the courts to find out what that company did, the courts should adopt the approach to finding out what that company did that the creators of the legal rule in question intended them to adopt for the purposes of applying that rule. 'This is always a matter of interpretation: given that [the rule in question] was intended to apply to a company, how was it intended to apply? Whose act . . . was *for this purpose* intended to count as the act . . . of the company? One finds the answer to this question by applying the usual canons of interpretation, taking into account the language of the rule (if it is a statute) and its content and policy.'[66]

So, in Lord Hoffmann's view, the *Tesco Supermarkets* case was decided the way it was because those who created the defence contained in s 24(1) of the Trade Descriptions Act 1968 did not intend the courts to treat Tesco as having failed to take care to ensure that its goods were not sold at a price higher than the advertised price if one of the Tesco store managers did not take such care. On the other hand, Lord Hoffmann argued, *Re Supply of Ready Mixed Concrete (No. 2)* was decided the way it was because an injunction against a company, requiring it not to enter into or give effect to unlawful price fixing and work allocation agreements with other companies, would be of little use if a company that was subject to such an injunction could not be held liable for breaching that injunction if its employees set up and operated an unlawful price fixing and work allocation agreement without the knowledge of the company's management.

It is not true to say, then, that there is a *general* rule, good for *all* situations, that what a company did at a particular time is to be ascertained by reference to what those who represented the company's 'guiding mind or will' at the time did. However, the Court of Appeal has recently affirmed that the 'guiding mind or will' approach to determining what a company did should be adopted unless there is a good reason why a different approach should be adopted (such as that Parliament intended that a different approach should be adopted in the context of determining whether a company committed a particular statutory offence).[67] If this is right, then the 'guiding mind or will' approach should still be adopted when we have to determine whether or not a company breached a *duty of care* that it owed to someone else.

So, on the view taken here, if ABC plc manufactures bottles of ginger beer and Beth, an employee of ABC's, deliberately inserts a snail into one of ABC's bottles, Beth's actions will not necessarily put ABC in breach of the duty it owes each potential consumer of its ginger beer to take care that it does not put into general circulation ginger beer that is unsafe to consume. While *Beth* has

---

[65] [1995] 2 AC 500.

[66] Ibid., 507.

[67] *Attorney-General's Reference (No. 2 of 1999)* [2000] QB 796, 814, 816: 'the primary "directing mind and will" rule still applies though it is not determinative in all cases.'

failed to take such care, *ABC* will only be held to have failed to take such care if its management – its 'guiding mind or will' – failed to take care to ensure that its ginger beer would be safe to consume.[68]

In every case where an artificial legal person owed someone else a duty we are confronted with the problem – Whose actions should we look at to determine whether or not that person breached that duty? In the case of companies that problem is solved, we suggest, by adopting the 'guiding mind or will' principle according to which we ascertain what a company did at a particular time by looking at what those who represented that company's 'guiding mind or will' at that time did. The same approach should be adopted in relation to artificial legal persons that are not companies, such as local authorities.

BURDEN OF PROOF

Generally speaking, the burden is on the claimant in a negligence case to prove that the defendant breached a duty of care owed to her. So, for example, in *Knight* v *Fellick*[69] the claimant was run down by the defendant driver. The claimant was so badly injured in the accident that she had no memory of how it happened. The claimant sued the defendant in negligence for compensation but her claim failed: she could not prove that the defendant was driving without due care and attention at the time he hit the claimant.

It was significant that the accident in *Knight* happened at night, on a road which had no street lighting and that the claimant was wearing dark clothing at the time of the accident. Suppose that Gary ran Nita over in his car during the day when visibility was perfect and Nita wants to sue Gary in negligence. In such a case, Nita will find it very easy to convince a court that Gary was not driving with due care and attention at the time of the accident. She will be able to argue, 'Gary hit me in broad daylight. What more proof do you need that he wasn't driving with due care and attention at the time of the accident? Had he been driving carefully, he would have managed to avoid me. The facts speaks for themselves: *res ipsa loquitur.*' Of course, it may be that Gary *was* driving with due care and attention – it may be that he hit Nita only because she dashed out into the middle of the road right in front of his car. But if Gary cannot prove that that is what happened, the court will find that Nita has discharged the burden on her and find that at the time of the accident, Gary was in breach of the duty of care that he owed Nita to take care not to drive dangerously.

This way of arguing that a defendant breached a duty of care owed to a claimant – what's called by lawyers a *res ipsa loquitur* argument – only works if the facts of the case are such that the most natural explanation of what

---

[68] Of course, there is a possibility that ABC could be sued by anyone harmed by the snail on the ground that it is vicariously liable for Beth's negligence. Whether ABC is vicariously liable or not will depend on whether there was a 'sufficiently close connection' between Beth's negligence and what she was employed to do: see below, pp. 650–1. Also ABC might be held liable for any harm done by the presence of the snail in the bottle under the Consumer Protection Act 1987: see below, pp. 760–76.

[69] [1977] RTR 316.

happened is that the defendant was careless.[70] So a *res ipsa loquitur* argument will be available to help establish that the defendant breached a duty of care owed to the claimant if: (1) the defendant performed a minor operation on the claimant's hand and after the operation was over, the claimant lost the use of his hand;[71] (2) the claimant was working in the defendant's factory and an electrical panel fell on his head;[72] (3) the claimant was injured when a coach driven by the defendant suddenly veered across the road into the claimant's path;[73] (4) the defendant cleaned a suit belonging to the claimant and the claimant suddenly developed dermatitis on wearing the suit again.[74] But such an argument will not be available in the case where a door on a moving train operated by the defendant suddenly opens and the claimant falls out.[75] The fact that the door opened suddenly does not of itself indicate that the defendant was careless in operating the train: the door could just as well have opened because of the fault of another passenger.

As we have said, the burden of proof in a negligence case normally falls on the claimant to show that the defendant breached the duty of care that he owed her. However, there are a couple of exceptions to this general rule. In such cases, the *defendant* will be required to show that he was careful. If he cannot, then the courts will find that he breached the duty of care that he owed the claimant.

(1) *Bailment.* If A holds goods on a bailment for B and those goods are lost, destroyed or damaged, it will be presumed – unless A can prove otherwise – that A breached the duty of care that he owed B to take reasonable steps to safeguard those goods.[76]

(2) *Criminal conviction.* If A owed B a duty of care and has been convicted of a criminal offence which A could not have committed had he fulfilled the duty of care that he owed B, in any civil proceedings between A and B it will be presumed – unless A can prove otherwise – that A breached the duty of care that he owed B.[77]

---

[70] The requirements that had to be satisfied before a *res ipsa loquitur* argument could be made in favour of the view that the defendant had breached a duty of care owed to the claimant were first set out by Erle CJ in *Scott* v *London and St Katherine Docks Company* (1865) 3 H & C 595, 601; 159 ER 665, 667: '... where the thing [which caused the accident complained of] is shewn to be under the management of the defendant ... and the accident is such as in the ordinary course of things does not happen if those who have the management use proper care, it affords reasonable evidence, in the absence of explanation by the defendants, that the accident arose from want of care.'

[71] *Cassidy* v *Ministry of Health* [1951] 2 KB 343.

[72] *Bennett* v *Chemical Construction (GB) Ltd* [1971] 1 WLR 1571.

[73] *Ng Chun Pui* v *Lee Chuen Tat* [1988] RTR 298 (note that no finding of negligence was ultimately made in this case – even though it looked at first as if the defendant had been careless in driving the coach, he had an explanation for his driving into the claimant's lane: he was trying to avoid a car that had cut in front of him).

[74] *Mayne* v *Silvermere Cleaners* [1939] 1 All ER 693.

[75] *Easson* v *London and North Eastern Railway Company* [1944] 1 KB 421.

[76] *Houghland* v *R R Low (Luxury Coaches) Ltd* [1962] 1 QB 694; *Port Swettenham Authority* v *T W Wu & Co.* [1979] AC 580.

[77] Civil Evidence Act 1968, s 11. On which, see *Stupple* v *Royal Insurance Co. Ltd* [1971] 1 QB 50.

TORTS INVOLVING THE INFLICTION OF CERTAIN KINDS OF HARM

If we take any two individuals, A and B, A will owe B a number of tortious duties that are *not* duties of care.

For instance, A will *normally* owe B a duty under the common law not to hit her. If A breaches this duty, he will commit the tort of *battery* (discussed in Chapter 10). Moreover, A will *normally* owe B a further duty under the common law that requires A to ensure that he does not intentionally or carelessly cause B to think that he is about to hit her. If A breaches this duty he will commit the tort of *assault* (again, see Chapter 10). Both these duties happen to be duties not to cause B to suffer a specific kind of harm – being hit in the case of the first duty and being put in fear of being hit in the case of the second duty. Let us call a duty not to cause another to suffer a specific kind of harm a 'harm-avoiding' duty.

There are many other harm-avoiding tortious duties that A may owe B. The existence of these duties accounts for the existence of the torts set out in this section – they all consist of the breach of a tortious duty owed to someone else not to cause that someone else to suffer a certain kind of harm. We have already touched on the torts of assault and battery. We can briefly mention the other torts discussed in this section.

(1) *False imprisonment.* If you take two individuals, A and B, A will owe B a common law duty to ensure that he does not voluntarily subject B to any form of bodily restraint which is not authorised by law. If A breaches this duty he will commit the tort of *false imprisonment* (discussed in Chapter 11).

(2) *Libel and slander.* If you take two individuals, A and B, A will *normally* owe B a common law duty to ensure that he does not publish to another a statement that is defamatory of B. (A statement will be defamatory of B if it is liable either to make right-thinking people think less well of B or to make right-thinking people feel unwilling to share B's company.) If A breaches that duty he will commit the tort of *libel* or the tort of *slander*, depending on whether the statement in question is published in permanent or non-permanent form. Both these torts are discussed in Chapter 12.

(3) *Harassment.* If you take two individuals, A and B, A will *normally* owe B a statutory duty under the Protection from Harassment Act 1997 to ensure that he does not treat B in a way which he knows or ought to know amounts to harassment. Section 3 of the 1997 Act makes it clear that if A breaches this duty he will commit a tort. While the tort which will be committed by A if he breaches this duty has no official name – the existence of the statutory duty created by the 1997 Act being a relative novelty – it seems natural to say that if A breaches this duty he will commit the tort of *harassment* (discussed in Chapter 13).

(4) *Wrongful disclosure of private information.* If you take two given individuals, A and B, A will *not* owe B a general duty not to intrude into B's privacy. So if A intrudes into B's privacy he will not normally commit a tort – even if he had no good reason for doing what he did. However, if A is in possession of private information about B, A will *normally* owe B a duty not to disclose that information to a third party. If A breaches this duty, he will commit the tort of *wrongful disclosure of private information.* This area of the law will be discussed in Chapter 14.

(5) *Conversion.* If B is in possession of, or has an immediate right to possess, certain goods, then A will *normally* owe B a duty to ensure that he does not do anything that will seriously interfere with B's possession of, or right to possess, those goods. If A breaches this duty, he will commit the tort of *conversion* (discussed in Chapter 15).[1]

(6) *Trespass to goods.* If B is in possession of certain goods, A will *normally* owe B a duty to ensure that he does not directly interfere with those goods. If A breaches this duty, he will commit the tort of *trespass to goods* (discussed in Chapter 16).

(7) *Trespass to land.* If B is in possession of a piece of land A will *normally* owe B a duty not to go onto that land. If he breaches that duty, he will commit the tort of *trespass to land* (discussed in Chapter 17).

(8) *Private nuisance.* If B has an interest in a piece of land, A will normally owe B a duty to ensure that he does not do anything that will unreasonably interfere with the amenity value of that land. Moreover, if there exists a state of affairs (not created by A) on land possessed by A which is unreasonably interfering with the amenity value of the land in which B has an interest, A will normally owe B a duty to take reasonable steps to bring that state of affairs to an end. If A breaches either of these duties, he will commit the tort of *private nuisance* (discussed in Chapter 18).

(9) *Inducing a breach of contract.* If B is in a contractual relationship of some kind with a third party, C, A will *normally* owe B a common law duty to ensure that he does not persuade C to breach his contract with B. If A breaches this duty, he will commit the tort of *inducing a breach of contract* (discussed in Chapter 19).

A couple of points remain to be made about the torts dealt with in this part of the book.

(1) *Lawful justification and excuse.* Obviously, A will not have a duty not to do *x* if the law allows him – or even requires him – to do *x*: the law cannot contradict itself. If A is legally allowed or required to do *x*, we can say that he has a *lawful justification or excuse* for doing *x*. So if A has hit B or walked onto B's land or harassed B, he will *not* have committed a tort in so doing if he had a lawful

---

[1] Cf. *Marfani & Co. Ltd* v *Midland Bank Ltd* [1968] 1 WLR 956, at 970–1 (per Diplock LJ): 'At common law, one's duty to one's neighbour who is the owner, or entitled to possession of any goods, is to refrain from doing any voluntary act in relation to his goods which is a usurpation of his proprietary or possessory rights in them.'

justification or excuse for acting in the way he did. No hard and fast rules can be laid down as to when someone will be able to establish that he had a lawful justification or excuse for acting in a particular way. However, a couple of observations may be made at this point.

(*a*) If A has done *x* and wants to establish that he had a lawful justification or excuse for doing *x*, it is not enough for him to show that it was *reasonable* for him to do *x*. He has to show that the decided cases or in-force statutes *specifically establish* that the law allowed or required him to do *x*. So suppose Eric is a policeman and suppose that Eric walked across Wendy's land searching for Gary, an escaped criminal. Suppose further that Wendy is now suing Eric for trespassing on her land. In such a case, Eric will *not* be able to establish that he had a lawful justification or excuse for acting as he did – and, therefore, that he did not commit a tort in walking across Wendy's land – merely by showing that it was reasonable, all things considered, for him to go onto Wendy's land in search of Gary. He will have to show that the in-force statutes and decided cases specifically establish that he was allowed to go onto Wendy's land in order to see whether Gary was on it. If he cannot show that this is the case then he will have committed a tort in going onto Wendy's land – no matter how reasonable it was for him to have walked across Wendy's land when he did. This contrasts with the law of negligence. Suppose John has done *x* and Beth wants to establish – for the purpose of suing John in negligence for compensation for some loss that she suffered as a result of John's doing *x* – that John owed her a duty to take care not to do *x*. As we have seen, John will be able to rebut Beth's claim that he owed her a duty to take care not to do *x* if he can show that it was reasonable, all things considered, for him to do *x*.[2]

(*b*) While A will not be able to establish that he had a lawful justification or excuse for doing *x* merely by showing that it was reasonable for him to do *x*, *as a general rule*, if it was *unreasonable* for A to do *x*, A will *not* be able to establish that he had a lawful justification or excuse for doing *x*. For example, suppose Paul attacked Ruth and Ruth hit him in self-defence. If Ruth acted unreasonably in defending herself – for example, she used excessive force in self-defence (say Paul slapped Ruth and Ruth responded by hitting Paul repeatedly with a baseball bat) – Ruth will *not* be able to establish that she had a lawful justification or excuse for hitting Paul in the way she did. The general rule set out above has two exceptions. First, if A hit B with B's consent then A will have had a lawful justification or excuse vis-à-vis B for acting as he did even if it was, all things considered, unreasonable for him to have hit B – that is, even if it was, all things considered, unreasonable for B to have consented to allow A to hit her. The same thing is true if A walked onto B's land with B's consent or if A interfered with B's watch with B's consent – in each case, A will be able to establish that he had a lawful justification or excuse vis-à-vis B for acting as he did even if, all things considered, it was unreasonable for him to have acted in the way he did. Secondly, if A did *x* but he was allowed by statute to act in this

---

[2] See above, pp. 76–80.

way, A will have had a lawful justification or excuse for having acted in the way he did – even if, all things considered, it was unreasonable for A to have done *x* when he did. So, for example, suppose Ian – a police officer – arrested Mary when he was allowed to do so under the Police and Criminal Evidence Act 1984. In this situation Ian will have had a lawful justification or excuse for arresting Mary – and this is so even if, all things considered, it was unreasonable of Ian to have arrested Mary when he did because there was a clear danger when Ian arrested Mary that his doing so would trigger a riot.

(2) *Strict liability.* Some of the tortious harm-avoiding duties set out above are *strict* in nature. A duty is strict in nature if someone can breach it without being at fault for doing so. So, for example, suppose that Lara is in possession of a piece of land – call it Blackacre – and, as a result, Carl owes Lara a duty to ensure that he does not walk onto Blackacre. This duty is strict: Carl can breach it without being at fault in any way for the breach. This will be the case if Carl walks onto Blackacre when he does not know that he is walking onto Blackacre and – due to lack of signs or fences – he has no reason to know that he is walking onto Blackacre. Carl is not to blame for the fact that he has walked onto Blackacre – but he will still be in breach of the duty he owes Lara not to walk onto Blackacre.

The fact that some tortious harm-avoiding duties are strict in nature creates a potential unfairness. This is because, as we have seen, the general rule in English law is that if A breaches a tortious duty owed to B, B will be entitled to sue A for compensation for the losses suffered by her as a result of A's breach.[3] So if A has breached a strict duty owed to B and A was not at fault for the breach, A will be held liable to compensate B for the losses suffered by her as a result of A's breach even though A was not at fault for the fact that B suffered those losses. In other words, A is held *strictly liable* to compensate B for the losses that she has suffered. This, it may be thought, is unfair.[4]

The point can be illustrated by reference to the case of *Newstead* v *London Express Newspaper Limited*.[5] In that case, the defendants were the publishers of the *Daily Express*. They published an account of a prisoner's trial for bigamy and referred to the prisoner as 'Harold Newstead, thirty-year old Camberwell man'. The claimant – whose name was Harold Newstead and who worked in Camberwell and was aged about 30 – sued the defendants for libel. Newstead won his case. The Court of Appeal held that the defendants had libelled Newstead and were liable to pay him compensatory damages. This was so even though, when the defendants published the piece complained of by Newstead, they had no intention of referring to him and no reason to know of his existence.[6]

---

[3] See above, p. 23.
[4] Which is not to say that strict liability cannot sometimes be justified: see below, p. 639.
[5] [1940] 1 KB 377.
[6] Fortunately for the defendants, a jury found that Newstead had suffered little or no loss as a result of the defendants' libel and awarded him one farthing in damages.

There are two ways of curing the potential unfairness created by the fact that some of the tortious harm-avoiding duties that may be owed by one person to another are strict in nature. The first is to reshape those harm-avoiding duties that are strict in nature and turn them into duties of care. So if Lara is in possession of Blackacre, the law could say that Carl owes Lara, not a common law duty to ensure that he does not walk onto Blackacre, but, rather, a duty *to take care* that he does not walk onto Blackacre. So Carl will do no wrong if he walks onto Blackacre when he did not know and had no reason to know that he was doing so.

The second is to make inroads into the English rule that if A breaches a tortious duty owed to B and B suffers loss as a result, A will normally be held liable to compensate B for that loss. So the law could say that if A breaches a strict tortious duty owed to B and B suffers loss as a result, A will *not* be held liable to compensate B for that loss if he can prove that he was not at fault for the breach. Section 1 of the Defamation Act 1996 provides an example of the law being reshaped in this way. It provides, among other things, that if A, a shopkeeper, libels B by selling someone a newspaper which contains a defamatory statement about B, B will not be able to sue A for compensation for whatever losses she is presumed to have suffered as a result of A's libel if A can prove that he did not know and had no reason to know that the newspaper sold by him contained the defamatory statement complained of by B.

10

ASSAULT AND BATTERY

Let's start with some definitions. First, A will have committed the tort of *battery* in relation to B if: (*a*) he directly applied force to B's person; (*b*) he did so intentionally or carelessly; and (*c*) he had no lawful justification or excuse for acting in the way he did.

Secondly, A will have committed the tort of *assault* in relation to B if: (1) he intentionally or carelessly caused B to think that he was about to do *x*; and (2) if A had done *x*, he would have committed the tort of battery in relation to B.

The definition of when someone will commit the tort of assault is therefore parasitic on the definition of when someone will commit the tort of battery. It therefore makes sense in this chapter to begin with the tort of battery and explain in more detail when someone will commit that tort, before we turn our attentions to the tort of assault.

BATTERY

It follows from what has just been said that if B wants to sue A for committing the tort of battery in relation to her, she will have to show that A directly applied force to her person; that he did so intentionally or carelessly; and that he had no lawful justification or excuse for acting as he did. Let's now look at the key terms in this definition.

Direct application of force

There are a variety of ways of directly applying force to someone's person:

(1) *Touch.* A will directly apply force to B's person if he voluntarily *touches* B. So Paul will commit the tort of battery if he puts dye on Wendy's hair when he has no lawful justification or excuse for doing so.[1]

(2) *Projectiles.* A will directly apply force to B's person if B is hit by something which A *threw or propelled*.[2] It does not matter whether or not A directed the thing in question at B. In *Scott* v *Shepherd*,[3] the defendant threw a lighted squib into a marketplace where it was thrown from trader to trader, each seeking to get rid of the squib, until the squib exploded in the claimant's face and put out one of his eyes. It was held that the defendant had committed the tort of

---

[1] *Nash* v *Sheen*, The Times, 13 March 1953.
[2] *Pursell* v *Horn* (1838) 8 Ad & El 602 (boiling water).
[3] (1773) 2 Black W 892, 96 ER 525.

battery; the fact that the defendant had not thrown the squib at the claimant was immaterial.

(3) *Unseating.* A will directly apply force to B's person if he *applies force to something on which B is sitting* with the result that B is unseated and falls to the ground. So Gary will commit the tort of battery if Beth is sitting on a chair and Gary pulls it out from under her, causing her to fall to the ground. (It is assumed that Gary has no lawful justification or excuse for pulling Beth's chair out from under her.) Similarly, Nita will commit the tort of battery if Ian is sitting on a horse and Nita wilfully strikes the horse with the result that Ian is unseated and falls to the ground.[4] (Again, it is assumed that Nita has no lawful justification or excuse for wilfully striking Ian's horse.)

So, Carl will directly apply force to Lara's person if he wipes shoe polish on a towel and then rubs the towel in Lara's face; but he will not directly apply force to Lara's person if he leaves the towel in Lara's bathroom and Lara uses it, thus getting shoe polish all over her face. Similarly, Sarah will directly apply force to Eric's person if she pushes Eric into a hole; but she will not directly apply force to Eric's person if she digs a hole in the road and Eric falls into it. Likewise, Alan will directly apply force to Karen's person if he pulls Karen away as she attempts to enter a room; but Alan will not directly apply force to Karen's person if, when she attempts to enter a room, he stands in the doorway to the room, blocking Karen's way.[5]

What is the position if Sarah is standing on a train which suddenly comes to a halt with the result that Sarah falls over and crashes into John, a fellow passenger? In such a case, Sarah will not have directly applied force to John's person – while she touched John, she did not do so voluntarily. So Sarah will not have committed the tort of battery in this situation. Similarly, if Vijay pushes Fred into Dawn, Fred will not have directly applied force to Dawn's person – again, his touching Dawn was involuntary. On the other hand, Vijay *will* have directly applied force to Dawn's person in this situation – Dawn was hit by a thing (Fred) that was propelled by Vijay. So, in this situation, Fred will not have committed the tort of battery, but Vijay probably will have.

The requirement of intentional or careless conduct

Suppose A has directly applied force to B's person. If we want to show that A committed the tort of battery in acting as he did, we must show that A *intentionally or carelessly* applied force to B's person.[6] This is the result of the decision in *Fowler* v *Lanning*.[7]

In that case, the claimant sued the defendant. His statement of claim merely alleged that the defendant shot him. Diplock J held that the claimant's statement of claim was inadequate – it did not disclose any cause of action. If the

[4] *Dodwell* v *Burford* (1670) 1 Mod 24, 86 ER 703.
[5] *Innes* v *Wylie* (1844) 1 C & K 257, 174 ER 800.
[6] For more detail, see Trindade 1982.
[7] [1959] 1 QB 426.

claimant wanted to make out that the defendant had committed the tort of battery in relation to him, he had to allege and prove not only that the defendant shot him but also that the defendant intentionally or carelessly shot him.

So suppose Tom was out shooting birds in the woods one day when he accidentally shot Ian, a poacher, who had hidden in some bushes. In such a case, Tom will not have committed the tort of battery in relation to Ian. While he *did* directly apply force to Ian's person – Ian was hit by something (a bullet) which was propelled by Tom – Tom did not apply that force to Ian's person either intentionally or carelessly.

Lawful justification or excuse

Let's now look at the main ways in which someone who has applied force to another's person can establish that he or she had a lawful justification or excuse for doing so.

Consent

Suppose that A has voluntarily touched B in some way. If B *validly consented* to A's touching her in the way he did, then A will not have committed a battery in this situation; he will have had a lawful justification or excuse for acting as he did.

In order to show that B validly consented to A's touching her in the way he did, it has to be shown that: (*a*) B agreed that A could touch her in the way he did; (*b*) at the time B agreed that A could touch her in the way he did, B's level of maturity, intelligence and understanding was such that B could be safely left to decide for herself whether or not A could touch her in the way he did; and (*c*) B did not agree that A could touch her in the way he did because she was forced to do so by anyone else. It does *not* have to be shown that: (*d*) B understood the risks, if any, that she would be exposed to if A touched her in the way he did. We will now look at each of these requirements in turn.

(1) *The need for agreement.* If A has touched B in some way, B will obviously not have validly consented to A's touching her in the way he did if B did not agree that A could touch her in the way he did. So suppose Ruth went to hospital for a tonsillectomy but her surgeon – due to an administrative mix-up – performed an appendectomy instead. In such a case, it could not be said that Ruth validly consented to her surgeon's touching her in the way he did.[8]

Even if B formally agreed that A could touch her in the way he did, it still cannot be said that she validly consented to A's touching her in that way, if, when she agreed, she did not really understand what A was proposing to do. So suppose Gary was a patient in a hospital and Lara, his doctor, proposed to Gary that they treat his condition by giving him an 'intrathecal injection of phenol solution nerve block'. If Gary agreed that Lara could do this but did not actually understand what Lara was proposing to do – because Lara did not bother

---

[8] *Chatterton* v *Gerson* [1981] 1 QB 432, 443.

to explain to Gary what such an injection involved – then it cannot be said that Gary validly consented to Lara's giving him such an injection.[9]

It should be noted that in the case of a continual touching which was *initially* agreed to, the touching can *become* unlawful if the person who is subject to it withdraws her consent to it. So suppose that Beth is incapacitated to such an extent that she requires continual medical treatment from Vijay to keep her alive. If, after a few months of being treated by Vijay, Beth loses her will to live and refuses any more treatment, Vijay will commit the tort of battery if he continues to treat Beth.[10]

(2) *The need for a sufficient degree of maturity, intelligence and understanding.* If A has touched B in some way with B's agreement, B will still not have validly consented to A's touching her in the way he did if, at the time B agreed that A could touch her in the way he did, B's level of maturity, intelligence and understanding was not such that B could be safely left to decide for herself whether or not A could touch her in the way he did.

If, at the time B agreed that A could touch her in the way he did, B was an adult (over 18) and not mentally unstable or acting under the influence of drugs or alcohol, it will be automatically presumed that B's level of maturity, intelligence and understanding was such that she could be safely left to decide for herself whether or not A could touch her in the way he did.

Section 8 of the Family Law Reform Act 1969 provides that 'the consent of a minor who has attained the age of sixteen years to any surgical, medical or dental treatment which, in the absence of consent, would constitute [a battery], shall be as effective as it would be if he were of full age . . .'. The effect of this is that if Tom medically treated Mary with Mary's agreement and Mary was between 16 and 18 when she agreed that Tom could treat her, it will be automatically presumed that Mary's level of maturity, intelligence and understanding at that time was such that she could be safely left to decide for herself whether or not Tom could treat her in the way he did – just as would have been the case if Mary had been over 18 when she agreed to being medically treated by Tom.

If, when B agreed A could touch her in the way he did, B was less than 16 years old then no fixed rules will apply – all the circumstances will have to be looked at to determine whether, when B agreed A could touch her in the way he did, B's level of maturity, intelligence and understanding was such that she could be safely left to decide for herself whether or not A could touch her in the way he did.[11]

(3) *The need for an unforced agreement.* If A has touched B in some way with B's

---

[9] Ibid. Cf. *R v Williams* [1923] 1 KB 340 where the defendant – who had been engaged to give singing lessons to one Vera Howley – persuaded Howley to allow him to have sexual intercourse with her by pretending that he was performing a surgical operation on her to improve her voice. He was convicted of rape; she had not validly consented to the defendant's having sex with her as she did not really understand what he was proposing to do when she agreed that he could have sex with her.

[10] *B v An NHS Hospital Trust* [2002] 2 All ER 449.

[11] *Gillick v West Norfolk and Wisbech Area Health Authority* [1986] AC 112.

agreement, B will still not have validly consented to A's touching her in the way he did if B was forced or pressured into agreeing that A could touch her in the way he did. So suppose, for example, that Gary performed an abortion on Wendy and Wendy only agreed to the abortion because Fred, her father, threatened to kill her if she did not have it. In such a case, it cannot be said that Wendy validly consented to Gary's performing the abortion on her.

(4) *No need for 'informed consent'.* English courts have consistently rejected the notion that if A has touched B in some way with B's agreement, B will only have validly consented to A's touching her in the way he did if her consent was 'informed' – that is, B will only have validly consented to A's touching her in the way he did if, at the time B agreed that A could touch her in that way, B knew of the risks, if any, that she would be exposed to if A touched her in that way.[12]

So, in *Chatterton v Gerson*[13] the claimant had an operation which left her with an extremely painful scar. The claimant consulted the defendant – who was a specialist in treating pain – and he suggested that she have an operation to block the sensory nerve behind the scar which was transmitting pain signals to her brain. The claimant agreed and the defendant carried out the operation. After the operation, the claimant discovered that the area around her scar was numb and she had suffered a loss of muscle power in that area. The claimant sued the defendant, claiming that the defendant had committed the tort of battery in operating on her. She argued that she had not validly consented to the operation performed by the defendant because she had not been informed that there was a risk she would experience numbness and loss of muscle power if she had that operation. This argument was rejected: as the claimant had known perfectly well the nature of the operation the defendant was proposing to carry out on her when she agreed that the defendant could carry out that operation, she validly consented to that operation's being carried out. The fact that she was unaware that the operation involved some risk for her did not vitiate her consent in any way.

Third party consent

Suppose that A touched B without B's consent but with the consent of a third party, C. As a general rule, C's consent will *not* make A's touching of B lawful. However, there are some exceptions to this general rule.

Suppose, for example, that Dawn medically treated Eric with the consent of Sarah, Eric's mother. Suppose further that Eric was under 18 when he was treated by Dawn and that Eric did not validly consent to his being treated by Dawn. In such a case, can it be said that Sarah's consent means that Dawn committed no battery in medically treating Eric in the way she did? The legal position is confused. On one view, Sarah's consent *does* mean that Dawn did *not* commit a battery

---

[12] *Chatterton v Gerson* [1981] 1 QB 432; *Sidaway v Board of Governors of the Bethlem Royal Hospital* [1984] QB 498, aff'd, [1985] AC 871; *Freeman v Home Office (No 2)* [1984] 1 QB 524.
[13] [1981] 1 QB 432.

in medically treating Eric – and this is so even if Eric or Eric's father objected to Dawn's treating Eric in the way she did.[14] On another view, Dawn will still have committed a battery in treating Eric *if* Eric objected to Dawn's treating him in the way she did *and* Eric was *either* over 16 when he was treated by Dawn *or* Eric was under 16 but his level of maturity, intelligence and understanding at the time he was treated was such that he could be safely left to decide for himself whether or not Dawn could treat him in the way she did – but if any of these conditions are not met, then Sarah's consent will have made Dawn's treatment lawful.[15]

The position is clearer if an under-age patient is a ward of court at the time he is treated.[16] In such a case, the patient's doctors will commit no battery in treating him if they have a court's permission to do so – and this is so even if the patient does not want to be treated.[17] Obviously, a court will only permit doctors to treat a patient medically if it is in the patient's best interests to be so treated[18] and, in deciding whether or not such treatment is in the patient's best interests, the courts will take into account the patient's wishes.[19] However, an under-age patient who is a ward of court will possess no veto over how she is treated – whatever her age and whatever her level of maturity, intelligence and understanding.

Voluntary assumption of risk

It is not a tort to apply force to someone else's person if he or she has voluntarily taken a risk that such force will be applied to his or her person.

So, for example, it is well established that A will commit no battery if he brushes past B in the street.[20] The reason is that, in walking the streets, B will have voluntarily taken the risk that he will be touched by people brushing past him. Similarly, it is well established that if Tom plays football with Carl, Tom will commit no battery if he touches Carl in tackling him so long as the tackle is within the rules of the game. The reason for this is that, in agreeing to play football with Tom, Carl will have voluntarily taken the risk that Tom would subject him to tackles that are within the rules of the game. What if Tom's tackle was a foul tackle? In such a case, the courts draw a distinction between the case where Tom's tackle amounted to a mere 'error of judgement' or a 'lapse' and cases where Tom's tackle showed a 'wanton' or 'reckless' disregard of Carl's safety.[21] Carl can be taken to have voluntarily taken the risk that he would be subjected to the former kind of tackle, but not the latter. So if Tom

---

[14] *Re R (a minor) (wardship: medical treatment)* [1992] Fam 11, 23–5 (per Lord Donaldson MR); *Re W (a minor) (medical treatment)* [1993] Fam 64, 76 (per Lord Donaldson MR), 87 (per Balcombe LJ).

[15] *Re R (a minor) (wardship: medical treatment)* [1992] Fam 11, 27 (per Staughton LJ). This view rests heavily on some *obiter dicta* of Lord Scarman's in *Gillick v West Norfolk and Wisbech Area Health Authority* [1986] AC 112, 188H–189A: '... I would hold that as a matter of law the parental right to determine *whether* or not their minor child below the age of 16 will have medical treatment *terminates* if and when the child achieves a sufficient understanding and intelligence to enable him or her to understand fully what is proposed' (emphasis added).

[16] Adults cannot be made wards of court.

[17] *Re R (a minor) (wardship: consent to treatment)* [1992] Fam 11.

[18] *Re B (a minor) (wardship: sterilisation)* [1988] 1 AC 199.

[19] *Re W (a minor) (medical treatment)* [1993] Fam 64.

[20] *Cole v Turner* (1704) 6 Mod 149, 87 ER 907; *Collins v Wilcock* [1984] 1 WLR 1172, 1177F.

[21] *Condon v Basi* [1985] 1 WLR 866; *Blake v Galloway* [2004] EWCA Civ 814.

tackled Carl in a way that showed a wanton or reckless disregard for Carl's safety, then Carl would be able to sue Tom for battery – but he would not if Tom technically committed a foul in tackling Carl, but the foul merely amounted to an error of judgement on Tom's part. Of course, if Tom punched Carl in the course of playing football with him, there is no doubt that Carl would be able to sue Tom for battery – it is not possible to argue that, in agreeing to play football with Tom, Carl voluntarily took the risk that he would be punched by Tom.[22]

Necessity

Suppose that A directly applied force to B's person. If it was *necessary* for A to do this to prevent a crime or protect someone from being physically harmed, then A *may* be able to argue that he acted lawfully in acting as he did.

(1) *Self-defence*. Under the common law, A will be allowed to use reasonable force against B to protect himself from being attacked by B. The case of *Cross v Kirkby*[23] provides an example of a case where such a defence was successfully made out. In that case, Kirkby was a farmer who allowed the local hunt to ride over his land while hunting foxes. Cross was a hunt sabo-teur. While the local hunt was riding over Kirkby's land, Cross walked onto Kirkby's land in an attempt to disrupt the hunt. Kirkby attempted to remove Cross from his land with the result that Cross attacked Kirkby with a base-ball bat, jabbing him in the chest and throat with the bat and eventually hitting Kirkby twice on the arm with the bat. Kirkby managed to grab the bat from Cross and hit Cross with it. Cross sustained a fracture of the skull as a result of the blow and sued Kirkby. Kirkby claimed that he had acted reasonably in self-defence in hitting Cross and had therefore done no wrong in hitting Cross.

The trial judge considered scientific evidence as to how heavy Kirkby's blow had been, found that the blow had been a 'heavy' one and held that Kirkby had used excessive force in striking Cross. He therefore found for Cross, awarding him £52,000 in damages. However, the Court of Appeal allowed Kirkby's appeal, finding that Kirkby *had* acted reasonably in self-defence. Beldam LJ – with the agreement of Otton LJ – thought that the correct test to apply, for the purpose of determining whether Kirkby acted reasonably in self-defence, was to ask: '[Did Kirkby] in a moment of unexpected anguish only [do] what he hon-estly and instinctively thought was necessary?' As Kirkby had only hit Cross in

---

[22] See *R v John William Billinghurst* [1978] Crim LR 553 where the defendant was held to have committed a battery in punching another player in an off-the-ball incident during a rugby foot-ball match. Willing participants in a fight will be held to have voluntarily taken the risk that they will be hit by their opponent, though if they are subjected to a blow that is particularly savage and unexpected, the defence of voluntary assumption of risk will not apply and the blow will amount to a battery: *Lane v Holloway* [1968] 1 QB 379. We speak here merely of *tort law*: in the interests of preventing disorder and unnecessary injury, under the *criminal law* a normal blow inflicted in the course of a fight between two willing participants will *normally* amount to a battery if the victim of the blow suffered actual bodily harm as a result: *R v Brown* [1994] 1 AC 212.

[23] The Times, 5 April 2000.

order to bring the attack on him to an end, the answer was 'yes'. All the Court of Appeal judges emphasised that the trial judge was wrong to find that Kirkby had used excessive force in hitting Cross because his blow was estimated to be 10 per cent harder than a blow delivered with average force. Beldam LJ remarked that 'the judge [in reaching such a finding] ... fell into the error ... [of] "using jeweller's scales to measure reasonable force" '. Judge LJ remarked that the victim of violence cannot be expected, when acting in self-defence, 'to measure [the force used by him in self-defence] with mathematical precision'.

(2) *Prevention of crime*. Section 3 of the Criminal Law Act 1967 provides that '[a] person may use such force as is reasonable in the circumstances in the prevention of crime, or in effecting or assisting in the lawful arrest of offenders or suspected offenders or of persons unlawfully at large'.[24] So if Alan attacks Helen, Helen will commit no battery if she uses reasonable force against Alan in an attempt to stop him attacking her. Similarly, if Sarah runs out of a store with some goods for which he has not paid, Vijay – one of the store's security guards – will commit no battery if he chases Sarah and wrestles her to the ground in an attempt to apprehend her.

(3) *Rescue of person to whom force is applied*. It is well established that if B is in danger of being hit by some moving object, A will commit no battery if he drags B out of the way. Similarly, it is well established that if B is brought *unconscious* into hospital, A, the attending doctor, will commit no battery if he gives B the medical treatment she needs to bring her back to good health.

In *Re F*,[25] the House of Lords gave formal expression to the principle underlying this last example and ruled that: if A has medically treated B, an adult, without her consent, A will *not* have committed a battery in so treating B if: (*a*) it was in B's best interests for A to treat her in the way he did; (*b*) B did not validly decline to be treated by A in the way he treated her;[26] and (*c*) B was incapable of validly consenting to be treated by A in the way he treated her

---

[24] See also the Education Act 1996, s 550A, which provides that 'A member of the staff of a school may use, in relation to any pupil at the school such force as is reasonable in the circumstances for the purpose of preventing the pupil from doing (or continuing to do) any of the following, namely – (a) committing any offence, (b) causing personal injury to, or damage to the property of, any person (including the pupil himself), or (c) engaging in any behaviour prejudicial to the maintenance of good order and discipline at the school or among any of its pupils, whether that behaviour occurs during a teaching session or otherwise.'

[25] [1990] 2 AC 1.

[26] Suppose Paul has carried out an operation X on Mary. Mary will have validly declined to have that operation carried out on her if: (*a*) Mary refused to undergo operation X in the knowledge of what carrying out operation X involved; (*b*) at the time Mary refused to undergo operation X, Mary's maturity, intelligence and understanding was such that she could be safely relied on to decide for herself whether or not she would undergo operation X; and (*c*) Mary did not refuse to undergo operation X because she was forced to do so. In order to establish that Mary validly declined to undergo operation X there is no need to show that Mary's refusal to undergo operation X was based on a full understanding of the costs and benefits involved in undergoing operation X: *Re T (adult: refusal of medical treatment)* [1993] Fam 95, 115. The incapacitated claimant in *B v An NHS Hospital Trust* [2002] 2 All ER 449, not wishing to live any more, declined to undergo any more of the treatment she needed to keep her alive. It was held that she was old enough and intelligent enough to decide for herself

(either because she was drunk or because she was mentally unstable[27] or because she was unconscious at the time she was treated by A).

In *Re F* itself, F was a voluntary in-patient in a mental hospital. She was 36 years old but had the mental age of a small child. When she showed signs that she was about to become sexually active, F's mother sought to have her sterilised on the grounds that it would be harmful to F's mental health if she became pregnant. The House of Lords held that the hospital staff at F's mental hospital would commit no battery if they sterilised F without her consent: it would be in F's best interests to be sterilised; F had not validly declined to be sterilised; and F's mental age meant that F was incapable of validly consenting to be sterilised.

In *Re T*,[28] T was injured in a car accident when she was 34 weeks pregnant. She was admitted into hospital where she went into labour. She was told that the baby would have to be delivered by Caesarean section and that it might be necessary to give her a blood transfusion to replenish her blood after the operation. After conversations with her mother, T told the hospital staff that she was a Jehovah's Witness and did not want to have a blood transfusion after her Caesarean. After the Caesarean was carried out, T's condition suddenly deteriorated and she was transferred to an intensive care unit where she was put on a ventilator and paralysing drugs were administered. She was then given a blood transfusion at the behest of T's father and boyfriend. The Court of Appeal had to decide whether the hospital had committed a battery in giving T a blood transfusion.

The court thought that the House of Lords' decision in *Re F* established that the hospital did *not* commit a battery in treating T in the way it did: the court thought that it had been in T's best interests to give her a blood transfusion (she might have died without it); T had not validly declined to be given a blood transfusion in the circumstances in which she was given it; and at the time the blood transfusion was administered T was incapable of validly consenting to its being given to her. The court gave two reasons for thinking that T had not validly declined to be given a blood transfusion in the circumstances in which she was given it. First, when T declined to be given a blood transfusion after her Caesarean she was simply declining to be given a blood transfusion in order to replenish her blood – she did not mean to indicate that if it was necessary for her to receive a blood transfusion to save her life, she still did not want to be given a blood transfusion. Secondly, when T declined to be given a blood transfusion after her Caesarean, she did so under pressure from her mother.

(4) *Rescue of person other than person to whom force was applied.* If A has applied force to B's body in order to save *someone other than B* from being physically

---

whether she wanted to continue to be treated and so her refusal to be treated any more was perfectly valid. Accordingly, the defence of necessity could not be invoked to justify continuing to treat her.

[27] If B was mentally unstable, A may have been authorised to treat her under ss 62 or 63 of the Mental Health Act 1983 (authorising treatment of patients detained in hospital on the ground that they suffer from a mental disorder).

[28] [1993] Fam 95.

harmed, will A ever be entitled to claim that he acted lawfully in acting as he did? The law in this area is still developing.

In *Re S*,[29] the President of the Family Division, Sir Stephen Brown, ruled that a doctor who performs a Caesarean section on a pregnant patient in order to save the life of her foetus will commit no battery *even if* the patient has validly *declined* to undergo a Caesarean section.[30] However, in *St George's Healthcare NHS Trust v S*,[31] the Court of Appeal held that Sir Stephen Brown was wrong: if a pregnant patient validly declines to undergo a Caesarean section, a doctor who performs such an operation on the patient will commit a battery even if it is necessary to perform the operation in order to save the life of the patient's foetus.

Re A[32] concerned a pair of conjoined twins, Jodie and Mary. Mary was much the weaker of the twins and relied on Jodie's heart and lungs to keep her alive. If an operation was not carried out to separate Mary from Jodie, Jodie's heart would fail within six months and they both would die. However, if such an operation were carried out, Mary would certainly die as a result. The Court of Appeal held that Mary and Jodie's doctors would act lawfully if they carried out the operation. The doctors were entitled to rely on a defence of necessity in this case as Mary posed a (passive) threat to Jodie's life and removing Mary from Jodie was the only way of saving Jodie's life. It is submitted that the decision is to be confined to its own facts – it does not, for example, authorise A to kill B if both are stranded in some wilderness and one needs to eat the other in order to survive; nor does it authorise a doctor to kill a terminally ill patient by removing his heart and lungs in order to give them to another patient who is in need of them.

Lawful chastisement

If A hits B to punish her for misbehaving, A will not usually be able to argue that he acted lawfully in hitting B. It used to be that there were two exceptions to this general rule. First, parents were allowed to use reasonable force to discipline their children. Secondly, a schoolteacher, acting *in loco parentis*, was allowed to use reasonable force to punish the children in his care if they misbehaved.

The second exception no longer survives: s 548 of the Education Act 1996 provides that 'Corporal punishment given by, or on the authority of, a member of staff to a child ... cannot be justified in any proceedings on the ground that it was given in pursuance of a right exercisable by the member of the staff by virtue of his position ...'[33] The first exception still survives: parents are still

---

[29] [1993] Fam 123.

[30] In so holding he was following a suggestion of Lord Donaldson MR's in *Re T (adult: refusal of medical treatment)* [1993] Fam 95, 102: 'An adult patient who ... suffers from no mental incapacity has an absolute right to choose whether to consent to medical treatment, to refuse it or to choose one rather than another of the treatments being offered. The only possible qualification is a case in which the choice may lead to the death of a viable foetus.'

[31] [1999] Fam 26.

[32] [2001] Fam 147.

[33] In *R (Williamson) v Secretary of State for Education and Employment* [2003] QB 1300 (noted, Eekelaar 2003), the Court of Appeal rejected a claim that this provision violated the applicants' rights to manifest their religion or beliefs under Art 9 of the European Convention on Human Rights and Art 2 of the First Protocol to the Convention.

allowed to use reasonable force[34] to discipline their children,[35] though this aspect of the law is under constant attack from those who think it unacceptable for force ever to be used on children.[36]

Acceptable contact

In *Collins* v *Wilcock*, Robert Goff LJ, as he then was, suggested that an application of force to another's person that is 'generally acceptable in the conduct of daily life'[37] will not amount to a battery.

So, on this view, if Beth touches Alan on the shoulder to get his attention, Beth will commit no battery – touching someone on the shoulder to get their attention is a generally acceptable thing to do. In *Collins* v *Wilcock* itself, a policewoman grabbed a prostitute by the arm to stop her from walking away while she was trying to question her. The Court of Appeal held that the policewoman committed the tort of battery in restraining the prostitute – the policewoman's conduct went some way beyond what is 'generally acceptable in the conduct of daily life'.

Further requirements?

A couple of cases have departed from the definition advanced here of when someone will commit the tort of battery.

In *Letang* v *Cooper*, Lord Denning MR – with the concurrence of Danckwerts LJ – suggested that in order to establish that A has committed the tort of battery in relation to B it had to be shown that A, in acting as he did, *intended to injure* B: '[if someone] does not inflict injury [on a claimant] intentionally, but only unintentionally, the claimant has no cause of action in [battery].'[38]

In *Wilson* v *Pringle*, the Court of Appeal held that if one wants to show that A committed the tort of battery in applying force to B's person, it must be shown that A acted in a *hostile* way in applying that force to B's person: 'for there to be . . . a battery there must be something in the nature of hostility.'[39]

---

[34] *Important note*. The courts are required under s 6 of the Human Rights Act 1998 to take positive steps to develop the law in such a way as to ensure that people are not 'subjected to torture or to inhuman or degrading treatment'. The reason for this is that if they do not, they will violate those people's rights under Art 3 of the European Convention on Human Rights not to be subjected to such treatment: see *A* v *United Kingdom* (1998) 27 EHRR 611. So, in deciding whether the force used by a parent on his child was 'reasonable', the courts are under an obligation to say that that parent's treatment of his child was *not* 'reasonable' if it amounted to 'torture or to inhuman or degrading treatment'.

[35] In judging what amounts to reasonable force, the courts must 'consider the nature and context of the defendant's behaviour, its duration, its physical and mental consequences in relation to the child, the age and personal characteristics of the child and the reasons given by the defendant for administering punishment': *R* v *H* *(assault of child: reasonable chastisement)* [2001] 2 FLR 431, at [31].

[36] See, for example, Bitensky 1998. At the time of writing (July 2004), it seems likely that the forthcoming Children Act 2004 will provide that 'battery of a child causing actual bodily harm to the child cannot be justified in any civil proceedings on the ground that it constituted reasonable punishment' (at the time of writing, this provision appears in clause 49(3) of the Children Bill).

[37] [1984] 1 WLR 1172, 1177G–H.

[38] [1965] 1 QB 232, 239G.

[39] [1987] 1 QB 237, 250C–D.

In *Wilson* v *Pringle* itself the claimant and the defendant were both schoolboys. The defendant was walking down a corridor behind the claimant when, as a joke, he pulled at the claimant's sports bag – which the claimant was carrying over his right shoulder. The claimant fell and injured his left hip. The claimant sued the defendant, claiming he had committed the tort of battery. He obtained summary judgment, the judge taking the view that the defendant had obviously committed a battery. The Court of Appeal reversed the judge's decision, holding that it was not completely clear that the defendant had committed the tort of battery on these facts – a hearing would be required to determine whether the defendant, in acting as he did, acted with the requisite degree of hostility.

The suggestions in these cases as to what has to be established in order to show that someone has committed the tort of battery have *not* been followed by the courts. The Court of Appeal in *Wilson* v *Pringle* ruled that '[an] intention to injure is not essential to an action for [battery]',[40] thereby disapproving Lord Denning MR's statement to the contrary in *Letang* v *Cooper*. In *Re F*, Lord Goff of Chieveley disapproved the suggestion in *Wilson* v *Pringle* that an application of force to another's person must be 'hostile' before it can amount to a battery:

> I respectfully doubt whether that is correct. A prank that gets out of hand; an over-friendly slap on the back; surgical treatment by a surgeon who mistakenly thinks that the patient has consented to it – all these things may transcend the bounds of lawfulness, without being characterised as hostile. Indeed the suggested qualification is difficult to reconcile with the principle that any touching of another's body is, in the absence of lawful excuse, capable of amounting to a battery . . .[41]

ASSAULT

Less needs to be said here about when someone will commit the tort of assault. Only a couple of points need be emphasised.

(1) *The need to be put in fear of imminent attack.* A will only commit the tort of assault if he leads B to believe that he is *about* to commit a battery on B. So in *Tuberville* v *Savage*[42] it was held that Tuberville did not commit an assault when he reacted to something Savage said by drawing his sword while saying 'If it were not assize-time I should not take such language from you.' As it *was* assize time, Tuberville did not lead Savage to believe that Tuberville was about to strike him with his sword.

In *Thomas* v *National Union of Mineworkers (South Wales Area)*,[43] the claimants were coal miners who wished to go to work during the miners' strike. As they entered the colliery where they worked they suffered abuse and threats from massed pickets at the colliery gates. They sought to obtain an injunction against the massed picketing, claiming among other things that the pickets were

---

[40] Ibid., 249H.
[41] [1990] 2 AC 1, 73B–C.
[42] (1669) 1 Mod 3, 86 ER 684.
[43] [1986] 1 Ch 20.

committing the tort of assault in abusing and threatening them as they entered the colliery. This claim was rejected by Scott J on the ground that the claimants were always driven into the colliery and were separated from the pickets by ranks of policemen – given this, it could hardly be said that the abuse and threats the claimants received when they entered the colliery put them in fear that they were *about* to be beaten up by the pickets.

(2) *Silence*. In *R* v *Ireland*,[44] the House of Lords ruled that someone can commit the tort of assault through mere silence. The defendant in that case made a series of malicious telephone calls to three women – when they answered he would remain silent. The women all developed psychiatric illnesses as a result of their treatment at the hands of the defendant. The defendant was charged with committing the offence of assault occasioning actual bodily harm and was convicted. The House of Lords upheld the conviction, holding that his silent telephone calls could have led the women in question to believe they were about to be attacked by whoever was on the other end of the line.

---

[44] [1988] AC 147.

11

FALSE IMPRISONMENT

A will commit the tort of false imprisonment in relation to B if he intentionally[1] 'imprisons' B when he has no lawful justification or excuse for doing so.

THE MEANING OF IMPRISONMENT

A will 'imprison' B if: (*a*) he completely restricts B's freedom of movement or (*b*) he restricts B's freedom of movement to within a defined area. So Vijay will 'imprison' Beth if he grabs Beth's arm so that she cannot go anywhere. Similarly, Sarah will 'imprison' Eric if she locks Eric in a room – Eric will be free to move within the room but will not be free to move outside.

In *Bird* v *Jones*,[2] a public right of way ran through an enclosure created by the defendants for the purpose of viewing a boat race. The claimant, in an attempt to use the right of way, entered the enclosure. The defendants prevented the claimant from walking through the enclosure and instead instructed him to turn back and use another route to reach his destination. The claimant refused to move and stayed in the enclosure for half an hour. The claimant sued the defendants, claiming that they had committed the tort of false imprisonment. The claim was rejected: the defendant had done nothing that completely restricted the claimant's freedom of movement or restricted that freedom of movement to within a defined area. The claimant had been free at all times to leave the enclosure and find another way of getting to where he wanted to go.

If A restricts B's freedom of movement to within a defined area, he will 'imprison' B whether or not B knows that his freedom of movement is restricted to the area in question. So, in *Meering* v *Grahame-White Aviation Company Ltd* Atkin LJ remarked:

> It appears to me that a person could be imprisoned without his knowing it. I think a person can be imprisoned while he is asleep, while he is in a state of drunkenness, while he is unconscious and while he is a lunatic. Those are cases where it seems to me that the person might properly complain if he were imprisoned, though the imprisonment began and ceased while he was in that state. Of course, the damages might

---

[1] Though there is no authority on the matter, most scholars think that a defendant must have acted *with the aim of* imprisoning a claimant before the defendant can be held to have committed the tort of false imprisonment in relation to the claimant: see W&J, 82 n. 19; Lunney & Mitchell 2002, 365; GS&Z, 568. So – on this view – if A locks a room when he ought to have known that B was inside, that will not necessarily amount to false imprisonment; he must have locked the room with the aim of imprisoning B before he can be held to have committed that tort.

[2] (1845) 7 QB 742, 115 ER 668.

be diminished and would be affected by the question of whether he was conscious of it or not.[3]

These *dicta* were endorsed by the House of Lords in *Murray* v *Ministry of Defence*.[4] So if Mary locks a room in which John is sleeping, Mary will 'imprison' John – the fact that John is completely unaware that he is in a locked room will be completely immaterial.[5]

What is the position if Ruth is in a particular room or building and Fred decides that if Ruth attempts to leave that room or building he will prevent Ruth from doing so but, because Ruth has not yet attempted to leave the room or building in question, Fred has not actually done anything yet to prevent her from leaving that room or building? Has Fred 'imprisoned' Ruth? One would think the answer must be 'no': whether or not Fred has 'imprisoned' Ruth cannot merely depend on Fred's mental state. The House of Lords confirmed that this view is correct in *R* v *Bournewood Community and Mental Health NHS Trust, ex parte L*.[6] That case concerned one L who had a history of mental health problems. Having spent 30 years being treated in Bournewood Hospital, L was discharged into the community in 1994 and looked after by paid carers. However, in 1997 after an incident in a day care centre, L became particularly agitated and voluntarily agreed to go back to Bournewood Hospital. Once there, he was kept in an unlocked ward and no attempts were made to restrain him from leaving. However, the staff there decided that if he attempted to leave they would section him under the Mental Health Act 1983 and prevent him from leaving. L did in fact eventually attempt to leave and was sectioned under the Act. When L was eventually discharged, he sued the hospital, claiming that its employees had falsely imprisoned him in the period between his entering the hospital and his being sectioned. The House of Lords dismissed L's claim. By a majority of three to two, they held that the staff at Bournewood Hospital had not imprisoned L during that time: the fact that during that time they were pre-pared to section L if he attempted to leave did not mean that they had 'imprisoned' him.

What is the position if A has caused a third party, C, to 'imprison' B? In such a case, can we say that *A* has 'imprisoned' B? The decision of the Court of Appeal in *Davidson* v *Chief Constable of North Wales*[7] indicates that the answer is 'yes' if A *persuaded, encouraged or requested* C to 'imprison' B, but otherwise the answer is 'no'. In that case, a store detective who was employed by the defendants thought that the claimant had left the store with a cassette for which she had not paid. The store detective reported his suspicions to the police and they arrested the claimant, thereby 'imprisoning' her. In fact the claimant did not steal the cassette in question – it had been paid for by a friend of hers. The claimant sued the defendants, claiming that the store detective, their employee,

---

[3] (1920) 122 LT 44, 53–54.
[4] [1988] 1 WLR 692, 701C–703B.
[5] Most jurisdictions in the United States take the view that a claim for false imprisonment could *not* be made here: GS&Z, 571.
[6] [1999] 1 AC 458.
[7] [1994] 2 All ER 597.

had falsely imprisoned her. The Court of Appeal dismissed the claimant's claim: the store detective did not persuade, encourage or request the police to arrest the claimant – all he did was report his suspicions to the police; he then left it up to the police to decide what to do.

LAWFUL JUSTIFICATION OR EXCUSE

If A has 'imprisoned' B, there are a number of different ways in which A could establish that he had a lawful justification or excuse for acting in the way he did.

Consent

Obviously, if A has imprisoned B with B's consent, then A will have had a lawful justification or excuse for acting as he did. So, for example, suppose that Peter is addicted to drugs and allows his parents to lock him in his room so that he can kick the habit that he has acquired. His parents will do no wrong in locking Peter up in his room. But what is the position if Peter is suffering such acute withdrawal symptoms that he begs his parents to let him out of his room? Will his parents commit the tort of false imprisonment if they do not let him out at that stage? It is hard to say. Perhaps the best analysis is that Peter is not in his right mind when he begs his parents to let him out of his room – so when he begs his parents to let him out, he does not withdraw the consent that he initially gave his parents to lock him up. On this analysis, Peter's parents will not commit the tort of false imprisonment if they do not let him out of his room in the situation we are considering.

Voluntary assumption of risk

Two cases seem to establish that A will have had a lawful justification or excuse for imprisoning B if B voluntarily took the risk that she would be imprisoned in the way she was.

The first case is *Robinson v Balmain New Ferry Company Ltd.*[8] In that case, the claimant wanted to take a ferry across a river. In order to get to the wharf from which the ferry would depart, he had to go through a turnstile operated by the defendants. As notices on either side of the turnstile made clear, the charge for using the turnstile to enter or exit the wharf was one penny. The claimant handed over a penny, went through the turnstile and waited on the wharf for the ferry to arrive and pick him up. The claimant then changed his plans and decided not to take the ferry at all. He attempted to go back through the turnstile but the defendants insisted that if he wanted to use the turnstile to leave the wharf, he had to pay them a penny – as was stipulated in the notices at the turnstile. When the claimant refused to pay the defendants the required penny, the defendants refused to let him use the turnstile, effectively trapping the claimant on the wharf. The claimant sued the defendants, claiming they had falsely imprisoned him, but his

---

[8] [1910] AC 295.

claim was dismissed by the Privy Council. One explanation of this decision is that when the claimant walked through the turnstile, he voluntarily took the risk that he would not be allowed to go back through the turnstile without paying a penny – he therefore voluntarily took the risk that if he did not pay a penny to go back through the turnstile, he would be imprisoned by the defendants on the wharf.

The second case is *Herd* v *Weardale Steel, Coal and Coke Company Ltd.*[9] In that case, the claimant, a miner, descended to the bottom of a pit at the start of his shift but then refused to do certain work and asked to be lifted up to the surface. The claimant was only allowed to go back up to the surface at the end of the morning shift and even then he was only permitted to go back up once all the miners on the morning shift had been taken to the surface. The claimant sued, claiming that he had been falsely imprisoned. The House of Lords dismissed his claim: when the claimant descended the mine at the start of the shift he voluntarily took the risk that if he did not do any work and wanted to be taken back up to the surface, he would be made to wait to be taken back up – so he voluntarily took the risk that he would be imprisoned at the bottom of the pit in the way he was.[10]

In *Sunbolf* v *Alford*,[11] the claimant ate a meal at the defendant's inn and attempted to leave without paying for it. The defendant forcibly restrained the claimant from doing so. The claimant sued the defendant, claiming that when the defendant prevented him from leaving the defendant's inn, the defendant falsely imprisoned him. The claimant's claim was allowed. However, the result might have been different if there had been a notice in the inn informing customers that they would be detained if they attempted to leave without paying for the food consumed by them in the inn. If this had been the case, the defendant could have argued that when the claimant chose to eat at his inn, he voluntarily took the risk that if he did not pay for his meal, he would be detained.[12]

Statutory authority

There are plenty of occasions when one person will be authorised or required by statute to imprison another. The most obvious example is provided by the Police and Criminal Evidence Act 1984 which sets out the rules governing when someone may be lawfully arrested for committing an offence.[13] Another

---

[9] [1915] AC 67.

[10] *Important note.* For criticism of these cases, see Tan 1981. He argues that 'no person can by imprisonment force another to abide by or conform to any condition, if that other does not consent do so, unless such compliance is required by law' (ibid., 168) – and this is so even if that other voluntarily took a risk that he would be imprisoned if he did not conform to that condition. Tan attempts to explain cases such as *Robinson* and *Herd* on the basis that someone who *initially* consents to be deprived of his liberty by a defendant for a certain amount of time may be prevented from withdrawing that consent if granting him his liberty immediately would be inconvenient for the defendant: ibid., 169. However, he doubts whether the inconvenience that would have been involved in freeing the claimants in *Robinson* and *Herd* was sufficiently serious as to justify or excuse the claimants' continued imprisonment.

[11] (1838) 3 M & W 248, 150 ER 1135.

[12] For a different view, see Tan 1981, 167: 'a creditor cannot imprison his debtor in the absence of statutory authority' (quoting Glanville Williams).

[13] For a detailed account of these rules, see any textbook on constitutional law.

example is provided by the Mental Health Act 1983, under which people suffering from mental disorders may in certain circumstances be arrested or detained in hospital.[14] A further example is provided by section 12(1) of the Prison Act 1952, which provides that '[a] prisoner, whether sentenced to imprisonment or committed to prison on remand or pending trial or otherwise, may be lawfully confined in any prison'.

This section does not, of course, authorise or allow the governor of a prison to detain a prisoner for longer than the period of his sentence or the time he is supposed to spend on remand.[15] So, for example, the prison governor in *R v Governor of Brockhill Prison, ex parte Evans (No. 2)*[16] was held to have committed the tort of false imprisonment when he held the claimant in that case in prison for 59 more days than she was supposed to spend in prison. Section 12(1) of the 1952 Act *does* allow the governor of a prison to detain a convicted prisoner *whether or not* that prisoner was rightly or wrongly convicted. So suppose Nita was wrongly convicted of committing murder and was sentenced to life imprisonment. Suppose further that Nita's conviction was overturned three years later and she was released. In such a case, Nita could not sue the prison authorities, claiming that the prison authorities falsely imprisoned her during the three years she spent in prison before she was released. The authorities will have had a lawful justification or excuse under s 12(1) of the 1952 Act for detaining Nita for those three years.[17]

The House of Lords' decision in *R v Deputy Governor of Parkhurst Prison, ex parte Hague*[18] seems to suggest that s 12(1) of the 1952 Act not only authorises the governor of a prison to detain a prisoner within the confines of the prison but also authorises the governor of a prison to choose *how* that prisoner is to be detained. The decision actually dealt with two cases – the *Hague* case and *Weldon v Home Office*. In the *Hague* case, the claimant – a prisoner at Parkhurst Prison – claimed he had been falsely imprisoned because he had been kept in isolation for 28 days, contrary to the Prison Rules 1964. In the *Weldon* case, the claimant – a prisoner at Leeds Prison – claimed he had been falsely imprisoned

---

[14] See for example s 136 of the Mental Health Act 1983, which provides that if 'a constable finds in a place to which the public have access a person who appears to him to be suffering from mental disorder and to be in immediate need of care or control, the constable may, if he thinks it necessary to do so in the interests of that person or for the protection of other persons, remove that person to a place of safety . . .'.

[15] Though see *Olotu v Home Office* [1997] 1 WLR 328. The claimant in that case was committed to custody for trial under a warrant that specified that she should be held in custody awaiting trial for a maximum of 112 days. The claimant was actually held in prison for 193 days. She brought a claim for false imprisonment against the governor of the prison in which she was detained. Her claim was dismissed on the ground that the prison governor was required by statute not to release her until ordered to do so by the courts.

[16] [2001] 2 AC 19.

[17] Nita will, however, be entitled to bring a non-tortious claim for compensation for the years she spent in prison under s 133 of the Criminal Justice Act 1988 (restrictively interpreted in *R (Christofides) v Secretary of State for the Home Department* [2002] 1 WLR 2769 as applying only to cases where an innocent person was convicted of a criminal offence and not to cases where a guilty person was convicted of a more serious offence than he should have been with the result that he was held longer in prison than he should have been).

[18] [1992] 1 AC 58.

because he had been detained in a strip cell. Lord Bridge remarked that the 'primary and fundamental issue' raised by the *Hague* and *Weldon* cases was: '[does] any restraint within defined bounds imposed upon a convicted prisoner whilst serving his sentence by the prison governor . . . but in circumstances where the particular form of restraint is not sanctioned by the prison rules, amounts for that reason to the tort of false imprisonment[?]'[19] The House of Lords answered this question in the negative and dismissed the claims of both the claimant in the *Hague* case and the claimant in the *Weldon* case. This result cannot be explained on the basis that a prisoner cannot be falsely imprisoned by the governor of his prison because he enjoys no liberty. The House of Lords was very clear that if A, a fellow prisoner of B's, locks B in a prison shed, then A will have committed the tort of false imprisonment.[20] Similarly, the House of Lords held that if A, a prison officer, locks B in a cell and does so in bad faith – knowing that he has no authority from the governor of the prison to do so – then A will have committed the tort of false imprisonment.[21] Both these findings presuppose that a prisoner *does* enjoy *some* liberty and *can* therefore be falsely imprisoned.

The reason the House of Lords gave for answering Lord Bridge's question in the negative was that if the governor of a prison detained a prisoner at that prison in some way (for instance, by putting him in a strip cell or an isolation unit), he could argue that he was allowed under s 12(1) of the 1952 Act to detain that prisoner in the way he did. So, in effect, the House of Lords took the view that s 12(1) of the 1952 Act permits the governor of a prison to determine how the prisoners in his charge will be detained. But this is patently untrue. If the governor of Parkhurst Prison breached the Prison Rules 1964 in keeping the claimant in the Hague case in isolation for 28 days, then he was plainly not authorised to detain that claimant in the way he did – whatever s 12(1) of the Prison Act 1952 says. Similarly, if the governor of Leeds Prison was not allowed under the Prison Rules 1964 to put the claimant in the Weldon case in a strip cell, then he was plainly not authorised to subject the claimant to that sort of detention. Perhaps a better explanation as to why the House of Lords answered Lord Bridge's question in the negative is that they feared that if they said that a governor of a prison would commit the tort of false imprisonment if she subjected a prisoner to a form of restraint that breached the Prison Rules 1964, governors of prisons would be swamped by claims from prisoners, each arguing that he had been subjected to a form of detention that technically breached the 1964 Rules and that he had therefore been falsely imprisoned.

Necessity

Suppose that A imprisoned B because it was *necessary* for him to do so. If B subsequently sues A for false imprisonment, will A be able to argue that he had a lawful justificaton or excuse for imprisoning B? The law on this issue is not terribly clear, but a number of different situations can be distinguished.

---

[19] Ibid., 162F–G.
[20] Ibid., 164C–D, 166H–167A, 178F.
[21] Ibid., 164D–E.

(1) *Public defence.* Suppose Karen locked Carl up in a room because she feared that, if she did not, Carl would assault Tom. In such a case, Karen could probably establish that she had a lawful justification or excuse for locking Carl up. Section 3 of the Criminal Law Act 1967 supports this view. That section, it will be recalled, provides that '[a] person may use such force as is reasonable in the circumstances in the prevention of crime . . .'.

(2) *Arrest under invalid byelaw.* In *Percy* v *Hall*,[22] the claimants were arrested over 150 times for trespassing on land in the vicinity of a military communications installation in North Yorkshire in breach of the HMS Forest Moor and Menwith Hill Station Byelaws 1986. These byelaws were actually invalid at the time the claimants were arrested because they were insufficiently precise. When this was discovered, the claimants sued the constables who had arrested them for breach of the byelaws, claiming that as the byelaws were invalid, the constables had committed the tort of false imprisonment in arresting them. The claimants' claims were dismissed by the Court of Appeal. How can we explain this result? As the byelaws were invalid at the time the claimants were arrested, they could not have supplied the constables who arrested the claimants with a lawful excuse or justification for arresting the claimants. However, when the constables arrested the claimants 'they were enforcing what at the time appeared to be perfectly valid byelaws; to have done otherwise [viz. not to have arrested the claimants] would seemingly have involved them in a clear breach of their duties'.[23] This fact was crucial to the Court of Appeal's finding that the constables did not falsely imprison the claimants when they arrested them. The constables had a lawful justification or excuse for arresting the claimants because, at the time the constables arrested the claimants, it was *necessary* for them to do so. If they had not, they would have been in breach of their duties – they would have failed to enforce apparently valid byelaws.

(3) *Unduly prolonged detention in prison.* Suppose that A is convicted of committing a criminal offence and sentenced to spend some time in prison. Suppose further that someone makes a mistake in determining how long A should spend in prison and as a result A is imprisoned for three months longer than he ought to have been. Can A sue the prison governor on the ground that he was falsely imprisoned for those three months? If it was the courts that made the mistake in calculating A's sentence, then A will *not* be able to sue the prison governor for falsely imprisoning him.[24] The prison governor will be able to argue that he was duty-bound to imprison A for as long as he did, and that he therefore had a lawful justification or excuse for imprisoning A for the extra three months that A should not have served.

---

[22] [1997] QB 924.

[23] Ibid., 945D–E.

[24] *Quinland* v *Governor of Swaleside Prison* [2003] QB 306. A will not be able to sue the *courts* for falsely imprisoning him by virtue of s 2(5) of the Crown Proceedings Act 1947, which provides that 'No proceedings shall lie against the Crown by virtue of this section in respect of anything done or omitted to be done by a person whilst discharging or purporting to discharge any responsibilities of a judicial nature vested in him, or any responsibilities which he has in connection with the execution of judicial process.'

If, however, it was the prison governor who made the mistake in calculating A's sentence, then A *will* be able to sue the prison governor for falsely imprisoning him – and this is so even if the prison governor's mistake was an entirely reasonable one to make. This was established by the House of Lords' decision in *R v Governor of Brockhill Prison, ex parte Evans (No. 2)*.[25] In that case, the claimant was a woman named Evans who was sent to prison to serve several terms of imprisonment, running concurrently. At the time Evans was sent to prison, the Divisional Court had ruled – in a case called *R v Governor of Blundeston Prison, ex parte Gaffney*[26] – that the release date of a prisoner serving several concurrent sentences should be calculated in a certain way (call this 'Method X'). The governor, abiding by the decision in *Gaffney*, applied Method X to determine when Evans should be released. However, while Evans was still in prison, she went to court and persuaded the Court of Appeal to rule that the governor should have used a different method for calculating her release date – let's call this method 'Method Y'.[27] The Court of Appeal thereby overruled the decision of the Divisional Court in *Gaffney*. According to Method Y, Evans should have *already* been released and, accordingly, she was released on the same day as the Court of Appeal overruled *Gaffney*. In fact, according to Method Y, Evans should have been released 59 days before she was actually released. Evans sued the prison governor, claiming that she had been falsely imprisoned in being detained for those 59 days. The House of Lords allowed her claim.

It is, however, hard to see why the prison governor was not allowed to rely on a defence of necessity in this case to defeat Evans's claim. Until *Gaffney* was overruled, the governor of Evans's prison was *required* to calculate Evans's release date using Method X and to detain Evans in prison until that date. So the governor of Evans's prison was duty-bound to detain Evans for as long as he did.[28] It was therefore necessary for the governor of Evans's prison to detain Evans for as long as he did. Given this, it could be argued that the governor of Evans's prison had a lawful justification or excuse for detaining Evans for as long as he did. Indeed, if the constables in *Percy v Hall* had a lawful justification or excuse for arresting the claimants in that case based on the fact that they were duty bound to arrest the claimants when they did, it is hard to see why the governor of Evans's prison did not have a lawful justification or excuse for detaining Evans for as long as he did based on the fact that he was duty bound to act in the way he did.[29]

---

[25] [2001] 2 AC 19 (noted, Cane 2001a).

[26] [1982] 1 WLR 696.

[27] *R v Governor of Brockhill Prison, ex parte Evans* [1997] QB 443.

[28] Cf. Judge LJ's remarks in the Court of Appeal in *R v Governor of Brockhill Prison, ex parte Evans (No. 2)* [1999] QB 1043, 1071B–C: 'The governor was blameless. Indeed if he had not continued to detain [Evans] he would have been acting in defiance of the earlier decisions of the Divisional Court . . . So in detaining [Evans] for as long as he did the governor was responsibly performing his duties.'

[29] All of which is not to say that Evans should not have been entitled to recover something for the extra days she was kept in prison. She should probably have been allowed to bring a non-tortious claim for compensation, just as people who are wrongly convicted of committing an offence and sent to prison are allowed to bring a non-tortious claim for compensation for the time they have spent in prison (see above, n. 17). See, to the same effect, Cane 2001a, 10.

12

DEFAMATION

We are concerned in this chapter with two torts – libel and slander – both of which are committed by *defaming* someone else. We will discuss the difference between libel and slander in detail later on, but for the time being it is enough to know that if A makes a defamatory statement about B while *talking* to someone else, that is *slander* and B will usually have to prove that A's statement caused him some harm before he will be allowed to sue A. On the other hand, if A makes a defamatory statement about B to someone else in *writing*, that is *libel* and B will be allowed to sue A even if he cannot show that A's statement caused him harm.

So much for the difference between libel and slander – we'll now look at what they have in common. If B wants to sue A for libel or slander, B will have to show *in either case*: (*a*) that A published a statement to a third party that was defamatory of B; *and* (*b*) that B is the sort of person who can sue someone else for libel or slander. But even if (*a*) and (*b*) are true, B will *not* be entitled to sue A if A has a *defence* to B's claim. All this needs more explanation.

WHAT IS DEFAMATORY?

Suppose A made a statement S to a third party, C.[1] When will B be able to establish that that statement was defamatory of her? The answer is: statement S will have been defamatory of B if:

(*a*) an ordinary, reasonable person who heard or read statement S would tend as a result to think less well of B as a person;[2] *or*

(*b*) an ordinary, reasonable person who heard or read statement S would tend as a result to think that B lacked the ability to do her job effectively and efficiently;[3] *or*

(c) an ordinary, reasonable person who heard or read statement S would tend as a result to shun and avoid B;[4] *or*

---

[1] *Important note.* One can, of course, make a statement by *conduct* as well as by *words*. See, for example, *Monson* v *Tussaud's* [1894] 1 QB 671. In that case the claimant was someone who had been charged with shooting someone with a gun; a Scottish jury returned a verdict of 'not proven' and the claimant was released. The defendants subsequently featured the claimant in their waxworks exhibition, placing a model of the claimant with a gun in his hand near their 'Chamber of Horrors'. The claimant successfully sued the defendants for libel, arguing that they had, in their exhibition, represented that he was guilty of the shooting.

[2] *Sim* v *Stretch* [1936] 2 All ER 1237, 1240 (per Lord Atkin).

[3] *Drummond-Jackson* v *British Medical Association* [1970] 1 All ER 1094, 1104 (per Lord Pearson). Cf *Cornwell* v *Myskow* [1987] 2 All ER 504 where a jury found that it is defamatory to say of an actress that 'she can't sing, her bum is too big and she has the sort of stage presence that jams lavatories'.

[4] *Youssoupoff* v *Metro-Goldwyn-Mayer Pictures Ltd* (1934) 50 TLR 581, 587 (per Slesser LJ).

(*d*) an ordinary, reasonable person who heard or read statement S would tend as a result to treat B as a figure of fun or as an object of ridicule.[5]

So, for example, it is defamatory of B to say that she has committed adultery (in which case (*a*) would be true) or that her work is usually shoddy (in which case (*b*) would be true) or that she has a communicable disease (in which case (*c*) would be true) or that she always insists on wearing a Chelsea shirt when making love (in which case (*d*) would be true).[6] A couple of cases illustrate how this test for determining whether a given statement was defamatory works.

In *Byrne* v *Deane*,[7] the claimant was a member of a golf club which was run by the two defendants. The defendants kept some automatic gambling machines on the premises of the golf club for the use of the members. It was illegal of the defendants to do this and someone within the golf club reported the existence of the machines to the police. When the police removed the machines, someone else posted up a poem on one of the walls of the golf club which plainly indicated that the claimant had been responsible for telling the police of the existence of the machines. The claimant sued the defendants, claiming that the poem was defamatory of him and they were responsible for its publication. The Court of Appeal held, by a bare majority, that the poem was not defamatory: an ordinary, reasonable person who read the poem would not tend to think less well of the claimant as a result – he would think the claimant was to be congratulated on ensuring that the law was observed. Greer LJ dissented; he thought an ordinary, reasonable person who read the poem would draw the conclusion from it that the claimant had acted in a disloyal and underhand fashion and would therefore tend to think less well of the claimant as a result.

In *Charleston* v *News Group Newspapers Ltd*,[8] the *News of the World* published an article on a pornographic computer game which had superimposed the faces of the claimants – two stars of the television series *Neighbours* – on the bodies of two persons engaged in various sexual activities. The article had as its headline 'Strewth! What's Harold up to with our Madge?' and the article carried two large stills from the computer game. The text of the article made it clear that the claimants' faces had been used without their knowledge or consent. The claimants sued the owners of the *News of the World*, claiming that the photographs and the headlines were defamatory – the claimants claimed that an ordinary, reasonable person who looked at the photographs and the headlines would have thought that the claimants had willingly participated in the production of the pornographic computer game in question and would therefore think

---

[5] It has long been acknowledged that statements which expose someone to ridicule are defamatory: see *Parmiter* v *Coupland* (1840) 6 M & W 105, 108, 151 ER 340, 341–2.

[6] *Important note*. It should be noted that a statement can be defamatory *even if it is true*. So if B *has* committed adultery it is still defamatory of her to say that she has committed adultery. Which is *not* to say that if B has committed adultery, she will be able to sue anyone who reports that fact to someone else. Anyone who says that B has committed adultery when she actually has committed adultery will be able to raise a defence of *justification* (discussed below, pp. 280–3) if B attempts to sue him or her for libel or slander.

[7] [1937] 1 KB 818.

[8] [1995] 2 AC 65.

less well of the claimants as a result. The House of Lords dismissed the claimants' claim: an ordinary, reasonable person who saw the headline and photographs complained of would also have read the article below the headlines and the photographs and would have realised that the claimants had nothing to do with the production of the computer game in question.

Let us now look in more detail at what sort of statements are defamatory.

Abusive words

It is often said that words of abuse are not defamatory if they are uttered and heard as such.[9] The reason is presumably that if an ordinary, reasonable person heard the words in question he would realise they were uttered in anger and merely to abuse and would therefore not take them seriously.[10] He would therefore not think less well of the person at whom the abuse was directed.

Offensive words

An offensive statement about B will not be defamatory *per se*; it will only be defamatory if an ordinary, reasonable person who heard the statement would tend either: (*a*) to think less well of B as a person; or (*b*) to think less well of V's ability to do his work; or (*c*) to shun and avoid B; or (*d*) to treat B as a figure of fun or an object of ridicule. Having said that, the courts have come close in a couple of cases to finding that words were defamatory *merely* because they were offensive.

In *Youssoupoff* v *Metro-Goldwyn-Mayer Pictures Ltd*,[11] the claimant sued the defendants, claiming that she had been libelled in a film released by the defendants. The film portrayed the life and death of Rasputin and suggested that Rasputin had enjoyed sexual relations with one 'Princess Natasha'. The claimant argued that an ordinary, reasonable person who saw the film would identify her with Princess Natasha and the suggestion that Rasputin had had sexual relations with the claimant/Princess Natasha would tend to make him think less well of the claimant. The defendants contended that there was nothing to associate Princess Natasha with the claimant and that there was therefore nothing in the film that would cause an ordinary, reasonable person to think less well of the claimant. The Court of Appeal rejected this claim, finding that an ordinary, reasonable person who watched the film would associate Princess Natasha with the claimant.

The defendants then contended that an ordinary, reasonable person who watched the film would gather from it that Rasputin *raped* the claimant/

---

[9] *Penfold* v *Westcote* (1806) 2 B & P (NR) 335, 127 ER 656; *Fields* v *Davis* [1955] CLY 1543.

[10] For the same reason, Handley & Davis 2001 argue that 'words are not defamatory if they are spoken in a context where it is clear that they are in jest'. It is not clear whether the English courts would accept this. If they did not, comedians' freedom of expression would be seriously interfered with: almost all satirical depictions of public figures would be defamatory and *prima facie* actionable.

[11] (1934) 50 TLR 581 (discussed, Treiger-Bar-Am 2000).

Princess Natasha and his feelings towards the claimant would not therefore be adversely affected by the film. (It was conceded that if an ordinary, reasonable person who watched the film would gather from it that Rasputin *seduced* the claimant/Princess Natasha then the film would be defamatory of the claimant – an ordinary, reasonable person would conclude that the claimant was of low morals and would therefore think less well of her.) The Court of Appeal held that even if it were true that an ordinary, reasonable person who watched the film would gather from it that Rasputin raped the claimant/Princess Natasha, the film would still be defamatory of the claimant.[12]

Scrutton LJ evidently regarded the argument that 'to say of a woman that she had been [raped] by a man of very bad character when as a matter of fact she never saw the man at all and was never near him is not defamatory of the woman' as outrageous, remarking that he had 'no language to express my opinion of that argument'.[13] Slesser LJ based his finding that it would be defamatory to say of a woman that she had been raped on the ground that an ordinary, reasonable person who heard or read that statement would tend to shun and avoid the woman in question: 'a lady of whom it has been said that she has been [raped will suffer] in social reputation and in opportunities of receiving respectful consideration from the world.'[14] This does not seem convincing. The Court of Appeal in *Youssoupoff* therefore offered little by way of argument in support of its view that it will be defamatory to say of a woman that she has been raped. Of course, it is grossly offensive to say of someone that he or she has been raped when he or she has not been raped and that may have been one consideration which motivated the Court of Appeal in *Youssoupoff* to find that such a statement would be defamatory.

In *Berkoff* v *Burchill*,[15] Steven Berkoff, the well-known actor, sued the journalist Julie Burchill for libel after she called him, in one review, 'hideous-looking' and, in another review, compared his appearance unfavourably with Frankenstein's monster. The Court of Appeal held, by a bare majority, that Burchill's suggestion in these reviews that Berkoff was 'hideously ugly' was defamatory of Berkoff. The decision is very hard to explain and it is hard to avoid the impression that the Court of Appeal was led to find that Burchill's reviews were defamatory of Berkoff because they were so offensive. Of course, the Court of Appeal did not say as much – but the reasons that the majority in the Court of Appeal did offer in support of its decision are singularly unconvincing.

Neill LJ found that Burchill's reviews gave the impression that Berkoff was 'not merely physically unattractive in appearance but actually repulsive'. He went on to suggest that 'to say this of someone in the public eye who makes his living, in part at least, as an actor, is capable of lowering his standing in the estimation of the public and of making him an object of ridicule'.[16] It is hard to see

---

[12] In fact both Greer LJ and Slesser LJ thought that an ordinary, reasonable person who watched the film would gather from it that Rasputin seduced the claimant/Princess Natasha (ibid., 586, 587).

[13] Ibid., 584.

[14] Ibid., 587.

[15] [1996] 4 All ER 1008.

[16] Ibid., 1018f–g.

why Neill LJ put such an emphasis on the fact that Burchill's reviews suggested that Berkoff was *repulsive* and the fact that Berkoff was, and is, an *actor*. Why should suggesting that someone is physically unattractive make him any the less an object of ridicule than suggesting that someone is actually repulsive would? And again – why should suggesting that an actor is repulsive make him any more an object of ridicule than suggesting that a painter or a teacher or judge is repulsive would? Turning to Phillips LJ's judgment, he expressly found that Burchill's reviews would *not* tend to cause ordinary, reasonable people to shun and avoid Berkoff. But, like Neill LJ, he found that Burchill's reviews could be defamatory of Berkoff because they could have the effect of making him an object of ridicule among ordinary, reasonable people. But such a finding shows a poor regard for ordinary, reasonable people – the suggestion that someone is 'hideously ugly' would surely *not* tend to cause ordinary, reasonable people to treat that someone as a figure of fun.

The repetition rule

Suppose Alan said to Karen, 'John thinks/John told me that Gary is a thief.' In such a case, it will be conclusively presumed that an ordinary, reasonable person who heard or read Alan's statement would have concluded that Gary was a thief. This rule of law is known as the 'repetition rule'. The repetition rule applies even if it would have been clear to an ordinary, reasonable person who heard or read Alan's statement that Alan was not necessarily endorsing John's opinion of Gary – as would be the case if Alan qualified his statement by saying that 'Of course, I have no way of knowing myself whether or not Gary is a thief.'[17] It follows that Alan's statement to Karen in the above case *will* be defamatory of Gary – it will be conclusively presumed that an ordinary, reasonable person who heard or read Alan's statement would have concluded from it that Gary was a thief and would as a result have thought less well of Gary.

A similar rule applies if Alan said to Karen, 'I think Gary is a thief.' Again, it will be conclusively presumed that an ordinary, reasonable person who heard or read Alan's statement would have concluded from it that Gary was a thief and would therefore have thought less well of Gary. It will therefore be conclusively presumed that Alan's statement to Karen was defamatory of Gary – and this is so even if an ordinary, reasonable person who heard or read Alan's statement could actually have been expected to think, 'Well, Alan thinks Gary is a thief, but his opinion is not necessarily correct and I should wait to make up my own mind about Gary instead of just blindly going along with Alan's opinions.'

Similarly, if Alan said to Karen, 'I have reasonable grounds to suspect Gary of being a thief', it will be conclusively presumed that an ordinary, reasonable person who heard or read Alan's statement would have concluded from it that there *were* reasonable grounds to suspect Gary of being a thief and would have thought less well of Gary as a result.[18] So, again, it will be conclusively

[17] *Stern* v *Piper* [1997] QB 123.
[18] *Shah* v *Standard Chartered Bank* [1999] QB 241.

presumed that Alan's statement to Karen was defamatory of Gary – and this is so even if an ordinary, reasonable person who heard or read Alan's statement could actually have been expected to think, 'Well, Alan may think he has reasonable grounds to believe that Gary is a thief – but what does he know? I should make up my own mind and judge Gary on the evidence presented to me.'

Community standards

In judging how an ordinary, reasonable person would react to a given statement about someone, one must take into account the current state of public opinion. So, for example, suppose Mary says of Fred that he is a homosexual. Is that defamatory? Thirty years ago, the answer would have been 'yes' – the state of public opinion at that time was such that an ordinary, reasonable person would have tended to think less well of someone if it were alleged that he was a homosexual.[19] Nowadays, it is more difficult to say – today, people generally are more tolerant of homosexuality and, given this, it is difficult to say that an ordinary, reasonable person would nowadays think less well of someone if it was alleged that he was a homosexual. This creates a problem for B if A says of him that he is a homosexual and B wants to sue A so as to establish publicly that he is in fact heterosexual – the courts may rule that A's allegation was not defamatory and thereby prevent B from suing A for libel or slander.

It follows from what has just been said that if B has higher standards of behaviour than the general public and A accuses B of engaging in conduct which is inconsistent with those high standards, B will find it difficult to show that A's words were defamatory for the purpose of suing A for libel or slander. So, for example, suppose Eric is a teetotaller but Sarah wrote to Wendy saying that she saw Eric drinking a pint of lager in a pub at the weekend. Sarah's statement to Wendy will not be defamatory – an ordinary, reasonable person who read Sarah's statement about Eric would not think any the worse of Eric as a result. However, it would be different if Eric was well known to be a temperance campaigner. In such a case, an ordinary, reasonable person who read Sarah's statement would tend to think that Eric was a hypocrite and would tend to think less well of Eric as a result. On these facts, then, a case could be made out for thinking that Sarah's statement to Wendy was defamatory of Eric.

Innuendo

A statement which is innocent on its face will still be defamatory of B if: (*a*) an ordinary, reasonable person *who was possessed of certain special knowledge* would tend on hearing or reading that statement to think less well of B; *and* (*b*) the statement in question was published to one or more people who were possessed

---

[19] In *R* v *Bishop* [1975] QB 274, the Court of Appeal expressed the view (at 281) that if A said that B was a homosexual 'a submission that [A's] words were incapable of a defamatory meaning would be bound to fail and a jury would generally be likely to find them defamatory'.

of that special knowledge. If (*a*) and (*b*) are true of a particular statement, lawyers say that the statement in question gave rise to an *innuendo* which was defamatory of B.

So, to take a well-known example, suppose that Paul said to Beth that he saw Carl coming out of a particular house. Suppose further that that house happened to be a brothel. So an ordinary, reasonable person who knew the house in question was a brothel would, on hearing Paul's statement, tend to think less well of Carl as a person – he would tend to think that Carl used prostitutes. Now, if Beth *knew* that the house in question was a brothel, Paul's statement, while innocent on its face, will have been defamatory of Carl. Note that, so far as Beth is concerned, all that has to be proved – for the purpose of establishing that Paul statement was defamatory of Carl – is that Beth knew that the house in question was a brothel. It does *not* also have to be shown that Beth concluded from Paul's statement that Carl used prostitutes or that Beth thought any the less of Carl as a person when she heard Paul's statement. It is enough that an ordinary, reasonable person who was possessed of the knowledge Beth had when she heard Paul's statement would have tended to think less well of Carl if he had heard Paul's statement.

In *Cassidy v Daily Mirror Newspapers Ltd*,[20] the *Daily Mirror* published a photograph of one Cassidy with a lady companion. The caption accompanying the photograph informed the reader that Cassidy and his companion had announced their engagement. In fact, Cassidy was married to the claimant. The claimant successfully sued the *Daily Mirror* for libel. The Court of Appeal found that: (*a*) an ordinary, reasonable person who knew the claimant and knew that she purported to be Cassidy's wife would tend to think on the basis of the caption that she was a liar and was not Cassidy's wife at all; therefore (*b*) an ordinary, reasonable person who knew the claimant and knew that she purported to be Cassidy's wife would, on seeing the caption beneath the *Daily Mirror*'s photograph, tend to think less well of her as a person; (*c*) people who knew the claimant and knew that she purported to be Cassidy's wife had seen the photograph and its accompanying caption; therefore (*d*) the caption beneath the *Daily Mirror*'s photograph, while innocent on its face, gave rise to an innuendo – that the claimant was not married to Cassidy and was therefore a liar – which was defamatory of her.

Defamatory statements which do not on their face specifically refer to the claimant

A defamatory statement which did not, on its face, specifically refer to B will still be defamatory of B if: (*a*) an ordinary, reasonable person who *knew of B and her circumstances* would have, on hearing or reading the statement in question, thought that it referred to B and would, as a result, have tended to think less well of B; *and* (*b*) the statement in question was published to one or more people *who thought that it referred to B*. If (*a*) and (*b*) are true then the statement

[20] [1929] 2 KB 331.

in question will be defamatory of B even though it did not, on its face, specifically refer to B.

We will usually have occasion to employ this test for determining whether a given statement was defamatory of a claimant in two kinds of situation. The first is the case where a defendant published a statement to another which defamed a particular individual (real or imaginary) and that statement could have been taken as referring to the claimant because people might have identified the claimant with the individual referred to in the statement. The second is the case where a defendant published a statement which defamed a particular class of people and that statement could have been taken as referring to the claimant because the claimant belonged to that class. Let us now look at how the courts have applied the above test in each of these situations.

Mistaken identity cases

In *E Hulton & Co.* v *Jones*,[21] the *Sunday Chronicle* carried an article describing a motor festival at Dieppe. The article featured described various figures who attended the festival including one 'Artemus Jones'. He was described as being a 'churchwarden at Peckham'. The article alleged that while he was at the festival he had consorted with a woman who was not his wife and that he was, in general, 'the life and soul of a gay little band that haunts the Casino and turns night into day, besides betraying a most unholy delight in the society of female butterflies'. The claimant was a barrister called Artemus Jones. He sued the defendants, the publishers of the *Sunday Chronicle*, for libel. His claim was successful. It was found that friends of the claimant had seen the article in question and thought it referred to the claimant. Moreover, it was found that an ordinary, reasonable person who knew the claimant would have thought, on reading the article, that it referred to him and would have tended as a result to think less well of him as a person. The fact that the claimant was a barrister and not a churchwarden at Peckham did not affect the issue. No doubt the fact that the claimant and the person referred to in the article shared such a distinctive name as Artemus Jones played a large part in the finding that an ordinary, reasonable person who knew the claimant would have thought on reading the article in question that it referred to him.

In *Newstead* v *London Express Newspaper Limited*,[22] the *Daily Express* published an account of a trial for bigamy, referring to the accused as 'Harold Newstead, thirty-year-old Camberwell man'. The claimant – who was called Harold Newstead and who worked in Camberwell and was aged about 30 – sued the publishers of the *Daily Express* for libel. His claim succeeded. It was found that some acquaintances of the claimant had read the account in the *Daily Express* and thought that it referred to the claimant. Moreover, it was found that an ordinary, reasonable person who knew the claimant would have – on reading the report of the trial – thought that the report referred to the claimant and would therefore have thought less well of the claimant as a person. It might have been different if the name of the prisoner who was accused of bigamy had been 'John

[21] [1910] AC 20.
[22] [1940] 1 KB 377.

Smith' and the prisoner had simply been described as 'John Smith, a thirty-year-old London man'.[23] In such a case, if another John Smith who came from London and was about 30 years old had sued the publishers of the *Daily Express* for libel, he would *not* have been able to establish that an ordinary, reasonable person who knew him would, on reading the report in the *Daily Express*, have thought that the report referred to the claimant and would therefore have tended to think less well of him: such an ordinary, reasonable person would have had no reason to identify the claimant with the prisoner named in the report in the *Daily Express* even though their names, ages and residences coincided.

In *Morgan* v *Odhams Press Ltd*,[24] the claimant took into his house a kennel girl who was helping a journalist with his inquiries into the activities of a dog doping gang. The claimant spent six days with the girl in his flat and in that period a few acquaintances of the claimant met him in the company of the girl. After the six days were up, the girl in question went to stay with the journalist she was helping. The journalist published his story about the dog doping gang in a Sunday newspaper and the story included a photograph of the kennel girl who had helped him break the story. The next day, *The Sun* published a story claiming that the kennel girl in question had been kidnapped by members of the gang. The claimant sued *The Sun* for libel, claiming: (*a*) that an ordinary, reasonable person who saw the kennel girl with the claimant during the six days that she spent with the claimant would, on reading the story in *The Sun*, think that the claimant was one of the dog doping gang who had kidnapped the girl and would therefore think less well of the claimant; and (*b*) that people who had seen the kennel girl with the claimant during the six days that she spent with the claimant had thought the story in *The Sun* referred to him. The claimant's claim was allowed: a jury found that (*a*) and (*b*) were true and the House of Lords declined to disturb the verdict, thinking that it was possible that an ordinary, reasonable person who read the story in *The Sun could* have thought, on the basis of having seen the claimant with the kennel girl, that the claimant had been involved in her kidnapping.

Defamation of a class

Suppose Tom said or wrote to Dawn that 'All lawyers are corrupt.' Suppose further that Vijay is a lawyer. If Vijay sues Tom for libel or slander his claim will certainly fail. No court will find that an ordinary, reasonable person who heard or read Tom's statement would have thought that it referred to Vijay and would have tended as a result to think less well of Vijay.[25] Why is this? The answer is presumably that generalisations always admit of exceptions and an ordinary, reasonable person who heard or read Tom's statement would not have thought that Tom's statement applied to *all lawyers without exception*. An ordinary, reasonable person who heard or read Tom's statement would

---

[23] Ibid., 391 (per MacKinnon LJ).

[24] [1971] 1 WLR 1239.

[25] *Eastwood* v *Holmes* (1858) 1 F & F 347, 349, 175 ER 758, 759: '[If] a man wrote that all lawyers were thieves, no particular lawyer could sue him unless there was something to point to the particular individual' (per Willes J).

therefore have had no reason to think that Vijay *in particular* was covered by Tom's statement.[26]

It would be different if Tom said or wrote to Dawn that 'All the lawyers employed by the firm Sue, Grabbit and Run are corrupt' and Vijay was employed by Sue, Grabbit and Run. In such a case, Vijay will probably be able to establish that Tom's statement was defamatory of him. An ordinary, reasonable person who heard or read Tom's statement would be entitled to think that Tom, in making that statement, was not making a sweeping generalisation but was instead making a specific allegation against *each and every* lawyer employed at Sue, Grabbit and Run. So an ordinary, reasonable person who heard Tom's statement would be entitled to think that Tom's statement indicated that Vijay was corrupt and would tend to think less well of Vijay as a result.

So, in *Knupffer v London Express Newspaper Ltd*[27] the *Daily Express* carried an article during the Second World War which accused members of the 'Young Russia' party of being willing to help Hitler by building up a pro-German movement within the Soviet Union. The claimant was the head of the British branch of the 'Young Russia' party. A number of people read the article and thought it referred to or reflected on the claimant. The claimant sued the publishers of the *Daily Express* for libel. His claim was dismissed by the House of Lords: an ordinary, reasonable person who read the *Daily Express* article would not have thought it referred to the claimant in particular. The accusations against members of the 'Young Russia' party contained in the *Daily Express* article were far too generalised to make it reasonable to think that they applied to the claimant in particular.

In contrast, in *Riches v News Group Newspapers Ltd*[28] the *News of the World* published a letter from a man who was holding his son and a woman hostage at gun point. The letter made various allegations against 'the Banbury CID' – including an allegation that members of the Banbury CID had raped his wife. Ten members of the Banbury CID sued the publishers of the *News of the World* for libel and were awarded substantial damages at first instance. The Court of Appeal held that the damages awarded to the claimants should be reassessed but did not question the propriety of awarding each of the claimants something by way of damages. Clearly, the Court of Appeal agreed with the court of first instance that the letter published in the *News of the World* was defamatory of *each* of the claimants. An ordinary, reasonable person who read the letter published in the *News of the World* would have thought that the allegations contained in the letter applied to *each and every* member of the Banbury CID – he would not have simply thought that those allegations merely amounted to sweeping generalisations which did not necessarily apply to each and every member of the Banbury CID.

---

[26] Cf. Lord Atkin's remarks in *Knupffer v London Express Newspaper Ltd* [1944] AC 116, 122: 'The reason why a libel published of a large or indeterminate number of persons described by some general name generally fails to be actionable is the difficulty of establishing that the claimant was, in fact, included in the defamatory statement, for the habit of making unfounded generalisations is ingrained in ill-educated or vulgar minds, or the words are occasionally intended to be a facetious exaggeration.'

[27] [1944] AC 116.

[28] [1986] 1 QB 256.

THE REQUIREMENT OF PUBLICATION

If B wants to sue A for libel or slander, B will have to show that A *published* a statement that was defamatory of him to a *third party*. So, obviously, if Mary said to Ian, 'I think you're a thief', Ian would not be entitled to sue Mary for libel or slander: her statement was not published to a third party. A number of points may be made about when this requirement will be satisfied.

(1) *Spouses.* Suppose John told his wife, 'I think Ruth is a thief.' Ruth will not be able to sue John for libel or slander. The reason is that the courts will *not* find that John's statement in this case was published to a *third party*.[29] The courts' attitude is a throwback to the days when a husband and wife were regarded as having a common identity. While we have, of course, abandoned the idea that a husband and wife share a common identity, the courts still seem to think that someone who makes a defamatory statement to his or her spouse does not publish that statement to a third party.

(2) *Secretaries.* If John dictates a letter to Wendy, his secretary, that is defamatory of Eric, Eric may be able to sue John even if the letter is never sent. John will have published the defamatory statements contained in the letter to a third party, namely Wendy. But if Wendy hands back the letter to John for checking, Eric will not be able to sue *Wendy*. Wendy's handing back of the letter to John for checking will not amount to a publication by Wendy to a third party of the defamatory statements contained in the letter.[30] It would be different, of course, if Wendy showed the letter to someone other than John or Eric – in that case, Eric may well be able to sue Wendy for libel.

(3) *Misunderstanding.* It seems to be generally acknowledged that if John made a statement to Gary that was defamatory of Karen, John will not be held to have published that statement to a third party if Gary did not understand what John said because, for example, he was deaf or illiterate.

(4) *Private notes.* Suppose that John wrote down on a piece of paper 'Lara is a thief' and locked the piece of paper in a desk drawer. Suppose further that Carl, a burglar, subsequently broke into the desk drawer and read the piece of paper. Lara will not be able to sue John for libel.[31] John did not publish the defamatory material to Carl: he did not show Carl the piece of paper or allow him to read it.

(5) *Unintended recipients.* If John sent a letter to Alan that was defamatory of Sarah and Helen opened the letter and read it, the courts will not hold that John published the letter to Helen *unless* it was *reasonably foreseeable* when John sent the letter that it would be opened and read by someone like Helen.

---

[29] *Wennhak v Morgan* (1888) 20 QBD 635. The same rule will apply, of course, if a wife tells her husband something that is defamatory of another.

[30] *Eglantine Inn Ltd v Smith* [1948] NI 29, 33.

[31] *Pullman v Hill & Co.* [1891] 1 QB 524, 527.

So: in *Pullman* v *Hill & Co.*,[32] the defendant sent a letter to the claimants at their firm which claimed that they had obtained money under false pretences. The letter was opened by a clerk in the claimants' firm and was read by him and two other clerks. It was held that the defendant had published his defamatory letter about the claimants to the clerks because it was reasonably foreseeable that they would open and read the letter, it being normal practice for the clerks in a firm to open and read all the correspondence addressed to the firm.

Similarly, in *Theaker* v *Richardson*[33] the defendant sent a letter to the claimant, a member of the local council, which accused her of shoplifting, of running a brothel, of being a prostitute and of having committed various acts of dishonesty in her position as a council member. The claimant's husband opened the letter and read it. The claimant sued the defendant for libel. A jury found for the claimant, holding that the defendant had published his letter to the claimant's husband – it had been reasonably foreseeable when the defendant sent his letter to the claimant that the claimant's husband would read the letter. The Court of Appeal declined to set aside the jury's verdict.[34]

In contrast, in *Huth* v *Huth*[35] the defendant sent a letter to his estranged wife which, the claimants claimed, was defamatory of them. The claimants were the defendant's children – they claimed the defendant's letter suggested that they were illegitimate. In order to sue the defendant they had to show that the defendant had published the letter to someone other than his wife. (The fact that the defendant published the letter to his wife was not, of course, enough to allow the claimants to sue the defendant – as we have already seen, if someone publishes a defamatory statement to his wife, that statement will not be regarded as having been published to a third party.) In fact, the butler in the house where the defendant's wife was staying when she received the letter had opened and read the letter before he handed it over to the defendant's wife. The Court of Appeal held that the defendant had not published his letter to the butler as it was not reasonably foreseeable that the butler would open and read his letter. The claimants could not therefore show that the defendant had published his letter to anyone other than his wife and their claims were dismissed.

(6) *Platforms*. If John put a statement that was defamatory of Nita on an electronic bulletin board that was maintained by Vijay, the courts will hold that *Vijay* – as well as John – published that statement to whoever accessed the bulletin board and read John's statement.[36] What is the position if John posted up a statement that was defamatory of Nita on some premises which were owned or run by Vijay? In such a case, the courts will hold that *Vijay* – as well as John – published the statement to the people who read it *if* there is some evidence that Vijay *approved* of the posting

---

[32] Ibid.

[33] [1962] 1 WLR 151.

[34] Note that the old-fashioned view that husbands and wives share a common identity does not extend to cases where A makes a defamatory remark about B to B's husband. In such a case, the courts will hold that the remark *has* been published to a *third party*. They will not regard A's remark as having just been made to B.

[35] [1915] 3 KB 32.

[36] *Godfrey* v *Demon Internet Limited* [2001] QB 201.

up of that statement.[37] Similarly, it is suggested, if John made a defamatory statement about Nita in the course of a meeting held on premises owned or run by Vijay, *Vijay* – as well as John – will be held to have published that statement to the people who attended the meeting if there is some evidence that he approved of the making of that statement.

(7) *Chinese whispers*. Suppose John made a defamatory statement about Beth to Fred. Suppose further that Fred repeated that statement to Mary. If John authorised or instructed Fred to repeat his statement about Beth to Mary, then *John* – as well as Fred – will be held to have published Fred's statement to Mary.

However, if Beth suffered some kind of loss as a result of the publication to Mary, and wishes to recover compensation for that loss from *John*, she will not necessarily have to show that John – as well as Fred – published Fred's statement to Mary. Beth could choose to sue John for his statement to Fred. If she can sue him for making that statement, then she can recover compensation for all the *reasonably foreseeable* losses that John's statement to Fred has *caused* her to suffer.[38]

So if Beth *can* sue John for making his statement to Fred, all she has to do – if she wants to recover compensation for the losses she suffered as a result of the publication to Mary – is show that John's statement *caused* her to suffer those losses and it was *reasonably foreseeable* that she would suffer those losses if John made his statement to Fred.[39] The causation requirement will be satisfied if Fred acted *reasonably* in repeating John's statement to Mary. The reasonable foreseeability requirement will be satisfied if it was reasonably foreseeable when John made his statement to Fred that Fred would repeat it to Mary and Beth would suffer loss as a result.

Of course, if John's statement to Fred was privileged in some way so that Beth cannot sue John for making that statement to Fred, the only way Beth will be able to sue John for the loss she has suffered as a result of the publication to Mary is to show that John – as well as Fred – published Fred's statement to Mary. And, as we have said, John will only be held to have published Fred's statement to Mary if he authorised or instructed Fred to make that statement to Mary.

---

[37] See *Byrne v Deane* [1937] 1 KB 818. An allegedly defamatory poem which was posted up on walls of golf club run by defendants held to have been published by defendants to whoever read the poem because there was some sign that they approved of its being posted up – the defendants had had the power to take the poem down, but none of them had. However, no claim could be made against the defendants because the poem was held not to be defamatory: see above, p. 266.

[38] *Slipper v BBC* [1991] 1 QB 283.

[39] See *McManus v Beckham* [2002] 1 WLR 2982. In that case, it was held that it was possible that Victoria Beckham could be held liable for the losses suffered by the claimant as a result of the media reporting her claims that the David Beckham autographs on memorabilia sold by the claimant were forged. The Court of Appeal held (at [43], per Laws LJ) that whether she could be sued or not for those losses would depend on whether it was reasonably foreseeable at the time she made her claims (that is, very likely or probable: see above, p. 70, n. 24) that those claims would be reported in the media (ibid., at [43], per Laws LJ). With respect, it would also depend on whether it was *reasonable* for the media to report Victoria Beckham's claims: see *Ward v Weeks* (1830) 7 Bing 285, 131 ER 81 and *Weld-Blundell v Stephens* [1920] AC 956. The claim in *McManus v Beckham* was subsequently settled, with the Beckhams paying the claimant a substantial sum in damages as well as giving him some more signed memorabilia to sell in his shop.

(8) *Shops*. If John sells a newspaper to Carl that contains a defamatory statement about Wendy, then John will be held to have published that statement to a third party. Similarly, if John helps print a newspaper that contains a defamatory statement about Wendy, the courts will hold that John published that statement to whoever read the newspaper once it was printed.[40]

TITLE TO SUE

If A has published a statement to another that was defamatory of B, B will only be entitled to sue A for libel or slander if B is the sort of person who can sue someone else for libel or slander.

If B is a *natural person* then there is no problem: a flesh and blood person may bring an action for libel or slander against a defendant if she feels that that defendant has defamed her. The case of *South Hetton Coal Company Ltd* v *North-Eastern News Association Ltd*[41] establishes that a *company* may be able to sue a defendant for libel or slander if the defendant publishes to another a statement that is defamatory of the company – but only if the statement in question has a tendency to damage the company's trading interests. What about a trade union? Section 10(1) of the Trade Union and Labour Relations (Consolidation) Act 1992 provides that a 'trade union is not a body corporate' – so a trade union does not enjoy sufficient personality to bring an action for libel or slander in respect of a statement that is defamatory of the trade union.[42]

If A publishes a statement to another that is defamatory of a *public body* – such as a local authority – the public body in question will *not* be entitled to sue A for libel or slander. This was established by the House of Lords' decision in *Derbyshire County Council* v *Times Newspapers Ltd*.[43] In that case, *The Sunday Times* printed a couple of articles which alleged that Derbyshire County Council had acted improperly in investing funds in its superannuation fund. Derbyshire County Council sued *The Sunday Times* for libel but its claim was dismissed by the House of Lords on the ground that an action for libel could not be maintained by a public body.

The House of Lords admitted that a public body could have a legitimate interest in bringing an action for libel or slander if it were the subject of a defamatory statement. As Lord Keith of Kinkel observed, the making of a defamatory statement about a public body 'might make it more difficult [for the body] to borrow or to attract suitable staff and thus affect adversely the efficient carrying out of its functions.'.[44] However, the House of Lords felt that freedom of speech would be unreasonably infringed if the law did not assure people that

---

[40] In each case, however, John may have a *defence* which would prevent Wendy from suing him for libel. See below, pp. 297–9.

[41] [1894] 1 QB 133.

[42] *EETPU* v *Times Newspapers Ltd* [1980] 3 WLR 98. A trade union used to enjoy sufficient legal personality to bring an action for libel or slander: *National Union of General and Municipal Workers* v *Gillian* [1946] KB 81.

[43] [1993] AC 534.

[44] Ibid., 547E.

they could criticise public bodies without fear of being made subject to actions for libel or slander as a result. Lord Keith remarked, 'it is of the highest public importance that a democratically elected governmental body, or indeed any governmental body, should be open to *uninhibited* public criticism. The threat of a civil action for [libel or slander] must inevitably have an inhibiting effect on freedom of speech.'[45]

The House of Lords did *not* go further in the *Derbyshire* case and say that a *politician* would have no right to sue for libel or slander if he felt that some criticism of his conduct in office was defamatory. Indeed, the House of Lords made it clear that if a defendant's criticism of a public body reflected badly on the people running the affairs of that body, those people might well be able to sue the defendant for libel or slander.[46] No doubt this can be explained on the basis that politicians have more of an interest in vindicating their reputation than public bodies do – a politician, after all, has a life inside and outside politics which can be seriously affected by the publication of a defamatory statement about him – and this warrants giving politicians a higher degree of protection from being defamed than the House of Lords was willing to afford to public bodies.

It is now clear that the *Derbyshire* decision extends to *political parties* and that a political party which feels that it has been defamed by some statement made by someone else will not be able to bring an action for libel or slander in respect of that statement,[47] though, of course, if the statement simultaneously defamed a member of that party, he or she might be able to sue for libel or slander.

DEFENCES

Suppose A published a statement to a third party that was defamatory of B and B is the sort of person who can sue someone for libel or slander. In such a case, B will still not be entitled to sue A for libel or slander if A has some kind of *defence* to B's claim. The sort of defences that someone may be able to raise to an action for libel or slander are set out below.

Consent

First of all, *consent* is a defence to an action for libel or slander. B will not be able to complain about A's publishing a defamatory statement about her to a third party if B consented to that publication in the first place.

For example, in *Chapman v Lord Ellesmere*[48] a stewards' inquiry held by the Jockey Club found that a horse trained by the claimant was doped when it ran a particular race. The Jockey Club disqualified the horse and 'warned' the claimant off the course where the horse ran. The Jockey Club's decision was published in the *Racing Calendar*, the Jockey Club's official journal. The claimant sued, claiming the

---

[45] Ibid., 547F–G.
[46] Ibid., 550D.
[47] *Goldsmith v Bhoyrul* [1998] QB 459.
[48] [1932] 2 KB 431.

publication was defamatory of him. The claimant's claim was dismissed – he had consented to that publication. He was held to have consented to the publication because when he obtained a trainer's licence, he agreed to abide by the rules of the Jockey Club, one of which rules specified that a decision of the Jockey Club could be published in the *Racing Calendar* if the Jockey Club thought it fit to do so.

Justification

Suppose A has published to another a statement that was defamatory of B because an ordinary, reasonable person who read or heard A's statement would have thought that *x* was true of B and would as a result have tended to think less well of B. In such a case, A will have a defence if B sues him for libel or slander if he can prove that *x was* true of B. If A can prove this, we say that he has a defence of *justification* to B's claim.

Notice that in order to raise this defence, it will *not* be enough for A to show that his words were *literally* true – he will have to show that the impression an ordinary, reasonable person would have gained of B from A's words was a correct one. So suppose John wrote a letter to Mary in which he remarked, 'I think Ian is a thief.' If Ian sues John for libel and John wants to raise a defence of justification to Ian's claim, it will not be enough for John to prove that *he actually did think* when he wrote the letter that Ian was a thief and therefore that his statement to Nita was literally true. It will be conclusively presumed that an ordinary, reasonable person who heard or read John's allegation would have thought on the basis of it that Ian *was* a thief[49] – given this, if John wants to raise a defence of justification to Ian's claim, he will have to prove that Ian *is* a thief.

Similarly, if Ian is suing John for libel because John wrote to Nita that 'Tom says that Ian is a thief', if John wants to raise a defence of justification to Ian's claim, it will not be enough for John to prove that *Tom actually said* to someone that Ian was a thief. As it will be conclusively presumed that an ordinary, reasonable person who heard or read John's allegation would have thought that Ian *was* a thief,[50] John will have to prove that Ian actually *is* a thief in order to raise a defence of justification to Ian's claim.

Again, suppose John wrote to Nita that 'I have reasonable grounds to suspect that Ian is a thief.' If Ian sues John for libel and John wants to raise a defence of justification to Ian's claim, it will not be enough for John to prove that he had reasonable grounds to suspect Ian of being a thief. So it will not be enough for John to prove that Tom told him that Ian was a thief and Tom had proved himself in the past to be honest and reliable so that Tom's statement to John gave John reasonable grounds for believing that Ian *was* a thief. As it will be conclusively presumed that an ordinary, reasonable person who heard or read John's statement would have thought as a result of hearing or reading that statement that there were reasonable grounds to suspect Ian of being a thief,[51]

---

[49] See above, pp. 269–70.
[50] Ibid.
[51] Ibid.

if John wants to establish a defence of justification to Ian's claim for libel, John will have to prove that there *are* reasonable grounds to suspect Ian of being a thief.

Sometimes there will be some dispute as to what impression an ordinary, reasonable man would have gained from hearing or reading a given statement. In *Lewis v Daily Telegraph Ltd*,[52] the defendants, the *Daily Mail* and the *Daily Telegraph*, both published front-page reports which alleged that the Fraud Squad was inquiring into the affairs of the claimant, Rubber Improvement Ltd. The claimant sued both newspapers for libel. It was admitted that the reports were defamatory: an ordinary, reasonable person who read the reports would have tended to think less well of the claimant as a result. The defendants sought to rely on a defence of justification to defeat the claimant's claim. The issue was: what would the defendants have to prove to raise such a defence? This turned on what impression of the claimant would have been gained by an ordinary, reasonable person who heard about or read the reports in the newspapers. The claimant argued that an ordinary, reasonable person who heard about or read the reports in question would have concluded from them that the claimant had operated in a dishonest or fraudulent manner – so the defendants would have to prove that the claimant *had* conducted its affairs in a dishonest way if they wanted to rely on a defence of justification to defeat the claimant's claim.

The House of Lords disagreed. At best, an ordinary, reasonable person would have concluded from the stories in the defendants' newspapers that the claimant had conducted its affairs in such a way as to give rise to a *suspicion* that it was guilty of some dishonest or fraudulent conduct. As Lord Reid observed – if someone, on reading the stories in the defendants' newspapers had observed 'Oh, if the fraud squad are after these people you can take it they are guilty' an ordinary, reasonable person would have rounded on him 'with such remarks as – "Be fair. This is not a police state. No doubt their affairs are in a mess or the police would not be interested. But that could be because [someone] has been very stupid or careless. We really must not jump to conclusions. The police are fair and know their job and we shall know soon enough if there is anything in it. Wait till we see if they [bring charges]. I wouldn't trust [the people involved in this company] until this thing is cleared up but, it is another thing to condemn [them] unheard." '[53] So, in order to establish a defence of justification to the claimant's claim, the defendants did *not* have to show that the claimant had operated its affairs in a dishonest or fraudulent manner; at best, the defendants were required to show that the claimant had operated its affairs in such a way as to give rise to a suspicion that it had acted dishonestly or fraudulently in the way it operated.

In *Wakley v Cooke and Healey*,[54] the claimant, a former journalist, was a coroner in Middlesex. The defendants published an article in the *Medical Times* which contained an attack on the claimant. The article observed, 'There can be

---

[52] [1964] AC 234.
[53] Ibid., 259–60.
[54] (1849) 4 Ex 511, 154 ER 1316.

no court of justice unpolluted which this libellous journalist [meaning the claimant] ... is allowed to disgrace with his presidentship.' The claimant sued the defendants for libel. It was held that an ordinary, reasonable man would gather from this statement that the claimant had been in the habit of libelling others when he was a journalist. So the defendants could not raise a defence of justification to the claimant's claim by showing that the claimant had on *one* occasion been found to have libelled someone else as a journalist; they would have to show that the claimant had on *many* occasions libelled other people when working as a journalist. As the defendants could not show this, the claimant's claim was allowed.

A few more points may be made about the defence of justification.

Partial justification

If A has published a statement to another that is defamatory of B, A does not have to prove – for the purpose of raising a defence of justification to any claim B might bring against him for libel or slander – that *every word* of what he said was correct; it is enough if he can show that what he said was *substantially correct.*

So in *Alexander* v *The North Eastern Railway Company,*[55] the defendant railway company reported that the claimant had been convicted of what would now be known as 'fare-dodging' and sentenced either to pay a fine of £9 or serve three weeks' imprisonment. In fact the claimant had actually been sentenced either to pay a fine of £1 or to serve two weeks' imprisonment. The claimant sued the defendants for libel. His claim was dismissed: while the defendants' report was inaccurate in its details, it was at the same time substantially correct – the claimant *had* been convicted of fare-dodging and had been sentenced either to pay a fine or spend time in jail. Similarly, suppose Paul told someone else that Tom beat his wife three times a week but in fact Tom beat his wife twice a week. In such a case, Paul will be able to raise a defence of justification to any claim Tom might bring against him for libel or slander – what Paul said was substantially true, even though he got it wrong as to how many times Tom beat his wife a week. It is impossible to formulate a test to determine whether a given defamatory statement will be 'substantially correct' or not; in the end, one has to use one's common sense to resolve the issue.

Section 5 of the Defamation Act 1952 provides that '[in] an action for libel or slander in respect of words containing two or more distinct charges against the claimant, a defence of justification shall not fail by reason only that the truth of every charge is not proved if the words not proved to be true do not materially injure the claimant's reputation having regard to the truth of the remaining charges'. So suppose Karen said to someone else, 'John is a rapist and a thief.' Suppose further that John sues Karen for libel or slander for saying that he is, one, a rapist, and two, a thief. Suppose finally that Karen can prove that John is a rapist, but she cannot prove that John is a thief. In such a case, Karen will not only have a defence of justification to John's claim against her for saying that he is a rapist, Karen will *also*

---

[55] (1865) 6 B & S 340, 122 ER 1221.

have a defence of justification under s 5 of the 1952 Act in respect of John's claim against her for saying that John is a thief. Now that it has been established that John is a rapist, Karen's statement that John is a thief could hardly further injure John's reputation in the eyes of ordinary, reasonable people – John's reputation in those people's eyes will have gone about as low as it possibly could go.

It would be different, of course, if Karen could prove that John is a thief but could not prove that John is a rapist. In such a case, Karen would have a defence of justification in respect of John's claim against her for saying that he is a thief, but she will *not* have a defence of justification in respect of John's claim against her for saying that he is a rapist. Section 5 of the 1952 Act cannot be invoked because it could hardly be said that now that it has been established that John is a thief, Karen's further charge that John is a rapist would not materially injure his standing among ordinary, reasonable people.

Staying with the above example but assuming again that Karen can prove John is a rapist but cannot prove that John is a thief – suppose John simply chooses to sue Karen for libel or slander in respect of her statement that he is a thief. Can Karen establish a defence of justification to John's claim by showing that John is a rapist? The answer, it seems, is 'no'.[56] However, if John leaves Karen's claim that he is a rapist unchallenged, he is not likely to be awarded much by way of damages to compensate him for the harm done by Karen's statement that he is a thief. The courts will take the view that a rapist does not have much of a reputation to lose and therefore suffers little harm if he is unjustly accused of being a thief.[57]

Criminal conviction

Suppose Lara told Ian, 'Vijay burned down Sarah's house.' In such a case, Lara will *normally* have a defence of justification to any claim Vijay might bring against her for libel or slander if she can prove that Vijay was criminally convicted for burning down Sarah's house and Vijay's conviction was not subsequently overturned. Lara will *not* have to go further and prove that Vijay *actually did* burn down Sarah's house, that is, she will not have to prove that Vijay was rightly convicted.[58]

However, if Sarah made her allegation about Vijay 'with malice' and Vijay's conviction for burning down Sarah's house counts as 'spent' under the Rehabilitation of Offenders Act 1974, then Vijay will be treated as though he never burned down Sarah's house and, therefore, Lara's statement to Ian will be conclusively presumed to have been untrue.[59] The result is that Vijay will be able to sue Lara for libel or slander: Lara will not be able to raise a defence of justification to Vijay's claim.

---

[56] *Polly Peck (Holdings) plc* v *Trelford* [1986] 1 QB 1000.

[57] See *Grobbelaar* v *News Group Newspapers Ltd* [2002] 1 WLR 3024 (£1 awarded in damages to Bruce Grobbelaar, the ex-Liverpool and Southampton goalkeeper, who – it was found – was justifiably accused by the defendant of taking bribes to 'throw' football matches but unjustifiably accused of acting on those bribes and actually throwing football matches).

[58] Civil Evidence Act 1968, s 13(1): 'In any action for libel or slander in which the question whether the claimant did or did not commit a criminal offence is relevant to an issue arising in the action, proof that at the time when that issue falls to be determined, he stands convicted of that offence shall be conclusive evidence that he committed that offence ...'

[59] Rehabilitation of Offenders Act 1974, ss 4(1), 8.

Fair comment

If A has published to another a statement S that was defamatory of B and B wants to sue A for libel or slander, A may be able to raise a defence of *fair comment* to defeat B's claim. A will be able to raise this defence if: (*a*) A was obviously expressing an *opinion*, rather than making a statement of fact, when he made statement S; *and* (*b*) A was expressing an opinion on a matter of *public interest*, rather than private interest, when he made statement S; *and* (*c*) A *honestly* held the opinion expressed by him when he made statement S and A *did not act maliciously* in expressing that opinion; *and* (*d*) the opinion that A expressed in making statement S was *not based on facts which were untrue*. All this needs more explanation.

Opinion and fact

The defence of fair comment only protects those who make defamatory statements that are, on their face, statements of opinion – the defence is not available to someone who makes a defamatory statement about another which is, on its face, a statement of fact.[60]

For example, if Helen said of a politician that 'he is a habitual liar and not fit to hold office' then the defence of fair comment will *not* be available to Helen if the politician in question decides to sue her for libel or slander – Helen's statement was, on its face, a statement of fact. But if Helen said of a politician that 'everything he has said and done in office tends to indicate that he is a habitual liar and is unfit to hold office' then, if the politician in question sues her for libel or slander, Helen *may* be able to take advantage of the defence of fair comment. Her statement was, on its face, a statement of opinion. In saying what she said, Helen was obviously expressing an opinion about what could be concluded from the politician in question's conduct in office.

In *London Artists Ltd* v *Littler*,[61] the defendant held a press conference in which he suggested that the claimants had attempted to force a play which he had been producing to close by persuading the four leading actors in the play to withdraw from it simultaneously. The claimants sued the defendant. The defendant attempted to defeat the claimants' claim by raising a defence of fair comment. He was not allowed to do so: his allegation that the claimants had plotted to close his play was, on its face, a statement of fact rather than a statement of opinion.

Two further points emerge from the cases. First, in judging whether a given defamatory statement was, on its face, a statement of opinion, *only* the statement may be taken into account. In *Telnikoff* v *Matusevitch*,[62] the claimant wrote an article in *The Daily Telegraph* which concerned the BBC Russian Service. In it the claimant observed that only about 10 per cent of those who worked for the BBC Russian Service would actually identify themselves as Russian and called on the BBC Russian Service to recruit more such people on

---

[60] For criticism of this limit on the defence, see Young 2000.
[61] [1969] 2 QB 375.
[62] [1992] 2 AC 343.

the ground that the BBC's radio broadcasts to Russia would be more effective if the people doing the broadcasting shared the same ethnic origin as the people at whom the broadcasts were directed. The defendant was infuriated by this article and wrote a letter to *The Daily Telegraph* which made a number of statements about the claimant's article – saying, among other things, that the claimant's article called for the use of blood tests to determine who should work for the BBC Russian Service.

The claimant sued the defendant for libel. The defendant sought to defeat the claimant's claim by raising a defence of fair comment. The claimant claimed that the defendant could not rely on this defence to defeat his claim because the statements in the defendant's letter were, on their face, statements of fact rather than statements of opinion. Now – anyone who read both the claimant's article and the defendant's letter would have realised that the defendant's statements about the claimant's article were statements of opinion: they were statements as to what the defendant *thought* was the effect of the claimant's article. However, the House of Lords held that the defendant's letter had to be read *in isolation* when determining whether the statements in the defendant's letter were, on their face, statements of fact or statements of opinion. Read in isolation, the statements in the defendant's letter could be said to have been, on their face, statements of fact – statements as to what the claimant's article *said*, rather than statements as to what the defendant *thought* were the implications of the claimant's article. The House of Lords ordered a new trial to be held on the issue of whether the statements in the defendant's letter were, on their face, statements of fact or statements of opinion.

Secondly, the courts will sometimes hold that a defamatory statement *was*, on its face, a statement of opinion even if it did *not* set out certain facts and then draw a conclusion from them. In *Kemsley v Foot*,[63] *Tribune* published an article by Michael Foot which criticised a particular newspaper. The article carried the headline 'Lower than Kemsley'. Lord Kemsley was a well-known newspaper proprietor and the point of the headline was to indicate that while the newspapers controlled by Lord Kemsley were contemptible, the newspaper criticised in the article was even more contemptible. Lord Kemsley sued for libel, claiming that the headline defamed him. Michael Foot attempted to defeat his claim by raising a defence of fair comment, claiming that the statement implicit in the headline that Kemsley's newspapers were contemptible was, on its face, a statement of opinion. Lord Kemsley applied to have the defence struck out. He argued that the statement in question was, on its face, a statement of fact and could not therefore be protected by a defence of fair comment. The House of Lords refused Lord Kemsley's application, holding that the statement was, on its face, a statement of opinion even though no facts were supplied along with the statement to support or justify that statement.

It is uncertain how far this decision goes. If Helen said of a particular politician, 'He is clearly in hock to various special interest groups' without supplying any supporting facts, could Helen – if she were sued by the politician

---

[63] [1952] AC 345.

for libel or slander – argue that her statement was, on its face, a statement of opinion rather than a statement of fact and on that basis attempt to raise a defence of fair comment to defeat the politician's claim? It is difficult to tell: perhaps the use of the word 'clearly' might tend to indicate that a statement of opinion was being made rather than a statement of fact.

Public interest

The defence of fair comment only operates to protect people who utter defamatory opinions on matters of *public interest*. So suppose Gary behaved in an ungentlemanly way during a tennis match with Tom and Tom wrote to Beth that 'Gary's behaviour was such that I do not think he is fit to mix in polite society.' If Gary chooses to sue Tom for libel, Tom will not be able to raise a defence of fair comment – his statement did not express an opinion on a matter of public interest. On the other hand, returning to an earlier example, suppose Helen observed of a particular politician that 'everything he has said and done in office establishes that he is a habitual liar and not fit to hold office'. If the politician in question chooses to sue Helen, Helen may well be able to raise a defence of fair comment to defeat the politician's claim. Helen's statement was a statement of opinion on a matter of public interest – the honesty and fitness for office of our politicians being a matter of public interest.

So what counts as a matter of public interest? In *London Artists Ltd* v *Littler*, Lord Denning MR offered a definition. According to Lord Denning, whenever 'a matter is such as to affect people at large, so that they may be legitimately interested in, or concerned, at what is going on; or what may happen to them or to others; then it is a matter of public interest on which everyone is entitled to make fair comment'.[64] So the quality of a West End play will count as a matter of public interest – people may be legitimately interested in how good the play is, so as to know whether or not to buy tickets for it or not. Given this, a critic's statements of opinion about the quality of a West End play may well be protected by the defence of fair comment. Similarly, someone who criticised a Fellow of an Oxbridge College, saying that the way he conducted his admissions interviews showed that he was biased against state school applicants, could probably take advantage of a defence of fair comment if he were sued by the Fellow in question for libel – his statement of opinion would be on a matter of public interest. People will be legitimately concerned that Fellows of Oxbridge Colleges not be biased in conducting admissions interviews.

Honesty and malice

If A has published to another an opinion which was defamatory of B, A will only be able to raise the defence of fair comment to defeat any claim made against him by B for libel or slander if: (*a*) A honestly held that opinion when he published it; and (*b*) A did not act maliciously in publishing that opinion.

Requirement (*a*) is probably a sub-requirement of requirement (*b*) in the sense that if requirement (*a*) is *not* satisfied, requirement (*b*) *cannot* be satisfied.

---

[64] [1969] 2 QB 375, 391B–C.

Suppose, for example, that Paul wrote a review of a new play by Lara and said that he thought the play was terrible. Suppose further that Paul did not honestly think the play was terrible. If this is so then Paul *must* have been acting maliciously in saying that the play was terrible – if he did not honestly think the play was terrible then why did he say it was?

But even if requirement (*a*) *is* satisfied, requirement (*b*) may *not* be. Suppose, again, that Nita published an article criticising the food and service at a particular restaurant run by Fred. Suppose when Nita wrote the article she honestly thought that the food and service at Fred's restaurant was terrible. Nita may still have acted maliciously in publishing her article – she may, for example, have decided to expose the poor food and service at Fred's restaurant to get revenge on Fred for breaking up with her.

Lawyers usually sum up the above by saying that the defence of fair comment only protects those who express opinions that are 'fair'. Someone who has expressed an opinion which he did not actually hold or who has acted maliciously in expressing an opinion will not be able to establish that the opinion expressed by him was 'fair' and will as a result not be able to take advantage of the defence of *fair* comment if the opinion in question was defamatory and he is sued for stating it. However, this usage is liable to confuse – it may make one think, wrongly, that the defence of fair comment only protects people who express opinions that are *fair-minded* or *reasonable*. Given this, the reader should try to avoid adopting this usage and, instead of thinking that the defence of fair comment will only protect people who express opinions that are 'fair', he or she should try to remember that the defence of fair comment will protect expressions of opinion that are made honestly and without malice – and this is so however unreasonable or outrageous or unfair the opinions in question happen to be.[65]

If A has expressed an opinion about B that is defamatory of B, it will usually be difficult to tell whether A *honestly* held that opinion when he expressed it. One way of determining whether this requirement is satisfied is to ask whether an honest man could *possibly* have held the opinion expressed by A.[66] If the answer is 'no' then it follows that A did *not* honestly hold the opinion that was expressed by him. If the answer is 'yes' then the matter remains open – it is possible that A honestly believed what he said, but it is, on the other hand, possible that he did not.

Turning to the question of when an expression of opinion will be held to have been published maliciously, the courts will find that A acted maliciously in expressing a defamatory opinion about B if he expressed that opinion out of spite or for some other evil or improper motive. Again, this will be hard to prove. In determining whether A acted maliciously in acting as he did, it will

[65] See Lord Nicholls's observations about the defence of fair comment in *Reynolds* v *Times Newspapers Ltd* [2001] 2 AC 127, 193: 'the time has come to recognise that in this context the epithet "fair" is now meaningless and misleading ... The true test [to determine whether an expression of opinion is protected by the defence of fair comment] is whether the opinion, however exaggerated, obstinate or prejudiced, was honestly held by the person expressing it.' See also *Branson* v *Bower* [2002] QB 737.

[66] Cf. the tests for determining whether an expression of opinion will fall within the ambit of the defence of fair comment advanced in *Merivale* v *Carson* (1887) 20 QBD 275, 281 and *Turner* v *Metro-Goldwyn-Mayer Pictures Ltd* [1950] 1 All ER 449, 461C–F.

be legitimate to take into account A's general demeanour towards B,[67] the language A used in expressing his opinion about B and how necessary it was for A to publish his opinion about B as widely as he did.

The above principles as to when someone will be able to take advantage of the defence of fair comment to defeat a claim against him for libel or slander are modified somewhat in the case where a newspaper has published a letter or column which contained opinions which were defamatory of B. In such a case, if B sues the newspaper for libel, the newspaper will be able to raise a defence of fair comment even if *it* did not hold the opinions expressed in the letter or column in question. Of course, the newspaper will not be able to take advantage of a defence of fair comment to defeat B's claim if it acted maliciously in publishing the letter or column in question.

Untrue facts

The defence of fair comment will not protect someone who has expressed a defamatory opinion about someone else which was based on untrue facts. This rule of law is subject to two qualifications.

First, suppose Ruth said of Eric, 'I think Eric is a disgrace as a human being – despite all his wealth, he has never done anything to assist his estranged wife and child or his destitute mother.' Suppose further that Eric sues Ruth for libel or slander – arguing that Ruth defamed him when she said that he is a disgrace as a human being. Suppose finally that while Eric does nothing to support his destitute mother, he does actually help to support his wife and child. If Ruth can show that, had she known the true facts, she would honestly still have thought that Eric was a disgrace as a human being, Ruth will be able to raise a defence of fair comment to defeat Eric's claim.[68] How can Ruth show that, had she known the true facts, she would honestly still have thought that Eric was a disgrace as a human being? One way is for Ruth to show that an honest man who knew the true facts *could* still have come to the conclusion that Eric was a disgrace as a human being. Of course, even if Ruth can defeat Eric's claim for damages arising out of her allegation that he is a disgrace as a human being, it will still be open to Eric to sue Ruth for libel or slander in respect of her allegation that Eric has never supported his estranged wife and child. As this is a statement of fact, not opinion, the defence of fair comment will not protect Ruth from being sued in respect of this allegation.

Secondly, if Vijay made an incorrect statement of fact about Mary on a privileged occasion and Wendy expressed an opinion on the basis of that statement of fact which was defamatory of Mary, the fact that Vijay's statement of fact was actually incorrect will not prevent Wendy from relying on the defence of fair comment to defeat any claim Mary might bring against her for libel or slander.[69]

---

[67] *Thomas* v *Bradbury, Agnew & Co. Ltd* [1906] 2 KB 627.

[68] See Defamation Act 1952, s 6, which provides that in 'an action for libel or slander in respect of words consisting partly in expressions of opinion, a defence of fair comment shall not fail by reason only that the truth of every allegation of fact is not proved if the expression of opinion is fair comment having regard to whether such of the facts alleged or referred to in the words complained of are proved'.

[69] *Grech* v *Odhams Press Ltd* [1958] 2 QB 275.

Privilege

If A has published a statement to C that is defamatory of B, B will *not* be entitled to sue A for libel or slander if the statement in question was *privileged*. Certain statements will *always* be privileged – such statements are said to be *absolutely privileged*. Other statements will only be privileged provided that certain conditions are met – these statements are said to be protected by *qualified privilege*. We will now look at what sort of statements will be absolutely privileged and what sort of statements will be protected by qualified privilege.

Absolute privilege

The law sometimes places such a high priority on people being able to say what they want without fear of being sued that it assures such people that what they say will always be privileged.

So, for example, the law places such a high priority on Members of Parliament being allowed to say what they want to say in Parliament without fear of being sued that it assures Members of Parliament that what they say in Parliament will always be privileged.[70] So if Alan is a Member of Parliament he will be able to say what he wants about Karen in Parliament without fear of being sued by Karen for libel or slander – if Karen attempts to sue him, based on what Alan said about her in Parliament, Alan will always be able to raise a defence to Karen's claim. And this is so even if Alan knowingly tells complete lies about Karen in Parliament: he cannot be sued.

In addition to statements made by Members of Parliament in Parliament, the following statements will also always be privileged:

(1) *Statements made in reports, papers and proceedings ordered to be published by Parliament.*[71]

(2) *Statements made in the course of judicial or quasi-judicial proceedings by anyone involved in those proceedings.* However, statements made in the course of judicial or quasi-judicial proceedings which have no relevance to those proceedings may not be privileged.[72] A court-martial will count as a 'judicial or quasi-judicial' proceeding;[73] as will disciplinary proceedings held by the Law Society.[74] So statements made in the course of either will be absolutely privileged. However, the holding of an industrial conciliation procedure will not count as a 'judicial or quasi-judicial' proceeding[75] and neither will an

---

[70] This follows from Art 9 of the Bill of Rights 1688 which states that 'the freedom of speech and debates or proceedings in Parliament ought not to be impeached or questioned in any court or place out of Parliament'. An exception to this rule was created by s 13 of the Defamation Act 1996 which provides that where 'the conduct of a person in or in relation to proceedings in Parliament is in issue during defamation proceedings, he may waive for the purpose of those proceedings, so far as concerns him, the protection of any enactment or rule of law which prevents proceedings in Parliament being impeached or questioned in any court or place out of Parliament'.

[71] Parliamentary Papers Act 1840, s 1.

[72] *Seaman v Netherclift* (1876) 2 CPD 53, 56.

[73] *Dawkins v Lord Rokeby* (1875) LR 7 HL 744.

[74] *Addis v Crocker* [1961] 1 QB 11.

[75] *Tadd v Eastwood* [1985] ICR 132.

investigation by the European Commission into alleged breaches of European competition law.[76]

(3) *Statements made by a witness to his solicitor in preparing his testimony for court.*[77] While it is certain that such statements will always be privileged, it is uncertain whether other kinds of statements that a client may make to his solicitor will always be privileged. The House of Lords left the matter open in *Minter* v *Priest*.[78] There does not seem to be any reason why they should be: there does not seem to be any reason why the law should go further than it currently does to ensure that a client will be able to talk to his solicitor free from the fear that he might be sued as a result of what he says to his solicitor.

(4) *Statements made in the course of being questioned by someone investigating a crime; statements made at the request of someone investigating a crime.*[79] It is unclear whether a statement which is *spontaneously* made to the authorities for the purpose of encouraging them to start an investigation will be absolutely privileged. In *Hasselblad (GB) Ltd* v *Orbinson*,[80] the Court of Appeal thought that a letter sent to the European Commission complaining that a particular firm was engaging in anti-competitive practices would be protected by absolute privilege; their reason for so holding was that it was extremely important that people should be able to report these sorts of practices to the European Commission free from fear that their doing so would result in their being sued. However, in *Mahon* v *Rahn (No. 2)*[81] Brooke LJ refused to decide whether an informant who spontaneously told the authorities that a particular investment adviser was guilty of fraud would always be able to claim that his statement to the authorities was privileged, preferring to leave the task of deciding that question to another day.[82]

(5) *Statements made in a report prepared by an expert which may be used in later criminal proceedings.*[83]

(6) *Statements made by an investigator to someone else in the course of investigating a crime.*[84]

(7) *Statements made by one officer of state to another for the purpose of discharging some official business.* There is some authority in favour of the view that such statements will always be privileged. In *Chatterton* v *Secretary of State for India in Council*,[85] the claimant, a captain in the Indian Army, sued the Secretary of

---

[76] *Hasselblad (GB) Ltd* v *Orbinson* [1985] QB 475.
[77] *Watson* v *M'Ewan* [1905] AC 480; *Evans* v *London Hospital Medical College (University of London)* [1981] 1 WLR 184, 191G. See below, p. 498.
[78] [1930] AC 558.
[79] *Mahon* v *Rahn (No. 2)* [2000] 1 WLR 2150.
[80] [1985] QB 475.
[81] [2000] 1 WLR 2150.
[82] Ibid., at [195].
[83] *X* v *Bedfordshire County Council* [1995] 2 AC 633, 755G. See below, p. 499.
[84] *Taylor* v *Director of the Serious Fraud Office* [1999] 2 AC 177. See below, p. 499.
[85] [1895] 2 QB 189.

State for India for libel; he claimed the Secretary of State had, in a letter to his Under-Secretary of State, claimed that the Commander-in-Chief of the Indian Army had recommended that the claimant be put on half-pay on the grounds that keeping him as a full-time member of the Indian Army would be extremely undesirable. The claimant claimed that the Commander-in-Chief had made no such recommendation and that the Secretary of State had lied in his letter to the Under-Secretary of State so as to induce the Under-Secretary of State to besmirch the claimant's reputation in Parliament where questions were to be asked about the Secretary of State's treatment of the claimant. The claimant's claim against the Secretary of State was dismissed on the ground that his letter to the Under-Secretary of State was absolutely privileged. However, it is uncertain whether the same principle applies to statements made by one civil servant to another[86] or by one officer in the army to another.[87]

(8) *Statements made in an internal memorandum circulated within a foreign embassy.*[88]

(9) *Statements made in a fair and accurate and contemporaneous report of proceedings in public before a UK court or the European Court of Justice or the European Court of Human Rights or any international crime tribunal.* Section 14(1) of the Defamation Act 1996 provides that such statements will always be privileged. Section 14(2) provides that a 'report of proceedings which by an order of the court, or as a consequence if any statutory provision, is required to be postponed shall be treated as published contemporaneously if it is published as soon as practicable after publication is permitted'.

Qualified privilege

A statement which is protected by *qualified privilege* will be privileged so long as it was *not made maliciously.* For the purposes of this area of the law, A will be held to have acted maliciously in making a statement about B if: (*a*) he knew that that statement was untrue when he made it; *or* (*b*) when he made that statement he did not care whether it was true or not; *or* (*c*) he made that statement for some improper or illegitimate reason.[89] The following kinds of statements will be protected by qualified privilege:

(1) *The duty/interest test.* If A has made a statement to C, that statement will be protected by qualified privilege if, *had the information contained in that statement been correct,* A would have had a moral or legal duty to pass that information on to C and C would have had an interest in receiving that information.

So: in *Watt v Longsdon,*[90] the claimant was the managing director of the

---

[86] Henn-Collins J thought not in *Szalatnay-Stacho v Fink* [1946] 1 All ER 303.
[87] The Court of Queen's Bench thought it would in *Dawkins v Lord Paulet* (1869) LR 5 QB 94.
[88] *Fayed v Al-Tajir* [1988] 1 QB 712.
[89] *Horrocks v Lowe* [1975] AC 135. See also Mitchell 1999; Murphy 2003, 514–18.
[90] [1930] 1 KB 130.

Morocco branch of the Scottish Petroleum Company. The manager of the Morocco branch wrote to the defendant, a director of Scottish Petroleum, accusing the claimant of being drunk, dishonest and immoral. The defendant showed the letter to the chairman of the board and also the claimant's wife. The claimant sued the defendant for libel in respect of both publications of the letter.

The allegations contained in the letter were untrue so the defendant could not defeat the claimant's action by raising a defence of justification. However, the publication to the chairman of the board was held to be privileged. Had the information contained in the letter been correct, the defendant would obviously have had a duty to show the letter to the chairman of the board and the chairman of the board would have had an interest in seeing the letter. This established that the publication to the chairman of the board was protected by qualified privilege and, as the defendant had not been acting maliciously in showing the letter in question to the chairman of the board, the publication of that letter to the chairman of the board was privileged.

It was different with the publication to the claimant's wife. Obviously, had the allegations in the letter been true, the claimant's wife would have had an interest in seeing the letter. However, the defendant could *not* establish that, had the allegations in the letter been true, he would have had a *duty* to show that letter to the claimant's wife. The Court of Appeal refused to be drawn on the question – If A has found out that B's husband has been cheating on her and generally engaging in disreputable activities, when will A have a duty to tell B of this fact? However, the Court of Appeal thought that the nature of the defendant's relationship with the claimant's wife was not such as to make it his place to tell the claimant's wife of what her husband was supposed to have been getting up to.

(2) *The common interest test.* If A has made a statement to C, that statement will be protected by qualified privilege if it served A's interests to make that statement to C and it served C's interests to hear it.

For example, in *Watt* v *Longsdon* the claimant also sued the defendant for libel in respect of a letter that the defendant wrote to the manager of the Morocco branch of Scottish Petroleum in which the defendant voiced his own suspicions about the claimant and asked the manager to obtain confirmation of the allegations contained in the manager's letter. The Court of Appeal held that the defendant's letter was protected by qualified privilege. This was because the defendant and the manager had a common interest in protecting the interests of Scottish Petroleum and this shared interest of the defendant and the manager's was served by the defendant's writing his letter to the manager and the manager's receiving it and acting on it. And as the defendant had not acted maliciously in writing to the manager, the letter was privileged.

Similarly, in *Hunt* v *Great Northern Railway Company*[91] the claimant worked as a guard for the defendant railway company. The defendants sacked the

---

[91] [1891] 2 QB 189.

claimant on the ground that he had been guilty of gross neglect of duty. The defendants inserted a notice in the monthly circular which was distributed to the defendants' employees saying that the claimant had been guilty of gross neglect of duty and had been sacked as a result. The claimant sued the defendants for libel but his case was dismissed on the ground that the statement in the monthly circular was privileged. It was protected by qualified privilege, the court held, because the publication of the statement in the monthly circular served the interests of both the defendants and the people to whom the statement was published, the defendants' employees – in both cases, because publication of the statement let the defendants' employees know that they would be sacked if they were guilty of gross neglect of duty. And as the defendants had not acted maliciously in publishing the statement in their monthly circular – they had not, for example, published the statement in order to make the claimant unemployable or published it in the knowledge that the claimant had not been guilty of a gross neglect of duty – that statement was privileged.

Lord Denning MR thought that what we might call the common interest test could be used to establish that statements made by an employer to his secretary in dictating a letter will be protected by qualified privilege. He argued in *Bryanston Finance* v *de Vries*[92] that as the employer and the secretary would both have an interest in getting the letter dictated by the employer written, any statements made to the secretary by the employer in dictating the letter would be protected by a qualified privilege. Such statements would therefore be privileged so long as the employer did not act maliciously in publishing them to his secretary. However, neither of the two other members of the Court of Appeal in *Bryanston Finance* agreed with Lord Denning MR on this point. They both thought the statements made in dictation would only be privileged if the publication to the intended recipient of the letter would also be privileged.

(3) *Statements made in self-defence.* It is well established that if someone attacks or criticises A verbally or in print, then any statements made by A in order to rebut that attack or criticism will be protected by qualified privilege.

So, in *Osborn* v *Thomas Boulter & Son*[93] the claimant – a publican – wrote to the defendants to complain about the quality of their beer. The defendants wrote back suggesting that the source of the claimant's problems with their beer was that he watered it down once it was delivered to him. The claimant sued the defendants for slander on the basis that the defendants' letter had been published not only to the claimant but also to the defendants' secretary when it was dictated to her. His claim was dismissed on the ground that the defendants' rebuttal of the claimant's attack on the quality of their beer was protected by qualified privilege and the defendants had not acted maliciously in making the allegations that they did.

In *Watts* v *Times Newspapers Ltd*,[94] *The Sunday Times* published a story which accused the claimant, Nigel Watts, of plagiarism. However, they accom-

---

[92] [1975] 1 QB 703.
[93] [1930] 2 KB 226.
[94] [1997] QB 650.

panied the story with a photograph of a quite different Nigel Watts, a property developer. This Nigel Watts complained and *The Sunday Times* printed an apology in its next edition which was dictated by Nigel Watts's solicitors, Schilling & Lom. The apology repeated the original defamatory story about the claimant. The claimant sued *The Sunday Times* for libel, claiming that the apology was defamatory of him. It was held that *The Sunday Times* could not claim that their apology was privileged as they were not publishing it to rebut an attack on themselves. *The Sunday Times* then sought to make a claim in contribution against Schilling and Lom on the ground that, having dictated the terms of the apology, they were also liable to pay damages to the claimant in respect of the publication of the apology. This claim was dismissed; it was held that, vis-à-vis Schilling & Lom, the apology was privileged as it had been dictated in order to rebut the attack which *The Sunday Times* had inadvertently made on their client.

(4) *The public interest test.* Statements made in an article published in a newspaper will be protected by qualified privilege if: (*a*) the article was on a matter of public concern or interest *and* (*b*) the newspaper acted responsibly in going ahead and publishing the article when they did and in the form that they did.[95] This is the effect of the decision of the House of Lords in *Reynolds* v *Times Newspapers Ltd*.[96]

In the *Reynolds* case, Lord Nicholls provided a list of factors which could be taken into account in determining whether a newspaper acted responsibly in publishing a particular article about someone when they did and in the form that they did:

[95] *Important note.* The House of Lords in *Reynolds* v *Times Newspapers Ltd* [2001] 2 AC 127 seemed to think that if (*a*) and (*b*) were satisfied then the article in question would be protected by qualified privilege because the 'duty-interest' test would be satisfied. (See, for example, ibid., at 197 (per Lord Nicholls). See also the decisions of the Court of Appeal in *Loutchansky* v *Times Newspapers Ltd* [2002] QB 321 and *Loutchansky* v *Times Newspapers Ltd (Nos 2–5)* [2002] QB 783.) However, it is unrealistic to think that the 'duty-interest' test covers the situation of qualified privilege considered here: if (*a*) and (*b*) are satisfied, the newspaper in question may be able to argue that it had a *duty* to publish the article in question; but will *all* the newspaper's readers really have had an *interest* in reading it? The House of Lords' attempt to argue that the 'duty-interest' test applies here may have been a result of its adopting an overly reductive view of when a statement will be protected by qualified privilege, under which a statement will *only* be protected by qualified privilege if the 'duty-interest' test is satisfied (such a view seems to be adopted by M&D, at 678). The truth is that there are *many different situations* where a statement will be protected by qualified privilege – and the 'duty-interest' test only identifies *one* of them. The *Reynolds* decision is best seen as adding a *new* category to the list of situations where a statement will be protected by qualified privilege to the list. Significantly, perhaps, when the Privy Council had to decide in *Bonnick* v *Morris* [2003] 1 AC 300 whether a newspaper article was protected by qualified privilege under *Reynolds*, it dropped all mention of the 'duty-interest' test and instead simply asked whether the article was on a matter of the public interest and whether the newspaper had acted responsibly in publishing it when they did and in the form that they did. Moreover, in *Kearns* v *General Council of the Bar* [2003] 1 WLR 1357, the Court of Appeal held that considerations that would be relevant in establishing that a statement was protected by qualified privilege under *Reynolds* (such as whether the publisher of that statement acted responsibly in making that statement) would *not* be relevant in establishing whether that statement was protected by qualified privilege under the 'duty-interest' test or the 'common interest' test.

[96] [2001] 2 AC 127 (noted, Williams 2000).

1. The seriousness of the [allegations made in the article]. The more serious the charge, the more the public is misinformed and the individual harmed, if [the allegations in the report were] untrue. 2. The nature of the information [in the article], and the extent to which the subject matter is a matter of public concern. 3. The source of the information. Some informants have no direct knowledge of the events. Some have their own axes to grind, or are being paid for their stories. 4. The steps taken to verify the information. 5. The status of the information. [The allegations made in the article] may already have been the subject of an investigation which commands respect. 6. The urgency of the matter. News is often a perishable commodity. 7. Whether comment was sought from the [subject of the article]. He may have information others do not possess or have not disclosed. [However, an] approach . . . will not always be necessary. 8. Whether the article contained the gist of the [subject of the article's] side of the story. 9. The tone of the article. A newspaper can often raise queries or call for an investigation. It need not adopt allegations as statements of fact. 10. The circumstances of the publication, including the timing.[97]

In the *Reynolds* case itself, *The Sunday Times* published an article which dealt with the resignation of Albert Reynolds, the Irish prime minister. The article alleged that Reynolds had deliberately and dishonestly misled the Irish Dáil on a particular matter and that Reynolds had been forced to resign when his colleagues found out about Reynolds's misconduct. In fact, this was not true: Reynolds never misled the Dáil and he resigned for other reasons. Reynolds sued *The Sunday Times* for libel and *The Sunday Times* claimed in its defence that its article was privileged. The House of Lords held that the article was not privileged. While there was no doubt that the article was on a matter of public concern and interest,[98] the House of Lords found that *The Sunday Times* did *not* act responsibly in publishing the article in the form that it did. The reason for this was that the article was unjustifiably one-sided in its presentation of the reasons why Reynolds resigned. No account was given of Reynolds's explanation of why he had resigned which Reynolds presented to the Irish Dáil on the day he resigned when, in fairness, one would have expected such an account to have been given. Indeed, the coverage of the story behind Reynolds's resignation had been much more balanced in the Irish editions of *The Sunday Times* and this must have counted against *The Sunday Times* in the eyes of the House of Lords in determining whether *The Sunday Times* acted responsibly in publishing its article about Reynolds's resignation in the form that it did.

Some hoped that the House of Lords would rule in *Reynolds* that 'political speech' – statements about or relating to political figures – will be protected by qualified privilege.[99] While the House of Lords refused to go that far – for

---

[97] Ibid., 205. The decision of the Court of Appeal in *Loutchansky* v *Times Newspapers Ltd* [2002] QB 321 makes it clear that, in judging whether a newspaper acted responsibly in publishing a particular article when it did and in the form that it did, one should only take into account the information available to the newspaper at the time it published the article. (The House of Lords refused to grant leave to appeal this ruling: [2002] 1 WLR 1592.)

[98] As Reynolds was one of the architects of the Northern Ireland 'peace' process, the reasons for his resignation were of public concern and interest in the UK.

[99] This is the position in the United States: *New York Times Co.* v *Sullivan* (1964) 376 US 254. In New Zealand, 'political speech' concerning past, present or prospective MPs is protected by qualified privilege: *Lange* v *Atkinson* [1998] 3 NZLR 424; *Lange* v *Atkinson (No. 2)* [2000] 3 NZLR 385. The position in Australia is much closer to that in England: *Lange* v *ABC* (1997) 189 CLR

reasons we will explore later[100] – the decision in *Reynolds* does go a long way towards ensuring that newspapers can publish articles on matters of public interest or concern free from the fear that they will be sued for libel as a result. So long as they act reasonably and non-maliciously in publishing articles on matters of public interest or concern – so long, that is, as they do not publish statements that they know to be false; or abuse their position to persecute certain people; or rush into print without checking the reliability of their sources; or refuse to allow those criticised in their articles to give their side of their story – then they should have nothing to worry about. Certainly, if *Reynolds* had been decided 25 years ago it is inconceivable that newspapers would have been deterred – as they were – by the prospect of a libel suit from going into print with their suspicions as to what the late Robert Maxwell was doing with the assets of pension funds under his control. Had *Reynolds* been decided 25 years ago, any newspaper which wanted to expose Maxwell's crimes would have known that provided it acted responsibly in dealing with the story – by doing such things as assuring itself of the reliability of its sources and giving Maxwell full opportunity to rebut the charges against him – it would have been able to raise a defence of qualified privilege to any subsequent action for libel launched against it by Maxwell.

Finally, it should be noted that there is no reason to think that this category of statements that are protected by qualified privilege only covers statements made in articles published in newspapers. This category will also cover statements made in books, television documentaries or news programmes. It will also cover statements made in articles that have been posted in a newspaper archive on the Internet.[101]

(5) *The Defamation Act 1996.* The Defamation Act 1996 confers the protection of qualified privilege on a wide range of statements made on a matter of public concern or interest.[102] The Act splits these statements into two groups.

First, the Act provides that certain statements on matters of public concern or interest will be protected by qualified privilege 'without explanation or contradic-

---

520 establishes that a defamatory story about a political figure will be protected by qualified privilege so long as the publishers of the story took reasonable care to ensure that it was true and gave the subject of the story a chance to respond to it before publication. Loveland 2000 expresses a preference (at 181–4) for the Australian position. He criticises the *Sullivan* ruling on the ground that it gives a corrupt politician who is accused of acting corruptly by a newspaper an excuse for not suing the newspaper in libel – thereby avoiding having a court of law test the truth of the allegations against him. The corrupt politician can plausibly argue that there is no point in suing the newspaper as the *Sullivan* ruling means that he will almost certainly lose his case.

[100] See below, pp. 304–6.

[101] *Loutchansky* v *Times Newspapers Ltd (Nos 2–5)* [2002] QB 783. The Court of Appeal held that a newspaper could not claim to have acted responsibly when it placed a defamatory article originally published in its print edition in an archive on the Internet without qualifying the article in any way to make it clear that its accuracy had been challenged. The House of Lords refused leave to appeal: [2002] 1 WLR 1552.

[102] Section 15(3) of the Defamation Act 1996 provides that the 1996 Act does not confer qualified privilege on matter published 'to the public, or a section of the public, . . . which is not of public concern and the publication of which [was] not for the public benefit'.

tion'. These include: (*a*) statements made in a fair and accurate report of proceedings in public of a legislature or a court or a public inquiry or an international organisation or an international conference located anywhere in the world; and (*b*) statements made in a fair and accurate copy of or extract from any matter published by a government or a legislature or an international organisation or an international conference located anywhere in the world.[103] Such a statement will be privileged so long as the person who published it did not act maliciously in doing so.[104]

Secondly, the 1996 Act provides that certain other statements on matters of public concern or interest will be protected by qualified privilege 'subject to explanation or contradiction'. What this means is that if A, a newspaper, has published such a statement and the statement in question is defamatory of B, A will *not* be able to claim – if B sues it for libel or slander – that the statement was privileged if: (*a*) A acted maliciously in publishing that statement;[105] *or* (*b*) A refused or neglected to publish in a suitable manner a 'reasonable letter or statement by way of explanation or contradiction' of the statement published by A when it was requested to do so by B.[106]

The 1996 Act provides that statements that will be protected by qualified privilege 'subject to explanation or contradiction' include:[107] (*a*) statements made in a fair and accurate report of proceedings at any lawful meeting held in the EU on a matter of public concern;[108] (*b*) statements made in a fair and accurate copy of or extract from matter issued by any member state of the EU or by any organisation performing governmental functions in a member state of the EU[109] or by the European Commission; (*c*) statements made in a fair and accurate report of proceedings at any general meeting of a UK public company; (*d*) statements made in a fair and accurate copy of or extract from any document circulated to the members of a UK public company by its board or its auditors; (*e*) statements made in a fair and accurate report of any decision or finding made by an organisation concerned to promote a trade or a profession or a business or a game or a charitable object or general interest in art or science or religion or learning.

Innocent dissemination

Section 1(1) of the Defamation Act 1996 provides that if A has published to another a statement which was defamatory of B, A will have a defence to any claim for damages B might bring against A if: (*a*) A was not the 'author, editor or publisher' of the statement in question; (*b*) A took reasonable care in relation to its publication; *and* (*c*) A did not know, and had no reason to believe, that

---

[103] For a full list, see Part I of Sch 1 of the Defamation Act 1996.
[104] Section 15(1).
[105] Ibid..
[106] Section 15(2).
[107] For a full list, see Part II of Sch I of the Defemation Act 1996.
[108] The House of Lords has now held that a report which fairly and accurately summarises the contents of a press release issued to accompany a press conference will be protected by qualified privilege under this head: *McCartan Turkington Breen* v *Times Newspapers Ltd* [2001] 2 AC 277.
[109] Defined in the Act as including 'police functions': Sch 1, Part II, para. 9(2).

what he did would cause or contribute to the publication of a defamatory state-ment.[110]

So the 'author, editor or publisher' of a defamatory statement will *not* be able to take advantage of the defence set out in s 1(1) of the 1996 Act. Section 1(2) makes it clear that the term 'author', as used in s 1(1) of the 1996 Act, 'means the originator of the statement [in question], but does not include a person who did not intend that his statement be published at all ... "editor" means a person having editorial or equivalent responsibility for the content of the state-ment [in question] or the decision to publish it ... [and] "publisher" means a commercial publisher, that is, a person whose business is issuing material to the public, or a section of the public, who issues material containing the statement [in question] in the course of that business'. Section 1(4) of the 1996 Act pro-vides that an employee or agent of someone who was the 'author, editor or publisher' of a defamatory statement according to the above definition will *also* be held to have been the 'author, editor or publisher' of the statement in ques-tion if he was 'responsible for the content of the statement in question or the decision to publish it'.[111]

For the avoidance of doubt, s 1(3) goes on to provide that a person:

> shall not be considered the author, editor or publisher of a statement if he is only involved – (a) in printing, producing, distributing or selling printed material con-taining the statement; (b) in processing, making copies of, distributing, exhibiting or selling a film or sound recording ... containing the statement; (c) in processing, making copies of, distributing or selling any electronic medium in or on which the statement is recorded, or in operating or providing any equipment, system or service by means of which the statement is retrieved, copied, distributed or made available in electronic form; (d) as the broadcaster of a live programme containing the statement in circumstances in which he has no effective control over the maker of the statement; (e) as the operator of or provider of access to a communications system by means of which the statement is transmitted, or made available, by a person over whom he has no effective control.

In *Godfrey* v *Demon Internet Ltd*,[112] the defendant was a company which ran an electronic bulletin board on the Internet. Someone posted a message on the Internet which was defamatory of the claimant and the message ended up on the defendant's bulletin board where it was accessed by various people. The claimant complained about the message to the defendant but even after he had

---

[110] It should be remembered that a statement can still be defamatory *even if it is true*. So suppose a bookseller sold a book which contained damaging allegations about Mary and Mary wants to sue the bookseller for libel. If we want to know whether the bookseller can take advantage of the defence set out in s 1(1) of the 1996 Act we ask – did the bookseller know, or have reason to know, that the book sold by him contained damaging allegations about Mary? If so, he will *not* be able to take advantage of the defence set out in s 1(1) of the 1996 Act. It will not matter whether or not the bookseller in question knew, or had reason to know, that the allegations in question were *untrue* – even if he did not know, and had no reason to know, that those alle-gations were untrue, he will still *not* be able to take advantage of the defence set out in s 1(1) of the 1996 Act if he knew, or ought to have known, that the book contained those allegations.
[111] Section 1(4).
[112] [2001] QB 201.

done so the defendant failed to remove the message from its bulletin board. The claimant sued the defendant for libel on the ground that it had published the message on its bulletin board to other people. The defendant sought to take advantage of the defence set out in s 1(1) of the 1996 Act to defeat the claimant's claim. It was held that the defendant could not take advantage of this defence.

Admittedly, the defendant was *not* the 'author, editor or publisher' of the message complained of – that was made clear by s 1(3) of the 1996 Act. However, the defendant could not show that in running its bulletin board it was unaware it was contributing to the publication of a statement that was defamatory of the claimant. The claimant *did* draw the defendant's attention to the presence of the message on its bulletin board and it was obviously defamatory of the claimant. From that moment onwards, the defendant was aware that it was contributing to the publication of a statement that was defamatory of the claimant in running its bulletin board without removing the message complained of by the claimant. Given this, s 1(1) of the 1996 Act did not operate to protect the defendant from being sued for libel in respect of any publications to third parties of the message on the defendant's bulletin board that took place after the presence of that message on the defendant's bulletin board was brought to the defendant's attention.

Offer to make amends

Suppose A has published to another a statement that was defamatory of B and B wants to sue A for libel or slander. If A cannot take advantage of one of the defences set out above to defeat B's claim, he may still be able to prevent B from suing him for libel or slander by making an 'offer to make amends' to B under s 2 of the Defamation Act 1996.

Section 2 of the Defamation Act 1996 provides that if A wants to make an 'offer to make amends' to B he *must* offer '(a) to make a suitable correction of the statement complained of and a sufficient apology to [B], (b) to publish the correction and apology in a manner that is reasonable and practicable in the circumstances, and (c) to pay [B] such compensation (if any), and such costs, as may be agreed or determined to be payable'.[113] If A offers to do only one or two of these things, then his offer will not amount to an 'offer to make amends' and will have no effect on B's right to sue A for libel or slander.

If A does make an 'offer to make amends' to B and B *accepts* the offer, B will be barred from suing A for libel or slander.[114] If B does *not* accept the offer, B will still be barred from suing A for libel or slander *unless*, when A published the statement which was defamatory of B: (*a*) he knew or had reason to believe that that statement referred to B or was likely to be understood as referring to B *and* (*b*) he knew or had reason to believe that the statement in question was both false and defamatory of B.[115] If (*a*) and (*b*) are true then A's 'offer to make

---

[113] If B accepts A's offer but then they find themselves unable to agree on what should be paid to B by way of compensation, the courts will decide for them: Defamation Act 1996, s 3(5).
[114] Section 3(2).
[115] Section 4. *Milne v Express Newspapers Ltd* [2004] EWCA Civ 664 makes it clear that (*b*) will only be true if A acted *recklessly* in publishing the statement in question. Merely showing that a

amends' will have no effect on B's right to sue A for libel or slander – unless, of course, B accepts the offer.

THE DIFFERENCE BETWEEN LIBEL AND SLANDER
The distinction

Having reviewed what libel and slander have in common, we can now return in more detail to the question of what the difference between them is.

Broadly speaking, if A has published to another a statement which is defamatory of B, the tort – if any – committed by A in publishing that statement will be *libel* if the statement in question was published in *permanent form*; if, on the other hand, the statement in question was published in *impermanent form* then the tort – if any – committed by A in the case we are considering will be *slander*.

So, for example, if Karen *says* to Ian 'Gary is a thief' then that is slander. However, if Karen sends Ian a letter saying 'Gary is a thief' then that is libel. If Karen dictated a letter to her secretary saying 'Gary is a thief' then that is slander. But if the letter is read out to a third party, that – it seems – will be libel.[116] It is submitted that if Karen records herself saying 'Gary is a thief' and then plays the recording back to Ian, that is libel; Karen's statement will have been published in a permanent form because it could be replayed.[117]

Some statutes provide that certain statements are to be treated as having been published in permanent form. So s 166 of the Broadcasting Act 1990 provides that for 'the purposes of the law on libel and slander ... the publication of words in the course of any programme included in a programme service shall be treated as publication in permanent form'. So if John gives a speech in a public hall in which he makes various defamatory allegations about Nita, that will be slander. But if John makes the same speech on television, that will be libel. Similarly, s 4 of the Theatres Act 1968 provides that, subject to one exception, for 'the purposes of the law on libel and slander ... the publication of words in the course of a performance of a play shall ... be treated as publication in permanent form'. Section 7 of the 1968 Act makes it clear that this rule will not 'apply in relation to a performance of a play given on a domestic occasion in a private dwelling'.

---

reasonable person in A's position would have realised that that statement was untrue and/or defamatory will not be enough.

[116] *Forrester* v *Tyrell* (1893) 9 TLR 257. However, in *Osborn* v *Thomas Boulter & Son* [1930] 2 KB 226, Scrutton and Slesser LJJ both thought that reading out a defamatory letter to a third party would amount to slander. Greer LJ disagreed.

[117] Cf. the discussion in *Youssoupoff* v *Metro-Goldwyn-Mayer Pictures Ltd* (1934) 50 TLR 581 as to whether the tort – if any – committed in playing a film which contained a defamatory statement in its soundtrack would be slander or libel. The Court of Appeal expressed no firm view on the issue – merely saying the statement would be libellous if it served to amplify or explain the visual images presented in the film: ibid., 587.

The significance of the distinction

The principal[118] significance of the distinction between libel and slander is that if A has committed the tort of libel in relation to B, it will be presumed that A's libel caused B to suffer some kind of loss and so B will be entitled to sue A for compensatory damages without having to prove that she has suffered any kind of loss as a result of A's libel. The rule is different if A has committed the tort of slander in relation to B.

Generally speaking, it will *not* be presumed that B suffered some kind of loss as a result of A's slander. B will therefore have to prove that she suffered some kind of loss as a result of A's slander if she wants to sue A for compensatory damages. There are exceptions to this rule. If A has committed the tort of slander in relation to B, it will be presumed that B suffered some kind of loss as a result of A's slander if A had slandered B by suggesting: (*a*) that she had committed a serious criminal offence; *or* (*b*) that she had a communicable disease;[119] *or* (*c*) that she was no good at her job;[120] *or* (*d*) that she was unchaste or had committed adultery.[121]

EVALUATION OF THE LAW ON DEFAMATION

A complete evaluation of the law on defamation is beyond the scope of this book.[122] In this section we will confine ourselves to discussing some limited aspects of this area of the law.

Truth

If A has published to another a statement that is defamatory of B and B wants to sue A for libel or slander, B will *not* have to prove that A's statement was *untrue*. Should she have to?

One argument can be advanced in favour of the view that B *should* be required to prove that A's statement was untrue if she wants to sue A for libel or slander. Under the present law, B cannot clear her name by suing A for libel or slander. Even if she is successful in her claim against A, that will not be because the court found that A's statement was untrue. The court will merely have found that A could not prove that his statement was true – which is a very different thing. If B were required to prove that A's statement was untrue before she could sue A for libel or slander, then the question of the truth or untruth of A's statement would be placed firmly before the courts and a finding that A did libel or slander B would have the effect of clearing B's name – the

---

[118] Another difference between libel and slander is that libel will sometimes amount to a crime, whereas slander will not.
[119] *Bloodworth v Gray* (1844) 7 Man & Gr 334, 135 ER 140.
[120] Defamation Act 1952, s 2.
[121] Slander of Women Act 1891, s 1.
[122] For further discussion, see Gibbons 1996; Mahoney 1997; Barendt 1999.

courts could only reach such a finding if they first found that B had proved that A's statement about her was untrue.

At the same time, three arguments can be advanced in favour of the position currently taken by the law. First, it can be very difficult to prove a *negative*. Suppose that A's statement alleged that B once committed adultery. If B were required to prove that A's statement was untrue before she could sue A for libel or slander, how could B satisfy this requirement in this case? How could B prove that she has never committed adultery? Secondly, if the law did require the victim of a defamatory statement to prove that that statement was untrue before allowing her any remedy against the publisher of that statement, then the effect might be to encourage the press to become even less responsible in checking and sourcing stories which they publish than they are now. A news-paper which was proposing to publish a damaging story about B would no longer have to ask itself, 'Do we think we could prove this story was true in a court of law if B sued us for libel?' and have to think twice about publishing its story about B if it thought the answer was 'no'. Thirdly, if A attacks B physi-cally, B will be allowed to sue A for damages unless *A* can prove that he had a lawful justification or excuse for attacking B – B will not have to prove that A did *not* have a lawful justification or excuse for attacking her before she will be allowed to sue A. Why should the rule be different if A attacks B verbally or in print? Why should B suddenly have to show that A's attack on her was unjus-tified before she will be allowed to sue A for libel or slander?

On balance, then, we would conclude that the law should *not* be changed so as to require the victim of a defamatory statement to prove that that statement was untrue before she will be allowed to obtain a remedy from the person who published that statement.

The liability of distributors

Under s 6(1) of the Human Rights Act 1998, the courts have a responsibility to ensure that the law on libel and slander is compatible with Article 10 of the European Convention on Human Rights, which stipulates that:

> Everyone has the right to freedom of expression. This right shall include [the] freedom ... to receive and impart information and ideas without interference by public authority ... [though this freedom may be] subject to such formalities, con-ditions, restrictions or penalties as are prescribed by law and are necessary in a democratic society ... for the protection of the reputation or rights of others ...

The courts have consistently held that the law on libel and slander in the UK is compatible with Article 10.[123] However, there is one aspect of the UK law on libel and slander which does, in our view, unnecessarily impinge on people's rights to freedom of expression.

---

[123] *Derbyshire County Council* v *Times Newspapers Ltd* [1993] AC 534, 551G (per Lord Keith of Kinkel); *Reynolds* v *Times Newspapers Ltd* [2001] 2 AC 127, 204 (per Lord Nicholls); *McCartan Turkington Breen* v *Times Newspapers Ltd* [2001] 2 AC 277, 300–1 (per Lord Cooke); *Loutchansky* v *Times Newspapers Ltd (Nos 2–5)* [2002] QB 783, at [74].

Suppose Tom has written a book that obviously makes defamatory alle-gations about Mary. Suppose further that Eric, a bookseller, is considering whether to stock and sell copies of Tom's book. Eric may well think, 'Well – if I do stock and sell copies of Tom's book and the allegations in the book prove to be incorrect, I could well be sued for libel by Mary. Section 1 of the Defamation Act 1996 will not protect me because that only applies to people who unwittingly distribute material that is defamatory – and I won't fall into that category. I can't be sure that the allegations in Tom's book are correct so I will definitely be taking a risk of being sued for libel by Mary if I stock and sell copies of Tom's book. All in all, it might be best if I did not stock Tom's book.' Now – if all booksellers react in the same way as Eric, Tom will be unable to find a market for his book – and this is so even if all the allegations contained in the book are correct. This is hardly satisfactory.

Similarly, suppose Karen runs an electronic bulletin board on the Internet. Suppose further that Tom has posted a message on the board which is obvi-ously defamatory of Mary. Mary complains to Karen about the message and requests her to withdraw it from the bulletin board. Again, Karen may well think, 'If I don't agree to Mary's request and the allegations made in Tom's message prove to be untrue, I could well be sued for libel by Mary. I won't be protected by s 1 of the Defamation Act 1996 because that only protects people who unwittingly distribute defamatory material – and I won't fall into this cat-egory of protected defendants if I keep Tom's message on the bulletin board now that my attention has been drawn to it and its defamatory nature. I have no idea whether the allegations contained in Tom's message are true or not so I will definitely be taking a risk of being sued for libel by Mary if I don't take Tom's message down. Given this, it might be better if I withdrew Tom's message from the bulletin board.' If Karen does think in this way, Tom's message will be withdrawn from Karen's bulletin board even if the allegations contained in that message were true. Again, this is hardly satisfactory.

In both these cases, the law on libel operates to 'chill' legitimate expression. In the first case, Tom's book will be rendered unmarketable by the law of libel even though it is perfectly accurate in what it says about Mary. In the second case, Karen will be encouraged by the law on libel to 'censor' Tom's message even though it is perfectly accurate in what it says about Mary. What can be done to ensure that the law on libel does not have this effect? Probably the most satisfactory solution would be to change the law so that it says that someone who disseminates defamatory material which has been created by a third party will have a defence to being sued for libel if he did not know and had no reason to know that the allegations contained in that material were untrue.

If the law were changed in this way then, in the first case described above, booksellers could stock Tom's book confident in the knowledge that if the alle-gations in Tom's book proved to be untrue and they were sued for libel by Mary, they would have a defence to Mary's claim based on the fact that they did not know and had no reason to know that Tom's allegations were untrue. Similarly, in the second case described above, Karen could refuse to withdraw Tom's message from his bulletin board, confident in the knowledge that if the allegations contained in that message proved to be untrue and Mary sued her for libel, she would have a defence to Mary's claim based on the fact that she did not know and had no reason to know that the allegations in Tom's message were untrue.

Political speech

As we have seen, in the United States statements about political figures are protected by qualified privilege. Courts in the United States have taken the view that speech about politicians would be unreasonably restricted if the law did not say that someone who has made a false and damaging statement about a politician cannot be sued in libel or slander for making that statement unless he made that statement maliciously.[124] If the law did *not* say this, it is argued, then someone who wanted to make a damaging allegation about a political figure might be inhibited from making that allegation – he would fear that his making that allegation would result in his being sued for libel or slander.

In awarding qualified privilege to statements about political figures, the law in the United States allows people to make allegations about politicians free from the fear that they will be sued as a result. So long as they do not act maliciously in making those allegations they will have nothing to worry about – their allegations will be privileged and there will be no way of making them the subject of an action for libel or slander. By way of contrast, in the United Kingdom, statements about political figures are *not* automatically protected by qualified privilege. The House of Lords confirmed that this was the case in *Reynolds* v *Times Newspapers Ltd.*[125] Their Lordships advanced a number of arguments in support of the United Kingdom position.

Lord Nicholls observed that if statements about political figures were protected by qualified privilege, a politician whose reputation had been unjustly sullied by a newspaper acting in good faith would have no means of clearing his name – he would be barred from suing the newspaper for libel.[126] Lord Nicholls did not think that this was satisfactory – '[once] besmirched by an unfounded allegation in a national newspaper, a reputation can be damaged for ever, especially if there is no opportunity to vindicate one's reputation. When this happens, society as well as the individual is the loser ... It is in the public interest that the reputation of public figures should not be debased falsely. In the political field, in order to make an informed choice, the electorate needs to be able to identify the good as well as the bad.'[127]

Both Lord Nicholls and Lord Cooke observed that if statements about politicians were automatically protected by qualified privilege, one could have no confidence that newspapers – especially the tabloid press – would act respon-

---

[124] See above, n. 99. A statement about any public figure – not necessarily a politician – will be protected by qualified privilege in the United States but in the section above we shall simply concentrate on the protection afforded by the law here and in the United States to 'political speech' – speech about politicians.

[125] [2001] 2 AC 127.

[126] Ibid., 201.

[127] Ibid., 201.

sibly in using this new-won freedom to make statements about politicians free from the fear that they would be sued as a result of what they said.[128] They did not elaborate on this point but they must have feared that the press would use this freedom to print damaging stories about political figures based on the slenderest of materials and to print damaging stories about politicians which were of no conceivable public interest.

Lords Cooke and Steyn observed that if political speech were protected by qualified privilege, a politician who was defamed by a story in a newspaper would find it very difficult to establish that the newspaper acted maliciously in publishing that story.[129] This is for two reasons. First, malice is in itself a difficult thing to prove. Secondly, English law makes it even more difficult to prove malice because it does not require newspapers to disclose the sources for their stories. So a politician who was defamed by a story in a newspaper and wanted to prove that the newspaper knew that the story was not true when it published it would not be able to get the newspaper to disclose the source of its story to see whether, given what the source said and his or her reliability, the newspaper could have believed its story to be true when it published it. Given these difficulties of proving malice, politicians would have very little protection against being defamed if political speech were protected by qualified privilege – such speech would be *de facto* absolutely privileged; a politician who was defamed by a particular story would in effect find it impossible to sue for libel in respect of that story.

Finally, Lord Steyn advanced another argument against holding that all statements about politicians are protected by qualified privilege. He thought that such a rule might violate the European Convention on Human Rights, under which the resolution of competing rights and interests – such as the right to freedom of speech and the interest in preserving one's reputation undamaged – is to be done on a case-by-case basis rather than by laying down general rules which apply in a wide variety of cases.[130]

While the law in the UK does not protect political speech *as such*, it does protect *some* statements about political figures.

If Paul has made a defamatory statement about Lara, a politician, Lara will not be allowed to sue Paul for libel or slander if: (*a*) Paul's statement was on its face a statement of opinion *and* (*b*) Paul did not act maliciously in making that statement; *and* (*c*) the facts on which Paul formed his opinion of Lara were true. In such a case, Paul will be able to raise a defence of fair comment to any claim made against him by Lara. Moreover, if the *Daily Herald* has published a damaging story about Lara and Lara wants to sue the *Daily Herald* for libel, the *Reynolds* decision means that the *Daily Herald* will be able to claim that its story was privileged if: (*a*) the story was on a matter of public interest; *and* (*b*) the *Daily Herald* did not act maliciously in publishing the story; *and* (*c*) the *Daily Herald* acted responsibly in publishing the story when it did and in the form that it did. (Let us call this the '*Reynolds* test for privilege'.)

---

[128] Ibid., 201–2 (per Lord Nicholls), 219 (per Lord Cooke).
[129] Ibid., 210 (per Lord Steyn), 219–20 (per Lord Cooke).
[130] Ibid., 211.

Given this, most forms of political speech will be protected under the law in the United Kingdom and those forms of political speech which will not be protected – malicious speech, tittle-tattle and the publication of irresponsible and untrue stories about politicians – are perhaps not worthy of protection. However, the House of Lords admitted in *Reynolds* that the law on libel and slander in the United Kingdom *could* have the effect of inhibiting or suppressing legitimate political speech. For example, suppose a newspaper has come into possession of a damaging story about a politician which concerns a matter of public interest. The newspaper wants to know whether the story will be privileged if it publishes it. As the *Reynolds* test for determining whether a story about a politician will be privileged is not exactly easy to apply, the newspaper will be left in some uncertainty as to whether or not its story will be privileged.

In such a case, the newspaper may well think, 'While we have checked out our story and think it is correct we cannot be sure that it is. So if we publish the story and are sued for libel as a result, we may not be able to make out a defence of justification to defeat the claim. And it is uncertain whether a court will hold that our story was privileged. Given this, we will definitely be running a risk of being successfully sued for libel if we publish this story. Perhaps it would be better to "sit" on the story rather than publish it – at least until we have incontrovertible proof that it is correct.' If the newspaper *does* decide to 'sit' on the story and the allegations contained in the story were actually *correct*, then the law on libel will have had the effect of 'chilling' legitimate political speech. The House of Lords admitted in *Reynolds* that the law in the United Kingdom on libel and slander could 'chill' legitimate political speech in exactly this way.[131]

However, the House of Lords did not think that the law in the United Kingdom would often have the effect of 'chilling' legitimate political speech in this way. If a newspaper came into possession of a damaging story about a politician which concerned the public interest, it would normally be able to tell what it would have to do in order to ensure that the story once published would be privileged under the *Reynolds* test for privilege. The newspaper would simply have to treat the story responsibly – check the reliability of the sources of the story, give the subject of the story an opportunity to give his version of events and so on – and it can hardly be supposed that the newspaper would not know how to do this given that all newspapers purport to act responsibly in publishing stories about other people.[132]

Given this, the House of Lords thought it unlikely that a newspaper which came into possession of a story about a politician which it believed to be true would ever be forced to 'sit' on the story for fear that publishing the story would result in their being successfully sued for libel. If this is right then the House of Lords was right to refuse to declare in *Reynolds* that political speech would always be protected by qualified privilege. The benefits of making such a declaration would have been marginal; at the same time, making such a declaration would have had the unpleasant side effect of encouraging irresponsible journalism.

---

[131] Ibid., 202 (per Lord Nicholls), 224 (per Lord Cooke). (See also the criticisms of *Reynolds* made by the New Zealand Court of Appeal in *Lange* v *Atkinson (No. 2)* [2000] NZLR 385.)
[132] Ibid., 202 (per Lord Nicholls).

13

HARASSMENT

Section 1(1) of the Protection from Harassment Act 1997 provides that, 'A person must not pursue a course of conduct – (a) which amounts to harassment of another, and (b) which he knows or ought to know amounts to harassment of the other.' It is clear that anyone who breaches this duty will commit a tort. Section 3(1) of the 1997 Act provides that: '[an] actual or apprehended breach of section 1 may be the subject of a claim in civil proceedings by the person who is or may be the victim of the course of conduct in question.' Only three points need be made about these provisions.

(1) *Course of conduct*. The duty created by s 1(1) of the 1997 Act can only be breached by someone who engages in a *course of conduct* which amounts to harassment. Section 7(3) of the Act provides that 'A "course of conduct" must involve conduct on at least two occasions.' The courts have taken a very liberal view of what amounts to a course of conduct, going so far as to hold that someone who loses his temper with his wife on two separate unconnected occasions can be said to have engaged in a 'course of conduct' that amounts to harassment.[1] In our view, this goes too far. One associates the concept of *conduct* with *intentional* behaviour. So A's repeatedly doing x can only be said to amount to a 'course of *conduct*' if A intended to do x each time he did it.[2] As people never intend to lose their temper, a repeated loss of temper cannot amount to a 'course of conduct'.

(2) *The notion of harassment*. Section 7(2) of the 1997 Act provides that 'References to harassing a person include alarming the person or causing the person distress.' So the duty set out in s 1(1) of the 1997 Act will be breached if someone engages in a course of conduct which alarms or distresses someone else and he knows or ought to know that his engaging in that conduct is having that effect.

(3) *Limits*. Section 1(3) of the 1997 Act qualifies the effect of s 1(1), providing as it does that s 1(1) 'does not apply to a course of conduct if the person who pursued it shows – (a) that it was pursued for the purpose of preventing or detecting crime, (b) that it was pursued under any enactment or rule of law or to comply with any condition or requirement imposed by any person under any

---

[1] *Pratt* v *DPP* [2001] EWHC Admin 483.
[2] Though the *repetition* need not have been intended for A's behaviour to amount to a 'course of conduct'. If A repeatedly rings up B because he is obsessed with her and needs to hear her voice every day, he engages in a 'course of conduct' just as much as someone who repeatedly rings up B with the object of making her life a misery.

enactment, or (c) that in the particular circumstances the pursuit of the course of conduct was reasonable'.

So a policeman will commit no tort under the 1997 Act if he camps outside the house of a known car thief every day, with the object of deterring the car thief from going out and stealing cars. Similarly, if A has lent money to B and repayment is long overdue, A will commit no tort under the 1997 Act if he regularly rings B up and demands payment of his money – so long, of course, as A rings B at a reasonable time and does not do it unreasonably often. (A could not, of course, establish that his regularly ringing B up to demand payment of his money was reasonable if his telephone calls were made at 4 am or if he rang B every five minutes.)

In determining whether or not a given course of conduct was 'reasonable' the courts have to be careful that they do not violate people's rights to freedom of expression under Article 10 of the European Convention on Human Rights.[3] So in *Thomas v News Group Newspapers Ltd*, Lord Phillips MR explained that a newspaper which instituted a campaign against a particular individual would only be held to have acted unreasonably in running that campaign if the campaign amounted 'to an abuse of the freedom of the press which the pressing social needs of a democratic society require should be curbed'.[4] As a test for determining when a newspaper will be held to have acted unreasonably in running a campaign against a particular individual, this is unsatisfactory: it is likely to have a 'chilling' effect on people's legitimately exercising their right to freedom of expression. This is because the test is so vague that a newspaper which is thinking of running a campaign against an individual will find it hard to know whether it will or will not be held liable under the 1997 Act if it runs the campaign. As a result, it may well choose to 'pull' the campaign rather than run it and take the risk of being sued under the 1997 Act.

It would have been more satisfactory if the Court of Appeal in *Thomas* had adopted the test set out in the second American Restatement of Torts for determining when the infliction of severe emotional distress will be tortious, and ruled that a newspaper which ran a campaign against a particular individual could only be held to have acted unreasonably in so doing if its running that campaign was so 'extreme and outrageous' that it went beyond 'all possible bounds of decency . . . and [was] utterly intolerable in a civilized society'.[5]

---

[3] Set out above, p. 302.

[4] [2001] EWCA Civ 1233, at [50]. It was conceded in *Thomas* that this test would be satisfied if a newspaper campaign was calculated to stir up racial hatred.

[5] Rest 2d, Torts, §46, Comment *d*. For a discussion of when this requirement will be satisfied, see GS&Z, 644–7.

14

INVASION OF PRIVACY

English law recognises privacy as a value which underpins various rules of tort law (for instance, parts of the torts of trespass to land, private nuisance, defamation, and malicious falsehood). However, English law has not elevated the protection of privacy to the status of a legal principle from which judges can directly derive conditions of tortious liability.[1] To put the same point another way, English law has *not* recognised a *general* 'over-arching, all-embracing cause of action for "invasion of privacy" '.[2] In the last decade, however, English law has developed a tort which deals with a *specific* form of invasion of privacy, and the first part of this chapter concentrates on this new tort which we will refer to as *the tort of wrongful disclosure of private information*. The remaining part of this chapter discusses whether English law ought to develop any further torts to deal with other specific forms of invasion of privacy.

WRONGFUL DISCLOSURE OF PRIVATE INFORMATION

The case of *Campbell* v *MGN*[3] concerned the publication in the *Daily Mirror* of the information that Naomi Campbell was a drug addict, was seeking treatment through Narcotics Anonymous, some details of her treatment, and a photograph of her at a place where a Narcotics Anonymous meeting took place. She conceded that the *Daily Mirror* was entitled to reveal that she was a drug addict and that she was seeking treatment, but contended that the defendant committed a tort in relation to her by publishing the other details and the photograph. The House of Lords unanimously confirmed that A will commit a tort[4] in relation to B if A unjustifiably discloses to C information which A knows or ought to know is private information about B. By a bare majority of three to two the House of

---

[1] In *Wainwright* v *Home Office* [2003] 3 WLR 1137, Lord Hoffmann suggested (at [31]–[33]) that English law should not give effect to a general principle such as 'the unjustified invasion of another's privacy is always actionable' because the detailed attention of a legislator would often be necessary in order to fashion conditions of liability and appropriate defences in the very different areas where the value of privacy might be invoked. He mentioned regulation of the use of images recorded by CCTV cameras as an example of an area where detailed legislation would be more appropriate than a judicial attempt to derive a solution from a broad principle.

[2] *Campbell* v *MGN Ltd* [2004] 2 WLR 1232, at [11] (per Lord Nicholls).

[3] Ibid. (henceforth, '*Campbell*').

[4] Strictly speaking, only one of their Lordships refers to the wrong as a 'tort' (Lord Nicholls at [14]). But in the next subsection we explain why we think that the wrong should be acknowledged as a tort. Any reader who does not accept this explanation can instead treat the first part of this chapter as dealing with *part of* an equitable wrong for pragmatic reasons. See above, p. 8, n. 13.

Lords held that the *Daily Mirror* had committed this tort in publishing the details of Naomi Campbell's treatment and the photograph.

The independence of the new tort

This new tort has its roots in the equitable wrong of breach of confidence. But whilst greater protection of privacy has been achieved *formally* under the cloak of this long-established wrong, it would be artificial to pretend that all that has happened is that breach of confidence 'has developed'. The traditional features of breach of confidence no longer play a significant role in deciding cases involving the unjustifiable disclosure of private information. For instance, the 'cause of action has now firmly shaken off the limiting constraint of the need for an initial confidential relationship'[5] and the narrow limits on the defences to the equitable wrong do not apply in cases protecting privacy.[6] Moreover, the principal influences on the future development if the civil wrong are likely to be human rights law and analogies with torts like libel and slander rather than any principles developed by the Courts of Equity. Thus we think that it makes most sense to treat the civil wrong committed in *Campbell* as a *new and independent tort* – the tort of wrongful disclosure of private information.[7]

An important influence on the development of the new tort has been and will be the right to privacy contained in Article 8 of the European Convention on Human Rights (ECHR). Although s 6 of the Human Rights Act 1998 does not impose a duty to act compatibly with Convention rights on *private individuals*,[8] the courts have held that 'the values underlying Articles 8 and 10 are not confined to disputes between individuals and public authorities'.[9] Indeed, Lord Hoffmann has said that he 'can see no logical ground for saying that a person should have less protection against a private individual than he would have against the state for the publication of personal information for which there is no justification'.[10] It is important to note, however, that the English courts have developed a *limited* new tort reflecting the values underlying Articles 8 and 10: they have *not* simply made violations of Article 8 actionable against private individuals.[11]

---

[5] Ibid., at [14] (per Lord Nicholls).

[6] *Theakston* v *MGN* [2002] EMLR 137, [66].

[7] One reason for this is that the equitable wrong of breach of confidence will continue to exist in a *separate* form in order to deal with situations where abstract information – such as a trade secret – is disclosed to someone else on the condition that it will remain confidential.

[8] See below, Chapter 43.

[9] *Campbell*, at [18] (per Lord Nicholls). Article 10 is, of course, the provision which defines the right to free expression in the ECHR.

[10] Ibid., at [50].

[11] This point is important because Article 8 protects privacy in contexts beyond the scope of the new tort, and in some of these contexts there are good reasons for providing a person with more protection against a public authority than against a private individual. For instance, the compilation of records about individuals by public authorities requires justification under Article 8(2) but it is doubtful that the same can be said when private individuals keep diaries, scrap books or photograph albums. See, for example, *Amann* v *Switzerland* (2000) 30 EHRR 843, where the European Court of Human Rights held that there was an interference with an applicant's right to respect for his private life under Article 8 when a file card recorded that he had supplied a depilatory appliance to a customer in the Soviet embassy.

The structure of the new tort

The new tort has an unusual structure because it exists at the meeting point of *two* human rights: A's disclosure to C of private information about B *may* infringe B's right to privacy, but a restriction on A making such a disclosure *may* infringe the right to free expression of both A and C.[12] Neither of these human rights is pre-eminent, so 'the proportionality of interfering with one has to be balanced against the proportionality of restricting the other'.[13]

The term 'balancing' is shorthand for a complex process. In order to impose tort liability only when that is appopriate given the competing rights at stake the court is likely to find it convenient to proceed by asking the following questions: (1) Is the information about B which A has disclosed[14] to C sufficiently *private* to come within the potential ambit of the tort? (2) If the information is sufficiently private, how important is it to protect this aspect of B's privacy? (3) Was A's disclosure of the information to C *expression* within the ambit of article 10? (4) If so, how important is it not to restrict this sort of expression?[15] (5) Given the answers to (2) and (4), will making A liable amount to a proportionate restriction on A's freedom of expression in order to protect B's privacy *or* will not holding A liable constitute a proportionate limit on the protection of B's privacy in order preserve freedom of expression? It may also be necessary to ask a further question: (6) Did A know, or ought A to have known, that the information was sufficiently private and its publication was not justifiable?

Private information

Suppose that A has disclosed information about B to C. When will that information be regarded as sufficiently private to come within the potential ambit of the tort discussed here?

The basic test
In answer to the question just posed, the basic test is whether B had a 'reasonable expectation of privacy' in relation to the information that A disclosed to C.[16]

Some simple points can be made about this test. First, in working out what this test means we think it is helpful to start by thinking of information as *private* if it is the sort of information which a person would expect to be able to control dissemination of.[17]

---

[12] It is important to remember that both *publisher* and *recipient* have a right to free expression.

[13] *Campbell*, at [140] (per Baroness Hale). See also [113] (per Lord Hope) and [167] (per Lord Carswell).

[14] Or, where B is seeking a pre-publication injunction, 'is intending to disclose'. On pre-publication injunctions see below, pp. 6–8.

[15] Importance must be assessed considering the interests of both *publisher* and *recipient*.

[16] *Campbell*, at [21] (per Lord Nicholls), [85] (per Lord Hope), [134] (per Baroness Hale)

[17] In *Campbell*, Lord Hoffmann said (at [51]) that the new tort 'focuses upon the protection of human autonomy and dignity – *the right to control the dissemination of information about one's private life* and the right to the esteem and respect of other people' (emphasis added).

Importantly, this means that B can have a 'reasonable expectation of privacy' even if the information is not totally *secret*. Usually[18] the information involved will have been known to *some* people other than B before A's involvement; for instance, because B permitted its disclosure to a *limited* circle.[19] Thus the relevant expectation is that B will be able to control whether, when and how the information is released beyond this circle.[20] Where, however, information has already been widely or indiscriminately disclosed B may be unable to claim that he has any *reasonable* expectation of controlling its further publication.[21]

Secondly, the expectation of privacy must be *reasonable*: 'The law of privacy is not intended for the protection of the unduly sensitive.'[22] Thus a claim cannot be based on the publication by A of the sort of information about B that a reasonable person would not be worried about maintaining any degree of control over. For example, if B is inexplicably sensitive about other people finding out the date of her birthday this will not mean that A will commit a tort if he discloses the date to C. The sensitivity rule is qualified to an extent, however, by the further rule that the reasonableness of the expectation of privacy as to information about a particular feature is judged from the perspective of people who share the same feature. Thus in the *Campbell* case the question whether it was reasonable for Naomi Campbell to expect that the details of her treatment should be kept private was assessed from the perspective of a *reasonable drug addict receiving treatment*.[23]

One problem with the reasonable expectation test is that it seems to be circular: B's *privacy* can be protected when B reasonably expects his *privacy* to be protected. A related second problem is that it is unclear what the *nature* of the expectation must be. It is difficult to conclude that it must be a *factual* expectation because very few celebrities could claim that they *in fact expected* tabloid newspapers not to publish salacious details obtained from former lovers or photographs of them in embarrassing poses.[24] Thus it seems that when judges ask about whether B had a 'reasonable expectation of privacy' they are really asking whether B *ought to be able to* expect privacy. But this, of course, is often a controversial question.

---

[18] There are a few exceptions; for instance, where A obtains and publishes B's private diary.

[19] For instance, to members of his close family or to close colleagues.

[20] Difficult cases can arise where information is *available* to all, but onerous to obtain. It seems that a person *may* have a reasonable expectation that people will not make such information easily available. For instance, a celebrity may have a reasonable expectation that a newspaper will not publish his address: *Mills* v *News Group Newspapers Ltd* [2001] EWHC Ch 412. But we suspect that celebrities object to the publication of their addresses because this facilitates *intrusion* rather than because the *publication itself* threatens their dignity or autonomy. Consequently, such cases might be better dealt with under a form of privacy tort other than that dealing with *wrongful disclosure of private information*. See below, pp. 326–7, for discussion of the question whether English law should develop a tort of invasion of privacy by *unreasonable intrusion*.

[21] In *Woodward* v *Hutchins* [1977] 2 All ER 751, 754–5, a case decided under the old wrong of breach of confidence, Lord Denning MR suggested that a claimant could not complain about wider publicity being given to an incident which took place at a well-attended dance or on a jumbo jet.

[22] *Campbell*, at [94] (per Lord Hope).

[23] Ibid., at [98] (per Lord Hope), [136] (per Baroness Hale).

[24] See below p. 314 for discussion of whether these examples fall within the scope of the tort.

Because of the difficulty of applying the reasonable expectation test in borderline cases some judges have advocated the use of a test based on a reasonable person's *reaction* to the publication. For instance, in the *Campbell* case Lord Hope stated that 'the broad test is whether disclosure of the information about the individual ("A") would give substantial offence to A, assuming that A was placed in similar circumstances and was a person of ordinary sensibilities.'[25] This echoes the suggestion of Gleeson CJ in the High Court of Australia that a 'useful practical test' is whether the 'disclosure or observation of information or conduct would be highly offensive to a reasonable person of ordinary sensibilities.'[26] However, this test was criticised by some of the other Lords in the *Campbell* case. For instance, Lord Nicholls was concerned that the 'highly offensive' test raised the threshold of liability higher than the 'reasonable expectation' test, and that a person's reaction to a publication might reflect factors relevant to the later stages of an inquiry into whether a defendant could be held liable for disclosing private information (for instance, whether the publication was justified by free speech values) and not just whether the information was potentially *private*.[27]

Our prediction is that many trial judges will proceed by (*a*) using the reasonable expectation test as the basic test; (*b*) checking their intuitions using Lord Hope's 'substantial offence' test; and (*c*) drawing analogies with the reasoning of appellate courts in similar *types* of cases.

Sexuality and health

Two categories of information about which individuals are generally agreed to have a reasonable expectation of privacy are sexuality and health. The category of 'sexuality' includes information about a person's gender identification, sexual orientation and sexual life,[28] whilst the category 'health' includes 'information about a person's health and treatment for ill-health'.[29]

Financial information

Many people keep information about their financial affairs, such as their wealth and earnings, private and would feel offended if it was disclosed to the public. But the connection between such information and an individual's sense of personhood and dignity is rather remote. In France, where a right to privacy was inserted into the Civil Code in 1970,[30] it has been held that the publication of purely financial information is not actionable.[31] The matter has not been considered, however, by the English courts.

---

[25] *Campbell*, at [92].
[26] *Australian Broadcasting Corporation* v *Lenah Game Meats Pty Ltd* (2001) 208 CLR 199, at [42].
[27] *Campbell*, at [22]. See also [135] (per Baroness Hale).
[28] *PG* v *United Kingdom* [2001] ECHR 546, at [56].
[29] *Campbell*, at [145] (per Baroness Hale). This does not, of course, mean that all publications about another's state of health are wrongful. In paragraph [157] of her speech Baroness Hale explained that, 'the privacy interest in the fact that a public figure has a cold or a broken leg is unlikely to be strong enough to justify restricting the press's freedom to report it'.
[30] Code Civil, article 9.
[31] Cass civ 1re, 28 May 1991, D 1992 Jur 213.

Relationship cases

Where A, who was in a relationship with B, publishes information about B relating to events during the relationship then the *nature of the relationship* will be an important factor in deciding whether B had a 'reasonable expectation of privacy'. At one end of the spectrum of relationships are those where the expectation is strongest (and most likely to be protected by law), such as marriage, and other relationships intended to be permanent. Relationships where there is an express contractual agreement not to publish any information are probably also close to the protective end of the spectrum. In *Campbell v Frisbee*[32] the Court of Appeal stated that it was at least arguable 'that a duty of confidentiality that has been expressly assumed under contract carries more weight, when balanced against the restriction of the right of freedom of expression, than a duty of confidentiality that is not buttressed by express agreement'. At the less protective end of the spectrum are relationships where the law is unlikely to treat any expectation as reasonable, such as 'a transitory engagement in a brothel'.[33] In *A v B* the Court of Appeal agreed with the opinion that the sexual relationship that Gary Flitcroft, a married footballer, had with a lap-dancer over the course of a year was at the 'outer limits of relationships which require the protection of the law'.[34]

The nature of the relationship is only one factor, however, and the nature of the information concerned must also be considered. Thus in *Theakston v MGN*[35] Ouseley J suggested that the claimant would not be able to establish that publication of details of his sexual activity during a visit to a brothel amounted to a violation of privacy, but would be able to prevent publication of photographs showing his appearance during the activity.

Information in a photograph

If a person goes to a public place then he clearly accepts that other people will be able to look at him and thereby obtain certain information about him. But a photograph taken of the person may capture *more* information than even a careful observer would perceive, will preserve that information in a potentially permanent form, and can be used to communicate *more* information *more* efficiently than mere words easily could. For instance, if John wanted to let Paul know about a dress that Mary wore to a child's birthday party (in order to criticise her for choosing to wear such a dress) then showing Paul a photograph of Mary wearing the dress would communicate more information about the dress more quickly and more convincingly than trying to describe it verbally.

If observers can *see* a person at a particular moment then how can he claim to have a reasonable expectation of privacy as to what would appear on a photograph taken at that moment? The answer to this is that one purpose of the new tort is to protect a person's right to control *access* to private information, and that by going where observers can *see* him a person only allows access to information about him *to a limited degree*: a person accepts that his appearance may

[32] [2003] ICR 141.
[33] *Theakston v MGN Ltd* [2002] EMLR 137, [62].
[34] [2003] QB 195, at [47].
[35] [2002] EMLR 137.

be seen and commented on by people in the vicinity, but not that a permanent record will be made and published to the world.[36] Where the only way in which a defendant can obtain such a photograph is by taking it surreptitiously this tends to emphasise that the person was not accepting such a degree of access.[37]

In many situations publishing a photograph of a person doing something innocuous in a public place will not be an invasion of privacy *despite* the difference in the degree of access to the information provided by the photograph. This is because the information contained in the image is unlikely to be the sort of information that a reasonable person would be worried about maintaining any degree of control over. Baroness Hale, for instance, suggested that there was nothing essentially private about what Naomi Campbell 'looks like if and when she pops out to the shops for a bottle of milk'.[38] But where a photograph does contain information that a reasonable person would want to maintain control over – for instance what the person looks like when in extreme distress or when eating messy food – then publication of a photograph of such an event might violate the person's privacy even though *looking at* them during the event would not. Lord Hoffmann has stated that 'the widespread publication of a photograph of someone which reveals him to be in a situation of humiliation or severe embarrassment, even if taken in a public place, may be an infringement of the privacy of his personal information'.[39]

A photograph taken of someone in a private place will also often contain information that a reasonable person might want to maintain control over and will thus infringe the subject's reasonable expectation of privacy. But in the *Campbell* case Lord Hoffmann went further than the other Lords and stated that 'the publication of a photograph taken by intrusion into a private place (for example, by a long-distance lens) may in itself be [an infringement of the privacy of personal information], even if there is nothing embarrassing about the picture itself'.[40] Clearly most people would describe being spied on in a private place with a long-distance lens as an invasion of privacy regardless of whether the spy obtained and then published any information that a reasonable person would want to maintain control over. But this demonstrates that the essence of such a violation is *not* the *publication* of the information obtained. Thus we think that Lord Hoffmann's example involves a different form of invasion of privacy from *wrongful disclosure of private information* and requires separate treatment.[41]

---

[36] *Campbell*, at [122] (per Lord Hope).

[37] In *Campbell*, Lord Hope attached importance (at [121] and [123]) to the fact that the relevant photograph was obtained covertly.

[38] Ibid., at [154].

[39] Ibid., at [76]. In *Von Hanover v Germany* (59320/00), 24 June 2004, unreported, the European Court of Human Rights considered a case arising from the publication in German magazines of photographs of Princess Caroline of Monaco. Although many of these photographs only showed Princess Caroline in everyday situations in public, for instance, doing her shopping, the Court held that publishing them interfered with her right to privacy (at [53]). It seems to us, however, that the essence of Princess Caroline's complaint was not that the photographs *disclosed* private information but that they were a product of systematic *intrusion* by paparazzi and *appropriation* of her image for public entertainment (at [44]). But cf. [59].

[40] *Campbell*, at [76].

[41] We think that the example involves invasion of privacy *by intrusion*. See below, pp. 326–7.

Sometimes a photograph may communicate information which is not contained in the image itself. For instance, in the *Campbell* case Baroness Hale thought that the photograph of Naomi Campbell outside the building where a Narcotics Anonymous meeting took place suggested that Naomi Campbell was being followed or betrayed.[42] However, although such a photograph might have communicated this to Naomi Campbell, and perhaps also to a shrewd tabloid reader, it is doubtful whether *this* was *private information* about Naomi Campbell which should have been withheld from the public.[43]

Iniquity

The wrong of breach of confidence took the view that there could be no protection for 'iniquity'.[44] It is not clear whether the courts will similarly maintain that a claimant cannot assert a reasonable expectation as to the privacy of information relating to 'iniquitous behaviour', or whether instead a defendant will have to establish a justification for publishing such information. In the *Campbell* case Lord Hoffmann said that 'use of drugs' was a matter in respect of which 'even a public figure would ordinarily be entitled to privacy'.[45] By contrast, in *X* v *Y* Mummery LJ held that a person's sexual activity in a transport café lavatory 'did not take place in his private life nor was it within the scope of application of the right to respect for it'[46] apparently because it amounted to a criminal offence.

The experience of other jurisdictions suggests that it might be an error to adopt the stark position that a person can never have a reasonable expectation in maintaining control over the *further* publication of details of his iniquitous behaviour. With the passage of time a person's legitimate interest in maintaining the benefit of successful rehabilitation may come to outweigh any possible public benefit to be gained by allowing further publication.

Companies

Should a company be able to sue for invasion of privacy, if, for instance, information about its private operations is published? The simplest way of answering this question would be to say 'yes' – tort law applies the same rules to claimants whether they are human beings or artificial legal persons. But if we look deeper then it seems that many of the reasons for creating a privacy tort, such as protecting human dignity and facilitating love, friendship and community, do not apply to artificial legal persons.

In *R* v *Broadcasting Standards Commission ex p BBC*[47] the Court of Appeal held that the Commission was entitled to uphold a complaint by Dixons (a company) that the BBC had infringed its privacy unjustifiably by carrying out

---

[42] *Campbell*, at [155].

[43] No doubt in *some* contexts the fact that a person was being betrayed or followed might be private information that a reasonable person would not want others to know about.

[44] *Gartside* v *Outram* (1857) 26 LJ Ch 113.

[45] *Campbell*, at [36].

[46] [2004] EWCA Civ 662, at [53]. See also [69]–[71] (per Dyson LJ). Brooke LJ dissented on this point.

[47] [2001] QB 885.

covert filming in one of its stores. Lord Woolf MR pointed out that companies could engage in private activities which should be protected from unwarranted intrusion, such as board meetings. But both he and Hale LJ drew attention to the fact that article 8 of the ECHR did not refer to a 'right to privacy' in general but only to a 'right to respect for his private and family life, his home and correspondence'. Thus the fact that Dixons succeeded in this case may not be a good guide to the scope of the new tort because its development has been strongly tied to Article 8. Extending the new tort to protect companies would also be inconsistent with the opinion of three members of the High Court of Australia who expressly held in *Australian Broadcasting Corporation* v *Lenah Game Meats* that Australia's emergent tort of invasion of privacy was for 'the benefit of natural, not artificial, persons'.[48] Similarly, companies are not protected under the United States Rest 2d, Torts, §652I: 'an action for invasion of privacy can be maintained only by a *living* individual whose privacy is invaded.'[49] By contrast, a rival textbook argues that companies should be able to sue for invasions of privacy because they can sue for libel and slander, and allowing them to sue for invasions of privacy will prevent them from seeking to distort other torts in order to prevent unwanted publications about their private activities.[50]

Measuring the importance of protecting privacy

The importance of protecting particular private information from publication can be measured by reflecting on the reasons which are commonly given for such protection: to protect human dignity[51] and personality,[52] and to facilitate the formation of *special* relationships such as love, friendship and community.[53] Generally, the significance of an affront to dignity and personality can be measured by considering how *intimate* the information was. Similarly, it can be assessed how far *control* over the distribution of such information is important in forming particular *special relationships*. An alternative approach, which can be used alongside the first, ranks the importance of privacy interests by estimating the *intensity of the offence* that a reasonable person in the claimant's position might be expected to suffer on the publication of such information. A further relevant factor in measuring the importance of preventing the publication of particular material is the likelihood that the publication will cause *other significant harm* to the claimant beyond distress. In the *Campbell* case the majority in the House of

---

[48] (2001) 208 CLR 199, at [132].

[49] American Law Institute (1965), emphasis added. It seems that the protection offered by article 8 of the ECHR does *not* end with an individual's death: see *Plon* v *France* (58148/00), 18 May 2004, unreported.

[50] M&D, 699.

[51] See, for example, Bloustein 1964, 1003, 'The man who is compelled to live every minute of his life among others and whose every need and thought, desire, fancy or gratification is subject to public scrutiny, has been deprived of his individuality and human dignity.'

[52] *Von Hanover* v *Germany* (59320/00), 24 June 2004, unreported, at [50]: 'the guarantee afforded by Article 8 of the Convention is primarily intended to ensure the development, without outside interference, of the personality of each individual in his relations with other human beings.'

[53] See, for example, Fried 1968; also Feldman 1997.

Lords attached particular weight to the fact that publication of the details of Naomi Campbell's treatment might cause *harm* by disrupting her treatment.[54]

Freedom of expression

What counts as expression?

Although it is *logical* to ask whether the defendant's disclosure of the information amounted to 'expression' within the ambit of article 10 we might expect it to be rare for the answer to be 'no'. One situation where the defendant's behaviour may not count as 'expression' is where the defendant unintentionally permits C to obtain the information, for instance by forgetfully leaving B's medical records on a train. But this example raises the awkward question of what is meant by 'disclosure' in the context of the new tort. Because the cases considered so far in England have all involved deliberate publication the courts have not provided any guidance on whether the tort covers accidental or careless disclosures.[55]

Measuring the importance of preserving freedom of expression

The courts have provided more guidance on how to measure the importance of not restricting expression. In the *Campbell* case Baroness Hale said: 'There are undoubtedly different types of speech, just as there are different types of private information, some of which are more deserving of protection in a democratic society than others. Top of the list is political speech. The free exchange of information and ideas on matters relevant to the organisation of the economic, social and political life of the country is crucial to any democracy. . . . This includes revealing information about public figures, especially those in elective office, which would otherwise be private but is relevant to their participation in public life. Intellectual and educational speech and expression are also important in a democracy, not least because they enable the development of the individuals' potential to play a full part in society and in our democratic life. Artistic speech and expression is important for similar reasons, in fostering both individual originality and creativity and the free-thinking and dynamic society we so much value.'[56] Expression which is not political, intellectual, educational or artistic, such as mere gossip, is still protected to an extent, because it may play an important role in preserving social networks and in making newspapers financially viable. But it will be far easier to justify a restriction on mere gossip[57] to protect privacy than a restriction on political debate.

[54] *Campbell*, at [98] and [119] (per Lord Hope), [130] and [165] (per Baroness Hale), [169] (per Lord Carswell).

[55] A parallel could be drawn with the legal rules on what counts as 'publication' for the purposes of the torts of libel and slander (above pp. 275–8). But these rules might be thought only to be tolerable from a free expression perspective because of the existence of the special statutory defence for 'innocent dissemination' and the 'offer to make amends' procedure (see above, pp. 297–300), and these provisions do not extend to liability for invasion of privacy.

[56] *Campbell*, at [148].

[57] In *Von Hanover v Germany* (59320/00), 24 June 2004, unreported, the European Court of Human Rights treated (at [65]) the preservation of freedom to publish photographs of Princess Caroline of Monaco's daily activities as relatively unimportant when 'the sole purpose was to satisfy the curiosity of a particular readership regarding the details of the applicant's private life,

Public interest

A potentially decisive factor in measuring the importance of preserving free expression is whether it is in the public interest for the information to be disclosed to the people to whom the defendant disclosed it. 'Public interest' is obviously a concept which it is impossible to *define* with any precision. In *A* v *B* the Court of Appeal suggested that 'in the majority of situations whether the public interest is involved or not will be obvious' and that where it is not obvious the factor is 'unlikely to be decisive'.[58] No doubt in time courts will reach predictable decisions on what private information it is in the public interest to publish by drawing analogies with previous cases. But until a body of cases has been decided it may be helpful to quote the Press Complaints Commission's Code of Practice which states that the 'public interest includes: (i) Detecting or exposing crime or a serious misdemeanour. (ii) Protecting health and safety. (iii) Preventing the public from being misled by some statement or action of an individual or organisation.' It may also be worth drawing attention to some of the old breach of confidence cases which held that it could be in the public interest to publish information: about the dangerous teachings of a cult,[59] casting doubt on the safety of criminal convictions,[60] and to assist in the prevention of crime.[61]

Public figures

If publication of the information is in the public interest then this will weigh heavily against liability, but it also seems that public figures must accept a greater degree of disclosure of information than ordinary individuals even when that disclosure is not justified by the public interest. In *A* v *B* Lord Woolf CJ made the following observations: '. . . because of his public position [a public figure] must expect and accept that his actions will be more closely scrutinised by the media. . . . Whether you have courted publicity or not you may be a legitimate subject of public attention. If you have courted public attention then you have less ground to object to the intrusion, which follows. In many of these situations it would be overstating the position to say that there is a public interest in the information being published. It would be more accurate to say that the public have an understandable and so a legitimate interest in being told the information.'[62]

In the *Campbell* case the Court of Appeal made clear that Lord Woolf CJ was not intending to say that once *a person* was identified as a legitimate subject of public attention then *any information of any type* about that person could be published. Rather, the cases have suggested that the public will have 'an understandable and so legitimate interest' where: (*a*) the information contradicts or clarifies information that C has published about the same aspect of his life; or (*b*) C is 'a role model whose conduct could well be emulated by others'.

[and the photographs] cannot be deemed to contribute to any debate of general interest to society despite the applicant being known to the public'.

[58] [2003] QB 195, at [11](viii).
[59] *Hubbard* v *Vosper* [1972] 2 QB 84.
[60] *Lion Laboratories* v *Evans* [1985] QB 526.
[61] *Hellewell* v *Chief Constable of Derbyshire* [1995] 1 WLR 804.
[62] [2003] QB 195, at [11](xii).

In *A* v *B* Lord Woolf CJ stated that, 'where a public figure chooses to make untrue pronouncements about his or her private life, the press will normally be entitled to put the record straight'.[63] This rule seems to be justified partly by the public interest in preventing the public from being misled, but also partly by the idea that if a person makes pronouncements about a particular aspect of his private life then it is fair to treat him as having waived his privacy to some extent. The second part of the justification is important because it explains why courts seem not to make any attempt to measure the benefit that the public might gain from avoiding being misled about some aspect of a celebrity's private life.

There are two grounds for being sceptical about the fairness of the rule which tips the balance against 'role models' even in circumstances where the defendant cannot establish that the public interest will be advanced by publication of the information. First, this seems harsh when it is applied to persons who have never *projected* themselves as positive 'role models' for others. In *A* v *B* Lord Woolf CJ suggested that *all* footballers were 'role models' whether they liked this or not. Perhaps where a person has *chosen* to enter a particular sphere of life where he might be treated as a 'role model', for instance by becoming a professional sportsman, a vicar or a teacher, he can be fairly taken to have consented to information about particular aspects of his life being published. But where a person has become a 'role model' unintentionally, for instance by saving a drowning dog or making a scientific discovery, the consequences for his privacy seem harder to justify.[64]

The second ground for scepticism is that the logic behind the rule is opaque: If 'role models' can influence young people then why should the law make it easier for the public to learn about their private misdeeds? In the *Campbell* case the Court of Appeal stated that it did 'not see why it should necessarily be in the public interest that an individual who has been adopted as a role model, without seeking this distinction, should be demonstrated to have feet of clay'.[65] The suggestion that publishing details of Gary Flitcroft's sex life or Naomi Campbell's drug addiction is useful in order to prevent members of the public being harmed by inappropriate 'role models' is unconvincing. A more plausible explanation of the sentiment that leads (some) people to think that such publications are fair seems to be that where individuals are admired for their *distinctive* talents and gifts it is fair for the ways in which they are *undistinguished* to be revealed. The ordinary recipient of such information values it because it reassures him that

---

[63] Ibid., at [43]. See also *Campbell*, at [58] (per Lord Hoffmann).

[64] The German courts have similarly argued that the public has a legitimate interest in being allowed to judge whether the personal behaviour of a 'figure of contemporary society *par excellence*' (*absolute Person der Zeitgeschichte*), the sort of person who might be treated as an idol or role model, convincingly tallies with his behaviour during official engagements. However, the European Court of Human Rights held in *Von Hanover* v *Germany* (59320/00), 24 June 2004, unreported, that the application of this doctrine to Princess Caroline of Monaco left her with insufficient protection for her right to privacy when 'the interest of the general public and the press is based solely on her membership of a reigning family whereas she herself does not exercise any official functions' (at [72]). The Court stated, at [77], that 'the public does not have a legitimate interest in knowing where the applicant is and how she behaves generally in her private life even if she appears in places that cannot always be described as secluded and despite the fact that she is well known to the public'.

[65] [2003] QB 195, at [41]. See also *Campbell*, at [151] (per Baroness Hale).

neither Gary Flitcroft nor Naomi Campbell is such a *superior* being after all, rather than because it protects him against being unduly influenced by the examples they set. No doubt the ordinary recipient's reaction is as *natural* as other aspects of *envy*, but we are not convinced that 'the public have an understandable and so legitimate interest' in the satiation of this *jealous* impulse.

Striking the balance between the protection of privacy and freedom of expression

Suppose that A has disclosed to C information about B that is sufficiently private to attract the protection of the tort considered here. How will the courts strike the balance between the desire, on the one hand, to protect B's privacy and the desire, on the other hand, not to limit disproprtionately A's freedom of expression? It is hard to give any useful *general* guidance on this issue. However, two points can be made.

(1) *The dual perspective approach.* In deciding which right is to prevail in this case – A's right to freedom of expression or B's right to privacy – a court must take account of the fact that *neither* right should be subjected to a disproportionate restriction. So if the court is considering making A liable –thus restricting A's right of freedom of expression in order to protect B's privacy – it must ask if the restriction it is considering imposing on A's right to freedom of expression is rational, fair, not arbitrary and the minimum restriction necessary to protect B's right to privacy. In order to decide whether this is the case it will often be helpful for the court *also* to consider the case from the converse perspective; that is, to consider: If B's privacy is *denied* protection in order to protect A's right to freedom of expression, will this restriction on the protection of B's privacy be rational, fair, not arbitrary and the minimum restriction necessary to protect A's right to freedom of expression? The reason for this is that since one right must prevail, and neither right should be subject to any disproportionate restriction, the court will *only* be able to hold A *liable* if doing so amounts to a proportionate restriction on A's right to freedom of expression in order to protect B's privacy; while, at the same time, it will *only* be able to hold that A is *not* liable if turning down B's claim amounts to a proportionate limit on the protection of B's privacy in order to protect A's right to freedom of expression. Adopting a dual perspective approach allows the court to compare the *relative merits* of these two possible conclusions.[66]

(2) *Practical reality.* In striking a balance between protecting people's privacy and people's rights to freedom of expression, the courts must be careful to ensure that they are not devising standards which real journalists cannot be reasonably expected to meet. For instance, a real journalist cannot be expected to produce a justification

---

[66] A summary of the dual perspective approach is set out by Baroness Hale in *Campbell*, at [141], and it also seems to have been the approach used by Lord Hope, at [105], with the agreement of Lord Carswell, at [167].

for every choice of phrasing or supporting detail. In the *Campbell* case all of their Lordships recognised 'the importance of allowing a proper degree of journalistic margin to the press to deal with a legitimate story in its own way, without imposing unnecessary shackles on its freedom to publish detail and photographs which add colour and conviction'.[67] Thus a judge setting the balance must be careful not to hold a defendant liable merely because he or she would have presented the story in a different way, and must take account of the advantages which come with detailed argument and hindsight.

Having made these points, let's consider two concrete examples so as to get a better 'feel' for how the courts are likely to strike a balance between people's rights to freedom of expression and people's interests in having their privacy protected.

(1) *The romantic politician.* Lara, a solicitor employed by Blandshire County Council, reveals to the *Daily Clarion* that she began a love affair with John, the Council leader, shortly before being appointed to the post. The *Daily Clarion* publishes this information in an article which also recounts Lara's recollections of John's performance as a lover.[68]

In this case John is likely to be able to establish that the details of his affair with Lara are sufficiently private to be entitled to be potentially protected unless the relationship was intended to be casual and transitory. Moreover, regardless of the nature of the relationship, intimate information about his physical appearance and behaviour when love-making will be sufficiently private. At the same time the *Daily Clarion* will be able to establish that its publication is a form of 'expression'. Given this, whether John can sue the *Daily Clarion* or not will turn on what balance the court strikes between John's interest in having his privacy protected on the one hand and the *Daily Clarion*'s right to freedom of expression on the other.

Looking at the importance of protecting John's right to privacy first, John will point to the value of preserving the sanctity and security of intimate relationships of the kind he had with Lara, and to the value of protecting him from the loss of dignity and humiliation likely to be caused by the revelation of intimate information about his physical appearance and behaviour when love-making. John may seek to identify *other* damage that will be caused to him by publication, such as damage to his marriage, but in the case of *A* v *B* Lord Woolf CJ instructed courts not to speculate as to whether it would be in a wife's interest to be kept unaware of the details of a husband's affair.[69]

Turning now to the importance of protecting the *Daily Clarion*'s freedom of expression in this case, the *Daily Clarion* might argue that it is in the public interest to reveal information suggesting that inappropriate factors influenced a public appointment. This, however, raises the difficulty that it would be defamatory for the *Daily Clarion* to make this suggestion directly and to avoid liability for libel the newspaper would probably have to rely on the defence of justification or qualified privilege. In this context it is worth noting that to rely on the

---

[67] Ibid., at [169] (per Lord Carswell). Lord Nicholls and Lord Hoffmann thought that this factor was decisive in favour of the defendants, but the majority disagreed.

[68] This example is based on one suggested by Lord Hoffmann in *Campbell*, at [60].

[69] [2003] QB 195, at [43](v).

form of qualified privilege that attaches to publications relating to matters of public concern the newspaper would have to establish that it acted responsibly in going ahead and publishing the article when it did and in the form that it did.[70] Thus if the *Daily Clarion* seeks to rely on the public interest in revealing information which might lead readers to draw a defamatory inference it is *arguable* that the newspaper ought to demonstrate that it acted responsibly in not seeking further information as to whether such an inference was justified.

As an additional or alternative argument, the *Daily Clarion* may suggest that the moral integrity of an elected politician, a public figure, is a subject of legitimate interest to the public, and that information about John's extramarital affair is relevant to his moral integrity. It must be noted, however, that this argument is unlikely to provide much support for publishing Lara's recollections of John's performance as a lover.

On balance, it seems that a court may regard treating the *whole* story as actionable as too great a restriction on the *Daily Clarion*'s freedom of expression and conclude that John must accept some invasion of his privacy in the interests of free expression because he is a public figure. But the court may also regard a duty not to publish Lara's recollections of John's performance as a lover as a proportionate limit on the *Daily Clarion*'s freedom of expression (and that of its readers) in the interests of protecting John's privacy.[71] In reaching this conclusion, the court will want to check that a reasonable newspaper editor can be expected to draw the line between the essential story which it should be free to publish and the salacious supporting details which invade John's privacy to an unacceptable extent.

(2) *The drunken student.* Sarah, a student, gets so drunk celebrating the end of her exams that she collapses in the street and has to be treated by paramedics. The incident is recorded by CCTV cameras belonging to Instown University, and the University later uses the images in a video it shows to students to warn them about the dangers of binge drinking.

Here, assuming that the case is argued as one of wrongful disclosure of private information,[72] Sarah will have to establish that the images contain information about her that a reasonable person would want to retain control over. If she is recognisable then it is likely that the images will convey what she looked like during a distressing and humiliating episode which is something that a reasonable person would want to retain control over, at least to the extent of preventing a permanent record of it being released to a wide audience. However, her willingness to expose this information about herself to those present in a public street will prevent her from claiming that her interest in maintaining control over the information is very weighty.

From the point of view of expression, Instown University may seek to argue that the violation of Sarah's privacy is proportionate to the public interest in expressing an important social message in a graphic and effective manner. The

---

[70] See above pp. 294–5, discussing *Reynolds v Times Newspapers Ltd* [2001] 2 AC 127.

[71] This seems to have been the conclusion envisaged by Lord Hoffmann.

[72] If Instown University is a public authority within the Human Rights Act 1998 Sarah could claim under that statute and thereby seek to circumvent the limits on the new tort. In this example we assume that it is a *private* institution.

court will want to investigate, however, whether it was *necessary* to violate Sarah's privacy in order to express this message effectively, or whether it was merely *convenient* to do so. In this context it will consider whether the same scene could have been equally well presented using actors or by disguising Sarah's identity.[73] On balance it seems unlikely that Instown University will be able to justify using the images.

The defendant's knowledge

Where a claim is brought against a publisher who has obtained the information *indirectly* the question may arise whether the publisher *knew or ought to have known* that the material it was publishing violated the subject's reasonable expectation of privacy.[74] Thus where A provides information about B to C, a newspaper, and C publishes this information, it will be C's knowledge which is in issue if B sues C.[75]

It seems, however, that the courts may define what a *media defendant* 'ought to know' so widely that the requirement will be rendered nugatory. In the *Campbell case,* the Court of Appeal held that 'the media can fairly be expected to identify confidential information about an individual's private life which, absent good reason, it will be offensive to publish'.[76] This suggests that a *professional* publisher will not be able to defend itself by relying on a misunderstanding as to what sorts of information the law potentially protects. But the court did not expressly consider the difficult situations which might arise where a defendant is misled as to the nature of the relationship between A and B or the circumstances in which a photograph was obtained.

The Court of Appeal in the *Campbell* case also said that, 'the media must accept responsibility for the decision that, in the particular circumstances, publication of the material in question is justifiable in the public interest',[77] meaning that a *professional* publisher cannot avoid liability by establishing an honest belief that publication was justifiable. But again, the court did not consider more difficult situations involving defendants who are understandably unfamiliar with the law or arguments relying on justifications other than the public interest, for instance a defendant's mistaken belief that the claimant had consented to the publication.

Evaluation of the new tort

Many torts are based on duties which reflect a balancing of the competing

---

[73] In *Peck* v *United Kingdom* (2003) 13 BHRC 669, the European Court of Human Rights held that a local authority's disclosure to the media of CCTV footage showing the applicant in a public place with a large knife in order to increase the effectiveness of a new CCTV system 'pursued the legitimate aim of public safety, the prevention of disorder and crime and the protection of the rights of others' (at [67]), but interfered with the applicant's privacy to a disproportionate extent because no attempt was made to secure his consent and too little was done to ensure that his identity was properly masked (at [85] and [87]).

[74] *Campbell*, at [85] (per Lord Hope), [134] (per Baroness Hale).

[75] Of course, if B only sues A then C's knowledge will be irrelevant.

[76] *Campbell* v *MGN Ltd* [2003] QB 633, at [68].

[77] Ibid.

interests of potential claimants and defendants in the light of concerns about what sorts of distinctions courts can cope with in practice. But the new tort of wrongful disclosure of private information is unusual in that it requires the court to carry out this balancing process in every case. A major advantage of this structure is that it gives the tort the flexibility to respond to new factors that may be raised in future cases, and to new combinations of factors which may not have been anticipated. A major disadvantage, however, is that, at least until a significant number of cases has been decided, it will be difficult to predict what the law demands in borderline cases. In the light of this disadvantage it might have been preferable for Parliament to have produced detailed legislation on the protection of privacy. But in the light of Parliament's apparent unwillingness to undertake this task, and its apparent willingness at the time of passing the Human Rights Act 1998 for the courts to take it on, it is difficult to criticise the courts for usurping the legislative role. That said, having taken on the task the courts can be criticised for: (*a*) having built the new tort around the unhelpfully circular concept of 'reasonable expectation of privacy'; (*b*) having provided no guidance on whether there will be liability for careless and accidental disclosures; (*c*) having developed a doctrine of 'legitimate interest in the behaviour of public figures' which seems to condone public pleasure at seeing the mighty humbled; (*d*) having given guidance on what must be shown as to the defendant's state of mind which is either inexplicably harsher than the law of libel or incomplete.

CASES NOT INVOLVING THE WRONGFUL DISCLOSURE OF PRIVATE INFORMATION

We have already mentioned that some aspects of privacy may be protected by torts dealt with elsewhere in the book (for instance, by the torts of trespass to land, private nuisance, defamation, and malicious falsehood). But these and the new tort discussed above do not between them provide comprehensive protection for privacy. For instance, most people would accept that being compelled to undress in front of a prison officer involves a violation of privacy, but the claimants in *Wainwright* v *Home Office*[78] were unable to establish that this behaviour fell within the ambit of any tort. Given that the House of Lords in the *Campbell* case confirmed their previous refusal in the *Wainwright* case to develop an 'over-arching, all-embracing cause of action for "invasion of privacy" ',[79] it is worth asking whether the courts are likely to develop any further *limited* torts to protect against other *specific* forms of invasion of privacy.

In the United States of America a fourfold division of forms of invasion of privacy is commonly used: (*a*) unreasonable intrusion into private situations; (*b*) unreasonable publication of private facts; (*c*) publicity unreasonably placing the claimant in a 'false light'; (*d*) appropriating the claimant's name or likeness for private advantage.[80] The second of these covers the forms of behaviour dealt with

---

[78] [2003] 3 WLR 1137 (discussed above, pp. 107–9).
[79] *Campbell*, at [11] (per Lord Nicholls).
[80] See, for instance, Prosser 1960; Rest 2d, Torts § 652A.

by the new English tort of wrongful disclosure of private information. Thus here we will briefly consider some of the difficulties which might be involved in creating *limited* torts to cover each of the other three forms. So far as there are *distinct* problems with developing each of the limited torts these will tend to confirm Lord Hoffmann's opinion that a *general* tort should not be created because of the need to fashion conditions of liability and appropriate defences reflecting the differences between the areas where the value of privacy may be invoked.[81]

Unreasonable intrusion

A tort covering this form of invasion would extend over behaviour such as watching a stranger giving birth, having a person remove his clothes in front of you, or taking a photograph of a person in a private place using a long-distance lens. The essence of this form of invasion of privacy is that the way in which the defendant behaves enables him to *gather* information about the claimant in violation of the claimant's asserted right to control when, how and to what extent such information is available to others. This can be usefully contrasted with the new tort of wrongful disclosure of private information where the essence is the defendant's *publication* of information about the claimant in violation of the claimant's asserted right to control when, how and to what extent such information is available to others.

It is at least arguable that if the claimant's right to control such information is to be protected at all then it ought to be protected against both unacceptable methods of *gathering* information and unacceptable *publication* of what has been gathered. In practice, however, it is easier to design liability rules dealing with *publication*. This is because rules relating to *publication* apply at a stage when we know what the information is and can measure the importance of it being kept private and of it being available to the public. By contrast, rules regulating methods of *gathering* information apply *before* we know what the defendant might discover by strip-searching the claimant or monitoring him in the street using a CCTV camera. Of course, it would not be impossible for the English courts to adapt the balancing approach at the core of the new wrongful disclosure tort in order to regulate intrusions. Thus the courts might ask if the likelihood of the defendant obtaining information by means of a particular gathering technique which it would be in the public interest to have available *outweighed* the extent to which use of such a technique would reduce the claimant's control over information which he might have a reasonable interest in maintaining control over. The outcome of such a balancing might be straightforward in many cases, in particular where the defendant was gathering information merely to satisfy prurient curiosity.[82] But there would also be con-

---

[81] *Wainwright* v *Home Office* [2003] 3 WLR 1137, at [31]–[33].

[82] An example of a case which might be covered is provided by *Kaye* v *Robertson* [1991] FSR 62, where agents of the defendants entered a hospital room where the claimant, an actor, was recovering from brain surgery, took photographs, and purported to conduct an interview.

[83] See *Jones* v *University of Warwick* [2003] 1 WLR 954, at [29], where the Court of Appeal apparently held that such filming violated article 8.

troversial cases involving, for instance, the use of covert filming in investigating possible insurance fraud[83] and the use of 'ambush' interviews in journalism.

We noted above that in the *Campbell* case Lord Hoffmann seemed willing to develop a tort to cover the *publication* of a photograph taken of a person in a private place by using a long lens even if the photograph contained no essentially private information.[84] It seems to us, however, that the essence of the wrong in such a case is the *intrusion* caused by *taking the photograph* and we will not be surprised if the courts develop a limited balancing-based tort to deal with such intrusions during the next decade.[85]

False light

A tort covering this form of invasion would extend over behaviour such as publishing the false information that the claimant was romantically involved with a celebrity or a false version of a dramatic event involving the claimant. Clearly if a newspaper published the information that Mary, a single woman, was dating Prince William, a single man, this would usually not be defamatory of Mary even if it was wholly false.[86] It would be likely, however, to subject Mary to a significant degree of unwanted public attention and it is easy to see why people might want to be protected from such attention. But the issue whether a tortious duty should be created to confer such protection raises two subsidiary questions. First, whether the degree of annoyance likely to be suffered by someone subjected to such attention is sufficiently significant to warrant such a step, given that there cannot be a duty to avoid all potentially annoying forms of conduct.[87] Secondly, whether the existence of such a duty might unduly restrict the activities of those who want to retell recent events in a dramatically engaging manner, such as the authors of docudramas and unauthorised biographies. It would certainly be a burden on modern historians and the unauthorised biographers if they could be liable for non-defamatory factual errors, and we think that the complexity of the web of common law and statute that makes up the law of libel provides a good reason why courts should be cautious about presuming that they have the capacity to develop a new privacy tort in this area.

Appropriation of personality

A tort covering this form of invasion would extend over behaviour such as using

---

[84] *Campbell*, at [76].

[85] Article 8 clearly entitles people to protection against intrusions into their privacy, and the European Court of Human Rights has repeatedly held that the article imposes a positive obligation on states which *may* require 'the adoption of measures designed to secure respect for private life even in the sphere of the relations of individuals between themselves' (for instance, *Von Hanover v Germany* (59320/00), 24 June 2004, unreported, at [57]). One way in which the United Kingdom could fulfil this obligation would be for the *courts* to develop a new tort making unreasonable intrusions actionable.

[86] It might be defamatory in unusual circumstances; for instance, if Mary was a nun.

[87] Such a duty would be unsatisfactory because it would impinge on so many aspects of ordinary social life. It would be extraordinarily ironic if many everyday encounters became subject to legal regulation in the interests of protecting *privacy*!

a photograph of a person in an advertisement without his consent. For instance, if an airline published an advertisement for its flights using the picture of a person recently involved in a criminal case with the slogan 'for a quick getaway fly with our airline'[88] then the person depicted might be able to claim. Similarly, this tort might cover a case where a photograph of a teenager taken in a public place without obtaining her consent was used to illustrate a magazine article.[89] From a privacy perspective the utility of the tort is that it gives a person control over *how* her image and identity is used, and prevents that image and identity being treated as a mere tool by others. In practice, however, such a tort can play an important role in helping to preserve for celebrities the rewards they can gain by carefully licensing their images and identities for use in advertising.[90]

One difficulty with creating a tort to cover this form of invasion of privacy would be defining the scope of a claimant's protected interest. Where a photograph of the claimant is used the matter is straightforward, but more difficult cases might involve use of a distinctive catchphrase, mannerism or vocal characteristic.[91] It might be possible to get round this problem by defining the tort so that it covered only *intentional* appropriation, but this would not avoid all difficulties.[92] A further difficulty would be defining the situations where use of a person's image without consent is legitimate. For instance, photographs are commonly used without the consent of those depicted to illustrate legitimate news stories, in protest and in satire.[93] In Germany a person's image is protected and in an important decision the Bundesgerichtshof had to determine when it was permissible for Greenpeace to use the name and picture of the president of a chemical company on a campaign poster.[94] No doubt English courts could solve similar disputes, but it is important to note that extending tort law to cover this form of invasion of privacy would be likely to involve a move away from the traditional preference for clear legal duties in commercial settings.[95]

---

[88] EasyJet issued similar advertisements during 2003.

[89] *Aubry* v *Editions Vice-Versa Inc.* [1998] 1 SCR 591.

[90] The extension of the tort of passing off in *Irvine* v *Talksport Ltd* [2002] 1 WLR 2355 (discussed below, p. 450) will protect the interest of a celebrity who has acquired a valuable reputation or goodwill from misrepresentations which enable a defendant to make use of or take advantage of that reputation (at [38], per Laddie J). The tort of passing off will not, however, protect an unknown teenager like the claimant in the *Aubry* case, above, and may not protect a claimant who has attained *notoriety*.

[91] Cases from the United States have involved the use of a television presenter's catchphrase to market a portable toilet (*Carson* v *Here's Johnny Portable Toilets Inc.*, 698 F 2d 831 (1983)), the use of a singer who sounded like Bette Midler to advertise cars (*Midler* v *Ford Motor Co.* 849 F 2d 460 (1988)), and the use of a robot dressed like a gameshow hostess to advertise video-recorders (*White* v *Samsung Electronics America Inc.*, 971 F 2d 1395 (1992)).

[92] For instance, if the defendant argued that he intended to invoke a *generic* athlete of the 1970s and the claimant argued that his individual image was appropriated.

[93] The short phrase 'for private advantage' used in the summary of the tort clearly does not go very far towards answering the difficult issues raised, since newspapers and satirists generally seek to make a profit.

[94] BGH, 12 October 1993, NJW 1994, 124 (Federal Court of Justice, Germany).

[95] In *Von Hanover* v *Germany* (59320/00), 24 June 2004, unreported, the European Court of Human Rights held (at [72]) that states have undertaken a 'positive obligation under the Convention to protect private life and the right to control the use of one's image' (emphasis added). See also [57]. One way in which the United Kingdom could fulfil this obligation would be for the *courts* to develop a new tort making appropriation of personality actionable.

15

CONVERSION

MODES OF CONVERSION

It is notoriously difficult to define when someone will commit the tort of conversion.[1] There seem to be at least[2] six different ways of committing this tort. A will have committed the tort of conversion in relation to B if –

(1) *Taking possession.* B was in possession of certain goods, or had an immediate right to possess certain goods, and A took possession of those goods with the intention of keeping them[3] when he had no lawful justification or excuse for doing so.

So, for example, suppose Fred steals some jewellery from Karen, and then sells it to Eric, who takes possession of it. In this case, both Fred and Eric will have committed the tort of conversion in relation to Karen – Fred in stealing the jewellery from Karen and Eric in taking possession of the stolen jewellery with the intention of keeping it. Eric, it should be noted, will have committed the tort of conversion in this situation even if he bought the jewellery from Fred in perfect good faith and had no idea it was stolen.

In *Tear* v *Freebody*,[4] the claimant unlawfully erected a building and the defendant was given the job of tearing the building down. The defendant did so and then took the bricks and so on out of which the building was made to a stone yard, intending to retain them until he was paid for the work he had done in tearing down the building. The defendant was not entitled to do this. It was held that the defendant committed the tort of conversion in taking possession of the bricks.

It is essential to show – for the purpose of showing that someone has committed the tort of conversion under this head – that he took possession of an item

---

[1] See Bramwell LJ in *Hiort* v *The London and North Western Railway Company* (1879) 4 Ex D 188, 194: 'I have frequently stated that I never did understand with precision what was a conversion ... I find it impossible to give an exhaustive description as to what was or was not a conversion.' Also Lord Nicholls in *Kuwait Airways Corpn* v *Iraqi Airways Co. (Nos 4 & 5)* [2002] 2 AC 883, at [39]: 'Conversion of goods can occur in so many different circumstances that framing a precise definition of universal application is well nigh impossible.' Probably the best definition – though necessarily imperfect – is that offered by Professor Tettenborn. See C&L, 729: '[C]onversion is an act of deliberate dealing with a chattel inconsistent with another's right whereby that other is deprived of the use or possession of it.'

[2] There may well be other ways of committing this tort: C&L, 741–2. However, a student reader of this book need not be troubled with these.

[3] The expression 'keeping' here covers both the situation where A took possession of the goods with the intention of keeping them for himself and the situation where A took possession of the goods with the intention of giving them to a third party.

[4] (1858) 4 CB (NS) 228, 140 ER 1071.

of property *with the intention of keeping it*.[5] For example, in *Fouldes* v *Willoughby*[6] the defendant operated a ferry that ran between Birkenhead and Liverpool. The claimant took two horses on board the ferry, which the defendant refused to carry. The claimant refused to take the horses off the ferry so the defendant took hold of them and led them off the ferry and onto the shore where the defendant's brother took charge of them. The claimant stayed on the ferry which took him to Liverpool where he sent for the horses. The horses were never returned to him. The claimant sued the defendant, claiming that in taking the horses off the ferry he had committed the tort of conversion. The court doubted whether this was true: when the defendant took the horses off the ferry, he had no intention of keeping them.

(2) *Refusal to hand over goods.* B had an immediate right to possess certain goods that were in A's possession and A refused to hand them over to B when he had no lawful justification or excuse for making such a refusal.[7]

For example, in *Howard E Perry* v *British Railways Board*,[8] the members of the Iron & Steel Trades Confederation went on strike. In order to support this strike, the employees of the British Railways Board (BRB) were instructed by their union – the National Union of Railwaymen (NUR) – not to assist in the transport of any steel. The claimants had some 500 tonnes of steel located at various depots owned by the BRB which the BRB could not transport because of the action of the NUR. The claimants asked the BRB if they could collect the steel themselves and transport it by road but the BRB refused because it feared that if it agreed it would be subjected to further industrial action by the NUR. The claimants sued the BRB, claiming that it had committed the tort of conversion in refusing to hand over the steel to them. The claimants succeeded in their claim: the BRB had no lawful justification or excuse for refusing to hand over the claimants' steel to the claimants.

It was different in *Clayton* v *Le Roy*.[9] In that case the claimant bought a watch

---

[5] See Lord Nicholls in *Kuwait Airways Corpn* v *Iraqi Airways Co. (Nos 4 & 5)* [2002] 2 AC 883, at [42]: 'To constitute conversion detention … must be accompanied by an intention to keep the goods.' So someone who picks up a wallet in the street will not commit the tort of conversion if he picks it up with the object of restoring it to its rightful owner: *Isaack* v *Clark* (1615) 2 Bulstr 306, 312, 80 ER 1143, 1148.

[6] (1841) 8 M & W 540, 151 ER 1153.

[7] *Marcq* v *Christie's* [2004] QB 286, at [33]. A couple of authorities may be interpreted as contradicting this. In *Miller* v *Jackson* [1977] QB 966, at 978, Lord Denning MR remarked that it is not conversion to refuse to give back a cricket ball that has been hit into your back garden. (Though, as we will see, it is if you pick the cricket ball up and give it to someone else or start playing with it.) However, this may be explained on the basis that if a cricket ball is hit into your back garden, you are legally entitled to refuse to give it back, so as to encourage people not to hit cricket balls onto your property. In *British Economical Lamp Co.* v *Empire Mile End (Limited)* (1913) 29 TLR 386, the claimants hired out some electrical lamps to the tenants of a theatre which was owned by the defendants. When the tenants moved out of the theatre, they left the lamps behind. At the end of the period for which the lamps had been hired out, the claimants demanded their lamps back from the defendants. The defendants refused to hand over the lamps or to allow the claimants to come onto their land to remove the lamps themselves. It was held that the defendants did not commit the tort of conversion in refusing to allow the claimants to get their lamps back. This case *is* very difficult to reconcile with the position taken here and we are forced to suggest that it was wrongly decided.

[8] [1980] 1 WLR 1375.

[9] [1911] 2 KB 1031.

from the defendant's shop. A few years later the watch was stolen. The claimant informed the defendant and asked him to keep an eye out for it. The watch went through a few people's hands before it was purchased by one B. B sent the watch to the defendant to be valued. The defendant recognised the watch as being the one which had been stolen from the claimant. He wrote to both the claimant and B informing them of the position and asking them what they wanted him to do. A few days later a representative of the claimant's solicitors went to the defendant's shop and demanded that he hand over the watch. The defendant refused. It was held that the defendant did not commit the tort of conversion in refusing to hand over the watch. He had been justified in acting as he did: '... a man does not act unlawfully in refusing to deliver up property immediately upon demand made. He is entitled to take adequate time to inquire into the rights of the claimant.'[10]

In order to show that A has committed the tort of conversion in relation to B under this head, it is essential to show that A *refused* to give B's property back to him. Merely showing that A failed to return B's property to him when he was supposed to is not enough. B must have demanded the property back and A must have refused to give it back or to allow B to get it back herself.[11]

(3) *Delivery into hands of third party.* B was in possession of certain goods, or had an immediate right to possess those goods, and A intentionally did something which resulted in their being delivered[12] into the hands of a third party when he had no lawful justification or excuse for doing so.

So, for example, Ian will commit the tort of conversion if he pledges[13] Ruth's property to Gary when he has no lawful justification or excuse for doing so.[14] Similarly, if B gives A some property to deliver to D and A gives it to C instead, A will normally be held to have committed the tort of conversion in relation to B.

In order to make out that A has converted B's property under this head it is not necessary to show that A *physically* handed over B's property to a third party – but it must be shown that a third party obtained possession of B's property as a result of something A did.

---

[10] Ibid., 1051 (per Fletcher Moulton LJ).

[11] *Barclays Mercantile Finance Ltd* v *Sibec Developments Ltd* [1992] 1 WLR 1253, 1258 (per Millett J); also *Kuwait Airways Corpn* v *Iraqi Airways Co.* (*Nos 4 & 5)* [2002] 2 AC 883, at [37] (per Lord Nicholls): '... mere unauthorised possession or detention is not an act of conversion. Demand and refusal to deliver up are required ...'

[12] It seems that for A to have committed the tort of conversion under this head, it is essential that his actions must have resulted in B's goods being *delivered* into the hands of a third party. So if A sells, or attempts to sell, B's goods to C, that will not *of itself* amount to conversion: it is only when the goods are actually handed over to C that the tort will have been committed. See, on this, *Lancashire Waggon Co.* v *Fitzhugh* (1861) 6 H & N 502, 158 ER 206; *Consolidated Company* v *Curtis & Son* [1892] 1 QB 495, 498; *Marcq* v *Christie's* [2004] QB 286, at [19]. *A fortiori*, if A goes about insisting that B's goods belong to A, that will not amount to conversion: see s 11(3) of the Torts (Interference with Goods) Act 1977 ('Denial of title is not of itself conversion').

[13] A will pledge B's property to C if he transfers possession of that property to C as security for a debt owed by A to C.

[14] Gary will also be held to have converted Ruth's property by accepting it as a pledge. See s 11(2) of the Torts (Interference with Goods) Act 1977, which provides that '[receipt] of goods by way of pledge is conversion if delivery of the goods is conversion'.

In *Ashby* v *Tolhurst*,[15] a thief stole the claimant's car from a private parking ground which was supervised by an attendant. It was claimed the attendant had committed the tort of conversion in allowing the thief to get away with the car. The claim was rejected. The thief did not obtain possession of the car as a result of anything the attendant did; all the attendant did was allow the thief to make good his escape once he had obtained possession of the claimant's car.

In contrast, in *Moorgate Mercantile Co. Ltd* v *Finch and Read*,[16] the hirer of a car under a hire purchase agreement lent his car to the defendant who, unknown to the hirer, used the car to smuggle watches into the country. When the defendant's activities were discovered, the car was forfeited and sold by the Customs and Excise authorities. The owners of the car argued that the defendant had committed the tort of conversion. The Court of Appeal agreed: Customs and Excise had obtained possession of the claimant's car as a result of what the defendant did – that is, smuggling watches in the claimant's car.

Similarly, in *R H Willis & Son* v *British Car Auctions Ltd*,[17] the claimants leased a car to one David Croucher under a hire purchase agreement under which he would become the owner of the car after making a certain number of hire payments. Before Croucher had made enough hire payments to become owner of the car, he took the car to the defendant firm of car auctioneers and asked them to auction it for him. The minimum he was willing to accept for the car was £450. Unfortunately, at auction, the highest bid was merely £400. The car was withdrawn but after the auction was over the auctioneers persuaded Croucher to sell the car to the highest bidder for £400 by agreeing to reduce their commission on the sale. The claimants sued the defendants, claiming that they had committed the tort of conversion in acting as they did. (Croucher was not worth suing as he was bankrupt.) The defendants were held liable: the Court of Appeal held that the claimants' car had been delivered into a third party's hands as a result of the actions of the defendants in reducing their commission on the sale.

(4) *Use.* B was in possession of certain goods, or had an immediate right to possess those goods, and A used those goods when he had no lawful justification or excuse for doing so.[18]

This has long been well acknowledged. As far back as 1591 it was observed: '[no] law compelleth him that finds a thing to keep it safely ... but if a man findeth a thing and useth it, he is answerable, for it is conversion.'[19] Rolle's *Abridgement* took the same view: '[if] a man takes my horse and rides it and then redelivers it to me nevertheless I may have an action against him, for this is a conversion ...'[20]

---

[15] [1937] 2 KB 242.
[16] [1962] 1 QB 701.
[17] [1978] 1 WLR 438.
[18] There seems to be an exception in the case where a bailee uses property which he holds on a bailment for another without denying the bailor's right to the return of the property: Murphy 2003, 57.
[19] *Mulgrave* v *Ogden* (1591) Cro Eliz 219, 78 ER 475.
[20] Rolle, *Abridgement*, Action sur Case, p 5.

(5) *Destruction*. B was in possession of certain goods, or had an immediate right to possess those goods, and A intentionally did something which resulted in those goods being destroyed.

In order to show that A has committed the tort of conversion under this head, it is necessary to show that A *destroyed* B's property – if A merely *damaged* the property, that is not enough. This can create difficulty because it is sometimes difficult to tell whether a given item of property has been damaged or destroyed. If a plank of wood is sawn in two that seems to be a case of damage rather than destruction.[21] But if a cask of wine is watered, that seems to be a case of destruction.[22]

(6) *Bailment*. A held goods as a bailee for B and A wrongfully allowed those goods to be lost or destroyed.[23]

Now that we have identified the six different ways in which the tort of conversion can be committed, three remaining issues need to be addressed.

First, what sort of things can be converted? We have been talking so far in terms of 'goods'. However, this is slightly misleading. There are some things that we would not normally think of as being 'goods' that can be converted; for example, cheques and body parts. So we need to clear up what sort of things can be converted. Secondly, we have already seen that – with the exception of the statutory form of conversion created by section 2(2) of the Torts (Interference with Goods) Act 1977 – A can only commit the tort of conversion in relation to B by interfering with an item of property that is either in B's *possession* or which B has an *immediate right to possess*. We need to explain what these terms mean. Thirdly, and finally, we need to explain when A will be able to claim that he has a lawful justification or excuse for acting in a way that would otherwise amount to conversion.

THINGS THAT MAY BE CONVERTED

Three points may be made under this heading.

First, things which are not items of property cannot be converted. For example, as a general rule, a corpse or part of a corpse does not count as an item of property.[24] So someone who removes a corpse from its grave does not commit the tort of conversion. A corpse or part of a corpse *will* count as an item of property if work has been done on it – either to alter it or to preserve it.[25] So if someone steals an Egyptian mummy from a museum, he will commit the tort of conversion. It is less clear what the position is in relation to tissues and body parts taken from living people. Presumably, if work has been done on tissue or a body part taken from a living person to alter it or preserve it then it will count

---

[21] *Simmons* v *Lillystone* (1853) 8 Ex 431, 155 ER 1417.
[22] *Richardson* v *Atkinson* (1723) 1 Stra 576, 93 ER 710.
[23] Torts (Interference with Goods) Act 1977, s 2(2).
[24] *Williams* v *Williams* (1882) 20 Ch D 659, 665.
[25] *Dobson* v *North Tyneside Health Authority* [1997] 1 WLR 596; *R* v *Kelly* [1999] QB 621. See, generally, Matthews 1983, 196–221.

as an item of property – just as would be the case if it had been taken from a dead person.[26]

Secondly, not all items of property are capable of being converted. Logically, only items of property that are capable of being possessed can be converted – if an item of property cannot be possessed then a claimant will not be able to establish that she possessed that item of property or had an immediate right to possess that item of property for the purpose of establishing that the tort of conversion has been committed in relation to her. So only items of property which have a 'corporeal' existence are capable of being converted. Intangible property which does not take a corporeal form – such as a copyright – cannot therefore be converted. But cheques, insurance policies and negotiable instruments can be converted – while they represent forms of intangible property, they take a corporeal form.

Thirdly, even though land is an item of property that can be possessed, land cannot be converted.

TITLE TO SUE

We have already seen that, in most cases, A can only commit the tort of conversion in relation to B if he interferes with an item of property[27] which is in B's *possession* or which B has an *immediate right to possess*. This raises two questions. First, when can we say that an item of property is in someone's possession? Secondly, when can we say that someone has an immediate right to possess an item of property?

Possession

Suppose that B wants to show that an item of property[28] was in her possession on 1 January 2005. To do this, she will have to show that she *acquired* possession of that item of property at some time before 1 January 2005 and *she* did not subsequently *lose* possession of that item in the intervening period between that time and 1 January 2005.[29] This definition raises two issues. First, when can we say

---

[26] For a wider view, see Matthews 1983, 221–9. In *Moore* v *Regents of University of California*, 271 Cal Rptr 146 (1990), the claimant argued that the defendant doctors at the UCLA Medical Center had committed the tort of conversion in using an enlarged spleen removed from the claimant's body to produce a cell-line which became the basis of a $3 billion dollar industry. The claim was dismissed. The decision can be explained on the basis that when the spleen was removed, it was not an item of property and was therefore not capable of being converted. After it was removed and worked on by the doctors at the UCLA Medical Center, it became an item of property, but at that point the claimant had no rights over the spleen which would entitle him to maintain an action for conversion against the doctors. Note that once the spleen became an item of property, the UCLA Medical Center – being in possession of the spleen – *would* have been entitled to bring a claim in conversion had someone stolen the spleen or cells taken from the spleen: ibid., at 168 (per Broussard J, dissenting). For a discussion of the decision in *Moore*'s case, see Harris 1986, 75–84.

[27] From now on, the term 'item of property' will *only* refer to an item of property that is capable of being converted.

[28] It should be remembered that we are *not* referring to land here. The question of when someone can claim to be in possession of a piece of land is dealt with in Chapter 17, below.

[29] Harris 1961, 73–4.

that someone has *acquired* possession of an item of property? Secondly, when can we say that someone has *lost* possession of an item of property?

Acquiring possession

B will acquire possession of an item of property if: (1) she takes control of that item of property with (2) the intention of preventing others from taking control of that item of property.

Someone will take control of an item of property if he takes as much control over that item of property as the nature of that item of property will admit. So, for example, in *Young* v *Hichens*,[30] the claimant was fishing for pilchards and had almost encircled a shoal of pilchards with his nets when the defendant rowed through a gap in the nets and prevented the claimant from capturing the pilchards. The claimant sued the defendant, claiming that he had been in possession of the pilchards and that the defendant had disturbed his possession of the pilchards. The claim was rejected: at no time did the claimant have the pilchards completely under his control.

In contrast, in *The Tubantia*,[31] the claimants attempted to salvage the cargo of a Dutch steamship which had been sunk in the First World War and lay under 100 feet of water. The claimants located the steamship in April 1922 and spent as many days exploring the ship and salvaging its cargo as the weather permitted until November 1922 when it became impracticable to continue exploring the ship during the winter. The claimants marked the location of the ship and returned in April 1923. They then spent about twenty-five days exploring the ship and salvaging the cargo until July 1923 when the defendants – encouraged by rumours that the ship had been carrying treasure at the time it was sunk – started to send divers down to the ship in an attempt to locate the treasure and take it for themselves. The claimants sued the defendants, claiming that they had possession of the ship and that the defendants were acting unlawfully in disrupting their possession of the ship. The claimants' claim was allowed: they had taken as much control over the Dutch steamship as the nature of the thing and its location allowed.

Someone who takes control of an item of property will not acquire possession of that item of property unless he intends, in taking control of that item of property, to prevent other people from taking control of that item of property. If he lacks this intention, he is said to have 'custody' of the item of property in question, not 'possession'. So, for example, if Sarah asks Fred to value a ring for her, when Sarah gives Fred the ring, Fred will acquire custody but not possession of the ring.[32] When Fred takes control of the ring to inspect it he does not intend, in taking control of the ring, to prevent other people from taking control of it. Again, it is often said that employees only have custody of their work tools – they do not possess their work tools. When an employee takes control of some tools that he has been given to work with, he does not intend, in taking control of those tools, to prevent other people from taking control of those tools.[33] Of

[30] *Young* v *Hichens* (1844) 6 QB 606, 115 ER 228.
[31] *The Tubantia* [1924] P 78.
[32] *Armory* v *Delamirie* (1721) 1 Stra 505, 93 ER 664.
[33] While this works to explain the rule that an employee only has custody of his work tools and does not possess them, the rule, it should be noted, has its origins in the definition of the now defunct

course, if an employee steals some work tools and takes them home he will acquire possession of those tools – he will have taken control of those tools with the intention of preventing other people from taking control of those tools.

Losing possession

If B has acquired possession of an item of property, B will lose possession of that item of property if: (*a*) someone else takes possession of that item of property; or (*b*) B intentionally abandons that item of property.

So B does *not* have to *retain control* of an item of property in order to retain possession of that item of property. For example, if Alan goes on holiday he retains possession of all the items of property in his house even though he does not have physical control over them while he is gone. Obviously, though, if someone breaks into Alan's house while he is gone and steals some items of property from Alan's house, Alan will lose possession of those items of property – someone else (the burglar) will have taken possession of those items of property. Again, suppose Alan employs Beth to perform some task for him and gives Beth the tools she will need to do the job. Alan will retain possession of the tools even after he has given them to Beth – and this is so even though Alan will not physically control the tools once he gives them to Beth. The reason why Alan will retain possession of the tools when he gives them to Beth is that when he gives the tools to Beth, Beth will merely acquire the custody of the tools: she will not possess them.

Immediate right to possess

Let us now answer the second of our two questions – When can we say that someone has an immediate right to possess an item of property? In order to answer this question, let us suppose that A is currently in possession of a watch. B will have an immediate right to possess the watch if she *currently* has a right to call on A to hand over possession of the watch to her. If she has no such right at the moment but will – other things being equal – acquire such a right in the future, that will not be enough: B will only have an immediate right to possess the watch if she *currently* has a right to call on A to hand over possession of the watch to her.

In *Gordon* v *Harper*,[34] the claimant leased a fully furnished flat to one B. B owed some money and the defendant sheriff – thinking that the furniture in the flat belonged to B – seized it and sold it in execution of the debt. The claimant sued the defendant in conversion. The claimant lost: he could not establish that at the time the defendant seized and sold the furniture in the

---

crime of larceny. Someone would commit the offence of larceny if he removed goods from the possession of their owner. Under this definition, an employee who had possession of his work tools would not commit the offence of larceny if he absconded with them – by definition, if he had possession of his work tools, he would not remove them from the possession of their owner (his employer) if he absconded with them. In order to ensure that employees who absconded with their employer's tools *did* commit the offence of larceny in so doing, the idea grew up that employees did not possess their work tools – they only had custody of them.

[34] (1796) 7 TR 9, 101 ER 828.

flat he had a right to call on B to hand over possession of the furniture to him. At the expiry of the lease, he would have acquired such a right but the lease had not expired at the time the defendant seized and sold the furniture in question. B, on the other hand, being in possession of the furniture at the time it was seized and sold, could have sued the defendant for selling the furniture.

Let's now look at a few categories of situations in which someone *may* have an immediate right to possess an item of property.

(1) *Theft*. If B is in possession of an item of property and A takes the property off B when he has no lawful justification or excuse for doing so, B will acquire an immediate right to possess that property. So, for example, suppose Carl found a watch in the street and then Ruth took the watch off Carl when she had no right to do so. In this case, Carl will acquire an immediate right to possession of the watch. But Carl will lose this right if the watch finds its way into the hands of its rightful owner; once this happens, Carl will obviously have no right to call on the rightful owner to hand over possession of the watch to him.

(2) *Stolen property*. Suppose that A was in possession of stolen goods and that those goods were seized by the police in pursuit of a criminal investigation.[35] Suppose further that the true owner of the goods is untraceable and and the police no longer have any statutory authority to retain those goods. In this situation, A will have an immediate right to possess the goods in question.[36] So if A demands that the police give him back the goods and the police refuse to do so, they will commit the tort of conversion.[37] It seems that this will be the case even if A actually stole the goods in question.[38]

(3) *Lost property*. If A has found an item of property on B's land which had been lost by a third party, B will have an immediate right to possess that item of property if: (*a*) A is B's employee and A found the item of property in question in the course of his employment;[39] *or* (*b*) A is a trespasser on B's land;[40] *or* (*c*) the item of property in question was buried on B's land;[41] *or* (*d*) B has 'manifested an intention to exercise control over his land and the things which may be upon it or in it'.[42] If none of (*a*)–(*d*) are made out, B will have no right to

---

[35] Section 19 of the Police and Criminal Evidence Act 1984 grants the police a statutory power to do this: see below, pp. 340–1.

[36] *Important note.* It must be emphasised that this will only be the case if the police remain in custody of the goods and the true owner of the goods cannot be traced. If the police have exercised a statutory power to transfer the stolen goods to a third party then A will no longer have any rights over the goods: *Buckley* v *Gross* (1863) 3 B & S 566. Similarly, if the stolen goods are still in the custody of the police, but the true owner can be identified, then A will have no right to demand that the goods be returned to him.

[37] *Costello* v *Chief Constable of Derbyshire Constabulary* [2001] 1 WLR 1437.

[38] Ibid., at [31].

[39] *City of London Corporation* v *Appleyard* [1963] 1 WLR 982; *Parker* v *British Airways Board* [1982] QB 1004, 1017G.

[40] *Hibbert* v *McKiernan* [1948] 2 KB 142; *Parker* v *British Airways Board* [1982] QB 1004, 1017E.

[41] *Waverley Borough Council* v *Fletcher* [1996] QB 334.

[42] *Parker* v *British Airways Board* [1982] QB 1004, 1018A–B.

possess the item of property found by A and A may keep it until, of course, the rightful owner turns up and claims the item of property in question.[43]

(4) *Bailment.* If A holds B's property as a bailee, B will have an immediate right to possess that property if the bailment on which A holds B's property is a bailment *at will* – that is, if B has reserved the right to reclaim her property from A at any time.

If A holds B's property on a fixed term bailment, B will normally only acquire a right to call on A to hand over possession of the property once the fixed term has elapsed. But if A misuses B's property before the term has elapsed, B may immediately acquire a right at that stage to call on A to hand over possession of the property. So, for example, suppose Eric rented out a car to Mary for six months. Two months later, Mary gave the car away to Ian. In such a case, Eric will probably be able to establish that when Mary gave the car away to Ian, Eric acquired an immediate right to possess the car. As a result, Eric will probably be able to establish that Mary and Ian both committed the tort of conversion in relation to Eric when Mary gave the car away to Ian and Ian took possession of the car.

(5) *Trusts.* Suppose A holds an item of property on trust for B. Will B have an immediate right to possess that item of property? If the property is held *solely* on trust for B then B will have a right – under the decision in *Saunders v Vautier*[44] – to call on A to hand over possession of the property to her.[45] One would have thought, then, that if A held the trust property solely on trust for B and then disposed of that property to C in breach of trust, B would be able to sue both A and C in conversion – and indeed one case held exactly that.

However, if the law *did* say this, then the rule in Equity that a *bona fide* purchaser of trust property disposed of in breach of trust cannot be sued for the value of that property[46] would be subverted.[47] A claim in conversion would lie against the *bona fide* purchaser. In order to prevent this happening, the Court of Appeal has ruled in *MCC Proceeds Inc.* v *Lehman Bros International (Europe)*[48] that if trust property which is held solely on trust for B is disposed of in breach of trust, a claim in conversion will *not* lie either against the trustee disposing of the property

---

[43] Of course, if A takes the property with the intention of keeping it for himself that will be conversion – A is only allowed to take the property if his intention in so doing is to restore it to its rightful owner: see above, p. 330.

[44] (1841) Cr & Ph 240, 41 ER 482.

[45] If A holds the property on trust for B and C, then B will only acquire a right to demand that A hand over the property to her if C agrees that she can do so. So B will not have an *immediate* right to demand possesion of the property.

[46] See *Pilcher* v *Rawlins* (1872) LR 7 Ch App 259.

[47] Though Tettenborn 1996 questions whether this is true (at 40–1). He argues that the real reason for maintaining that the beneficiary under a trust cannot bring a claim for conversion when the property is misappropriated is that to allow such a claim would expand the liabilities of: (*a*) innocent donees of trust property; (*b*) people who innocently assist a trustee to dispose of trust property; *and* (*c*) trustees who innocently commit a breach of trust by disposing of trust property to another.

[48] [1998] 4 All ER 675, distinguishing *International Factors* v *Rodriguez* [1979] 1 QB 751.

or the recipient of the property. While B might have an immediate right to possess the trust property, that right, being *equitable* in nature, is not sufficient to allow B to bring a claim in conversion. What has to be established is that B had an immediate right to posses the trust property *under the common law* – and this B cannot do, as she merely had an equitable interest in the trust property.

LAWFUL JUSTIFICATION OR EXCUSE

Let us now turn to the question of when someone will have a lawful justification or excuse for doing something that would otherwise amount to conversion. Such lawful justification or excuse will exist in the following situations.

Consent

Obviously, if B consents to A's interfering with an item of property which is in her possession or which she has an immediate right to possess, then A will have a lawful justification or excuse for doing so. So John will not commit the tort of conversion if he rides Karen's horse with her consent. Similarly, Wendy will not commit the tort of conversion if she takes some goods off the shelves of Ian's supermarket and puts them in her shopping basket (though she probably will if she puts them in her pocket).

The Animals Act 1971

The Animals Act 1971 authorises the occupier of land in certain cases to detain or destroy animals which trespass on his land. For example, s 7(2) of the 1971 Act provides that 'Where any livestock strays on to any land and is not then under the control of any person the occupier of the land may detain it.' Section 7(4) provides that 'Where livestock has been detained in pursuance of this section for a period of not less than fourteen days the person detaining it may sell it at a market or by public auction, unless proceedings are then pending for the return of the livestock . . .'

Section 9(1)(a) of the 1971 Act provides that in any civil proceedings against a person for killing or causing injury to a dog it shall be a defence to prove 'that the defendant acted for the protection of any livestock [on his land][49] and was a person entitled to act for the protection of that livestock'. A defendant who has killed or injured a dog 'shall be deemed . . . to [have acted] for the protection of any livestock [on his land] if, and only if, either – (a) the dog [was] worrying or [was] about to worry the livestock and there [were] no other reasonable means of ending or preventing the worrying; or (b) the dog [had been] worrying livestock, [had] not left the vicinity and [was] not under the control of any person and there [were] no practicable means of ascertaining to whom it belongs'[50] or (c) the defendant reasonably believed (a) or (b) were true.[51]

---

[49] Animals Act 1971, s 9(2).
[50] Section 9(3).
[51] Section 9(4).

Distress damage feasant

If an inanimate item of property of B's is on A's land without permission and is causing damage to A's land or disrupting the operation of A's business on that land, A will be allowed: (*a*) to take steps to move that item of property so that it no longer causes any damage or disruption, and then (*b*) to detain it until B fairly compensates him for the damage or disruption caused by the presence of that item of property on his land.[52] This remedy is known as 'distress damage feasant'.[53]

Recaption

If B is in possession of an item of property that rightly belongs to A, then A may be allowed to seize the item of property in question and take it into his possession.

This will be the case for example if Vijay steals Lara's goods and Lara arrests him while they are still on his person – Lara will be entitled to seize the goods and take them into her possession.[54] What if a watch that rightly belongs to Lara is on Vijay's land? When will Lara be allowed to go onto Vijay's land and seize the watch and take it into her possession? The position is unclear. If Vijay stole the watch from Lara, Lara will be allowed to go onto Vijay's land and reclaim it.[55] But where Vijay came by the watch innocently, the position is far more uncertain. In *Anthony* v *Haney*,[56] Tindal CJ suggested in some *obiter dicta* that if, in the situation we are considering, the watch came to end up on Vijay's land without any wrongdoing on his part, Lara will only be entitled to go onto Vijay's land and reclaim the watch if: (*a*) the watch ended up on Vijay's land by accident; *or* (*b*) someone stole the watch from Lara; or (*c*) Lara has already asked Vijay to return the watch to her and Vijay has wrongfully refused to comply with that demand.

The Police and Criminal Evidence Act 1984

Under s 19 of the Police and Criminal Evidence Act 1984, any constable who is lawfully on any premises[57] 'may seize anything which is on the premises if he has reasonable grounds for believing – (a) that it has been obtained in consequence of the commission of an offence; and (b) that it is necessary to seize it in order to prevent it being concealed, lost, damaged or destroyed'.[58] Moreover,

---

[52] See, for example, *The Ambergate, Nottingham and Boston and Eastern Junction Railway Company* v *The Midland Railway Company* (1853) 2 E & B 793, 118 ER 964.

[53] The remedy of distress damage feasant also used to be available when an animal of B's strayed onto A's land and caused damage or destruction: see, for example, *Sorrell* v *Paget* [1950] 1 KB 252. But s 7(1) of the Animals Act 1971 provided that the 'right to seize any animal by way of distress damage feasant is hereby abolished'.

[54] *Whatford* v *Carty*, The Times, 29 October 1960.

[55] *Patrick* v *Colerick* (1838) 3 M & W 483, 150 ER 1235.

[56] (1832) 8 Bing 186, 131 ER 372.

[57] Section 19(1).

[58] Section 19(2).

a constable who is lawfully on any premises may also 'seize anything which is on the premises if he has reasonable grounds for believing – (a) that it is evidence in relation to an offence which he is investigating or any other offence; and (b) that it is necessary to seize it in order to prevent it being concealed, lost, damaged or destroyed.'[59]

Returning goods

If A has B's goods and B has an immediate right to possess those goods, A will of course do no wrong if he returns the goods to B. What if A gives the goods to a third party, C, with instructions to return them to B? A will be allowed to do this so long as it is *reasonable* to give the goods to C for the purpose of returning them to B.

In *Elvin & Powell Ltd* v *Plummer Roddis Ltd*,[60] a conman approached the claimants – a firm of coat makers – and ordered about £350 worth of coats, asking them to be delivered to the defendants' shop. The coats were sent and the conman sent a telegram to the defendants in the claimant company's name, saying 'Goods despatched to your branch in error. Sending van to collect.' When the coats arrived at the defendants' shop, the conman turned up in a van and took the coats from them. He then disappeared. The claimants sued the defendants, claiming that they had committed the tort of conversion in handing the coats over to the conman. The claim was rejected – the defendants had only handed the coats to the conman because they wanted to return them to the claimants and it had been reasonable for them to hand the coats over to the conman for the purpose of returning them to the claimants.

This defence was not available to the defendants in *Hiort* v *Bott*.[61] In that case, the claimants mistakenly sent the defendants an invoice for barley together with a delivery order. The defendants had not in fact ordered any barley from the claimants but the invoice stated that the defendants had ordered the barley through one G. The defendants got in touch with G. He said there had been a mistake and asked them to endorse the delivery order to him so that he could have the barley delivered to the customer who actually ordered it. This the defendants did. G then used the delivery order to obtain the barley himself and absconded with it. The claimants sued the defendants, claiming that the defendants, in endorsing the delivery order, had committed the tort of conversion. The court agreed: the defendants had delivered the barley into G's hands without the claimants' consent and they had no lawful justification or excuse for doing so. They could not argue that they had delivered the barley into G's hands in order to return it to the claimants as the barley was already in the claimants' hands at the time they signed the delivery order.

---

[59] Section 19(3).
[60] (1934) 50 TLR 158.
[61] (1874) LR 9 Ex 86.

The principle in *Hollins* v *Fowler*

In *Hollins* v *Fowler*, Blackburn J argued:

> I cannot find it anywhere distinctly laid down, but I submit to your Lordships that on principle, one who deals with goods at the request of the person who has the actual custody of them, in the bona fide belief that the custodier is the true owner, or has the authority of the true owner, should be excused for what he does if the act is of such a nature as would be excused if done by the authority of the person in possession ... Thus a warehouseman with whom goods had been deposited is guilty of no conversion by keeping them, or restoring them to the person who deposited them with him, though that person turns out to have had no authority from the true owner.[62]

So if Carl steals Lara's dog and, pretending to Ruth that the dog is his, asks Ruth to look after it over the weekend, Ruth will not commit the tort of conversion in relation to Lara if she gives the dog back to Carl at the end of the weekend.[63] Again, suppose Fred steals Gary's painting and, pretending that the painting is his, hands it over to Sarah so that she can find a buyer for it. If Sarah cannot find a buyer and hands the painting back to Fred, she will not commit the tort of conversion in relation to Gary in so doing.[64]

Common currency

In the interests of ensuring the smooth running of the economy, the law provides that someone who accepts stolen money paid over to him as common currency will not be liable for conversion: 'Conversion does not lie for money, taken and received as currency ...'.[65] So if Tom steals some money out of Mary's wallet he will commit the tort of conversion. But if Tom takes that money and uses it to pay for some goods in Paul's store using that money, Paul will not commit the tort of conversion in accepting that money.

---

[62] (1875) LR 7 HL 757, 766–7.

[63] What would be the position if Carl instructed Ruth at the end of the weekend to give the dog to Tom? Would Ruth commit the tort of conversion in relation to Lara if she handed the dog over to Tom? The Privy Council's decision in *Maynegrain Pty Ltd* v *Compafina Bank* (1984) 58 ALJR 389 could be read as suggesting that the answer is 'no'. However, that case may rest on technicalities of the law of agency which do not apply in Ruth's case. For further discussion, see W&J, 614.

[64] *Marcq* v *Christie's* [2004] QB 286. However, if Sarah had found a buyer for the painting, and sold and delivered it to Mary, that would be conversion: W&J, 615.

[65] *Lipkin Gorman* v *Karpnale Ltd* [1991] 2 AC 548, 559 (per Lord Templeman). For similar reasons, the law provides that a bank that accepts a stolen cheque will not be liable in conversion so long as it acted in good faith and without negligence in accepting the cheque: Cheques Act 1957, s 4.

16

TRESPASS TO GOODS

A will have committed the tort of trespass to goods in relation to B if: (*a*) he directly interfered with goods in B's possession; (*b*) he did so intentionally or carelessly;[1] *and* (*c*) he had no lawful justification or excuse for acting as he did. Only three points need to be made about this tort.

(1) *The requirement of direct interference*. It is easier to provide illustrations of situations in which someone's goods[2] will be directly interfered with than it is to define what directly interfering with someone's goods involves. So if Paul beats Ruth's cat, he will directly interfere with it;[3] but he will not if he kills Ruth's cat by laying down some poison which Ruth's cat eats. Ian will directly interfere with Mary's car if he places a wheel clamp on it;[4] but he will not if he finds Wendy's car on his land and he locks the gates to his land so that Wendy's car cannot be driven off his land.[5] If Lara gets on Eric's horse and rides away on it, she will directly interfere with the horse; but she will not if her dog escapes her control, runs up to Eric's horse and makes it run away by barking at it.

(2) *Lawful justification or excuse*. Suppose A has directly interfered with B's goods. Not much needs to be said on the issue of when A will be able to establish that he had a lawful justification or excuse for interfering with B's goods. The previous chapter on the tort of conversion will have given the reader a good idea as to the sort of situations in which such a lawful justification or excuse will exist. Only a couple of cases which deal with this issue need be mentioned here.

In *Arthur* v *Anker*,[6] the defendants wheel-clamped the claimants' cars, which were parked at the time in a private car park without the permission of the

---

[1] This seems to follow from *Fowler* v *Lanning* [1959] 1 QB 426. See *National Coal Board* v *J E Evans & Co. (Cardiff) Ltd* [1951] 2 KB 861, where the defendant contractors struck an underground cable belonging to the claimants when digging a trench on land belonging to the local county council. The claimants sued the defendants, claiming that they had committed the tort of trespass to goods in damaging the cable. Held: no trespass, even though the defendants had directly interfered with the claimants' cable – they had not intended to damage the cable and had not carelessly damaged the cable as they did not know and had no reason to know it was under the land on which they were digging.

[2] For the sake of convenience, in this chapter when goods are referred to as 'someone's goods' or some equivalent expression is used, what is meant is *not* that those goods belong to that someone but that that someone is in possession of those goods.

[3] *Slater* v *Swann* (1730) 2 Stra 872, 93 ER 906.

[4] *Arthur* v *Anker* [1997] QB 564; *Vine* v *Waltham Forest LBC* [2000] 1 WLR 2383.

[5] *Hartley* v *Moxham* (1842) 3 QB 701, 114 ER 675.

[6] [1997] QB 564.

occupiers of the car park. The claimants sued the defendants, claiming that they had committed the tort of trespass to goods in clamping the claimants' cars. The claimants' claims were rejected: the defendants had had a lawful justification or excuse for clamping the claimants' cars. The claimants knew when they parked their cars in the car park without permission that there was a risk that their cars would be clamped: there were very visible signs in the car park warning that cars that were not authorised to park in the car park would be clamped. So the claimants voluntarily took the risk that their cars would be clamped. As a result, the defendants had a lawful justification or excuse for clamping the claimants' cars.

It was different in *Vine* v *London Borough of Waltham Forest*.[7] In that case the claimant was driving her car along the road when she suddenly felt extremely ill. She pulled off the road, got out of the car and after she had walked a little way she was violently sick. After a few minutes she felt better and returned to her car only to find it had been clamped – she had parked in a parking space reserved for employees of Railtrack. The defendants were responsible for her car being clamped. The claimant sued them, claiming that they had committed the tort of trespass to goods in clamping her car.

The claimant succeeded in her claim. An attempt to justify the clamping on the ground that the claimant had voluntarily taken the risk that her car would be clamped failed: the claimant had not seen the sign which warned that her car was liable to be clamped if she parked where she did; it had been obscured by another car which had been parked nearby. What would have been the position if the claimant had seen the sign? In such a case, it would still have been difficult to establish that the claimant *voluntarily* took the risk that her car might be clamped given that the claimant only parked where she did because she was in great distress and needed to be sick. Given this, it is submitted that the claimant's claim should still have succeeded even if she saw the sign warning that cars parked where her car was would be clamped. These two cases raise a few issues which we will now deal with.

First, in *Arthur* v *Anker*, Sir Thomas Bingham MR suggested that a wheel clamping firm would not be able to justify or excuse its clamping someone's car if it charged an exorbitant price for releasing the car.[8] This seems too strong. Suppose Dawn parked her car in a private car park, knowing that she had no authorisation to park there. Suppose further that the car park had very visible signs warning that 'Unauthorised vehicles will be clamped and may be towed away' and Dawn saw these signs. Suppose finally that John, someone who works for a wheel clamping firm, clamped Dawn's car and charged her an exorbitant amount of money – say £2,000 – to release it. In such a case, John will *not* be able to excuse or justify his clamping Dawn's car. When Dawn parked her car, she did not expect that if her car were clamped she would have to pay £2,000 to release it – so it will not be possible to argue

[7] [2000] 1 WLR 2383.
[8] [1997] QB 564, 573C.

that Dawn voluntarily took the risk that her car would be detained until she produced £2,000 to release it.

But suppose that the signs in the car park warned that 'Unauthorised vehicles will be clamped and may be towed away – a fee of £2,000 will be charged for their release'. If this was the case, it *will* be possible to argue that when Dawn parked her car, she voluntarily took the risk that it would be detained until she produced £2,000 to release it. Given this, it *will* be possible to argue that John committed no trespass to Dawn's car in clamping it and charging Dawn £2,000 for its release. On the other hand, it might be argued that when Dawn saw the signs she did not seriously think that if her car were clamped she would *actually* be charged £2,000 to get her car back. In other words, it might be argued that Dawn thought that the warning that owners of clamped cars would be charged £2,000 for their release was for 'show' only, to deter people from parking in the car park without authorisation. If this were the case, it would be harder to establish, in the case we are considering, that Dawn voluntarily took the risk that her car would be clamped until she found £2,000 to release it.

Secondly, what is the position if Dawn parks her car in a particular place and, due to carelessness or stupidity, Dawn does not see the clearly visible signs nearby that warn that parking in the place where Dawn has parked is not permitted and cars parking in the place where Dawn has parked may be clamped and towed away? If John clamps Dawn's car will he be able to establish that he had a lawful justification or excuse for clamping her car? On the facts as we have presented them, it is hard to argue that Dawn voluntarily took the risk that her car would be clamped – as Dawn did not see the signs warning her that her car was liable to be clamped, she did not know she was taking a risk that his car might be clamped.

It might be thought that if, in this case, John's clamping Dawn's car will amount to a trespass to the car, then someone whose car had been clamped would find it very easy to establish that the clamping amounted to a trespass to his car: he could simply claim that he did not see any signs warning him that his car was liable to be clamped if it were parked where it was. However, he would find it hard to convince a court that he did *not* see any such signs if such signs were clearly visible in the area where he parked the car. As Roch LJ remarked in the *Vine* case: '[to] show that the car owner consented to or willingly assumed the risk of his car being clamped, it has to be established that the car owner was aware of the consequences of parking his car . . . That will be done by establishing that the car owner saw and understood the significance of a warning notice or notices that cars in that place without permission were liable to be clamped. *Normally* the presence of notices which are posted where they are bound to be seen . . . will lead to a finding that the car driver had knowledge of and appreciated the warning.'[9]

Thirdly, if John clamps Dawn's car and the clamping amounts to a trespass to Dawn's car, Dawn will be entitled to take reasonable steps to release her car from the clamp. However, if John proposes to charge Dawn a reasonable sum to release the clamp, Dawn will act unreasonably if, instead of paying the sum demanded and getting her car back that way, she releases her car from the

---

[9] *Vine* v *Waltham Forest LBC* [2000] 1 WLR 2383, 2390 (emphasis added).

clamp by breaking it.[10] So if John proposes to charge Dawn a reasonable sum to release the clamp, Dawn will not be entitled to break the clamp on her car and will commit the tort of trespass to goods *herself* if she does break the clamp on the car. But if John makes it clear that he will only release the car if Dawn pays him an exorbitant sum of money, then it might be reasonable for Dawn to break the clamp so as to free his car from the unlawful clamping – and if this is the case, Dawn will commit no trespass if he breaks the clamp.

(3) *The requirement of possession.* As we have said, A will commit the tort of trespass to goods in relation to B if he directly interferes with goods in B's *possession* when he has no lawful justification or excuse for doing so. But it is not always necessary for B to show that goods that have been interfered with were in her possession before she can sue for a trespass to them.

First, if B held goods on trust for C and C was in possession of them at the time A, without lawful justification or excuse, directly interfered with them, A will have committed the tort of trespass to goods in relation to B as well as C.[11]

Secondly, if A, without lawful justification or excuse, directly interfered with a deceased's goods, A will have committed the tort of trespass to goods in relation to the deceased's executors or administrators even if they had not taken possession of the goods at the time A interfered with them.[12]

Thirdly, if B is the owner of a franchise (as will be the case, for example, if B has the right to the goods on a shipwreck), A will commit the tort of trespass to goods in relation to B if he, without lawful justification or excuse, directly interferes with the goods covered by that franchise – and this is so even if B has not yet taken possession of those goods.[13]

[10] *Lloyd* v *DPP* [1992] 1 All ER 982, 992c–e.
[11] *White* v *Morris* (1852) 11 CB 1015, 138 ER 778; *Barker* v *Furlong* [1891] 2 Ch 172.
[12] *Tharpe* v *Stallwood* (1843) 5 M & G 760, 134 ER 766.
[13] *Bailiffs of Dunwich* v *Sterry* (1831) 1 B & Ad 831, 109 ER 995.

17

TRESPASS TO LAND

DEFINITION

A will commit the tort of trespass to land in relation to B if he crosses the boundary of B's land[1] when he has no lawful justification or excuse for doing so. A will also commit the tort of trespass to land in relation to B if he directly causes some object or matter to pass onto B's land when he has no lawful justification or excuse for doing so.

THE MENTAL ELEMENT REQUIRED TO COMMIT THE TORT

Suppose A at some time crossed the boundary of B's land. In order to establish that A committed the tort of trespass to land in so doing, B does *not* have to prove: (*a*) that when A crossed the boundary he intended to trespass on B's land; *or* (*b*) that when A crossed the boundary, he knew or ought to have known that there was a risk he would trespass on B's land. Indeed, A will have committed the tort of trespass to land in relation to B even if, when he crossed the boundary of B's land, he honestly believed that he was remaining on land where he was permitted to be. An honest mistake by A is not a defence to the tort of trespass to land.

The paragraph above discusses what state of mind A must have in order to commit the tort of trespass to land. It is important to distinguish this from the separate question of what state of mind A must be shown to have in order to make him liable to pay compensation for all the *consequences* of a trespass. The tort of trespass to land is actionable *per se*, which means that it is actionable regardless of whether B suffers any consequential damage.[2] This means that A does not have to anticipate any consequential damage in order to commit the tort. But where the tort does lead to consequential damage A's state of mind *will* be relevant to whether A is held liable for that damage.

For instance, suppose that Ruth parked her car in John's car park without John's permission. Suppose further that whilst the car was parked there, the car – without any fault on Ruth's part – burst into flames and damaged the car park. On such facts, it is obvious that Ruth committed the tort of trespass to land, but this does not mean that Ruth will be held liable for all the *consequences*

---

[1] The degree of connection that has to be established between B and the land necessary before B can sue A for trespassing on it cannot be simply summarised and will be discussed in detail below, pp. 350–2.

[2] See below, pp. 663–4.

of her trespass. It is a matter of dispute what rule will be applied to determine whether Ruth is liable for the fire damage done to John's car park. On one view, Ruth will only be held liable if she intended the car to burst into flames or it was reasonably foreseeable that it would burst into flames when she parked it in the cark park.[3] On another view, Ruth will be held liable for the fire damage done to John's car park even if it was unintended and unforeseeable *if* it was a direct result of Ruth's trespass and Ruth knew when she parked in John's car park that she did not have his permission to park there.[4] Whichever view one takes, it is clear that whether Ruth will be held liable for the fire damage done to John's car park will depend a great deal on what her state of mind was when she parked her car in John's car park. But her state of mind at the time she parked her car is *not* relevant to the issue of whether she committed the tort of trespass to land in relation to John when she parked her car.

THE DEGREE OF CONTROL REQUIRED TO COMMIT THE TORT

Suppose again that A at some time crossed the boundary of B's land. A will only have committed the tort of trespass to land in relation to B when he crossed the boundary of B's land if he was in control of his own body when he crossed the boundary. In *Smith* v *Stone*,[5] the defendant pleaded that he had been carried across the boundary of the claimant's land by the force and violence of others. Roll J held that this meant that the defendant had *not* committed the tort of trespass to land in relation to the claimant. The same judge later held that the defendant would have been liable if he had crossed the boundary under duress.[6] It might be different, however, if a threat caused A to leap across the boundary of B's land in an instinctive panic.[7]

With regard to the case where A has caused some object or matter to pass onto B's land, a distinction is drawn between crossings which are *direct* (and thus within the scope of the tort) and those which are *indirect* consequences of

---

[3] This is the normal rule that is applied to determine the extent of a defendant's liability when he or she has committed a non-intentional tort (that is, a tort which can be committed non-intentionally): see below, pp. 557–60.

[4] This was the view preferred by the New Zealand Court of Appeal in *Mayfair Ltd* v *Pears* [1987] 1 NZLR 459, from which our hypothetical example is drawn. (The court went on to find that the fire damage caused by the car bursting into flames in that case was *not* a *direct* result of the defendant's parking his car in the claimant's building so it held that – in the absence of proof that the car's bursting into flames was intended or reasonably foreseeable at the time the defendant parked his car – the defendant could not be held liable for the fire damage suffered by the claimant.) Some support for the New Zealand Court of Appeal's approach comes from Lord Nicholls's judgment in *Kuwait Airways Corpn* v *Iraqi Airways Co. (Nos 4 & 5)* [2002] 2 AC 883. Lord Nicholls suggested that while the normal rule is that someone who converts another's goods should only be liable for the reasonably foreseeable consequences of his conversion, if A knowingly converts B's goods, A should be held liable for *all* the losses suffered by B that were a direct consequence of A's conversion: ibid, at [103]-[104]. There is no reason to think that he would apply a different rule if A knowingly trespassed on B's land.

[5] (1647) Style 65, 82 ER 533.

[6] *Gilbert* v *Stone* (1647) Style 72, 82 ER 539.

[7] *Braithwaite* v *South Durham Steel Co. Ltd* [1958] 1 WLR 986.

A's behaviour (and thus outside the tort) in accordance with the extent to which A's behaviour can be said to have controlled the crossing by the object or matter. Thus where A has thrown or fired an object across the boundary of B's land A will have committed trespass to land in relation to B. But where A has released some substance into the atmosphere which has then emanated across the boundary of B's land (for instance, the case where A's operations release acid fumes which then drift on the breeze across the boundary of B's land) A will not have committed trespass to land, though B will still gain redress if he can establish that A committed the tort of private nuisance in acting as he did.[8] The distinction between crossings which are *direct* and those which are *indirect* consequences is *not* the same as the distinction between crossings which are *intentional* and those which are *unintended*. In some circumstances the connection between A's voluntary behaviour and the unintended crossing of an object onto B's land will be so close that A will be unable to deny that he had a sufficient degree of control. For instance, if Brian hits golf balls towards Chloe's land with the intention that they should land and stop just before the boundary then he is likely to be unable to claim that any ball which crosses was beyond his control. The outcome might be different, however, if Brian is an excellent golfer who uncharacteristically slices a golf ball off a golf course and onto Chloe's land.

A landowner is not generally treated as having sufficient control over things on his land so as to make him liable for trespass if they cross onto B's land as a result of ordinary natural processes. Thus where the roots or branches of a tree on A's land gradually grow so that they cross onto B's land no trespass will be committed but A may be guilty of committing the tort of private nuisance by encroachment.[9]

The law on when A will commit a trespass to land in relation to B if his animals cross over onto B's land is complicated. The possessor of livestock which strays onto another's land is strictly liable for damage done by that livestock to the land or that other's property which is on the land.[10] But this liability, although it is the statutory replacement for the common law wrong known as 'cattle trespass',[11] is best understood as part of the law relating to the keeping of dangerous things[12] rather than part of the law on when someone will commit the tort of trespass to land. The Animals Act 1971 also makes the keepers of dangerous animals liable for the damage that they cause[13] and consequently in such cases it is not usually necessary to determine whether the keeper is liable for having committed trespass to land through the animal.

In *Buckle* v *Holmes*,[14] the Court of Appeal held that where an animal did not fall within either the class of dangerous animals or the class of livestock, and was of a

---

[8] For the tort of private nuisance, see below, Chapter 18.
[9] *Lemmon* v *Webb* [1895] AC 1. See below, p. 358.
[10] Animals Act 1971, s 4.
[11] Section 1(1)(c).
[12] See below, Chapter 44.
[13] Section 2.
[14] [1926] 2 KB 125. (The defendant's cat strayed onto the claimant's property and killed the claimant's pigeons and poultry.) In *Tutton* v *A D Walter Ltd* [1986] QB 61 the judge refused to treat unwanted straying bees as trespassers for the purpose of deciding whether a landowner owed their owner a duty to take care not to harm them. Suppose Tom, a beekeeper, released bees which

class not generally confined and unlikely to cause substantial damage on straying, such as dogs and cats, the owner of the animal would not commit the tort of trespass to land if the animal strayed onto someone else's land. But whilst this rule clearly applies to a dog or cat acting of its own volition, equally clearly it would be a tort for A to *send* an animal onto B's land. In *League Against Cruel Sports* v *Scott*,[15] Park J held that the master of a hunt would be liable for trespass to land if 'he either intended that the hounds should enter the land or by negligence he failed to prevent them from doing so'.[16] In so far as this makes a huntsman liable for *sending* hounds onto another's land it is uncontroversial. But the suggestion that a huntsman is liable in trespass for negligently allowing hounds to stray is not easy to reconcile with *Buckle* v *Holmes*.[17] Our view is that an owner of a pet dog will not commit the tort of trespass to land if he negligently fails to prevent it from straying onto someone else's land,[18] but that Park J was correct to state that if such straying frequently happened and the owner was apparently indifferent to it, this might give rise to an inference that the owner intended the dog to cross the boundary.[19]

TITLE TO SUE

B will be able to sue someone for trespassing on a particular piece of land if she was in *possession* of the land at the time of the alleged trespass.[20] But it is important to note that possession of land is a legal concept, and is not synonymous with physical occupation. Thus squatters may be in physical occupation but will not gain possession of the land unless the owner in some way acquiesces to their presence.[21] Whether a licensee (someone with permission to be on land but not with an interest in the land) is treated as being in possession for the purposes of suing a third party for trespass[22] depends on the terms of the

---

strayed onto Lara's land and Tom knew they were likely to do this when he released the bees. Will Tom have committed the tort of trespass to land in relation to Lara? The doctrine expounded in *Buckle* v *Holmes* indicates that the answer is 'no'. We think it *would* be trespass to land, however, to put bees through Lara's letterbox, or otherwise send them onto Lara's property.

[15] [1986] QB 240.

[16] Ibid, 251H–252A. A difficult case would arise if a master of hunting dogs negligently lost control of the dogs but they then strayed to a place that he would not have expected them to go. In such a case it would be difficult to argue that the crossing of the other's boundary was a sufficiently *direct* consequence of the master's behaviour to constitute trespass to land by the master.

[17] One possibility is that a huntsman is considered to be sufficiently in control of the crossing by the straying pack of hounds because he *sent* the pack *close to* the boundary.

[18] The owner might, however, be liable for any consequential damage, in the tort of negligence, or under Animals Act 1971, ss 2, 3 or 8.

[19] *League Against Cruel Sports* v *Scott* [1986] QB 240, 252E–F.

[20] An oddity which is worth a footnote is the fact that the holders of certain rights over land known as *profits à prendre* can also sue for trespass to land. Thus a holder of a right to herbage, a liberty of hunting or a fishery can sue for a trespass to the land which damages the right. This rule has been applied in a modern context to hold that the company which 'owned' a genetically-modified crop being grown on another's land was entitled to sue third parties for trespass to land: *Monsanto* v *Tilly* [2000] Env LR 313. By contrast, a person entitled to an easement, such as a right of way, will *not* be able to claim that A committed the tort of trespass to land in relation to her if A interfered with that right; but she may be able to claim that A committed the tort of private nuisance in relation to her in so acting: see below, p. 358.

[21] *McPhail* v *Persons, Names Unknown* [1973] Ch 447.

[22] Where the licensor throws the licensee off the land, or tries to do so, the question is generally whether the licensee has become a trespasser (after failing to leave) and not whether the licensee

licence.[23] A person who was in possession before being ousted by the alleged trespasser can also sue.[24] Similarly, a person with a right to immediate possession can seek a summary remedy to obtain possession.[25] Such a claim is the modern equivalent of an old form of trespass action.[26] Further, when a person with a right to immediate possession enters into possession that person is treated as having been in possession for the whole time that he has had the right to enter and can claim damages from the time that he had the right to enter.[27]

Where land is held on a lease it is the tenant who is in possession and can sue for trespass. But a reversioner can also sue for trespass to land where there is: (*a*) damage to the property which the reversioner will in time gain the right to possess; or (*b*) injury of such a permanent nature as to be necessarily prejudicial to the reversion.[28] The right of a reversioner to bring an immediate action is useful because the reversioner might be more willing to take the risks of litigation than a tenant with a time-limited interest and there are occasions when it is desirable for a claim in trespass to be brought sooner rather than later. This will be the case where a trespass to land has caused damage to the land and it is desirable to have the damage repaired now rather than later, when the reversioner has obtained possession. This will also be the case where there is a continuing trespass to land: if a trespass were allowed to continue for many years before the reversioner could gain possession and could bring an action, the courts might at that stage become unwilling to grant an injunction and bring the trespass to an end.

Where B is in possession of land, A cannot successfully defend an action for trespass to land on the basis that someone else has a title superior to B's,[29]

---

can sue *for* trespass to land. The question often arises where the licensee sues for a trespass to the person committed in throwing him off the land and the licensor relies on the justification of using reasonable force to expel a trespasser. For when a licensee becomes a trespasser, see below, p. 353.

[23] In *Hill* v *Tupper* (1863) 2 H & C 121, 159 ER 51 the claimant was granted the 'sole and exclusive right or liberty' to put pleasure boats on the Basingstoke Canal, but this was held to be insufficient. By contrast in *Manchester Airport plc* v *Dutton* [2000] QB 133, the claimant was granted the right to enter and occupy the land concerned and this was held to be sufficient to allow it to obtain an order for possession against third parties who were squatting, partly on the basis that if the claimant had already entered under such a licence then it would have had sufficient possession to seek such an order. This strongly suggests that the claimant, although a licensee, would have had sufficient possession to sue for trespass. *Manchester Airport plc* v *Dutton* [2000] QB 133 was distinguished in *Countryside Residential (North Thames) Ltd* v *Tugwell* [2000] 34 EG 87, where a claimant seeking an order for possession against protesters who were camping on the site only had a licence to enter and carry out investigatory work and not one which granted 'effective control over the land'.

[24] Indeed, where one co-owner ousts the other the ousted co-owner can sue for trespass: *Murray* v *Hall* (1849) 7 CB 441, 137 ER 175.

[25] Civil Procedure Rules Part 55, III (Interim possession orders). Such orders are not available against a tenant 'holding over' after the expiration of the lease.

[26] This old form of action was known as ejectment, or, at an earlier stage, trespass *de eiectio firmae*. The form of trespass dealing with those who crossed the boundary of a person who remained in possession was trespass *quare clausum fregit*.

[27] This is referred to as the doctrine of *trespass by relation*. See, for example, *Ocean Accident & Guarantee Corp.* v *Ilford Gas Co.* [1905] 2 KB 493.

[28] *Mayfair Property Co.* v *Johnston* [1894] 1 Ch 508 (trespass by foundations of wall); *Jones* v *Llanrwst UDC* [1911] 1 Ch 393 (trespass by deposit of faecal matter on riverbank).

[29] This defence is commonly referred to as the defence of *ius tertii*. The question whether the defence of *ius tertii* can be raised when the claimant is seeking possession is unsettled: W&J, para 13.17 suggests that the better view is that the defence *cannot* be raised, whilst C&L, para 18–76 suggests that it can be raised where the claimant is not relying on his own prior possession.

unless A can establish that *he* has a superior title, or that he crossed the boundary with the permission of the person with a superior title.[30] This means that B can usually safely sue if *in fact* she is in possession, even if as a matter *of law* she has no title or formal interest in the land.

What counts as land

One question that has attracted some attention is how far B can claim to be in possession of the airspace above his property so as to be able to object to A's crossing that airspace or placing something in it. The original principle was often said to be that 'the man who has land has everything above it, or is entitled at all events to object to anything else being put over it'.[31] Thus possessors of land have successfully objected to, for instance, overhanging signs[32] and cranes.[33] Modern cases have suggested, however, that passing over land at a height at which there can be no interference with the ordinary use of that land is not a trespass, and that all members of the public have an equal right to use this airspace.[34] Thus the modern principle seems to be that the possessor of the surface's interest only extends to superjacent airspace which must be controlled if the possessor is to be able to reasonably enjoy the land and put it to purposeful use.[35] Even if the modern principle represents the law, it is merely a presumption, since often in a multi-storey building one owner's rooms on a higher floor will protrude over the rooms owned by another on the ground floor.[36]

Just as the tort of trespass to land can be committed by intruding into the airspace immediately above B's land, it can also be committed by intruding into the ground beneath it.[37]

LAWFUL JUSTIFICATION OR EXCUSE

If A has crossed the boundary of B's land, there are many different ways in which A could establish that he had a lawful justification or excuse for crossing that boundary. We will not attempt to catalogue them here. A may, for instance, seek to establish that, in acting as he did, he was merely making lawful use of a highway[38] or private right of way, or that he had a licence to enter, or

---

[30] *Nicholls* v *Ely Beet Sugar Factory* [1931] 2 Ch 84, 86.
[31] *Wandsworth Board of Works* v *United Telephone Co. Ltd* (1884) 13 QBD 904, 919, Bowen LJ. This doctrine is often presented in Latin as *cujus est solum ejus est usque ad coelum*.
[32] *Kelsen* v *Imperial Tobacco Co.* [1957] 2 QB 334.
[33] *Anchor Brewhouse Developments Ltd* v *Berkley House Ltd* [1987] 2 EGLR 173.
[34] *Bernstein* v *Skyviews* [1978] QB 479. (An overflight by a civil aircraft at a reasonable height is immune from liability under the Civil Aviation Act 1982, s 76(1).)
[35] Ibid. See also Gray 1991.
[36] *Corbett* v *Hill* (1870) LR 9 Eq 671.
[37] For instance, by foundations or mining. As has already been observed (see above, p. 349), encroaching tree roots are treated as a form of private nuisance.
[38] The public's right to use a highway is limited: In *DPP* v *Jones* [1999] 2 AC 240 the majority held that the public's right was not limited to passing, repassing and ancillary uses, and accepted that *at least some* other reasonable, peaceful and non-obstructive uses were lawful (at 257, per Lord Irvine; 281, per Lord Clyde; and 286–7, per Lord Hutton). The person in possession of land across which a highway runs is treated as being in possession of the soil under the highway and

that statute[39] or common law[40] conferred on him a power to enter.[41] Here we will discuss only two instances where A might be able to establish that he had a lawful justification or excuse for crossing the boundary of B's land.

Licence (consent)

Suppose A enters B's land. A will not commit the tort of trespass to land in so doing if B has licensed him to enter. A may commit the tort of trespass to land, however, if he either exceeds the terms of the licence[42] or fails to leave within a reasonable time after the licence is withdrawn. Sometimes a contract will restrict B's power to withdraw a licence. But it is important to distinguish between cases where the withdrawal is wrongful (a breach of contract) but still effective and those where the withdrawal is ineffective.[43] If the withdrawal is effective, then A must leave B's land within a reasonable period of time – if he does not, then he will commit the tort of trespass to land in relation to B. If, on the other hand, the withdrawal is ineffective, A will *not* commit the tort of trespass to land if he stays on B's land.

Necessity

In *Southport Corporation* v *Esso Petroleum*,[44] the defendant ship owners dumped some oil from their ship into the sea when their ship ran aground. The defendants dumped the oil because they feared that the ship would break its back and the crew would be endangered if they did not. The oil washed up onto the claimants' foreshore. The claimants sued the defendants, claiming that they had committed the tort of trespass to land in dumping the oil.

Devlin J thought that the defendants could rely on the defence of *necessity* to justify their dumping the oil.[45] He also held, however, that the defendants

---

consequently entitled to sue for trespass a person who uses the highway in an unauthorised way: *Harrison* v *Duke of Rutland* [1893] 1 QB 142.

[39] For example, police officers have statutory powers under ss 17 and 18 of the Police and Criminal Evidence Act 1984 to enter premises in order to make an arrest and to search after making an arrest.

[40] For example, the common law confers powers to enter premises in order to reclaim wrongfully taken personal property, in order to abate a nuisance (though sometimes notice may be required), and in order to preserve person or property from immediate danger.

[41] Where a person who is authorised by law to enter for a particular purpose afterwards abuses that authority he may be treated as a trespasser *ab initio*, that is, he may be treated as if the initial entry was unlawful. The doctrine is associated with *The Six Carpenters' Case* (1610) 8 Co Rep 146a, 77 ER 695. Although Lord Denning MR thought in *Chic Fashions Ltd* v *Jones* [1968] 2 QB 299 that the doctrine should be interred with the bones of the old forms of action, he later used the doctrine in *Cinnamond* v *BAA* [1980] 1 WLR 582.

[42] The picturesque illustration commonly given is that a person licensed to walk down the stairs becomes a trespasser if he slides down the banisters.

[43] A textbook on tort is not the appropriate place to explore when licences cannot be revoked and when they will bind third parties. The interested reader should consult a standard textbook on land law.

[44] [1953] 2 All ER 1204. This judgment was reversed by the Court of Appeal but restored by the House of Lords: [1956] AC 218.

[45] See also *Cope* v *Sharpe (No. 2)* [1912] 1 KB 496.

would not be permitted to rely on the defence if the predicament was a result of their own negligence.[46] The defence is only available in cases of immediate danger or emergency. So in *Southwark LBC* v *Williams*,[47] the Court of Appeal held that the defence did not stretch to cover the case of homeless people who made an orderly entry into empty property.

The fact that in some circumstances necessity seems to make the defendant's decision to cause harm to the claimant justifiable does not mean that the defendant should necessarily be free from an obligation to pay compensation for the harm that he has caused. For instance, in *Vincent* v *Lake Erie Transportation Co.*[48] the defendant's boat was moored at the claimant's dock when a severe storm arose. The crew acted to prevent the boat from getting away from the dock and being lost, but with the result that the vessel was repeatedly thrown against the dock and damaged it. A majority of the Supreme Court of Minnesota held that the claimant was entitled to compensation for the damage done. One explanation for such an outcome is that there is an *incomplete* privilege to perform an act which would otherwise be a tort in a situation of necessity – that is, the act may be performed and the claimant cannot resist or prevent this, but liability is still imposed for any *material* harm done.[49] An alternative explanation is that while the availability of a defence of necessity meant that the defendant could not be held liable to compensate the claimant in *tort* for the damage done to the dock, the defendant could still be held liable in *restitution* for the damage done to the dock.[50]

[46] *Southport Corporation* v *Esso Petroleum* [1953] 2 All ER 1204, 1210A. See also *Rigby* v *Chief Constable of Northamptonshire* [1985] 1 WLR 1242.
[47] [1971] 1 Ch 734. See also *Monsanto* v *Tilly* [2000] Env LR 313.
[48] 124 NW 221 (1910).
[49] Bohlen 1926, 313. The reference to 'material' harm is intended to denote that the claimant cannot recover *simply* for the 'invasion of the right'. See also *Burmah Oil* v *Lord Advocate* [1965] AC 75, where the House of Lords treated a situation where oil installations were destroyed in wartime to prevent them falling into enemy hands as one where the acts were performed in the lawful exercise of the Royal prerogative but there was nonetheless an obligation to pay compensation.
[50] See below, p. 696; also Weinrib 1995, 196–203.

18

PRIVATE NUISANCE

DEFINITION

A will commit the tort of private nuisance in relation to B if he creates, authorises, adopts or continues a state of affairs which unreasonably interferes with the use and enjoyment of land in which B has a sufficient interest. A will also commit the tort of private nuisance in relation to B if he creates, authorises, adopts or continues a state of affairs which unreasonably interferes with some natural right or easement that B enjoys. This needs a lot more explanation. However, before we go on to explain some of the key terms in the above definitions, it may be useful to distinguish the tort of private nuisance from the tort of trespass to land. Two points help to distinguish the two torts.

First, if A *directly* interferes with B's land,[1] the tort, if any, committed by A in so acting will be trespass to land. If, on the other hand, A *indirectly* interferes with B's land, the tort, if any, committed by A in so acting will be private nuisance.

Secondly, trespass to land does *not* cover cases where no person or physical object crosses the boundary onto B's land. Because of this second distinction, the tort of trespass to land does not cover situations where B's land is invaded by, for instance, noise, heat or vibrations. Further, where A's interference is with a natural right or an easement[2] the situation is covered by private nuisance and not by trespass to land.

These distinctions are not easy to apply in practice. It is easy to disagree over what counts as a *direct* interference and what counts as an *indirect* interference, and over what is a physical object and what is not. It is only rarely, however, that it will matter to a defendant whether a claimant describes her claim as being for trespass to land or for private nuisance. From the defendant's perspective, if a claimant sues her for private nuisance instead of trespass to land, then the claimant will have to prove two additional things: (*a*) that the defendant's interference with the claimant's land was unreasonable and (*b*) that the defendant's interference caused damage.[3]

---

[1] When we use the phrase 'B's land' in this context we intend the word 'land' to include not just the earth itself but also things attached to it, such as buildings, which count as real property. The statement that the land must be 'B's' is shorthand for the fact that in order to claim B must have a particular relationship with the land. The precise nature of that necessary relationship is discussed below, pp. 381–2. At this stage an adequate summary may be that the land will count as 'B's land' if B has a legally-recognised interest in it, and in certain circumstances it may be sufficient that B has exclusive possession of the land.

[2] These concepts are familiar to land lawyers, and we do not want to try to duplicate the discussions of them which will be found in textbooks devoted to that subject. Examples of natural rights and easements include: rights to the passage of light, rights to support from neighbouring land or buildings, and rights to use particular paths across another's land.

[3] It will be recalled that in Chapter 17 we stated that any crossing onto someone else's property, no matter how trivial, could be a trespass, and that trespass to land was actionable *per se*, that

Consequently, as a rule of thumb, where there is uncertainty about which tort is applicable it is safer for a claimant to sue for private nuisance, because this will not be to the defendant's disadvantage.[4] We will now look at these two distinctions in more detail.

(1) *Direct and indirect.* The most important factor in drawing this distinction seems to be the defendant's degree of control over the thing which caused the interference. For example, if Eric crosses onto Mary's land this will be a direct interference and trespass, while if the roots or branches of Eric's tree cross over onto Mary's land this will be an indirect interference and private nuisance. The reason for the distinction between these two cases seems to be that Eric has direct control over how his own body moves but he does not have the same degree of control over how the roots or branches on his tree grow.

Similarly, if Eric throws rubbish onto Mary's land that is trespass, but if Eric releases acid smuts into the air which drift across onto Mary's land then that is private nuisance. Difficulties arise, however, where Eric releases something in a place where he knows that it will almost inevitably be carried onto Mary's land. Is the interference in that case *direct* or *indirect*? There are cases which suggest that if A puts something in a river where it will be carried by the flow onto B's land, A's interference with B's land will be sufficiently direct to amount to a trespass.[5]

(2) *Physicality.* All emanations for which A is responsible which do not involve the projection of a physical object onto B's land are treated as within the tort of private nuisance. Thus if A screams over B's garden fence or creates vibrations which rock B's house, B will have to try to show that A has committed the tort of private nuisance in so acting if she wants to sue A. She will not be able to claim that A's actions amount to a trespass to her land.

This second distinction can also be used to explain why some interests in land are *only* protected by private nuisance, in particular natural rights and easements. The reason is that if B has an easement, for instance a private right of way over C's land, an interference with that right of way is not treated as involving any physical thing crossing onto B's land.[6]

---

is, without proof of damage. The tort of private nuisance is not, generally speaking, actionable *per se.*

[4] Although it might be objected that modern rules of civil procedure relieve the claimant of the burden of *identifying* exactly which tort is supposed to have been committed, what facts have to be established for the claimant's claim to succeed will still depend on what sort of tort is supposed to have been committed in the claimant's case.

[5] See, for example, *Jones v Llanrwst UDC* [1911] 1 Ch 393.

[6] It might be thought obvious that nothing crosses onto B's land because the right of way is across C's land. But here we must remind ourselves that in some circumstances B will be able to sue for trespass to land, even though the land belongs to C and B only has certain rights over it. Thus not only the person in possession of the soil but also those with certain rights over the land can sue for a trespass to land, e.g. the holders of hunting and fishing rights, and the owners of growing crops (see, above, p. 350).

TYPES OF INTERFERENCE

It is useful to classify the types of interference which can amount to a private nuisance for two reasons. First, such a classification will help us to describe the *range* of situations which the tort of private nuisance can cover. Secondly, the tests which determine whether an interference is unreasonable vary depending on the type of interference involved. For example, it is far easier to establish that an interference is unreasonable when it involves an encroachment on someone's land than when it merely reduces the amenity value of someone's land.

Two systems of classification are worth discussing. The first classifies a given interference according to what *effect* it has on the person whose land is being interfered with. The second classifies a given interference according to *how* it arose.

Encroachment, physical injury, reducing amenity value

In *Hunter* v *Canary Wharf Ltd*, Lord Lloyd said that 'Private nuisances are of three kinds. They are (1) nuisance by encroachment on a neighbour's land; (2) nuisance by direct physical injury to a neighbour's land; and (3) nuisance by interference with a neighbour's quiet enjoyment of his land.'[7] Because this statement was given such prominence in a House of Lords' speech and has such an attractive simplicity, we feel that we must discuss it. Our opinion, however, is that it is dangerously misleading unless *five* modifications are made.

First, we think that the word 'another' should be substituted for 'neighbour' each time that it occurs. The word 'neighbour' in this context tends to suggest that the defendant must have an interest in neighbouring land, and, as we will explain below, we think that this is incorrect.[8]

Secondly, we think that the statement needs some reworking to make clear that (1), (2) and (3) are three forms of *interference*,[9] and that such interferences will only be private nuisances if they are *unreasonable*.

Thirdly, we think that the word 'indirect' should be substituted for the word 'direct' in (2). As we have explained above,[10] one of the crucial distinctions between the torts of trespass to land and private nuisance is that in private nuisance the effect on the claimant's land is *indirect*. If A damages B's land *directly*, for instance by throwing a rock through B's greenhouse or taking an axe to her front door, then the situation falls within the tort of trespass to land and not private nuisance.

Fourthly, we think that the phrase 'quiet enjoyment' is best avoided in (3) because it is a phrase which has a different meaning in landlord and tenant law. We would also prefer to avoid the word 'interference' because under our definition (1), (2) and (3) are *all* forms of interference. In its place we would substitute the phrase 'reducing the amenity value', a phrase Lord Lloyd used later in his speech[11] to explain (3).

---

[7] [1997] AC 655, 695.
[8] See below, pp. 372–3.
[9] Lord Lloyd acknowledged this point later in his speech [1997] AC 655, 696: 'the essence of private nuisance is easy enough to identify, and it is the same in all three classes of private nuisance, namely, interference with land or the enjoyment of land.'
[10] See above, pp. 355–6.
[11] [1997] AC 655, 696.

Fifthly, we think that 'or his rights over land' should be added to (3) since otherwise the definition will not cover actionable interferences with natural rights and easements.

With these modifications the statement reads: 'Private nuisances can be divided into three kinds in accordance with the type of *unreasonable* interference involved. They are (1) nuisance by encroachment on another's land; (2) nuisance by indirect physical injury to another's land; and (3) nuisance by reducing the amenity value of another's land or his rights over land.' This modified version of Lord Lloyd's statement helpfully classifies the types of interference that can amount to a private nuisance according to their effect on the person whose land is being interfered with. It is also useful, however, to consider an alternative system for classifying the different kinds of interference that can amount to a private nuisance. This system divides up these kinds of interference according to *how* they arise.

Emanation, encroachment, obstruction and withdrawal, affront

If we divide types of interference according to *how* they arise then they fall into four categories. We will look at each category before considering a relevant aspect of the decision of the House of Lords in *Hunter* v *Canary Wharf Ltd*.[12]

(1) *Emanation*. Most cases of private nuisance involve interference caused by things that *emanate* onto a claimant's land. Thus typical cases involve the *emanation* of noise, smells, vibrations, acid smuts, and sewage onto a claimant's land.

(2) *Encroachment*. When the thing which crosses onto a claimant's land is something such as growing branches or tree roots lawyers tend to refer to the process as being one of *encroachment* rather than emanation.

(3) *Obstruction and withdrawal*. A more difficult category covers cases where the complaint is that A has *obstructed* or *withdrawn* some benefit which B could otherwise have expected to enjoy. For instance, A might obstruct the wind that would otherwise have passed over A's land and onto B's land and powered B's windmill. Or A might obstruct the groundwater that would otherwise have passed through A's land and percolated onto B's land, filling B's reservoir. Alternatively, A might withdraw the support that his land previously offered B's house. In these cases B must establish a *right* to the benefit passing to him free from unreasonable interruption before he can complain about A's obstruction or withdrawal.

Sometimes this is straightforward: B may be able to demonstrate that she has a private right of way across A's land and will then be able to complain if that right of way is unreasonably interfered with by A. But in some cases the need to show a right to the benefit will pose a considerable obstacle for B because English land law is so cautious about holding that landowners are subject

---

[12] [1997] AC 655.

to obligations to allow benefits to pass over, across or through their land. In particular, English land law has always been reluctant to recognise such obligations where they cannot be precisely defined. Saying that a landowner must not unreasonably interfere with a private right of way along a path or with the passage of a river which flows in a defined channel is one thing, but saying that he or she must not interfere with the wind, or percolating groundwater, or invisible electromagnetic signals is another. Alongside the problem that such obligations can often not be precisely defined is the further difficulty that such benefits could easily be obstructed by activities that the law would not want to discourage. Thus almost any building might interfere with wind, groundwater and signals. The consequence of all this is that if B alleges unreasonable interference by obstruction of a benefit or withdrawal of support she may often lose simply because she can prove no entitlement to the benefit passing unobstructed or the support continuing.[13]

There are two matters on which English land law has taken a firm view. First, a person cannot usually claim a right to an uninterrupted view across another's land, and consequently it is not a private nuisance to interfere with a claimant's view. In the United States some courts have been willing to draw a distinction between obstructing a view (which is not usually actionable) and positively creating an ugly sight (which can be treated as analogous to an emanation). But English law has not adopted this distinction. Nonetheless, although a claim cannot be based on obstruction of a view in certain circumstances it can be based on an obstruction of light.[14] Secondly, a person cannot automatically claim a right to his neighbour's land continuing to support his building (as opposed to his land) but must acquire an easement to gain such a right. This means that in the absence of such an easement a defendant is permitted to excavate on his own land even if the result is that the claimant's building collapses.[15]

(4) *Affront.* The fourth way in which A can commit the tort of private nuisance in relation to B is by *affront*, though English law has made only tentative moves towards acceptance of the notion that this form of interference can amount to an actionable nuisance. It seems that in the cases which fall within this category the interference is caused not by any emanation, encroachment or obstruction but by the affront that comes from the knowledge that nearby land is being used for a particular

---

[13] A famous example is the decision of the House of Lords in *Bradford Corporation* v *Pickles* [1895] AC 587 where because the Corporation could not establish any right to the percolating groundwater passing to them without interruption they could not complain even about Pickles's malicious interference with it.

[14] See below, p. 362.

[15] *Dalton* v *Angus* (1881) 6 App Cas 740, 804 (per Lord Penzance): 'It is the law, I believe I may say without question, that at any time within twenty years after the house is built the owner of the adjacent soil may with perfect legality dig that soil away, and allow his neighbour's house, if supported by it, to fall in ruins to the ground.' See also *Ray* v *Fairway Motors (Barnstaple) Ltd* (1969) 20 P & CR 261. Similarly, a landowner can extract percolating groundwater from beneath his own land even if this drains water from beneath another's land and causes damage: *Popplewell* v *Hodkinson* (1869) LR 4 Ex 248; *Langbrook Properties Ltd* v *Surrey CC* [1970] 1 WLR 161.

purpose. In England this form of claim has been used principally against brothels, pornographic cinemas and sex shops.[16] But in practice such claims are rare because in order to succeed a claimant must demonstrate not only that he has suffered interference by affront but also that it was unreasonable for the defendant to create, authorise, adopt or continue the state of affairs which is causing the affront. It is only likely to be in unusual circumstances that a court will be able to conclude that a defendant is acting *unreasonably* in expecting a landowner to tolerate a lawful business[17] which causes no interference more severe than psychic affront. Nonetheless, the doctrine that there can be such a thing as a private nuisance by affront is sometimes attacked for allowing the majority in a locality to impose its moral views on minorities.

A doctrine similar to the doctrine that interference by affront can amount to an actionable nuisance might explain a group of cases in which extreme dangers, such as warehouses of gunpowder, were held to be nuisances even before they had caused any physical harm.[18] It might be said that in such cases there was an existing nuisance from the fear and anxiety caused to those living in the vicinity.[19] There is a tension, however, between these cases and the rule that a claimant can only obtain an injunction to restrain an *anticipated* tort when such a tort is 'highly probable' and 'imminent'.[20] There is also a risk that claimants will be able to rely on this sort of reasoning to obtain a remedy even though there may be no rational basis for their fears and anxiety.[21]

(5) *Interference with television reception.* One of the complaints in *Hunter* v *Canary Wharf Ltd*[22] was that the building of the Canary Wharf Tower inter-

---

[16] See, for example, *Laws* v *Florinplace* [1981] 1 All ER 659, where ten residents of an area of Pimlico, London, which was claimed to enjoy an attractive village atmosphere, sought an injunction against the 'Victoria Sex and Video Centre'. Vinelott J held that even if the defendant changed the business's name and altered its signs and displays, it was still arguable that the 'profound repugnance' caused to the claimants by knowledge of nearby trade in hard pornography could amount to sufficient interference for the purposes of the tort. In the United States 'nuisance by affront' is regularly relied on against undertakers.

[17] In *Laws* v *Florinplace* [1981] 1 All ER 659, 668, Vinelott J treated it as relevant to whether to grant an interim injunction that the defendant's business was 'at least near the boundary of the criminal law' and thought that at a full trial of the action it would be necessary to decide whether the business was lawful or not.

[18] *R* v *Lister* (1856–7) Dears & B 209, 169 ER 979; *Hepburn* v *Lordan* (1865) 2 H & M 345, 71 ER 497; *R* v *Chilworth Gunpowder Co.* (1888) 4 TLR 557.

[19] In *R* v *Lister* (1856–7) 7 Dears & B 209, 227, 169 ER 979, 987, Lord Campbell CJ stated that, 'the well-founded apprehension of danger which would alarm men of steady nerves and reasonable courage, passing through the street in which the house stands, or residing in adjoining houses, is enough to show that something has been done which the law ought to prevent'. It is unclear whether a series of claims in the nineteenth century against smallpox hospitals and asylums are best explained as 'nuisance by anxiety', 'nuisance by affront', or both.

[20] The Court of Appeal in *Hooper* v *Rogers* [1975] Ch 43 treated this rule as requiring no more than that the degree of probability was sufficient to make an injunction just, and the application was not premature, but even this softened version of the rule seems more stringent than the approach taken in the gunpowder factory cases.

[21] The nuisance claim against the operators of a smallpox hospital which gave rise to the appeal in *Managers of the Metropolitan Asylum District* v *Hill* (1881) 6 App Cas 193 is often raised in this context. Although the claimants' evidence included allegations as to the emanation of smells from the morgue and of a disproportionate infection rate in the vicinity of the hospital it seems that many of the fears were exaggerated.

[22] [1997] AC 655.

fered with the claimants' television reception because it stood between their homes and the Crystal Palace transmitter. In *Bridlington Relay Ltd* v *Yorkshire Electricity Board*,[23] Buckley J had suggested that interference with television reception could not constitute a legal nuisance because it was interference with a purely recreational facility, as opposed to interference with the health or physical comfort or well-being of the claimants. In *Hunter* the House of Lords expressed some doubts as to whether such reasoning was still convincing in the light of the increased social importance of television.[24] The majority held, however, that interference with television reception merely by building on one's own land was not actionable, relying on an analogy with the fact that interference with a view cannot give rise to a claim in private nuisance in the absence of an agreement.[25] Thus the case supports the proposition set out above that obstruction of a benefit that would otherwise pass onto a claimant's land is not actionable unless the claimant can establish a right to have the benefit come onto her land.[26]

UNREASONABLE INTERFERENCE

Our definition of private nuisance states that there must be an *unreasonable* interference. Consequently it is necessary to examine how the law determines whether a particular interference is an *unreasonable* one. The easiest point to make is that not all interferences are unreasonable. Ordinary social living requires a degree of 'give and take'. Your neighbours have to put up with your singing in the shower; you, in turn, have to put up with their wailing baby.

The form of the interference is an important factor in determining whether it is unreasonable. If we consider this point using the categorisation of interferences in terms of the *effect* on the claimant then: (*a*) it seems that all encroachments are unreasonable (though in practice many occupiers tolerate overhanging branches and straying roots);[27] (*b*) not all indirect physical damage is unreasonable – for instance, an interference will not be unreasonable if it was only capable of indirectly damaging unusually delicate property;[28] (*c*) it is generally easier to establish that an interference causing indirect physical damage was unreasonable than that an interference only reducing amenity value was.

Looking at the matter using the division of types of interference in terms of *how* they arise, a special feature in cases of interference by obstruction or withdrawal of a benefit is that sometimes the benefit to which a claimant is itself entitled is defined in such a way as to incorporate already a factor of

---

[23] [1965] Ch 436.
[24] [1997] AC 655, at 684–5 (per Lord Goff), 708 (per Lord Hoffmann), 722 (per Lord Cooke).
[25] Ibid., at 685 (per Lord Goff), 699 (per Lord Lloyd), 709 (per Lord Hoffmann), 726–7 (per Lord Hope).
[26] Consequently, the question whether an *emanation* of electromagnetic waves *onto* B's land which interferes with B's television reception can be actionable is still open.
[27] The question whether the occupier will be responsible for an encroachment is separate from the question whether the encroachment is an unreasonable interference.
[28] *Robinson* v *Kilvert* (1889) 41 Ch D 88. See below, p. 365.

reasonableness. For instance, a claimant cannot acquire by prescription a right to a continuance of present levels of light, but only a right to freedom from such obstruction of light as would interfere with the ordinary occupations of life.[29] In such a case *any* interference with the right, so defined, would be unreasonable. Usually, however, benefits are defined in more absolute terms. For instance, Beth may have a private right of way along a path across Carl's land. In such a case Beth would not be able to base a claim on any trivial interference with her use of the path, but would have to show that the interference was *unreasonable*. Beth could not claim, for instance, if Fred also had a private right of way along the same path and slowed Beth down by pushing a heavy cart up it.

What one must put up with is not simply a matter of the *degree* of interference. It is also relevant *why* the interference was caused. Thus if I have builders in to replace the floorboards in my house then my neighbour will be expected to put up with the inevitable loud noises. It would probably be unreasonable, however, for me to make exactly the same amount of noise by banging on trays and kicking the furniture. In particular, it would almost certainly be unreasonable for me to make the same amount of noise if my purpose was to annoy my neighbour.[30] The point that the reason for the interference is relevant is sometimes made by saying that a defendant cannot be liable for interference stemming from a 'reasonable user'. It is important to note, however, that this is not the same as saying that the defendant cannot be liable for interference stemming from a 'careful user'. What is a 'reasonable user' does not turn wholly on the degree of risk to neighbours and the cost of precautions but on the extent to which the user is an ordinary part of social living.

Sometimes it may not be unreasonable even to cause an intolerable disturbance. An example of this is provided by the case of *Southwark London Borough Council v Tanner*.[31] In that case, the claimants were tenants who lived in old houses with inadequate soundproofing. They could hear everything their neighbours did, 'their coming and going, their cooking and cleaning, their quarrels and their love-making'.[32] Lord Millett accepted that '[life] in these conditions must be intolerable'.[33] But the House of Lords unanimously found that there was not an actionable private nuisance. Despite the 'intolerable' effect of their everyday noises it was not unreasonable for the claimants' neighbours to make such noises – they were made as part of those neighbours' reasonable and ordinary use of their property.

Lord Millett stated that there could be no liability if the acts causing the interference were *necessary for the common and ordinary use and occupation of land and conveniently done*.[34] The test of necessity is weak here: *common and ordinary* is the phrase which governs. Babies, televisions and washing machines are not strictly necessary for occupation of land, but they are all part of *common and*

---

[29] *Colls v Home & Colonial Stores Ltd* [1904] AC 179.
[30] See below, pp. 369–71.
[31] [2001] 1 AC 1.
[32] Ibid., 7.
[33] Ibid., 18.
[34] Ibid., 21.

ordinary occupation, and they will not ordinarily be treated as involving unreasonable interference. *Conveniently done* is an important qualification here, however. The point seems to be that babies, televisions and washing machines must not be arranged so as to expose neighbours to maximum noise where it would be equally convenient to arrange them otherwise. Thus, if there was nowhere in his house that a defendant could put the washing machine without it disturbing his neighbours then the noise caused by the washing machine would not amount to an unreasonable interference with the neighbours' use and enjoyment of their land, but if it only disturbed the neighbours because he chose to put it in an alcove where the wall between the houses was particularly thin then the interference so caused might be unreasonable.

Much academic ink has been spilled trying to explain the distinction between the test for unreasonableness in private nuisance and the test for unreasonableness in negligence. We think that this distinction can best be illustrated by thinking about a case where a chemical works operated by Vijay emits acid which damages the shrubs in the garden of a cottage used by Wendy as a weekend country retreat and causes an unpleasant smell in the cottage's dining room. It seems clear that it could be concluded that the operation of Vijay's chemical works is unreasonably interfering with Wendy's use and enjoyment of her land without any need to investigate whether the chemical works are being carelessly operated or not. No doubt if the chemical works are emitting the acid because Vijay is operating them in a careless[35] manner that would make it easy to show that the interference is unreasonable. But, to put the point firmly, it is *not necessary* to show careless operation in order to establish unreasonable interference.[36]

Most commentators agree with the analysis so far, but some say that nonetheless there is a type of carelessness in such a case: carelessness not in the operation of the chemical works but in locating it in such a place that it can interfere with Wendy's use and enjoyment of her cottage. We think that this view is wrong and that the chemical works can be found to be causing an unreasonable interference even if there is evidence that it is located in by far the most sensible place. We think that even if everyone is agreed that such chemical works are valuable for society, and that this one has been located where it will interfere with the smallest number of people to the least extent, it can still be said that the interference that it causes is unreasonable. How can this be? How can what seems valuable and sensible be castigated as unreasonable and wrong? The answer we think is that the chemical works and its location is valuable and sensible *from the perspective of society as a whole*, but is unreasonable *from the perspective of Wendy*, who has had her shrubs damaged and her dining room made

---

[35] It is worth noting that there is some ambiguity even in the word 'careless' in this context. Thus in the tort of negligence carelessness often refers to the degree of risk being created, whilst here one may just mean that Vijay is not meeting the standards of comparable chemical works operators.

[36] For instance, in *Dennis v Ministry of Defence* [2003] EWHC 793, it was found that the circuit flying of Harrier jump-jets from RAF Wittering caused a private nuisance to Mr Dennis, a neighbouring landowner, but it was not suggested that the jets were being flown carelessly or that the Ministry of Defence had carelessly chosen to train its pilots in an inappropriate way.

unpleasant. Wendy can quite fairly argue that it is unreasonable to expect her to put up with *all* the consequences of the chemical works without any redress and the common law accepts this point of view.[37]

One way of thinking about what the common law is doing is to think of Wendy and Vijay as having *equal* rights to use and enjoy their land.[38] If both have bought their land then surely they both have equal rights to exploit it for uses which are ordinary in the locality. But if Vijay argues that the importance of his chemical works for society as a whole means that he should be able to continue operating in such a way as to render Wendy's land far less valuable for her ordinary purposes then he will not be respecting her *equal* right. Almost everyone would agree that Vijay should not be permitted to seize Wendy's cottage and evict her without redress merely because it would be valuable and sensible to extend the chemical works onto the land occupied by the cottage. Seizing the cottage would clearly be a tort. Private nuisance exists to cover the situation where Vijay has not seized the cottage directly but is indirectly causing damage or reducing the extent that it can be used and enjoyed.

If we have identified the test for unreasonableness in private nuisance correctly then we can confront the difficult question of whether this test is *strict*. Here we run into trouble with the confusion surrounding the label *strict liability*. We can certainly say that the liability is strict in the sense that it is not sufficient answer to Wendy's claim for Vijay to prove that he took reasonable care. The interference may still be unreasonable even if reasonable care was taken in siting and operating the chemical works. Liability is not strict, however, in the sense that the unreasonableness rule is just about the efficient absorption of loss and no moral opprobrium attaches to its breach. Even if it is valuable and sensible to locate a chemical works where it will damage a cottage owner's shrubs it is still *wrongful* to damage the shrubs. It is wrongful to treat a neighbour's shrubs as something which can be destroyed without redress just because it is convenient or expedient to destroy them.

In summary, the standard of unreasonableness relies on a compromise between the competing interests of land users. The governing test is not what is careless or what is not socially useful but what goes beyond the standards set by reasonable compromise. And as the *Southwark* case shows, the standards set by reasonable compromise take account of a complex combination of factors.

---

[37] The argument in this paragraph demonstrates why we would not want to adopt Conor Gearty's suggestion that *all* cases involving physical damage to land should be dealt with by the tort of negligence (or under the rule in *Rylands* v *Fletcher*, discussed below, pp. 739–50) rather than in private nuisance: see Gearty 1989. In contrast to Gearty, Lee 2003 argues that the label 'unreasonable' is 'unnecessary and misleading' in situations where a court is considering whether an interference which has caused physical damage to land is actionable because all that the court is really considering is whether strict liability should apply to a particular *activity*. As we have explained above we do not believe that all that courts do in such cases is classify *activities*. For instance, they may also have to consider if an activity, although ordinary, was *conveniently done*, and whether the damage was merely trivial or a result of hypersensitivity.

[38] A defendant and a claimant will not have equal rights in *all* private nuisance cases. We argue below (pp. 372–3) that a defendant may be held liable even if he has no right to use the land where he creates the nuisance. We have merely chosen an example where a defendant and a claimant have equal rights in order to illustrate the necessity for compromise.

What neighbours must put up with in the context of living in terraced houses without soundproofing is wholly different from what they must put up with in an estate of widely-spaced modern villas. Below we identify some of the factors that the case law suggests are most relevant.

Hypersensitivity

First, an interference will only be unreasonable if it would affect an ordinary occupier. If an interference would only harm a hypersensitive occupier then it will not be unreasonable.[39] According to the leading case, for an interference to be actionable it must be '[an] inconvenience materially interfering with the ordinary comfort . . . of human existence, not merely according to elegant or dainty modes of living, but according to plain and sober and simple notions among the English people'.[40]

The principle applies to interference with 'dainty trades' as well as with 'dainty modes of living'. Thus in *Robinson* v *Kilvert*,[41] the claimant complained that brown paper he had been storing had been damaged by the defendant's overheating of the room below. The court held that there had not been an unreasonable interference because the heat could only have had a detrimental effect on an 'exceptionally delicate trade'.

It is important, however, to distinguish the test for liability from the question of the extent of a defendant's liability in a private nuisance case. This distinction means that once it has been established that a defendant's acts would have unreasonably interfered even with a *reasonably robust* trade, a claimant can claim even though she actually operates a delicate trade. Thus in *McKinnon Industries* v *Walker*,[42] the Privy Council held that the claimant could obtain a remedy for the noxious fumes and sulphur dioxide emitted from the defendant's plant. The fumes would have damaged any reasonably robust neighbouring trade so it did not matter that what had actually been interfered with was the claimant's delicate trade as an orchid grower.

Type of damage – the nature of the locality

A second factor, the nature of the locality, is important when the interference causes a reduction in amenity value rather than indirect damage to the land. The effect on the claimant was identified as a significant distinction in this context by the House of Lords in *St Helen's Smelting* v *Tipping*.[43] In that case

---

[39] In *Network Rail Infrastructure Ltd* v *CJ Morris* [2004] EWCA Civ 172, the Court of Appeal suggested that it was no longer necessary to determine whether particular uses were hypersensitive since this issue had been subsumed in the more general question whether the defendant's behaviour was 'reasonable between neighbours'. We believe that the Court was wrong to say this since the general question is far too loose for lawyers to use in a predictable and consistent manner. Sub-rules have developed to foster predictability and consistency, and the hypersensitivity rule is one of these sub-rules which is used when deciding whether an interference for which the defendant is responsible is an *unreasonable* interference.

[40] *Walter* v *Selfe* (1851) 4 De G & Sm 315, 322, 64 ER 849, 852 (per Knight Bruce V-C).

[41] *Robinson* v *Kilvert* (1889) 41 Ch D 88.

[42] [1951] 3 DLR 577.

[43] (1865) 11 HLC 642.

Lord Westbury LC suggested that where there was an interference with personal sensibilities by, for instance, noise or smell, the question whether the interference was unreasonable would have to be judged taking into account the nature of the locality, while there would be no need to consider the nature of the locality if the interference resulted in material injury to the property.

Unfortunately, the *St Helen's* case left some loose ends. First, Lord Westbury LC at one point talks about 'material injury to property' being the condition for ignoring the locality, but later talks about 'sensible injury to the *value* of property' being the condition.[44] If the latter were right, then the distinction would virtually disappear, because most interferences with ordinary sensibilities will cause at least a temporary reduction in land value. Nobody is likely to pay as much for a bad-smelling house or for one with a noisy factory next door. This suggests that the distinction should be between interferences which cause indirect physical damage and interferences which reduce amenity value. The degree of noise, smell and the like which one should tolerate as part of the social rules of 'give and take' may vary with locality, but such rules cannot justify doing something which physically damages another's reasonably robust land. If A's activity causes physical damage to B's reasonably robust land, A cannot argue that he is respecting B's equal right to the use and enjoyment of her land. Lord Hoffmann and Lord Cooke both mentioned *St Helen's Smelting* and the locality rule in *Hunter* v *Canary Wharf*,[45] and both expressed the distinction as between 'material injury to the property' and 'sensible personal discomfort'.[46] Lord Lloyd used a similar distinction, though he did not expressly link it to *St Helen's*.[47]

The second issue raised by Lord Westbury's distinction is that there are difficulties in identifying and classifying localities. The famously quotable observations on locality, such as that of Byles J, during argument in *Hole* v *Barlow*, that '[a] swine-style might not be considered a nuisance in Bethnal Green: but it certainly would be so in Grosvenor Square'[48] do not subdivide localities in any detail. *Gaunt* v *Fynney*[49] provides a fairly typical example of the 'broad brush' sometimes used by the judiciary in classifying localities: in this case Lord Selborne went no further than categorising Leek, Staffordshire, as a 'manufacturing town'. By contrast, in *Adams* v *Ursell*[50] the evidence suggested that most of Silver Street was 'in the lowest district of Dursley . . . but that the plaintiff's house and others near it were of a much better character'. In these circumstances Swinfen Eady J granted an injunction against the defendant preventing him from operating a fried fish shop in a building adjoining the claimant's, but refused to extend the injunction so as to prevent him from opening such a shop elsewhere on the street.

---

[44] Ibid., at 650–1.
[45] [1997] AC 655.
[46] Ibid., 705H (per Lord Hoffmann), 712B (per Lord Cooke).
[47] Ibid., 695B–C.
[48] (1858) 4 CB NS 334, 340, 140 ER 1113, 1116.
[49] (1870) LR 8 Ch App 8.
[50] [1913] 1 Ch 269.

One suggestion that has gathered some momentum is that in classifying localities reference should be made to the opinions of planning authorities. The orthodox view, however, is that planning permission cannot authorise a nuisance. The right to bring an action in private nuisance is a matter of private right, and planning permission cannot remove private rights. Thus in *Wheeler* v *JJ Saunders Ltd*, a case involving swine-styles in the Mendips, Peter Gibson LJ stated, 'The court should be slow to acquiesce in the extinction of private rights without compensation as a result of administrative decisions which cannot be appealed and are difficult to challenge.'[51] This view also received some support from Lord Hoffmann in *Hunter* v *Canary Wharf*, who said, 'It would, I think, be wrong to allow the private rights of third parties to be taken away by a permission granted by the planning authority to the developer. The Court of Appeal rejected such an argument in this case and the point has not been pursued in your Lordships' House.'[52]

This orthodox view had to be reconfirmed in *Wheeler* and *Hunter* because some doubt had been cast on it by the case of *Gillingham BC* v *Medway (Chatham) Dock Co. Ltd.*[53] This case involved unusual facts in that the council which was claiming that the dockyard was a nuisance had previously authorised the development. The case is now taken to stand for the principle that whilst a grant of planning permission cannot directly authorise a nuisance, it may nonetheless have the effect of changing the character of the neighbourhood or locality. Thus *Gillingham* suggests that the decisions of planning authorities may help to define the nature of a locality for the purposes of deciding whether an interference is unreasonable. If this is correct, then, for example, if planning permission was given for the development of an industrial park on a green-field site, a neighbour would no longer be able to claim on the basis that the level of noise was inappropriate for a green-field, but in order to establish private nuisance would have to show that the level of noise was inappropriate for an industrial park. Lord Cooke felt it necessary to apply the *Gillingham* principle to explain why an interference with television reception was not actionable in *Hunter* v *Canary Wharf*.[54] But none of the other Law Lords used this approach.

The problem with the *Gillingham* principle, however, is that it allows an administrative decision *indirectly* to redefine and reduce private rights without compensation. If such decisions are sometimes made without all interested parties being represented, can be based on incomplete information and are difficult for third parties to challenge, then allowing them to redefine private rights is objectionable regardless of whether the effect is indirect or direct. Even if this fundamental criticism of the *Gillingham* principle is not accepted, its restricted scope must always be borne in mind.

First, it seems that planning permission is only likely to 'change the nature of the locality' when it is permission relating to a major development. Even Lord Cooke suggested that the principle would only apply to a 'strategic planning decision

---

[51] [1996] Ch 19, 35.
[52] [1997] AC 655, 710D. Similarly Lord Cooke said at 722C: 'compliance with planning controls is not itself a defence to a nuisance action.'
[53] [1993] QB 343.
[54] [1997] AC 655, 722.

affected by considerations of public interest'.[55] This suggests that a routine grant of small-scale planning permission will not trigger the principle. Secondly, it is important to remember what planning permission actually permits. If Alan applies for permission to build an extension on the back of his house, the planning authority will not be considering how much noise Alan is going to make in the extension if Alan decides to practise his electric guitar in there, nor what pungency of smell Alan is going to emit if he uses the extension for making fibre-glass sculptures. In simple terms, if Alan gets planning permission for building a particular structure, that does not mean that the planning authority regards it as reasonable in the locality for Alan to do whatever he may choose to do in the structure.

Joanne Conaghan and Wade Mansell have argued that the locality principle conceals judicial prejudice and is an essentially class-based exercise.[56] We think, however, that it is necessary to reflect carefully on what this criticism means. It is certainly true that the locality principle has been used to protect the well-heeled from fish and chip shops,[57] but it has also been used to protect blue-collar residential districts from industrial noise.[58] The core of the criticism is probably that the locality principle tends to lead to inhabitants of working-class housing areas having to put up with greater degrees of interference than inhabitants of more expensive areas. There is a risk here, however, of treating the social reality that the locality principle reflects as if it was a *consequence* of the principle.[59] Furthermore, it is worth noting that the locality principle applies equally to both claimants and defendants. Thus if it is established that Gary cannot use his property as a fish and chip shop because of the locality, then equally Gary is protected against others carrying on activities similar to fish frying which might reduce the utility value of his land. Further, if it is found that in a particular locality it is reasonable for Ian to interfere with Nita's use and enjoyment of her land by using his land for light industry, then equally it will be reasonable for Nita to interfere with other people's use and enjoyment of *their land* by using *her* land for light industry. Thus while the locality principle means that there are inequalities between owners of property situated in different places, at the same time all owners in a particular locality have equal opportunities and restrictions on their use and enjoyment of land.

Time, duration, regularity

The third factor is largely a matter of common sense. In assessing whether an activity reduces the amenity value of a piece of land to an unreasonable extent, the courts will consider the time, duration and regularity of the interference in question. Night-time noise which interferes with sleep is far more likely to be held a nuisance than day-time noise. The unreasonableness of interfering with

[55] Ibid., 722E.
[56] Conaghan & Mansell 1999, 137.
[57] *Adams* v *Ursell* [1913] 1 Ch 269.
[58] *Halsey* v *Esso Petroleum* [1961] 1 WLR 683.
[59] To put the same point another way – housing is more affordable in such localities *because* they are areas which are understood to be noisy, etc., rather than the law allowing such areas to be subjected to additional noise, etc., because that is where the affordable housing is.

sleep was a major consideration in the case of *Rushmer* v *Polsue & Alferi*,[60] where a disgruntled resident persuaded North J to close down the printing presses of Fleet Street at night. When dawn breaks and when night begins are clearly matters of degree. In *Metropolitan Properties Ltd* v *Jones* Goddard LJ held that an electric motor which started at 8 am was a nuisance since 'after [that] hour an elderly gentleman is quite entitled to stay in bed, if he wants to, and have a restful time'.[61] On the other hand, in the case of *Vanderpant* v *Mayfair Hotel*,[62] the judge only granted an injunction against a hotel's noise-making between 10 pm and 8 am. Locality is probably a relevant factor. In agricultural areas no doubt the day begins rather earlier than it does in most student flats.

On duration, the courts have held that the temporary disturbances associated with building-works are not a nuisance, provided that the works are carried on with reasonable care and skill. In *Andreae* v *Selfridge & Co. Ltd*,[63] the claimant's hotel on Wigmore Street, London, was affected by a major development by Selfridges. Lord Greene MR stated that reasonable care required restricting the hours of work, and 'using proper scientific means of avoiding inconvenience', but that it was not unreasonable to use pneumatic hammers for six days to break up rein-forced concrete. Even the most innocent of noises may become a nuisance if it is repeated too often. Thus in the case of *Soltau* v *De Held*,[64] the claimant succeeded in obtaining an injunction against a Roman Catholic church in Clapham which rang its chapel bell at 5 am and 6.45 am every morning, its steeple bell at 8.45 am, 6.45 pm and 7.15 pm every day, with occasional additional peals of all its bells at weekends.

Malice

An important, and much disputed, question concerns whether if A interferes with B's use and enjoyment of land out of malice, this will make the interference unreasonable.

In *Christie* v *Davey*[65] the defendant was unfortunate enough to live next door to a 'musical family' in Brixton.[66] He found that the lessons disturbed his con-centration and responded to them by knocking on a party wall, beating on trays, whistling, shrieking and imitating what was being played. North J decided that this alternative symphony was an unreasonable interference and granted an injunction, stating that 'what was done by the Defendant was done only for the purpose of annoyance and in my opinion it was not a legitimate use of

---

[60] [1906] 1 Ch 234.
[61] [1939] 2 All ER 202, 204b.
[62] [1930] 1 Ch 138.
[63] [1938] Ch 1.
[64] (1851) 2 Sim NS 133, 61 ER 291.
[65] [1893] 1 Ch 316.
[66] Mrs Christie was a teacher of music and singing; her daughter was a medallist at the Royal Academy of Music and gave lessons on violin and piano; her lodger was also a medallist in music; and her son was in the habit of playing the cello in the kitchen up until 11 at night. Only Mr Christie was not musical. As North J observed, Mr Christie 'perhaps fortunately for himself, is very deaf' (ibid., 324).

the Defendant's house to use it for the purpose of vexing and annoying his neighbours'.[67] It may be useful to compare this case with the *Southwark*[68] case where a comparable degree of disturbance was not actionable because it was a product of ordinary domestic living.

A similar conclusion to that in *Christie* was reached in *Hollywood Silver Fox Farm Ltd* v *Emmett*.[69] Here the claimant bred silver foxes and put up a sign advertising this fact. The defendant was developing one of his fields as plots for bungalows and took the view that people were less likely to buy a bungalow plot if they knew it was a mere 29 yards from where foxes were being bred. When the claimant refused to remove the sign the defendant carried out a threat to shoot with 'black powder' to frighten the foxes and disturb their breeding. Macnaghten J held that this firing had amounted to a nuisance, emphasising the use of bird-scaring cartridges, and that the defendant's intention in firing the cartridges was to harm the claimant.

The difficulty for the suggestion that malice *is* a relevant factor is that it seems to be in tension with the decision of the House of Lords in *Bradford Corporation* v *Pickles*.[70] In this case it was alleged that Pickles had interfered with the groundwater percolating under his land principally because he wanted to force the Corporation, which used the water for its waterworks, to buy his land for an inflated price. In deciding the case against the Corporation their Lordships treated the question whether Pickles was malicious as irrelevant. Lord Watson, for instance, said that 'No use of property, which would be legal if due to a proper motive, can become illegal because it is prompted by a motive which is improper or even malicious.'[71]

It can be argued, however, that *Bradford* v *Pickles* can be distinguished from *Christie* and *Hollywood Silver Fox*, because the *Bradford* case involved interference by *obstruction* of a benefit, whilst *Christie* and *Hollywood Silver Fox* involved interference by the *emanation* of noise.[72] It is important to remember that in an *obstruction* case a claimant can only sue if she can show that she has a right to receive the benefit that has been obstructed. Now – the claimants in *Bradford* v *Pickles* could not establish that they had a right to the water which the defendant obstructed. Thus it did not matter that the defendant had acted maliciously in obstructing the water. If the claimants had no right to receive the water, they had no claim in private nuisance. So the House of Lords' broad statements about malice in *Bradford* v *Pickles* could be seen as being limited to situations where A unreasonably prevented something going onto B's land

---

[67] Ibid., 326–7.

[68] *Southwark LBC* v *Tanner* [2001] 1 AC 1.

[69] [1936] 2 KB 468.

[70] [1895] AC 587. For suggestions that the decision in the *Bradford* case is inconsistent with the decision in the *Hollywood Silver Fox Farm* case, see MacDonald 1936-1938; Cross 1995, 453–5; Simpson 1995, 74; S&H, 62. Cane 1996 attempts to reconcile the two cases by arguing (at 265–6) that the defendant in *Bradford* was acting out of 'self-interest', while the defendant in *Hollywood* was acting out of 'spite'. This does not work: as our explanation of the facts in *Hollywood* shows, the defendant in that case was acting out of the plainest self-interest in attempting to disrupt the claimant's operations.

[71] [1894] AC 587, 598.

[72] See Taggart 2002, 189.

which B had no right to receive. *By contrast*, in an *emanation* case the lawfulness of the defendant's activity can only be ascertained by considering whether the claimant should be expected to tolerate such interference and, obviously, the fact that no valuable interests were served by creating the interference – indeed there were only reprehensible reasons for doing so – is *highly* relevant to the inquiry into whether the emanation had unreasonably interfered with the claimants' use and enjoyment of their land. There is no reason why a claimant should be expected to put up with an interference with her use and enjoyment of land created by a malicious emanation onto her land.

Defence against a common enemy

In *Arscott* v *The Coal Authority*[73] the Court of Appeal confirmed that it is reasonable for an owner or occupier of land to take convenient steps to protect her land against a 'common enemy', for instance flooding, even if the reasonably foreseeable consequence of these steps is to displace the problem onto a neighbour's land.[74] This rule is subject to three exceptions, however. First, a defendant is not permitted to protect her land by altering an established watercourse. Secondly, the rule only permits a defendant to take steps in *anticipation* of a threat from a 'common enemy' and does not permit a defendant to cure a problem that has *already* arisen on her land by exporting the misfortune.[75] Thirdly, while a court will not seek to weigh up whether each and every protective measure was necessary and proportionate, it may still find that the defendant's actions were unreasonable if the protective measures were clearly excessive and the harm to the claimant was caused by their excess.

CREATING, AUTHORISING, ADOPTING OR CONTINUING

Everybody has a duty not to *create* a private nuisance or to *authorise* others to create a private nuisance. It is the duty of an occupier[76] of land who knows (or can be presumed to know) that a private nuisance has been created or arisen on that land to take reasonable steps to eliminate the problem. This second duty is often referred to as the duty not to *adopt or continue* a private nuisance.

---

[73] [2004] EWCA Civ 892. The defendants were held not liable for raising the level of a playing field situated on a flood plain in order to protect it from flooding even though raising the field caused a flood to affect the claimants' houses more severely than it might otherwise have done.

[74] The parties in the *Arscott* case were content to treat the 'common enemy' rule as existing independently of the question whether the defendant had *unreasonably* interfered with the use and enjoyment of land in which B has a sufficient interest. We believe, however, that the 'common enemy' situation is merely one where the courts have developed clear guidance as to what is reasonable; a view apparently shared by Laws LJ: ibid., at [40].

[75] *Whalley* v *Lancashire and Yorkshire Railway Co.* (1884) 13 QBD 131.

[76] In *L E Jones (Insurance Brokers) Ltd* v *Portsmouth City Council* [2003] 1 WLR 427 the Court of Appeal held that this duty was not limited to occupiers. We discuss this further below, pp. 337–8.

Creating

If A *creates* a state of affairs that causes an unreasonable interference with B's land then it seems straightforward that A should be liable.

One doubt, however, might stem from the common assertion that private nuisance is a tort committed between *neighbours*. This might be read as suggesting that only a neighbouring *landowner* can be held liable in nuisance, and not someone who creates an unreasonable interference but not on his own land. In *Hussain v Lancaster City Council*[77] the Court of Appeal relied on a thesis that Professor Newark was 'prepared ... to nail ... to the doors of the Law Courts and to defend against all comers'. The thesis states that 'the term "nuisance" is properly applied only to such *actionable user of land* as interferes with the enjoyment by the claimant of rights in land'.[78] Unfortunately, the Court of Appeal took this to mean that the essence of private nuisance required that 'the defendant's use *of the defendant's land* interferes with the claimant's enjoyment of the claimant's land'.[79] Thus the Court held against the claimants because the harassment by the tenants of the defendant that was being complained about did not involve the tenants using their own premises. Rather the tenants were carrying out the harassment from the street and from open ground which they did not have any rights over.

The Court of Appeal's view is not orthodoxy. Indeed, in our opinion, it is nonsense. There are plenty of cases to suggest that a defendant can be held liable for creating an unreasonable interference with another's land even if he does not own or have a tenancy over the land that he creates it on. Thus a defendant can be liable if he creates the interference on a highway, or on land that he does not own but merely occupies or uses.[80] Quite apart from these cases, there is no reason in principle to make a claimant's degree of protection turn on the status of the person who creates the interference. A landowner deserves protection from an over-noisy neighbour regardless of whether that neighbour is owner, tenant, lodger or squatter. As Sir Christopher Staughton has pointed out,[81] it is not self-evident why a defendant who plays his stereo loudly at home may

---

[77] [2000] QB 1. The facts of the case are discussed in more detail under the next subheading.

[78] Newark 1949, 489 (emphasis added). This thesis was approved by Lord Goff in *Hunter v Canary Wharf*, but, of course, in that case the focus was on the second part of the thesis – that the interference had to be with rights in land.

[79] [2000] QB 1, 23E (emphasis added). It will not have escaped the notice of the observant reader that Professor Newark only insists that nuisance must involve *user of land*, and not that it must involve *the defendant's use of the defendant's land*.

[80] Cases suggesting that the defendant does not have to possess or own the land that he creates the nuisance from include: *Halsey v Esso Petroleum* [1961] 1 WLR 683 (nuisance created from highway); *Hall v Beckenham Corp.* [1949] 1 KB 716 (nuisance created from public park); *Bernstein v Skyviews* [1978] QB 479 (nuisance created from air). There is also a series of cases supporting the view that picketing can be a private nuisance, at least if it involves obstruction, violence, intimidation, molestation or threats (*J Lyons & Sons v Wilkins* [1899] 1 Ch 255, 267, 271–2; *Hubbard v Pitt* [1976] QB 142, 177B–C, 183D–F, 189A; *Thomas v NUM (South Wales Area)* [1986] Ch 20, 65D), and none of these suggests that the pickets must be using their own land in order to commit the tort. For *dicta* pointing the other way, see *Esso Petroleum v Southport Corp.* [1954] 2 QB 182, 196–7 (per Denning LJ), [1956] AC 218, 242 (per Lord Radcliffe), suggesting that private nuisance cannot be committed from the sea.

[81] *Lippiatt v South Gloucestershire CC* [2000] QB 51, 65B.

commit the tort of private nuisance in relation to his neighbour but a defendant who plays his car stereo loudly while parked outside his neighbour's house will not. Further, acceptance of the Court of Appeal's opinion in *Hussain* would lead to an undesirable distinction between this tort and the tort of trespass to land. Clearly a defendant can commit trespass to land without using his own land.[82]

Someone can *create* a nuisance even if he or she did not *intend* to bring about the situation which amounted to a nuisance. In *R* v *Moore*,[83] a gunmaker possessed land that he encouraged his customers to use for shooting at pigeons. Some of the pigeons were not brought down by his customers and a nuisance resulted from the large number of people who gathered outside his premises to shoot at the strays. In response to the argument that the gunmaker had not committed nuisance because he had not invited this crowd, Littledale J asserted that 'If the experience of mankind must lead any one to expect the result, he will be answerable for it.'[84]

Authorising

A1 can commit the tort of private nuisance by *authorising* A2 to create a state of affairs that causes an unreasonable interference with B's land. This principle can play an important role in attaching liability to owners of land who are not in occupation, for instance because they have granted a lease.

In *Hussain* v *Lancaster City Council*,[85] Malazam Hussain and his partner Linda Livingstone bought a shop on the Ryelands Estate in Lancaster. Thereafter they were subjected to over 2,000 racist attacks. Their claim listed several hundred attacks on their property (including use of petrol bombs), assaults and thefts, and named 106 alleged culprits. Many of these alleged culprits were tenants of Lancaster City Council on the Ryelands estate. Importantly, the council had power to evict these tenants from their homes if they were causing a nuisance to their neighbours, but had not done so. The claimants' case was that in these circumstances the council was liable for the state of affairs being created by its tenants.

One difficulty with the claim was that it sought to make the council liable for the racist attacks even though it was clearly not the council which was carrying them out. Can a landlord be held responsible for a state of affairs resulting from the deliberate misbehaviour of its tenants? The usual answer given by English law, found in cases such as *Rich* v *Basterfield*,[86] is that a landlord is *only* liable for a state of affairs created by his *tenants* if he has *authorised* its creation. In *Southwark London Borough Council* v *Tanner*, Lord Millett expressed the general

---

[82] The inconvenience of the distinction can best be appreciated by remembering that it is a trespass to land to throw something directly onto B's land, and a private nuisance to release something so that it indirectly drifts onto B's land and causes an unreasonable interference. If the Court of Appeal's view was confirmed then B would seek, whenever A created an emanation from land other than his own land, to argue that the emanation was *direct* (and thus a trespass to land).

[83] (1832) 3 B & Ad 184, 110 ER 68.

[84] Although *R* v *Moore*, above, was a case of public nuisance the same principle has been applied in cases of private nuisance, for example, *Walker* v *Brewster* (1867) LR 5 Eq 25 ('assemblage of idle and dissolute persons' outside a house used by defendant for twice weekly fetes with fireworks).

[85] [2000] QB 1.

[86] (1847) 4 CB 783, 136 ER 715.

rule when he said that, 'The person or persons directly responsible for the activities in question are liable; but so too is anyone who authorised them. Landlords have been held liable for nuisances committed on this basis. It is not enough for them to be aware of the nuisance and to take no steps to prevent it.'[87]

What will suffice for authorising? Lord Millett clearly asserts that knowing about a problem and not trying to solve it is insufficient. But what if the landlord knew when the lease was granted that the tenant was very likely to create a nuisance? In *Smith* v *Scott*,[88] Pennycuick V-C stated that this could be enough so long as the nuisance was certain to result from the purposes for which the property was let.[89] Subsequently, in *Tetley* v *Chitty*,[90] Medway Borough Council was held liable for the noise nuisance caused by go-karts when they had leased land with (at least) implied permission to use the land as a go-kart track, and when noise nuisance was an ordinary and necessary consequence of such a use. In that case, however, McNeill J pointed out that there was some inconsistency in the previous cases as to what degree of knowledge or foresight a claimant would have to prove that the landlord had. McNeill J seemed attracted by the possibility that proving mere reasonable foreseeability of nuisance might be enough.[91] We think, however, that there is a significant gulf between foreseeing that something might possibly happen and *authorising* it. Nonetheless, even if later cases follow the generous view of McNeill J, this will not be enough to help claimants in the same position as those in *Hussain*. In that case it would have been difficult to prove that a campaign of racial persecution was a reasonably foreseeable, still less a necessary, consequence of the granting of ordinary local authority tenancies.

Adopting or continuing

Hussain can be contrasted with the case of *Lippiatt* v *South Gloucestershire CC*,[92] where a group of travellers allegedly set up camp on land belonging to the council and used that camp as a 'launching pad' for a series of damaging invasions of a neighbouring farmer's property. In this case the Court of Appeal held that the council was arguably liable for the nuisance resulting from the state of affairs on its land. A crucial distinction from *Hussain* is that in *Lippiatt* the travellers were *not* tenants of the council, and consequently the council continued to occupy the land. Orthodoxy holds that the responsibility of an occupier for a state of affairs which he did not create goes beyond responsibility for what he authorised, and extends to any state of affairs that he continued or adopted.[93]

---

[87] [2001] 1 AC 1, 22.

[88] [1973] Ch 314.

[89] Ibid., 321. He stated that such a degree of 'high probability' was necessary in order to infer that the nuisance was impliedly authorised.

[90] [1986] 1 All ER 663.

[91] Ibid., 671.

[92] [2000] QB 51.

[93] For criticism of this area of the law, see Bright 2001, arguing that a landowner should only be held liable for actions of people on his land if he authorised or encouraged those actions.

So what must B prove in order to establish that A continued or adopted a state of affairs arising on land A occupied that unreasonably interfered with B's use and enjoyment of his land?

In *Sedleigh-Denfield* v *O'Callaghan*,[94] the defendants owned and occupied land on which there was a drainage ditch. Middlesex County Council decided to use this ditch to drain water from a new residential development and substituted a culvert[95] for the ditch. The County Council's action was both lawless – it did not obtain permission from the owners – and incompetent – it failed to take the sensible precaution of putting in a grid to prevent the culvert becoming blocked. Three years later the culvert did block, and water which could not escape down it instead flooded the claimant's property. The House of Lords found that the defendant occupiers of the land were liable even though the state of affairs which led to the flood had been created by the trespassing and incompetent County Council. Viscount Maugham stated that an occupier in such a situation would be liable if he had 'continued' or 'adopted' the nuisance, and explained that, 'an occupier of land "continues" a nuisance if, with knowledge or presumed knowledge of its existence, he fails to take any reasonable means to bring it to an end, though with ample time to do so. He "adopts" it if he makes use of the erection, building, bank or artificial contrivance which constitutes the nuisance.'[96] On the facts, Viscount Maugham found that the defendants had both 'continued' and 'adopted' the nuisance. The other Lords did not draw such a stern distinction between 'continuing' and 'adopting'. They did, however, stress the importance of 'knowledge' or 'presumed knowledge' of the nuisance or the potential for nuisance before the occupier could be liable.

In *Sedleigh-Denfield* the potential for interference with the claimant's land could have been easily and cheaply rectified by the defendants' putting a grid in front of the pipe's orifice. Moreover, the claimants might well have been able to obtain the cost of installing the grid from the County Council. More difficult questions are raised, however, where it will be costly to remove the potential for nuisance, and where those costs may not be recoverable from a third party, for instance because the potential for nuisance has been caused by an unidentified malefactor or by natural forces.

These more difficult questions had to be addressed by the Court of Appeal in *Leakey* v *National Trust*.[97] In this case the defendant owned and occupied a cone-shaped hill in Somerset called Burrow Mump. The claimants lived in converted cottages beneath the mump. In 1976 the Mump was badly affected by the hot summer and wet autumn and a crack appeared, making it likely that the Mump would collapse onto the claimants' houses. Rendering the Mump stable was likely to prove expensive and consequently the National Trust adopted the attitude that it was not responsible for a state of affairs created by the wondrous workings of nature. The Court of Appeal, however, held that the National

---

[94] [1940] AC 880.
[95] In less obscure language, a fifteen-inch pipe.
[96] [1940] AC 880, 894.
[97] [1980] QB 485.

Trust, as a landowner in occupation,[98] was responsible. Megaw LJ (with whom Cumming-Bruce LJ agreed) held that the *Sedleigh-Denfield* principle applied to a potential nuisance caused by the workings of nature,[99] and that if the defendant knew or ought to have known of the potential for nuisance, it was obliged to take reasonable steps to eliminate the problem. Importantly, however, the Court of Appeal also said that in judging whether particular steps were reasonably required, the defendant's capacity to find the money would be relevant; and alongside this could be considered the claimants' capacity to protect themselves from damage by erecting a barrier or providing funds for agreed works. While the duty to act reasonably is clearly subjective to this extent, Megaw LJ stressed that he did not envisage that it would be necessary to assess the wealth of the parties in anything other than an impressionistic manner.[100]

The nature of the occupier's duty with regard to natural forces was further explored in the case of *Holbeck Hall Hotel Ltd* v *Scarborough Borough Council*.[101] In this case a cliff on land belonging to the defendant council gave way and as a consequence a hotel on neighbouring land belonging to the claimant was destroyed. The case was particularly difficult because while the defendant ought to have foreseen some minor slips causing damage to the claimant's rose garden and lawn, there was no reason why it ought to have foreseen such an exceptional event as the massive slip which destroyed the hotel. In these circumstances, the Court of Appeal held that an occupier which failed to meet the measured duty to take reasonable steps to prevent a nuisance occurring on its land should only be liable to the extent of the damage that ought to have been foreseen.[102] Further, the Court of Appeal suggested that in the circumstances where the hazard was a result of the forces of nature and the defendant would have gained little benefit from preserving its own land against the hazard, the defendant might well have fulfilled the duty to act reasonably by informing the claimants of the risk and sharing any information relating to it.

The expansion of the rule that an occupier will be held to have continued a nuisance if he ought to have known of it and has failed to take reasonable steps to deal with it has led to some tension between the law of torts and established principles of land law. In particular, it is a basic principle of land law that a person whose land is subject to an easement is not obliged to undertake any repairs to the land so as to facilitate continued enjoyment of the easement, but instead the beneficiary of the easement has a right to enter the land to carry out

---

[98] In fact there were some doubts as to whether the National Trust really occupied the Mump, but for the purposes of the litigation it conceded that it did: ibid., 509.

[99] Ibid., 517–24.

[100] Ibid., 526–7. In *Abbahall* v *Smee* [2003] 1 WLR 1472, in circumstances where defendant and claimant occupied different floors of a building beneath a leaking roof, and the defendant sought to argue that because of her relative poverty she should not have to contribute towards the repairs, the Court of Appeal held that such an approach would be 'unjust to the point of absurdity' [57] and that the costs should normally be divided in proportion to the benefit that each party would gain from the work [41]. The problems which may arise where a nuisance causes consequential damage whilst the parties are squabbling about contributions have not yet been addressed by the courts.

[101] [2000] QB 836.

[102] This contrasts with the usual rule of remoteness of damage (see below, p. 557) that a defendant is liable for all damage of the same *type* as ought to have been foreseen, regardless of the *extent*.

works necessary to protect his right.[103] It seems that in light of the development of wider liability for adopting a nuisance this principle of land law can no longer be treated as an exhaustive summary of the law, at least when a failure to repair the land will lead to physical damage to the claimant's land.[104]

Nuisance or negligence?

Given that the question whether an occupier will be liable for consequences resulting from a state of affairs he did not create is answered by considering whether he has fulfilled a measured duty of care it is sometimes suggested that this group of cases properly forms part of the tort of negligence.[105] We would reject this suggestion. Such a suggestion is not merely one about the appropriate distribution of topics within textbooks. If the *Sedleigh-Denfield* doctrine was treated as *only* being part of the tort of negligence then this would make it difficult for a claimant to bring an action when a defendant occupier had failed to deal with a state of affairs which merely had the effect of reducing the amenity value of the claimant's land.[106] We think that the true position is that a breach of the duty can lead to a claim for continuing a private nuisance, but that there is also a parallel duty of care breach of which will amount to the tort of negligence.[107]

Occupiers

The case of *LE Jones (Insurance Brokers) Ltd v Portsmouth City Council*[108] raised the question whether the duty to take reasonable steps to abate a nuisance arising on some land will be owed by anyone other than the occupier of that land. The case involved damage caused by a tree which was situated on land vested in the highway authority but which the defendant council had agreed to maintain. Dyson LJ stated that 'the basis for the liability of an occupier for a nuisance on his land is not his occupation as such. Rather, it is that, by virtue of his occupation, an occupier usually has it in his power to take the measures

---

[103] *Jones v Pritchard* [1908] 1 Ch 630, 637–8.

[104] *Bradburn v Lindsay* [1983] 2 All ER 408.

[105] This view is advanced by Gearty 1989, who writes of *Sedleigh-Denfield* (at 237): 'This was negligence pure and simple, confused by an ill-fitting and woolly disguise of nuisance.' See also Weir 1998a, 102–3: 'that the defendant's liability in nuisance [in *Sedleigh-Denfield*] [was] affected by considerations relevant in the tort of negligence seems beyond doubt.'

[106] An example of such a case might be an occupier failing to deal with regular noisy trespassers, or with smelly rotting rubbish tipped onto his land by trespassers. In such a case the type of damage suffered by the claimant would not normally give rise to a claim in the tort of negligence but could give rise to a claim in private nuisance.

[107] See above, pp. 176–8. The scope of the negligence duty may be important. Compensation for personal injuries can never be recovered in the tort of private nuisance (see below, pp. 383–4), but can of course sometimes be recovered in the tort of negligence. Although Megaw LJ expressed the opinion that if an occupier breached a *Goldman v Hargrave*-type duty of care owed to his neighbour and his neighbour suffered a personal injury as a result, then the neighbour should be able to sue the occupier for damages in negligence (see *Leakey v National Trust* [1980] QB 485, at 523) there is currently no binding authority as to whether 'personal injury' suffered as a result of the breach of a *Goldman v Hargrave*-type duty of care will count as the 'right kind of loss' to be actionable in negligence. Our view is that it does not: see above, p. 176, n. 41.

[108] [2003] 1 WLR 427.

that are necessary to prevent or eliminate the nuisance. He has sufficient control over the hazard which constitutes the nuisance for it to be reasonable to make him liable for the foreseeable consequences of his failure to exercise that control so as to remove the hazard.'[109] Dyson LJ's test, which focuses instead on *control* over the *hazard*, rather than *occupation* of the land, has the potential to catch not just occupiers, but also independent contractors managing hazards on land on behalf of occupiers, and possibly also non-occupiers which have power to intervene and deal with hazards. We suspect, however, that the courts will be very cautious about extending liability much beyond those in occupation,[110] and have therefore in the interests of simplicity continued to use the phrase 'occupiers' to describe those who may be found to have adopted or continued a private nuisance.

Three defences

It is appropriate at this point to mention three defences which may prevent a defendant from being held responsible for a state of affairs or its consequences.

(1) *Necessity*. In the case of *Southport Corporation* v *Esso Petroleum Ltd*, a tanker got into difficulties, and fearing for the ship and the safety of his crew, the captain discharged his cargo of oil to make the tanker lighter. The oil polluted the claimant's beach. At first instance Devlin J suggested *obiter* that it would be a defence to create a nuisance in order to save human life, but that he was unwilling to hold that one could damage another's property in order to save one's own property, without providing compensation.[111] The Court of Appeal split on the defence of necessity. Singleton LJ suggested that there was a defence of necessity to claims for creating a nuisance, and that the defendant could rely on it unless he was negligent in creating the necessity.[112] Denning LJ also suggested that there was a defence of necessity, but he felt that it was for the defendant to prove that the necessity was unavoidable.[113] In the House of Lords[114] the decision concentrated on the pleadings, but Lord Radcliffe suggested *obiter* that there was a defence of necessity in nuisance, unless it was the defendant's carelessness which brought about the necessity.[115]

One reason for the divergence in judicial opinion is that where the necessity was brought about by circumstances for which neither party was responsible, the principal issue is which of two innocents should bear the cost. Had the ship

---

[109] Ibid., at [11].
[110] Many of the principles applied, for instance that which relates contributions to the cost of dealing with the state of affairs to the degree of benefit that claimant and defendant will gain from the state of affairs being dealt with, are difficult to apply to defendants who are not occupiers.
[111] [1953] 3 WLR 773.
[112] [1954] 2 QB 182, 194.
[113] Ibid., 197. Strictly speaking, Denning LJ only discussed *public* nuisance, but his reasoning on necessity, which relied on a parallel with the tort of trespass to land, can be applied equally to *private* nuisance.
[114] [1956] AC 218.
[115] Ibid., 242.

been caught in freak weather which itself led to the spillage of the oil, the defendant would probably have been held not to have *created* the pollution. Should we treat the case differently if the defendant responds reasonably to freak weather and was not at fault in exposing himself to the risk in the first place? Whatever the final judicial answer to this question, it is already clear that the courts will not countenance the development of a wide defence of necessity. In *Andreae v Selfridge & Co. Ltd*, Bennett J was scathing about a plea that it was necessary for builders to create severe disturbance in order to complete the work swiftly. He referred to a line from *Paradise Lost*: 'So spake the Fiend, and with necessity, the tyrant's plea, excused his devilish deeds.'[116]

(2) *Act of third party*. There seems little doubt that a defendant will avoid liability if he can prove that any unreasonable interference arising on his land was caused by a wholly unpredictable act of a trespasser. Where, however, a state of affairs created by a trespasser does not immediately cause an unreasonable interference, or continues to cause an interference over an extended period, an occupier of land may be held liable if he knew or ought to have known of the state of affairs and failed to take reasonable steps to rectify the situation.[117]

Further, where the trespasser's intervention was not wholly unpredictable a landowner may be held liable in negligence for failing to take reasonable precautions against the intervention. The question of how predictable an intervention must be before the landowner will be under a duty to take reasonable steps to prevent it is difficult to answer with confidence. The decision of the House of Lords in *Smith v Littlewoods Organisation Ltd*[118] provides no single clear answer. Lord Mackay LC stated that a landowner would only have had a duty to take reasonable steps to prevent a trespasser acting in some way if it was reasonably foreseeable that if he failed to take such steps then damage to the claimant would be probable, and that to establish that damage was probable it would be necessary to consider carefully both how likely the trespasser's intervention was and how likely it was that such an intervention would cause damage to the claimant.[119] By contrast, Lord Goff argued that a landowner would only owe his neighbour a duty to take reasonable steps to prevent a trespasser causing harm to his neighbour if: (*a*) the landowner has assumed a responsibility to his neighbour; *or* (*b*) the landowner is responsible for controlling the trespasser in question;[120] *or* (*c*) the landowner has negligently caused or permitted to be created a source of danger which it is reasonably foreseeable that a trespasser may 'spark off';[121] *or* (*d*) the landowner knows or ought to know that the trespasser in question has created a fire risk.[122]

---

[116] [1936] 2 All ER 1413, 1422.
[117] *Sedleigh-Denfield v O'Callaghan* [1940] AC 880. Discussed above, p. 375.
[118] [1987] 1 AC 241.
[119] Ibid., 261.
[120] Ibid., 272.
[121] Ibid., 273–4. Lord Goff's example is the storage of a quantity of fireworks in an unlocked garden shed.
[122] Ibid., 274. Here the duty seems to be parallel to the measured duty of care that is considered in cases of *continuing* a private nuisance (see above, p. 376).

(3) *Act of God*. A defendant will avoid liability in private nuisance if he can prove that any unreasonable interference was caused by a wholly unpredictable and uncontrollable natural force. In *Sedleigh-Denfield* v *O'Callaghan*, Lord Maugham stressed that the defendants had not tried to argue that the rainfall which caused the flood was so heavy as to give rise to a defence of 'Act of God'. He suggested that such a defence would, in any case, only have been available if the rain had been 'so exceptional in amount that no reasonable man could have anticipated it'.[123] A defendant may be liable if the force of nature was reasonably foreseeable, or if the state of affairs created by the force did not *immediately* lead to the interference. In the latter situation, if the defendant is an occupier, then he will be liable if he fails to take reasonable steps to deal with a known risk.[124]

A TORT TO LAND

In *Hunter* v *Canary Wharf Ltd*,[125] the House of Lords re-emphasised that the essence of private nuisance is that it is 'a tort to land'.[126] Lord Hoffmann, for instance, said that '[private nuisance] is a tort against land'.[127] The House of Lords did not, of course, mean by this that if A creates a private nuisance by unreasonably interfering with the use and enjoyment of a certain piece of land, he breaches a duty owed to that piece of land – that would be absurd. What they seemed to mean by this was two things.

First, A will only commit the tort of private nuisance *in relation to B* if he creates, authorises, adopts or continues a state of affairs which unreasonably interferes with the use and enjoyment of a piece of land with which B is linked by virtue of the fact that B has *an interest* in that land. If, then, Mary created, authorised, adopted or continued a state of affairs which unreasonably interfered with the use and enjoyment of a piece of land in which Tom had *no* interest, Tom will not be able to establish that Mary – in acting as she did – committed the tort of private nuisance in relation to *him*. He will, in consequence, have to find some other ground to sue Mary if he wants to sue her for damages in respect of the harm suffered by him as a result of Mary's activities.

Secondly, if A has committed the tort of private nuisance in relation to B by unreasonably interfering with the use and enjoyment of Blackacre, a piece of land in which B has an interest, the duty breached by A in so acting will have been imposed on A to help ensure that B's *interest in Blackacre was not damaged*.

---

[123] [1940] AC 880, 886.

[124] This is another situation where the relevant duty is the measured duty of an occupier to take reasonable steps to prevent conditions on his land causing nuisance to his neighbour. *Goldman* v *Hargrave* [1967] 1 AC 645 provides a good example of a state of affairs created by a uncontrollable force of nature (red gum set alight by lightning) only causing harm to a neighbour after the occupier had a reasonable opportunity to abate the risk.

[125] [1997] AC 655.

[126] This phrase comes from Newark 1949, 482, where he wrote that the essence of private nuisance was that 'it was a tort to land. Or to be more accurate it was a tort directed against the claimant's enjoyment of rights over land . . .' This passage was commended by Lord Goff in *Hunter* [1997] AC 655, at 687H as the clearest expression of the basic position.

[127] Ibid., 702H.

So B will only be entitled to sue A for damages in respect of the harm done by A's interference *to his interest in Blackacre*. He will not be entitled to sue A for damages in respect of *any other type of harm* that he has suffered as a result of A's interference – for example, personal injury.[128]

We will now look at each of these propositions in more detail before considering some of the criticisms that have been made of this aspect of the House of Lords' decision in *Hunter* v *Canary Wharf*.

Title to sue

It seems to be correct, in English law at any rate, that A will only commit the tort of private nuisance in relation to B if he creates, authorises, adopts or continues a state of affairs which unreasonably interferes with a piece of land in which B has an interest. However, two difficult questions must be addressed. First, what sort of interests count as interests *in land*? Second, if A has unreasonably interfered with a particular piece of land and B wants to sue A on the basis that A in so acting committed the tort of private nuisance in relation to her, does B have to *prove* that she has a legally-recognised interest in the land in question – and, linked with that, will B be barred from suing A if A can show that B did not have a legally-recognised interest in the land?

Interests in land[129]
English land law draws a distinction between interests *in land* and *personal* interests. The main distinction between these is that interests *in land* can bind third parties while *personal* interests generally do not. A person with a fee simple in possession over Greenacre has an obvious interest *in land* while a person who has purchased a ticket from the owner of Greenacre entitling him to visit Greenacre Hall for a guided tour has only a *personal* (contractual) interest. Consequently, if Greenacre Hall is blighted by intolerable noise created by Paul, the person with a fee simple in possession can sue for private nuisance but the visitor on the guided tour cannot. If Greenacre Hall is leased to a tenant then that tenant has an interest in land and is able to sue for private nuisance. The reversioner (that is, the person who will take back Greenacre Hall at the end of the tenancy) may also sue if the private nuisance has any effect on *his own* interest in land.[130] The interests of two classes of persons are particularly difficult to classify: (*a*) licensees, and (*b*) the spouses and children of people with interests in land. With regard to licensees, if the licence grants exclusive possession then the licensee will often be able to sue because of the *de facto* possession rule discussed in the next section. With regard to family members, it is clear that they will not be treated as having interests *in land* if they merely occupy the house as a home.[131]

---

[128] See below, pp. 383–4 and 570–1.
[129] We will not attempt to list *all* the interests which may qualify as interests *in land*. The interested reader should consult a standard textbook on land law.
[130] If, for instance, the noise is sufficiently loud to damage the windows and the tenant is not obliged to repair them, then the noise damages the reversioner's interest in the land.
[131] *Hunter* v *Canary Wharf Ltd* [1997] AC 655.

De facto possession

A person who *in fact* enjoys or asserts exclusive possession over a piece of land will not be required to *prove* that he has a right to that possession in order to sue a defendant in private nuisance for unreasonably interfering with the use and enjoyment of that land. Moreover, the defendant will only be permitted to rely on the fact that the possessor has *no* right to possess the land in question[132] if either the defendant has the right to possession of that land, or the defendant created the nuisance with the authority of the person with the right to possession. This rule has several consequences.

First, a person enjoying exclusive possession in fact, but who has a defective title, will still be able to sue.[133] Secondly, a licensee enjoying exclusive possession may be able to sue without having to convince the court that a licence granting exclusive possession creates an interest *in land*. Thirdly, a person asserting exclusive possession over something which cannot be owned as land may be able to sue.[134]

Because most[135] of those who qualify as having a title to sue in nuisance under the first rule – on the ground that they have an interest *in the land* being interfered with – will also qualify under the second rule – on the ground that they enjoy *de facto* exclusive possession of the land interfered with, it might be thought to be a sensible simplification to treat the law as simply saying that a person who enjoys *de facto* exclusive possession of a piece of land can sue in nuisance if his use and enjoyment of that land is unreasonably interfered with. Our view, however, is that this simplification should be resisted.

First, such a simplification ignores the fact that a reversioner can sue for interference with *his own* interest in land. Secondly, such a simplification risks obscuring the point that a defendant who is being sued in nuisance for unreasonably interfering with another's use and enjoyment of land will have a good defence if he can demonstrate that he has the right to possession of the land in question or is acting on the authority of the person with that right. Thirdly, such a simplification may be confusing when it comes to assessing what remedy to grant. There would be a particular problem if the court wanted to award damages compensating for *future* interferences in lieu of an injunction[136] but it was not clear who would suffer those future interferences.[137]

---

[132] This is often referred to as the defence of *ius tertii*.

[133] See, for example, *Pemberton v Southwark London Borough Council* [2000] 1 WLR 1672. In *Metropolitan Properties Ltd v Jones* [1939] 2 All ER 202 the claimant, Jones, had been a tenant of the flat affected by the nuisance, but he had assigned the tenancy (and hence the right to occupy) to a person called Storer, before returning to live in the flat when Storer disappeared, leaving him (Jones) still liable for the rent. Lord Hoffmann suggested in *Hunter v Canary Wharf Ltd* [1997] AC 655, 704E, that Jones should have been allowed to sue on the basis of his *de facto* possession.

[134] In *Foster v Warblington UDC* [1906] 1 KB 648 the claimant sued for the pollution of oyster ponds on the foreshore.

[135] The obvious exception is a reversioner.

[136] For this remedy see below, pp. 713–17.

[137] The fact that someone *presently* enjoys exclusive possession does not mean that such possession is likely to continue in the future.

Recoverable harm

Given that the test for liability is different in the torts of negligence and private nuisance it becomes important to consider whether there are any situations where there will be an awkward overlap. In *Hunter* v *Canary Wharf* the House of Lords limited the possibility of overlap by reasserting the traditional rule that only those with an interest in land can sue in private nuisance. Lord Lloyd and Lord Hoffmann went further, however, in eliminating the prospect of overlap and both stated that damages for personal injuries could not be recovered in private nuisance.[138] Lord Goff raised this issue but did not express any concluded opinion on it, preferring to say no more than that actions for interference with interests in land were the *typical* form of private nuisance.[139]

If damages for personal injuries could be recovered in private nuisance then the anomalous situation would arise that a person would find it easier to recover personal injury damages if injured when in a garden that she owned than if injured in the street or at work. Further, because only a claimant with an interest in land can sue in private nuisance, there would then be a second anomaly. A landowner who was injured in her garden by an emanation would be able to sue the creator of that emanation in nuisance for damages in respect of her injury without having to prove that the creator of the emanation acted carelessly; on the other hand, if the landowner's infant son (who would not have an interest in the land affected by the emanation) were injured by the same emanation, he would have to prove carelessness on the part of the creator of the emanation before he could sue for damages in respect of his injuries. One possible solution to the second anomaly would be to let those without interests in land sue in private nuisance. But the House of Lords rejected this solution, and ruled that it was inconsistent with the *function* of the tort which is to protect interests in land. The Lloyd–Hoffmann solution to both anomalies was to deny that anyone could sue in private nuisance for compensation in respect of personal injuries.

It may be worth noting, however, that by excluding personal injuries from private nuisance a third apparent anomaly arises. If foul-smelling acidic smoke created by Gary drifts across land belonging to Lara, Lara will find it easier to sue Gary for the bad smell carried by the smoke than she will if the smoke physically burns her nostrils. If the bad smell reduces the amenity value of Lara's land then she will be able to sue Gary in nuisance for compensation for that without having to prove carelessness on Gary's part. On the other hand, carelessness must be established on Gary's part before Lara can sue him for compensation in respect of the harm to her nostrils.

A fourth anomaly might also arise, depending on how damage to chattels on the land is treated. Lord Hoffmann suggested that if Dawn committed the tort of private nuisance in relation to Carl by flooding Carl's land with the result that some cows belonging to Carl were drowned, Carl might be able to recover damages for the loss of those cows.[140] While it is easy to appreciate the convenience of such a rule, and its attraction in avoiding a need to distinguish between

---

[138] *Hunter* v *Canary Wharf Ltd* [1997] AC 655, 696D, 707H.
[139] Ibid., 692.
[140] Ibid., 706.

crops (which might count as part of the land itself) and cows (which would not), it would have the unattractive consequence of drawing a distinction between the level of protection given to cows and that given to people.

Evaluation of the decision in *Hunter* v *Canary Wharf Ltd*[141]

The majority in *Hunter* v *Canary Wharf Ltd*[142] insisted that there had to be a clear distinction between the *function* of the tort of private nuisance and the *function* of the tort of negligence in order to explain the differences between the torts.[143] These differences were said to flow from the fact that private nuisance protects a claimant's interests in land, while negligence protects the personal safety of all persons regardless of whether they have interests in land. The argument, in summary, is that if those without interests in land were allowed to sue in private nuisance that would 'transform it from a tort to land into a tort to the person'[144] and blur the distinction between the two torts.

This transformation would also conflict with the way a majority of their Lordships thought that damages should be assessed for *past* harm[145] in private nuisance cases. Lords Lloyd, Hoffmann and Hope all insisted that the appropriate measure of damages for an interference with the use and enjoyment of land in cases not involving physical damage to the land is the diminution in the amenity value of the land caused by the nuisance.[146] This amenity value is an amount relative to the land, not relative to how many people live on it. Lord Hoffmann said, 'Damages for nuisance recoverable by the possessor or occupier may be affected by the size, commodiousness and value of his property but cannot be increased merely because more people are in occupation and therefore suffer greater discomfort.'[147]

Their Lordships also treated both the weight of the 'transformation' argument and the persuasiveness of the damages point as reinforced by the symmetry which would consequentially exist between the three different forms of interference which can constitute private nuisance: encroachment on land, indirect[148]

---

[141] The ruling in this case relating to interference with television reception has already been discussed above, pp. 360–1.

[142] [1997] AC 655.

[143] Lord Hope pointed out one difference (ibid., at 724A–B), that 'the tort of nuisance is a tort of strict liability in the sense that it is no defence to say that the defendant took all reasonable care to prevent it' and Lord Hoffmann noted another (ibid., at 707H), that 'the law of negligence gives no remedy for discomfort or distress which does not result in bodily or psychiatric illness'.

[144] Ibid., 693D–E.

[145] Damages may be claimed for *past* harm. Further, where an injunction is claimed, a court may decide to award damages for anticipated *future* harm *in lieu* of an injunction. For more details, see Chapter 41, below.

[146] [1997] AC 655, 696B–C (per Lord Lloyd), 706E–F (per Lord Hoffmann), 724G–H (per Lord Hope).

[147] Thus both Lord Hoffmann (ibid., at 706D–707B) and Lord Lloyd (ibid., at 698D–699A) expressly disapproved of the suggestion in *Bone* v *Seale* [1975] 1 WLR 797 that damages for private nuisance by smell might be assessed by drawing an analogy with awards in personal injury cases for loss of the sense of smell. Lord Hope's views were less clear.

[148] Their Lordships talked about *direct* physical damage instead of *indirect* physical damage, but we have explained above (at p. 357) why this was an error.

physical damage to land and reduction in amenity value. Where interference is by encroachment on or physical damage *to land* it seems obvious that the person who should be able to sue is the person with the interest in the land. Equally it seems obvious that if that person claims damages then these should be calculated to compensate him for the diminution in the value of his interest in the land. Accepting that only those with interests in land can sue for interferences with sensibilities, and that *all* they can sue for is reduction of the amenity value *of the land*, means that whatever the form of interference, only those with interests in land can sue and their damages should reflect the damage done to their interest.

Lord Goff provided two additional practical reasons why liability in private nuisance should only extend to those with interests in land. First, he pointed out that potential claimants often reach compromises with potential defendants, for instance permitting the nuisance to continue for a fixed period in exchange for payment. Lord Goff feared that the likelihood of such sensible arrangements would be reduced if potential defendants had to identify and deal with not just those with interests in the land but all the occupiers of each property affected by their activities.[149] Secondly, he suggested that if the range of liability in private nuisance extended beyond the clear category of those with interests in land it would prove impossible to find any other easily definable limit. Thus he raised the awkward cases of lodgers, au pairs, resident nurses, and employees.[150]

Of the Lords who heard the *Hunter* case, only Lord Cooke argued against the traditional rule. His dissent urged that there was no *logical* reason why those who had actually been enjoying the amenities of a home should be unable to sue for an unreasonable interference with those amenities and that consequently a judicial determination of the issue depended on a policy choice.[151] In approaching this choice he expressed a preference for utility and justice over symmetry and tidiness,[152] discounted Lord Goff's concerns about sensible compromises and au pairs,[153] and concluded, 'occupation of the property as a home is, to me, an acceptable criterion, consistent with the traditional concern for the sanctity of family life and the Englishman's home'.[154] A tolerable paraphrase of Lord Cooke's reasoning might be that in modern society a domestic house, a home, is more than just a piece of investment property. No doubt if the home is invaded by noxious fumes or bad vibrations the owner's investment is harmed, and only the owner should be able to claim for that damage *to the investment*. But equally without doubt is the fact that other occupants of the home will have suffered – their lives will have been rendered less restful and fulfilling – and so far as they are concerned, they should be compensated for their loss. In doctrinal terms, Lord Cooke might be said to have been arguing that

[149] [1997] AC 655, 692H–693C.
[150] Ibid., 693C–F.
[151] Ibid., 711C–D.
[152] Ibid., 711B–C.
[153] Ibid., 718A–D.
[154] Ibid., 718B–C.

the interest that the tort of private nuisance should protect is not merely an interest in land but a wider 'interest in a home'.

We think that Lord Cooke is unfair to the majority when he portrays the divergence as turning on whether one prefers symmetry and tidiness or utility and justice. We think that the majority was motivated by the need to set down clearly who is protected by the law on private nuisance and for what harm damages can be recovered if A commits the tort of private nuisance in relation to B. Clarity on these issues is important for settling disputes and also for those who want, in advance of any dispute, to negotiate permission to develop and use land in ways which may inconvenience neighbours. On the other hand, we also think, that the majority's treatment of 'homes' as simply *investments in property* fails to reflect the way in which most members of our society value 'homes'. The question of who is protected by the law on private nuisance is part of a more general dispute in the law of torts between the desire to draw bright-lines which will allow people to plan around the law and the desire to decide each case on its individual merits. There are no easy answers to the question of how to balance these two desires. In the area under discussion, it would be very helpful to have more evidence about whether those who carry out activities which *may* create a nuisance generally *try* to negotiate in advance, or not, before deciding whether the balance struck by the majority is preferable to the balance struck by Lord Cooke.[155]

Article 8 of the European Convention of Human Rights

Article 8(1) of the ECHR provides that 'Everyone has the right to respect for his private and family life, his home and his correspondence.' The European Court of Human Rights has held that this right can be violated by 'homes' being exposed to extreme noise or environmental pollution,[156] and that even when the State has not directly created the noise or pollution it may nonetheless be responsible for the violation if it has failed properly to regulate private industry.[157]

Several lawyers have argued that s 6 of the Human Rights Act 1998 obliges the English courts to develop the common law so as to make it compatible with the Convention,[158] and that they should fulfil this obligation by extending the tort of private nuisance so that *all* those who reside in a 'home' can sue (regardless of whether they have a sufficient interest in the land) if their use and enjoyment of the 'home' has been unreasonably interfered with and damages should be available for 'distress' caused by such interferences.[159] Two problems

---

[155] If such negotiating in advance is very rare we think this would strengthen the case for accepting Lord Cooke's views.

[156] Though interference with a person's 'home' by noise or pollution can be justified under Article 8.2 if the interference is prescribed by law and necessary in a democratic society.

[157] *Powell & Rayner* v *United Kingdom* (1990) 12 EHRR 355; *Lopez Ostra* v *Spain* (1995) 20 EHRR 277; *Guerra* v *Italy* (1998) 26 EHRR 357; *Hatton* v *United Kingdom* (2003) 37 EHRR 28.

[158] See, for example, Hunt 1998.

[159] Wright J 2001, 194. In *McKenna* v *British Aluminum*, The Times, 25 April 2002, Neuberger J thought that it was arguable that the English courts would accept this argument.

with this argument are worth mentioning here. First, although the English courts are obliged to act compatibly with the Convention, the cases before the European Court of Human Rights have *not* established that a failure by a State to create private law actions for children and other non-owners to bring against polluters is incompatible with Article 8. The cases have established that a failure of the State to prevent such pollution by regulation is incompatible with Article 8, but that is not the same as saying that such regulation must be by the provision of private law actions. Secondly, extending the tort of private nuisance may actually provide children and non-owners with *far more* than Article 8 requires. As we have seen, the tort of private nuisance allows the owner of a house in a luxurious residential district to sue when the premises are subjected to the smell of frying fish,[160] but it seems highly unlikely that the European Court of Human Rights would regard such an owner's children as victims of a human rights violation.[161]

REMAINING POINTS

Three points remain to be made about the tort of private nuisance.

(1) *Some unusual forms of private nuisance.* There are some other torts which are treated as forms of private nuisance though they do not fit within the definition of what committing the tort of private nuisance involves which was advanced at the start of this chapter. For example: the tort of organising a rival market within 6½ miles of a franchise or statutory market;[162] or the tort of organising a ferry service which rivals that of a person with a franchise right to operate a ferry. Such torts have often developed their own esoteric rules, like that making the distance of 6½ miles significant, and consequently can claim to be treated as independent torts rather than forms of private nuisance. We think that it is likely, however, that a judge asked to resolve any uncertainty about the rules applying to these torts would draw strong analogies with the tort of private nuisance.

(2) *The relationship between private nuisance and public nuisance.* Although the word 'nuisance' is common to both wrongs it is important to remember that private nuisance and public nuisance are *separate* forms of unlawful conduct.[163] In some situations they may overlap, but not every defendant who commits the tort of private nuisance will create a public nuisance and not every defendant who creates a public nuisance will commit the tort of private nuisance.

---

[160] *Adams* v *Ursell* [1913] 1 Ch 269.
[161] In *Dennis* v *Ministry of Defence* [2003] EWHC 793 (QB), Buckley J held that the amount he was awarding a landowner for private nuisance caused by noise was sufficient to amount to 'just satisfaction' of the claim by the landowner and *his wife* that their rights under Article 8 had been infringed. It seems, however, that he reached this conclusion after using the wrong method to assess damages for private nuisance, and without considering whether the amounts would always coincide. See further, Bagshaw 2004a, 41.
[162] *Tamworth BC* v *Fazeley Town Council* (1978) 77 LGR 238; *Sevenoaks DC* v *Vinson Ltd* [1984] Ch 211; *Stoke-on-Trent City Council* v *W & J Wass Ltd* [1988] 1 WLR 1406.
[163] Public nuisance is discussed below, in Chapter 46.

At this stage in the chapter it will be clear that if A commits the tort of private nuisance in relation to B, he will usually do so by unreasonably interfering with the use and enjoyment of land in which B has an interest. In contrast, creating a public nuisance involves interfering with a *public right* or acting in a way which is generally *contrary to the public interest*. In many situations, such as when there is an actionable interference with the public right to free passage along a highway, there can be a public nuisance even though nobody's interests in land have been affected. Private individuals can seek redress, including damages, for public nuisances where they have suffered 'special damage'. But one can show that one has suffered 'special damage' without showing that land in which one has an interest has been unreasonably interfered with or damaged. Where a public nuisance *does* lead to a person suffering 'special damage' in the form of damage to land in which he has an interest there will be an *overlap* between private nuisance and a possible individual claim for public nuisance. It seems, however, that it would not be to the private individual's advantage to sue for *public* nuisance in such a case.[164]

(3) *The relationship between private nuisance and the rule in Rylands v Fletcher.*[165] The rule in *Rylands* v *Fletcher* imposes liability on a defendant who has brought onto, or kept on, some land an *exceptionally dangerous or mischievous thing in extraordinary or unusual circumstances*, when the thing has escaped from that land and damaged the claimant's land.[166] There is some controversy over the relationship between the rule and the tort of private nuisance. Following the opinion of Lord Macmillan that '*Rylands* v *Fletcher* . . . derives from a conception of mutual duties of adjoining or neighbouring landowners, and its cogenors are trespass and nuisance',[167] and the assertion of Lord Goff that '*Rylands* v *Fletcher* was essentially concerned with an extension of the law of nuisance to cases of isolated escape',[168] a majority of the House of Lords in *Transco plc* v *Stockport Metropolitan Borough Council*[169] stated that the rule in *Rylands* v *Fletcher*, like the torts of trespass to land and private nuisance, can only be relied on by those who have interests in land,[170] and cannot be used to claim compensation for personal injuries. Although this classification of the rule in *Rylands* v *Fletcher* is now authoritative, our view is that it is misguided and was adopted by the House of Lords without sufficient attention to the issues involved.[171] Consequently we will postpone discussion of liability under the rule in *Rylands* v *Fletcher* until Chapter 44.

---

[164] A person choosing to sue in public nuisance instead of private nuisance would impose on herself the additional burdens of proving both that the state of affairs affected a sufficient proportion of the community and that she had suffered 'special damage'.

[165] (1866) LR 1 Ex 265; (1868) LR 3 HL 330.

[166] For what we mean by 'the claimant's land' in this context see above, n. 1.

[167] *Read* v *J Lyons & Co.* [1947] AC 156, 173.

[168] *Cambridge Water Co.* v *Eastern Counties Leather Plc* [1994] 2 AC 264, 304E.

[169] [2003] 3 WLR 1467.

[170] In practice those who have exclusive possession of land can often claim. See above, p. 382.

[171] We present our reasons for this view below, pp. 741–2.

19

INDUCING A BREACH OF CONTRACT

DEFINITION

A will have committed the tort of inducing a breach of contract in relation to B *if*: (1) B had a contract with a third party, C; *and* (2) A induced C to breach that contract;[1] *and* (3) A was in a certain state of mind – defined below – when A induced C to breach that contract; *and* (4) A had no justification for acting as he did.

So, in *Lumley* v *Gye*,[2] Johanna Wagner, a well-known soprano, made a contract with Lumley to sing at Her Majesty's Theatre, and not to sing anywhere else. Gye, a rival opera impresario, was alleged to have persuaded Wagner to sing for him at the Royal Italian Opera – and therefore to break her contract with Lumley. The Court of Queen's Bench held that if Gye *had* persuaded Wagner to break her contract with Lumley then Gye would have committed a tort in relation to Lumley.[3]

The tort in *Lumley* v *Gye* is usually described as 'the tort of inducing a breach of contract'. But, as we will see below,[4] it now seems clear that the tort can be committed without a *breach* of contract actually being engineered. This has led some writers to refer to the tort discussed here as the tort of *interference with a contract* instead.[5] The problem with this name, however, is that there seems to be an important difference between *direct* and *indirect* interference with a contract. If A has *indirectly* interfered with a contract between B and C to B's detriment, A will *not* have committed a tort in relation to B *unless* he used *unlawful means* to interfere with B's contract with C *and* his object in interfering with the contract was to harm B,[6] and even then the tort A will have committed in relation to B is 'the tort of using unlawful means to harm another'.[7] Consequently, we think that to call the tort discussed here 'interference with a contract' is potentially dangerous, because one might then be tempted to view cases of tortious *indirect* interference with a contract as instances of the tort

---

[1] *Important note.* The term 'induce' as used in this chapter does not bear its normal meaning of 'cause' or 'bring about'. We will discuss when someone will be held to have 'induced' a breach of contract below at pp. 393–9.

[2] (1853) 2 E & B 216, 118 ER 749.

[3] In fact, at the later trial of the facts, a jury found that Gye had not committed the tort because he had honestly believed that Wagner was at liberty to terminate her agreement with Lumley: for further details, see Waddams 2001.

[4] See below, pp. 399–402.

[5] For instance, Fleming 1998, 756–7; W&J, 635–6.

[6] *Torquay Hotel* v *Cousins* [1969] 2 Ch 106, 139A, per Lord Denning MR.

[7] This tort is discussed below, in Chapter 20.

discussed here when they are properly viewed as instances of the tort of 'using unlawful means to harm another'.

THE MENTAL ELEMENT REQUIRED TO COMMIT THE TORT

Suppose A induced C to breach a contract that she had made with B. A will not have committed the tort of inducing a breach of contract in so acting unless he was in a *certain state of mind* when he brought about the breach. For example, if A merely brought about the breach *carelessly*, he will not have committed the tort of inducing a breach of contract in causing C to breach her contract with B. So what sort of state of mind does it have to be shown A was in before we will find that A committed the tort of inducing a breach of contract in inducing C to breach her contract with B?

It does *not* have to be shown that A *intended to harm* B when he acted as he did. This follows from the decision in *Lumley* v *Gye*. The Court of Queen's Bench held that if Gye persuaded Wagner to sing for him, he would have committed a tort – the tort of inducing a breach of contract – in relation to Lumley. It did not hold that it *also* had to be established that Gye acted as he did in order to harm Lumley. So suppose Gye persuaded Wagner to sing for him and breach her with Lumley because he thought he could make a lot of money if Wagner sang for him. In such a case, Gye would have committed a tort – the tort of inducing a breach of contract – in relation to Lumley. And this is so even though Gye was not trying to harm Lumley in acting as he did but was rather trying to make some money for himself.[8]

So what *does* have to be shown? Many cases and textbooks rely on the statement of Jenkins LJ in *D C Thomson* v *Deakin* that it is necessary to show that a defendant acted 'with knowledge of the contract and the intention of bringing about its breach'.[9] But this statement must be discussed further because the concept of 'intention' is used in different ways in different areas of the law.

In this context, the word 'intention' is used in quite a loose way. Strictly speaking, a defendant can only be said to have *intended* to induce a breach of contract when he did *x* if his *object* or *aim* in doing *x* was to bring about a breach of contract. But if we try to reconstruct what was being alleged about Gye's state of mind when he sought to persuade Johanna Wagner to sing at the Royal Italian Opera we are unlikely to conclude that the allegation was that his *aim* in persuading Wagner to sing for him was to cause her to *breach her contract* with Lumley. If Wagner could have sung for Gye without breaching her contract with Lumley, Gye would have been perfectly happy – Gye's aim or object in

---

[8] *Important note.* We can test whether Gye was trying to harm Lumley in the scenario we have just described by asking: If it turned out that Lumley was not made worse off as a result of Wagner's going off to sing for Gye – say Lumley was insured against the consequences of Wagner's walking out on him – would Gye have been disappointed or upset? The answer, in the scenario we have just described, is plainly 'no' – Gye's motivation in persuading Wagner to sing for him was to enrich himself, not to harm Lumley.

[9] [1952] Ch 646, 694. See also *Merkur Island Corp.* v *Laughton* [1983] 2 AC 570, 608G.

persuading Wagner to sing for him was not therefore to get Wagner to breach her contract with Lumley; his aim or object was to get Wagner to sing for him and, ultimately, to make some money by getting Wagner to sing for him.

Of course, if Gye knew that Wagner had entered a valid contract with Lumley not to sing elsewhere than Her Majesty's Theatre then he must also have known that a *side effect* of his getting Wagner to sing at the Royal Italian Opera would be that she would breach her contract with Lumley. But if you acted in a certain way knowing that a side effect of your acting in that way was that event E would happen, that does not mean you acted in the way you did with the *intention* of causing event E to happen.[10] So when the courts say that a defendant will have committed the tort of inducing a breach of contract in bringing about a breach of contract if and only if he acted 'with knowledge of the contract and the intention of bringing about its breach' they use the term 'intention' in a weak (and inaccurate) way. They will find that the defendant intended to bring about a breach of contract if *he knew that his conduct would result or was likely to result in a breach of contract.*[11]

So suppose that B had a contract with C and A induced C to commit a breach of that contract. In clarifying the mental element that A must have possessed before he will be found to have committed the tort of inducing a breach of contract in this situation, it may be helpful to follow Jenkins LJ and distinguish between the state of mind A must have had towards the existence of the contract between B and C and the state of mind A must have had towards C's breach of that contract.

State of mind towards the contract

As to the state of mind towards the contract, there seems little doubt that A must have been *aware* of the contract between B and C before he will be found to have committed the tort of inducing a breach of contract in inducing C to breach it. It is clear from the cases, however, that A will *not* have had to know the *precise terms* of the contract between B and C. Moreover, A will still be found to have been aware of the contract between B and C if he 'turned a blind eye' to the existence of the contract.[12] Indeed A can be *deemed* to have known of the contract if contracts are almost always found in the particular commercial context in which B and C were operating and A has general expertise in that area.[13]

---

[10] Compare: suppose that you ran out into the rain to buy a newspaper, knowing that a side effect of your doing so was that you would get wet. It would be strange to say that when you ran out into the rain to buy the newspaper, you intended to get wet.

[11] See, for example, *Millar* v *Bassey* [1994] EMLR 44.

[12] *Torquay Hotel* v *Cousins* [1969] 2 Ch 106, 138E (per Lord Denning MR).

[13] See, for instance, *Merkur Island Shipping Corp.* v *Laughton* [1983] 2 AC 570, 608G–609C where Lord Diplock approved Sir John Donaldson MR's statement (at 591E–G) that the defendants' knowledge could be deemed where the defendants were officials of a trade union with expert knowledge of shipping contracts and their target was a laden ship about to leave port so that there would almost certainly exist contracts of carriage to which the shipowners were parties.

State of mind towards the breach

As to the state of mind that A must have possessed towards C's breach, it follows from what has already been said that for A to be found to have committed the tort of inducing a breach of contract in the case we are discussing, it does not have to be shown that A acted as he did with the *aim* or *object* of causing C to breach her contract with B. It is enough if, when A acted as he did, he knew that his acting in that way *would or was likely to have* the effect of causing C to breach her contract with B. Indeed, the cases go further and suggest that A can be liable even if he did *not* know that his actions were likely to result in C breaching her contract with B: it may be enough if A knew that his actions *could* result in C breaching her contract with B and he did not care whether or not his actions had that effect.

In *Emerald Construction* v *Lowthian*[14] the defendants, the officers of a building trade union, sought to persuade the main contractor on the project to build the Fiddlers Ferry power station to terminate a labour-only subcontract. The defendants knew of the subcontract but were not aware of its terms. The main contractor did terminate the subcontract and committed a breach of contract in so doing – the main contractor was not allowed under the subcontract to terminate the subcontract in the way he did. The subcontractors sued the defendants, claiming that they had committed the tort of inducing a breach of contract. The defendants were held liable even though they had not actually been aware that the main contractor would commit a breach of the subcontract if he terminated it. Lord Denning MR remarked, 'if the officers deliberately sought to get this contract terminated, heedless of its terms, regardless of whether it was terminated by breach or not, they would do wrong. For it is unlawful for a third person to procure a breach of contract knowingly, or recklessly, indifferent whether it is a breach or not.'[15]

Summary

So: before we can find that A committed the tort of inducing a breach of contract in inducing C to breach her contract with B, it will have to be established that when A acted as he did: (1) he was aware that there was a contract between B and C; *and* (2) he knew that his actions were very likely to result in C breaching that contract, or he knew that his actions could result in C breaching that contract and he did not care whether or not his actions had that effect.

[14] [1966] 1 WLR 691.
[15] Ibid., 700H–701A. Carty 2001 states (at 51–3) that there are 'strong policy reasons' for rejecting Lord Denning MR's view on this point. She argues that B ought to have to show that A acted as he did with the *aim* or *object* of causing C to breach her contract with B, since otherwise the tort may interfere too much with competition and industrial action. We believe, however, that the scope of the tort can be sufficiently limited by carefully defining when A will be held to have *induced* C to breach her contract with B.

WHEN WILL SOMEONE BE HELD TO HAVE *INDUCED* A BREACH OF CONTRACT?

It is not easy to define when someone will be held to have *induced* someone else to commit a breach of contract. Perhaps a good starting point is to say that if A has *persuaded* C to break a contract with B then A will be held to have induced C to breach that contract. Some commentators have argued that the tort should extend no further: 'liability should attach under *Lumley* v *Gye* only when the defendant has persuaded the [claimant's] contractor deliberately to break his contract.'[16] However, there are some cases when A has been held to have induced C to breach her contract with B even though it would be difficult to describe the part he played in bringing about that breach as *persuasion*.[17]

Advice

Suppose that Lara has contracted to sing at Paul's theatre in London and that Lara's aunt, Mary, has advised her not to go to London to sing because a wealthy relative is dying, and this relative is only likely to give bequests to family members who pray at his bedside. If Lara takes this advice and breaks her contract, should Mary be held to have induced the breach?

Those who argue that Mary should not be held to have induced Lara to breach her contract assert that there is an important distinction between *creating* a reason to break a contract and *pointing out* that a reason exists.[18] But Winn LJ showed no sympathy for such a distinction when it was pressed in *Torquay Hotel* v *Cousins*, and suggested that a father who told his daughter that her fiancé had been convicted of indecent exposure would have induced her to break her engagement even if the information was true.[19] Certainly there would be a risk, if the courts drew a distinction between persuasion and advice, that the line between making a soprano a generous offer to *persuade* her to break her contract and merely *advising* her that such an offer was likely to be available if she broke her contract would be difficult to draw in practice.

'Harbouring'

Can A be said to have induced a breach of a contract between B and C if C's breach of that contract happened *before* A became involved? Suppose, for example, that Beth, a soprano, contracted to perform exclusively for Ian. Suppose that Beth then walked out on Ian in breach of contract and was later engaged by Gary. Can Gary

---

[16] Weir 1997, 35 (quoted approvingly by Carty 2001, at 61). Weir treats 'persuasion' in this context as involving persuasion with either 'stick or carrot': Weir 1997, 34.

[17] These are conveniently listed by Jenkins LJ in *D C Thomson* v *Deakin* [1952] Ch 646, 694–5.

[18] S&H, 353; Carty 2001, 47.

[19] [1969] 2 Ch 106, 147D–E. Of course, in such a case the father might be able to rely on the defence of justification. See below, pp. 402–3. In *Camden Nominees Ltd* v *Slack (or Forcey)* [1940] Ch 352, Simonds J was equally clear that 'advice which is intended to have persuasive effects is not distinguishable from inducement', but also held that a person who provided advice could rely on the defence of justification if the law recognised a moral duty to give the advice.

be said to have induced Beth to breach her contract with Ian? It seems that the English courts have taken the view that Gary *can* be held liable if Beth's breach of her contract with Ian was still 'retrievable'.[20] This is often referred to as liability for 'harbouring' – the idea being that in the case just described, Gary, by providing Beth with a 'harbour', made it less likely that Beth would return and perform for Ian.[21]

Facilitating

In *British Motor Trade Association* v *Salvadori*[22] C sold a car to A, in breach of a contractual undertaking that C had made with B that he would not sell the car to anyone within a year after purchasing it. A argued that C had been willing to sell the car and break his contract with B without any influence from him, and that consequently he could not be said to have induced the breach. Roxburgh J held, however, that C could not break the contract not to sell without *someone* being willing to buy, and that 'any active step taken by a defendant . . . by which he facilitates a breach' was sufficient to fall within the scope of the tort.[23] Some commentators, however, have expressed strong doubts about this statement because the courts have refused to adopt a general principle that anyone who assists another to commit a tort will be held liable.[24] But, for reasons that we explain further below, we are not convinced that the tort of inducing breach of contract must conform to some set of *general* principles of secondary civil liability.[25]

Inconsistent dealing

If A has caused C to breach her contract with B by what is called 'inconsistent dealing' it can sometimes be very difficult to say whether A should be held to have induced C to breach her contract with B. Two examples may be given to illustrate the kind of problems that arise.

First, Wendy contracts with Carl that no building will be erected during Carl's lifetime on a particular plot of land ('Whiteacre') that Wendy owns. Wendy then sells Whiteacre to Karen. Would it be a tort for Karen to build on Whiteacre with the knowledge that to do so would bring about a breach of Wendy's contract with Carl?[26]

---

[20] *Blake* v *Lanyon* (1795) 6 TR 221, 101 ER 521; *De Francesco* v *Barnum* (1890) 63 LT 514.

[21] If there was no doubt that Beth would never have returned to perform for Ian then Ian might be unable to sue Gary because Gary's wrong would not have caused him any actionable loss: *Jones Brothers (Hunstanton) Ltd* v *Stevens* [1955] 1 QB 275.

[22] [1949] Ch 556.

[23] Ibid., 565.

[24] See, for example, C&L, 24–9, pointing to the decisions of the House of Lords in *Credit Lyonnais Bank Nederland NV* v *Export Credit Guarantee Department* [2000] 1 AC 486 and *CBS Songs Ltd* v *Amstrad Consumer Electronics plc* [1988] AC 1013.

[25] See, below, pp. 403–4. Contrast the opinion of Carty 2001, at 271–3.

[26] This example is similar to the situation in *Sefton (Earl)* v *Tophams* [1965] Ch 1140, where Stamp J found that the defendant would have committed the tort of inducing a breach of contract if he built. The Court of Appeal continued an injunction against the defendant, requiring him not to build, without finding that the defendant would commit the tort of inducing a breach of contract if he did build, and the House of Lords did not consider this point: *Sefton (Earl)* v *Tophams* [1967] 1 AC 50.

Secondly, Wendy owns a boat (the *Prima Donna*) which she hires to Carl for two years. During this period, Wendy sells the *Prima Donna* to Karen. Would it be a tort for Karen to take possession of the *Prima Donna* before the two years for which Carl has hired the *Prima Donna* are up, with knowledge that she would thereby bring about a breach of the contract of hire that Wendy entered into with Carl?

It is important to note that if these matters came before the courts *before* Wendy had transferred Whiteacre or the *Prima Donna* to Karen then the central question might not be whether Karen's building on Whiteacre/repossessing the *Prima Donna* will amount to a tort. The issue might instead be: (*a*) Can Carl obtain a remedy to prevent *Wendy* putting herself in a position where she might be put in breach of her contract with Carl (such as an injunction ordering Wendy not to transfer Whiteacre/the *Prima Donna* to Karen)? (*b*) Can a court refuse to grant Karen specific performance of her contract with Wendy to purchase Whiteacre/the *Prima Donna* if the effect of granting such an order will almost certainly be that Wendy ends up in breach of her contract with Carl? The answer to both these questions is 'yes'.[27]

Even if Whiteacre or the *Prima Donna* has already been transferred to Karen, the first relevant question may not be whether Karen will commit a tort by building on Whiteacre or by claiming possession of the *Prima Donna*. Two other sets of rules must be considered. First, there is a special set of rules about when a covenant relating to land can be enforced against a subsequent owner of the land.[28] Secondly, where a contract between A and B creates an equitable interest in an item of property then this will bind a subsequent purchaser of the property unless he was a bona fide purchaser for value without notice.[29] A significant point to note about this second set of rules is that if the purchaser has *constructive notice* then he will be bound by the equitable interest, even though a stronger degree of knowledge is necessary in order to commit the tort of inducing a breach of contract.[30] This has encouraged courts to be wary about recognising equitable interests in commercial settings.

If neither of these special sets of rules applies then it becomes necessary to ask whether Karen may be liable for having induced a breach of the contract between Wendy and Carl by 'inconsistent dealing'. In determining whether there has been culpable 'inconsistent dealing' it seems particularly important to consider whether Wendy's *contracting* with Karen, or *performing her contract with Karen*, was *in itself* a breach of the contract between Wendy and Carl. If

---

[27] For discussion see Treitel 2003, 1019–46. For relevant case law on (1) see *Lumley* v *Wagner* (1852) 1 De G M & G 604, 42 ER 687; *Manchester Ship Canal Co.* v *Manchester Racecourse Co.* [1901] 2 Ch 37; *Sefton (Earl)* v *Tophams* [1965] Ch 1140. For case law on (2) see *Willmott* v *Barber* (1880) 15 Ch D 96; *Warmington* v *Miller* [1973] QB 877.

[28] For these rules see, Smith 2002, chapter 21.

[29] *Swiss Bank Corp.* v *Lloyd's Bank Ltd* [1982] AC 584, 598A–B, 613B–E. When such an equitable interest will arise is a controversial question. Compare *Lord Strathcona SS Co.* v *Dominion Coal Co.* [1926] AC 108 with *Port Line Ltd* v *Ben Line Steamers Ltd* [1958] QB 146.

[30] It was argued on p. 391 above that a defendant could be liable if he 'turned a blind eye' to the existence of the contract, but it is commonly thought to be easier to establish 'constructive notice' than this 'Nelsonian knowledge'.

this is the case, as it would be if Wendy had, for instance, promised in a contract with Carl not to sell Whiteacre to anyone but Carl and then sold it to Karen, then Karen may be held to have committed the tort of inducing a breach of contract in relation to Carl if she had the requisite mental element when she contracted to buy Whiteacre from Carl or sought performance of it.[31]

Where neither the making of the contract between Wendy and Karen nor the performance of it was in itself a breach of the contract between Carl and Wendy, and the breach was instead the result of Karen later exercising the rights that she acquired as owner, then it seems correct that Karen should not be liable.[32] One possible explanation for this would be to treat Karen as *justified* in putting her own rights, as owner, ahead of Carl's right that Wendy fulfil her contract with him.[33] An alternative, however, would be to look at the claim that Karen, after becoming owner, should be obliged to act so as to enable Wendy to perform her contract with Carl as a claim that Karen should *assist* Wendy to fulfil that contract. As we will see below, there are good reasons for thinking that the law in this area does not extend so far as to impose on people a duty to *assist* others to fulfil their contracts.[34]

Preventing performance

Suppose A *prevented* C from performing a contract with B and B suffered some kind of financial loss as a result.

If someone who has prevented another from performing a contract can be held to have *induced* that other to breach that contract, then B will be able to establish that A committed the tort of inducing a breach of contract in acting as he did – providing, of course, that he can also show that A acted with the requisite mental element when he acted as he did and that A had no justification for acting as he did.

If someone who has prevented another from performing a contract *cannot* be held to have induced that other to breach that contract, then B will *not* be able to establish that A committed the tort of inducing a breach of contract in acting as he did. So if this is the case then if B wants to establish that A committed a tort in relation to her in the situation we are discussing, B will have to show that A, in acting as he did, committed the tort discussed in the next chapter – the tort of using unlawful means to harm another. But in order to establish that A committed *that* tort in acting as he did, B will have to show: (*a*) that A used unlawful means to prevent C performing her contract with B; *and* (*b*) that A acted as he did with the aim or object of harming B. If B cannot show that (*a*) and (*b*) are true, then she will have no claim against A.

Tony Weir has argued that A will only have induced C to break a contract with B if he *persuaded* C to do so when C was free not to break that contract.[35] Looking at the same point from the other side, Weir's argument is that if A acts so as to

---

[31] This seems to follow from *British Motor Trade Association* v *Salvadori* [1949] Ch 556, discussed in the previous section.

[32] This view is also advanced by Bright 2000, 411–12. If this view is correct it follows that Karen should not be held liable for *inducing a breach of contract* in either of our two examples.

[33] Professor Treitel seems to prefer this view: see Treitel 2003, 623. See also Smith 1977. For the defence of justification see below, pp. 402–3.

[34] See below, pp. 400–2.

[35] Weir 1997, 35.

make it *impossible* for C to perform then this is not a case of inducing C to breach her contract with B; it is a case of *preventing* C from performing her contract, and *preventing* C from performing does not count as *inducing a breach of contract*.

The two main arguments[36] in favour of drawing a line between persuading and preventing are that it is easier to draw this line than the principal alternative[37] and that there is a moral difference between seducing C into committing a wrong and merely rendering C unable to perform.[38] But, the clarity of the persuasion/prevention distinction should not be exaggerated: there are some forms of behaviour which must be assessed, such as *harbouring, facilitating* and *inconsistent dealing,* which cannot be easily described as either *persuasion* or *prevention.* Similarly, the significance of the moral difference should not be overplayed: B may find it difficult to share the philosopher's view that if A persuades C to break her contract with B by threatening to have her tied up[39] he commits a different wrong from D who keeps C away by actually tying her up.

Some English judges have identified a distinction between *direct* and *indirect* interference with contracts instead.[40] Following this approach, if A has performed an act which *directly prevented* C from performing her contract with B then A *will* have induced C to breach her contract with B – so A will have committed the tort of inducing a breach of contract in acting as he did provided, of course, that he acted with the requisite mental element and that he had no justification for acting as he did.[41]

So suppose Nita contracted to sing for Gary one evening and John *unlawfully* tied her up so that she could not perform for Gary. Now if John acted as he did *with the aim of causing harm to* Gary, Gary will be able to sue John on the basis that John committed the tort of using unlawful means to harm another in acting as he did.[42] But even if John did not try to harm Gary in acting as he did,[43] Gary will still be able to establish that John committed the tort of inducing a breach of contract in acting as he did provided, of course, that John acted with the requisite mental element in acting as he did.[44] John will be held to have induced

---

[36] A wider range of arguments for and against such a distinction are reviewed in Bagshaw 2000.

[37] The principal alternative is to draw a line between *direct* and *indirect* interferences with contract.

[38] Simester and Chan 2004 argue (at 152) that *persuading* C to break a contract is essentially different from *preventing* C from performing because only the former 'attacks the very status of [the contractual] undertaking as a reason-generating promise'. But whilst this argument identifies a way in which *persuasion* is different from *prevention* it does not explain why the law of torts ought to *use* the distinction.

[39] Recall that for Weir *persuasion* can involve 'carrot or stick': see above, n. 16.

[40] *Torquay Hotel* v *Cousins* [1969] 2 Ch 106.

[41] The example of direct interference which is most commonly mentioned involves A 'preventing by means of actual physical restraint, [C] from being where he should be, or doing what he should do, under the contract', *D C Thomson* v *Deakin* [1952] QB 646, 695, per Jenkins LJ. In *The Nadezhda Krupskaya* [1997] 2 Lloyd's Rep 35, the defendant shipowners 'withdrew' a ship and thereby prevented a charterer of it from performing its contract to sub-charter it to the claimants. Rix J held that this constituted the tort of procuring [inducing] the breach of the sub-charter.

[42] Unlawfully tying up Nita was the *unlawful means,* and doing so *with the aim of causing harm to* Gary fulfilled the necessary mental element for the tort of *using unlawful means to harm another.*

[43] For instance, because he tied Nita up in order to rob her.

[44] That mental element being that (*a*) John was aware that there was a contract between Nita and Gary; and (*b*) he knew that his actions were very likely to result in Nita breaching that contract or he knew that his actions could result in Nita breaching that contract and he did not care

Nita to breach her contract with Gary because he *directly* prevented Nita from performing that contract. Indeed, Gary would still be able to sue John for inducing a breach of contract if Nita had asked John to tie her up, so that his direct prevention of performance did not involve any use of *unlawful means*.

In contrast, if A has *indirectly* prevented C from performing a contract with B, B will *not* be able to establish that A committed the tort of inducing a breach of contract in acting as he did – A will not be held to have induced C to breach her contract with B.[45] So if B wants to sue A, B will have to establish that A committed the tort of using unlawful means to harm another in acting as he did.

It is not easy to define precisely what the difference is between *directly* interfering with the performance of a contract and *indirectly* interfering with the performance of a contract. Indeed, this difficulty is one of Tony Weir's strongest points against the distinction. The most helpful guidance may be the statement of Slade J that 'the phrase "direct interference" covers the case where the intervener, either by himself or his agents, speaks, writes or publishes words or does other acts which communicate pressure or persuasion to the mind or person of one of the contracting parties themselves, while "indirect interference" refers to the case where, without actually doing any of these things, the intervener nevertheless procures or attempts to procure a situation which will result or may result in a breach of the contract'.[46] Applying this guidance, if Eric persuaded Ruth to break her contract with Lara, intending that this would lead Lara to break her contract with Fred, then Eric would have interfered *directly* with the contract between Ruth and Lara, but only *indirectly* with the contract between Lara and Fred.

Omissions[47]

Should A be said to have induced C to commit a breach of contract if A 'caused' the breach by doing nothing; that is, if A merely omitted to act in a way which would have helped C to perform a contract that she had with B?

For example, if Vijay thought that he would be able to buy a particular car from Dawn and consequently agreed to supply the same car to Helen, but

---

whether or not his actions had that effect. See below, pp. 399–400, for discussion of the significance of the fact that in this example the contract between Nita and Gary might be *frustrated*.

[45] An example of indirect interference (with a contract between B and C) involves A persuading D's employees to break their contracts of employment with the result that D cannot perform a contract with C, and C is as a result prevented from performing a contract with B.

[46] *Greig* v *Insole* [1978] 1 WLR 302, 334A–B. We would be tempted to extend the phrase 'mind or person' to 'mind or person or property' in order to cover the case of *GWK Ltd* v *Dunlop Rubber Co.* (1926) 42 TLR 376, where the defendant prevented a car manufacturer from performing a contract to display the claimant's tyres by removing them. See also *The Nadezhda Krupskaya* [1997] 2 Lloyd's Rep 35, discussed above, n. 41.

[47] It is important to note that omissions usually operate to *prevent* performance. Consequently, if the courts ever retreat from their view (discussed in the previous section) that someone who *directly* prevents performance of a contract will be held to have induced a breach of that contract, then the question about whether an omission can ever be held to have induced a breach of contract is likely to disappear.

Dawn refused to sell the car to Vijay, so that, inevitably, Vijay broke his contract with Helen, would we want to say that Dawn had induced Vijay to breach his contract with Helen and could therefore be liable to Helen? Alternatively, suppose that Vijay entered into a contract to purchase a particular car of Dawn's *before* he contractually agreed to sell the car on to Helen, and then after Vijay entered into his contract with Helen, Dawn failed to deliver the car to Vijay with the result that Vijay breached his contract with Helen. Again, would we want to say that Dawn had induced Vijay to breach his contract with Helen and could therefore be held liable to Helen?

Perhaps we should draw a distinction between these two examples and say that there *can* be liability for an omission where there was a duty to act (as in the variation where there was a pre-existing contract between Vijay and Dawn) but not where there was no such duty.[48] In *Millar* v *Bassey*[49] the Court of Appeal thought that it was arguable that A *could* be held liable for inducing a breach of contract if she broke her own contract with C, knowing that this would deprive C of the essential services that he required in order to perform his contract with B. But the court did not consider what the position might have been if A had not been in a contract with C. In our opinion it is most unlikely that a court would ever find that A could be liable for merely omitting to act (in the absence of a duty to do so) where she knew that C would be unable to perform a contract with B in the absence of A's action. This is because to find liability in such a case would be tantamount to imposing a *positive* duty on A to assist in the performance of C's contract.[50]

THE DEGREE OF INTERFERENCE WITH A CONTRACT REQUIRED TO COMMIT THE TORT

Is inducing a *breach of contract* a necessary element of the tort discussed here? There are three difficult questions to be confronted here.

(1) *Force majeure and frustration.* Will A have committed the tort discussed here if he directly prevented C from performing her contract with B but there was a

---

[48] It will be apparent that the definition of 'direct interference' which we presented under the previous subheading requires an *act* by the defendant or his agent. The definition could obviously be amended to include *omissions* where there was a duty to act owed to the party said to have been induced to breach the contract. Of course, where there is a legal duty to act an omission to perform the duty will amount to 'unlawful means'. Thus, even if we conclude that omitting to perform a duty *cannot* count as 'inducing' it may count as 'use of unlawful means' for the purposes of the tort of using unlawful means to harm another.

[49] [1994] EMLR 44.

[50] Direct authority on this point is sparse. In *Stocznia Gdanska SA* v *Latvian Shipping Co. and others (No. 3)* [2001] 1 Lloyd's Rep 537, [252], Thomas J held that the conscious decision of a company not to fund its subsidiary with the consequence that the subsidiary breached a contract was not a direct inducement of the breach in the absence of any obligation to fund the subsidiary. This conclusion was not challenged when the case was dealt with by the Court of Appeal (see [2002] 2 Lloyd's Rep 436) though the company was found liable for committing the tort of using unlawful means to harm another. Further, whilst courts have granted injunctions against defendants to prevent them from acting so as to bring about a breach they have refused to order defendants to act so as to prevent a breach occurring. See, for example, *Law Debenture Corp.* v *Ural Caspian Ltd* [1993] 1 WLR 138 (reversed on a different point, [1995] Ch 152).

force majeure clause in C's contract with B that provided that C could not be held liable if she was prevented from performing her contract with B in the way that A did? It is fairly clear the answer to this question is 'yes'. In *Torquay Hotel v Cousins*[51] the Court of Appeal held that someone who induced another not to perform his primary obligations[52] under a contract *could* be held liable for committing the tort of inducing a breach of contract even if a term in the contract meant that the non-performer could not be held liable to pay damages for his non-performance.[53]

If the tort can be committed by A preventing C from performing the primary obligations she owes under a contract with B then it seems that it can be committed by A even when his acts lead to the frustration of the contract. So, if C agreed to make a particular music hall that she owned available to B for a series of concerts in exchange for a payment of £100 per concert, and A, with knowledge of the contract and intending to prevent its performance, set fire to the music hall causing its destruction, A would have committed the tort discussed in this chapter in relation to B.

(2) *Termination.* Will A have committed the tort discussed here if he persuaded C to terminate her contract with B in a *lawful* manner? It is difficult to say. There is little doubt that it is *not* a tort for A to persuade C *not* to make a contract with B. In the famous case of *Allen v Flood*[54] the defendant persuaded the employers of Flood and Taylor not to re-engage them the next morning, and a majority of the House of Lords was clear that no tort was committed because the defendant did not induce a breach of contract and did not make use of unlawful means. Without the defendant's intervention it seems certain that Flood and Taylor would have been re-engaged the next morning, but they had no contractual right to a new engagement. This seems very similar to the situation of a contract which one party can lawfully terminate. In such a situation there is *no right* that it should not be terminated.

However, judicial opinion is divided on the question of whether persuading another lawfully to terminate a contract can amount to a tort. In *Torquay Hotel Co. Ltd v Cousins*, Winn LJ stated *obiter*, 'For my part I think that it can at least be said, with confidence, that where a contract between [B and C] exists which gives [C] an optional extension of time or an optional mode for his performance

---

[51] [1969] 2 Ch 106.

[52] Lord Diplock famously analysed contracts in terms of primary and secondary obligations in *Photo Production Ltd v Securicor Transport Ltd* [1980] AC 827, at 848–9. (See also Lord Diplock in *Moschi v Lep Air Services Ltd* [1973] 1 AC 331, at 350.) In a very simple contract to deliver 100 barrels of oil, the primary obligation would be to deliver the oil. The secondary obligation, which *might* arise if this primary obligation went unfulfilled, would be to pay damages for failing to deliver. The analysis in *Torquay Hotel* is that a defendant who has induced the non-performance of the primary obligation will have committed the tort of inducing a breach of contract, even if a *force majeure* clause prevented a secondary obligation to pay damages from arising.

[53] Support for this view can be found in the observation that when parties put a *force majeure* clause into their contract they probably do not intend this to give third parties greater scope to interfere with the contract lawfully. For the reasons why parties include such clauses in their contracts see, Treitel 1994, 427–8.

[54] [1898] AC 1.

of it, or of part of it, but, from the normal course of dealing between them, [B] does not anticipate such postponement, or has come to expect a particular mode of performance, [inducing C] to exercise such an option should, in principle, be held actionable if it produces material damage to [B].'[55] This view was contrary, however, to that expressed by Morris LJ in *DC Thomson & Co. Ltd* v *Deakin*.[56]

We think, for reasons given below, that Morris LJ was correct on this point, and would only support Winn LJ's position in situations where before A's intervention C had already waived the right to postpone or to select an option.[57] An analogous question is whether it is a tort to persuade someone to rescind a contract that is voidable.[58] In *Greig* v *Insole*, Slade J found that the authorities relevant to this question conflicted, but decided to assume that it was not a tort to induce a person who is entitled to rescind a contract to exercise that right.[59] We think that Slade J was correct to treat this as the law.

Our support for Morris LJ and Slade J is based on the opinion that the essence of the tort in *Lumley* v *Gye* is bringing about *the violation of contractual rights*. So if A has persuaded C to terminate, vary or rescind a contract with B, the decisive question – for the purpose of determining whether A committed the tort discussed here in acting as he did – is whether B had a *right* that C not terminate, vary or rescind the contract in the way she did. If B had no such right, then B will not be able to establish that A committed the tort discussed here in acting as he did – though B will still be able to establish that A committed the tort of using unlawful means to harm another in acting as he did if: (*a*) A used unlawful means to persuade C to terminate, vary or rescind her contract with B; *and* (*b*) A's aim in persuading C to act in this way was to harm B.

(3) *Diminished profits.* Will A have committed the tort discussed here if he did not prevent C from performing her contract with B but *directly* made C's performance of that contract less profitable for B? It follows from what has just been said that the answer to this question is 'no'. Because B has *no right* to earn a certain level of profits from C's performance of her contract with B, A cannot commit the tort discussed here if he directly interferes with the contract in such a way as to make C's performance of the contract less profitable for B.

In *RCA Corp.* v *Pollard*, Slade LJ said that he could find no support for the principle 'that A may be liable to B under this head of tort merely because A does an act (even an illegal act) which he knows is likely to render less valuable certain contractual rights of B as against C without actually interfering with the

---

[55] [1969] 2 Ch 106, 147C.

[56] [1952] Ch 646, 702. The High Court of Australia accepted in *Sanders* v *Snell* (1998) 196 CLR 329, at [23], that Morris LJ had correctly stated the law on this point.

[57] In *Boxfoldia Ltd* v *National Graphical Association (1982)* [1988] ICR 752 it was accepted that a trade union would not commit a tort by persuading employees of the claimant to give notice that they wished to terminate their contracts of employment.

[58] There is clear authority that someone will not commit the tort discussed here if he induces someone not to perform a contract which is void: *Joe Lee Ltd* v *Lord Dalmeny* [1927] 1 Ch 300.

[59] [1978] 1 WLR 302, 333A–G.

performance by C of the contractual obligations owed by him to B'.[60] We agree with Slade LJ, but would highlight that his proposition was about the tort of inducing a breach of contract: if A's act is illegal and was done with the intention of *harming* B, B *will* be able to establish that A committed the tort of using unlawful means to harm another in acting as he did.

JUSTIFICATION

Suppose A has induced C to breach her contract with B. Suppose further that A acted with the requisite mental element when he induced C to breach that contract. If A had a *justification* for inducing C to breach her contract with B, the courts will *not* find that A committed the tort of inducing a breach of contract in acting as he did. It is important to note that the question is not whether C's breach was justified but whether A's inducing C to breach her contract was justified.

English law has recognised the validity of both legal and moral justifications for inducing a breach. A can claim to have had a legal justification if he had a legal right which was inconsistent with B's contractual rights and was superior or equal in status to those contractual rights. A simple example of this situation would be if Johanna Wagner had foolishly made two contracts with rival impresarios promising to sing exclusively for each. In such circumstances either impresario would be justified in seeking to persuade Johanna Wagner to break her contract with the other.

A more complex example was provided by *Edwin Hill* v *First National*.[61] In this case the defendant was a finance company which had loaned money to a property developer to enable him to purchase Wellington House for development. Unfortunately the project stalled and the developer became unable to repay. This meant that the defendant had the power to force the sale of Wellington House. Instead of exercising this power of sale, the defendant agreed to finance the project itself, but, as a condition of doing so, insisted that the property developer should break his contract with the architects who he had previously engaged. The architects then sued the defendant for inducing the developer to breach this contract. The defendant claimed that it had been justified in doing so.

The complexity in the case comes from the fact that although the defendant had a (superior) legal right in the form of its power to force the sale of Wellington House it had not actually exercised *this* power. It had instead used the bargaining position that this power provided in order to put together a different deal (which included the breach of contract). Despite this complexity the Court of Appeal thought that the defendant could rely on the defence of justification. Two explanations were provided. First, the court identified the legal right which the defendant had which might justify it in interfering with the architects' contractual right as the right to receive payment of what was due. Given this, one could say that the defendant acted reasonably[62] to protect its right to be

---

[60] [1983] Ch 135, 156G.
[61] [1989] 1 WLR 225.
[62] The reasonableness of changing architects was not considered in detail. But it should have been, because it is important to establish some inconsistency between the architect's right to the continuation of his contract and the defendant's right to be repaid.

repaid the money it had lent the developer. Secondly, the court pointed out that the end result was no worse for the architects than if the power to force the sale had been exercised and that in such circumstances it made no sense for the law to prohibit a different deal which was better for both defendant and developer.

To establish a defence of moral justification the defendant must show that he was impelled to act by a sense of moral duty. It is not sufficient merely to claim that there were good reasons for inducing a breach or that the person breaking the contract might gain some valuable benefit from doing so: 'The fact that their motives were good in the interests of those they moved to action does not form any answer to those who have suffered from the unlawful act.'[63] In practice the defence of moral justification has been successfully deployed only rarely. An example is provided by *Brimelow* v *Casson*,[64] where the defendant induced theatre proprietors to break their contracts with a stage show producer in order to pressurise him into paying higher wages to the chorus girls he engaged. The supposed moral necessity was provided by the belief that the wages were so low that his employees were being forced into lives of immorality and prostitution.

IS INDUCING A BREACH OF CONTRACT A TORT?

Hazel Carty and Philip Sales have suggested that liability for inducing a breach of contract is not an *independent* tort but is actually a form of *secondary* liability – the defendant is held liable because he participated in the contract-breaker's wrong.[65] This point has been used as a foundation for arguing that liability for inducing a breach of contract should be studied alongside liability for participating in torts committed by others, and should be reformulated to make it conform to a *general* model of secondary liability for torts.[66]

We have four reasons for rejecting this understanding of liability for inducing a breach of contract. (1) The courts regularly refer to inducing breach of contract as a tort. Thus if it is not a tort the courts must have been erroneously using inappropriate language for many years. (2) Suppose that A has induced C to breach her contract with B. If A's liability to B in this situation is genuinely *secondary* in nature – and does not arise out of the fact that A committed a tort in relation to B in acting as he did – then it follows that A's liability should not exceed C's. But there is no reason to think that A's liability will be so limited.[67] (3) Suppose that A induces B to breach her contract with C – and that A, in so acting, was acting in the course of his employment by E. If A's

---

[63] *South Wales Miners' Federation* v *Glamorgan Coal Co. Ltd* [1905] AC 239, 252 (per Lord James). See also *Greig* v *Insole* [1978] 1 WLR 302, 341.

[64] [1924] 1 Ch 302.

[65] See Carty 2001, 272; Sales 1990, 503–4. The law on when someone will be held secondarily liable for a tort committed by someone else is dealt with (under the title 'Vicarious Liability') in Chapter 35, below.

[66] Carty 1999, 506–10; Carty 2001, 272–3.

[67] The cases where damages have been assessed do not seem to have proceeded by considering how much would be awarded in an action for breach of contract. See eg *Goldsoll* v *Goldman* [1914] 2 Ch 603, 615–16. In *Lumley* v *Gye* (1853) 2 E & B 216, 230, one of the reasons that Crompton J gave for the existence of the tort was that the measure of damages might be different from that in an action for breach of contract.

liability for inducing B to breach her contract with C were genuinely secondary in nature then C could not sue *E* for damages in respect of the losses suffered by him as a result of B's breach.[68] But it seems likely that E *would* be held liable in this situation, on the ground that A committed a tort in relation to B in acting as he did, and that E is vicariously liable in respect of that tort. (4) If a defendant's liability in an inducing breach of contract case is genuinely *secondary* it seems odd that the defendant can rely on a defence of *justification* to escape being held liable even when the contract-breaker has undoubtedly committed the wrong of breach of contract, and that the defendant can be liable even when there has been no actionable breach of contract.[69]

EVALUATING THE TORT

Some legal commentators[70] have criticised the existence of the tort of inducing a breach of contract. The foundation for their criticisms is that if A has committed the tort by inducing C to breach her contract with B, B will usually[71] be able to make a claim for breach of contract against C. Why, they ask, should B be given a claim against A as well?

Part of the answer may be that occasionally a claim against A will be more attractive than a claim against C. For instance, in *South Wales Miners' Federation* v *Glamorgan Coal Co. Ltd*[72] the defendant organisation had persuaded miners in South Wales to break their contracts with the coal companies which employed them and stop working for a one-day protest. Regardless of what we may think about such protests, we can easily imagine why the coal companies did not want to sue the people who had broken their contracts, the miners. It would not have been good for labour relations to have made legal claims against the minors as soon as they returned to work. There might also have been doubts about whether the miners would have had the money to pay for any losses suffered through stopping production for a day. Furthermore, from the point of view of the coal companies we can see why the defendant organisation might appear to have been 'the real authors of the mischief'.[73] The miners would not have stopped work for the protest without the encouragement of the defendant organisation. To use a biblical metaphor, the defendant organisation played a role similar to that of the serpent in the Garden of Eden.

But showing why victims of a breach of contract would like a tort of inducing a breach of contract to exist is not enough to satisfy all of its critics. One common criticism is that the tort fails to advance economic efficiency because

---

[68] This follows from the decision of the House of Lords in *Credit Lyonnais NV* v *ECGD* [2000] 1 AC 486 (discussed below, pp. 658–9).

[69] Carty 2001 admits (at 72) that in order to establish that liability for inducing a breach of contract is actually a form of *secondary* liability, cases suggesting that there is liability for facilitating, inconsistent transactions, or interferences which do not cause breach, must be rejected as having been wrongly decided.

[70] See, for example, Howarth 1995, at 484: '*Lumley* v *Gye* was wrongly decided'.

[71] For an exception see above, pp. 399–400.

[72] [1905] AC 239.

[73] Ibid., 246 (per Lord Macnaghten).

it tends to discourage 'efficient breach' of contracts. A second common criticism is that the tort reduces the capacity of workers to organise effective industrial action and consequently facilitates oppression by powerful employers. Can these criticisms be answered?

Efficient breach

The notion of 'efficient breach' is based on the idea that it may be better for the wealth of society as a whole if particular contracts are broken.[74] Suppose, for example, that Tom owns the only widget in the world and he has contracted to sell it to Ruth, who will use it to generate forty units of wealth each year. Tom discovers that Eric could use the widget to generate fifty units of wealth each year and is therefore willing to pay Tom more for the widget than Ruth is. In such a case, *it might be thought* that it would be better for Tom to break his contract with Ruth, pay her compensation for her expectation loss, and sell the widget to Eric instead.[75] But the existence of the tort of inducing a breach of contract means that it would be wrongful for Eric (or anyone else) to *encourage*[76] Tom to break his contract with Ruth in order to ensure that the widget goes to the person who can make the most productive use of it.

So far it looks as if the critics of the tort have a good case. But we have ignored two things. First, the tort does not stop Eric negotiating with Ruth and Tom[77] to try to persuade them to cancel their contract so that it can be sold to him – and if Eric can make more money than Ruth using the widget then Eric should be capable of making very attractive offers to both Ruth and Tom. Secondly, in our discussion we have assumed that everyone knows how much Eric and Ruth can make with the widget. In real life such information is often not available. In particular, it is unlikely that Tom, if approached by Eric, will be in any position to know who is likely to make best use of the widget. Consequently, it might again be better to encourage Eric to negotiate with both Ruth and Tom. A further benefit of encouraging such negotiations rather than allowing Eric to persuade Tom to break his contract with Ruth is that it will avoid the courts having to spend valuable time and effort calculating how much by way of damages Tom should pay Ruth in the aftermath of his breaching his contract to sell the widget to her.[78]

---

[74] For a presentation of the doctrine of 'efficient breach' see Posner 2003, 119–21. But note that Posner has argued that the existence of the tort can be justified in most of the circumstances in which it is used: Landes & Posner 1987, 224.

[75] See, for example, Perlman 1982, at 128, 'In cases of [inducing breach of contract by] otherwise lawful acts, tort liability works at cross-purposes with contract policies. Contract remedies seem to promote efficiency, whereas the addition of inducer liability inhibits efficient outcomes.'

[76] As we have seen, the tort of inducing breach of conduct might also cover Eric's behaviour if he enters into a contract with Tom which is inconsistent with the contract between Tom and Ruth.

[77] If Eric wants the identical widget which Tom has contracted to supply to Ruth he may be able to negotiate solely with Ruth – but in other cases, where, for instance, Tom has contracted to supply the output of his widget factory to Ruth, and Eric instead wants Tom's factory to make slightly different widgets for him, all three parties will have to be involved in the negotiations.

[78] See Macneil 1982, at 957–60, for discussion of how it can only be determined whether a breach will be 'efficient' in the light of 'transaction costs' – that is, broadly speaking, the relative costs of negotiations and of sorting out breaches.

Industrial action and oppression

One answer to the second criticism advanced above of the tort of inducing a breach of contract might be that the tort of inducing a breach of contract only has a role to play where there is a contract between two parties. Now – an employee must have voluntarily (to the extent that the law of contract demands) agreed to the terms of his contract of employment. Given this, there is only limited scope for the employee to argue that it is oppressive not to allow others to encourage him to break his contract. But this argument only really works at a formal level. In practice we know that in many circumstances employees (and others) have little control over the terms of the contracts that they enter. The South Wales miners had little opportunity when applying for jobs to influence the terms of any employment offered. Parliament has recognised that in practice employees are empowered by the possibility of collective industrial action and has provided a statutory immunity for economic torts committed in the furtherance of trade disputes.[79] There is no doubt, however, that the law in this area does still restrict liberty. The core issue is whether this restriction on liberty is justified by the protection that this area of the law provides for contractual rights. Our view is that for many people and companies their contractual rights are one of their most valuable assets, and that consequently it makes sense for the law to offer them some protection.[80]

TORTS ANALOGOUS TO THE TORT OF INDUCING A BREACH OF CONTRACT

We argued above that the essence of the tort in *Lumley* v *Gye* is the bringing about of the violation of contractual rights. This raises the question of whether there are similar torts covering the bringing about of the violation of other types of rights. In *Lumley* v *Gye* Erle J did not confine his statement of principle to contractual rights, and asserted that, 'the procurement of the violation of a right is a cause of action in all instances where the violation is an actionable wrong'.[81] It is clear, however, that English law has not treated this principle as applying to *all* types of rights.

Generally, English cases have applied the principle only to rights which have some similarity to contractual rights. For example, the Court of Appeal held in a case involving an employment relationship that was governed by statute rather than contract, that it could be a tort to induce the violation of statutory rights that are enforceable by a civil action.[82] It has also been held that it is a

---

[79] This immunity is now conditional on certain procedures being followed in the organisation of the industrial action: see below, p. 497.

[80] See further, Bagshaw 2000, at 132–7.

[81] (1853) 2 E & B 216, 232, 18 ER 749, 755.

[82] *Associated British Ports* v *Transport and General Workers' Union* [1989] 1 WLR 939; *Meade* v *Haringey LBC* [1979] 1 WLR 637. Where a claim is based on the fact that the defendant induced another to breach a statutory duty, the claimant must be able to make a civil claim for compensation against the person actually breaking the duty: *Associated British Ports* v *Transport and General Workers' Union* [1989] 1 WLR 939, 952E–F, 959H–960A, 964H–965B.

tort to induce the violation of a right to a particular private law remedy.[83] By contrast, in *Metall und Rohstoff AG v Donald Lufkin & Jenrette Inc.*,[84] the Court of Appeal refused to recognise that it was a tort to induce someone to commit a breach of trust, principally to avoid any conflict with the well-developed equitable wrong of dishonestly assisting another to commit a breach of trust.[85] Similarly, in *F v Wirral MBC*[86] the Court of Appeal refused to recognise that it is a tort to interfere directly with parental rights.[87] Again, it is not a tort to induce or assist someone to commit a tort[88] – however, it is important to note that if A *persuades* or *authorises* C to commit a tort in relation to B, then B will be able to sue A for damages on the basis that C's tort was committed by *A*, as well as C.[89]

In our opinion the courts have been wise not to apply Erle J's principle beyond situations which involve someone's inducing the violation of rights which have some similarity to contractual rights. This is because the tort of inducing breach of contract is based on a duty designed to protect claimants against a particular type of harm, and the form of the duty may not be appropriate to protect claimants against very different types of harm.

---

[83] This was assumed by the Court of Appeal in *Law Debenture Corp. v Ural Caspian Ltd* [1995] Ch 152, although it went on to hold that there was no right to an equitable remedy until it had been granted.

[84] [1990] 1 QB 391, at 481G–H.

[85] *Royal Brunei Airlines v Tan* [1995] 2 AC 378.

[86] [1991] Fam 69.

[87] At common law there existed torts which allowed a spouse to sue a third party who enticed the other spouse to leave, and a head of household to sue a third party who seduced or enticed away a child. These torts, however, came to be seen as unwelcome remains of outmoded social ideas and were abolished by Paliament: see above, p. 20. The Court of Appeal in *F v Wirral Metropolitan Borough Council* [1991] Fam 69 was understandably reluctant to create any similar head of liability.

[88] *CBS Songs Ltd v Amstrad Consumer Electronics plc* [1988] AC 1013; *Credit Lyonnais Bank Nederland NV v Export Credits Guarantee Department* [2000] 1 AC 486.

[89] See Oliver LJ's judgment in *John Hudson & Co. Ltd v Oaten*, 19 June 1980 (unreported), quoted with approval by the House of Lords in *Credit Lyonnais NV v ECGD* [2000] 1 AC 486, 497–8; also Carty 1999, 500–1.

TORTS INVOLVING THE INTENTIONAL INFLICTION OF HARM

DEFINITIONS

In this section, we will look at some torts which are committed by intentionally harming someone else. When can we say that someone has *intentionally* harmed someone else? The answer is quite simple.[1] A will have intentionally harmed B if: (*a*) A acted in a particular way in order to cause B to suffer some kind of harm; *and* (*b*) B suffered that kind of harm as a result of A's acting in the way he did. To put it another way – A will have intentionally harmed B if: (*a*) A acted in a particular way; *and* (*b*) one of A's purposes in acting in that way was to cause B to suffer a particular kind of harm; *and* (*c*) B suffered that kind of harm as a result of A's acting in the way he did. We can illustrate the point by contrasting a couple of cases.

In *Allen* v *Flood*,[2] Allen caused two shipwrights, Flood and Taylor, to be dismissed from their jobs repairing the woodwork of a ship by threatening their employer that forty boilermakers also employed by the employer would walk out if Flood and Taylor were not dismissed. The reason why Flood and Taylor were singled out for this treatment was that they had done some metal work on another ship and the boilermakers regarded such work as falling exclusively within their province. On one reading of the case, Allen made his threats in order to punish Flood and Taylor for acting as they did. On another reading, Allen bore no personal ill-will towards Flood and Taylor but was seeking to have them dismissed in order to discourage other shipwrights from taking on boilermakers' work in the future. On either reading, Allen intentionally harmed Flood and Taylor – he acted as he did in order to cause them to be dismissed and his actions succeeded in having that effect.

In *CBS Songs* v *Amstrad Consumer Electronics plc*,[3] Amstrad, it will be recalled, sold stereos with twin cassette decks which could be used – and were used – to create 'pirate' copies of music tapes sold in the shops. As a result, CBS Songs lost money – it was deprived of the royalties it could have earned if members of the public had to buy tapes in the shops instead of making pirate copies of tapes bought by someone else. In this case, Amstrad did *not* intentionally harm CBS Songs – it was no part of Amstrad's purpose in marketing their stereos to deprive CBS Songs of any royalties. Amstrad may have known that it was inevitable that their marketing their stereos would result in CBS Songs losing money but they did not intentionally harm CBS Songs – they did not market their stereos *in order to* diminish the amount of money CBS Songs would earn by way of royalties on music tapes sold in the shops.[4]

---

[1] For an excellent discussion, see Finnis 1991; also White 1991, chapter 4.
[2] [1898] AC 1.
[3] [1988] AC 1013.
[4] Woolf LJ suggested in *Lonrho plc* v *Fayed* [1990] 2 QB 479, at 494C–D, that if A did *x* knowing that B would be harmed as a result, then A can be said to have intended to harm B when he did *x*.

INTENTIONAL INFLICTION OF HARM AS AN INDEPENDENT TORT

If A does intentionally cause B to suffer harm, A will sometimes commit one of the torts already discussed in this book. For example, if A intentionally shoots B, A will obviously have committed the tort of battery in relation to B.[5] Again, as we have seen, A will commit the tort of private nuisance if he makes a lot of noise around his house simply in order to annoy his neighbour B.

However, A's intentionally causing B to suffer harm may amount to a tort even if he – in acting in this way – does not commit one of the torts already discussed in this book. When will this be the case? Well, the decided cases establish that if you take two individuals, A and B: (*a*) A will owe B a common law duty to ensure that he does not intentionally harm B *using unlawful means* to do so; *and* (*b*) A will owe B a common law duty to ensure that he does not *in conjunction with other people* intentionally harm B *for no good reason*. So A will commit a tort in relation to B if he intentionally harms B *using unlawful means to do so*.[6] Also, A will commit a tort in relation to B if he *joins forces* with a third party, C, and they *together* intentionally harm B *for no good reason*.

On this view, Amstrad *can* be said to have intended to harm CBS Songs when it marketed its stereos. However, Woolf LJ's suggestion is incorrect (for criticism, see Sales & Stilitz 1999, 425–30) and, in this context, cannot be condemned strongly enough. (Criminal lawyers adopt a looser definition of intention than that advanced here, according to which someone can be said to have intended to kill when he did *x* if he knew that death was virtually certain to result from his doing *x*. However, in *that* context, such a (mis)reading of the concept of intention is justified as it allows those who have shown a depraved indifference to the value of human life to be convicted of murder, even though they may not have acted with the actual aim or purpose of killing someone else.)

[5] It might also be argued that he committed the tort of negligence: see above pp. 62–3. However, as we have seen, some people believe that A will only have committed the tort of negligence in relation to B if: (*a*) A breached a duty of care owed to B; *and* (2) A, in breaching that duty of care, did *not* intend to harm B. Such people will baulk at saying that A committed the tort of negligence in the situation considered in the text.

[6] *Important note.* We will call the tort committed by A here the tort of *using unlawful means to harm another*. However, lawyers will often give a more specific name to the tort committed by A here, depending on what *sort* of unlawful means were used by A to harm B. So, for example, A will be said to have committed the tort of *intimidation* here if he intentionally harmed B by making unlawful *threats* to a third party. Some call the generic tort that is committed by someone who intentionally harms another using unlawful means to do so, the tort of *unlawful interference with trade* (Carty 2001, 1, 21–2; Murphy 2003, 163; Fridman 1993, 99) or the tort of *interference with trade by unlawful means* (W&J, 656). However, this is a mistake: see Sales & Stilitz 1999, 430–1. There is no reason to think that this tort can *only* be committed by interfering with someone's *trade or business*. The tort will be committed if you cause someone to suffer *any kind of harm* using unlawful means to do so. See, for example, *Allen v Flood* [1898] AC 1, at 137: 'It is said the essence of the wrong in this case [*Tarleton v M'Gawley* (1793) Peake 270, 170 ER 153] was that the claimant was disturbed in his trade. I do not think so. Can it be doubted that if the shipowner had desired the presence of persons on board his ship for any other purpose [other than business], and the same wrongful act had deterred them from approaching the ship, the shipowner might have maintained a[n] . . . action to recover damages for any loss or inconvenience to which he had been put owing to the wrongful act of the defendant?' (per Lord Herschell); and *Crofter Hand Woven Harris Tweed Co. v Veitch* [1942] AC 435, at 446–7: 'Although most of the cases have dealt with trade rivalry in some form or other, I do not see why the proposition as to the conditions under which [intentionally causing another to suffer loss] becomes a tort should be limited to trade competition' (per Viscount Simon LC).

ALTERNATIVES TO THE CURRENT LAW

The extreme position

Why have the courts not gone further and taken the *extreme position* that if you take two individuals, A and B, A will owe B a common law duty to ensure that he does not intentionally harm B – with the result that A will *always* commit a tort in relation to B if he intentionally harms B?[7] There are probably four reasons why the courts have not adopted this extreme position.

(1) *Justification*. First and foremost, the courts have refused to adopt the extreme position set out above because they recognise that there are occasions when A *ought* to harm B. So, for example, if Eric is attacking Wendy on the street, and Fred is in a position to knock Eric out then Fred *ought*[8] to knock him out. Similarly, if Tom has been tried and convicted of sexually abusing his daughter, then Karen – the judge presiding at Tom's trial – *ought* to send him to prison for a long time. Obviously, we would not want it to be illegal for Eric to hit Fred or for Karen to send Tom to jail – but it would be if the courts adopted the extreme position set out above.

(2) *Competition*. The courts have also refused to adopt the extreme position set out above because they have tended to think that competition in the marketplace would be unacceptably limited if they took this position. True, not all competition in the marketplace takes the form of one trader intentionally causing another trader to suffer harm. If John is in business selling mousetraps and Dawn invents and markets a better mousetrap with the result that John goes out of business, Dawn will not have intentionally caused John to suffer harm. While it might have been inevitable that John would go out of business as a result of Dawn's activities, putting John out of business formed – we presume – no part of Dawn's purpose in marketing her mousetrap.

However, some competition in the marketplace *does* take the form of one trader intentionally causing another trader to suffer harm. This is the case where John and Dawn are both in the business of selling mousetraps and Dawn attempts to drive John out of business by deliberately cutting the price of her mousetraps to uneconomic levels. If Dawn succeeds in driving John out of business in this way – at which point Dawn, having captured John's customers, will raise her prices again to an economic level – Dawn will have intentionally caused John to suffer harm. If the courts took the extreme position set out above, this sort of competitive practice would be proscribed under the common law – Dawn would owe John a common law duty to ensure that she did not *intentionally* drive John out of business – and the courts have, rightly or wrongly,[9]

---

[7] The legal philosopher John Finnis seems to take this position: see Finnis 2002, 46: 'A sound tort law identifies as tortious every act *intended* precisely to cause harm to another person . . .' (emphasis in original).

[8] Morally, that is; the legal position is that Fred will have no duty to intervene absent special circumstances. See above pp. 197–8.

[9] Wrongly, in the view of Gronow 1995.

thought in the past that the law would unacceptably limit competition in the marketplace if it made this sort of competitive practice illegal.[10]

(3) *Legitimate reason.* There are other occasions – outside competition in the marketplace – when A may have a perfectly legitimate reason for wanting to harm B. If the courts took the extreme position set out above, A would not be permitted on these occasions to harm B. But the courts have taken the view that A *should be allowed* to harm B in these situations so long as his method of harming B is not independently unlawful, and have therefore rejected the extreme position set out above.

For example, suppose that Carl wants to stop ABC plc from testing the perfumes it makes on animals. Carl thinks that the best way of bringing pressure to bear on ABC to stop its testing is to organise a boycott of its products. The courts take the view in this case that as Carl has a perfectly legitimate reason for wanting to organise a boycott of ABC's products and organising the boycott is not independently unlawful, Carl should be allowed to organise his boycott – something which he would not be allowed to do were the courts to adopt the extreme position set out above.

Again, when the case of *Allen* v *Flood* was being argued, one of the judges asked: If a cook, wishing no longer to work alongside her master's butler because she did not get on with him, said to her master 'I will leave you at the end of my current engagement unless you dismiss the butler at the end of his' and the master, in consequence, dismissed the butler at the end of his engagement, will the cook have committed a tort?[11] The majority of the House of Lords thought the answer was 'no'.[12] The cook in this example had a perfectly legitimate reason for wanting to see the butler dismissed and the House of Lords thought that she should therefore be allowed to do what she could to get the butler dismissed so long as her means of doing so were not independently unlawful.

(4) *Freedom.* The courts have also been forced to reject the extreme position set out above because they have long recognised that people enjoy certain *absolute freedoms.* If A possesses an absolute freedom to do *x* then he is free to choose whether to do *x* irrespective of the consequences that his doing *x* will have for other people. Because the courts recognise that people enjoy certain absolute freedoms, they *cannot* take the extreme position set out above. The courts cannot at one and the same time say: (*a*) A has an absolute freedom to do *x*; *and* (*b*) A will owe B a common law duty not to do *x* if his object in doing *x* is to cause B to suffer some kind of harm. If A has an absolute freedom to do *x*, it follows that he must be allowed to do *x* even if his object

---

[10] The courts now stand corrected on this point by Parliament. See the Competition Act 1998, as amended by the Enterprise Act 2002.

[11] [1898] AC 1, 36 (per Cave J), 179 (per Lord James). Lord Herschell (at 138–9) and Lord Shand (165–6) had a different recollection of what was said in argument: they thought it had been asked what the position would be if a butler threatened not to renew his contract with his master unless the cook were let go.

[12] It would, of course, be different if the cook had encouraged the master to dismiss the butler *before* the end of his engagement and the master had acted on that encouragement. In such a case the cook would have committed the tort of inducing a breach of contract: see above, Chapter 19.

in doing *x* is to harm B. In other words, if A has an absolute freedom to do *x*, his doing *x* cannot ever be said to be wrongful – and this is so even if his object in doing *x* is to harm B.

So, for example, the courts recognise that an owner of land has an absolute freedom to extract water that flows under his land in undefined channels. As a result the courts have always held that a landowner will do no wrong if he intentionally harms someone else by extracting water that flows under his land in undefined channels. This was the result in *Bradford Corporation* v *Pickles*[13] where, it will be recalled, the defendant, Pickles, intercepted water flowing under his land in undefined channels that would otherwise have flowed into the claimant's reservoirs. Pickles plainly intended by doing this to cause the claimant inconvenience – Pickles had no use for the intercepted water himself. By inconveniencing the claimant in this way Pickles hoped, it seems, to give the claimant an incentive either to buy his land or to pay him to restore the water supply. Either way, Pickles, in acting as he did, intentionally harmed the claimant. The House of Lords refused to find that Pickles had owed the claimant a common law duty not to act in the way he did. Pickles had an absolute freedom to extract the water from under his land even if his object in so doing was to harm the claimant. Pickles did not therefore commit a tort in acting as he did.

The American position

It is easy to see why the English courts have not adopted the extreme position set out above. But they also haven't adopted the *American position*, under which A will commit a tort in relation to B if A intentionally harms B when he has no lawful justification or excuse for doing so.[14]

Suppose, for example, that Lara ran a corner shop selling newspapers and so on. Suppose further that Alan disliked Lara's political views so much that he resolved to ruin Lara by setting up a rival shop beside hers, selling the same goods that Lara sold but at much lower, and uneconomic, prices. Suppose finally that Lara soon went out of business under the pressure of this competition. The ruling in *Allen* v *Flood* makes it clear that because Alan used lawful means to drive Lara out of business, she will not be able to establish that Alan committed a tort in relation to her in acting as he did. But why don't the English courts adopt the American position and rule that Alan committed a tort in relation to Lara when he intentionally drove her out of business when he had no lawful justification or excuse for doing so? Four reasons can be given.

(1) *The difficulty of ascertaining someone's motives.* Whether A had a lawful justification or excuse for intentionally harming B can often turn on what his *motives*

---

[13] [1895] AC 587.

[14] See Restatement 2d, Torts, §870: 'One who intentionally causes injury to another is subject to liability to the other for that injury, if his conduct is generally culpable and not justifiable under the circumstances' (American Law Institute, 1979). See also *Tuttle* v *Buck*, 119 NW 946 (1909) (defendant banker was held liable to the claimant when he set out, for malicious reasons, to drive the claimant out of business as a barber by setting up a barber's shop near the claimant's shop and undercutting the claimant's prices).

were for harming B.[15] So, for example, in the above case we say that Alan had no lawful justification or excuse for acting as he did because he acted as he did out of a dislike for Lara's political views. Now – it is often very difficult to ascertain what someone's motives were for acting as he did.

Take the example of the cook and the butler, considered above. The cook secured the dismissal of the butler not out of spite but because she just didn't want to work with him any more. We know that because the situation was presented in that way. But if such a case were to occur in the real world it would be very difficult to tell whether the cook acted as she did because she disliked the butler and wanted to see him harmed (in which case, she would have had no lawful justification or excuse for procuring the butler's dismissal) or whether the cook acted as she did because she wanted to work alongside colleagues she liked and the butler did not fit the bill (in which case, she would have had a lawful justification or excuse for procuring the butler's dismissal).

Similarly with the case considered above where Carl wants to organise a boycott of ABC's products so as to put pressure on ABC to give up testing its perfumes on animals. In the real world, it would be very difficult to tell whether Carl's boycott is being organised for that reason (in which case Carl would have a lawful justification or excuse for organising the boycott) or whether Carl's boycott is being organised because Carl wishes to punish ABC for experimenting on animals (in which case Carl would not have a lawful justification or excuse for organising the boycott).

So if the courts adopted the American position, they would find it very difficult in a case where A has intentionally harmed B to determine *why* A set out to harm B, for the purpose of determining whether A had a lawful justification or excuse for harming B.[16] The ruling in *Allen* v *Flood* has the merit of ensuring that the law on whether A committed a tort in this case is easy to apply – one simply looks to see whether A employed lawful or unlawful means to harm B. It is far from clear that this area of the law would be just as easy to apply if the English courts took the American position and said that it is a tort to harm someone else intentionally when you have no lawful justification or excuse for doing so.

(2) *The legitimacy of motives.* Suppose that A has intentionally harmed B and we know *why* A harmed B. If the courts adopted the American position, then they would hold that A committed a tort in harming B if he had no lawful justification or excuse for acting as he did. However, the question of whether A had a lawful justification or excuse for acting as he did given the reasons for which he acted

---

[15] See Restatement 2d, Torts, §870, Comment *i*.

[16] Had *Allen* v *Flood* [1898] AC 1 gone the other way, in any case where a defendant intentionally harmed a claimant, it would have been – at that time – up to a jury to determine why the defendant acted in the way he did. Undoubtedly one of the reasons why *Allen* v *Flood* was decided in the way it was, was that the House of Lords did not think that a jury could be trusted to act responsibly in determining why a defendant intentionally harmed a claimant. The fear was that a jury would be influenced by its own personal likes and dislikes to put either the worst or best possible construction on a defendant's motives for intentionally harming a claimant. See ibid.., at 26 (per Mathew J), 118 (per Lord Herschell).

will often be very difficult and controversial to resolve.[17] For example, suppose A harmed B because B beat up his son – would A have had a lawful justification or excuse for acting in the way he did? What if A acted as he did because B seduced A's wife, or offered A's daughter drugs? These are very difficult questions and it is not clear the courts are the right institutions to answer them.[18] Under the ruling in *Allen* v *Flood* these questions never arise. If A sets out to ruin B using unlawful means to do so he will commit a tort – the question of whether or not A has a lawful justification or excuse for doing this never arises because it cannot be justifiable or excusable to break the law in order to inflict harm on someone else.[19] If A sets out on his own to ruin B using lawful means to do so then A will *not* commit a tort – whether or not A has a lawful justification or excuse for acting in this way.

(3) *Certainty*. The third reason why the English courts have not adopted the American position emerges out of the first two: if the law said that A will commit a tort in relation to B if he intentionally harms B when he has no justification or excuse for doing so, the law would become intolerably uncertain. Take the example of the cook and butler that we have already considered twice before. Were the law to take the American position, the cook would not be able to tell with any degree of certainty whether or not her procuring the butler's dismissal would amount to a tort. Maybe it would, maybe it wouldn't – it would all depend on how the courts, acting after the event, construed her motives and how much sympathy they had for the reasons why she acted as she did. This is unsatisfactory: as Tony Weir points out, 'Is it not important that people should be able to be told in advance what they may or may not do . . .?'[20]

(4) *Freedom*. In *Wainwright* v *Home Office*,[21] the House of Lords considered whether they should recognise that A would commit a tort in relation to B if he intentionally caused B distress when he had no lawful justification or excuse for doing so. Lord Hoffmann, delivering the leading judgment, thought that they should not take such a step: 'In institutions and work-places all over the country, people constantly do and say things with the intention of causing distress and humiliation to others. This shows lack of consideration and appalling manners but I am not sure that the right way to deal with it is always by litigation . . . [It] might not be in the public interest to allow the law to be set in motion for one boorish incident.'[22] The fear underlying Lord Hoffmann's judgment here is that were English law to take

---

[17] See Weir 1997, 74–5.

[18] Again (see above, n. 16), had *Allen* v *Flood* [1898] AC 1 gone the other way, it would have been – at that time – up to a jury to determine these issues. And again, undoubtedly one of the reasons why *Allen* v *Flood* was decided in the way it was, was that the House of Lords did not think that juries could be trusted to act responsibly in deciding whether or not someone had had a lawful justification or excuse for intentionally harming someone else: ibid., at 26 (per Mathew J), 118 (per Lord Herschell).

[19] Though Parliament has taken the view that a trade union official who uses unlawful means to inflict harm on an employer in the course of a trade dispute should not be held liable for so acting: see the Trade Union and Labour Relations (Consolidation) Act 1992, s 219 (summarised below, p. 497).

[20] Weir 1997, 68.

[21] [2003] 3 WLR 1137.

[22] Ibid., at [46].

the step of recognising that it is a tort intentionally to cause someone else distress (or some other kind of harm) when one has no lawful justification or excuse for so doing, then our freedom to do and say what we like would be radically curtailed.[23] Under the ruling in *Allen* v *Flood*,[24] no such concern arises. If A intentionally causes B to suffer some kind of harm, A will only commit a tort in relation to B if the means he uses to inflict that loss are *already* means that he is forbidden to use. So *Allen* v *Flood* does not have the effect of curtailing our liberties in any way at all.

So there is a lot to be said for the English courts' refusal to adopt the American position.[25] Having said that, the English courts *have* adopted a variation of the American position in cases where A *joins forces with someone else* – call him C – to inflict harm on B. In such a case, A will be held to have committed a tort in relation to B if A and C had *no good reason* for wanting to harm B. Whether or not lawful means were used to harm B will be irrelevant – if A and C used lawful means to harm B but they had no good reason for wanting to harm B, then A (and C) will have committed a tort in relation to B. Two criticisms may be made of this aspect of the law.

(1) *Paradox*. It does seem paradoxical that if A, acting alone, sets out to ruin B because he dislikes his political views he will commit no tort so long as his method of ruining B is lawful in nature; but, if A and C combine to ruin B because they dislike his political views, A will commit a tort even if A and C's chosen method of ruining B is lawful in nature.[26]

(2) *Difficulty*. Just as the courts would find it difficult to apply the law if it said that A will commit a tort if he intentionally causes B to suffer harm when he has no lawful justification or excuse for doing so, the courts have found this area of the law difficult to apply and for precisely the same reasons. As the law stands at the moment, if A and C joined forces and intentionally caused B to suffer harm using lawful means to do so, A will have committed a tort in so acting if he and C had no good reason for acting as they did. However, as we will see, it is sometimes difficult to determine *why* A and C acted in the way they did in order to see whether they had a good reason for acting as they did; and even if one knows why A and C acted in the way they did, it is often very difficult to determine whether or not that means they had a good reason for seeking to ruin B.

---

[23] In the United States, where a tort of intentionally causing another emotional distress without lawful justification or excuse is recognised, this concern is addressed by requiring that the defendant's conduct has been so 'extreme and outrageous' that it goes beyond 'all possible bounds of decency ... and [is] utterly intolerable in a civilized community': see Rest 2d, Torts, §46, Comment *d*.

[24] Strangely, *Allen* v *Flood* was not cited at all in *Wainwright* v *Home Office* even though, had the House of Lords declared that it is a tort intentionally to cause another distress without lawful justification or excuse, they would have created a large exception to the principles laid down in *Allen* v *Flood*.

[25] For an alternative view, see Finnis 1995; also Dietrich 2000.

[26] *Lonrho Ltd* v *Shell Petroleum (No. 2)* [1982] AC 173, 188H: 'Why should an act which causes economic loss to [B] but is not actionable at his suit if done by [A] alone become actionable because [A] did it pursuant to an agreement between [A] and C?' (per Lord Diplock).

20

USING UNLAWFUL MEANS TO HARM ANOTHER

INTRODUCTION

A will have committed the tort of *using unlawful means to harm another* in relation to B if: (*a*) A caused B to suffer some kind of harm; *and* (*b*) the means by which A caused B to suffer that harm were *unlawful*; *and* (*c*) A acted in the way he did with the *aim or object* of harming B.[1]

The usefulness of this tort

Two elements make this tort particularly useful. First, it can be used to claim redress for pure economic loss. In particular, it can be used to recover for economic losses *not* associated with the violation of contractual *rights*.[2]

Secondly, it can be used by a claimant to claim for losses that he has suffered as a result of a wrong done to a third party. For instance, if Dawn runs down a well-known footballer, Tom, with the aim of causing economic loss to the football club, Greatchester FC, which employs Tom, then Greatchester FC will be able to make a claim against Dawn on the basis that Dawn, in acting as she did, committed the tort of using unlawful means to harm another in relation to Greatchester FC. Such a claim will be supplementary to Tom's claim for the wrong done to *him* when Dawn ran him down. Moreover, such a claim is permitted even though Greatchester FC could not claim for its losses if all that happened was that Dawn *negligently* ran down Tom. It is a crucial feature of the tort that Dawn must have acted as she did with the *aim or object* of harming Greatchester FC.

Why are 'unlawful means' needed?

The requirement of 'unlawful means' was established in the important case of *Allen* v *Flood*.[3] In this case, Allen, a representative of the Ironworkers' Trade

---

[1] Fridman 1993 suggests (at 113) that for this tort to be committed, 'It is only necessary to show that the defendant's acts caused the loss of which the [claimant] complains, and that the defendant knew, or presumably could have appreciated, that such would be the effect or consequence of his acts.' (To the same effect, see S&H, 346.) This is wrong: if it were right, then *Lonrho* v *Shell Petroleum (No. 2)* [1982] AC 173 (summarised below, pp. –) would have been decided differently.

[2] In *JT Stratford & Son Ltd* v *Lindley* [1965] AC 269, Lord Reid said, 'In addition to interfering with existing contracts the respondents' action made it practically impossible for the appellants to do any new business with the barge hirers. It was not disputed that such interference with business is tortious if any unlawful means are employed' (ibid., 324).

[3] [1898] AC 1.

Union, went to an employer and said that unless the employer ceased to employ the claimants, Flood and Taylor, members of the Ironworkers' Trade Union would not work for the employer the next day. It is crucial that at the time all the employers' workers were employed on day-to-day contracts. Thus Flood and Taylor had no enforceable contractual right to be employed beyond the end of the day and equally the members of the Ironworkers' Trade Union were under no enforceable obligation to work for the employer the next day. So Allen's threat that his members would walk out if Flood and Taylor were not dismissed was not unlawful, and when the employers failed to re-engage Flood and Taylor the next day they were doing nothing unlawful. Flood and Taylor argued, however, that Allen had committed a tort in relation to them since he had maliciously caused them loss. Allen responded that there was no such tort.

Eventually[4] a majority of the House of Lords concluded that Allen was correct and that a tort of 'maliciously causing loss' did not exist. The majority thought that the law would be too uncertain if liability turned solely on the question whether the defendant was malicious. In this corner of the law many claims arise from fierce competition between traders and from bitter industrial disputes, and it would clearly be difficult to draw the line between vigorous pursuit of self-interest and malice.[5] By contrast, the majority thought that there was a 'chasm' between lawful and unlawful means.[6] Competitors and participants in industrial disputes would know where they stood if the rule was simply that they could use any means that were not unlawful. The justification based on certainty will only hold water, however, if 'unlawful means' is clearly defined.

Defining 'unlawful means'

In defining what amounts to 'unlawful means' for the purpose of the tort of using unlawful means to harm another, the law draws on definitions of what is unlawful found in other areas of the law. Thus there seems little doubt that if A has caused B to suffer some kind of harm by committing a *tort* in relation to C, A will be found to have caused B to suffer that harm through unlawful means – with the result that A will be found to have committed the tort of using unlawful means to harm another in relation to B if he acted as he did with the aim or object of harming B. Indeed, it seems that this is so even if C will not be able to sue A because A's tort did not cause him to suffer any kind of actionable loss.[7]

---

[4] For an account of the litigation see Heuston 1986.

[5] A further concern at the time of *Allen* v *Flood* was that as the law then stood the question whether there had been malice would usually have been left to a jury.

[6] *Rookes* v *Barnard* [1964] AC 1129, 1168–9, per Lord Reid, 'I agree with Lord Herschell [in *Allen* v *Flood* [1898] AC 1, at 121] that there is a chasm between doing what you have a legal right to do and doing what you have no legal right to do.' See also *Allen* v *Flood* [1898] AC 1, 139, per Lord Herschell, 'In my opinion a man cannot be called upon to justify either act or word merely because it interferes with another's trade or calling; any more than he is bound to justify or excuse his act or word under any other circumstances, *unless it be shewn to be in its nature wrongful*, and thus to require justification' (emphasis added).

[7] This was decided in *Lonrho* v *Fayed* [1990] 2 QB 479 where it was alleged that the defendant had caused loss to the claimant by making a deceitful statement to the Secretary of State for Trade and Industry, but it was not alleged that the Secretary of State had suffered any actionable loss as a result of the deceit.

The question whether a *breach of contract* will amount to 'unlawful means' for the purposes of the tort discussed here might seem to be more difficult. If A has breached a contract with C in order to harm B, one can clearly castigate what A has done as unlawful vis-à-vis C, but is there any reason to treat A's action as unlawful vis-à-vis B? The law of contract would not, after all, usually give B any right to insist on the contract being performed.[8] Nonetheless, it was decided in *Rookes* v *Barnard*[9] that a threat to break a contract was an unlawful threat for the purposes of the tort of intimidation. A major strand in the reasoning which supported this conclusion was that there was 'no difference in principle between a threat to break a contract and a threat to commit a tort'.[10] So it seems likely that a breach of contract will count as unlawful means for the purposes of the tort discussed here.[11]

Will the commission of a *criminal offence* count as 'unlawful means' for the purposes of the tort discussed here? This question does not cause any problems when the behaviour that constitutes the crime could also be actionable as a tort, because we have already seen that all torts count as unlawful means. The question is difficult, however, when we think about minor crimes such as regulatory offences. Here the main controversy flows from the fact that the definition of 'unlawful means' helps to determine what, for instance, traders can do to each other by way of competition, while Parliament may have defined certain things as minor crimes for reasons completely different from any considerations of what should be legitimate behaviour between competitors.

For example, many competitors try to persuade each others' customers to switch allegiances by sending out small free gifts with advertising slogans. If John decided to try and take customers from Lara by sending Lara's customers free calculators, would we want this to say that John committed the tort of using unlawful means to harm another in relation to Lara if it later turned out that the batteries in these calculators contained a dangerous chemical so that it was a statutory offence to supply them? The dilemma here is that 'unlawful means' is meant to be a clearly defined concept and consequently there are grounds for saying that *all* violations of statutes should count as 'unlawful means'. On the other hand, however, if the role of the tort is to define what methods it is wrongful for A to use against B in an attempt to harm B, it makes nonsense of the tort to make it cover methods which nobody thinks are improper. Does anyone think if Tom sends Lara's customers defective

---

[8] For an exception see the Contracts (Rights of Third Parties) Act 1999.

[9] [1964] AC 1129.

[10] Ibid., 1168 (per Lord Reid).

[11] But this suggests that if A breaks a contract with B *with the aim of harming* B, he will have committed the *tort* of using unlawful means to harm another. As a result, B will be allowed to sue A in *tort* for compensation for the losses suffered by her as a result of A's breach, thereby circumventing the ordinary remoteness rules which apply to actions for breach of contract (set out above, p. 9). In an attempt to get round this point, Carty 2001 argues (at 111) that an actual breach of contract should only constitute 'unlawful means' in a case involving *three* parties. Similarly, Sales & Stilitz 1999 argue (at 424) that in a case only involving *two* parties, a threat to break a contract should constitute 'unlawful means' but an actual breach of contract should not. To the same effect, W&J, 657.

calculators (instead of some other advertising gift) he is behaving wrongfully vis-à-vis Lara?

The question whether the breach of a statutory duty will count as 'unlawful means' for the purposes of the tort discussed here if a breach of the duty in question is *not* civilly actionable[12] has divided the judges. In *Lonrho v Fayed*, Dillon LJ suggested *obiter* that the breach of a statutory duty would only constitute 'unlawful means' if 'on its true construction the statute which imposed the prohibition gave rise to a civil remedy'.[13] But in *Associated British Ports v Transport and General Workers' Union* Stuart-Smith LJ concluded that 'at the very least it is strongly arguable that where the unlawful act relied on in this tort is a breach of statute, it is not necessary that it should be one that is actionable in tort at the suit of the claimant'.[14] In the recent case of *Michaels v Taylor Woodrow Developments Ltd*, Laddie J looked at all the relevant authorities and expressed a preference for Dillon LJ's view.[15]

There have been suggestions in a few cases that some things that are not torts, breaches of contract or crimes may nonetheless be unlawful means. Thus Lord Denning MR stated once that 'interference with the freedom of the press is so contrary to the public interest that it is to be regarded as the employment of unlawful means'.[16] Our opinion is that it is important that there should be a clear line between lawful and unlawful means, and consequently it would be best not to define 'unlawful means' in terms of a vague concept like 'the public interest'.

NOMINATE TORTS AND THE 'GENUS' TORT

The tort of using unlawful means to inflict harm on another is sometimes referred to as a 'genus of torts'[17] or 'the genus tort'. The main purpose of this label is to explain this tort's relationship with some other torts which have their own names – such as, intimidation and indirectly inducing a breach of contract.

---

[12] The breach of a statutory duty will be civilly actionable if: (*a*) its breach amounts to a tort, a breach of contract or an equitable wrong; *or* (*b*) its breach amounts to some kind of interference with a public right which causes someone to suffer special damage. See Chapters 27 and 28, below, for a discussion of when the breach of a statutory duty owed to another will amount to a tort. In Chapter 46, below, we discuss when an unlawful interference with a public right will be civilly actionable.

[13] [1990] 2 QB 479, 488F. Dillon LJ's views on this question have not been consistent, however, and in *Williams v Department of Transport*, The Times, 7 December 1993, when considering an injunction granted to prevent interference with trade by unlawful means he stated that, 'any thing which is illegal under any statute provides the unlawful means'.

[14] [1989] 1 WLR 939, 966H. Butler-Sloss LJ was of the same opinion (at 961G), but Neill LJ was more doubtful: see 954H–955B. We would certainly agree with Stuart-Smith LJ *to some extent*, in that there is no necessity that 'unlawful means' are actionable *by the claimant*. In many cases of using unlawful means to cause harm the 'unlawful means' consist in a wrong committed in relation to a third party, in an attempt to harm the claimant.

[15] [2001] Ch 493, at [65]. This view is also preferred by Carty 2001, 127–8 and 274–6 (the later pages reveal Carty's preference for the policy she has outlined in the earlier pages).

[16] *Associated Newspapers Group v Wade* [1979] ICR 664, 691C.

[17] *Merkur Island Shipping Corp. v Laughton* [1983] 2 AC 570, 609H (per Lord Diplock).

The suggestion is that the named torts are species within the wider genus. They fit the same general pattern but have their own spheres of operation.

The 'genus tort' has been influential in two main ways. First, it has encouraged expansion of the scope of liability beyond arbitrary limits. Thus it has helped to reinforce the idea that *indirect* interference with contractual interests by unlawful means is actionable even where there is no hint of a breach of contract. Secondly, the 'genus tort' has encouraged some co-ordination of the features of the torts which are thought to fit within it. There is no obvious reason, for instance, why different parts of the genus should require different mental elements.

In the next section we discuss some of the major nominate torts which fit within the genus. It should be noted, however, that the more loosely the genus is defined the greater the number of nominate torts it is possible to squeeze within it. Equally, some authors have sought to redefine the features of certain nominate torts in order to facilitate fitting them within the genus.[18]

Indirect interference with a contract

In Chapter 19 we discussed the tort of inducing a breach of contract and the difficult question of whether that tort extended to cover the case where someone prevented another from performing a contract.[19] We concluded that if A has prevented C from performing her contract with B, A will *only* be held to have committed the tort of *inducing breach of contract* in relation to B if A *directly* prevented C from performing her contract with B.

If, on the other hand, A *indirectly* prevented C from performing her contract with B, B will *not* be able to establish that A committed the tort of inducing a breach of contract in acting as he did. However, if A used *unlawful means* to prevent C from performing her contract with B *and* A acted as he did with the object of harming B, then B will still be able to establish that A committed a tort in relation to B in acting as he did – the tort of *indirect interference with a contract*.

Although many judges confusingly treat this tort as an instance of the wider tort of inducing a breach of contract, this tort is most naturally seen as an instance of the tort discussed in this chapter – the tort of using unlawful means to harm another. This classification is not simply a question of elegance. This classification explains why if A *indirectly* interferes with a contract of B's, A will *only* be held to have committed a tort in relation to B in so acting if: (*a*) A used 'unlawful means' to interfere with B's contract; *and* (*b*) A acted as he did with the aim or object of harming B.

It is not possible to catalogue all the ways in which one person will *indirectly* interfere with a contract. A common situation in the cases, however, goes as follows. A persuaded C's employees to break their contracts with C. As a result, C was forced to break its contract with B and B suffered harm as a result. In this situation A's actions will have *indirectly* interfered with the contract between C and B.[20] It follows that if A acted as he did with the object of

---

[18] Weir 1997 attempts to redefine the tort of inducing a breach of contract so that it will fit within the genus tort of using unlawful means to harm another. For criticisms of this attempt, see Bagshaw 1998.

[19] On this question see above, pp. 396–8.

[20] See above, p. 398.

harming B, A will have committed the tort of indirect interference with a contract in relation to B.[21]

We said at the start of this chapter that one of the features which makes the tort of using unlawful means to harm another useful is the fact that it covers forms of economic loss not associated with breach of contract. So suppose A persuaded C's employees to break their contracts with C and walk out on C. As a result, C was prevented from *entering into* a new contract with B because it did not have the workforce to fulfil the contract. Suppose further that B suffered harm as a result – he could not get anyone else to enter into the contract in C's place. If A's aim in persuading C's employees to walk out was to harm B in this way, then A will have committed a tort in relation to B in acting as he did. Of course, the tort which will have been committed in this scenario cannot easily be referred to as *indirect interference with a contract* because no existing contract was interfered with here. However, the tort committed here might instead be labelled *indirect interference with trade by unlawful means*.

In some cases the interference is far more indirect than these simple examples above. Thus in *Merkur Island Shipping Corp.* v *Laughton*,[22] the claimants owned a ship, the *Hoegh Apapa*, which docked at Liverpool. The defendant union officials persuaded the employees of a tug company to break their contracts of employment with the tug company by refusing to assist the tug company in fulfilling its obligation to tow the ship from its berth. This prevented the claimants from performing their charter-contract with C to 'prosecute ... voyages with the utmost despatch'. Under the terms of the charter-contract C was not obliged to pay hire for the days when the ship was trapped in Liverpool. The claimants sued the defendants, arguing that the defendants had committed a tort in indirectly interfering with the claimants' ability to perform their charter-contract and that the defendants were therefore liable to compensate the claimants for the loss of hire suffered by them as a result of the defendants' interference. The House of Lords agreed, referring to the tort committed by the defendants as 'the common law tort of actionable interference with contractual rights'.[23] But the House of Lords also acknowledged that the case would fit within the genus of 'interfering with the trade or business of another person by doing unlawful acts'.[24] Persuading the tug company's employees to break their contracts of employment was identified as the necessary 'unlawful means'.

Intimidation

In some circumstances A will not have to *use* unlawful means to inflict harm on B; he will be able to do so merely by *making threats* that he will act unlawfully.

---

[21] A has used 'unlawful means' to harm B here because in persuading C's employees to break their contracts of employment, he committed the tort of inducing a breach of contract in relation to C.

[22] [1983] 2 AC 570.

[23] Ibid., 609.

[24] Ibid.

So suppose that A threatens C that he will burn down his house unless he ceases to trade with B. Suppose further that C ceases to trade with B as a result of A's threat. In such a case, A will have harmed B without A's actually having to *do* anything unlawful to harm him. This is because a threat of the sort made by A here is not *in itself* unlawful.[25] If I say to you, 'I am going to cut down all the trees in your garden next week' then I probably do not commit any kind of crime or tort. It is abundantly clear, however, that if B has suffered some kind of harm because A threatened to act unlawfully towards C, A will commit a tort in relation to B – so long, of course, as A's object or aim in acting in the way he did was to harm B. The tort that A will have committed in this situation is usually referred to as the tort of *three-party intimidation*.[26] It can be fitted within the genus tort discussed in this chapter provided that we stipulate that the genus tort covers not just cases where someone intentionally causes another harm through the use of unlawful means but also cases where someone intentionally causes another harm through the use of *threats* to use such means.

Conspiracy to cause harm using unlawful means

If two or more people conspired together to cause B to suffer some kind of harm they will have committed a tort in relation to B if the means by which they caused B to suffer that harm were unlawful. The tort is known as the tort of *conspiracy to cause harm using unlawful means* or *unlawful means conspiracy* for short. This tort is distinct from the tort which we will call 'the tort in *Quinn* v *Leathem*' and which we will look at in the next chapter. While the tort in *Quinn* v *Leathem* also involves two or more people conspiring together to cause someone to suffer some kind of harm, there are two differences between the tort of conspiracy to cause harm using unlawful means and the tort in *Quinn* v *Leathem*.

First, two or more people who conspire together to cause B to suffer some kind of harm may commit the tort in *Quinn* v *Leathem* even though the means

---

[25] This point would not hold, though, if A had threatened to beat C up if he did not stop trading with B. It is both a tort and a crime to put someone in fear that they will be shortly beaten up: see above, p. 244.

[26] *Important note.* This name suggests that there may also be a tort of *two-party intimidation*. If this tort exists it would cover the situation where A makes a threat to B in order to persuade B to harm himself (for example: 'I will burn down your house unless you give me your priceless Rembrandt self-portrait'). There is some support for the existence of this tort in the case law. See, for example, *Rookes* v *Barnard* [1964] AC 1129, 1183 (per Lord Evershed), 1205 (per Lord Devlin); *Huljich* v *Hall* [1973] 2 NZLR 279, 285; *Godwin* v *Uzoigwe* [1993] Fam Law 65. But there are two reasons why the courts ought to be very cautious in developing such a tort. Firstly, the existence of such a tort might encourage victims to give in to threats too easily. Secondly, the law of contract and the law of restitution have developed rules and principles (such as the law on duress) to deal with situations where people are pressurised either into making contracts with others or into handing over money or goods to others. Judges ought to be reluctant to develop tort law in any way which might undermine these rules and principles. This said, there are cases where the harm that B subjects himself to as a result of the unlawful threat cannot be remedied by the law of contract or the law of restitution (for example: 'I will burn down your house unless you *destroy* your priceless Rembrandt self-portrait') and in such cases the tort of *two-party intimidation* can play a useful role.

they use to inflict that harm on B are *not* independently unlawful. Secondly, it is traditionally said that two or more people who conspired together to cause B to suffer some kind of harm will only have committed the tort in *Quinn* v *Leathem* in so doing if their *predominant purpose* in organising together was to harm B.[27] In contrast, if two or more people have conspired together to cause B to suffer some kind of harm, it does not have to be shown, for the purpose of establishing that they committed the tort of unlawful means conspiracy in acting as they did, that their predominant purpose in organising together was to harm B. They may still have committed the tort of unlawful means conspiracy in relation to B even if they only tried to harm B in order to achieve some other goal or end.[28] All that has to be shown is that the aim or object of the conspiracy was to harm B and the means used in order to harm B were independently unlawful.

One question which is sometimes asked is whether conspiracy to cause harm using unlawful means is really a separate tort, or simply a species of the general tort of using unlawful means to inflict harm on another. The main argument for treating it as a separate tort is that a person can commit the conspiracy tort even if he does not himself *use* unlawful means to harm another.[29] For example, suppose Fred, Paul and Mary agreed that Mary should inflict some kind of harm on Karen using some kind of unlawful means to do so. Suppose further that Mary carried out the plan and Karen suffered loss as a result. In this situation, Fred, Paul and Mary will all have committed the tort of unlawful means conspiracy in relation to Karen even though *Mary* was the only one who actually used unlawful means to harm Karen.[30] Consequently, one cannot pretend that this form of conspiracy can be fully merged with the genus tort discussed in this chapter. That said, many of the rules that govern this form of conspiracy, such as what counts as the meaning of 'aim or object' should be the same as the rules of the genus tort. 'Unlawful means', should be the same as the rules of the genus tort.

In *Michaels* v *Taylor Woodrow Developments Ltd*,[31] Laddie J accepted the principle that 'unlawful means' should be defined in the same way for the tort of conspiracy to cause harm using unlawful means and the other torts involving

---

[27] We question whether this traditional view of the ambit of the tort in *Quinn* v *Leathem* is actually correct below, at p. 431.

[28] *Lonrho* v *Fayed* [1992] 1 AC 448, 465H-466A; *Kuwait Oil Tanker Co. SAK* v *Al Bader (No. 3)* [2000] 2 All ER (Comm) 271, at [118] (per Nourse LJ): 'in order to establish an unlawful means conspiracy, it is necessary to establish an intention to injure the claimant but not a predominant intention or purpose to do so.'

[29] In practice, the unlawful means conspiracy tort is often alleged where (a) the claimant cannot tell which of a group of parties ranged against him actually performed the relevant unlawful act, or (b) many parties have committed the same unlawful act concertedly against the claimant and the claimant finds it easier to attribute the losses he has suffered to the concerted behaviour rather than to particular acts. Establishing a conspiracy may also be beneficial from an *evidential* standpoint, since the admissions of one conspirator may be used as evidence against another.

[30] A difficult situation will arise if Fred, Paul and Mary agreed that Mary should inflict some kind of harm on Karen but their agreement left it open as to what means Mary would use to inflict that harm. If Mary then used unlawful means to harm Karen, can Fred and Paul be said to have committed the tort of unlawful means conspiracy in relation to Karen? There is no authority on the point but we venture to suggest that if the conspirators agreed that Mary *could* use unlawful means to harm Karen if it was necessary to do so, then Fred and Paul should be found to have committed the tort of unlawful means conspiracy in relation to Karen.

[31] [2001] Ch 493.

using unlawful means to harm another, except where there was binding precedent requiring a different conclusion.[32] The precise question which he had to consider was whether a breach of a statutory duty which did not itself give rise to a private law action for damages could none-the-less amount to 'unlawful means' for the purpose of the tort of conspiracy to cause harm using unlawful means. He concluded that such a breach could not amount to 'unlawful means' since otherwise it would be too easy for claimants to outflank the decision that the particular statutory duty was not one the breach of which will amount to a civil wrong.

In reaching this conclusion Laddie J stated that 'in a conspiracy by unlawful means the means must be actionable in its own right against at least some of the conspirators'.[33] This, of course, suggests that 'unlawful means' may not be defined in the same way for the two torts after all because, as we have seen, other courts have held that if A intentionally harmed B by committing a tort in relation to C, A will have committed the 'genus tort' of using unlawful means to harm another in relation to B – and this is so even if C cannot sue A for committing the tort in question because, for example, he has suffered no loss as a result of its being committed.[34] Thus it would appear that these other courts have concluded that the commission of a tort can amount to 'unlawful means' even if it is not 'actionable in its own right'. In practice, it seems unlikely that Laddie J's requirement will make the unlawful means conspiracy tort *narrower* than the genus tort because if conspirators have agreed that one of the conspirators should use means which are unlawful means *under the genus tort* then the means used will be actionable against one of the conspirators – since that conspirator will have committed the genus tort. It has been argued, however, that Laddie J's requirement reveals that the theoretical framework supporting the unlawful means conspiracy tort is different from that supporting the genus tort: the unlawful means conspiracy tort exists to enable a claimant to sue secondary parties who have participated in another's *actionable* wrongdoing.[35]

---

[32] In *Rookes* v *Barnard* [1964] AC 1129, at 1210 Lord Devlin expressly left open the question whether a conspiracy to harm someone by bringing about a breach of contract would be tortious. It is possible that his reason for doing this was a worry that a newly-recognised tort of conspiracy to commit a breach of contract might conflict with the well-established tort of inducing a breach of contract.

[33] Ibid., at [66].

[34] See above, p. 418.

[35] Sales 1990; Carty 2001, 24–6.

21

THE TORT IN *QUINN* V *LEATHEM*

A PROBLEM OF TERMINOLOGY

It seems well acknowledged now that if A joins forces with a third party, C, and they together intentionally cause B to suffer harm for no good reason, then A will commit a tort. The tort has no good name.

Names which have been suggested in the past – such as *conspiracy* or *conspiracy to injure* – do not seem adequately to distinguish the tort discussed here from the tort (discussed in the previous chapter) which A will commit if he joins forces with C and they intentionally cause B harm using unlawful means to do so. In her book on the economic torts, Hazel Carty calls the tort discussed in this chapter, *simple conspiracy*.[1] However, that name suggests that you will commit the tort discussed here if you *simply* combine together with another to make someone else worse off; but that is not true – you must have acted as you did for no good reason to have committed the tort discussed here.

We will simply call the tort discussed in this chapter – *the tort in Quinn v Leathem*. The name comes from the first case in which a defendant was held to have committed a tort by virtue of the fact that he – acting in combination with someone else – intentionally caused someone else to suffer harm for no good reason.[2]

THE NEED FOR AGREEMENT

So – A will have committed the tort in *Quinn* v *Leathem* in relation to B if: (1) A joined forces with C and they together intentionally caused B to suffer some kind of harm; *and* (2) they did so for no good reason.

(1) is established by showing that A and C *agreed* that they would take steps to harm B and that they put that agreement into effect. So (1) will *not* be established in the case where A sets out to cause B harm and orders his employees to engage in various actions which will have that effect – as there is no *agreement* between A and his employees that they will take steps to harm B, it cannot be said that A and his employees have joined forces against B.[3]

---

[1] Carty 2001, 16.

[2] *Quinn* v *Leathem* [1901] AC 495.

[3] See *Crofter Hand Woven Harris Tweed Co.* v *Veitch* [1942] AC 435, 468 (per Lord Wright). On the other hand, see Viscount Simon LC, at 441: 'It was argued that the [defendant] Mackenzie should not be regarded as acting in combination with the [defendant] Veitch, so as to establish the element of agreement between them in the tort of conspiracy, because Veitch held the responsible position of Scottish area secretary to the union, whereas Mackenzie was only branch secretary for Stornoway. This, I think, is an unsound contention. The respective position of the two men in the heirarchy of

GOOD REASON

Suppose that A and C joined forces and they intentionally caused B to suffer some kind of harm. When will the courts hold that they had no good reason for acting as they did? The following guidance can be gleaned from the cases:

(1) *Business*. If A and C were businessmen, A and C will have had a good reason for acting in the way they did if they acted as they did in order to protect or promote their business interests.

In *Mogul Steamship Co. v McGregor, Gow & Co.*,[4] the defendant shipowners formed a cartel and sought to secure exclusively for themselves all the carrying trade at a particular loading port. The claimant shipowner was not a member of the cartel but nevertheless sent ships to the loading port in question and attempted to pick up cargoes there. The defendants resolved to eliminate this threat to their cartel and sought to drive the claimant out of business. They did so by drastically cutting their own rates for carrying cargo so that the claimant, to remain competitive, had to cut his own rates and trade at a loss. Moreover, they offered local shippers and agents who would agree to deal exclusively with them a rebate of 5 per cent on their normal rates for carrying cargo. The House of Lords held that the defendants had committed no tort in acting as they did. While they set out to cause the claimant to suffer harm, they did so in order to capture a larger share of the carrying business at the loading port where the claimant was attempting to pick up cargoes.

In *Sorrell v Smith*,[5] a union of retail newsagents attempted to limit the number of retail newsagents operating in any given area by adopting a policy of refusing to deal with wholesalers who supplied retail newsagents who had opened for business without the union's permission. R, a wholesaler, fell foul of the policy when he supplied a particular retail newsagent with newspapers when the newsagent had not obtained permission to trade from the union. In accordance with the policy, S – a retail newsagent within the union – withdrew his custom from R and switched it to W, another wholesaler who was prepared to abide by the union's demands. The defendants were members of a committee representing the proprietors of newspapers. They took the view that the union – in attempting to limit the number of retail newsagents trading in a given area – was acting contrary to their interests and weighed in on the side of R in an attempt to disrupt the union from achieving its aims. The defendants threatened not to supply W with any newspapers unless S switched his custom back to R. The House of Lords held that the defendants committed no tort in acting in this way. While they may have set out to cause S to suffer harm in acting as they did – in the sense that they were trying to make S do something he did not want to do – they had a good reason for doing so: they were trying to protect their business interests.

---

trade union officials has nothing to do with it. *Even if Mackenzie could be regarded as only obeying orders from his superior, the combination would still exist if he appreciated what he was about'* (emphasis added).
[4] [1892] AC 25.
[5] [1925] AC 700.

(2) *Trade unions.* If A and C were trade union officials, A and C will *usually* have had a good reason for acting as they did if they acted as they did in order to further the interests of their trade union or its members.

In *Crofter Hand Woven Harris Tweed Co. Ltd* v *Veitch*,[6] the defendants were officials of the Transport and General Workers' Union. All the dockers at Stornoway, the main port of the Isle of Lewis, and the great majority of the workers employed in the spinning mills on the Isle of Lewis, were members of the TGWU. The workers employed in these spinning mills would produce yarn that would be given out to the crofters on the Isle of Lewis. The crofters would weave the yarn into tweed cloth which would then be finished in the mills and sold as 'Harris tweed' by the mill owners. The claimant also sold 'Harris tweed' but he had a different method of manufacturing it. The claimant imported yarn from the mainland, handed it out to the crofters on the Isle of Lewis to weave into tweed cloth and then sent the tweed cloth back to the mainland for finishing. As a result, the claimant's 'Harris tweed' was cheaper than the mill owners' 'Harris tweed'. The mill owners resolved to do something about this and persuaded the defendants to order the dockers at Stornoway to refuse to handle yarn imported from the mainland – the intended effect being to drive the claimant out of business.

The House of Lords held that the defendants committed no tort in so acting. There was some ambiguity about why the defendants acted as they did. On one reading of the case, the defendants agreed to drive the claimant out of business in order to keep the mill owners' business competitive, thus guaranteeing that those of their members who were employed by the mill owners would not lose their jobs. On another reading of the case, the defendants struck a deal with the mill owners under which the mill owners would – in return for the defendants' assistance in putting the claimant out of business – allow the creation of a 'closed shop' in the spinning mills on the Isle of Lewis the effect of which would be that someone could only obtain employment in those mills if they were a member of the TGWU. On either reading, the defendants had a good reason for acting as they did: they did so in order to promote the interests of their members.

However, if A and C are officials of a trade union and they set out to cause B to suffer harm in order to promote the interests of their union or its members, it will *not* always be the case that they had a good reason for seeking to harm B.[7] In the *Crofter* case, Viscount Simon LC observed: 'If ... the mill-owners in the present case had promised a large subscription to the trade union funds as an inducement to bribe the [defendants] to take action to smash the [claimant's] trade, I cannot think that the [defendants] could excuse themselves for combining to inflict this damage merely by saying that their ... purpose was to benefit the funds of the union thereby.'[8]

---

[6] [1942] AC 435.

[7] Contra, Gronow 1995, who takes an unduly pessimistic view of the current scope of this tort.

[8] [1942] AC 435, 446. This view was supported by Viscount Maugham (at 451). What if the defendants in the *Crofter* case *had* acted as they did because the mill owners had promised to allow the creation of a closed shop in the mills in return for the trade union's assistance in ruining the claimant? It is hard to see a distinction between that case and the case where a trade union assists in ruining a third party's competitor because the third party promised to give a handsome sum to the trade union's funds in return for such assistance. Viscount Simon LC did not have

In *Giblan* v *National Amalgamated Labourers' Union of Great Britain and Ireland*,[9] the claimant was once the treasurer of the defendant union. There were some irregularities in the way the claimant handled the union's finances and it was alleged that the claimant had kept for himself some money which he should have handed over to the union. The claimant agreed to pay the money over to the union but never did. As a result, officials of the union resolved to make life difficult for the claimant. Accordingly, whenever he found employment, the union officials would threaten his employer with reprisals unless he discharged the claimant. In this way the union officials secured on four different occasions the claimant's dismissal from some job he had found.

It is difficult to tell whether the officials acted in this way to punish the claimant for acting as he did (in which case they would not have had a good reason for acting as they did – see (4), below) or because they wished to compel him to pay the debt he owed the trade union. However, the Court of Appeal was prepared to find that even if the latter was the case – and that therefore the trade union officials were acting as they did to protect and promote the interests of the trade union – the trade union officials had no good reason for acting as they did and therefore committed the tort in *Quinn* v *Leathem* in acting as they did.[10] Even if the trade union officials acted as they did to compel the claimant to pay his debt, they still had no good reason for doing what they did as they had a perfectly good legal remedy available to them to compel the claimant to pay the union what he owed it. They had no need to take the extra-legal measures they did to compel him to pay up.

(3) *Public interest.* In *Scala Ballroom (Wolverhampton) Ltd* v *Ratcliffe*,[11] the claimants were proprietors of a ballroom. They operated a colour bar, excluding coloured visitors from the dancefloor. At the same time, they allowed coloured musicians to play in the orchestra. The defendants were officials of the Musicians' Union. They attempted to bring the colour bar to an end by warning the claimants that members of the Musicians' Union would not be allowed to play at the claimants' ballroom while the colour bar was in place. The Court of Appeal held that the defendants had committed no tort in so acting. While they had, in acting as they did, sought to harm the claimants – in the sense of seeking to make the claimants do something they did not want to do – they had had a good reason for doing so. The Court of Appeal found that the defendants had, in acting as they did, sought to promote the interests of the coloured members of their union. However, we would submit, even if the defendants' union had had no coloured members they would still have had a

---

to confront this difficulty: he found, on the facts, that the defendants had not acted as they did because the mill owners had promised in return to allow the creation of a closed shop in the mills (at 439) but had instead acted 'to benefit their ... members by preventing under-cutting and unregulated competition, and so helping to secure the economic stability of the island industry'.

[9] [1903] 2 KB 600.

[10] The only tort that the trade union officials could have committed was the tort in *Quinn* v *Leathem*; the union officials had employed no unlawful means in their attempts to make life difficult for the claimant and they did not induce any of his employers to discharge him in breach of contract.

[11] [1958] 1 WLR 1057.

good reason for acting as they did. If the defendants honestly felt that what the claimants were doing was wrong, then there seems no reason why the defendants should not have been allowed to organise together to attempt to induce the claimants to give up their colour bar.

(4) *Punishment.* If A and C acted as they did because they wanted to punish B for something she did or for the fact that she held certain views, then A and C will *not* have had a good reason for acting as they did *unless* they thought that punishing B was necessary to safeguard their business interests or to protect the interests of their trade union.

In *Quinn* v *Leathem*,[12] Leathem was a butcher. The Belfast Journeymen Butchers and Assistants' Association was upset that Leathem did not exclusively employ men who belonged to that union. In fact, none of Leathem's employees belonged to that union and neither did Leathem. Leathem attended a meeting of the union and offered to make his employees members of the union. The union insisted that he dismiss his employees and employ existing members of the union instead. Leathem refused to do this. The defendants, officials of the union, resolved to punish Leathem for taking this stand and did so by threatening Leathem's customers that union members employed by those customers would walk out on their jobs if they continued to deal with Leathem. As a result, Leathem lost a lot of custom. On these facts, the House of Lords held that the defendants had committed a tort. They had organised together and intentionally caused Leathem to suffer loss and had no good reason for doing so – they did not act as they did to advance the interests of their union or the members of the union, but simply out of a vindictive desire to see Leathem punished for acting as he did.

In *Huntley* v *Thornton*,[13] the claimant was employed in a shipyard in Hartlepool when he received a notice from his union to stop work for 24 hours in support of a wage claim. The claimant refused to abide by this instruction and went to work as usual. The defendants, members of the Hartlepool district committee of the union, recommended that the claimant be expelled from the union (a recommendation not acted on by the union's executive council) and then embarked on a campaign to prevent the claimant finding alternative employment by threatening anyone who employed him, or thought of employing him, with industrial action. It was found, at first instance, that the defendants had committed a tort in so acting. They had intentionally harmed the claimant and had done so for no good reason. In acting as they did, Harman J held, the defendants were not acting to promote the interests of their trade union. Rather, the defendants sought to harm the claimant for showing 'an arrogant attitude' towards them; in acting as they did, the defendants 'entirely lost sight of what the interests of the union demanded, and thought only of their own ruffled dignity'.[14]

---

[12] [1901] AC 495.
[13] [1957] 1 WLR 321.
[14] Ibid., 341.

Some have sought to sum up the above by saying that if A and C join forces and intentionally cause B to suffer some kind of harm, they will have committed a tort if their *predominant purpose* in causing B to suffer that harm was to injure B.[15]

This formulation is apt to confuse. In all the cases we have looked at so far the defendants' purpose was to injure the claimant and in all the cases we have looked at so far the defendants' purpose was to injure the claimant to achieve some other end – either to advance the defendants' business interests (as in the *Mogul* case) or to advance the interests of the defendants' union (as in the *Crofter* case) or to assuage the defendants' sense of resentment or outrage towards the claimant (as in *Quinn v Leathem* and in *Huntley v Thornton*). How can one say, then, that in *Quinn* and *Huntley* the defendants' predominant purpose was to injure the claimant; but in *Mogul* and *Crofter* the defendants' predominant purpose was not to injure the claimant?

Moreover, the formulation under scrutiny here – that if A and C join forces and intentionally cause B to suffer some kind of harm, they will have committed a tort if their predominant purpose was to harm B – is apt to mislead. It may lead us to think that if trade union officials set out to cause – and succeed in causing – B to suffer some kind of harm they will not commit the tort in *Quinn v Leathem* so long as their primary intention in so acting was to promote the interests of the officials' trade union. However, we have already seen that there may be cases where trade union officials who intentionally cause another harm may be guilty of committing the tort in *Quinn v Leathem* even though their ultimate object in so acting was to promote the interests of their trade union. This was the case in the *Giblan* case and may be the case where trade union officials set out to ruin an individual in return for a promised contribution to trade union funds.

For these reasons, we would reject the view that if A and C join forces and intentionally cause B to suffer some kind of harm, whether or not they have committed the tort in *Quinn v Leathem* will depend on whether or not A and C's predominant purpose in so acting was to injure B. This view is confusing and misleading. The touchstone of liability in this context, we submit, is whether or not A and C had 'just cause or excuse for the action taken'.[16]

THE PROBLEM OF MIXED MOTIVES

So far we have been dealing with the situation where A and C join forces and intentionally cause B to suffer some kind of harm for no good reason – in such a case, A and C will commit the tort in *Quinn v Leathem*. We must now deal with two questions. (1) What is the position if A and C joined forces and intentionally caused B to suffer some kind of harm and A had a good reason for acting in the way he did but C did not? Will A have committed a tort in this

---

[15] *Crofter Hand Woven Harris Tweed Co. v Veitch* [1942] AC 435, 445 (per Viscount Simon LC); *Lonrho plc v Fayed* [1992] 1 AC 448, 465H (per Lord Bridge of Harwich).

[16] *Sorrell v Smith* [1925] AC 700, 712 (per Viscount Cave LC). See also *Crofter Hand Woven Harris Tweed Co. v Veitch* [1942] AC 435, 451–2 (per Viscount Maugham).

situation? (2) What is the position if A and C joined forces and intentionally caused B to suffer some kind of harm and C had a good reason for acting in the way he did but A did not? Will A have committed a tort in this situation?

The answer to question (1) is 'no' unless A *knew* of C's reasons for seeking to cause B to suffer harm.[17] So, in *Huntley* v *Thornton*,[18] when the claimant left Hartlepool and moved to Teesside in an attempt to escape the attentions of the Hartlepool district committee of the claimant's union and find work, the Hartlepool district committee persuaded two union officials in the Teesside district to join with them in helping prevent the claimant find work. However, the two union officials in question committed no tort in so acting – they had been led to believe that safeguarding the interests of the union required them to take steps against the claimant and had no idea that the Hartlepool district council were engaged in a petty and vindictive campaign against the claimant.

The answer to question (2) seems to be 'no' unless C knew of A's reasons for seeking to cause B to suffer harm. If C did know, then both A and C will have committed a tort in organising together to harm B. Why will *C's* ignorance – if he is ignorant of A's purposes – absolve *A*? The answer, it seems, is that an agreement – a conspiracy – to inflict harm on another cannot be unlawful unless *at least* two parties to it are acting unlawfully. So if C cannot be held to have acted unlawfully – committed a tort – in agreeing with A that they would seek to cause B to suffer some kind of harm, then that agreement with A could not have been unlawful. But if the agreement with A was not unlawful, then A could not have acted unlawfully in being party to it. So A could not have committed a tort in agreeing with C that they would seek to cause B to suffer some kind of harm.

This line of reasoning, while superficially attractive, has nothing to recommend it. If A wishes for no good reason to cause B to suffer some kind of harm there is no reason why the law should not enjoin him from joining forces with someone else to cause B to suffer that harm – whatever the motivations of that someone else. According to the orthodox view summed up above, if A wishes for no good reason to cause B to suffer some kind of harm, the law only requires A not to join forces with a third party, C, to inflict that harm on B if C *also* has no good reason for wanting to harm B. It is hard to see why the law would take such an odd position.

---

[17] Ibid., at 495 (per Lord Porter).
[18] [1957] 1 WLR 321.

TORTS INVOLVING THE DECEPTION OF OTHERS

The trio of torts collected here – deceit, malicious falsehood and passing off – do not fit under any of the categories of torts that we have studied so far.

None of these torts are committed by breaching a duty of care owed to someone else. The tort of *deceit* owes its existence to the fact that if we take any two individuals, A and B, A will owe B a common law duty not to induce B to act in some way by lying to him or her. If A breaches this duty we say he has committed the tort of deceit in relation to B. The tort of *malicious falsehood* owes its existence to the fact that if we take any two individuals, A and B, A will owe B a common law duty to ensure that he does not cause B to suffer any loss by lying to other people about B. If A breaches this duty we say he has committed the tort of malicious falsehood in relation to B. We use the term *passing off* to describe the breach of a number of different common law duties that one person will owe another – none of them a duty of care. So, for example, suppose that A and B are both in business producing and selling jeans. A will owe B a common law duty not to mislead the public into thinking that A's jeans are made by B.[1] If A breaches this duty we say that A has committed the tort of passing off in relation to B. Likewise, A will owe B a common law duty not to mislead the public into associating A's jeans with B or B's jeans if the effect of A's doing this would be to harm B's reputation or the reputation of B's jeans. Again, if A breaches this duty we say that A has committed the tort of passing off in relation to B.

It should be obvious from the discussion in the previous paragraph that none of the three torts under scrutiny here involve the breach of a 'harm-avoiding' duty (a duty not to cause another to suffer a specific kind of harm) – so it would be wrong to categorise any of these torts as 'torts involving the infliction of a certain kind of harm'.

Likewise, each of the three torts discussed here can be committed in the absence of an intention to cause someone else to suffer harm – so none of these torts can be categorised as 'torts involving the intentional infliction of harm'. Suppose, for example, that Carl thought that Wendy would do herself a favour if she bought shares in XYZ plc. Suppose further that, in order to convince Wendy to invest in XYZ, Carl told Wendy some lies about XYZ – exaggerating

---

[1] Why will A owe B such a duty? The answer is that B will have spent time and trouble building up a reputation for her jeans and it would be wrong for A to appropriate the goodwill B has earned for her jeans and use it to sell his own brand of jeans. On the other hand, if B has spotted a gap in the market and moved to fill it, A will do nothing wrong if he copies B's example and attempts to corner that part of the market himself: while it is wrong for A to appropriate the goodwill that is specifically attached to B's products, there is nothing wrong in A's borrowing B's good ideas. See, on this, *Cadbury Schweppes Pty Ltd* v *Pub Squash Co. Pty Ltd* [1981] RPC 429 (held, no tort committed by defendant who marketed a sports drink aimed at the same kind of consumer as the claimant's sports drink); also Cane 1996, 80–1.

its current profitability and future prospects. Suppose finally that Wendy was induced by those lies to invest in XYZ and lost her money. On these facts Carl will have committed the tort of deceit in relation to Wendy – even though he never intended to cause Wendy any harm when he acted as he did.[2] Similarly, suppose that Eric sold a story about Ruth to the newspapers for a large sum of money. Suppose further that this story was false and Eric knew it was when he sold it to the newspapers. Suppose finally that when the story was published Ruth lost her job. On these facts Eric will have committed the tort of malicious falsehood – even if his sole intention in selling the story to the newspaper was to earn money and not to harm Ruth. Finally, suppose that Gary marketed his goods in such a way as to mislead the public into thinking that his goods were made by Helen. Gary will, in so acting, have committed the tort of passing off – even if his only object in marketing his goods in this way was to increase the attractiveness of his goods to the general public.

The three torts gathered here therefore have two things in common: they do not fit inside any of the categories of torts that we have already discussed and – as should be obvious from what has already been said – they are all committed by deceiving people. Beyond that, these three torts have very little in common. One of them (passing off) can be committed quite innocently; the other two (deceit and malicious falsehood) can only be committed by deliberately deceiving someone else. One of them (deceit) is committed by deceiving the victim of the tort; the other two (passing off and malicious falsehood) are committed by deceiving people other than the victim of the tort. However, these three torts have enough in common – by virtue of the fact that they are all committed by deceiving people – to warrant grouping them together.

---

[2] See *Polhill* v *Walter* (1832) 3 B & Ad 114, 110 ER 43. The fact that the tort of deceit can be committed without any intention to harm the victim of the deceit means that Weir 1964 (at 226), Cane 1996 (at 152, n. 9) and Sales & Stilitz 1999 (at 432) are *wrong* to suggest that deceit can be seen as an instance of the tort of using unlawful means to harm another.

22

DECEIT

DEFINITION

A will have committed the tort of deceit (or fraud) in relation to B if: (1) he made a representation of fact to B which was untrue; *and* (2) when he made that representation to B he did not honestly believe that it was true; *and* (3) he intended, in making that representation to B, to induce B to act in a particular way; *and* (4) B was induced to act in that way by A's representation. We will now look at each of these elements in turn.[1]

UNTRUE REPRESENTATION OF FACT

Types of representation

A representation of fact may be distinguished from a representation of opinion, a representation of intention and a representation of law. However, the distinction between these different kinds of representations is not ultimately of great significance to the law on deceit. This is because a representation of opinion or a representation of intention or a representation of law always carries with it a representation of fact.

If A says to B, 'I think that *x* is true' he makes a representation that it is a fact that he thinks *x* is true. So if A says to B 'I think that *x* is true' when he does not actually think *x* is true then A makes an untrue representation of fact to B – he represents to B that he thinks *x* is true and this is not true. Some judges have gone further and said that if A says to B 'I think that *x* is true' when A is in a much better position than B to know whether or not *x* is true, then A's representation 'I think that *x* is true' will amount to a representation of fact that there is *good reason* to believe that *x* is true.[2] Some judges have gone even further than this and said that in such a case, A's representation 'I think that *x* is true' will amount to a representation of fact that *x is* true.[3]

If A says to B, 'I intend to do *x*', he makes a representation that it is a fact that he currently has an intention to do *x*. So if A says to B 'I intend to do *x*' when he has no such intention, A makes an untrue representation of fact – he represents to B that it is currently his intention to do *x* when this is not true. For example, in *Edgington* v *Fitzmaurice*,[4] the directors of a company issued a

---

[1] There is no further requirement that A's representation must have been made in a commercial context: *P* v *B* [2001] 1 FLR 1041 (action for deceit brought by claimant against his ex-girlfriend, claiming that she had lied to him in telling him that he was the father of her child).
[2] *Brown* v *Raphael* [1958] 1 Ch 636.
[3] *Bisset* v *Wilkinson* [1927] AC 177.
[4] (1885) 29 Ch D 459.

prospectus inviting subscriptions for debentures issued by the company. The prospectus stated that the object of the issue was to raise money to allow the company to complete alterations in the buildings of the company, to purchase horses and vans and to develop the company's trade. In fact the directors intended to use the money raised to pay off some of the company's debts. It was held that the directors had made an untrue representation of fact in the prospectus – they had represented that it was their intention to invest the money raised by the issue of debentures when it was actually their intention to use the money to pay off some of the company's debts. Bowen LJ put the point memorably: '[t]here must be a misstatement of an existing fact [for an action in deceit to be maintained]: but the state of a man's mind is as much a fact as the state of his digestion.'[5]

Similarly, in *East* v *Maurer*,[6] the defendant ran two hairdressing salons in neighbouring areas. The defendant decided to sell one of the salons and devote all his efforts to working in the other salon. The claimants were interested in purchasing the salon the defendant wanted to sell and, in order to encourage them to buy the salon, the defendant assured them that he did not intend to work regularly in the other salon. In so assuring the claimants, the defendant made an untrue representation of fact: he represented that he had no intention of working regularly in his other salon when, in fact, he had every intention of doing so.

Finally, if A tells B that 'the law says *x*', he makes a representation that it is a fact that he thinks the law says *x*. So if A tells B that 'the law says *x*' when he does not believe that the law says *x*, he will make an untrue representation of fact to B.[7]

Ways of making representations of fact

The easiest, and most obvious, way of making a representation of fact is in *words* or in *writing*.[8] However, it is also possible to make a representation of fact by *conduct*. If A conducted himself in such a way that B *reasonably* inferred from A's conduct that *x* was true, then it is fair to say that A represented to B that *x* was true.

In *Ward* v *Hobbs*,[9] Hobbs sold pigs to Ward at the Newbury market. Ward later discovered that the pigs were suffering from typhoid fever; all but one of the pigs died and some other pigs of Ward's also died, having been infected by the pigs bought from Hobbs. Ward sued Hobbs claiming, *inter alia*, that Hobbs had committed the tort of deceit. The claim failed: Hobbs had made no representation that his pigs were free from illness and of good quality. Ward argued that Hobbs's act of

---

[5] Ibid., 483.
[6] [1991] 1 WLR 461.
[7] *Beattie* v *Lord Ebury* (1872) LR 7 Ch 777.
[8] For the purposes of the law on deceit, it will not normally make a difference whether an untrue representation was made orally or in writing. However, if someone makes a false representation as to someone else's financial standing, that representation will only be actionable in deceit if it is made in writing and signed: Statute of Frauds Amendment Act 1828, s 6.
[9] (1878) 4 App Cas 13.

driving the pigs to market when he had a statutory duty not to do so if they were suffering from a contagious disease meant that he represented to Ward that his pigs were free from disease. However, even if Ward inferred from Hobbs' driving his pigs to market that the pigs were free from disease, this was not a reasonable inference to draw; it was not *reasonable* to think that Hobbs would observe his statutory duty and not drive his pigs to market if they were suffering from a contagious disease. As Lord Selborne remarked: '[t]o say that every man is always to be taken to represent, in his dealings with other men, that he is not, to his knowledge, violating any statute, is a refinement which . . . would not I think appear reasonable to any man.'[10]

In *Gordon* v *Selico Co. Ltd*, it was held at first instance that if a landlord deliberately covers up dry rot in a flat before showing it to a prospective tenant, then the landlord makes a representation to the tenant that the flat does not suffer from dry rot.[11] This ruling was not challenged on appeal.[12] The ruling at first instance is authority for the proposition that if A does a positive act *y* with the object of inducing B to believe that *x* is true, then A represents to B that *x* is true.

What is the position if a flat which A wanted to let suffered from dry rot and A did not cover it up but simply did not mention the existence of the dry rot to prospective tenants? Did he thereby represent to the prospective tenants that the flat did not suffer from dry rot? The answer is 'no': one cannot make a representation of fact by silence.[13] This is so even if A had a moral or legal obligation to mention the existence of any dry rot in the flat to prospective tenants looking round the flat.[14] Even if A had such a moral or legal obligation, it would not have been reasonable to take A's failure to say that the flat had any dry rot as an indication that the flat did not suffer from dry rot, just as it was not reasonable in *Ward* v *Hobbs* for Ward to think that Hobbs's driving his pigs to market when he had a statutory duty not to do so if they suffered from an infectious disease indicated that Hobbs's pigs did not suffer from an infectious disease.[15]

LACK OF HONEST BELIEF

In *Derry* v *Peek* Lord Herschell observed: 'in order to establish an action of deceit, there must be proof of fraud, and nothing short of that will suffice . . . [F]raud is proved when it is shewn that a false representation has been made

---

[10] Ibid., 29.

[11] [1985] 2 EGLR 79.

[12] [1986] 1 EGLR 71, 75J.

[13] *Bradford Third Equitable Building Society* v *Borders* [1941] 2 All ER 205, 211B–C per Viscount Maugham.

[14] Though see Lord Blackburn in *Brownlie* v *Campbell* (1880) 5 App Cas 925, 950: 'it is my opinion, where there is a duty or obligation to speak, and a man in breach of that duty or obligation holds his tongue and does not speak, and does not say the thing he was bound to say, if that was done with the intention of inducing the other party to act upon the belief that the reason why he did not speak was because he had nothing to say, I should be inclined to hold that that was fraud.'

[15] Of course, if A failed to mention the existence of the dry rot affecting the flat to a prospective tenant, when he owed the prospective tenant a *legal* duty to do so, and the prospective tenant suffered loss as a result, the prospective tenant could sue A for breaching that legal duty and would have no need to sue A in deceit.

(1) knowingly, or (2) without belief in its truth, or (3) recklessly, careless whether it be true or false.'[16]

It should be noted that A can make an untrue representation of fact to B 'recklessly, careless whether it be true or false' even if he honestly believes that his representation is correct. This will be the case where A makes an untrue representation of fact to B, honestly believing in its truth, but he would still have made that representation to B even if he had known that it was untrue.

So suppose that Vijay sold a car to Beth and, in order to persuade Beth to buy the car, he told Beth that the car had never been involved in an accident when in fact it had been. Vijay may have honestly believed that the car had never been involved in an accident – but his representation would still have been made 'recklessly, careless whether it be true or false' if, had he known that the car had been involved in a previous accident, he would *still* have told Beth that the car had never been involved in an accident.

So in any given case where A makes an untrue representation of fact to B, (3) may be true even if (1) and (2) are not. However, Lord Herschell did not take this point and went on to observe: 'Although I have treated the second and third as distinct cases, I think the third is but an instance of the second, for one who makes a statement under such circumstances can have no real belief in the truth of what he states.'[17] It would be more accurate to say that (2) is an instance of (3) – if A told B that a car he was selling had never been involved in an accident and, when he made that representation, he had not formed any view on whether the car had or had not been involved in an accident (he thought: 'It might have been involved in an accident, it might not have been – I don't know one way or the other'), then, by definition, he made that representation to B 'recklessly, careless whether it be true or false'. Be that as it may, Lord Herschell thought that (3) was really an instance of (2).

So, according to Lord Herschell, A could only be said to have committed the tort of deceit in making an untrue representation of fact to B, if: (1) he knew that that representation was untrue when he made it; *or* (2) when he made that representation he did not honestly believe that that representation was true. This is generally accepted to state the law as it is today.[18] At this point we can note that (1) is just an instance of (2) – someone who makes an untrue representation of fact knowing that it is untrue does not, in making that representation, honestly believe that it is true.

So the law can be stated more simply if we say that: A can only be said to have committed the tort of deceit in making an untrue representation of fact to B if, when he made that representation, he did not honestly believe that it was true. So, suppose that Beth bought a car from Vijay after Vijay told her that it had never been involved in an accident. Suppose further that this was untrue:

---

[16] (1889) 14 App Cas 337, 374.

[17] Ibid.

[18] Cf. *Bradford Third Equitable Building Society* v *Borders* [1941] 2 All ER 205, 211: 'the representation must be made with a knowledge that it is false ... or at least made in the absence of any genuine belief that it is true [before an action in deceit can be maintained]' (per Viscount Maugham).

the car had been involved in an accident. If we want to find out whether Beth can sue Vijay in deceit we have to ask: When Vijay told Beth that the car had never been involved in an accident, did he honestly believe that what he was saying was true? If the answer is 'yes' then Vijay *cannot* have committed the tort of deceit in telling Beth that the car had never been involved in an accident. If the answer is 'no' – either because, at the time of Vijay's representation, he knew that the car had been involved in an accident or had no idea whether it had been or not – then Vijay *may* have committed the tort of deceit in telling Beth that the car had never been involved in an accident.

INTENTION

A will intend to induce B to act in a certain way by making a representation of fact to B if A's object or purpose in making that representation to B is to induce B to act in that way.

On this definition it seems doubtful whether the reasoning employed in the case of *Brown Jenkinson & Co.* v *Percy Dalton (London) Ltd*[19] was correct. In that case, the defendant had a quantity of orange juice which he wished to ship to Hamburg. The owner of the ship on which the orange juice was to be shipped noticed that the barrels containing the orange juice were old and frail. The defendant needed the shipowner to issue a 'clean' bill of lading for the orange juice – a bill of lading which stated that the orange juice was shipped in good order and condition – otherwise the person he was shipping the orange juice to in Hamburg would not have paid for it. But if the shipowner issued a 'clean' bill of lading he would be held liable to the buyer of the orange juice for any orange juice that was lost during the voyage to Hamburg – the shipowner would be prevented by virtue of the fact that he issued a 'clean' bill of lading from denying that it was his fault the orange juice was lost during the voyage. The defendant persuaded the shipowner to issue a 'clean' bill of lading – stating that the orange juice was shipped in barrels that were in good order and condition – by promising to indemnify the shipowner against any liabilities he would incur to the buyer of the orange juice as a result of his issuing a 'clean' bill of lading. When the barrels of orange juice arrived in Hamburg, they were leaking and the shipowner had to compensate the buyer for the lost orange juice. The shipowner then sought to recover the money he had paid out to the buyer from the defendant.

The defendant claimed that his promise to indemnify the shipowner was unenforceable because it was made in order to persuade the shipowner to commit the tort of deceit. The Court of Appeal agreed, holding that the shipowner, in issuing a 'clean' bill of lading, had committed the tort of deceit. This does not seem right. The shipowner, in issuing a 'clean' bill of lading in respect of the orange juice shipped by him, *did* make an untrue representation of fact to the buyer of that orange juice: he represented that the orange juice was shipped in barrels that were in good order and condition when they were

[19] [1957] 2 QB 621.

not. When the shipowner made this representation of fact, he was aware that it was not true. The buyer was induced by this representation of fact to pay for the orange juice shipped by the shipowner. But the shipowner did not issue a 'clean' bill of lading *in order to* induce the buyer to pay for the orange juice: whether or not the buyer paid for the orange juice was a matter of complete indifference to him. Rather, he issued the 'clean' bill of lading in order to help the defendant out.

The Court of Appeal found otherwise and held that the shipowner had issued the 'clean' bill of lading with the object of inducing the buyer to agree to buy the orange juice shipped by the shipowner. The decision probably rests on a discredited notion of intention according to which if A did *y* knowing that B would do *x* as a result, A is held to have done *y* with the intention of inducing B to do *x*.[20] This is clearly nonsensical: if Tom steals diamonds from a jewellery store, he knows that the police will attempt to apprehend him as a result but Tom can hardly be said to have stolen the diamonds with the intention of inducing the police to attempt to apprehend him.[21]

INDUCEMENT

A's making a representation of fact to B will have induced B to do *x* if A's representation *played some part* in B's decision to do *x*.

In *Smith* v *Chadwick*,[22] the claimants claimed that they were induced to buy shares in a company because its prospectus falsely represented that G was a director of the company. This claim was dismissed: the claimants could not have been induced to buy shares in the company by the representation in the prospectus that G was a director of the company because, by their own admission, the claimants had never heard of G before the prospectus was issued: the representation in the prospectus that G was a director of the company could not therefore have played any part in the claimants' decision to take up shares in the company.

In *JEB Fasteners Ltd* v *Marks Bloom & Co.*[23] (*not* a deceit case) the claimants started negotiations to take over a company which had recently started trading in the same products as the claimants. In the course of negotiations, the defendants drew up and showed to claimants the company's accounts, which accounts gave a false picture of the financial health of the company. The claimants decided to take over the company. When the takeover proved

---

[20] Cf. Morris LJ's observation in the *Brown Jenkinson* case at [1957] 2 QB 621, 631: 'if the shipowner both knows that a clean bill ought not be issued and that the bill will be relied upon by others, it seems to me impossible to contend that the shipowner does not make a representation with the intention that it should be acted upon.'

[21] All of which is *not* to say that the shipowner should have been allowed to recover on the defendant's indemnity: it is merely to say that it was not satisfactory to hold that the indemnity was unenforceable on the ground that it had been made to persuade the shipowner to commit the tort of deceit. Clearly, indemnities such as the one made by the defendant in that case should be unenforceable so as to better ensure that shipowners cannot be persuaded to issue 'clean' bills of lading which they know to be false.

[22] (1884) 9 App Cas 187.

[23] [1983] 1 All ER 583.

unsuccessful the claimants sued the defendants, claiming that they had been induced to take over the company by the misrepresentations as to the company's profitability contained in the company's accounts. The claimants' claim was dismissed. The judge was satisfied that the company's accounts had played *no* part in the claimants' decision to take over the company. Two considerations played a large part in this finding. First, the claimants' main object in taking over the company was to secure the services of the company's two directors. Secondly, the claimants knew before they took over the company that its accounts were unreliable.

It must be emphasised that the test for whether a false representation of fact made by A to B induced B to do *x* is: Did the representation made by A *play some part* in B's decision to do *x*? It is *not*: Would B have done *x* had A not made the representation he made to B or had A told B the truth? In *Downs* v *Chappell*,[24] the claimants were looking to buy a business to see them through to their retirement, having found that running their existing business – a newsagent's shop – was becoming too much of a strain. They looked at a number of businesses, including a bookshop run by the defendant. The defendant showed the claimants the bookshop's accounts. These accounts 'showed a business with a very healthy, and growing turnover, with a substantial gross profit margin which would cover [the claimants'] financing costs and leave them with enough to live on'.[25]

The claimants decided to buy the business and then discovered, when they started running the bookshop, that the accounts they had been shown had – to the defendant's knowledge – given an exaggerated picture of the bookshop's financial health. The claimants sued the defendant, claiming that he had committed the tort of deceit. The Court of Appeal allowed the claimants' claim: the defendant had made a false representation to the claimants which he knew to be false for the purpose of inducing them to buy his bookshop and they had been induced by the defendant's representation to buy his bookshop. On the last point, it was *immaterial* that the claimants would probably have bought the bookshop anyway if they had been shown a true set of accounts for the bookshop – which accounts would have shown the bookshop to be making a profit, albeit much smaller than the profit which the accounts the claimants saw said the bookshop was making. Clearly, the state of the accounts the claimants saw played a substantial part in the claimants' decision to buy the defendant's bookshop, and this was enough to establish that the claimants had been induced by the state of those accounts to buy the bookshop.

Sometimes it is very difficult to know whether a given person was induced to act in a certain way by a representation that was made to him or her. So, for example, suppose Beth bought a car from Vijay. Suppose further that, while Beth was inspecting the car before making up her mind whether or not to buy it, Vijay told Beth that the car had just passed its MOT. Did that representation induce Beth to buy the car? In other words, did that representation play any

---

[24] [1997] 1 WLR 426.
[25] Ibid., 431E.

part in Beth's decision as to whether or not to buy the car? It is very hard to say.

To assist them in resolving difficult questions like this, the courts have adopted a principle that if: (*a*) A made a representation to B with the object of inducing B to do *x*; *and* (*b*) it would have been reasonable for B to have taken that representation into account in deciding whether or not to do *x*; *and* (*c*) B did *x* after A made that representation to him; *then* (*d*) it is presumed that A's representation induced B to do *x*.[26] This principle allows us to presume in the situation just discussed that Beth *was* induced to buy the car from Vijay by Vijay's representation that it had just passed its MOT. Vijay made that representation in order to induce Beth to buy the car; it would have been reasonable for Beth to have taken Vijay's representation into account in deciding whether or not to buy the car; and Beth did buy the car.

SOME DIFFICULT CASES

Having clarified the conditions that have to be satisfied before we can say that someone committed the tort of deceit, we can now look at how the law deals with some cases where it is difficult to say whether or not those conditions are satisfied.

Untrue representations that later come true

Suppose that A made a representation of fact to B intending to induce B to do *x* and B was induced to do *x* by that representation. Suppose further that A's representation of fact was – to A's knowledge – untrue at the time he made it, but, by the time B came to do *x*, A's representation of fact was no longer untrue. What is the position? The question came up in *Ship* v *Crosskill*.[27] In that case, a company issued a prospectus which said, *inter alia*, that more than half the capital of the company had been subscribed. At the time the prospectus was issued, this was not true. However, by the time the claimant applied for, and was sold, shares in the company, this was true. It was held that the claimant could not bring an action in deceit to recover the money he had paid for shares in the company. At the time he bought the shares in the company, he was not deceived.

Ambiguous representations

In *Smith* v *Chadwick*,[28] a company's prospectus claimed that the 'present value of the turnover or output of the entire works is over £1,000,000 per annum'. This was ambiguous: it could have meant that the company's entire works had actually produced £1,000,000's worth of produce in one year (which was not true) or it could have meant the company's entire works were capable of

---

[26] *Smith* v *Chadwick* (1884) 9 App Cas 187, 196 per Lord Blackburn: 'if it is proved that the defendants with a view to induce the claimant to enter into a contract made a statement to the claimant of such a nature as would be likely to induce a person to enter into a contract, and it is proved that the claimant did enter into the contract, it is a fair inference of fact that he was induced to do so by the statement.'
[27] (1870) LR 10 Eq 73.
[28] (1884) 9 App Cas 187.

producing £1,000,000's worth of produce in one year (which was true). The claimant was induced by this statement to buy shares in the company. He then sued the directors of the company in deceit, seeking to recover the money he had paid for the shares.

To succeed in his claim the claimant would have had to have shown: (*a*) that he understood the statement in the company's prospectus to mean that the company's entire works had actually produced £1,000,000's worth of produce in one year;[29] (*b*) that – by saying that the company's turnover was over £1,000,000 per annum – the directors intended to encourage people to think that the company's entire works had actually produced £1,000,000's worth of produce in one year; (*c*) the directors did not honestly believe that the company's entire works had actually produced £1,000,000's worth of produce in one year;[30] and (*d*) the directors intended, by encouraging people to believe that the company's entire works had actually produced £1,000,000's worth of produce in one year, to induce people to buy shares in the company. As things turned out, the claimant's claim failed: he could not prove that (*a*) was true.

Representations later discovered to be untrue

Suppose A made a representation of fact to B intending to induce B to do *x* and B was induced to do *x* by that representation. Suppose further that at the time he made that representation A honestly believed that it was true but A later discovered that that representation was untrue. What is the position?

The law, as it stands now, seems to say that if A discovered the truth before B did *x* and he did not warn B in time that his representation was untrue, then A committed the tort of deceit.[31] So, it will be recalled, in *East* v *Maurer*[32] the defendant assured the claimants – who were interested in buying one of his hairdressing salons – that he did not intend to work regularly at his other salon. This assurance induced the claimants to buy the defendant's salon, just as the defendant intended. The defendant was held to have committed the tort of deceit – at the time he gave the assurance he had every intention of working regularly at his other salon. The result would have been the same if the defendant had been telling the truth when he assured the claimants that he did not intend to work regularly at his other salon, but before the sale went through he – without telling the claimants – changed his mind and decided that he would after all work regularly at his other salon.

---

[29] The claimant's claim could not have succeeded if he had understood the statement in the company's prospectus to mean that the company's entire works were capable of producing £1,000,000's worth of produce in one year because, in that case, the claimant would not have been deceived when he bought shares in the company – just like the claimant in *Ship* v *Crosskill*.
[30] *Akerhielm* v *De Mare* [1959] AC 789, 805.
[31] *Brownlie* v *Campbell* (1880) 5 App Cas 925; *Briess* v *Woolley* [1954] AC 333.
[32] [1991] 1 WLR 461.

23

MALICIOUS FALSEHOOD

As a general rule, A will commit the tort of malicious (or injurious) falsehood in relation to B if he maliciously makes a false statement to C that refers to B or B's property and B suffers loss as a result.

The term 'maliciously' needs some explanation. A will have acted maliciously in making a false statement to C if: (*a*) he knew the statement was untrue when he made it; *or* (*b*) he did not care whether or not the statement was true when he made it; *or* (*c*) he made that statement for some dishonest or improper reason.[1]

A couple of examples of this tort being committed can be given from the case law. In *Ratcliffe* v *Evans*,[2] the *County Herald*, a Welsh newspaper, incorrectly said that the claimant had ceased to trade as an engineer and boilermaker and that the claimant's firm had ceased to trade. As a result the claimant experienced a loss of business. He was held entitled to sue the *County Herald* on the ground that it had committed the tort of malicious falsehood. The *County Herald* had not acted in good faith in publishing its story about the claimant and the claimant had suffered loss as a result of its publication.

In *Khodaparast* v *Shad*,[3] the claimant was an Iranian woman who worked in an Iranian community school. She had an affair with the defendant and when she brought it to an end the defendant sought to take some revenge by circulating photocopies of pages from pornographic magazines which appeared to contain photographs of the claimant advertising telephone sex services. In fact the claimant had nothing to do with telephone sex services; the defendant's photocopies were made by photocopying pages from pornographic magazines on which he had artfully superimposed revealing pictures of the claimant that he had taken during their affair. As a result of the defendant's circulating these photocopies, the claimant was dismissed from her job. The claimant successfully sued the defendant for committing the tort of malicious falsehood – the defendant had, through his photocopies, maliciously misled people into thinking that the claimant was involved in telephone sex services and the claimant had suffered loss as a result.[4]

A variety of points can be made about the tort of malicious falsehood:

(1) *Malicious falsehood and privacy.* In *Kaye* v *Robertson*,[5] Gorden Kaye, the well-known comedian, was recovering in hospital from being hit on the head by a piece of wood during a big storm in 1990. Representatives of the *Sunday Sport*

---

[1] *Dunlop* v *Maison Talbot* (1904) 20 TLR 579.
[2] [1892] 2 QB 524.
[3] [2000] 1 WLR 618.
[4] The House of Lords refused leave to appeal: [2001] 1 WLR 126.
[5] [1991] FSR 62.

gained access to his room and conducted an interview with him, which interview the *Sunday Sport* proposed to publish in its next edition. Kaye's injuries were such that he was in no condition to grant an interview – Kaye had no recollection of talking to the *Sunday Sport*'s representatives 15 minutes after the interview ended – and he sought an injunction preventing the *Sunday Sport* from publishing the interview, claiming, *inter alia*, that the *Sunday Sport* would commit the tort of malicious falsehood if it published the interview. The Court of Appeal agreed and granted the injunction.

The Court of Appeal's reasoning was that in publishing the interview the *Sunday Sport* would implicitly represent that Kaye had chosen to give an 'exclusive' interview to the *Sunday Sport*; this was not true and the *Sunday Sport* knew that this was not true, and Kaye would suffer loss as a result because other newspapers would be inclined to pay Kaye less for an interview with him about his accident if the *Sunday Sport* had already published an 'exclusive' interview with him on the same topic. So if the *Sunday Sport* published its interview with Kaye it would make a statement to its readers which it knew was untrue and Kaye would suffer loss as a result. The reasoning is a little strained and probably the true explanation of the case is that the Court of Appeal wanted to prevent the *Sunday Sport* from invading Kaye's privacy by publishing its interview with him and its finding that the *Sunday Sport* would commit the tort of malicious falsehood if it went ahead and published its interview was simply a means of giving it a legal basis for restraining the *Sunday Sport* from invading Kaye's privacy.

(2) *The difference between malicious falsehood and defamation.* The case of *Ratcliffe v Evans* illustrates one difference between the torts of libel and slander and the tort of malicious falsehood. A cannot commit either the tort of libel or the tort of slander by making a false statement to C that refers to B unless that statement is defamatory of B. In contrast, A *may* commit the tort of malicious falsehood by making a false statement to C that refers to B even if that statement is not defamatory of B. The statement in *Ratcliffe v Evans* was not defamatory of the claimant – right-thinking people would not think less well of the claimant on hearing that he had closed down his business – but that did not prevent a finding that the defendant had committed the tort of malicious falsehood in making that statement.

There are two other differences between the torts of libel and slander and the tort of malicious falsehood. First, to bring an action for malicious falsehood you have to prove that the statement you are complaining of was untrue; to bring an action in defamation, all you need do is prove that the statement you are complaining of was defamatory – it is for the defendant to prove that it was true. Secondly, to bring an action for malicious falsehood you have to prove that the defendant acted maliciously in making the statement which you are complaining about; in an action for libel or slander, you will not normally need to show that the defendant acted maliciously to succeed in your claim.

Of course, it is possible that you may be able to sue someone for malicious falsehood and defamation at the same time. This will be the case if a defendant maliciously published a false and defamatory statement about you to someone else and you suffered loss as a result. In such a case you will be able to sue either for malicious falsehood or defamation, depending on which way of presenting your action is more advantageous.[6]

(3) *Presumption of loss.* The normal rule in a malicious falsehood case is that the claimant has to prove that the defendant's statement caused her to suffer some kind of loss. However, section 3(1) of the Defamation Act 1952 qualifies this rule. It provides that, 'In an action for malicious falsehood, it shall not be necessary to allege or prove ... damage – (a) if the words upon which the action is founded are calculated to cause pecuniary damage to the claimant and are published in writing or other permanent form; or (b) if the said words are calculated to cause pecuniary damage to the claimant in respect of any office, profession, calling, trade or business held or carried on by him at the time of the publication.'

(4) *An exception to the rule.* There is one well-established exception to the rule that A will commit the tort of malicious falsehood if he maliciously makes a false statement to C that refers to B and B suffers some kind of loss as a result.

If Carl is a trader and he lures some business away from his rivals by making the groundless boast that his goods are superior to those of his rivals, he will *not* commit the tort of malicious falsehood. This is so even though Carl's boast refers to his rivals' goods, is unjustified, made maliciously and results in damage to his rivals' business. Why does Carl's conduct in this case not amount to a tort? The reason for this is as follows.

Suppose the law *did* say that a trader in the marketplace will owe his rivals a common law duty not to cause them loss by maliciously representing that their goods are inferior to his when they are not; in other words, suppose the law *did* say that a trader in the marketplace *will* commit the tort of malicious falsehood if he causes his rivals to lose business by maliciously boasting that his goods are superior to those of his rivals when they are not. If this *were* the law then if a trader boasted that his goods were superior to his rivals, and his rivals suffered loss as a result, the rivals would have grounds to sue the trader and the courts would be given the unenviable task of deciding whether or not the trader's goods *were* superior to those of his rivals – a question which would often be too difficult or too controversial for the courts to resolve.[7]

However, Carl *will* commit the tort of malicious falsehood if he lures some customers away from Lara, one of his rivals, by maliciously alleging that Lara's product suffers from defects x, y and z when it does not.[8] The law *does* say that

---

[6] *Joyce* v *Sengupta* [1993] 1 WLR 337.

[7] See the remarks of Lord Herschell LC in *White* v *Mellin* [1895] AC 154, 164–5: 'My Lords, I cannot help saying that I entertain very grave doubts whether any action could be maintained for an alleged disparagement of another's goods, merely on the allegation that the goods sold by the party who is alleged to have disparaged his competitor's goods are better either generally or in this or that particular respect than his competitor's are ... I think it is impossible not to see that ... a very wide door indeed would be opened to litigation, and that the Courts might be constantly employed in trying the relative merits of rival productions, if an action of this kind were allowed.'

[8] *De Beers Abrasive Products Ltd* v *International General Electric Co.. of New York* [1975] 1 WLR 972.

a trader in the marketplace will owe his rivals a common law duty not to cause them loss by maliciously alleging that his rivals' goods suffer from certain defects when they do not suffer from those defects. In taking this stand the law does not impose an impossible burden on the courts. If a trader lures business away from one of his rivals, by alleging that the rival's product suffers from defects x, y and z, and the rival chooses to sue the trader for malicious falsehood, the courts should have no problem determining whether or not the trader's allegations were justified.

24

PASSING OFF

It is probably impossible to supply a general definition of when someone will commit the tort of passing off.[1] Two main forms of the tort can be identified.

(1) *Appropriation of goodwill.* The first form of the tort is committed if A *appropriates* the *goodwill* attached to B's name or business when he was not entitled to do so. What is 'goodwill'? Lord Macnaghten supplied a definition in *Inland Revenue Commissioners* v *Muller & Co.'s Margarine Ltd*, observing that goodwill 'is a thing very easy to describe, very difficult to define. It is the benefit and advantage of the good name, reputation, and connection of a business. It is the attractive force which brings in custom.'[2]

So A will commit this form of the tort if he markets his goods or services in such a way as to create a substantial risk that people will purchase those goods or services in the belief that they are B's goods or services.[3] If he does this he will mislead people into thinking that his goods or services are supplied by B and in so doing appropriate the goodwill attached to B's name or business. This is what happened in *Reddaway* v *Banham*.[4] The claimant had for some years made belting and sold it as 'Camel Hair Belting'. As a result, the name 'Camel Hair Belting' was used in the trade to refer to the belts manufactured by the claimant. The defendant began to manufacture belts

---

[1] Characteristically, Lord Diplock attempted a general definition in *Erven Warnink Besloten Vennootschap* v *J Townend & Sons (Hull) Ltd* [1979] AC 731, 742D–E. For criticisms of the definition see McBride & Bagshaw 2001, at 385–6; also *Consorzio del Prosciutto di Parma* v *Marks & Spencer plc* [1991] RPC 351, at 368 (per Nourse LJ); and Carty 2001, 180. Lord Diplock himself admitted that his general definition did not quite cover all the situations that might give rise to an action for passing off: [1979] AC 731, 742F.

[2] [1901] AC 217, 223–4. Lord Macnaghten went on to say that goodwill is a form of property (albeit intangible): ibid. If this is right, there is a case for dealing with passing off alongside other torts involving an interference with property such as conversion, trespass to goods, trespass to land and private nuisance. However, we have chosen for the time being to continue to deal with passing off as a 'deception' tort.

[3] See, in addition to the cases cited in the text, *Parker-Knoll Ltd* v *Knoll International Ltd* [1962] RPC 265 (held it would be passing off to market furniture under the name 'Knoll International' because doing so would create a substantial risk that people would purchase that furniture in the belief that it was marketed by Parker-Knoll); *Norman Kark Publications Ltd* v *Odhams Press* [1962] 1 WLR 380 (held the defendants would not commit the tort of passing off in relation to the claimants – the publishers of a magazine called 'Today' – if they published a magazine called 'Today, the New John Bull'; there was no substantial risk that people would be confused into purchasing the defendants' magazine in the mistaken belief that it was the claimants'); *Alain Bernardin et Compagnie* v *Pavilion Properties Ltd* [1967] RPC 581 (held the defendants did not commit the tort of passing off in relation to the claimants when they opened a nightclub in London called 'The Crazy Horse Saloon'; while the claimants ran an identically named nightclub in Paris, the Paris nightclub was not so well known that people in London were liable to go the defendants' nightclub in London in the mistaken belief that it was run by the claimants).

[4] [1896] AC 199.

made of the yarn of camel's hair and stamped the words 'Camel Hair Belting' on them. He was held to have committed the tort of passing off – in stamping 'Camel Hair Belting' on his belts he had created a substantial risk that people would purchase his belts in the belief that they were manufactured by the claimant.

Similarly, in *Reckitt & Colman Products Ltd* v *Borden Inc*,[5] the House of Lords held that Borden would commit the tort of passing off if it sold its lemon juice in lemon shaped bottles. Reckitt & Colman had been selling its Jif lemon juice in lemon shaped bottles for thirty years and as a result consumers tended to think that lemon shaped bottles contained Jif lemon juice. There was therefore a substantial risk that if Borden sold *its* lemon juice in lemon shaped bottles, consumers would purchase Borden's lemon juice in the belief that it was Jif lemon juice. Borden could not, it was found, eliminate this risk by labelling its lemon shaped bottles to make it clear that they did not contain Jif lemon juice; the House of Lords found that, when selecting a lemon juice from a range of bottles of lemon juice on sale in a supermarket, shoppers tended not to look at the labels on the bottles of lemon juice in making their choice. So Borden's labelling its lemon shaped bottles to make it clear that they did not contain Jif lemon juice would not eliminate the risk that shoppers would purchase Borden's lemon juice in the belief that it was Jif lemon juice.

It should be emphasised that this form of the tort may *also* be committed in situations *outside* the one we have just been considering: to establish that A committed this form of the tort it does *not* have to be established that he marketed his goods or services in such a way as to create a substantial risk that his customers would think those goods or services were B's. It merely has to be shown that A appropriated the goodwill attached to B's name or business when he was not entitled to do so.

So it has been held that if A markets his goods or services in such a way as to mislead people into thinking that they are of the *same quality* as B's goods or services, he will commit the tort of passing off[6] – if A markets his goods by making people think that his goods are as good as B's when they are not, A will appropriate the goodwill attached to the products marketed by B when he is not entitled to do so. It has also been held that a charity will commit the tort of passing off if it solicits donations under a name which is liable to make people think that they are donating money to a quite different, and well-established, charity.[7] It has further been held that a radio station committed the tort of

[5] [1990] 1 WLR 491.

[6] See *J Bollinger* v *Costa Brava Wine Co.* [1960] 1 Ch 262 (held that the defendants committed the tort of passing off in relation to the claimant champagne manufacturers when they sold wine made in Spain or from grapes produced in Spain as 'champagne' or as 'Spanish champagne', thereby appropriating the goodwill attached to the claimants' business when they were not entitled to do so – the defendants' wine not being as good as genuine champagne); also *Erven Warnink Besloten Vennootschap* v *J Townend & Sons (Hull) Ltd* [1979] AC 731 (held that it was passing off for the defendants to manufacture a mixture of dried egg powder and Cyprus sherry under the name 'Keeling's Old English Advocaat'; if the defendants marketed their product under this name, they would appropriate the goodwill attached to genuine advocaat when they were not entitled to do so – genuine advocaat, which is made out of brandy, egg yolks and sugar, being far superior to the defendants' product).

[7] See *British Diabetic Association* v *Diabetic Society Ltd* [1995] 4 All ER 812 (held that it would be passing off for a charity to solicit contributions under the name 'The Diabetic Society' because there was a substantial risk that people would make donations to the charity in the belief that they were donating money to the quite distinct British Diabetic Association).

passing off when it misled potential advertisers into thinking that Eddie Irvine, the Formula One driver, was a fan of the station, thereby appropriating the goodwill associated with Eddie Irvine's name when it was not entitled to do so.[8]

It should also be noted that this form of the tort can be committed quite innocently.[9] Suppose, for example, Paul opened a video shop in Bristol and decided to call it 'Videodrome' after the famous David Cronenberg film of that name. Suppose further that Karen had already had the same idea and had run for a number of years a well-regarded video shop in London, also called 'Videodrome'. In this situation Paul may well have committed the tort of passing off in relation to Karen – and this is so even if Paul had no idea Karen's shop existed and had no intention, in naming his shop 'Videodrome', of appropriating any of the goodwill that had become attached to Karen's shop.

(2) *Endangering goodwill.* The second form of the tort of passing off is committed if A markets his goods or services in such a way as to create a danger that the goodwill attached to B's name or business will be unjustifiably damaged.

This is what happened in *Associated Newspaper plc* v *Insert Media Ltd.*[10] In that case, the defendant inserted advertising material into the claimant's newspapers without the claimant's consent. The Court of Appeal held that the defendant, in so acting, had committed the tort of passing off. There was a substantial risk that people would think that the defendant's advertising material was inserted with the claimant's consent. There was therefore a substantial risk that people would associate the defendant's advertising material with the claimant and would hold it against the claimant if the advertising material proved to be dishonest or inaccurate.

Similarly, in *Mirage Studios* v *Counter-Feat Clothing Company Ltd,*[11] the claimants were owners in copyright of the 'Teenage Mutant Ninja Turtles'. A major part of the claimants' income came from licensing other people to use images of the 'Teenage Mutant Ninja Turtles' on products manufactured by those people. The defendants sought to cash in on the craze for the Teenage Mutant Ninja Turtles by drawing pictures of humanoid turtles and licensing various garment manufacturers to use those pictures on T-shirts and jogging clothes. It was held that the defendants had committed the tort of passing off in so acting. There was a substantial risk that people would mistake the defendants' drawings for images of the Teenage Mutant Ninja Turtles and would think that the claimants – the owners of the Teenage Mutant Ninja Turtle image – had licensed the use of those drawings on the items of clothing on

---

[8] *Irvine* v *Talksport Ltd* [2002] 1 WLR 2355.
[9] It used to be a matter of debate whether someone who innocently committed the tort of passing off could be held liable to pay anything more than nominal damages to the victim of his tort, with the House of Lords reserving its position on the issue in *Marengo* v *Daily Sketch and Sunday Graphic* (1948) 65 RPC 242. However, in *Gillette UK Ltd* v *Edenwest Ltd* [1994] RPC 279, Blackburne J held that no special rule existed for defendants who innocently committed the tort of passing off: they would be held liable to pay damages to the victims of their torts in the same way as any other tortfeasors. See, on this, Carty 2001, 211–12.
[10] [1991] 1 WLR 571.
[11] [1991] FSR 145.

which they appeared. There was therefore a substantial risk that people would associate the claimants with the items of clothing on which the defendants' drawings appeared and would therefore hold it against the claimants if those items of clothing proved to be of poor quality.

Again, in *Clark v Associated Newspapers Ltd*,[12] the *Evening Standard* was held to have committed the tort of passing off when it published a weekly column called 'The Secret Diary of Alan Clark MP'. The column was written in the same manner as Alan Clark's published diaries and amounted to a witty and exaggerated weekly fantasy as to what Alan Clark might have written in his diary that week. Although it was made clear that the diary entries were written by Peter Bradshaw, an *Evening Standard* journalist, it was held that there was a substantial risk that people would think that the diary entries were written by Alan Clark and that people would think less well of Alan Clark as a result.

[12] [1998] 1 WLR 1559.

TORTS INVOLVING THE MISUSE OF POWER

The torts gathered together in the following two chapters owe their existence to the fact that someone who possesses power over someone else will *sometimes* owe that someone else a common law duty not to misuse that power. In fact, the occasions when someone who possesses power over someone else will owe that someone else a common law duty not to misuse that power are few and far between. This is for two reasons.

First, when we had separate Courts of Law and Courts of Equity, the Courts of Law would generally do nothing to ensure that private persons did not misuse the powers they possessed over other people; instead, the Courts of Equity took on the function of imposing duties on private persons who possessed powers over other people, requiring them not to misuse those powers. The result is that nowadays if A, a private person, possesses some kind of power over B, any duty that A will owe B not to misuse that power is likely to be an *equitable* duty rather a *common law* duty. So, for example, suppose Lara mortgages her house to Big Bank plc but then fails to keep repaying the money she owes the bank. In such a case the bank will usually be entitled to sell Lara's house so as to recoup the money she owes the bank. Now if the bank does have the power to sell off Lara's house, it will owe her a duty to take care that it does not misuse this power by, for example, selling the house for much less than it is worth.[1] But this duty will be an equitable duty, not a common law duty.

Secondly, the courts have been loath to adopt the position that a public official who possesses some kind of power over someone will owe that someone a common law duty not to misuse that power. (Let us call this the *extreme position*.) This is for two reasons. First, the courts have thought that if they adopted the extreme position set out above, public officials would become unduly cautious in exercising their powers because they would fear that they would be sued if they overstepped the mark in exercising their powers. Secondly, the courts have thought that if they adopted the extreme position set out above, public officials would be swamped with litigation from people who were affected by the way they exercised their powers, all claiming that the officials in question misused their powers in acting as they did and as a result public officials would not be able to get on with their jobs of serving the public. For similar reasons, the courts have been loath to adopt the position that a public official who possesses some kind of power over someone will owe that someone a common law duty *to take care* that he does not misuse that power. It will be recalled that considerations such as those mentioned above led the Court of Appeal to deny in *Harris* v *Evans*[2] that a health inspector who inspects

---

[1] *Cuckmere Brick Co.*. v *Mutual Finance* [1971] Ch 949.
[2] *Harris* v *Evans* [1998] 1 WLR 1285; see above, p. 212.

a business will owe that business a duty to take care that he does not interfere unnecessarily with the running of that business.

Instead, the courts have – very broadly speaking – adopted the position that a public official who possesses some kind of power over someone will owe that someone a common law duty to ensure that he does not *knowingly or maliciously* misuse that power.[3] (Let us call this the 'moderate position'.) So, for example, suppose Eric occupied a public office which gave him the power to bring criminal prosecutions against people. Suppose further that Eric misused this power – he brought a criminal prosecution against Karen when he had no cause to do so. Eric will not necessarily have committed a tort in this situation – he will not have owed Karen a common law duty to *ensure* that he did not misuse his powers in prosecuting her. But Eric *will* have committed a tort in the situation just described if he knowingly or maliciously misused his powers in prosecuting Karen – this is because he will have owed Karen a common law duty to ensure that he did not knowingly or maliciously misuse his powers in prosecuting her. More generally, and again broadly speaking, if Eric is a public official and he possesses some kind of power over Karen, he will commit a tort – the tort of *misfeasance in public office* – if he knowingly or maliciously misuses that power.

It is easy to see why the courts are happy to take the moderate position set out above. First, their taking this position will not result in public officials becoming unduly cautious in exercising their powers. A public official who acts honestly and in good faith in exercising his powers will know that even if it turns out that he misused his powers, those who suffered loss as a result will not be able to sue him successfully to be compensated for that loss; they will not be able to prove that he knowingly misused his powers or that he acted maliciously in misusing his powers. So he will have no reason to be unduly cautious in exercising his powers. Secondly, it is unlikely that the courts' taking the moderate position set out above will result in public officials being swamped with litigation that would disrupt their ability to serve the public. Someone who wishes to sue a public official because he suffered loss as a result of that official's misusing his powers will find it very hard to get a case off the ground; he will not only have to prove that the official misused his powers – he will also have to show that the official knowingly or maliciously misused those powers.

It is to be expected that the courts' adoption of the moderate position set out above will encourage them to develop the law on when a *private person* who possesses some kind of power over someone else will owe that someone else a common law duty not to misuse that power, so as to ensure that the law does not discriminate arbitrarily between public officials and private persons. For example, go back to the situation considered above where Eric occupied a public office which enabled him to bring criminal prosecutions against other people and he misused his powers by bringing a prosecution against Karen

---

[3] A note on the terminology adopted here. A public official will have knowingly misused his powers if he consciously misused them – that is, when he misused his powers he was aware his conduct involved a misuse of his powers. A public official will have maliciously misused his powers if he was acting for an illegitimate purpose when he misused his powers.

when he had no cause to do so. As we have seen, the law says that in this situation, Eric will have owed Karen a common law duty to ensure that he did not knowingly or maliciously misuse his powers in prosecuting Karen. So Eric will have committed a tort – the tort of *malicious prosecution* – in prosecuting Karen if he knew when he prosecuted her that he had no cause to prosecute her or if he acted maliciously in prosecuting her.

Now what is the position if Eric brought a criminal prosecution against Karen when he had no cause to do so, but this time Eric brought the prosecution *in his capacity as a private citizen*? If the law is not to discriminate arbitrarily between private citizens and public officials, then it must say that in this situation too Eric owed Karen a common law duty to ensure that he did not knowingly or maliciously misuse his power to prosecute her. And indeed the law does say this. The result is that Eric *will* have committed a tort in the situation we are considering if Eric knew when he brought his private prosecution against Karen that he had no cause to bring that prosecution or if Eric acted maliciously in bringing his private prosecution against Karen.

However, the law – in its current form – *does* arbitrarily discriminate between public officials and private persons in other respects. For example, suppose that Fred worked in the legal department of a local authority and as such had the power to sue people in the name of that local authority. Suppose he misused that power: he sued Wendy in the name of the local authority when he had no cause to do so. As we have seen, the law says that Fred will have committed a tort in this situation – the tort of misfeasance in public office – if Fred knew when he sued Wendy that he had no cause to do so or he acted maliciously in suing Wendy. But what is the position if Ian, *a private person*, sued Beth when he had no cause to do so? Will Ian have committed a tort in suing Beth if: (*a*) he knew he had no cause to sue Beth when he sued her; or (*b*) he acted maliciously in suing Beth? The answer is 'no'. The courts have so far set their face against saying that a *private person* will commit a tort in relation to someone else if he knowingly or maliciously sues that someone else when he has no cause to do so. But this creates an arbitrary distinction between private persons and public officials – a private person who knowingly or maliciously sues someone when he has no cause to do so will *not* commit a tort, but a public official who has the power to bring civil suits on behalf of a public body *will* commit a tort if he knowingly or maliciously sues someone on behalf of that body when he has no cause to do so. In order to eliminate this arbitrary distinction in our law, the courts should develop the law on when a private person who possesses some kind of power over someone else will owe that someone else a common law duty not to misuse that power so that it says: If you take two given individuals, A and B, A will owe B a common law duty to ensure that he does not knowingly or maliciously sue B when he has no cause to do so. If the law said this then a private person who knowingly or maliciously sued someone else when he had no cause to do so would commit a tort.

25

MALICIOUS PROSECUTION AND ANALOGOUS TORTS

MALICIOUS PROSECUTION

A will have committed the tort of malicious prosecution in relation to B if: (1) A prosecuted B for committing a criminal offence; *and* (2) the prosecution ended in B's favour;[1] *and* (3) A had no reasonable and probable cause to prosecute B for that offence; *and* (4) A acted maliciously in prosecuting B for committing that offence.[2]

Prosecution

In order to show that A has committed the tort of malicious prosecution in relation to B, it is first necessary to show that A prosecuted B for committing a criminal offence. This requirement will obviously be satisfied if A is a private citizen and brings a private prosecution against B for committing an offence. Similarly, if A works for the Crown Prosecution Service and in that capacity prosecutes B for committing an offence.

Outside these simple cases, the House of Lords has made it clear that A will be held to have prosecuted B for committing a criminal offence if he was *directly responsible* for B's being prosecuted for committing that offence.[3] So, for example, suppose that A supplied information to the police which indicated that B had committed some offence and B was subsequently prosecuted for that offence. When will A be held to have prosecuted B for committing that offence? The Court of Appeal's decision in *Mahon* v *Rahn (No. 2)* makes it clear that A will only be held to have prosecuted B in this situation if: (1) A supplied his information to the police with the intention of persuading the police to prosecute B; *and* (2) the facts of B's case were such that it was impossible for the police to exercise any independent judgement as to whether or not A should be charged with an offence.[4]

Both these requirements were satisfied in *Martin* v *Watson*.[5] In that case, the defendant complained that the claimant had indecently exposed himself to her. The claimant was charged with committing the offence of indecent exposure but, when

---

[1] That is, B was not found guilty of committing that offence or B was found guilty of committing that offence but her conviction was subsequently reversed.
[2] For a general discussion of the tort, see Fridman 1963.
[3] *Martin* v *Watson* [1996] 1 AC 74.
[4] [2000] 1 WLR 2150, at [269].
[5] [1996] 1 AC 74.

the case came to trial, no evidence was offered against the claimant; the defendant had declined to give evidence. The claimant was cleared and sued the defendant, claiming she had committed the tort of malicious prosecution. The House of Lords agreed. It held that the defendant was directly responsible for the claimant's being prosecuted for committing that offence. She had claimed that the claimant had committed the offence of indecent exposure with the intention of persuading the police to prosecute the claimant and only the defendant could know whether or not the claimant had committed that offence. As a result, it was virtually impossible for the police officers who charged the claimant to exercise their own judgement as to whether or not the claimant had committed the offence. Given this, it was fair to say that the defendant was responsible for the claimant's being prosecuted.

Termination of prosecution in the claimant's favour

The courts will refuse to say that A committed the tort of malicious prosecution in prosecuting B for committing a particular criminal offence if B was found guilty of committing that offence and her conviction has not yet been reversed. Technically, whether or not A acted wrongfully in prosecuting B for committing a particular offence cannot depend on the exigencies of whether or not that prosecution ended in B's favour. However, the courts will refuse to say that A committed the tort of malicious prosecution in prosecuting B for committing a particular criminal offence if B was found guilty of committing that offence and has not yet had her conviction reversed. The courts will take this stand so as to prevent B from re-opening the question of whether or not her conviction was valid by bringing an action for malicious prosecution against A.[6]

In *Basébé v Matthews*,[7] the defendant claimed that the claimant assaulted her. He was found guilty and was fined 40s. He had no right to appeal against the decision and so when he sued the defendant for malicious prosecution – claiming that the defendant's claims had been false and made maliciously – his conviction had not been reversed. The Court of Appeal refused to find that the defendant committed the tort of malicious prosecution. Byles J remarked: 'there is [no] doubt that the criminal proceeding must be determined in favour of the accused before he can maintain an action for malicious prosecution. If this were not so, almost every case would have to be tried over again upon its merits ... [I]t makes no difference that the party convicted has no power of appealing.'[8]

Reasonable and probable cause

If A prosecuted B for committing a particular criminal offence he will not have had reasonable and probable cause to prosecute B for committing that offence if: (1) A did not think, in prosecuting B, that B probably committed that

---

[6] As a general rule, if B claims that A has committed a tort in relation to her by acting in some way, B will be barred from suing A for damages if her doing so would bring into question the correctness of an earlier judicial decision: see below, pp. 500–1.

[7] (1867) LR 2 CP 684.

[8] Ibid., 687.

offence; *or* (2) A thought that B probably committed the offence for which he prosecuted B, but it was unreasonable for him to think this, given the evidence available to him at the time he prosecuted B.

It used to be thought that A would, in prosecuting B for committing a criminal offence, not have reasonable and probable cause to prosecute B if he did not think that B was guilty of committing that offence. So if A, in prosecuting B, lacked an honest belief in B's guilt, he would not have reasonable and probable cause to prosecute B.[9] However, we would submit, this is not the law. As Lord Denning observed in *Glinski* v *McIver*: 'in order to have reasonable and probable cause a man who brings a prosecution, be he a police officer or a private individual [need not] believe in the *guilt* of the accused . . . [I]n truth he has only to be satisfied that there is a proper case to lay before the court.'[10] In an earlier case, Denning LJ, as he was then, remarked: 'There are many justifiable prosecutions where the prosecutor has not himself formed any concluded belief as to the guilt of the accused. If he is a very fair-minded man he may well say to himself "The case is so black against the man that I feel I must prosecute, but I am not going to believe him to be guilty unless the court finds him to be so." Such a man would, I should have thought, have reasonable and probable cause for instituting a prosecution even though he did not affirmatively believe the man to be guilty.'[11] The law is as we have stated it: If A prosecutes B for committing a particular criminal offence, A will not have reasonable and probable cause to prosecute B for committing that offence if he does *not* think, in prosecuting B, that B is *probably* guilty of that offence. So if A prosecutes B for committing a particular offence while thinking at the time that B is probably innocent of that offence, A will lack reasonable and probable cause to prosecute B for committing that offence.[12]

Even if A did think, when he prosecuted B for committing a particular criminal offence, that B was probably guilty of committing that offence, A will have lacked reasonable and probable cause to prosecute B for committing that offence if A's view that B was probably guilty of committing that offence was, on the evidence available to him, an unreasonable one to take: '. . . there must [have been] cause (that is, sufficient grounds . . .) for thinking that [B] was probably guilty of the offence imputed.'[13] Whether or not A's view that B was probably guilty of com-

---

[9] *Hicks* v *Faulkner* (1878) 8 QBD 167, 171 (per Hawkins J), approved in *Herniman* v *Smith* [1938] AC 305.

[10] [1962] AC 726, 758.

[11] *Tempest* v *Snowden* [1952] 1 KB 130, 139.

[12] See Lindley J in *Shrosbery* v *Osmaston* (1877) 37 LT 792, 794: '. . . if a man believes that another is not guilty of a criminal charge, and prosecuted unsuccessfully, I confess I have the greatest difficulty in seeing that such a man can be held to have reasonable and probable cause for prosecuting.'

[13] *Glinski* v *McIver* [1962] AC 726, 766 (per Lord Devlin). So it is enough for A – to establish that he had reasonable and probable cause to prosecute B for committing a particular offence – to show that he thought and that it was reasonable to think, on the basis of the evidence available to him, that B probably did commit that offence. Of course, for B to be convicted of committing that offence it has to be shown *beyond a reasonable doubt* that B committed that offence. This means that A might have had reasonable and probable cause to prosecute B for committing a particular offence even if the evidence available to him at the time he prosecuted B was not enough to secure a conviction. This would be the case where the evidence available to A at the time he prosecuted B was such that it would convince a reasonable man that B *probably* committed the offence for which A prosecuted him but not such that it would convince a reasonable man that B *definitely* committed that offence. See *Dawson* v *Vansandau*

mitting the offence for which A prosecuted B was reasonable or not is judged by reference to the evidence available to him at the time of the prosecution – it does not matter if some of the evidence was flawed or incorrect: '[A must] be judged not on the real facts but on those which he honestly, and however erroneously, [believed]; if he [acted] honestly upon fiction, he can claim to be judged on that.'[14]

What is the position if: (1) John *committed* a particular offence; *and* (2) Ruth prosecuted John for committing that offence; *but* (3) Ruth did so on the basis of evidence that would not have led a reasonable man to think that John probably committed that offence? Would Ruth have had reasonable and probable cause to prosecute John in this case (assuming, of course, that Ruth did believe at the time she prosecuted that John probably did commit the offence for which she prosecuted him)? In principle, the answer should be 'no': whether or not Ruth had reasonable and probable cause to prosecute John must be judged on the basis of the evidence available to her at the time she prosecuted.[15] However, in *Heslop* v *Chapman*[16] two judges departed from this position. The facts of that case were as follows. Heslop was sued by Hinde for the price of some barley which Heslop was alleged to have purchased from Hinde. Chapman appeared as a witness for Hinde. Heslop accused Chapman of committing perjury. At his trial, Chapman was acquitted and he subsequently sued Heslop for malicious prosecution. Chapman's claim was successful. It was held that Heslop had not had reasonable and probable cause to prosecute Chapman for perjury. However, both Jervis CJ and Pollock CB held that if Chapman had *actually* perjured himself in giving evidence against Heslop then Heslop would have had reasonable and probable cause to prosecute Chapman for perjury, whatever Heslop's state of mind or state of knowledge at the time he prosecuted Chapman.[17] We would submit that this is not the law[18] and that in the hypothetical case we have been considering, Ruth will not have had reasonable and probable cause to prosecute John.[19]

Whether or not it was reasonable for A to think, on the basis of the evidence available to him at the time he prosecuted B for committing a particular

---

(1863) 11 WR 516, 518: '[There may be] evidence sufficient to make out a *prima facie* case, and warrant the preferring of a criminal charge, though it might not be sufficient evidence upon which to convict.'

[14] *Glinski* v *McIver* [1962] AC 726, 776 (per Lord Devlin).

[15] But if John did actually commit the offence for which Ruth prosecuted him, even if John could make out a case that Ruth – in prosecuting him – committed the tort of malicious prosecution, John would not – we think – be entitled to recover anything by way of damages from Ruth.

[16] (1853) 23 LJ QB 49.

[17] Ibid.., 52: '[I]f Chapman had sworn falsely ... then there was reasonable and probable cause. That is so, whether [Heslop] believed him guilty or not' (per Jervis CJ); 'I agree with the Chief Justice in thinking that if Chapman had sworn falsely, though [Heslop] thought he had not, there was reasonable and probable cause for the prosecution' (per Pollock CB).

[18] See *Delegal* v *Highley* (1837) Bing NC 950, 132 ER 677 (action for malicious prosecution against defendant; defence that claimant actually guilty of the offence for which the defendant prosecuted him; held defence was bad in law because it did not allege that defendant was actually aware of the claimant's guilt – or the facts which established the claimant's guilt – when he launched the prosecution against the claimant).

[19] A will also not have had reasonable and probable cause to prosecute B for committing an offence which B actually committed if, at the time A prosecuted B for committing that offence, A did not believe that B probably did commit that offence.

criminal offence, that B probably did commit that offence will depend on all the circumstances.

In *Hicks* v *Faulkner*,[20] the defendant sued one of his tenants for rent due under the lease. The claimant, the tenant's son, swore that before the rent became due the tenant had given up the lease by surrendering to the defendant the key to the premises let by the defendant to the tenant. The defendant did not remember this happening and charged the claimant with perjury. The claimant was acquitted of having committed this offence and he sued the defendant, claiming that the defendant had committed the tort of malicious prosecution. The claimant's claim failed; the court held that the defendant had had reasonable and probable cause to prosecute the claimant for perjury. The reason was that it had been reasonable for the defendant to think, given the state of his memory, that the claimant had perjured himself: '[i]f a man has never seen reason to doubt, but on the contrary, has ever had reason to trust, the general accuracy of his memory, and that memory presents to him a vivid apparent recollection that a particular occurrence took place in his presence within a recent period of time, is it not reasonable to believe in the existence of it?'[21] So it would have been different if, to the defendant's knowledge, his memory was generally faulty and unreliable: in such a case it would not have been reasonable for him to believe, on the basis of his memory of things, that the claimant had probably committed the offence of perjury.

In *Dawson* v *Vansandau*,[22] the defendant prosecuted the claimant on a charge of conspiring to defraud his creditors on the basis of a statement made to him by B, one of the parties to the alleged conspiracy. When the claimant was acquitted of the charge he sued the claimant for malicious prosecution. The claimant won his claim at first instance but the verdict was annulled on the basis that it might have been reasonable for the defendant to have thought – on the basis of B's statement – that the claimant had probably conspired to defraud his creditors: '[a]n accomplice, or a tainted witness, may give evidence sufficient to make out a *prima facie* case, and warrant the preferring of a criminal charge.'[23]

In *Abbott* v *Refuge Assurance Co. Ltd*,[24] the claimant took out an endowment policy with the defendants for his wife. A few years later, the defendants were tricked into handing over the surrender value of the policy (£2,415) to the claimant's secretary, who impersonated the claimant's wife and led the defendants to believe that she wanted to surrender the policy in return for its surrender value. The claimant's secretary confessed to what she had done and implicated the claimant in the plot. Counsel advised the defendants that the secretary's statement was sufficient evidence on which to prosecute the claimant. The defendants brought a private prosecution against the claimant for conspiracy to defraud – the Director of Public Prosecutions having declined

---

[20] (1878) 8 QBD 167.
[21] Ibid., 172–3.
[22] (1863) 11 WR 516.
[23] Ibid., 518.
[24] [1962] 1 QB 432.

to prosecute – but the prosecution failed. The claimant sued the defendants for malicious prosecution but his claim failed.

It was held, among other things, that the defendants, having taken the advice of counsel, had had reasonable and probable cause to prosecute the claimant. In the terms advanced here, it had been reasonable for the defendants to believe counsel's advice that the secretary's statement indicated that the claimant probably did conspire to defraud them and therefore it had been reasonable for the defendants to believe, given that advice, that the claimant probably did conspire to defraud them. However, while the opinion of counsel was a 'potent' factor in establishing that the defendants had reasonable and probable cause to prosecute the claimant, it was 'not ... conclusive'.[25] As a matter of common sense, it would not have been reasonable for the defendants to believe counsel's advice if it had been obviously incompetent or based on a desire to please the defendants; nor would it have been reasonable for the defendants to believe counsel's advice that the claimant probably committed the offence of conspiracy to defraud if that advice was based on an incorrect summary of the available evidence.[26] None of those possibilities were actually made out in the *Abbott* case and so the defendants *did* have reasonable and probable cause to prosecute the claimant.

Malice

It seems that A will act maliciously in prosecuting B for committing a criminal offence if his predominant purpose in prosecuting B for committing that offence is not to ensure that justice is done to B.[27] So if A had no reasonable and probable cause to prosecute B for a particular criminal offence because, when he prosecuted B, he did not think that B was probably guilty of that offence, it may be inferred that A acted maliciously in prosecuting B for committing that offence. If he did not think that B was probably guilty of committing that offence then A probably did not prosecute B for committing that offence with the primary aim of ensuring that justice would be done to B.[28] (Note that the reverse is not true: 'even from the most express malice, want of probable cause ... is not to be inferred.'[29] Even if A's primary aim in prosecuting B was not to ensure that justice would be done to B, A could still believe

---

[25] Ibid., 450 (per Ormerod LJ).

[26] *Malz v Rosen* [1966] 1 WLR 1008.

[27] See Alderson B's observation in *Stevens v Midland Counties Railway* (1854) 10 Ex 352, 356; 156 ER 480, 482: 'Any motive other than that of simply instituting a prosecution for the simple purpose of bringing a person to justice, is a malicious motive on the part of the person who acts in that way.'

[28] This might not always be true. Suppose Vijay is suspected of murdering Carl. Vijay, in his defence, claims that Carl committed suicide. Sarah, the prosecutor in charge of the case, thinks – on the basis of Vijay's demeanour and history – that Vijay probably did not murder Carl. Nevertheless she acknowledges she might be wrong and decides to put Vijay on trial for Carl's murder in order to allow a jury to sort out the issue of Vijay's guilt. The jury acquit Vijay and Vijay sues Sarah for malicious prosecution. Sarah will have lacked reasonable and probable cause to prosecute Vijay by virtue of the fact that she thought that Vijay probably did not murder Carl. However, it is impossible to say that Sarah acted maliciously in prosecuting Vijay in this case. Sarah, in prosecuting Vijay, was actuated by a desire to see that justice was done to Vijay – to see that Vijay would be punished if he were (contrary to Sarah's belief) actually guilty of murdering Carl.

[29] *Glinski v McIver* [1962] AC 726, 744 (per Viscount Simonds).

– and it could be reasonable for A to believe – that B probably committed that offence.)

If A thought that B committed a particular offence and prosecuted B for committing that offence because he was angrey at B for committing that offence he will not, it is submitted, have acted maliciously in prosecuting B. His predominant purpose in prosecuting B will still have been to ensure that justice was done to B – in other words, to see that B was punished for the offence A believed she had committed.[30] On the other hand, if A was angry at B for acting against his interests and saw his chance to get some revenge by prosecuting B for committing a particular criminal offence, which A thought that B had committed, it is submitted that A *did* act maliciously in prosecuting B. It formed no part of A's purpose in prosecuting B in this case to see that justice was done to B. A would, in the case just described, have been happy to see B punished even if she did not commit the offence for which A prosecuted her.

This was the case in *Glinski* v *McIver* where – it was suggested – the police prosecuted the claimant for conspiracy to defraud not 'in order to bring him to justice for that offence, but . . . [in order] to punish the claimant for having a week before given evidence, which the police believed then to have been perjured, for the defence in the case of *Reg* v *Comer*'.[31] On another reading of the facts in *Glinski* v *McIver*, the police prosecuted the claimant in order to induce him to admit that he had perjured himself in the *Comer* case the week before. Even on this reading, the police acted maliciously in prosecuting the claimant: their object in prosecuting the claimant was not to ensure that justice was done to the claimant – if the claimant had admitted his perjury, they would have dropped the prosecution.

In *Heslop* v *Chapman*[32] it was alleged that the reason Heslop charged Chapman with perjury was to stop Chapman giving evidence for another person also indicted for perjury at Heslop's suggestion. If this were true then Heslop, we would submit, acted maliciously in prosecuting Chapman for perjury; Heslop's object in prosecuting Chapman would not have been to ensure that justice was done to Chapman: Heslop would not have cared whether or not Chapman was actually guilty of perjury but would only have prosecuted him to prevent him from acting contrary to Heslop's interests in another case.

It should be noted that even if A does not prosecute B with the predominant aim of ensuring that justice is done to B, A may still not act maliciously in prosecuting B if he is only prosecuting B because the law requires him to do so. In *Abbott* v *Refuge Assurance Co. Ltd*, the defendants prosecuted the claimant for conspiracy to defraud because it was a rule at the time that if A's property had been taken from him as a result of B's committing a felony, then before A could sue B to recover the value of his property from B, he had to prosecute B first for committing that felony. So the defendants prosecuted the claimant for con-

---

[30] See *Brown* v *Hawkes* [1891] 2 QB 718, 722 (per Cave J): 'so far from [anger] being a wrong . . . motive, it is one of the motives on which the law relies to secure the prosecution of offenders against the criminal law.'

[31] *Glinski* v *McIver* [1962] AC 726, 766 (per Lord Devlin).

[32] (1853) 23 LJ QB 49.

spiracy to defraud so as to put themselves in a position to launch civil proceedings against the claimant to recover the value of the money they lost as a result of the fraud practised on them. The Court of Appeal held that the defendants had not acted maliciously in prosecuting the claimant for this reason.[33] The Court of Appeal reasoned that while the defendants' predominant aim in prosecuting the claimant was to get their money back, they only prosecuted the claimant because the law made their doing so a precondition of their getting their money back from the claimant, and the defendants could not have acted maliciously in simply doing what the law required them to do.

ANALOGOUS TORTS

It seems well established that:

(1) *Arrest warrant.* A will commit a tort if he maliciously and without reasonable and probable cause procures the issue of a warrant for B's arrest.[34]

(2) *Search warrant.* A will commit a tort if he maliciously and without reasonable and probable cause procures the issue of a search warrant authorising the police to search B's premises.[35]

(3) *Liquidation proceedings.* A will commit a tort if he maliciously and without reasonable and probable cause starts liquidation proceedings against a trading company or bankruptcy proceedings against an individual.[36]

(4) *Disciplinary proceedings.* There is no tort of maliciously and without reasonable and probable cause instituting disciplinary proceedings against someone else. So if A maliciously and without reasonable cause institutes disciplinary proceedings against B and does not in doing so commit one of the torts mentioned in this book, he will not commit a tort.[37]

(5) *Civil proceedings.* There is no tort of maliciously and without reasonable and probable cause bringing a civil action against someone else. So if A maliciously and without reasonable cause brings a civil action against B and does not in doing so commit one of the torts mentioned in this book, he will not commit a tort.[38]

Does this make sense? Why will the law protect B from having arrest warrants issued against her for no good reason or from her being subject to unwarranted bankruptcy proceedings while it does not take any special steps to ensure that B is not subjected to groundless disciplinary proceedings or to ensure that B is not the victim of unjustified civil suits? The traditional explanation for the distinctions drawn by the law in this area is that the law in this area is designed to

---

[33] [1962] 1 QB 432, 452–3, 461–2, 469.
[34] *Roy* v *Prior* [1971] AC 470.
[35] *Reynolds* v *Commissioner of Police of the Metropolis* [1984] 3 All ER 649.
[36] *Quartz Hill Consolidated Gold Mining Co.* v *Eyre* (1863) 11 QBD 674.
[37] *Gregory* v *Portsmouth City Council* [2000] AC 419, 432.
[38] *Metall und Rohstoff AG* v *Donaldson Lufkin & Jenrette Inc.* [1990] 1 QB 391, 471H–472D; *Gregory* v *Portsmouth City Council* [2000] AC 419, 432–3.

prevent people suffering three kinds of harm: damage to their reputation, damage to their person and damage to their property (or wallet).[39] So where B is liable to suffer one of these kinds of harm as a result of proceedings being taken against her, A will owe B a common law duty to ensure that he does not maliciously start such proceedings when he has no reasonable and probable cause to do so.

So B's being subject to a criminal prosecution is liable to harm both her reputation and her person (if she might be imprisoned as a result of the prosecution); consequently, A will owe B a common law duty to ensure that he does not maliciously prosecute B for committing a criminal offence when he has no reasonable and probable cause to do so. The issue of a warrant for B's arrest or to search B's premises is liable to harm her reputation and – in the case of a warrant for B's arrest – her person; consequently, A will owe B a common law duty to ensure that he does not maliciously procure the issue of a warrant for B's arrest when he has no reasonable and probable cause to do so. B's being subject to bankruptcy proceedings is liable to damage B's reputation (her credit); consequently, A will owe B a common law duty to ensure that he does not maliciously start bankruptcy proceedings against B when he has no reasonable and probable cause to do so.

Given this, it is hard to see why the law does *not* say that: (1) A will owe B a common law duty to ensure that he does not maliciously institute disciplinary proceedings against B when he has no reasonable and probable cause to do so; *and* (2) A will owe B a common law duty to ensure that he does not maliciously bring a civil action against B when he has no reasonable and probable cause to do so. The bringing of disciplinary proceedings against B is liable to damage her reputation and her income. While being subject to civil litigation is, generally speaking, not liable to damage one's reputation, it *is* liable to injure one's property in the sense that it is liable to cost one a lot of money to defend. This was denied by Bowen LJ in *Quartz Hill Consolidated Gold Mining Co.* v *Eyre* who observed that: '[t]he bringing of [a civil] action does not as a natural or necessary consequence involve any injury to a man's property, for this reason, that the only costs which the law recognises, and for which it will compensate him, are the costs properly involved in the action itself. For those the successful defendant will have been already compensated, so far as the law chooses to compensate him.'[40] However, this is not true. The costs awarded to a successful defendant to a civil action will always be less than the true costs incurred by the defendant in defending that action.

In *Gregory* v *Portsmouth City Council*, the House of Lords expressed some unease at the state of the law in this area but refused to disturb it. It thought the jump from imposing common law duties on people not to start *legal proceedings* maliciously and without reasonable and probable cause to imposing common law duties on people not to start *private disciplinary proceedings* maliciously and without reasonable and probable cause was too large a jump for the law to take.[41] It thought that there was a stronger case for changing the law so as to protect people from being subjected to malicious and groundless civil

---

[39] The threefold division of the harms concerned to be prevented by the law in this area goes back to a *dictum* of Holt CJ's in *Savill* v *Roberts* (1698) 12 Mod Rep 208, 88 ER 1267.
[40] (1863) 11 QBD 674, 690.
[41] [2000] AC 419, 431–2.

actions but expressed the hope that the existing network of common law duties that people owe to each other not to defame each other or tell malicious lies about each other or conspire to injure each other would suffice to ensure that people would not be subjected to such civil actions and that the remedies for the breach of one or more of these common law duties would be available to someone who did suffer harm because he was subjected to a malicious and groundless civil action.[42]

42 Ibid., 432–3.

26

MISFEASANCE IN PUBLIC OFFICE

Public officials have a special capacity to cause harm by abusing their official powers[1] or neglecting their official duties.[2] 'The rationale of the tort [of misfeasance in public office] is that in a legal system based on the rule of law executive or administrative power "may be exercised only for the public good" and not for ulterior and improper purposes.'[3] In many situations a public official who abuses his or her powers will commit one of the other torts discussed in this book. For instance, if a public official physically detains someone when he has no lawful authority to do so, he will commit the tort of false imprisonment. Similarly, a public official will commit the tort of conversion if she seizes someone else's property when she has no lawful authority to do so. But in some situations an abuse of power by a public official will not fall within the ambit of any other tort. This will be the case, for example, if a public official refuses to grant a licence to someone when such a licence would normally have been granted, or orders someone not to carry out a profitable activity when such an order should not have been given. The tort of misfeasance in public office is normally the only tort which could have been committed in these situations.

A, a public official, will commit the tort of misfeasance in public office in relation to B if: (1) in bad faith he misuses his powers or neglects his duties with the specific intention of injuring B; *or* (2) in bad faith he acts in a way that he knows is beyond his powers or inconsistent with his duties and he knows that his acting in that way is likely either to injure B or to injure a class of people of which B is a member. In the case of *Three Rivers DC* v *Bank of England (No. 3)*[4] the

---

[1] Many of the cases on misfeasance in public office involve abuses of licensing powers. For example, *Roncarelli* v *Duplessis* [1959] SCR 121 involved an abuse of the power to grant liquor licences to restaurants, *David* v *Abdul Cader* [1963] 1 WLR 834 involved an abuse of the power to licence cinemas, and *Three Rivers DC* v *Governor and Company of the Bank of England (No. 3)* [2003] 2 AC 1 (henceforth, *Three Rivers (No. 3)*) involved allegations of abuse of the power to license banks. Another group of cases involve alleged abuses of planning powers: see, for example, *Dunlop* v *Woollahra MC* [1982] AC 158 and *Barnard* v *Restormel BC* [1998] 3 PLR 27.

[2] Some of the claims in *Three Rivers (No. 3)* involved allegations that the defendant had deliberately decided not to perform the duties imposed on it by the statutes which made it the regulator of deposit-taking institutions. In *Odhavji Estate* v *Woodhouse* [2003] 3 SCR 263, the Supreme Court of Canada expressly rejected the argument that the tort only covered the abuse of powers. The Court held (at [30]) that the tort should cover both abuse of powers and neglect of duty because they were 'equally inconsistent with the obligation of a public officer not to intentionally injure a member of the public through deliberate and unlawful conduct in the exercise of public functions'.

[3] *Three Rivers (No. 3)* [2003] 2 AC 1, 190 (per Lord Steyn, quoting Nourse LJ in *Jones* v *Swansea CC* [1990] 1 WLR 54, 85F).

[4] [2003] 2 AC 1. The House of Lords dealt with the issues raised in two separate sets of speeches that are reported sequentially in [2003] 2 AC. Only the second set of speeches used numbered paragraphs. Thus our references to the first set of speeches use page numbers and our references to the second set use paragraph numbers.

members of the House of Lords expressed different views as to whether (1) and
(2), above, amount to two different forms of the tort or not. Lord Steyn suggested
that it was 'conducive to clarity to recognise' that (1) and (2) are alternative forms
of the tort with a 'unifying element of conduct amounting to an abuse of power
accompanied by subjective bad faith'.[5] By contrast, Lord Millett argued that 'the
two limbs are merely different ways in which the necessary element of intention
is established'.[6] On this question we prefer the view of Lord Steyn because we
doubt whether anything properly called intention can be inferred from the proof
of (2). We would describe the relationship between the two forms in this way –
form (2) is an *extension* of the scope of the tort beyond form (1).

Several elements of the definition are worth further discussion.

(1) *Public official.* This is defined broadly. Best CJ was of the opinion that 'every
one who is appointed to discharge a public duty, and receives a compensation in
whatever shape, whether from the Crown or otherwise, is constituted a public
officer'.[7] Most cases involve officers who are members of the executive, but the
Court of Appeal of New Zealand has held that the tort can also be committed by
a judge.[8] Public bodies, such as local councils, can be liable, as well as individual
public officials.[9] If A is a public official, he can commit the tort of misfeasance in
public office by abusing any of the powers attached to his post. 'It is not the nature
of the power which matters. Whatever its nature or origin, the power may be exercised only for the public good. It is the office on which everything depends.'[10]
Thus an official who works for a particular public body can commit the tort by
abusing the powers which come from the public body being a landlord,[11] or which
come from the fact that the body has the capacity to make contracts, and not just
by abusing the special statutory and prerogative powers that the public body may
have. Indeed, it seems that a public official can also commit the tort by using his
or her position to lay claim to powers that he or she does not legally have. In the
Australian case of *Northern Territory* v *Mengel*,[12] the defendant public officials
committed the tort of misfeasance in public office by asserting a power to stop the
Mengels transporting their cattle to market when, in fact, they did not have such
a power.

(2) *Acts and omissions.* Obviously, a public official may commit the tort of misfeasance in public office if he performs a *positive act* that is unlawful, such as
issuing an unlawful order. If B wants to claim that A committed the tort of misfeasance in public office by performing some kind of positive act, it will be

---

[5] Ibid., 191–2.
[6] Ibid., 235.
[7] *Henly* v *Mayor of Lyme* (1828) 5 Bing 91, 107; 130 ER 995, 1001.
[8] *Rawlinson* v *Rice* [1998] 1 NZLR 454.
[9] Further, a public body may be held vicariously liable if one of its employees commits the tort of
   misfeasance in public office: *Racz* v *Home Office* [1994] 2 AC 45. For the rules governing when
   an employer will be vicariously liable in respect of a tort committed by one of his employees, see
   below, Chapter 35.
[10] *Jones* v *Swansea CC* [1990] 1 WLR 54, 85F, per Nourse LJ.
[11] As was the case in *Jones* v *Swansea CC* where the claimant alleged that the council had maliciously refused to allow a change of user of premises that she leased from the council.
[12] (1995) 185 CLR 307.

important for B to identify the act in question since a pivotal issue will be A's state of mind in performing the act in question.[13]

A difficult question is whether the tort also covers situations where a public official *fails to act*, knowing that this is likely to lead to B suffering some kind of harm. Different members of the House of Lords gave different answers to this question in *Three Rivers (No. 3)*, where some of the claims were based on *failure* to revoke a licence.[14] Lord Hobhouse stated that 'If there is a legal duty to act and the decision not to act amounts to an unlawful breach of that legal duty, the omission can amount to misfeasance for the purpose of the tort . . . What is not covered is a mere failure, oversight or accident.'[15] This answer suggests that two separate conditions must be fulfilled before an omission can amount to misfeasance: There must be (1) a breach of a *legal duty* to act, and (2) a *decision* not to act. Lord Hutton also seemed to support (2) and said that where the claim was based on an omission it 'must be a deliberate one involving an actual decision'.[16] By contrast, Lord Hope stated 'I would reject the argument that proof of conscious decisions to act or not to act is required. In my view the tort extends to a deliberate or wilful failure to take those decisions.'[17] There can be little doubt that condition (1) is required in a claim based on an omission because the tort of misfeasance requires *unlawful* behaviour and an omission will not be unlawful unless there was a duty to act. It is important to remember, however, that public law insists that where an official has a *power* to act: (*i*) that official will be under a legal *duty* to exercise the power if, in the circumstances, it would be utterly unreasonable[18] not to do so, and (*ii*) that official will be under a legal duty *to consider* whether to use that power or not. Lord Hope's reason for rejecting condition (2) was that he thought it would benefit a defendant who repeatedly procrastinated and refused to make a decision. But it seems at least arguable that such a defendant could be described as having *decided* to breach legal duty (*ii*).[19]

(3) *State of mind.* The state of mind which it must be proved a public official had at the time of his unlawful act or omission is different for the two forms of the tort. To prove that A has committed form (1) of the tort in relation to B, B must prove that A 'specifically intended' to injure B (or a class of persons of which B

---

[13] *Calveley v Chief Constable of the Merseyside Police* [1989] AC 1228, 1240.

[14] *Three Rivers (No. 3)* [2003] 2 AC 1 involved claims that the Bank of England, as regulator of deposit-taking institutions, was liable to compensate depositors who lost money on the collapse of the Bank of Credit and Commerce International (BCCI). The claims alleged that the Bank of England had acted unlawfully in licensing BCCI and in not intervening sooner to control its activities.

[15] Ibid., 230. See also 237, per Lord Millett.

[16] Ibid., 228.

[17] Ibid., [69].

[18] Those who have studied administrative law will be familiar with this concept being called '*Wednesbury* unreasonableness', after the case of *Associated Provincial Picture Houses Ltd* v *Wednesbury Corp.* [1948] 1 KB 223.

[19] The House of Lords in *Three Rivers (No. 3)* [2003] 2 AC 1 split 3:2 over whether the claims should be permitted to proceed to trial. The dissentients, Lord Hobhouse, at [172]–[173], and Lord Millett, at [191], regarded the claims based on omissions to revoke the licence as flawed by a failure to establish a legal duty to revoke. Lord Hope was willing to allow the case to proceed on the basis of the general allegation that 'the Bank deliberately ran away from its responsibility as the relevant supervisory authority' (at [68]).

was a member) when he misused his powers or neglected his duty. It is probably also necessary to show that A knew that it was not lawful to injure B – otherwise the tort might cover cases where a public official honestly believed that punishing someone else was legally authorised.[20]

Suppose now that B wants to establish that A, in acting beyond his powers or inconsistently with his duties, committed form (2) of the tort of misfeasance in public office. What will B have to prove was A's state of mind when he acted in this way? In addressing this question, it is important to distinguish between what must be shown to have been A's state of mind towards the unlawfulness of his act and what must be shown to have been A's state of mind towards B. As to the first, in the *Three Rivers (No. 3)* case Lord Steyn said that 'only reckless indifference in a subjective sense will be sufficient'.[21] So, at the very least, B will have to 'prove that [A] acted with a state of mind of reckless indifference to the illegality of his act'.[22] This means that B must show that A knew that the act was unlawful, or suspected that the act was unlawful but did not bother to check further because he or she did not care whether it was or not. As to A's state of mind towards B, Lord Steyn said that at the very least B must prove that A acted 'in the knowledge that his act would probably injure [B] or a person of a class of which [B] was a member'.[23] But again, proof of actual knowledge is not necessary and it would be sufficient for B to prove that A suspected that injury[24] to B would probably be caused but did not bother to check further because he or she did not care.

In *Akenzua* v *Secretary of State for the Home Department*[25] the Court of Appeal had to consider whether Lord Steyn's statement that A must know that 'his act would probably injure [B] or a person of a class of which [B] was a member' meant that the tort could not catch a defendant who unlawfully acted in a way which imperilled people indiscriminately. The Court held that it did not matter whether the defendant could contemplate harm to a particular *group of persons* provided that the *way in which the harm was caused* was the same sort of way as the defendant had in contemplation at the time of his unlawful act or omission. Thus if A unlawfully released C knowing him to be an arsonist, A might be liable to B if she was injured by a fire started by C, but not if she was injured by C's negligent driving.

---

[20] The formulation of the tort in *Three Rivers (No. 3)* [2003] 2 AC 1 does not mention this element, but both forms of the tort require 'bad faith' and in our opinion it is obvious that 'bad faith' and 'malice' require not just an intention to injure but also knowledge that such injury is not lawful.

[21] Ibid., 193.

[22] Ibid.

[23] Ibid., 196.

[24] In this context 'injury' means *either* harm such as personal injury, property damage and economic loss, *or* the violation of one of B's constitutional rights. Thus a public official can commit the tort by opening a prisoner's correspondence with his lawyer (thus violating the prisoner's constitutional right of access to the courts) even if there was no likelihood that his doing this would cause the prisoner any harm: *Watkins* v *Secretary of State for the Home Department* [2004] EWCA Civ 966.

[25] [2003] 1 WLR 741. The case involved the allegation that an immigration official had unlawfully arranged for a dangerous person to be released from custody so that he could become a police informer. The claimants were the personal representatives of a person who was subsequently murdered by the dangerous person.

(4) *Bad faith.* The speeches in *Three Rivers (No. 3)* have not settled the role of 'bad faith' in the context of the tort. Lord Hope suggested that 'bad faith' was *demonstrated* by proof of the relevant state of mind.[26] Thus, for him at least, 'bad faith' was not an *additional* ingredient. By contrast Lord Hutton treated 'bad faith' as requiring an evaluation of the defendant's *motive*.[27] If a bad motive is an additional ingredient then a public official who knowingly acted unlawfully, and knew of the risk of probable harm to the claimant, could nonetheless be not liable if he acted for the purest of motives, for instance, because he believed that the unlawful behaviour was in the public interest. This has been criticized on the ground that 'there should be no encouragement given to [public officials] to dream up arguments as to why it was a good idea to deliberately choose not to comply [with legislation]'.[28] But Lord Hutton's view seems to give more weight to the function of the tort as being to control *abuse* of the official's position. The official's pure motive clearly cannot make his unlawful behaviour lawful, but we think that it may be sufficient to prevent it from falling within this tort.

(5) *Lord Steyn's error?* In *Three Rivers (No. 3)* Lord Steyn stated that 'in both forms of the tort the [state of mind] required *must be directed at the harm complained of,* or at least to harm of the type suffered by the plaintiffs'.[29] If Lord Steyn's view is correct then two things follow from it. Suppose A misused his powers intending[30] B to suffer a particular kind of harm – harm H – and thereby committed the tort of misfeasance in public office. Suppose further that in fact B did not suffer harm H as a result of A's misusing his powers but instead suffered a quite different kind of harm. In such a case, applying Lord Steyn's rule, A will not be held liable to compensate B for the harm suffered by her as a result of A's act of misfeasance. This result is contrary to the usual rules as to the extent of a defendant's liability in the case where a defendant has committed an intentional tort.[31] Moreover, Lord Steyn did not expressly consider what the correct legal outcome should be in this case. Consequently there are grounds for arguing that Lord Steyn made an error. In our opinion, he should have said that in order to commit the tort of misfeasance in public office in relation to B, A must, when misusing his powers, intend B to suffer harm, or know that B will probably suffer harm, or suspect that B will probably suffer harm and not care, but that if A has committed the tort, the separate and further question of what damages are recoverable should be governed by the usual rules governing the extent of an intentional tortfeasor's liability.[32]

---

[26] *Three Rivers (No. 3)* [2003] 2 AC 1, [44].
[27] Ibid., [121]–[125].
[28] Stanton 2003, 134.
[29] *Three Rivers (No. 3)* [2003] 2 AC 1, 195–6 (emphasis added).
[30] Or knowing or suspecting that B would suffer a particular kind of harm – harm H.
[31] An intentional tort is one which can only be committed deliberately. On the rules governing the extent of an intentional tortfeasor's liability, see below, pp. 563–4.
[32] In each case the word 'harm' could be replaced with 'injury' so as to better accommodate the situation where the defendant knew or suspected that his behaviour was likely to violate one of the claimant's constitutional rights. See above, n. 24.

TORTS INVOLVING THE BREACH OF A STATUTORY DUTY OWED TO ANOTHER

We have already seen some examples of situations where someone will commit a tort if he or she breaches a statutory duty. For example, an occupier of premises will commit the tort of negligence if he breaches the statutory duty he owes his visitors under the Occupiers' Liability Act 1957 to take reasonable steps to see that they will be reasonably safe in visiting his premises. Again: A will commit the tort of harassment in relation to B if he breaches the duty he will normally owe her under the Protection from Harassment Act 1997 not to engage in a course of conduct that amounts to harassment of B and which he knows or ought to know amounts to harassment of B. Finally, if A sets out to harm B and does so by breaching a statutory duty, B will usually[1] be able to establish that A committed a tort in relation to her in so acting – the tort of using unlawful means to harm another.

We are concerned in this part of the book with situations where A has breached a statutory duty but A has not – in breaching that duty – committed one of the torts we have already come across. Three such situations can be distinguished.

(1) *Breach of duty owed to claimant.* If A has breached a statutory duty owed to B[2] and B has suffered loss as a result, B will be entitled to sue A for compensation for that loss if: (*a*) the duty breached by A was imposed on him in order to help ensure that B did not suffer that kind of loss;[3] *and* (*b*) A committed a tort in breaching that duty.

(2) *Breach of duty owed to third party.* If A has breached a statutory duty owed to C and B has suffered loss as a result, B will not normally be entitled to sue A for compensation for that loss.[4] For example, in *Wingrove* v *Prestige & Co. Ltd*,[5] the claimant was a clerk of works employed by Middlesex County Council to supervise the defendants as they built a school for the council. The claimant was blinded in both eyes as a result of an accident on the construction site. The accident occurred because the defendants committed a breach of a statutory duty: they had a statutory duty to ensure that 'suitable and safe scaffolds shall be provided for all work that cannot be safely done on or from the ground or from part of the building . . .'.[6] The claimant sued the defendants for compensation for his injury but his claim was dismissed. The statutory duty that the

---

[1] For a possible exception, see above, pp. 419–20.
[2] That is, the duty breached by A was imposed on him for B's benefit.
[3] *Gorris* v *Scott* (1874) LR 9 Ex 125 (discussed below, p. 566).
[4] If A committed a tort in breaching the duty owed to C, then B may exceptionally be entitled to sue A for compensation for the losses suffered by her as a result of A's breach under the principles set out below in Chapter 34.
[5] [1954] 1 WLR 524.
[6] Building (Safety, Health and Welfare) Regulations 1948, reg 5.

defendants breached had been imposed for the benefit of the defendants' employees, not the claimant.[7]

(3) *Breach of duty owed to no one in particular.* If A has breached a statutory duty which was imposed on him for the benefit of the community as a whole and B has suffered loss as a result, B will only be entitled to sue A for compensation for that loss if A's breach amounted to a *public nuisance*[8] and B suffered *special damage* as a result of A's breach.[9]

For example, in *Lonrho Ltd v Shell Petroleum (No. 2)*,[10] the claimants in that case owned an oil pipeline which ran into Southern Rhodesia. Oil companies would pay the claimants to use the oil pipeline to transport oil into Southern Rhodesia. When Southern Rhodesia unilaterally declared itself independent of the UK, the UK government made it illegal to supply oil to Southern Rhodesia and the claimants' pipeline fell into disuse. The defendants secretly continued to supply oil to Southern Rhodesia, in breach of the sanctions applied by the UK government to Southern Rhodesia. Had they not, it was likely that the Southern Rhodesian government would have collapsed sooner than it did; that the sanctions against Southern Rhodesia would have been lifted earlier than they were; and that the claimants' pipeline would not have been out of use for as long as it was. Let us say that the defendants' unlawful conduct caused the claimants' pipeline to be put out of use for an extra nine months. The claimants sued the defendants for compensation for the profits they would have made had oil companies been allowed to use their pipeline during those nine months. The claimants' claim was dismissed. The statutory duty breached by the defendants in this case was imposed for the benefit of the UK as a whole, which had an interest in bringing down the Southern Rhodesian government through the use of sanctions. The duty breached by the defendants was therefore owed to no one in particular. So it followed that the claimants could only sue the defendants for compensation for the losses suffered by them as a result of the defendants' breach of statutory duty if the defendants' breach amounted to a public nuisance – which it did not.[11]

The statutory duty that was breached in *Lonrho* was clearly imposed for the benefit of the community as a whole, and not for any particular individual's benefit. However, not all cases are so clear cut. For example, in *X v Bedfordshire County Council*,[12] the claimants were five children who suffered years of abuse at home. Despite being alerted to this, the relevant local authority failed to ini-

---

[7] For further examples, see W&J, 275; Grubb 2002, 672–3.

[8] For an account of the law on public nuisance, see Chapter 46, below.

[9] It was suggested in the Australian case of *Beaudesert Shire Council v Smith* (1966) 120 CLR 145, at 160 that B would *also* be able to sue A if A intentionally breached the statutory duty in question and the loss suffered by B was an inevitable consequence of that breach. However, the House of Lords ruled in *Lonrho v Shell Petroleum (No. 2)* [1982] AC 173, at 188 that this was *not* the law in England. (Nor is it now the law in Australia: *Northern Territory v Mengel* (1995) 185 CLR 307.)

[10] [1982] AC 173.

[11] Note that the claimants could not sue the defendants for compensation on the ground that the defendants had committed the tort of using unlawful means to harm another in acting as they did. While the defendants knew perfectly well that their conduct would inevitably harm the claimants, their *aim* or *object* in breaking sanctions was not to harm the claimants.

[12] [1995] 2 AC 633.

tiate proceedings to take the claimants into care, thereby breaching various statutory duties which required it to intervene to protect 'at risk' children. The claimants sued the local authority for compensation in respect of the losses they had suffered as a result of the local authority's breaches of statutory duty. It follows from what has already been said that the claimant's claim for compensation could only succeed if the statutory duties breached by the local authority had been imposed on the local authority for the benefit of the claimants. One would have thought this requirement was easily satisfied in this case, but the House of Lords held that the statutory duties that were breached in *X* were 'all concerned to establish an administrative system designed to promote the social welfare of the community'.[13] So the statutory duties that the local authority breached in *X* were *not* owed to the claimants, but were rather owed to no one in particular. The claimants' claims for compensation were accordingly dismissed.

So – if A has breached a statutory duty and B has suffered loss as a result, and that breach does not amount to a public nuisance, B will normally only be able to sue A for compensation for the loss suffered by her as a result of A's breach if: (1) the duty breached by A was owed to B; *and* (2) the duty breached by A was imposed on him in order to help ensure that B did not suffer the kind of loss that she has suffered; *and* (3) A committed a tort in breaching that duty.[14]

It follows that if you are confronted with a situation where A has committed a breach of a statutory duty and B has suffered loss as a result and are asked to determine whether B can sue A for compensation for that loss, you should first ask: Did A's breach amount to a public nuisance? If it did, then B can sue for compensation if she suffered special damage as a result of A's breach. If it did not, then you must next ask: Was the duty breached by A imposed on A for B's benefit? If it was not, then B's claim for compensation will fail. If it was, then you must next ask: Did B suffer the kind of loss as a result of A's breach that the duty breached by A was imposed on him in order to avoid? If the answer is 'no', then B's claim for compensation will fail. If the answer is 'yes', then you must next ask: Did A commit a tort in breaching the statutory duty that he breached? If he did, then B's claim for compensation will succeed. If he did not, then B's claim for compensation will fail.

It is this last question that is always the most difficult to answer. If we recall the lessons taught in Chapter 1, a breach of a statutory duty will amount to a tort if Parliament, in creating the duty, intended that a breach of that duty

---

[13] Ibid., 747 (per Lord Browne-Wilkinson).

[14] For a *dictum* indicating that (1) and (2) must be satisfied before B can sue A see *South Australia Asset Management Corporation* v *York Montague Ltd* [1997] AC 191, 211 (per Lord Hoffmann): 'A plaintiff who sues for breach of a duty imposed by the law (whether in contract or tort *or under statute*) must do more than prove that the defendant has failed to comply. He must show that the duty was owed to him and that it was a duty in respect of the kind of loss which he has suffered' (emphasis added). There are plenty of *dicta* in favour of the view that (3) must also be satisfied before B will be allowed to sue A – that is, in favour of the view that B will not necessarily be allowed to sue A even if the duty breached by A was owed to B and B has suffered the kind of loss that the duty breached by A was imposed on him in order to avoid. See, for example, *Pickering* v *Liverpool Daily Post* [1991] 2 AC 370, 420 (per Lord Bridge).

should be treated in the same way as the breach of a non-contractual common law duty owed to another to do something other than pay money. Let's say that if Parliament created a statutory duty with that intention, it intended that a breach of that duty should be *actionable in tort*. So the breach of a statutory duty will amount to a tort if Parliament intended when it created that duty that a breach of that duty should be actionable in tort. In the following chapter we will lay down some basic guidelines that you can use to determine whether Parliament intended that the breach of a statutory duty created by it should be actionable in tort. In Chapter 28, we will set out some statutory duties breach of which *will* amount to a tort because it is clear that Parliament intended that a breach of these duties should be actionable in tort when it created them.

27

BASIC PRINCIPLES

We are concerned in this chapter with the situation where A has breached a statutory duty owed to B and as a result B has suffered the kind of loss which the statutory duty breached by A was imposed on him in order to avoid.[1] As we have seen, B will be entitled to sue A for compensation for the loss that she has suffered if Parliament intended, when it created the statutory duty breached by A, that a breach of that duty should be actionable in tort.

If Parliament has made its intentions clear on the matter, then there is no problem. If Parliament expressly said that a breach of the statutory duty breached by A should be actionable in tort then B will be entitled to sue A.[2] If Parliament expressly said that it should not be, then B will not be entitled to sue A.[3]

The difficulty arises if Parliament did *not* make it clear – when it created the statutory duty breached by A – whether or not a breach of that statutory duty should be actionable in tort. How do we ascertain Parliament's intentions in that kind of case? Lord Denning MR thought that in such a case it was impossible to tell what Parliament's intention was: 'you might as well toss a coin to decide.'[4] Others take the view that it *is* possible to discern Parliament's intention, but to do so one must consider 'the whole Act [that created the statutory duty breached by A] and the circumstances, including the pre-existing law, in which it was enacted'.[5] However, it is unlikely that this approach – which Keith Stanton calls the 'construction approach' – to discerning Parliament's intention will often be successful: in many cases the courts will be 'seeking to discover something which is not there'.[6] Given this, we favour a different approach to

---

[1] If, in an attempt to save time, you have skipped the introduction to this section of the book (see above, pp. 471–4), we recommend that you go back and read it before proceeding any further.

[2] This will be the case if the statutory duty breached by A arose under s 17 of the Race Relations Act 1976 (which provides that an educational establishment will owe someone applying for a place to study at that establishment a statutory duty not to discriminate against him on the grounds of his race). Section 57 of the 1976 Act makes it clear that a breach of that duty will be actionable in tort: 'A claim by any person ("the claimant") that another person ("the respondent") . . . has committed an act of discrimination against the claimant which is unlawful by virtue of [s 17 of the 1976 Act] . . . may be made the subject of civil proceedings in like manner as any other claim in tort . . .'

[3] This will be the case if the statutory duty breached by A arose under s 9 of the Post Office Act 1969 (which provides that 'It shall be the duty of the Post Office . . . to provide throughout [the British Islands] . . . such services for the conveyance of letters . . . as satisfy all reasonable demands for them'). Section 9(4) of the Act makes it clear that a breach of this duty will *not* be actionable in tort: 'Nothing in this section shall be construed as imposing upon the Post Office . . . any form of . . . liability enforceable by proceedings before any court.'

[4] *Ex parte Island Records* [1978] 1 Ch 122, 135A.

[5] *Cutler* v *Wandsworth Stadium Ltd* [1949] AC 398, 407 (per Lord Simonds).

[6] Stanton 2003, 24. Students, in particular, are likely to find the 'construction approach' unhelpful in attempting problem questions involving the breach of a statutory duty owed to another. This

the question of whether Parliament intended that a breach of the statutory duty breached by A should be actionable in tort. Stanton calls this approach 'the presumption approach'.[7] It goes as follows.

We start off by making a basic presumption that Parliament intended, when it created the statutory duty breached by A, that it should be actionable in tort. The argument in favour of making this presumption has seven stages. It goes as follows. (*a*) The law should be consistent – it should treat like cases alike. (*b*) There is no fundamental difference between judge-made duties that are owed to others and statutory duties that are owed to others. (*c*) Given this, the law should treat someone who breaches a statutory duty owed to another in the same way as it does someone who breaches a judge-made duty owed to that other. (*d*) Someone who breaches a judge-made duty owed to another will be routinely ordered to pay compensation to the victim of his breach. (*e*) Given this, someone who breaches a statutory duty owed to another should be ordered to pay compensation to the victim of his breach. (*f*) We presume that Parliament, when it created the statutory duty breached by A, wished to respect the basic dictate that the law should treat like cases alike and therefore intended that if A breached that duty he should be held liable to pay compensation to the victim of his breach. (*g*) We therefore presume that when Parliament created the statutory duty breached by A, it intended that a breach of that duty should be actionable in tort.[8]

Having made this basic presumption, we then see if that presumption can be rebutted. That is, we see if there is some indication that Parliament did *not*

---

is because the statutory duty in question is very likely to have been made up by the examiner. As a result, there simply will not exist any legislative history relating to that statutory duty for the student to consult in an attempt to determine whether Parliament intended that a breach of that duty should be actionable in tort.

[7] Ibid., 25–6.

[8] *Important note.* This argument only makes sense if it is accepted that (*d*) is true: that is, if it is accepted that someone who breaches a judge-made duty owed to another will be routinely ordered to pay damages to the victim of his breach. As we have seen (see above, pp. 18–20), many academics do *not* accept that a defendant who is held liable to pay damages to another in negligence or deceit or private nuisance or defamation is held liable because he has breached a judge-made duty owed to another. Let's call such an academic, a *duty-minimalist*. A duty-minimalist will take a very restrictive view of what judge-made duties we owe each other: she will tend to think that the *only* judge-made duties we can be said to owe each other are duties to pay other people money in certain situations. Unfortunately, someone who breaches *that kind of duty* – a duty to pay money to another – will *not* be routinely ordered to pay damages to the victim of his breach. So a duty-minimalist will *not* accept that (*d*) is true and will therefore reject the presumption approach altogether. Moreover, a duty-minimalist will find it hard to understand why the breach of a statutory duty owed to another should *ever* give rise to liability in tort. This is because as soon as one starts denying that all the other causes of action in tort (in negligence, deceit, private nuisance, defamation and so on) are based on the fact that the defendant has breached a duty owed to the claimant, actions in tort which arise out of the fact that a defendant has breached a statutory duty owed to another will start to look anomalous and out of place. It is therefore unsurprising – given the current (and completely undeserved) popularity of duty-minimalism among tort academics – that so many of them should be hostile to the existence of the action for breach of statutory duty. See, for example, Fleming 1998, 134; M&D, 361; and Davis 1998, applauding the Canadian Supreme Court's decision to abolish the action in *R v Saskatchewan Wheat Pool* [1983] 1 SCR 205.

intend that a breach of the statutory duty breached by A should be actionable in tort. How do we do this?

(1) *Did Parliament provide what should happen on breach of the statutory duty?* We first of all see if Parliament specified what should happen if someone breached the duty breached by A. If it did, and it did not specify that a breach of that duty should be actionable in tort, then that provides some indication that Parliament did *not* intend that a breach of the duty breached by A should be actionable in tort. The reason behind this is that if Parliament had intended that a breach of the duty breached by A should be actionable in tort, we would have expected Parliament to make that clear when it specified what should happen if someone breached the duty breached by A.

So, for example, in *Scally* v *Southern Health and Social Services Board*,[9] the question was raised: If an employer owes an employee of his a statutory duty under s 4(1) of the Contracts of Employment and Redundancy Payments Act (Northern Ireland) 1965 to give that employee a written statement detailing the particulars of his contract of employment, will the employer commit a tort if he breaches that duty? The House of Lords thought the answer was 'no'. In s 5(1) of the 1965 Act, Parliament specified what should happen in the situation we are considering – if an employer owed his employee a duty under s 4(1) of the 1965 Act to give that employee a written statement detailing the particulars of his contract of employment and he breached that duty, the employee would have a right to have the particulars of his contract of employment specified by a tribunal. The fact that Parliament did not at the same time make it clear that a breach of duty under s 4(1) of the 1965 Act should be actionable in tort tended to show that Parliament did *not* intend that a breach of a duty arising under s 4(1) of the 1965 Act should be actionable in tort.

However, if Parliament specified what should happen if someone breached the duty breached by A and did not in doing so specify that a breach of that duty should be civilly actionable, that does not provide a *conclusive* indication that Parliament did *not* intend, when it created that duty, that a breach of that duty should be actionable in tort. For example, in *Groves* v *Wimborne*,[10] the claimant was injured by some unfenced cog-wheels. In leaving the cog-wheels unfenced, the claimant's employer, the defendant, breached the statutory duty he owed the claimant under s 5 of the Factory and Workshop Act 1878 to ensure that all dangerous machinery used by the claimant was securely fenced. Section 82 of the 1878 Act provided that an employer who breached a statutory duty owed to one of his employees under s 5 of the 1878 Act would be liable to be fined. Parliament did not further specify that the breach of a statutory duty under s 5 of the 1878 Act would be actionable in tort. Despite this, the Court of Appeal still found that when Parliament created the statutory duty contained in s 5 of the 1878 Act, it intended that a breach of that duty should be actionable in tort. Vaughan Williams LJ observed that: 'where . . . a remedy is provided in cases of

---

[9] [1992] 1 AC 294.
[10] [1898] 2 QB 402.

nonperformance of the statutory duty, that is a matter to be taken into consideration for the purpose of determining whether [Parliament intended that breach of that duty should be actionable in tort], or whether [Parliament] intended that there should be no other remedy than the statutory remedy; *but it is by no means conclusive or the only matter to be taken into consideration for that purpose.*'[11]

(2) *Common sense*. Secondly, we ask: As a matter of common sense, can it really be contemplated that Parliament intended that a breach of the duty breached by A should be actionable in tort? If the answer is 'no' then that provides a strong indication that when Parliament created the duty breached by A it did *not* intend that a breach of that duty should be actionable in tort.

For example, in *R v Deputy Governor of Parkhurst Prison, ex parte Hague*,[12] it was claimed that a prison governor would commit a tort if his treatment of a prisoner violated the Prison Rules 1964. So, for example, a prison governor will owe a prisoner of his a statutory duty under rule 43 of the Prison Rules 1964 not to put that prisoner into isolation for more than 24 hours without the authority of the board of visitors or the Secretary of State. It was claimed in *ex parte Hague* that a governor who breached this duty would commit a tort in so doing. This claim was rejected by the House of Lords. As a matter of common sense, it could hardly be supposed that Parliament intended, when it authorised the creation of the Prison Rules, that a prisoner who was the victim of a technical breach of the Prison Rules should be allowed to sue the governor of the prison in which he was held for compensatory damages, as would happen if breaches of the Prison Rules were actionable in tort.[13]

(3) *Does the duty depend on someone's having a certain state of mind?* Thirdly, we ask: Is the existence of the duty breached by A dependent on the state of mind of the person who is subject to that duty? If the answer is 'yes' that indicates that when Parliament created the duty breached by A it did *not* intend that a breach of that duty should be actionable in tort.

For example, s 2(2) of the Child Care Act 1980 provided that: 'Where it appears to a local authority with respect to a child in their area ... that his parents are ... prevented ... from providing for his proper accommodation, maintenance and upbringing ... [and] that the intervention of the local authority ... is necessary in the interests of the welfare of the child, it shall be the duty of the local authority to receive the child into care.' In *X v Bedfordshire*

---

[11] Ibid., 416 (emphasis added). See also *Phillips v Britannia Hygienic Laundry Co..* [1923] 2 KB 832, 841 (*per* Atkin LJ).

[12] [1992] 1 AC 58.

[13] Another possible reason for not allowing a prisoner to bring an action for breach of statutory duty if he was treated in a way that violated the Prison Rules is that the statutory duty that was breached in his case was not imposed for his benefit but for the benefit of the community as a whole, which has an interest in seeing that its prisons are well run. See ibid., at 172 (per Lord Jauncey of Tullichettle): 'The [Prison Rules] are wide-ranging in their scope covering a mass of matters relevant to the administration and good government of a prison ... The rules are regulatory in character, they provide a framework within which the prison regime operates but they are not intended to protect prisoners against loss, injury and damage nor to give them a right of action in respect thereof.'

County Council,[14] the House of Lords had to decide – among many other things – whether a breach of this statutory duty would amount to a tort. The House of Lords thought that it would not: it thought that when Parliament enacted the 1980 Act it did not intend that a breach of this statutory duty should be actionable in tort. One of the reasons for this was that a local authority would only incur a duty under s 2(2) of the 1980 Act to take a child in its area into care if it *thought* that the child's parents were incapable of bringing the child up properly and that taking the child into care was necessary to protect the child's interests. Given this, if a breach of the statutory duty under s 2(2) of the 1980 Act *were* actionable in tort in tort the following paradoxical result would obtain.

A local authority that thought a child in its area needed to be taken into care but then failed to take that child into care would be liable to pay compensatory damages to that child: as soon as it thought the child needed to be taken into care, it would have incurred a duty to take the child into care under s 2(2) of the 1980 Act and it would have breached that duty by failing to take the child into care, thereby committing a tort in relation to that child. On the other hand, a local authority which perversely refused to acknowledge that a child needed to be taken into care would *not* be liable to pay compensatory damages to that child when it failed to take that child into care: it would never have incurred a duty to take the child into care under s 2(2) of the 1980 Act and would therefore have done no wrong in failing to take that child into care. When Parliament created the statutory duty contained in s 2(2) of the 1980 Act, it could not have intended to produce such a paradoxical result. It follows that when Parliament created the statutory duty contained in s 2(2) of the 1980 Act, it could not have intended that a breach of that duty should be actionable in tort.

Again, s 65 of the Housing Act 1985 provides that if a housing authority '[is] satisfied that [an applicant for accommodation] has a priority need and [is] not satisfied that he became homeless intentionally, [it] shall . . . secure that accommodation becomes available for his accommodation'. In *O'Rourke v Camden London Borough Council*,[15] Lord Hoffmann thought that when Parliament enacted this section, it could not have intended that a breach of this duty should be actionable in tort. If it *had* had such an intention then the following 'anomalous' result would obtain: 'a housing authority which accepts it has a duty to house the applicant but does so inadequately will be liable in damages, but an authority which perversely refuses to accept it has any such duty will not.'[16] As Lord Hoffmann observed, 'This seems to me wrong.'[17]

(4) *Oppressiveness.* Fourthly, we ask: Would finding that a breach of the duty breached by A is actionable in tort impose an oppressive burden on whoever is subject to that duty? If the answer is 'yes' then that tends to indicate that when Parliament created the duty breached by A, it did *not* intend that a breach of that duty should be actionable in tort.

[14] [1995] 2 AC 633.
[15] [1998] AC 188.
[16] Ibid., 196.
[17] Ibid.

For example, in *Atkinson* v *The Newcastle and Gateshead Waterworks Company*,[18] the defendants supplied Newcastle and surrounding towns with water. Under the Waterworks Clauses Act 1847, they had a statutory duty to install fire hydrants and supply water to those hydrants at a certain pressure. They breached this duty with the result that firemen could not obtain any water from one of the defendants' fire hydrants to put out a fire in the claimants' house. As a result, the claimants' house burned down. The claimants sued the defendants claiming that they had committed a tort in breaching their statutory duty under the 1847 Act. The claimants' claim was rejected. The Court of Appeal thought that when Parliament created the duty breached by the defendants it could not have intended that a breach of that duty should be actionable in tort:

> it certainly appears a startling thing to say that a company undertaking to supply a town like Newcastle with water, would not only be willing to be put under [a statutory] duty to supply gratuitously for the purpose of extinguishing fire an unlimited quantity of water at a certain pressure ... but would further be willing in their contract with [P]arliament to subject themselves to the liability to actions by any number of householders who might happen to have their houses burnt down in consequence [of the company's non-performance of this duty]; and it is, a priori, equally improbable that [P]arliament would think it a necessary or reasonable bargain to make ... [T]he company would virtually become gratuitous insurers of the safety from fire, so far as water is capable of producing that safety, of all the houses within the district over which their powers were to extend.[19]

(5) *Public interest.* We ask, fifthly: Would finding that a breach of the duty breached by A is actionable in tort seriously interfere with the performance of some important public function? If the answer is 'yes' then that again indicates that when Parliament created the duty breached by A, it did *not* intend that a breach of that duty should be actionable in tort.

This was one of the considerations that led the House of Lords to conclude in *X* v *Bedfordshire County Council*[20] that when Parliament imposed duties on local authorities to safeguard the welfare of children in their jurisdiction in the Children and Young Persons Act 1969, the Child Care Act 1980 and the Children Act 1989, Parliament did not intend that the breach of those duties should be actionable in tort. As Lord Browne-Wilkinson observed:

> ... the Acts in question are all concerned to establish an administrative system designed to promote the social welfare of the community. The welfare sector involved is one of peculiar sensitivity, involving very difficult decisions how to strike the balance between protecting the child from immediate feared harm and disrupting the relationship between the child and its parents. Decisions often have to be taken on the basis of inadequate and disputed facts. In my judgment in such a context it would require exceptionally clear language to show a parliamentary intention that those responsible for carrying out these difficult functions should be liable in damages if, on subsequent investigation with the benefit of hindsight, it was shown that they had

[18] (1877) 2 Ex D 441.
[19] Ibid., 445–6.
[20] [1995] 2 AC 633.

reached an erroneous conclusion and therefore failed to discharge their statutory duties.[21]

Again, as we have seen, the House of Lords thought in *R* v *Deputy Governor of Parkhurst Prison, ex parte Hague*[22] that Parliament could not have intended that a breach of a statutory duty owed to a prisoner under the Prison Rules 1964 should be actionable in tort when it authorised the creation of the Prison Rules. It is hard to resist the impression – though it must remain an impression as the point was not explicitly acknowledged – that one of the main reasons the House of Lords reached this conclusion was that if a breach of a statutory duty owed to a prisoner under the Prison Rules were actionable in tort, prisoners could severely disrupt the conduct of prison life by making compensation claims on the ground that they had been the victims of technical breaches of the Prison Rules.

(6) *Useful purpose.* Sixthly, we ask: Would finding that a breach of the duty breached by A is actionable in tort serve some useful purpose? If the answer is 'no' then that indicates that when Parliament created the duty breached by A, it did *not* intend that a breach of that duty should be actionable in tort.

For example, in *McCall* v *Abelesz*[23] the claimant let a room in a house owned by the defendants. Through no fault of the claimant the authorities cut off the supply of gas and electricity to his room and the defendants did nothing to get the supply reconnected in the hope that if the gas and electricity supply to the claimant's room remained cut off, the claimant would be persuaded to take up alternative accommodation that they were offering him. The defendants owed the claimant a statutory duty under s 30(2) of the Rent Act 1965 not to act in this way and the claimant sued the defendants, claiming that in breaching this duty they had committed a tort.[24] The Court of Appeal dismissed the claimant's claim. They thought that when Parliament enacted the 1965 Act, it did not intend that a breach of the duty set out in s 30(2) of that Act should be actionable in tort. One of the reasons the Court of Appeal gave for reaching this conclusion was that little useful purpose would be served if a breach of the duty set out in s 30(2) of the 1965 Act were actionable in tort. If a breach of this duty were *not* actionable in tort, a tenant who was subjected to harassment from his landlord designed to induce him to give up his tenancy would still have a perfectly good set of remedies against that landlord because the harassment would amount to a breach of contract. So a tenant would not be afforded any greater protection against being harassed by his landlord if a breach of the duty set out in s 30(2) of the 1965 Act *were* actionable in tort.

In *Cullen* v *Chief Constable of the Royal Ulster Constabulary*,[25] the claimant was arrested under suspicion of being involved in an act of terrorism. During his time in police custody, the police denied him access to a solicitor and in doing

---

[21] Ibid., 747C–E.

[22] [1992] 1 AC 58.

[23] [1976] 1 QB 585.

[24] Section 30(2) of the Rent Act 1965 provided that: 'If any person with intent to cause the residential occupier of any premises ... does acts calculated to interfere with the peace or comfort of the residential occupier ... or persistently withdraws or withholds services reasonably required for the occupation of the premises as a residence, he shall be guilty of an offence ... '

[25] [2003] 1 WLR 1763.

so committed a breach of statutory duty. The claimant suffered no loss as a result of being denied access to a solicitor but still sued the police for nominal damages. A bare majority of the House of Lords held that the claim should be dismissed. The majority thought that Parliament had not intended that a breach of this kind of statutory duty should be actionable in tort even if the victim of the breach suffered no loss as a result of the breach. The best explanation of this decision is that no useful purpose would be served if denial of access to a solicitor were actionable *per se* – that is, actionable in tort without the claimant having to prove that he had suffered any loss as a result of the denial of access. Of course, if unlawfully denying someone access to a solicitor were actionable *per se*, then someone who was denied access to a solicitor could bring a claim in tort against the police straightaway, without having to wait for the denial of access to cause him some kind of loss. He would thereby be provided with a speedy means of getting a court to determine whether or not he was entitled to a solicitor. However, someone who is denied access to a solicitor while in custody *already* has a speedy means of getting a court to determine whether or not he is entitled to see a solicitor – he can make an application for judicial review of the decision to deny him access.[26]

Suppose, having looked at all these matters, we get the impression that when Parliament created the duty breached by A, it did *not* intend that a breach of that duty should be actionable in tort. If this is the case, we will of course conclude that Parliament did *not* intend that a breach of the duty breached by A should be actionable in tort when it created that duty. We will therefore find that B is not entitled to sue A for compensation for the loss suffered by her as a result of A's breach. If, on the other hand, having taken everything into consideration, we do *not* get the impression that Parliament did *not* intend that a breach of the duty breached by A should be actionable in tort when it created that duty, our initial presumption that Parliament *did* intend that a breach of that duty should be actionable in tort when it created that duty will remain unrebutted and we will conclude that A committed a tort in breaching that duty. B will therefore be entitled to sue A for compensation for the loss suffered by her as a result of A's breach.

Let's now apply this method for determining whether a breach of a statutory duty amounts to a tort to a concrete case. In *Monk v Warbey*,[27] Warbey allowed one Knowles to drive his car when Knowles was not insured against third party

---

[26] Ibid., at [34] – [40] (per Lord Hutton). Lords Bingham and Steyn dissented, on the ground that someone who is denied access to a solicitor will hardly be in a position to make an application for judicial review to get a court to determine whether the denial of access is lawful or not: ibid, at [20]. However, it is hard to see how being allowed to sue for nominal damages would assist such a detainee – the lack of access to a solicitor would make it just as difficult for him to bring a claim in tort against the police. The only possible advantage of allowing claims for nominal damages to be made in cases like *Cullen* is that if such claims could be made, then a detainee who was denied access to a solicitor while in custody would be able to bring a claim in tort against the police months or years after he was detained for the *sole* purpose of having it established in a public forum whether or not the police acted lawfully in denying him access to a solicitor. But it is hard to see what *useful* purpose would be served in allowing him to do this.

[27] [1935] 1 KB 75.

risks (risks of being held liable to third parties) in driving that car. In doing so, Warbey breached the statutory duty that he was subject to under s 35(1) of the Road Traffic Act 1930, which provided that 'it shall not be lawful for any person ... to permit any other person to use a motor vehicle ... unless there is in force in relation to the user of the vehicle ... such a policy of insurance or such a security in respect of third-party risks as complies with the requirements of this Part of this Act'. Knowles negligently injured Monk in driving Warbey's car but because Knowles was uninsured, he was not worth suing. Instead, Monk sued Warbey for compensation for the loss that he had suffered as a result of Warbey's breach of statutory duty in allowing Knowles to drive his car.

Monk had no problem showing that the duty breached by Warbey was imposed for his benefit. The duty was of course imposed for the benefit of other drivers on the road like Monk. Moreover, Monk had no problem showing that he had suffered the kind of loss which the duty breached by Warbey had been imposed on him in order to avoid. The duty was imposed on Warbey in order to help ensure that other drivers on the road did not suffer harm to their persons or property that were not covered by a liability insurance policy – and Monk suffered exactly that kind of harm. So whether Monk could sue Warbey came down to whether Warbey committed a tort in allowing Knowles to drive his car. This, in turn, depended on whether Parliament intended – in creating the duty breached by Warbey – that a breach of that duty should be actionable in tort. The Court of Appeal concluded that it did: there was nothing to displace the initial presumption that Parliament intended that a breach of the statutory duty imposed by s 35(1) of the Act should be actionable in tort when it created that duty.

True, the 1930 Act specified that someone who breached the duty under s 35(1) could be fined or imprisoned and did not mention at the same time that his breach would be actionable in tort. But this did not conclusively indicate that Parliament did *not* intend that a breach of the statutory duty imposed by s 35(1) of the Act should be actionable in tort. And there was no other indication that Parliament did not intend that a breach of the statutory duty imposed by s 35(1) of the Act should be actionable in tort: (*a*) it was not silly or ludicrous to think that Parliament intended, when it created the statutory duty imposed by s 35(1), that a breach of that duty should be actionable in tort; (*b*) the duty's existence did not depend on Warbey's state of mind; (*c*) if a breach of the statutory duty imposed by s 35(1) were actionable in tort, an oppressive burden would not be imposed on car owners: it was quite easy for car owners to avoid breaching the duty; (*d*) finding that a breach of the statutory duty imposed by s 35(1) was actionable in tort would not have any detrimental effect on the performance of any valuable public functions; and (*e*) it was impossible to say that no significantly useful purpose would be served if a breach of the statutory duty imposed by s 35(1) were actionable in tort – if a breach of the statutory duty imposed by s 35(1) were actionable in tort then someone who was negligently knocked down by a car driven by someone other than its owner would have a remedy against the owner if the driver had no insurance against third party risks and was therefore judgment-proof.

28

SOME EXAMPLES

We saw in the previous chapter how one determines whether or not the breach of a statutory duty owed to another will amount to a tort. Let's now look at some specific examples of statutory duties, breach of which will amount to a tort.

HEALTH AND SAFETY AT WORK

We have already seen that an employer will not commit a tort if he breaches the general duty that he will owe all of his employees under s 2 of the Health and Safety at Work Act 1974 'to ensure, so far as is reasonably practicable, the health, safety and welfare at work of all his employees'. This is because s 47(1)(a) of the 1974 Act provides that '[nothing in this Act] shall be construed . . . as conferring a right of action in any civil proceedings in respect of any failure to comply with [the] duty imposed by [s] 2'. However, s 15 of the 1974 Act gave the government power to introduce statutory regulations governing health and safety in the workplace and s 47(2) of the 1974 Act provided that a breach of a duty arising under these regulations should be actionable in tort unless the regulations provide otherwise. Section 15 has been used to introduce a huge number of regulations governing health and safety in the workplace, such as the Workplace (Health, Safety and Welfare) Regulations 1992, the Personal Protective Equipment at Work Regulations 1992, the Construction (Health, Safety and Welfare) Regulations 1996, the Fire Precautions (Workplace) Regulations 1997, the Provision and Use of Work Equipment Regulations 1998 and the Control of Substances Hazardous to Health Regulations 2002.[1] Particularly significant are the Management of Health and Safety at Work Regulations 1999, which require an employer, among other things, to make a 'suitable and sufficient assessment of . . . the risks to the health and safety of his employees to which they are exposed whilst they are at work' and to take 'preventive and protective measures' to protect the health and safety of his employees on the basis of that risk assessment.[2] It used to be that a breach of duty under the 1999 Regulations was not actionable in tort[3] but the Management of Health and Safety at Work and Fire Precautions (Workplace) (Amendment) Regulations 2003 now provide that a breach of duty under the 1999 Regulations *will* be actionable in tort.[4] As virtually

---

[1] Most of these regulations have been introduced in response to EU Directives.
[2] Regs 3–4.
[3] This was by virtue of Reg 22(1), which provided that 'Breach of a duty imposed by these Regulations shall not confer a right of action in any civil proceedings.'
[4] The 2003 Regulations do this in a somewhat backhanded way, amending Reg 22 of the 1999 Regulations so that it says: 'Breach of a duty imposed on an employer by these Regulations shall not

any accident at work can be said to be attributable to an employer's failure to implement a 'suitable and sufficient' risk assessment, it is likely that the 1999 Regulations will provide a fertile source of litigation in the future.

HIGHWAYS

Under s 41(1) of the Highways Act 1980, the highway authority for a particular highway will owe the users of that highway 'a [statutory] duty to maintain the highway'.[5] Section 41(1A) provides that 'In a particular, a highway authority are under a duty to ensure, so far as is reasonably practicable, that safe passage along a highway is not endangered by snow or ice.'[6] A highway authority which breaches its duty to maintain the highway will commit a tort; the 1980 Act clearly contemplates that if a user of a highway is injured because the relevant highway authority breached the statutory duty it owed him to maintain the highway, he will be entitled to sue the highway for damages.

Section 58(1) of the 1980 Act provides that in 'an action for damages against a highway authority in respect of damage resulting from their failure to maintain a highway ... it is a defence ... to prove that the authority had taken such care as in all the circumstances was reasonably required to secure that the part of the highway to which the action relates was not dangerous for traffic'. So, in effect, a user of a highway who is injured or whose property has been harmed[7] because the relevant highway authority failed to ensure that the highway was properly maintained will not be able to sue the highway authority for damages in respect of his injuries if the highway authority can prove that it took reasonable steps to see that the highway in question would be reasonably safe to travel on.

BUILDING WORK

Section 1(1) of the Defective Premises Act 1972 provides that:

> A person taking on work for or in connection with the provision of a dwelling (whether the dwelling is provided for by the erection or by the conversion or enlargement of a building) owes a duty – (a) if the dwelling is provided to the order of any

---

confer a right of action in any civil proceedings insofar as that duty applies for the protection of persons not in his employment.' Thus, but only by implication, a breach of a duty arising under the 1999 Act *will* be actionable if an *employee* was affected by the breach. The somewhat grudging wording of the new Reg 22 is no doubt attributable to the fact that the government was forced into changing the old Reg 22 on the ground that the old Reg 22 failed properly to implement EU health and safety directives.

[5] It has been held that this duty does not go so far as to require the highway authority to erect traffic signs along the highway to reduce the risk of accidents: *Lavis* v *Kent County Council* (1992) 90 LGR 416; *Gorringe* v *Calderdale MBC* [2004] UKHL 15.

[6] This provision was inserted by s 111 of the Railways and Transport Safety Act 2003 and has the effect of reversing the decision of the House of Lords in *Goodes* v *East Sussex County Council* [2000] 1 WLR 1356, which held that a highway authority will *not* be required under s 41 to keep the highways under its jurisdiction free from ice.

[7] It appears no action can be brought under the Highways Act 1980 for pure economic loss resulting from a highway authority's breach of its duty to maintain the highway: *Wentworth* v *Wiltshire CC* [1993] QB 654.

person, to that person; and (b) without prejudice to paragraph (a) above, to every person who acquires an interest (whether legal or equitable) in the dwelling; to see that the work which he takes on is done in a workmanlike or, as the case may be, professional manner, with proper materials and so that as regards that work the dwelling will be fit for habitation when completed.[8]

It is quite clear that someone who breaches this duty will commit a tort: both ss 1(5) and 2(1) of the 1972 Act contemplate that someone who breaches this duty may be sued by a victim of the breach who has suffered loss as a result. Three points may be made about this statutory duty.

(1) *Approved scheme.* Section 2(1) of the 1972 Act provides that if someone breaches the duty set out in s 1(1) in doing work on a dwelling, no action may be brought against him for breaching the duty set out in s 1(1) if the dwelling in question is covered by an 'approved scheme' which protects people who acquire interests in houses which prove to suffer from structural defects. For a long time, most houses in the UK were covered by an approved scheme operated by the National House Building Council with the result that during that time most people who discovered they lived in houses which suffered from structural defects because of the way they were built were barred from suing for breach of the statutory duty owed to them under s 1(1) of the 1972 Act. However, the National House Building Council no longer submits its scheme for approval and so the existence of this scheme no longer stands in the way of an action being brought in respect of a breach of the duty set out in s 1(1) of the 1972 Act.

(2) *Who is subject to the duty?* Because the National House Building Council's scheme worked for a long time to prevent actions being brought for breach of the duty set out in s 1(1) of the 1972 Act, there is no case law on this section. So it remains uncertain *who* is subject to the duty set out in s 1(1): the duty could apply not only to builders and engineers but also to architects and surveyors. Section 1(4) provides that a 'person who – (a) in the course of a business which consists of or includes providing or arranging for the provision of dwellings or installations in dwellings; or (b) in the exercise of a power of making such provision or arrangements conferred by or by virtue of any enactment; arranges for another to take on work for or in connection with the provision of a dwelling shall be treated for the purposes of this section as included among the persons who have taken on the work'.

(3) *Work done to order.* Section 1(2) of the 1972 Act provides that if A takes on work in connection with the provision of a dwelling on B's behalf and does so

---

[8] Why did we not mention this duty when setting out the situations in which it has been established one person will owe another a duty of care? (See above, Chapters 4–7.) The reason is that the duty set out in s 1(1) of the 1972 Act is *not* a duty of care – it is much stricter than that. It requires someone who takes on work in connection with the provision of a dwelling to *ensure* that the work is done in a workmanlike manner, with proper materials and done in such a way that the house will be fit for habitation.

on the understanding that he is to do that work in accordance with B's instructions, A will be treated as having discharged the duty set out in s 1(1) of the 1972 Act if he does the work in accordance with B's instructions.

EQUALITY

The law imposes a raft of statutory duties on employers, businesses and schools requiring them not to discriminate against people on grounds of their sex, race, disability, sexual orientation, religion or belief. Breach of *most* of these duties will amount to a tort.

Duties arising under the Race Relations and Sex Discrimination Acts

The Sex Discrimination Act 1975

Part III of the Sex Discrimination Act 1975 provides that:

(1) *Education.* If B applies to study at an educational establishment, the educational establishment will normally owe B a statutory duty not to discriminate against him or her on grounds of his or her sex either in the terms on which it offers to admit B or by refusing to admit him or her.[9]

Moreover, if B studies at an educational establishment, the educational establishment will normally owe B a statutory duty not to discriminate against him or her on grounds of his or her sex 'in the way it affords [him or her] access to any benefits, facilities or services, or by refusing ... to afford [him or her] access to them, or ... by excluding [him or her] from the establishment or subjecting [him or her] to any other detriment'.[10]

(2) *Goods and services.* If A provides goods, facilities or services to the public which B wants to purchase, A will normally owe B a statutory duty not to discriminate against B on grounds of his or her sex *either* by refusing to deal with B *or* by refusing to provide B with goods, facilities or services of the same quality as he would provide to people of the opposite sex *or* by refusing to provide B with goods, facilities or services on the same terms as he would deal with members of the opposite sex.[11]

(3) *Land.* If A has the power to dispose of premises to other people and B wishes to acquire those premises, A will normally owe B a statutory duty not to discriminate against B on grounds of his or her sex 'in the terms on which he offers [B] those premises, or by refusing [B's] application for those premises, or in his treatment of [B] in relation to any list of persons in need of premises [fitting the description of the premises disposed of by B]'.[12]

---

[9] Sex Discrimination Act 1975, s 22.
[10] Ibid.
[11] Section 29.
[12] Section 30.

Section 66 of the 1975 Act makes it clear that a breach of any of these duties will amount to a tort: 'A claim by any person ("the claimant") that another person ("the respondent") . . . has committed an act of discrimination which is unlawful by virtue of Part III . . . may be made the subject of civil proceedings in like manner as any other claim in tort.'

The Race Relations Act 1976

Part III of the Race Relations Act 1976 imposes on people and institutions statutory duties not to discriminate against people on grounds of their race which are identical to the duties set out in Part III of the Sex Discrimination Act 1975.[13] Again, s 57 of the 1976 Act makes it clear that a breach of any of these duties will amount to a tort in terms identical to those employed by s 66 of the 1975 Act.

The scope of liability under these Acts

Suppose A owed B one of the statutory duties we are discussing here – that is, a duty of some description not to discriminate against B on grounds of his or her sex or race. In determining whether A breached this duty, we do not just look at A's behaviour. We are also required by ss 41(1) of the 1975 Act and 32(1) of the 1976 Act to look at the behaviour of A's employees, if he has any. Section 41(1) of the 1975 Act provides that: '[a]nything done by a person in the course of his employment shall be treated for the purposes of this Act as done by his employer as well as by him, whether or not it was done with the employer's knowledge or approval.' Section 32(1) of the 1976 Act says the same thing. It seems that an employee will be taken to have been acting 'in the course of his employment' by A for the purpose of the 1975 and 1976 Acts when he did *x* if he did *x while he was working for A*.

So in *Jones* v *Tower Boot Co. Ltd*,[14] the claimant worked in the defendant's shoe factory. The claimant was of mixed parentage and this resulted in his being subjected to unremitting abuse from his fellow employees while he worked at the factory. He claimed that the defendant had subjected him to a detriment because of his race contrary to s 4(2)(c) of the Race Relations Act 1976. The claimant's claim was upheld. True, *the defendant* had not *personally* subjected the claimant to any kind of detriment because of his race. However, the defendant's *employees* had: they had subjected the claimant to abuse because of his race. And the defendant's employees were regarded, for the purposes of the 1976 Act, as having acted in the course of their employment when they abused the claimant: they were working for the defendant when they abused the claimant. The defendant was therefore treated under s 32(1) of the

---

[13] See Race Relations Act 1976, ss 17 (statutory duties not to discriminate on grounds of race owed by educational establishment to applicants and students at that establishment), 20 (statutory duty not to discriminate on grounds of race against a customer for goods, facilities or services offered to public), 21 (statutory duty not to discriminate on grounds of race owed by person disposing of premises to person seeking to obtain those premises).

[14] [1997] ICR 254. This was *not* a tort case but is illustrative of the point being made here.

1976 Act as though *he* had racially abused the claimant and had therefore subjected the claimant to some kind of detriment because of his race.

Duties arising under the Disability Discrimination Act 1995 and the Employment Equality Regulations 2003

The Disability Discrimination Act[15] 1995,[16] the Employment Equality (Religion or Belief) Regulations 2003[17] and the Employment Equality (Sexual Orientation) Regulations 2003[18] all work in the same way. They require certain classes of people not to discriminate or harass members of other classes of people on the ground that they are, respectively, disabled,[19] of a certain religious or philosophical persuasion,[20] or have a certain sexual orientation.[21] The relevant classes are: (*a*) employers – employees/applicants for jobs;[22] (*b*) employers – contract workers;[23] (*c*) appointments committees – potential office holders;[24] (*d*) barristers/barristers' clerks – tenants/pupils/applicants for a tenancy or pupillage;[25] (*e*) firms – partners/employees being considered for partnership;[26] (*f*) trade organisations – members of the organisation/potential members;[27] (*g*) qualifications bodies – those seeking to obtain a qualification;[28] (*h*) providers of vocational training – trainees/potential trainees;[29] (*i*) employment agencies – temps/potential temps;[30] (*j*) institutions of further and higher education – students/potential students.[31] The Disability Discrimination Act 1995 also provides that: (1) it is unlawful for a provider of services to discriminate against a disabled person;[32] (2) it is unlawful for anyone who provides employment services to harass a disabled person on the ground that he is disabled;[33] and (3) it is unlawful for anyone with the power to dispose of any premises to discriminate against a disabled person.[34]

The 1995 Act and 2003 Regulations make it clear that a breach of one of the duties mentioned in the preceding paragraph will be actionable in tort[35] – and that damages for injury to feelings may be awarded.[36] The Act and the

---

[15] Henceforth, 'DDA'.
[16] As amended by the Disability Discrimination Act 1995 (Amendments) Regulations 2003.
[17] Henceforth, 'ROBR'.
[18] Henceforth, 'SOR'.
[19] DDA ss 3A–3B
[20] ROBR, regs 3–5.
[21] SOR, regs 3–5.
[22] DDA, s 4; ROBR (and SOR), reg 6.
[23] DDA, s 4A; ROBR (and SOR), reg 8.
[24] DDA, s 4D; ROBR (and SOR), reg 10.
[25] DDA, s 7A; ROBR (and SOR), reg 12.
[26] DDA, s 6A; ROBR (and SOR), reg 14.
[27] DDA, s 13; ROBR (and SOR), reg 15.
[28] DDA, s 14A; ROBR (and SOR), reg 16.
[29] ROBR (and SOR), reg 17.
[30] ROBR (and SOR), reg 18.
[31] ROBR (and SOR), reg 20.
[32] DDA, s 19.
[33] DDA, s 21A.
[34] DDA, s 22.
[35] DDA, ss17A, 25; ROBR (and SOR), regs 30–31.
[36] DDA, ss17A(4), 25(2); ROBR (and SOR), reg 31(3).

Regulations also provide that 'Anything done by a person in the course of his employment shall be treated for the purposes of this Act as also done by his employer, whether or not it was done with the employer's knowledge or approval.'[37] However, they also go on to provide that 'In proceedings ... against any person in respect of an act alleged to have been done by an employee of his, it shall be a defence for that person to prove that he took such steps as were reasonably practicable to prevent the employee from – (a) doing that act; or (b) doing, in the course of his employment, acts of that description.'[38]

INTELLECTUAL PROPERTY

Patents

If B takes out a patent on an invention of hers, A will owe B a statutory duty under the Patents Act 1977 not to infringe B's patent. Section 60 of the 1977 Act provides that subject to certain exceptions:

(1) *Product.* If B's invention is a product, A will infringe B's patent if he 'makes, disposes of, offers to dispose of, uses or imports the product or keeps it whether for disposal or otherwise' without B's consent.

(2) *Process.* If B's invention is a process, A will infringe B's patent if: (*a*) A, without B's consent, 'uses the process or he offers it for use in the United Kingdom when he knows, or it is obvious to a reasonable person in the circumstances, that its use there without [B's consent] would be an infringement of the patent' *or* (*b*) A, without B's consent, 'disposes of, or offers to dispose of, uses or imports any product obtained directly by means of that process or keeps any such product whether for disposal or otherwise'.

(3) *Product or process.* If B's invention is a product or a process, A will infringe B's patent if he, acting without B's consent, supplies someone who is not 'entitled to work [B's] invention with any of the means, relating to an essential element of the invention, for putting the invention into effect when he knows, or it is obvious to a reasonable person in the circumstances, that those means are suitable for putting, and are intended to put, the invention into effect in the United Kingdom'.

If A breaches the statutory duty he owes B not to infringe B's patent, he will commit a tort: s 61 of the Patents Act 1977 provides that 'civil proceedings may be brought in the court by the proprietor of a patent in respect of any act alleged to infringe the patent'. However, if A infringes B's patent when he 'was not aware, and had no reasonable grounds for supposing that [B's] patent existed', B will be barred from suing A for damages in respect of any loss suffered by her as a result of A's infringement of her patent or damages in respect of any profit made by A in infringing B's patent.[39]

---

[37] DDA, s 58(1); ROBR (and SOR), reg 22(1).
[38] DDA, s 58(5); ROBR (and SOR), reg 22(3).
[39] Patents Act 1977, s 62(1).

Copyright

If B owns the copyright in some kind of work, A will owe B a statutory duty under the Copyright, Designs and Patents Act 1988 not to infringe B's copyright in that work. It is not possible to summarise the various ways in which someone can infringe another's copyright in some kind of work: the interested reader should consult ss 16–76 of the 1988 Act and specialist works on intellectual property law. But *very roughly* if B owns the copyright in some kind of work, A will infringe that copyright if: (*a*) he makes a copy of that work without B's consent; *or* (*b*) he reproduces that work in any material form without B's consent; *or* (*c*) he issues copies of that work without B's consent; *or* (*d*) he rents or lends the work to the public without B's consent; *or* (*e*) he performs, shows or plays the work in public without B's consent.

If A infringes B's copyright in some kind of work, A will commit a tort: s 96 of the 1988 Act provides that '[an] infringement of copyright is actionable by the copyright owner' and '[in] an action for infringement of copyright all such relief by way of damages, injunctions, accounts or otherwise is available to the claimant as is available in respect of the infringements of any other property right'. However, if A has infringed B's copyright in a work when he 'did not know, and had no reason to believe, that copyright subsisted in [that] work', B will be barred from suing him for compensatory damages in respect of any losses suffered by her as a result of A's infringing her copyright.[40]

Design right

If a design X is the sort of design that can be protected by a design right[41] and B owns the design right over design X, A will owe B a statutory duty under the Copyright, Designs and Patents Act 1988 not to infringe B's design right in design X. Section 226 of the 1988 Act provides that, subject to certain exceptions, A will infringe B's design right in design X if: (*a*) he reproduces articles to design X; *or* (*b*) he makes a design document recording design X for the purpose of enabling articles to be made to design X.

If A infringes B's design right in design X he will commit a tort: s 229 of the 1988 Act provides that '[an] infringement of design right is actionable by the design right owner' and '[in] an action for infringement of design right all such relief by way of damages, injunctions, accounts or otherwise is available to the claimant as is available in respect of the infringement of any other property right'. But if A has infringed B's design right in design X when he did not know and had no reason to believe that design X was protected by a design right, B will be barred from suing A for compensatory damages in respect of any losses suffered by her as a result of A's infringement.[42]

---

[40] Copyright, Designs and Patents Act 1988, s 97(1).
[41] Section 213 of the Copyright, Designs and Patents Act 1988 specifies what sort of designs may be protected by a design right.
[42] Copyright, Designs and Patents Act 1988, s 233(1).

PART III

—

REMEDIES

COMPENSATORY DAMAGES: BASIC PRINCIPLES

In the following five chapters, we will set out the principles that determine when the victim of a tort can sue the person who committed that tort for compensation in respect of the losses that she has already suffered or may suffer in the future as a result of that tort being committed – and if she can, how much she will be able to recover by way of damages.

Suppose that A has committed a tort in relation to B. If B wants to sue A for compensatory damages, she must first show that A's tort has *caused* her to suffer some kind of loss. She must next show that this loss is *actionable*. If she can do both these things, then she will usually be entitled to sue A for compensation in respect of that loss. However, A may be able to raise a *defence* to B's claim for compensation; if he is, then B will not be able to sue A. But if A's tort caused B to suffer some kind of actionable loss and A has no defence to B's claim for compensation in respect of that loss, then A will be held liable to pay B a *sum sufficient* to compensate her for that loss. However, the damages payable to B may in certain circumstances be *reduced* beneath the level necessary to compensate her for the loss she has suffered as a result of A's tort. This will happen if, for example, B was partly to blame for the fact that she suffered that loss or because B obtained a benefit as a result of A's tort which offset in part the loss she suffered as a result of that tort having been committed.

In Chapter 29, we will explain when someone who has committed a tort will have a defence to being sued for compensation by the victim of that tort. Chapter 30 explains when the victim of a tort will be able to establish that that tort caused her to suffer some kind of loss. Chapter 31 deals with the law on when a loss that has been suffered by the victim of a tort will be actionable. In Chapter 32 we will explain how the courts assess how much should be paid by way of compensation to the victim of a tort who has suffered various actionable losses as a result of that tort having been committed. Finally, in Chapter 33 we will set out the law on when the damages payable to the victim of a tort to compensate her for the actionable losses she has suffered as a result of that tort having been committed will be reduced below the level necessary to compensate her fully for the fact that she has suffered those losses.

29

LIMITS ON THE RIGHT TO SUE

If A has committed a tort in relation to B, B may – depending on the circumstances – be barred from suing A for compensatory damages. This will be true in the following situations.

SPECIAL DEFENCES

If A has committed a tort in relation to B and A has a *special defence* to being sued by B for compensatory damages, B will – obviously – be barred from suing A for such damages.

In Part II of this book – which dealt with when someone will be held to have committed a tort – we noted some occasions when a tortfeasor would have a special defence to being sued for damages by the victim of his tort. So, for example, if Paul runs a newsagents and has committed a tort in relation to Lara by selling a newspaper which contains a defamatory statement about Lara, Paul will be able to raise a defence to any claim Lara might make against him for damages if he can show that when he sold the newspaper he did not know, and had no reason to know, that it contained a defamatory statement about Lara.[1] Similarly, if John commits a tort in relation to Wendy by infringing the patent that she holds on some invention, Wendy will be barred under s 62(1) of the Patents Act 1977 from suing John for compensatory damages if, at the time John infringed Wendy's patent, he 'was not aware, and had no reasonable grounds for supposing that [her] patent existed'.[2]

DEATH

It used to be the rule at common law that if A committed a tort in relation to B and A subsequently died, B would be barred from suing A (or, more accurately, A's estate) for compensatory damages. Similarly, it used to be the rule at common law that if A committed a tort in relation to B and B subsequently died, B (or, more accurately, B's estate) would be barred from suing A for compensatory damages in respect of the losses suffered by B as a result of A's tort before she died. These rules were, for the most part, abolished by s 1(1) of the Law Reform (Miscellaneous Provisions) Act 1934. However, the 1934 Act left the old common law rules intact in one respect. Section 1(1) of the 1934 Act provides that 'this subsection shall not apply to causes of action for defamation'.

[1] See above, pp. 297–9.
[2] See above, p. 490.

496

So suppose that Ruth libelled Eric and shortly after this happened Eric died. In such a case, Eric's estate will be barred from suing Ruth for compensatory damages in respect of the losses suffered by Eric as a result of Ruth's libel before he died. Alternatively, suppose that Ruth died shortly after she libelled Eric. Again, Eric will be barred from suing Ruth's estate for compensatory damages.

CROWN IMMUNITY

It used to be the rule at common law that 'the Crown could do wrong'. So it was simply not possible to sue a body which exercised the powers of the Crown (such as a government department or a branch of the armed forces) in tort for damages. However, the Crown Proceedings Act 1947 abrogated this rule to some extent.

Suppose that the Ministry of Public Works – a public body which exercises the powers of the Crown – has committed a tort in relation to Gary and Gary has suffered some loss as a result. In this case, Gary will *not* be barred from suing the Ministry in tort for compensation for the loss he has suffered if: (1) the Ministry was Gary's employee and it breached one of the common law duties of care it owed Gary as his employer; *or* (2) the tort committed by the Ministry consisted in the breach of a common law duty that it owed to Gary by virtue of the Ministry's 'ownership, occupation, possession or control of property'; *or* (3) the tort committed by the Ministry consisted in the breach of a statutory duty which is binding on persons 'other than the Crown and its officers'.

If none of (1), (2) or (3) are true in the case we are considering, the old common law rule will still hold sway and Gary will be unable to sue the Ministry in tort for compensation for the loss he has suffered.[3]

TRADE UNION IMMUNITY

If A, a trade union member, has committed a tort in relation to B, B will be barred from suing A for compensatory damages under s 219 of the Trade Union and Labour Relations (Consolidation) Act 1992 Act *if*: (1) A committed that tort in the 'contemplation or furtherance of a trade dispute';[4] *and* (2) the tort committed by A was one of the following torts: inducing a breach of contract, interfering with the performance of a contract, interfering with B's business using the unlawful means of threatening a breach of contract, the tort in *Quinn v Leathem*; *and* (3) none of the qualifications to s 219 of the 1992 Act apply in A's case.[5]

---

[3] Of course, if Gary can establish that it was not only the Ministry that committed a tort in relation to him in the situation we are considering, but also one of the Ministry's employees, Gary will still be able to sue the Ministry for compensation for the harm that he has suffered under the law on vicarious liability: Crown Proceedings Act 1947, s 2(1)(a).

[4] Section 244 of the 1992 Act defines a 'trade dispute' as involving a 'dispute between workers and their employer which relates wholly or mainly' to such things as – the workers' terms and conditions of employment, the employer's actions in firing or refusing to engage one or more workers; matters of discipline; a worker's membership or non-membership of a trade union; facilities for officials of trade unions.

[5] *Very broadly speaking*, s 219 will not work to protect A from being sued by B if: (1) A's tort was committed by him in the course of picketing which was not rendered lawful by s 220 of the 1992 Act (s 219(3)); (2) A's tort was committed because B proposed to employ a non-union member

WITNESS IMMUNITY

B will be barred from suing A for damages in respect of anything said by A about B as a witness in judicial proceedings. This immunity from liability – known in legal circles as *witness immunity* – applies even if A *knowingly* gave false testimony about B. Even in this case, B will be barred from suing A for libel or slander or malicious falsehood. Why is this? The reason is that the law regards it as supremely important that witnesses in judicial proceedings should be able to say what they want in court free from the fear that they might be sued for what they say. So the law makes witnesses completely immune from being held liable for what they say in court, thereby assuring witnesses that there is no prospect that they could be successfully sued for what they say in court.[6]

The policy underlying the existence of witness immunity means that its ambit has had to be extended to statements made *outside* court. After all, witnesses would hardly be encouraged to say what they want in court if someone who was displeased with what they said could sue them not for what they said in court but for what they said to their lawyers in preparing their testimony. So in *Watson* v *M'Ewan*,[7] Jessie M'Ewan brought divorce proceedings against Thomas M'Ewan. The defendant made various defamatory statements about Jessie M'Ewan to Thomas M'Ewan's barrister when he was collecting evidence about the case. These statements came to Jessie M'Ewan's attention and she sued the defendant. The House of Lords held that she was barred from suing the defendant – his statements to Thomas M'Ewan's barrister were protected by witness immunity.[8]

Again, the policy underlying the existence of witness immunity means that its ambit has had to be widened to protect witnesses from being sued not for what they have *said* but for what they are alleged to have *done*. For instance, a witness would hardly be encouraged to say what he wanted in court if he knew that someone who was displeased with his evidence could sue him, alleging that he had unlawfully conspired with his lawyers or some other third parties to injure the claimant by giving false evidence about him in court. Because of this, the law on witness immunity was extended by the Court of Appeal in *Marrinan* v *Vibart*[9]

---

or refused to discriminate against a non-union member (s 222); (3) A's tort was committed because B dismissed an employee for unofficial trade union action (s 223); (4) B was not party to the trade dispute in the furtherance of which A's tort was committed (s 224, though A will still be protected if his tort was committed in the course of lawfully picketing B's premises); (5) A's tort was committed in order to pressure B into recognising a trade union (s 225).

[6] Witnesses who knowingly give false testimony in court are, of course, liable to be prosecuted for perjury. However, the prospect of a prosecution for perjury is not likely to have any 'chilling' effect on what (honest) witnesses say in court. Witnesses will know that prosecutions for perjury are very rare and are only brought in blatant cases of dishonesty, so there is little or no likelihood of a witness who gives his testimony in good faith being prosecuted for perjury.

[7] [1905] AC 480.

[8] What is the position if someone makes a statement to a lawyer in preparing his testimony for court but he is never actually called as a witness? It seems that he will still be immune from being sued for what he said in his statement: *Evans* v *London Hospital Medical College (University of London)* [1981] 1 WLR 184, 191G. Similarly, if one side in a civil case commissions an expert witness to prepare a report on the merits of their case, that report will be protected by witness immunity even if it is never used in court but is merely used as the basis for arriving at a settlement of the dispute: *Stanton* v *Callaghan* [2000] QB 75.

[9] [1963] 1 QB 528.

to say that a witness who has given testimony in court cannot be sued on the basis that in giving that testimony he was engaged in an unlawful conspiracy to injure the claimant.

Attempts have been made to extend the ambit of witness immunity to cover statements made by investigators in investigating possible offences on the basis that investigators must be able to feel free to say what they want in the course of investigating possible offences and investigators would feel inhibited in making statements in the course of their investigations if they thought that their statements could be used as the basis of making claims for libel or malicious falsehood or negligence against them. These attempts have proved largely successful. In *X* v *Bedfordshire County Council*, Lord Browne-Wilkinson held that a psychiatrist who was employed by the police to determine who had sexually abused a child could not be sued in negligence for mistakenly reporting that the child had been sexually abused by the child's mother's lover; her report was protected by witness immunity.[10] In *Taylor* v *Director of the Serious Fraud Office*,[11] the defendant was a lawyer in the Serious Fraud Office. She suspected that the claimant, a lawyer practising on the Isle of Man, was engaged in a major fraud with one F. She wrote to the Attorney-General of the Isle of Man, requesting his assistance in her investigation. When F was eventually charged and prosecuted, the Serious Fraud Office's files on him were disclosed to F. These files included a copy of the defendant's letter which F showed to the claimant. The claimant sued the defendant for libel. The claim was dismissed; it was held that the statements made in the letter were protected by witness immunity.

The protection given to investigators in making statements in the course of their investigations would be easily subverted if the law said that an investigator who made a statement in the course of his investigations could be sued on the ground that in making that statement he was engaged in a conspiracy to injure the claimant. If the law said this then an investigator – so the argument goes – would be inhibited in making statements in the course of his investigations; he would know that someone who was adversely affected by a statement made by him in the course of his investigations could sue him, alleging that in making that statement he was engaged in a conspiracy to injure the claimant. Given this, the law probably does protect investigators from being sued on the basis that *in making statements in the course of their investigations* they were engaged in a conspiracy to injure the claimant. But the recent case of *Darker* v *Chief Constable of the West Midlands Police*[12] makes it clear that the law does not go any further than this – it does not protect an investigator from being sued on the basis that he committed a tort *by encouraging other people to fabricate evidence or by concealing evidence*. So if Gary and Mary, two police officers, falsely alleged that they saw Ian steal jewellery from a store, Ian will be prevented from suing Gary and Mary for libel or conspiracy or misfeasance in public office; their statement will be protected by witness immunity.

[10] [1995] 2 AC 633, 755G.
[11] [1999] 2 AC 177.
[12] [2001] 1 AC 435.

But if Gary and Mary induce a third party, Tom, to allege falsely that he saw Ian steal jewellery from a store, Ian will be able to sue Gary and Mary for conspiracy or misfeasance in public office. They will not be protected by witness immunity.

ABUSE OF PROCESS

If A has committed a tort in relation to B, B will sometimes be barred from suing A for compensatory damages on the ground that B will only be able to establish that she is entitled to sue A for such damages by bringing into question – in other words, by making a *collateral attack* on – the correctness of an earlier decision of the courts. In such a case, B may be barred from suing A for compensatory damages on the ground that bringing such an action would involve an *abuse of process*. It is hard to tell *when* B will be barred from suing A on this basis but the following test may be suggested: B will be barred from suing A on the ground of abuse of process if it would not be legitimate to allow B to challenge the correctness of the earlier judicial decision by bringing a claim in tort against A.

For instance, in *Hunter* v *Chief Constable of the West Midlands Police*,[13] the claimants were the Birmingham Six. They had been convicted of causing two bomb explosions which killed 21 people and injured 161 others. They were convicted largely on the basis of written and oral confessions that they made while in police custody. At their trial, they had claimed that these confessions had been beaten out of them. The trial judge held a hearing on the matter and concluded that the claimants had not been beaten by the police and held that their confessions were admissible in evidence. After the claimants were convicted, they sued the police for assault. Their claims were struck out on the ground that they involved an abuse of process. The claimants' claims sought to challenge the correctness of the trial judge's decision that the claimants had not been beaten and, in the absence of any fresh evidence that was unavailable to the trial judge at the time he made his decision, it would not be legitimate to allow the claimants to attack the correctness of that earlier decision by bringing a claim in tort against the police.

Similarly, in *Smith* v *Linskills (a firm)*,[14] the claimant was convicted of aggravated burglary at the Crown Court and sent to prison. On his release, the claimant sued the defendants, the solicitors who had acted for him during his trial, claiming that they had breached the duty they owed him to represent him with a professional degree of care and skill. The claimant's claim was dismissed on the ground that it amounted to an abuse of process. The claimant's claim involved an attack on the correctness of his conviction – he could only show that the defendants' negligence had caused him to suffer some kind of loss by showing that 'if his criminal defence had been handled with proper care he would not, and should not, have been convicted.'[15] In the absence of any fresh evidence that was unavailable to the Crown Court when the claimant was

---

[13] [1982] AC 529.
[14] [1996] 1 WLR 763.
[15] Ibid., 768H–769A.

convicted, it would not be legitimate to allow the claimant to cast doubt on the correctness of his conviction by bringing a claim in tort against the defendants.

In contrast, in *Walpole* v *Partridge & Wilson (a firm)*,[16] the claimant was convicted of obstructing a veterinary officer in the execution of his duty in that he tried to prevent the officer taking blood samples from the pigs at his farm. The claimant instructed the defendants, his solicitors, to appeal against the decision. He thought that as the officer had no reason to suspect that his pigs were diseased, he had not committed any offence in attempting to prevent the officer taking blood samples from them. The defendants failed to lodge an appeal in time and the claimant sued them in negligence. The Court of Appeal refused to strike out the claimant's claim on the ground that it amounted to an abuse of process. While the premise of the claimant's claim was that his conviction would have been overturned on appeal and therefore that he should not have been convicted in the first place, the claimant's claim that he should not have been convicted in the first place was based on a point of law which was not considered by the court which convicted the claimant. Given this, it was not illegitimate to allow the claimant to bring a claim in tort against the defendants even though the bringing of such a claim would inevitably challenge the correctness of his conviction.

All these cases concerned claimants who claimed to have been convicted of some *criminal* offence due to the negligence of their lawyers. What is the position if, say, A, a barrister, represented B in a *civil case* and B lost her case. What is the position: could B sue A in negligence for damages, alleging that A failed to conduct her case with a professional degree of care and skill and that had A conducted her case properly, she would have won the case? The question was considered in *Arthur J S Hall* v *Simons*,[17] which established that a barrister who represented a client in court would owe that client a duty to represent that client with a reasonable degree of care and skill. Lord Hoffmann thought that in the situation just described, any claim by B would *not* normally be struck out as involving an abuse of process.[18]

---

[16] [1994] QB 106.

[17] [2002] 1 AC 615.

[18] Ibid., 706–7. He did suggest one exception. Suppose Carl represented Nita in a defamation case where Karen was suing Nita for defaming her. Suppose further that Nita admitted that her statements about Karen were defamatory but claimed that they were true. Suppose finally that Carl did not do a very good job of arguing Nita's case with the result that the court found that Nita's statements were not true and found for Karen. In such a case, Lord Hoffmann suggested, if Nita then sought to sue Carl in negligence, her claim might be struck out on the ground that it amounted to an abuse of process. In order to make out her claim against Carl, Nita would have to show that but for Carl's negligence, the courts would have accepted that her statements about Karen were true. So Nita's claim would amount to an attack on the correctness of the court's decision that her statements about Karen were not true. Lord Hoffmann thought it might be improper to allow Nita to attack this decision. This must be right: it would surely be wrong to allow Nita to bring an action against Carl which, if successful, would have the effect of blackening Karen's name without giving Karen any opportunity to defend herself.

VOLENTI NON FIT INJURIA

The general rule

If A has committed a tort in relation to B and B has suffered some kind of loss as a result, B will normally be barred from suing A for compensation for that loss on the ground that *volenti non fit injuria* if she willingly took the risk that *she would suffer that kind of loss in the way that she suffered it.*[19]

For example, in *Morris* v *Murray*,[20] Morris and Murray went drinking together. At the end of the evening Murray suggested that they go for a ride in his light aircraft. Both men were quite drunk at this stage but Morris agreed to Murray's suggestion. Once both men were inside the plane, Murray – in his drunken state – just managed to get the plane airborne but it crashed soon after. Morris was badly injured and Murray was killed. Morris sued Murray's estate for damages in respect of his injuries, claiming that Murray had been negligent in the way he had piloted the plane. The Court of Appeal dismissed Morris's claim.[21] In climbing into the plane he had willingly taken a risk that Murray would fail to pilot the plane properly and that he would be injured as a result. It would have been different, it might be suggested, if – once Morris and Murray were airborne – Murray had suddenly been overcome by suicidal feelings and had deliberately targeted the plane at the ground. While Morris willingly took the risk when he climbed into the plane that he would be injured as a result of the plane being badly piloted, he did not willingly take the risk that he would be injured as a result of Murray's deliberately crashing the plane into the ground. Given this, in our alternative scenario, Morris would not have been barred from suing Murray's estate for damages on the ground that *volenti non fit injuria*.

That this is correct is confirmed by the decision of the Court of Appeal in *Slater* v *Clay Cross Co. Ltd.*[22] In that case, the defendants operated a railway which passed through a tunnel. For many years, local residents walked through the tunnel to get to a village. One day the claimant happened to be walking through the tunnel when she was hit by one of the defendants' trains and was injured. The claimant sued the defendants, claiming that the defendants' driver had been negligent in the way he had driven the train; he had not kept a proper lookout and so on. The defendants argued that the claimant's claim should be dismissed on the ground that when the claimant walked through the tunnel she had voluntarily taken a risk that she would be hit by an oncoming train. However, the Court of Appeal dismissed this argument, holding that when the claimant walked through the tunnel she did not willingly take a risk that a train driver would *negligently* run into her.[23]

---

[19] Jaffey 1985 takes a much narrower view of the defence, arguing that it will only be available if B expressly agreed that A's conduct would not be actionable before he did what he did. However, this view is too narrow; it is certainly not consistent with the authorities mentioned below.

[20] [1991] 2 QB 6.

[21] The House of Lords refused leave to appeal: [1991] 1 WLR 1362.

[22] [1956] 2 QB 264.

[23] See also *Blake* v *Galloway* [2004] EWCA Civ 814: claimant who participated in good-natured game which involved friends throwing twigs and pieces of bark at each other willingly took the risk that he might be hit by a piece of bark; though not if the piece of bark was thrown with the intention of harming the participant or was thrown in such a way as to evince a reckless disregard for the claimant's safety.

It should be emphasised that for the *volenti* defence to be raised, it must be shown that the claimant – who is seeking compensation for some loss that she has suffered – *willingly* took the risk that she would suffer that loss in the way that she did. So in *Haynes* v *Harwood*,[24] the defendant negligently left some horses unattended in the street.[25] A boy threw a stone at the horses and as a result they bolted. The claimant, a nearby police constable, threw himself in the way of the horses and seized their reins and brought them under control – but in doing so he suffered various personal injuries. The claimant successfully sued the defendant in negligence for compensation for his injuries. The Court of Appeal held that the defence of *volenti non fit injuria* was not available here. While the defendant had taken the risk when he tried to stop the horses bolting that he would be injured, he did not *willingly* take that risk – he had only acted as he did because it was an emergency.

Exceptions to the general rule

A couple of exceptions to the general rule set out above are worth mentioning.

(1) *Paternalistic duties*. If A owes B a duty to stop B harming herself, then if A breaches that duty with the result that B harms herself, A will not be able to defeat B's claim for damages on the ground that *volenti non fit injuria*. While B – when she harmed herself – willingly took the risk that she would suffer that harm in the way she did, if the *volenti* defence were available to A here A's duty would become meaningless. A would be completely free to breach it, safe in the knowledge that if B took advantage of his breach to harm herself, he would be able to raise a *volenti* defence to any subsequent claim she might bring against him for compensation for the harm she had suffered.[26]

(2) *Traffic accidents*. In *Pitts* v *Hunt*,[27] the claimant and defendant stole a motor-bike and took it for a joyride. The defendant drove the motorbike and the claimant rode in the bike's pillion car. The defendant – with the encouragement of the claimant – drove the bike faster and faster, and finally crashed the bike. The claimant was injured in the crash and sued the defendant for compensation. The defendant sought to raise a *volenti* defence to the claimant's claim. The Court of Appeal held he could not.[28] While the claimant had willingly taken a risk that he would be injured in the way he was when he encouraged the defendant to drive faster and faster, the equivalent of what is now s 149(3) of the Road Traffic Act 1988 applied to prevent the defendant

---

[24] [1935] 1 KB 146.

[25] Why 'negligently'? Well, it was reasonably foreseeable that the horses might bolt and injure passers-by if they were left unattended in the street. As a result, the defendant owed those passers-by a duty to take care not to leave the horses unattended in the street under the physical danger principle set out above, pp. 66–85.

[26] *Reeves* v *Commissioner of Police of the Metropolis* [2000] 1 AC 360, 375–6 (per Lord Jauncey of Tullichettle).

[27] [1991] QB 24.

[28] The claimant's claim for damages was, however, dismissed on the ground of illegality: see below, n. 74.

from relying on a *volenti* defence to defeat the claimant's claim. Section 149(3) of the 1998 Act provides that, 'The fact that a [passenger] has willingly accepted as his the risk of negligence on the part of the [driver] shall not be treated as negativing any ... liability of the user.'[29]

The 'fireman's rule'

Some American states have adopted what is known as the 'fireman's rule' under which someone whose job involves running the risk of suffering a particular kind of loss cannot seek to recover compensatory damages if he actually suffers that kind of loss in doing his job.[30]

So if A negligently starts a fire in his house and B, a fireman, is injured in the course of fighting the fire, then – under the 'fireman's rule' – B will be barred from suing A for compensatory damages in respect of the injuries suffered by him as a result of A's negligence. Again, the 'fireman's rule' would operate to bar a policeman who developed a psychiatric illness as a result of what he saw or heard in dealing with a particularly traumatic incident from suing for compensatory damages in respect of that illness.

The reason for the fireman's rule is clear enough: if you have been paid to run a particular risk, you should not complain if that risk materialises and you suffer loss as a result. However, in *Ogwo* v *Taylor*, the House of Lords refused to adopt the 'fireman's rule' in English law and allowed a fireman to sue a householder for damages in respect of injuries suffered by him in fighting a fire negligently started by the householder.[31] The House of Lords had another opportunity to adopt the 'fireman's rule' in *White* v *Chief Constable of South Yorkshire Police*[32] where – it will be recalled – the claimant policemen sought to recover damages in respect of the psychiatric illnesses they claimed to have developed as a result of the work they did helping out in the aftermath of the Hillsborough tragedy. However, their Lordships again showed no sign that they were in any way inclined to adopt the 'fireman's rule'.

CONTRACTUAL EXCLUSION OF LIABILITY

Suppose A has committed a tort *x* in relation to B. Suppose further that, before A committed that tort, A and B entered into a contract under which B undertook not to sue A for compensation if she suffered loss as a result of A's committing tort *x* (in which case we say A and B's contract contained an

---

[29] So the result in *Morris* v *Murray* would have been different if Murray had invited Morris to come for a drive in his car and had driven the car so badly that it crashed with the result that Morris was injured. In such a case, s 149(3) of the Road Traffic Act 1988 would have applied to prevent Morris's claim being barred on the ground that *volenti non fit injuria*.

[30] California: *Walters* v *Sloan*, 571 P 2d 609 (1977); Michigan: *Kreski* v *Modern Wholesale Electric Supply Co.*, 415 NW 2d 178 (1987) (though see also *Miller* v *Inglis*, 567 NW 2d 253 (1997) and *Gibbons* v *Caraway*, 565 NW 2d 663 (1997), holding that the 'fireman's rule' does not apply in cases where defendant wilfully and wantonly created a risk that the claimant would be injured).

[31] [1988] AC 431, 449C, approving *Salmon* v *Seafarer Restaurants Ltd* [1983] 1 WLR 1264.

[32] [1999] 2 AC 455.

exclusion clause).[33] In such a case, B will be barred from suing A for compensatory damages *so long as* A is not himself barred from taking advantage of the exclusion clause in his contract with B to prevent B from suing him for such damages. As a general rule, A *will* be entitled to take advantage of the exclusion clause in his contract with B. Parliament has, however, created a number of exceptions to this general rule:

(1) *Business liability for negligently inflicted death or personal injury.* Under s 2(1) of the Unfair Contract Terms Act 1977, 'A person cannot by reference to any contract term ... exclude or restrict his [business][34] liability for death or personal injury resulting from negligence'. Under s 1(1) of the Act, a person is 'negligent' if he breaches a 'common law duty to take reasonable care or exercise reasonable skill or care' or a duty of care imposed on him by the Occupiers' Liability Act 1957.

So suppose Tom agreed to perform some medical operation on Dawn for a substantial fee. Suppose further that before performing the operation, Tom and Dawn contractually agreed that if Tom negligently injured Dawn in the course of the operation, he would not be held liable to compensate her for her injuries. Suppose finally that Tom performed the operation so negligently that Dawn suffered severe brain damage as a result. In such a case, Dawn would not be barred from suing Tom for compensatory damages; Tom would not be allowed to take advantage of the exclusion clause in his contract with Dawn to prevent her from suing him for such damages.

(2) *Business liability for negligently inflicted harm not resulting from death or personal injury.* Under s 2(2) of the Unfair Contract Terms Act 1977, 'in the case of [loss other than that resulting from death or personal injury] a person cannot exclude or restrict his [business] liability for negligence except in so far as the term [excluding or restricting that liability] satisfies the requirement of reasonableness'.

---

[33] Of course, if A and B did enter into a contract with each other before A committed tort *x*, there may be a dispute over whether A and B's contract contained an exclusion clause. This will be the case, for example, if, when A contracted with B, he intended that his contract with B should contain an exclusion clause, but B had no intention of agreeing to such a clause. And if A and B did enter into a contract with each other before A committed tort *x* and that contract *did* contain an exclusion clause, there may be a dispute over whether that exclusion clause operated to exclude A's liability to pay compensatory damages to B in the event of his committing tort *x*. This will be the case, for example, if the exclusion clause in A and B's contract was drafted using such vague language that it is debatable whether it excludes A's liability to pay compensation to B in the event of her being harmed as a result of his committing tort *x*. It is outside the scope of this book to explain how the courts resolve these disputes. The interested reader should consult a specialist book on the law of contract for such an explanation.

[34] Unfair Contract Terms Act 1977, s 1(3): 'In the case of both contract and tort, sections 2 to 7 apply only to business liability, that is liability for breach of obligations or duties arising – (a) from things done or to be done by a person in the course of a business (whether his own business or another's); or (b) from the occupation of premises used for business purposes of the occupier; and references to liability are to be read accordingly but the liability of an occupier of premises for breach of an obligation or duty towards a person obtaining access to the premises for recreational or educational purposes, being liability for loss or damage suffered by reason of the dangerous state of the premises, is not a business liability of the occupier unless granting that person such access for the purposes concerned falls within the business purposes of the occupier.'

So suppose Karen, a professional car mechanic, agreed to repair Paul's car. Suppose further that under the terms of their agreement Karen would not be held liable for any damage done by her to the paintwork of Paul's car in the course of repairing it. Suppose finally that Karen negligently damaged the paintwork of Paul's car while repairing it. In such a case, Paul would *only* be barred from suing Karen for compensation for the damage done to his paintwork if the exclusion clause in the contract between Paul and Karen was 'reasonable'.

How do we judge whether the exclusion clause in the contract between Paul and Karen was 'reasonable' or not? In *Smith* v *Eric S Bush*, Lord Griffiths provided some guidance.[35] He suggested that we should ask the following questions. (*a*) Were Paul and Karen of equal bargaining power? Did Paul have the ability to object to this term and the bargaining power to get Karen to withdraw it? If so then the term might be 'reasonable' – Paul has only himself to blame if he did not use his bargaining power to insist that this term was not part of the contract. (*b*) Could Paul have gone elsewhere to have his car repaired? If so, the term might again be regarded as 'reasonable' – if Paul did not want to be subject to this term then he could have gone elsewhere and the fact that he did not might go to show that Paul regarded the term as fair. (*c*) How difficult was it for Karen to repair Paul's car without scratching the paintwork? If very difficult, it might have been 'reasonable' for Karen to make it clear that she would not be held liable if she scratched the paintwork while repairing Paul's car. (*d*) What would be the practical consequences of declaring this sort of term to be 'unreasonable'? Would car mechanics be exposed to liabilities which, being unpredictable in size, would be difficult to insure against? Would it make more commercial sense to throw the burden of bearing the cost of any damage done to the paintwork of a car while it is being repaired on the owner of the car (and his insurer) rather than the repairer? If the answer is 'yes' then, again, the term might be regarded as 'reasonable'.

However, Lord Griffiths emphasised that 'it is impossible to draw up an exhaustive list of the factors that must be taken into account when a judge is faced with [the] very difficult [task of deciding whether a given exclusion clause is "unreasonable"]'.[36] The four questions set out above were merely questions which he thought 'should . . . always be considered'.[37]

(3) *Misrepresentation*. Under s 3 of the Misrepresentation Act 1967, 'If a contract contains a term which would exclude or restrict – (a) any liability to which a party to a contract may be subject by reason of any misrepresentation made by him before the contract was made; or (b) any remedy available to another party to the contract by reason of such a misrepresentation, that term shall be of no effect except in so far as it satisfies the requirement of reasonableness as

---

[35] [1990] 1 AC 831, at 858–9.
[36] Ibid., 858.
[37] Ibid.

stated in section 11(1) of the Unfair Contract Terms Act 1977;[38] and it is for those claiming that the term satisfies that requirement to show that it does.'

So if, for example, the defendant in *Saunders* v *Edwards*[39] had insisted that the contract for the sale of his flat to the claimants included a term to the effect that he would not be held liable for any misrepresentations, innocent or otherwise, made by him to the claimants in the course of negotiations over the sale of the flat, the claimants would only have been barred from suing the defendant for compensatory damages in respect of the losses suffered by them as a result of the fraudulent misrepresentation made by him in the course of negotiations (that a right to use the roof terrace which the flat overlooked came with the flat) if the defendant had been able to show that that exclusion clause was reasonable.

It is worth noting that s 3 of the Misrepresentation Act 1967 – unlike s 2 of the Unfair Contract Terms Act 1977 – does *not* just apply when someone seeks to rely on a contract term to exclude or restrict some 'business liability' of his. Section 3 of the 1967 Act applies even in cases (as in *Saunders* v *Edwards*) where a defendant made a misrepresentation outside the course of business.

(4) *Unfair terms.* Under the Unfair Terms in Consumer Contracts Regulations 1999, if a contract made between a consumer and a seller or supplier of goods or services acting in the course of business contains an 'unfair' term then that term is not valid and cannot therefore be relied on in any litigation between the consumer and the seller or supplier in question.[40]

So, for example, suppose Vijay employed Mary – a professional surveyor[41] – to value a particular house for him that he was thinking of buying. Suppose further that Mary's contract with Vijay specified that if Vijay suffered any loss as a result of Mary's valuation, Mary would not be held liable to compensate Vijay for that loss. Suppose also that Mary negligently overvalued the house because she failed to spot that the house suffered from certain structural defects and, as a result, Vijay, having bought the house on the basis of Mary's valuation, suffered various losses. If, under the 1999 Regulations, the exclusion clause in Mary and Vijay's contract was 'unfair' then it would be invalid and Vijay would be

---

[38] Section 11(2) specifies that 'In determining ... whether a contract term satisfies the requirement of reasonableness, regard shall be had to matters specified in Schedule 2 of the Act . . .' Schedule 2 of the 1977 Act instructs the courts to take into account the following matters in judging the reasonableness of a term: (*a*) the relative strength of the bargaining power of the parties to the contract; (*b*) whether the customer received an inducement to agree to the term or could have entered into a similar contract with someone else without having to agree to that term; (*c*) whether the customer knew or ought to have known of the term; (*d*) if the term excluded a defendant's liability for acting in a particular way, how reasonable it was to expect the defendant to avoid acting in that way; (*e*) (in the case of a contract for the sale of goods) whether the goods were manufactured, processed or adapted to the special order of the customer.

[39] [1987] 1 WLR 1116.

[40] Unfair Terms in Consumer Contracts Regulations 1999, reg 8.

[41] The Regulations apply only to terms in contracts between consumers and sellers or suppliers (reg 4) where a 'seller or supplier' is defined by the Regulations as meaning 'any natural or legal person who [in contracting with another] is acting for purposes relating to his trade, business or profession, whether publicly owned or privately owned' (reg 3(1)).

allowed to sue Mary for compensation for the losses suffered by him as a result of Mary's negligence. (Of course, Mary may in any case be barred from relying on the exclusion clause in her contract with Vijay to defeat his claim against her for compensation under s 2(2) of the Unfair Contract Terms Act 1977.)

The exclusion clause in Mary and Vijay's contract will not be regarded as being 'unfair' if it was 'individually negotiated'.[42] If it was not – say it was a term which was included in Mary's standard form contract for doing surveying work for another – then it will be regarded as being 'unfair' if the term, contrary to the requirement of 'good faith', caused a 'significant imbalance' in Mary's and Vijay's rights and obligations under the contract to the detriment of Vijay.[43] The definition of what amounts to an 'unfair' term is so loose that it is hard to predict, in any given case, whether or not the courts will hold that an exclusion clause in a contract between two people is 'unfair' and therefore invalid under the 1999 Regulations.[44]

(5) *Traffic accidents.* Under s 149 of the Road Traffic Act 1988, if (*a*) A drives B in his car; *and* (*b*) A is required, under s 143 of the 1988 Act, to carry third party insurance (liability insurance) in driving that car; then (*c*) if A and B agree that A will not be held liable to compensate B if she is harmed as a result of A's driving that car negligently, the agreement between A and B will be of no effect.

Three party cases (1)

Let us now consider a more complex situation. Suppose that John employed XYZ plc to build an extension on his house. John's contract with XYZ specified that if XYZ or 'any subcontractor' employed by XYZ to help in the construction of John's extension unintentionally damaged John's house or its contents in doing such work, John would not seek to sue the person responsible. XYZ subcontracted the work of wiring the extension to Ruth. While Ruth was doing the wiring, she carelessly caused a fire to start which damaged John's house. John now wants to sue Ruth in negligence for damages to compensate him for the fire damage done to his house. Can Ruth take advantage of the exclusion clause in the contract between John and XYZ and thereby prevent John from suing her for such damages?

Until recently, Ruth would *only* have been able to take advantage of the exclusion clause in the contract between XYZ and John if she could show that she was a party to the contract between XYZ and John by, for example, showing that XYZ was acting as her agent in entering into the contract with

---

[42] Regulation 5.

[43] Regulation 5(1).

[44] Witness, for example, the history of the litigation in *Director General of Fair Trading* v *First National Bank plc* where a term requiring a defaulting borrower to pay interest on his loan until he had paid off the loan was judged to be unfair under the Regulations by the Director General of Fair Trading (who is given power under the Regulations to direct companies to remove terms which are unfair under the Regulations from their standard form contracts); fair by Evans-Lombe J at first instance ([2000] 1 WLR 98); unfair by the Court of Appeal ([2000] QB 672); and, finally, fair by the House of Lords ([2002] 1 AC 483).

John.[45] (Of course, even if this were true Ruth might still have been barred by statute from taking advantage of the exclusion clause in the contract between ABC and John.) It is hard to understand why the courts should have taken such a position. John indicated in his contract with ABC that if one of ABC's sub-contractors unintentionally damaged his house, he would be happy to forgo any rights he might otherwise have to sue the responsible subcontractor for damages. Given this, it is hard to see why the courts should have gone out of their way to allow John to sue Ruth for damages in respect of the unintentional damage done by Ruth to John's house.[46]

The courts took the above position because they thought that the doctrine of *privity of contract* dictated that Ruth should not be allowed, in the situation we are considering, to take advantage of the exclusion clause in the contract between John and XYZ if she was not a party to that contract. However, the doctrine has now been reformed by the Contracts (Rights of Third Parties) Act 1999. Under that Act, if A and B have entered into a contract to which C is not a party, C may 'enforce' a term in the contract *if*: (1) C is expressly identified by the contract – whether by name or as a member of a class or as answering to a particular description – as someone who may 'enforce' that term; *or* (2) (*i*) the term purports to confer a benefit on C *and* (*ii*) C is expressly identified by the contract, whether by name or as a member of a class or as answering to a particular description *and* (*iii*) when A and B entered into the contract they did *not* intend that C should *not* be able to 'enforce' that term. Under s 1(6) of the Act 'Where a term of a contract excludes or limits liability in relation to any matter references in [the 1999] Act to the third party enforcing the term shall be construed as references to his availing himself of the exclusion or limitation.'

So in the situation we were considering, Ruth would probably be able, under the provisions of the 1999 Act, to take advantage of the exclusion clause in the contract between John and XYZ, thereby preventing John from suing her for compensation for the fire damage done to his house. This term purported to confer a benefit on Ruth; Ruth – as a 'subcontractor' – was expressly identified in the contract between John and ABC; and there is no evidence that John and ABC did *not* intend that Ruth should be able to take advantage of that term in the situation under consideration here.

However, it should be noted that under s 3(6) of the 1999 Act, Ruth will *not* be allowed to take advantage of the exclusion clause in the contract between John and ABC if, had Ruth been a party to that contract, she would *not* have been allowed, under the Unfair Contract Terms Act 1977 or some other

---

[45] *Scruttons Ltd* v *Midland Silicones Ltd* [1962] AC 446.

[46] Ibid., 488–9 (per Lord Denning, dissenting). Perhaps recognising this, the courts sometimes went out of their way to prevent people like John suing people like Ruth through such devices as: (1) finding that there was a contract, collateral to the ones between John and XYZ and XYZ and Ruth, under which John undertook not to sue Ruth in negligence if she unintentionally damaged John's house (see *New Zealand Shipping Co. Ltd* v *A M Satterthwaite & Co. Ltd, The Eurymedon* [1975] AC 154); or (2) finding that when Ruth worked on John's house, she did not owe him a duty to take care not to damage the house or its contents (see *Norwich City Council* v *Harvey* [1989] 1 WLR 828).

statutory provision, to take advantage of that exclusion clause to prevent John from suing her for compensatory damages.

Three party cases (2)

Now let us turn to see what the position is in another three party situation. Suppose that Fred committed a tort in relation to Lara by doing x. Suppose further that before Fred did x, Fred entered into a contract with Wendy under which they agreed that he would not be held liable if he did x. Suppose finally that Lara wants to sue Fred for damages to compensate her for the losses she has suffered as a result of Fred's doing x. Will Fred be able to take advantage of the exclusion clause in his contract with Wendy and prevent Lara from suing him for such damages?[47] As a general rule the answer to this question is 'no'. This is not surprising. It is hard to see why an agreement between Fred and Wendy should ever have the effect of prejudicing Lara's rights against Fred. However, there are some exceptions to the general rule just set out.

Bailment

Suppose that Lara bailed goods to Wendy and Wendy sub-bailed those goods to Fred, telling him that they belonged to Lara. Suppose further that Fred and Wendy agreed that Fred would not be held liable if Lara's goods were destroyed or damaged while in Fred's care. Suppose finally that Lara's goods *were* destroyed because Fred failed to take proper precautions to keep them safe from harm.

There is no doubt that Fred has committed a tort in relation to Lara here. In this situation, he owed Lara a duty to take reasonable steps to ensure that Lara's goods were not destroyed or damaged[48] and he breached that duty. However, if Lara authorised Wendy to sub-bail her goods to Fred on the terms which Wendy agreed with Fred, Lara will be barred from suing Fred for compensation for the loss of her goods: Lara will be bound by the exclusion clause in the contract between Fred and Wendy.[49]

---

[47] In posing this question we assume, of course, that Lara is not a party to the contract between Fred and Wendy. If she were then it would be straightforward to find that Fred could take advantage of the exclusion clause in his contract with Wendy and prevent Lara from suing him for compensatory damages. Lara, as a party to the Fred-Wendy contract, would be bound by the terms of that contract.

[48] See above, pp. 181–2. It is crucial that when Fred took the goods, he knew they were Lara's. If Fred had taken possession of the goods in the belief that they were Wendy's, it is doubtful whether he would have owed *Lara* a duty to take reasonable steps to keep the goods from harm. It is therefore doubtful that Fred would have committed a tort in relation to Lara in failing to keep her goods safe: see *The Pioneer Container* [1994] 2 AC 324, 342.

[49] *Morris* v *C W Martin* [1966] 1 QB 716, 729 (per Lord Denning MR); *The Pioneer Container* [1994] 2 AC 324. We assume of course that Fred is not barred by statute from taking advantage of the exclusion clause in his contract with Wendy to prevent Lara suing him. It is more difficult to know what the position is if: (1) Lara authorised Wendy to sub-bail the goods on the basis that the sub-bailee would not be held liable for the loss of the goods; *and* (2) Fred destroyed the goods in this case through an act of *positive carelessness*. In this case, Lara will not need to rely on the existence of any bailment relationship between her and Fred to sue Fred: she can simply say that Fred owed her a duty under the 'property harm principle' set out above (at pp. 110–19) to take care not to destroy her goods; that he breached that duty; and that he is liable for the loss that she

Other cases

Suppose that Fred took on the job of drawing up Wendy's will and that Lara stood to receive a substantial bequest under that will. Suppose further that Fred carelessly failed to draw up the will in such a way that it would be valid and this fact was only discovered after Wendy's death. The result was that Lara did not receive her bequest. It is well-established now that Fred will have committed the tort of negligence in relation to Lara in this case and Lara will normally be entitled to sue Fred for damages to compensate her for the loss of the legacy that she would have received under Wendy's will had it been correctly drawn up.[50]

But what is the position if Wendy's contract with Fred specified that Fred was not to be held liable in the event of his carelessly drawing up an ineffective will for Wendy? In such a case, it seems that Lara will be barred from suing Fred for damages: she will be bound by the exclusion clause in Fred and Wendy's contract.[51] The reason for this is that any claim brought by Lara against Fred for compensatory damages in the situation we are considering will be founded on the fact that Fred took on the task of preparing Wendy's will. Elementary fairness dictates that if Lara wants to take advantage of this fact and sue Fred for damages in respect of the losses suffered by her as a result of the way Fred performed that task, Lara must make allowance for the fact that Fred only took on that task on the understanding that he would not be held liable at all if he carelessly drew up an ineffective will for Wendy. Given this, it would be unfair to allow Lara to sue Fred unless, of course, Fred is barred by statute anyway from relying on the exclusion clause in his contract with Wendy to defeat Lara's claim.

Now suppose that Lara wanted a house built for her and she engaged Wendy to build it for her. Lara – having been impressed by a presentation from Fred – ordered Wendy to subcontract the work of laying the floors of the house to Fred; which Wendy duly did. The contract between Wendy and Fred specified that he would not be held liable if the floors of the house started to crack up more than a year after they were laid. Fred failed to do a good job of laying the floors of Lara's house and after two years the floors began to suffer from serious cracks. Now – there is no doubt in this situation that Fred has committed the tort of negligence in relation to Lara. He owed her a duty to lay the floors of her house with reasonable skill and care under the extended principle in *Hedley Byrne* and he breached that duty.[52] However, Lord Roskill thought in *Junior Books Ltd* v *Veitchi Co. Ltd* that in the case just described, Lara would be bound by the terms of the subcontract between Fred and Wendy 'in some circumstances'.[53] As that contract specified that Fred could

---

has suffered as a result of Fred's breach. In such a case, will Fred be able to argue that Lara is bound by the exclusion clause in his contract with Wendy – or does the principle established in *Morris* v *C W Martin* only apply to cases where an owner of goods' claim against a sub-bailee for the loss of his goods is based on a claim that there existed a bailment relationship between her and the sub-bailee? It is very difficult to say. For a discussion of the point, see Treitel 1999, 135–7.

[50] See above, pp. 148–51.

[51] *White* v *Jones* [1995] 2 AC 207, 268 (per Lord Goff). Again, this assumes that Fred will not be barred under the Unfair Contract Terms Act 1977 or some other statutory provision from taking advantage of the exclusion clause in his contract with Wendy to prevent Lara from suing him for damages.

[52] *Junior Books Ltd* v *Veitchi Co. Ltd* [1983] 1 AC 520, discussed above, pp. 130–1.

[53] Ibid., 546E-F.

not be held liable if Lara's floors cracked up more than a year after they were laid, Lara might therefore be barred from suing Fred for compensation for the losses she has suffered as a result of the floors cracking up *two* years after they were laid.[54]

Lord Roskill did not make it clear in *what* circumstances Lara would be bound by the terms of the Fred-Wendy contract. It seems to us that Lara would only be bound by those terms if Fred warned Lara before she ordered Wendy to subcontract the flooring work to him that he was only willing to lay her floors on the basis that he could not be held liable if the floors cracked up more than a year after they were laid.[55] If Lara was willing to take the risk that she would have no remedy against Fred if the floors of her house cracked up after a year, there seems little reason why the courts should assist Lara to obtain such a remedy.[56] However, if Lara had no idea that the Fred-Wendy contract would contain an exclusion clause under which Fred would be free from liability if the floors of Lara's house started to crack up more than a year after they were laid, it is hard to see why Lara's rights against Fred should be limited by such a clause.

ILLEGALITY

Suppose that A has committed a tort in relation to B and B has suffered various losses as a result. Suppose further that A's tort or B's losses arose out of, or in connection with, B's committing a criminal offence. In this case, A *may* be able to raise a defence of *illegality* (otherwise known as the defence of *ex turpi causa non oritur actio*)[57] to prevent B suing him for damages.

The law in this area has been complicated somewhat by the enactment of s 329 of the Criminal Justice Act 2003, which is intended to *supplement*[58] the common law (judge-made law) on when A will be entitled to rely on a defence of illegality to prevent B suing him for damages.[59] We will begin our discussion of this area of the law by explaining when A will be able to raise a defence of illegality under the common law to defeat B's claim. We will then discuss when A will be able to raise a defence under s 329 of the 2003 Act to defeat B's claim against him.

---

[54] We assume of course that Fred is not barred by statute from taking advantage of the exclusion clause in his contract with Wendy to prevent Lara suing him.

[55] Of course, if Fred warned Lara that he could not be relied on to do a very good job of laying the floors, Lara would probably not be able to sue Fred at all. Fred will only have owed Lara a duty to lay the floors with the degree of care and skill that he indicated to her that he could be relied on to lay them with (see above p. 130). So if Fred warned Lara he could not be relied on to do a very good job of laying the floors, Lara will face severe difficulties showing that he breached the (minimal) duty of care that he owed her in laying the floors.

[56] The same reason explains why Lara will not be allowed to sue Fred if Wendy sub-bails Lara's goods to Fred and agrees – with Lara's consent – that Fred will not be held liable if he fails to take reasonable steps to keep Lara's goods safe from harm and they are destroyed or damaged as a result.

[57] No action will arise out of an illegal act.

[58] This is made clear by s 329(6), which provides that the defence made available by s 329(4) 'is without prejudice to any other defence'.

[59] Section 329 will only come into force when the government makes an order bringing it into force (see s 336) and at that time of writing no such order has been made.

The position at common law[60]

Let's go back to the basic situation we were considering. That is, suppose that A has committed a tort in relation to B and B has suffered various losses as a result. And suppose further that A's tort or B's losses arose out of, or in connection with, B's committing a criminal offence. The courts have found it hard to agree in this situation on when *exactly* A will be entitled to rely on a defence of illegality to prevent B suing him in tort for damages. This is hardly surprising: *whatever* the exact circumstances of A and B's case, there will *always* be good reasons for *both* denying *and* allowing B's claim for damages here.

If the courts allowed B's claim here, they would offend people's sense of fairness. They would rightly say, 'Why should B be allowed to take advantage of our laws when she is not willing to abide by them? She should not be allowed to pick and choose. If she thought it was all right to break the law when she committed her criminal offence, she should not now be allowed to take advantage of the law and sue A for damages in respect of the losses she has suffered as a result of A's tort.' If, on the other hand, the courts did *not* allow B to sue A here, they might be seen to be winking at wrongdoing. They would treat A more leniently than other wrongdoers and in doing so might send out a message that what A did was 'not really' wrong, or not so wrong that A should be treated in the same way as other wrongdoers.

Given these competing imperatives, the courts have usually[61] attempted in illegality cases to steer a middle way between them, sometimes allowing the defence to be raised, sometimes not.[62] *Generally speaking,*[63] in the case we are considering, A *will* be allowed to rely on the defence of illegality to defeat any claim B might bring against him for compensation for the losses she has suffered as a result of his tort *if*: (1) the criminal offence committed by B was a serious one;[64]

---

[60] See, generally, Glofcheski 1999.

[61] Though see Sedley LJ's dissenting judgment in *Vellino v Chief Constable of Greater Manchester Police* [2002] 1 WLR 218, which suggests that in illegality cases a defendant should *never* be allowed to raise the defence of illegality to defeat a claim for damages that has been made against him. Instead, the damages payable to the claimant should be reduced for contributory negligence in appropriate situations: 'It is clear that since the passage of the Law Reform (Contributory Negligence) Act 1945 the power to apportion liability between claimant and defendant in tort actions of all kinds has afforded a far more appropriate tool for doing justice than the blunt instrument of [the defence of illegality]' (ibid., at [55]). It is significant that Sedley LJ is plainly contemptuous of public feelings that it would be unfair to allow a claimant in a tort case to sue for damages if the tort in question or the claimant's losses arose out of, or in connection with, the claimant's committing a criminal offence: 'The public conscience, an elusive thing, as often as not turns out to be an echo-chamber inhabited by journalists and public moralists' (ibid., at [60]). Such a judge will, of course, see little reason why a defendant in a tort case should ever be allowed to rely on the illegality defence.

[62] See *Saunders v Edwards* [1987] 1 WLR 1116, at 1134 (per Bingham LJ).

[63] *Important note.* There is one important exception to the rule set out in the text. This is that A will *not* be allowed to rely on the illegality defence if doing so would permit him to appropriate B's property in circumstances where he has no statutory authority to do so: *Webb v Chief Constable of Merseyside Police* [2000] QB 427.

[64] Defined by Sir Murray Stuart-Smith in *Vellino v Chief Constable of Greater Manchester* [2002] 1 WLR 218 as being one which is punishable with imprisonment (at [70]).

and (2) there was a very close connection between B's committing that offence *and* A's tort *or* the losses suffered by B as a result of A's tort.[65]

A case where this test was clearly *not* satisfied was *Saunders* v *Edwards*.[66] In that case, the defendant sold a second floor flat of his and all its contents to the claimants. The flat overlooked a flat roof which the defendant had converted into a roof terrace accessible from his flat. The defendant represented to the claimants that a right to use the roof terrace came with the flat. In fact, as the defendant knew, the defendant had no right to use the roof terrace and his landlord had frequently objected to his doing so. The defendant's fraudulent representation played a large part in the claimants' decision to acquire the flat. The defendant and the claimants agreed that the flat and its contents were worth £45,000. The claimants persuaded the defendant to agree to sell them the contents for £5,000 – far more than they were worth – so as to minimise the price paid by them for the flat. The claimants did this in an illegal attempt to avoid paying the higher rate of stamp duty on the flat which would have been payable had they purchased the flat for more than £40,000. After the claimants moved in they discovered the defendant's fraud and sued him in deceit for the loss of wealth they suffered in paying too much for the defendant's flat. The defendant argued that the claimants' illegal attempt to avoid paying the correct rate of stamp duty on the purchase of the flat meant they were barred from suing him for compensatory damages. Unsurprisingly, this argument was dismissed. There was no real connection between the defendant's tort and the claimants' tax evasion.

Two cases where this test clearly *was* satisfied were *Clunis* v *Camden and Islington Health Authority*[67] and *Vellino* v *Chief Constable of Greater Manchester Police*.[68] In the *Clunis* case, the claimant, who had a history of mental disorder and violent behaviour, stabbed Mr Jonathan Zito to death at a tube station. He pleaded guilty to manslaughter on grounds of diminished responsibility and was detained under the Mental Health Act 1983. The claimant sought to sue the defendant health authority in negligence so as to recover compensatory damages for the losses suffered by him in being detained under the 1983 Act. He claimed that the defendant health authority had owed him a duty to treat his mental health problems with a professional degree of care and skill and that had the defendant health authority not breached this duty – as he claimed it had – he would not have stabbed Mr Zito to death and been detained under the Mental Health Act. The Court of Appeal held that even if the defendant health authority had owed the claimant a duty of care and breached that duty, the claimant's claim for damages still could not succeed: it was barred on the ground of illegality.[69] There was obviously a very close connection between the serious criminal act committed by the claimant in this case – manslaughter

[65] Ibid.; see also *Cross* v *Kirkby*, The Times, 5 April 2000.
[66] [1987] 1 WLR 1116.
[67] [1998] QB 978 (followed in *Worrall* v *British Railways Board* [1999] CLY 1413).
[68] [2002] 1 WLR 218.
[69] The House of Lords refused leave to appeal: [1998] 1 WLR 1093.

– and the losses for which the claimant was seeking compensation – that is, the losses associated with the claimant's being imprisoned for manslaughter.[70]

In the *Vellino* case, it will be recalled, the claimant was a career criminal who was seriously injured when, in an attempt to escape police custody, he jumped out of the kitchen window of his flat. His claim for damages was dismissed on the ground that the police had not owed him a duty to stop him trying to escape. However, Sir Murray Stuart-Smith went on to hold that even if the police had owed him such a duty and breached it, the claimant would still have been barred from suing the police for damages in respect of his injuries on the ground of illegality. There was obviously again a very close connection between the serious criminal offence that the claimant committed in the *Vellino* case – that is, attempting to escape police custody – and the injuries for which the claimant was seeking compensation.

However, not all cases are as easy as these. The following cases are generally regarded as being more marginal: whether or not the defence of illegality can be pleaded in these kinds of cases will depend on all the circumstances.

(1) *Provocation.* Suppose that Tom provoked Dawn to shoot him by burgling her house. Suppose further that Dawn's shooting Tom cannot be justified on the ground of self-defence. If Tom sues Dawn for damages in respect of the injuries he sustained as a result of Dawn's shooting him, will Dawn be able to raise a defence of illegality to his claim? The Court of Appeal made it clear in *Cross* v *Kirkby*[71] that Dawn will only be able to rely on the defence of illegality if there was a sufficiently close connection between Tom's burgling Dawn's house and Dawn's shooting him.

Such a connection was not made out in *Revill* v *Newbery*.[72] In that case, it will be recalled, the claimant was shot by the defendant when he attempted to break into a shed on the defendant's allotment. The Court of Appeal held that the claimant was *not* barred from suing the defendant for compensatory damages on the ground of illegality. The Court of Appeal explained this decision in *Cross* v *Kirkby* on the basis that there wasn't a sufficiently close connection between the claimant's attempting to break into the defendant's shed and the defendant's shooting him. In shooting the claimant, the defendant was guilty of a gross overreaction to the claimant's conduct.

It might have been different in *Revill* if the claimant had been breaking into the shed in order to beat up the defendant. In such a case, while it might have been unreasonable – and therefore tortious – for the defendant to have shot the claimant, one would still be able to understand why the defendant acted in the

---

[70] The decision in *Clunis*, it should be noted, runs counter to that in *Meah* v *McCreamer* [1985] 1 All ER 367. In that case, the claimant was involved in a car crash that was caused by the defendant's negligence. The injuries sustained by the claimant in the car crash had the effect of changing the claimant's personality for the worse, with the result that he sexually assaulted two women. The claimant was imprisoned and recovered damages from the defendant for the losses suffered by him as a result of his being imprisoned. However, unaccountably, the judge in *Meah* v *McCreamer* was not invited to dismiss the claimant's claim on the ground of illegality. Had the judge been so invited, he would – one would hope – have accepted the invitation and dismissed the claimant's claim.

[71] The Times, 5 April 2000.

[72] [1996] QB 567.

way he did. There would then have been a sufficiently close connection between the claimant's criminal act in breaking into the shed and the defendant's shooting him so as to allow the defendant to rely on the defence of illegality to defeat the claimant's claim for damages.

Some support for this comes from the case of *Cross v Kirkby* itself. In that case, it will be recalled, Cross – a hunt saboteur – attacked Kirkby – a farmer who was allowing the local hunt to ride across his lands – with a baseball bat. Kirkby seized the baseball bat and hit Cross with it on the head. When Cross sued Kirkby, the Court of Appeal dismissed Cross's claim on the ground that Kirkby had acted reasonably in self-defence in striking Cross. The Court of Appeal went on to hold that even if Kirkby *had* acted unreasonably in striking Cross, they would have still allowed Kirkby to rely on the defence of illegality to defeat Cross's claim for damages. There would still have been a sufficiently close connection between Cross's conduct and Kirkby's striking him.

(2) *Joint venture.* In *National Coal Board v England*, Lord Asquith considered what the position would be if 'A and B, agree to open a safe by means of explosives, and A so negligently handles the explosive charge as to injure B'.[73] His Lordship thought that in this case A would be able to raise a defence of illegality to any claim B might make against A for damages. In this case there would be a very close connection between A's tort and the illegal venture that A and B were engaged on at the time A committed his tort, as that tort was committed in the course of furthering the illegal venture.[74] Lord Asquith thought it would be different if 'A and B are proceeding to . . . premises which they intend burglariously to enter, and before they enter them, B picks A's pocket and steals his watch'.[75] In this sort of case there would be less of a connection between A's tort and the illegal venture that A and B were engaged on; accordingly, Lord Asquith thought that in this second case, A would *not* be entitled to rely on a defence of illegality to defeat B's claim against him for damages.

(3) *Illegal employment.* In *Hewison v Meridian Shipping Services Pte Ltd*,[76] the claimant worked for the defendant shipping company as a crane operator. The claimant suffered from epilepsy and should therefore not have been put in charge of a crane. However, the claimant concealed his epilepsy from the defendants, thereby committing a criminal offence under s 16 of the Theft Act 1968.[77] Due to the defendants' negligence, the claimant was injured on the job. The injuries suffered by the claimant caused him to have three epileptic fits. As a result, the defendants became aware of the claimant's condition and were forced to dismiss

---

[73] [1954] AC 403, at 429.
[74] The decision of the Court of Appeal in *Pitts v Hunt* [1991] 2 QB 24 bears out Lord Asquith's point. The claimant and defendant in that case went joyriding on a motorbike – the defendant drove the bike and the claimant travelled in the pillion car attached to the motorbike. The claimant urged the defendant to drive faster and faster and when the defendant complied, he crashed the bike and the claimant was injured. The claimant's claim for damages in respect of his injuries was thrown out on the ground of illegality – there was a very close connection between the defendant's negligent driving and the joint illegal venture which the claimant and the defendant were engaged on at the time the defendant negligently crashed the bike.
[75] [1954] AC 403, at 429.
[76] [2002] EWCA Civ 1821.
[77] The offence of obtaining a pecuniary advantage by deception.

him. The claimant sued the defendants for damages in respect of the losses that their negligence had caused him to suffer.

The Court of Appeal allowed the claimant to sue for damages in respect of the physical injuries he had suffered as a result of the defendants' negligence. No defence of illegality could be raised to prevent the claimant suing for such damages – and this was so even though the claimant would not have suffered those injuries had he not committed a serious criminal offence in lying to the defendants about his medical condition.[78] The Court of Appeal obviously thought there wasn't a sufficiently close connection between the claimant's lies and either the defendants' negligence or the injuries suffered by the claimant as a result of the defendants' negligence.

But the Court of Appeal reached a different conclusion when it considered the claimant's claim to be compensated for the money he would have earned working for the defendants in the future had he not been negligently injured by the defendants. (Had he not been injured, he argued, his epilepsy would not have become known to the defendants and he would not have been sub-sequently dismissed by the defendants.) In order to earn that money, the claimant would have had to continue deceiving the defendants about his medical condition, and in so doing he would have committed a serious criminal offence. So the loss of (future) earnings suffered by the claimant as a result of the defendants' negligence was inextricably linked to his willingness to commit a serious criminal offence in the future. Given this, the Court of Appeal ruled by 2 to 1 that the defendants would be entitled to raise a defence of illegality to the claimant's claim to be compensated for that loss.[79]

The position under s 329 of the Criminal Justice Act 2003

Section 329 of the 2003 Act provides that if: (1) B is suing A for damages on the basis that A committed the tort of assault, battery or false imprisonment in relation to B by doing x;[80] *and* (2) B's actions round about the time A did x resulted in B's being convicted of an imprisonable offence;[81] *and* (3) A did x because he honestly believed at the time: (*i*) that B was about to commit an offence or had committed an offence or had just committed an offence and because he honestly believed that it was necessary; *and* (*ii*) that it was necessary to do x in order to protect himself or another person; or to protect or to recover property; or to prevent the commission or continuance of an offence; or to

---

[78] Had he not lied, he would not have been employed by the defendants and would therefore not have been in a position to be injured as a result of their negligence.

[79] It is hard to see why Ward LJ, who dissented, thought the claimant's claim for this loss of (future) earnings might have merit. After all if Ian beat up a burglar, Gary, so badly that Gary had to give up his 'career' as a burglar, he could hardly be allowed to sue for the money he would have made in the future had he been allowed to continue burgling people's houses. Perhaps the real reason for Ward LJ's dissent was that he did not think that the claimant's offence in lying about his health was actually that serious.

[80] Section 329(1)(a), (8)(a).

[81] Section 329(1)(b). If conditions (*a*) and (*b*) are satisfied, then B will have to secure a court's permission before he is allowed to sue A: s 1(2).

apprehend B or secure B's conviction of having committed an offence;[82] *and* (4) A's doing *x* was not grossly disproportionate to whatever B did, then A will be able to raise a defence to B's claim against him.[83]

Two points may be made about this provision. First, it is unlikely that it adds anything to the existing law on when someone will be entitled to rely on a defence of illegality to defeat a claim in tort that has been made against him. Suppose, for example, that Lara wants to sue Eric in tort for damages for some loss that she has suffered. Suppose further that Eric is not entitled to rely on a defence of illegality under the common law to defeat Lara's claim because he cannot establish that there was a very close connection between Lara's committing a serious offence and Eric's tort or the losses suffered by Lara as a result of Eric's tort. In such a case, it is unlikely that Eric would be able to rely on s 329 to defeat Lara's claim against him for damages.

Secondly, the fact that s 329 only operates in cases where a claimant sues a defendant for damages on the ground that the defendant committed the tort of assault or battery or false imprisonment in relation to her makes s 329 very easy to evade. Suppose, for example, that Gary breaks into Karen's house and in order to defend her property, Karen shoots Gary in the leg. Obviously, if Gary sues Karen for damages on the basis that she committed a battery by shooting him in the leg, then s 329 will come into play. However, Gary could easily evade the effect of s 329 by suing Karen in negligence, claiming that 'You owed me a duty not to discharge your gun in my direction.' The fact that Karen shot Gary *deliberately* would not of course stop Gary suing Karen in negligence – a deliberate action can amount to negligence.[84]

LIMITATION

Suppose A has committed a tort in relation to B and B has suffered various losses as a result. If B delays too long before suing A for damages to compensate her for the fact that she has suffered these losses, she may be barred on *grounds of limitation* from suing A for such damages. There are two reasons B will be barred from suing A for damages if she delays too long before bringing an action against A. First, it would be unfair on A if B could sue him for damages in respect of the losses that he caused her to suffer many years after he caused her to suffer those losses. A would constantly have the threat of litigation hanging over his head and, as a result, would find it difficult to make long-term plans or decisions about the future.

Secondly, the interests of justice would not be served if B were free to sue A for damages in respect of the losses that A caused B to suffer many years after A caused

---

[82] Section 329(4)(a), (5).

[83] Section 329(4)(b).

[84] See above, pp. 62–3. If this were not so, it is hard to see what tort would be committed if A deliberately left out a poisoned drink for B to drink and B was made sick drinking it. The decision of the House of Lords in *Wainwright* v *Home Office* [2003] 3 WLR 1137 means that one can no longer say, 'the tort in *Wilkinson* v *Downton*': see above, p. 64, n. 18. The tort committed by A in this situation must be negligence, or nothing.

B to suffer those losses. It is in the interests of justice that suits be brought promptly when witnesses with evidence relevant to the suit are still available, when documents relevant to the suit are still easily to hand and when the memories of all involved in the suit are still fresh and uncorrupted by the passage of time. The longer the period of time before a claim is brought to court, the more likely that relevant witnesses will have died or disappeared, that relevant documents will have been destroyed or lost and that the memories of those involved in the case will have become stale and unreliable. Thus: the longer the period of time before a claim is brought to court, the harder it is likely to be to decide correctly whether or not that claim has any merit.

A detailed account of when the victim of a tort will be barred on grounds of limitation from suing the person who committed that tort for compensatory damages is beyond the scope of this book. However, a brief summary of the law in this area can be given. The *general rule* is that if A has committed a tort in relation to B, B will be barred from bringing an action against A in respect of that tort if she does not sue A within *six years* of the date she was first entitled to obtain a remedy in respect of A's tort.[85]

However, this general rule is subject to various qualifications.

(1) *Ignorance.* What if B was first entitled to obtain a remedy in respect of A's tort on 4 July 2005 – but she only found out that she was entitled to obtain such a remedy on 1 August 2011? As a general rule, if it was A's fault that B did not know she was entitled to sue A for committing his tort until 1 August 2010, then the limitation period will be extended and B will have six years from 1 August 2010 to bring an action against A, not six years from 4 July 2005.[86]

If it wasn't A's fault that B was left in ignorance for so long that she was entitled to sue A, then B will normally be stuck – the limitation period for suing A having elapsed on 4 July 2011, she will be barred from suing A for damages. However, it is different if the tort committed by A was negligence and A's negligence caused B to suffer various actionable losses which B only found out about on 1 August 2011. In such a case, B will have three years to sue A from the date that she could first have reasonably been expected to find out about those losses. So if B could only have been reasonably expected to find out about the actionable losses which A's tort caused her to suffer on 15 June 2009, she will have until 15 June 2012 to sue A.[87]

---

[85] Limitation Act 1980, s 2. Assume that A committed his tort on 1 January 2005. If that tort was actionable *per se* (that is, the tort committed by A was actionable even if it did not cause B to suffer any actionable loss), then B will *normally* have until 1 January 2011 to sue A for committing that tort. The reason for this is that because A's tort was actionable *per se* B was entitled to obtain a remedy in respect of that tort as soon as it was committed. If, on the other hand, A's tort was not actionable *per se* (that is, the tort committed by A was only actionable if it caused B to suffer an actionable loss), then B will *normally* have six years from the date she first suffered an actionable loss as a result of A's tort to sue A for committing that tort. So if A's tort was not actionable *per se* and B first suffered an actionable loss as a result of A's tort on 25 December 2010, B will *normally* have until 25 December 2016 to sue A for committing that tort. The reason for this is that because A's tort was not actionable *per se*, the first time B was entitled to obtain a remedy in respect of A's tort was on 25 December 2010.

[86] Limitation Act 1980, ss 32(1)(b), 32(2). It appears this qualification to the general rule does not apply to actions under the Defective Premises Act 1972: *Warner* v *Basildon Development Corp.* (1991) 7 Const LJ 146.

[87] Limitation Act 1980, s 14A. This rule is not meant to prejudice the limitation period for suing A that

(2) *Physical injury.* If A has committed a tort in relation to B and B has suffered some kind of physical injury as a result, a special limitation regime will sometimes apply to B's action against A. This will be the case if A's tort involved 'negligence, nuisance or [a] breach of duty'.[88] If it did, then B will normally have three years from the date she was injured as a result of A's tort to sue A for damages in respect of that injury. There are two exceptions to this rule. First, if – once B was injured – it took some time for her to find out that A had caused her to suffer that injury, she will have three years from the date she found out that A had injured her to sue him.[89] Secondly, if the applicable limitation period for suing A in respect of B's injury has elapsed, the courts may nevertheless allow B to sue A for compensation for her injury if it would be 'equitable' to do so.[90]

(3) *Defamation, malicious falsehood and deceit.* If A has committed one of these torts in relation to B, a special limitation period will apply. In cases of defamation and malicious falsehood, B will normally have only a year to sue A from the moment she was first entitled to obtain a remedy in respect of A's tort.[91] In the case of deceit, B will have six years from the time A's deceit first came to light to sue A.[92]

THE IMPACT OF ARTICLE 6 OF THE EUROPEAN CONVENTION ON HUMAN RIGHTS

Thus stands the law at the moment on when the victim of a tort will be barred from suing the person who committed that tort for compensatory damages. However, for the sake of completeness we should note one further point. Suppose that A has committed a tort in relation to B but he has a defence to being sued for damages by B. Call the defence that A can raise to any claim B might make against him, *defence x*. In such a case, B may be able to argue that allowing A to rely on defence *x* to defeat her claim for damages will violate her

---

B would enjoy under the general rule. So if A breached a duty of care owed to B on 1 January 2005 and B first suffered an actionable loss as a result of that breach on 1 April 2006 and she could have reasonably been expected to find out about that loss on 1 March 2008, B will have until 1 April 2012 to sue A for the losses suffered by her as a result of his negligence – she won't have to bring her action against A by 1 March 2011. It should also be noted that the extension of time for bringing an action in negligence afforded by this section is subject to a 'long stop' limitation period which will expire 15 years after the victim of another's negligence was first entitled to obtain a remedy in respect of that negligence: s 14B. So if A breached a duty of care owed to B on 1 January 2005 and B first suffered an actionable loss as a result of that breach on 1 April 2006, but B could not reasonably have been expected to find out about that loss until 1 February 2020, B will only have until 1 April 2021 to sue A – the limitation period for suing A will not be extended until 1 February 2023.

[88] Limitation Act 1980, s 11(1). The House of Lords held in *Stubbings* v *Webb* [1993] AC 498 (discussed above, pp. 18–19) that this provision does not cover cases where A has committed a tort involving a trespass to B's person.

[89] Limitation Act 1980, s 11(1).

[90] Section 33.

[91] Section 4A. However, the limitation period may be extended under s 14A, discussed above at pp. 519–20. If the applicable limitation period for B's suing A has expired, the courts may still allow B to sue A if it would be 'equitable' to do so: s 32A.

[92] Section 32(1)(a).

rights under Article 6(1) of the European Convention on Human Rights.[93] If this is right, then the courts will be required under s 6 of the Human Rights Act 1998 not to allow A to rely on defence *x* to defeat B's claim.

If B wants to establish that her Article 6(1) rights will be violated if A is allowed to rely on defence *x* to defeat B's claim against him for damages, she will have to do two things. First of all, she will have to show that allowing A to rely on defence *x* to defeat B's claim *could* violate her rights under Article 6(1). If she can do this, let's say that her case is *covered* by Article 6(1). If she can show that her claim is covered by Article 6(1), she will then have to show *either* that allowing A to rely on defence *x* to defeat her claim will serve no legitimate purpose *or* that allowing A to rely on defence *x* to defeat her claim will serve a legitimate purpose but in a disproportionate way. If she can do this, then B's Article 6(1) rights *will* be violated if A is allowed to rely on defence *x* to defeat B's claim.

When will a claimant who wants to sue someone else but is unable to do so be able to establish that her case is covered by Article 6(1)? This is a very difficult question and the cases on this issue are currently in a state of some confusion. However the following points can be made.

(1) A claimant cannot argue that her Article 6(1) rights have been violated just because she has not been allowed to sue a defendant.[94]

(2) The law on the scope of Article 6(1) draws a distinction between cases where a claimant has been prevented from suing a defendant because the domestic law governing her case put a *procedural* bar in the way of the claimant suing the defendant and cases where a claimant has been prevented from suing a defendant because the domestic law governing her case put a *substantive* bar in the way of her suing the defendant.

(3) A claimant who has been prevented from suing a defendant will be able to argue that her case is covered by Article 6(1) if she was prevented from suing the defendant because the law put a *procedural* bar in the way of her suing the defendant.[95] So, for example, a prisoner who was prevented from suing his prison governor for libel because, under UK law, he was not allowed access to a solicitor was able to establish that Article 6(1) covered his case.[96] Similarly, the case of a claimant who was sexually abused by the defendant as a child and was prevented from suing him for damages on grounds of limitation was held to be covered by Article 6(1).[97] The law on limitation of actions created a procedural bar to her claim.[98]

---

[93] Article 6(1), of course, provides that 'In the determination of his civil rights and obligations ... everyone is entitled to a fair and public hearing within a reasonable time by an independent and impartial tribunal established by law.'

[94] *Z* v *United Kingdom* [2001] 2 FLR 612, at [88].

[95] *James* v *United Kingdom* (1986) 8 EHRR 123, at [81].

[96] *Golder* v *UK* (1975) 1 EHRR 524, discussed above, pp. 84–5. The prisoner's Article 6(1) rights were found to have been violated.

[97] *Stubbings* v *United Kingdom* [1997] 1 FLR 105. The European Court of Human Rights went on to find that the claimant's Article 6(1) rights had not actually been violated: the laws on limitation which prevented the claimant suing the defendant pursued a legitimate goal and in a proportionate way.

[98] See *Matthews* v *Ministry of Defence* [2003] 1 AC 1163, at [128] (per Lord Walker): 'Bars arising from statutes of limitation are ... generally regarded as procedural.'

(4) By contrast, Article 6(1) will not cover the case where a claimant has been prevented from suing a defendant because the law put a *substantive* bar in the way of her suing the defendant. If the claimant's claim against the defendant failed because she had *no right* to sue the defendant under the law applicable to her claim, then we would *normally* say that there existed a *substantive* bar which prevented her from suing the defendant. However, it is clear from the decided cases that a claimant whose claim against a defendant has failed because she had no right to sue him will *sometimes* be able to argue that the bar on her suing the defendant that existed in her case was actually *procedural* in nature and *not* substantive.

(5) The European Court of Human Rights (ECtHR for short) has held in a number of cases that a claimant who has been prevented from suing a defendant because she had no right to sue him will be able to argue that a *procedural* bar stood in the way of her suing the defendant if the reason why she had no right to sue him was that the domestic law governing her claim conferred an *immunity* on the defendant from being sued by the claimant.[99] These cases take their inspiration from the following *dictum* of the ECtHR in *Fayed* v *United Kingdom*: 'it would not be consistent with the . . . basic principle underlying Article [6(1)] . . . – namely that civil claims must be capable of being submitted to a judge for adjudication – if, for example, a State could, without restraint or control by the Convention enforcement bodies, remove from the jurisdiction of the civil courts a whole range of civil claims or confer immunities from civil liability on large groups or categories of persons . . .'[100]

(6) The ECtHR has never explained when exactly a defendant can be said to enjoy an *immunity* from being sued by a claimant. A close examination of the relevant case law seems to suggest that a defendant will enjoy an immunity from being sued by a claimant if: (*a*) the claimant wants to bring an action against the defendant which is well recognised under the domestic law governing her case; *and* (*b*) the domestic law governing the claimant's case provides that the claimant has no right to bring such an action against the defendant, but it does so for reasons that have nothing to do with the merits of the claimant's case.[101] If (*a*) and (*b*) are made out then, according to the ECtHR, the claimant will be able to argue that the domestic law governing her case has put a *procedural* bar in the way of her suing the defendant and that therefore her case is covered by Article 6(1).[102]

---

[99] *Tinnelly & Sons Ltd* v *United Kingdom* (1998) 27 EHRR 249, at [71]–[72]; *Al-Adsani* v *United Kingdom* (2002) 34 EHRR 273, at [46]–[48]; *Fogarty* v *United Kingdom* (2001) 34 EHRR 302, at [25]–[26], *McElhinney* v *Ireland* (2001) 34 EHRR 322, at [23]–[25].

[100] (1994) 18 EHRR 393, at [65]. It may be that the ECtHR was, in saying this, attempting to transform Article 6(1) into a European equivalent of the Fourteenth Amendment to the Constitution of the United States, which provides that no State shall 'deny to any person within its jurisdiction the equal protection of the laws'.

[101] See cases cited above, n. 99.

[102] It could be argued that our account of the scope of Article 6(1) is inconsistent with the decision of the ECtHR in *Powell and Rayner* v *United Kingdom* (1990) 12 EHRR 355. In that case the claimants were prevented from suing the defendants in private nuisance because of s 76(1) of the Civil Aviation Act 1982, which provides that no claims in private nuisance can brought in respect of 'the flight of an aircraft over any property at a height above the ground which is . . .

(7) The House of Lords has, however, taken a much narrower view than the ECtHR as to when a claimant who has no right to sue a defendant can argue that the bar which the law places on her suing the defendant is procedural in nature, rather than substantive.

In *Matthews v Ministry of Defence*,[103] the claimant was a sailor who suffered various asbestos related injuries as a result of working in the Royal Navy between 1955 and 1968. He sued the Ministry of Defence for compensation. Under the law that was applicable to his claim, he would have had no right to sue the Ministry of Defence for compensation *if*: (*a*) his injuries were suffered as a result of the condition of any ship used by the armed services; *and* (*b*) the relevant Secretary of State issued a certificate to that effect.[104] Such a certificate was issued in the claimant's case and as a result his claim for damages was thrown out.[105]

The claimant argued that his rights under Article 6(1) were violated when his claim was thrown out. The House of Lords disagreed: they held the bar which prevented the claimant suing the Ministry of Defence in this case was substantive, not procedural, in nature and that therefore the claimant's case was not covered by Article 6(1). The House of Lords was prepared to admit that a *no right* case might in certain circumstances be covered by Article 6(1). At the same time, it is clear that their Lordships took a very narrow view of what those circumstances might be. Lord Hoffmann suggested that a *no right* case would be covered by Article 6(1) if the reason why the claimant had no right to sue a defendant was that the government had been given an 'arbitrary power' to declare that the claimant had no right to sue the defendant and thereby stop her case in its tracks.[106] Lord Millett took the view that a *no right* case would be covered by Article 6(1) if the reason why the claimant had no right to sue the defendant was that the government had passed a statute stripping people like

---

reasonable'. It was held that the bar on the claimants' suing the defendants here was a substantive one and that Article 6(1) did not therefore cover the claimants' case. However, two points can be made in response to this. First, it is not clear that the bar which existed in *Powell and Rayner* had nothing to with the merits of the claimants' case: if the flight of aircraft over the claimants' property was 'reasonable' then that would weaken the strength of the claimants' claim that they were entitled to sue the defendants in private nuisance. Secondly, even if the first point does not hold good, the decision in *Powell and Rayner* antedated the decision in *Fayed*, and it may well be that if a case like *Powell and Rayner* came up again today, the decision would be very different. (Contrast, for example, *Agee v United Kingdom* (1976) 7 D&R 164, where the European Commission of Human Rights ruled pre-*Fayed* that the absolute privilege enjoyed by MPs from being sued in libel or slander was not covered by Article 6(1) because it created a substantive bar to such claims being brought against MPs, and *A v United Kingdom* (2003) 36 EHRR 51, decided post-*Fayed*, where the ECtHR was content to assume that Article 6(1) applied to cases where a claimant was prevented from suing an MP in libel on grounds of absolute privilege.)

[103] [2003] 1 AC 1163.

[104] Crown Proceedings Act 1947, s 10. This provision was later repealed by the Crown Proceedings Act 1987, and therefore does not figure in our account of the scope of Crown immunity set out above, at p. 497. As the claimant's injuries in *Matthews* were suffered by him as a result of his working in the Royal Navy between 1955 and 1968, his claim for compensation for those injuries was governed by s 10.

[105] Though the issuing of the certificate meant that the claimant became entitled to a pension which would help compensate him for the injuries he had suffered.

[106] [2003] 1 AC 1163, at [35].

her of the right to sue people like the defendant for reasons which were unrelated to the reason why people like her had a right to sue people like the defendant in the first place.[107]

In so ruling, the House of Lords took the view that the object of Article 6(1) is to prevent the government arbitrarily interfering with people's enjoyment of the rights that they are afforded under the law – either through using procedural tricks designed to prevent them getting a full hearing of their case or by using its legislative power to strip people of rights to sue that they would otherwise enjoy. Seen in this way, it was obvious that the claimant's case in *Matthews* was not covered by Article 6(1). Section 10 of the Crown Proceedings Act 1947 was not intended to deprive people of any rights that they previously enjoyed under statute or the common law. Instead it preserved, in part, the old rule that people had *no rights* to sue the Crown, while at the same time ensuring – through the certification procedure – that those prejudiced by the preservation of that rule would obtain an alternative means of compensation for the harm they had suffered through the award of a pension.[108]

(8) The difference between the position taken by the ECtHR as to when a *no right* case will be covered by Article 6(1) and the position taken by the House of Lords in *Matthews* v *Ministry of Defence* may be better appreciated through the use of a concrete example. We have already seen that if Paul libels Karen and subsequently dies, Karen will not be allowed to sue Paul's estate for damages.[109] Whether or not Karen will be able to argue that this violates her rights under Article 6(1) will depend on whether the bar on Karen's suing Paul's estate here is procedural or substantive in nature.

It is not hard to imagine that the ECtHR would rule that the bar here is *procedural* in nature: Karen wants to sue Paul's estate for damages in defamation – a cause of action which is well acknowledged in UK law – but she is prevented from doing so by s 1(1) of the Law Reform (Miscellaneous Provisions) Act 1934 and for reasons which have nothing to do with the merits of her claim. So the ECtHR might well rule that Article 6(1) covers Karen's claim here.[110] Equally, it seems to follow from the decision in *Matthews* that the House of Lords would rule that there exists a *substantive* bar in the way of Karen's suing Paul's estate here. Section 1(1) of the 1934 Act does not deprive people like Karen of any rights that people like her previously enjoyed. Instead it preserves, in part, the old rule that the victim of a tort would have *no rights* to sue the person who committed that tort if he died after he committed that tort. So the House of Lords – if asked – might well rule that Article 6(1) does *not* cover Karen's case here, with the result that Karen will *never* be able to claim that the

---

[107] Ibid., at [79].

[108] Ibid., at [73] (per Lord Hope).

[109] See above, pp. 496–7.

[110] Of course, if Article 6(1) does cover Karen's case here, dismissing Karen's claim will not necessarily violate her Article 6(1) rights: it depends on whether dismissing her claim will serve a legitimate purpose and in a proportionate way. It is hard to think that it will. Given this, the issue of whether Article 6(1) covers Karen's claim becomes vitally important – if it is conceded that Article 6(1) covers Karen's claim, it seems that dismissing Karen's claim against Paul's estate *will* violate her Article 6(1) rights.

courts will violate her Article 6(1) rights if they throw out her claim, no matter how silly or disproportionate the rule embodied in s 1(1) of the 1934 Act is.

Now that we have a firmer grasp of what sort of cases are covered by Article 6(1), we can return to our original case – where A has committed a tort in relation to B but can raise a defence *x* to any claim that B might make against him for damages. When will B be able to argue that her claim against A is covered by Article 6(1)? It is clear that if the defence relied on by A to defeat B's claim is a limitation defence then B's case will be covered by Article 6(1). B will have no problem establishing that the bar on her suing A created by that defence is procedural in nature. It is much more uncertain what the position is in relation to the other defences that A might raise to defeat B's claim. Normally one would think that these defences create a substantive bar to B's suing A: if A is able to take advantage of any of these defences, B will have *no right* to sue A. But, as we have seen, even some *no right* cases will be treated by the courts as cases where the law has placed a *procedural* bar in the way of a claimant suing a defendant. Can any of the defences considered here be treated as creating a procedural bar in the way of B's suing A?

If we follow the ECtHR's approach to the question of when a *no right* case will involve a procedural bar, then the following defences might well be regarded as creating a procedural bar to B's suing A if they are relied upon by A to defeat B's claim: Crown immunity, witness immunity, trade union immunity and abuse of process. All of these defences will operate to prevent B from bringing a tort claim for damages against A – a claim which is well acknowledged under UK law – and for reasons that have nothing to do with the merits of B's claim. The defences of volenti, exclusion of liability and illegality will also prevent B bringing a tort claim for damages against A but the defences in those cases will be centrally concerned with the merits of B's claim.

If, on the other hand, we follow the House of Lords' approach to this question, then trade union immunity is probably the only defence (other than the obvious one of limitation) that could be said to raise a procedural bar to B's suing A. It could be argued that Parliament, in creating this immunity, stripped people of rights they previously enjoyed under the common law. If this is right then, under the House of Lords' approach to the scope of Article 6(1), cases where a defendant is able to take advantage of the defence of trade union immunity may well be covered by Article 6(1). An employer who is prevented from suing a trade union for damages under s 219 of the Trade Union and Labour Relations (Consolidation) Act 1992 might therefore be able to argue that his Article 6(1) rights have been violated – though whether they have or not will depend on whether s 219 serves a legitimate purpose in a proportionate way.[111] By contrast, it is hard to argue that the existence of defences such as witness immunity, crown immunity, volenti, exclusion of liability and illegality strip people of rights that they previously enjoyed before those defences were created. The defences came with the rights: they did not post-date them.

So it is still uncertain what effect Article 6(1) of the European Convention

---

[111] It is likely, though, that s 219 would survive this process of scrutiny, given that it is so severely qualified.

on Human Rights will have on the availability of the defences dealt with in this chapter. If the House of Lords' view as to the scope of Article 6(1) is correct, then the effect should be very small – Article 6(1) will not prevent a tortfeasor relying on most of the defences set out in this chapter. If the ECtHR's view is followed, then the impact of Article 6(1) should be more far-reaching.

30

CAUSATION

Suppose that A has committed a tort in relation to B. If B wants to sue A for compensatory damages, the very first thing she will have to show is that A's tort *caused* her to suffer some kind of loss. Before we go on to describe the principles that the courts will use to determine whether or not A's tort has caused B to suffer any kind of loss, it is worth cataloguing the different kinds of loss that A's tort might have caused B to suffer.

TYPES OF LOSS

There are many different kinds of loss that A's tort may have caused B to suffer.

(1) *Physical injury*. A's tort could have caused B to suffer some kind of physical injury. The term 'physical injury', as it is used here, is fairly straightforward. B will suffer a form of physical injury if her leg breaks or she develops cancer. She will also – seemingly – suffer a form of physical injury if she becomes pregnant.[1] However, the concept of 'physical injury', as it is used here, does not cover *death*.[2] If A commits a tort in relation to B and B dies *instantaneously* as a result, B will not – for our purposes here – suffer a physical injury or, indeed, any other kind of loss. It makes no sense to say that B's dying means that she *has* suffered a loss as a result of A's tort – B is no longer around for her to experience her death as a loss. However, if A stabs B and B dies of her wounds six months later, then A's tort in stabbing B will have caused B to suffer a form of physical injury and associated losses such as distress; and an action can be brought for compensation for these losses even after B's death.[3]

(2) *Property damage*. A's tort could have caused property in which B had an interest to be destroyed or damaged.[4]

---

[1] See above, p. 70.

[2] It will be recalled that the term 'physical injury' *does* cover death in the context of the physical danger principle, which we identified as underlying the decision in *Donoghue* v *Stevenson* [1932] AC 562: see above, p. 67.

[3] See above, p. 496.

[4] The fact that property damages counts as a loss in its own right helps to explain why a claimant whose property has been wrongfully damaged will still be entitled to sue for substantial damages even if she has not actually suffered any loss *as a result* of the property being damaged: see *Mediana (Owners of Steamship)* v *Comet (Owners of Lightship)* [1900] AC 113 (the claimants' lightship was damaged as a result of the defendants' negligence and had to be taken out of service to be repaired, during which time its place was taken by a substitute lightship maintained by the defendants for exactly this purpose: the claimants were held entitled to sue the defendants for substantial damages to compensate them for the (temporary) loss of their lightship, even though they did not suffer any further loss as a result of suffering that loss).

(3) *Psychiatric illness.* A's tort could have caused B to develop a psychiatric illness – that is, a form of mental harm that is regarded as amounting to a psychiatric illness by the medical profession.

(4) *Damage to reputation.* A's tort could have caused B's good name to be impaired or ruined.

(5) *Imprisonment.* A's tort could have caused B to be locked up. This will obviously be the case if the tort committed by A was false imprisonment. But A could have caused B to be locked up by committing some other kind of tort. In *Meah* v *McCreamer*,[5] it will be recalled, the claimant was involved in a car crash that was negligently caused by the defendant. (The claimant was in the defendant's car and the defendant was drunk at the time of the car crash.) The claimant sustained serious head injuries in the accident that caused his personality to change for the worse. The claimant went on to attack two women and was sent to prison as a result. The court held that the defendant's negligence had caused the claimant to be locked up and the claimant (wrongly, in our view)[6] recovered damages for his imprisonment.

(6) *Distress.* A's tort could have caused B distress. We use the term 'distress' here to cover not only anxiety and upset but also pain and suffering. There are a variety of ways in which A's tort could have caused B distress. A's tort could have caused B to suffer some kind of personal injury with the result that B experienced some degree of pain and suffering. Similarly, A's tort could have caused B's property to be damaged with the result that B suffered a great deal of distress.[7] Alternatively, A's tort could have caused B to suffer a *pure* form of distress: that is, one which was not consequent on A's tort causing B to suffer some kind of personal injury or property damage. So, for example, suppose A upset B by repeatedly making aggressive telephone calls to her, thereby committing the tort of harassment. In this case, A's harassment will have caused B to suffer a pure form of distress.

(7) *Inconvenience.* A's tort could have caused B to suffer hassle or inconvenience. Again, the most obvious way in which A's tort could have caused B to suffer this kind of loss is if A's tort caused B to suffer some form of personal injury which made it difficult for B to get around. Another obvious way in which A's tort could have caused B to suffer hassle or inconvenience is if A's tort caused her to suffer some other kind of loss such as personal injury or property damage and B sued A for compensation for that loss. The very act of bringing litigation will involve hassle or inconvenience for B and B will reasonably be able to argue that A's tort caused her to suffer that hassle or inconvenience.[8]

(8) *Loss of amenity.* A's tort could have caused B to suffer a loss of amenity. This will be the case if A's tort has prevented B from enjoying some pleasurable

---

[5] [1985] 1 All ER 367.
[6] See above, p. 515.
[7] Though in this case, B will not be able to claim damages for her distress; the distress suffered by her as a result of her property being damaged will not be an actionable loss: see below, p. 584–5.
[8] However, B will not be able to claim damages for that hassle or inconvenience. It is regarded as non-actionable.

experience that she would otherwise have experienced. So suppose A's tort caused B's leg to break with the result that B could not go on holiday. In such a case, A's tort will have caused B to suffer a loss of amenity.[9]

(9) *Wasted expenditure.* There are many different types of economic loss that A's tort could have caused B to suffer. This is the first: A's tort could have caused B to spend money on something which she would not otherwise have spent money on or had occasion to spend money on. So if A's tort caused B to lose the use of her legs with the result that B had to spend money on a wheelchair and having a lift installed in her house, A's tort will have caused B to suffer the form of economic loss discussed here: A's tort will have caused B to spend money on things that she would not otherwise have spent money on.

(10) *Loss of a chance.* Another form of economic loss that A's tort could have caused B to suffer is the loss of a chance of obtaining some benefit or avoiding some harm. This loss of a chance counts as a form of economic loss because a chance of obtaining some benefit or avoiding some harm is something of monetary value, that is, something which people would be willing to spend money on. The claimant in *Chaplin* v *Hicks*[10] (*not* a tort case) suffered this form of economic loss. The claimant was a contestant in a beauty competition organised by a newspaper. She had passed the preliminary stages of the competition and the defendant had arranged to meet her to see if she should make the final of the competition. The defendant – in breach of contract – never turned up and the final went on without the claimant. The defendant's breach of contract deprived the claimant of the chance to win the beauty contest and, as such, caused the claimant to suffer a form of economic loss, for which she was entitled to claim compensation in an action for breach of contract.

(11) *Loss of income.* Obviously, A's tort will have caused B to suffer a form of economic loss if B's earnings are now less than they would have been had A not committed that tort.

(12) *Interception of benefit.* A's tort will also have caused B to suffer some kind of economic loss if it has prevented B from obtaining money that she would otherwise have obtained. The claimants in *White* v *Jones*[11] suffered this form of economic loss. In that case, it will be recalled, the defendants were instructed to draw up a will under which the claimants would have received £9,000 each. The defendants dallied too long over drawing up the will and the testator died before the will was signed and witnessed. The defendants' negligence – they had owed the claimants a duty to draw up the will with reasonable skill and care – caused the claimants to suffer a form of economic loss; the defendants'

---

[9] One of the puzzling features of the law of tort as it stands at the moment is that a victim of a tort who is in an irreversible coma as a result of that tort being committed will be entitled to bring a claim for loss of amenity: see *Wise* v *Kaye* [1962] 1 QB 638; *H West & Sons Ltd* v *Shepherd* [1964] AC 326; *Lim* v *Camden Area Health Authority* [1980] AC 174. It is difficult to see why such damages can be claimed: they can be of no earthly benefit to the victim of the tort.
[10] *Chaplin* v *Hicks* [1911] 2 KB 786.
[11] [1995] 2 AC 207.

negligence prevented the claimants receiving the money which they would otherwise have received under the will.

(13) *Pure economic loss*. This form of economic loss is not actually distinct from the other kinds of economic loss set out above. We describe any form of economic loss as being 'pure' if the person suffering it did not suffer it as a result of his being injured or his property being damaged or his developing a psychiatric illness.

The case of *H West & Sons Ltd* v *Shepherd*[12] provides a good illustration of the different kinds of loss that might be suffered by the victim of a tort. In that case, the claimant, then aged 41, was knocked down by a motor lorry that was driven negligently by the defendant. The claimant sustained severe head injuries resulting in cerebral atrophy and paralysis of all her limbs. She was unable to speak but could communicate by moving her eyes, face and hands. She was only expected to live for another five years after the accident and might have appreciated what sort of condition she was in.

We can isolate five different losses that the defendant's negligence caused the claimant to suffer in this case. First, physical injury: the defendant's negligence caused the claimant to sustain head injuries. Secondly, distress: the defendant's negligence caused the claimant to suffer distress in two ways: first, the claimant experienced pain and suffering when she was knocked down; second, the claimant suffered distress as a result of knowing what her condition was. Thirdly, inconvenience: the claimant had to put up with the hassle and inconvenience involved in trying to live her life in a paralysed condition. Fourthly, loss of amenity: as a result of the defendant's negligence, the claimant could not enjoy many of the pleasures of life that she would have enjoyed but for the defendant's negligence. Fifthly, economic loss: the defendant's negligence caused the claimant to suffer a loss of income.

THE BASIC PRINCIPLE

Suppose that A has committed a tort in relation to B and B wants to establish that A's tort has caused her to suffer some kind of loss – say, some form of physical injury. To do this, B will *normally* have to show that she would not have been injured in the way she was *but for* A's tort *and* nothing happened *after* A committed his tort to *break the chain of causation* between A's tort and B's injury. This needs more explanation.

The 'but for' test

Suppose A breached a duty of care owed to B.[13] Suppose it is alleged that A's negligence caused B to develop cancer.[14] A's negligence will *not* have caused B

---

[12] [1964] AC 326.

[13] There is no significance in the fact that we are supposing here that A has committed the tort of negligence in relation to B. We could have easily based our discussion of the principles of causation around a case where A committed the tort of defamation or private nuisance in relation to B. Many textbooks on tort confusingly give an account of the law of causation straight after their account of the tort of negligence. (In some cases, presenting the law of causation as *part of* the law on negligence.) This may lead the unwary reader to think that the principles governing

to develop cancer if B would still have developed cancer in the way she did even if A had not been negligent. If we are to show that A's negligence caused B to develop cancer, we will normally have to show that B would not have developed cancer in the way she did[15] *but for* A's negligence.[16]

Examples of the application of the 'but for' test

In *Barnett* v *Chelsea & Kensington Hospital Committee*,[17] three nightwatchmen presented themselves at a hospital casualty department, complaining that they had started vomiting after drinking some tea. The casualty officer on duty told the men to go to bed and call their own doctors. The men followed his advice and five hours later one of them died from arsenic poisoning. It was held that the casualty officer's failure to treat the man who died (in breach of the duty of care he owed him to treat him with a reasonable degree of care and skill) did not cause his death; he would have died anyway, even if he had been treated by the casualty officer.

In *Jobling* v *Associated Dairies Ltd*,[18] the claimant was employed by the defendants in their butchers' shop. In 1973 he slipped on the floor of the shop because the defendants had failed (in breach of their duty under the Office, Shops and Railway Premises Act 1973) to keep the floor free from slippery substances. The claimant

---

the law on causation apply only in negligence cases – in fact, they apply across the board, in *all* cases where someone has committed a tort in relation to someone else.

[14] Again, no significance is attached to the fact that the loss we are supposing B suffered here is a form of physical injury; another kind of loss would have served just as well.

[15] *Important note.* The qualifier 'in the way she did' is important. In the case where B has suffered some sort of loss and it is alleged that A's tort caused her to suffer that loss, you have to look at *how* B suffered that loss and ask – would she have suffered that loss *in the way she did* but for A's tort? If you do not, your causal judgments will soon go awry. For example, suppose that Karen is walking down the street and she is attacked by Paul, who breaks both her legs. Obviously in this case Paul's attack caused Karen's legs to be broken – *and this is so even if, had Paul not attacked Karen, John would have done so and broken both her legs.* Karen's legs would not have been broken *in the way they were* had Paul not attacked her. It is irrelevant – at any rate, when making judgments about causation – that Karen's legs would have been broken anyway by John had Paul not attacked her. Of course, when it comes to assessing how much Paul should pay Karen by way of damages for the fact that he broke her legs, it would usually be highly relevant that Karen's legs were 'doomed' to be broken in any case. However, if the damages payable to Karen were reduced significantly in this case to take account of the fact that her legs were 'doomed', then she would be seriously undercompensated for the fact that her legs were broken. She could not sue Paul for substantial damages; and she could not sue John for anything, given that he committed no tort in relation to her (though he was going to do so). Given this, the courts could be expected to disregard the fact that Karen's legs were 'doomed' when Paul broke them, and allow Karen to sue Paul for substantial damages designed to compensate her *in full* for the pain and suffering and so on that she suffered as a result of her legs being damaged. See the discussion of *Baker* v *Willoughby* [1970] AC 467 below, at pp. 545–6.

[16] *Important note.* Once it is understood that it has to be shown under the 'but for' test that B would not have developed cancer *in the way she did* but for A's negligence, the 'but for' test can be seen to provide a perfectly adequate starting point for determining whether A's negligence caused B's cancer. There is certainly no need (as Stapleton 2003 suggests, at 393) to abandon the 'but for' test in favour of some other test for causation such as the NESS test (propounded by Hart & Honoré 1985; R. Wright 1985, 1988, 2001), under which A's negligence will be held to have caused B's cancer if it was a *N*ecessary *E*lement in a *S*et of circumstances that would have been *S*ufficient to cause B to contract cancer. The NESS test for causation suffers from formidable difficulties of its own: for example, the NESS test produces false positives and false negatives when it is applied to determine whether a tort that was committed by *failing to act* in a particular way caused the victim of the tort to suffer some kind of harm: see Fischer 1992.

[17] [1969] 1 QB 428.

[18] [1982] AC 794.

suffered a back injury which was somewhat disabling. In 1976 the claimant's back became completely disabled because he developed a condition called myelopathy. The myelopathy was completely unconnected with the claimant's accident in 1973. It was held that while the defendants' failure to keep the floor of their shop free from slippery substances had caused the claimant's disablement between 1973 and 1976, that failure had not caused any of the claimant's disablement after 1976. If the defendants had kept the floor of their shop free from slippery substances, the claimant would still have been completely disabled from 1976 onwards.

In *McWilliams* v *Sir William Arrol & Co.*,[19] the claimant's husband was working for the defendant, his employer, on a steel lattice tower when he fell to his death. It was found that the defendant's failure to provide the husband with a safety belt (in breach of his duty under s 36(2) of the Factories Act 1937) did not cause the husband's death. If the defendant had supplied the husband with a safety belt he would not have worn it so it could not be said that but for the defendant's failure to supply the husband with a safety belt the husband would not have fallen to his death.[20]

Divisible losses

It is sometimes possible to divide up a loss that has been suffered by the victim of a tort and say in relation to one part of the loss that had the tort not been committed she would still have suffered that part of the loss in the way she did; while holding in relation to the other part that had the tort not been committed, the victim of the tort would not have suffered that part of the loss in the way she did. In such a case, the person who committed the tort in question will be held to have caused the victim to suffer the second part of the loss she has suffered, but not the first.

So, for example, in *Holtby* v *Brigham & Cowan (Hull) Ltd*,[21] Holtby worked for 24 years as a marine fitter. For twelve of those years he worked for the defendants. Holtby's work meant that he was frequently exposed to asbestos dust. None of his employers – including the defendants – took any special precautions to protect him against the asbestos dust and Holtby eventually developed asbestosis. He sued the defendants and the trial judge found that Holtby's asbestosis would have been 75 per cent less severe if the defendants had provided him with proper protection against asbestos dust in the years that he worked for them. So had the defendants not been negligent, Holtby would still have suffered a quarter of the asbestosis that he was currently suffering from. Accordingly, it was held that the defendants only caused Holtby to suffer 75 per cent of the asbestosis he was suffering from and they were held liable to compensate Holtby

---

[19] [1962] 1 WLR 295.

[20] It might have been different if the defendant had owed the claimant's husband a duty not only to supply him with a safety belt but *also* to take steps to ensure that he wore it. In that case, it could have been argued that had the defendant supplied the claimant's husband with a safety belt *and* taken steps to ensure that he wore it, the claimant's husband would have worn a safety belt while he was working and would not have fallen to his death. It could therefore have been argued that the defendant's breach of the duty he owed the claimant's husband to supply the claimant's husband with a safety belt *and* to take steps to ensure that he wore it caused the claimant's husband to die. See, for example, *Nolan* v *Dental Manufacturing Co. Ltd* [1958] 1 WLR 936.

[21] [2000] 3 All ER 421.

for that loss – with the compensation being assessed by determining what sum would fully compensate Holtby for the asbestosis suffered by him and knocking 25 per cent off that figure. The Court of Appeal upheld the trial judge's award.[22]

It may seem a little unreal that Holtby's asbestosis could have been divided up in this way. Indeed, the courts sometimes seem overeager to divide up a loss that the victim of a tort has suffered and hold the person who committed that tort liable for a portion of that loss. For example, in *Rahman* v *Arearose Ltd*,[23] the claimant was attacked by some thugs while he worked in a burger bar. One of his eyes was injured in the attack and needed to be operated on. He was taken to the defendants' hospital but the operation on the eye was so badly performed that he was blinded in that eye. In the aftermath of these experiences, the claimant developed a psychiatric illness. The Court of Appeal held, on the basis of 'expert' evidence, that the claimant's psychiatric illness could be divided up – the court held that part of the claimant's psychiatric illness would have been suffered anyway even if the defendants had not been negligent and so the defendants could only be held liable for that part of the claimant's psychiatric illness that he would not have suffered had the defendants not been negligent. It seems unlikely that it was possible to divide up the claimant's psychiatric illness in this way. A better way of deciding the case would have been to find that the claimant would not have developed his (indivisible) psychiatric illness *in the way he did* but for the defendant's negligence and therefore hold the defendant liable for the *whole* of the psychiatric illness suffered by the claimant. However, in assessing the damages payable to the claimant to compensate him for that illness, it would have been legitimate to knock something off to take account of the fact that when the claimant went into hospital, he was probably 'doomed' anyway to suffer some form of psychiatric illness – even if he had been treated impeccably by the defendants.

Difficulties of proof

It is sometimes difficult, for the purposes of applying the 'but for' test, to determine what would have happened had a tort not been committed. That is, if A has committed a tort in relation to B and B has subsequently suffered some kind of loss, it is sometimes difficult to determine whether B would have

---

[22] See also *Allen* v *British Rail Engineering Ltd* [2001] ICR 942, where an employee who contracted Vibration White Finger (VWF) condition as a result of using vibrating tools in the course of his employment by the defendant was allowed to recover damages in respect of that part of his condition that he would not have suffered from had the defendant not wrongfully failed to assess his employees for the incidence of VWF among them. The decisions in *Holtby* and *Allen* implicitly cast doubt on the correctness of the decision of the House of Lords in *Bonnington Castings Ltd* v *Wardlaw* [1956] AC 613. In that case the claimant's employer exposed the claimant to excessive quantities of silica dust at work, in breach of a statutory duty that he owed the claimant. The claimant later developed a lung disease and sued his employer for compensation for the disease, claiming that the employer's breach of statutory duty had caused him to develop that disease. The House of Lords held for the claimant, finding that the employer's breach of statutory duty had 'materially contributed' to the disease – by which, presumably, they meant the employer's breach had made the claimant's lung disease more serious than it would otherwise have been. But if this is right, then the claimant should only have been awarded damages to compensate him for the 'extra' lung disease that he was suffering from that was attributable to the employer's breach of statutory duty. However, the claimant was actually awarded damages to compensate him for the *whole* of his lung disease.
[23] [2001] QB 351.

suffered that loss anyway in the way she did had A not committed his tort. How the courts handle these cases depends on the type of loss that B has suffered.

(1) *Physical injury cases*. Suppose that A has committed a tort in relation to B and B subsequently developed cancer. Suppose further that it is claimed that A's tort caused B to develop cancer. Suppose finally that it is hard to tell whether B would have developed cancer in the way she did had A not committed his tort. In this sort of case, the courts determine whether the 'but for' test is satisfied by using a *balance of probabilities* test. They ask: Is it more likely than not that B would not have developed cancer in the way she did had A not committed his tort?[24] If the answer is 'yes' then the courts will find that B would not have developed her cancer but for A's tort and A will usually be held liable to compensate B for the fact that she has developed cancer. If the answer is 'no' then the courts will find that B would have developed her cancer in the way she did even if A had not committed his tort, with the result that A will usually not be held liable to compensate B for her cancer.[25]

For instance, in *Hotson v East Berkshire Health Authority*,[26] the claimant fell when climbing a tree and one of his hips sustained an acute traumatic fracture. He was taken to hospital but the defendants (in breach of the duty of care they owed him) failed to diagnose his injury and sent him home. After five days the claimant was taken back to the hospital and this time his injury was correctly diagnosed. As things turned out the hip fracture resulted in the claimant being permanently disabled. The claimant claimed that the defendants' failure to treat him properly caused him to be permanently disabled. It was impossible to tell with any certainty whether or not the claimant would have been permanently disabled even if the defendants had correctly diagnosed and treated his injury when he first went to the hospital. If the claimant's fall had damaged a certain proportion – call it x per cent – of the blood vessels in his hip then the claimant would have been permanently disabled whatever the defendants had done when he first went to hospital. If the fall had damaged less than x per cent of the blood vessels in his hip then the defendants would have been able to prevent the claimant becoming permanently disabled had they acted promptly when the claimant first went to hospital. No one could tell with any degree of certainty what proportion of blood vessels in the claimant's hip were damaged by his fall and therefore no one could tell with any degree of certainty whether or not the claimant would have been permanently disabled even if the defendants had treated his injuries when he first came to the hospital.

The courts in *Hotson* resolved this uncertainty by asking – Was it more likely than not that the claimant's fall damaged less than x per cent of the blood vessels in his hip? If the answer was 'yes' then they would have held that the claimant would not have become permanently disabled but for the defendants' negligence. But if the answer was 'no' then the courts would have held that the claimant would have become permanently disabled in the way he did even if the defendants had not been

---

[24] In other words: Is the probability that B would not have developed cancer in the way she did had A not committed his tort over 50%?

[25] Though there is an exception to this, dealt with below, at pp. 547–8.

[26] [1987] AC 750.

negligent. As things turned out, the answer was 'no'. It was found that the probability that the claimant's fall damaged less than x per cent of the blood vessels in his hip was only 25%. It was therefore more likely than not that the claimant's fall damaged at least x per cent of the blood vessels in his hip and therefore more likely than not that the defendants' negligence made no difference to the claimant's becoming permanently disabled. The claimant's claim for damages therefore failed: he could not show that the defendants' negligence caused him to become permanently disabled.

Some academics have suggested that the claimant in *Hotson* should have been allowed to bring a claim for the *chance* he lost of avoiding injury as a result of the defendants' negligence.[27] But did the defendants' negligence actually cause the claimant to lose a chance of avoiding injury? It is important to remember that in *Hotson* it was *possible* that when the claimant went into hospital, he had a (very good) chance of avoiding injury. But it was *also possible* that when he went into hospital, he had *no chance* of avoiding injury: that is, it was *also possible* that he was *doomed* to become permanently disabled. So it was uncertain whether or not the defendants' negligence actually caused the claimant to lose a chance of avoiding injury. Again, we resolve this uncertainty by applying a balance of probabilities test and ask – when the claimant went into hospital, was it more likely than not that he was *doomed* to become permanently disabled? The answer is 'yes' – it was 75 per cent likely that when the claimant went into hospital more than x per cent of the blood vessels in his hip had been damaged and he was therefore doomed to be permanently disabled. So *Hotson* was not a case where a claim for a loss of a chance of avoiding injury could have been brought:[28] the claimant in *Hotson* simply could not have established that the defendants' negligence caused him to lose a chance of avoiding injury.

The issue of whether damages for the loss of a chance of avoiding injury can ever be awarded was raised squarely in the case of *Gregg* v *Scott*.[29] In that case, the claimant suffered from a cancerous tumour. The tumour went undetected for almost a year due to the negligence of the claimant's doctor. Had the tumour been detected and treated when it should have been, the claimant would have had a 42 per cent chance of being cured. However, the year's delay in detecting and treating the tumour allowed it to spread, with the result that the claimant now only had a 25 per cent chance of being cured.[30] The claimant sued for compensation for the loss of a chance

---

[27] See, most recently, Peel 2003b, 627, and references contained therein.

[28] Contra, M&D, 199; Porat & Stein 2003, 679; Tettenborn 2003, 580; Weir 2004, 214–15, all of whom seem to suggest that the fact that the House of Lords awarded the claimant in *Hotson nothing* means that *Hotson* is authority for the proposition that damages for loss of a chance of avoiding physical injury cannot be claimed in negligence. As the majority of the Court of Appeal recognised in *Gregg* v *Scott* [2002] EWCA Civ 1471 (at [39], per Latham LJ and at [78], per Mance LJ) this is nonsense – the facts of the case in *Hotson* were such that the claimant simply could not bring a claim for loss of a chance against the defendants. See, to the same effect, Reece 1996; also Hill 1991. Fleming 1997 puts the point quite well (at 69): '[A] 25% probability that there was a chance [of avoiding injury cannot] be conflated into a 25% chance [of avoiding injury].'

[29] [2002] EWCA Civ 1471.

[30] To clarify what these figures mean: 42 out of 100 patients with the kind of cancerous tumour that the claimant had will survive if the tumour is detected and treated speedily. The rest will die. 25 out of 100 patients with the kind of cancerous tumour that the claimant had will survive even if the tumour goes untreated for a year. The rest will die if their tumours go untreated for a year. So 17 out of 100 patients with the kind of cancerous tumour that the claimant had will die if the tumour goes untreated for a year when they would have survived had the tumour been treated speedily.

of being cured that his doctors' negligence caused him to suffer. His claim was dismissed by the Court of Appeal.[31] At the time of writing, the case is being appealed to the House of Lords – and by the time this book is published, the House of Lords will have released its decision in the case. The interested reader will find a summary of, and comments on, the decision on the McBride and Bagshaw website.[32]

(2) *Economic loss cases.* The courts adopt a different approach in cases where it is uncertain whether or not the victim of a tort would have obtained a particular amount of money had that tort not been committed. Suppose that Gary and Ian were two professional footballers and that, when they were playing football together, Ian negligently injured Gary with the result that Gary became permanently disabled. Suppose that, at the time of the accident, a big club was interested in signing Gary. The transfer would have earned Gary a large amount of money in signing on fees and publicity deals and so on – let's say that if Gary had been transferred he would have made £1,000,000 in all. Of course, after Gary's accident, the big club in question lost interest in signing him. In this sort of case, it is difficult to tell whether or not Gary would have earned £1,000,000 but for Ian's negligence. Had Ian not injured Gary, the big club might have decided not to sign Gary anyway. In this sort of case, the courts will *not* find that Ian's negligence caused Gary to lose £1,000,000. And this is so even if the prob-

---

[31] *Important note.* Latham LJ would have allowed the claimant's claim on the basis that the defendant's negligence caused the claimant to suffer a physical injury (the spread of his tumour) and that the claimant *did* suffer a loss of a chance of being cured as a result of suffering that physical injury. Latham LJ rejected the idea that it was more likely than not that the claimant was doomed to die when he was first seen by his doctor, so that the doctor's negligence did not deprive him of a chance of being cured. He took the view that *every* cancer patient has a chance of being cured, and that his or her chances of being cured will diminish the longer the delay in treating him or her. Mance LJ was not so confident of this: he thought that we simply do not know whether someone who is diagnosed with cancer always has a chance of being cured, or whether it is the case that some people who get cancer are simply doomed to die, while others have an excellent chance of being cured provided that they are properly treated. Mance LJ thought that it came down to a matter of policy whether we decide cases like *Gregg* v *Scott* on the basis that everyone who gets cancer has a chance of being cured (as Latham LJ did); or on the basis that some people who get cancer are doomed to die, and require people like the claimant in *Gregg* v *Scott* to show that it was more likely than not that he was *not* doomed to die when he was first seen by his doctor. Mance LJ thought that the public interest in ensuring that people could not bring speculative claims against doctors dictated that we should decide cases like *Gregg* v *Scott* on the latter basis. He accordingly ruled against the claimant on the ground that the claimant could not prove (and could never prove) that it was more likely than not that he was *not* doomed to die when he first saw his doctor. Both Latham and Mance LJJ would have been in favour of dismissing the claimant's claim had it been a claim for a *pure* loss of a chance – that is, not consequent on the enlargement of the claimant's tumour, which everyone acknowledged was caused by the defendant's negligence. The third judge in the Court of Appeal in *Gregg* v *Scott* was Simon Brown LJ. By coincidence, he had been willing at first instance to allow the claimant in *Hotson* to sue the defendants in that case on the basis that the defendants' negligence had caused him to lose a chance of avoiding injury. Perhaps influenced by the fact that the House of Lords in *Hotson* had overturned his decision in favour of the claimant, he ruled in *Gregg* v *Scott* that the House of Lords' decision in *Hotson* meant that claims for loss of a chance of avoiding injury could not be brought in negligence and accordingly dismissed the claimant's claim. However, as we have seen, this is to misread the House of Lords' decision in *Hotson* – the issue of whether damages for loss of a chance of avoiding injury can be awarded in negligence simply did not arise in *Hotson* because the claimant in that case could not establish that he *ever* had a chance of avoiding injury.

[32] See above, p. xiv, for details.

ability that Gary's transfer would have gone ahead was 80 per cent – making it more likely than not that Gary would have earned £1,000,000 had he not been injured by Ian. Instead, the courts will find that Ian's negligence deprived Gary of a chance to make £1,000,000 and will award Gary damages designed to compensate Gary for that loss of a chance.[33] So if the probability that the transfer would have gone through was 80 per cent then Gary will be awarded £800,000 in damages; if the probability was 20 per cent, £200,000.[34]

Break in the chain of causation

Suppose that A committed a tort in relation to B. Suppose further that B suffered some kind of loss as a result[35] of A's tort. Even if this is true, it may be wrong to say that A's tort *caused* B to suffer that loss.

To take an obvious example, suppose that Paul beat Mary up and Mary was so angered by this that she burned down the offices where Paul worked. Mary was subsequently imprisoned for committing arson. Now – here Mary has suffered a loss (being imprisoned) which she would not have suffered but for Paul's beating her up, but no one would say that Paul's beating Mary up caused her to be imprisoned. In this sort of situation, we say that there has been a *break*

---

[33] See, for example, *Blue Circle Industries plc* v *Ministry of Defence* [1999] Ch 289. The claimants owned land next to land owned by the Atomic Weapons Establishment (AWE). The claimants were in negotiations to sell the land for about £10.5m to a third party when it was discovered that the land was contaminated with nuclear waste from the AWE's land. The third party broke off negotiations and the claimants set about cleaning up their land. The property market collapsed in the meantime and once the claimants' land was cleaned up and marketable again, it was only worth £5m. The claimants sued the defendants for damages, claiming that the defendants had committed a tort in contaminating their land. The trial judge found that there was a 75% chance that, had the defendants not committed their tort, the third party would have bought the claimants' land for £10.5m and therefore that there was a 75% chance that, but for the defendants' tort, the claimants would have been £5.5m better off than they were. The judge did *not* go on to find that, because it was more likely than not that the claimants would have been £5.5m better off than they were but for the defendants' tort, the claimants *would* have been £5.5m better off than they were but for the defendants' tort. He merely found that the defendants' tort deprived the claimants of a 75% chance of being made better off by £5.5m and awarded them 75% of £5.5m as compensation for the fact that the defendants' tort deprived the claimants of that chance. See also *Allied Maples Group Ltd* v *Simmons & Simmons* [1995] 1 WLR 1602 (claimants bought share capital of K, a subsidiary of G, in order to acquire leases held by K; the claimants' solicitors – the defendants – conducted the negotiations with G over the terms of the share deal; they negligently failed to tell the claimants that the terms of the share deal did not protect them against the risk that they would have to meet any liabilities incurred by K's subsidiaries; the claimants successfully argued that had they been told this, there was a chance they would have successfully renegotiated the deal with G to obtain such protection, and were allowed to sue the defendants for damages to compensate them for the fact that they lost that chance to renegotiate as a result of the defendants' negligence).

[34] *Important note.* Note that even if the probability of the transfer going through was only 20%, one would *not* say that it was more likely than not that the transfer was *doomed* not to go through. Clearly there *was* a (smallish) chance that the transfer would go through, for which Gary can be compensated. Because the football club that was thinking about buying Gary when he was injured possessed free will – and was therefore free to choose to buy Gary – we would always say that there *was* a *chance* that the transfer would go through.

[35] From here on *in this chapter*, a loss will be said to have been suffered 'as a result of' a tort having been committed if that loss would not have been suffered in the way it was *but for* that tort having been committed.

in the chain of causation between the tort committed by Paul in beating Mary up and Mary's being imprisoned.[36]

So – when will we be able to say that there was a break in the chain of causation between someone's tort and a loss suffered by the victim of that tort? To clear the ground, we can immediately identify three kinds of events that could *never* break the chain of causation between someone's tort and a loss suffered by the victim of that tort.

(1) *Events preceding a tort.* Suppose that Carl's wife beat him up so badly that he underwent a personality change and developed an obsessive hatred of women. As a result, one day Carl attacked Karen in the street and this caused Karen to develop a psychiatric illness. In this case, the beating Carl received from his wife could not possibly have broken the chain of causation between the tort committed by Carl in attacking Karen and Karen's developing her psychiatric illness. This is because Carl's wife beat him up *before* Carl attacked Karen. For an event to break the chain of causation between someone's committing a tort and the victim of that tort's suffering some kind of loss, that event *must* occur between the time that tort was committed and the time the victim of the tort suffered that loss.

(2) *Events that make no difference.* Suppose that Tom raped Dawn and Dawn developed a psychiatric illness as a result. Suppose further that after Dawn had been raped but before her psychiatric illness developed, she went to the police to complain that she had been raped and was treated in an insensitive manner by the police. Suppose finally that the manner in which Dawn was treated by the police had nothing to do with her developing her psychiatric illness, which was entirely attributable to the rape. In this case, the manner in which the police treated Dawn could not possibly have broken the chain of causation between Tom's rape of Dawn and Dawn's developing a psychiatric illness. The reason is the police's treatment of Dawn did not contribute towards her developing her psychiatric illness. For an event to break a chain of causation between someone's committing a tort and the victim of that tort's suffering some kind of loss as a result, that event *must* have contributed in some way to the victim's suffering that loss.

(3) *Omissions.* Suppose that Vijay was driving at a very high speed down the road and as a result he negligently knocked Ruth, a little girl, off the bike that she was riding in the road. Ignoring her wails, Vijay drove off. Ruth made her way home and told her mother, Lara, that she had been hit by a car and that her head felt 'funny'. Lara told Ruth not to make a fuss and packed her off to bed. During the night, Ruth suffered a brain haemorrhage. She survived the haemorrhage – she was immediately rushed to hospital as soon as the problem become obvious – but suffered permanent

---

[36] See, however, Stapleton 2001, arguing (at 166) that the rules dealt with in this section should not be presented as part of the law on causation, and that to do so gives a 'misleadingly factual flavour to a collection of rules based on normative concerns'. Against this, one could observe that someone approaching Paul's case without any normative concerns at all (such as a concern to protect Paul from being subjected to excessive liabilities) would still find it odd to say that Paul's assault *caused* the offices where Paul worked to be burned down.

brain damage as a result. Had Lara taken Ruth to hospital as soon as Ruth came in complaining that she had been hit by a car, then the brain haemorrhage and consequent brain damage could have been avoided.

In this situation, Lara's failure to take Ruth to hospital could not possibly have broken the chain of causation between Vijay's negligence in knocking Ruth down and the brain damage suffered by Ruth as a result of being knocked down. The reason is that *omissions do not break chains of causation.*[37] So Vijay's negligence will be held to have caused Ruth's brain damage. But Lara has also committed a tort here. As Ruth's mother, she owed Ruth a duty to take reasonable steps to see that Ruth did not come to any physical harm[38] and she breached that duty when she failed to take Ruth to hospital when Ruth told her that she had been knocked down. Lara's negligence *also* caused Ruth's brain damage because Ruth would not have suffered her brain damage had Lara not been negligent.

So Vijay *and* Lara will *each* be held in this case to have committed a tort in relation to Ruth which caused Ruth to become permanently brain damaged. The result is that Ruth will be entitled to sue either Vijay or Lara or both for compensation for her brain damage. If she chooses to sue Vijay (the obvious choice), Vijay will be entitled to make a claim in contribution against Lara to make her share some of the burden of compensating Ruth for her brain damage.

The same point about omissions not breaking chains of causation also applies in cases where the victim of a tort fails to take steps to save herself suffering some loss which she was put in danger of suffering as a result of that tort's being committed. Her failure to save herself from suffering that loss will not break the chain of causation between that loss and the tort that was committed in relation to her. However, she will probably be prevented from suing for compensation for that loss on the ground that she only suffered it because she *failed to mitigate* the losses flowing from the tort that was committed in relation to her.[39]

For example, in *McAuley* v *London Transport Executive*,[40] the claimant suffered an accident at work as a result of the defendants' negligence. The claimant's left wrist was cut in the accident. The claimant was taken to hospital but he refused to have an operation on his wrist which would have gone some way towards restoring the claimant's left hand and wrist to full working order. Without an operation, the condition of the claimant's left wrist deteriorated and he lost the use of his left hand. In this case, the defendants' negligence caused the claimant to lose the use of his left hand: the claimant's failure to agree to the operation that would have saved his hand did not break the chain of causation between

---

[37] One case which seems to contradict this is *Mann* v *Coutts & Co.* [2004] 1 All ER (Comm) 1. In that case the claimants suffered loss as a result of acting on a letter supplied by the defendants relating to an agency with whom the claimants had dealings. Their claim in negligence for compensation for that loss was dismissed on the ground that they would not have suffered that loss had they not failed to investigate the agency and that failure broke the chain of causation between the loss suffered by the claimants and the letter supplied by the defendants. However, the decision was at first instance and the judge seems not to have realised that the same result could have been reached by reference to the law on mitigation of damage, dealt with below, at pp. 581–3.

[38] See above, pp. 183–4.

[39] The victim of a tort's so-called 'duty to mitigate' the losses suffered by her as a result of that tort's being committed is discussed further below, at pp. 581–3.

[40] [1958] 2 Lloyd's Rep 500.

the defendants' negligence and the claimant's losing the use of his left hand. However, the claimant was still barred from suing for compensation for the loss of the use of his left hand: he only lost the use of his left hand because he failed to mitigate the losses suffered by him as a result of the defendants' negligence.

Now that we have clarified what sort of events will *not* break chains of causation, we can go on to discuss what kind of event – known in the legal literature as a *novus actus interveniens – will* break a chain of causation. Two kinds of event will have this effect. First, an unexpected and natural event. Second, a deliberate and unreasonable act. Let's now look at each in turn.

Unexpected and natural events

The standard example of an unexpected and natural event is a lightning strike. So: suppose that Alan beats Eric up with the result that Eric needs to be taken to hospital in an ambulance. On the way to the hospital, the ambulance is struck by lightning and Eric is electrocuted. We would not say here that Alan's beating Eric up caused Eric to be electrocuted. The lightning strike, which occurred after Alan's beating Eric up and contributed to Eric's being electrocuted, broke the chain of causation between Alan's beating Eric up and Eric's being electrocuted.

In *Carslogie Steamship Co. Ltd* v *Royal Norwegian Government*,[41] the claimants' ship, the *Heimgar*, was damaged in a collision with the *Carslogie*, which was owned by the defendants. The collision occurred because of the defendants' negligence. The *Heimgar* was on its way to port to have the damage it had suffered in the collision with the *Carslogie* repaired permanently when it was involved in a violent storm which rendered the *Heimgar* unseaworthy. The *Heimgar* limped into port where it spent 30 days having both the storm damage and the damage done in the collision with the *Carslogie* repaired simultaneously. If the *Heimgar* had not suffered any storm damage it would have taken ten days to repair the damage done in the collision with the *Carslogie*. It was held that the defendants' negligence did not cause the *Heimgar* to suffer the storm damage which resulted in its being detained in port for 30 days. While the *Heimgar* would not have suffered that storm damage had the defendants' not been negligent, the violent storm – an unexpected and natural event – broke the chain of causation between the defendants' negligence and the storm damage suffered by the *Heimgar*. Given this, the defendants did not cause the *Heimgar* to be detained in port for the 30 days that it was detained and they were therefore not liable for the profits which the claimants could have made had the *Heimgar* been available to them in that period.

Deliberate and unreasonable acts

It is well established that, as a general rule, *deliberate and unreasonable acts break chains of causation*. We have already seen this with the example of Dawn's burning down the offices in which Paul worked to get revenge on him for beating her up. Paul's beating Dawn up did not cause her to be imprisoned because her deliberate and unreasonable act in burning down the offices where Paul worked broke the

---

[41] [1952] AC 292.

chain of causation between Paul's beating Dawn up and Dawn's being imprisoned. Let's now look at a number of cases that illustrate this principle at work.

In *Haynes* v *Harwood*,[42] it will be recalled, the defendant left some horses unattended in a street. The horses bolted and the claimant, a policeman, dashed out and attempted to stop the horses. He was injured in doing so. It was held that the defendant's negligence in leaving the horses unattended in the street had caused the claimant to be injured. True, the claimant was only injured as a result of the defendant's negligence because he deliberately ran out and attempted to stop the defendant's horses bolting. However, it had been reasonable for the claimant to do this.

In *Hyett* v *Great Western Railway Company*,[43] a fire broke out in a train wagon which had been left by the defendants – the wagon's owner – in a railway siding. The fire broke out because of the defendants' negligence in leaving a number of leaking paraffin drums in the wagon. The claimant – who was employed to do work on the wagons in the railway siding – saw the fire and tried to deal with it. While a friend of his went for assistance, the claimant attempted to remove a number of the paraffin drums from the wagon. While he was doing so one of the drums exploded and the claimant was injured. It was held that the defendants' negligence had caused the claimant to be injured. While the claimant was only injured as a result of the defendants' negligence because he deliberately chose to try to remove some of the paraffin drums in the wagon, as it was reasonable for the claimant to do this, this deliberate act of his did not break the chain of causation between the defendants' negligence and his being injured.

In *Lagden* v *O'Connor*,[44] the claimant's car was damaged as a result of the defendant's negligence and needed to be repaired. While his car was out of action, the claimant hired a replacement car. The claimant could not afford to hire a car from a normal car hire firm. Instead he hired a car from a credit hire company called Helphire which – crucially – did not charge him anything upfront for the hire of the car. Instead, Helphire allowed him to hire the car on credit – the idea being that when the claimant succeeded in his claim against the defendant, the damages payable to the claimant would cover the cost of renting a car from Helphire, and the defendant would be able to pay off his debt to Helphire out of that portion of the damages. The claimant ended up owing £659 to Helphire for the hire of their car; and he sought to recover that sum from the defendant. Now – a normal car hire firm would have charged the claimant a lot less to use one of their cars for an equivalent period of time: Helphire's rates were a lot higher because they were hiring their cars out on credit and their hire charges included charges designed to cover the cost of helping the claimant to sue the defendant for damages and the cost of taking out an insurance policy to pay off the claimant's debt to Helphire should his claim against the defendant fail. A majority of the House of Lords held that the claimant was allowed to recover damages from the defendant to cover the cost

---

[42] [1935] 1 KB 146.
[43] [1948] 1 KB 345.
[44] [2004] 1 AC 1067.

of renting a car from Helphire. The fact that he had chosen to rent a car from Helphire rather than a normal car hire firm did not break the chain of causation between the defendant's negligence and the claimant's owing Helphire £659 for the use of one of their cars. This is because – given the claimant's impecuniosity – the claimant had acted quite reasonably in hiring a replacement car from Helphire rather than a normal car hire firm, despite the fact that Helphire's rental charges were a lot higher than a normal car hire firm's would have been.[45] Of course, it would have been different if the claimant had been rich enough to afford to hire a replacement car from a normal car hire company. Had this been the case, his decision to hire a replacement car from Helphire would have been unreasonable and would have broken the chain of causation between the defendant's negligence and the claimant's owing Helphire £659 for the use of one of their cars.[46]

In *Knightley* v *Johns*,[47] the defendant drove his car dangerously down a tunnel, in breach of the duty of care he owed other users of the tunnel. As a result, the car overturned near the exit to the tunnel. The police turned up but failed to close the entrance to the tunnel to oncoming traffic. A police inspector at the exit to the tunnel realised the omission and told the claimant – a police constable on a motorcycle – to ride through the tunnel to the entrance and close off the entrance to oncoming traffic. The claimant did so, travelling against the traffic coming through the tunnel, and was hit by a car as he came round a bend in the tunnel. It was held that the defendant's dangerous driving did not cause the claimant's accident, even though the accident would not have happened but for the defendant's dangerous driving. The defendant's dangerous driving only resulted in the claimant being injured because the police inspector deliberately and unreasonably instructed the claimant to ride back through the tunnel against the flow of the traffic. Given this, the defendant's dangerous driving did not cause the claimant's injury – the police inspector's instruction broke the chain of causation between the defendant's dangerous driving and the claimant's accident. It would have been different, of course, if the inspector's instruction had been a reasonable one to give: in that case, the giving of the instruction would not have broken the chain of causation between the defendant's dangerous driving and the claimant's accident.

---

[45] It was suggested in *The Liesbosch* [1933] AC 449 that damages could not be recovered by the victim of a tort in respect of economic losses incurred by him because of his impecuniosity. However, this was not followed by the House of Lords in *Lagden* v *O'Connor*, and quite right too.

[46] This was the majority's (surprising) explanation of the House of Lords' decision in *Dimond* v *Lovell* [2002] 1 AC 384. The facts in *Dimond* were identical to those in *Lagden* v *O'Connor* except for the fact that the claimant in *Dimond* 'could have found the money needed to hire a replacement car until she was reimbursed by [the defendant in that case] or his insurers' (*Lagden* v *O'Connor* [2004] 1 AC 1067, at [5], per Lord Nicholls). It was held that the defendant could not recover anything from the defendant for the cost of hiring a replacement car from a credit hire company because her credit agreement with the credit hire company was not binding under the Consumer Credit Act 1974. However, the majority of the House of Lords went on to observe that even if the agreement had been binding, the claimant would *not* have been entitled to sue the defendant for more than whatever a normal car hire firm would have charged her to hire a replacement car from them. For an explanation of the majority's reasoning in *Dimond* that actually reflects what was said by the majority in *Dimond*, see either McBride & Bagshaw 2001, 516–18, or Lord Scott's powerful dissenting judgment in *Lagden* v *O'Connor*.

[47] [1982] 1 WLR 349.

In *The Oropesa*[48] two steam vessels, *The Manchester Regiment* and *The Oropesa*, collided. The collision was, in part, due to the negligence of the defendants, who were in charge of *The Oropesa*. Although *The Manchester Regiment* was badly damaged in the collision, its master thought it could be salved and set out in a boat with 16 men to go to *The Oropesa* and to discuss what could be done to rescue *The Manchester Regiment*. Before the boat could reach *The Oropesa* it capsized in rough weather and nine of the men in the boat were drowned. It was held that the collision between *The Manchester Regiment* and *The Oropesa* had caused the death of the nine men in the boat. While the defendants' negligence only resulted in the nine men dying because the master of *The Manchester Regiment* voluntarily set out to sea with those nine men – and seven more – the master acted reasonably in doing so and therefore his voluntarily setting out to sea did not break the chain of causation between the negligence of the defendants and the men's deaths.

In *Wieland* v *Cyril Lord Carpets Ltd*,[49] the claimant was injured in a traffic accident caused by the defendant's negligence. She was taken to hospital where a collar was fitted to her neck. The collar made it difficult for the claimant to move her head and as a result she was unable to use her bifocal glasses with her normal skill. The result was that shortly afterwards, when she was descending some stairs with the assistance of her son, she became confused as to the position of the stairs and fell. Her ankles were damaged in the fall. It was held that the defendant's negligence had caused the damage to the claimant's ankles. Admittedly, the defendant's negligence only resulted in the claimant's ankles being fractured because: (1) the hospital put a collar on the claimant which made it difficult for the claimant to use her bifocals; and (2) the claimant chose to walk down a flight of steps while it was difficult for her to use her bi-focals. However, it was obviously reasonable for the hospital to do (1) and it was reasonable for the claimant to do (2) given that she walked down the stairs with the assistance of her son and so there was no break in the chain of causation between the defendant's negligence and the claimant's ankles being fractured.

It was different in *McKew* v *Holland & Hannen & Cubitts (Scotland) Ltd*.[50] In that case, the claimant was employed by the defendants. The claimant suffered certain injuries as a result of the defendants' negligence. The claimant's injuries meant, among other things, that his left leg was prone to give way suddenly. A few days later the claimant and a few members of his family inspected a flat which he was thinking of renting. On leaving the flat, the claimant, unassisted, walked down some steep stairs which had no handrail. The claimant's left leg suddenly gave way and he fell down the stairs with the result that he fractured one of his ankles. The House of Lords held that the defendants' negligence did not cause the claimant's ankle fracture. The defendant's negligence only resulted in the claimant suffering an ankle fracture because the claimant chose to walk down a steep staircase which had no handrail without any assistance. This was an unreasonable thing to do and so the claimant's decision to walk

---

[48] [1943] P 32.
[49] [1969] 3 All ER 1006.
[50] [1969] 3 All ER 1621.

down the staircase without any assistance broke the chain of causation between the defendant's negligence and the claimant's ankle fracture.

In *Lynch* v *Knight*,[51] the defendant warned the claimant's husband that the claimant was a 'notorious liar' and that she took 'delight in causing disturbances' wherever she went and that her behaviour could be attributed to one Dr Casserley who 'all but seduced' the claimant. The claimant's husband reacted to these words by divorcing the claimant. The claimant sued the defendant in slander for compensation for the fact that her husband had divorced her. It was admitted that the defendant's words amounted to slander, but it was held that the husband's decision to divorce the claimant had broken the chain of causation between the defendant's words and the break-up of the claimant's marriage: it had not been reasonable for the claimant's husband to react to the defendant's words in the way he did.

A couple of further points need to be made about this kind of *novus actus interveniens*.

(1) *Private medical treatment.* Suppose that Beth negligently injured John and John chose to pay someone to treat his injuries. Beth's negligence will have caused John to incur this expenditure if it was reasonable for John to incur that expense. In attempting to establish that it was *unreasonable* for John to incur this expense, Beth will *not* be able to argue that as John could have had his injuries treated free on the National Health Service it was unreasonable for John to 'go private' and pay someone to treat his injuries. Section 2(4) of the Law Reform (Personal Injuries) Act 1948 provides that in 'an action for damages for personal injuries . . . there shall be disregarded, in determining the reasonableness of any expenses, the possibility of avoiding those expenses or part of them by taking advantage of facilities available under the National Health Service . . .'.

(2) *Acts performed under the influence of mental illness.* If A commits a tort in relation to B which causes B to develop some kind of mental illness, it seems that if B performs some act under the influence of that mental illness and suffers some further loss as a result, B's act will *not* have the effect of breaking the chain of causation between A's tort and B's suffering that further loss. This is so however deliberate and unreasonable B's act might have been.

For example, in *Pigney* v *Pointer's Transport Services Ltd*,[52] the claimant's husband worked for the defendants. He suffered head injuries at work due to the defendants' negligence. As a result of suffering those injuries he developed an acute anxiety neurosis and after one and a half years he committed suicide. It was held that the defendants' negligence had caused the claimant's husband's death. The defendant's negligence had only resulted in the claimant's husband's dying because the claimant chose to kill himself, but because that choice was made under the influence of a mental illness it did not have the effect of breaking the chain of causation between the defendant's negligence and the claimant's death.

---

[51] (1861) 9 HLC 577, 11 ER 854.
[52] [1957] 1 WLR 1121.

In *Meah* v *McCreamer*,[53] it will be recalled, the claimant was a passenger in a car driven by the defendant, who was drunk at the time. The car was involved in an accident caused by the defendant's negligence and the claimant sustained serious head injuries which caused his personality to change. Before the accident the claimant had no history of being violent towards women. After the accident he developed aggressive tendencies towards women which resulted in him sexually assaulting and wounding two women four years after the accident. The claimant was sent to jail for committing these offences. It was held that the defendant's negligence had caused the claimant to be sent to jail. While the defendant's negligence only resulted in the claimant's being sent to jail because the claimant chose to attack two women, that choice was made under the influence of a mental illness triggered by the car accident which the defendant's negligence caused and as such did not break the chain of causation between the defendant's negligence and the claimant's being sent to jail.[54]

QUALIFICATIONS TO THE BASIC PRINCIPLE

There are some cases in which the victim of a tort was allowed to sue for compensation for a loss suffered by him or her even though, strictly speaking, he or she could not establish that the commission of that tort *caused* him or her to suffer that loss. In this section we will look at these cases.

Baker

In *Baker* v *Willoughby*,[55] the claimant was crossing the main highway when he was struck by the defendant's car. The accident happened due to the defendant's negligence. As a result of the accident the claimant suffered fairly severe injury to his left leg and ankle. The accident occurred in 1964. The claimant sued the defendant so as to be compensated for the fact that the defendant's negligence had caused him to lose the use of his left leg. In 1967 – before the claimant's case against the defendant had been tried – the claimant was shot in the left leg during an armed robbery and the claimant's left leg had to be amputated immediately. The House of Lords awarded damages against the defendant on the basis that the defendant's negligence had caused the claimant to lose the use of his left leg *for the rest of his life*. This is puzzling. Had the defendant not been negligent, the claimant would have only enjoyed the use of his left leg for three more years, until 1967 when his left leg would have been amputated. So the defendant's negligence only caused the claimant to lose the use of his left leg for *three years* – the three years between 1964 and 1967.

Why then did the House of Lords proceed on the basis that the defendant's negligence had caused the claimant to lose the use of his left leg for the rest of his life? One explanation goes as follows. *Had* the House of Lords held that the

---

[53] [1985] 1 All ER 367.
[54] If the defendant's actions were performed under the influence of a mental illness, why was the defendant not found not guilty by reason of insanity? It can only be supposed that the defendant's mental illness was not so severe as to deprive him of the ability to know what he was doing and that what he was doing was wrong.
[55] [1970] AC 467.

defendant's negligence only caused the claimant to lose the use of his left leg for the three years between 1964 and 1967, the claimant would not have been entitled to sue *anyone* for compensation for the loss of the use of his left leg experienced by him from 1967 onwards. Even if the criminals who had shot the claimant were found, he could not have claimed – for the purpose of suing them for damages – that their shooting him in the leg caused him to lose the use of his left leg between 1967 and the rest of his life because his left leg was already useless at the time of the shooting. But it would have been unjust if the claimant had only been entitled to sue for the loss of the use of his left leg between 1964 and 1967. The criminals and the defendant *together* robbed the claimant of the use of his left leg from 1964 to the end of his life. The claimant should therefore have been entitled to sue *someone* – either the criminals or the defendant – for compensation for the fact that between 1967 and the end of his life he would have to get along without a left leg. So, the argument goes, the House of Lords held that the defendant's negligence caused the claimant to lose the use of his left leg for the rest of his life so as to ensure that the claimant would be able to sue *someone* – in this case, the defendant – for compensation for the loss of the use of his left leg that he would experience post-1967. No injustice was done to the defendant by the House of Lords in so holding: if the claimant had not been shot in the armed robbery, the claimant would have been entitled to sue the defendant on the basis that the defendant's negligence had caused him to lose the use of his left leg for the rest of his life.

The decision in *Baker* is to be confined to its own facts. It has no application to the situation presented in *Jobling* v *Associated Dairies Ltd*,[56] where – it will be recalled – the defendants' negligence in 1973 resulted in the claimant's back becoming disabled and then three years later the claimant developed a condition which would have disabled the claimant's back anyway. The House of Lords held that the defendants' negligence only caused the claimant's back to become disabled between 1973 and 1976 and assessed the damages payable by the defendants to the claimant on that basis. No injustice was done to the claimant as a result of the House of Lords' decision: this was not a case where two tortfeasors, working independently of each other, caused the claimant to lose the use of his back from 1973 onwards and applying the rules on causation strictly would result in the claimant only having a remedy against them for the loss of his back between 1973 and 1976. It may be noted, by the way, that while the House of Lords in *Jobling* subjected the House of Lords in *Baker* to some criticism for the *way* in which they reached their decision, their Lordships overall seemed to think the House of Lords in *Baker* reached the right *result*. So, for example, Lord Edmund-Davies said in *Jobling* that he could 'formulate no convincing juristic or logical principles supportive of the decision' in *Baker* but at the same time conceded that the decision in *Baker* might have been 'acceptable on its own facts'.[57]

---

[56] [1982] AC 794.
[57] Ibid., 808H–809D.

Fairchild

Fairchild v *Glenhaven Funeral Services Ltd*[58] concerned three cases. In each of them an employee (C) was 'employed at different times and for differing periods by both A and B ... A and B were both subject to a duty to take reasonable care to prevent C inhaling asbestos dust because of the known risk that asbestos dust (if inhaled) might cause a [form of cancer called] mesothelioma ... [Both] A and B [breached] that duty ... during the periods of C's employment by each of them with the result that during both periods C inhaled excessive quantities of asbestos dust'.[59] C subsequently developed mesothelioma and sought to recover damages from either A or B for his mesothelioma. It was impossible to tell who C was working for when C inhaled the fatal dust that triggered his mesothelioma. Moreover, C could not show that it was more likely than not that he developed his mesothelioma as a result of either A or B's breach of the duty of care they owed him to see that he did not inhale asbestos dust.[60] So he could not show that either A's or B's negligence caused him to develop his mesothelioma.

Despite this, the House of Lords held that C *would* be entitled to sue either A or B or both for compensation for his mesothelioma.[61] Why was this? Two arguments seem to have led the House of Lords to reach this conclusion.

The first – which we can call the *fairness argument* – goes as follows. If we applied the strict rules on causation to cases such as C's, then it seems that employees who worked for *one* bad employer and contracted mesothelioma as a result would be much better off than employees who worked for *two or more* bad employers and contracted mesothelioma as a result. An employee who worked for one bad employer would have no problem establishing that it was his employer's negligence that triggered his mesothelioma and would therefore have no problem obtaining full compensation for his mesothelioma from that employer. An employee who worked for two or more bad employers would find it very difficult to establish which of his employers' negligence caused his mesothelioma and would therefore find it very difficult to identify anyone whom he was entitled to sue for compensation for his mesothelioma. This is unfair: why should an

---

[58] [2003] 1 AC 32 (discussed, Stapleton 2002b, Morgan 2003).

[59] Ibid., at [2] (per Lord Bingham).

[60] This is because we have *no idea* how asbestos dust triggers mesothelioma. It could be that mesothelioma is triggered by long exposure to asbestos dust; or it could be that mesothelioma is triggered by one fatal fibre being inhaled. So even if C worked for A for 10 years and for B for one year, it is not possible to say that it was more probable than not that C's working for A triggered C's mesothelioma. It could *equally* well be the case that the year that C worked for B tipped the balance and caused his mesothelioma to develop. We simply do not know. See, further, Stapleton 2002b, 280–1, 299.

[61] One question which was not addressed by the House of Lords is whether, in the case we are considering, C would be entitled to sue A *or* B *or* both for damages designed to compensate him *fully* for his mesothelioma or whether the damages payable by A and B would in each case be reduced to take account of the proportion of asbestos dust C was exposed to in working for them. If the latter, and C was exposed to equal amounts of asbestos dust in working for A and B, A and B would each only be held liable to pay C 50% of the damages required to compensate C fully for his mesothelioma; so if C wanted to obtain full compensation for his mesothelioma he would have to sue *both* A *and* B (and if one of them were insolvent, C would not be able to obtain full compensation for his mesothelioma). The Court of Appeal's decision in *Barker* v *Saint Gobain Pipelines Ltd* [2004] EWCA Civ 545 indicates that the former approach is the correct one: so, so long as *either* A *or* B was solvent, C would be able to obtain *full* compensation for his mesothelioma.

employee who worked for one bad employer be in a much better position to obtain compensation for his mesothelioma than an employee who worked for two or more bad employers?[62] To avoid this unfairness, we have to waive the strict rules on causation in the case where an employee who has contracted mesothelioma worked for two or more employers and allow the employee to sue his employers for compensation for his mesothelioma even though we cannot establish *which* of his employers' negligence caused that mesothelioma to develop.[63]

The second argument – which we can call the *sanction argument* – goes as follows. If we do not allow C to sue A and B for compensation for his mesothelioma in this sort of case, then the duties that employers owe their employees to take reasonable steps to see that they do not inhale asbestos dust will become essentially empty. An employer will know that if he breaches that duty and one of his employees subsequently develops mesothelioma, he will not be held liable so long as he can show that that employee was also exposed to asbestos dust during the course of his working life while working for someone else.[64] We have to ensure that employers do not feel free to breach the duties of care that they owe their employees – and so in this sort of case we have to make it clear that an employer who has negligently exposed an employee to asbestos dust will be held liable to pay that employee compensation if the employee subsequently develops mesothelioma and this is so even if it cannot be shown that it was the employer's negligence that caused the employee to develop his mesothelioma, because the employee was also exposed to asbestos dust while working for other people.[65]

---

[62] [2003] 1 AC 32, at [36]: '[Holding that C could not obtain compensation for his mesothelioma] would be deeply offensive to instinctive notions of what . . . fairness demands' (per Lord Nicholls).

[63] It could be argued against this that it is unfair to hold a negligent employer liable for mesothelioma developed by a claimant when it was more likely than not that his negligence did not cause that mesothelioma to develop. However, their Lordships were able to overcome this objection, arguing that if they had a choice between being unfair to an innocent claimant and being unfair to a negligent employer, they would rather be unfair to the wrongdoing employer: ibid., at [33] (per Lord Bingham), [39]–[42] (per Lord Nicholls), [155] (per Lord Rodger).

[64] Ibid., at [33]: 'Were the law [not to allow C's claim in the kind of case we are considering], an employer exposing his employee to asbestos dust could obtain complete immunity against mesothelioma . . . claims by employing only those who had previously been exposed to excessive quantities of asbestos dust. Such a result would reflect no credit on the law' (per Lord Bingham); at [62]: 'a rule requiring proof of a link between the defendant's asbestos and the claimant's disease would, with the arbitrary exception of single-employer cases, empty the duty of content. If liability depends upon proof that the conduct of the defendant was a necessary condition of the injury, it cannot effectively exist' (per Lord Hoffmann); at [155]: 'if the law did [here] impose a standard of proof that no [one claiming compensation for mesothelioma] could ever satisfy, then, so far as the civil law is concerned, employers could with impunity negligently expose their workmen to the risk of . . . mesothelioma. The substantive duty of care would be emptied of all practical content so far as victims are concerned' (per Lord Rodger).

[65] This argument is actually quite weak in this context. This is for two reasons. First, the argument's success in this context depends on a verbal sleight of hand. The argument only works in this context if one says that the duty of care that C's employers owed him, and breached, was a duty to take reasonable steps to see that he did not inhale asbestos dust – the argument being that if C were not allowed to sue A and B here, then employers generally would be left free to breach this duty of care. But if one characterises the duty of care that C's employers owed him, and breached, in wider terms – as a duty to take reasonable steps to see that he did not come to any physical harm in working for him – then not allowing C to sue *in this situation* would not mean that employers generally would be free to breach this wider duty of care. Secondly, even if *Fairchild* had gone the other way, employers would hardly have had *carte blanche* to expose their

How far does *Fairchild* go in releasing the victim of a tort from the necessity of proving that that tort caused her to suffer a particular loss? Four situations can be considered.

(1) *The two hunters.* In the Canadian case of *Cook* v *Lewis*,[66] two hunters negligently fired their guns in the direction of the claimant. The claimant was hit and injured by a pellet fired from one of the hunters' guns – but it was impossible to tell from whose gun the pellet had come. The Supreme Court of Canada held that, in this situation, each of the hunters should have been held liable to compensate the claimant for his injury.[67] It is clear that the House of Lords thought the same conclusion should be reached under English law.[68] A finding of liability on the part of both hunters in this case can probably be justified by the fairness argument.[69] If a claimant was hit by a pellet negligently fired from a gun, he would have no problem suing for compensation for his injuries if only one gun was fired in his direction just before he was hit – so it would seem unfair to deprive him of a remedy if two guns were fired in his direction just before he was hit.

(2) *The dangerous drug.* In the American case of *Sindell* v *Abbott Laboratories*,[70] the claimant's mother was given a drug called diethylstilbesterol (DES for short) while she was pregnant with the claimant. The drug was designed to prevent her having a miscarriage. After the claimant was born, she developed a cancerous tumour in her bladder as a result of being exposed to DES while she was in her mother's womb. Whoever manufactured the DES taken by the claimant's mother knew or ought to have known that there was a danger that taking DES would have this effect, and was therefore liable in negligence to compensate the claimant for the cancer she had developed as a result of her mother's taking that DES.

Unfortunately, the claimant could not identify *who* had manufactured the DES taken by her mother – there were about 200 companies that manufactured DES at the time her mother was pregnant and the DES taken by the claimant's mother could have come from any one of them. The Supreme Court of California overcame this difficulty by holding that the claimant was entitled to sue *all* the manufacturers of DES at the relevant time for compensation for her cancer, with each manufacturer being held liable to compensate the claimant

---

employees to excessive amounts of asbestos dust. An employer acting in this way would be: (1) subject to criminal sanctions; and (2) held liable to an employee who contracted asbestosis after working for him (the idea being that the employer's negligence in exposing the employee to asbestos will have either caused the employee to develop asbestosis or made the asbestosis 'worse' – in which case the employer will be held liable to compensate the employee for that 'part' of the asbestosis which is attributable to the employer's negligence: see above, p. 533.

[66] [1951] SCR 830.

[67] The Supreme Court of California reached an identical conclusion in *Summers* v *Tice*, 199 P 2d 1 (1948). See GS&Z, 257–62.

[68] *Fairchild* v *Glenhaven Funeral Services Ltd* [2003] 1 AC 32, at [39] (per Lord Nicholls), [169] (per Lord Rodger).

[69] The sanction argument will not apply here: if a claimant were not allowed to sue in a two hunters situation, it is unlikely that people firing guns would feel free to fire them wherever they wanted.

[70] 607 P 2d 924 (1980).

for her cancer in proportion to the share of the market for DES that it enjoyed at the time the claimant's mother was pregnant.[71] Lord Hoffmann did not think that the decision in *Fairchild* had any implications for how a *Sindell*-type case would be decided under English law. In *Fairchild*, he said, A and B each *increased* the risk that C would develop mesothelioma by exposing him to excessive quantities of asbestos dust. In contrast, in *Sindell*, all the other manufacturers of DES who did not manufacture the DES taken by the claimant's mother did nothing to increase the risk that the claimant would develop cancer.[72] But it seems doubtful whether this distinction is of any real significance – the fact that A and B *both* did something to increase the risk that C would develop mesothelioma has very little to do with why A and B were each held liable in *Fairchild* to compensate C for his mesothelioma.

Having said that, it *is* doubtful whether an English court would go as far as the Supreme Court of California did in *Sindell*. Neither the fairness argument nor the sanction argument require that *all* the manufacturers of a dangerous drug should be held liable for the harm done by that drug to a claimant if the company that manufactured that drug cannot be identified.[73]

(3) *The dirty cleaner.* In *McGhee* v *National Coal Board*,[74] the claimant was employed by the defendants to clean out some brick kilns. This was hot and dirty work which exposed the claimant to clouds of abrasive brick dust. The defendants (in breach of the duty of care they owed the claimant as his employers) failed to provide the claimant with any on-site washing facilities which would allow him to wash off the brick dust as soon as he knocked off work. Instead, the claimant had to cycle home and wash there. After some days of working in the brick kilns, the claimant was found to be suffering from dermatitis. The claimant claimed that the defendants' breach of the duty of care they owed him had caused him to develop dermatitis. To make out this claim he normally would have had to have shown that he would not have developed dermatitis had the defendants provided him with on-site washing facilities. This was impossible to show. Despite this, the House of Lords found that the defendants' failure to provide the claimant with on-site washing facilities did cause the claimant to develop dermatitis and allowed the claimant's claim.

The House of Lords in *Fairchild* clearly thought that *McGhee* was correctly decided: indeed, their Lordships relied on *McGhee* heavily as authority in favour of the view that, on the facts of *Fairchild*, C was entitled to sue both A and B for compensation for his mesothelioma.[75] The decision in *McGhee* can probably be justified

---

[71] A manufacturer who could affirmatively prove that it was not his DES that triggered the claimant's cancer would, however, not be held liable. See, generally, GS&Z, 900–13.

[72] [2003] 1 AC 32, at [78].

[73] The point is, though, somewhat academic. A claimant who was harmed by a dangerous drug could bring an action for compensation under the Consumer Protection Act 1987 and, if the manufacturer of that drug could not be identified, the last identifiable person who was involved in the chain of supply of that drug would normally be held liable: see below, p. 762.

[74] [1973] 1 WLR 1 (discussed, Hope 2003).

[75] [2003] 1 AC 32, at [33] (per Lord Bingham), [44] (per Lord Nicholls), [64]–[66] (per Lord Hoffmann), [151]–[153] (per Lord Rodger).

by reference to the sanction argument.[76] If the claimant had not been allowed to sue in *McGhee* on the ground that he could not prove that the defendants' negligence caused him to develop dermatitis, an employer who, in breach of the duty of care he owed his employees, did not guard against the risk that his employees would develop dermatitis in working for him by providing his employees with showering facilities would never face any sanction for his negligence. Even if one or more of his employees developed dermatitis, they would never be able to prove that the failure to provide showering facilities caused them to develop dermatitis.

(4) *The premature baby.* In *Wilsher* v *Essex Area Health Authority*,[77] the claimant was a baby that was born prematurely. Shortly after he was born, he developed a serious eye condition called retrolental fibroplasia (RLF for short) and was blinded as a result. The claimant may have developed RLF because he was exposed to excess oxygen by the defendants. However, the claimant also suffered from four medical conditions that could have accounted for his developing RLF. Given this, he could not show that it was more likely than not that he developed RLF because he was given too much oxygen by the defendants. The House of Lords held that the claimant's action against the defendants in negligence for compensation for the fact that he was blind could not succeed: he could not show that the defendants' actions had caused him to go blind.

Four of the Law Lords in *Fairchild* thought that *Wilsher* was correctly decided.[78] Why is this case so different from *Fairchild*? Three of those four Law Lords drew a formalistic distinction between *Wilsher* and *Fairchild*, arguing that in *Fairchild* there was only one possible agent which could have caused the claimant to develop mesothelioma: asbestos dust. In contrast, in *Wilsher* there were five different agents that could have caused the claimant to develop RLF.[79] However, this again does not seem to be a very significant difference – the reasons why the defendants were held liable in *Fairchild* had very little to do with the fact that there was only one possible agent that could have caused the claimant to develop mesothelioma. Lord Hoffmann made much the same point, saying that he did not think that the distinction drawn by the other Law Lords between *McGhee* and *Wilsher* was 'a principled distinction. What if [one of the claimants in *Fairchild*] had been exposed to two different agents – asbestos dust and some other dust – both of which created a material risk of the same cancer and it was equally impossible to say which had caused the fatal cell mutation? I cannot see why this should make a difference.'[80] Instead, Lord Hoffmann argued that the reasons why the defendants were held liable in *Fairchild* simply did not

[76] [1973] 1 WLR 1, at 9: '[Not to hold for the claimant] would mean that the [defendants] were under a legal duty which they could, in the present state of medical knowledge, with impunity ignore' (per Lord Simon of Glaisdale); and at 12: '[Not to hold for the claimant] would mean that in the present state of medical knowledge and in circumstances such as these (which are by no means uncommon) an employer would be permitted by the law to disregard with impunity his duty to take reasonable care for the safety of his employees' (per Lord Salmon).
[77] [1988] AC 1074.
[78] Ibid., at [22] (per Lord Bingham), [70] (per Lord Hoffmann), [118] (per Lord Hutton), [149] (per Lord Rodger). The fifth judge, Lord Nicholls, expressed no opinion on the matter.
[79] Ibid., at [22] (per Lord Bingham), [118] (per Lord Hutton), [170] (per Lord Rodger).
[80] Ibid., at [72].

apply in *Wilsher*. In particular, the sanction argument did not apply in *Wilsher*: it could not be said that if the defendants were not held liable in *Wilsher* then doctors would be free to breach the duties of care that they owed their patients.[81]

Three cases involving a duty to act

In *Reeves* v *Commissioner of Police of the Metropolis*,[82] a man named Lynch hanged himself while in the defendants' custody. Lynch was known to be a suicide risk and the defendant police force therefore owed him a duty to take reasonable steps to ensure that he did not commit suicide. The defendant police force breached this duty. Lynch – who was of sound mind and knew what he was doing – took advantage of the defendants' negligence to hang himself. The claimant sued the defendants under the Fatal Accidents Act 1976, claiming that their negligence had caused Lynch's death and that the defendants were there-fore liable to compensate her for the loss of support that she and her child by Lynch suffered as a result of Lynch's death. It was argued that the defendants' negligence had not caused Lynch's death: there was a break in the chain of cau-sation between the defendants' negligence and Lynch's death because Lynch deliberately and unreasonably chose to take advantage of the defendants' negli-gence by hanging himself. The House of Lords refused to find that the defendants' negligence had not caused Lynch's death: '[If] the law [has imposed] a duty [on someone] to guard against loss caused by the free, deliberate and informed act of a human being . . . [it] would make nonsense of the existence of this duty if the law were to hold that the occurrence of the very act which ought to have been prevented negatived [the existence of a] causal connection between the breach of duty and the loss.'[83] In other words, if a police force owed a sane person in its custody a duty to take reasonable steps to ensure that he did not commit suicide, they would be able to ignore that duty with impunity if it were the law that if they breached this duty and the prisoner took advantage of this breach to kill himself, their breach would not have caused the prisoner's death.

The decision in *Stansbie* v *Troman*,[84] can be explained on a similar basis.[85] The defendant in that case was employed to decorate the claimant's house. The claimant's wife left the defendant alone in the house on the understanding that the defendant would take reasonable steps to lock the house securely if he had reason to leave it. The Court of Appeal found that once the claimant's wife left

---

[81] Ibid., at [69] (per Lord Hoffmann). However, if one characterised the duty of care owed, and breached, in *Wilsher* more narrowly as being a duty to take reasonable steps not to expose the premature baby to excess oxygen the sanction argument might apply. One could argue that if hospitals are not held liable in *Wilsher*-type situations, then they will be free to breach the duties of care that they owe premature babies in their care not to expose them to excess oxygen. Whether this argument works or not will depend on whether exposing a premature baby to excess oxygen might cause the baby any ill effects – other than developing RLF – which could not also be attributed to medical complications arising out of the baby's premature birth.

[82] [2000] 1 AC 360.

[83] Ibid., at 367 (per Lord Hoffmann).

[84] [1948] 2 KB 48.

[85] As can the decision in *Dorset Yacht Co. Ltd* v *Home Office* [1970] AC 1004 (defendants held liable for deliberate criminal damage done by Borstal boys under the defendants' control).

the defendant alone in the house the defendant owed the claimant a duty to take reasonable steps to lock the house up securely every time he left it.[86] The defendant breached that duty: he went to fetch some wallpaper but failed to take adequate steps to lock the house up securely when he did so. In his absence, a thief entered the claimant's house and stole a diamond bracelet and some clothes. The Court of Appeal held the defendant liable in negligence for the loss of the diamond bracelet and the clothes, holding that the defendant's negligence had caused the claimant to lose these items of property. But if we apply the principles of causation set out above, it is hard to see how one could say that the defendant's negligence *caused* the claimant to lose the bracelet and the clothes. While those items of property would not have been stolen but for the defendant's negligence, surely the deliberate and unreasonable act of the thief in stealing the bracelet and clothes broke the chain of causation between the defendant's negligence and the loss of those items of property? However, the decision in *Stansbie* can be justified in the same way as the decision in *Reeves* was. If the defendant had *not* been held liable here, the duty that the defendant owed the claimant to take reasonable care to lock up the house would have had no force whatsoever: the defendant would have been free to breach that duty and if some thief took advantage of his breach to steal from the claimant, the defendant could argue that he was not liable for the loss suffered by the claimant as a result of the theft because the thief's acts broke the chain of causation between his breach and that loss. In order, then, to ensure that the defendant could not ignore with impunity the duty he owed the claimant to take reasonable care to lock up the claimant's house, the Court of Appeal had to disregard the normal rules of causation in *Stansbie v Troman* and hold that the defendant's negligence *had* caused the theft of the claimant's bracelet and clothes.

It is more difficult to explain the result in *Ward v Cannock Chase District Council*.[87] In that case the defendant council damaged the claimant's house so badly that he had to move out of the house. The defendants admitted liability for the damage done to the house and acknowledged that they were liable to repair it. However, they failed to repair the house and the vandals took advantage of this delay to break into the house and do further damage to the house. Scott J held that the council was liable to compensate the claimant for this further damage. Why was this? The council obviously committed a tort in failing to repair the claimant's house and it was true that if the council had not committed that tort the claimant's house would not have been vandalised – had the council done its duty and repaired the house, the claimant would have been allowed to move back into the house and stop anyone breaking into it. But surely the fact that the vandals *deliberately and unreasonably* vandalised the claimant's house meant there was a break in the chain of causation between the council's tort and the damage done to the claimant's house by the vandals? Scott J held that there had been no break in the chain of causation because it

---

[86] Although the decision in *Stansbie v Troman* antedated the decision in *Hedley Byrne v Heller* [1964] AC 465 we would nowadays support this aspect of the decision in *Stansbie v Troman* by reference to the extended principle in *Hedley Byrne*, discussed above, at pp. 127–35.

[87] [1986] Ch 546.

had been *reasonably foreseeable* that the claimant's house would be vandalised if the council delayed in repairing it.[88] It is doubtful whether this is correct – and one cannot justify the decision by reference to the 'sanction' argument which underlay the decision in *Reeves* and which justifies the decision in *Stansbie*. If the council had *not* been held liable for the damage done by the vandals to the claimant's house, the council would not have been left free to disregard the duty it owed the claimant to repair his house.

PRESUMPTION OF LOSS

Before we leave the topic of causation, we should note that if A has committed a tort in relation to B, the courts will sometimes *presume* that A's tort caused B to suffer some kind of loss.[89]

So, for example, we have already seen that if A has committed the tort of libel in relation to B, the courts will presume that A's libel caused B to suffer some kind of loss.[90] In contrast, it will be recalled, if A has committed the tort of slander in relation to B, the courts will only presume that A's slander caused B to suffer some kind of loss if: (1) A slandered B by publishing to another words that suggested B had committed a criminal offence; *or* (2) A slandered B by publishing to another words that suggested B had a contagious or infectious disease; *or* (3) A slandered B by publishing to another words that were calculated to disparage B in an office, profession, calling, trade or business held or carried on by B at the time of the publication; *or* (4) A slandered B by publishing to another words that suggested B was unchaste or adulterous (though this will only hold true if B is a woman).

Similarly, as we have already seen,[91] if A has committed the tort of malicious falsehood in respect of B, the courts will presume that A's falsehood caused B to suffer some kind of loss if: (1) A's falsehood was calculated to cause pecuniary damage to B and was published in writing or other permanent form; *or* (2) A's falsehood was calculated to cause pecuniary damage to B in respect of any office, profession, calling, trade or business held or carried on by him at the time of the publication of the falsehood. Again, if A caused B to suffer some kind of personal injury by committing a tort in relation to B, the courts will naturally presume that the infliction of that injury caused B to suffer some kind of pain and suffering.

---

[88] Ibid., 571. In judging whether it was reasonably foreseeable that the claimant's house would be vandalised if the council delayed in repairing it, Scott J asked whether a reasonable person in the position of the council would have realised that it was 'very likely' that the claimant's house would be vandalised if the council did not take prompt steps to repair it: ibid., at 570. It should be remembered that such a high level of foreseeability will always be required in cases where we are determining whether it was reasonably foreseeable that a third party would act in a particular way.

[89] Damages which are awarded to compensate the victim of a tort for a loss which he is *presumed* to have suffered as a result of that tort being committed are known as 'general damages'. Damages which are awarded to compensate the victim of a tort for a loss which he had to prove that he suffered as a result of that tort being committed are known as 'special damages'.

[90] See above, p. 301.

[91] See above, p. 446.

31

ACTIONABILITY

Suppose that A has committed a tort in relation to B and that tort caused B to suffer some kind of loss. B will only be entitled to sue A for compensation for that loss if it is *actionable*. This chapter explains when this condition will be satisfied.

However, before we can set out the rules governing when a loss will be actionable, we must first make a distinction between the kinds of losses that might be suffered by the victim of a tort. All these losses can be divided up into *primary losses* and *secondary losses*. Suppose for example that A has committed a tort in relation to B and B has suffered various losses as a result.[1] If we take one of the losses suffered by B as a result of A's tort, that loss will be a primary loss if she did *not* suffer that loss because she suffered some other kind of loss as a result of A's tort; in contrast, that loss will be a *secondary* loss if B's suffering that loss was a consequence of B's suffering some other kind of loss as a result of A's tort.[2] (See Diagram 2, overleaf.)

So, for example, suppose that A negligently crashed into B's car. B's car was badly damaged in the collision and she had to spend £1,000 having it repaired. B's leg was also broken in the crash. At the time of the crash, B was on her way to a job interview but was unable to make the interview as she had to be taken to hospital to have her leg treated; the job went to someone else. B's heart was so set on getting this job that she became extremely depressed. In this situation B has suffered six losses. First, property damage: her car was damaged. Secondly, economic loss: B had to spend £1,000 having her car repaired. Thirdly, physical injury: B's leg was broken. Fourthly, distress: B will have suffered a great deal of pain as a result of her leg being broken. Fifthly, economic loss, again: B lost the chance of getting a job as a result of A's crashing into her car. Sixthly, distress, again: B became extremely depressed as a result of losing the chance to get the job she had set her heart on. The property damage and physical injury suffered by B here will count as *primary* losses: B did not suffer those losses because she suffered some other kind of loss as a result of A's tort. The other losses suffered by B will count as *secondary* losses: they were all suffered because B suffered some other kind of loss as a consequence as a result of A's tort. The money B spent on having her car repaired was spent because her car was damaged. The pain B suffered in the aftermath of the crash was suffered because her leg was broken. The chance B lost to get the job she wanted

---

[1] From now on in this book, a loss suffered by the victim of a tort will be said to have been suffered 'as a result of' that tort having been committed if the commission of that tort *caused* the victim of that tort to suffer that loss.

[2] An alternative term for 'secondary losses' which enjoys some popularity is *consequential losses*.

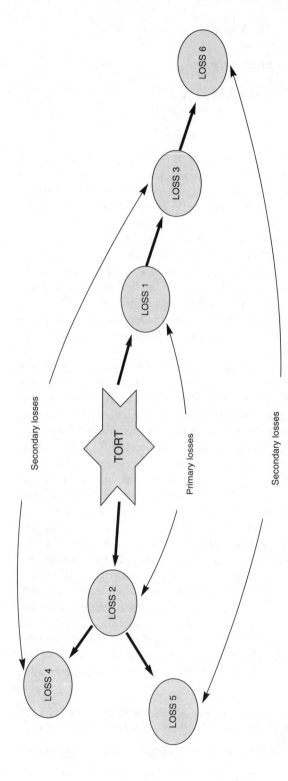

Diagram 2. The distinction between primary and secondary losses. (The thick straight arrows indicate chains of causation.)

was lost because her leg was broken. And the depression B went through was suffered because she lost the chance of getting that job.

Now that we are familiar with the distinction between primary and secondary losses, we are in a good position to understand the rules governing when a loss suffered by the victim of a tort as a result of that tort's having been committed will be actionable. Basically, if A has committed a tort in relation to B and B has suffered some kind of loss as a result, that loss will be non-actionable if: (*a*) it was a *remote* consequence of A's tort;[3] *or* (*b*) it is a *primary* loss and is the *wrong kind of loss*; *or* (*c*) it would be contrary to *public policy* to allow B to sue A for compensation for that loss; *or* (*d*) it is regarded as being *automatically non-actionable* for some reason. If none of these things are true of the loss that B has suffered, then that loss will be actionable. Let's now look at these four different reasons why a loss might be non-actionable.

REMOTENESS

The foreseeability test

Suppose A has committed a tort in relation to B and B has suffered some kind of loss as a result. *Normally* that loss will count as a remote consequence of A's tort if it was *not* reasonably foreseeable at the time A committed his tort that *someone like B would suffer that kind of loss as a result of A's committing that tort.*[4] Let's call this the *foreseeability test* for determining whether a loss suffered by the victim of a tort was a remote consequences of that tort.[5] The foreseeability test

---

[3] *Important note.* There is a paper, or even a monograph, to be written on the mania for unification that afflicts most lawyers and causes them to try and unify what are in fact disparate legal rules or doctrines, with invariably disastrous results. We have seen, and will see, many examples of this. For example: the idea that the various torts recognised in English law can be reduced to one or two or three 'master torts' (see above, pp. 21–3); Lord Atkin's insistence that there *must* exist *one* principle or test which accounts for the existence of *all* the duties of care recognised in English law (see above, pp. 65–6); the popular misconception that *all* cases where a claimant may sue another in negligence for pure economic loss fall under the 'principle in *Hedley Byrne*' (see above, pp. 139–40); the continual hankering after a rule or principle that would unify the 'economic' torts dealt with in Chapters 19–24 of this book (on which, see Weir 1997 and Bagshaw 1998); the insistence of some restitution scholars that in *all* cases where restitutionary damages are awarded against a defendant who has committed a tort, he is *always* stripped of the gains he has made by committing that tort (see below, p. 686); and the insistence, recently endorsed for no good reason by the House of Lords in *Transco plc* v *Stockport MBC* [2003] 3 WLR 1467, that the rule in *Rylands* v *Fletcher* is an outgrowth, or part, of the law on private nuisance (see below, pp. 741–2). This mania for unification has caused many tort scholars to treat the law on remoteness of damage as being part of the law on causation: see, for example, W&J, 223f; M&D, 201f; Murphy 2003, 299f, GS&Z, 265f. Increasingly, it is being recognised that this is a mistake and that the law on remoteness of damage has *nothing to do* with the law on causation: the law on causation determines what losses can be said to have been caused by a defendant's committing a tort; the law on remoteness of damage helps to determine for which of those losses the defendant will be held liable. See, for example, Stapleton 2003, at 389, congratulating the authors of the *Restatement (Third) of Torts: Liability for Physical Harm (Basic Principles)* (though not the authors of the first edition of this book, where exactly the same move was made) for taking the 'bold and necessary' step of clearly distinguishing between the law on causation and the law on the 'scope of liability for consequences', of which the law on remoteness of damage forms part.

[4] *Hughes* v *Lord Advocate* [1963] AC 837.

[5] Cases in which the foreseeability test was adopted to determine whether a loss suffered by the victim of a tort was a remote consequence of that tort include: *Overseas Tankship (UK) Ltd* v

---

may seem straightforward to apply, but it is not. The reason is that whether or not the foreseeability test is satisfied in a given case depends a great deal on how we describe what kind of loss it was that the claimant suffered. And in a lot of cases there will be room for dispute as to what is the appropriate way of describing what kind of loss it was that the claimant suffered – especially as, *in this context*, we describe *what* kind of loss it was that a claimant suffered by reference – in part – to *how* that loss was suffered.[6]

For example, in *Jolley* v *Sutton London Borough Council*[7] a council owned a piece of amenity land near a block of flats. A boat had been left lying on this land for about two years. The boat was in a poor condition and anyone playing about on the boat was liable to put a foot through the rotten timbers of the boat and suffer an injury. Given this – and given the fact that children playing on the amenity land were liable to clamber onto the boat and run the risk of being injured – the council owed children going onto the amenity land a duty under the Occupiers' Liability Act 1957 to take reasonable steps to remove the boat from the land. The council breached this duty when they did nothing about the boat for two years. In that time, the claimant and a friend of his – both children – saw the boat and decided to repair it so they could go sailing in it. They used a car jack to elevate one side of the boat and, crawling underneath, repaired some of the holes in the hull of the boat. Unfortunately, one day when the claimant was working under the boat, the car jack gave way and the boat fell on the claimant's back, causing him severe spinal injuries. The claimant sued the council for damages. The case turned on whether the claimant's injuries were a remote consequence of the council's admitted negligence under the foreseeability test.

Now whether or not you think that the foreseeability test was satisfied here will depend a great deal on how you describe what kind of loss it was that the claimant suffered. Remembering that, in this context, we describe what kind of loss it was that the claimant by reference – in part – to how it was suffered, you might say that the kind of loss suffered by the claimant here was 'Physical injury resulting from meddling with the boat'. If you say *that* then the foreseeability test was plainly satisfied here. It was reasonably foreseeable that if the defendants did

---

    Morts Dock & Engineering Co. Ltd, The Wagon Mound [1961] AC 388 (a negligence case); *Overseas Tankship (UK) Ltd* v *Miller Steamship Co. Pty, The Wagon Mound (No. 2)* [1967] 1 AC 388 (private nuisance); and *Slipper* v *British Broadcasting Corpn* [1991] 1 QB 283 (libel).

[6] *Important note.* For example, in *Doughty* v *Turner* [1964] 1 QB 518, the claimant was very badly burned in an explosion that occurred at the defendants' factory when a cement cover was carelessly knocked into a cauldron of molten liquid. The claimant sued the defendants in negligence for compensation for his injuries but his claim was dismissed. One of the grounds for doing so was that the kind of loss suffered by the claimant here was *burns caused in an explosion* and it was not reasonably foreseeable at the time that knocking a cement cover into the molten liquid would result in the claimant suffering *that* kind of loss. (It was not known at the time that putting cement into the molten liquid in the cauldron would trigger an explosive reaction.) It would have been different had some of the molten liquid escaped from the coverless cauldron and splashed onto the claimant's skin, burning it. In that case, the kind of loss suffered by the claimant would have been *burns caused by splashing* – and the claimant would have been able to show that it was reasonably foreseeable at the time the cover was knocked into the cauldron that doing this would result in the claimant suffering *that* kind of loss.

[7] [2000] 1 WLR 1082 (noted, Nolan 2001).

not remove the boat from their land, someone like the claimant would 'meddle' with the boat and would suffer physical injury as a result. However, you could adopt a narrower description and say that the kind of loss suffered by the claimant here was 'Physical injury resulting from the boat falling on him'. But if you say *that* then it is unlikely that you will conclude that the foreseeability test was satisfied here: it was not really reasonably foreseeable that if the defendants left the rotten boat on their land that it would *fall* on someone like the claimant. The trial judge and the House of Lords adopted the first description of what kind of loss it was that the claimant suffered here and accordingly found that the foreseeability test was satisfied. In contrast, the Court of Appeal adopted the second description of what kind of loss it was that the claimant suffered here and dismissed his claim on the basis that his injuries were a remote consequence of the council's negligence.[8] What accounts for the difference? It is impossible to say for certain but it is hard to resist the impression that the sympathy for the claimant and the fact that the council was a 'deep pockets' defendant must have influenced the way the trial judge and the House of Lords approached the case.

So the foreseeability test is not a self-executing test. In some cases such as the *Jolley* case, it will allow an imaginative judge room for manouevre. This, and the fact that any finding as to whether the foreseeability test is satisfied in a given case will always turn on a detailed scrutiny of the facts of that case,[9] means there is little point in our going through the decided cases where the

---

[8] [1998] 1 WLR 1546.

[9] An example of a situation where this was true is provided by the *Wagon Mound* litigation. The litigation arose out of a fire that started when the defendants negligently allowed a lot of oil to spill into Sydney Harbour. The oil spread and drifted close to the first claimants' wharf, where the first claimants were doing some welding work on a ship called the *Corrimal*, which belonged to the second claimants. A piece of molten metal from the welding work dropped into the oil and set it on fire. The wharf and the *Corrimal* suffered severe fire damage. The first claimants sued the defendants in negligence for compensation for the fire damage done to their wharf in *Overseas Tankship (UK) Ltd* v *Morts Dock & Engineering Co. Ltd, The Wagon Mound* [1961] AC 388. Their claim failed because it was held that it was not reasonably foreseeable at the time that if the defendants spilled any oil into the harbour it would ignite and set the first claimants' wharf on fire. (Why then did the defendants owe the first claimants a duty to take care that they did not spill any oil into the harbour? The reason is that it *was* reasonably foreseeable that if the defendants spilled any oil into the harbour it would spread and foul the first claimants' wharf.) When the second claimants subsequently sued the defendants for the fire damage done to the *Corrimal* (in *Overseas Tankship (UK) Ltd* v *Miller Steamship Co. Pty, The Wagon Mound (No. 2)* [1967] 1 AC 388) they introduced a lot of scientific evidence to show that it *was* reasonably foreseeable at the time the defendants negligently spilled the oil into Sydney Harbour that it could ignite and start a fire and convinced the courts that the fire damage to the *Corrimal* was a reasonably foreseeable consequence of the defendants' spilling oil into Sydney Harbour. Why didn't the first claimants press this evidence on the courts in the original *Wagon Mound* case? Two reasons can be given. First, they did not think that they had to: they assumed that if they showed that the defendants were negligent, the defendants would be held liable for *all* the losses that were a *direct* result of the defendants' negligence, however unforeseeable. This was the rule laid down by the Court of Appeal in *Re Polemis* [1921] 3 KB 560. This rule was, however, overturned in the first *Wagon Mound* case, with the Privy Council ruling that a negligent defendant could not be held liable for a loss suffered by a claimant if that loss was not a reasonably foreseeable consequence of the defendant's negligence. Secondly, it would have harmed the first claimants' claim for compensation if they had admitted that it was reasonably foreseeable that the oil that the defendants spilled into Sydney Harbour could ignite. If it *was* reasonably foreseeable, then the first claimants would have been partly to blame for the fire damage done to their wharf, having carried on doing welding work on the *Corrimal* while oil was lapping around their wharf. And if the first claimants

foreseeability test has been applied to determine whether or not a loss suffered by a victim of a tort was a remote consequence of that tort or not.[10] Instead, we will note a number of exceptions that exist to the foreseeability test.

Exceptions to the foreseeability test

There seem to be five exceptions to the foreseeability test for determining whether a loss suffered by the victim of a tort was a remote consequences of that tort.

(1) *The eggshell skull rule.* The *eggshell skull rule* says that if A has committed a tort in relation to B and it was reasonably foreseeable that B would suffer some kind of physical injury if A committed that tort but – because B suffered from a pre-existing condition – B actually suffered a very different and much worse form of physical injury as a result of A's tort, the injury suffered by B will *not* have been a remote consequence of A's tort, however unforeseeable it might have been that someone like B would suffer that kind of injury as a result of A's tort.[11]

The eggshell skull rule will also apply in cases where A commits a tort in relation to B and B develops a psychiatric illness as a result. If it was reasonably foreseeable that B would develop some kind of psychiatric illness as a result of A's tort, but – because B suffered from some pre-existing condition – B in fact developed a very different and much more serious psychiatric illness as a result of A's tort, B's psychiatric illness will *not* have been a remote consequence of A's tort, however unforeseeable it might have been that B would develop that kind of mental illness in the aftermath of A's tort.[12]

---

were partly to blame for the fire damage done to their wharf, the damages payable to compensate them for that fire damage would have been reduced on the grounds of contributory negligence.

[10] See Lord Steyn's observation in *Jolley* v *Sutton London Borough Council* [2000] 1 WLR 1082, 1089: '[In] this corner of the law the results of decided cases are inevitably very fact-sensitive. Both counsel nevertheless at times invited your Lordships to compare the facts of the present case with the facts of other decided cases. That is a sterile exercise.' The leading cases applying the foreseeability test include, in addition to *Jolley* and the *Wagon Mound* cases: *Hughes* v *Lord Advocate* [1963] AC 837, *Doughty* v *Turner Manufacturing Co.* [1964] 1 QB 518 (discussed above, n. 6) and *Tremain* v *Pike* [1969] 1 WLR 1556. For a detailed account of these cases, see McBride & Bagshaw 2001, 493–4.

[11] See *Smith* v *Leech Brain* [1962] 2 QB 405, where the claimant's husband was struck on the lip by a piece of molten metal as a result of his employer's negligence. The ensuing burn caused the tissues in the husband's lip to turn cancerous and the husband eventually died from the cancer. It was, of course, *not* reasonably foreseeable that the defendants' negligence would cause the claimant's husband to develop cancer but the Court of Appeal still held that the cancer was not a remote consequence of the defendant's negligence: the eggshell skull rule applied.

[12] See *Brice* v *Brown* [1984] 1 All ER 997, where the claimant was involved in a car accident with her daughter; the accident was caused by the defendant's negligence. The claimant had suffered from a hysterical personality disorder from early childhood and developed a severe mental illness as a result of the accident, in which the claimant was slightly injured and the daughter more seriously so, though she made a swift recovery. Stuart Smith J held that the claimant's illness was not a remote consequence of the defendant's negligence even though it had not been reasonably foreseeable that the claimant would suffer a psychiatric illness as severe as the one she developed as a result of the accident in which she and her daughter were involved. It was enough that it had been reasonably foreseeable that the claimant would develop *a* psychiatric illness as a result of being involved in the car accident. (It should be noted that nowadays the claimant would not even need to show that it was reasonably foreseeable that she would suffer a psychiatric illness as a result of being involved in the accident: it would be enough for her to show that it was reasonably foreseeable that she would suffer some kind of physical injury as a result. See *Page* v *Smith* [1996] AC 155, discussed below, pp. 561–2.)

(2) *Economic loss consequent on physical injury.* A rule analogous to the eggshell skull rule says that if A has committed a tort in relation to B, and B has suffered some kind of physical injury as a result, if B can recover compensation for the physical injury that she has suffered as a result of A's tort, she will be able to sue A for compensation in respect of the economic losses that she has suffered as a result of sustaining that injury without having to prove that it was reasonably foreseeable at the time A committed his tort that she would suffer those economic losses as a result. Scrutton LJ made the point graphically in *The Arpad*: 'In the cases of claims in tort, damages are constantly given for consequences of which the defendant had no notice. You negligently run down a shabby-looking man in the street, and he turns out to be a millionaire engaged in a very profitable business which the accident disables him from carrying on [. . . you will be held liable for the economic loss so caused].'[13]

The same rule will *not* apply if A commits a tort and B suffers some damage to *property* of hers which causes her to suffer various consequential economic losses. If B wants to recover compensation for those economic losses, she will have to show that it was reasonably foreseeable at the time A committed his tort that if A committed that tort she would suffer those kinds of losses as a result.[14] So, for example, suppose Fred negligently ran down and killed Rover, a dog which belonged to Nita. Suppose further that a film company was going to pay Nita £50,000 to use Rover in one of its films. Nita will not be able to sue Fred for compensation for the loss of this £50,000 unless it was reasonably foreseeable at the time Fred ran over and killed Rover that his doing so would prevent Nita making money by hiring Rover out to the film company. However, Nita *will* be entitled to sue Fred for compensation for the fact that Rover has been killed – and this compensation will equal Rover's market value at the time he was killed.[15] So if Rover was especially valuable because he was trained to perform all kinds of tricks, Fred *will* be held liable to pay more to Nita by way of compensatory damages than he would have had Rover been a normal dog.

(3) *Page v Smith.*[16] In this case, the defendant negligently ran into the claimant's car while the claimant was in it. As a result,[17] the claimant developed chronic fatigue syndrome (CFS).[18] The House of Lords held, by a bare majority, that the claimant's CFS was *not* a remote consequence of the defendant's negligence. Two of the Law Lords who made up the majority in *Page v Smith* held that it was reasonably foreseeable at the time the defendant

---

[13] [1934] P 189, 202. To the same effect, see *Smith v London and South Western Railway Co.* (1870) LR 6 CP 14, 22–23 (per Blackburn J).

[14] Scrutton LJ disagreed with this in *The Arpad* [1934] P 189, at 202–3; but he was in a minority on this issue and his views have not been followed since. See, for example, *Saleslease Ltd v Davis* [1999] 1 WLR 1664.

[15] Cf. *Horne v Midland Railway* (1873) LR 8 CP 131, 140 (per Blackburn J). See below, p. 597.

[16] [1996] AC 155.

[17] It was found in *Page v Smith (No. 2)* [1996] 1 WLR 855 that the claimant's CFS was indeed attributable to his being involved in the crash.

[18] The collision was quite trivial but the claimant – having suffered from CFS in the past – was liable to develop CFS again as a results of incidents such as these.

negligently ran into the claimant's car that if he did so the claimant would develop a psychiatric illness as a result.[19] But they *also* expressed their agreement with the opinion of Lord Lloyd, the third member of the majority, and *he* said that the claimant would be entitled to recover for his psychiatric illness even if it was *not* reasonably foreseeable at the time the defendant crashed into the claimant's car that the claimant would suffer a psychiatric illness as a result.[20]

Lord Lloyd's view is hard to justify. He seemed to take the view that even if the claimant's psychiatric illness was not a reasonably foreseeable consequence of the defendant's negligence, the claimant's psychiatric illness would *not* count as a remote consequence of the defendant's negligence under the foreseeability test because psychiatric illness counts as a form of physical injury[21] and it *was* reasonably foreseeable that the claimant would suffer *that kind of loss* if the defendant crashed into the claimant's car.[22] However, it is hard to see why we should treat psychiatric illnesses and physical injuries as being the same kind of loss in this context when in almost every other context we recognise that there is a distinction between them.[23] Perhaps recognising this, the courts seem to be very unwilling to apply *Page* v *Smith* outside the area of traffic accidents.[24]

For example, in *Coleman* v *British Gas*[25] the claimants had a gas heater that had been negligently installed by one of the defendants' employees. As a result of the way it had been installed, carbon monoxide leaked out of the claimants' heater and into their living room for eight years; at which point the fault with the heater was discovered and repaired. The claimants were medically examined and it was found that they had not suffered any ill effects as a result of the

---

[19] [1996] AC 155, 170 (per Lord Ackner), 181–2 (per Lord Browne-Wilkinson).

[20] Though he too thought that at the time the defendant crashed into the claimant's car, it was reasonably foreseeable that the claimant would develop a psychiatric illness as a result: ibid., at 197. The two dissenting Law Lords in *Page* v *Smith* thought that the crash had not been serious enough as to make it reasonably foreseeable that the claimant would suffer a psychiatric illness as a result: ibid., at 169–70 (per Lord Keith of Kinkel), 180 (per Lord Jauncey of Tullichettle).

[21] Ibid., at 197: 'There is no justification for regarding physical and psychiatric injury as "different kinds of damage".'

[22] That was after all the main reason why the defendant owed the claimant a duty to take care not to run into his car in the first place.

[23] For example, a duty of care will normally be owed if it is reasonably foreseeable that someone else will suffer a form of physical injury as a result of your actions – but the same is not necessarily true if it reasonably foreseeable that someone else will suffer a form of psychiatric illness as a result of your actions: see above, p. 88.

[24] *Important note*. Having said that, in *Donachie* v *Chief Constable of Greater Manchester* [2004] EWCA Civ 405, *Page* v *Smith* was applied to allow a claimant police officer to sue for the hypertension that he had suffered as a result of being made by the defendants to make nine trips to a suspect's car to attach a tagging device to the underside of the car (the tagging device was faulty and it took nine trips to make it work). It was held that the defendants had owed the claimant a duty of care not to make him make so many trips to the car because it was reasonably foreseeable that he would suffer some kind of physical injury at the hands of the suspect if he were made to do so. It was held that the claimant could sue for the psychiatric illness that he had suffered as a result of the defendants' breach of this duty of care even though it was not foreseeable that he would suffer such an illness as a result of the defendants' breach; it was enough that it was reasonably foreseeable that the claimant would suffer some kind of physical injury as a result of the defendants' carelessness.

[25] 27 February 2002 (Toulson J), unreported.

heater being defective. However, the claimants became convinced that they had suffered carbon monoxide poisoning and became so worried about this that they each developed a full-blown psychiatric illness. The claimants' claim for compensation in respect of their psychiatric illnesses was dismissed on the ground that it was not reasonably foreseeable at the time the employee fitted the heater that if he fitted it badly the claimants would develop a psychiatric illness as a result. The claimants had argued that this did not matter. They argued – *á la* Lord Lloyd in *Page* v *Smith* – that it had been reasonably foreseeable that they would suffer some form of physical injury if the heater was defectively installed and they had suffered *that kind of loss* as a result of the heater being defectively installed when they developed their psychiatric illnesses. However *Page* v *Smith* was distinguished on the ground that the defendant's negligence in that case had caused the claimant in that case to receive a shock to his system – here, there had been no equivalent shock, just a growing sense of anxiety.[26] The distinction seems quite tenuous and bespeaks an underlying unease with applying *Page* v *Smith* at all.[27]

Given this, one should be careful in applying *Page* v *Smith* outside the context of traffic accidents.[28] Within that context, one can say with some confidence that if A negligently causes a traffic accident in which B was involved *and* (*a*) B was injured in the accident and developed a psychiatric illness as a result; *or* (*b*) B was not injured in the accident but so frightened by it that she developed a psychiatric illnesss, B's psychiatric illness will not have been a remote consequence of A's negligence so long as it was reasonably foreseeable that B would suffer some kind of physical injury as a result of the accident occurring. Outside the context of traffic accidents, it is hard to know in what situations, if any, *Page* v *Smith* will apply to relieve the victim of a tort who has suffered a psychiatric illness from the necessity of showing that it was reasonably foreseeable that she would suffer that illness.

(4) *Intentional torts*. The foreseeability test for determining whether the loss

---

[26] Ibid., at [57].

[27] See also *Group B Plaintiffs* v *British Medical Council* [2000] Lloyd's Rep Med 161 (discussed, O'Sullivan 1999) where the claimants were negligently injected with human growth hormone (HGH) that might have contained a virus that could trigger Creutzfeld-Jakob Disease (CJD). Here it was reasonably foreseeable that the claimants would suffer a physical injury as a result of being given the HGH (that was why the defendants who injected the claimants owed them a duty in the first place not to give them the HGH) but the claimants developed psychiatric illnesses instead as a result of worrying about whether they would develop CJD in the future. The claimants were allowed to recover compensation for their psychiatric illnesses but Morland J held that they would *not* have been entitled to recover if their psychiatric illnesses had not been a reasonably foreseeable consequence of the defendants' negligence: in other words, he did not think *Page* v *Smith* applied in this kind of case.

[28] Though see *Essa* v *Laing* [2004] EWCA Civ 02, where the defendant committed the statutory tort of racial discrimination (discussed above, p. 488) in relation to the claimant and the claimant suffered a psychiatric illness as a result. Held, on the basis of *Page* v *Smith*, that the claimant could sue for damages in respect of his psychiatric illness even if it was not a foreseeable consequence of the defendant's tort: it was enough that it was reasonably foreseeable that the claimant would suffer distress as a result of the defendant's tort. Rix LJ dissented on this point.

suffered by the victim of a tort was a remote consequence of that tort does not seem to apply to cases where someone commits an *intentional tort*.

We should explain that an intentional tort is *not* a tort that is committed intentionally. An intentional tort is a tort that can *only* be committed intentionally – that is, by someone who knows what he or she is doing. So most of the torts we have studied – such as negligence, battery, false imprisonment, defamation and private nuisance – are examples of *non-intentional torts*. All these torts can be committed unintentionally or inadvertently.[29] In contrast, malicious falsehood is an example of an intentional tort: it can only be committed intentionally – by *maliciously* making a false statement about someone to a third party which results in that someone suffering loss. Other examples of intentional torts are: the intentional infliction of harm using unlawful means, the tort in *Quinn v Leathem*, deceit and malicious prosecution.

It seems the remoteness rule that applies to intentional torts goes as follows. If A has committed an intentional tort in relation to B and B has suffered some kind of loss as result, that loss will not have been a remote consequence of A's tort if it was a *direct*[30] consequence of A's tort.[31] So A may be held liable to compensate B for the loss she has suffered even if it was *not* reasonably foreseeable at the time A committed his tort that B would suffer that kind of loss as a result. Why is this? Why do the courts treat people who commit unintentional torts more favourably than they do people who commit intentional torts?

The reason must be that the courts recognise that people can commit non-intentional torts quite innocently, and accordingly attempt to ensure that the liability of someone who commits a non-intentional tort does not get out of all proportion to his fault for committing that tort. They attempt to do this by holding someone who has committed a non-intentional tort liable only for the reasonably foreseeable consequences of his tort. In contrast, someone who commits an intentional tort will always be very wicked and there is no reason why we should try to put a limit on such a person's liabilities. Accordingly, someone who commits an intentional tort will be held liable for all the losses that were suffered by the victim of his tort as a direct result of that tort being committed – however unforeseeable those losses were.[32]

---

[29] Though of course they can also be committed intentionally. See above, pp. 62–3 for a discussion of whether the tort of negligence can be committed intentionally.

[30] 'Direct' here probably means 'without the intervention of any other cause'. So the fire damage that resulted from the defendant's parking his car without authority in the claimants' car park in *Mayfair Ltd v Pears* [1987] 1 NZLR 459 (discussed above, p. 348) was not a direct consequence of the defendant's intentional trespass on the claimants' land: the defendant's trespass only resulted in the claimants' car park suffering fire damage because the car caught on fire.

[31] *Doyle v Olby (Ironmongers) Ltd* [1969] 2 QB 158 and *Smith New Court v Scrimgeour Vickers (Asset Management) Ltd* [1997] AC 254 confirm that this is the position in relation to the tort of deceit. Lord Lindley confirmed that this is the position in regard to the tort in *Quinn v Leathem* in *Quinn v Leathem* itself: [1901] AC 495, 527.

[32] *Important note.* Of course, if A has *deliberately* committed a non-intentional tort, it is hard to see why the courts should treat him any more indulgently than it does people who commit intentional torts. Given this, there is a strong case for saying that the remoteness rule which applies to people who commit intentional torts should also be applied to people who deliberately commit non-intentional torts. (To the same effect, see Gordley 1998.) Under this approach, if A has deliberately committed a non-intentional tort in relation to B and B has suffered some kind of loss as a direct result of A's committing that tort, that loss would not be a remote con-

(5) *Statutory torts.* In *Essa* v *Laing*,[33] the Court of Appeal held that if A has committed a tort by breaching a statutory duty owed to B and B has suffered some kind of loss as a result, the foreseeability test will not necessarily apply to determine whether the loss suffered by B was a remote consequence of A's tort. To see whether the test will apply or not, one simply has to interpret the Act or Regulations that created the statutory duty breached by A.[34] In *Essa*, the defendant committed a tort under the Race Relations Act 1976 by racially abusing the claimant. The claimant developed a psychiatric illness as a result of the abuse he had suffered. Pill and Clarke LJJ held that – given the language of, and policy underlying, the 1976 Act – the foreseeability test should *not* be applied to determine whether the claimant's psychiatric illness was a remote consequence of the defendant's tort. It seems that Pill LJ might have taken a different view had the defendant's tort been committed unintentionally,[35] whereas Clarke LJ took the view that the foreseeability test should *never* apply in race discrimination cases. The third judge in the *Essa* case – Rix LJ – thought that the foreseeability test should apply in race discrimination cases: there was no reason to adopt a more relaxed remoteness rule given that a tort can be committed under the 1976 Act even if one has no intention of doing so.[36] Taken together, the judgments in the *Essa* case are deeply unsatisfactory. They have created a great deal of uncertainty over what remoteness rules will apply in respect of the various statutory torts recognised in English law – and, because each of the judges in *Essa* took a different view on the issue, they do not even have the merit of establishing once and for all what remoteness rule will apply in race discrimination cases.

WRONG KIND OF LOSS

The basic principle

Suppose A has committed a tort by breaching a duty owed to B. Suppose further that the duty breached by A was imposed on him in order to help ensure

---

sequence of A's tort – even if it was not reasonably foreseeable that B would suffer that kind of loss when A committed his tort. There is some authority in favour of the view that the remoteness rule that applies to people who commit intentional torts should also be applied to people who intentionally commit non-intentional torts. Lord Nicholls indicated he thought that a defendant who intentionally converted another's goods should be held liable for all the losses suffered by that other as a direct result of the defendant's act of conversion in *Kuwait Airways Corpn* v *Iraqi Airways Co. (Nos 4 & 5)* [2002] 2 AC 883, at [103]–[104]; and the New Zealand Court of Appeal held in *Mayfair Ltd* v *Pears* [1987] 1 NZLR 459 that a defendant who intentionally trespasses on another's land should be held liable for all the losses suffered by that other as a direct result of the defendant's trespass. See also Pill LJ's judgment in *Essa* v *Laing* [2004] EWCA Civ 2, discussed below.

[33] [2004] EWCA Civ 2
[34] Ibid., at [46], [48] (per Clarke LJ)
[35] Ibid., at [39].
[36] Ibid., at [98], [105]. Rix LJ was unenthusiastic about the idea that the foreseeability test should apply in cases of non-intentional racial discrimination but not in cases of intentional race discrimination: ibid., at [106].

that B did not suffer a certain kind of loss. Suppose finally that one of the *primary losses* suffered by B as a result of A's tort was a different kind of loss from the loss which the duty breached by A was imposed on him in order to avoid. If this is true then it seems that that primary loss will be non-actionable on the ground that it amounts to the *wrong kind of loss*.[37]

Examples of the principle at work

A number of cases show this principle – which we can call the *wrong kind of loss principle* – in action.

(1) *Breach of a statutory duty owed to another*.[38] In *Gorris* v *Scott*,[39] the claimant's sheep were transported to a foreign port on the defendant's ship. Under the Contagious Diseases (Animals) Act 1869, the defendant had a statutory duty to ship the claimant's sheep in pens. However, he did not bother doing this. As a result, the claimant's sheep were swept out to sea when a wave crashed onto the defendant's ship; had they been placed in pens at the time, the sheep would have been perfectly safe. The claimant sued the defendant for compensation for the loss of his sheep but his claim was dismissed.

The duty breached by the defendant in this case was imposed on him *not* in order to stop the claimant's sheep from drowning but in order to help ensure that if some of the claimant's sheep contracted some kind of disease mid-voyage the disease would not spread to the rest of the claimant's sheep; if the claimant's sheep were kept separated in pens the sheep in one pen would not be able to pass on any disease they were suffering from to the sheep in the other pens. So the primary loss suffered by the claimant in this case – the loss of his sheep through drowning – was non-actionable because it was the wrong kind of loss; not the kind of loss which the duty breached by the defendant in this case was imposed on him in order to avoid.

---

[37] While academics are only now starting to take seriously the idea that a loss suffered by the victim of a tort will not be actionable if it is the wrong kind of loss (thanks mainly to Lord Hoffmann's judgment in *South Australia Asset Management Corporation* v *York Montague Ltd* [1997] AC 191) there is good reason to think that this idea underlies the existence of the foreseeability test for remoteness of damage in negligence. See, for example, Machin 1954 and Stauch 2001, both of whom advance wrong kind of loss-type arguments in favour of a foreseeability test of remoteness in negligence. (The idea being that if A owes B a duty of care because it is foreseeable that B will suffer loss X if A is careless, then if A is careless and B suffers a different and unforeseeable loss Y as a result of A's carelessness, B should not be allowed to sue for compensation for loss Y: it is the wrong kind of loss, not the kind of loss that A's duty of care was imposed on him in order to avoid.) Machin's article was truly ahead of its time, anticipating by seven years the Privy Council's decision in *The Wagon Mound* [1961] AC 388.

[38] See Stanton 2003, 303–5.

[39] (1874) LR 9 Ex 125. See also *Nicholls* v *F Austin (Leyton) Ltd* [1946] AC 493 (claimant was hit and injured by a piece of wood flying out of a piece of machinery that had been inadequately fenced, in breach of s 14(1) of the Factories Act 1937; held, the claimant could not sue her employer for damages because s 14(1) was designed to prevent the claimant coming into contact with dangerous machinery, not to prevent her being hit by something that had been ejected from a machine).

(2) *Dangerously defective buildings.* Suppose that Karen commissioned Tom to build a house for her. Tom built the house but he carelessly failed to ensure that the house was built on adequate foundations. However, when the house was built it seemed to be fine and Karen was very happy with it. After a few years, she sold the house to Eric, who subsequently sold the house to Wendy. A few months after Wendy moved in, the problem with the foundations became apparent and it soon became clear that the house was actually dangerous to live in. Wendy spent £10,000 on having the foundations strengthened, thereby making the house safe to live in again. Can Wendy sue Tom for compensation for the £10,000 she has spent on making the house save to live in?

Now – there is no doubt that in this situation, Tom owed Wendy a duty to take care not to build the house in such a manner that it would become physically dangerous to live in it.[40] There is no doubt either that he breached this duty and that his breach caused Wendy to lose £10,000.[41] Moreover, the economic loss suffered by Wendy was not a remote consequence of Tom's negligence – it was eminently foreseeable at the time Tom built the house that if he built the house in such a way that it would become dangerous to live in, a future occupant of the house down the line would have to spend money having the house repaired. But the decisions of the House of Lords in *D & F Estates* v *Church Commissioners*[42] and *Murphy* v *Brentwood DC*[43] make it clear that Wendy will *not* be entitled to sue Tom in negligence for compensation for the economic loss she has suffered here.[44]

One explanation why Wendy will not be entitled to sue Tom here is that she has suffered the wrong kind of loss. The duty of care that Tom breached here

---

[40] The existence of this duty can be justified under the physical danger principle set about above, pp. 66–85.

[41] Wendy acted perfectly reasonably in spending £10,000 on having the house made safe to live in so her decision to spend that money did *not* amount to a *novus actus interveniens*, breaking the chain of causation between Tom's negligence and the economic loss suffered by Wendy.

[42] [1989] AC 177.

[43] [1991] 1 AC 398.

[44] *Important note.* The position taken by the House of Lords is not without its critics (see, for example, Cooke 1991; Fleming 1997, 59–60) and it is clear that in other common law jurisdictions Wendy *would* be entitled to sue Tom in negligence for compensation for the economic loss she has suffered: see *Bryan* v *Moloney* (1995) 182 CLR 609 (Australia); *Winnipeg Condominium Corporation No. 36* v *Bird Construction Co. Ltd* [1995] 1 SCR 85 (Canada). It may be that the criticism of the House of Lords' stance rests on a false premise. The critics say that in the situation we are considering Wendy *ought* to be able to sue Tom for the money she has spent on making her house safe; *therefore* she ought to be able to sue Tom in *negligence*. But this assumes that the *only* cause of action available to Wendy in this situation is a claim in negligence. There is no reason to think that this is true. See Moran 1997 for an interesting argument that Wendy would be able to bring a claim in *restitution* against Tom to recover the money she has spent in making her house safe to live in. There are a number of American cases which support Moran's argument: see *City of New York* v *Keene Corp.*, 505 NYS 2d 782 (1986) (aff'd, 513 NYS 2d 1004 (1987)) (claimants allowed to sue defendants in restitution for cost of removing potentially toxic asbestos which defendants had installed in claimants' schools); *Adams-Araphoe School District No. 28-J* v *Celotex Corp.*, 637 F Supp 1207 (1986) (ditto); *Drayton Public School District No. 19* v *WR Grace & Co.*, 728 F Supp 1410 (1989) (ditto); *City of New York* v *Lead Industries Ass'n, Inc.*, 644 NYS 2d 919 (1996) (claimants allowed to sue manufacturers of potentially toxic paint in restitution for cost of removing paint from their city buildings).

was imposed on him in order to help ensure that people like Wendy would not be *physically injured* as a result of living in the house built by Tom. But in this situation the only loss that Wendy has suffered as a result of Tom's breach was that she had to spend money on having her house repaired – a completely different kind of loss from the kind of loss which the duty breached by Tom was imposed on him in order to avoid. It would therefore have been different if – after Wendy moved in – the problem with the foundations caused part of the house to fall down and Wendy was injured as a result. In such a case, Wendy would have suffered the right kind of loss as a result of Tom's breach of the duty of care that he owed her and would therefore have no problem suing Tom for compensation for her injury.[45]

Similarly, a different result would have been reached in Tom and Wendy's case if Tom had owed Wendy a duty under s 1 of the Defective Premises Act 1972 to ensure that his work was done in a workmanlike manner and with proper materials so that the house built by him would be fit for habitation. If Tom had owed Wendy such a duty, she *would* have been able to sue him under the 1972 Act for the £10,000 she spent on repairing her house. This is because the duty imposed on those undertaking work in connection with the provision of a house is not just imposed on them in order to help ensure that future occupants of the house will not be injured; the duty is also imposed in order to help ensure that the future occupants of the house will not have to spend money making the house safe to live in. So the £10,000 spent by Wendy on making the house safe to live in would *not* have counted as the wrong kind of loss.

(3) *Power cut*. In *Spartan Steel & Alloys Ltd* v *Martin & Co. (Contractors) Ltd*,[46] the defendants negligently damaged an electric power cable that supplied electricity to the claimants' factory, thus causing the claimants' factory to be shut down for about 14 hours. The claimants manufactured stainless steel in that factory. Among other things they would melt metal in furnaces in order to turn it into stainless steel ingots. The power cut caused the claimants to suffer two primary losses. First of all, the 'melts' that were being processed at the time of the power cut were damaged. Secondly, because the defendants could not operate their factory, they suffered an economic loss of £1,767: this was the profit they would have made if they had been allowed to work for the 14 hours the factory was out of action. The claimants were allowed to sue the defendants in negligence for compensation in respect of the first loss, but not the second. The wrong kind of loss principle explains why.

The defendants had owed the claimants a duty to take care not to cut off the power to their factory because it was reasonably foreseeable that if they did so the claimants' property would be damaged.[47] So the duty of care that the defendants breached in this case was imposed on them in order to help ensure that

---

[45] See *Rimmer* v *Liverpool City Council* [1985] QB 1; *Targett* v *Torfaen Borough Council* [1992] 3 All ER 27.
[46] [1973] 1 QB 27.
[47] See above, pp. 110–11.

the claimants did not suffer any harm to their property. So the damage to the 'melts' that the claimants suffered as a result of the defendants' negligence in *Spartan Steel* counted as the right kind of loss and was therefore actionable: it was the kind of loss which the duty breached by the defendants had been imposed on them in order to avoid. By contrast, the loss of profits suffered by the claimants in *Spartan Steel* as a result of their factory being shut down counted as the wrong kind of loss and was therefore non-actionable: the duty breached by the defendants was not imposed on them in order to help ensure that the claimants did not experience any interruption in the running of their business.

(4) *Negligently inflicted pure distress.* In *Hicks* v *Chief Constable of South Yorkshire Police*,[48] the claimants were representatives of Sarah and Victoria Hicks, two football fans who were suffocated to death in the Hillsborough tragedy. Sarah and Victoria Hicks were standing at the front of a full spectator pen in the Leppings Lane end of the Hillsborough ground waiting to watch the start of the FA Cup semi-final between Liverpool and Nottingham Forest. In order to get Liverpool fans who were still waiting outside Hillsborough into the ground, the police decided to open the outer gate to the Leppings Lane end of the ground without first cutting off access to the spectator pen where Sarah and Victoria Hicks were standing. As a result, Liverpool fans rushed into the back of that spectator pen and Sarah and Victoria Hicks were crushed and suffocated to death, as were 93 other fans.

The police who were in charge at Hillsborough clearly owed the Hickses a duty not to act as they did – it was reasonably foreseeable that people like Sarah and Victoria Hicks would be killed or injured if the police opened the outer gate at the Leppings Lane end of the ground without first shutting the gate to the spectator pen where the Hickses were standing. Equally clearly the police breached that duty. So the claimants sued the police in negligence for damages in respect of the losses that Sarah and Victoria Hicks suffered before they died. The House of Lords found that the police's negligence only caused the Hickses to suffer one kind of loss before they died: distress. The House of Lords found that the Hickses suffered no physical injury before the moment of their deaths through crushing[49] and so the only loss suffered by the Hickses before their death was the anxiety, pain and suffering they experienced as their situation grew more and more desperate at the front of the pen. The House of Lords went on to hold that the claimants could not sue for compensation in respect of this distress that Sarah and Victoria Hicks had experienced before they died.

The wrong kind of loss principle explains why the Hickses' distress was non-actionable. The duty of care breached by the police in this case was imposed on them in order to help ensure that people like Sarah and Victoria Hicks were not killed or injured. But the police's breach of that duty resulted in the Hickses suffering a completely different kind of primary loss: distress.

[48] [1992] 2 All ER 65.
[49] [1992] 2 All ER 65, 68j–69c.

Acordingly, that distress was non-actionable under the wrong kind of loss principle.

(5) *Private nuisance.* Adapting the facts of *Malone* v *Laskey*[50] somewhat, suppose that Dawn and Gary are neighbours. Suppose further that Gary committed a tort of private nuisance in relation to Dawn by running an engine on his land to produce electricity which was so noisy and produced such large vibrations that Dawn's use and enjoyment of her land was seriously interfered with. Suppose finally that one day while Gary's engine was running, the walls of Dawn's house began to shake with the result that a shelf fell off one of the walls of Dawn's house and hit her on the head.

Now in this case, Dawn has suffered two primary losses as a result of Gary's committing the tort of private nuisance – and let us suppose that both of them were equally foreseeable consequences of Gary's tort. First of all, she suffers a form of economic loss: Gary's running of his engine on his land diminishes the value of her land. Secondly, Dawn suffered a physical injury: the injury to her head. Now Dawn will be entitled to sue Gary in private nuisance for damages in respect of the interference with the value of her land that she has suffered as a result of his tort. But what about the physical injury she has sustained? In *Hunter* v *Canary Wharf Ltd*, Lords Hoffmann and Lloyd made it clear that they thought that Dawn would *not* be entitled to sue Gary in private nuisance for compensation in respect of the injury to her head.[51]

The wrong kind of loss principle explains why this is. The duty breached by Gary in committing the tort of private nuisance here was imposed on him in order to help ensure that the use-value of Dawn's land was not unreasonably interfered with – so the diminution in the value of Dawn's land that has resulted from Gary's running his engine counts as the right kind of loss, the kind of loss that the duty breached by Gary here was imposed on him in order to avoid. That loss is therefore actionable in private nuisance. In contrast, the physical injury suffered by Dawn here counts as the wrong kind of loss: the duty breached by Gary in committing the tort of private nuisance was *not* imposed on him in order to help ensure that Dawn would not be physically injured. So that loss is not actionable in private nuisance.

Of course it is probable that Gary, in running his engine, also committed the tort of negligence. If it was reasonably foreseeable that Dawn would be injured as a result of Gary's running his engine, then Gary would almost certainly have owed Dawn a duty not to run that engine.[52] If he did then Dawn *would* be entitled to sue Gary in *negligence* for compensation for the head injury she suffered as a result of his running his engine. That injury would count as a foreseeable consequence of Gary's negligence and, moreover, no wrong kind of loss objection could be made to Dawn's suing Gary in negligence for compensation in respect of her head injury because the duty of care that Gary breached

[50] [1907] 2 KB 141.
[51] [1997] AC 655, 696D (per Lord Lloyd), 707H (per Lord Hoffmann).
[52] This is under the physical danger principle discussed above, at pp. 62–85.

in this case *was* imposed on him in order to help ensure that Dawn would not be physically injured.

Three important points

Three important points remain to be made about the wrong kind of loss principle.

(1) *Duties that are not imposed to prevent someone suffering a particular kind of loss.* The wrong kind of loss principle only bites in the case where A has committed a tort by breaching a duty owed to B that was imposed on him in order to help ensure that B would not suffer a particular kind of loss. But there are plenty of duties that A might owe B that are not like this. Such duties are *not* imposed on A in order to help ensure that B does not suffer a *particular* kind of loss; rather, they are imposed on A for B's *general advantage*. So if A breaches one of these duties, then the wrong kind of loss principle simply will not apply to determine whether the primary losses suffered by B as a result of A's breach are non-actionable.

For example, suppose that A agreed to perform a particular task for B and as a result he owed her a duty to perform that task with a reasonable degree of care and skill under the extended principle in *Hedley Byrne*. Suppose further that A breached this duty and B suffered one primary loss as a result: some kind of economic loss. Suppose finally that B is not barred from suing A for compensation in respect of this loss under the *SAAMCO* principle – part of the reason why A was given the job of performing the task that he took on was to help ensure that B did not suffer that loss.[53]

The duty breached by A here does not seem to have been imposed on him in order to help ensure that B would not suffer a particular kind of loss – rather the duty that A owed B here was imposed on him for B's general advantage. So the wrong kind of loss principle simply will not apply here and the question of whether the economic loss suffered by B as a result of A's negligence is actionable will depend on whether it was reasonably foreseeable that B would suffer that loss when A breached his duty of care; whether it would be contrary to public policy to allow B to sue A for compensation for that loss; and whether the economic loss suffered by B is automatically non-actionable.[54]

---

[53] The *SAAMCO* principle is discussed above, at pp. 135–8.

[54] *Important note.* So if A undertook to do some work for B with the result that A owed B a duty to perform that work with a reasonable degree of care and skill under the extended principle in *Hedley Byrne*, B will usually be able to sue A if A breaches that duty and she suffers a form of pure economic loss as a result so long as one of the reasons why A was given the job of doing that work in the first place was to help ensure that B did not suffer that kind of loss, thus satisfying the *SAAMCO* principle. The same point applies if B suffers some kind of pure distress as a result of A's breach of a duty that A owed B under the extended principle in *Hedley Byrne* to perform a task with a reasonable degree of care and skill. So long as one of the reasons A had been given the task that he failed to perform properly was to help ensure that B did not suffer that distress – thus satisfying the *SAAMCO* principle – there is no fundamental reason why B should not be allowed to sue A in negligence for compensation for her distress. These conditions were satisfied in the case of *Farley v Skinner* [2002] 2 AC 732 (*not* a tort case). In that case, the

(2) *Secondary losses.* It important to remember that the wrong kind of loss principle only applies to determine whether a *primary* loss suffered by the victim of a tort is actionable. It does not apply to *secondary* losses.[55]

So, for example, in *Attia v British Gas*[56] the defendants negligently burned down the claimant's house when they did work on her house. The claimant came home to see her house burning down and suffered a psychiatric illness as a result. In this case, the claimant suffered a primary loss (damage to her house) and a secondary loss (psychiatric illness) that flowed from this primary loss. The primary loss was actionable under the wrong kind of loss principle: the duty of care breached by the defendants in this case had been imposed on them in order to help ensure that the claimant's house was not damaged or destroyed. The wrong kind of loss principle did not apply to the claimant's psychiatric illness because that illness counted as a secondary loss. So it could not be argued that the claimant's psychiatric illness was not actionable because the duty breached by the defendants in this case was not imposed on them in order to help ensure that the claimant would not suffer a psychiatric illness. So long, then, as the claimant's psychiatric illness was not a remote consequence of the defendants' negligence – because it was not reasonably foreseeable at the time they burned down the claimants' house that she would suffer a psychiatric illness as a result – the claimant's psychiatric illness was actionable.[57]

(3) *A rogue case.* We should note one case in which a claimant was allowed to recover compensation in respect of a primary loss suffered by him as a result of the defendant's tort even though that loss was non-actionable under the wrong kind of loss principle.[58]

---

claimant was thinking of buying a house in Sussex which was 15 miles away from Gatwick Airport. He paid the defendant surveyor to tell him whether the house would be unduly affected by the noise of aeroplanes taking off and landing. The surveyor reported back that, essentially, the claimant had nothing to worry about and the claimant subsequently bought the house. He then discovered that the house was substantially affected by aircraft noise because it was located near a beacon that planes would circle while they were waiting to land. The claimant brought an action for breach of contract against the defendant surveyor, claiming damages designed to compensate him for the fact that the time he spent in the house was made miserable through the amount of aircraft noise he had to endure. The claim was allowed. It is hard to imagine that the result would have been any different had the claimant sued the defendant in *negligence*, claiming that his distress was a result of the defendant's breach of a duty of care that the defendant owed the claimant under the extended principle in *Hedley Byrne*. In particular, the *SAAMCO* principle would not have stood in the way of the claimant suing the defendant for his distress here as the whole point of his getting the defendant to survey his house was to avoid suffering that distress.

[55] Though any secondary losses suffered by a claimant because she suffered a primary loss which is non-actionable under the wrong kind of loss principle will themselves be non-actionable: see below, pp. 585–6.

[56] [1988] QB 304.

[57] The other two tests for determining whether a loss is actionable did not apply here: it would not have been contrary to public policy to allow the claimant to recover for her psychiatric illness and there was no reason why the claimant's psychiatric illness was automatically non-actionable.

[58] *Important note.* There are also a couple of rogue *dicta* which indicate that if A carelessly creates a danger to other people's health and B is compelled by law to spend money eliminating that danger, then B will be entitled to sue A in negligence for compensation for the fact that she has had to spend that money: see *Murphy v Brentwood DC* [1991] 1 AC 398, 495 (per Lord Bridge); *The Orjula* [1995] 2 Lloyd's Rep 395, 403 (per Mance J). These *dicta* are inconsistent with the wrong kind of loss

In *Morrison Steamship Co. Ltd* v *Greystoke Castle (Cargo Owners)*,[59] two ships – the *Greystoke Castle* and the *Cheldale* – collided. The collision was due in part to the negligence of the defendants who were in charge of the *Cheldale*. As a result of the collision the *Greystoke Castle* had to put into port to be repaired. Before the *Greystoke Castle* could be repaired, its cargo had to be unloaded. After the *Greystoke Castle* was repaired, its cargo was reloaded onto the ship. The claimants were owners of cargo on board the *Greystoke Castle* and the owners of the *Greystoke Castle* charged the claimants – as they were entitled to do under the terms of the contract of carriage between them and the claimants – for some of the expense they had incurred (called a 'general average expenditure') in unloading and reloading the claimant's goods. The claimants successfully sued the defendants in negligence so as to be compensated for the pure economic loss that this charge caused them to suffer.

No complaints can be made about the court's finding that the defendants had owed the claimants a duty to take care not to collide with the *Greystoke Castle*; or that the defendants breached that duty; or that the defendants' negligence caused the claimants to incur the economic loss for which they were suing; or that that economic loss was a non-remote consequence of the defendants' negligence. However, the economic loss suffered by the claimants was non-actionable under the wrong kind of loss principle. The duty of care breached by the defendants in this case was imposed on them in order to help ensure that the claimants' property was not damaged: a completely different kind of loss from the loss that the claimants suffered here. It is therefore a bit of a puzzle why the claimants were allowed to sue the defendants in this case. However, it should be noted that only a bare majority (three to two) of the Law Lords who decided the *Greystoke Castle* case were in favour of holding the defendants liable to compensate the claimants and subsequent judicial reaction to the *Greystoke Castle* case has been tepid to say the least.[60]

PUBLIC POLICY

Suppose that A has committed a tort in relation to B and B suffered some kind of loss as a result. Obviously, the courts will hold that that loss is not actionable if it would be contrary to public policy to allow B to sue A for compensation in respect of that loss.

In *Pritchard* v *J H Cobden Ltd*,[61] the claimant was severely injured in a road traffic accident caused by the defendant's negligence. He suffered brain

---

principle: even if A breached a duty of care owed to B in creating the danger in question, that duty was imposed on A to save B from being physically harmed, not in order to save her from having to incur the expense of cleaning up the danger created by A. It may be that the judges in these cases got their causes of action mixed up and instead of saying that B could sue A in *negligence* for the cost of eliminating the danger created by A they should have said that B could sue A in *restitution*: see above, n. 44.

[59] [1947] AC 265.

[60] See *Murphy* v *Brentwood DC* [1991] 1 AC 398, 468F (per Lord Keith of Kinkel): '[The *Greystoke Castle*] case, which was decided by a narrow majority, may . . . be regarded as turning on specialities of maritime law concerned in the relationship of joint adventurers at sea.'

[61] [1988] Fam 22.

damage which meant he experienced a complete change in personality. As a result, his marriage broke down and his wife divorced him. The claimant sued the defendant, seeking to be compensated for the economic loss that he had suffered when his assets were divided up between him and his wife in the divorce. The Court of Appeal held that the economic loss suffered by the claimant in *Pritchard* was not actionable. The reason was that it would be contrary to public policy to allow the claimant to sue the defendant so as to be compensated for this loss of wealth.

There were a number of reasons why this was so. First, allowing this sort of claim could lead to abuse. Suppose Vijay and Sarah were a married couple who were going to divorce when Vijay was involved in an accident negligently caused by Ian. If the sort of claim made by the claimant in *Pritchard* were allowed, Vijay and Sarah could easily collude with each other and claim that, when they divorced each other, they did so because of the effects of the accident. Vijay would then be allowed to recover from Ian, and split with Sarah the value of the assets that he lost in the divorce.

Secondly, allowing this sort of claim could undermine marriages. Suppose that Fred was happily married to Beth when he was involved in an accident that was negligently caused by Paul, and that the injuries sustained by Fred in the accident had a damaging effect on his personality. If the sort of claim made by the claimant in *Pritchard* were allowed then Fred would know that if Beth divorced him because of his change in personality he would suffer no financial prejudice whatsoever: he would be able to claim the value of any assets he lost in the divorce. He would then have less incentive to try and moderate the effect of the accident on his personality for the sake of preserving his marriage.

Thirdly, if this sort of claim were allowed, then in the case we have just been considering – where Fred was happily married to Beth when he was negligently injured by Paul – if Beth wanted to divorce Fred because of the effect that his injuries have had on his personality, *Paul* would be entitled to be represented in any proceedings dealing with how Fred and Beth's assets should be divided. This is because such proceedings would have an effect on his legal liabilities. So the divorce court dealing with Fred and Beth's divorce would have to have regard not to their interests, but also Paul's interests, in deciding how Fred and Beth's assets should be divided between them.

Another case where public policy was invoked as a reason for finding that a loss suffered by the victim of a tort was non-actionable was *Meah v McCreamer (No. 2)*.[62] We have already come across the first *Meah v McCreamer* case.[63] In *that* case, it will be recalled, the defendant negligently crashed a car that he was driving. The claimant was a passenger in the car and suffered severe head injuries as a result. The claimant's injuries caused his personality to change for the worse. Before the accident, he had been involved in various scrapes with the law but did not have a history of being violent. After the accident, he developed

---

[62] [1986] 1 All ER 943.
[63] *Meah v McCreamer* [1985] 1 All ER 367. See above, pp. 515, 545.

a tendency to attack women. As a result, he sexually assaulted two women and was sent to prison.

In the first *Meah* v *McCreamer* case, the claimant sued the defendant for compensation for the fact that he had been sent to prison and Woolf J allowed his claim, awarding the claimant £45,500 in damages. This decision caused something of a public outcry, which had the useful side effect of letting the two women who had been attacked by the claimant know that the claimant now had some money and was worth suing. Accordingly, they sued the claimant in tort for compensation in respect of the harm they had suffered when he attacked them and between them they obtained £17,000 in damages.[64] The claimant then sued the defendant again in *Meah* v *McCreamer (No. 2)*, arguing that the defendant was liable to compensate him for the damages he had had to pay out to the women he had attacked.

This time round, Woolf J – perhaps wary of the outcry that had attended his first decision[65] – dismissed the claimant's claim. He held that it would be contrary to public policy to allow the claimant to sue the defendant for the £17,000 he had had to pay in damages to the victims of his sexual assaults.[66] Why would it have been contrary to public policy to allow the claimant to sue the defendant here? Woolf J did not say much in support of his finding on this issue, remarking only that it would be 'distasteful' to allow the claimant to sue.[67] However, it can be inferred from other parts of his judgment that he was concerned that if the claimant's claim was allowed here then the defendant's liability to the claimant might become unlimited in nature – with the defendant being held liable for any harm caused by the claimant's personality disorder.

A third case in which public policy was invoked to explain why a loss suffered by the victim of a tort was non-actionable was *Spartan Steel & Alloys Ltd* v *Martin & Co. (Contractors) Ltd*.[68] In that case, it will be recalled, the claimants were not allowed to sue for compensation in respect of the loss of profits they experienced when the power to their factory was negligently cut off by the defendants. The finding that the claimants' loss of profits was non-actionable can be justified by reference to the wrong kind of loss principle, but Lord

---

[64] *W* v *Meah, D* v *Meah* [1986] 1 All ER 935.

[65] In *Meah* v *McCreamer (No. 2)* [1986] 1 All ER 943, Woolf J – somewhat defensively – attempted to justify his decision in the first *Meah* v *McCreamer* case on the ground that the claimant had a wife and child who had suffered a loss of support as a result of the claimant's being locked up. So allowing the claimant to recover compensation for his being imprisoned would help him support his wife and child while he was in prison: ibid., 951f–h. (Dependants of the victim of a tort who have suffered a loss of support as a result of that tort are entitled to sue the tortfeasor for compensation in respect of the loss of support that they have experienced, but only if the tort caused the victim of the tort to die: see below, p. 623.)

[66] He also found that the payout to the victims of the claimants' sexual assaults was a remote consequence of the defendant's negligence ([1986] 1 All ER 943, 950d) but that finding is impossible to reconcile with his decision in *Meah* v *McCreamer* [1985] 1 All ER 367: if the claimant's imprisonment was *not* a remote consequence of the defendant's negligence in that case then the claimant's being sued for damages for the things he did which got him imprisoned could not have been a remote consequence of the defendant's negligence either.

[67] [1986] 1 All ER 943, 950h–j.

[68] [1973] 1 QB 27, discussed above, pp. 568–9.

Denning MR also thought it would be contrary to public policy to allow the claimants to recover for their loss of profits.[69]

He had three reasons for thinking that it would be contrary to public policy to allow this element of the claimants' claim. First, allowing claims such as the claimants' to succeed could lead to abuse. Someone whose business was disrupted by a negligently caused power cut would be tempted to exaggerate the profits he could have made had his business not had its power cut off if he knew that he could claim compensation for the profits he would have made if his business had not been disrupted. Secondly, allowing claims such as the claimants' to succeed could sap people's capacity for self-reliance. Someone whose business was disrupted by a negligently caused power cut would have less incentive to make up the profits he could have made had the power cut not occurred if he knew that he could claim compensation for the loss of those profits from whoever was responsible for the occurrence of the power cut. Moreover, someone running a business would have less incentive to take steps to guard against having his business disrupted by a negligently caused power cut (by, for example, installing a back-up power system) if he knew that should his business be disrupted by a negligently caused power cut, he could recover compensation for the profits he would have made had his business not been disrupted. Thirdly, allowing claims such as the claimants' to succeed would result in the courts being clogged with claims for compensation for losses suffered as a result of power cuts, thus making it harder for more important and more deserving cases to be dealt with speedily.

LOSSES THAT ARE AUTOMATICALLY NON-ACTIONABLE

Some kinds of losses that might be suffered by the victim of a tort are automatically regarded as being non-actionable. They are as follows.

The cost of bringing up a child

Suppose A committed a tort in relation to B and B ended up giving birth to a child that she would not otherwise have had.[70] It is well established that in this situation B will be entitled to sue A for compensation in respect of the inconvenience that she suffered in the run-up to giving birth, the pain and suffering that she went through in labour, any economic losses that she suffered before giving birth as a result of

---

[69] Ibid., 38E–39A.

[70] The two most common situations where this will happen are as follows. (1) B's partner, C, asks A to perform a vasectomy on him; A fails to carry out the vasectomy properly; B and C, not knowing this, have unprotected sex; B becomes pregnant as a result and chooses to carry the baby to term (in this situation, A will have owed *B* a duty to perform the vasectomy with a reasonable degree of care and skill under the principle in *White v Jones* [1995] 2 AC 207: see above, p. 152). (2) B becomes pregnant and A, B's doctor, negligently fails to tell B that B's baby will be seriously disabled when it is born when had B known this she would have chosen to have an abortion (s 1(1)(d) of the Abortion Act 1967 allows an abortion to be performed 'if there is a serious risk that if the child were born it would suffer from such physical or mental abnormalities as to be seriously handicapped'); as a result B gives birth to a baby that she would not have had but for A's negligence.

taking time off work, having to spend money on new clothes to fit her as she grew larger and so on.[71] But if B attempts to sue A for compensation in respect of the money she is going to have to spend on bringing up the child, she will usually find that that loss is regarded as being automatically non-actionable by the courts.[72] In order to understand *when* this loss will be held to be non-actionable, we have to distinguish between the case where B's child is healthy and the case where B's child is born disabled.

(1) *Healthy child.* The House of Lords ruled in *McFarlane v Tayside Health Board*[73] that if B and her child are both healthy then the cost of bringing up the child will be automatically non-actionable.[74] In a subsequent case – *Rees v Darlington Memorial Hospital NHS Trust*[75] – the House of Lords placed a 'gloss' on the ruling in *McFarlane*, holding that while B would not be entitled to sue A for damages representing the cost of bringing up her child, B *would* be entitled to sue A for a fixed sum of £15,000 to compensate her for the disruption to her life that bringing up her child will involve. Two issues arise out of this: (*a*) Why is B *not* allowed to sue A for the cost of bringing up her child? (*b*) Why *is* B allowed to sue A for a fixed sum of £15,000 to compensate her for the disruption to her life that bringing up her child will involve?

On the first issue, a number of reasons were advanced by the Law Lords in both *McFarlane* and *Rees* as to why the cost of bringing up B's child should be held to be non-actionable. First, it would be wrong, in assessing the damages payable to B for the fact that she had given birth to an unwanted child, to disregard the benefits B would reap from bringing that child up. It would be morally offensive to think that those benefits are worth less than the cost of bringing up B's child – to think that would be to think that bringing B's child

---

[71] *McFarlane v Tayside Health Board* [2000] 2 AC 59, 74A–E (per Lord Slynn), 81F–G (per Lord Steyn), 87B–E (per Lord Hope), 102F–H (per Lord Clyde). It is unclear why, in a type (2) (see n. 70, above) situation, B will be entitled to sue A for compensation in respect of these losses – it could be argued that she willingly took the risk that she would suffer these losses when she became pregnant. See, on this, Mason 2002, 50.

[72] The cost of bringing up B's child will be regarded as actionable in Australia: *Cattanach v Melchior* (2003) HCA 38 (noted, Cane 2004).

[73] [2000] 2 AC 59 (henceforth, '*McFarlane*').

[74] For criticisms of this ruling, see Hoyano 2002. An attempt to get round this ruling was made in *Greenfield v Irwin* [2001] 1 WLR 113, where the claimant – who had given birth to a baby that she would not have had but for the defendants' negligence – did not sue the defendants for the cost of bringing up the baby, but rather sued to be compensated for the loss of income she had experienced as a result of giving up work to look after the baby full-time. The claim was dismissed on the ground that if it were allowed, a coach and horses would be driven through the House of Lords' ruling in *McFarlane*. Another attempt to get round *McFarlane* was made in *Rees v Darlington Memorial Hospital NHS Trust* [2004] 1 AC 309, where a woman who was near-blind decided that she would be incapable of bringing up a baby properly and as a result had the defendants perform a sterilisation operation on her. The defendants performed the operation incompetently and the claimant subsequently conceived, and gave birth to, a healthy baby boy. It was argued that while the claimant's boy was perfectly healthy, the fact that the *claimant* was disabled meant that *McFarlane* did not apply, and that the claimant should at the very least be allowed to recover the *extra* cost of bringing up the boy that was attributable to the fact that *she* was disabled. The House of Lords rejected this claim by 4:3, holding that *McFarlane* applies across the board to *all* cases where someone gives birth to a healthy child as a result of another's negligence.

[75] *Rees v Darlington Memorial Hospital NHS Trust* [2004] 1 AC 309 (henceforth, '*Rees*').

up is more trouble than it is worth. Given this, it must be taken that the benefits of bringing B's child up outweigh the costs and therefore no claim can be made for the cost of bringing up that child.[76] Secondly, the benefits B will reap from bringing her child up are incalculable, but they must be taken into account in judging how much B should be paid by way of damages. The only fair way of taking these benefits into account is to assume that they at least equal the cost of bringing up B's child and therefore no claim can be brought for damages in respect of the cost of bringing up B's child.[77] Thirdly, to make A liable for the cost of bringing up B's child would impose on A a liability far out of proportion to his fault in causing B to conceive in the first place.[78] Fourthly, if A were required to compensate B for the cost of bringing up her child, the funds would in all probability come out of the hard-pressed coffers of the National Health Service; and the general public would think it wrong for that money to be used to subsidise the upbringing of B's child as opposed to using it to treat patients.[79] Fifthly, were B to be compensated for the cost of bringing up her child, then the amount of damages payable to B would depend on how rich she is – the richer she is, the more she could be expected to spend on bringing her child up and therefore the greater the damages that would be payable to B. It would be 'unseemly' for the law to allow B's award to depend on how rich or poor she is.[80]

Moving on to the second issue, why will B be allowed to sue A for a fixed sum of £15,000 in the situation we are considering? The House of Lords divided 4:2 in *Rees* over the issue of whether B should be allowed to make such a claim against A.[81] The majority thought that it would be wrong if the law did nothing to compensate B for the 'loss of autonomy' that she had suffered as a result of giving birth to a child.[82] They thought that awarding B £15,000 would afford her some compensation for this 'loss of autonomy'.[83] Lords Steyn and Hope criticised the majority ruling on this issue. Lord Steyn took the view that the courts simply did not have the power to make awards designed to compensate individuals for intangible fancies such as 'loss of autonomy' – let alone to rule that such awards would be fixed across the board at £15,000, whatever the circumstances of a claimant who gave birth to an unwanted healthy baby as a result of someone else's negligence.[84] Lord Hope criticised the majority ruling on this issue on the basis that he could not understand why the majority was proposing to compensate for the 'loss of autonomy' suffered by a claimant who gave birth to an unwanted healthy baby as a result of someone's negligence through the

---

[76] *McFarlane*, at 82 (per Lord Steyn), 111 (per Lord Millett); *Rees*, at [28] (per Lord Steyn), [112] (per Lord Millett).

[77] *McFarlane*, at 97 (per Lord Hope); *Rees*, at [51] (per Lord Hope), [138] (per Lord Steyn).

[78] *McFarlane*, at 91 (per Lord Hope); *Rees*, at [16] (per Lord Nicholls).

[79] *Rees*, at [6] (per Lord Bingham).

[80] *McFarlane*, at 82 (per Lord Steyn).

[81] Lord Hutton, sitting in *Rees*, did not express an opinion on the issue.

[82] *Rees*, at [8] (per Lord Bingham), [17] (per Lord Nicholls), [123] (per Lord Millett), [148] (per Lord Scott).

[83] Though confusingly Lord Bingham took the view that the award of £15,000 is not designed to *compensate* B for any loss that she has suffered: ibid., at [8]. But, as Lord Hope pointed out in dissent at [74], if the award is not compensatory in nature, what is it?

[84] Ibid., at [45].

award of a *fixed* sum of £15,000. If such an award is meant to be compensatory, then why should such a claimant not be entitled to say, 'The value of *my* loss of autonomy comes to much more than £15,000, and so I should be awarded much more than the fixed sum the majority in *Rees* said I should be given'?[85]

(2) *Disabled child.* Let's now consider what the position is if, in the situation we are considering, the child that B has given birth to is *disabled*. The House of Lords' decision in *McFarlane* did not deal with that issue at all – it was purely concerned with what the position would be if a claimant such as B gave birth to a healthy child. After *McFarlane* was decided, the Court of Appeal ruled in *Parkinson v St James and Seacroft University Hospital NHS Trust* that if, in the situation we are considering, B gave birth to a disabled baby, B would be entitled to sue A for the *extra cost of raising the child that is attributable to the fact he was born disabled.*[86] So, on this view, the normal costs of raising B's child, that B would have incurred whether or not the child was disabled, would still be non-actionable. But any extra expenses that B would have to incur in raising her child because he is disabled would be actionable.

In *Rees*, the House of Lords found themselves split on the issue of what the position should be in the case where B gives birth to a disabled child. Lords Steyn, Hope and Hutton took the view that *Parkinson* was correctly decided.[87] Lords Bingham and Nicholls took the view that *Parkinson* was wrongly decided and that, in the situation we are considering, A's liability to B should not depend on whether B's child was born healthy or disabled. In *both* cases, B should not be allowed to claim *anything* for the cost of bringing up the child: instead, all she will be entitled to sue A for (in addition to damages for the pain of pregnancy and so on) is a fixed sum of £15,000 to compensate her for her 'loss of autonomy'.[88] Lord Scott took the view that we may have to distinguish between: (*i*) the case where A was employed to stop B becoming pregnant because she was fearful that any baby she had would be disabled; and (*ii*) the case where A was employed to stop B becoming pregnant because she did not want to have another baby. He thought that the Court of Appeal's ruling in *Parkinson* should only be allowed to apply in case (*i*). So he thought that if (*ii*) were true, B should not be allowed to sue for *anything* in respect of the cost of bringing up her child.[89] As the issue of whether *Parkinson* was rightly decided did not arise for decision in *Rees*, Lord Millett preferred to leave the question 'open'.[90] He went on to observe that while, in 'strict logic', a claimant who gave birth to a disabled child should not be allowed to claim anything for the cost of bringing up the child,[91] he himself did not think that the Court of Appeal's

---

[85] Ibid., at [71]–[73].
[86] [2002] QB 266.
[87] [2004] 1 AC 309, at [35] (per Lord Steyn), [57] (per Lord Hope), [91] (per Lord Hutton).
[88] Ibid., at [9] (per Lord Bingham), [18] (per Lord Nicholls).
[89] Ibid., at [145].
[90] Ibid., at [112].
[91] Because – following the logic underlying Lord Millett's judgments in *McFarlane* and *Rees* on the issue of whether a claim for the cost of bringing up a healthy child should be allowed – if one did allow such a claim to be made in the case where a claimant gave birth to a disabled child, one *would* be saying that bringing up a disabled child *is* more trouble than it is worth; which can hardly be right.

ruling in *Parkinson* was 'morally offensive'. At the same time, he expressed himself fearful that allowing B to sue for the extra cost of bringing up her child attributable to the fact that her child was born disabled might 'prove difficult to achieve without introducing nice distinctions and unacceptable refinements of a kind which tend to bring the law into disrepute'.[92]

What a mess! However, as *Parkinson* was not overruled in *Rees*,[93] *Parkinson* will remain binding on all courts up to and including the Court of Appeal until the House of Lords readdresses the issue of whether *Parkinson* was correctly decided. As this is not likely to happen any time soon, we can safely assume that, for the foreseeable future, the Court of Appeal's decision in *Parkinson* will determine how much a claimant is entitled to sue a defendant for in a disabled child case. So if B gives birth to a child as a result of A's negligence, and that child proves to be disabled, B will be entitled to sue A for compensation in respect of any extra expenses that she will have to incur in raising the child because he is disabled.[94] This ruling gives rise to a couple of complications that need to be addressed.

First of all, what is the difference between a disabled child and a healthy child? Suppose for example that, due to Carl's negligence, Ruth gives birth to a baby boy, Alan. As Alan grows up, it becomes clear that he is short-sighted and will need to wear glasses. Will Ruth be able to sue Carl for the cost of providing those glasses? It depends on whether Alan counts as being 'disabled' or not: if he is a 'healthy' child, then Ruth will not be able to recover *any* of the costs of raising him, including the cost of providing him with spectacles. In the *Parkinson* case, Hale LJ suggested that a child will be held to be disabled if 'he is blind, deaf or dumb or suffers from mental disorder of any kind or is substantially and permanently handicapped by illness, injury or congenital deformity ...'.[95] On this definition, Alan would probably not count as being disabled and so Ruth would not be able to sue Carl for the cost of providing him with glasses.

Secondly, what is the position in the following case? Dawn negligently performs a vasectomy on Lara's husband, Tom. Thinking (incorrectly) that the operation has been a success, Lara and Tom have unprotected sex. As a result Lara becomes pregnant. She decides to carry the child to term but, six months into her pregnancy, she is involved in a car accident due to the negligence of the driver of another car, Eric. Lara survives the car accident but her doctors tell her that, as a result of the accident, her baby is liable to be severely brain damaged when he is born. Nevertheless Lara decides to carry on with pregnancy and three months later she gives birth to a baby boy, John, who suffers from severe brain damage.[96] Will Dawn be liable for the extra cost that Lara will

---

[92] *Rees*, at [112].

[93] Nor could it have been as the correctness of the Court of Appeal's ruling in *Parkinson* was not at issue in *Rees*.

[94] Though this point was not addressed by any of the Law Lords in *Rees*, it is presumably the case that B would *also* be entitled to sue A for a fixed sum of £15,000 to compensate her for the 'loss of autonomy' suffered by her as a result of A's negligence.

[95] [2002] QB 266, at [91] (quoting s 17(11) of the Children Act 1989).

[96] In this situation, Eric will be liable to compensate John for the fact that he was born disabled under the Congenital Disabilities (Civil Liability) Act 1976: see below, p. 631.

have to incur in raising John that is attributable to the fact that he has been born brain damaged? One would have thought not but in *Parkinson* the Court of Appeal held that Dawn *would* be liable so long as Eric's negligence did not break the chain of causation between Dawn's negligence and Lara's giving birth to John.[97] As Eric's negligence did not have that effect, Dawn will be liable.[98]

Avoidable losses

The duty to mitigate
Suppose that A has committed a tort in relation to B and B has suffered some kind of loss as a result. That loss will be non-actionable if B could have done something after A committed his tort to avoid suffering that loss but she unreasonably failed to do so. B has a 'duty to mitigate'[99] the losses suffered by her as a result of A's tort and will be barred from suing A for damages in respect of any losses that she has only suffered as a result of A's tort because she breached that 'duty'.[100]

We have already seen an example of this principle at work in the case of the workman who unreasonably refused to have an operation which would have saved his left hand, the hand having been originally injured by the defendants' negligence.[101] He was not allowed to sue the defendants for compensation in respect of the loss of his left hand because the loss of that hand was attributable to his failure to mitigate the losses suffered by him as a result of the defendants' negligence.

Avoidable births and the duty to mitigate
What is the position in the following case? Suppose Lara and Gary were married, and they asked Paul, a surgeon, to carry out a vasectomy on Gary so

---

[97] [2002] QB 266, at [53] (per Brooke LJ) and [92] (per Hale LJ).

[98] Eric's negligence was not a *novus actus interveniens* because it was not deliberate. Could it be argued that Lara's failure to have an abortion when she was told that John would be born severely brain damaged broke the chain of causation between Dawn's negligence and Lara's giving birth to John? No – it must be remembered that omissions do not break chains of causation (see above, pp. 538–40). Could it be argued, alternatively, that Lara is barred from suing Dawn for the extra cost of raising John that is attributable to the fact that he has been born with brain damage because, by failing to have an abortion, she failed to mitigate the losses suffered by her as a result of Dawn's negligence? The answer is 'no' – see below, pp. 581–2.

[99] This is, of course, not a real duty – B cannot be compelled to mitigate the losses suffered by her as a result of A's tort or sued if she fails to mitigate those losses.

[100] It seems, in light of the decision of the Privy Council in *Geest plc* v *Lansiquot* [2002] 1 WLR 3111, that the burden of proving that B has breached this 'duty' will fall on A. So if B has suffered some kind of loss as a result of A's tort that she could have avoided, B will still be able to claim compensation for that loss unless A can show that B acted *unreasonably* in failing to avoid that loss. In an earlier case, the Privy Council took the opposite view, holding that in the situation just described, B would not be able to claim compensation for the loss that she has suffered unless *she* could show that she acted *reasonably* in failing to avoid that loss: *Selvanayagam* v *University of West Indies* [1983] 1 WLR 585. There is something to be said for the position taken by the Privy Council in *Selvanayagam*: it will surely be easier for B to demonstrate that she acted reasonably in failing to avoid the loss in question than it will be for A to show that B acted unreasonably in failing to avoid that loss.

[101] *McAuley* v *London Transport Executive* [1958] 2 Lloyd's Rep 500, discussed above, pp. 539–40.

that Lara and Gary could have sexual relations without using contraceptives. Paul performed the operation but (in breach of the duty of care he owed Lara and her husband) he failed to carry it out properly and the operation was as a result ineffective. Thinking, however, that the operation had been a success, Lara and her husband began to have unprotected sexual intercourse and Lara eventually fell pregnant. Nine months later, Lara gave birth, experiencing a lot of pain and suffering in doing so. Lara also had to take time off work during the pregnancy and spent money on new clothes that would fit her in the latter stages of her pregnancy. Suppose she wants to sue Paul for damages in respect of these forms of economic loss and the pain and suffering experienced by her in labour, arguing that Paul's negligence caused her to suffer these forms of loss.

Could Paul argue that Lara is barred from suing him for damages in respect of these losses on the ground that she could have avoided these losses by having an abortion? Obviously, the answer is 'no'. It cannot be argued that Lara acted *unreasonably* in not having an abortion – so it cannot be said that her failure to have an abortion put her in breach of her 'duty to mitigate' the losses suffered by her as a result of Paul's negligence. Astonishingly, in *Emeh* v *Kensington Area Health Authority*[102] Park J, at first instance, took the opposite line and suggested that, in the case we are considering, Lara *might* be barred from suing Paul for damages in respect of the losses that her pregnancy caused her to suffer on the ground that she could have avoided those losses by having an abortion. Fortunately, good sense has prevailed in the courts: Park J's views have been firmly rejected by both the Court of Appeal in *Emeh*'s case and by the House of Lords in *McFarlane*.[103]

Having said that, in the case of *Richardson* v *LRC Products Ltd*,[104] Ian Kennedy J suggested that if Lara was warned by Paul that Gary's vasectomy had been unsuccessful the day after Gary impregnated her, then Lara might be barred from suing Paul for damages in respect of the losses suffered by her as a result of her pregnancy if she failed to bring that pregnancy to a halt by taking a 'morning-after' pill. In such a case he thought it could be said that Lara had failed to mitigate the losses suffered by her as a result of Paul's negligence.[105]

---

[102] [1985] 1 QB 1012.

[103] [2000] 2 AC 59, 74 (per Lord Slynn), 81 (per Lord Steyn), 104 (per Lord Clyde), 112–13 (per Lord Millett).

[104] [2000] Lloyd's Rep Med 280.

[105] The case actually concerned a claim under the Consumer Protection Act 1987: a married couple claimed that the wife had become pregnant as a result of their using a defective condom which split while they were making love. Ian Kennedy J rejected the claim that the condom was defective but held that, even if it were, the claimants still had no case because the wife – knowing that the condom had split – could have easily avoided suffering any loss as a result by taking a 'morning-after' pill. The decision is not easy to reconcile with the views expressed by the Court of Appeal in *Emeh* and the House of Lords in *McFarlane*. Is there a distinction between taking a 'morning-after' pill and having an abortion? Munby J thought there was in *R (Smeaton)* v *Secretary of State for Health* [2002] 2 FLR 146 (*not* a tort case), ruling that the 'morning-after' pill was not an abortifacient under the Abortion Act 1967.

White v *Jones* and the duty to mitigate[106]

An unusual case which raised a 'duty to mitigate' point – though it was not argued as such in the case – was *Gorham* v *British Telecommunications plc*.[107] That case, it will be recalled, concerned a man, G, who was given some bad pensions advice by the defendants. As a result, the claimants, G's wife and two young children, were left worse off after G's death than they would have been had the defendants advised G properly. Had the defendants advised G properly, G would have joined his employer's pension scheme, instead of taking out a pension plan with the defendants. And had G joined his employer's pension scheme, the claimants would have obtained a lump sum on his death.

The claimants sued the defendants for compensation and it was held that the defendants had owed them a duty of care in advising G under the principle in *White* v *Jones* and that the defendants had breached that duty of care. However, it was held that the claimants could not sue for the lump sum that they would have received on G's death had he been properly advised by the defendants. The reason was that some time after being badly advised by the claimants, G discovered that his employer's pension scheme was superior to the pension plan that he had taken out with the defendants, but he then failed to join his employer's pension scheme. Had he done so, the claimants would have received the lump sum on G's death that they were suing the defendants for not receiving. In other words, G failed to mitigate the loss that the defendants' negligence caused the claimants to suffer on G's death.

It is not surprising that G's failure to mitigate the claimants' loss should have been held against the claimants. If the principle in *White* v *Jones* is (as we contend)[108] concerned with situations where A has been *prevented* by B's actions from conferring a benefit on C no action should be available to C under *White* v *Jones* if B's actions did not actually *prevent* A from conferring that benefit on C.

Losses caused in the course of a rescue

In *The Tojo Maru*, Lord Reid considered what would be the position in the following situation: 'Suppose a house is on fire. It contains a valuable collection of, say, china. There is little or no hope of saving the collection but a passer-by, with or without the consent of the owner, goes in and brings most of the collection to safety. But owing to some gross negligence on his part some of the china is smashed.'[109]

---

[106] For a straightforward *White* v *Jones* case which raised a duty to mitigate point, see *Walker* v *Medlicott & Son* [1999] 1 WLR 727, where the defendant firm of solicitors failed to draft a will properly with the result that the claimant was not left a house in the will which the testatrix had intended to leave to the claimant; the claimant's claim for compensation was dismissed because he could have applied to have the will rectified under s 20(1) of the Administration of Justice Act 1982 and so had failed to mitigate the loss suffered by him as a result of the defendants' negligence.

[107] [2000] 1 WLR 2129 (discussed above, pp. 151–2).

[108] See above, pp. 151–2.

[109] [1972] AC 242, 268.

In principle, one would have thought that the passer-by could be sued for the loss of the smashed china: when he went into the house, he owed the owner of the china a duty to take care not to smash it, he breached that duty, and the china was destroyed as a result of that breach. However, subject to a couple of qualifications that we will set out below, Lord Reid thought the loss of the china in this case would be non-actionable: he said it would be 'most unjust'[110] if the passer-by were held liable for the destruction of the china.

In this sort of situation we can say that the passer-by is entitled to take advantage of a 'I did more good than harm' defence[111] to being sued for the loss of the china.[112] What are the limits on this defence? Lord Reid said that the passer-by should not be allowed the defence if he deterred other people from rescuing the china by rushing in to rescue it himself; or if there was no immediate emergency requiring the china to be saved.[113] It is also doubtful whether the passer-by could take advantage of the defence if he – having seized the china in an attempt to rescue it – deliberately smashed one cup to see what noise it would make when it broke.

Losses associated with the destruction or damage of property

It seems that the following losses – each of which might be suffered by the victim of a tort if that tort causes his property to be destroyed or damaged – will be automatically non-actionable.

(1) *Distress.* Suppose that A negligently runs over B's cat and B suffers a great deal of distress as a result. Will B's distress be actionable? The question has not been much addressed but it seems implict in *Attia* v *British Gas*[114] that the answer is 'no'.[115] After all, if B could sue for compensation in respect of her distress here, it is hard to see why the claimant's claim in *Attia* v *British Gas*[116] for

---

[110] Ibid.

[111] The name we have given the defence is a bit of a misnomer because the loss of the china would still be non-actionable under Lord Reid's principle even if the passer-by did more harm than good, by – for example – destroying a complete set of dinner plates while managing to save one teacup. And in fact the loss of the china would not be actionable under Lord Reid's principle if the passer-by did no good whatsoever: which would be the case if he picked up the china, and then smashed it all carelessly and walked out of the house with nothing.

[112] Notice that the passer-by could not argue that his liability should be very small because the destroyed china was 'doomed' anyway (see above, pp. 531–2 and below, p. 596). It was not: had the passer-by not been negligent, the china would have been saved. Notice also that the passer-by could not argue either that his liability to compensate for the loss of the china should be reduced to take account of the benefits obtained by the owners of the china as a result of his negligence (see below, p. 600). The owners of the china obtained no benefit from his carelessly smashing the china – they only obtained a benefit from his rushing in and rescuing the china (in the course of which he smashed some of it).

[113] [1972] AC 242, 268.

[114] [1988] QB 304 (discussed above, p. 572).

[115] Of course, distress suffered by the victim of a tort who has been *physically injured* as a result of that tort's being committed will be actionable as a matter of routine so long as the victim's physical injury is actionable. So if A negligently ran over B and B suffered pain and suffering as a result, B would have little difficulty in recovering for compensation for that pain and suffering. Moreover, if B was so badly injured as a result of A's hitting him that his expectation of life was shortened, B would be able to recover damages for the distress suffered by him as a result of knowing that he did not have long to live: Administration of Justice Act 1982, s 1(1)(b).

[116] [1988] QB 304.

compensation in respect of the psychiatric illness that she developed as a result of seeing her house burn down was thought to be problematic.[117]

(2) *Cost of repair.* Though the point is not made anywhere, it seems to us that if A has committed a tort in relation to B and in doing so caused B's property to be damaged and B has spent money on repairing that property, then the economic loss suffered by B in having the property repaired will *not* be actionable. The reason is that if it *were* actionable then B would be able, other things being equal, to sue A for compensation in respect of (*a*) the damage done to her property; *and* (*b*) the money she spent on repairing that property. But if B were allowed to sue A for (*a*) *and* (*b*), she would be overcompensated. This is because the courts, in awarding B damages for the damage done to her property, will customarily give her damages equal to the cost of repairing that property.[118] So if B is allowed to sue A for (*a*) *and* (*b*) she will recover the cost of repairing the property that A damaged twice over. This cannot be right. This possibility is avoided if we say that the money spent by B on repairing the damage done to her property is non-actionable.

(3) *Cost of replacement.* For the same reason, if A has tortiously destroyed B's property and B has spent money buying a replacement item of property, it seems to us that the money spent on the replacement will be non-actionable. If it were actionable then B would be entitled to sue A for compensation for the loss of her property *and* the cost of its replacement, and in so doing would recover the cost of replacing the item of property in question twice over (giving B the replacement cost of the item of property being the standard way of compensating B for the loss of that property). This possibility is avoided if we say that the money B actually laid out in obtaining a replacement for the item of property that A's tort destroyed will be non-actionable.

Losses suffered as a result of the infliction of a non-actionable loss

Suppose that A has committed a tort in relation to B and B suffered some kind of loss as a result of A's tort. Suppose further that because B suffered that loss, she went on to suffer a further loss. If the first loss suffered by B is non-actionable then the second loss suffered by B – which proceeded from the first – will also be non-actionable.

The point is perhaps too obvious to require support. Suppose, for example, that Ian negligently ran down Helen's cat and Helen was so grief-stricken by

---

[117] See *Essa* v *Laing* [2004] EWCA Civ 02, at [40]–[42] (per Pill LJ), [54]–[55] (per Clarke LJ), [112]–[116] (per Rix LJ), considering what the position would be if: (*i*) A committed a tort in relation to B; (*ii*) B suffered a psychiatric illness as a result; and (*iii*) had B suffered pure distress as a result of A's tort, she would have been entitled to sue A for damages in respect of that distress. Pill and Clarke LJJ thought – on the basis of the decision in *Page* v *Smith* [1996] AC 155 – that B would be able to sue A for damages in respect of her psychiatric illness *without* having to show that her *psychiatric illness* was a foreseeable consequence of A's tort: it is enough that it was reasonably foreseeable that B would suffer pure distress as a result of A's tort. Rix LJ dissented on this point.
[118] See below, p. 595.

this that she was unable to go to work for a year and suffered a consequent loss of income. If Helen's grief is non-actionable,[119] then nobody would suggest that the loss of income suffered by Helen as a result of her being grief-stricken *is* actionable. So we will move on to mention one possible exception to the rule stated above.

In *Dulieu* v *White & Sons*,[120] the defendants carelessly drove a van into a pub. The claimant was serving behind the bar. The claimant was not hit by the van but she received such a fright at the sight of the van crashing into the pub that she fell ill. The claimant sued the defendants in negligence for compensation in respect of her illness. In principle, one would have expected the court to have ruled that the claimant's illness was non-actionable. There was no doubt that the defendants owed the claimant a duty to take care not to drive the van into the pub where she was working[121] and that they breached that duty. However the claimant suffered two losses as a result of the defendant's breach: shock and fright (which counted as a primary loss); and physical illness (which counted as a secondary loss flowing from the shock and fright suffered by the claimant).

There is no doubt that the shock and fright suffered by the claimant was non-actionable[122] under the wrong kind of loss principle: the duty breached by the defendants in this case was imposed on them in order to help ensure that the claimant was not physically injured, not in order to help ensure that she did not become frightened. However, the claimant was still allowed to sue the defendants for compensation in respect of her illness – that loss was declared to be actionable, even though it flowed from the claimant's suffering a loss that was in itself non-actionable. In reaching its conclusion, the court was probably influenced by the fact that if the defendants' van had *hit* the claimant when it crashed into the pub, she would have been entitled to sue the defendants in respect of the injuries suffered by her as a result. The court may have thought that it should make no difference to the claimant's right to recover that the physical injury suffered by the claimant here was suffered by her not because she was *hit* by the defendant's van but because she thought that she was *going to be hit* by the defendant's van.

---

[119] Which is our view: see above, pp. 569–70.

[120] [1901] 2 KB 669.

[121] This is justified under the physical danger principle set out above at pp. 66–85: it was plainly foreseeable that someone like the claimant would be injured if the defendants drove the van into the pub.

[122] One can test this by asking: what would have happened if the claimant had not fallen ill in the aftermath of the defendants' crashing the van into the pub but had merely been shaken up by the experience? Would she have been entitld to sue the defendants for compensation in respect of the pure distress that she had suffered as a result of the defendants' negligence? The answer is 'no': see above, pp. 569–70.

32

QUANTIFICATION OF LOSS

Suppose that A has committed a tort in relation to B and A's tort has caused B to suffer at least one actionable loss. So B is entitled to sue A for compensatory damages. But how much will B be entitled to sue A for? This chapter and the next are concerned with that question. In this chapter we explained *how much* B will normally be entitled to sue A for – what we can call the *prima facie measure of liability*. In the next chapter we will explain when the damages payable to B will be *reduced* below this *prima facie* level.

THE LUMP SUM RULE

The *prima facie* measure of liability is assessed in the following way. The courts will aim – in awarding damages to B – to award B a *lump sum* sufficient to compensate B for the losses[1] that A's tort *has caused* her to suffer and the losses that A's tort *may* cause B to suffer in the future.

So suppose that John negligently runs Mary over and one of Mary's legs has to be amputated as a result. Mary currently works in an office and her terms of employment are unaffected by the fact that she has lost one leg, though she did of course have to take some time off work to have her injuries treated. In this situation John's tort *has caused* Mary to suffer three kinds of losses. First, physical injury – Mary was injured in the accident caused by John's negligence and one of her legs had to be amputated. Secondly, distress – Mary will have experienced a great deal of pain and suffering as a result of being injured in the accident, as well as distress at the fact that she will now have to live with having only one leg. Thirdly, economic loss – as a result of the fact that she had to take time off work to have her injuries treated, Mary will have suffered some kind of diminution in income. However, in this situation, John's tort *may cause* Mary to suffer a further kind of loss *in the future*. If Mary loses her current job in the future, the fact that she has only one leg may make it difficult for her to find alternative employment. So Mary may suffer economic loss in the future as a result of John's tort.

So the lump sum payable to Mary in this situation will be designed to compensate her for: (*a*) the fact that John's tort has *caused* her to suffer physical injury, distress and economic loss; (*b*) the fact that John's tort *may* cause her to suffer economic loss in the future because her capacity to find alternative employment if she loses her current job has been diminished.[2] Inevitably, in awarding

---

[1] By 'losses' we mean here and from now on, *actionable* losses.

[2] Damages that are designed to compensate the victim of a tort for the fact that she may suffer economic loss in future because the tort has reduced her capacity to find alternative

damages designed to compensate Mary for (*b*), she will not be awarded damages equal to the full amount of money she would lose if she lost her job and found it difficult, because of her disability, to find alternative employment. Because there is a chance that she will not lose her job, the damages payable to Mary will be *discounted* to take account of that chance. However, this creates a problem.

The problem arises out of the fact that once Mary is awarded a lump sum in damages that is designed to compensate her for (*a*) and (*b*), that is it. If the lump sum proves inadequate to cover the losses that Mary has suffered as a result of John's tort, she will not be able to go to court to obtain a larger amount. Similarly, if it proves that John has overpaid and the lump sum award turns out in fact to be larger than was necessary to compensate Mary for the losses that she has suffered as a result of John's tort, then John will not be able to go to court to claw back the overpayment.

Now – because the lump sum payable to Mary in this case will be designed in part to compensate her for (*b*), that lump sum will *inevitably* either undercompensate or overcompensate Mary for the losses she has suffered as a result of John's tort.[3] Either Mary will at some stage in the future lose her job and find it difficult to find alternative employment because she only has one leg – in which case the lump sum award will undercompensate her because that part of the award which was designed to compensate her for the fact that this might happen was discounted to take account of the possibility that Mary might *not* lose her job. Or Mary will never lose her current job and will sail on to retirement, with her earning capacity undisturbed by the fact that she only has one leg – in which case Mary will be overcompensated, because the lump sum paid to her included an element designed to compensate her for the possibility that she might suffer a loss that, as things turned out, she never did.

Given this problem one might think it would be sensible for the law to move to a system of making provisional awards of damages to the victim of a tort – under which system, the victim of a tort would be awarded a sum designed to compensate her for the losses that she has suffered as a result of that tort being committed; and then if it turns out that tort has caused her to suffer some further losses, she would be able to go back to court and sue for further damages, designed to compensate her for those losses. And indeed such provisional awards may be made in certain cases to the victim of a tort.[4] However,

---

employment are known as damages for 'loss of earning capacity' or '*Smith* v *Manchester* damages' after one of the cases in which such damages were awarded: *Smith* v *Manchester* (1974) 17 KIR 1. In the situation we are considering, such damages will only be awarded to Mary if there is in fact a *real or substantial* risk that she will lose her job in the future and that her disability will make it difficult for her to find alternative employment: *Moeliker* v *Reyrolle* [1977] 1 All ER 9.

[3] See Lord Scarman's remarks in *Lim* v *Camden Area Health Authority* [1980] AC 174, at 182H–183B: '[There are] insuperable problems implicit in a system of compensation for personal injuries which (unless the parties agree otherwise) can yield only a lump sum assessed by the court at the time of judgment. Sooner or later . . . if the parties do not settle, a court (once liability is admitted or proved) has to make an award of damages. The award, which covers past, present, and future injury and loss, must, under our law, be of a lump sum assessed at the conclusion of the legal process. The award is final; it is not susceptible to review as the future unfolds, substituting fact for estimate. Knowledge of the future being denied to mankind, so much of the award as is to be attributed to future loss and suffering – in many cases the major part of the award – will almost surely be wrong. There is really only one certainty: the future will prove the award to be either too high or too low.'

[4] Supreme Court Act 1981, s 32A allows the courts in a personal injury case to make a provisional award of damages which would be later topped up with further awards of damages if 'there is

there are good arguments against allowing the courts to award damages in this way.

First, all the parties to litigation will have an interest in not letting litigation 'drag on'. The victim of a tort's ability to get on with her life will be impeded if she is left in constant uncertainty as to how much compensation she will get in respect of the losses suffered by her as a result of that tort being committed. At the same time, the tortfeasor (or his insurer) will have an interest in knowing as soon as possible what his total liability to the victim of his tort is going to be for the purpose of financial planning. Secondly, the victim of a tort may well have other reasons for preferring to receive a lump sum award designed to compensate her for *all* the losses that she has suffered as a result of that tort being committed and the losses that she may suffer in the future as a result of that tort being committed, rather than receiving small periodic payments designed to compensate her for the losses that, it turns out, she has suffered as a result of that tort being committed. She will be able to do more things with a lump sum: for instance, armed with a lump sum award of damages, she could purchase a business which would be out of her financial reach if she received her damages in small periodic payments over a number of years.[5]

Let's now look at some typical cases where the victim of a tort might sue the person who committed that tort for compensatory damages and see how the courts assess how large the lump sum that is payable to the victim of the tort should be.

PHYSICAL INJURY CASES

The standard case

Let us consider first a standard case where A negligently caused a car crash in which B was injured. B's injuries were such that she has become permanently disabled and, as a result, she has had to take a job which pays less than the job she was working in before the crash. B had to take six months off work so as to have her injuries treated with the result that she did not receive any wages for those six months. B opted to have her injuries privately treated and as a result she incurred substantial medical bills.

So A's negligence will have caused B to suffer the following losses. (1) *Physical injury*: B was injured in the car crash caused by A. (2) *Distress*: B will

---

proved or admitted to be a chance that at some definite or indefinite time in the future the injured person will, as a result of the act or omission which gave rise to the cause of action, develop some serious disease or suffer some serious deterioration in his physical or mental condition.'

[5] At the same time, the victim of a tort who has suffered large losses as a result of that tort being committed might not want to shoulder the burden of managing the large lump sum that she will be awarded to compensate her for her losses. If this is the case *and* liability is undisputed *and* the person who committed the tort in question is insured, the victim of the tort will have the option of entering into what is called a 'structured settlement' with the tortfeasor's insurer. Under this arrangement, a proportion of the damages that would be paid to the victim of the tort in a lump sum if she went to court are paid over to the victim of the tort upfront and the rest is invested by the tortfeasor's insurer in annuities that will produce a regular, tax-free, yearly income for the victim of the tort.

have suffered pain and suffering as a result of being injured in the car crash. (3) *Inconvenience*: now that B is disabled, it is more difficult for her to get around and cope with life generally. (4) *Loss of amenity*: B's disability will almost certainly mean that B now gets less enjoyment out of life than she used to. (5) *Economic loss*: A's negligence caused B to suffer two kinds of economic loss. First, B had to take six months off work to have her injuries treated and suffered a loss of income as a result. Secondly, B opted to have her injuries privately treated and thereby incurred substantial medical bills. (6) *Future economic loss*: A's negligence will also almost certainly cause B to suffer a further economic loss in the future: B's disabilities mean that she has had to take a job which pays less than the job she was working in before she was injured.

Now, how do we assess how much of a lump sum B should be paid to compensate her for the fact that she has suffered losses (1)–(5) and for the fact that she will almost certainly suffer loss (6) in the future?

Non-pecuniary losses
Let us deal first with the non-pecuniary losses suffered by B: that is, losses (1)–(4) above. The courts will normally take these items of loss together in determining how much compensation should be paid to B for the fact that B has suffered them.

Inevitably, the process of determining how much B should be paid to compensate her for the fact that she has suffered losses (1)–(4) is arbitrary in the sense that there is no demonstrably correct answer as to how much B should be awarded so as to compensate her for the fact that she has suffered these losses. We could easily award B £10,000 or we could award her £20,000; neither figure seems more appropriate. In assessing the figure payable, the courts will merely seek to be *consistent*. So if someone in a previous case who suffered a similar injury to B was awarded £15,000 in respect of that injury and consequential non-pecuniary loss, then the courts will almost certainly award the same amount to B. Moreover, if someone in a previous case who suffered a much more serious injury than B was awarded £20,000 in respect of that injury and consequential non-pecuniary loss, the courts will not give B more than that. In this way, a body of case law has been built up on how much will be customarily awarded to compensate people who suffer certain 'standard' injuries and consequential non-pecuniary losses, details of which can be found in advanced works on damages. At the prompting of the Law Commission, the Court of Appeal has sought to update this case law, finding that in the past personal injury victims have been undercompensated by the courts for the non-pecuniary losses suffered by them as a result of their injuries. From now on, if the victim of a tort who has suffered a personal injury as a result of a tort being committed would have been entitled – under the old case law – to sue for more than £10,000 in respect of that injury and consequential non-pecuniary losses, her award should be increased by up to one-third, depending on what she would have obtained under the old case law.[6]

---

[6] *Heil* v *Rankin* [2001] QB 272.

Whatever sum is payable to B to compensate her for the fact that she has suffered losses (1)–(4), it will normally be discounted somewhat to take account of the possibility that had B not become disabled as a result of A's negligence, she might have become disabled at some stage in the future. So if B was 'doomed' to become disabled even if A had not been negligent, then the damages payable to B to compensate her for the fact that she has suffered losses (1)–(4) will be substantially reduced.[7]

Pecuniary losses

In considering how much B should be paid so as to compensate her for the pecuniary losses that she has suffered or may suffer in the future as a result of A's negligence, we should draw a distinction between the pecuniary losses that B *has* suffered as a result of A's negligence – that is, loss (5) – and the pecuniary losses that B will almost certainly suffer in the future as a result of A's negligence – that is, loss (6).

(1) *Past loss.* It is quite easy to determine how much B should be paid to compensate her for the loss of wages suffered by her when she had to take time off work to have her injuries treated. She should be paid a sum equivalent to the *net* loss suffered by her: that is, a sum equal to how much B would have taken home after tax had she not had to take time off work. Again, it is not difficult to determine how much B should be paid to compensate her for the fact that she incurred medical bills as a result of having her injuries treated. She should be paid a sum equivalent to the amount she was charged for medical treatment.[8]

(2) *Future loss.* Assessing the amount payable to B in respect of the future loss of income that she will probably suffer as a result of A's negligence is much more problematic. Let us suppose that before she was injured B was earning £20,000 a year net of tax. B's disability means that she is now in a job where she earns £12,000 a year net of tax. Let us further assume that B was 40 when she was injured.

It is *not* possible to say that had B not been injured she would probably have earned £8,000 a year more than she is currently earning up until retirement age (65) and that she should therefore be awarded (£8,000 x (65−40) =) £200,000 to compensate her for the future loss of income that she will probably suffer as a result of A's negligence. This is for three reasons.

First, B might not live until 65. If B's medical health is such that an actuary would predict that B will not survive beyond 60, then the damages payable to B in respect of the loss of income that she will probably suffer in the future as a result of A's negligence should be assessed on the basis that B will die at 60.

---

[7] *Jobling* v *Associated Dairies Ltd* [1982] AC 794. For an exceptional situation where the damages payable to the victim of a tort who was injured as a result of that tort being committed will not be reduced, even though she was 'doomed' to suffer those injuries anyway at some stage in the future, see above, pp. 545–6.

[8] Though the sum payable will be reduced if the medical bills covered the cost of food and laundry: see below, pp. 600–1.

Secondly, B might not have continued to earn £20,000 a year net of tax but for A's negligence for the rest of her expected working lifespan. B might have been sacked, or been made redundant and found it difficult to find alternative employment. The damages payable to B to compensate her for the loss of income that she will probably suffer in the future as a result of A's negligence should be adjusted to take account of these possibilities.

Thirdly, suppose that we estimate that B will probably work for 20 more years and that, but for A's negligence, B would have earned £8,000 a year more over those years than she actually will. The damages paid to B *now* in respect of the loss of income that she will probably suffer in the future as a result of A's negligence should not equal the total amount of extra income B would probably have earned over her expected working lifespan, that is, (£8,000 x 20 =) £160,000. If they did, then B could invest the damages and earn a yearly income with them – made up of interest plus yearly withdrawals of portions of the capital sum invested – which would exceed the yearly income loss suffered by her as a result of A's negligence. So awarding B damages equal to the total amount of extra income B would have obtained over her expected lifespan had A not negligently injured her would overcompensate B: it would make B better off than she would have been had A not been negligent. To avoid this possibility, the damages payable to B should amount to a capital sum which, when properly invested, will yield B an annual income – made up of interest plus a proportion of the capital sum – equivalent to £8,000 a year for 20 years; at the end of which twenty years the capital sum will be used up. This capital sum will be considerably smaller than £160,000.

So one way of assessing how much B should be paid to compensate her for the loss of income that she will probably suffer in the future as a result of A's negligence would be to proceed as follows. First, ask: What is the difference between what B is earning now net of tax and what she would have been earning now net of tax had A not been negligent? (Say this is £8,000.) Then ask: How much of a working life has B probably got left to her? (Say this is 20 years.)

Next, multiply £8,000 by 20 to get a rough idea of how much the total loss of income will be that B will suffer over the rest of her working life as a result of A's negligence: this gives us £160,000. Next, discount that sum to take account of the possibility that had A not been negligent B would have been sacked or made redundant and might not have earned as much as £8,000 a year more over the rest of her working life than she will now earn over the rest of her working life. So if we discount it by 25 per cent, this gives us a figure of £120,000, equivalent to a loss of income of £6,000 a year over the rest of B's expected working life.

Then we assess what sort of capital sum, properly invested, would produce a yearly income stream – made up of interest plus a proportion of the capital sum – of £6,000 a year over 20 years. Obviously this depends a lot on how we might expect B to invest the capital sum awarded. If we can only expect B to invest the money in very safe investments which produce a low rate of interest, then more of a capital sum must be awarded to B to produce the necessary income stream. If, on the other hand, we can expect B to invest her money in more risky investments which produce a higher rate of interest, then less of a capital sum must be awarded to B to produce the necessary income stream. In *Wells* v *Wells*,[9] the House of Lords ruled that in assessing the damages payable in respect of future loss of income it must be assumed that the payee will invest the damages in very safe, low-interest investments such as government index-linked bonds. The capital sum we finally come up with (say £112,000) is the sum B should be paid to compensate her for the loss of income that she will probably suffer in the future as a result of A's negligence.

Instead, the courts adopt a slightly different method of assessing how much B should be paid by way of damages to compensate her for the loss of income that she will probably suffer in the future as a result of A's negligence. This method is known as the *multiplier method*. What the courts do is assess the difference between what B now earns net of tax and what she would have been earning now net of tax had A not been negligent. This figure (here £8,000) is known as the *multiplicand*. They then multiply the multiplicand by a figure (known as the *multiplier*) which takes into account: (*a*) the number of years that B can be expected to suffer that yearly loss of income; (*b*) the possibility that B would not actually have earned as much in the future as she was earning at the time A injured her; and (*c*) the fact that B is being awarded damages *now* in respect of future income loss and can therefore be expected to earn interest with those damages which will help to cover that future income loss.

The end result is exactly the same as is yielded by the approach suggested in the above paragraph (the courts might be expected to apply a multiplier of about 14 in the above case,[10] resulting in a damages award of £112,000). The multiplier approach simply represents a slightly different way of going about assessing the damages payable to B in respect of the loss of income that she will probably suffer in the future as a result of A's negligence.

The case where an injury results in a loss of life expectancy

Suppose A has negligently injured B. Suppose further that B was 35 when she was injured and before she was injured she could have been expected to live to 70. However, B's injury now means that she can only be expected to live to 45.

B will, of course, be entitled to sue A for damages in respect of: her injury and any consequential non-pecuniary losses suffered by her as a result of that injury; any medical expenses incurred by her as a result of being injured; and any loss of income that she has suffered or is likely to suffer as a result of A's negligently injuring her between the date of her injury and the date of her death (now anticipated to occur at 45).

It is, however, well established that B will *also* be entitled to sue A for damages in respect of the money she could have earned during the years that

---

[9] [1999] AC 345.
[10] Of course, if B had been younger when she was injured, a higher multiplier would be used to assess the damages payable to her. In practice, the courts will rarely apply a multiplier greater than 17 or 18 in assessing how much should be paid to compensate someone for a future loss of income.

are now 'lost' to her as a result of A's negligence.[11] This is a bit puzzling: what earthly good would awarding B such damages do her? However, the point of awarding B such damages is *not* actually to compensate B but to ensure that any dependants of B – who would have been supported by B in the years that are now 'lost' to her – do not lose out as a result of B's expectation of life being reduced.[12] B can sue for damages in respect of the money she would have earned in the years that are now lost to her and thereby create a fund which will help to support her dependants after she dies.[13]

How do we assess how much B should be entitled to recover in respect of this loss of income? The courts again use a 'multiplier' approach. They first assess how much B could have been expected to earn per year net of tax in the years that are now 'lost' to her: say this is £50,000. They then deduct from that the yearly amount B would have spent on supporting herself in the years that are now 'lost' to her: call this £35,000.[14] £15,000 (the difference between £50,000 and £35,000) is the multiplicand used by the courts to determine how much B should be paid in damages. The courts then arrive at a multiplier, which takes into account the following factors: (*a*) the fact that B could have been expected to earn money for 20 of the 25 years that are now 'lost' to her as a result of A's negligence; (*b*) the fact that had B not been injured she might not have earned £50,000 per year in the years that are now 'lost' to her: she might have been made redundant and found it difficult to find alternative employment; (*c*) the fact that any damages award to B can be invested and produce an income stream which will help replace the yearly net amount that B would have earned and not spent on herself in the years that are now 'lost' to her. They then multiply the multiplier and multiplicand together to arrive at the figure B should be

---

[11] *Pickett* v *British Rail Engineering Ltd* [1980] AC 126, overruling *Oliver* v *Ashman* [1962] 2 QB 210. Section 1(1)(a) of the Administration of Justice Act 1982 prevents victims of torts who have suffered a 'loss of expectation of life' suing for damages to compensate them for that fact (so no action for loss of amenity can be brought in respect of the pleasures that a victim of a tort would have enjoyed in the years that are now 'lost' to her as a result of that tort being committed). However, s 1(2) of the same Act provides that s 1(1)(a) does not apply to actions for 'damages in respect of loss of income'.

[12] However, B will be entitled to sue A for damages in respect of the money she would have earned in the years that are now lost to her even if she has no dependants who would have been supported by her in those years.

[13] See Lord Diplock's explanation of the decision in *Pickett* v *British Rail Engineering Ltd* in *Gammell* v *Wilson* [1982] AC 27, at 64E–65A. An alert student might raise the following objection to this explanation. 'Surely after B dies, B's dependants will be entitled in any case to bring a claim for loss of support against A under the Fatal Accidents Act 1976? So why would the law go to such lengths to allow B to protect her dependants while she is still alive?' However, if B sues A for damages before she dies, B's dependants will lose any rights they might otherwise have had to sue A under the 1976 Act – and B will almost certainly want and need to sue A before she dies in order to get some compensation for the losses that she is *currently* suffering as a result of A's negligence.

[14] This is consistent with the reason why B is allowed to sue A for damages in respect of the money she would have earned in the years that are now 'lost' to her. As the object of awarding her such damages is really to compensate B's dependants, if any, for the loss of support that they will suffer on B's premature death, there is no reason to allow B to claim damages in respect of any income that she would have earned in the years that are now 'lost' to her that she would merely have spent on supporting herself.

awarded in damages to compensate her for the money she would have made in the years that are now 'lost' to her.

PROPERTY DAMAGE CASES

Let us now consider what the position is if A commits a tort in relation to B and thereby causes property belonging to B to be destroyed or damaged. Assuming that this loss is actionable, how do we go about determining how much B should be paid so as to compensate her for the fact that she has suffered this loss?

Damage to property

Suppose first that A has negligently damaged B's property and that the damage done to B's property amounts to an actionable loss. How much should B be paid so as to compensate her for the fact that her property has been damaged? The courts' answer is: *As a general rule*, B should be paid damages equal to the amount of money it would have cost B to repair the property in question had she repaired that property at the time it was first reasonable for her to do so.

So, for example, in *Dodd Properties (Kent) Ltd* v *Canterbury City Council*[15] the defendants built a multi-storey car park beside a building owned by the claimants. The building work took place in 1968. Due to the defendants' negligence in carrying out pile-driving operations for the foundations, serious structural damage was done to the claimants' building. The earliest time the claimants could have repaired the building was in 1970 when it would have cost £11,375 to repair the building. However, the claimants could not easily raise the funds to do the repairs at that date and were in any case uncertain as to whether or not they would be able to claim back the cost of the repairs from the defendants. Given this, they decided to hold off doing any repairs until they had sued the defendants. The claimants' case was heard in 1978, by which time the cost of doing the repairs had risen to £30,327. The Court of Appeal held that the claimants had acted reasonably in delaying repairing their building until they had sued the defendants and therefore held that the claimants should be awarded damages in respect of the damage done to their property equal to the cost of repairing the building in 1978. The Court of Appeal therefore awarded the claimants £30,327 in damages.[16]

The general rule set out above is subject to three exceptions.

(1) *Cheaper to replace.* If, when B's property was damaged, it would have been cheaper to replace it rather than repair it then the compensation for the damage done to B's property will *usually* be assessed by reference to the cost of replacing it rather than repairing it. The cost of repair measure of compensation will still be used if the property in question was so special to B that it would

---

[15] [1980] 1 WLR 433.
[16] See also the Privy Council decision in *Alcoa Minerals of Jamaica Inc.* v *Broderick* [2002] 1 AC 371, which endorsed the decision in *Dodd Properties*.

have been unreasonable to expect her to have replaced it rather than repaired it.

So in *O'Grady* v *Westminster Scaffolding Ltd*,[17] the defendant negligently damaged the claimant's 1938 MG motor car. The claimant could have bought a replacement car for about £185 but his MG was his 'pride and joy' and so he decided to keep it and spent about £250 repairing it. It was held that the claimant was entitled to damages for the damage done to his car assessed according to the cost of repair measure: given his special attachment to his car, it would have been unreasonable to expect him to have scrapped it and bought a replacement car.

It was different in *Darbishire* v *Warran*.[18] In that case, the claimant's car was badly damaged in a collision caused by the defendant's negligence. The claimant had owned the car for about four years and it had always proved reliable. Rather than look for a replacement – which would have cost about £80 – the claimant chose, more out of inertia than anything, to have the car repaired instead. The repairs cost him about £192. The court held that the claimant was entitled to damages for the damage done to his car assessed according to the cost of replacement measure: it would not have been unreasonable to expect the claimant to have bought a new car rather than have his old, damaged, one repaired. So the claimant was awarded £80 as compensation for the damage done to his car, with the result that he was left out of pocket by £112.

(2) *Valueless property*. The second qualification to the general rule stated above is that if the property that was damaged by A's negligence was valueless to B – for example, B was going to scrap it – then B will, of course, not be entitled to recover the cost of repairing that property from A.

(3) *Property in need of repair*. The third qualification is that if the property that was damaged by A's negligence was in need of repair anyway and performing that repair work would at the same time repair the damage done by A's negligence, B will not be entitled to recover anything for the damage done to her property by A's negligence.

So in *Performance Cars Ltd* v *Abraham*,[19] the defendant negligently drove his car into the claimant's Rolls-Royce. The front wing of the claimant's Rolls-Royce was damaged as a result. It was agreed that in order to repair the damage the whole of the lower part of the Rolls-Royce would need to be resprayed. However, at the time of the collision, the rear wing of the Rolls-Royce was already damaged and *that* damage could only be repaired by respraying the whole of the lower part of the Rolls-Royce. The Court of Appeal held that the claimant was not entitled to sue the defendant for anything by way of damages: at the time of the accident, the Rolls-Royce was already in need of a respray and carrying out that respray would, as well as repairing the damage to the rear wing

[17] [1962] 2 Lloyd's Rep 238.
[18] [1963] 1 WLR 1067.
[19] [1962] 1 QB 33.

of the Rolls-Royce, at the same time repair the damage done by the defendant to the front wing of the Rolls-Royce.

Destruction of property

Now suppose that A has negligently destroyed B's property. Again, we can assume that the destruction of B's property amounts to an actionable loss. How much should B be paid so as to compensate her for the fact that her property has been destroyed? The courts' answer is: B should be paid damages equal to how much it would have cost her to replace the property that was destroyed if she had obtained such a replacement at the time it was first reasonable for her to do so.[20]

DEFAMATION CASES

Suppose that A has libelled or slandered B and it is found (or presumed) that A's libel/slander caused B to suffer some damage to her reputation. This damage will of course be an actionable consequence of A's libel/slander. How do we determine how much B should be paid so as to compensate her for the fact that she has suffered this damage to her reputation?

Normally a jury will have the job of determining how much B should be paid – an action for libel or slander will be tried in front of a jury if either party wishes it to be.[21] If a jury *is* given the job of determining how much B should be paid then its first problem – in the case where it is presumed that B has suffered some damage to her reputation as a result of A's libel/slander – will be to determine how much damage it is willing to presume has been done to B's reputation. Because juries do not have to justify their decisions, it is hard to tell what they take into account in doing this, but it seems to follow as a matter of common sense that the worse the libel/slander in question, the more damage it will be presumed was done to B's reputation as a result of A's publishing that libel/slander. But if B was generally of low reputation anyway, the jury will be entitled to find that little damage was done to B's reputation on the grounds that she had little reputation to lose in the first place.[22] And if only a few of the people to whom the libel/slander in question was published actually knew that it referred to B, then it can be presumed that little damage was done to B's general reputation as a result of the publication of that libel/slander.[23]

Having determined how much damage (real or presumed) was done to B's reputation as a result of the publication of A's libel/slander, the jury's next task

---

[20] Though of course if the property in question was valueless to B at the time it was destroyed, then very little will be awardable in respect of its destruction.

[21] Though the Supreme Court Act 1981, s 69(1) provides that a jury trial should not be allowed if 'the court is of the opinion that the trial [will require] any prolonged examination of documents or accounts or any scientific or local investigation which cannot conveniently be made with a jury'.

[22] *Plato Films Ltd* v *Speidel* [1961] AC 1090. The damages payable in such a case are known as 'derisory' or 'contemptuous' (*not* 'nominal': see below, p. 664) because the fact that they are so low indicates that the jury thought that the claimant had very little reputation to lose.

[23] *Morgan* v *Odhams Press* [1971] 1 WLR 1239.

will be to determine how much B should be paid so as to compensate her for that damage. Again, as juries do not have to justify their decisions, it is hard to know what factors a jury will take into account in determining how much the victim of a libel or slander should be paid so as to compensate her for the damage (real or presumed) that has been found to have been done to her reputation. Juries have tended to put a high value on reputation and have in the past awarded damages for loss of reputation which are far in excess of the damages that someone could hope to recover for a broken leg or the loss of an eye.

To take some examples from previous cases: Lord Aldington was awarded £1.5m by a jury when he sued the authors of a pamphlet which suggested that he had participated in a war crime at the end of the Second World War;[24] the wife of the Yorkshire Ripper was awarded £600,000 by a jury when *Private Eye* published a story which suggested that she had known of her husband's guilt before he was arrested;[25] Esther Rantzen was awarded £250,000 by a jury when the *Daily Mirror* suggested that she had knowingly shielded a child abuser from prosecution;[26] and Elton John was awarded £350,000 by a jury when the *Daily Mirror* accused him of being bulimic.[27]

Both Parliament and the courts have acted on mounting concerns that juries tend to award excessive amounts to compensate the victims of libels and slanders for the damage done to their reputation. First, s 8 of the Courts and Legal Services Act 1990 gives the Court of Appeal the power to reduce a jury's award in a libel or slander case if they think it 'excessive', a power which was exercised in the Rantzen case (damages reduced to £110,000) and in the Elton John case (damages reduced to £50,000).[28] Secondly, in *John* v *MGN Ltd*[29] the Court of Appeal developed the law on what guidance a trial judge could give a jury in a libel or slander case to help them in their deliberations as to what amount of damages should be awarded. The position now is that while a trial judge cannot tell the jury of awards that other juries have made in other cases, he can tell them of awards that have been approved or substituted by the Court of Appeal.

---

[24] *Tolstoy Miloslavsky* v *United Kingdom* (1995) 20 EHRR 442 (the European Court of Human Rights held that the award – being disproportionately large – violated the authors' rights of freedom of expression under Article 10 of the European Convention on Human Rights).

[25] *Sutcliffe* v *Pressdram Ltd* [1991] 1 QB 153.

[26] *Rantzen* v *MGN (1986) Ltd* [1994] QB 670.

[27] *John* v *MGN Ltd* [1997] QB 586. Admittedly, a large proportion of this award (£275,000) was made up of exemplary damages, damages designed to punish the *Daily Mirror* for the way it acted in publishing the story about Elton John.

[28] The decision of the Court of Appeal in *Kiam* v *MGN Ltd* [2003] QB 281 provides the latest guidance as to when the courts will exercise this power. The following points emerge from the decision in that case: (1) The question of whether an award was 'excessive' will be determined by asking whether 'a reasonable jury could have thought the award necessary to compensate the claimant and re-establish his reputation' (ibid., at [48], per Simon Brown LJ). (2) The fact that a claimant in a libel case has been made an award which is much greater than he might be awarded were he to suffer a serious physical injury does not necessarily indicate that it is 'excessive' (ibid., at [60], per Waller LJ). (3) In judging whether an award is 'excessive' the courts should show great deference to the decision of the jury (ibid., at [53], per Simon Brown LJ; and [60], per Waller LJ). (4) Even if an award is judged to be 'excessive', it should only be set aside if it 'substantially [exceeds] the most that any jury could reasonably have thought appropriate' (ibid., at [49], per Simon Brown LJ).

[29] [1997] QB 586.

He may also tell them of how much would be awarded in different kinds of personal injury case. Furthermore, he may tell them how much he thinks it might be appropriate to award for the damage done to the claimant's reputation.[30]

OTHER CASES

It is beyond the scope of this book to explain how we determine how much the victim of a tort should be paid by way of damages to compensate him for the fact that the commission of a tort has caused him to suffer some kind of loss other than the types of loss dealt with above, for example, a temporary loss of liberty. The interested reader should consult detailed works on the law of damages for such an explanation.

---

[30] Ibid., 611–16.

33

REDUCTION IN LIABILITY

We are concerned in this chapter with the situation where A has committed a tort in relation to B and B is entitled to sue A for compensatory damages. Let's say that A's *prima facie* measure of liability in this case is £10,000 – that is, other things being equal, B will be entitled to sue A for £10,000 in compensatory damages. In certain situations, the damages payable to B will be reduced below this level. In this chapter we explain what those situations are.

RECEIPT OF BENEFIT

If, in the situation, we are considering, B obtained some kind of benefit as a result of A's tort, the damages payable to B by A may be reduced to take account of that fact.[1] However, it is important to emphasise that the damages payable *may* be reduced: they will not always be. It is hard to formulate a principle which will tell us when a benefit that has been received by the victim of a tort as a result of that tort being committed will be taken into account in determining the damages payable to the victim. Perhaps all that can be said is that receipt of a benefit by the victim of a tort as a result of that tort being committed will operate to reduce the damages payable to the victim unless there is a good reason why the damages payable should not be reduced.

Situations where the receipt of a benefit will be taken into account

In the following situations, the fact that the victim of a tort received some benefit as a result of that tort being committed will be taken into account in assessing the damages payable to him or her.

Savings on food and other necessities
Suppose that Dawn negligently injured Eric, with the result that Eric had to stay for a few weeks in a private hospital, having his injuries treated. Suppose

---

[1] There is a difficult line to be drawn between this kind of case and cases where we determine how much of a loss has been suffered by B as a result of A's tort. For example, suppose B was employed on a job which paid £50,000 a year when she was negligently injured by A. As a result, B had to leave her job and obtained alternative employment which paid a salary of £30,000 a year. No one would treat this as a reduction of liability case – that is, no one would say that A is *prima facie* liable to compensate B for the fact that she no longer earns £50,000 a year but A's liability is reduced to take account of the fact that as a result of A's negligence, B is now earning £30,000 a year. Instead, we simply say that B has suffered and will suffer in the future a drop in salary of £20,000 a year for which loss A is *prima facie* liable to compensate her. However, it is hard to see why this isn't treated as a reduction of liability case – but the convention is to treat it as a quantification of loss case.

further that while he was in the hospital, the hospital provided him with meals. Dawn will of course be *prima facie* liable to pay Eric a sum sufficient to compensate him for the medical bills he has incurred in being treated.

However, in this situation Dawn's negligence will have resulted in Eric receiving a benefit: while he was in hospital, he did not have to buy his own food. Dawn's liability will be reduced to take account of this saving that Eric has made.[2] So suppose that Eric's medical bills came to £10,000; but in the time Eric was in hospital, he would have spent £500 on buying food for himself. On these figures, Dawn will only be liable to pay Eric £9,500 in compensatory damages – Dawn's *prima facie* liability to pay Eric £10,000 in damages will be reduced to take account of the fact that Eric saved £500 that he would otherwise have spent on buying food for himself while he was in hospital.[3]

The same point will apply if, had Eric not been in hospital, he would have spent money on necessities that were provided by the hospital, such as washing Eric's clothes. The damages payable to Eric will be reduced to take account of this saving.

Compensation payments from other defendants liable in tort

Suppose that A committed a tort in relation to B and B suffered losses worth £10,000 as a result of that tort being committed. Suppose further that C was also liable *in tort* to compensate B for the fact that she suffered these losses. Suppose finally that C made a compensation payment to B – that is, a payment designed to compensate B in full or in part for the losses that she suffered in this situation.[4] In this situation the damages payable by A to B will be reduced: the compensation payment will count as a benefit that B received as a result of A's tort.

The difficult question is by how much A's liability to B will be reduced. Obviously, if C's compensation payment to B came to £10,000, then A will not be liable to pay B anything. B will be fully compensated for the losses that she suffered as a result of A's tort and will therefore not be entitled to sue A for anything.[5] But what if C's compensation payment only came to £7,000? The normal rule is that B will be entitled to sue A for £3,000 – the balance of the uncompensated loss that she suffered as a result of A's tort. However, there are two situations in which C's compensation payment to B of £7,000 will have the effect of extinguishing entirely A's liability to B.

(1) *Joint liability.* It used to be the case that if A and C were *jointly liable*[6] to compensate B for the losses suffered by her, then C's compensation payment

---

[2] *Shearman* v *Folland* [1950] 2 KB 43.

[3] Of course, Eric's medical bills will almost certainly include a charge for the food Eric received while he was in hospital but that is immaterial. At the same time as Eric was paying the hospital for the food that the hospital served him, he was saving money which he would have spent had Dawn not injured him on buying food for himself.

[4] The payment could have been made either in order to settle B's claims against C or because a court ordered C to make that payment to B.

[5] However, C will be entitled to make a claim in contribution against A, forcing A to shoulder a 'just and equitable' share of the burden of compensating B for the losses she has suffered: see above, pp. 26–7.

[6] *Important note.* A and C will be *jointly* liable in respect of the losses suffered by B *if*: (1) they each caused her to suffer those losses by committing a tort in relation to her and A and C's torts were each committed as a part of a *joint venture* which they were engaged on; *or* (2) C is liable in tort to

to B would have had the effect of discharging A's liability to B. However, the position nowadays is a bit more complicated.

If C's compensation payment was made because B won a judgment against C, then C's payment will not have the effect of extinguishing B's rights to sue A for compensation: A will therefore be liable to pay B £3,000 in damages.[7] If, on the other hand, C's compensation payment was made to B under a settlement that he reached with B, then the old rule will apply – and A's liability to B will be extinguished – *unless* B's settlement with C preserved her rights to sue A for damages in respect of the losses suffered by her:[8] in which case, A will again be liable to pay B £3,000 in damages.

(2) *Payment treated by the claimant as fully compensating her.* Even if A and C were *jointly and severally* liable to compensate B for the losses suffered by her, C's compensation payment to B will have the effect of extinguishing A's liability to B if B treated C's payment of £7,000 to her as fully compensating her for the losses she has suffered.[9]

---

compensate B for the losses suffered by her as a result of A's tort because C persuaded or authorised A to commit that tort (with the result that A's tort is regarded as having been committed by C, as well as A: see above, p. 407); *or* (3) C is liable in tort to compensate B for the losses suffered by her as a result of A's tort because C is vicariously liable for A's tort. (See, on this, Carty 1999.) If none of these conditions are satisfied then A and C will be *jointly and severally* liable to compensate B for the losses suffered by her. An example of joint and several liability is provided by *The Koursk* [1924] P 140. In that case, two ships – the *Clan Chisholm* and the *Koursk* – collided with each other. The collision occurred as a result of the negligence of both the owners of the *Clan Chisholm* and the negligence of the defendants, the owners of the *Koursk*. As a result of the collision, the *Clan Chisholm* collided with the claimants' vessel, the *Itria*, which sank. In this case the owners of the *Clan Chisholm* and the defendants, the owners of the *Koursk*, were each liable in tort to compensate the claimants for the loss of the *Itria*: each of them committed the tort of negligence in relation to the claimants and the *Itria* would not been sunk had not each of them been negligent. However, as their negligent acts were not performed as part of a joint venture, the owners of the *Clan Chisholm* and the defendants were not *jointly* liable to compensate the owners of the *Itria* for the loss of the *Itria*; they were jointly and severally liable. So when the owners of the *Clan Chisholm* made a compensation payment to the owners of the *Itria*, that did not have the effect of extinguishing the liability of the defendants to the owners of the *Itria*. The defendants were still liable to compensate the owners of the *Itria* for the balance of the uncompensated loss that they had suffered as a result of the sinking of the *Itria*.

[7] Civil Liability (Contribution) Act 1978, s 3: 'Judgment recovered against any person liable in respect of any . . . damage shall not be a bar to an action . . . against any other person who is . . . jointly liable with him in respect of the same . . . damage.'

[8] *Gardiner* v *Moore* [1969] 1 QB 55.

[9] *Jameson* v *CEGB* [2000] 1 AC 455. That case concerned the following situation. A and C each committed a tort in relation to B and B was injured as a result. A and C were *jointly and severally* liable to compensate B for that injury. A made a compensation payment to B which did not have the effect of fully compensating B for that injury but was treated by both parties as fully compensating B for his injury. B then died of his injury and B's widow brought an action against C for loss of support under the Fatal Accidents Act 1976, arguing that C committed a tort that caused B to die and at the time B died, he was entitled to sue C for compensation in respect of the injury suffered by him as a result of C's tort. Now: if C were held liable to compensate B for her loss of support here, he would have been entitled to bring a claim in contribution against A, thereby making A shoulder some of the burden of compensating B's widow for her loss of support. It was thought that this would be unfair on A because A had already made a compensation payment to B and that payment would not be taken into account in assessing the damages payable to B's widow to compensate her for the loss of support she had experienced. (Although that compensation payment passed to B's widow on B's death, s 4 of the Fatal Accidents Act 1976 provides that 'In assessing damages in respect of a person's death in an action under this Act, benefits which have accrued . . . to any person from his estate . . .

Redundancy payments

Suppose that Fred negligently injured Ruth and as a result Ruth was unable to continue in her job and was made redundant. Any redundancy payment received by Ruth on leaving her job will operate to reduce the damages payable by Fred to Ruth.[10]

Social security payments

Suppose that Carl negligently injured Beth and Beth was incapacitated as a result. Suppose that as a result of her being incapacitated, Beth received quite a lot of money in social security payments. The Social Security (Recovery of Benefits) Act 1997 establishes that the social security payments that Beth received as a result of her being incapacitated in the first *five* years after Tom injured her will be taken into account in determining the damages payable to Beth; however any subsequent social security payments will be disregarded. At first sight, the Act seems to work in Tom's favour. However, the Act also provides that if Tom makes a compensation payment to Beth, he will be liable to compensate the State for *all* the social security payments that Beth received as a result of her being incapacitated. This can cause injustice if Tom is not wholly to blame for the fact that Beth was injured.

Situations where the receipt of a benefit will not be taken into account

There are many situations where the damages payable to the victim of a tort will *not* be reduced even though she received a benefit as a result of that tort being committed.

Gifts

Suppose that Sarah negligently injured Tom and as a result Tom was laid up for a while. Tom's friend, Nita, heard his bad news and sent him £100 'to help you out until you are back on your feet.' Nita's gift will *not* have the effect of reducing the damages payable to Tom by £100. There are two reasons for this.

First, if the damages payable to Tom *were* reduced, then Nita's gift would end up benefiting Sarah and not Tom. As Nita intended her gift to be for Tom's sole benefit, this would be unfair. Secondly, if the damages payable to people like Tom were reduced to take account of any gifts that he received as a result of being injured, then people like Nita would be discouraged from helping out people like Tom: if Nita knew any gift she gave Tom would simply benefit Sarah and not Tom, she would see little point in making a donation.[11]

---

as a result of his death will be disregarded.') In order to avoid this unfairness, it was held that A's compensation payment to B had had the effect of extinguishing B's rights to sue C for compensation in respect of his injury because A's payment was treated by B as fully compensating him for his injury. The decision is hardly principled and as a result may not survive being tested in the courts.

[10] *Colledge* v *Bass Mitchells & Butlers Ltd* [1988] 1 All ER 536.

[11] See *Parry* v *Cleaver* [1970] AC 1, 14A–D (per Lord Reid).

Insurance payments

In *Bradburn* v *Great Western Railway Co.*,[12] the defendant railway company's negligence caused the claimant to be injured while he was travelling on the defendants' line. The claimant sued the defendants for compensatory damages. Compensation for the actionable losses suffered by the claimant as a result of his injuries was assessed at £217. However, the claimant had received, on account of his injuries, £31 from his insurance company, the Accidental Insurance Company. The question was whether the claimant was entitled to recover £217 or (£217 − £31 =) £186 in compensatory damages from the defendants. It was held that even though the £31 received by the claimant was a benefit which he received as a result of the defendants' negligence − had the defendants not been negligent he would never have received that £31 − the claimant was still entitled to recover £217 from the defendant in compensatory damages.[13]

Why didn't the court hold that the claimant could only sue the defendants for £186? The reason is that had they done this all the premiums paid by the claimant on his insurance policy with the Accidental Insurance Company would have gone to waste. He would have obtained no benefit from them. Instead, the defendants would have been the ones who benefited from the insurance premiums paid by the claimant. As the claimant paid those premiums for his benefit and not for the benefit of anyone else, this would have been unfair. As Asquith LJ remarked in *Shearman* v *Folland*: 'If the wrongdoer were entitled to set-off what the wrongdoer was entitled to recoup or had recouped under his policy, he would, in effect, be depriving the claimant of all benefit from the premiums paid by the latter and appropriating that benefit to himself.'[14]

Three points may be made about this. First, there could have been no objection if the Court in *Bradburn* had held that the claimant would only be entitled to recover £186 in compensatory damages from the defendants *if* the defen-

---

[12] (1874) LR 10 Ex 1.

[13] The claimant − having obtained those damages − would have been entitled to keep the damages for himself. What is the position if A negligently destroys B's property, B obtains the value of the property from her property insurer, and then sues A for damages equal to the value of the property? B will be entitled to recover the full value of the property from A − for the reasons set out below, the damages payable to B will not be reduced to take account of the insurance payment that B has already obtained in respect of the destruction of her property − but B's insurance company will then have a charge over those damages for the value of the insurance money it paid out to B: *Lord Napier and Ettrick* v *Hunter* [1993] AC 713. The reason why B's insurance company will have a charge over the damages is to prevent double recovery. (For the same reason, if A tortiously causes B to suffer some kind of pure economic loss that B was insured against, B will be entitled to claim on her insurance policy but will then hold any damages obtained against A subject to a charge for the insurance company.) The reason why contracts of insurance against physical injury − such as the contract of insurance in *Bradburn* − are 'different' is that the concern to prevent double recovery will not apply in the cases where a claimant suffers physical injury as a result of someone's committing a tort in relation to her. The courts acknowledge that it is impossible to determine what would amount to an 'adequate' level of compensation for the physical injury suffered by the claimant − so people should be left free to insure their persons so as to 'boost' the amount of money they will be able to recover if someone physically injures them.

[14] [1950] 2 KB 43, 46.

dants repaid all the premiums paid by the claimant on his insurance policy with the Accidental Insurance Company.[15] However, it probably did not occur to the court to decide the *Bradburn* case in this way.

Secondly, what would have been the position if the *defendants* had paid the insurance premiums on the claimant's insurance policy with the Accidental Insurance Company? Say, for example, that the claimant had been an employee of the defendants and they had taken out the insurance policy for his benefit to protect him against the risk of being killed or injured while he worked for them. Recent authority indicates that if this had been the case, then the claimant would have been limited to suing the defendants for £186.[16] This is quite right: in the case just described, no injustice would have been done to anyone if the defendants had been allowed to take advantage of the premiums paid on the claimant's insurance policy – after all, they paid those premiums in the first place.

Thirdly, what would have been the position if someone other than the claimant – call him John – or the defendants had paid the premiums on his insurance policy with the Accidental Insurance Company for him? If this had been the case, should the court have held that the claimant could only sue the defendants for £186? Subsequent authorities seem to say that the answer to this question is 'yes'.[17] However, it is more complex than that. We can imagine two variations on the situation we are now imagining obtained in *Bradburn*, where John paid the insurance premiums on the claimant's policy with the Accidental Insurance Company. In the first case, John intended, when he paid the premiums, that the claimant and no one else should get the benefit of those premiums. If this had been the case, it would have been unfair – unfair on John – for the court to allow the defendants to take advantage of the payment of those premiums and hold that the claimant was only entitled to recover £186 in compensatory damages from the defendants. The right decision would have been to hold that the claimant could sue the defendants for £217. In the second case, John paid the premiums because he was contractually obliged to do so under an arrangement with the claimant – say John was the claimant's employer – and, in paying the premiums, had no intention one way or the other as to who should benefit from the payment of those premiums. If this had been the case, it would *not* have been unfair for the court to allow the defendants to take advantage of the payment of those premiums and hold that the claimant could sue the defendants for £186. Given this, that is what the court should have held.

Pension payments[18]

In *Parry* v *Cleaver*,[19] the claimant was prevented from carrying on working as a police constable as a result of injuries he sustained in a traffic accident caused by the defendant's negligence. At the time of the accident the claimant was 35

---

[15] *Bristol & West Building Society* v *May May & Merrimans (No. 2)* [1998] 1 WLR 336, 356.
[16] *Pirelli General plc* v *Gaca* [2004] EWCA Civ 373.
[17] *Hussain* v *New Taplow Paper Mills* [1988] 1 AC 514, 527G–H; *Hodgson* v *Trapp* [1989] 1 AC 807, 819H; *Bristol & West Building Society* v *May May & Merrimans (No. 2)* [1998] 1 WLR 336, 358–9.
[18] See Lewis 1999, 81–6.
[19] [1970] AC 1.

years old and had worked as a police constable for 12 years. Throughout his time in the force the claimant had made a weekly contribution to the police pension fund. On being invalided out of the force, the claimant obtained an invalidity pension of £204 a year. It was found that had the claimant not been injured, he would have continued working as a police constable until the age of 48 and would then have retired on a pension of £515 a year and found work in the civilian sector. As it was, the claimant's injury meant he had to find work in the civilian sector at the age of 35 and he did not receive a retirement pension at all.

So the defendant's negligence caused the claimant to suffer two losses: (1) the loss of the extra money the claimant would have earned net of tax between the ages of 35 and 48 had he continued working for the police and not been forced to work in the civilian sector (say this loss was worth £5,000); (2) the loss of the extra pension money the claimant would have received from the age of 48 until the end of his life had he not been invalided out of the police force (this was worth £311 a year: the difference between the retirement pension that the claimant would have received had he stayed on in the police force until he was 48 and the invalidity pension that the claimant actually did receive as a result of being invalided out of the police force).

However, the defendant's negligence also meant that the claimant would receive a benefit between the ages of 35 and 48: an invalidity pension payment of £204 a year. Had the defendant not been negligent, the claimant would not have received that payment. The House of Lords held that this benefit should not be taken into account in determining the damages payable to the claimant, on the ground that if it were then the claimant would lose the benefit of his 12 years' worth of contributions to the police pension fund that he made before he was injured.[20]

Parry v *Cleaver* was followed in *Smoker* v *London Fire Authority*.[21] In that case, the claimant was employed as a fireman by the defendants. Under the terms of his employment, he was a member of a pension scheme to which he contributed approximately 11 per cent of his wages. The defendants contributed twice as much as the claimant towards his pension. In 1985 the claimant was disabled as a result of the defendants' negligence and his disability meant he had to retire from the force in December 1985. Had the defendants not been negligent, the claimant would have continued to work as a firefighter until December 1987, when he was due to retire.

The defendants' negligence therefore resulted in the claimant suffering a loss of income: the money the claimant would have earned in the two years between December 1985 and December 1987 had he been allowed to continue to work

---

[20] This is not quite true. The claimant was allowed to sue the defendant for the extra pension money he would have received after the age of 48 had he not been invalided out of the police force and that extra pension money would have been payable in part because of the 12 years' worth of contributions that the claimant made to the police pension fund. So the claimant would still have obtained something for those 12 years' worth of contributions even if the damages payable to him had been reduced to take account of the invalidity pension payments he was going to receive between the ages of 35 and 48 as a result of the defendant's negligence.

[21] [1991] 2 AC 502.

for the defendants. This loss was worth about £13,500. At the same time the defendants' negligence resulted in the claimant obtaining a benefit during those two years. The claimant received about £10,000 in invalidity pension payments in the two years between December 1985 and December 1987. These payments were made out of the claimant's pension scheme in consideration of the contributions that he and the defendants made to that pension scheme.

The House of Lords held, following *Parry v Cleaver*, that the invalidity pension payments made to the claimant between December 1985 and December 1987 were not to be taken into account in calculating the damages payable to the claimant. So the claimant was entitled to recover £13,500 in compensatory damages from the defendants in respect of the loss of income suffered by him between December 1985 and December 1987: no deduction would be made to take account of the fact that the claimant had in fact received a benefit of about £10,000 in invalidity pension payments as a result of the defendants' negligence during those two years. This decision can be criticised. The pension payments that the claimant received between December 1985 and December 1987 could be split into two. One third of those payments (approximately £3,300) were attributable to the contributions that the claimant made to his pension scheme. Two thirds (approximately £6,700) were attributable to the contributions that the defendants made to the claimant's pension scheme.

Now it might be conceded that the £3,300 that the claimant received in pension payments between December 1985 and December 1987 and that were attributable to the claimant's contributions to his pension scheme should not have been taken into account in determining the damages payable to the claimant, on the ground that if they were that would be unfair on the claimant. However, it would not have been unfair – on the claimant or the defendants – to deduct the remaining pension payments, that were attributable to the *defendants'* contributions to the claimant's pension scheme, from the damages payable to the claimant.

The House of Lords recognised the strength of this point in the case of *Hussain v New Taplow Paper Mills Ltd.*[22] In that case the claimant was injured in an accident due to the negligence of the defendants, his employers, and was unable, due to his injuries, to continue working for the defendants. For 15 months after the accident, the defendants continued to pay the claimant his full pay – even though he was not doing any work for them – under their 'permanent health insurance scheme'. This scheme was paid for by the defendants: the defendants' employees, including the claimant, made no contribution to this scheme. The claimant sued the defendants in negligence for damages to compensate him for the loss of income that he had suffered as a result of the defendants' negligence.

The House of Lords held that the health insurance payments that the claimant had received for 15 months after he had stopped work should be taken into account in determining the damages payable to the claimant. The House of Lords held that deducting these payments from the damages payable to the

---

[22] [1988] 1 AC 514.

claimant would not be unfair on the claimant. The claimant could not claim that making such a deduction would result in him receiving no benefit from the contributions he had made to the defendants' health insurance scheme: the claimant made no such contributions.

Windfall payments

In *Needler Financial Services Ltd* v *Taber*,[23] the defendants negligently advised the claimant to switch pension schemes. The claimant did so and lost out as a result: the pension scheme that he switched into (with the Norwich Union) was not as profitable as his original pension scheme. He sued the defendants for damages. The defendants admitted liability but claimed that the damages payable to the claimant should be reduced because the claimant received a windfall payment of about £7,800 when the Norwich Union demutualised. Sir Andrew Morritt V-C held that this benefit – which the claimant had received as a result of the defendants' negligent advice – should *not* be taken into account in determining the damages payable to the claimant. It is hard to understand why it should not have been. However, one possible explanation is that the claimant might have already spent the windfall payment that he received from the Norwich Union. If he had, then taking that windfall payment into account in determining the damages payable to the claimant would have made him, through no fault of his own, worse off overall – which would have been unfair to the claimant.

Gains made through the exercise of skill and judgment

In *Hussey* v *Eels*[24] the defendants fraudulently induced the claimants to buy their house. The house was, to the defendants' knowledge, affected by subsidence but the defendants told the claimants that to their knowledge the property had not been subject to subsidence. The claimants purchased the defendants' house for approximately £53,000. The true value of the house was about £36,000 as repairing it would cost in excess of £17,000. So the defendants' fraud caused the claimants to lose £17,000. However, the claimants, having discovered the problem with subsidence, then began to turn things around. They decided not to have the house repaired. Instead, they demolished it and sought planning permission to build two bungalows on the vacant plot. This was granted and the claimants then sold the land to a developer with the planning permission for £78,500.

So – having initially lost £17,000, the claimants' ingenuity meant that they made a gain of £42,500 on selling the land on which their house was originally built: they obtained £78,500 in return for an asset which was originally worth £36,000 in their hands. The claimants then sued the defendants for the original £17,000 that they had lost in buying the defendants' house. The defendants claimed that the £42,500 profit that the claimants made on selling the land on which the house was built should be taken into account in assessing

[23] [2002] 3 All ER 501.
[24] [1990] 2 QB 227.

the damages payable to the claimants. So in effect they argued that they should not be held liable to the claimants at all. The Court of Appeal rejected the defendants' claim. This was quite right: had the claimants' profit been taken into account, all the work and planning they did in improving the value of their land would have redounded to the benefit of the defendants. So the defendants were correctly held liable to pay the claimants £17,000 in damages.

Psychic benefits

In *Wise* v *Kaye*, Sellers LJ remarked that: 'The complete loss of sight may bring, and I think often does, a serenity and calm of life which might lead to a happiness hitherto unknown, but I cannot think that a defendant is entitled to pray that in aid in order to reduce the damages he has to pay to the sufferer. [Similarly if] [i]nfirmity which cripples and incapacitates a man ... [brings] him a sympathy and attention which reveals in him an inward comfort which he has never previously known [making him] happier than he has ever been.'[25]

CONTRIBUTORY NEGLIGENCE

Section 1(1) of the Law Reform (Contributory Negligence) Act 1945 provides that where 'any person suffers damage as the result partly of his own fault and partly of the fault of any other person or persons ... the damages recoverable in respect thereof shall be reduced to such extent as the court thinks just and equitable having regard to the claimant's share in the responsibility of the damage'. Section 4 of the 1945 Act provides that ' "fault" means negligence, breach of statutory duty or other act or omission which gives rise to liability in tort or would, apart from this Act, give rise to a defence of contributory negligence'.

The basic effect of the 1945 Act is this. Suppose A has committed a tort in relation to B. Suppose further that B suffered losses worth £50,000 as a result of A's tort and she wants to sue A for compensation in respect of those losses. A will usually have a defence of *contributory negligence* to B's claim if B was partly to blame for the fact that she suffered the losses that she has suffered.[26] B will be partly to blame for the fact that she suffered those losses if she would not have suffered those losses had she not acted unreasonably[27] in some

---

[25] [1962] 1 QB 638, 651.

[26] Although the defence is known as the defence of *contributory negligence*, there is no reason to think that the defence will not be available in the case where B *deliberately* did something that resulted in her suffering the losses that she suffered as a result of A's tort. In such a case, the losses suffered by B will still be partly her fault. The House of Lords ruled that the defence of contributory negligence would cover cases where a victim of a tort's deliberate act contributed to her suffering the losses she did in *Reeves* v *Commissioner of Police of the Metropolis* [2000] AC 360, at 370 (per Lord Hoffmann), 377 (per Lord Jauncey), 383 (per Lord Hope), 385 (per Lord Hobhouse).

[27] *Important note.* In judging whether B acted reasonably, one asks whether a reasonable person of B's age (*Yachuk* v *Oliver Blais Co. Ltd* [1949] AC 386; *Gough* v *Thorne* [1966] 1 WLR 1387) and in B's physical condition (*Daly* v *Liverpool Corporation* [1939] 2 All ER 142) would have acted in the way B did. Although there is authority to the contrary (*Baxter* v *Woolcombers Ltd* (1963) 107 SJ 553), it is hard to believe that B's mental condition will not also be taken into account in judging whether B acted unreasonably – so that if a reasonable person with B's mental condition would have acted in the same way, B will *not* be found to have acted unreasonably. So, for example, if B kills himself while in police custody because he is mentally ill, it would not be

way.[28] If A can take advantage of a defence of contributory negligence in meeting B's claim, the damages payable to B will be reduced to take account of the fact that B was partly to blame for the fact that she suffered those losses. So B will not be able to claim £50,000 from A by way of damages: she will only be entitled to claim some lesser amount.

A number of points need to be made about the scope and effect of the defence of contributory negligence.[29]

(1) *Assessment of reduction: two party cases.* If A has committed a tort in relation to B but can raise a defence of contributory negligence to reduce the damages payable to B in respect of the losses suffered by B as a result of A's tort, the courts determine by how much the damages payable to B should be reduced by assessing the *comparative blameworthiness* of A and B for the losses suffered by B. So if they were equally to blame for the fact that B suffered those losses, the damages payable will be reduced by 50 per cent;[30] if A was four times as much to blame as B for the losses suffered by B, the damages will be reduced by 20 per cent.[31]

(2) *Assessment of reduction: three party cases.* The position is a bit more complicated in a case which involves two tortfeasors. Suppose that A and B each committed a tort in relation to C and C suffered various losses as result but C was partly to blame for the fact that he suffered those losses. We determine by how much the damages payable to C should be reduced by lumping A and B together and asking: as compared to C, how much to blame were A and B *together* for the losses suffered by C?

So in *Fitzgerald* v *Lane*,[32] the claimant walked across a road when the lights were against him. He was struck by a motor car being negligently driven by the first defendant. While he was lying in the road he was struck by a motor car which was negligently driven by the second defendant. It was held that the first defendant and second defendant both caused the claimant to suffer the injuries

---

appropriate to reduce any damages payable to B's dependants for contributory negligence. (So far as we know, no such reduction has ever been made in a case where a mentally ill person killed himself in police custody.)

[28] Of course if A's tort only resulted in B suffering the losses she did because B deliberately and unreasonably did *x after* A committed his tort then B will usually be *barred* from suing A for damages in respect of those losses, either on the ground that B's deliberate and unreasonable act broke the chain of causation between A's tort and the losses suffered by B or on the ground that B had a duty to mitigate the losses suffered by her as a result of A's tort and she only suffered the losses she did because she breached that duty. So A will only really need to take advantage of the defence of contributory negligence in the following cases: (1) where B only suffered the losses she did because B did something unreasonable *before* A committed his tort; (2) where B only suffered the losses she did because she did something unreasonable *after* A committed his tort but she did not act deliberately when she acted as she did; (3) where B only suffered the losses she did because she deliberately did something unreasonable *after* A committed his tort but there is some policy reason why B's act should not be held to have broken the chain of causation between A's tort and B's suffering those losses.

[29] On which, see, generally, Gravells 1977.

[30] The deduction made in *Reeves* v *Commissioner of Police of the Metropolis* [2000] AC 360 (prisoner took advantage of defendants' negligence to commit suicide).

[31] The deduction made in *Froom* v *Butcher* [1976] QB 286 (claimant's failure to wear seat belt contributed to the injuries she suffered in car accident caused by defendant's negligence).

[32] [1989] AC 328.

he suffered as a result of the second collision[33] and so the claimant was entitled to sue either the first defendant or the second defendant or both for compensation for the fact that he received those injuries. However, the claimant was partly to blame for the fact that he suffered those injuries: he would not have suffered those injuries had he not acted unreasonably by walking across the road when the lights were against him. Given this, the damages payable to the claimant were liable to be reduced for contributory negligence. It was found that the claimant in this case was twice as much to blame as each of the defendants for the injuries that he suffered in the second collision. It followed that he was just as much to blame for the injuries that he suffered as the two defendants *together*. The damages payable to the claimant were therefore reduced by 50 per cent.

(3) *100 per cent reduction?* Could the defence of contributory negligence have the effect of reducing the damages payable to the victim of a tort to *zero*? The Court of Appeal doubted in *Pitts* v *Hunt*[34] whether the 1945 Act could ever have this effect. After all, if A has committed a tort in relation to B and B has suffered various losses as a result, it is hard to imagine that B could ever be 100 per cent to blame for the fact that she suffered those losses – after all they were triggered in part by A's committing a tort.

However, in *Reeves* v *Commissioner of Police of the Metropolis* one judge in the Court of Appeal found that a prisoner who hanged himself while in the custody of the police was 100 per cent to blame for his death and held as a result that if the prisoner had survived his suicide attempt, he would not have been entitled to sue the police for anything.[35] When *Reeves* went to the House of Lords, their Lordships found that the police and the prisoner were equally to blame for the prisoner's death and accordingly reduced the damages payable to the prisoner's dependants by 50 per cent.[36] But they did not go so far as to say that it would never be possible to find that the victim of a tort was 100 per cent to blame for the losses that she suffered as a result of that tort being committed. The point must therefore be regarded as still open to argument.

(4) *Torts to which the defence is inapplicable.* The defence of contributory negligence will not be available in *all* cases where A commits a tort in relation to B and B suffers losses as a result for which B was partly to blame. If the tort committed by A was conversion or amounted to an intentional trespass to B's goods, then the defence will

---

[33] How was it that the *first* defendant's negligence caused the claimant to suffer the injuries that he suffered in the *second* collision? The claimant would not have suffered those injuries but for the first defendant's negligence and the second defendant's negligence did not break the chain of causation between the first defendant's negligence and the injuries suffered by the claimant in the second collision: while the second defendant acted unreasonably in running over the claimant, he did not *deliberately* run over the claimant. He was careless, not malicious.

[34] [1991] 2 QB 24.

[35] [1999] QB 169, 195 (per Morritt LJ). Of the other two judges, Buxton LJ did not think the defence of contributory negligence was available (ibid., 182–3), and Lord Bingham CJ thought that the damages payable should be reduced by 50%, but in order to produce a result with which at least two members of the court agreed, he held that the damages payable should not be reduced at all (ibid., 198).

[36] [2000] AC 360.

not apply;[37] nor will it if the tort committed by A was deceit[38] or involved dishonesty of any kind[39] (as will be the case if the tort committed by A was conspiracy or inducing a breach of contract). In *Standard Chartered Bank* v *Pakistan National Shipping Corporation (Nos 2 and 4)*, Lord Rodger of Earlsferry stated that 'contributory negligence [has] never been a defence open to a defendant who . . . intended to harm the [claimant].'[40] However, this may be too wide.

(5) *Contributory negligence and Hedley Byrne.* Two problems need to be addressed under this heading. First, will a defendant who has breached a duty of care owed to another under one of the principles in *Hedley Byrne* be entitled to rely on the defence of contributory negligence to reduce the damages payable to that other? Secondly, if he is, how does the defence of contributory negligence interact with the limit placed by the *SAAMCO* principle on what damages can be sued for in a *Hedley Byrne* case?

On the first question, suppose that A advised B that a car that she was thinking of buying was in good condition and that he indicated to her that she could safely rely on his advice. Suppose further that she did rely on A's advice and bought the car. However the car later proved to be so defective that it was not worth repairing and had to be given away to some scrap metal merchants. If B sues A in negligence, can A attempt to raise a defence of contributory negligence to B's claim on the basis that she was partly to blame for the fact that she lost the money she spent on the car because it was very foolish of her to rely on his advice? It is unlikely that A would be allowed to make such an argument.[41] Having earlier indicated to B that she could safely rely on his advice, it is likely that A would be prevented (estopped) from subsequently arguing that B was foolish to rely on his advice for the purpose of raising a defence of contributory negligence to her claim for damages.

However, if the *extent* of the losses suffered by B as a result of acting on A's advice were partly B's fault, then there is no reason why A should not be allowed to raise a defence of contributory negligence to reduce the damages payable to B. This what happened in *Platform Home Loans* v *Oyston Shipways Ltd*,[42] a case which also dealt with the interaction between the *SAAMCO* principle and the defence of contributory negligence. Simplifying the facts of the case slightly, the claimant lent £1m to a Mr Hussain secured by a mortgage of Hussain's home. The home was negligently valued by the defendant as being worth £1.5m: it was in fact worth only £1m. Four years later, Hussain defaulted on repaying the loan and the

---

[37] Section 11 of the Torts (Interference with Goods) Act 1977 provides that 'Contributory negligence is no defence in proceedings founded on conversion, or on intentional trespass to goods.'

[38] *Alliance & Leicester Building Society* v *Edgestop Ltd* [1993] 1 WLR 1462; *Standard Chartered Bank* v *Pakistan National Shipping Corporation (Nos 2 and 4)* [2003] 1 AC 959.

[39] *Corporacion Nacional de Cobre* v *Sogemin* [1997] 1 WLR 1396.

[40] [2003] 1 AC 959, at [45], querying whether Lord Denning MR was right to think in *Murphy* v *Culhane* [1977] 1 QB 94 that the defence would be available in a case where A beat B up in response to provocation from B (ibid., at 98–9).

[41] See *Gran Gelato Ltd* v *Richcliff (Group) Ltd* [1992] Ch 560, 574 (per Sir Donald Nicholls V-C), doubting whether the damages payable to a claimant in a *Hedley Byrne* case could be reduced for contributory negligence where it was alleged that the claimant was contributorily negligent because she should not have done the very thing that she was advised to do by the defendant.

[42] [2000] 2 AC 190.

claimant sought to recoup the money he had lent by selling Hussain's house, which was only worth £400,000 at that stage. So the claimant lost £600,000 as a result of the defendant's negligence.[43] But two points complicated the case.

The first was that under the *SAAMCO* principle, the defendant should only have been entitled to sue the claimant for £500,000 – that was the loss which the defendant had suffered that was attributable to the fact that it had loaned money to Hussain on inadequate security.[44] The second point was that the claimant was – as compared with the defendant – 20 per cent to blame for the fact that he lost the money he did on the loan to Hussain. The reasons for this were: (*a*) he had failed to check whether or not Hussain was a credit risk; and (*b*) he had loaned Hussain more than was reasonable given the defendant's valuation of Hussain's house. So the defendant was entitled to raise a defence of contributory negligence to reduce the damages that he had to pay the claimant.

The problem faced by the courts in the *Platform Home Loans* case was – how did these two points relate to each other? Do you say that the defendant was *prima facie* liable to pay the claimant £600,000, deduct 20 per cent for contributory negligence, turning the defendant's liability into one to pay the claimant £480,000, and then allow the claimant to claim for the whole of that on the basis that doing so would not violate the *SAAMCO* principle (under which the most the claimant could have sued the defendant for was £500,000)? Or do you say that the *SAAMCO* principle means that the defendant was *prima facie* liable to pay the claimant £500,000 and then knock 20 per cent off *that* figure, turning the defendant's liability into one to pay the claimant £400,000? The Court of Appeal preferred the latter approach;[45] but the House of Lords ruled that the former approach was correct. In so doing, the House of Lords reinterpreted the *SAAMCO* principle as one which does not determine *which* of the losses suffered by a claimant in a *Hedley Byrne* case can be sued for by that claimant, but as one which places a 'cap' on the potential liability of a defendant to a claimant in a *Hedley Byrne* case. It is, however, doubtful whether that interpretation of the *SAAMCO* principle is reconcilable with the reasons for its adoption by Lord Hoffmann in the *SAAMCO* case.

(6) *Contributory negligence and White v Jones.* Suppose that A asked C to prepare a will for him under which B would inherit £9,000. C prepared the will but had only one person witness A's signing the will, thus making the will invalid. A – who had some knowledge of the law relating to wills – thought that more than one witness was required but did not raise any objections because he thought

---

[43] It was established that if the defendant had taken care in his valuation, he would have accurately valued the house as being worth only £1m; as a result, the defendants would have offered to lend Mr Hussain only £700,000 and he would have declined the loan.

[44] Had the claimant lent the £1m to Hussain on adequate security – that is, in return for a mortgage of a house worth £1.5m – when Hussain defaulted, the security would have been worth £900,000 and the claimant would have lost £100,000 on the loan. So £100,000 of the £600,000 loss suffered by the claimant would have been suffered by the claimant anyway, even if he had lent Hussain money on adequate security. Therefore, £500,000 of the money lost by the claimant was lost by the claimant because he lent money to Hussain on inadequate security.

[45] [1998] Ch 466.

C 'knew best'. Shortly afterwards, A died and his will was declared to be invalid with the result that B did not receive her legacy. B will, of course, be able to sue C for damages under the principle in *White* v *Jones*,[46] but will C be able to raise a defence of contributory negligence to her claim on the basis that *A* was partly to blame for the fact that B did not receive her legacy? The question was raised in *Gorham* v *British Telecommunications plc*.[47] Of the three members of the Court of Appeal who decided that case, Pill and Schiemann LJJ preferred to leave the matter to be decided another day,[48] though Pill LJ thought the argument that a defence of contributory negligence should be available in this kind of case had its 'attractions'.[49] Sir Murray Stuart-Smith thought that the defence *would* be available in this kind of case.[50]

(7) *One final limit.* Suppose that A has committed a tort in relation to B and B has suffered various losses as a result, for which she was partly to blame – she would not have suffered those losses had she not acted unreasonably in some way. It seems to be the case that if the reason why B suffered those losses has nothing to do with the reason why it was unreasonable for B to act in the way she did, A will not be able to raise a defence of contributory negligence to B's claim to be compensated for those losses.

So, for example, in *Jones* v *Livox Quarries Ltd*[51] Denning LJ considered whether the defence would be available in the following case. A negligently fires a gun and the bullet fired from the gun happens to hit and injure B while she was dangerously perched on the back of a moving lorry. Now – it was clearly unreasonable for B to stand on the back of the lorry and had she not done this she would not have been hit by the bullet: it was because she was on the lorry that she was in the wrong place at the wrong time. Does this mean that A can raise a defence of contributory negligence to any claim B makes against him for damages? Denning LJ thought not.[52] But the only explanation as to why the defence would not be available here is that the reason why it was unreasonable for B to perch on the back of the lorry had nothing to do with the reason why B was hit by the bullet.

In *Westwood* v *The Post Office*,[53] the claimant worked for the Post Office at a telephone exchange. His place of work was a three storey building with a flat roof. Workers at the exchange, including the claimant, would frequently take short breaks on the roof although they were not authorised to do so and not permitted to gain access to the roof. While on his way back from one such break on the roof, the claimant fell through a defective trapdoor and was injured. The claimant sued the Post Office for damages in respect of his injuries, claiming that he had been injured because the Post Office had breached the duty it owed

[46] [1995] 2 AC 207.
[47] [2000] 1 WLR 2129.
[48] Ibid., 2144 (per Pill LJ), 2145 (per Schiemann LJ).
[49] Ibid., 2144.
[50] Ibid., 2149.
[51] [1952] 2 QB 608.
[52] Ibid., 616.
[53] [1974] AC 1.

him under s 16 of the Offices, Shops and Railway Premises Act 1963 to ensure that the floors in the claimant's workplace were of sound construction. The Post Office admitted liability but sought to raise a defence of contributory negligence to the claimant's claim. The Post Office argued that the claimant was partly to blame for his injuries because he would not have been injured had he not acted unreasonably in trespassing on the flat roof of the telephone exchange. The House of Lords held that no defence of contributory negligence could be raised here: the reason why the claimant was injured (he trod on a trapdoor which was not soundly constructed) had nothing to do with the reason why it was unreasonable for the claimant to trespass on the flat roof of the telephone exchange (he had no business being up there).

LIMITATION CLAUSE

We have already come across the concept of an exclusion clause – a clause in a contract which provides that someone will not be held liable if he commits a tort in relation to someone else. A limitation clause is a clause in a contract which provides that if someone commits a tort, the most he can be held liable for is a certain sum of money. So if A has committed a tort in relation to B and B has suffered losses worth £50,000 as a result, A's liability to B will be reduced to £5,000 if there exists a limitation clause which he is entitled to rely on which provides that A's liability to B in the event of his committing a tort in relation to B will be limited to £5,000. The same rules that apply to determine whether a tortfeasor can rely on an exclusion clause to escape being held liable to the victim of his tort[54] also apply to determine whether a tortfeasor can rely on a limitation clause to limit his liability to the victim of his tort, so we need say no more about the validity of limitation clauses here.

---

[54] Discussed above, pp. 504–12.

COMPENSATORY DAMAGES: THIRD PARTIES

We are concerned in this section of the book with two questions. First, when will a third party to a tort[1] be able to obtain compensation for a loss that he has suffered as a result of that tort being committed? Secondly, if a tort has been committed, when will a third party to the tort be held liable to compensate those who suffered loss as a result of that tort being committed? Let's briefly look at how the law answers these two questions.

THE FIRST QUESTION

Occasionally, the law will allow the victim of a tort to sue for damages that are essentially designed to compensate a third party for a loss that she has suffered because that tort was committed. We have already seen an example of this.

If A has committed a tort in relation to B and B has been so badly injured as a result that her expectation of life has been reduced, she will be allowed to sue A for damages in respect of the money she would have earned and not spent on herself in the years that are now 'lost' to her.[2] The point of allowing B to sue for such damages is essentially to ensure that any dependants that B has, who would have been supported by her in the years that are now 'lost' to her, do not lose out as a result of A's tort. By allowing B to sue A for damages in respect of the money she would have earned in the years that are now 'lost' to her, the law enables B to set up a fund which will look after her dependants after she has died.

Another example is provided by what we can call the principle in *Donnelly* v *Joyce*.[3] This principle applies in the following kind of situation. Suppose that A negligently injured B and B, as a result, was incapacitated and needed to be looked after. Suppose further that C – a friend[4] of B's – looked after B without charging her anything for the work done by him in looking after her.[5] The

---

[1] Someone will be a 'third party' to a tort if he neither committed the tort in question nor was he the victim of that tort.

[2] See above, pp. 593–4. Though no such damages will be awarded if B is so young that any estimate as to how much she earned in the years that are now 'lost' to her would be purely speculative: *Gammell* v *Wilson* [1982] AC 27, 78E–G (per Lord Scarman, suggesting there might be an exception in the case where a child was already earning money at the time her expectation of life was cut short as a result of someone's negligently injuring her; which would be the case if the child was a movie star).

[3] [1974] QB 454.

[4] The principle will equally apply if C was a relative of B's. It is uncertain whether the principle in *Donnelly* v *Joyce* will apply in the situation where a complete stranger looks after the victim of a tort without charging her anything for doing so. In Scotland, only care provided by a relative is covered by their version of the principle in *Donnelly* v *Joyce*: Administration of Justice Act 1982, s 8.

[5] If C had *charged* B for looking after her, then A would of course be liable to compensate B for the money she spent on getting C to look after her – so long, of course, as the money she paid C for looking after her was reasonable.

principle in *Donnelly* v *Joyce* says that in this situation, B will be entitled to sue A for damages equal to the value of the work that C did in looking after B.[6] That such damages are designed to compensate C for the effort he put in looking after B is shown by two things. First, the damages payable will depend on what sort of sacrifices were incurred by C in looking after B; the greater the sacrifices, the greater the damages payable.[7] Secondly, if B does sue A for damages equal to the value of the work done by C in looking after her, she will hold those damages on trust[8] for C.[9] (It is a difficult question whether B will also hold her *right to sue* A for those damages on trust for C; if she does, then C will be allowed to *compel* B to sue A for those damages.[10])

There are other situations where the victim of a tort will be entitled to sue for damages in respect of losses suffered by third parties to that tort – though it must be emphasised that these situations are exceptional in nature; the normal rule is that the victim of a tort is confined to suing for compensatory damages in respect of the losses that *she* has suffered as a result of that tort being committed. So: if A negligently injures a housewife with the result that she can no longer do any housework, she will be entitled to sue A for damages in respect

---

[6] So – in *Donnelly* v *Joyce* [1974] QB 454 itself, the claimant was a child who was negligently injured by the defendant and as a result needed to spend six months at home having his injuries treated. The claimant's mother took time off work to look after the claimant. The claimant was allowed to sue the defendant for damages equal to the value of the work done by the claimant's mother in looking after him.

[7] *Housecroft* v *Burnett* [1986] 1 All ER 332, 343e–f. However the damages payable will not be allowed to exceed the going market rate for the kind of services that C provided B: ibid. So, for example, suppose Paul negligently injured Mary and Mary's injuries were so serious that she needed to be looked after 24 hours a day for six months. Mary's husband – who earned £400 an hour working as a lawyer – decided to quit his legal practice to look after Mary full-time for the six months she was laid up, thereby forgoing roughly £400,000. Mary would not be able to sue Paul for that £400,000; instead she will be limited to suing Paul for the market value of the services provided by her husband in looking after her. The reason why Mary will not be able to sue Paul for £400,000 under the principle in *Donnelly* v *Joyce* is that by having her husband look after her, she and her husband failed to mitigate the loss suffered by them as a result of Paul's tort: it would have been much cheaper to hire a nurse to look after Mary and have Paul carry on working.

[8] Property is held 'on trust' for another when the legal owner of that property is under an obligation – equitable in nature – to apply that property for the benefit of another. In such a case, we say that the property is held on trust for that other, who is known as a *beneficiary* or a *cestui que trust*.

[9] *Hunt* v *Severs* [1994] 2 AC 350 (the defendant in that case negligently injured his girlfriend in a car crash and then spent a lot of time looking after her; when she sued him for damages (which would, in effect, have been paid by the defendant's liability insurer), it was held that she could not recover damages in respect of the work the defendant had done in looking after her because if such damages were awarded her, they would have to be paid straight back to the defendant). (For another example of this principle at work – which we can call the principle against *circuity of actions* – see *Hyundai Heavy Industries Co. Ltd* v *Papadopolous* [1980] 1 WLR 1129.) The logic of the decision is impeccable, but it has been criticised on the ground that its effect is to encourage a husband who has negligently injured his wife to contract out her care to a complete stranger rather than looking after her himself. The Law Commission has accordingly recommended that the result in *Hunt* v *Severs* be reversed: Law Commission No. 262, *Damages for Personal Injury* (1999), paras 3.67 – 3.76.

[10] Degeling 2003 takes the view that, as the law stands, C will not be able to compel B to sue. However, she goes on to argue that C *should* be subrogated to B's rights to sue A for damages in respect of the cost of caring for her – which would allow C to sue A for such damages in B's name.

of the work done by any members of her family in filling in for her.[11] Similarly, if B regularly looked after C, a family member, but is now no longer able to do so because she was negligently injured by A, with the result that another family member has to look after C, B will be entitled to sue A for damages equal to the value of the work she used to do looking after C.[12] If A negligently damages B's car and C – a friend of B's – lends B a replacement car while his car is being repaired, then B may be entitled to sue A for damages equal to the rent that he would normally have had to pay to rent that kind of replacement car.[13]

These are all cases where the victim of a tort will be entitled to sue the person who committed that tort for damages in respect of the losses suffered by a third party to that tort as a result of that tort being committed. When will a third party to a tort be entitled to sue *in her own right* for compensation in respect of the losses she has suffered because that tort was committed? *Normally,* she never will be.[14] However, there are some exceptions to this rule and they are set out in the next chapter.

THE SECOND QUESTION

Not much needs to be said at this stage on this issue. If A has suffered various losses as a result of a tort that B committed, A will normally only be allowed to sue *B* for compensation in respect of those losses.[15] However, the law on vicarious liability creates an exception to this rule. If C is vicariously liable in respect of B's tort, then if A is entitled to sue B for compensation in respect of the losses suffered by him as a result of B's tort, then he will also be entitled to sue C for such compensation as well.[16] In Chapter 35, we will set out the situations in which one person will be held vicariously liable in respect of a tort committed by someone else.

---

[11] *Daly* v *General Steam Navigation Co. Ltd* [1981] 1 WLR 120. But if A negligently injures a businessman and as a result the businessman can no longer run his business and has his wife fill in for him, he will not be able to sue A for damages in respect of the work done by his wife running the business for him: *Hardwick* v *Hudson* [1999] 1 WLR 1770.

[12] *Lowe* v *Guise* [2002] QB 1369. Rix LJ suggested in that case (at [38]) that the damages, once paid over, 'may' be held on trust for the family member who took B's place in looking after C. What if C responded to B's being incapacitated by paying someone else to look after him, C? Presumably in that case the damages payable to B might then be held on trust for C.

[13] The point was left open in *Giles* v *Thompson* [1994] 1 AC 142, at 166G–167A. However, it is implicit in the House of Lords' decision in *Dimond* v *Lovell* [2002] 1 AC 384 that such a claim will be available to B, and may even be available where C was not a friend but a complete stranger. No such claim could be made on the facts of *Dimond* v *Lovell*, however – where the replacement car was provided by a finance company under a hire agreement that was void under the Consumer Credit Act 1974 – because to allow such a claim would have subverted the 1974 Act.

[14] See above, at pp. 24, 89 and 471–2, for examples of situations where a claimant sued for compensation in respect of losses suffered by her because a tort was committed, but her claim was thrown out because she was a third party to that tort.

[15] And as we have seen, A will not normally be allowed to sue the person who committed that tort for compensation in respect of the losses he has suffered if he was a third party to that tort – that is, if he was not the victim of that tort.

[16] Of course, he cannot recover twice over for the losses that he has suffered: he will lose all his rights to sue once C or B has fully compensated A for the losses that he has suffered.

34

LIABILITY TO THIRD PARTIES

Suppose A has committed a tort in relation to B. Suppose further that C, a third party, has suffered some kind of loss as a result. As a general rule, C will *not* be entitled to sue A[1] for compensatory damages in respect of the loss he has suffered as a result of A's tort. However, there are some exceptions to this rule.

THE FATAL ACCIDENTS ACT 1976

The major exception is created under the Fatal Accidents Act 1976. That Act covers the situation where A has committed a tort in relation to B, B has died as a result and a dependant of B's has suffered loss as a result. In such a case, that dependant *may* be entitled to sue A for damages under the 1976 Act. Whether he will or not depends on the principles set out below.

General conditions for bringing a claim under the 1976 Act

If A has committed a tort in relation to B, and C wants to bring a claim against A under the 1976 Act, C will only be entitled to sue A if: (1) A's tort caused B to die; (2) B's death was not a remote consequence of A's tort;[2] (3) C was a 'dependant' of B's; (4) had B not died, she would have been entitled to sue A for compensatory damages; *and* (5) the limitation period for C's bringing a claim against A under the 1976 Act has not elapsed. We have already looked at the law on causation and remoteness; but requirements (3), (4) and (5) deserve some further consideration.

Who is a dependant?
It is common for students to think that C will have been a dependant of B's if he was financially dependent on her. However, the definition of 'dependant' set out in the 1976 Act is quite different.

Section 1(3) of the Act provides that if someone commits a tort that causes another to die, the deceased's dependants will be: (*a*) the wife or husband or

---

[1] Or anyone who is vicariously liable in respect of A's tort.
[2] The Act does not explicitly state that this is a condition of C's being entitled to bring an action against A under the 1976 Act: s1(1) of the Act merely says that 'If death is *caused* by any wrongful act ... the person who would have been liable had death not ensued shall be liable to an action for damages ...' (emphasis added). However, it would seem to make sense that C will not be entitled to bring an action against A under the 1976 Act if B's death was a remote consequence of A's tort. See, on this issue, Law Com. No. 263, *Claims for Wrongful Death* (1999), para 2.4.

former wife or husband of the deceased; (*b*) any person who was living with the deceased at the time of the deceased's death as the deceased's husband or wife and had been living with the deceased in such a capacity for at least two years before the deceased's death; (*c*) any parent or other ascendant of the deceased; (*d*) any person who was treated by the deceased as being his or her parent; (*e*) any child or other descendant of the deceased; (*f*) if the deceased was married to someone else and started a family with that someone else, any person who was treated by the deceased as being a member of that family; *and* (*g*) anyone who was, or was the issue of, the deceased's brother, sister, uncle or aunt.[3]

The parasitical nature of claims under the Act

Suppose that A committed a tort in relation to B and A's tort caused B to die and B's death was not a remote consequence of A's tort. Suppose further that C was a dependant of B's. C will only be entitled to bring a claim against A under the 1976 Act *if* had B not died she would have been entitled to sue A for compensatory damages. In this sense, C's right to sue A for damages under the Act is parasitical on B's right: if B would not have been able to sue A for damages had she survived his tort, then C will have no right to sue A for damages under the Act. This limit on C's right to sue A under the Act covers – somewhat uneasily – two entirely different situations, which need to be considered separately.

(1) *Instantaneous death.* Suppose that A's tort caused B to die instantaneously. Suppose, for example, that A shot B in the head. In order to see whether C is entitled to sue A under the 1976 Act, we have to ask: had B survived the shooting and merely been injured by it, would she have been entitled to sue A for compensatory damages? The answer will usually be 'yes' – in which case, C will be entitled to bring a claim against A under the 1976 Act. However, it may be 'no' – in which case, C will not be able to bring a claim against A under the 1976 Act. This will be the case if, had B merely been injured, A would have been able to raise a defence of illegality to any claim B might have brought against him for damages.[4]

---

[3] The most notable omission from this list is people who were involved in a stable homosexual relationship with the deceased and it may be that the definition of 'dependant' needs updating to eliminate this omission. The Law Commission has recommended that the definition of 'dependant' under the 1976 Act be altered to cover to cover anyone who was being maintained on a non-business basis by the deceased at the time of his or her death and was likely to have continued being maintained on that basis by the deceased had he or she not died: ibid., para 7.7.

[4] See *Murphy* v *Culhane* [1977] 1 QB 96. In that case, Culhane struck Murphy on the head with a plank of wood and killed him. Murphy's widow brought an action against Culhane, seeking to recover compensation for the loss of support that she had experienced as a result of Murphy's death. Her claim could not succeed if, had Murphy survived Culhane's attack, Murphy would not have been entitled to sue Culhane for damages. It was alleged that Culhane had struck Murphy only after Murphy, along with some other men, had attempted to attack Culhane. The Court of Appeal held that if that allegation were made out then the widow's claim would fail. On the facts as they were alleged to be, had Murphy survived Culhane's attack and merely been injured by it, he would *not* have been allowed to sue Culhane for damages: had he attempted to do so, Culhane would have been able to raise a defence of illegality to defeat Murphy's claim. Presumably the court thought in this case that there would have existed a sufficiently close connection between Murphy's threatening to beat Culhane up and Culhane's attacking Murphy: see above, pp. 515–6.

(2) *Tort causing injury which results in death some time after.* Suppose that A's tort caused B to suffer some kind of injury and B died some time after that because she suffered that injury. In order to see whether C is entitled to sue A under the 1976 Act we have to ask: had B not died when she did but had lived a little longer, would she have been entitled to sue A for damages in respect of her injury? So – if before she died, B had already obtained a compensation payment from A in respect of her injury, then the answer will be 'no' and C will not be entitled to bring a claim against A under the 1976 Act.[5] Because A had already compensated B once for the injury suffered by her as a result of his tort, she could not have gone to court to try to sue him for more compensation.[6]

If B did *not* obtain a compensation payment from A before she died, then we simply look to see whether B could have sued A at the time she died for damages in respect of the injury she suffered as a result of A's tort. If she could have, then C might be able to bring a claim against A under the 1976 Act. If she could not – because, for example, B's injury was a non-actionable consequence of A's tort or because, before she died, B obtained a compensation payment from someone else in respect of her injury which had the effect of extinguishing A's liability to compensate B for the fact that she suffered that injury[7] – then C will not be able to bring a claim against A under the 1976 Act.

Limitation period

Section 12(2) of the Limitation Act 1980 provides that, in the case where the victim of a tort has died as a result of that tort having been committed, a claimant will not be able to bring an action under the 1976 Act more than three years after the *later* of the following two dates: (*a*) the date the victim of the tort died; (*b*) the date the claimant first learned, or could have reasonably been expected to learn, that the victim of the tort had died. Section 33 of the Limitation Act 1980 creates an exception to this rule: it provides that a claimant who attempts to bring a claim under the 1976 Act outside the limitation period set out in s 12(2) may be allowed to do so if it would be 'equitable' to do so.

The sort of claims that can be brought under the 1976 Act

There are basically three kinds of claims that can be brought under the 1976 Act by a dependant who has suffered loss as a result of a victim of a tort's death:

---

[5] See, for example, *Read v The Great Eastern Railway Company* (1868) LR 3 QB 555. In that case, the claimant's husband was injured as a result of the defendant railway company's negligence. The claimant's husband died of his wounds but not before he accepted a sum of money from the defendants in full and final settlement of all his claims against the defendants. Once the claimant's husband died the claimant brought a claim for loss of support against the defendants. Her claim was dismissed: at the time of her husband's death, he was not entitled any more to sue the defendants for damages.

[6] See above, p. 602.

[7] Which was the case in *Jameson v CEGB* [2000] 1 AC 455, discussed above, pp. 602–3.

(1) a claim for loss of support; (2) a claim for bereavement; (3) a claim for funeral expenses.

Loss of support

Suppose that A committed a tort in relation to B and B died as a result. Suppose further that C was a dependant of B's. In this case, C will be entitled to bring a claim for *loss of support* against A under the 1976 Act *if*: (1) the basic conditions that have to be satisfied before C can sue A under the 1976 Act are satisfied; *and* (2) C can show that there was a *reasonable prospect* that had B not died, he would have obtained some kind of financial benefit in the future; *and* (3) C would have obtained that benefit *by virtue of the fact that he was B's dependant*. The following cases demonstrate the above rule in action.

In *Franklin* v *The South Eastern Railway Company*,[8] the claimant's son was killed as a result of the defendants' negligence. At the time his son was killed, the claimant was getting old and infirm but was not receiving any assistance from his son, who was earning 3s 6d a week at the time he was killed. It was held that had the son not been killed there was a reasonable prospect that as the claimant grew older and weaker, the son would have paid the claimant some money so as to assist him financially. As a result the claimant was held entitled to bring an action for loss of support against the defendants.

In *Barnett* v *Cohen*,[9] the claimant's four-year-old son was killed as a result of the defendant's negligence. The claimant brought an action for loss of support against the defendant, claiming that had his son not been killed and had instead grown up to earn a living, his son would have paid him some money to assist him financially. The claim was dismissed: the claimant had not established that there was a reasonable prospect he would have received such assistance from his son had his son not been killed and grown up instead. This was for two reasons. First, the age of the claimant's son when he was killed made it impossible to predict what would have happened had he not been killed as a result of the defendant's negligence. Secondly, the claimant was a very wealthy man (earning £1,000 a year at the time of his son's death) and it was therefore hardly likely that the claimant's son would have had any reason to give the claimant anything by way of financial assistance if he had been allowed to grow up.

In *Davies* v *Taylor*,[10] the claimant's husband was killed in a road accident that was caused by the defendant's negligence. At the time the claimant's husband died, the claimant and her husband were separated and the claimant's husband was in the process of divorcing the claimant for adultery. The claimant brought an action for loss of support against the defendant, claiming that had her husband not been killed, there was a reasonable prospect her husband would have spent money on her. The claimant's claim was dismissed: had the claimant's husband not been killed, the claimant's husband would only have spent money on the claimant if they had been

[8] (1858) 3 H & N 211, 157 ER 448.
[9] [1921] 2 KB 461.
[10] [1972] 1 QB 286.

reconciled and the claimant had not established that there was a reasonable prospect that she and her husband would have been reconciled had he not been killed as a result of the defendant's negligence. While it was *possible* that they would have been reconciled had the claimant's husband not been killed, the chances of their being reconciled were not so high as to make it reasonable to think that the claimant and her husband would have been reconciled had her husband not been killed.

In *Berry* v *Humm*,[11] the defendant negligently knocked down and killed the claimant's wife. At the time of her death, the claimant's wife stayed at home and did all the domestic chores while her husband worked in the docks. Had the claimant's wife not been killed there was every prospect that the claimant's wife would have continued to do work around the claimant's house for free, thereby conferring a financial benefit on the claimant. As a result, the claimant was held entitled to bring a claim for loss of support against the defendant.

In *K* v *JMP Co. Ltd*,[12] a man and a woman lived together and had three illegitimate children. The father covered all the family expenses on things such as rent, food, electricity and holidays. The father was killed as a result of the defendants' negligence. The children were, of course, entitled to sue the defendants for damages in respect of the money their father would have spent on them had he not been killed. It was held that in assessing how much money the father would have spent on his children had he not been killed, account should be taken of the money the father would have spent enabling the mother to come on holiday with him and the children: this money could fairly be regarded as money the father would have spent *on the children* as the point of spending money to enable the mother to come on holiday would have been to enhance the children's enjoyment of their holidays.

In *Burgess* v *Florence Nightingale Hospital for Gentlewomen*,[13] the claimant and his wife were professional dance partners. The claimant's wife was killed as a result of the defendant's negligence. There was a reasonable prospect that had the wife not been killed the claimant and his wife would have continued to dance together and would have earned a certain amount of prize money. It was held that the claimant – in bringing a claim against the defendant for loss of support – could not sue for the prize money he would have earned in the future had his wife not been killed. The reason was that the prize money that the claimant would have earned if his wife had not been killed would not have been obtained by him by virtue of the fact that he was one of his wife's dependants. That money would have been obtained by him because he was his wife's *dancing partner*, not because he was *married* to her.[14] The claimant *was*, however, entitled, in bringing a claim for loss of support against the defendant, to sue the defendant for damages in respect of the money his wife would have

---

[11] [1915] 1 KB 627.

[12] [1976] QB 85.

[13] [1955] 1 QB 349.

[14] See also *Cox* v *Hockenhull* [2000] 1 WLR 750. The claimant's wife was killed in a car accident that the defendant negligently caused. The claimant's wife was disabled and at the time of the accident the claimant was her full-time carer and as such received an invalidity care allowance. Held: the claimant could not sue the defendant for the loss of the invalidity care allowance that he experienced after his wife's death as that allowance had not been received by the claimant because he was his wife's husband but because he was his wife's carer.

given him as a contribution towards their household expenses had she not been killed. *That* money *would* have been obtained by him as a result of the fact that he was married to his wife and therefore one of his wife's dependants.

In *Malyon* v *Plummer*,[15] the claimant and her husband ran a business selling and distributing portable electrical machinery to builders and farm machinery suppliers in East Anglia. The business was run through a company which paid the claimant a salary of about £600 a year. The claimant did not do much work for the company in return for her salary; the claimant's husband did most of the work drumming up business and collecting and processing orders. In fact, the value of the work done by the claimant for the company came to only about £200 a year: the remaining £400 a year paid to the claimant essentially amounted to a gift to the claimant. When the claimant's husband was killed in a car crash caused by the defendant's negligence, the business collapsed. The company through which the business was run went into insolvency and the claimant lost her £600 a year salary.

Of course, had the claimant's husband not been killed there was every prospect that the family business would have flourished and the claimant would have continued to draw a salary of £600 a year from their company, but £200 of that £600 a year salary would have been obtained by the claimant by virtue of the work done by her for the company she and her husband owned; only £400 of that £600 a year salary would have been paid to her by virtue of, or in recognition of, the fact that the claimant was married to her husband and therefore one of her husband's dependants. The claimant could therefore only bring a claim for loss of support against the defendant in respect of two-thirds of the £600 a year salary she would have continued to draw had her husband not been killed. In other words, she could only sue the defendant for damages in respect of that proportion of the salary she would have continued to draw had her husband not been killed which was attributable to the fact that she was married to her husband and therefore one of her husband's dependants.

Two limits on a dependant's ability to bring a claim for loss of support under the 1976 Act should be noted.

(1) *Illegality*. In the case we are considering, C will be barred from bringing an action for loss of support against A if the financial benefit that he would have received had B not died would have represented the proceeds of crime.

In *Burns* v *Edman*,[16] the claimant's husband was killed in a motor accident caused by the defendant's negligence. The claimant's husband had never had a job and what money he gave her (£20 a week) invariably represented the proceeds of crime. The claimant brought an action for loss of support against the defendant but her claim was dismissed. While there was more than a reasonable prospect that the claimant would have received an allowance of £20 a week from her husband had he not been killed, there was no prospect that that weekly allowance would have represented anything but the proceeds of crime.

---

[15] [1964] 1 QB 330.
[16] [1970] 2 QB 541.

(2) *No loss of benefit.* In the case we are considering, C will of course be barred from bringing a claim for loss of support against A if B's death did not actually prevent C receiving the financial benefit that he would have received had B not died.

In *Auty* v *National Coal Board*,[17] the claimant's husband was killed due to the defendants' negligence. Her husband was 55 when he died. When he died the claimant received a widow's pension under the Mineworkers' Pension Scheme. Had the claimant's husband not been killed, there was a reasonable prospect that he would have died before retiring at 65 and the claimant would have received a widow's pension. The claimant brought an action for loss of support against the defendants and included in her claim a claim for the fact that had her husband not been killed as a result of the defendant's negligence, there was a reasonable prospect he would have been killed before retiring and she would have received a widow's pension. This element of her claim was thrown out: her husband's death had not actually prevented her from receiving a widow's pension as when he died as a result of the defendants' negligence, she received a widow's pension.

In light of this, the decision of the Court of Appeal in *Hay* v *Hughes*[18] is difficult to understand. In that case, the parents of two boys were killed in a motor accident caused by the defendant's negligence. Had the parents not been killed the boys would have received a financial benefit: they would have been cared for until the age of their majority. But in fact the parents' deaths did not prevent the boys obtaining that benefit: the boys' grandmother took them in and looked after them. Despite this, the boys were still held entitled to bring a claim for loss of support against the defendant to compensate them for the loss of the free of charge care that they would have received from their parents until the age of their majority.

Perhaps the best explanation of the result in this case (and others similar to it)[19] is that if A has committed a tort in relation to B and B has died as a result, B's children (if any) will *not* be entitled to bring a claim for bereavement against A so as to console them for the loss of B.[20] So in *Hay* v *Hughes* the two boys were not entitled to claim any damages for bereavement from the defendant so as to console them for the loss of their parents. This might have seemed unfair to the Court of Appeal in *Hay* v *Hughes* and allowing the boys to sue the defendant for damages equivalent to the value of the care they would have received from their parents until the age of their majority might have seemed to the Court of Appeal an acceptable way of giving the boys something to console them for the loss of their parents.

Section 3(3) of the 1976 Act creates an exception to the rule that, in a case where the victim of a tort has died as a result of that tort being committed, a claimant

---

[17] [1985] 1 WLR 784.
[18] [1975] 1 QB 790.
[19] See *Regan* v *Williamson* [1976] 1 WLR 305; *Mehmet* v *Perry* [1977] 2 All ER 529; *Creswell* v *Eaton* [1991] 1 WLR 1113; *Corbett* v *Barking Havery and Brentwood Health Authority* [1991] 2 QB 408; *R* v *Criminal Injuries Compensation Board, ex parte Kavanagh* [1998] 2 FLR 1071.
[20] See below, pp. 627–8.

cannot bring a claim for loss of support under the Act if the victim's death has not actually prevented him receiving a financial benefit that he would have received had the victim not died. Section 3(3) provides that if in 'an action under this Act ... there fall to be assessed damages payable to a widow in respect of the death of her husband there shall not be taken into account the re-marriage of the widow ...'. So suppose Carl was married to Lara and Carl supported Lara: he would pay for all the common household expenses as well as paying for Lara's clothes and so on. Suppose further that John committed a tort in relation to Carl and Carl died as a result. Suppose finally that shortly after Carl's death, Lara remarried and her new husband supported her to the same extent as Carl used to. In such a case, John's tort will not have caused Lara to suffer any loss of support but Lara will still be able to bring a claim for loss of support against John: the fact that Lara has remarried and is being supported by her new husband will be disregarded and Lara will be able to sue John on the basis that John's tort *did* cause her to suffer a loss of support.

This aspect of the law, it should be noted, discriminates between widows and widowers in favour of widows. If you cause a married woman to die by committing a tort in relation to her and her husband remarries shortly afterwards and consequently suffers no loss of support as a result of your tort, the husband will have no action against you under the 1976 Act: s 3(3) does not instruct the courts to disregard the husband's remarriage in assessing the damages payable to him as a result of his first wife's death.

Bereavement

The second kind of action that can be brought under the 1976 Act is a claim for bereavement. Section 1A of the Fatal Accidents Act 1976 provides that – so long as the general conditions that have to be satisfied before a claim can be brought under the 1976 Act are satisfied – this sort of claim can be made in two kinds of situations.

The first is where A commits a tort in relation to B, B dies as a result, and at the time B died she was married. In such a case, B's spouse will be able to bring a claim for bereavement against A.[21] The second kind of case where a claim for bereavement can be brought is where the victim of a tort who has died as a result of that tort being committed was not married and was a minor at the time he or she died. In such a case, the victim's parents (if the victim was legitimate) or the victim's mother (if the victim was illegitimate) will be entitled to bring an action for bereavement under the 1976 Act against whoever committed that tort.[22]

The damages payable for bereavement are fixed at £10,000:[23] if A has committed a tort in relation to B and B has died as a result, and C is entitled to claim damages for bereavement, the damages payable to C will not be increased if he was especially upset by B's death and they will not be reduced if C was indifferent to the fact that B died. This leads Tony Weir to argue that the damages payable for bereavement are 'not designed as compensation for grief but [are] simply ... a

---

[21] Section 1A(2)(a).
[22] Section 1A(2)(b).
[23] Damages for Bereavement (Variation of Sum) (England and Wales) Order 2002 (S.I. No. 644).

replacement in money for a life lost. The lump sum is standard because people are equal, not because they are equally regrettable.'[24] However, it may be argued that these damages *are* designed to compensate for grief but the damages payable are fixed so as to avoid the courts having to make intrusive and distasteful inquiries into *how* grief-stricken a particular claimant is. £10,000 is the maximum someone can be held liable to pay by way of damages for bereavement; so if more than one person is entitled to claim such damages,[25] the lump sum has to be shared out between them.[26]

Funeral expenses

Section 3(5) of the 1976 Act provides that 'If the dependants [of the victim of a tort who was killed as a result of that tort being committed] have incurred funeral expenses in respect of the deceased, damages may be awarded in respect of those expenses.' Such a claim will of course only be available if the conditions that have to be satisfied before a claim can be brought under the 1976 Act are satisfied.

Reduction in liability

Suppose that A has committed a tort in relation to B, B has died as a result and C – a dependant of B's – is entitled to bring some kind of claim against A under the 1976 Act.

The damages payable to C will be reduced if B was partly to blame for the fact that she died. Section 5 of the Fatal Accidents Act 1976 provides that where 'any person dies as the result partly of his own fault and partly of the fault of any other person or persons, and accordingly if an action were brought for the benefit of the estate under the Law Reform (Miscellaneous Provisions) Act 1934 the damages recoverable would be reduced under s 1(1) of the Law Reform (Contributory Negligence) Act 1945, any damages recoverable in an action ... under this Act shall be reduced to a proportionate extent.'[27]

However, the damages payable to C will *not* be reduced to take account of any benefit that he might have received as a result of B's death. Section 4 of the Fatal Accidents Act 1976 provides that 'In assessing damages in respect of a person's death in an action under this Act, benefits which have accrued or will or may accrue to any person from his estate or otherwise as a result of his death shall be disregarded.'[28]

---

[24] Weir 2001, 196.

[25] This will only be the case where a legitimate minor has been killed as a result of someone else's tort: in such a case both parents will be entitled to sue for damages for bereavement.

[26] Fatal Accidents Act 1976, s 1A(4).

[27] This was the position in *Reeves* v *Commissioner of Police of the Metropolis* [2000] AC 360 (damages payable under 1976 Act to partner of deceased who committed suicide in custody – when police in breach of the duty of care they owed the deceased failed to take reasonable steps to prevent him committing suicide – were reduced by 50% because the deceased was partly to blame for his own death).

[28] The Social Security (Recovery of Benefits) Act 1997 (discussed above, p. 603) does not seem to apply to actions brought under the Fatal Accidents Act 1976. So: suppose Eric committed a tort in relation to Wendy and Wendy died as a result. Suppose further that had Wendy not died, Sarah – a dependant of Wendy's – would have received a financial benefit worth £14,000 which she is not now going to receive. Suppose also that because Wendy died, Sarah was paid social security benefits

So – in *Pidduck* v *Eastern Scottish Omnibuses Ltd*,[29] the claimant's husband was killed as a result of the defendants' negligence. Before the claimant's husband was killed he received money from a pension scheme, two thirds of which he spent on the claimant. The payments under the pension scheme ceased when the claimant's husband was killed but the claimant started to receive a widow's allowance instead. The claimant brought an action for loss of support against the defendants on the basis that had her husband not been killed there was a reasonable prospect that he would have continued to receive a pension for a good few years and would have spent two thirds of that pension money on the claimant.

The defendants argued that the damages payable to the claimant should be reduced to take account of the fact that as a result of her husband's death she was now in receipt of a widow's allowance. The defendants' argument was rejected and no reduction in the damages payable to the claimant was made. The result was that the claimant was left better off (financially) than she would have been had her husband not died; she not only obtained from the defendant damages equivalent to the value of all the pension money she would have received had her husband not been killed, she also enjoyed the benefit of the widow's allowance that she would *not* have received had her husband not been killed.

In two situations, the courts have shown themselves willing to disregard the rule set out in s 4 of the 1976 Act:

(1) *Receipt of benefit from defendant.* If, in the situation we are considering, C received a benefit worth £5,000 from *A* as a result of B's death, the damages payable to C under the 1976 Act will be reduced by £5,000. The reason is that the benefits conferred by A on C as a result of B's death are regarded as partially compensating C for the losses suffered by him as a result of B's death.

So – in *Hayden* v *Hayden*,[30] the claimant's mother was killed because of the negligence of the defendant, the claimant's father, in driving a car in which the claimant's mother was a passenger. The defendant gave up his job to look after the claimant. The claimant brought an action for loss of support against the defendant (in reality, the defendant's liability insurer), claiming that had his mother not been killed as a result of the defendant's negligence, his mother would have looked after him free of charge until he was 18. The damages payable to the claimant were reduced to take account of the value of the care the claimant had received from the defendant as a result of his mother's death.

(2) *Adoption.* In *Watson* v *Willmott*,[31] the claimant's mother was killed in a car accident caused by the defendant's negligence. The claimant's father, depressed at the death of his wife, committed suicide and the claimant was

---

worth £10,000. It seems that so long as the conditions that have to be satisfied before Sarah can bring a claim for loss of support against Eric under the 1976 Act are satisfied, Sarah will be entitled to sue Eric for £14,000 in damages; the 1997 Act will not reduce the damages payable to Eric to £4,000.

[29] [1990] 1 WLR 993.
[30] [1992] 1 WLR 986.
[31] [1991] 1 QB 140.

adopted. The claimant brought an action for loss of support against the defendant, seeking to obtain compensation for the fact that he would not now, thanks to the defendant's negligence, be looked after free of charge by his father and mother until he was 18.

The damages payable to the claimant were reduced to take account of the value of the benefit he had received and would receive as a result of the defendant's negligence: the value of the care he had received and would receive from his adoptive parents. The court felt it was authorised to depart from the rule set out in s 4 of the 1976 Act by virtue of para 3 of Sch 1 of the Children Act 1975 under which '[a]n adopted child shall be treated in law ... where the adopters are a married couple, as if he had been born as a child of the marriage'. As such, the decision in *Watson* v *Willmott* is to be confined strictly to the case where a child's parents have been killed as a result of a tort committed in relation to them and the child has been subsequently adopted.

RECOVERY OF LOSSES SUFFERED BY THE STATE

In two situations, the State is allowed to sue someone who has committed a tort for compensation in respect of the losses that it has suffered as a result of that tort being committed.

(1) *The Social Security (Recovery of Benefits) Act 1997. Roughly speaking*, this Act provides that someone who has made a compensation payment to the victim of a tort will be held liable to the State for the value of *all* the social security payments that have been made to the victim of that tort as a result of her being a victim of that tort.[32]

(2) *The Road Traffic (NHS Charges) Act 1999*.[33] This Act covers the situation where a motorist negligently causes a traffic accident in which B is injured and B's injuries are treated on the National Health Service. The Act provides that if the motorist makes a compensation payment to B, he (or, in reality, his liability insurer) will be liable to pay the NHS a sum representing the cost of treating B's injuries on the NHS.

THE CONGENITAL DISABILITIES (CIVIL LIABILITY) ACT 1976

The basic idea

This Act is primarily designed to cover the situation where A committed a tort in relation to B while she was pregnant and as a result her child was born disabled *when it would otherwise have been born healthy*. In this situation, B's child

---

[32] Space does not allow us to say more than this. For a *very* detailed treatment of the Act, see Lewis 1999, 113–222.
[33] For a fuller discussion, see ibid., 223–32.

will normally be entitled to sue A under the Congenital Disabilities (Civil Liability) Act 1976 for compensation for the fact that it was born disabled.[34]

Torts committed before conception

The Act also covers two other situations:

(1) *Torts affecting a woman's ability to bear a healthy child.* If A commits a tort in relation to B before she gets pregnant which affects her ability to have a healthy child and, as a result, she gives birth to a disabled child, that child will normally be able to sue A for damages under the 1976 Act. However, there is one limit on this. If B knew that A's tort had affected her ability to have a healthy child but she nonetheless went on to get pregnant and carried the child to term, the child – if born disabled – would not be able to sue A for damages under the 1976 Act.[35]

(2) *Torts committed in the course of fertility treatment.* If B went to A for fertility treatment, and A breached the duty of care that he owes B as his patient by implanting in her a defective embryo or defective sperm or defective eggs and – as a result – the child that B subsequently gave birth to was disabled, that child will be entitled to sue A for damages under the 1976 Act.[36] There is, again, one limit on this. If B willingly took the risk that the embryo, sperm or eggs implanted inside her would turn out to be defective – and therefore willingly took the risk that she would, as a result of being given that embryo, sperm or eggs, give birth to a disabled child – then B's child will not be able to sue A for damages under the 1976 Act.

Actions for wrongful birth

The 1976 Act does not cover situations where a child *that was always going to be born disabled* was born as a result of someone's committing a tort in relation to the child's mother before she gave birth to the child.

For example, in *McKay* v *Essex Area Health Authority*[37] the claimant was born disabled because her mother suffered rubella (or German measles) while the claimant was in her womb. The defendant doctor had – in breach of the duty of care he owed the claimant's mother in treating her – failed to inform the claimant's mother that she had been infected with rubella. Had he told her that she had been infected with rubella, she would probably have had an abortion. While the 1976 Act was not in force at the time of these events, the Court of Appeal unanimously held that had the 1976 Act been in force at the time these

---

[34] The baby's right to sue A is parasitic on B's. So if A would be able to rely on an exclusion clause to defeat any claim for damages that B might make against him in respect of his tort, then he will similarly be entitled to rely on that clause to defeat any claim that B's baby makes against him under the 1976 Act: s 1(6). Similarly, if A would be entitled to raise a defence of contributory negligence to any claim B might make against him for damages in respect of his tort, A will also be entitled to rely on that defence if B's baby sues him for damages under the 1976 Act: s.1(7).

[35] Section 1(4).

[36] Section 1A(1), (2).

[37] [1982] 1 QB 1166.

events occurred, the claimant would *not* have been entitled to sue the defendant doctor for damages designed to compensate her for the fact that she was born disabled.[38]

Why does the 1976 Act not cover this kind of situation – which we can call a 'wrongful birth' case?[39] The answer is simple. In a case like *McKay* any damages award made to the claimant would be designed to compensate her for the losses she suffered as a result of the defendant's tort. But what losses has she suffered as a result of his tort? Had he not committed his tort, the claimant would never have been born. As a result of his tort, the claimant was born and not aborted. So to award the claimant damages here would be to say that she suffered a loss as a result of being born. In other words, to award the claimant damages here would be to say that she would have been better off dead. Understandably, the courts are unwilling to accept that anyone would be 'better off dead' on the grounds that to do so would undermine the sanctity of human life. In any case, an 'I would have been better off dead' argument could only have any plausibility in the case of a claimant who was born with such severe disabilities that she was constantly racked in pain and unable to garner any enjoyment from life whatsoever – and not many claimants in a 'wrongful birth' case would be able to satisfy this requirement.

THE LATENT DAMAGE ACT 1986

Section 3 of the Latent Damage Act 1986 covers the situation where A committed a tort in relation to B and B's property was damaged as a result, but before the damage was discovered B transferred the property to C. In such a case, s 3 provides that if B would have been entitled to sue A for damages in respect of the damage done to his property had he discovered it in time, C will be entitled to sue A for damages in respect of the damage done to that item of property.

THE PRINCIPLE OF TRANSFERRED LOSS

In *The Aliakmon*, it will be recalled, Leigh & Sillavan Ltd suffered a loss as a result of Aliakmon Shipping Co. Ltd's breaching a duty of care owed to Kinso-Mataichi Corp.[40] They had agreed to buy some steel coils from Kinso-Mataichi. The coils were to be shipped to them by Aliakmon Shipping. During shipment the coils still belonged to Kinso-Mataichi. The coils were damaged during shipment due to Aliakmon Shipping's negligence and Leigh & Sillavan suffered loss as a result; they ended up paying far more for the coils than they were, in their damaged state, actually worth.

In the Court of Appeal, Robert Goff LJ, dissenting, held that Leigh &

---

[38] Ibid., 1178A–C (per Stephenson LJ), 1186H–1187B (per Ackner LJ), 1192C (per Griffiths LJ).
[39] 'Wrongful birth' because the claimant in *McKay* would not have been born but for the defendant's wrong.
[40] *Leigh & Sillavan Ltd v Aliakmon Shipping Co. Ltd, The Aliakmon* [1986] AC 785 (discussed above, p. 116).

Sillavan *were* entitled to sue Aliakmon Shipping for compensatory damages sufficient to compensate them for the loss they had suffered as a result of Aliakmon Shipping's negligence, even though that negligence had consisted in the breach of a duty of care owed not to Leigh & Sillavan but rather to Kinso-Mataichi. Robert Goff LJ suggested that English law should recognise a 'principle of transferred loss' according to which if 'A owes a duty of care in tort not to cause physical damage to B's property, and commits a breach of that duty in circumstances in which the loss of or physical damage to the property will ordinarily fall on B but (as is reasonably foreseeable by A) such loss or damage, by reason of a contractual relationship between B and C, falls upon C, then C will be entitled, subject to the terms of any contract restricting A's liability to B, to bring an action in tort against A in respect of such loss or damage to the extent that it falls on him, C'.[41]

When *The Aliakmon* fell to be decided by the House of Lords they roundly rejected the idea that English law should give effect to this principle of transferred loss. Lord Brandon of Oakbrook remarked: 'With the greatest possible respect to Robert Goff LJ, the principle of transferred loss ... is not only not supported by authority, but is on the contrary inconsistent with it.'[42] In *White* v *Jones* (*not* a case which was covered by the principle of transferred loss)[43] Lord Goff (as he had by then become) did not renew the attempt he made in *The Aliakmon* to introduce the principle of transferred loss into English law, beyond observing that recognition of such a principle might serve to fill some lacunae in English law.[44] Subsequently, in the case of *Alfred McAlpine Construction Ltd* v *Panatown Ltd*, Lord Goff seemed to disown the principle of transferred loss entirely, remarking that the principle 'is not an easy one for a common lawyer to grasp' and observing that he did not feel 'sufficiently secure' in his understanding of how it would apply to employ it in deciding the case at hand.[45] With Lord Goff now retired from the bench, it must be doubted whether anyone else will attempt to introduce the principle of transferred loss into English law and thereby create another exception to the general rule that if A has committed a tort in relation to B and a third party, C, has suffered loss as a result, C will *not* be entitled to sue A for damages in respect of that loss.

---

[41] [1985] 1 QB 350, 399E–G. For discussion of this principle and how it works, see Cane 1996, 327–9.

[42] [1986] AC 785, 820E–F.

[43] In *White* v *Jones* [1995] 2 AC 207, it will be recalled, a father instructed his solicitor to make a will under which his daughters would receive £9,000 each. The solicitor was unacceptably tardy in drawing up the will and it was not signed and witnessed by the time the father died. As a result the father's daughters did not receive their bequests. In this case, the father did *not* suffer any loss as a result of his solicitor's negligence which was then passed on to his daughters.

[44] Ibid., 264–6.

[45] [2001] 1 AC 518, 557.

35

VICARIOUS LIABILITY

THE NATURE OF VICARIOUS LIABILITY

Suppose that Mary has committed a tort in relation to Fred. We say that Lara is *vicariously liable* in respect of Mary's tort if the law treats Lara as though she committed that tort along with Mary. So although Lara did not actually do anything wrong,[1] she is treated as though she did. The result is that if Fred is entitled to sue *Mary* for compensation in respect of the losses that he has suffered as a result of Mary's tort, Fred will also be entitled to sue *Lara* for such compensation.[2]

To say that Lara is *vicariously* liable in respect of Mary's tort is slightly misleading because it suggests that Mary's liability to pay damages to Fred is shifted[3] onto Lara.[4] The reality is that *both* Mary *and* Lara will be liable to pay damages to Fred and he will be free to choose to sue one or the other or both of them. Because Lara is treated as though she committed Mary's tort along with Mary, they will be *jointly liable* to compensate Fred for the losses suffered by him as a result of Mary's tort.[5] So if Fred releases Mary from liability, all his rights to sue Lara for compensation will usually also be extinguished.[6]

We should be careful to distinguish *vicarious liability* from *personal liability*. In the above case, Mary is personally liable to compensate Fred for the losses that he has suffered because *she* committed a tort in relation to Fred and thereby caused him to suffer those losses. Lara's liability is merely vicarious in nature because she herself did not commit a tort in the situation we are considering; she is liable to Fred because she is treated *as though* she committed a tort in this situation – the same tort that Mary committed.

So suppose Wendy entrusted her mink coat to Karen's care and Karen gave the coat to Paul to look after. Suppose further that Paul stole the coat. It is well established in this situation that Wendy will be entitled to sue Karen for compensation for the loss of her coat.[7] At first sight, this looks like an example of

---

[1] Some would argue (though we would disagree) that if Lara is held liable here it is because Lara *did* do something wrong: see Williams 1956.

[2] Likewise, if a third party has suffered loss as a result of Mary's tort for which he is entitled to sue Mary, he will also be entitled to sue *Lara* for compensation for that loss.

[3] See Birks 1995, 41: 'A "vicarious" liability is a liability which one person takes over from another, and as such [is] not his but that other's, just as a "vicar" was originally a person in holy orders who occupied a place which was not his but the rector's whose substitute he was.'

[4] Some commentators use the term 'secondary liability' instead of 'vicarious liability' to describe Lara's liability here, but that is also misleading because it suggests that Lara is only liable if Fred has no effective remedy against Mary.

[5] See above, pp. 601–2.

[6] See above, p. 602.

[7] *Morris v C W Martin & Sons Ltd* [1966] 1 QB 716.

vicarious liability.[8] Karen, it may be argued, is liable to compensate Wendy for her coat because Karen is vicariously liable in respect of the tort of conversion that Paul committed when he stole Wendy's coat. But appearances mislead. The real reason that Karen is liable to Wendy here is that she owed Wendy a non-delegable duty[9] to take reasonable steps to safeguard Wendy's coat and Paul's actions put her in breach of this duty.[10] So as Karen has acted wrongfully in this situation, she is *personally*, not vicariously, liable to compensate Wendy for the loss of her coat.

Again, suppose that XYZ plc runs a nuclear power plant. Suppose further that, in order to save money, the managing directors of XYZ decide not to pay for their employees to have regular medicals, so as to detect at an early stage whether any of them are showing signs that they are developing cancer as a result of working in the power plant. Suppose further that Nita develops cancer as a result of working in XYZ's power plant and she can show that had she had a regular medical in all probability her cancer would have been detected early enough to have been treated successfully. In this situation Nita will be able to sue XYZ for compensation. Again, this is not an example of vicarious liability. XYZ are personally liable here to compensate Nita for her injuries because XYZ – acting through those representing its 'guiding mind or will' – did something wrong and Nita suffered injury as a result. XYZ owed Nita a duty to take reasonable steps to see that she would be reasonably safe working for XYZ[11] and it breached that duty when it failed to arrange regular medicals for Nita.

Sticking with the same company, suppose that Carl was employed by XYZ and he was racially abused by his fellow employees while he was working with them. In this case, Carl will be entitled to sue XYZ for damages under Part III of the Race Relations Act 1976.[12] Again, this may look like an example of vicarious liability – we may suppose that Carl's fellow employees did something wrong in racially abusing him and that XYZ is held vicariously liable in respect of that wrong.[13] But, again, appearances mislead. Whether or not Carl's fellow employees did anything wrong in racially abusing him is immaterial. XYZ are held liable here because the 1976 Act provides that when XYZ's employees racially abused Carl they put XYZ in breach of the duty it owed Carl not to subject him to unfavourable treatment because of his race.[14] So XYZ's liability to Carl here is personal in nature. XYZ is held liable here because *it* did something wrong – not because it is vicariously liable in respect of any wrongs that

---

[8] It was assumed that this is an example of vicarious liability in *Lister* v *Hesley Hall Ltd* [2002] 1 AC 215, at [19] (per Lord Steyn), [46] (per Lord Clyde), [57] (per Lord Hobhouse), [75]–[76] (per Lord Millett). See also *Dubai Aluminium Co. Ltd* v *Salaam* [2003] 2 AC 366, at [129] (per Lord Millett).

[9] Any reader currently unacquainted with the concept of a non-delegable duty of care should read pp. 227–32, above, before proceeding further.

[10] See Weir 2001, 102. Also *New South Wales* v *Lepore* [2003] HCA 4, at [127] (per Gaudron J) and at [147], [161] (per McHugh J).

[11] See above, p. 180.

[12] See above, pp. 488–9.

[13] Markesinis, Johnston & Deakin fall into the trap of thinking that XYZ's liability to Carl here is an example of vicarious liability: see M&D, 584.

[14] Section 32(1). See above, pp. 488–9.

its employees might have committed in relation to Carl when they racially abused him.

SITUATIONS OF VICARIOUS LIABILITY

There are many different[15] situations in which one person will be vicariously liable in respect of a tort committed by another:

(1) *Employment*. If A is B's *employer*, A will be vicariously liable in respect of a tort committed by B if that tort is committed by B 'in the course of his employment'.[16] On the other hand, if A gets B to do some work for him as an *independent contractor*, A will *never* be vicariously liable in respect of a tort committed by B, even if B commits that tort in the course of doing the work that A has hired him to do.[17]

(2) *Police*. If A is the chief police officer in charge of an area in which B, a police officer, is working, A will be vicariously liable in respect of a tort committed by B in performing his functions as a police officer.[18]

(3) *Agency*. If A appoints B to act as his agent,[19] and B commits a tort while acting within the actual or ostensible scope of her authority as A's agent, A will be vicariously liable in respect of B's tort.[20]

(4) *Car owners*. Suppose that A requested B to perform some task for him which required B to drive A's car. Suppose further that in performing that task B negligently crashed A's car and in so doing injured C. It has been held – perhaps by analogy to the above rule dealing with vicarious liability for the acts of one's

---

[15] It should be noted that the Supreme Court of Canada takes the view that these situations are not so different and that there is a general rule underlying all these instances of vicarious liability, namely that A may be held vicariously liable for a tort committed by B if the relationship between A and B at the time B committed his tort was 'sufficiently close as to make a claim for vicarious liability appropriate': see *KLB* v *British Columbia* [2003] 2 SCR 403, at [18] (per McLachlin CJ). In order to judge whether this requirement is satisfied, we must determine whether B was ' "acting on his own account" or acting on behalf of [A]' at the relevant time (ibid, at [21]) – and this in turn will depend, in part, on how much 'control' A exerted over B at the relevant time (ibid, at [22]). Accordingly, it was held in the *KLB* case (Arbour J dissenting) that the government could not be held vicariously liable for various assaults that a foster parent committed on a child placed in his care by the government: foster families do not operate under 'close government control' and, as a result, while they do 'indeed [act] in the service of a public goal, their actions are too far removed from the government in the sense necessary to justify vicarious liability' (ibid, at [23], [25]).

[16] It used to be the case that if an employee of the Crown committed a tort in the course of his employment, the Crown would not be held vicariously liable in respect of that tort. That rule has now been abolished by s 2(1)(a) of the Crown Proceedings Act 1947.

[17] Of course, if A was subject to a non-delegable duty and he gave B – an independent contractor – the job of discharging that duty, then B might put A in breach of that duty and A might incur some sort of liability as a result. However, as has already been made clear, that liability will be personal in nature, not vicarious.

[18] Police Act 1996, s 333.

[19] An 'agent' is someone who acts as someone else's representative for legal purposes.

[20] *Lloyd* v *Grace, Smith & Co.* [1912] AC 716 (for an alternative explanation of the decision in this case, see above, pp. 230–1); *Uxbridge Permanent Building Society* v *Pickard* [1939] 2 KB 248; *Armagas Ltd* v *Mundogas Ltd, The Ocean Frost* [1986] AC 717. For a full discussion, see Fridman 1996, 315–25.

agents – that in this situation, A will be vicariously liable in respect of B's negligence.[21]

(5) *Partnership*. Under s 10 of the Partnership Act 1890, the partners in a firm will be vicariously liable in respect of a tort committed by one of the partners in that firm so long as the partner in question was acting 'in the ordinary course of the business of the firm'.[22]

(6) *Joint venture*.[23] If A and B embark on a joint venture, and B commits a tort in the course of furthering that venture, then A will be vicariously liable in respect of B's tort.

So in *Brooke* v *Bool*,[24] the defendant let to the claimant a shop on the ground floor of a house next door to the defendant's home. The claimant agreed, that each day, the defendant could enter the shop after the claimant had left it to check that it was securely locked up. One night a lodger in the defendant's home told the defendant that he thought he could smell gas coming from the claimant's shop. The defendant and the lodger both went to investigate. They inspected a gas pipe which passed down a wall in the claimant's shop, the defendant inspecting the lower half of the pipe and the lodger the upper half. The lodger used a naked light to inspect his half of the gas pipe. Unfortunately, the upper half of the gas pipe was leaking gas and when the gas came into contact with the lodger's light there was an explosion which damaged the claimant's goods. The lodger had been negligent in using a naked light to inspect the gas pipe and the defendant was held to be vicariously liable in respect of the lodger's negligence: he and the lodger had been engaged in a joint venture (checking for a gas leak) and the lodger had been attempting to further that venture when he acted as he did.

Of these six situations in which one person will be held vicariously liable in respect of a tort committed by someone else, the most important by far is the first, which we will now discuss in detail.

---

[21] See *Ormrod v Crosville Motor Services Ltd* [1953] 1 WLR 1120 (criticised, Brooke-Smith 1954). The defendant asked O to drive his car down to Monte Carlo so that the defendant could drive it in a motor rally there. In doing so, O negligently crashed the car into a bus. It was held that the defendant was vicariously liable in respect of O's negligence. *Ormrod* did *not* apply in *Klein v Caluori* [1971] 1 WLR 619, where F borrowed the defendant's car without his consent; when the defendant discovered this, he told F to bring the car back. As F was driving the car back, he negligently crashed into the claimant's car. Held, the defendant was not vicariously liable in respect of F's negligence because F was not performing a task for the defendant in bringing the car back – the job of bringing the car back was always F's to perform, not the defendant's. Neither did it apply in *Morgans* v *Launchbury* [1973] AC 127, where the defendant's husband went to the pub in the defendant's car. Realising he was too drunk to drive himself home, he had C drive him home in the defendant's car. On the way home, C drove the car so negligently that the claimants were injured. It was held that the defendant was not vicariously liable in respect of C's negligence as the defendant did not ask C to drive her husband home. See also *Nelson v Raphael* [1979] RTR 437.

[22] It is worth noting that vicarious liability used to arise in the context of a very different kind of partnership: a husband used to be held vicariously liable in respect of any torts committed by his wife, but that rule was abolished by s 3 of the Law Reform (Married Women and Joint Tortfeasors) Act 1935.

[23] See Carty 1999, 496–500.

[24] [1928] 2 KB 578.

VICARIOUS LIABILITY FOR EMPLOYEES' TORTS

It is well established that an employer will be vicariously liable in respect of a tort committed by one of his employees if that tort was committed 'in the course' of the employee's employment. This rule raises three questions. First of all, *why* does this rule exist? Secondly, when can we say that someone is another's *employee*? Thirdly, when can we say that an employee who has committed a tort did so in the *course* of his employment?

Rationale of the law

Suppose that A employs B and B commits a tort in the course of his employment by A. Nobody really understands why A will be held vicariously liable in respect of B's tort in this situation.[25] A number of different explanations of the law in this area have been advanced[26] but none of them really stand up to even the mildest critical scrutiny.[27]

(1) *Deep pockets.* It has been argued that A will be held vicariously liable in respect of B's tort because B is not likely to be worth suing. So making A vicariously liable in respect of B's tort will help to ensure that those who have suffered loss as a result of B's tort will be able to sue someone of substantial means for compensation for their losses.[28] But this does not explain why A's liability in respect of B's tort is dependent on it being shown that B's tort was committed *in the course of his employment*. The 'deep pockets' rationale of an employer's vicarious liability for the torts committed by his employees justifies his being held liable for *all* the torts committed by his employees, whether they were committed within or without the course of their employment.[29]

(2) *Deterrence.* It is also said that holding A vicariously liable in respect of B's tort here will encourage him to take steps to see that his employees do not act

---

[25] Cf. *Hollis* v *Vabu Pty Ltd* (2001) 207 CLR 21, at [35] (per Gleeson CJ, Gaudron, Gummow, Kirby and Hayne JJ): 'a fully satisfactory rationale for the imposition of vicarious liability . . . has been slow to appear . . .'; also *New South Wales* v *Lepore* [2003] HCA 4, at [106] (per Gaudron J, remarking on the 'absence of a satisfactory and comprehensive jurisprudential basis for the imposition of liability on a person for the harmful acts or omissions of others'), and [299] (per Kirby P: 'The history of the imposition of vicarious liability demonstrates that the foundation of such liability has been uncertain and variable').

[26] See, generally, Fleming 1998, 410.

[27] Which is not to say that the law on vicarious liability should not be reformed so that it gives effect to one of the rationales identified below. We personally are in favour of the law on vicarious liability being reformed so it gives effect to the 'enterprise risk' rationale set out below, at p. 639.

[28] Cf. *Limpus* v *London General Omnibus Company* (1862) 1 H&C 526, 529; 158 ER 995, 998: 'It is well-known that there is virtually no remedy against the driver of an omnibus, and therefore it is necessary that, for injury resulting from an act done by him in the course of his master's service, the master should be responsible; for there ought to be a remedy against some person capable of paying damages to those injured by improper driving' (per Willes J). Also Baty 1916, 152; Atiyah 1967, 22; Feldthusen 1998, 224–5.

[29] Fleming 1998 argues (at 410) that the law does not hold employers liable for torts committed by their employees outside the course of their employment because it does not want to 'foist an undue burden on business enterprise'. But there is more than a whiff of *ex post facto* rationalisation about this explanation.

wrongfully while they work for him.[30] But if this is correct, one would expect the law to say that A will be held vicariously liable in respect of B's tort if A could possibly have done something to prevent that tort being committed. But it does not say this and it has never said this.

(3) *Enterprise risk.* Another explanation as to why A will be vicariously liable in respect of B's tort goes as follows. Elementary fairness dictates that if you seek to make money from engaging in some activity and other people suffer loss as a result of your engaging in that activity, you should compensate them for that loss – if you want to obtain the gains resulting from engaging in that activity, then you should bear the losses as well.

This principle of fairness applies here:[31] A set up in business for himself and as a result of his doing so other people – the people who were harmed by B's tort – have suffered loss as a result. It is only fair that A should compensate those people for the loss they have suffered and the law's way of ensuring that A does so is to make A vicariously liable in respect of B's tort.[32]

But if this is right, it is hard to understand why someone who carries on his business using independent contractors to work for him is not held vicariously liable in respect of the torts committed by those independent contractors in the course of working for him. Moreover, this explanation does not explain why the law on vicarious liability applies as much to government agencies and private foundations that do not seek to make money from their activities as it does to people who set up businesses to earn money.[33]

---

[30] Cf. *Bazley* v *Curry* [1999] 2 SCR 534, at [32]-[33]: 'Fixing the employer with responsibility for the employee's wrongful act, even where the employer is not negligent, may have a deterrent effect. Employers are often in a position to reduce accidents and intentional wrongs by efficient organization and supervision ... Beyond the narrow band of employer conduct that attracts direct liability in negligence lies a vast area where imaginative and efficient administration and supervision can reduce the risk [of wrongdoing by the employer's employees]. Holding the employer vicariously liable for the wrongs of its employee may encourage the employer to take such steps and, hence, reduce the risk of future harm' (per McLachlin J). Also *New South Wales* v *Lepore* [2003] HCA 4, at [305] (per Kirby P); Pollock 1882, 130.

[31] It may also underlie the Consumer Protection Act 1987, in so far as it makes a manufacturer who manufactures goods for profit liable for the harm caused by any of his goods being defective. See Stapleton 1994, 185–217; Waddams 1998, 124–5. The 1987 Act is discussed in detail below, in Chapter 45. The rule in *Rylands* v *Fletcher* (discussed below, at pp. 739–50), might also be said to rest on this principle of fairness: Cane 1999b, 202.

[32] Cf. *Dubai Aluminium* v *Salaam* [2003] 2 AC 366, at [21]: 'The ... legal policy [underlying the law on vicarious liability] is based on the recognition that carrying on a business enterprise necessarily involves risks to others. It involves the risk that others will be harmed by wrongful acts committed by the [employees] through whom the business is carried on. When those risks ripen into loss, it is just that the business should be responsible for compensating the person who has been wronged' (per Lord Nicholls). See also *Lister* v *Hesley Hall Ltd* [2002] 1 AC 215, at [65] (per Lord Millett); *Bazley* v *Curry* [1999] 2 SCR 534, at [22], [30] (per McLachlin J); *New South Wales* v *Lepore* [2003] HCA 4, at [303] (per Kirby P); Pollock 1882, 122; W&J, 703.

[33] However, it could be argued (as Kirby P did in *New South Wales* v *Lepore* [2003] HCA 4, at [303]) that as the *community as a whole* seeks to profit from the activities of government agencies, the community as a whole should bear the losses caused by someone who committed a tort while working for a government agency if it was predictable that the person doing that kind of work would commit that kind of tort. One way of doing this is to hold the government agency vicariously liable in respect of the tortfeasor's tort: the government can then spread the cost of paying compensation for the losses caused by the tort among the community as a whole through higher taxes or increased

(4) *Relative blame.* In *Hern* v *Nichols*, Holt CJ explained that an employer will be vicariously liable in respect of a tort committed by an employee in the course of his employment because 'seeing somebody must be a loser [as a result of a tort committed by an employee] it is more reason that he that employs and puts a trust and confidence in [the employee] should be a loser than a stranger'.[34] But if this is right it is again hard to see why someone who engages someone else to work for him as an independent contractor should not be vicariously liable in respect of any torts committed by that contractor in doing the work he is engaged to do.

(5) *Loss-spreading.* Finally, it has been said that A will be held vicariously liable in respect of B's tort because doing this will allow the losses caused by B's tort to be effectively spread among the community at large. If A is held vicariously liable in respect of B's tort, the losses caused by B's tort will be shifted onto A's shoulders and A will then be able to spread the losses – either by charging his customers slightly higher prices or by making a claim on his liability insurance.[35]

But this does not explain why an employer will not be held vicariously liable in respect of a tort committed by one of his employees if that tort was not committed in the course of the employee's employment. In such a case, there is just as much of a need to spread the losses caused by the employee's tort as there would be if he committed it in the course of his employment, but the law does not respond to this need by making the employer vicariously liable in respect of his employee's tort. Why not?

Employee

Suppose that A commits a tort while working for B. When can we say that A is an employee of B's? The answer is – A will be an employee of B's if A contracts[36] to do work for B under a *contract of service*, as opposed to a *contract for services*.

The distinction between a contract of service and a contract for services is easy to grasp but hard to express. We can grasp the distinction by looking at two cases. In the first, A contracts to build a greenhouse for B in B's back

---

borrowing. This argument will not work to justify holding private foundations that do not seek to make money from their activities vicariously liable for torts committed by their employees as they cannot pass any losses resulting from their being held vicariously liable onto the community. Despite this, the Supreme Court of Canada refused to find that such foundations should be given any special exemption from the rules on vicarious liability in *Bazley* v *Curry* [1999] 2 SCR 534, at [47]–[56].

[34] (1700) 1 Salk 289, 91 ER 256. See also *Bazley* v *Curry* [1999] 2 SCR 534, at [50] and [54] (per McLachlin J).

[35] Cf. *Bazley* v *Curry* [1999] 2 SCR 534, at [31]: 'the employer is often in the best position to spread the losses [caused by an employee's tort] through mechanisms like insurance and higher prices, thus minimizing the dislocative effect of the tort within society' (per McLachlin J).

[36] Obviously, if A is at a given time under no contractual obligation to do any work for B then A cannot be an employee of B's at that time: *Carmichael* v *National Power plc* [1999] 1 WLR 2042 (tour guides who worked for defendant on casual basis, turning up for work as and when they were required to do so, could not claim to be employees of the defendant as they were under no obligation to turn up for work when they were asked to do so).

garden. In the second, A contracts to work in B's factory making glass panes for greenhouses. In the first case, A's contract with B is a contract for services. So, in the first case, B will not be A's employer, or, to put it another way, A will not be B's servant or employee; rather, he will be an independent contractor vis-à-vis B. In the second case, A's contract with B will be a contract of service. So, in the second case, B will be A's employer and A will be B's employee or servant.

It is far harder to put one's finger on what makes a given contract to do work for another a contract of service or a contract for services.[37] Traditionally, the courts adopted a 'control test' to differentiate between contracts of service and contracts for services. According to the 'control test', if A contracts to do work for B, that contract will be a contract of service if B has the power under the contract to dictate *how* A will do his work; if, on the other hand, B does not have the power under the contract to dictate how A will do his work but merely specifies *what* work is to be done by A and leaves it up to A to determine how he will do that work, then that contract will be a contract for services.[38]

In *Performing Right Society Ltd* v *Mitchell & Booker (Palais de Danse) Ltd*,[39] the defendants owned a dance hall and engaged a band to play in it. On one occasion the band performed some dance music which was protected by copyright. The copyright on the music in question belonged to the claimants and the band did not have the claimants' permission to play that music when they did so. The claimants sued the defendants, claiming that the defendants were vicariously liable in respect of the band's violation of the claimants' copyright. The case turned on whether the band were employees of the defendants when they played in the dance hall or whether they were in fact independent contractors. The court applied the control test and found that the band were employees of the defendants when they played in the defendants' dance hall: 'the contract [gave] to the defendants the right of continuous, dominant and detailed control on every point, including the nature of the music to be played [by the band].'[40]

In *Mersey Docks & Harbour Board* v *Coggins & Griffith (Liverpool) Ltd*,[41] the first defendants, a harbour authority, let a mobile crane to the second defendants, a firm of stevedores, for loading a ship. The harbour authority had one of their employees, a man named Newall, operate the crane for the second defendants. Due to Newall's negligence in operating the crane, the claimant was injured. The claimant sued the first and second defendants, claiming that

---

[37] See Kidner 1995.
[38] Cf. *Yewens* v *Noakes* (1880) 6 QBD 530, 532–3: 'A servant is a person who is subject to the command of his master as to the manner in which he shall do his work' (per Bramwell LJ). See also *Honeywill and Stein Ltd* v *Larkin Brothers Ltd* [1934] 1 KB 191, 196: 'The determination whether [someone] is a servant ... on the one hand or an independent contractor on the other depends on whether or not the employer not only determines what is to be done, but retains control of the actual performance, in which case the doer is a servant ...; but if the employer, while prescribing the work to be done, leaves the manner of doing it to the control of the doer, the latter is an independent contractor' (per Slesser LJ).
[39] [1924] 1 KB 762.
[40] Ibid., 771.
[41] [1947] AC 1.

one of them was vicariously liable in respect of Newall's negligence. The question was: who was Newall's employer at the time he operated the crane for the second defendants? The House of Lords held that it would be presumed that the first defendants were Newall's employers at the time he operated the crane for the second defendants unless the first defendants could show that in fact the second defendants were Newall's employers at the relevant time. The House of Lords, applying the control test, held that the first defendants had failed to discharge this burden: they could not show that when Newall worked for the stevedores the stevedores had the power to control *how* Newall did his job in operating the crane; all the stevedores had the power to do was to tell Newall what to lift and drop with his crane, not to tell Newall how to operate the crane.[42]

More recently, the courts have rejected the 'control test' as an unsatisfactory means of differentiating between contracts of service and contracts for services.[43] For example, suppose that A contractually undertakes to do work for B and the work which A is supposed to do for B is of such a technical character that B – in his ignorance as to how that work should be done – is in no position to dictate to A how that work should be done. In such a case, under the control test, it will be impossible to find that A is employed by B. But this is counter-intuitive: there are plenty of cases where we would say that B is A's employer even though the work to be done by A under the contract between him and B is of such a complex character that B is in no position to tell him how to do it. For example, the master of a ship is plainly employed by the owners of the ship even though the owners are in no position to dictate to him how he should navigate the ship.[44] Similarly, a surgeon may well be employed by the hospital at which he works even though the hospital authorities are in no position to dictate to him how he should conduct his operations.[45] If the 'control test' is no longer a useful test for differentiating between contracts of service and contracts for services, what test should we adopt in its place? The courts have suggested a variety of alternative tests.

(1) *Ordinary person.* In *Cassidy* v *Ministry of Health*, Somervell LJ suggested that a given contract to do work for another would be a contract of service if an ordinary person would regard it as being a contract of service and that it would be a contract for services if an ordinary person would regard it as being a contract for services.[46]

---

[42] Another reason for holding that Newall was not employed by the stevedores at the time he worked for them was that there was no evidence that there was any contractual nexus between Newall and the stevedores at the time he worked for them.

[43] Which is not to say that considerations of control are not sometimes taken into account by the courts in judging whether someone is an employee or not. See, for example, *Montgomery* v *Johnson Underwood Ltd* [2001] ICR 819 (held, a temp. is not employed by the employment agency which places her with various employers on a temporary basis because the employment agency had no control over how she did her work).

[44] *Gold* v *Essex County Council* [1942] 2 KB 293, 305 (per Mackinnon LJ).

[45] *Cassidy v Ministry of Health* [1951] 2 KB 343.

[46] Ibid., 352–3.

This test for differentiating between contracts of service and contracts for services – which we can call the 'ordinary person' test – is of severely limited usefulness. There are many instances of contracts to do work for another which an ordinary person would be hard pressed to classify as being contracts of service or contracts for services. For instance, in *Argent* v *Minister of Social Security*[47] a drama school engaged Argent to work for them as a part-time teacher. Argent was paid on an hourly basis. The school did not dictate to Argent what he should do in his classes. Occasionally, Argent would cease giving classes at the school in order to work full-time as an actor in various theatre productions. Would an ordinary person say that Argent's contract with the drama school was a contract of service or a contract for services? It is difficult to imagine he would have any firm view on the matter.[48] Given this, it is doubtful whether the 'ordinary person' test provides much of a guide as to whether a given contract to do work for another amounts to a contract of service or a contract for services.

(2) *Integration.* In *Stephenson Jordan & Harrison Ltd* v *MacDonald & Evans*, Denning LJ suggested that 'under a contract of service, a man is employed as part of the business and his work is done as an integral part of the business: whereas under a contract for services his work, although done for the business, is not integrated into it but is only accessory to it'.[49] Shortly afterwards, in *Bank voor Handel en Scheepvart NV* v *Slatford*, Denning LJ rephrased this test – which we can call the 'integration' test – for differentiating between contracts of service and contracts for services. In that case, he suggested 'the test of being a servant does not rest nowadays on submission to orders. It depends on whether the person is part and parcel of the organisation.'[50]

The integration test for differentiating between contracts of service and contracts for services is again, because of its vagueness, of very limited usefulness. MacKenna J criticised the test in *Ready Mixed Concrete (South East) Ltd* v *Minister of Pensions and National Insurance*, arguing that it 'raises more questions than I know how to answer. What is meant by being "part and parcel of an organisation"? Are all persons who answer this description servants? If only some are servants, what distinguishes them from the others . . .?'[51]

(3) *Four indicia.* In *Short* v *J W Henderson Ltd*, Lord Thankerton suggested that a contract under which A undertakes to do work for B will amount to a contract of service if: (1) B selected A to do work for him; (2) under the contract A is to be paid wages for the work done by him; (3) B has the right under the contract to control the way in which A does the work contracted for; (4) B has the right to suspend or dismiss A.[52]

---

[47] [1968] 1 WLR 1749.
[48] In fact, it was found that he was not an employee but was employed under a contract for services.
[49] (1951) 69 RPC 10, 22.
[50] [1953] 1 QB 248, 295.
[51] [1968] 2 QB 497, 524.
[52] (1946) 62 TLR 427, 429.

This test for determining whether or not a contract to do work for another is a contract of service or a contract for services – which we can call the 'four *indicia*' test – is not particularly helpful. First of all, the fact that (1) and (4) are true of a particular contract to do work for another does not indicate that that contract is a contract of service: (1) and (4) may well be satisfied even if the contract in question is a contract for services. Secondly, as we have seen, if (3) is not true of a particular contract to do work for another that does not necessarily mean that that contract is not a contract of service. However, the 'four *indicia*' test does highlight *a* difference between a contract of service and a contract for services. A person who does work for another under a contract of service is usually paid *wages* or a *salary* for the work done by him. A person who does work for another under a contract for services is usually paid a *fee* for the work done by him.

(4) *Principal obligation.* In *WHPT Housing Association Ltd* v *Secretary of State for Social Services*, Webster J suggested that 'the difference between a contract of service and one for services must reside, essentially, in the terms of the principal obligation agreed to be undertaken by the employee – a word which I use without begging the question. In a contract of service ... the principal obligation undertaken by the employee is to provide himself to serve: whereas in a contract for services the principal obligation is not to provide himself to serve the employer but his services for the use of the employer'.[53]

This test – which we can call the 'obligation' test – seems to capture *a* difference between a contract of service and a contract for services. If A enters into a contract for services with B, the contract will *normally* specify that A must do a specific piece of work for B; how long A takes over the work is left up to A.[54] If A enters into a contract of service with B, the contract will normally specify that A must work a certain number of hours for B doing a particular kind of work and A will have no flexibility over how long he can take working for B.

Related to this is another difference that seemingly exists between contracts of service and contracts for services. A contract of service is *personal*: if A enters into a contract of service with B, A will not be able to discharge his obligations under the contract by getting C to fill in for him and fulfil his duties under his contract with B. As a general rule, a contract for services is *impersonal*: if A enters into a contract for services with B, A will – as a general rule[55] – be able to discharge his obligations under the contract through other people.[56] So, for example, if A contracts to build a greenhouse in B's back garden, he will dis-

---

[53] [1981] ICR 737, 748.

[54] There are obvious exceptions to this point. For example, if B hires A to clean his house for four hours a week, the contract will still be a contract for services even though A's contractual obligation is to work for a certain amount of time for B.

[55] Again, there are some obvious exceptions to this point. If B hires A to paint her portrait, the contract will be a contract for services even though it is personal in nature; A will not be able to discharge his obligations to B under the contract by getting a third party to paint B's portrait.

[56] This is why when B hires a company to do some work for him one could never say that the company does that work as B's employee. The company – being incapable of doing the work itself – will always do that work through other people; that is, its own employees.

charge his obligation to build that greenhouse in B's back garden if he gets C to build the greenhouse requested by B.

(5) *Independence*. In *Market Investigations Ltd* v *Minister of Social Security*, Cooke J suggested that 'the fundamental test to be applied [to determine whether a given contract is a contract of service or a contract for services] is this: "Is the person who has engaged himself to perform these services performing them as a person in business on his own account?" If the answer to that question is "yes" then the contract is a contract for services. If the answer is "no" then the contract is a contract of service.'[57]

We can call this the 'independence' test for differentiating between contracts of service and contracts for services. Cooke J then went on to say that a variety of factors would have to be taken into account in judging whether or not someone who has engaged himself to perform services for another will perform them in business on his own account: 'control will no doubt always have to be considered, although it can no longer be regarded as the sole determining factor; ... factors which may be of importance are such matters as whether the man performing the services provides his own equipment, whether he hires his own helpers, what degree of financial risk he takes, what degree of responsibility for investment and management he has, and whether and how far he has an opportunity of profiting from sound management in the performance of his task.'[58] In *Lee Ting Sang* v *Chung Chi-Keung*, the Privy Council explicitly endorsed Cooke J's approach in the *Market Investigations* case to the question of whether a given contract is a contract of service or a contract for services, holding that the appropriate approach to this question had 'never been better put than by Cooke J in *Market Investigations Ltd ...*'.[59]

Again, this test does capture *a* difference between a contract of service and a contract for services. If A works for B under a contract of service, to some extent A's economic welfare is bound up with B's: if B does not do well, then that imperils A's economic welfare. On the other hand, if A works for B under a contract for services, then A's economic welfare is relatively independent of B's. Instead, A's economic welfare is bound up with the quality of the work he does for B: if his work is bad, he will not be paid; if it is good, then he will be paid. In other words, if A works for B under a contract of service, A's and B's interests will coincide: A will have an interest in seeing that B's interests are promoted. If A works for B under a contract for services, A will not necessarily have an interest in seeing that B's interests are promoted.

In light of the above, we can propose a 'five *indicia*' test for determining whether a given contract to do work for another amounts to a contract of service or a contract for services. Under this test, if A has entered into a contract with B under which he undertakes to do work for B, that contract will be a contract *of service* if *most* of the following five requirements are met: (1) Under the contract, B has the

---

[57] [1969] 2 QB 173, 184.
[58] Ibid., 185.
[59] [1990] 2 AC 374, 382.

power to control how A does his work; (2) A is required under the contract to work for B for a set period of time; (3) A is due to be paid wages or a salary for the work done by him under his contract with B; (4) A's obligations under his contract with B are personal to him and cannot be discharged by having a third party perform them; (5) the terms of A's contract with B indicate that A, in working for B, is not engaged in some business on his own account. If *most* of these requirements are *not* met then A's contract with B will be a contract for services.

Course of employment

Suppose that A was an employee of B's when he committed a tort. When can we say that A committed that tort 'in the course of his employment' by B? The law on this question has undergone a dramatic transformation since the publication of the previous edition of this book.

The Salmond test

Before the decision of the House of Lords in *Lister* v *Hesley Hall Ltd*,[60] one would use the *Salmond test* to determine whether an employee's tort was committed in the course of his employment. Under this test – set out by the great tort lawyer Sir John Salmond in the first edition of his *Law of Torts* – an employee's tort will have been committed in the course of his employment if it was:

> either (a) a wrongful act authorised by [the employee's employer], or (b) a wrongful and unauthorised mode of doing some act authorised by [the employee's employer][61]

To put the test another way, under the Salmond test, an employee's tort will have been committed in the course of his employment if *the employee did something he was employed to do by committing that tort*.

So suppose that Gary, who was employed by Ruth, drove a car from point A to point B at 100 mph, thereby breaking the speed limit. And suppose further that Ian was injured as a result of Gary's dangerous driving. Under the Salmond test, Ruth would be vicariously liable in respect of Gary's negligence if Gary was employed by her to drive from point A to point B.[62] If he was, then he did something he was employed to do by driving the car at 100 mph. It may be that he was not authorised to break the speed limit in driving from point A to point B but that is immaterial under the Salmond test: the only thing that counts is whether Gary was employed to drive from point A to point B. If he was not, then Ruth would not be vicariously liable in respect of Gary's negligence under the Salmond test.[63] Gary would not have done anything he was employed to do by driving from point A to point B at 100 mph.

---

[60] [2002] 1 AC 215.

[61] Salmond 1907, 83.

[62] See *Limpus* v *London General Omnibus Company* (1862) 1 H&C 526; 158 ER 995 (bus company vicariously liable for bus driver's breaking of speed limit while driving buses on route); also *Rose* v *Plenty* [1976] 1 WLR 141 (defendant employers vicariously liable in respect of milkman's negligent driving in driving milk float on his round).

[63] See *Storey* v *Ashton* (1869) LR 4 QB 476 (two employees of defendant's went by horse and cart to deliver some wine to a customer of the defendant's; on the way back, one employee persuaded

Similarly, suppose Gary intentionally hit Ian while he, Gary, was employed by Ruth. Under the Salmond test, Ruth would only be vicariously liable in respect of the tort committed by Gary in hitting Ian if Gary did something he was employed to do by hitting Ian. So suppose Gary was employed by Ruth to work in a bar and was charged with the general responsibility of keeping order in the bar. If Ian was making a nuisance of himself in the bar and Gary hit him to shut him up, then Gary would have done something he was employed to do by hitting Ian and Ruth would be vicariously liable in respect of Gary's tort under the Salmond test.[64] If, on the other hand, Gary – in hitting Ian – was merely taking revenge on him for some slight which Gary suffered at Ian's hands in the past, then, under the Salmond test, Ruth would not have been vicariously liable in respect of the tort committed by Gary in hitting Ian.[65] Gary would not have done anything he was employed to do by hitting Ian.

A difficulty in applying the Salmond test

For the most part, the Salmond test for determining whether or not an employer would be vicariously liable in respect of a tort committed by one of his employees was straightforward to apply. However, in certain marginal cases there were difficulties – arising out of the fact it is not always clear how widely or narrowly we should characterise what an employee was employed to do. For example, in *London County Council* v *Cattermoles (Garages) Ltd*[66] the defendants employed one Preston to work in their garage. One of Preston's duties was to

---

the other to make a diversion and pick up a cask of wine from the first employee's brother-in-law; held, defendant not vicariously liable in respect of negligent way in which second employee drove horse and cart on the way to the home of the first employee's brother-in-law as second employee not employed to drive horse and cart to that destination); also *Conway* v *George Wimpey & Co. Ltd* [1951] 2 KB 266 (defendant building contractor appointed to do work at airport; had employee drive lorry around perimeter of airport and pick up and drop off any of defendant's employees who were working in the airport and wanted a lift to a different part of the airport; employee gave a lift to someone who was not working for defendant and drove lorry so negligently that passenger injured; held, defendant not vicariously liable in respect of employee's negligent driving as employee did not do anything he was employed to do by giving passenger a lift).

[64] Contra, O'Sullivan 2002, who seems to take the view (at 94) that the Salmond test can *never* be satisfied in a case of intentional wrongdoing. In support of our view, see *Poland* v *John Parr & Sons* [1927] 1 KB 236 (carter employed by defendants to accompany wagon of sugar as it travelled through Liverpool; carter hit claimant schoolboy who he mistakenly thought was trying to steal some sugar off the wagon; held, defendants vicariously liable in respect of carter's battery as carter did something he was employed to do – defend the wagon from theft – by hitting the claimant).

[65] See *Warren* v *Henleys Ltd* [1948] 2 All ER 935 (a petrol pump attendant struck a customer in the course of an altercation about whether or not the customer had paid for petrol taken from the petrol pump; held, that the employers of the attendant were not vicariously liable in respect of the battery committed by the attendant as the attendant did not do anything he was employed to do by striking the passenger); *Keppel Bus Co.* v *Sa'ad bin Ahmed* [1974] 1 WLR 1082 (bus conductor swore at passenger and then hit him when the passenger protested; held, bus company not vicariously liable in respect of conductor's battery as he did not do anything he was employed to do in hitting the passenger); *Aldred* v *Nacanco* [1987] IRLR 292 (defendant employer not vicariously liable for tort committed by employee in trying to startle fellow employee; first instance decision in *Harrison* v *Michelin Tyre Co. Ltd* [1985] 1 All ER 918, holding defendant employer vicariously liable in respect of tort committed by employee in causing fellow employee to lose footing and fall, disapproved); *Deatons Pty Ltd* v *Flew* (1949) 79 CLR 370 (defendant hotel owners not vicariously liable in respect of tort committed by employee tending bar in hotel when she reacted to lewd suggestion by patron of bar by throwing beer, and subsequently an empty glass, in his face).

[66] [1953] 1 WLR 997.

move cars that had been left at the garage when they were in the way of other cars using the garage. He was told to move any cars by hand as he did not have a driving licence. Preston was instructed to move a van which was obstructing access to the defendants' petrol pumps. Preston got into the van and drove it into the road. However, he did not keep a proper lookout in driving the van into the road and it collided with the claimant's vehicle. The claimant sued the defendants claiming that they were vicariously liable in respect of Preston's negligence.

The case turned on the question: What was Preston employed to do? If he was employed to move cars in the defendants' garage *by hand* then Preston did *not* do anything he was employed to do by *driving* the van into the road without keeping a proper lookout. If he was simply employed to *move* cars in the defendants' garage, then Preston *did* do something he was employed to do by driving the van into the road without keeping a proper lookout. The Court of Appeal took a wide view of what Preston was employed to do in this case and found that Preston was employed to move cars in the defendants' garage. So the court concluded that Preston *was* acting in the course of his employment when he drove the van into the road without keeping a proper lookout.

Other cases are more difficult. For example, suppose Alan was an employee of Acme Co. and one day he drove to work at 100 mph, with the result that he negligently crashed into Dawn's car. Could we say – for the purposes of applying the Salmond test to determine whether Acme are vicariously liable in respect of Alan's negligence – that Alan was doing something he was employed to do when he drove to work at 100 mph? The House of Lords addressed this issue in the case of *Smith* v *Stages*.[67] Lord Lowry sought to deal with it by setting out some guidelines which are worth setting out in full:

1. An employee travelling from his ordinary residence to his regular place of work, whatever the means of transport and even if it is provided by the employer is not on duty and is not acting in the course of his employment, but, if he is obliged by his contract of service to use the employer's transport, he will normally, in the absence of an express condition to the contrary, be regarded as acting in the course of his employment while doing so.

2. Travelling in the employer's time between workplaces (one of which may be the regular workplace) or in the course of a peripatetic profession, whether accompanied by goods or tools or simply in order to reach a succession of workplaces . . . will be in the course of the employment.

3. Receipt of wages (though not receipt of a travelling allowance) will indicate that the employee is travelling in the employer's time and for his benefit and is acting in the course of his employment, and in such a case the fact that the employee may have discretion as to the mode and time of travelling will not take the journey out of the course of his employment.

4. An employee travelling in the employer's time from his ordinary workplace to a workplace other than his regular workplace or in the course of a peripatetic profession or to the scene of an emergency (such as a fire, an accident or mechanical breakdown of plant) will be acting in the course of his employment.

[67] [1989] 1 AC 928.

5. A deviation from or interruption of a journey undertaken in the course of employment (unless the deviation or interruption is merely incidental to the journey) will for the time being (which may include an overnight interruption) take the employee out of the course of his employment.

6. Return journeys are to be treated as on the same footing as outward journeys.[68]

Estoppel and the Salmond test

It should also be noted that the application of the Salmond test in particular cases to determine whether an employer was vicariously liable in respect of a tort committed by one of his employees was sometimes affected by the following legal rule: In any proceedings between a claimant and an employer of an employee who has committed a tort, the employer will be *estopped* (or prevented) from denying that the employee in question was employed to do *x* if the employer led the claimant to believe that the employee was employed to do *x* and the claimant relied on that belief.

So, in *Conway* v *George Wimpey & Co. Ltd*[69] the defendant building company took on some construction work at an airport and to help out their employees, they had some of their employees drive lorries around the perimeter of the airport – the idea being that if any of the defendants' employees wanted a lift to another area of the airport, they could hitch a lift on one of these lorries. The claimant – who was not one of the defendants' employees – hitched a ride on one of these lorries and was injured as a result of the fact that the driver was negligent in driving the lorry. The Court of Appeal applied the Salmond test and held that the defendants were *not* vicariously liable in respect of their driver's negligence because he was not employed to give rides to people like the claimant: he was only employed to give rides to the defendants' employees of the defendant company who were working at the airport.

But it would have been different if the defendants had led the claimant to believe that their drivers were employed to give rides to *anyone* working in the airport and the claimant had relied on that belief by hitching a ride on one of the defendants' lorries. In such a case – when the claimant sued the defendants on the basis that they were vicariously liable in respect of their driver's negligence – the defendants would have been estopped (or prevented) from denying that their driver was employed to give rides to people like the claimant. The defendants would therefore have been unable to deny that their driver was acting in the course of his employment when he drove the claimant to his chosen destination in a negligent fashion. As it happened, the defendant company had done nothing to induce the claimant to believe that its lorry driver was employed to pick up people like him and give them lifts to where they wanted to go and so the defendant company was not estopped from denying that its lorry driver was employed to pick up people like the claimant.

This principle of estoppel is often said[70] to underlie the decision of the House of Lords in *Lloyd* v *Grace, Smith & Co.*[71] In that case, the claimant owned two cottages. She was dissatisfied with the income she received from her assets and

---

[68] Ibid., 955–6.

[69] [1951] 2 KB 266. See above, n. 63.

[70] See *Dubai Aluminium Co. Ltd* v *Salaam* [2003] 2 AC 366, at [28] (per Lord Nicholls); *New South Wales* v *Lepore* [2003] HCA 4, at [108] – [111] (per Gaudron J) and [232] (per Gummow and Hayne JJ).

[71] [1912] AC 716. For an alternative explanation of the case, see above, pp. 230–1.

consulted the defendant firm of solicitors for advice. Her case was handled by one Sandles, the managing clerk of the firm. He tricked her into transferring the two cottages to him. The House of Lords held that the defendants were liable to compensate the claimant for the losses suffered by her as a result of Sandles's deceit. It is possible to argue that the source of the defendants' liability in this case was that they were vicariously liable in respect of Sandles's deceit – and the reason why they were vicariously liable in respect of Sandles's deceit was that they were estopped from denying that Sandles did something he was employed to do when he persuaded the claimant to sign over her cottages to him. After all, the defendants did lead the claimant to believe that Sandles was acting with their authority in *whatever* he did in relation to the claimant's affairs and the claimant relied on that belief by allowing Sandles to handle her affairs.

The *Lister* decision

We are now in a position to understand the radical change in the law that was brought about by the decision of the House of Lords in *Lister* v *Hesley Hall Ltd*.[72] In that case, the defendants ran a boarding house for children who attended a nearby school. The defendants employed a married couple, Mr and Mrs Grain, to run the boarding house and maintain discipline. Unfortunately, Mr Grain used his position to sexually abuse a number of the children staying at the boarding house. They sued the defendants for compensation, claiming that the defendants were vicariously liable in respect of the torts committed by Grain when he sexually abused them.

Had the Salmond test been applied to determine whether or not Grain was acting in the course of his employment when he sexually abused the claimants, the claimants' claims for compensation would certainly have been dismissed. There was no way it could be said that Grain did something he was employed to do by sexually abusing the claimants. Indeed, in an earlier case the Court of Appeal had applied the Salmond test to determine whether a local education authority was vicariously liable in respect of the torts committed by a deputy headmaster in sexually assaulting a student when they were on a school trip together, and had concluded that the deputy head had not been acting in the course of his employment when he sexually assaulted the student.[73]

However, the Salmond test was *not* applied in the *Lister* case to determine whether or not Grain was acting in the course of his employment when he sexually abused the claimants. The House of Lords swept that test away. In its place, the House of Lords adopted a quite different test for determining whether or not an employee was acting in the course of his employment when he committed a tort. This test was first adopted by the Supreme Court of Canada in the cases[74] of *Bazley* v *Curry*[75] and *Jacobi* v *Griffiths*.[76] Under this test, an employee will be held to have acted in the course of his employment

---

[72] [2002] 1 AC 215 (noted, Giliker 2002).
[73] *Trotman* v *North Yorkshire County Council* [1999] LGR 584.
[74] Noted, Cane 2000.
[75] [1999] 2 SCR 534.
[76] [1999] 2 SCR 570.

when he committed a tort if that tort was 'so closely connected with his employment that it would be fair and just to hold the [employee's employer] vicariously liable [in respect of that tort]'.[77] The House of Lords held that under *this* test – what we might call the 'sufficiently close connection' test, Grain *had* acted in the course of his employment when he sexually abused the claimants.[78] Their main reason for so finding was that the defendants had owed the claimants a duty to look after them; that they tried to discharge that duty by having Grain look after the claimants; and Grain conspicuously failed to look after the claimants when he sexually abused them.[79]

Critique of the decision in *Lister*

Three criticisms may be made of the House of Lords' decision in *Lister*:

(1) *Constitutionality*. It may be wondered whether the House of Lords acted entirely constitutionally in sweeping aside a test for determining whether an employee acted in the course of his employment when he committed a tort that had stood the test of time for almost a century. It was surely a job for Parliament, acting in conjunction with the Law Commission, to bring about such a radical change in the law on vicarious liability.[80]

Perhaps recognising this, their Lordships in *Lister* attempted to argue that there was nothing *new* about the 'sufficiently close connection' test that they adopted in *Lister*.[81] They argued that there were plenty of cases where this test had *already* been used to determine whether an employee acted in the course of his employment in committing a tort. Unfortunately, it could be argued that two of the cases mentioned – *Morris* v *C W Martin & Sons Ltd*[82] and *Photo Production* v *Securicor*[83] – are not vicarious liability cases at all but cases where

---

[77] *Lister* v *Hesley Hall Ltd* [2002] 1 AC 215, at [28] (per Lord Steyn). See also [70] (per Lord Millett: 'What is critical is ... the closeness of the connection between the employee's duties and his wrongdoing'). An alternative formulation of the same test was offered by Lord Nicholls in *Dubai Aluminium Co. Ltd* v *Salaam* [2003] 2 AC 366, at [23]: 'the wrongful conduct must be so closely connected with acts the ... employee was authorised to do that, for the purpose of the liability of the ... employer to third parties, the wrongful conduct *may fairly and properly be regarded* as done by the [employee] while acting in the ordinary course of the ... employee's employment' (emphasis in original).

[78] They also found that under this test the deputy headmaster in the *Trotman* case (see above, p. 650) *had* been acting in the course of his employment when he sexually assaulted the student in that case and, accordingly, the House of Lords overruled the Court of Appeal's decision in that case that the local education authority was not vicariously liable in respect of the torts committed by the deputy head in sexually assaulting the student.

[79] [2002] 1 AC 215, at [25]–[28] (per Lord Steyn), [50] (per Lord Clyde), [59]–[61] (per Lord Hobhouse), [82]–[83] (per Lord Millett).

[80] It was argued by counsel for the defendants that 'Any radical expansion or development of liability in this area of law should be left to Parliament' (ibid, at 218) but that argument was ignored by their Lordships.

[81] Ibid, at [15] (per Lord Steyn), [69] (per Lord Millett). Cf. *New South Wales* v *Lepore* [2003] HCA 4, at [319]: '[The House of Lords] did not depart from precedent in establishing the "close connection" analysis. They merely developed and elaborated the traditional approach' (per Kirby P). Academic support for this line can be found in W&J, 720 (expressing surprise that the Court of Appeal refused to find vicarious liability in *Lister*).

[82] [1966] 1 QB 716.

[83] [1980] AC 827.

the defendant was put in breach of a non-delegable duty of care by the acts of one of his employees.[84] A similar analysis could be made of the third case mentioned by their Lordships – *Lloyd* v *Grace, Smith & Co.*[85] But even if that case *is* regarded as a vicarious liability case, the decision in that case is compatible with the Salmond test for determining whether an employee acted in the course of his employment in committing a tort and cannot be read as supporting the 'sufficiently close connection' test adopted by their Lordships in *Lister*.

(2) *Necessity*. Had the House of Lords wanted to rule in favour of the claimants in *Lister*, they had no need to alter the law on vicarious liability to do so. They could have easily found that the defendants in *Lister* were *personally* liable to compensate the claimants for the harm they suffered as a result of being sexually abused by Grain. Their Lordships could have reached this conclusion using the device of a non-delegable duty of care. They could have ruled that: the defendants owed the claimants a non-delegable duty of care to look after them; the defendants gave Grain the job of looking after the claimants; and Grain put the defendants in breach of the non-delegable duty of care that they owed the claimants when, by sexually abusing the claimants, he failed to look after the claimants properly. It is hard to understand why the House of Lords did not decide *Lister* in this way – particularly as these were the *very* reasons why the House of Lords found that there *was* a 'sufficiently close connection' between the torts committed by Grain in the *Lister* case and what he was employed to do so as to make the defendants *vicariously* liable in respect of those torts.[86]

(3) *Certainty*. The third criticism that may be made of the House of Lords' decision in *Lister* is that the 'sufficiently close connection' test is so vague and open-ended that it is now very hard to tell when exactly an employee will be held to have committed a tort in the course of his employment.[87] As Lord Nicholls observed in *Dubai Aluminium Co. Ltd* v *Salaam*, the ' "close connection" test ... affords no guidance on the type or degree of connection which will normally be regarded as sufficiently close to prompt the legal conclusion

---

[84] For such an explanation, see above, pp. 229–30, 231.
[85] [1912] AC 716. See above, pp. 649–50.
[86] See Glofcheski 2004, 27; also *New South Wales* v *Lepore* [2003] HCA 4, at [208]: 'The analyses of Lord Hobhouse and Lord Millett [in *Lister*] have strong echoes of non-delegable duties' (per Gummow and Hayne JJ).
[87] Cf. Callinan J's criticisms of the 'sufficiently close connection' test for determining whether an employee committed a tort in the course of his employment in *New South Wales* v *Lepore*: '[If such a test were to be adopted in Australia] [d]istinguishing between [cases where there was a "sufficiently close connection" between an employee's tort and what he was employed to do and cases where there was not] would be very difficult. Cases would, as a practical matter, be decided according to whether the judge ... thought it "fair and just" to hold the employer liable. Perceptions of fairness vary greatly. The law in consequence would be thrown into a state of uncertainty. I would not therefore be prepared to adopt their Lordships' or any like test' (ibid, at [345]). Only one of the seven judges who decided *New South Wales* v *Lepore* in the High Court of Australia expressed any enthusiasm for the 'sufficiently close connection' test (Kirby P). Callinan, Gaudron, Gummow, Hayne JJ and (less clearly) Gleeson CJ all held that Australian courts should continue to use the Salmond test to determine whether an employee committed a tort in the course of his employment. McHugh J declined to express an opinion on the issue.

that the risk of the wrongful act occurring, and any loss resulting from the wrongful act, should fall on the firm or employer rather than the third party who was wronged ... [Under the 'sufficiently close connection' test, the] crucial feature or features, either producing or negativing vicarious liability, [will] vary widely from one case or type of case to the next. Essentially the court makes an evaluative judgment in each case, having regard to all the circumstances ...'[88]

It is not clear that the judges who decided *Lister* would regard the lack of certainty inherent in the 'sufficiently close connection' test as a problem; they might even regard it as a virtue. It is obvious that in the *Lister* case, their Lordships wanted to come up with a test for when an employee would be held to have acted in the course of his employment in committing a tort that would allow them to do 'practical justice'[89] in individual cases.[90] But as Lord Millett observed in *Lister*, it is doubtful whether anyone can come up with a test that is sufficiently flexible as to allow the courts to do 'practical justice' in individual cases but at the same time is sufficiently precise as 'to enable the outcome of a particular case to be predicted'.[91] Any test which did work in a predictable fashion would be 'rigid and possibly inappropriate ... as a test of liability' in particular cases.[92]

However, in their desire to do 'practical justice' in individual cases, the Law Lords who decided *Lister* forgot or disregarded the primary responsibility that they owe the public at large, which is to ensure that the law is stated in clear and certain terms, so that we can all know where we stand when we get involved in disputes with other people. For this reason, it is to be hoped that a future House of Lords will abandon the 'sufficiently close connection' test for determining whether an employee committed a tort in the course of his employment in favour of another test which will work in a more predictable fashion.[93]

---

[88] [2003] 2 AC 366, at [25]–[26].
[89] [2002] 1 AC 215, at [16] per Lord Steyn.
[90] For a fine critique of judicial attempts to do 'practical justice' in individual cases, see Beever 2003b.
[91] [2002] 1 AC 215, at [66].
[92] Ibid.
[93] *Important note.* Such a test would have to identify exactly *when* it is 'fair and just' to hold an employer vicariously liable in respect of a tort committed by one of his employees in terms which make it possible to predict with a fair degree of success in any given case whether an employer will be held vicariously liable in respect of a tort committed by one of his employees. The Supreme Court of Canada attempted to come up with such a test in *Bazley* v *Curry* [1999] 2 SCR 534, holding that 'the policy purposes underlying the imposition of vicarious liability on employers are served *only* where the wrong *is so connected with the employment that it can be said that the employer has introduced the risk of the wrong* (and is thereby and usefully charged with its management and minimization)' (at [37], per McLachlin J, emphasis added). However, members of the High Court of Australia expressed themselves doubtful in *New South Wales* v *Lepore* [2003] HCA 4 whether that test was expressed in sufficiently clear terms as to make its application predictable: see [126] (per Gaudron J) and [212] (per Gummow and Hayne JJ). If it is not possible to identify in clear and certain terms *when* it would be 'fair and just' to hold an employer vicariously liable in respect of a tort committed by one of his employees (and Lord Millett seemed to think in *Lister* that it was not: see above, p. 653), a 'second-best' test would have to be formulated which worked in a predictable fashion *and* served to make employers vicariously liable for their employees' torts in *most* situations where it would be 'fair and just' to make them so liable. It may be that the only such 'second-best' test on offer is the Salmond test.

How will the new test work in practice?

Until that day comes, in any case where an employee has committed a tort, the courts will have to determine whether the employee committed that tort in the course of his employment by asking – Was there a sufficiently close connection between the employee's tort and what he was employed to do so as to make it 'fair and just' that the employer should be held vicariously liable in respect of the employee's tort? When are the courts likely to find that this test is satisfied? The available case law on the matter offers the following guidance.

(1) *The Salmond test*. It seems clear that if an employer would have been held vicariously liable in respect of a tort committed by one of his employees under the old Salmond test, then the courts will hold that there is a 'sufficiently close connection' between the employee's tort and what he was employed to do.[94]

(2) *Delegation*. It seems to follow from the *Lister* decision that if an employer was under a duty to do *x*, and he instructed one of his employees to discharge that duty, then if the employee failed to follow instructions and in so doing committed a tort, there will exist a 'sufficiently close connection' between the employee's tort and what he was employed to do.[95]

In order to show a 'sufficiently close connection' under this head, it is crucial to show that the employee in question was entrusted with the job of discharging a duty of his employer's. So it was vital that the employee in the *Lister* case was employed to discharge the duty that the defendants were under to look after the children staying at their boarding house. Had the claimants in *Lister* been abused by a handyman who was employed by the defendants merely to do odd jobs around the boarding house, then it is unlikely that the House of Lords would have found a 'sufficiently close connection' between the torts committed by the handyman in abusing the claimants and what he was employed to do.[96] It could not have been said that the defendants employed the handyman to discharge the duty they were under to look after the children staying at their boarding house.

(3) *Opportunity*. It seems well acknowledged that if an employee was given the opportunity to commit a tort by virtue of his being employed to do a certain kind of work, that fact *on its own* will *not* be enough to establish that there was

---

[94] It can hardly be supposed that for nearly 100 years before *Lister* was decided the courts acted unfairly or unjustly by holding employers vicariously liable for their employees' torts when the Salmond test was satisfied. But see Lord Millett's observation in *Dubai Aluminium Co. Ltd* v *Salaam* [2003] 2 AC 366 that 'the Salmond test is only that – a test. It is not a conclusive definition of the circumstances in which vicarious liability arises. *Even if it is satisfied, the facts, taken as a whole, may nevertheless show that the employee was not acting in the course of his employment*' (at [128], emphasis added).

[95] See [2002] 1 AC 215, at [50] (per Lord Clyde), [59] (per Lord Hobhouse), [82] (per Lord Millett). The House of Lords did not feel it necessary to explain *why* it is 'fair and just' to hold an employer vicariously liable in respect of a tort committed by one of his employees in this situation: Lord Steyn thought that it was a clear case where vicarious liability should be imposed (at [28]).

[96] See *Jacobi* v *Griffiths* [1999] 2 SCR 570, at [45] (per Binnie J); also *EDG* v *Hammer* [2003] 2 SCR 459, at [36] (per Arbour J).

a 'sufficiently close connection' between the employee's tort and what he was employed to do.[97]

So in *Jacobi* v *Griffiths*,[98] the defendants set up a club for children. They employed a Harry Griffiths to act as programme director at the club. His job was to organise recreational activities at the club and the occasional outing. Griffiths used his position to befriend a couple of the children who used the club and he ended up inviting them to his home, where he sexually assaulted them. The Supreme Court of Canada held, by four to three, that there was *not* a 'sufficiently close connection' between what Griffiths was employed to do and the torts that he committed in sexually assaulting the children. The fact that Griffiths had been employed to work at the club had of course given him the opportunity to sexually assault the children, but that was not enough to establish the requisite connection between his torts and what he was employed to do.[99]

(4) *Special risk*. In the *Lister* case, Lord Steyn made clear that the decisions of the Supreme Court of Canada in *Bazley* v *Curry* and *Jacobi* v *Griffiths* should form the 'starting point' of any inquiry into whether there was a 'sufficiently close connection' between what an employee was employed to do and a tort committed by the employee.[100] Those decisions indicate that if an employee is employed to do a particular job and there is a *special risk*[101] associated with that job that he will commit a particular kind of tort, then if the employee in question commits that tort there will be a 'sufficiently close connection' between the employee's tort and what he was employed to do.[102]

This requirement was held to be satisfied in *Bazley* v *Curry*, where the defendants unknowingly employed a paedophile to work in a home for disturbed children and the paedophile used his position to sexually abuse some of the children in the home. It was held that there was a special risk that people who work in children's homes will sexually assault the children there. This is because, McLachlin J explained, people who work in children's homes occupy a position of 'power and intimacy' in relation to the children at the homes – as a result, if they have paedophiliac tendencies, they will feel emboldened to

---

[97] *Lister* v *Hesley Hall Ltd* [2002] 1 AC 215, at [45] (per Lord Clyde), [59] (per Lord Hobhouse), [65] (per Lord Millett). Also *Bazley* v *Curry* [1999] 2 SCR 534, at [40] (per McLachlin J); and *Jacobi* v *Griffiths* [1999] 2 SCR 570, at [81] (per Binnie J).

[98] [1999] 2 SCR 570.

[99] If the same case occurred in the United Kingdom, could a court find the defendants vicariously liable for the programme director's acts of sexual abuse using the 'delegation' idea set out above? It depends on whether it could be said that the programme director in *Jacobi* v *Griffiths* was employed by the defendants in that case to discharge the duty they owed the children at the club to take reasonable steps to see that they were reasonably safe in using the club.

[100] [2002] 1 AC 215, at [27].

[101] The decisions actually talk in terms of an 'increased or materially enhanced . . . risk' (*Bazley* v *Curry* [1999] 2 SCR 534, at [39] (per McLachlin J)) but we prefer to use the term 'special risk'.

[102] The Supreme Court thought that the enterprise risk and deterrence rationales for vicarious liability set out above, at pp. 638–9, implied that it would be 'fair and just' to hold an employer vicariously liable in respect of a tort committed by one of his employees in this situation. See, to the same effect, Feldthusen 1998.

sexually abuse the children in their care and the children in their care will be more likely to submit to being assaulted without complaint.[103]

In contrast, the special risk requirement was held not to be satisfied in *Jacobi* v *Griffiths* where, as we have seen, the programme director at a children's club used his position to sexually abuse the children at the club. There was no special risk that someone employed in such a capacity would sexually abuse children who used the club because there was no special reason to think that someone employed to work as a programme director at a children's club would develop a relationship of 'power and intimacy' with the children at the club that might embolden him to assault the children at the club and lead them to submit to the assaults without complaint.[104]

The fact that the Supreme Court of Canada divided four to three in *Jacobi* over whether the special risk requirement was satisfied in that case indicates that it will often be very difficult to tell – in a given case where an employee has committed a tort – whether or not there was a special risk associated with what he was employed to do that he would commit that kind of tort. For example, in *Heasmans* v *Clarity Cleaning Co.*,[105] the claimants engaged the defendant cleaning company to clean its offices. One of the cleaners employed by the defendants to clean the claimants' offices made a number of long-distance telephone calls on the claimants' telephones while cleaning their offices, thereby committing the tort of conversion. The claimants sued the defendants, claiming that they were vicariously liable in respect of their cleaner's acts of conversion. The claim was dismissed on the ground that under the Salmond test, the cleaner did not act in the course of his employment when he made his international telephone calls.[106] But were the same case to occur today, could it be argued that there was a special risk that the cleaner would make international telephone calls while cleaning the claimants' offices and that there was therefore a 'sufficiently close connection' between the cleaner's acts of conversion and what he was employed to do so as to make the defendants vicariously liable in relation to the cleaner's acts of conversion? It is very hard to tell.

---

[103] [1999] 2 SCR 534, at [44]. See also *New South Wales* v *Lepore* [2003] HCA 4, at [216] (per Gummow and Hayne JJ). The result in *Weir* v *Chief Constable of Merseyside Police* [2003] EWCA Civ 111 may also be justified in this way. The defendant chief constable in that case was held vicariously liable in respect of an assault committed by an off-duty police officer on the claimant in a police van which the officer had borrowed in order to help a friend move some belongings. (The police officer suspected that the claimant had attempted to pilfer some of the friend's belongings while they were awaiting removal.) The Court of Appeal's main reason for finding the defendant vicariously liable in respect of the officer's assault was that, before he took the claimant into the police van and assaulted him, 'he . . . confirmed to, and the [claimant] understood, that he was a police officer' (at [12], per Rt. Hon. Sir Denis Henry). It may be that there is a special risk that police officers will commit assaults on ordinary citizens whenever they act in their capacity as police officers: they may feel that they are more likely to 'get away' with assaulting people when they act in their official capacity.

[104] [1999] 2 SCR 570, at [79]–[86] (per Binnie J).

[105] [1987] ICR 949.

[106] This was obviously right: the cleaner did not do anything he was employed to do by making the telephone calls.

(5) *Revenge attacks.* Until recently, it seemed well acknowledged in the cases dealing with the 'sufficiently close connection' test that the test would not be satisfied in the case of an employee who attacks someone else in revenge for some perceived slight or harm.[107]

However, in *Mattis* v *Pollock*[108] the claimant was stabbed by a nightclub bouncer employed by the defendants; the bouncer had earlier had an altercation with the claimant and was seeking to take revenge on him for this. The Court of Appeal held that the defendants *were* vicariously liable in respect of the bouncer's attack on the claimant. The court held that a 'close and direct' connection was established between the bouncer's attack and what he was employed to do because: (*a*) using violence on other people was part of his job; *and* (*b*) the earlier altercation between the bouncer and the claimant had arisen out of the bouncer's doing what he was employed to do and the bouncer's stabbing the claimant was directly linked to the earlier altercation. It is suggested that the decision is to be confined to its own facts,[109] and that the general rule remains that the 'sufficiently close connection' test will *not* be satisfied where an employee carries out a revenge attack on someone who has annoyed him or her.

FURTHER POINTS

A couple of further points about the law on vicarious liability remain to be made.

(1) *Contribution and indemnity.* Suppose that Beth has committed a tort and John is vicariously liable in respect of that tort. Suppose further that John is held liable to compensate someone who has suffered loss as a result of that tort. In such a case John will be entitled to bring a claim in contribution against Beth under the Civil Liability (Contribution) Act 1978 because they were both liable to make the compensation payment that John made. This will allow John to recover from Beth a 'just and equitable' *proportion* of the compensation payment that he made.

However, if the reason why John was vicariously liable in respect of Beth's tort was that Beth was his employee and she committed her tort in the course of her employment by John, then John will be entitled to bring a claim for

---

[107] *Bazley* v *Curry* [1999] 2 SCR 534, at [21] and [42] (per McLachlin J); *Lister* v *Hesley Hall Ltd* [2002] 1 AC 215, at [81] (per Lord Millett, endorsing the result in *Deatons Pty Ltd* v *Flew* (1949) 79 CLR 370, summarised above at n. 65); *Attorney-General* v *Hartwell* [2004] 1 WLR 1273, at [16]-[17] (police officer saw his ex-girlfriend in a bar with her new lover; he fired four shots into the bar with a gun issued to him by the police authority for whom he worked; one of the shots hit the claimant; 'clear-cut' that police authority not vicariously liable for police officer's actions).

[108] [2003] 1 WLR 2158 (reversing the decision of Judge Seymour QC at [2002] EWHC 2177).

[109] For a similar case where a finding of vicarious liability was also made by the Court of Appeal, see *Fennelly* v *Connex South Eastern Ltd* [2001] IRLR 390 (an initial altercation between a passenger and a ticket inspector over the passenger's failure to produce his ticket escalated and the ticket inspector ended up putting the passenger into a headlock; held, the inspector's employers were vicariously liable in respect of the tort committed by the inspector in laying his hands on the passenger).

breach of contract against Beth as she will have invariably breached her contract of employment in committing her tort. If he does bring a claim for breach of contract against Beth, he will be allowed to sue Beth for damages equal to the *entire* compensation payment that he has had to make as this payment will count as a loss that John has suffered as a result of Beth's breach of contract.

So – in *Lister v Romford Ice and Cold Storage Co. Ltd*,[110] Lister, who was employed by the claimants as a lorry driver, drove his lorry into a slaughterhouse yard to pick up some waste. Lister's father accompanied him and got out of the lorry before Lister had parked it. In parking the lorry, Lister negligently knocked down and injured his father. Lister's father sued the claimants, claiming that they were vicariously liable in respect of his son's negligence, and recovered £1,600 from the claimants in compensatory damages. The claimants then sued Lister, claiming that he had breached his contract of employment when he negligently knocked down his father and that they were therefore entitled to sue him for damages equal to the £1,600 that they had to pay out to Lister's father as a result of Lister's negligence. The House of Lords allowed the claim, agreeing that Lister had breached his contract of employment in negligently knocking down his father: they found that there was an implied term in Lister's contract of employment with the claimants that he would perform his duties under his contract of employment with reasonable skill and care and that when Lister negligently knocked down his father he breached that implied term.

(2) *Vicarious vicarious liability.* Suppose that Mary is vicariously liable in respect of a tort committed by Vijay. And suppose that Mary is vicariously liable in respect of Vijay's tort because she did various things in the course of her employment by Tom. Will Tom be vicariously liable along with Mary in respect of Vijay's tort?

The House of Lords gave a negative answer to this question in *Credit Lyonnais Bank Nederland NV v Export Credit Guarantee Department*.[111] In that case, the claimants were defrauded of a substantial amount of money by one Mr Chong. The fraud worked like this. Chong forged some bills of exchange and offered them for sale to the claimants. Obviously, the claimants – before buying the bills of exchange – wanted some assurance that they would be paid the monies payable under the bills. So Chong approached one Mr Pillai, who was employed by the defendants, a government agency. He bribed Pillai – who was well aware that Chong's bills of exchange were forged – to arrange for the defendants to guarantee that they would pay the claimants 90 per cent of the face value of the bills of exchange if sums payable under the bills of exchange remained unpaid three months after payment was due. Because they had this guarantee, the claimants bought the bills of exchange from Chong for over £10m.

Chong disappeared with the money paid him by the claimants and the claimants asked the defendants to fulfil their guarantee. However, the defen-

---

[110] [1957] AC 555.
[111] [2000] AC 486.

dants' guarantee was conditional on the claimants having taken all reasonable steps to satisfy themselves that the bills of exchange were valid and enforceable. As the claimants had failed to do this, the guarantee was not binding on the defendants and the claimants were left out of pocket. The claimants sued the defendants, seeking to recover the £10m that they had lost as a result of purchasing Chong's bills of exchange. The claimants argued that they were entitled to sue the defendants because the defendants were vicariously liable in respect of Chong's deceit. As Chong had no connection with the defendants, the claimants were forced to argue that: (1) Pillai was vicariously liable in respect of Chong's deceit (which was true: Pillai and Chong had engaged in a joint venture – defrauding the claimants – and Chong committed the tort of deceit in furthering that venture) *and* (2) because Pillai's acts, which made him vicariously liable in respect of Chong's deceit, were performed in the course of his employment by the defendants, the defendants were vicariously liable along with Pillai in respect of Chong's deceit.

The House of Lords thought that (2) was not true: one can only be vicariously liable in respect of *torts* committed by one's agents, one's employees, one's partners and those with whom one is engaged in a joint venture. As Chong fell within none of these categories, the defendants could not be vicariously liable in respect of Chong's deceit, even if one of their employees *was* vicariously liable in respect of Chong's deceit by reason of things done by him in the course of his employment. The fact that Pillai had not himself committed a tort[112] – but was merely vicariously liable in respect of the tort committed by Chong – was crucial. If Pillai had committed a tort in assisting Chong in his scheme to defraud the claimants then the claimants might have been able to argue that the defendants were vicariously liable in respect of Pillai's tort. But, in fact, Chong was the only tortfeasor here and it was impossible to find that the defendants were vicariously liable in respect of the tort committed by him.

---

[112] See above, p. 407.

NON-COMPENSATORY DAMAGES

We saw much earlier in the book that many people believe – wrongly – that the function of tort law is to determine when one person will be entitled to sue another for compensation in respect of some loss that he has suffered.[1] Let's say that Paul is one such person. Paul will find it difficult to understand the areas of law that we are going to look at in the next few chapters. For these areas of law allow a claimant to sue a defendant in tort for damages that are *not* designed to compensate the claimant for some losses that he has suffered, but instead serve some other function. So these areas of law represent a problem for Paul, a problem which he will characteristically react to in one of three ways.

First, Paul might attempt to ignore or minimise these areas of law, to brush over them as not very important.

Secondly, Paul might attempt to distort these areas of law – to argue that the kinds of damages that are awarded to claimants under these areas of law are *really* compensatory in nature. One sees this reaction in, for example, the Law Commission's analysis of aggravated damages, according to which aggravated damages are designed to *compensate* the victim of a tort for any *distress* she might feel at the way the tort was committed.[2] Again one sees this reaction among academics who argue that when B – whose property has been used by A without B's permission – is allowed to sue A for *restitutionary damages* designed to make A pay B a reasonable sum for the use he's enjoyed of B's property, those damages are really designed to *compensate* B for the fact that A, in using B's property, wrongfully deprived B of the *right to bargain* with A for a fee for using her property.[3] And you again see this reaction in Lord Nicholls's analysis of what is happening when B – whose property has been converted by A – is allowed to sue A for damages equal to the value of that property at the time it was converted. According to him, the damages payable to B here are really *compensatory* in nature, designed to compensate B for the fact that A did not return B's property to him, instead of converting it.[4]

Thirdly, Paul might condemn these areas of law as 'anomalous' and call for their abolition. One sees this reaction in Lord Scott's speech in *Kuddus v Chief Constable of Leicestershire*, which called for the abolition of awards of exemplary damages in tort cases on the ground that 'the function of an award of damages in our civil justice system is to compensate the claimant for a wrong done to him. The wrong may consist of a breach of contract, or a tort, or an interference with some right of the claimant under public law. But whatever the wrong

---

[1] See below, p. 666.

[2] Law Com No. 247, *Aggravated, Exemplary and Restitutionary Damages*, para 2.1; Tettenborn 2003, 30. Beever 2003a contends, alternatively, that aggravated damages are designed to compensate the victim of a tort for any injury to his moral dignity that he suffered as a result of the way that tort was committed.

[3] Sharpe & Waddams 1982; also Tettenborn 2003, 48–9.

[4] *Kuwait Airways Corpn v Iraqi Airways Company (Nos 4 and 5)* [2002] 2 AC 883, at [67] (per Lord Nicholls).

may consist of the award of damages should be compensatory in its intent. Measured by this fundamental principle of damages, an award of exemplary damages, the intention of which is not to compensate the victim of a wrong but to punish its perpetrator, is an anomaly.'[5]

Whichever way Paul reacts to the areas of law dealt with in the following chapters, he will fail to do them justice. These areas of law are important: they cannot be brushed under the carpet. Moreover, the kinds of damages awarded to tort claimants under these areas of law cannot be explained away on the basis that they are really compensatory in nature: to say that is fundamentally to misunderstand their nature and rationale. Finally, to call for the abolition of – say – awards of exemplary damages on the ground that they do not fit with the speaker's preconceived vision of what tort law says or does is to condemn them for no good reason whatsoever.

The only way to avoid falling into this trap that Paul has fallen into is to recognise that the function of tort law is *not* to determine when one person can sue another for compensation in respect of some loss that he has suffered. Rather, tort law serves two functions: it helps determine what specific duties we owe each other; and it determines what remedies will be available when someone breaches one of those duties.[6] Once you realise this, you will be able to do justice to these areas of law – to appreciate their importance, to understand them correctly, and to take a reasoned view as to how, if at all, these areas of law should be reformed. That is what we will try to do in the following chapters.

---

[5] [2002] 2 AC 122, at [95]. Weir 2001 rightly ridicules Lord Scott's argument (at 202) as 'a fine example of question-begging, that is, assuming what you are setting out to prove, otherwise known as *petitio principii* . . .'

[6] See above, p. 36.

36

NOMINAL DAMAGES

Suppose A has committed a tort in relation to B but B has not suffered any actionable loss as a result of A's tort. Obviously, in this situation, B will not be entitled to recover anything by way of compensatory damages from A. However, B may be entitled to sue A for *nominal damages*, that is a nominal sum equal to £5.[1] Whether B will be entitled to sue A for such damages will depend on whether the tort committed by A is 'actionable *per se*'.

The following torts are actionable *per se*: torts involving a trespass to someone's person;[2] trespass to land; private nuisances involving an interference with someone's right to light or other rights attached to his land.[3] The classic example of a tort that is *not* actionable *per se* is negligence. So if A drives recklessly down the street and almost runs over a nearby pedestrian, that pedestrian will not be entitled to sue A for nominal damages. Private nuisances not involving an interference with someone's right to light or other rights attached to his land do not seem to be actionable *per se*. It is unclear whether the tort of trespass to goods is actionable *per se*, but what authority there is on the matter indicates that it is not.[4] Recent authority indicates that the tort of misfeasance in public office will be actionable *per se* in cases where the tort involves an interference with a 'constitutional right'.[5] It seems that it will be very rare for the breach of a statutory duty owed to another to be actionable *per se*.[6]

Libel is often said to be a tort that is actionable *per se*. This is because if A publishes to C a statement referring to B that is defamatory of B, B will still be entitled to sue A for a small sum in damages even if she cannot show that she

---

[1] £5 is currently the conventional figure awarded in making an award of nominal damages: see, for example, *Brandeis Goldschmidt & Co.* v *Western Transport* [1981] QB 864, 874A; *Watkins* v *Secretary of State for the Home Department* [2004] EWCA Civ 966, at [61]. Until the 1980s, the conventional sum awarded in making an award of nominal damages was £2: see, for example, *Child* v *Stenning* (1879) 11 Ch D 82; *Sykes* v *Midland Bank Executor & Trustee Co.* [1971] 1 QB 113.

[2] That is, assault, battery and false imprisonment.

[3] See *Nicholls* v *Ely Beet Sugar Factory Ltd (No. 2)* [1936] 1 Ch 343, 348–9.

[4] *Slater* v *Swann* (1730) 3 Stra 872, 93 ER 906.

[5] *Watkins* v *Secretary of State for the Home Department* [2004] EWCA Civ 966, at [48] (per Brooke LJ). The Court of Appeal adopted (at [50]) the definition of a 'constitutional right' offered by Laws J in *R* v *Lord Chancellor ex p Witham* [1998] QB 575, 581: 'a constitutional right ... cannot be abrogated by the state saved by specific provision in an Act of Parliament, or by regulations [passed under] legislation specifically [conferring] the power to abrogate that right'. Under this definition, the right to vote and the right of access to the courts count as constitutional rights.

[6] In *Cullen* v *Chief Constable of the Royal Ulster Constabulary* [2003] 1 WLR 1763 (discussed above, pp. 481–2), Lord Hutton held that the breach of a statutory duty owed by A to B might be actionable *per se* if the statutory duty was contained in a written constitution, but if the duty in question was imposed by an ordinary statute, A's breach of that duty would only be actionable if it caused B to suffer 'loss or injury of a kind for which the law awards damages': ibid., at [47], quoting *Pickering* v *Liverpool Daily Post* [1991] 2 AC 370, at 420 (per Lord Bridge).

suffered any loss as a result of A's publication. However, the damages payable to B in such a case will often be much smaller than £5, the sum which is normally recoverable by the victim of a tort that is actionable *per se* who has not suffered any actionable loss as a result of that tort being committed.[7] The better analysis of what is going on in a libel case such as B's is that B does not have to *prove* that she has suffered any loss as a result of A's libel. Instead, it will be *presumed* that she did suffer some loss as a result of A's libel and it will be up to a jury or a judge to put a figure on how much of a loss that she suffered. If the loss suffered by B seems to the jury or judge to be very small because, for example, C did not believe A's statement or because B was of such bad character that she had no reputation to lose, then B will not be awarded very much by way of damages[8] – but the damages paid to her will still be *compensatory* in nature, not *nominal*.

Why, it might be wondered, would the victim of a tort ever sue the person who committed that tort for nominal damages? Three reasons may be given.

(1) *Setting the record straight*. If A has committed a tort that is actionable *per se* in relation to B but B has suffered no actionable loss as a result, B might want to sue A for nominal damages in order to have it publicly established that A committed a tort in acting as he did. This is why, for example, if A defames B, B might want to sue A even though she has suffered no loss as a result of A's defaming her: she will want it to be publicly established that whatever A said about her was untrue.[9]

(2) *Assertion of right*. If A has committed a tort that is *actionable per se* in relation to B by doing *x* but B has suffered no actionable loss as a result, B might still want to sue A for nominal damages because if she does not sue him for doing *x*, he might acquire a *licence* to do *x* in the future.

Suppose, for example, that A regularly walks across B's land without her permission but she does not suffer any loss as a result of his walking across her land. Because A's conduct amounts to the tort of trespass to land, B will be entitled to sue A for nominal damages here. Now: B will have an incentive to sue A for such damages, because if she does not A might – if he continues to walk across her land – acquire a *right by prescription* to walk across B's land.

Similarly, in *Bower* v *Hill*[10] the defendant blocked a drain which lay between the claimant's land and a nearby river. In so doing he committed a tort: the claimant had a right of way over the drain. The claimant did not suffer any loss as a result of the defendant's blocking the drain as it was already choked with mud. However, the claimant still sued the defendant for nominal damages (as he was entitled to do as the tort committed by the defendant in blocking the

---

[7] In *Newstead* v *London Express Newspaper* [1940] 1 KB 377 the claimant was awarded one farthing. In *Reynolds* v *Times Newspapers Ltd* [2001] 2 AC 127 the claimant was awarded one penny.

[8] If the damages payable to B are extremely small because she had no reputation to lose when A libelled her, they will be known as *contemptuous* or *derisory* damages.

[9] Of course, a finding of liability in a defamation case does not indicate that what the defendant said about the claimant was untrue; it merely indicates that the defendant could not prove that what he said about the claimant was true (see above, pp. 301–2).

[10] (1835) 1 Bing NC 549, 131 ER 1229.

drain was actionable *per se*) because, as Tindal CJ noted, if '[the claimant] acquiesced in [the blockage of the drain] for twenty years, [that] would become evidence of a renunciation and abandonment of the [claimant's] right of way'[11] and everyone would, after that time, be free to block the drain.

(3) *Punishment.* If A commits a tort that is actionable *per se* in relation to B but B has suffered no actionable loss as a result, B might want to sue A for nominal damages as a way of punishing A for committing that tort. The punishment would not of course consist in having to pay B £5 in nominal damages; the punishment would consist in having to repay the legal costs incurred by B in bringing her case against A – which would, obviously, come to a lot more than £5. However, such a plan might well backfire on B: if the courts thought that B's sole motivation in suing A for nominal damages was to inflict a bill for her legal costs on him, then they might well refuse to award B costs and she would have to bear those costs herself.[12]

---

[11] Ibid., 555, 1231.

[12] See Devlin J's remarks in *Anglo-Cyprian Agencies* v *Paphos Industries* [1951] 1 All ER 873, at 874D–G doubting whether a claimant who has obtained nominal damages from a defendant should always be entitled to recover the costs incurred by him in suing the defendant for such damages.

37

AGGRAVATED DAMAGES

THE NATURE OF AGGRAVATED DAMAGES

Suppose that A has committed a tort in relation to B and B is entitled to sue A as a result for either compensatory damages or nominal damages. In such a case, B will *also* be entitled to sue A for *aggravated damages* if: (*a*) A acted in an arrogant and high-handed way in committing his tort or in dealing with B's claims to be compensated for the actionable losses that she suffered as a result of A's committing that tort; *and* (*b*) the tort committed by A is the sort of tort in respect of which aggravated damages may be claimed.

What are aggravated damages? There is some dispute over this question. The dominant view is that aggravated damages are designed to compensate the victim of a tort, who has been treated in an arrogant and high-handed way by the person who committed that tort, for the distress suffered by her as a result of being treated in that way.[1] On this view, aggravated damages are a form of compensatory damages, though they are unusual in that they can sometimes be awarded to the victim of a tort not to compensate her for the actionable losses suffered by her as a result of that tort being committed but to compensate her for losses suffered by her as a result of the way the person who committed the tort in question treated her *after* he committed that tort.[2]

The better view, we would submit, is that aggravated damages are awarded in order to assuage the anger and outrage felt by the victim of a tort who has been treated in an arrogant and high-handed way by the person who committed that tort. On this view, aggravated damages are not a form of compensatory damages; they are not awarded in order to compensate the victim of a tort for any distress suffered by her

---

[1] *Rookes* v *Barnard* [1964] AC 1129, 1221 (per Lord Devlin); *McCarey* v *Associated Newspapers Ltd (No. 2)* [1965] 2 QB 86, 104G–105A (per Pearson LJ); *Broome* v *Cassell & Co. Ltd* [1972] AC 1027, 1124 (per Lord Diplock); *Archer* v *Brown* [1985] QB 401, 424–5 (per Peter Pain J); *Thompson* v *Commissioner of Police of the Metropolis* [1998] QB 498, 512. Windeyer J criticised this view of aggravated damages in the Australian case of *Uren* v *John Fairfax & Sons Pty Ltd* (1965–66) 117 CLR 118, 151: 'The theory is that [aggravated] damages are ... compensatory because the more insulting or reprehensible the defendant's conduct the greater the indignity that the claimant suffers and the more he should receive for the outrage to his feelings ... This ... explanation is convenient, but not altogether convincing. Two objections may be made. First, the satisfaction that the claimant gets is that the defendant has been made to pay for what he did ... Secondly, conceding an indignity suffered must be paid for, why is the degree of indignity that the claimant suffers to be measured by considering what was in the mind of the defendant, the malice or motive that moved him?'

[2] This may be why Birks 1996a argues that in aggravated damages cases, *two* torts have been committed – the primary tort committed by the tortfeasor and a secondary tort, committed by insulting the victim of the primary tort.

666

but in order to pacify her.[3] There is some support for this view in the cases.[4] In *Duffy* v *Eastern Health and Social Services Board*,[5] the defendants acted unlawfully in failing to appoint one of their employees, the claimant, to a permanent position because she was Catholic. The claimant was awarded £15,000 in compensation for the distress she suffered as a result of the defendants' conduct. But she was *also* awarded £5,000 in aggravated damages because of the high-handed and arrogant way she had been treated by the defendants in, first of all, blatantly discriminating against her on grounds of her religion and, secondly defending her claim to be compensated for the actionable losses that she had suffered as a result of their discrimination.

Clearly, the aggravated damages awarded to the claimant in *Duffy* were not awarded to her in order to compensate her for the distress suffered by her as a result of the way in which she was treated by the defendants: the award of £15,000 fully compensated her for that distress. Rather, aggravated damages were awarded to the claimant in *Duffy* in order to assuage the anger she felt towards the defendants as a result of the way they treated her both in discriminating against her and in attempting to frustrate her attempts to obtain some redress in respect of that discrimination.[6]

In *AB* v *South West Water Services Ltd*,[7] the Court of Appeal addressed the question: can aggravated damages be awarded in a negligence case? Answering this question in the negative, Sir Thomas Bingham MR remarked: 'I know of no precedent for awarding damages for indignation aroused by a defendant's conduct [where the defendant has merely acted negligently or committed some other non-intentional tort].'[8] Clearly, Sir Thomas Bingham MR took the view that when aggravated damages are awarded to the victim of a tort, they are

---

[3] In *Merest* v *Harvey* (1814) 5 Taunt 442, 128 ER 761, the claimant was shooting game on his land when the defendant, who was drunk and happened to be passing by the claimant's land, asked the claimant if he could join the claimant's shooting party. The claimant refused and warned the defendant not to trespass on his land or shoot his game. The defendant took umbrage at this and walked onto the claimant's land and started shooting at the claimant's game. The claimant sued the defendant for trespass and was awarded £500 damages by a jury. The £500 award was clearly intended to punish the defendant for his conduct, the actual loss suffered by the claimant as a result of the defendant's trespass was minimal. The jury's award was upheld on appeal. Heath J remarked: 'It goes to prevent the practice of duelling if juries are permitted to punish insult by [making awards of exemplary] damages' (Ibid.). On the view of aggravated damages taken here, he could have said the same of awards of aggravated damages.

[4] See, in addition to the authorities mentioned in the text, *Deane* v *Ealing London Borough Council* [1993] ICR 329, where it was conceded that aggravated damages are entirely distinct from damages awarded to the victim of a tort in order to compensate her for any distress suffered by her as a result of that tort being committed: Ibid., 335C.

[5] [1992] IRLR 251.

[6] See also *Prison Service* v *Johnson* [1997] ICR 275 where the claimant, who was the victim of unlawful racial discrimination by the defendants, was awarded £20,000 to compensate him for the distress suffered by him as a result of the defendants' conduct *and* £7,500 in aggravated damages.

[7] [1993] QB 507.

[8] Ibid., 532. It is necessary to insert the passage in square brackets because otherwise Sir Thomas Bingham's remarks may be read as indicating that aggravated damages may *never* be awarded to the victim of a tort. Cf. Smith J's remarks in *Prison Service* v *Johnson* [1997] ICR 275, at 286H–287B: '[It has been suggested] that Sir Thomas Bingham MR was [in *AB* v *South West Water Services Ltd*] making a statement of general application that there is not or should not be any such thing as an award of aggravated damages ... [However it must be] realised that those remarks were made in the context of a claim for damages ... based upon the torts of negligence, non-intentional nuisance and non-intentional breach of statutory duty ... [Sir Thomas Bingham MR's] dicta were not [therefore] of general application and were not intended to change the law relating to aggravated damages ...'

awarded to her in recognition of the anger felt by her at the way she was treated by the person who committed the tort in question.

THE AVAILABILITY OF AGGRAVATED DAMAGES

To recap: if A has committed a tort in relation to B and B is entitled to sue A for either compensatory damages or nominal damages as a result, then B will also be entitled to sue A for aggravated damages if: (*a*) A acted in an arrogant and high-handed way in committing his tort or in dealing with B's claims to be compensated for the actionable losses suffered by her as a result of A's committing that tort; *and* (*b*) the tort committed by A is the kind of tort in respect of which aggravated damages may be claimed. These two preconditions on B's being able to sue A for aggravated damages need some explanation.

Arrogant and high-handed conduct

In discussing when a tortfeasor will be held to have acted in an arrogant and high-handed way towards the victim of his tort, we have to distinguish between cases where the tortfeasor is alleged to have acted in an arrogant and high-handed way *in committing his tort* and cases where a tortfeasor is alleged to have acted in an arrogant and high-handed way *after committing his tort*.

(1) *Conduct in committing the tort.* Suppose A has committed a tort in relation to B. When can we say that A acted in an arrogant and high-handed way in committing that tort? The available authorities provide some guidance.

They indicate that someone who has *knowingly* committed a tort can be said to have acted in an arrogant and high-handed way in committing that tort. So – in *Thompson* v *Hill*,[9] the claimant's business as a tailor was disrupted when the defendant built some extra floors on his house, thus blocking off the light to the premises on which the claimant conducted his business. The defendant knew that his building the extra floors on his house would prevent the claimant's premises receiving any light and he also knew that the claimant had a right to receive such light. He therefore knew when he built the extra floors on his house that his doing so would amount to a private nuisance. Aggravated damages were awarded against the defendant and the award was upheld on appeal. Again, in *McMillan* v *Singh*[10] the claimant was a tenant of the defendant's, paying £16 a week rent. The defendant realised that if the claimant left, he could rent out the claimant's room for £26 a week. As a result the defendant threw the claimant out along with his belongings. The defendant knew that he had no right to do this and therefore knew that in throwing the claimant and his belongings out of his room, he was committing a tort. Aggravated damages were awarded against the defendant.

The authorities also indicate that someone who has unknowingly committed a tort can still be said to have acted in an arrogant and high-handed way in commit-

[9] (1870) LR 5 CP 564.
[10] (1984) 17 HLR 120.

ting that tort if he humiliated or insulted the victim of that tort in committing the tort in question. So, for example, in *Thompson v Commissioner of Police of the Metropolis*[11] the Court of Appeal held that police officers who commit the tort of false imprisonment by arresting someone when they are not entitled to do so can be sued for aggravated damages if, in making the arrest, they humiliated the person being arrested or otherwise behaved in a 'high-handed, insulting, malicious or oppressive manner [in conducting] the arrest',[12] and this is so even if the police officers thought they were entitled to make the arrest in question and therefore did not knowingly commit the tort of false imprisonment in making the arrest.

(2) *Conduct after the tort was committed.* Again, suppose A has committed a tort in relation to B. When can we say that A acted in an arrogant and high-handed manner in dealing with B's claims to be compensated for the actionable losses suffered by her as a result of A's tort? Again, the authorities provide some guidance.

In *Sutcliffe v Pressdram Ltd*,[13] the Court of Appeal held that if A has wrongfully defamed B, A will act in an arrogant and high-handed manner in dealing with B's claims to be compensated for the actionable losses suffered by her as a result of A's defaming her if: (*a*) he fails to make any or sufficient apology for and withdrawal of his defamatory statement; (*b*) he repeats the statement; (*c*) he tries to deter B from proceeding with her claim against A; (*d*) he tries to defeat B's claims by persisting, 'by way of a prolonged or hostile cross-examination of [B] or in turgid speeches to the jury, in a plea of justification which is bound to fail';[14] (*e*) he tries to give wider publicity to his defamatory statement in the preliminaries to the trial of B's action against A or in the trial itself; (*f*) he engages in a general persecution of B.[15]

In *Ley v Hamilton*,[16] the claimant libelled the defendant by publishing to some business partners of the defendant a letter which alleged that the defendant had embezzled money. This was completely untrue. When the claimant sued the defendant for libel, the defendant unsurprisingly did not seek to rely in his pleadings on a defence of justification but instead claimed that his statement to the claimant's business partners was protected by qualified privilege. However, when the case came to trial and the defendant was cross-examined, he persisted in claiming that the claimant *had* embezzled money. The claimant won his case and was awarded aggravated damages as well as damages to compensate him for the actionable losses suffered by him as a result of the defendant's libel. The award of aggravated damages was upheld by the House of Lords.

In *Alexander v Home Office*,[17] the Court of Appeal held that if A commits a tort by unlawfully discriminating against B on grounds of her race, A will act in an arrogant and high-handed way in dealing with B's claims to be compensated

---

[11] [1998] QB 498.
[12] Ibid., 516.
[13] [1991] 1 QB 153.
[14] Ibid., 184E–F.
[15] Ibid., 184D–G.
[16] (1935) 153 LT 384.
[17] [1988] 1 WLR 968.

for the actionable losses suffered by her as a result of A's discrimination if: (*a*) he makes untrue and injurious allegations about B in an attempt to establish that his acts of discrimination against B were not racially motivated; *or* (*b*) he conspicuously fails to acknowledge that his acts of discrimination against B were unjustified.[18] Similarly, if A commits the tort of false imprisonment by arresting B when he had no right to do so, he will act in an arrogant and high-handed way in dealing with B's claims to be compensated for the losses suffered by her as a result of A's falsely imprisoning her if he attempts, through making untrue allegations about B, to justify his arrest of B.[19]

The torts in respect of which aggravated damages may be awarded

It has been established that aggravated damages may be awarded against someone who has committed one of the following torts: assault or battery, false imprisonment, libel or slander, trespass to land, private nuisance, using unlawful means to harm another, deceit, malicious falsehood, malicious prosecution, unlawfully discriminating against another on grounds of race contrary to the Race Relations Act 1976 and unlawfully discriminating against another on grounds of sex contrary to the Sex Discrimination Act 1975.[20]

It has also been established that aggravated damages may *not* be awarded in a negligence case.[21] There seems no good reason why this should be so. In *Kralj v McGrath*, Woolf J explained that 'it would be wholly inappropriate to introduce into claims ... for ... negligence, the concept of aggravated damage. [Making such damages available in negligence cases would] be wholly inconsistent with the general approach to damages in this area, which is to compensate the [claimant] for the loss that she has actually suffered, so far as it is possible to do so, by the award of monetary compensation and not to treat those damages as being a matter which reflects the degree of negligence ... of the defendant.'[22] This is, of course, no explanation at all.[23]

---

[18] Ibid., 979C.

[19] *Thompson v Commissioner of Police of the Metropolis* [1998] QB 498, 518.

[20] Assault or battery: *W v Meah* [1986] 1 All ER 935. False imprisonment: *Thompson v Commissioner of Police of the Metropolis* [1998] QB 498. Libel or slander: *Ley v Hamilton* (1935) 153 LT 384; *Sutcliffe v Pressdram Ltd* [1991] 1 QB 153. Trespass to land: *Drane v Evangelou* [1978] 1 WLR 455, 461H, 462E; *McMillan v Singh* (1984) 17 HLR 120. Private nuisance: *Thompson v Hill* (1870) LR 5 CP 564. Intentionally inflicting harm on another using unlawful means: *Messenger Newspapers Group Ltd v National Graphical Association* [1984] IRLR 397. Deceit: *Archer v Brown* [1985] QB 401, 426D–G. Malicious falsehood: *Khodaparast v Shad* [2000] 1 WLR 618. Malicious prosecution: *Thompson v Commissioner of Police of the Metropolis* [1998] QB 498. Discriminating against another on grounds of race: *Prison Service v Johnson* [1997] ICR 275. Discriminating against another on grounds of sex: *Ministry of Defence v Meredith* [1995] IRLR 539.

[21] *Kralj v McGrath* [1986] 1 All ER 54; *AB v South West Water Services Ltd* [1993] QB 507.

[22] [1986] 1 All ER 54, 61e-g.

[23] Cf. Lord Scott's 'explanation' (set out above, p. 662) why exemplary damages should not be awarded in tort cases in *Kuddus v Chief Constable of Leicestershire* [2002] 2 AC 122, at [95].

Further points

A couple of further points need to be made about the circumstances in which one person will be entitled to sue another for aggravated damages:

(1) *Aggravated damages and artificial legal persons.* Suppose that A has committed a tort in relation to B and A acted in an arrogant and high-handed manner in committing that tort. Suppose further that B is a company or some other kind of artificial legal person such as a local authority. Because B is an artificial legal person, it will be incapable of feeling anger or distress at the way it was treated by A. Given this, it would seem strange to allow B to sue A for aggravated damages, whatever view one takes as to the nature of aggravated damages.

However, in *Messenger Newspapers Group Ltd* v *National Graphical Association*[24] Caulfield J remarked 'aggravated damages can be awarded against inanimate legal entities like limited companies, and I cannot see any reason why the same legal entities cannot be awarded aggravated ... damages'.[25] On the other hand, in *Columbia Picture Industries Inc.* v *Robinson*[26] the defendants wrongfully and arrogantly seized a number of video tapes which were on sale in a video shop run by one Robinson and a company controlled by him. Scott J held that Robinson and the company were entitled to sue the defendants for damages. Robinson was allowed to sue the defendants for compensatory damages and aggravated damages. The company was only allowed to sue the defendants for compensatory damages. The reason why the company was only allowed to sue the defendants for compensatory damages but not aggravated damages was that 'contumely and affront affect individuals, not inanimate corporations'.[27]

(2) *Lack of awareness of arrogant and high-handed conduct.* Suppose that A has committed a tort in relation to B and A acted in an arrogant and high-handed manner in committing that tort. If B is unaware that A acted in an arrogant and high-handed manner in committing the tort in question then there will be no reason to award her aggravated damages.[28] In such a case, B will not feel angry or distressed at the manner in which A acted.

In *Ministry of Defence* v *Meredith*,[29] the defendants unlawfully sacked the claimant when she became pregnant. The claimant sued the defendants for compensatory *and* aggravated damages. As part of her case, she sought to obtain discovery of documents that would indicate whether or not the defendants had known they were acting unlawfully in sacking her because she was pregnant. The Employment Appeal Tribunal held that the claimant was not entitled to discovery of those documents as they had no relevance to her claim.

---

[24] [1984] IRLR 397.
[25] Ibid., at [77].
[26] [1987] 1 Ch 38.
[27] Ibid., 88H.
[28] Again, this will be true whatever view one takes as to the nature of aggravated damages.
[29] [1995] IRLR 539.

They obviously had no relevance to her claim for compensatory damages; and they had no relevance to her claim for aggravated damages as she would only have been entitled to claim such damages from the defendants if she *already* knew that the defendants had acted in an arrogant and high-handed manner in sacking her.

38

EXEMPLARY DAMAGES

THE AVAILABILITY OF EXEMPLARY DAMAGES

Suppose that A has committed a tort in relation to B and B is entitled to sue A for either compensatory damages or nominal damages. In this situation, B may also be entitled to sue A for *exemplary damages* – that is, damages that are designed to *punish* A for committing his tort.[1]

B will only be allowed to sue A for such damages if three conditions are fulfilled.[2] First, it must be shown that A deserves to be punished for committing his tort. Secondly, it must be shown that if exemplary damages were not awarded against A, he would not be adequately punished for committing his tort. Thirdly, it must be shown that awarding exemplary damages against A would not fall foul of the limits that the House of Lords' decision in *Rookes* v *Barnard*[3] placed on when such awards could be made.[4] Let's now look at each of these conditions in turn.

---

[1] Another name for exemplary damages is *punitive damages*. English courts refer to the kind of damages discussed here as 'exemplary damages': see *Broome* v *Cassell & Co. Ltd* [1972] AC 1027, 1073–4 (per Lord Hailsham LC)). Courts in the United States and Canada refer to the kind of damages discussed here as 'punitive damages'. The American usage is preferable because it makes clearer why the kind of damages discussed here are awarded: to punish someone who has committed a tort for committing that tort. However, we will refer to the kind of damages discussed here as 'exemplary damages' in order to avoid any confusion.

[2] See, generally, Ghandi 1990.

[3] [1964] AC 1129.

[4] *Important note*. It used to be that a *fourth* condition had to be fulfilled before an award of exemplary damages could be made against A. It had to be shown that the tort committed by A was the *right kind of tort* – that is, the kind of tort in respect of which exemplary damages could be awarded. However, that condition was abolished by the House of Lords in *Kuddus* v *Chief Constable of Leicestershire* [2002] 2 AC 122. For reasons that are best forgotten, the Court of Appeal ruled in *AB* v *South West Water Services Ltd* [1993] QB 507 that a tort would only count as the right kind of tort if there existed some case pre-dating the decision of the House of Lords in *Rookes* v *Barnard* in which exemplary damages were awarded against a defendant who had committed that tort. This meant, for example, that exemplary damages could *not* be awarded against a public servant who committed the tort of misfeasance in public office as there was no case decided before 1964 in which exemplary damages were awarded against someone who committed that tort. *Kuddus* was a misfeasance in public office case in which exemplary damages *were* claimed. The House of Lords refused to follow the decision of the Court of Appeal in the *AB* case and held that the claim for exemplary damages could not be struck out on the basis that there was no case decided before 1964 in which exemplary damages were awarded against a defendant who committed the tort of misfeasance in public office. Subject to one doubt, it seems then that there is now no limit on the kinds of torts in respect of which exemplary damages can be awarded: for confirmation of this point see, for example, [2002] 2 AC 122, at [45] (per Lord Mackay), [60] (per Lord Nicholls), [120] (per Lord Scott). The one doubt arises in the case where a tort involved the breach of a statutory duty owed to another. In *Kuddus*, Lord Mackay thought (at [46]) that exemplary damages could only be awarded against someone who breached a statutory duty owed to another if the statute that created that duty expressly authorised exemplary damages to be awarded against someone who breached that duty. However, it is not clear whether the other Law Lords who decided *Kuddus* agreed with him on that point.

The tortfeasor must deserve to be punished

One might think that all tortfeasors deserve to be punished for their behaviour because they have acted unlawfully. However, this is an extreme view. For example, suppose that a police officer arrests someone thinking that he is entitled to do so. However, he was not in fact entitled to make the arrest and his arrest was therefore wrongful. It is hard to argue in this case that the police officer deserves to be punished: while he acted wrongfully, he also acted with the best intentions and attempted to stay the right side of the law.[5]

So the fact that someone has acted wrongfully does not necessarily mean that he or she deserves to be punished for acting as he or she did. Something more is required before we can conclude that punishment is deserved.[6] What that 'something more' must be divided the Privy Council in *A v Bottrill*.[7] The claimant in that case had four cervical smear tests over four years. In each case, the smear test was examined by the defendant pathologist and in each case he gave the claimant a clean bill of health. However, the defendant failed in each case to inspect the claimant's smear test with a proper degree of care and skill. Had the defendant done so, he would have spotted that the claimant was in danger of developing cervical cancer and the claimant would have received treatment that would have prevented the cancer developing. However, because the claimant's smear tests were not properly examined, the claimant's condition went untreated and she developed cervical cancer.

The claimant sued the defendant for exemplary damages.[8] Now it was possible that the defendant was not aware at the time he examined the claimant's smear test that he was doing anything improper or negligent in examining the claimant's smear test in the way he did. At the same time, the method used by the defendant to examine smear tests such as the claimant's resulted in his having a spectacularly high error rate in examining smear tests: on average, for every two smear tests that he received which revealed signs that the patient from whom the smear test was taken was in danger of developing cervical cancer, he would report one of them as 'normal'. So it was possible that the defendant was not *conscious* at the time he examined the claimant's smear test that he was doing anything wrong in examining the smear test. At the same time, the defendant's conduct in examining the claimant's smear test fell so far below the standard expected of people in the defendant's position that it was *outrageous* for him to behave in the way he did.

The majority in the Privy Council thought that an award of exemplary damages could properly be made against a tortfeasor such as the defendant

---

[5] See *Holden v Chief Constable of Lancashire* [1987] 1 QB 380, 388E.

[6] The criminal law acknowledges this point. To commit a criminal offence – and thereby render yourself liable to be punished under the criminal law – it is usually not enough for you to commit a wrongful act (an *actus reus*); you usually also have to have committed that wrongful act with a guilty mind (a *mens rea*).

[7] [2003] 1 AC 449.

[8] As the case occurred in New Zealand, she was not allowed to sue the defendant for compensation for the fact that she developed cervical cancer: that was covered under the New Zealand Accident Compensation Scheme (summarised below, pp. 791–2). However, s 396 of the Accident Insurance Act 1998 preserved the powers of the courts in New Zealand to award exemplary damages against defendants in personal injury cases.

whose conduct was so outrageous as to call for condemnation. Lords Millett and Hutton dissented, arguing that exemplary damages should only be awarded against a tortfeasor who consciously acted unlawfully: they therefore thought exemplary damages should only be awarded against the defendant if he was aware when he was examining the claimant's test that the method employed by him in examining that test fell short of the standards expected of him.

Decisions of the Privy Council are not binding on the English courts, but there is no reason to think that the majority's approach in *Bottrill* will not be adopted by the English courts in deciding whether or not an award of exemplary damages is warranted in a particular case. So if A has committed a tort in relation to B, the first thing B is likely to have to establish if she wants to sue A for exemplary damages is that A's conduct was so outrageous that it deserves condemnation. If that is true, then A will deserve to be punished for his behaviour.

An award of exemplary damages must be required

Even if A does deserve to be punished for his behaviour, exemplary damages will not be awarded against him if it is not necessary to award such damages against him to ensure that he is adequately punished for his behaviour.

So, for example, if A has already been criminally punished for committing his tort, then exemplary damages will not be awarded against him. In *Archer* v *Brown*,[9] for instance, a defendant defrauded the claimant of £30,000, thereby committing the tort of deceit in relation to the claimant. Peter Pain J held that exemplary damages could not be awarded against the defendant because he had already been sent to prison for defrauding the claimant.[10] Similarly, if A has lost his job or incurred disciplinary proceedings from his employer for committing his tort, it is unlikely that an award of exemplary damages will be made against him.[11] Even if none of these things have happened to A, exemplary damages will still not be awarded against A if allowing B to sue A for compensatory damages and – if available – aggravated damages – would adequately punish A for committing his tort.[12]

---

[9] [1985] QB 401.

[10] In light of this, it is doubtful whether the case of *Ashgar* v *Ahmed* (1984) 17 HLR 120 was correctly decided. In that case, the Court of Appeal held that the claimant – a tenant who was unlawfully evicted by his landlord, the defendant – was entitled to sue the defendant for £1,000 in exemplary damages even though the defendant had already been punished under the Protection from Eviction Act 1977 for evicting the claimant. (The defendant was fined £750 for evicting the claimant.)

[11] *Thompson* v *Commissioner of Police of the Metropolis* [1998] QB 498, 518.

[12] See Lord Devlin's speech in *Rookes* v *Barnard* [1964] AC 1129, at 1228 (jury is only allowed to award exemplary damages against a defendant in a tort case if 'the sum which they have in mind to award as compensation (which may, of course, be a sum aggravated by the way in which the defendant has behaved . . .) is inadequate to punish him for his outrageous conduct . . .').

Rookes v *Barnard*

Suppose that A has committed a tort in relation to B, that A deserves to be punished for committing that tort and that if B is not allowed to sue A for exemplary damages A will not be adequately punished for committing that tort. Even if all this is established, B will still not be allowed to sue A for exemplary damages if she is not allowed to do so under the decision of the House of Lords in *Rookes* v *Barnard*.[13]

In that case, the House of Lords set very tight limits on when exemplary damages may be awarded against a defendant in a tort case. They[14] held that if A has committed a tort, exemplary damages can *only* be awarded against him if: (1) A was a 'servant of the government' at the time he committed his tort and he acted in an 'oppressive, arbitrary or unconstitutional' manner in committing that tort;[15] *or* (2) A committed his tort because he figured that he would make more money committing that tort than he would have to pay out in damages to the victim of that tort; *or* (3) statute law authorises an award of exemplary damages to be made against someone who has committed the kind of tort that A committed. If A's case does not fall into one of these categories, then exemplary damages cannot be awarded against him.

Let's now look at each of these categories in turn.

The first category

Two points need to be made under this heading.

First, it is clear from the judgments in *Broome* v *Cassell & Co. Ltd* that the phrase 'servant of the government' should be construed broadly: it covers anyone 'purporting to exercise powers of government, central or local, conferred on them by statute or at common law'.[16] So the police would be counted for these purposes as being servants of the government, as would officials of a local authority. In *AB* v *South West Water Services Ltd*, the Court of Appeal held that a nationalised corporation which supplied water to the inhabitants of Camelford was not a 'servant of the government' for the purpose of determining whether or not it could be sued for exemplary damages; it did not exercise any governmental powers but was merely a commercial operation.[17]

Secondly, suppose that A – a 'servant of the government' – has committed a tort in relation to B. The decision of the Court of Appeal in *Holden* v *Chief Constable of Lancashire*[18] makes it clear that A will have committed his tort in an 'oppressive, arbitrary or unconstitutional' manner if he acted oppressively in committing that tort *or* if he acted arbitrarily in committing that tort *or* if he

---

[13] Ibid.

[14] Or rather Lord Devlin: he was the only Law Lord in *Rookes* v *Barnard* to address the issue of when exemplary damages could be awarded against a defendant in a tort case. The other Law Lords were content to indicate that they agreed with this aspect of Lord Devlin's judgment.

[15] Ibid., 1226.

[16] [1972] AC 1027, 1130 (per Lord Diplock). See also 1077–8 (per Lord Hailsham LC) and 1087–8 (per Lord Reid).

[17] [1993] QB 507, 525 (per Stuart-Smith LJ), 532 (per Sir Thomas Bingham MR).

[18] [1987] 1 QB 380.

acted unconstitutionally in committing that tort. In other words, it is not necessary, for the purposes of establishing that A acted in an 'oppressive, arbitrary or unconstitutional' manner in committing his tort, to show that A acted oppressively in committing that tort. In the *Holden* case itself, a police officer wrongfully arrested the claimant for 20 minutes. He did not act oppressively in doing so: he merely held on to the claimant's arm for 20 minutes. The Court of Appeal held that it could be argued that the police officer acted in an 'oppressive, arbitrary or unconstitutional' manner in wrongfully arresting the claimant. The fact that the defendant wrongfully arrested the claimant established that he acted unconstitutionally in arresting the claimant.

The second category

Lord Devlin made it clear in his judgment in *Rookes* v *Barnard* that this category does not just cover cases where someone deliberately commits a tort because he thinks that he will make more money by committing that tort than he will have to pay the victim of the tort in compensatory damages: 'It extends to cases in which [someone deliberately commits a tort in order] to gain . . . some object – perhaps some property which he covets – which either he could not obtain at all or not obtain except at a price greater than he wants to put down.'[19]

So – in *Drane* v *Evangelou*,[20] the defendant let some premises to the claimant. He then unlawfully evicted the claimant from the premises so that they could be occupied by his in-laws. It was held that the case fell within *Rookes* v *Barnard*'s second category of situations where exemplary damages could be awarded: the defendant deliberately committed the tort of trespass because he thought he would gain more by committing that tort – possession of the premises occupied by the claimant – than he would have to pay the claimant in damages.

Suppose that A has committed a tort in relation to B and we want to establish that A committed that tort because he figured he could make more money by committing that tort than he would have to pay out in damages to B. In order to establish this, we do *not* have to show that A did a precise calculation before he committed his tort of how much he would gain by committing that tort and how much he would have to pay out to B in damages if he committed that tort.[21] It is enough to show that when A committed his tort he did so because he knew or hoped he would obtain some kind of material gain from committing that tort: from this it can be inferred that A calculated that he would gain more by committing that tort than he would have to pay B in damages.[22] So if the *Daily Herald* deliberately libels Karen in order to boost its sales, Karen may well be allowed under *Rookes* v *Barnard* to sue the *Daily Herald* for damages. But, on the other hand, if the *Daily Herald* deliberately libels Karen for non-mercenary reasons – say, because it wants to victimise Karen – Karen will *not* be able to

---

[19] [1964] AC 1129, 1227.
[20] [1978] 1 WLR 455.
[21] *Broome* v *Cassell & Co. Ltd* [1972] AC 1027, 1078–9 (per Lord Hailsham LC), 1094 (per Lord Morris).
[22] *John* v *Mirror Group Newspapers Ltd* [1997] QB 586, 619A.

sue the *Daily Herald* for exemplary damages. Her case will fall foul of the *Rookes v Barnard* limits on when an award of exemplary damages may be made.

Statutory authorisation

There are very few examples of statutes which authorise the victim of a tort to sue the person who committed that tort for exemplary damages. Perhaps the only example is provided by s 13(2) of the Reserve and Auxiliary Forces (Protection of Civil Interests) Act 1951, which provides that exemplary damages may be awarded against someone who converts goods that are covered by the Act.

FURTHER POINTS

Some further points need to be made about this area of the law.

Assessment of damages

Suppose A has committed a tort in relation to B and B is – according to the principles set out above – entitled to sue A for exemplary damages. How much will A be required to pay B by way of exemplary damages? As a general rule, the answer is: just enough to bring the entire amount of damages A has to pay B up to a level sufficient to punish A for committing his tort.[23]

So, for example, in *Duffy v Eastern Health and Social Services Board*,[24] the defendants unlawfully discriminated against the claimant on grounds of her religion. The claimant was entitled to sue the defendants for £15,000 in compensatory damages and for £5,000 in aggravated damages. The court held that the claimant was entitled to sue the defendant for exemplary damages and found that the defendants would only be sufficiently punished for behaving in the way they did if they were made to pay the claimant £25,000 in damages. So they held that the claimant was entitled to sue the defendant for £5,000 in exemplary damages.

This general rule is subject to two qualifications.

(1) *Contributory negligence.* In *Holden v Chief Constable of Lancashire* the Court of Appeal held that the exemplary damages payable to the victim of a tort might be reduced if he or she provoked the person who committed that tort into committing that tort.[25]

(2) *Mass torts.* Suppose that Carl's doing *x* means that he has committed a tort in relation to Nita, Lara and Wendy. Suppose further that Nita, Lara and Wendy are each – according to the principles set out above – entitled to sue Carl for exemplary damages. The decision of the Court of Appeal in *Riches v News Group Newspapers*[26] says that one should use the following method to determine how much Carl must

---

[23] What level of damages will be sufficient to punish A for committing his tort will, of course, depend on his means and how badly he behaved in committing his tort: *Rookes v Barnard* [1964] AC 1129, 1228.
[24] [1992] IRLR 251.
[25] [1987] 1 QB 380, 388E (per Purchas LJ).
[26] [1986] 1 QB 256.

pay Nita, Lara and Wendy in exemplary damages. One first adds up the sums Nita, Lara and Wendy are each entitled to sue Carl for compensatory and aggravated damages. Say that Nita is entitled to sue Carl for £1,000; that Lara is entitled to sue Carl for £2,000; and that Wendy is entitled to sue Carl for £5,000. Added up, these sums come to £8,000. One then works out what sort of sum Carl should be made to pay to punish him for doing x – say that this is £11,000. £3,000 (the difference between £11,000 and £8,000) will therefore represent the *total* amount of exemplary damages that Carl should be made to pay to Nita, Lara and Wendy *together*. Nita, Lara and Wendy will *each* be entitled to a third of this lump sum, so Carl will be liable to pay each of them £1,000 in exemplary damages.[27]

Standard of proof

Suppose that events X, Y and Z are alleged to have occurred and if they did occur, then B would be entitled to sue A for exemplary damages under the principle set out above. As this is a civil case, the courts will find that events X, Y and Z occurred if it is *more probable than not* that those events occurred.[28] They will *not* require it to be proved *beyond a reasonable doubt* that those events occurred. But this is very odd. If it were alleged that events X, Y and Z occurred for the purpose of establishing that A committed a criminal offence, and is therefore liable to be punished criminally, the courts *would* require it to be proved beyond a reasonable doubt that those events occurred. So why is a lower standard of proof required in a case where establishing that events X, Y and Z occurred will result in an award of exemplary damages being made against A? The same standard of proof should apply in both cases.[29]

Vicarious liability

Suppose that A committed a tort in relation to B and, on the principles set out above, B is entitled to sue A for exemplary damages. Suppose further that A's employer, C, is vicariously liable in respect of A's tort. Could B sue *C* for exemplary damages? One would have thought the answer must be 'no': why on earth would we punish C for something that A did?[30]

However, there are some authorities that indicate that B may well be able to sue C for exemplary damages in this situation. For example, in *Lancashire*

---

[27] Notice that if Carl's doing x had not affected Lara and Wendy, Carl would have had to pay Nita £10,000 in exemplary damages – £9,000 more than he is liable to pay her under the facts assumed above.

[28] For another example of a situation where the courts apply a 'balance of probabilities' test to resolve what happened, see above, pp. 533–5.

[29] The OJ Simpson saga in the United States provides a graphic illustration of this point. OJ Simpson was charged with murdering his ex-wife Nicole Brown Simpson and her friend Ron Goldman. He was acquitted on the ground that it could not be proved beyond a reasonable doubt that he murdered Nicole Brown Simpson and Ron Goldman. Ron Goldman's estate then sued OJ Simpson in tort. It was found that it was more probable than not that OJ Simpson had murdered Ron Goldman and Ron Goldman's estate was held to be entitled to sue OJ Simpson for $33.5m, most of which was exemplary damages.

[30] Under the criminal law, of course, an employer would *not* be held criminally liable if one of his employees committed a crime in the course of his employment.

County Council v *Municipal Mutual Insurance Ltd*[31] the question arose: could a local authority insure against the possibility that it would be held liable to pay someone exemplary damages? The Court of Appeal held that the answer was 'yes'. Its reason for so finding was that if the local authority were ever held liable to pay someone exemplary damages, that would be because it was vicariously liable in respect of a tort committed by one of its employees. So allowing the local authority to insure against the risk that it would be held liable to pay someone exemplary damages would not offend against the general principle of law that no one should be allowed to insure himself against the risk of being held liable for engaging in criminal conduct. The significance of the decision here lies in the fact that the Court of Appeal clearly assumed that the victim of a tort committed by a local authority employee in the course of his employment might be able to sue the local authority for exemplary damages, depending on whether he is entitled to sue the employee for such damages.

The same assumption was made by the Court of Appeal in *Thompson* v *Commissioner of Police of the Metropolis*.[32] In that case, the court went so far as to hold that, in the situation we are considering, the exemplary damages payable by C could *exceed* the damages payable by A. The reason for this is that as exemplary damages are designed to punish a defendant for his behaviour, how much the defendant will be held liable to pay the claimant by way of exemplary damages will depend a great deal on his means. If the defendant is very wealthy, then the exemplary damages awardable against him will have to be correspondingly large, to ensure that they 'smart'. If he is very poor, then not much need be awarded against him by way of exemplary damages to ensure that he is punished for what he did. Now – the Court of Appeal made it clear in *Thompson* that if, in the situation we are considering, B made a claim for exemplary damages against *C*, then the damages payable should be assessed by reference to *C*'s means, not *A*'s.[33] So C – who is presumably much wealthier than A – may be held liable to pay B a sum in exemplary damages that far exceeds what B would have been able to recover from A had she sued him for exemplary damages.

In *Kuddus* v *Chief Constable of Leicestershire*,[34] the claimant called the police, complaining that some of his property was stolen. The police constable who dealt with the case later falsely reported that the claimant had withdrawn his complaint. He committed the tort of misfeasance in public office in so doing. The claimant was entitled to sue the police constable for exemplary damages.[35] Instead, he sued the chief constable for such damages on the basis that he was vicariously liable for the police constable's tort.[36] The House of Lords invited

---

[31] [1997] QB 897.

[32] [1998] QB 498.

[33] Ibid., 517. Lord Mackay doubted whether this could be correct in *Kuddus* v *Chief Constable of Leicestershire* [2002] 2 AC 122, at [47], but as the point was not argued, he expressed 'no concluded view upon it'.

[34] [2002] 2 AC 122.

[35] The case fell into the first *Rookes* v *Barnard* category of situations where exemplary damages may be awarded against a defendant in a tort case.

[36] See above, p. 536.

counsel to address them on the issue of whether exemplary damages could be awarded against someone who was merely vicariously liable in respect of a tort committed by someone else. However, counsel declined the opportunity,[37] preferring instead to concentrate on the issue of whether exemplary damages could ever be awarded in a misfeasance in public office case.[38] As a result, all but one of the Law Lords who decided *Kuddus* declined to express a view on whether exemplary damages could properly be awarded in a vicarious liability case. The exception was Lord Scott who expressed the strong view – which we share – that it is improper to award such damages against someone who is vicariously liable for another's tort.[39]

Death

Suppose that A has committed a tort in relation to B and B is entitled to sue A for exemplary damages. Section 1(2)(a)(i) of the Law Reform (Miscellaneous Provisions) Act 1934 provides that if B dies before she has had a chance to sue A for damages, her right to sue A for exemplary damages will die with her. Her estate will not be able to sue A for such damages.[40] This is puzzling. If A's conduct is worthy of punishment, then it is still worthy of punishment even after B has died. So why should B's death have the effect of letting him off the hook? What makes the law in this area even more puzzling is that it seems that if B has a right to sue A for *aggravated* damages, then that right *will* survive her death. But there is no reason why her estate should be allowed to sue A for aggravated damages. The whole point of awarding aggravated damages is to pacify the victim of a tort – so if B is no longer around to be pacified, there is no reason for aggravated damages to be awarded against A any more. So the law in this area has got things completely backwards – it allows B's right to sue A for exemplary damages to die with her, when it should survive her death; and it allows B's right to sue A for aggravated damages to survive her death, when it should die with her.

OPTIONS FOR REFORM

It is likely that the law on exemplary damages will be reformed in one way or the other in the next few years. While the government has declined the opportunity to reform the law on exemplary damages through statutory means,[41] it is

---

[37] [2002] 2 AC 122, at [125].
[38] To which the answer was 'yes' – see above, n. 4.
[39] [2002] 2 AC 122, at [137]. Interestingly, in a subsequent misfeasance in public office case, which involved prison officers interfering with the claimant's right of access to court, counsel for the claimant did *not* seek an award of exemplary damages against the Home Office, but only against the prison officers. The Court of Appeal thought that counsel had acted 'prudently' in not pursuing a claim for exemplary damages against the Home Office: *Watkins* v *Secretary of State for the Home Department* [2004] EWCA Civ 966, at [54].
[40] Though it will be able to sue A for damages in respect of the actionable losses suffered by B before she died: see above, p. 496.
[41] Hansard (HC Debates), 9 November 1999, col. 502.

plain that the House of Lords in the *Kuddus* case was keen to take a fresh look at the law on exemplary damages and was only prevented from making some radical changes to the law in this area because counsel in that case declined to invite them to do so. So it may be worth spending some time canvassing the various options for reform that are available.

(1) *Abolish exemplary damages.* The first option is to abolish the availability of exemplary damages in tort cases.[42] Clearly, Lord Devlin was in favour of doing this in *Rookes* v *Barnard*.[43] However, he felt constrained by precedent from doing so and instead sought – as a second-best solution – to confine awards of exemplary damages to situations where there was clear precedent for their being awarded: hence the *Rookes* v *Barnard* limits on when exemplary damages may be awarded.[44] Lord Scott also announced a clear preference for abolishing exemplary damages in *Kuddus* v *Chief Constable of Leicestershire*.[45]

If we can get past non-arguments[46] in favour of the abolition of exemplary damages (for example, that awards of such damages are 'anomalous'[47] or that they confuse the respective functions of the criminal law and the civil law[48]) the primary[49] argument against such awards being made is that if the victim of a tort is ever allowed to sue the person who committed that tort for exemplary damages, that person may be punished for his behaviour without being afforded any of the protections that we would normally accord to someone who

---

[42] For a fuller discussion of the case for and against abolishing exemplary damages, see Burrows 1996 and McBride 1996.

[43] [1964] AC 1129.

[44] See Lord Reid's remarks in *Broome* v *Cassell & Co. Ltd* [1972] AC 1027, 1088: 'I freely admit that [saying that exemplary damages may be awarded against a "servant of the government" who has acted in an "oppressive, arbitrary or unconstitutional" manner in committing a tort but that exemplary damages may not be awarded against a private individual who has acted in a similar manner in committing a tort] is illogical. The real reason for the distinction was, in my view, that the cases showed that it was firmly established with regard to servants of "the government" that damages could be awarded against them beyond any sum justified as compensation, whereas there was no case except one which was overruled where damages had been awarded against a private bully or oppressor to an amount that could not be fairly regarded as compensatory . . . Again I freely admit there is no logical reason [for saying that exemplary damages may be awarded against someone who has deliberately committed a tort if he committed that tort because he thought he would make more money by committing that tort than he would have to pay out in compensatory damages but not if he committed that tort out of malice towards the victim of the tort]. The reason for [this] is simply that firmly established authority required us to accept [that exemplary damages could be awarded against someone who deliberately committed a tort in order to make a gain] however little we might like it, but did not require us to go further.'

[45] [2002] 2 AC 122, at [111].

[46] These are non-arguments because they assume the very thing they are trying to show, namely that awards of exemplary damages should not be made in tort cases.

[47] [2002] 2 AC 122, at [95] (per Lord Scott).

[48] See Lord Reid's remark in *Broome* v *Cassell & Co. Ltd* [1972] AC 1027, 1086: 'I . . . think that [allowing the victim of a tort to sue the person who committed that tort for exemplary damages] is highly anomalous. It is confusing the function of the civil law which is to compensate with the function of the criminal law which is to inflict deterrent and punitive penalties.' For a more sophisticated version of this argument see Beever 2003a, 105–10.

[49] Another argument is that awarding exemplary damages to a claimant confers an undeserved windfall on him. But what is wrong with giving someone a windfall if doing so serves some valuable social purpose (here, ensuring that people who flagrantly breach the law are punished)? Is that not what happens every time someone wins on the National Lottery?

is subject to criminal punishment.[50] This is not only objectionable in principle; it might also be argued that a consequence of this is that awarding exemplary damages against tortfeasors will violate their rights under Article 1 of the Second Protocol to the European Convention on Human Rights.[51] If that is true, then the courts would be duty-bound under the Human Rights Act 1998 to cease awarding exemplary damages in tort cases. However, the fact that tortfeasors who are sued for exemplary damages are not given as much protection as people who are prosecuted for committing criminal offences does not mean that we should not award exemplary damages in tort cases – rather, it suggests that we should do more than we do now to protect defendants who are sued for exemplary damages.[52]

So there is no very strong argument *in favour* of the *complete abolition* of awards of exemplary damages. There is, on the other hand, a very strong argument *against* the complete abolition of such awards. If the law were changed so that it said that the victim of a tort can never sue the person who committed that tort for exemplary damages, people would have less incentive to abide by the law and the rule of law would be correspondingly weakened. As Lord Devlin observed in *Rookes* v *Barnard*, 'an award of exemplary damages can serve a useful purpose in vindicating the strength of the law'.[53] In the *Kuddus* case, Lord Nicholls also pointed to the useful role awards of exemplary damages make in helping to ensure that the rule of law is maintained: 'The availability of exemplary damages has played a significant role in buttressing civil liberties, in claims for false imprisonment and wrongful arrest ... On occasion conscious wrongdoing by a defendant is so outrageous, his disregard of the plaintiff's rights so contumelious, that something more is needed to show that the law will not tolerate such behaviour. Without an award of exemplary damages, justice will not have been done.'[54] Lord Hutton agreed: 'the power to

---

[50] [1972] AC 1027, at 1087 (per Lord Reid): 'I think that the objections to allowing juries to go beyond compensatory damages are overwhelming. To allow pure punishment in this way contravenes almost every principle which has been evolved for the protection of offenders. There is no definition of the offence except that the conduct punished must be oppressive, high-handed, malicious, wanton or its like – terms too vague to be admitted to any criminal code worthy of the name. There is no limit to the punishment except that it must not be unreasonable ... [T]here is no effective appeal against sentence . . .'

[51] This provides that 'Every natural or legal person is entitled to the peaceful enjoyment of his possessions. No one shall be deprived of his possessions except in the public interest and subject to the conditions provided for by law . . .' Lord Scott hinted in the *Kuddus* case that awards of exemplary damages might violate Article 6 of the ECHR: [2002] 2 AC 122, at [110], but it is hard to see that Article 6 extends this far. Article 6(3) sets out various minimum rights which those charged with a criminal offence are to enjoy – but of course, in a case where exemplary damages are awarded no one is charged with a criminal offence. Article 5 provides that 'No one shall be deprived of his liberty save ... in accordance with a procedure prescribed by law' and Article 7 provides that 'No one shall be held guilty of any criminal offence on account of any act or omission which did not constitute a criminal offence under national or international law at the time when it was committed' – but neither of these Articles seem apt to cover the case where exemplary damages are awarded against a defendant in a tort case.

[52] For a discussion of when defendant in the United States will be able to argue that an award of exemplary damages has violated his constitutional rights, see GS&Z, 970–84.

[53] [1964] AC 1129, 1226.

[54] [2002] 2 AC 122, at [63].

award exemplary damages ... serves to uphold and vindicate the rule of law because it makes clear that the courts will not tolerate such conduct.'[55]

Given this, it is hard to see that there is any case for pursuing the first option for reform.[56]

(2) *Overrule Rookes v Barnard.* If this second option for reform were pursued, exemplary damages would be awarded if a tortfeasor deserved to be punished for committing his tort and he would not be adequately punished for committing that tort if an award of exemplary damages were not made against him. The *Rookes* v *Barnard* limits on when exemplary damages may be awarded would be abolished.

The attractions of reforming the law on exemplary damages in this way are obvious. Everyone agrees that the *Rookes* v *Barnard* limits on when exemplary damages may be awarded are 'illogical'.[57] This was the major criticism made of *Rookes* v *Barnard* by the Court of Appeal in *Broome* v *Cassell & Co. Ltd.*[58] Lord Denning MR observed that 'If exemplary damages for libel can be awarded against the greedy seeker after profit, surely they should be able to be awarded against the wicked inventor of calumnies.'[59] And Salmon LJ asked:

> Why should exemplary damages be recoverable only for outrageous conduct by servants of the Crown? The public equally requires protection against such conduct if it is perpetrated by ... nationalised industries . . ., trade unions, large corporations and indeed by anyone, especially if in a position of power ... There is ... no sensible reason why the defendant's precise standing should be the criterion of his legal li-ability to pay exemplary damages. There exists an even more serious objection ... The doctrine that the executive is subject to extraordinary legal liabilities is dangerous. It is but a short and natural step from that doctrine to the doctrine that the executive may enjoy corresponding legal rights. This is entirely contrary to one of the fundamental principles of the common law, namely that it regards all men indifferently. The cabinet minister by virtue of his office has no greater legal rights or liabilities than his humblest constituent. All are equal before the law.[60]

This criticism was revived by Lord Nicholls in the *Kuddus* case. He was 'respectfully inclined to doubt the soundness of [the] distinction[s]' drawn in

---

[55] Ibid., at [79].

[56] Which is *not* to say that the courts will *not* abolish awards of exemplary damages in the future. They may be required to do so by the European Court of Human Rights. Moreover, some of our more *communautaire*-minded judges may take the view that as awards of exemplary damages are unheard of in France and Germany, they should not be allowed here. Certainly, any attempt to bring English private law more into line with private law on the Continent would see exemplary damages being jettisoned.

[57] *Broome* v *Cassell & Co. Ltd* [1972] AC 1027, 1088 (per Lord Reid). It is noticeable that no other common law jurisdiction has followed *Rookes* v *Barnard*.

[58] [1971] 2 QB 354.

[59] Ibid., 381. See also Taylor J's criticism of this aspect of *Rookes* v *Barnard* in the Australian case of *Uren* v *John Fairfax & Sons Pty Ltd* (1965–66) 117 CLR 118, 138: 'I am quite unable to see why the law should look with less favour on wrongs committed with a profit-making motive than upon wrongs committed with the utmost degree of malice or vindictively, arrogantly or high-handedly with a contumelious disregard for the claimant's rights.'

[60] [1971] 2 QB 354, 386.

Rookes v *Barnard* between the cases where exemplary damages could be awarded and the cases where they could not be.[61]

The case for abolishing the *Rookes* v *Barnard* limits on when exemplary damages may be awarded seems unanswerable. However, a word of caution is in order. *In the current climate* it seems likely that abolishing the *Rookes* v *Barnard* limits would result in an undesirable explosion in litigation, most of it frivolous and unmeritorious. Given this, it might be that the third option for reform discussed below might prove a better choice.

(3) *Incremental reform.* This third option for reform would involve removing some of the existing patent defects in the law on exemplary damages that have already been identified above – such as the fact that (seemingly) exemplary damages can be awarded against people who are vicariously liable for other people's torts and the fact that the death of the victim of a tort will extinguish any right she held while she was alive to sue the tortfeasor for exemplary damages. However, the *Rookes* v *Barnard* limits on when exemplary damages may be awarded would *not* be abolished until there was some assurance that the dramatic expansion in the range of situations where exemplary damages may be awarded that that would entail would not trigger an undesirable explosion in unmeritorious litigation. Until that time, the existing law on when exemplary damages may be awarded would remain basically unchanged.

---

[61] [2002] 2 AC 122, at [66].

39

RESTITUTIONARY DAMAGES

THE NATURE OF RESTITUTIONARY DAMAGES

It is important not to fall into the trap of thinking that all the cases collected together in this chapter are the same. In some of these cases damages were awarded against a tortfeasor that were designed to strip him of some benefit that he obtained by committing that tort. We will call such damages, *type one restitutionary damages*.[1] In the rest of the cases discussed here, damages were awarded against a tortfeasor that were designed to make him pay the victim of his tort a reasonable sum for some benefit he obtained by committing that tort. We will call such damages, *type two restitutionary damages*.[2] Though these are different types of damages, they are both 'restitutionary' in nature because they are each awarded with the object of holding someone liable for the fact that he has obtained a benefit by committing a tort.[3]

---

[1] Some dislike the term 'restitutionary damages', thinking that the word 'damages' denotes an award which is *compensatory* in function: see *Attorney-General v Blake* [2001] 1 AC 268, 284 (per Lord Nicholls, who prefers to use the term 'account of profits' to describe what we have called 'type one restitutionary damages') and McGregor 1996, 203. But no one objects to using the term 'exemplary *damages*' to describe a money award which is punitive in function; so it is hard to see what is so objectionable about using the term restitutionary damages to describe a money award which is designed to hold someone liable for the fact that he has obtained a benefit by committing a wrong in relation to someone else.

[2] Some academics fail to acknowledge the existence of type two restitutionary damages and attempt to analyse *all* the cases gathered together in this chapter as being cases where type one damages were awarded against a tortfeasor: see, for example, Burrows 2002a, 455–62; Cane 1996, 298–300. However, most restitution scholars recognise that this is far too simplistic: see, for example, Dagan 1997, 13–14; Edelman 2002b, 65–87; McInnes 2003, 710, 712; Tettenborn 2003, 48–50. And so, apparently, do the courts: see *Experience Hendrix LLC v PPX Enterprises Inc.* [2003] EWCA Civ 323 (noted, Edelman 2003) where the Court of Appeal drew a distinction between awards of type one and type two restitutionary damages, refusing to award the first but awarding the second against a contract-breaker.

[3] Though one could, of course, confine the term 'restitutionary' to type one awards and find another term for type two awards. (Edelman 2002b takes the opposite line, arguing that the term 'restitutionary damages' should be used to describe a type two award, while the term 'disgorgement damages' should be used to describe a type one award.) Clearly, when Lord Lloyd said in *Inverugie Investments Ltd v Hackett* [1995] 1 WLR 713, at 718, that an award of type two restitutionary damages 'need not be characterised as exclusively compensatory, or exclusively restitutionary, it combines elements of both' he was thinking that the term 'restitutionary' only properly described a type one award: an award designed to strip a wrongdoer of the benefits he had gained from his wrong.

THE AVAILABILITY OF RESTITUTIONARY DAMAGES

Type one restitutionary damages

Type one restitutionary damages may be awarded against a defendant if he has obtained a benefit by committing one of the following torts.

(1) *Conversion.* In *Kuwait Airways Corpn* v *Iraqi Airways Co. (Nos 4 & 5)*, Lord Nicholls remarked that 'all those who convert [someone else's goods] should be accountable for the *benefits* they receive';[4] and indeed it has long been established that type one restitutionary damages may be claimed against someone who commits the tort of conversion.

So, for example, in *Oughton* v *Seppings*,[5] the defendant, a sheriff's officer, received a warrant authorising him to seize the property of one Winslove and sell it in order to pay off a debt which Winslove owed. The defendant met Winslove driving a pony cart. The defendant seized the pony cart and the pony and sold both items of property. In selling the pony, the defendant committed the tort of conversion as the pony belonged to the claimant, Winslove's landlord, and not Winslove, at the time it was sold. The claimant was held entitled to sue the defendant for the money he obtained in return for the claimant's pony.

In *Oughton*, the defendant converted the claimant's property by selling it. Could type one restitutionary damages be awarded against a defendant who converts another's property by *using* it? There is no English authority where type one restitutionary damages have been awarded against someone who has converted another's property by using it.[6] However, there is an American case where such damages were awarded. In *Olwell* v *Nye & Nissen*,[7] the defendant converted a machine belonging to the claimant by using it in his factory. It was held that the claimant was entitled to sue the defendant for the profits the defendant had made by using that machine.

(2) *Passing off.* Type one restitutionary damages may be awarded against someone who has *deliberately* committed the tort of passing off.[8] So in *My Kinda Town* v *Soll*,[9] the defendants deliberately dressed up their restaurant in such a way that people would be deceived into thinking that the defendants' restaurant was a branch of a chain of restaurants run by the claimants. Slade J held that the claimants were entitled to sue the defendants for the money they had made by passing off their

---

[4] [2002] 2 AC 883, at [79] (emphasis added).
[5] (1830) 1 B & Ad 241, 109 ER 776. See also *Lamine* v *Dorrell* (1701) 2 Ld Raym 1216, 92 ER 303 (defendant who committed the tort of conversion by selling debentures belonging to claimant's estate held liable to hand over money he had received for the debentures to estate); and *Powell* v *Rees* (1837) 7 Ad & E 426, 112 ER 530 (defendant who committed tort of conversion by selling claimant's coal held liable for money made by selling the coal).
[6] See McInnes 2003, at 712: '[The] precedents consistently indicate that while the defendant is required to give up his entire gain if he wrongfully *sells* the claimant's property, he merely is required to pay a hiring fee [viz. type two restitutionary damages] for improper *usage*' (at 712). See also, to the same effect, Mason & Carter 1995, 649–52.
[7] 173 P 2d 652 (1946).
[8] *Edelsten* v *Edelsten* (1863) 1 De G J & S 185, 46 ER 72.
[9] [1982] FSR 147 (rev'd on other grounds, [1983] RPC 407).

restaurant as being one of the claimants' restaurants. But the claimants were only entitled to sue the defendants for the money they had made by deceiving people into believing that their restaurant was run by the claimants: the claimants were not entitled to sue the defendants for the money they had made from customers who had not entered the defendants' restaurant in the belief that it was run by the claimants. Quantifying how much money the claimants could sue the defendants for therefore proved a very difficult exercise: the court had to estimate how many of the defendants' customers had walked into the restaurant in the belief that it was run by the claimants and what the profits were on the meals sold to those customers.

(3) *Infringement of intellectual property rights.* Type one restitutionary damages may be awarded against someone who infringes another's copyright[10] or someone who infringes another's design right.[11] In the case where a defendant has infringed another's patent, type one restitutionary damages may be awarded if the defendant knew or ought to have known of the existence of the patent at the time he infringed it.[12]

It is not clear whether type one restitutionary damages will be awardable against a defendant who commits any other kind of tort. The question of whether type one restitutionary damages may be awarded against someone who commits a tort such as trespass to land,[13] battery, negligence, defamation or the new tort of wrongful disclosure of private information[14] has simply not been addressed

---

[10] Copyright, Designs and Patents Act 1988, s 96(2). It is not thought that s 97(1) of the 1988 Act affects this point. That subsection provides that: 'Where in action for infringement of copyright it is shown that at the time of the infringement the defendant did not know, and had no reason to believe, that copyright subsists in the work to which the action relates, the claimant is not entitled to damages against him, but without prejudice to any other remedy.' It is thought that the reference to *damages* in this section is a reference to *compensatory* damages.

[11] Section 229(2). Again, it is not thought that s 233(1) of the 1988 Act – which provides that the owner of a design right which has been infringed will not be entitled to sue the person who infringed the design right for damages if he did not know of, and had no reason to know of, the existence of the design right infringed by him – affects this point.

[12] Patents Act 1977, s62(1).

[13] *Important note.* But see the American case of *Edwards* v *Lee's Administrators*, 96 SW 2d 1028 (1936), which concerned a long cave that contained some very interesting rock formations. The entrance to the cave was on the defendants' land and they would charge people to enter the cave and look around. Unfortunately, a third of the cave stretched under the claimants' land. So the defendants committed the tort of trespass to land whenever they allowed customers to view that part of the cave that was under the claimants' land. The claimants were held entitled to sue the defendants for damages equal to the money the defendants had made by allowing people to look at that part of the cave that was under the claimants' land. McInnes 2003 is however doubtful whether this authority would be followed in England: '[It] is quite likely that an English claimant, in the same circumstances, would be limited to reasonable rental value [viz. type two restitutionary damages]' (at 712); to the same effect, Cooke 1994, 428–9; also *Severn Trent Water Ltd* v *Barnes* [2004] EWCA Civ 570 (disallowing an award against a defendant who had trespassed on the claimant's land by laying a water mains under the land that would have given claimant a proportion of profits made by the defendant as a resulting of committing that trespass).

[14] Type one restitutionary damages are routinely awarded (under the name 'account of profits') against someone who commits the equitable wrong of breach of confidence (see, for example, *Attorney-General* v *Guardian Newspapers Ltd (No. 2)* [1990] 1 AC 109) but it is not clear whether such damages will also be awarded against someone who commits this new tort, which emerged out of the equitable wrong. Could a newspaper that commits this tort by publishing some pho-

by the courts. However, the Court of Appeal has ruled that there are two torts in respect of which type one restitutionary damages *cannot* be awarded.

(1) *Private nuisance*. The decision of the Court of Appeal in *Stoke-on-Trent City Council* v *Wass*[15] indicates that type one restitutionary damages will not be awarded against someone who commits the tort of private nuisance.[16]

(2) *Deceit*. In *Halifax Building Society* v *Thomas*,[17] the Court of Appeal denied that type one restitutionary damages could be awarded against someone who committed the tort of deceit. In that case, one Mr Thomas obtained a mortgage advance from the Halifax Building Society to finance the purchase of a flat by making misrepresentations as to his identity and creditworthiness. After making some repayments of the money he owed the Halifax, Thomas defaulted. The Halifax exercised its right under the mortgage to sell the flat and thereby recouped the value of the money it loaned Thomas. However, the value of the flat had increased since Thomas bought it so there was some money left over from the sale of the flat once the debt to the Halifax was paid off, £10,500 in all. Normally, as the flat belonged to Thomas when it was sold, Thomas would have been entitled to this £10,500; the owner of property is entitled to whatever is obtained in exchange for that property.[18] However, the Halifax argued that they were entitled to the £10,500 as this money represented money made by Thomas as a result of his committing the tort of deceit. The Court of Appeal rejected the Halifax's claim: they held that Thomas was entitled to the £10,500; the fact that this money was made by Thomas as a result of his committing the tort of deceit was irrelevant.[19]

---

tographs of a naked celebrity really be held liable for the value of the increase in sales it experienced that day as a result of publishing the photographs?

[15] [1988] 1 WLR 1406. The private nuisance in this case took the anomalous form of an interference with the claimant's monopoly right to hold a market in a particular area.

[16] Restitution scholars sometimes point to *Carr-Saunders* v *Dick McNeil Associates Ltd* [1986] 1 WLR 922 as authority for the proposition that type one restitutionary damages may be awarded against someone who commits the tort of private nuisance: see, for example, Birks 1989, 471; Edelman 2002b, 136. However, that case was one where the claimant was denied an injunction to stop the defendant committing a nuisance and was awarded damages in *lieu*. It well established that in awarding such damages, the courts will take into account any profits that the defendant has or will make from engaging in the conduct which the claimant wanted to be enjoined. See below, p. 714.

[17] [1996] Ch 217.

[18] *Taylor* v *Plumer* (1815) 3 M & S 562, 105 ER 721; *Lipkin Gorman* v *Karpnale Ltd* [1991] 2 AC 548, 573 (per Lord Goff); *Trustee of the Property of F C Jones & Sons* v *Jones* [1997] Ch 159; *Foskett* v *McKeown* [2001] 1 AC 102, 127 (per Lord Millett).

[19] It would have been different if the Halifax, instead of exercising its right under the mortgage to sell the house to recoup the money it lent Thomas, had *avoided* the mortgage contract on the ground that they had entered into it on the strength of misrepresentations made by Thomas. This would have had the effect of making the mortgage transaction null and void with the result that Thomas would have been treated in law as having purchased the flat with money that *belonged to the Halifax* and not with money that the Halifax had loaned to Thomas and which therefore belonged to Thomas. The Halifax could then have invoked the principle that the owner of property is entitled to whatever is purchased with his property and established: (*a*) that the flat when it was purchased belonged to the Halifax and (*b*) that the Halifax was therefore entitled to whatever monies were obtained in return for the flat when it was sold. Unfortunately, the Halifax never avoided the mortgage contract but chose to assert its rights under it. See *Halifax Building Society* v *Thomas* [1996] Ch 217, 226G–H.

Type two restitutionary damages

Type two restitutionary damages may be awarded against a defendant who has committed one of the following torts.

(1) *Conversion.* It is well established that type two restitutionary damages may be awarded against someone who has committed the tort of conversion.[20]

So, for example, if A has converted B's property by using it, B will be entitled to sue A for damages designed to make A pay B a reasonable sum for the use he has made of B's property.[21] What if A did not *use* B's property but converted it by doing something to prevent B getting hold of it? It does not matter: B will still be entitled to sue A for damages designed to make A pay B a reasonable sum for the *dominion* he has enjoyed over B's property.[22]

(2) *Trespass to land.* It is also well established that type two restitutionary damages may be awarded against someone who has committed the tort of trespass to land.

So – if A occupies a house leased by B and then stays in the house beyond the term of the lease, B will be entitled to sue A for a reasonable sum – known as *mesne profits* – for the use A made of B's house by staying in it beyond the term of his tenancy.[23] More generally, if A commits the tort of trespass to land by using B's land without his consent for some purpose, B will be entitled to sue A for damages designed to make A pay B a reasonable sum for the use he has made of B's land.[24]

What if A commits the tort of trespass to land not by using B's land but by preventing B gaining access to his land? A will still have to pay B a reasonable sum for the dominion he has enjoyed over B's land while B was kept out. So in *Inverugie Investments Ltd v Hackett,*[25] the claimant leased 30 apartments in a hotel in the Bahamas but was then kept out of them for 15 years by the defendants, who owned the hotel. During those 15 years, the defendants let the apartments out to guests but at any one time only about 40 per cent of the

---

[20] See *Kuwait Airways Corpn v Iraqi Airways Co. (Nos 4 and 5)* [2002] 2 AC 883, at [87] (per Lord Nicholls).

[21] See, for example, *Strand Electric Engineering Co. Ltd v Brisford Entertainments* [1952] 2 QB 246 (defendants converted claimants' switchboards by using them in various theatre productions staged at the defendants' theatre; they were held liable to pay the claimants a reasonable sum for the use they had made of the switchboards).

[22] So if A takes one of B's chairs away for a year but does not use it, B will be entitled to sue A for damages designed to make A pay B a reasonable sum for the dominion he has enjoyed over the chair for a year – and this is so even if B did not miss the chair at all in the year A had it: *Mediana (Owners of Steamship) v Comet (Owners of Lightship)* [1900] AC 113, 117 (per Earl of Halsbury LC).

[23] *Swordheath Properties v Tabet* [1979] 1 WLR 285; *Ministry of Defence v Ashman* [1993] 2 EGLR 102; *Ministry of Defence v Thompson* [1993] 2 EGLR 107.

[24] See *Whitwham v Westminster Brymbo Coal & Coke Company* [1896] 2 Ch 538 (defendants who committed the tort of trespass to land by tipping refuse from their colliery onto the claimants' land held liable to pay the claimants a reasonable sum for the use they had made of the claimants' land); and *Penarth Dock Engineering Co. v Pounds* [1963] 1 Lloyd's Rep 359 (defendant committed the tort of trespass to land by keeping his boat tied up in the claimants' docks; he was held liable to pay the claimants a reasonable sum for the use he had made of their land).

[25] [1995] 1 WLR 713.

apartments were let out. So the defendants only used about 40 per cent of the claimant's apartments during the 15 years they kept him out of them. However, during those 15 years they enjoyed dominion over all the claimant's apartments, 365 days a year. Accordingly, it was held that the claimant was entitled to sue the defendants for damages designed to make the defendants pay the claimant the going rate for renting apartments like the claimant's 365 days a year, for 15 years.

(3) *Inducing a breach of contract*. It seems that type two restitutionary damages may be awarded against someone who commits the tort of inducing a breach of contract. So, for example, in *Lightly* v *Clouston*[26] the defendant persuaded the claimant's apprentice to work as a mariner on his ship instead of working on board the claimant's ship. Mansfield CJ held that the claimant was entitled to compel the defendant to pay him a reasonable sum for the work that his apprentice did for the defendant.[27]

Again, it is unclear whether type two restitutionary damages may be awarded against a defendant who has committed any other kind of tort.

Four points

Four points remain to be made about the availability of these two kinds of awards.

(1) *Change of position*. Suppose that B acquired title to money that belonged to A, but the money was transferred to B under a mistake or some other kind of vitiating factor. In this case, A will be entitled to sue B for that money back.[28] However, A's right to sue B may be subject to a defence of *change of position*.

This defence works in the following way. First of all, find out how much money was received by B – say it was £100. Next, see by how much B was enriched as a result of receiving that £100 *when she first found out that that money was transferred to her under a vitiating factor*. Call this amount £x. If £x is higher than £100 then A will be entitled to sue B for £100. But if £x is lower than £100 then A will only be entitled to sue B for £x; B will have a defence of change of position to A's claim for the remaining £(100 – x). The effect of this defence is to ensure that if A sues B for his money back B will normally not be made worse off than she would have been had she never received A's money.[29]

Now – will the defence of change of position operate to protect someone who would otherwise be liable to pay type one restitutionary damages to the victim of his tort?[30] For example, take the sheriff in *Oughton* v *Seppings*. Could he have

---

[26] (1808) 1 Taunt 112, 127 ER 774.
[27] See also *Foster* v *Stewart* (1814) 3 M & S 191, 105 ER 582.
[28] A's right to sue B does not of course arise out of a tort but out of the fact that if B does not give the money – or its equivalent – back, she will be *unjustly enriched*.
[29] The exception arises if B squandered the amount by which she was enriched as a result of receiving the £100 *after* she found out that that money was transferred to her under a vitiating factor.
[30] For a good discussion of the various academic views on this matter, see Burrows 2002a, 524–7.

argued, 'I know that I converted the claimant's pony and obtained £10 [say] for it. But I then handed the £10 over to Winslove's creditor. So holding me liable to pay the claimant £10 here will make me, someone who has acted throughout in complete good faith, worse off than I would have been had I not sold the claimant's horse.'

It might be thought that such an argument could not succeed because the sheriff in *Oughton* v *Seppings* was a wrongdoer: as Lord Goff remarked in *Lipkin Gorman* v *Karpnale*, 'it is commonly thought that the defence [of change of position] should not be open to a wrongdoer'.[31] However, in *Kuwait Airways Corpn* v *Iraqi Airways Co. (Nos 4 & 5)* Lord Nicholls suggested that the defence of change of position *would* be open to someone who converted another's property and was as a result held liable for the benefits he obtained by converting that property.[32] If this is right[33] then were *Oughton* v *Seppings* to be decided

---

[31] [1991] 2 AC 548, 580.

[32] [2002] 2 AC 883, at [79]. Though, presumably, he did not think that the defence should be open to someone who *knowingly* converted another's property and then squandered the enrichment that he obtained by converting that property.

[33] Lord Nicholls's suggestion is subject to one doubt created by the decision of the House of Lords in *Foskett* v *McKeown* [2001] 1 AC 102. Suppose that Eric steals John's Rolex watch and gives it to Beth as a birthday present. (Beth is unaware the watch is stolen.) Suppose the watch is worth £500 and because she no longer needs her old watch (worth £50), Beth gives that watch to her cousin, Mary. It is well established that in this situation John will be entitled to sue Beth for the watch or its value. The result is that Beth will be £50 worse off than she would have been had she never received the watch. However, that is neither here nor there: there is no defence of change of position to the sort of claim that John is bringing here (Ibid., 129 (per Lord Millett)). But what sort of claim is John bringing here? John's claim is not based on *unjust enrichment* – John is not saying that Beth is liable to him here because she would otherwise be unjustly enriched. John's claim is, instead, *property-based* – John is saying that Beth is liable to him here because she's got *his property*. (Notice that A's claim against B in the case where B acquires £100 that originally belonged to A and was transferred to B under some vitiating factor is not property-based because the £100 in B's hands belongs to B. Instead, as was noted above (at n. 28), B's liability to A is based on *unjust enrichment*.) Now suppose that the facts of the case we are considering were slightly different. After Beth was given the Rolex watch by Eric, she decided she didn't like it and sold it to Fred; in return for the watch, Fred gave Beth a motorbike that he no longer wanted and which was worth £600. Now when Beth sold the watch to Fred she converted it, and as a result John will be entitled to sue Beth for what she obtained in return for his watch – that is, the motorbike or its value. Suppose that after Beth received the motorbike, she no longer needed the bicycle that she previously used to get around and she gave that bicycle (which was worth £200) to her cousin Mary. When John sues Beth for the motorbike or its value, Beth will try to raise a defence of change of position to his claim and argue that her liability to him should be reduced by £200 – because she is now only enriched by £400 as a result of the receipt of the motorbike. While Lord Nicholls's dictum in the *Kuwait Airways* case suggests that he thought the defence should be available to Beth in this case, *Foskett* v *McKeown* suggests that the availability of the defence will depend on whether John's claim for the motorbike or its value is based on *unjust enrichment* (in which case the defence will be available) or whether John's claim for the motorbike or its value is *property-based* (in which case the defence will not be available, any more than it was in our original scenario where John sued Beth for the watch or its value): ibid. In *Foskett* v *McKeown* the House of Lords ruled that John's claim against Beth in this kind of case is *property-based* (Ibid., 109 (per Lord Browne-Wilkinson), 127 (per Lord Millett)) – John is allowed to sue Beth for the motorbike or its value because that motorbike, having been acquired in return for his Rolex, *belongs to him*. (See Burrows 2001 for criticism of this aspect of the decision in *Foskett* v *McKeown*; though his arguments have been dismissed as 'unconvincing and unsustainable': Grantham & Rickett 2003, 173, n. 59.) So it seems that Beth would *not* be entitled to rely on a defence of change of position to reduce her liability to John in this case. However, there is nothing in *Foskett* v *McKeown* which prevents a defendant who has obtained a benefit by innocently converting

---

today, the sheriff might well not have been held liable to pay the claimant any-thing by way of restitutionary damages. However, he would of course still have been held liable to compensate the claimant for the loss of her pony.

(2) *Assessment of type two restitutionary damages.* As we have seen, if A – a tenant of B's – has stayed on B's land beyond the expiry of his tenancy, then B will be entitled to compel A to pay him a reasonable sum for the use he made of B's land in staying on that land beyond the expiry of his tenancy. But how do we assess what amounts to a reasonable sum?

The usual approach is to assess what the going market rate would have been to rent B's land for the period on which A stayed on it.[34] However, the Court of Appeal departed from this approach in *Ministry of Defence v Ashman*.[35] In that case, Flight Sergeant Ashman, his wife – the defendant – and their two children took up accommodation in married quarters made available by the Ministry of Defence to members of services stationed at RAF Hulton. They were charged £95.41 a month for the accommodation, a rate far below what they would have had to pay for equivalent accommodation on the open market. It was made clear to Ashman that he was only entitled to remain in the married quarters so long as he remained a serving member of the RAF, living with his wife, and that he would be required to remove his family from the accommodation if he sep-arated from his wife. On 14 February 1991, Ashman deserted the defendant and his children. Having nowhere else to go – the defendant was too impecu-nious to move out and rent accommodation on the open market – Ashman's family stayed on in the married quarters until 26 April 1992 when they were found alternative local authority accommodation.

The claimants, the Ministry of Defence, sued the defendant, seeking to obtain a reasonable sum for the use of the claimants' accommodation that the defendant and her children had enjoyed between 14 February 1991 and 26 April 1992. There was no question that the claimants were entitled to claim such a sum from the defendant; the question was how that reasonable sum should be assessed. The claimants claimed that the defendant should be made to pay them a sum equivalent to the rent she would have had to pay had she rented equivalent accommodation on the open market between 14 February 1991 and 26 April 1992, that is, £435.72 a month. However, the Court of Appeal thought that it would be inappropriate to make the defendant pay that much. To make her pay that much for the use of the claimants' accommo-dation that the defendant and her children had enjoyed between 14 February 1991 and 26 April 1992 would have been to punish the defendant for the fact that the local authority could not promptly rehouse the defendant and her chil-dren: had the local authority been able to offer her and her children alternative accommodation, she would have moved out into that accommodation and paid

---

another's property relying on the defence of change of position if: (*a*) she has given the benefit away (as happened in *Oughton v Seppings*); or (*b*) she obtained the benefit by *using* that other's property, rather than *selling* it (as happened in *Olwell v Nye & Nissen*, discussed above, p. 687).

[34] *Swordheath Properties Ltd v Tabet* [1979] 1 WLR 285.

[35] [1993] 2 EGLR 102. See also *Ministry of Defence v Thompson* [1993] 2 EGLR 107.

the going rate for that accommodation. In order to ensure that the defendant was not disadvantaged as a result of the local authority's failure to rehouse the defendant and her children promptly, the Court of Appeal held that the claimants were only entitled to sue the defendant for a sum equivalent to the rent the defendant would have paid the local authority between 14 February 1991 and 26 April 1992 had she and her children been rehoused by the local authority as soon as Ashman deserted them.

(3) *Election.* In *Strand Electric Engineering Co. Ltd* v *Brisford Entertainments*,[36] the defendants used some electrical switchboards belonging to the claimants when they were not entitled to do so and were held liable to pay the claimants a reasonable sum for the use of the switchboards that they had enjoyed. Now – suppose that the claimants could have rented out those switchboards had they been returned to the claimants when they should have been. If this is right, then the defendants' act of conversion in using the switchboards caused the claimants to suffer an actionable loss – the rent that the claimants could have obtained for the switchboards had the defendants not converted them. Could the claimants have sued the defendants for compensatory damages in respect of this loss *and* type two restitutionary damages on top? The answer is 'no': the claimants would have had to *choose* which remedy to pursue.[37]

This rule – namely, that you cannot sue for both restitutionary damages and compensatory damages – seems to apply only in cases where the victim of a tort suffered an actionable loss that was an *inevitable* result of that tort being committed. This was true in the case we have just been considering – once the defendants decided to keep the switchboards and use them, it was inevitable that the claimants would not be able to rent them out to anyone else and would suffer loss as a result. But if the victim of a tort is entitled to sue the person who committed that tort for restitutionary damages, she will also be entitled *on top of that* to sue him for compensatory damages in respect of any actionable losses suffered by her as a result of that tort being committed that were *not* an inevitable consequence of that tort being committed. So, for example, if one of the switchboards in the *Strand Electric* case had been damaged while it was being used by the defendants, the claimants would have been entitled to sue the defendants for compensation in respect of that damage *in addition to* suing the

---

[36] [1952] 2 QB 246.

[37] The claimants would of course have opted to pursue the most lucrative remedy. In a situation where the victim of a tort has to choose between suing the person who committed a tort for compensatory or restitutionary damages, the law goes out of its way to ensure that she makes the 'right' choice and does not elect to sue the defendant for restitutionary damages when she would have been better off suing for compensatory damages or *vice versa*. So she is allowed to sue the defendant for both kinds of damages and put off the moment of choosing which kind of damages she wants to recover from the defendant until she knows how much she will be allowed to recover from the defendant under each measure: *United Australia Ltd* v *Barclays Bank Ltd* [1941] AC 1. And if she – not knowing that she would be better off suing the defendant for restitutionary damages – successfully sues the defendant for compensatory damages, she will be allowed to reverse her decision and sue him for restitutionary damages instead (though the damages already paid will be taken into account in judging how much more the defendant should pay under the restitutionary measure): *Tang Man Sit* v *Capacious Investments* [1996] AC 514.

defendants for type two restitutionary damages: the damage was not an inevitable result of the defendants' keeping and using the switchboards.[38]

(4) *Restitution without wrongdoing?* Daniel Friedmann raises an interesting question – could someone obtain an award analogous to an award of type one restitutionary damages or type two restitutionary damages *without being the victim of a wrong?*[39] That is, can one have restitution without wrongdoing?[40]

How you answer this question will depend on why you think tortfeasors are sometimes held liable to pay restitutionary damages to the victims of their torts. If you think that when the law holds a tortfeasor liable to pay restitutionary damages, it does so in order to give effect to the principle that 'no man shall profit from his wrong',[41] then you will find it difficult to understand why anyone would think that an award analogous to the kind of awards under discussion here could ever be made against someone who has *not* committed a wrong.

But it may be that the law in this area is *not* actually based on the principle that 'no man shall profit from his wrong'. If it were, it is difficult to understand why the courts have sometimes refused to make awards of type one restitutionary damages against people who have obtained benefits by wronging others – as they did in *Stoke-on-Trent City Council* v *Wass*[42] and in *Halifax Building Society* v *Thomas.*[43] A more plausible explanation of the law in this area is that it is concerned to give effect to moral principles such as 'An owner of property is entitled to the fruits of that property' and 'You should not use another man's property without paying him for it'.[44] This explains why, if A sells B's car for £1,000, B will be entitled to sue A for that £1,000 – as the £1,000 represents the 'fruits' of B's property, B is entitled to it.[45] Similarly, this explains why if A uses B's land without her permission, B will be entitled to sue A for a reasonable sum for the use he has made of her land – A, having

---

[38] [1952] 2 QB 246, 254 (per Denning LJ).

[39] He thinks the answer is 'yes': see Friedmann 1998. (For criticisms, see Andrews 1998.)

[40] Clearly one can have restitution without wrongdoing in the case where a benefit is transferred from A to B under a vitiating factor: in that case, A will normally be allowed to sue B for the benefit back without having to prove that B did anything wrong in obtaining that benefit. (This is known among restitution scholars as an action based on 'unjust enrichment by subtraction'.) The question posed in the text is really concerned with situations where B has received a benefit which was not obtained by subtraction from A – the question is whether *in this context*, one can have restitution without wrongdoing: that is, can A can sue B for the benefit that she has obtained without having to prove that B obtained that benefit by committing a wrong in relation to A?

[41] See Burrows 2002a, 480.

[42] [1988] 1 WLR 1406.

[43] [1996] Ch 217.

[44] Jackman 1989 attempts to explain the fact that this area of law is mainly concerned with proprietary torts by arguing (at 304) that restitutionary damages are awarded when it is necessary to do so to protect 'facilitative institutions' such as 'contracts, trusts and private property'. But it is not clear why the law would regard such institutions as worthy of greater protection than people's persons or reputations.

[45] Arguably, the decision of the House of Lords in *Foskett* v *McKeown* [2001] 1 AC 102, in rejecting the view that B's right to the £1,000 arises out of 'unjust enrichment' but is instead a matter of 'property law', can be read as supporting this analysis of the basis of B's right.

used B's land, has a moral obligation to pay B something for the use he has made of her land.[46]

If this latter analysis of the cases gathered together in this chapter is correct, it may well be that the courts *could* make an award analogous to an award of type one or type two restitutionary damages against someone who has not actually committed a wrong. Take, for example, the facts of *Vincent* v *Lake Erie Transportation Co.*[47] In that case, the defendants kept their ship moored to the claimants' dock against the claimants' will during a storm which repeatedly threw the defendants' ship against the dock. The dock sustained a great deal of damage as a result and the claimants sued the defendants for compensation. It was held that while the defendants did nothing wrong in keeping their ship moored to the defendants' dock,[48] they were still liable to compensate the claimants for the damage done to the dock. This could be interpreted as a case where the courts allowed restitution without wrongdoing in order to give effect to the moral principle that 'You should not use another man's property without paying him for it.' The defendants used the claimants' dock here and therefore had a moral obligation to pay them a reasonable sum for the use they had made of it – which sum, naturally, took into account the damage the defendants did to the claimants' dock by using it.[49]

OPTIONS FOR REFORM

Let's now canvass two options for reforming this area of the law.

(1) *Abolish restitutionary damages.* So far as we know no one is in favour of this option: unlike exemplary damages, the place of restitutionary damages in the

---

[46] Cf. the Court of Appeal's attempted synthesis in *Stoke-on-Trent City Council* v *Wass* [1988] 1 WLR 1406 of the authorities on when type two restitutionary damages could be awarded against a tortfeasor as being based on a 'user principle'; which principle did not apply on the facts of the *Wass* case because the defendants in that case did not *use* anything belonging to the claimants: Worthington 1999, 229–30. See also Grantham & Rickett's analysis of *Edwards* v *Lee's Administrators* (discussed above, n. 13): 'The characterisation of trespass [the tort committed in *Edwards*] as a wrong must not displace the focus of Lee's claim, [which was] *that his property was being used*': Grantham & Rickett 2003, 174 (emphasis added).

[47] 124 NW 221 (1910).

[48] While the defendants would normally have committed a trespass to land in keeping their ship moored to the claimants' dock against the claimants' wishes, it could be argued that they had a defence of necessity in this case which meant that they were allowed to keep their ship moored to the claimants' dock even though the claimants had objected to its being kept there: see above, pp. 353–4.

[49] On the other hand, we should note the existence of a significant anti-restitution without wrong-doing case in *McKenna & Armistead Pty Ltd* v *Excavations Pty Ltd* (1957) 57 SR (NSW) 483 (criticised in Palmer 1991, 234–5). In that case the defendant sold three earth-moving machines to the claimant and then, before he was due to deliver them to the claimant, he continued to use them in his business. The claimant sued the defendant for a reasonable sum for the use he had made of the machines after selling them to the claimant. The New South Wales Court of Appeal held that as the defendant had not committed a tort in using the machines after he sold them to the claimant (there was no conversion because the claimant did not have possession of, or an immediate right to possess, the machines as soon as they had been sold to him), the claimant's claim could not be allowed.

firmament of remedies for wrongs is assured; indeed the courts have started to liberalise the rules on when such damages may be awarded.[50]

(2) *Make type one restitutionary damages available for all torts that are committed intentionally*. This is the view advanced in Goff and Jones's *Law of Restitution*.[51] The case for expanding the range of situations where type one restitutionary damages may be awarded is that doing so will help discourage people from breaching the duties they owe other people: anyone planning to wrong someone else in order to make some kind of gain will know that he will not be allowed to retain that gain.[52] Moreover, there seems little reason why type one restitutionary damages should not be made more widely available. For example, expanding the range of situations where restitutionary damages may be awarded would not – we think – trigger an explosion in frivolous and unmeritorious litigation.

---

[50] In *Attorney-General* v *Blake* [2001] 1 AC 268, the House of Lords held that restitutionary damages could be awarded against someone who committed a breach of contract, though only in 'exceptional cases, where [the normal] remedies [for breach of contract] are inadequate' (Ibid., at 285, per Lord Nicholls). Lord Nicholls went on to observe that in judging whether an award of restitutionary damages is appropriate in a breach of contract case, '[the courts] will have regard to all the circumstances, including the subject matter of the contract, the purpose of the contractual provision which has been breached, the circumstances in which the breach occurred, the consequences of the breach and the circumstances in which relief is being sought. A useful general guide, although not exhaustive, is whether the [claimant] had a legitimate interest in preventing the defendant's profit-making activity and, hence, in depriving him of his profit' (Ibid.).

[51] G. Jones 2002, 784; see also Birks 1989, 328–9.

[52] *Important note*. Some restitution scholars make a different case for expanding the range of situations where type one restitutionary damages may be awarded against a tortfeasor. They argue that the law as it stands is incoherent and illogical: that it makes no sense, for example, for the law to allow someone whose property has been converted to sue another for type one restitutionary damages while it does not allow such damages to be claimed by someone whose character has been unjustly defamed. This kind of argument was made by Lord Nicholls in *Attorney-General* v *Blake* [2001] 1 AC 268 in support of his ruling that type one restitutionary damages should be available in the case where someone has committed a breach of contract: 'it is not easy to see why, as between the parties to a contract, a violation of a party's contractual rights should attract a lesser degree of remedy than a violation of his property rights' (Ibid., 283); 'it would be only a modest step for the law to recognise openly that, exceptionally, an account of profits may be the most appropriate remedy for breach of contract. It is not as though this step would contradict some recognised principle applied consistently throughout the law to the grant or withholding of the remedy of an account of profits. No such principle is discernible' (Ibid., 285). However, this argument only works if one assumes that the law in this area, *as it currently stands*, seeks to discourage people from committing torts. But, as we have noted, it is at least as arguable that the law in this area attempts to give effect to certain moral precepts applying to the ownership of property. If this is right, then the law in this area *as it stands* is not at all illogical or incoherent.

40

DAMAGES FOR CONVERSION

GENERAL PRINCIPLES
The normal rule

If A has converted B's property,[1] B will *normally* be entitled to sue A for: (1) damages equal to the value of B's property at the time it was converted;[2] *and* (2) damages sufficient to compensate B for any actionable losses – other than the loss of her property – that B has suffered as a result of A's converting her property.[3] Let's call the first set of damages, 'market value damages'; let's call the second set of damages, 'damages for consequential loss'. This chapter is mainly concerned with when someone whose property has been converted by another will be entitled to sue that other for market value damages.

Are market value damages compensatory?

Lord Nicholls has made it clear that he thinks damages for conversion are compensatory in nature. In *Kuwait Airways Corpn* v *Iraqi Airways Co. (Nos 4 & 5)*, he said:[4]

> The fundamental object of an award of damages in respect of this tort,[5] as with all wrongs, is to award just compensation for loss suffered. Normally ('prima facie') the measure of damages is the market value of the goods at the time the defendant expropriated them. This is the general rule, because generally this measure represents the amount of the basic loss suffered by the defendant. He has been dispossessed of his goods by the defendant. Depending on the circumstances some other measure, yielding a higher or lower amount, may be appropriate.

If this is right then market value damages are compensatory – if A has converted B's property, then B will only be entitled to sue A for market value damages if

---

[1] As in Chapter 15, the term 'B's property' will be used as shorthand for 'property which was in B's possession or which B had an immediate right to possess'.

[2] If the property in question was a cheque, the value of the property converted by A is assessed by reference to the value of the cheque *not* the value of the paper on which the cheque was written: *Morison* v *London County Westminster Bank* [1914] 3 KB 356.

[3] *Bodley* v *Reynolds* (1846) 8 QB 779, 115 ER 1066; *Re Simms* [1934] 1 Ch 1.

[4] See [2002] 2 AC 883, at [67].

[5] Lord Nicholls is referring here to the tort of 'wrongful interference with goods' (ibid.), but there is in fact no such tort in English law. Section 1 of the Torts (Inteference with Goods) Act 1977 uses the term 'wrongful interference with goods' to refer to conversion, trespass to goods, acts of negligence that result in damage to goods and 'any other tort [that] results in damage to goods' but this was merely for convenience: the 1977 Act did not purport to subsume all these different torts within a 'master tort' of 'wrongful interference with goods'.

A's act of conversion caused B to lose the property that was converted by A. But is this true?

Take the facts of the *Kuwait Airways* case. In that case, Iraq took possession of four planes belonging to the claimants (the Kuwait Airways Corporation) when it invaded Kuwait in 1990. The planes were then handed over to the defendants (the Iraqi Airways Company) and became part of its fleet. The planes were subsequently destroyed in coalition bombing of Iraq. The House of Lords held that had those events happened in England, the defendants would have been held liable for converting the claimant's aircraft and would have been held liable for the market value of the planes at the time the defendants converted them by incorporating them into their fleet.[6]

But it is hard to understand why market value damages would have been awarded in this case *if* damages for conversion are genuinely compensatory. It could hardly be said that the defendants' incorporating the claimants' planes into their fleet caused the claimants to lose those planes. Had the defendants not converted the claimants' planes, they would still have been destroyed in coalition bombing. Lord Hoffmann thought this point was 'irrelevant'.[7] However, that just begs the question of why, *if* awards of market value damages are designed to be compensatory, is it not relevant to consider what would have happened to the claimants' property had it not been converted by the defendants?

Lord Nicholls sought to get round this point by saying that the wrong involved in conversion is 'wrongfully [excluding] the owner from possession of his goods'.[8] So the damages awardable in a conversion case are assessed by asking – what position would the claimant have been in had the defendant not wrongfully excluded the claimant from possession of his goods?[9] Now: if the defendants in the *Kuwait Airways* case had not wrongfully excluded the claimants from their planes – that is, if the defendants had given the claimants their planes back, rather than incorporating them into their fleet – the claimants would obviously not have lost their planes. So, on this view, the market value damages awarded to the claimants in the *Kuwait Airways* case *were* compensatory in nature – the damages compensated the claimants for the loss that they suffered as a result of the defendants' wrongfully excluding them from their planes.

However, it is not at all clear that one can say here that the defendants *excluded* the claimants from their planes *by accepting them*. The fact is the defendants *never had the option* of returning the claimants' planes to them. No doubt they happily accepted the planes when they did – and that is why they were liable for converting the planes[10]

---

[6] Iraq actually took ten of the claimants' planes and handed them over to the defendants. The other six – that we have ignored in the main text – were not destroyed. They were smuggled into Iran and eventually returned to the claimants in return for $20m. Market value damages could not be claimed in respect of these planes because one of the established exceptions to the normal rule set out above is that market value damages will not be payable to a claimant whose property has been converted by someone else if that property has been returned to her: see below, pp. 700–1.

[7] Ibid., at [129].

[8] Ibid., at [82].

[9] Ibid., at [83].

[10] Had they been forced at gunpoint to accept the planes, no doubt they might have been able to raise a defence of necessity to being sued for conversion.

– but had they not been happy to accept the planes and attempted to return them to the claimants, the Iraqi government would not have allowed them to do so.

So we remain to be convinced that *as the law stands* market value damages are genuinely compensatory in nature – hence the location of this chapter in the book. It may be that the stand taken by their Lordships' in the *Kuwait Airways* case over the nature of damages for conversion will in due course mean that market value damages will only be awarded to someone whose property has been converted if it can be shown that she lost her property as a result of that act of conversion. However, the *result* in the *Kuwait Airways* case shows that that remains a remote prospect.

So – as the law stands at the moment, someone whose property has been converted by another will normally be entitled to sue that other for market value damages; and this is so even if she cannot show that that act of conversion caused her to lose the item of property in question. However – recognising the anomalous and perhaps unjustifiable[11] nature of this rule – the courts have created many exceptions to it. It is to these that we now turn.

SPECIAL CASES

If A has converted B's property, B will sometimes *not* be entitled to sue A for market value damages. This will be the case in the following situations.

Return of the property

Subject to what is said below, if A has converted B's property, but that property was subsequently returned to B, B will only be entitled to sue A for damages equal to the difference between the value of the property at the time it was converted and its present value.

For example, in *BBMB Finance (Hong Kong) Ltd* v *Eda Holdings Ltd*[12] the defendants came into possession of shares belonging to the claimants and sold them for $5.75 a share when they had no lawful justification or excuse for doing so; it should be noted, though, that the defendants never received any money for the shares. When they realised what they had done, they bought an equivalent number of shares to replace the shares they had sold and gave them to the

---

[11] *Important note.* Tettenborn 1993 canvasses a variety of explanations of the rule discussed here but finds all of them wanting. Weir 2004 argues (at 483–86) that this whole area of law is based on a historical accident. As he sees it, conversion started off as a tort which allowed B to sue A if A had her goods. Liability was strict because if A has B's goods, and B is suing A for them, it is no defence for A to say 'But it's not my fault I've got your goods!' If A had B's goods – and had no defence to B's claim against him – then B would naturally be entitled to sue A for the value of her goods (though if money damages were not as good as the goods themselves, specific restitution could be ordered: see pp. 721–2, below). At some point, the law lost touch with the idea that A had to *have* B's goods if he was to be held liable to her in conversion; instead, the law substituted a requirement that A had to have dealt with B's goods in such a way as to 'deny B's title' to the goods. But while the conditions of liability changed, the nature of the liability – irrationally – remained the same. Liability for conversion remained strict, and it remained the case that if A were liable to B for converting her goods, B would be entitled to sue A for the value of her goods.

[12] [1990] 1 WLR 409.

claimant. The market in the shares in question had collapsed so the defendants only had to pay $2.40 per share to replace the shares that they had sold. The claimants were held entitled to sue the defendants for damages equal to the difference between the value of the shares at the time they were sold by the defendants (assessed at $5.75 a share) and the value of the replacement shares the claimants got back from the defendants (assessed at $2.40 a share).[13]

Similarly, suppose Paul steals Mary's car and sells it to Eric. Suppose further that Eric crashes the car and as a result its value drops from £5,000 to £500. Suppose finally that police investigating Eric's car crash find out that the car is stolen and return it to Mary. Mary will be entitled to sue Paul for £4,500 in damages: the difference between the market value of his car when it was stolen and its present market value.

Unlawful detention

If A has converted B's property by refusing to hand it over to B when he had no lawful justification or excuse for doing so, B will only be entitled to sue A for damages sufficient to compensate her for the actionable losses she suffered as a result of A's unlawfully detaining her goods.

For example, in *Brandeis Goldschmidt & Co. Ltd* v *Western Transport Ltd*[14] the defendants wrongfully refused to hand over the claimants' copper to them. The defendants eventually relented and handed over the copper to the claimants. By that time the copper had diminished in value. The claimants sued the defendants but it was held that they could only sue the defendants for damages sufficient to compensate them for the actionable losses that the defendants' wrongful detention of the copper had caused them to suffer. As the claimants could not show that the detention had caused them any kind of loss – there was no evidence, for example, that had the defendants not unlawfully detained that copper, they would have sold the copper before it declined in value – they could not sue the defendants for anything by way of compensatory damages.[15]

Limited interest

In *Wickham Holdings Ltd* v *Brooke House Motors Ltd*,[16] the claimants let a car to one Mr Pattinson under a hire purchase agreement. The car was sold without their authority when they had received £615 for the car under the hire purchase agreement: the total hire-purchase price was £889. The claimants sued the

---

[13] Note that in this case the claimants suffered no loss as a result of the defendants' converting their shares, but the claimants were still entitled to sue the defendants for substantial damages. Lord Nicholls sought to distinguish this case in the *Kuwait Airways* case, arguing that the defendants in the *BBMB* case were *really* held liable to pay the claimants type one restitutionary damages: [2002] 2 AC 883, at [89]. This is unconvincing as it is not clear that the defendants benefited in any way from selling the claimants' shares.

[14] [1981] QB 864.

[15] The claimants were, however, entitled to sue the defendants for nominal damages: conversion is a tort that is actionable *per se*.

[16] [1967] 1 WLR 295.

purchasers of the car, claiming damages equal to the value of the car when it was sold: £415. The Court of Appeal held that the claimants were only entitled to sue for the actionable losses that they had suffered as a result of the car being sold without their authority: £274.[17] The expressed basis for the decision was that as the claimants had only a 'limited interest' in the car when it was sold, they were not entitled to claim market value damages; they could only sue for compensation in respect of the actionable losses that they had suffered because their car was sold.[18] However, a more straightforward explanation of the decision is that had the claimants been allowed to recover damages equal to the value of the car at the time it was sold, they would have been unjustly enriched: they would have received, in all, £1,030[19] for a car which was only ever worth £889.

Receipt of benefit

If A has converted B's property and as a result of A's converting his property, B has obtained some benefit, the damages payable to B will *sometimes* be reduced to take account of this fact. For example, in *Plevin v Henshall*,[20] the defendant converted goods worth £947 that belonged to the claimant. He converted them by detaining them on premises let by T, a landlord. The claimant was liable for the rent on these premises. T seized the goods detained by the defendant, claiming that he was owed £118 in unpaid rent. The defendant, in order to get the goods back, paid the rent owed. It was held that the claimant could only sue the defendant for £829 in damages – the market value of the goods converted by the defendant (£947) *minus* the value of benefit that the claimants indirectly received as a result of the defendant's detaining his goods on T's premises (£118).

Improvement

Suppose Dawn stole a car worth £500 from Vijay and sold it to Gary, who purchased it in good faith. Gary then made a number of improvements to the car, thereby increasing its market value to £750, and sold the car to Wendy for that amount. If Vijay sues Gary on the ground that he converted Vijay's car when he sold it to Wendy, Vijay will *not* be entitled to sue Gary for £750, the value of Vijay's car when it was sold to Wendy. Section 6(1) of the Torts (Interference with Goods) Act 1977 provides that 'If in proceedings for [conversion] against a person (the "improver") who has improved the goods, it is shown that the improver acted in the mistaken but honest belief that he had a good title to them, an allowance shall be made for the extent to which, at the

---

[17] Had the car not been sold without their authority, Pattinson would have continued paying the hire purchase instalments and they would have received £274 more for the car than they had at the time it was sold.

[18] [1967] 1 WLR 295, 299H–310A (per Lord Denning MR).

[19] The sum of £615 and £415.

[20] (1853) 10 Bing 24, 131 ER 814.

time as at which the goods fall to be valued in assessing damages, the value of the goods is attributable to the improvement.' So, in the situation we are considering, Vijay will only be entitled to sue Gary for £500 in damages: while it was worth £750 when Gary converted it by selling it to Wendy, £250 of the car's worth was attributable to the fact that Gary improved it.[21]

Bailment

If Alan converts goods that Nita held on a bailment at will for Lara, Alan will have committed the tort of conversion in relation to both Nita and Lara.[22] Now – if Nita sues Alan for damages equal to whatever Lara's goods were worth when they were converted by Alan, Lara will be barred from suing Alan for such damages.[23] The same is true if Lara sues Alan for market value damages; in such a case, Nita will be barred from bringing a similar claim against Alan.[24]

Multiple claimants

Suppose goods belonging to Karen were stolen from her by Tom. Suppose further that Tom abandoned Karen's goods and they were found by Ruth, who took them. Suppose finally that they were then stolen from Ruth by John. In such a case, John will have committed the tort of conversion in relation to Ruth *and* Karen.[25] Ruth and Karen will not *each* be allowed to sue John for market value damages. This is the effect of ss 7 and 8 of the Torts (Interference with Goods) Act 1977.

If Ruth and Karen both sue John *at the same time* for converting Karen's goods, John's *total* liability to Ruth and Karen *together* will not exceed the value of Karen's goods at the time they were converted by John.[26] The courts will decide how to apportion that liability between Ruth and Karen.[27]

If Ruth – but not Karen – sues John in conversion for market value damages, Ruth will be required under Rules of Court to give particulars of her title to the

---

[21] What if Vijay sues *Wendy* for converting his car by buying it? In principle, if he sues Wendy, he should be entitled to sue her for the value of the car at the time she bought it: £750. Once he recovers that from Wendy, will Gary be entitled to bring a claim against Vijay, arguing that £250 of the £750 that Vijay has recovered from Wendy is attributable to the work that Gary did on Vijay's car? Lord Denning MR thought that Gary could: see *Greenwood v Bennett* [1973] QB 195, at 202. Phillimore LJ in the same case seemed to agree with Lord Denning MR (ibid., at 202–3) but Cairns LJ disagreed: ibid., at 203.

[22] See above, p. 333.

[23] *The Winkfield* [1902] P 42, 61. No injustice will be done to Lara as a result of this rule – Nita will hold the damages she has recovered from Alan on trust for Lara: ibid., 55.

[24] *O'Sullivan* v *Williams* [1992] 3 All ER 385.

[25] At the time John stole the goods, Ruth was in possession of them and Karen had an immediate right to possession of them.

[26] Torts (Interference with Goods) Act 1977, s 7(2): 'In proceedings to which any two or more claimants are parties, the relief shall be such as to avoid double liability of the wrongdoer as between those claimants.'

[27] Presumably, the courts will award Karen market value damages and give Ruth nothing. But what is the position if, after John stole Karen's goods, Karen recovered them? In such a case, Karen would not be entitled to sue John for market value damages (see above, pp. 700–1) and it would be open to the courts to award *Ruth* market value damages instead (as happened in *Wilson* v *Lombank Ltd* [1963] 1 WLR 1294). But this would give Ruth an undeserved windfall.

goods at the time they were converted by John and disclose any information she has as to who else had a claim to the goods at the time they were converted by John.[28] If it becomes evident that the goods were Karen's when they were converted, then John can ask the court to direct that Karen be joined to Ruth's action. If his application is successful and Karen joins Ruth's action, John's liability to Karen and Ruth will be assessed as above. If his application is successful and Karen for some reason *fails* to join Ruth's action, Karen may be stripped of any right she might otherwise have had to sue John for converting her goods.[29]

If it is not evident that the goods converted by John belonged to someone other than Ruth at the time they were converted,[30] Ruth will be entitled to sue John for market value damages.[31] However, Karen will then be entitled to sue Ruth for whatever proportion of the damages recovered by Ruth that Karen would have been awarded had she and Ruth sued John together for converting Karen's goods.[32] The 1977 Act clearly contemplates that Karen will, alternatively, be allowed to sue John but it is unclear what will happen if she does. The better view, we would submit, is that Karen will not be allowed to recover more from John by way of damages than she would have recovered if she had sued John with Ruth for converting her goods. If Karen's claim against John is successful, then John will be entitled to recoup from Ruth whatever he has had to pay out to Karen by way of damages.[33]

Successive conversions

Suppose Sarah stole Fred's goods and sold them to Carl. To keep things simple, let us assume the goods were never returned to Fred. In such a case, both Sarah and Carl will have committed the tort of conversion in relation to Fred.[34]

If Fred sues *Sarah* for market value damages, Fred will *not* then be entitled to sue *Carl* for such damages. This is because of s 5 of the Torts (Interference with Goods) Act 1977, which provides that if Fred recovers damages in conversion from Sarah, Fred's title to his goods will be extinguished – presumably, from the date that Sarah converted Fred's goods. So once Fred sues Sarah in conversion for market value damages, history is rewritten: the goods that Sarah

---

[28] Torts (Interference with Goods) Act 1977, s 8(2).

[29] In such a case, will Ruth be entitled to sue John for market value damages? It is unclear: see W&J, 608. On the one hand, s 8(1) of the 1977 Act says that a defendant in a conversion case may raise as a defence the fact that someone else had a better title than the claimant to the goods that were converted (the defence of *ius tertii*). On the other hand, this seems inconsistent with section 7, which clearly contemplates that, in the right circumstances, Ruth will be entitled to sue John for market value damages: see, for example, s 7(4).

[30] Say, for example, that Ruth can make out a plausible case for thinking that the goods converted by John were abandoned when she found them.

[31] This point is unaffected by section 8(1) because John will not be able to establish in this case that someone other than Ruth had a better title to the goods that he converted.

[32] Torts (Interference with Goods) Act 1977, s 7(3).

[33] Section 7(4).

[34] See above, pp. 329–30.

sold to Carl are treated as though they were Sarah's when they were sold; the result is that Carl can no longer be said to have converted *Fred's* goods when he bought them. So Fred will no longer have any right to sue Carl for converting his property.

What if Fred sues Carl first and then Sarah? Section 5 will not work to prevent Fred doing this. However, it is submitted that if Fred sues Carl first and recovers market value damages from him, Fred will be barred from bringing a similar claim against Sarah. Instead, Fred will only be entitled to sue Sarah for damages equal to the depreciation in value, if any, that his goods experienced between the time they were stolen by Sarah and the time they were sold to Carl. In this way, Fred will be allowed to recover damages equal to whatever his goods were worth at the time they were stolen from him but no more than that – if he were allowed to recover more, he would obtain an undeserved windfall.

REMEDIES DESIGNED TO PREVENT
SOMEONE COMMITTING A TORT

Those who peddle the line that the function of tort law is to determine when one person will be held liable to compensate another for some loss that that other has suffered usually have the grace, and the intelligence, to acknowledge that this view of tort law is not wholly accurate.[1] So, for example, the legal historian David Ibbetson observes that 'tort [law] . . . is *primarily* reactive to events that have occurred in the past . . . [it is] *hardly at all* concerned with facilitating the orderly regulation of individuals' affairs . . .'.[2] The qualifiers 'primarily' and 'hardly at all' are inserted here because of the existence of the remedies dealt with in the next two chapters of this book. These remedies are not at all concerned with *loss-compensation*. They are concerned, rather, with *wrong-prevention*:[3] they are awarded in order to stop someone committing a tort. These remedies *are* therefore concerned with facilitating the orderly regulation of individuals' affairs; they *do* look to determine what will happen in the future, not to unpick a mess that has been created in the past. The existence of these remedies establishes definitively that committing a tort involves breaching a duty owed to another.[4] It is this fact that sets a natural limit to tort law's jurisdiction: if committing a tort involves breaching a duty owed to another, it follows that *no one* can be held liable *in tort* to compensate A for some loss that A has suffered if no *civil wrong* was committed in causing A to suffer loss. It is therefore wrong to think that tort law is concerned *generally* to determine when one person will be held liable to compensate another for some loss that that other has suffered: if that loss was not wrongfully inflicted, tort law has nothing to say on the issue, one way or the other. And if this is right, it is wrong to think that the function of tort law is to determine when one person will be held liable to compensate another for a loss that that other has suffered. Rather, the function of tort law is to help determine what specific duties we owe each other and to determine what remedies will be available when one of those duties is breached.[5]

---

[1] Of course, a statement that is not *wholly* accurate is not accurate *at all*.

[2] Ibbetson 2003, 475 (emphasis added).

[3] *Important note.* Some would prefer to say 'loss-prevention' at this point: see M. Jones 2002, 1; W&J, 1; S&H, 13. But if it is not legally wrong for A to cause B loss in a certain situation, why on earth would the courts try to prevent A causing B loss in that situation? Why would they not allow A to inflict the loss and then, if it is appropriate to do so, require A to compensate B for that loss? The *only* possible reason why the remedies dealt with in the next two chapters might be awarded against a given defendant is that the defendant proposes to commit a civil wrong; that is, he proposes to do something that involves the breach of a duty owed to another.

[4] See above, n. 3.

[5] To the same effect, see GS&Z, 3: 'tort law articulates legal responsibilities or duties that persons owe to one another, and provides victims of conduct breaching those duties with redress against those who have wronged them.'

41

INJUNCTION

Suppose that A will commit a tort in relation to B if he does x. Suppose further that A is likely to do x unless he is prevented from doing so. In such a case, B may be able to obtain an injunction[1] against A, requiring him not to do x.[2] If such an injunction were issued against A and he ignored it then he would commit a contempt of court and render himself liable to be criminally punished.

CLASSIFICATION OF INJUNCTIONS
Mandatory and prohibitory injunctions

If an injunction instructs someone to take positive action, for example, to repair a wall, then the injunction is called a *mandatory* injunction. On the other hand, if an injunction instructs someone to cease behaving in a particular way the injunction is called a *prohibitory* injunction. The distinction is one of substance rather than form. A good rule of thumb is that if fulfilling an injunction requires the expenditure of money then the injunction is, in substance, *mandatory*. English courts are more cautious about granting mandatory injunctions than prohibitory injunctions.[3]

Quia timet injunctions

Most injunctions will instruct someone either not to continue committing a tort or to undo the consequences which followed the commission of a tort. It is also possible, however, for someone to obtain an injunction if she can establish that she is *about* to be the victim of a tort to be committed by A. Such an injunction, known as a *quia timet* injunction, will order A not to commit the tort. For example, in *Litchfield-Speer* v *Queen Anne's Gate Syndicate (No. 2) Ltd*,[4] Lawrence J held that the claimants were entitled to an injunction to restrain the defendants from erecting a new building, which, had it been built, would have amounted to a private nuisance because its presence would have unreasonably interfered with the claimants' right to light.

---

[1] An injunction is 'a court order prohibiting a person from doing something or requiring a person to do something', Civil Procedure Rules, glossary.
[2] The general authority of the High Court to grant injunctions is found in Supreme Court Act 1981, s 37(1).
[3] The reasons for this are explained below, pp. 712–13.
[4] [1919] Ch 407.

Interim and final injunctions

Injunctions granted as a remedy at the conclusion of a trial are referred to as *final* or *perpetual* injunctions. English civil procedure also allows a party to seek an injunction to protect his or her position before trial. Such injunctions are referred to as *interim* (formerly *interlocutory*) injunctions.

WHEN WILL AN INJUNCTION BE GRANTED?

Interim injunctions

Interim injunctions are particularly important where A proposes to do *x* which will cause damage to B *before* there is any opportunity to hold a trial to determine whether A's doing *x* will be a tort to B, and the damage which will be caused is of a type which could not be properly reversed by a payment of damages. In such a case, B may be able to obtain an *interim* injunction against A, requiring him not to do *x* until some future time.

The 'balance of convenience' test[5]

The general rule requires B to do three things before an interim injunction will be granted. First, she must establish that there is a serious question to be tried as to whether if A does *x*, he will commit a tort to B.[6] Secondly, she will have to undertake that if an interim injunction is granted against A and it is later found that *x* would not have involved A committing a tort to B, she will compensate A for any losses suffered by him as a result of that injunction's being granted.[7] Thirdly, she will have to convince the court that the 'balance of convenience' favours granting an interim injunction.

The 'balance of convenience' is determined by balancing the claimant's need to be protected against any injury for which she could not be adequately compensated in damages recoverable in the action against the defendant's need to be protected against any injury from being prevented from doing *x* for which he could not be adequately compensated in damages under the claimant's undertaking. Thus if Vijay wanted to cut down an old tree, and Beth claimed that the old tree was on her land so cutting it down would be a tort to her, then the court would balance the extent to which Beth could be compensated by damages if the tree was cut down but it turned out that this did involve Vijay committing a

---

[5] This test was set out by Lord Diplock in *American Cynamid* v *Ethicon Ltd* [1975] AC 396, and is commonly referred to as 'the *American Cynamid* test'. For its detailed application, and some of the criticisms that have been made of it, the reader is advised to consult a specialist book on civil procedure.

[6] This is not a high hurdle. In *American Cynamid* v *Ethicon Ltd* [1975] AC 396, Lord Diplock suggested (at 407) that there was a 'serious question to be tried' if the court was satisfied that the claim was not 'frivolous or vexatious'. He also stated that, 'It is no part of the court's function at this stage of the litigation to try to resolve conflicts of evidence on affidavit as to facts on which the claims of either party may ultimately depend nor to decide difficult questions of law which call for detailed argument and mature considerations. These are matters to be dealt with at the trial.'

[7] Civil Procedure Rules, Practice Direction 25, 5.1(1).

tort to her, against the extent to which Vijay could be compensated by damages if he was prevented from cutting down the tree until trial when it turned out that cutting it down was not a tort. In such circumstances a pivotal issue would be what injury, if any, Vijay might suffer if he had to delay cutting down the tree.

Exceptions

There are three situations which commonly arise in tort cases where the courts will not use the 'balance of convenience' test. First, in some situations ordering A not to do something until trial will effectively preclude him from ever doing it, since he may only want to do it at a particular time. Consequently, in some tort cases the question whether an interim injunction will be granted effectively determines the whole dispute. An example might be where Carl seeks an order that Nita should not organise some industrial action. By the time of any trial the dispute which generated the threat of industrial action may have been resolved, and neither party may have much desire to determine whether the previously proposed action would have been lawful. In such an exceptional case a judge who is asked to grant an interim injunction should not consider merely whether there is a serious question to be tried, but whether Carl would have been likely to obtain a *final* injunction if the case had been fully tried.[8]

Secondly, 'the importance of leaving free speech unfettered is a strong reason in cases of libel for dealing most cautiously and warily with the granting of interim injunctions'.[9] This caution is reflected in the rule that interim injunctions will not generally be granted in cases where B claims that a proposed publication by A will libel or slander her[10] but A intends to argue at trial that his statement is not defamatory,[11] or intends to put forward a defence of justification,[12] fair comment on a matter of public interest,[13] or privilege.[14] If, however, it is clear that the defence is doomed to fail, an interim injunction may still be granted.[15]

Section 12(3) of the Human Rights Act 1998 provides that 'No such relief [affecting the exercise of the Convention right to freedom of expression] is to be granted so as to restrain publication before trial unless the court is satisfied that the applicant is likely to establish that publication should not be allowed.' The common law rule discussed in the previous paragraph, which applies in cases of libel and slander, is more protective of free expression than this

---

[8] *NWL Ltd* v *Woods* [1979] 1 WLR 1294, 1306–7.

[9] *Bonnard* v *Perryman* [1891] 2 Ch 269, 284 (per Lord Coleridge).

[10] Similar rules probably apply to the tort of malicious falsehood, and courts will be careful not to allow the rules to be evaded by claims that the publication may amount to some other tort, such as the tort in *Quinn* v *Leathem* (discussed in Chapter 21, above): see *Gulf Oil (Great Britain) Ltd* v *Page* [1987] Ch 327, 333–4; *Femis-Bank* v *Lazar* [1991] Ch 391.

[11] *Coulson* v *Coulson* [1887] 3 TLR 846.

[12] *Bonnard* v *Perryman* [1891] 2 Ch 269.

[13] *Fraser* v *Evans* [1969] 1 QB 349, 360.

[14] *Quartz Hill Consolidated Mining Co.* v *Beal* (1882) 20 Ch D 501; *Harakas* v *Baltic Mercantile and Shipping Exchange Ltd* [1982] 1 WLR 958.

[15] *Holley* v *Smyth* [1998] QB 726, holding that a claimant is allowed to adduce evidence to show that a defence of justification is bound to fail; *Herbage* v *Pressdram* [1984] 1 WLR 1160, 1164, discussing a situation where there was overwhelming evidence of malice which would negate a defence of qualified privilege.

statutory rule.[16] But the statutory rule may have a significant role to play where the interim injunction is sought to prevent the commission of some other tort involving publication, such as the tort of invasion of privacy by wrongful disclosure of private information.[17] The Court of Appeal has ruled that the word 'likely' in the statutory phrase 'the applicant is likely to establish that publication should not be allowed' does *not* mean 'more probable than not', and the court *may* grant an interim injunction if it finds that the claim has 'a real prospect of success, convincingly established'.[18] The approach under s 12(3) is distinct from that under the ordinary 'balance of convenience' test not only because it asks whether the claim has 'a real prospect of success' instead of whether there is 'a serious question to be tried', but also because under s 12(3) the court must seek to resolve disputes of fact and questions of law in order to reach a view on the merits of the claim.[19] In considering the merits the court must consider not merely the likelihood of the claimant establishing the defendant's *liability* but also the likelihood of the claimant convincing the court that a *final* injunction is appropriate.

The third exception is where A claims that his proposed course of action will be performed in contemplation or furtherance of a trade dispute. In such a case, before granting an interim injunction a court must consider the likelihood that A will be able to establish the defence of trade union immunity[20] at trial.[21]

Final injunctions

The general rule

The general rule is that courts will grant a *final* injunction to prevent the continuation or repetition of any tort where there is a sufficient basis for believing that without an injunction there will be a continuation or repetition of that tort. In practice this means that injunctions are far more common where certain types of tort are alleged. Torts which are usually committed by isolated impacts, such as negligence, are unlikely to give rise to claims for injunctions,[22]

---

[16] In *Coys Ltd* v *Autocherish Ltd* [2004] EWHC 1334, Tugendhat J held that the statutory rule did not indicate that the courts should now reduce the level of protection provided for free expression at common law and grant interim injunctions more readily in cases of alleged libel or slander. This opinion coincides with that expressed by Milmo 2003, 797–8.

[17] Discussed in Chapter 14, above. In *A* v *B plc* [2003] QB 195, [11], the Court of Appeal set out guidelines for judges asked to decide whether an interim injunction should be granted to prevent commission of this tort.

[18] *Cream Holdings Ltd* v *Banerjee* [2003] Ch 650, [12] (Simon Brown LJ).

[19] Ibid., [56] (Simon Brown LJ), [121]–[123] (Arden LJ).

[20] The immunity is found in Trade Union and Labour Relations (Consolidation) Act 1992, ss 219–220. These provisions are discussed above, at p. 497.

[21] Trade Union and Labour Relations (Consolidation) Act 1992, s 221(2).

[22] Cf Lord Denning MR's remark in *Miller* v *Jackson* [1977] QB 966, 980: 'there is no case, so far as I know, where [an injunction] has been granted to stop a man being negligent.' This is disputed, however, in McBride 2004, pointing to the American cases of *Shimp* v *New Jersey Bell Telephone Co.*, 368 A 2d 408 (1976) and *Smith* v *Western Electric Co.*, 643 SW 2d 10 (1982), where in each case an injunction was granted against an employer, compelling him to comply with the duty of care he owed his employees to take reasonable steps to see that they would be reasonably safe in working for him.

while torts which are often committed by interference over a longer period with someone's interests, such as private nuisance, commonly give rise to such claims. It is worth noting, however, that because injunctions are intended to deal with future continuation or repetition of the wrongful behaviour, a claimant seeking an injunction will often *also* claim damages for past injury – and where a court finds that A has committed and is committing a tort by engaging in a continuous course of conduct, it will often award *both* an injunction against A to prevent the tort being committed in the future *and* damages for past injury caused by A's tort.

The remedy of injunction was initially developed in the Courts of Equity and consequently it conforms to general equitable principles about remedies. The central general principle is that remedies developed by the Courts of Equity (known as 'equitable remedies') are discretionary. What this means is that even where a claimant has established the conditions sufficient to be awarded a remedy the courts will not necessarily grant it – they can still refuse. In practice, the courts' choices as to whether or not to grant someone an equitable remedy are usually directed by well-developed rules. Thus an injunction will not be awarded where justice can be done by ordering the defendant to pay damages to the claimant,[23] where granting the injunction would be oppressive,[24] where the claimant seeking the injunction does not have 'clean hands',[25] where the claimant seeking the injunction is unwilling to 'do equity',[26] where the claimant initially allowed the defendant to do what she is now seeking an injunction against,[27] or where there has been unacceptable delay on the part of the claimant in seeking an injunction against the defendant. But even beyond these rules there exists a degree of residual flexibility.

Courts are generally more cautious about granting mandatory injunctions than prohibitory injunctions for two principal reasons. First, if a mandatory injunction is awarded against a defendant, the court must specify what the defendant must do to comply with it. Where it is impossible to state clearly what it is that the defendant is being required to do a mandatory injunction will be refused.[28]

Secondly, there is a concern that if a mandatory injunction is awarded against A for B's benefit, A may be compelled to spend more money complying with

---

[23] Damages are generally not thought to be adequate where the harm caused is to non-pecuniary interests, such as health or amenity, or where the damages would be hard to quanitfy. Consequently, this basis for refusing an injunction is rarely relied on in tort cases.

[24] This concept is discussed in detail below, pp. 714–15.

[25] This basis for refusing an injunction allows a court to take account of any misconduct by a claimant seeking an injunction. Of course, the courts will not refuse to grant an injunction because of a trivial act of misconduct by the claimant.

[26] This basis for refusing an injunction allows a court to consider whether the claimant is willing to perform any duties that she owes the defendant.

[27] An injunction might be refused on this basis if, for instance, B stood by and watched A expend money on a project before objecting to it and seeking an injunction. In *Jaggard* v *Sawyer* [1995] 1 WLR 269 the claimant warned the defendant that the defendant's proposed action was wrongful but did not seek an interim injunction. The Court of Appeal treated this failure to seek an interim injunction as relevant to the decision whether to grant a final injunction: 283 (Sir Thomas Bingham MR), 289 (Millett LJ).

[28] *Redland Bricks Ltd* v *Morris* [1970] AC 632.

that injunction than B will gain from that injunction being complied with. This might be regarded as wasteful. Consequently, it is necessary to pay particular attention to whether damages will be an *adequate* remedy for any future harm, and how much it will cost a defendant to obey a mandatory injunction.[29] However, if the cost to A of complying with the injunction that B is seeking far outweighs whatever benefits B will reap from that injunction being awarded against A, an injunction may still be awarded against A if A has acted with wanton disregard of B's interests.

Injunctions affecting freedom of expression

Where a court is considering whether to grant any relief which, if granted, might affect the exercise of the Convention right to freedom of expression then:

> The court must have particular regard to the importance of the Convention right to freedom of expression and, where the proceedings relate to material which the respondent claims, or which appears to the court, to be journalistic, literary or artistic material (or to conduct connected with such material), to –
> (a) the extent to which –
> (i) the material has, or is about to, become available to the public; or
> (ii) it is, or would be, in the public interest for the material to be published;
> (b) any relevant privacy code.[30]

Clearly an injunction may affect freedom of expression to a greater extent than an award of damages. Thus, before granting an injunction which will interfere with freedom of expression a court will want to be convinced that the proposed interference is supported by 'relevant and sufficient grounds', will respond to a 'pressing social need' and will not interfere to any extent greater than necessary to meet the legitimate aim pursued.[31] The Court of Appeal has held that s 12(4) does not require a court to attribute *extra* weight to the listed factors but 'does no more than underline the need to have regard to contexts in which [the European Court of Human Rights'] jurisprudence has given particular weight to freedom of expression, while at the same time drawing attention to considerations which may none the less justify restricting that right'.[32] Equally, s 12(4) is not intended to give one Convention right (Article 10, freedom of expression) pre-eminence in a case where another Convention right (e.g. Article 8, privacy) is also involved.[33]

Damages in lieu of final injunctions

If B applies to a court for a final injunction which would require A not to commit a particular tort in relation to B, the choice for the court which is considering B's application is not a straightforward one between granting an injunction and leaving B without any remedy. The court may refuse to award

[29] Ibid.
[30] Human Rights Act 1998, s 12(4).
[31] See, for example, *In re S (a child) (identification: restrictions on publication)* [2004] Fam 43, [54].
[32] *Ashdown v Telegraph Group Ltd* [2002] Ch 149, [27].
[33] *Douglas v Hello! Ltd* [2001] QB 967, [133]–[137] (per Sedley LJ). See also, *Campbell v MGN Ltd* [2004] 2 WLR 1232, [111] (Lord Hope).

B an injunction but at the same time award B damages *in lieu of* (instead of) an injunction.[34]

The effect of such an award will be to give A a *right* to commit the tort complained of by B; in return, A is made to pay B a reasonable sum for the privilege of being allowed to commit that tort. If the court dealing with B's application does decide to award B damages in lieu of an injunction it will assess how much B should be paid by way of damages in lieu by asking: How much would a reasonable person in B's shoes charge A for the privilege of being allowed to commit the tort complained of by B?[35] The figure the court comes up with will be the amount it awards B by way of damages in lieu. So suppose the court dealing with B's application has decided to deny her application for an injunction and decided to award her damages in lieu of an injunction instead. In determining how much B should be paid by way of damages in lieu, the court will take into account how much B stands to lose if A is allowed to commit the tort complained of by B *and* how much money A will make if he is allowed to commit the tort complained of by B.[36] A reasonable man in B's shoes would take both matters into account in determining how much to charge A for the privilege of being allowed to commit the tort complained of by B.

So an award of damages in lieu of an injunction in effect amounts to a forced sale of B's rights against A. Consequently, the courts have traditionally been cautious about using their power to award damages in lieu of injunctions. In the leading case of *Shelfer* v *City of London Electric Lighting Co.*,[37] A. L. Smith LJ stated, 'In my opinion it may be stated as a good working rule that – (1) If the injury to the claimant's legal rights is small, (2) And is one which is capable of being estimated in money, (3) And is one which can be adequately compensated by a small money payment, (4) And the case is one in which it would be oppressive to the defendant to grant an injunction: – then damages in substitution for an injunction may be given.'[38] A. L. Smith LJ then went on to suggest that, regardless of the four factors, a defendant who had acted in reckless disregard of the claimant's rights would be unable to ask the Court to award damages in lieu of injunction.[39]

In *Jaggard* v *Sawyer*,[40] the Court of Appeal treated A. L. Smith LJ's list of four factors as having 'stood the test of time'.[41] Indeed, Lord Bingham MR favoured a narrow interpretation of the fourth factor and said, 'It is important

---

[34] The Chancery Amendment Act 1858, better known as Lord Cairns's Act, allowed the Court of Chancery to award damages in lieu of an injunction. This statute has been repealed, but s 50 of the Supreme Court Act 1981 preserves the court's jurisdiction to award damages in lieu of an injunction.

[35] *Jaggard* v *Sawyer* [1995] 1 WLR 269.

[36] *Carr-Saunders* v *Dick McNeil Associates Ltd* [1986] 1 WLR 922.

[37] [1895] 1 Ch 287.

[38] Ibid., 322–3.

[39] Ibid., 323. In *Ketley* v *Gooden* (1996) 73 P & CR 305, the Court of Appeal awarded damages in lieu of an injunction despite the fact that the defendant had recklessly disregarded the claimant's rights because of delay by the claimant in starting proceedings and the minor nature of the damage.

[40] [1995] 1 WLR 269.

[41] Ibid., 287 (per Millett LJ).

to bear in mind that the test is one of oppression, and the court should not slide into application of a general balance of convenience test.'[42] Millett LJ did not doubt the utility of A. L. Smith LJ's four factors, but he also observed that they were not to be treated as an exhaustive list of the situations when it would be appropriate to award damages in lieu of an injunction.[43] Most probably he was referring here to the general equitable principles, which may make a court reluctant to grant an injunction.

It is worth drawing attention to the fact that A. L. Smith LJ's four factors do not make any reference to the question whether awarding an injunction will be contrary to the *public interest*. The question whether the claimant should be able to obtain an injunction which might close down an enterprise operating in the public interest is controversial. In *Shelfer*, Lindley LJ expressed the strong view that, 'the Court has always protested against the notion that it ought to allow a wrong to continue simply because the wrongdoer is able and willing to pay for the injury he may inflict. Neither has the circumstance that the wrongdoer is in some sense a public benefactor (e.g., a gas or water company or a sewer authority) ever been considered a sufficient reason for refusing to protect by injunction an individual whose rights are being persistently infringed.'[44] Thus the court was willing to grant an injunction against the Bankside power station in London. Similarly, in *Manchester Corporation v Farnworth*,[45] an injunction was granted closing one of Manchester's main power stations.

A contrasting view was adopted by the majority of the Court of Appeal in *Miller v Jackson*.[46] The action in *Miller* was brought by owners of a new house bordering a cricket field in County Durham seeking an injunction ordering the village cricket club not to conduct games without first taking adequate steps to prevent balls being struck out of the ground. Such an order would effectively have prevented cricket being played, since the club had already erected a 15-foot-high chain-link fence (they could not build a higher one because of the wind) and even that was insufficient to prevent half a dozen balls a season escaping onto the new estate.[47]

---

[42] Ibid., 203.

[43] Ibid., 287.

[44] [1895] 1 Ch 287, 315–16.

[45] [1930] AC 171. In this context it is also common to cite the Irish case of *Bellew* v *Cement Ltd* [1948] IR 61 where the quarry which provided 80% of the cement in the Republic of Ireland was stopped from blasting by injunction at a time of national rebuilding. It is important to note, however, that whilst under the ordinary law injunctions may be granted against such activities as power stations and sewage works this has not meant that such activities have had to cease. Rather, operators of such works have had to seek statutory authority for causing the disturbance that they inevitably cause. Such statutory authority effectively renders such activities immune from tort claims arising from such inevitable disturbance, but it is often a condition of the grant of such authority that compensation must be paid to those worst affected. From this perspective, the question whether courts should take the public interest into account when deciding whether to grant injunctions is really a question about the appropriate forum and procedure for deciding what is in the public interest: Parliament or the courts.

[46] [1977] QB 966.

[47] The club had offered to take other measures, such as putting a net over the Jacksons' garden, or fitting their windows with shutters and unbreakable glass, but those offers were rejected by the Jacksons on the ground that they were measures which would not prevent the nuisance in the garden but would merely limit the resulting damage.

A majority of the Court of Appeal found that the club's activities constituted a private nuisance, with Lord Denning MR dissenting. But Cumming-Bruce LJ then joined Denning MR to form a majority in favour of taking into account the interests of the public generally when deciding whether to grant an injunction. Cumming-Bruce LJ said, 'a court of equity must seek to strike a fair balance between the right of the claimants to have quiet enjoyment of their house and garden without exposure to cricket balls occasionally falling like thunderbolts from the heavens and the opportunity of the inhabitants of the village in which they live to continue to enjoy the manly sport which constitutes a summer recreation for adults and young persons, including one would hope and expect the [claimants'] son'.[48] Striking this balance, the injunction was refused. The trial judge had awarded £174.14 for past damages as well as granting an injunction. The Court of Appeal substituted an award of £400 to cover both past and future loss.

This decision understandably attracted criticism from those who shared the views expressed by Lindley LJ in *Shelfer*. When a similar point arose four years later, in *Kennaway v Thompson*,[49] the Court of Appeal returned to the orthodox view. In that case, the claimant owned a house next to a lake. A motor boat racing club frequently held races on the adjoining lake, and the noise disturbed the claimant's enjoyment of her house. She brought a claim against the club in private nuisance for an injunction and damages. The trial judge held that the races held by the club on the lake were so frequent that they amounted to a nuisance but denied an injunction on the ground that it was in the public interest for the club to be allowed to carry on with its activities. On appeal, the Court of Appeal reversed the trial judge and granted the claimant an injunction.

Lawton LJ said, 'We are of the opinion that there is nothing in *Miller v Jackson*, binding on us, which qualifies what was decided in *Shelfer*. Any decisions before *Shelfer*'s case (and there were some at first instance . . .) which give support to the proposition that the public interest should prevail over the private interest must be read subject to *Shelfer*'s case.'[50] The Court of Appeal therefore held that the trial judge should have granted an injunction restricting the noise made by the motor boat racing club. Importantly, however, the Court of Appeal in *Kennaway* stressed that the injunction should be carefully drafted to deal with the nuisance, and should not outlaw the whole activity. The injunction which the court drafted recognised that while motor boat racing every weekend from March to November was a nuisance, a reasonable inhabitant of a lakeside house could be expected to tolerate some motor boat racing. The injunction thus allowed the club to have one three-day international event, two two-day national events and three one-day club events each year, with a further rule that no boat emitting more than 75 decibels was to be used at any event.

---

[48] [1977] QB 966, 988G–H.
[49] [1981] QB 88.
[50] Ibid., 93G.

In the United States, the American Law Institute's Restatement 2d of Torts, §936(1) advocates an approach somewhere between those adopted in *Miller* and *Kennaway* respectively. Thus the Institute recommends determining the appropriate remedy by taking into account a list of factors including the nature of the claimant's interest, the relative adequacy of damages and injunction, the relative hardship involved in granting or refusing an injunction and the effects on the interest of third parties and the public generally.

In England, however, it seems that in almost all cases since *Kennaway* the courts have reverted to applying *Shelfer*. For instance, in *Elliott* v *London Borough of Islington*,[51] a case involving private nuisance by encroaching tree roots, Lord Donaldson MR said, 'I would only be echoing the authorities, and in particular *Shelfer*'s case, if I say that it is not the function of the courts to licence breaches of the rights of citizens. Compulsory purchase under statute is a well-known concept and is subject to well-known protections, but it is not for the courts to add to that burden on the citizen a system whereby, as in this case, they will grant, for a fee [i.e. damages in lieu of injunction] payable to the claimant, a compulsory lease of land to accommodate the roots of this tree in addition to putting up with the nuisance it creates.'[52] Where there is a risk that an injunction will harm the public interest, however, it is very common for the injunction to be *suspended* for a time sufficient to give the defendant time to make alternative arrangements.

Alternatives to injunctions other than damages

Damages are not the only alternative to awarding an injunction. In situations where there is no doubt that the defendant will voluntarily comply with the law as soon as it has been clarified the court may choose to make a declaration rather than granting an injunction. Similarly, the defendant may volunteer to give a formal undertaking that he will behave in a particular way rather than the court having to order him to do so.

One other situation where a court might refuse an injunction is where future damage can reasonably be eliminated by the defendant providing the victim of his tort with some form of protection. The best illustration of this is the unusual New Zealand case of *Bank of New Zealand* v *Greenwood*.[53] In that case, the defendant had built a shopping centre with a glass-roofed walkway. Unfortunately, the angle of the glass roof was such that it reflected the glare of the sun in the windows of the Bank of New Zealand, to the discomfort of staff and customers. The judge found that this amounted to a private nuisance, but that the defendant did not have to alter the roof, which would have cost the defendant $20,000. Instead, the defendant could provide 'venetian blinds' for the Bank.

The precise nature of this remedy is not easy to classify. Hardie Boys J insisted that he was not awarding damages in lieu of an injunction, but was merely pointing out

---

[51] [1991] 1 EGLR 167.
[52] Ibid., 168K.
[53] [1984] 1 NZLR 525.

a way in which the defendant could leave the claimant without a claim. It is probably best to treat the case as exemplifying a principle that an injunction can be refused when the defendant has offered to provide the victim of his tort with a reasonable way of eliminating future damage and the victim of his tort has refused this offer.

This principle will only be applied, however, where it would be wholly unreasonable for the victim to reject the offer and insist on an injunction. In *Elliott* v *London Borough of Islington*,[54] the owners of a tree with encroaching roots offered to rebuild the claimant's wall on a pre-cast concrete bar raised above the ground, so that the roots could pass underneath it without causing any damage.[55] This solution, however, would not have eliminated the private nuisance by encroachment, but merely reduced its effects, and the Court of Appeal held that Elliott was still entitled to an injunction.

Reform of the law concerning the availability of final injunctions

It is important to note that a court's decision to grant a final injunction to B ordering A not to do *x* does not necessarily determine whether *x* will eventually be done. If A believes that it will be profitable for him to do *x*, then even if B has obtained an injunction against him, ordering him not to do *x*, he can still try to reach an accommodation with B and buy the right to do what would otherwise be a tort.

One question which has excited legal economists is whether the approach of courts to questions of remedies is likely to lead to *x* being done when it is efficient to do *x* rather than *y* (some activity which the doing of *x* prevents), and *x* not being done when it is *not* efficient to do *x* rather than *y*. For instance, it has been asked whether the law concerning remedies for the tort of private nuisance is likely to lead to land being used as productively as possible.

Professor Coase argued in a famous article[56] that if 'bargaining costs' were ignored, then the initial decision in a private nuisance case would have no effect on how land was actually used. Whatever the decision, the parties would end up using their land in the most profitable way.[57] All the decision

---

[54] [1991] 1 EGLR 167.
[55] Lord Donaldson MR described this as 'the arboreal equivalent of a cat-flap' (ibid., 168B).
[56] Coase 1960.
[57] It may be worth spelling this out. Suppose that if A does *x* on his land then B will be prevented from doing *y* on her land. Suppose further that A will make £10,000 if he is allowed to do *x* on his land while B will only make £3,000 if she is allowed to do *y* on her land. If this is the case, then if the courts decide that A's doing *x* on his land will *not* amount to a private nuisance, A will end up doing *x* on his land: B will only be prepared to pay A up to £2,999 not to do *x* on his land, but A will need to be offered more than £10,000 to make it worth his while not to do *x*. If, on the other hand, the courts decide that A's doing *x* on his land *will* amount to a private nuisance and award an injunction against A, A will still end up being allowed to do *x* on his land. The money A stands to make from doing *x* on his land is such that he will be able to pay B enough money to convince B to agree to allow him to do *x* and still turn a profit. Now suppose that B's doing *y* on her land will actually be more profitable than A's doing *x* on his: B will make £10,000 if she is allowed to do *y* on her land while A will only make £3,000 if he is allowed to do *x* on his land. If this is the case, then if the courts decide that A's doing *x* on his land will *not* amount to a private nuisance, A will not, in the end, do *x* on his land and B will as a result be allowed to do *y* on her land. The reason for this is that the money B stands to make from doing *y* on her land exceeds the money A will make from doing *x* on his land. So B will be able to afford to pay A enough money to get him to agree not to do *x* on his land and still turn a profit. If, on the other hand, the courts decide that A's doing *x* on his land *will* amount to a private nuisance and award an injunction against A, A will not in the end

would determine is how the profits garnered from using the land in that way would be shared between them.[58] In the real world, however, there are 'bargaining costs', and these make it important whether a court dealing with a dispute chooses to grant an injunction or merely damages in lieu.

Suppose, for example, that Tom wants to hold very noisy concerts on his land and Wendy wants to run a hotel on her land, which is next to Tom's. Suppose further that if Tom holds concerts on his land, no one will want to stay at Wendy's hotel and so Wendy will have to close it down. Suppose further that Tom will commit the tort of private nuisance in relation to Wendy if he holds concerts on his land. If the courts grant an injunction to Wendy – requiring Tom not to hold concerts on his land – then if Tom wants to hold concerts on his land, he will have to pay Wendy to release him from the injunction that she has obtained against him. Now if the costs of bargaining with Wendy are high, then Tom may be unable to reach an agreement with Wendy to obtain the right to be allowed to hold concerts on his land even if he stands to make more money by holding concerts on his land than Wendy will make if she is allowed to run a hotel on her land.

Now suppose, instead, that the courts grant damages in lieu of an injunction to Wendy. In assessing how much Wendy should be paid by way of damages in lieu the courts will, of course, take into account how much money Wendy will lose if Tom is allowed to hold concerts on his land. If it really is more profitable for Tom to hold concerts on his land than it is for Wendy to run a hotel on her land, then Tom will pay the damages in lieu and get on with holding concerts on his land: the right result from the point of view of economic efficiency. Holding concerts on his land will give Tom enough money to pay Wendy her damages in lieu – damages which will at least cover the losses that Wendy will suffer – and still have something left over. If, on the other hand, the money Wendy would make if she were allowed to run a hotel on her land exceeds the money Tom will make by holding concerts on his land, then Tom will decline to hold any concerts on his land: again, the right result from the point of view of economic efficiency. Tom will not make enough money out of holding concerts on his land to cover the damages in lieu that he will have to pay Wendy if he presses ahead.

Now – it costs time and money for a court to calculate, for the purpose of determining how much Wendy should be awarded by way of damages in lieu of an injunction.[59] So a court will only want to do this if it is necessary. Taking these matters together, legal economists[60] commonly argue that if 'bargaining costs' between Tom and Wendy are low, an injunction against Tom should be

---

be allowed to do *x* on his land and B will as a result be left free to do *y* on her land. A will not be able to afford to pay B enough money to persuade her to release him from the injunction. B would have to be offered more than £10,000 to release A from his injunction, while it is not in A's interests to offer her more than £2,999. So *whatever the courts decide*, if A's doing *x* on his land will be more profitable than B's doing *y* on hers, then A will end up doing *x* on his land. Similarly, if B's doing *y* on her land will be more profitable than A's doing *x* on his land: *whatever the courts decide*, A will not in the end do *x* on his land and B will as a result be allowed to do *y* on her land.

[58] Of course, the fairness of the distribution of the profits is a perfectly legitimate concern for English law. It is worth remembering throughout this section that economic efficiency is not all-important.

[59] For how such damages are calculated see above, p. 714.

[60] See, for instance, Ogus & Richardson 1977; Tromans 1982.

granted. This way, the courts will not have to spend time calculating how much Wendy will lose if Tom is allowed to hold concerts on his land. If Tom will really make more money holding concerts on his land than Wendy will make if she runs a hotel on her land, Tom will have little difficulty in buying the right to hold concerts on his land from Wendy anyway. If, however, 'bargaining costs' are high, it may be better to refuse to grant Wendy an injunction and instead award her damages in lieu of an injunction. As long as these damages are calculated correctly, Tom will only end up holding concerts on his land if he will make more money holding concerts on his land than Wendy would make if she were able to run a hotel on her land. If this is not the case, then Tom will undertake not to hold concerts on his land.

So legal economists commonly suggest that unless 'bargaining costs' are low between parties in private nuisance cases, English law should not be so willing to grant injunctions in such cases: the granting of injunctions in private nuisance cases will sometimes give rise to economically inefficient results if the 'bargaining costs' between parties in private nuisance cases are high. Unfortunately, what evidence there is suggests that 'bargaining costs' between parties in private nuisance cases *are* high. A recent study of twenty American nuisance cases found that there was no serious bargaining after judgment in any of them.[61] This was in part because the litigation seemed to have resulted in animosity between the parties; also, winning claimants often seemed unwilling to treat their rights – for example, to freedom from noise, or freedom from smell – as things which could be commodified and sold. Consequently, there is some basis for suggesting that English courts should be more willing to grant damages in lieu of injunctions in private nuisance cases.

42

SPECIFIC RESTITUTION OF GOODS

As we have seen, if A is in possession of certain goods and B has an immediate right to possess those goods, A will commit a tort – the tort of conversion – if he refuses to hand those goods over to B.[1] If A refuses to hand those goods over to B, s 3(2)(a) of the Torts (Interference with Goods) Act 1977 gives the courts the power to order A to do what he ought to do and hand those goods over to B.

One would have thought that if A is in possession of B's goods and has unlawfully refused to hand those goods over to B, the courts would *automatically* order A to hand those goods over to B. In fact, the courts will only order A to hand those goods over to B if those goods are unique or are of some special value. If they are not, then the courts will simply order A to hand over the goods *or* pay B damages equal to the value of the goods unlawfully detained by him, and it will be up to A to decide whether or not he will give B his goods back.[2] As Swinfen Eady MR observed in *Whiteley Limited* v *Hilt*: 'the power vested in the Court to order the delivery up of a particular chattel is discretionary and ought not to be exercised when the chattel is an ordinary article of commerce and of no special value or interest, and not alleged to be of any special value to the [claimant], and where damages would fully compensate.'[3]

In *Howard E Perry & Co. Ltd* v *British Railways Board*,[4] it will be recalled, the defendant board was in possession of steel belonging to the claimants. Industrial action prevented the defendant board from transporting the steel to the claimants' customers. At the same time the defendant board did not want to hand the steel over to the claimants for fear that doing so would trigger more industrial action. The defendants had no right to withhold the claimants' steel from the claimants and the claimants asked the courts to order the defendants to hand over the steel. The order was granted. The industrial action that obtained at the time the case was heard meant that steel was a very rare commodity. As a result, awarding the claimants damages equal to the market value of the steel detained by the defendants would not have allowed the claimants to purchase substitute supplies of steel that they could use instead of the steel detained by the defendants. Given this, the courts thought that the only appropriate remedy was to order the defendants to hand the claimants' steel over to the claimants.

---

[1] See above, pp. 330–1.
[2] Torts (Interference with Goods) Act 1977, s 3(2)(b).
[3] [1918] 2 KB 808, 819. See also *IBL Ltd* v *Coussens* [1991] 2 All ER 133, 137h–j (per Neill LJ).
[4] [1980] 1 WLR 1375.

It was argued that as the claimants merely wanted the steel to sell it to their customers, they should simply be awarded damages equal to the money they would have made by selling the steel. However, this argument was rejected on the ground that awarding the claimants such damages and nothing more would not adequately safeguard the claimants' interests. The claimants had an interest in keeping their customers supplied with steel because their customers would become insolvent if they did not receive regular supplies of steel, and if the claimants' customers became insolvent, they would be in no position to do business with the claimants in future. This interest of the claimants' in keeping their customers supplied with steel would therefore not have been served at all if the claimants had merely been awarded damages designed to compensate them for the money they would have made if they had sold the steel detained by the defendants.

PART IV

ALTERNATIVE SOURCES OF COMPENSATION

INTRODUCTION

In this part of the book we leave tort law behind and explore some other areas of the law which someone who wants to obtain compensation for some loss that he has suffered might be able to take advantage of. If he's entitled to bring such a claim for compensation under one of these areas of law, we can say that he's entitled to bring a *non-tortious claim for compensation*. The mark of a non-tortious claim for compensation is that whether or not someone is entitled to bring such a claim does *not* depend on whether a tort has been committed. In contrast, if someone wants to sue in tort for compensation for some loss that she has suffered, she will only be entitled to make such a claim – a *claim in tort* – if a tort has been committed.

Tortious and non-tortious claims for compensation can overlap: there are occasions when someone who has suffered a loss will be entitled to bring both a tortious claim for compensation in respect of that loss and a non-tortious claim. For example, suppose that A, a policeman, falsely imprisoned B for some considerable period of time. B will, of course, be entitled to bring a claim in tort against A for compensation for the loss that she suffered when she was locked up.[1] But B may also be entitled under the Human Rights Act 1998 to make a non-tortious claim against A for compensation for the loss that she suffered as a result of her being falsely imprisoned.[2] B may be able to argue that: (1) When A imprisoned me, he acted inconsistently with my right to liberty under Article 5 of the European Convention on Human Rights; (2) A was a 'public authority' at the time he unlawfully imprisoned me; (3) A's conduct in imprisoning me was therefore unlawful under s 6 of the Human Rights Act 1998 which provides that it 'is unlawful for a public authority to act in a way which is incompatible with a Convention right'; (4) I am therefore entitled, under s 8 of the 1998 Act, to sue A for damages sufficient to compensate me for the loss that I suffered as a result of A's locking me up.[3]

Again – to take an extreme example – suppose that B was walking round A's zoo when she was savaged by a tiger which had escaped from its cage when one of A's employees carelessly left it open. B will, of course, be entitled to bring a claim in tort against A for compensation for the losses – pain and suffering, loss of salary, cost of medical treatment – that she suffered as a result of being mauled by A's tiger. She will be able to establish that A's employee was negligent in relation to her in acting as he did and that A is vicariously liable in

---

[1] See Chapter 11, above.

[2] B will have a free choice as to which claim – the claim in tort or the non-tortious claim under the Human Rights Act 1998 – to pursue. Section 11 of the 1998 Act provides that 'A person's reliance on a Convention right does not restrict . . . his right to make any claim or bring any proceedings which he could make or bring apart from ss 7 to 9.'

[3] In fact, s 8 of the 1998 Act places strict limits on when damages may be awarded against a public authority that has acted inconsistently with someone's rights under the European Convention on Human Rights. See below, pp. 733–6.

respect of that employee's negligence. But B will also be entitled under the Animals Act 1971 to bring a non-tortious claim against A for compensation for the loss that she suffered as a result of being mauled by B's tiger. Section 2(1) of the 1971 Act provides that '[where] any damage is caused by an animal which belongs to a dangerous species, any person who is a keeper of the animal is liable for the damage . . .'.

We have just noted that the same set of facts can give rise to a claim in tort and a non-tortious claim for compensation. However, there are occasions when the only remedy available to someone who has suffered loss of some kind is to bring a non-tortious claim for compensation in respect of that loss. For example, suppose that the police knew that Fred, a criminal on the loose, was very likely to attack Sarah if he were not apprehended and, due to the police's carelessness, they did not manage to arrest Fred before he attacked Sarah. Suppose further that Sarah wants to sue the police for compensation for the losses suffered by her as a result of her being attacked by Fred. (Fred will probably not be worth suing.)

As the law currently stands, Sarah will not be able to bring a claim in tort against the police: the police will not have owed her a duty to take reasonable steps to arrest Fred before he attacked Sarah.[4] However, Sarah may be able to make a non-tortious claim against the police under the Human Rights Act 1998 for the compensation she wants. She may be able to argue that: (1) the police acted inconsistently with Sarah's right to liberty and security under Article 5 of the European Convention on Human Rights when they carelessly failed to apprehend Fred before he attacked Sarah; (2) the police are a 'public authority' under the Human Rights Act 1998; (3) the police therefore acted unlawfully under s 6 of the 1998 Act when they carelessly failed to apprehend Fred before he attacked Sarah; (4) Sarah is therefore entitled under s 8 of the 1998 Act to sue the police for damages sufficient to compensate her for the losses that she suffered as a result of Fred attacking her.

Again, suppose that John was injured when he used a product manufactured by Lara that was dangerously defective. Suppose further that Lara took all reasonable steps to ensure that the product in question would not be dangerously defective – say Lara had a very strict quality control regime in her factory but somehow the product that injured John managed to slip through the net and into general circulation. John will obviously want to sue Lara for compensation for his injuries but he will not be able to bring a claim in tort against her for such compensation. This is because he will not be able to show that Lara was negligent in manufacturing the product that harmed him. At the same time he *will* be able to bring a non-tortious claim against Lara for compensation for the fact that he was injured under the Consumer Protection Act 1987.

---

[4] See above, pp. 201–3.

43

THE HUMAN RIGHTS ACT 1998

Section 6(1) of the Human Rights Act 1998 makes it unlawful for a 'public authority to act in a way which is incompatible with a Convention right', except where s 6(2) applies. If A, a public authority, acts in a way which is incompatible with a 'Convention right' in circumstances where s 6(2) does not apply and B suffers loss as a result, B may be able to claim damages from A under s 8 of the 1998 Act in respect of that loss. In making such a claim B will not have to allege that A committed a tort; as we have already seen, acting incompatibly with a 'Convention right' will not, of and in itself, amount to a tort.[1] All this raises four issues which we will deal with in this chapter. First, what is a public authority? Secondly, when will a public authority be held to have acted in a way which was incompatible with a 'Convention right'? Thirdly, when will s 6(2) apply? Fourthly, if A, a public authority, acts in a way which is incompatible with a 'Convention right' and B suffers loss as a result, when will B be able to claim damages in respect of that loss?

WHAT IS A PUBLIC AUTHORITY?

The Human Rights Act 1998 does not define 'public authority'. It states that courts and tribunals *are* 'public authorities',[2] and that neither of the Houses of Parliament, nor any person exercising functions in connection with proceedings in Parliament, is a 'public authority'.[3] Beyond these classes, however, the Act merely provides that the term 'public authority' *includes* 'any person certain of whose functions are functions of a public nature'[4] but that such a person will not be a 'public authority' by virtue only of this provision when carrying out an act of a private nature.[5]

After reading this provision it might be thought that the question whether A is a 'person certain of whose functions are functions of a public nature' is the principal test for whether A is a 'public authority'. This, however, is not what Parliament intended.[6] Parliament intended that there should be two classes of 'public authorities'. First, *core* or *pure* public authorities, such as government

---

[1] See above, p. 11.

[2] Human Rights Act 1998, s 6(3)(a). The special problems arising from liability for judicial acts are discussed below, pp. 737–8.

[3] Section 6(3)(b).

[4] Ibid.

[5] Section 6(5).

[6] When interpreting a statute it is Parliament's intention which is crucial. Here, however, the best evidence of Parliament's intentions is the statements of government ministers who were involved in steering the Human Rights Act 1998 onto the statute book.

departments, local authorities, the police and the armed forces,[7] which are treated as 'public authorities' for *all* activities. Secondly, *hybrid* or *functional* authorities, which are only treated as 'public authorities' when their acts are part of their public functions.[8] In the parliamentary debates concerning the 1998 Act, Railtrack[9] was regularly used as an example of a *hybrid* or *functional* authority. Thus the Lord Chancellor suggested that Railtrack would have to act compatibly with 'Convention rights' when carrying out its *public* functions in relation to safety, but not when carrying out its *private* functions as a property developer.[10] The Home Secretary identified the churches and the governing bodies of certain sports as further authorities which might be treated as mixed.[11] Another example might be a doctor who worked partly for the NHS and partly for private patients.

How do the courts determine whether a particular function is public? In *Aston Cantlow* v *Wallbank*, Lord Nicholls said that 'clearly there is no single test of universal application given the diverse nature of governmental functions and the variety of means by which these functions are discharged today'.[12] Whilst there is no test it is possible to list factors which can be indicators that a function is public: 'receiving money from public funds, having activities controlled (or perhaps merely monitored) by state bodies, and providing services which allow clients or customers to secure their legal (including Convention) rights',[13] '[providing] a public service, the degree to which it is supported or underpinned by government, and whether it has special statutory powers'.[14]

---

[7] These are the examples given by Lord Nicholls in *Aston Cantlow and Wilmcote with Billesley Parochial Church Council* v *Wallbank* (henceforth '*Aston Cantlow* v *Wallbank*') [2004] 1 AC 546, at [7]. Oliver 2000 suggests (at 492) that the test for a *core* public authority should 'place emphasis on whether it enjoys special powers and authority, and whether it is under constitutional duties to act only in the public interest which are "enforceable", *inter alia*, via mechanisms of democratic accountability'.

[8] In *Aston Cantlow* v *Wallbank* [2004] 1 AC 546 the two classes are referred to (at [11]) as 'core public authorities' and 'hybrid public authorities'. In the report of the Joint Committee on Human Rights, *The Meaning of Public Authority under the Human Rights Act, Seventh Report of the Session 2003–4* (HL Paper 39, HC 382), 10, the terms 'pure' and 'functional' are preferred. For evidence that two classes were intended see, for example, Lord Irvine of Lairg LC, Hansard (HL Debates), 24 November 1997, col. 784, 'There are obvious public authorities ... which are covered in relation to the whole of their functions by [s 6(1)]. Then there are some bodies some of whose functions are public and some private. If there are some public functions the body qualifies as a public authority but not in respect of acts which are of a private nature.' See also Jack Straw MP, Home Secretary, Hansard (HC Debates), 16 February 1998, col. 775.

[9] The now defunct private company that maintained the railway track and stations making up the British railway system. In 2002, Railtrack was replaced by a not-for-profit company, Network Rail.

[10] Hansard (HL Debates), 24 November 1997, col. 784.

[11] Hansard (HC Debates), 20 May 1998, col. 1020. He suggested that 'two most obvious examples' of churches carrying out public functions 'relate to marriages and to the provision of education in Church schools'. Despite some pressure Parliament did not exclude churches from the scope of s 6 but instead sought to allay some concerns by accepting an amendment which became s 13 Human Rights Act 1998. In *Aston Cantlow* v *Wallbank* [2004] 1 AC 546 the House of Lords confirmed that parochial church councils, an emanation of the Church of England, were a hybrid body.

[12] [2004] 1 AC 546, at [12].

[13] Feldman 2002, 97. The phrase 'providing services which allow clients or customers to secure their legal (including Convention) rights' is intended to cover functions such as providing legal aid or education.

[14] Oliver 2000, 492; see also Bamforth 1999.

Controversy has arisen over when private companies and charities delivering services under contracts with pure public authorities, particularly local government bodies, are *functional* 'public authorities'.[15] The Court of Appeal appears to have decided that a private body will not be found to be performing a public function *merely* because the function is being paid for out of public funds and if the private body did not perform the function then a public body would be obliged to do so.[16] To identify the function as public the other factors on the list will also be influential, as well as how far 'the acts that could be of a private nature are enmeshed in the activities of a public body'.[17] Critics of this approach believe that the focus should be on the body's capacity to interfere with human rights rather than the body's administrative links with institutions of the State.[18]

WHEN WILL A PUBLIC AUTHORITY ACT INCOMPATIBLY WITH A 'CONVENTION RIGHT'?

The scope of this book does not allow us to deal with this issue in detail; the interested reader should consult a standard work on the Human Rights Act 1998. However, a few preliminary points may be made here.

Convention rights

The term 'Convention rights' refers to the rights and fundamental freedoms set out in Articles 2 to 12 and 14 of the Convention for the Protection of Human Rights and Fundamental Freedoms ('the European Convention on Human Rights') and in Articles 1 to 3 of the First Protocol and Articles 1 to 2 of the Sixth Protocol.[19]

These include: the right to life (Article 2), the right not to be subjected to torture or to inhuman and degrading treatment (Article 3), the right not to be enslaved or compelled to perform forced labour (Article 4), the right to liberty and security of person (Article 5), the right to a fair trial (Article 6), the right not to be retrospectively convicted of committing an offence (Article 7), the right to respect for private and family life (Article 8), the right to freedom of thought, conscience and religion (Article 9), the right to freedom of expression (Article 10), the right to freedom of peaceful assembly and freedom of association (Article 11), the right to marry (Article 12), the right not to be

---

[15] The relevant cases include *Poplar Housing and Regeneration Community Association Ltd* v *Donoghue* [2002] QB 48; *R (A)* v *Partnerships in Care Ltd* [2002] 1 WLR 2610; *R (Heather)* v *Leonard Cheshire Foundation* [2002] 2 All ER 936; *R (Beer)* v *Hampshire Farmers' Markets Ltd* [2004] 1 WLR 233. The *Poplar* and *Leonard Cheshire* cases are criticised in Craig 2002.

[16] This is stated most clearly in *Poplar Housing and Regeneration Community Association Ltd* v *Donoghue* [2002] QB 48, [58]–[59]. The case concerned the provision of housing.

[17] Ibid., [65].

[18] Joint Committee on Human Rights, *The Meaning of Public Authority under the Human Rights Act, Seventh Report of the Session 2003–4* (HL Paper 39, HC 382), para 16–17: 'A serious gap has opened in the protection which the Human Rights Act was intended to offer.'

[19] These articles are all set out in Sch 1 to the Human Rights Act 1998.

discriminated against in the enjoyment of the other rights and freedoms (Article 14), the right to peaceful enjoyment of possessions (First Protocol, Article 1), the right to education (First Protocol, Article 2), and the right to free elections (First Protocol, Article 3).

Many of these 'Convention rights' stretch beyond the interests currently protected by the law of tort. To pick one example, there is no tort designed to protect directly a person's right to a fair trial (Article 6) or a person's right to marry (Article 12). Further, some of the 'Convention rights' offer greater protection for particular interests than is provided by the law of tort.[20] Consequently, it seems likely that there will be attempts to claim damages under s 8 of the Human Rights Act 1998 for violations of many, if not all, of these 'Convention rights'.[21]

It is important to bear in mind that not all of these rights are *absolute*. Many of the rights *expressly* permit restrictions, provided that such restrictions can be demonstrated to be 'prescribed by law' and 'necessary in a democratic society' in order to fulfil certain listed purposes. Where a public authority's act goes no further than a permitted restriction or interference it will not be incompatible with a 'Convention right'.

Acts and omissions

'Failures to act' by a public authority are treated as 'acts' for the purpose of determining whether it has acted in a way which is incompatible with a 'Convention right'.[22] This provision is particularly important in those contexts where it has been held that the Convention imposes a *positive* obligation on states to protect 'Convention rights'.

For instance, in *Osman* v *United Kingdom*[23] the European Court of Human Rights ruled that Article 2 imposed a positive obligation on a state to protect an individual whose life was at risk from criminal acts, and that this included an obligation on the police to 'do all that could be reasonably expected of them to avoid a real and immediate risk to life of which they have or ought to have knowledge'.[24] Similarly, in *Z* v *United Kingdom*[25] the European Court of Human Rights held that there was a parallel positive obligation under Article 3 on local authorities to take all steps that could reasonably be expected of them to avoid a real and immediate risk of ill-treatment of children of which they knew or ought to have had knowledge.[26] In *Anufrijeva* v

---

[20] A good example is provided by Art 2, the right to life. In *Osman* v *United Kingdom* [1999] 1 FLR 193, the European Court of Human Rights suggested that Article 2 puts a broader duty on police to take steps to deal with threats to life by criminals than is imposed on the police by the common law.

[21] Of course, in practice, some of the 'Convention rights' are violated by public authorities far more often than others.

[22] Human Rights Act 1998, s 6(6).

[23] [1999] 1 FLR 193.

[24] Ibid., 223G–H. On the facts, though, the European Court of Human Rights found that there had not been a violation of Article 2.

[25] [2001] 2 FLR 612.

[26] Ibid., at [73].

Southwark LBC[27] the Court of Appeal accepted that Article 8 also imposed a positive obligation which extended beyond the obligation under Article 3 where a family unit was involved.[28] The Court offered the following guidance on when inaction would constitute a lack of respect for private and family life:

> ... [T]here must be some ground for criticising the failure to act. There must be an element of culpability. At the very least there must be knowledge that the claimant's private and family life were at risk ... Where the domestic law of a state imposes positive obligations in relation to the provision of welfare support, breach of those positive obligations of domestic law may suffice to provide the element of culpability necessary to establish a breach of article 8, provided that the impact on private or family life is sufficiently serious and was foreseeable.[29]

Although the Human Rights Act 1998 generally covers omissions as well as acts, s 6(6) makes it clear that a failure to introduce a proposal for legislation or to make a remedial order cannot be treated as an unlawful 'act'.

WHEN WILL SECTION 6(2) APPLY?

Section 6(2) of the 1998 Act provides that a public authority will not be liable for an act which violates a 'Convention right' if '(a) as the result of one or more provisions of primary legislation, the authority could not have acted differently; or (b) in the case of one or more provisions of, or made under, primary legislation which cannot be read or given effect in a way which is compatible with the Convention rights, the authority was acting so as to give effect to or enforce those provisions.' This provision means that a public authority will not be liable for performing a statutory duty, even if this leads to a violation of a 'Convention right'. In such circumstances the most that an English court will be able to do is to declare that the statutory provision is incompatible with a Convention right.[30] Similarly, a public authority will not be liable for enforcing or giving effect to an incompatible statute or delegated legislation, where that legislation cannot be given effect to in any way which is compatible.

THE AVAILABILITY OF COMPENSATORY DAMAGES
The 'victim' requirement[31]

If B has suffered loss as a result of a public authority's acting incompatibly with a 'Convention right', B will not be able to claim damages in respect of that loss

---

[27] [2004] 2 WLR 603.

[28] Ibid., at [43]. The Court suggested that where only an individual's welfare was involved it was unlikely that Art 8 would require the state to provide positive support unless the individual's predicament was sufficiently severe to engage Article 3.

[29] Ibid., at [45]. This passage clearly involves a jumble of conditions. It seems that the Court of Appeal intended that three elements should be relevant (the degree to which the public authority was at fault, whether the inaction breached a statutory duty, and the effect on the claimant) and that a decision whether there had been a breach of Article 8 should turn on the combined effect of these three elements.

[30] Human Rights Act 1998, s 4.

unless he was a 'victim' of the public authority's unlawful act.[32] The Human Rights Act 1998 expressly relies on the definition of 'victim' developed in individual claims to the European Court of Human Rights under Article 34 of the European Convention on Human Rights.[33] A person will have no difficulty in establishing that she is a 'victim' if she has been 'directly affected' by the public authority's unlawful act. In certain circumstances, however, the European Court of Human Rights has also allowed claims by 'indirect victims', for instance, close relatives of a person whose right to life was violated.[34] Companies and other associations with legal personality can be 'victims',[35] but core public authorities cannot be.[36]

Courts able to award damages

Where a court finds that a public authority has acted incompatibly with a 'Convention right' it may only award damages if it is a type of court which can award damages in civil proceedings.[37]

Principles relevant to awards of damages[38]

Section 8(3) of the Human Rights Act 1998 states that a court should not award damages unless, taking account of all the circumstances of the case, it 'is satisfied that the award is necessary to afford just satisfaction to the person in whose favour it is made'. In considering whether it is necessary to make such an award, and if so, the amount, courts are instructed to 'take into account the principles applied by the European Court of Human Rights in relation to the award of compensation under Article 41 of the Convention'.[39] This instruction is relatively loose since it is an instruction 'to take into account', not 'to follow', and it refers to 'principles', not to 'detailed practice'. Thus English courts have a degree of leeway to develop their own approach. A domestic approach may be particularly important, because the English courts have available a range of remedies *other* than damages which is different from the range available to the European Court of Human Rights.

Before the Human Rights Act 1998 came into force the Law Commission carried out a survey of the 'principles' applied by the European Court of Human Rights.[40] It found that 'the only principle which is clearly stated in the Strasbourg case-law is that of *restitutio in integrum*'.[41] That is: the victim should

---

[31] See, generally, Miles 2000.
[32] Human Rights Act 1998, s 7(1).
[33] Section 7(7).
[34] *Mrs W* v *United Kingdom* (1983) 32 D & R 10.
[35] Provided that the right that they are asserting is one which can be enjoyed by such a body.
[36] *Aston Cantlow* v *Wallbank* [2004] 1 AC 546 at [8], 'A core public authority seems inherently incapable of satisfying the Convention description of a victim' (per Lord Nicholls).
[37] Human Rights Act 1998, s 8(1). This is thought to prevent awards by magistrates and the Crown Court. The position of the Court of Appeal (Criminal Division) is unclear.
[38] See, generally, Fairgrieve 2001; also McGregor 2003, 1541–9.
[39] Section 8(4).
[40] Law Com. No. 266, *Damages Under the Human Rights Act 1998* (2000).

be returned, as far as possible, to the position that he or she would have been in had there not been a breach of a 'Convention right'. The Court of Appeal has described this as 'the fundamental principle' and has derived from it the proposition that 'where the breach of a Convention right has clearly caused significant pecuniary loss, this will usually be assessed and awarded'. Despite describing the *restitutio in integrum* principle as 'fundamental' the Court of Appeal has also emphasised the further principle that, 'in considering whether to award compensation and, if so, how much, there is a balance to be drawn between the interests of the victim and those of the public as a whole'.[42] This means that the claimant's interest in receiving compensation must be weighed against the interest of the wider public in the continued funding of public services.

The Law Commission identified five specific factors which seem to have been regularly taken into account by the European Court of Human Rights in determining whether or not to make an award of damages.[43]

(1) *A finding of a violation may constitute 'just satisfaction'.* Where an applicant has not suffered pecuniary loss as a result of a breach, the European Court of Human Rights has often concluded that the mere decision that there was a violation is sufficient to constitute 'just satisfaction'. This factor has been most influential in cases where convicted criminals have claimed that while they were being investigated or tried there were violations of a procedural type.

(2) *The degree of loss suffered must be sufficient to justify an award of damages.* Although the European Court of Human Rights has generally been more willing to award damages for non-pecuniary losses than English courts dealing with tort claims, it has also insisted that something beyond mere annoyance or frustration must be shown before an award of damages will be appropriate.[44] In *R (KB) v London and South and West Region Mental Health Review Tribunal*,[45] Stanley Burnton J concluded that mental health patients who had suffered frustration and distress because of inordinate delay in processing their claims to mental health review tribunals in violation of Article 5(4) were only entitled to compensation for significant distress, of the level that might be recorded in clinical notes.

(3) *The seriousness of the violation will be taken into account.* Generous awards have been made for both pecuniary and non-pecuniary losses where there has been a serious violation, for instance, deliberate torture.[46] At the same time, however, the European Court of Human Rights has expressly refused to award 'aggravated damages'[47] and 'exemplary damages'.[48] It seems that despite this refusal the European Court of Human Rights does take account of 'aggravating

---

[41] Ibid., para 3.78.
[42] *Anufrijeva v Southwark LBC* [2004] 2 WLR 603 at [56].
[43] *Law Com. No 266*, para 4.44.
[44] *Silver v United Kingdom* (1991) 13 EHRR 582.
[45] [2003] 3 WLR 185.
[46] *Aksoy v Turkey* (1997) 23 EHRR 553.
[47] Discussed in Chapter 37, above.

features' in assessing damages, and is generally more generous in awarding damages for distress, anxiety and injury to feelings than English courts are in dealing with tort claims.

(4) *The conduct of the public authority may be taken into account.* This may include both the conduct giving rise to the application and a record of previous violations by the state. Although the European Court of Human Rights has expressly refused to award 'exemplary damages' in cases where someone's Convention rights have been violated it tends to be more generous in compensating for non-pecuniary loss when the behaviour of the public authority in question has been particularly reprehensible[49] or forms part of a pattern of violations.[50] In *Anufrijeva v Southwark LBC*[51] the Court of Appeal treated the wording of s 8 as precluding an award of exemplary damages.[52]

The question has been asked whether a claimant will have to show that a breach of Convention rights was the result of a public authority's carelessness in order to claim damages.[53] The simple answer to this question must be 'no'. The more detailed answer will add the qualifications that *in some circumstances* the claimant will have to show fault on the part of the public authority in order to establish that the authority acted incompatibly with a particular Convention right,[54] and *in some circumstances* the fault of the public authority may be decisive in demonstrating that an award of compensation is necessary as 'just satisfaction' and reflects the appropriate balance between the interests of the victim and those of the public as a whole.

(5) *The conduct of the applicant will be taken into account.* An award will be reduced where the applicant's conduct made a violation more likely or contributed to the damage suffered as a result of a violation.[55] There is some evidence of a general reluctance to compensate criminals for violations of their 'Convention rights'.[56]

---

[48] Discussed in Chapter 38, above.
[49] Two cases involving the United Kingdom provide good examples of this factor in action: *Halford v United Kingdom* (1997) 24 EHRR 523 (£10,000 awarded for stress caused by phone-tapping); *Smith and Grady v United Kingdom* (2000) 29 EHRR 493 (£19,000 awarded for non-pecuniary loss suffered as a result of investigation and dismissal from the armed forces because of sexual orientation).
[50] Cases involving excessive length of legal proceedings in Italy provide the best example of this factor in action: Law Com. No. 266, paras 3.52–3.53.
[51] [2004] 2 WLR 603.
[52] Ibid. at [55].
[53] Fairgrieve 2001, at 698.
[54] For instance, where the Convention right imposes a positive obligation to take *reasonable* steps, a claimant will only be able to show that an omission to take steps was incompatible if it would have been *reasonable* to take such steps.
[55] In *McCann v United Kingdom* (1996) 21 EHRR 97, the European Court of Human Rights found a violation of Article 2 (right to life) with respect to three IRA terrorists suspected of planning a bomb attack on Gibraltar, but refused to award compensation because of the applicants' behaviour.
[56] Law Com. No. 266, para. 3.57 discusses the different views on this matter.

Quantification of damages[57]

With regard to the quantification of damages the Law Commission concluded that 'in many cases – probably the majority of cases – the terms of section 8, read in the light of our review of the Strasbourg case-law, will not require [a court] awarding damages under the [Human Rights Act 1998] to apply measures which are significantly different to those it would reach were the claim one in tort'.[58] As we have noted above, however, the European Court of Human Rights seems to be more ready to award damages for non-pecuniary losses such as distress, anxiety and loss of relationship than English courts dealing with tort claims, and maintains a broad and flexible discretion in assessing damages which 'takes account of a range of factors including the character and conduct of the parties, to an extent which is hitherto unknown in English law'.[59]

Before the Human Rights Act 1998 came into force Lord Woolf expressed the view, extrajudicially, that awards made by English courts under s 8 for non-pecuniary losses should be 'moderate',[60] and this comment has been judicially endorsed.[61] Where an award is to be made for a kind of harm which is not commonly compensated for by common law damages, courts have been instructed to consider the level of awards for such harm commonly made by the Parliamentary Ombudsman and Local Government Ombudsman.[62]

Liability for judicial acts

Section 9(3) of the Human Rights Act 1998 states that 'In proceedings under this Act in respect of a judicial act done in good faith, damages may not be awarded otherwise than to compensate a person to the extent required by Article 5(5) of the Convention.' Article 5(5) provides that 'Everyone who has been the victim of arrest or detention in contravention of the provisions of this Article [5] shall have an enforceable right to compensation.' In practice, the European Court of Human Rights has not interpreted Article 5(5) as requiring that every victim of a violation of Article 5 must be awarded compensation. Indeed, the Strasbourg Court has often ruled that the finding that Article 5 was violated is itself sufficient 'just satisfaction'.

Section 9(3) may be important, however, in that it precludes an award of damages for a good faith violation by a judge of, for instance, Article 6 (right to a fair trial) or Article 8 (right to respect for private or family life). To an extent, it may be possible to circumvent this by attributing the violation to the act of

---

[57] See, generally, McGregor 2003, 1549–72.
[58] *Law Com. No. 266*, para 4.97.
[59] Ibid., para 4.96.
[60] Woolf 2000, 434.
[61] *Anufrijeva v Southwark LBC* [2004] 2 WLR 603 at [73]. Lord Woolf also stated extrajudicially that awards should be 'normally on the low side by comparison to tortious awards', but in the same paragraph that endorsed his view that awards should be 'moderate' the Court of Appeal said that the 'on the low side' comment 'should in future be ignored'.
[62] Ibid., [74].

some other public authority, for instance, a public prosecutor. This will not always be possible, however, because s 9(5) defines 'judicial act' as including 'an act done on the instructions, or on behalf, of a judge'.

Liability for legislative acts

For the avoidance of doubt it is worth stating that because 'public authority' does not include 'either House of Parliament or a person exercising functions in connection with proceedings in Parliament'[63] there will be no liability under s 8 of the Human Rights Act 1998 for legislation which violates a 'Convention right'. Further, because 'act' does not include 'a failure to (a) introduce in, or lay before, Parliament a proposal for legislation, or (b) make any primary legislation or remedial order',[64] there will be no liability under s 8 of the Human Rights Act 1998 for a ministerial failure to correct legislation which violates a 'Convention right'.

[63] Human Rights Act 1998, s 6(3)(b).
[64] Section 6(6).

44

LIABILITY FOR DANGEROUS THINGS

If A keeps, stores or uses a dangerous thing that escapes from A's control with the result that B suffers some kind of harm, B may be entitled to bring a non-tortious claim against A so as to be compensated for the harm that she has suffered under: (1) the rule in *Rylands* v *Fletcher*; (2) some liability rule analogous to the rule in *Rylands* v *Fletcher*; or (3) the Animals Act 1971.[1]

THE RULE IN *RYLANDS* V *FLETCHER*

There is continuing debate over the scope of the rule in *Rylands* v *Fletcher*. However, the recent decision of the House of Lords in *Transco plc* v *Stockport Metropolitan Borough Council*[2] seems to establish that the rule applies where A has brought onto, or kept on, some land an *exceptionally dangerous or mischievous thing in extraordinary or unusual circumstances*. Let's call the thing in question 'T' and the land which that thing was brought onto, or kept on, 'Blackacre'. The rule in *Rylands* v *Fletcher* – as interpreted by the House of Lords in *Transco* – says that if T *escapes* from Blackacre and consequently *damages B's land*[3] then B will be entitled to sue A for compensation for that damage unless A can raise a *defence* to B's claim.[4] Importantly, in order to sue A for compensation under the rule in *Rylands* v *Fletcher*, B will *not* have to prove that A was at fault for the fact that T escaped from Blackacre.

Rylands v *Fletcher*: the litigation[5]

In the 1860s John Rylands was the leading textile manufacturer in England. He arranged for contractors to build a reservoir to provide water for the steam engines which powered the looms in one of his mills. The reservoir was built

---

[1] B's claim for damages under any of these heads of liability will be non-tortious in nature because, in order to succeed in bringing a claim for damages under any of these heads, she will *not* have to prove that A committed any kind of legal wrong in relation to her either in keeping, storing or using the dangerous thing which harmed her or in failing to ensure that that dangerous thing did not harm her.

[2] [2003] 3 WLR 1467 (noted, Bagshaw 2004b). We will refer to this case hereafter as '*Transco*'.

[3] When we use the phrase 'B's land' in this context we intend the word 'land' to include not just the earth itself but also things attached to it, such as buildings, which count as real property. The statement that the land must be 'B's' is shorthand for the fact that in order to claim B must have a particular relationship with the land. The precise nature of that necessary relationship is discussed below, p. 743. At this stage an adequate summary is that the land will count as 'B's land' if B has a legally-recognised interest in the land, and in certain circumstances it may be sufficient that B has exclusive possession of the land.

[4] This statement of the rule is based on the formulation of Lord Bingham in *Transco*, at [11].

[5] The crucial judgments in this litigation are those of Blackburn J for the Court of Exchequer Chamber (at (1866) LR 1 Exch 265) and of the House of Lords (at (1868) LR 3 HL 330).

over old mine-shafts which had been filled with earth, but one of these plugs of earth gave way and water escaped from the reservoir into the mine-workings. It flowed through some abandoned mine-workings and flooded a mine worked by Thomas Fletcher.

In the Court of Exchequer Martin B found that Rylands was not liable to compensate Fletcher for the flooding to his mine.[6] He stated that 'the making of a pond for holding water is a nuisance to no one'.[7] This seems correct. A pond does not *in itself* interfere unreasonably with the interests of neighbours. But Martin B went on to say that even when the water in a pond escaped the owner of the land on which it was built should not be liable, because 'To hold the defendants liable would ... make them insurers against the consequences of a lawful act upon their own land when they had no reason to believe or suspect that any damage was likely to ensue.'[8] As it was not reasonably foreseeable that building a reservoir on Rylands's land could result in Fletcher suffering any harm, it could not be argued that Rylands owed Fletcher a duty not to build a reservoir on his land. So it was not possible to argue that Rylands committed any kind of wrong – let alone a tort – in building the reservoir on his land.

On appeal, however, the Court of Exchequer Chamber decided the case in favour of the claimant, Fletcher. Blackburn J said, 'We think the rule of law is, that the person who, for his own purposes, brings on his land and collects and keeps there anything likely to do mischief if it escapes, must keep it in at his peril; and if he does not do so, is *prima facie* answerable for all the damage which is the natural consequence of its escape. He can excuse himself by showing that the escape was owing to the claimant's default; or perhaps that the escape was the consequence of *vis major*, or the act of God.' He went on to explain the justice of this rule: 'It seems but reasonable and just that the neighbour who has brought something onto his own property (which was not naturally there), harmless to others so long as it is confined to his own property, but which he knows will be mischievous if it gets on his neighbour's, should be obliged to make good the damage which ensues if he does not succeed in confining it to his own property.'[9]

In the House of Lords Lord Cairns LC quoted the rule and the explanation for it then stated, 'I must say I entirely concur.'[10] Lord Cranworth similarly supported Blackburn J's exposition of the law.[11] However, Lord Cairns LC suggested that the rule of liability formulated by Blackburn J would *only* apply to someone who had in the course of a *non-natural use* of his land brought onto or stored on his land something which was liable to do damage if it escaped.[12]

---

[6] *Rylands v Fletcher* (1865) 3 H & C 774, 159 ER 737.
[7] Ibid., 792, 745.
[8] Ibid., 793, 745.
[9] (1866) LR 1 Ex 265, 279–80.
[10] (1868) LR 3 HL 330, 340.
[11] Ibid. Three Law Lords heard the appeal in *Rylands v Fletcher* but there is some mystery as to who the third Law Lord was. See, generally, Heuston 1970.
[12] (1868) LR 3 HL 330, 339.

This limit on the application of the rule in *Rylands* v *Fletcher* – as originally formulated by Blackburn J – has been followed ever since.

The rationale of the rule in *Rylands* v *Fletcher*

Lord Hoffmann has explained that 'it is tempting to see, beneath the surface of the rule, a policy of requiring the costs of a commercial enterprise to be internalised; to require the entrepreneur to provide, by insurance or otherwise, for the risks to others which his enterprise creates'.[13] But in most contexts English law has rejected this policy and has insisted that entrepreneurs (and others) should only be liable for damage caused by their *wrongs*. Thus, quoting Lord Hoffmann again, 'with hindsight, *Rylands* v *Fletcher* can be seen as an isolated victory for the internalisers. The following century saw a steady refusal to treat it as laying down any broad principle of liability.'[14]

Given that the policy beneath the rule has been rejected in most contexts we might ask why the House of Lords has resisted calls to abolish the rule. One explanation is simply that to overturn a case which has been part of English law for so long is 'too radical a step' for judges to take.[15] A second explanation, however, is that the fairness of liability without the need to prove fault where a defendant has created an extraordinary risk still appeals to some judges.[16]

The combination of the refusal to abolish the rule in *Rylands* v *Fletcher* with the 'refusal to treat it as laying down any broad principle of liability' has led to the rule being restricted within narrow limits. These limits, however, have proved difficult to define with any precision. The High Court of Australia castigated them as so uncertain that 'the practical application of the rule in a case involving damage caused by the escape of a substance is likely to degenerate into an essentially unprincipled and *ad hoc* subjective determination'.[17] One of the principal aims of the speeches in the House of Lords in *Transco* was to 'restate [the rule] so as to achieve as much certainty and clarity as attainable'.[18]

Current scope of the rule

The relationship with private nuisance
Many of the limits on the scope of the rule in *Rylands* v *Fletcher* flow from the supposed relationship between that rule and the tort of private nuisance. A majority of the House of Lords recently classified the rule as 'a sub-species of nuisance',[19] 'an aspect of the law of private nuisance'[20] or 'a species, or special

---

[13] *Transco plc* v *Stockport Metropolitan Borough Council* [2003] 3 WLR 1467, at [29].
[14] Ibid.
[15] Ibid., at [43] (per Lord Hoffmann).
[16] For instance, ibid. at [6] (per Lord Bingham) and [110] (per Lord Walker).
[17] *Burnie Port Authority* v *General Jones Pty Ltd* (1994) 179 CLR 520, 540 (per Mason CJ, Deane, Dawson, Toohey and Gaudron JJ)
[18] *Transco plc* v *Stockport MBC* [2003] 3 WLR 1467, at [8] (per Lord Bingham).
[19] Ibid., at [9] (per Lord Bingham).
[20] Ibid., at [52] (per Lord Hobhouse).

case, of nuisance'.[21] This followed the earlier opinion that *Rylands* was part of the law concerning 'the mutual duties of adjoining or neighbouring landowners'.[22] If this classification is correct then it is one which will determine who can be liable, who can claim, and what types of damage can be claimed for under the rule.

We have three reasons for believing that this classification was misguided. First, private nuisance is a tort. In contrast, liability under the rule in *Rylands* v *Fletcher* does not arise in response to someone's committing a tort: a defendant does not have to commit any kind of legal *wrong* in order to be held liable under the rule in *Rylands* v *Fletcher*.[23] Secondly, the original rationale behind *Rylands* – internalisation of costs to commercial enterprises[24] – provides no justification for distinguishing between costs from damage to neighbouring land and costs from other types of damage, for instance personal injuries. Instead this rationale suggests that the rule has more in common with the other liability rules discussed in this chapter, most of which cover types of damage beyond damage to neighbouring land. Thirdly, the reasons recently provided by the House of Lords for preserving the rule in *Rylands* v *Fletcher*[25] provide no justification for limiting its operation to compensating for damage to land. Unfortunately, it seems that the erroneous classification is too firmly woven into the speeches of a majority of their Lordships in *Transco* for any court below the House of Lords to ignore it. Consequently in the paragraphs that follow we will assume that the erroneous classification is the current law.

Who can be held liable under the rule?

The proposition that *Rylands* is part of the law concerning 'the mutual duties of adjoining or neighbouring landowners'[26] might be taken to mean that only *an owner* of land from which a dangerous thing escapes can be held liable. Weighing against this suggestion, however, are several cases where defendants who neither owned the land, nor were tenants of it, were held liable.[27] These cases suggest that liability can attach to any occupier of land from which the dangerous thing escaped.[28] Some *dicta* seem to go further and suggest that the person responsible for storing or collecting the mischievous substance can be liable regardless of his relation to the land.[29] Our view, consistent with our view as to who can be liable in private nuisance,[30] is that it is these *dicta* which correctly express the law.

---

[21] Ibid., at [92] (per Lord Walker).

[22] *Read* v *J Lyons & Co. Ltd* [1947] AC 156, 173 (per Lord Macmillan).

[23] See above, pp. 31–2.

[24] See above, p. 741.

[25] See above, p. 741.

[26] *Read* v *J Lyons & Co. Ltd* [1947] AC 156, 173 (per Lord Macmillan).

[27] *Eastern & South African Telegraph Co.* v *Cape Town Tramways Co.* [1902] AC 381; *West* v *Bristol Tramways Co.* [1908] 2 KB 14; *Charing Cross Electricity Supply Co.* v *Hydraulic Power Co.* [1914] 3 KB 772; *Rainham Chemical Works Ltd* v *Belvedere Fish Guano Co. Ltd* [1921] 2 AC 465; *Shiffman* v *Order of St John* [1936] 1 All ER 557.

[28] In *Transco*, at [11], Lord Bingham's restatement uses the phrase 'occupier of land' to refer to the potential defendant.

[29] In *Rainham Chemical Works* v *Belvedere Fish Guano Co. Ltd* [1921] 2 AC 465, Lord Sumner said (at 479) 'they cannot escape any liability which otherwise attaches to them on *storing it* [explosives] there merely because they have no tenancy or independent occupation' (emphasis added). In *Powell* v *Fall* (1880) 5 QBD 597 the escape was from the highway.

[30] See above, pp. 372–3.

Who can claim under the rule?

The conclusion that liability under *Rylands* arises out of the law on private nuisance means that the question of who can claim under the rule should be answered in line with the way that the House of Lords answered the question who can sue in private nuisance in *Hunter* v *Canary Wharf*.[31] Thus to sue under *Rylands*[32] a claimant must have a legally-recognised interest in the land[33] or must be in exclusive possession of the land,[34] and such a claimant can only sue for physical harm caused to the land, harm to its amenity value and consequential damage to chattels, not for personal injuries.[35]

A claimant cannot therefore rely on *Rylands* to recover compensation for pure economic losses that he has suffered as a result of a dangerous thing's escaping off someone's else land. In *Cattle* v *Stockton Waterworks Co.*, Blackburn J was clear that in the *Rylands* case a claim could not have been made 'by every workman and person employed in the mine, who in consequence of its stoppage made less wages than he would otherwise have done'.[36] This should not be taken to mean, however, that *all* economic losses are irrecoverable under the rule in *Rylands* v *Fletcher*. Compensation for any diminution in the amenity value of land and compensation for economic losses *consequential on* physical damage to the claimant's land may be recovered under the rule in *Rylands* v *Fletcher*.[37]

An exceptionally dangerous or mischievous thing

Blackburn J spoke of the rule in *Rylands* v *Fletcher* as covering 'anything likely to do mischief if it escapes'. For a time, however, courts seemed to insist that this meant that the rule only extended to things which were 'inherently dangerous'. Thus in *Hale* v *Jennings Bros*[38] the Court of Appeal discussed whether a fairground 'chair-o-plane' was inherently dangerous, and concluded that it was because it was intended for use by 'ignorant people' who would be unaware of the dangers of fooling about in flying chairs.

It is difficult to disagree, however, with Professor Stallybrass who exhaustively examined the cases and concluded that a condition of 'inherent

---

[31] [1997] AC 655 (discussed above, pp. 381–2).

[32] This would have caused problems for the claimant in *Eastern & South African Telegraph Co.* v *Cape Town Tramways Co.* [1902] AC 381 because it was claiming for damage done to its submarine cable.

[33] Such as a fee simple in possession, a tenancy, or a reversionary interest. A more detailed presentation of what interests in land the law recognises is to be found in the chapter on the tort of private nuisance, above, pp. 381–2.

[34] Exclusive possession will be sufficient *unless* the defendant has the right to possess the land, or acted with the authority of the person with the right to possess. But exclusive possession is not necessary because, for instance, a reversioner may be able to sue. Unfortunately, in *Transco*, [9] and [11], Lord Bingham seems to have oversimplified when he stated that the claimant only had to be an 'occupier' of the land.

[35] A majority in *Transco plc* v *Stockport MBC* [2003] 3 WLR 1467 expressly states that claims cannot be brought for personal injuries under the rule in *Rylands* v *Fletcher*: see [9] (Lord Bingham), [35] (Lord Hoffmann), and [52] (Lord Hobhouse).

[36] (1875) LR 10 QB 453, 457.

[37] The claimants' claim in *Cambridge Water Co.* v *Eastern Counties Leather* [1994] 2 AC 264 was a claim to be compensated for economic loss suffered by them as a result of their land suffering some kind of physical damage: see below, p. 748.

[38] [1938] 1 All ER 579.

dangerousness' was unhelpful because 'just as there is nothing which is at all times and in all circumstances dangerous so it seems that there is scarcely anything which is in all circumstances safe'.[39]

In *Transco* Lord Bingham reasserted the importance of the 'dangerousness' condition. He said that 'It must be shown that the defendant has done something which he recognised, or judged by the standards appropriate at the relevant place and time, he ought reasonably to have recognised, as giving rise to an exceptionally high risk of danger or mischief if there should be an escape, however unlikely an escape may have been thought to be.'[40] Moreover, he stated that he did not think that 'the mischief or danger test should be at all easily satisfied'.[41] However, whilst Lords Hoffmann and Walker agreed with Lord Bingham that 'creation of an exceptional risk' was a relevant factor in the application of the rule, they both treated the matter as more relevant to the requirement of 'an extraordinary use of land'.[42]

Extraordinary use

The rule in *Rylands* v *Fletcher* as originally formulated by Blackburn J only applied to cases where someone brought onto land or kept on land something 'which was not naturally there'. As we have seen, in the House of Lords, Lord Cairns LC built on this statement and drew a distinction between defendants who use their land 'for any purpose for which it might in the ordinary course of the enjoyment of land be used . . . what I may term the natural user of land' and those who 'not stopping at the natural use of their close, had desired to use it for any purpose which I may term a non-natural use'.[43] So Lord Cairns LC seemed to think: (*a*) that liability under the rule in *Rylands* v *Fletcher* was limited to cases where someone used his land in a 'non-natural' way; *and* (*b*) that someone would use his land in a 'non-natural' way if he used it in an *extraordinary* way.

The early cases do not provide any clear answer as to the original meaning of 'non-natural user'. Since the House of Lords upheld the decision in favour of Fletcher their Lordships must have concluded that a reservoir was a sufficiently non-natural use of land. Moreover, the reasoning in Blackburn J's judgment suggested that the rule would also cover straying cattle and an escape of sewage.[44] Other early cases treated the rule as covering poisonous yew trees,[45] creosote,[46] and large quantities of electricity.[47] In *Wilson* v *Waddell*,[48] however,

---

[39] Stallybrass 1929, 387.
[40] [2003] 3 WLR 1467, at [10].
[41] Ibid.
[42] Ibid., at [49] (per Lord Hoffmann), [103] (per Lord Walker).
[43] (1868) LR 3 HL 330, 339.
[44] In *Smeaton* v *Ilford Corp.* [1954] Ch 450, Upjohn J stated that 'To collect into a sewer a large volume of sewage, inherently noxious and dangerous and bound to cause great damage if not properly contained, cannot be described, in my judgment, as a natural use of land' (ibid., 472).
[45] *Crowhurst* v *Amersham Burial Board* (1878) 4 CPD 5. The rule does not, apparently, cover thistles which are 'the natural growth of the soil': *Giles* v *Walker* (1890) 24 QBD 656, 657.
[46] *West* v *Bristol Tramways Co.* [1908] 2 KB 14.
[47] *Eastern & South African Telegraph Co.* v *Cape Town Tramways Co.* [1902] AC 381.
[48] (1876) 2 App Cas 95.

Lord Blackburn (as he had by then become) stated that use of land for ordinary mining operations was a natural use.

In *Rickards* v *Lothian*[49] the Privy Council held that an escape of water from ordinary plumbing[50] did not fall within the scope of the rule in *Rylands* v *Fletcher*. Lord Moulton said, 'It is not every use to which land is put that brings into play that [rule]. It must be some special use bringing with it increased danger to others, and must not merely be the ordinary use of land or such a use as is proper for the general benefit of the community.'[51] The last portion of this statement – 'not merely ... such a use as is proper for the general benefit of the community' – can be interpreted to suggest that only *improper* uses of land should fall within the scope of the rule in *Rylands* v *Fletcher*. Such an interpretation could be used by those who disliked the rule in *Rylands* v *Fletcher* to restrict its scope severely. Thus in *Read* v *J Lyons & Co.*[52] two members of the House of Lords suggested that use of land for a munitions factory in wartime might not be a 'non-natural user',[53] and in *Cambridge Water* v *Eastern Counties Leather* the trial judge held that the use of chemical solvents by a tannery in an industrial village was not a non-natural user given the benefits for local employment.

Shortly before the judgment of the House of Lords in *Cambridge Water* we could have described the meaning of 'non-natural user' as journeying from 'not naturally there' to 'improper', via 'extraordinary'. But in his judgment in that case Lord Goff spoke against any broad reading of Lord Moulton's phrase. Four points made by Lord Goff in this part of his judgment are worth particular attention. First, he made clear that in his opinion 'the storage of substantial quantities of chemicals on industrial premises should be regarded as an almost classic case of non-natural use'.[54] Secondly, he stated that the creation of employment could not be sufficient of itself to establish that a particular use of land was 'natural or ordinary'.[55] Thirdly, he suggested that because in the same case the House of Lords was deciding that there could be no liability under the rule in *Rylands* v *Fletcher* for unforeseeable consequences of escapes, it would

---

[49] [1913] AC 263.

[50] The line is not easy to draw between ordinary and extraordinary plumbing but it seems to lie somewhere between *Western Engraving Co.* v *Film Laboratories Ltd* [1936] 1 All ER 106, where the Court of Appeal held that the use of large quantities of water for film-washing was a non-natural user, and *Peters* v *Prince of Wales Theatre* [1943] KB 73 where a differently constituted Court of Appeal suggested that connection of water to a sprinkler system in a theatre was an ordinary and usual user. In *Transco* [2003] 3 WLR 1467 a water pipe carrying sufficient water for 66 flats was treated as 'entirely normal and routine' (at [13]) and thus not an 'extraordinary use', though Lord Bingham complicated the matter somewhat by stating that in his opinion the volume of water in a domestic plumbing system was also insufficient to amount to a sufficiently dangerous thing (at [10]).

[51] [1913] AC 263, 280.

[52] [1947] AC 156, 169–70 (per Viscount Simon), 173–4 (per Lord Macmillan).

[53] In the earlier case of *Rainham Chemical Works* v *Belvedere Fish Guano Co. Ltd* [1921] 2 AC 465, the House of Lords had shown no hesitation in finding that making munitions during the First World War was 'certainly not the common and ordinary use of the land': ibid., 471 (per Lord Buckmaster).

[54] [1994] 2 AC 264, 309.

[55] Ibid.

be less necessary *in future* to interpret the phrase 'non-natural user' narrowly in order to limit the scope of liability.[56] Fourthly, he thought that the historic relationship between the rule in *Rylands* v *Fletcher* and the tort of private nuisance meant that in future the concept of 'non-natural user' might develop alongside the concept of 'reasonable user' in private nuisance.[57] The fourth point is particularly important because it suggests that the main activities which should be excluded from the scope of 'non-natural user' are those which create risks which are generally accepted as part of ordinary social give-and-take.

In *Transco* Lord Bingham stated that: 'I think it is clear that ordinary user is a preferable test to natural user, making it clear that the rule in *Rylands* v *Fletcher* is engaged only where the defendant's use is shown to be extraordinary and unusual. This is not a test to be inflexibly applied: a use may be extraordinary and unusual at one time or in one place but not so at another time or in another place . . . I also doubt whether a test of reasonable user is helpful, since a user may well be quite out of the ordinary but not unreasonable, as was that of *Rylands*, *Rainham Chemical Works* or the tannery in *Cambridge Water*. Again, as it seems to me, the question is whether the defendant has done something out of the ordinary in the place and at the time when he does it. In answering that question, I respectfully think that little help is gained (and unnecessary confusion perhaps caused) by considering whether the use is proper for the general benefit of the community.'[58]

Whilst Lord Bingham cast doubt on the utility of tests asking whether particular uses were unreasonable or improper he offered little guidance on how to draw the line between the ordinary and extraordinary. Indeed Lord Hoffmann seemed to regard a test based around 'ordinary uses of land' as 'rather vague'.[59] He offered 'a use creating an increased risk' as the 'converse' of 'natural use',[60] stated that 'the criterion of exceptional risk must be taken seriously',[61] and, most exceptionally, asserted that a 'useful guide in deciding whether the risk has been created by a "non-natural" user of land is . . . to ask whether the damage which eventuated was something against which the [claimant] occupier could reasonably be expected to have insured himself'.[62]

An approach which distinguishes between ordinary and extraordinary uses of land in terms of the degree of risk posed to neighbours in the event of an escape seems as easy to apply and attractive as any. But we cannot offer any support for Lord Hoffmann's extraordinary proposition about insurability. It seems to us that insurability of the claimant's property is *irrelevant* to the correct classification of the defendant's activitiy. When a property owner insures a terraced house against destruction such insurance generally does not distinguish

---

[56] Ibid.
[57] Ibid., 299.
[58] [2003] 3 WLR 1467, at [11]. Lord Scott agreed with Lord Bingham's judgment. Lord Walker expressly commended Lord Bingham's discussion of this requirement, but also commended the different approach of Lord Hoffmann!
[59] Ibid., at [37].
[60] Ibid., at [44].
[61] Ibid., at [49].
[62] Ibid., at [46].

between a car swerving into the front wall or the local fireworks factory exploding, but that surely cannot make the local fireworks factory into an ordinary use of land in the locality?

Furthermore, in many situations, as Lord Hoffmann realises,[63] *both* the person responsible for the activity *and* the neighbouring property owners will be insured. In such circumstances it is doubtful whether leaving losses with the property owners will be economically efficient.[64] Moreover, as Lord Hobhouse pointed out, the issue is not solely about efficiency but also about whether it is fair to make potential claimants pay the insurance premiums which cover the risk of damage as a result of such incidents. Lord Hoffmann's argument that most property losses should be dealt with by self-insurance rather than by claims against those responsible for the activity looks remarkably like an argument *against* internalisation of costs to the activity, and thus an argument against the existence of *Rylands* v *Fletcher* liability, rather than a criterion for determining *when* costs should be internalised.

It is worth briefly making two further points about the 'extraordinary use' requirement. First, it seems that where statute has authorised a particular use of land that use will be considered as 'natural and ordinary' unless there has been negligence.[65] Secondly, Blackburn J's original formulation of the rule stated that the collection of the dangerous thing had to be 'for his own purposes'.[66] A court would be unlikely to use this phrase to protect a defendant whose activity was intended to benefit the public generally, but might use it to protect a defendant whose activity was intended to benefit both himself and the claimant. In such circumstances, however, there is often an overlap with the defence of consent.

Escape

In *Read* v *J Lyons & Co.*[67] the claimant was an inspector at a munitions factory who was injured by an exploding shell. The House of Lords determined that the rule in *Rylands* v *Fletcher* did not apply in these circumstances because the explosive had not escaped from the defendant's premises, but merely from its control. An escape from the defendant's land was treated as logically necessary because, in the words of Lord Macmillan, 'the doctrine of *Rylands* v *Fletcher*, as I understand it, derives

---

[63] Ibid., at [39].

[64] Leaving the potential claimant to bear the loss might be efficient if *either:* (*a*) the claimant was better placed to avoid the harm caused by an escape than the defendant to prevent the escape; *or* (*b*) the claimant was better placed to evaluate and insure against the risk of his suffering loss as a result of an escape from the defendant's land and *only* he carried insurance to guard against that risk eventuating. Neither of these conditions are likely to be satisfied. One might think that by leaving the loss with the potential claimant at least the legal costs of determining whether the defendant is liable will be saved. But because a *negligence* claim can certainly be brought when a careless escape has caused personal injury or damage to personal property, and probably *can* be brought if a careless escape has caused damage to land, the costs saved by preventing claims under the rule in *Rylands* v *Fletcher* where land has been damaged by an escape will be small. To spell the point out, the costs saved in not pursuing a claim under the rule in *Rylands* v *Fletcher* will often be spent instead determining whether there is a good claim in negligence.

[65] *Transco* [2003] 3 WLR 1467, at [30]–[31] (per Lord Hoffmann), [89] (per Lord Scott).

[66] See quotation above, p. 740.

[67] [1947] AC 156.

from a conception of mutual duties of adjoining or neighbouring landowners, and its cogenors are trespass and nuisance'.[68] A requirement of an escape from the defendant's premises ensures that the *Rylands* rule does not become entangled with the rules concerning the liability of an occupier to his or her visitors.

Transco involved an escape of water from one part of the defendant's premises to another part of the premises where it threatened to damage a gas pipe which the claimant had a right to run across the defendant's premises. Lord Scott was adamant that even if the claimant's right to run the pipeline across the defendant's land was a proprietary right, an easement, the claimant still could not sue the defendant because there had been no escape from the defendant's land.[69]

Reasonable foreseeability

Suppose A brought a dangerous thing, T, onto his land in the course of an extraordinary use of his land and T then escaped off A's land with the result that B suffered some kind of damage to her land. In *Rylands* v *Fletcher*, Blackburn J seemed to be of the opinion that B would be entitled to sue A for compensation for the harm suffered by her so long as her suffering that harm was a 'natural' consequence of T's escaping from A's land.[70] However, the House of Lords made it clear in *Cambridge Water Co.* v *Eastern Counties Leather*[71] that, in the case we are considering, B will *only* be entitled to sue A under the rule in *Rylands* v *Fletcher* for compensation for the harm that she suffered as a result of T's escaping from A's land if it was *reasonably foreseeable* that someone like B would suffer *that kind of harm* if T escaped from A's land.

The facts of the *Cambridge Water* case illustrate the point. The defendants ran a tanning business which used large quantities of chemicals. Some of these chemicals got spilled from time to time on the defendants' factory floor and they seeped through the factory floor and into the ground beneath the defendants' factory. The chemicals then flowed along impermeable strata until they reached a borehole owned by the claimants which was located over a mile away from the defendants' factory. The claimants used this borehole to obtain water which they would then supply to nearby residents. The chemicals from the defendants' factory contaminated this borehole with the result that the claimants were forbidden to extract any more water from the borehole.[72] The claimants sued the defendants under the rule in *Rylands* v *Fletcher* for compensation for the costs incurred by them in creating a new borehole.[73] The House of Lords dismissed the claimants' claim on the ground that no one could have

---

[68] Ibid., 173.

[69] [2003] 3 WLR 1467, at [78]–[80].

[70] (1866) LR 1 Ex 265, 279–80.

[71] [1994] 2 AC 264.

[72] The water in fact remained perfectly drinkable despite the contamination. However, the water fell foul of legislation that had been introduced pursuant to a silly EC Directive, banning the supply of water which contained even the slightest traces of the kind of chemicals that had contaminated the claimants' borehole.

[73] This claim did not fall foul of the rule in *Cattle* v *Stockton Waterworks* (1875) LR 10 QB 453 that compensation for pure economic loss may not be recovered under the rule in *Rylands* v *Fletcher*. The economic loss for which the claimants wanted to be compensated in *Cambridge Water* was consequential on the claimant's property (their borehole) being damaged.

foreseen that the claimants' borehole would be contaminated if the chemicals that the defendants used escaped from their land.

It should be noted that in the case we are considering, B will not have to show that it was reasonably foreseeable that T *would escape* from A's land in order to bring a claim under the rule in *Rylands* v *Fletcher* for compensation for the harm that she suffered as a result of T's escaping from A's land. All B will have to show is that it was reasonably foreseeable that *if* T escaped, someone like her would suffer the kind of harm for which she wants compensation. So suppose that Alan kept some explosives on his land. Suppose further that Alan used elaborate precautions to ensure that the explosives would not escape from his land and as a result it was not reasonably foreseeable that the explosives would escape from his land. Suppose further that the explosives – against all expectation – managed to detonate and damaged Betty's neighbouring land.

In such a case, the fact that it was not reasonably foreseeable that the explosives would escape from Alan's land would not be fatal to Betty's claim under the rule in *Rylands* v *Fletcher* to be compensated for the harm suffered by her. All Betty would have to show – for the purposes of satisfying the requirement of reasonable foreseeability of damage under the rule in *Rylands* v *Fletcher* – is that it was reasonably foreseeable that someone like her would suffer damage to her land *if* the explosives escaped from Alan's land. This was, of course, eminently foreseeable.[74]

Defences

Suppose something that A brought onto his land escaped from that land and harmed B. If B sues A for compensation for that harm under the rule in *Rylands* v *Fletcher*, there are a number of different defences that A may be able to raise to B's claim.

(1) *Act of a stranger.* A will have a defence to B's claim for compensation under the rule in *Rylands* v *Fletcher* if the escape resulted from the act of a person whom A could not control.[75] It seems to be assumed that a landowner has a sufficient degree of control over the anticipated activities[76] of independent contractors who he engages to bring the dangerous thing onto his premises or to store it there.[77] A defendant will not be liable, however, for an escape resulting from the deliberate and malicious act of a stranger, unless such an act ought to have been anticipated and guarded against. So in *Perry* v *Kendricks Transport Ltd*[78] a couple of boys threw a lighted match into the petrol tank of a motor coach that was standing on the defendants' land. The coach blew up and the

---

[74] However, Betty's claim under the rule in *Rylands* v *Fletcher* for compensation for the damage suffered may still be defeated if a defence is available to Alan.

[75] *Box* v *Jubb* (1879) 4 Ex D 76; *Rickards* v *Lothian* [1913] AC 263; *Perry* v *Kendricks Transport Ltd* [1956] 1 WLR 85.

[76] Where the independent contractor behaves in a wholly unanticipated way A may be able to avoid liability. This has certainly been the position in the analogous cases involving fire. See below, p. 751.

[77] In *Rylands* v *Fletcher* itself the escape seems to have been caused by the carelessness of the independent contractors who built the reservoir.

[78] [1956] 1 WLR 85.

claimant, who was standing outside the defendants' land at the time of the explosion, was injured. The defendants were not held liable to compensate the claimant for his injuries under the rule in *Rylands* v *Fletcher*.[79]

(2) *Act of God.* In the situation we are considering, A will have a defence to B's claim for compensation under the rule in *Rylands* v *Fletcher* if the escape resulted from a wholly extraordinary natural event.[80]

(3) *Fault of the claimant.* In the situation we are considering, A will have a defence to B's claim for compensation under the rule in *Rylands* v *Fletcher* if B was wholly at fault for the fact that she suffered the harm for which she is seeking compensation.[81]

(4) *Consent.* In *Peters* v *Prince of Wales Theatre*[82] the Court of Appeal held that where a tenant took premises knowing that a particular water system was installed in the landlord's adjoining premises the tenant consented to the existence of the system and could not complain if water escaped from it. An analogy was drawn with the rule that if A has granted possession of a parcel of land to B, and it is contemplated at the time of the grant that A will continue to use adjoining property for a particular purpose, B will not be able to complain that A's using the adjoining premises for that purpose will amount to a nuisance.[83]

LIABILITY RULES ANALOGOUS TO THE RULE IN *RYLANDS* V *FLETCHER*

Fire

It is commonly believed that the ancient common law made an occupier of premises liable for any damage caused by fire escaping from those premises. This stern rule was altered by statute and s 86 of the Fire Prevention (Metropolis) Act 1774 now states that no action can be brought 'against any person in whose house, chamber, stable, barn or other building, or on whose estate any fire shall ... accidentally begin'. But the interpretation and application of this provision is not straightforward.

In order to explain the current pattern of an occupier's liability for the spread of fire it may be helpful to distinguish three types of situation: (1) a fire

---

[79] It is now clear that the claimant's claim under the rule in *Rylands* v *Fletcher* should also have failed because the rule does not apply in personal injury cases: see above, p. 743.

[80] *Nichols* v *Marsland* (1876) 2 Ex D 1, where a rainstorm was said to have been the heaviest in human memory. A different heavy storm was judged insufficiently unusual in *Greenock Corporation* v *Caledonian Railway Co.* [1917] AC 556. In *Transco* [2003] 3 WLR 1467, at [59], Lord Hobhouse stated that the phrase 'Acts of God' was 'used to describe those events which involved no human agency and which it was not realistically possible for a human to guard against: an accident which the defendant can show is due to natural causes, directly and exclusively, without human intervention and could not have been prevented by any amount of foresight, pains and care, reasonably to be expected of him.'

[81] *Rylands* v *Fletcher* (1868) LR 1 Ex 265, 280.

[82] [1943] KB 73.

[83] *Vanderpant* v *Mayfair Hotel Co. Ltd* [1930] 1 Ch 138, 162–3; *Thomas* v *Lewis* [1937] 1 All ER 137.

is deliberately started on A's property and then spreads to B's property; (2) a fire is negligently started on A's property and then spreads to B's property; (3) natural forces start a fire on A's property and it then spreads to B's property.

Situation (2) may be the simplest to start with. It has been held that the statute does not protect the occupier from liability when the fire has been started 'negligently' rather than 'accidentally'.[84] Importantly, this exception from the statute's protection applies even when the negligence was not the negligence of the occupier or his employee but of a guest or independent contractor. Thus a claimant who wishes to sue the occupier in such circumstances will gain by relying on the ancient common law rule rather than the tort of negligence.[85] The occupier will not be liable, however, if the fire was started by the negligence of a 'stranger'. In this context 'a "stranger" is anyone who in lighting a fire . . . acts contrary to anything which the occupier could anticipate that he would do'.[86] In rare circumstances a guest or independent contractor may become a 'stranger' for the purposes of this rule 'if his conduct in lighting a fire is so alien to your invitation that he should *qua* the fire be regarded as a trespasser'.[87]

By way of illustration, in *Ribee* v *Norrie*,[88] the defendant owned a hostel and rented out bedrooms in it to various people. A fire started in the hostel's sitting room, probably as a result of a tenant dropping a smouldering cigarette onto the settee. The fire spread and damaged the adjoining house which belonged to the claimant. The defendant was held liable for the fire damage done to the claimant's house. He was held to have been in occupation of the hostel's sitting room when the fire started. The fire was negligently started in the sitting room by a tenant who had permission from the defendant to use the sitting room. Finally, the tenant's conduct was not 'so alien' that he could '*qua* the fire be regarded as a trespasser' because the defendant could reasonably have anticipated that a tenant using the sitting room 'might inadvertently drop a smouldering cigarette onto the settee eventually setting it on fire'.[89]

Liability in situation (1), where the fire is started deliberately, depends on the *type* of fire involved and *why it spread*. The *type* of fire involved is relevant because it has been held that some deliberate fires involve the 'extraordinary use' of land and potentially fall within the ambit of the rule in *Rylands* v *Fletcher*. If the type of fire does fall within the ambit of this rule then the occupier may be liable for its escape even if the escape was not a result of anyone's negligence. But lighting an ordinary domestic fire in a fireplace is not an 'extraordinary use', so there will be no liability for the accidental escape of such a fire.[90] The reasons *why the fire spread* are relevant because where the fire spread because of

---

[84] *Balfour* v *Barty-King* [1957] 1 QB 496.

[85] The claimant can, of course, seek to sue the guest or the contractor for the tort of negligence.

[86] *H & N Emmanuel Ltd* v *GLC* [1971] 2 All ER 835, 839a (per Lord Denning MR).

[87] Ibid.

[88] (2001) 33 HLR 777.

[89] Ibid., at [26] (per Ward LJ).

[90] *Sochacki* v *Sas* [1947] 1 All ER 344; *J Doltis Ltd* v *Issac Braithwaite & Sons (Engineers) Ltd* [1957] 1 Lloyd's Rep 522; *Johnson* v *BJW Property Developments Ltd* [2002] 3 All ER 574, at [31].

the negligence of the occupier, his employee, his guest or his independent contractor, it has been held that the statute does not protect the occupier against
liability.[91] Again, the occupier's liability is broader than ordinary vicarious liability for negligence, but does not stretch to cover liability for the negligence
of a 'stranger'.[92]

Where natural forces (or, indeed a 'stranger') start a fire on A's premises and
it subsequently escapes to damage B's neighbouring premises – situation (3) –
it seems that s 86 of the Fire Prevention (Metropolis) Act 1774 will prevent A
being held liable unless the claim can be brought under the rule in *Rylands* v
Fletcher or the rule in *Goldman* v *Hargrave*.[93] In order to show that the rule in
Rylands applies here, it will have to be shown that the fire started on the occupier's premises because he used those premises in an extraordinary way. This
requirement would probably be satisfied if the occupier stored large quantities
of inflammable chemicals on his land which accidentally caught fire.[94] But the
'extraordinary use' requirement will probably not be satisfied if what happened
was that A parked his car on his land and the petrol in the tank accidentally
caught fire.[95] *Goldman* v *Hargrave*[96] may assist a neighbour in claiming against
an occupier for damage caused by the spread of a natural fire from his land if
he failed to take reasonable steps to stop the fire spreading onto the neighbour's
property. Whether the occupier will be held to have taken such reasonable steps
will depend on factors such as his interests and resources, and the relative
interests and resources of anyone imperilled by the fire.[97]

Finally we should consider how far the liability rules that we have summarised are 'analogous to the rule in *Rylands* v *Fletcher*' since this may determine
questions such as who can claim and what types of damage they can claim for.[98]
Straightforwardly, we can say that those cases where it is necessary to prove
that the type of fire involved or the collection of inflammable material was an

---

[91] *H & N Emmanuel Ltd* v *GLC* [1971] 2 All ER 835. This seems to be the opinion of Lord
Denning MR (ibid., at 838b–g, though he later evinces a reluctance to classify the liability rule
at 839d–e) and also the opinion of Phillimore LJ (ibid., at 842). See also *Johnson* v *BJW Property
Developments Ltd* [2002] 3 All ER 574.

[92] *H & N Emmanuel Ltd* v *GLC* [1971] 2 All ER 835, 838-9 (per Lord Denning MR).

[93] *Goldman* v *Hargrave* [1967] 1 AC 645. See above, p. 175.

[94] In *Mason* v *Levy Auto Parts* [1967] 2 QB 530, MacKenna J found that the storage of a large
number of motor spares coated in oil or wrapped in waxed paper was a non-natural user of land.
The fact that it is not the inflammable material which escaped but the fire is not legally
important. In cases of explosion courts have similarly not treated it as important whether the
explosive chemicals *themselves* escaped (as opposed to mere shockwaves). See, for example,
Rainham Chemical Works Ltd v *Belvedere Fish Guano Co. Ltd* [1921] 2 AC 465.

[95] Admittedly, in *Musgrove* v *Pandelis* [1919] 2 KB 43, the Court of Appeal held that a motor car
and its petrol tank were a 'dangerous thing' to which the rule in *Rylands* v *Fletcher* could apply,
but paid less attention to the question whether storage of a car in a garage was an extraordinary
user. The better view, which accords with the opinion of Romer LJ in *Collingwood* v *Home &
Colonial Stores Ltd* [1936] 3 All ER 200, 209, must be that parking a car in a garage attached to
residential property is not an extraordinary use of land. Indeed in *Transco* [2003] 3 WLR 1467,
[107] Lord Walker used the *Musgrove* case to illustrate how the 'extraordinary use' test changes
though time. It might still be arguable that to park a petrol tanker on land is an 'extraordinary
user': see *Perry* v *Kendricks Transport Ltd* [1956] 1 WLR 85.

[96] [1967] 1 AC 645.

[97] See above, p. 220.

[98] For these matters under the rule in *Rylands* v *Fletcher* see above, p. 743.

'extraordinary use' of land actually fall within the rule in *Rylands* and do not depend on a special analogous rule relating to fire at all. Further, the rule in *Goldman* v *Hargrave* seems to form part of both the tort of negligence and the tort of private nuisance and need not be treated as analogous to the rule in *Rylands*. What remains to be classified is that remnant of the ancient common law rule relating to the escape of fire which has survived the 1774 statute. From one perspective this remnant is analogous to the rule in *Rylands* because it makes an occupier liable for escapes of fire which were the consequence of the negligence of a guest or independent contractor. But two distinctions may also be worth mentioning. First, under the remnant the occupier will avoid liability if he can prove that the escape was 'accidental', in the sense of not involving negligence. This is a broader defence than any available under the rule in *Rylands*.[99] Secondly, it is not clear that the ancient common law rule *only* protects neighbours against damage to their land.[100] One of the best known ancient authorities for the rule involves a claim for damage to chattels[101] and more recent judgments have also assumed that such claims were possible.[102]

Cattle trespass

Under s 4 of the Animals Act 1971, if livestock[103] belonging[104] to any person strays[105] onto land in the ownership or occupation of another, the person to whom the livestock belongs is liable for any damage[106] caused by the livestock to the land and property on it and for expenses reasonably incurred in impounding the livestock,[107] tracing who owns it and keeping it pending return. There is no defence covering escapes of livestock caused by malicious strangers or Acts of God. However, s 5(1) of the 1971 Act provides that a 'person [will not be] liable under [s 4] for any damage which is due wholly to the fault of the person suffering it'.[108]

Someone who has suffered harm as a result of straying livestock may not have to rely on s 4 of the Animals Act 1971 to obtain compensation for that harm:

---

[99] For defences under the rule in *Rylands* v *Fletcher* see above, pp. 749–50.

[100] See above, p. 743, for the limits on who can sue and for what under the rule in *Rylands* v *Fletcher*.

[101] *Beaulieu* v *Finglam* (1401) YB 2 Hen IV fo. 18, pl. 6.

[102] *Sochacki* v *Sas* [1947] 1 All ER 344, 345A, 'If I happen to be on somebody else's land at a time when a fire spreads to that land and my motor car or property is destroyed, I have just as much right against the person who improperly allows the fire to escape from his land as the owner of the land on which I happen to be' (per Lord Goddard CJ).

[103] This is broadly defined in s 11. It includes cattle, horses, sheep, pigs and poultry.

[104] Animals Act 1971, s 4(2): 'For the purposes of this section any livestock belongs to the person in whose possession it is.'

[105] There is no liability where livestock strays from a highway which it was being driven along or across: Animals Act 1971, s 5(5), following the common law rule in *Tillett* v *Ward* (1882) 10 QBD 17. There could be liability in negligence if the drovers were careless, or under s 2 of the Animals Act 1971 if the livestock in question was known to have an unusual and dangerous tendency.

[106] Not limited to damage to land.

[107] See Animals Act 1971, s 7.

[108] Damages can also be reduced for contributory negligence: s 10.

he may be entitled to bring a claim in tort for such compensation. So if A sends livestock onto B's land, he will commit the tort of trespass to land and B will be entitled to sue A in trespass for compensation for the harm caused by the livestock while it was on her land. Again, if A carelessly allows livestock to stray when it is reasonably foreseeable that it will do harm to B if it is allowed to stray, A will commit the tort of negligence and if B suffers foreseeable harm as a result of the livestock straying, B will be entitled to sue A in negligence for damages sufficient to compensate her for that harm.[109]

Escape of water from the mains

Where an escape of water, however caused,[110] from a pipe vested in a water undertaker causes loss or damage, the undertaker shall be liable for the loss or damage.[111]

Nuclear installations

The licensee of a nuclear installation is liable for injuries to persons and damage to the property of others caused by occurrences involving nuclear matter or the escape of ionising radiation.[112] Licensees cannot escape liability by showing that the occurrence was the result of an Act of God or of an uncontrollable third party, though there is a defence for incidents caused by 'hostile action in the course of armed conflict'.[113] The courts, however, have defined the forms of damage covered by the statutory liability narrowly,[114] and some claimants seeking to rely on it have been unable to prove causation.[115]

THE ANIMALS ACT 1971

Antecedents of the Act

Under the common law the keeper of an animal which had a tendency to do harm would be liable for any damage that it caused if he knew that that animal had a tendency to do harm.[116] Animals were divided by species into two classes.

---

[109] In this context the tort of negligence will straightforwardly allow B to claim for personal injury or property damage.

[110] There is an exception where the escape was due wholly to the fault of the person who sustained the loss or damage: Water Industry Act 1991, s 209(2).

[111] Water Industry Act 1991, s 209(1). There are some exceptions to this liability in s 209(3) and (6). Claims are not limited to claims for damage to land.

[112] Nuclear Installations Act 1965, ss 7 and 12. Thus for there to be liability under the Act there does not have to be an escape from the land occupied by the licensee.

[113] Nuclear Installations Act 1965, s 13(4).

[114] In *Merlin* v *BNFL* [1990] 2 QB 557, Gatehouse J held that a fall in the value of a house as a result of radioactive contamination was not 'damage' to property, and suggested *obiter* that 'the presence of alpha-emitting radionuclides in the human airways or digestive system or even in the bloodstream merely increases the risk of cancer to which everyone is exposed from both natural and artificial radioactive sources. They do not *per se* amount to injury' (ibid., 572–3).

[115] *Reay* v *BNFL*, *Hope* v *BNFL* [1994] PIQR P171.

[116] *Important note*. In this context 'harm' covers both physical injury and property damage.

If an animal belonged to a *dangerous species*, it would be conclusively presumed to have a tendency to do harm, its keeper would be conclusively presumed to know that it had a tendency to do harm,[117] and its keeper would be held liable for any damage that it caused. If, on the other hand, an animal which belonged to a species that was by nature harmless or generally tamed or domesticated caused harm, then its keeper would only be held liable for the harm under the above liability rule if it could be specifically proved that the animal had a tendency to do such harm and that its keeper knew that it had a tendency to do such harm. The Animals Act 1971 abolished the above common law rule[118] and put in its place the following set of liability rules.

The Animals Act 1971

The liability rules created by the Act
The liability rules created by the 1971 Act can be summarised as follows:

(1) *Liability of the keeper of an animal belonging to a dangerous species.* Section 2(1) of the 1971 Act provides that the keeper of an animal which belongs to a dangerous species is liable for the damage that it causes unless a relevant defence applies.

(2) *Liability of the keeper of an animal that does not belong to a dangerous species.* Section 2(2) of the 1971 Act provides that the keeper of an animal which does not belong to a dangerous species will be liable for damage that has been caused by that animal if three conditions are satisfied and no relevant defence applies. The three conditions are as follows. First, *either* the animal, unless restrained, must have been likely[119] to cause that kind of damage *or* it must have been likely that, if the animal ever caused that kind of damage, it would do so to a severe degree. Secondly, *either* the damage[120] must have been attributable to the animal having characteristics not normally found in animals of the same species *or* the damage must have been attributable to the animal having characteristics not normally found except at particular times or in particular circumstances. Thirdly, the keeper of the animal must have known that the animal had these characteristics.[121]

---

[117] Thus for the purposes of the common law, elephants were treated as wild and dangerous, even if individual elephants were docile and tame: *Behrens* v *Bertram Mills Circus Ltd* [1957] 2 QB 1.

[118] Section 1 of the Animals Act 1971 provides that the 'provisions ... of this Act replace ... the rules of the common law imposing a strict liability ... for damage done by an animal on the ground that the animal is regarded as ferae naturae or that its vicious or mischievous propensities are known or presumed to be known.'

[119] In *Mirvahedy* v *Henley* [2003] 2 AC 491, at [95]-[97], Lord Scott suggested that in this context damage would only be 'likely' if it was 'to be reasonably expected'. But the other Law Lords did not express an opinion on this point.

[120] The statute says that it is 'the likelihood of the damage or of its being severe' which must be 'due to' the abnormal characteristics of the animal, but in *Curtis* v *Betts* [1990] 1 WLR 459, the Court of Appeal suggested that the provision should be treated as if it read 'the damage' must be 'attributable to' the abnormal characteristics.

[121] It is sufficient to prove that the characteristics were known to someone who had charge of the animal as the keeper's servant, or to someone under 16 years old who was a member of the keeper's household and was also a keeper: Animals Act 1971, s 2(2)(c).

(3) *Liability of the keeper of a dog that has killed or injured livestock.* Section 3 of the 1971 Act provides that the keeper of a dog is liable for damage it causes by killing or injuring livestock unless a relevant defence applies.

(4) *Liability of person in possession of livestock for the damage done by that livestock.* Section 4 of the 1971 Act provides that the possessor of livestock is liable for certain types of damage and expenses caused by that livestock straying onto land in the ownership or occupation of another person unless a relevant defence applies.[122]

Interpretation

Certain terms in this summary require further discussion.

(1) *Keeper.* The keeper of an animal that has caused harm may be held liable for that harm under ss 2 and 3 of the 1971 Act. Who counts as being a keeper of an animal? Section 6(3) of the 1971 Act provides that 'a person is a keeper of an animal if – (a) he owns the animal or has it in his possession; or (b) he is the head of a household of which a member under the age of sixteen owns the animal or has it in his possession'. Section 6(4) of the 1971 Act qualifies this by providing that someone who takes an animal into his possession 'for the purpose of preventing it from causing damage or of restoring it to his owner' will not thereby become a keeper of that animal. Section 6(3) goes on to provide that 'if at any time an animal ceases to be owned by or to be in the possession of a person, any person who immediately before that time was a keeper thereof by virtue of the preceding provisions of this subsection [will continue] to be a keeper of the animal until another person becomes a keeper thereof by virtue of those provisions'.

(2) *Dangerous species.* For the purposes of applying s 2(1) of the 1971 Act, an animal belongs to a dangerous species if two conditions are met. The conditions are that the species is not commonly domesticated in the British Isles and that fully grown animals of that species have characteristics making it likely that they will cause severe damage, or that if they cause damage it is likely to be severe.

(3) *Knowledge of abnormal characteristics.* The second liability rule set out above summarises the effect of s 2(2) of the 1971 Act. Several judges have complained about the difficulty of interpreting this provision. Its wording has been described by Lord Denning MR as 'very cumbrously worded',[123] by Ormrod LJ as 'remarkably opaque',[124] and by Slade LJ as 'somewhat tortuous'.[125] In

---

[122] This provision replaces the old common law rules on liability for cattle trespass and is discussed above, p. 349.

[123] *Cummings* v *Grainger* [1977] QB 397, 404.

[124] Ibid., 407.

[125] *Curtis* v *Betts* [1990] 1 WLR 459, 462F–G.

[126] [2003] 2 AC 491. This followed the approach of the Court of Appeal in *Cummings* v *Grainger* [1977] QB 397 and *Curtis* v *Betts* [1990] 1 WLR 459, and rejected the opinions of Lloyd and Oliver LJJ in *Breeden* v *Lampard*, 21 March 1985, unreported.

Mirvahedy v *Henley*[126] the House of Lords split 3:2 over how to interpret the second condition in s 2(2), that dealing with abnormal characteristics.

In that case the claimant had been injured by a horse which had escaped onto a dual carriageway. The horse had apparently stampeded out of its field, pushing through an electric fence, because it had been subjected to a severe fright.[127] The parties agreed that such behaviour was unusual for a horse, but that it was not wholly unusual for a horse subjected to a severe fright. This made it necessary to interpret s 2(2)(b) which requires that: 'the ... damage ... was due to characteristics of the animal which are not normally found in animals of the same species or are not normally so found except at particular times or in particular circumstances.' The crucial issue was whether the phrase 'or are not normally so found except at particular times or in particular circumstances' was intended to create strict liability when an animal behaved in an unusual way even though that behaviour was usual in the particular circumstances (e.g. a normally docile bitch biting to protect its pups) or was intended only to prevent keepers of animals that they knew were abnormally vicious trying to argue that all such animals are vicious in some circumstances (e.g. a keeper of a dog which bites all strangers arguing that the characteristic is not abnormal because all dogs will bite strangers when poked with sticks). A bare majority of the House of Lords favoured the first interpretation of the phrase, and thus held that the keeper of the escaped horse was liable, because the horse's behaviour was unusual (horses do not usually stampede), even though it was usual in the particular circumstances (having been terrified).

The strongest objection to this reading of the statute is the argument that almost any circumstances in which a domesticated animal causes harm can be presented as involving a 'characteristic' only exhibited in 'particular circumstances', thus potentially leading to liability. Lord Scott gave the example of a police horse which kicked an innocent passer-by after a miscreant jabbed a sharp instrument into its rump. On the majority's approach 'kicking out' would be a characteristic not normally displayed by horses, but it would be normal in the 'particular circumstances' of being jabbed in the rump, and the keeper would be likely to know this.[128] Lord Nicholls, who was in the majority, suggested that this objection was exaggerated and that liability would still not attach if, for instance, a cow slipped and fell on someone, because the dangerous characteristic (its weight) would *not* be one found only in particular circumstances.[129] But the force of Lord Scott's argument is that a clever lawyer could present *even this* as exceptional: for instance, by arguing that the dangerous characteristic was 'the cow's tendency to lose its balance' and this was limited to the 'particular circumstances' of 'walking on wet mud'.[130]

---

[127] It was never discovered what caused the horse to panic.

[128] *Mirvahedy* v *Henley* [2003] 2 AC 491, at [115].

[129] Ibid., [46].

[130] Similar problems concerning what can count as a 'characteristic' arose in *Gloster* v *Chief Constable of Greater Manchester* [2000] PIQR 114, where the Court of Appeal discussed whether a police dog which had bitten the claimant had exhibited the characteristic of 'having been trained to bite people it thought it was chasing' (unusual for a German shepherd) or 'being trainable' (usual for a German shepherd). Pill LJ appeared to think that only the latter was a characteristic of the dog.

The effect of the House of Lords' ruling on the interpretation of s 2(2)(b) has been to extend the potential scope of liability for injuries caused by animals which are normally domesticated. Consequently, more attention than ever may be focused on the possible defences.

Defences

There are a number of defences open to someone who is sued under the 1971 Act.

(1) *Wholly at fault.* If B sues A for compensation for harm suffered by her under any of the liability rules set out above, A will have a defence to B's claim if B was wholly at fault for the fact that she suffered that harm.[131]

(2) *Voluntary assumption of risk; trespass.* If B has been harmed by an animal and seeks to sue A for compensation for that harm under s 2(1) or s 2(2) of the 1971 Act, A will have a defence to B's claim if B voluntarily took the risk that she would be harmed by that animal.[132] A will also have a defence if: (*a*) the animal in question harmed B while she was trespassing on premises on which that animal was kept; *and* (*b*) *either* that animal was *not* kept on the premises for the protection of persons or property *or* that animal *was* kept on the premises for the protection of persons or property and the keeping of the animal on those premises for that purpose was not unreasonable.[133] The question whether a trespasser injured by an animal might be able to sue the occupier of the premises (rather than the animal's keeper) under the Occupiers' Liability Act 1984 is not straightforward, and depends on the scope of this Act.[134]

(3) *Straying livestock.* Suppose livestock belonging to B strayed onto land belonging to someone else and was attacked there by a dog. If B sues A – the dog's keeper – for compensation for the damage done to her livestock by the dog under s 3 of the 1971 Act, A will have a defence to B's claim if: (*a*) the dog belonged to the occupier of the land on which the livestock was attacked; *or* (*b*) the dog was authorised to be on the land on which the livestock was attacked.[135]

(4) *No defences of act of a stranger and Act of God.* If an animal has caused B to suffer some kind of harm, and B seeks to sue A – the keeper of that animal – for compensation for that harm under the Animals Act 1971, it seems that the fact that the animal acted in the way it did because of the malicious act of a stranger or an Act of God will afford A no defence to B's claim. Consequently,

---

[131] Animals Act 1971, s 5(1). The defence of contributory negligence also applies: s 10.
[132] Section 5(2).
[133] Section 5(3). In *Cummings* v *Grainger* [1975] 1 WLR 1330, O'Connor J thought that it was unreasonable for a scrap metal dealer to keep an untrained alsatian with a known propensity to attack black people as protection for his yard, but the Court of Appeal disagreed: [1977] QB 397. It is worth noting, however, that the case arose before the Guard Dogs Act 1975 made it unlawful to keep an uncontrolled guard dog.
[134] On which see above, pp. 170–4.
[135] Animals Act 1971, s 5(4).

the potential liability of the keeper of a dangerous animal is wider than the potential liability of the keeper of an inanimate dangerous thing.

45

THE CONSUMER PROTECTION ACT 1987

ANTECEDENTS OF THE ACT

If you suffer some kind of harm as a result of a product being defective, you may be entitled to sue the 'producer' of that product for compensation under the Consumer Protection Act 1987.[1] Your claim for compensation under the 1987 Act will be non-tortious in character: in order to make out your claim, you will not have to show that the producer of the product committed any kind of legal wrong in manufacturing the product that harmed you.

The Consumer Protection Act 1987 has a European origin. It was passed to give effect to Council Directive 85/374/EEC ('the Directive') which required each Member State of the European Union to take steps to ensure that under their national laws the producer of a defective product would be held liable on a 'no-fault' basis for the damage done by that product – that is, would be held liable without the necessity of showing that the producer was at fault for the existence of the defect in the product in question. On its face, the object of the Directive was to harmonise the laws on product liability across the European Union because 'existing divergences may distort competition and affect the movement of goods within the [European Union's] common market'.[2] The idea was that producers of products in a particular country might gain an unfair competitive advantage if they were subject to product liability rules that were less harsh than those applied to producers of similar products in other countries within the European Union.[3] The Directive has signally failed to achieve this objective for three reasons.

First, the Directive sought only to harmonise the laws on when the producer of a defective product would be held liable in respect of damage done by that product to people or property 'intended for private use or consumption'.[4] National laws on when the manufacturer of a defective product would be held liable in respect of damage done by that product to *commercial property* were left untouched by the Directive.

Secondly, European Union governments did not have to implement *all* aspects of the Directive; they had some latitude to pick and choose which parts of the Directive they would implement. For example, the Directive provides that the

---

[1] The Act has now been amended by the Consumer Protection Act 1987 (Product Liability) (Modification) Order 2000 (S.I. No. 2771).

[2] Preamble to Council Directive 85/374/EEC.

[3] For this reason, the European Court of Justice has ruled that the Directive is a 'maximum harmonisation' directive – that is, national governments are not allowed to give effect to a products liability regime which is *stricter* than that contemplated by the Directive. See *EC* v *Greece*, C-154/00, 25 April 2002; *EC* v *France*, C-52/00, 25 April 2002; *Sanchez* v *Medicina Asturiana* SA, C-183/00, 25 April 2002.

[4] Directive, Art 9.

producer of a defective product should not be held liable as a result of that product being defective if 'the state of scientific and technical knowledge at the time when he put the product into circulation was not such as to enable the existence of the defect to be discovered'.[5] However, national governments were allowed, in implementing the Directive, to choose whether or not to implement this particular provision: Article 15(1)(b) of the Directive gives national governments the power to provide 'that the producer [of a defective product] shall be liable even if he proves that the state of scientific and technical knowledge at the time when he put the product into circulation was not such as to enable the existence of [the] defect to be discovered'. Again, Article 16(1) of the Directive provides that '[any] Member State *may* provide that a producer's total liability for damage resulting from a death or personal injury and caused by identical items with the same defect shall be limited to an amount which may not be less than 70 million ECU'.[6] So national governments were free to choose, in passing legislation which implemented the Directive, whether or not to put a cap on the liability that might be incurred by a manufacturer of a defective product under that legislation.

Thirdly, the Directive did nothing to harmonise the remedies that would be available if someone was killed or injured as a result of a product being defective; for instance, the Directive did nothing to harmonise the law on whether – if someone was killed as a result of a product being defective – the deceased's dependants would be able to bring an action for damages in respect of the loss of support suffered by them as a result of the deceased's death.

Given this, it may be suspected that the real reason for the 1985 Directive was *not* to harmonise the law on products liability across the European Union; rather, the Directive was adopted in order to help ensure that a 'citizen' of the European Union who suffered harm to his person or property as a result of a product being defective would be able to recover compensation for that harm without having to prove: (*a*) that anyone was at fault for the fact that he suffered that harm; or (*b*) that that harm was suffered by him as a result of someone's committing a legal wrong in relation to him.[7] Whatever the objectives that were sought to be achieved by adopting the 1985 Directive, as the Consumer Protection Act 1987 was enacted in order to implement that Directive the courts are required to take the Directive into account in interpreting the provisions of the 1987 Act and to interpret those provisions in such a way as will give effect to the Directive and promote its objectives.[8] It is to the provisions of the 1987 Act that we now turn.

---

[5] Ibid., Art 7(e). This is known as the 'development risks defence'. On which, see below, pp. 772–3.
[6] Emphasis added.
[7] Given this, the European Court of Justice's ruling that national governments are not allowed to introduce products liability regimes which are *more favourable* to an injured consumer than that contemplated by the Directive (see above, n. 3) may represent something of an own-goal. Significantly, the Council of the European Union has reacted to this ruling by calling for an assessment as to whether the Directive should be amended so as to allow national governments to hold *suppliers* of defective products liable for the harm done by those products *outside* the situations where the Directive currently contemplates suppliers of defective products may be held liable: Council Resolution of 19 December 2002, 2003/C 26/02.
[8] Consumer Protection Act 1987, s 1(1).

THE BASIC RULE

Section 2 of the Consumer Protection Act 1987 sets out the basic rule which under-lies the Act. It provides that if 'any damage is caused wholly or partly by a defect in a product'[9] then, as a general rule, 'the producer of the product'[10] *and* 'any person who, by putting his name on the product or by using a trade mark or other distin-guishing mark in relation to the product, has held himself out to be the producer of the product'[11] *and* 'any person who has imported the product into a member State from a place outside the member States in order, in the course of any business of his, to supply it to another'[12] will be held jointly and severally[13] 'liable for the damage'.[14]

The supplier of the product will also be 'liable for the damage' if: '(a) the person who suffered the damage requests the supplier to identify one or more of the persons (whether still in existence or not) [mentioned in the previous sentence]; (b) that request is made within a reasonable period after the damage occurs and at a time when it is not reasonably practicable for the person making the request to identify all those persons; and (c) the supplier fails, within a reasonable period after receiving the request, either to comply with that request or to identify the person who supplied that product to him.'[15] All this needs more explanation.

Product

Section 1(2) of the 1987 Act provides that ' "product" means any goods or electricity and includes a product which is comprised in another product, whether by virtue of being a component part or raw material or otherwise'. So the term 'product' covers not only *manufactured products* (like cars, radios and computers)[16] but also *natural products* (like coal, flowers and animals).

There is some debate over whether body parts and blood count as 'products' under the Act. It seems likely that they do – 'goods' is defined in the Act as including 'substances',[17] which would cover body parts and blood products; and Article 2 of the Directive defines the term 'product' as covering 'all move-ables', which again would cover body parts and blood products. Indeed, it was conceded in the important case of *A v National Blood Authority* that contami-nated blood did count as a 'product' under the Act.[18]

Opinion is more divided on the issue of whether an inaccurate map or some faulty software will count as a defective product under the 1987 Act.[19] The

---

[9] Section 2(1).
[10] Section 2(2)(a).
[11] Section 2(2)(b).
[12] Section 2(2)(c).
[13] Section 2(5).
[14] Section 2(1).
[15] Section 2(3).
[16] But not buildings: s 46(3).
[17] Section 45(1).
[18] [2001] 3 All ER 289, at [17]. Blood and other human body parts and tissues are not generally regarded as 'products' under American products liability laws: see GS&Z, 842.
[19] See, generally, Whittaker 1989. For a negative view, see Stapleton 1994, 333–4; for a positive view, see Mullis & Oliphant 2003, 207–8. Nolan 2002 suggests (at 823) that someone who is

problem is that the map or software *qua* physical item will not be deficient in any respect. It is the information *on* the map or *in* the software that is deficient and that information does not seem to count as a 'substance' or a 'moveable'. This question has yet to be settled by the courts. It would seem an arbitrary result if, for example, an inaccurate map was not counted as being a defective product under the 1987 Act while, for example, a faulty pair of boots was regarded as defective under the Act: the danger posed by each to a mountaineer is the same. However, it may be that the language of the 1987 Act and the Directive will leave the courts with little choice but to reach such a conclusion.

Producer

Section 1(2) of the 1987 Act also specifies who the 'producer' of a product will be. If the product was manufactured, the 'producer' of that product will be the person who manufactured it. If the product in question was not manufactured but was instead 'won or abstracted' – say the product in question was coal – 'the person who won or abstracted it' will be the producer of the product.[20] The 1987 Act goes on to specify that 'in the case of a product which has not been manufactured, won or abstracted but essential characteristics of which are attributable to an industrial or other process having been carried out (for example, in relation to agricultural produce), the person who carried out that process' will be the 'producer' of that product.

Defect

Certainly the most important and difficult provision in the 1987 Act is s 3, which explains when a product will count as being defective under the Act.

The legitimate expectations test
Section 3 follows the Directive[21] in adopting a 'legitimate expectations' test for determining whether a given product is defective. It provides that:

(1) ... there is a defect in a product ... if the safety of the product is not such as persons generally are entitled to expect ...
(2) In determining ... what persons generally are entitled to expect in relation to a product all the circumstances shall be taken into account, including –

---

harmed as a result of relying on inaccurate information provided by a product will not be able to sue under the 1987 Act; but if inaccurate information provided by a product causes damage directly without any intervening human agency, then a claim may lie under the 1987 Act. But is it sensible to draw a distinction between the case where a plane crashes because the software installed in the plane misled the pilots as to their altitude and the case where a plane crashes because the software installed in the plane caused a system failure?

[20] What is the position if John dies and a surgeon, Wendy, takes out his heart for transplantation purposes and the heart is given to Fred in a heart transplant operation? If the heart proves to be defective (say, for example, it is cancerous), who will count as being the 'producer' of the heart? Stapleton 1994 suggests (at 310–11) that John will be the producer because he 'manufactured' the heart. However, this seems unreal: a heart is not a manufactured product but a natural product. The better view is that Wendy is the producer because she 'won or abstracted' the heart.

[21] See Art 6(1).

(a) the manner in which, and purposes for which, the product has been marketed, its get-up, the use of any mark in relation to the product and any instructions for, or warnings with respect to, doing or refraining from doing anything with or in relation to the product;

(b) what might reasonably be expected to be done with or in relation to the product; and

(c) the time when the product was supplied by its producer to another ...

This definition is far from easy to understand or apply. How, for example, do we determine whether a product's safety is such as persons 'generally are *entitled* to expect'? Fortunately, there is a growing body of case law which provides a good deal of guidance as to how the 'legitimate expectations' test will operate in practice.[22] But before we look at this case law, it might be helpful to distinguish between six different types of product that *might* be regarded as defective under the 1987 Act. We will then be able to look at when each type of product *will* be regarded as defective under the Act.

A typology of products that may be defective under the Act

The six types of product are as follows:

First: a manufactured product that does not conform to its intended design and as a result is more dangerous to use than would otherwise be the case. It is customary to say that such a product suffers from a *manufacturing defect*.[23] An example of such a product is a tin of food where the inner lining of the tin is scratched, making the food inside dangerous to eat.

Second: a manufactured product that conforms to its intended design but it could be designed to a higher safety standard. It is customary to say that such a product suffers from a *design defect*. An example of such a product is a car that is not fitted with airbags.

Third: a manufactured product that is dangerous to use but which cannot be made any safer than it is. We can say that such a product is *inherently dangerous*. An example of such a product is a cigarette.

Fourth: a natural product that is contaminated or infected with some dangerous substance, or otherwise diseased in some way. As the product is natural, and therefore not designed or manufactured, it would be inappropriate to say that it suffers from a *manufacturing defect*, though it is analogous to such a product. Instead, we will say that such a product is *dangerously abnormal*. An example of such a product is a cancerous kidney or a dog that is infested with fleas.

Fifth: a product that does not carry a warning as to how it should be used. We can say that such a product suffers from a *marketing defect*. An example of such a product is a box of paracetamol that does not warn that the paracetamol should not be taken in conjunction with other medicine or by those who suffer kidney problems.

---

[22] See also the useful discussion in Stoppa 1992.

[23] Note that we use the term 'defect' here and below without prejudice to the issue of whether this kind of product is *actually* defective under the 1987 Act.

Sixth: a product that *may* be dangerous to use but it is impossible to tell whether it is or is not. We can say that such a product is *potentially harmful*. An example of such a product is a bag of blood that may or may not carry a virus that will trigger Creutzfeld-Jakob Disease (CJD) in a patient who is given the blood. The blood may be perfectly safe or it may be deadly but it is impossible to tell which it is.[24]

Doubtless there are other types of product that may be regarded as defective under the Act, but it is these six that we will concentrate on in discussing the case law that deals with the ambit of s 3 of the 1987 Act.

The case law

The most important case dealing with the issue of whether a product will be defective under the Act is *A* v *National Blood Authority*.[25] The claimants were people who had been infected with the hepatitis C virus as a result of receiving blood transfusions containing blood donated by people who had hepatitis C. At the time the claimants were infected, no test existed to detect whether a given bag of blood contained the hepatitis C virus. The claimants sued the National Blood Authority (the NBA) for compensation under the 1987 Act, claiming that the blood that they were given was defective under the 1987 Act.

Counsel for the NBA must have thought they had a good case for arguing that the blood given to the claimants was *not* defective under the 'legitimate expectations' test set out in s 3. After all, at the time the claimants were infected there was no way of ensuring that the bags of blood given to the claimants were free of the hepatitis C virus. Given this, how could it be said that 'persons generally were *entitled* to expect' that the bags of blood given to the claimants would be free of hepatitis C? Surely they could not be entitled to expect the impossible? However, if this argument were accepted then it would seem to follow that a product that suffered from a manufacturing defect would not be defective if it was not possible to detect the existence of that manufacturing defect. But such a finding would be inconsistent with the intentions of the framers of the Directive who clearly intended that producers of products that suffer from manufacturing defects should be held liable for the harm done by those defects irrespective of whether those defects could be discovered or not.

Faced with this problem, Burton J brushed aside the arguments of counsel for the NBA and held that the 'avoidability' of the harm suffered by a claimant in a products liability case is not to be taken into account in judging whether

---

[24] Of course, if we give the blood to a patient and he subsequently develops symptoms of CJD, we will know that the blood was dangerous. In such a case, the blood that was given to the patient will have been *both* potentially harmful (it was impossible to tell at the time the blood was given to the patient whether it was dangerous) *and* dangerously abnormal (it was a natural product that was contaminated with a CJD-triggering virus). This example shows that a given product may well fall into more than one of the categories of product listed above. So a cup of coffee served in a restaurant may suffer from a design defect (it could have been made safer by serving it at a lower temperature); at the same time it may also suffer from a marketing defect (it did not carry a warning that it was hot or that harm might be caused if the cup was spilled). In order to determine whether such a cup of coffee is defective under the Act, it is necessary first to ask whether it is defective because it suffered from a design defect; and if the answer is no, then ask whether it is defective because it suffered from a marketing defect.

[25] [2001] 3 All ER 289 (noted, Howells & Mildred 2002).

the product that harmed the claimant was defective or not under the Act.[26] Burton J went on to hold that the blood given to the claimants was defective under the Act. His reasoning went as follows. He held that the bags of blood given to the claimants were 'non-standard products ... They were different from the norm which the producer intended for use by the public.'[27] He further held that 'Where, as here, there is a harmful characteristic in a non-standard product, a decision that it is defective is likely to be straightforward, and I ... make my decision accordingly.'[28] However, Burton J conceded that the result might have been different had the public been generally aware at the time the claimants were infected that there was a risk that someone receiving a blood transfusion might contract hepatitis C. In such a case, it might have been diffi-cult to contend that at the time the claimants were infected 'persons generally were entitled to expect' that supplies of blood were free of hepatitis C.[29] However, that was not the case here. At the time the claimants were infected, people generally did *not* know that there was a risk they might contract hepa-titis C if they were given a blood transfusion.

Burton J's judgment represents the outcome of a struggle to reconcile the 'legitimate expectations' test for defectiveness that is set out in the Act with the policy objectives which underlie the Act – in particular, the objective of ensuring that producers of products that suffer from manufacturing defects are held liable for the harm caused by their products on a 'no-fault' basis. The policy behind the Act was allowed to trump the 'legitimate expectations' test when Burton J ruled that 'avoidability' of harm was not to be taken into account in judging whether a product is defective under the Act. But the 'legit-imate expectations' test was reintroduced into the equation when Burton J acknowledged that had there been widespread public knowledge of the risk that blood supplies might be contaminated with hepatitis C, a bag of blood which was contaminated with hepatitis C might not have counted as a defective product under the Act.

So, Burton J's judgment in *A* v *National Blood Authority* establishes in relation to the first and fourth type of products in our typology – that is, man-ufactured products that suffer from a manufacturing defect and natural products that are abnormally dangerous – that such products, being non-stan-dard in nature, will *always* be regarded as defective under the Act unless the possibility of such products being non-standard is widely acknowledged and accepted.

What of the other types of product in our typology?

(1) *Design defect.* When will a product that suffers from a design defect be regarded as defective under the Act? The 'legitimate expectations' test indicates that a product that purports to be designed to a higher safety standard than it actually is will be defective under the Act – it will not be as safe as 'persons gen-

---

[26] [2001] 3 All ER 289, at [63].
[27] Ibid., at [65].
[28] Ibid., at [66].
[29] Ibid., at [65].

erally are entitled to expect' given the product's 'get-up' and the way it 'has been marketed'. So a coat which has been marketed as 'suitable for all weathers' will be defective under the Act if it turns out not to be waterproof and its wearer catches influenza as a result; and this is so even if it was not actually designed to be waterproof.

What is the position if the product does not purport to be designed to a higher safety standard than it actually is? For example, what if a car obviously does not come with an airbag equipped? Or what if a condom – that has been designed in such a way that there is a 0.01 per cent chance that it will split – does not promise to be 100 per cent effective but warns the user that it is liable to split? When will such a product be held to be defective under the Act? Common sense indicates that such products cannot *automatically* be held to be defective under the Act. Otherwise every car would have to be equipped with every conceivable safety feature in order to avoid being held to be defective under the Act. Instead, it is suggested, such a product should be held to be defective under the Act if it was *unreasonable* not to design that product to a higher safety standard, given the costs and benefits involved.[30]

The available case law seems to adopt this line of thinking. In *Abouzaid* v *Mothercare (UK) Ltd*,[31] it will be recalled, the claimant was injured when he attempted to fit a sleeping bag onto a pushchair. The sleeping bag was to be attached to the pushchair by passing two elasticated straps attached to the sleeping bag around the back of the pushchair and buckling them together. Unfortunately, the claimant let go of one of the elasticated straps and the buckle at the end of the strap hit him in the eye. He sued the defendants who marketed the sleeping bag under their name for compensation in negligence and under the 1987 Act. The sleeping bag was held to be defective under the Act. The sleeping bag suffered from a design defect: it could have been designed to a higher safety standard, either by making the straps attached to the sleeping bag non-elasticated or by having one continuous elasticated strap stretch from one side of the sleeping bag to the other. And it was unreasonable not to design the sleeping bag to such a higher safety standard: it would have been quite easy to make the sleeping bag safer to use at no added cost.[32]

In contrast, in *B (a child)* v *McDonald's Restaurants Ltd*[33] the claimants sued McDonald's for compensation under the 1987 Act when they were scalded by McDonald's coffee that was spilled on them. The coffee suffered from a design defect: it would not have scalded the claimants so badly had it been served at

---

[30] *Important note*. It might be objected that questions of reasonableness should be irrelevant under a 'no fault' products liability regime. However, the point is that it is impossible *not* to attend to questions of reasonableness in determining whether a product that suffers from a design defect is defective – otherwise we end up with a liability regime which condemns almost all but the most expensive, top quality cars as being defective. So a pure 'no fault' liability regime is an impossibility – in certain cases, some fault-related considerations will *have* to be taken into account in judging whether or not a given product is defective.

[31] The Times, 20 February 2001. See above, p. 76.

[32] The fact that no one had any reason to know that there was any need to modify the sleeping bag was highly relevant to the claim against the defendants in negligence; but was irrelevant to the question of whether the sleeping bag was defective under the 1987 Act. So even in a design defect case, a defendant's fault is not *entirely* relevant to the question of whether he will be held liable under the Act.

[33] [2002] EWHC 490.

55°C rather than the 90°C that it was actually served at. However, Field J refused to find that the coffee was defective under the Act. He held that the costs involved in serving the coffee at this lower temperature – in the shape of a loss in custom – outweighed the benefits: '... coffee served at between 55°C and 60°C would not have been acceptable to McDonald's customers. Indeed, on the evidence, I find that the public want to be able to buy ... coffee served hot, that is to say at a temperature of at least 65°C [the temperature at which coffee will cause a severe burn if spilled on skin] even though they know ... that there is a risk of a scalding injury if the drink is spilled.'[34]

(2) *Inherently dangerous*. It might be thought that a product that is inherently dangerous *cannot* be defective under the 'legitimate expectations' test – how can persons generally be entitled to expect an average cigarette to be safer to use or consume when such a cigarette cannot possibly be made any safer to use or consume? However, Burton J in the *A* case ruled that if 'avoidability' of harm was not something to be taken into account in judging whether a 'non-standard' product is defective under the Act, then 'avoidability' cannot be taken into account either in judging whether a 'standard' product is defective under the Act.[35] So it seems that a product that is inherently dangerous may be defective under the Act. Whether it will be or not may depend on whether persons generally are aware that the product is inherently dangerous. If they are then it will be difficult to argue that the product's safety is not such as 'persons generally are entitled to expect.' But if they are not – if persons generally think that the product in question is safer than it actually is – then a finding that the product is defective under the Act should be straightforward. So cigarettes nowadays would almost certainly not count as being defective under the Act – though it might have been different 60 years ago, when the risks attached to cigarette smoking were less well understood.

(3) *Marketing defect*. If a product does not carry a warning as to how it should be used, it *cannot* be the law that it is *automatically* defective under the Act. Otherwise, we would be in the ridiculous position of saying that a knife will be defective if it does not carry a warning that it is sharp and that a cup of coffee is defective if it does not carry a warning that it is hot. Something more must be required before a product that does not carry a warning as to how it should be used will be held to be defective under the Act. It must be shown,

---

[34] Ibid., at [33]. For another design defect case where it was held that the offending product was not defective under the Act, see *Richardson* v *LRC Products Ltd* [2000] Lloyd's Rep Med 280 where the claimant fell pregnant after having sex with her husband using a condom that split. The claimant sued the defendant manufacturers of the condom for compensation under the 1987 Act. However, the condom was held not to be defective. An attempt to argue that the condom was defective because it suffered from a manufacturing defect failed: it was argued that the condom was unusually brittle because it was exposed to too much sunlight in the factory, but it could not be proved that the signs of excessive exposure to sunlight were not attributable to the claimant having stored the condom near a window after it split. And it was held that the fact that the condom could have been designed in such a way as to make it less liable to split did not make it defective under the Act. It did not purport to be more reliable than it was and making it less liable to split would have adversely affected its quality and marketability to little benefit.

[35] [2001] 3 All ER 289, at [71].

we would suggest, that it was *reasonable to expect* that product to carry a warning as to how it should be used, given the purposes for which the product might have been used, who might have been expected to use the product or get their hands on it, and the extent of the damage that might have been suffered had the product been misused. Under this test, a failure to give a warning of an obvious danger attached to the use of a product will not make the product defective under the Act – it is not reasonable to expect the producer of a product to spend time and trouble warning people against dangers which are obvious to everyone.[36]

(4) *Potentially harmful.* In *A* v *National Blood Authority*, it was argued that at the time the claimants contracted hepatitis C, *every* bag of blood in the UK was defective under the Act because at that time any given bag of blood was potentially harmful – any given bag of blood might have contained the hepatitis C virus and it was impossible to tell which ones did and which ones did not. However, Burton J rejected this argument, holding that only bags of blood which *did* contain the hepatitis C virus were defective under the Act.[37]

If this is right, then a product which is merely potentially harmful will not count as being defective under the Act. So, for example, in the case of *Group B Plaintiffs* v *Medical Research Council*[38] the claimants were all treated with human growth hormone (HGH) that, they subsequently discovered, might have been contaminated with a virus that triggers CJD in adults. Each of the claimants developed a psychiatric illness as a result of worrying about the fact that they might develop CJD in the future. Had the 1987 Act been in force at the time they were injected with the human growth hormone, could they have sued for compensation for their psychiatric illnesses under the Act?[39] On Burton J's approach, the answer is 'no.' In the absence of any evidence that the HGH that they were given was *actually* contaminated with a CJD-triggering virus, they would not have been able to establish that that HGH was defective. The fact that HGH was potentially harmful would not have been enough to establish that it was defective under the Act.

Complex products

Suppose that Eric was driving along in his new car when one of the tyres on the car blew out with the result that Eric crashed the car and suffered severe injuries. In this situation, Eric will be able to sue the producer of the car *and* the producer of the tyre under the 1987 Act for compensation for his injuries. Eric can sue the producer of the car because the car was defective under the 1987 Act – it was not as safe as persons generally are entitled to expect (persons generally are entitled

---

[36] *B (a child)* v *McDonald's Restaurants Ltd* [2002] EWHC 490, at [66] (McDonald's failure to warn its customers that its coffee is hot and liable to scald if spilled does not make it defective as 'its customers [can] be taken to know that the coffee they [are] buying [is] hot and could cause a nasty scalding injury if spilled on someone').

[37] [2001] 3 All ER 289, at [65].

[38] [2000] Lloyd's Rep Med 161.

[39] Note that psychiatric illnesses are actionable under the Act: see below, n. 40.

to expect when they buy a new car that the tyres on the car will not be faulty) – and Eric sustained his injuries because the car was defective. Similarly, Eric can sue the producer of the tyre which blew out because the tyre was defective under the 1987 Act and A sustained his injuries because the tyre was defective.

It should be noted that the person who sold the car to Eric – Mary – will only be treated as having supplied the *car* and not the *tyre* to Eric. Section 1(3) of the 1987 Act makes it clear that 'a person who supplies any product in which products are comprised . . . shall not be treated by reason only of his supply of that product as supplying any of the products so comprised'. So Mary will *not* be held liable under s 2(3) of the 1987 Act to compensate Eric for the injuries sustained by him if she is unable to tell Eric who manufactured the *tyre* on Eric's car or who supplied that *tyre* to her. This is, of course, something which Mary may well not be in a position to know. Eric will only be entitled to request Mary to tell him who manufactured Eric's *car* and so Mary will only be held liable under s 2(3) of the 1987 Act to pay Eric damages in respect of his injuries if she does not tell Eric who manufactured Eric's car or who supplied that car to him.

Damage

Section 5(1) of the 1987 Act provides that ' "damage" means death or personal injury or any loss of or damage to any property (including land)'. So only harm to someone's person or property is actionable under the Act.[40] However, s 5 goes on to set out three situations in which someone will not be entitled to recover compensation under the 1987 Act for harm done to his property by a defective product.

First, s 5(2) provides that a 'person shall not be liable [under the Act] in respect of any defect in a product for the loss of or any damage to the product itself or for the loss of or any damage to the whole or any part of the product which has been supplied with the product in question comprised in it'. So, returning to the example we considered above – where Eric was involved in a car crash because a tyre blew out on his new car while he was driving it – Eric will be able to sue the manufacturer of the car and the manufacturer of the tyre for compensation in respect of the injuries suffered by him in the car crash. On the other hand, s 5(2) means that Eric will not be able to sue them for compensation for the damage done to his car in the crash.

What is the position if Karen bought a car and then later refitted the car with new tyres, one of which suffered from a manufacturing defect which caused it to blow out while Karen was out driving with the result that Karen crashed the car and suffered various injuries? Karen will *not* be able to sue the manufacturer of the *car* for compensation for her injuries or the damage done to her car: the manufacturer will have a defence to any claim brought by Karen on the ground that the car was not defective when it left his hands.[41] But Karen *will* be able to sue the manufacturer of the *tyre* for damages to compensate her for the injuries that she sustained in the car crash *and* the damage done to her car. As the defective tyre was not supplied *with* the

---

[40] *Important note.* 'Personal injury', as defined in the Act, not only covers physical injury but also psychiatric illness. See s 45(1): ' "personal injury" includes any disease and any other impairment of a person's physical *or mental condition* . . .' (emphasis added).

[41] See below, p. 772.

car Karen will not be barred by s 5(2) from suing the tyre manufacturer for damages in respect of the damage done to her car by that tyre: that damage will not amount to damage done to a product which was supplied with the tyre *comprised in it*.

Secondly, s 5(3) provides that a 'person shall not be liable [under the Act] for any loss of or damage to any property which, at the time it is lost or damaged, is not – (a) of a description of property ordinarily intended for private use, occupation or consumption; and (b) intended by the person suffering the loss or damage mainly for his own private use, occupation or consumption'. So if a defective product damages a lathe in a factory, damages will not be recoverable under the 1987 Act in respect of the damage done to the lathe: lathes are not ordinarily intended for private (as opposed to commercial) use and the lathe here was not intended for private use. What if a defective product damages a company car? Could the company sue under the 1987 Act for damages in respect of the damage done to its car? It cannot: while the car counts as property that is *ordinarily* intended for private use, occupation or consumption, the car is *in fact* not intended by the company which has suffered the loss of the car to be privately used.

Thirdly, s 5(4) provides that no 'damages shall be awarded to any person [under this Act] in respect of any loss of or damage to any property if the amount which would fall to be so awarded to that person ... does not exceed £275'.

DEFENCES

Let us suppose that A has suffered some kind of actionable 'damage' as a result of a product being defective and B was the producer of that product. As a general rule, A will be entitled under the 1987 Act to sue B for damages in respect of the harm suffered by him. However, A will not be entitled to sue B for such damages if B can raise a *defence* to A's claim. Someone who is sued in respect of a defect in a product will have a defence if he can show:

(1) *That the defect was attributable to compliance with any requirement imposed by or under any enactment or with any Community obligation.*[42]

(2) *That he did not put the product into circulation.*[43] So say Lara manufactures a car which is then stolen from Lara's factory before it is shipped out. The car is then sold to Gary who is injured because the car suffers from some manufacturing defect. If Gary attempts to sue Lara for damages in respect of his injuries under the 1987 Act, Lara will have a defence to Gary's claim: she did not put the car into circulation.

(3) *That he did not supply the product to another in the course of business and he did not produce, brand or import it with a view to profit.*[44] So if Dawn bakes some cakes for a school fair and Ian, having bought them at the fair, is poisoned by them, Ian will not be entitled to sue Dawn for damages under the 1987 Act: Dawn

---

[42] Section 4(1)(a); Article 7(d).
[43] Section 4(1)(b); Article 7(a).
[44] Section 4(1)(c); Article 7(c).

did not supply the cakes to the fair organisers in the course of a business of hers and she did not supply those cakes for profit.

(4) *That the defect did not exist in the product at the time he supplied the product to someone else.*[45]

(5) *That the state of scientific and technical knowledge at the time when he put the product into circulation was not such as to enable the existence of the defect to be discovered.*[46] The classic case where this defence – known as the 'development risks defence' – will be available is where A puts into circulation some drug that has a dangerous side effect which no one[47] could have known about at the time the drug was marketed. Those who have suffered harm as a result of the drug's having that side effect will not be able to sue A for compensation under the 1987 Act.

It is now clear from the decision in *A* v *National Blood Authority* that the defence may also be available in a manufacturing defect case. Suppose A manufactures a product that suffers from some kind of manufacturing defect and B suffers some kind of actionable damage as a result. If it was simply not possible at the time the product was manufactured to detect the existence of this manufacturing defect, then A may be able to take advantage of the development risks defence to defeat B's claim for compensation under the Act.

However, Burton J placed one very important limit on the availability of the defence in this case. He held that A will not be able to take advantage of the defence if *he was aware at the time he manufactured the product that there was a risk that it might not conform to its intended design in the way it did.*[48] This limit severely curtails the availability of the development risks defence in manufacturing defect cases. For example, suppose that Eric manufactures tyres on a mass scale. Suppose further that he knows that his manufacturing process is imperfect and as a result it is likely to produce one faulty tyre in 10,000 – however, there is no way he can detect which of his tyres are faulty. Suppose finally that Eric's manufacturing process produces a faulty tyre which is then fitted on Wendy's car; and because the tyre was faulty it blew out when Wendy

---

[45] Section 4(1)(d); Article 7(b).

[46] Article 7(e). The equivalent provision in the 1987 Act – s 4(1)(e) – might appear to be somewhat narrower. That provides that someone who is sued in respect of a defect in a product under the Act will have a defence if the 'state of scientific and technical knowledge at the relevant time was not such that a *producer or producers of products of the same description as the product in question might be expected to have discovered the defect ...*' (emphasis added). This led the European Commission to bring an action against the UK, claiming that the UK had failed in s 4(1)(e) correctly to implement the Directive. However, the European Court of Justice expressed itself content with the wording of s 4(1)(e), holding that 'there is nothing ... to suggest that the courts in the United Kingdom, if called upon to interpret s 4(1)(e), would not do so in light of the wording and purpose of the Directive so as to achieve the result it has in view': *European Commission* v *UK* [1997] All ER (EC) 481, at [33].

[47] If, at the time A put the drug into circulation, an academic had published a paper in Manchuria revealing that the drug had this side effect, that – it seems – would not be enough to deprive A of the development risks defence: see the opinion of the Advocate-General in [1997] All ER (EC) 481, at [24]. It has to be shown that the state of *accessible* scientific and technical knowledge at the time the drug was circulated was not such as to allow the existence of the side effect to be discovered: ibid., at [23].

[48] [2001] 3 All ER 289, at [74].

was driving her car at high speed and she was injured as a result. If Wendy sues Eric for compensation under the Act, Eric will *not* be able to take advantage of the development risks defence to defeat Wendy's claim. While it was not possible to detect beforehand that the tyre was faulty, Eric was aware that there was a risk that every one in 10,000 tyres manufactured by him would suffer from such a fault.[49]

Burton J's limit on the applicability of the development risks defence also meant that it was unavailable to the defendants in the *A* case. They sought to argue that the defence was available to them because the state of scientific and technical knowledge at the time the claimants contracted hepatitis C was not such as to enable them to detect which of their bags of blood were contaminated with hepatitis C. Burton J held that even if this were true, the defence was unavailable because the defendants were aware at the time the claimants contracted hepatitis C that there was a risk that the blood supplied by them to people like the claimants might be contaminated with hepatitis C.

(6) *That the defect – (i) constituted a defect in a product ('the subsequent product') in which the product in question was comprised; and (ii) was wholly attributable to the design of the subsequent product or to compliance by the producer of the product in question with instructions given by the producer of the subsequent product.*[50]

It is often said that this defence will cover the case where, say, a lorry manufacturer fits tyres on one of his lorries which are completely unsuitable for that lorry with the result that when the lorry is driven the tyres blow out and an accident is caused. It is said that the tyre manufacturer will be able to take advantage of this defence if he is sued by the people involved in the accident under the 1987 Act. But it is difficult to see how he could be sued in any case by the people involved in the accident: surely his tyres were never defective?

It is worth mentioning two defences that are *not* available to the producer of a defective product:

(1) *Voluntary assumption of risk.* Suppose that Helen goes to her doctor for some botox injections into her face. Helen's doctor warns her against having the operaton, telling her that he has heard 'on the grapevine' that there are some stocks of botox that are infected with CJD-triggering viruses. Helen insists on going ahead with the operation. If the botox injected into Helen's face *is* contaminated with CJD-triggering viruses and Helen develops CJD as a result then Helen will be entitled to sue the manufacturer of the botox for compensation under the 1987 Act. It will be no defence for the manufacturer to say that

---

[49] It would be different if, at the time Eric manufactured the faulty tyre on Wendy's car, he believed that his manufacturing process was perfect and that every single tyre manufactured by him would be fault-free. In such a case, Eric would be allowed to take advantage of the development risks defence to defeat Wendy's claim against him for compensation (provided, of course, that he could show that the state of scientific and technical knowledge at the time he manufactured the tyre was such that he could not have detected that the tyre was faulty).

[50] Section 4(1)(f); Article 7(f).

Helen voluntarily took the risk that she would contract CJD when she had her injections.

(2) *More good than harm.* As we have seen,[51] there is some authority that a negligent defendant will in certain circumstances be able to take advantage of an 'I did more good than harm' defence. But no such defence is available to an action under the 1987 Act. So suppose that Nita is admitted to hospital in desperate need of a heart transplant. A donor heart is tracked down and is transplanted into Nita. Unfortunately, and unknown to everyone, the heart is cancerous and Nita develops cancer as a result of the heart transplant operation. Nita wants to sue the 'producers' of the heart for compensation. It seems likely that her claim will succeed: the heart was defective under the 1987 Act (it was cancerous) and Nita suffered actionable damage as a result of the heart being defective (she developed cancer). The producers of the heart will not be able to defeat Nita's claim for compensation by pointing out that her having the heart transplant operation did her more good than harm – that is, had she not had the operation, she would be dead now.

REMEDIES

A number of points may be made here about the remedies that will be available under the 1987 Act to someone who has suffered some actionable 'damage' as a result of a product being defective.

(1) *Consumers and third parties.* Although the title of the 1987 Act is the *Consumer* Protection Act, the Act operates to protect *anyone* who has suffered actionable 'damage' as a result of a product being defective. So say John drives a car and one of the tyres on the car blows out because it suffers from some kind of manufacturing defect. Suppose further that the blow-out causes John to crash the car with the result that both John and a passer-by, Mary, are injured. Both John and Mary will be entitled to sue the tyre manufacturer for damages under the 1987 Act to compensate them for their injuries: the fact that John is a consumer and Mary a third party is irrelevant.

(2) *Range of liability.* Having said that, the 1987 Act is completely silent on the issue of whether any limits should be drawn on the range of third parties who will be entitled to sue for damages under the 1987 Act. Suppose, for example, that in the above example, John's car crash had an adverse effect on his personality with the result that he eventually raped Wendy. Will Wendy be able to sue the manufacturer of the defective tyre that caused John's car crash for damages under the 1987 Act to compensate her for the fact that she was raped by John? There is nothing in the Act to guide us one way or the other on this issue. Suppose, alternatively, that John was so severely injured in the car crash that his wife, Ruth, had to give up her job and look after John. She was eventually so worn down by the strain of looking after John that she suffered a nervous

---

[51] See above, pp. 583–4.

breakdown. If she sued the tyre manufacturer in negligence for compensation for her breakdown, she would lose: she would not be able to establish that the tyre manufacturer owed her a duty of care in manufacturing the tyre.[52] But could she instead sue the tyre manufacturer for compensation for her breakdown under the 1987 Act? Again, there is nothing in the Act to give us any guidance on this issue.

(3) *Fatal accidents*. Section 6(1) of the 1987 Act provides that any 'damage for which a person is liable under [the Act] shall be deemed to have been caused – (a) for the purposes of the Fatal Accidents Act 1976, by that person's wrongful act, neglect or default'. So, if Paul has been killed by a defective product and had he not been killed but merely injured by that product he would have been entitled to sue its producers for damages under the 1987 Act, Paul's dependants may be entitled to sue those producers for damages under the Fatal Accidents Act 1976. Whether they will or not depends on who they are and what sort of loss they have suffered as a result of Paul's death.

(4) *Exclusion/limitation clauses*. If A has suffered some actionable 'damage' as a result of a product being defective, A will be entitled to sue B – the 'producer' of that product – for damages under the 1987 Act. This is so even if there exists a contract between A and B which purports to exclude or limit B's liability to A under the 1987 Act. Section 7 of the 1987 Act provides that the 'liability of a person [under this Act] to a person who has suffered damage caused wholly or partly by a defect in a product, or to a dependant or relative of such a person, shall not be limited or excluded by any contract term . . .'.

(5) *Assessment of liability*. If A has suffered some actionable 'damage' as a result of a product being defective, the 1987 Act is almost completely silent on the issue of how the damages payable in respect of that damage should be assessed. Presumably, A will not just be entitled to recover damages in respect of the damage suffered by him: he will also be entitled to recover damages in respect of the consequential losses suffered by him as a result of his sustaining that damage. So if A's leg is broken by a defective ski, A will not just be entitled to sue the manufacturer for damages to compensate him for the bare fact that his leg has been broken; he will also be entitled to sue him for damages in respect of the medical bills and loss of earnings, if any, incurred by him as a result of his leg being broken. But will A be entitled to sue the manufacturer for all the *foreseeable* losses suffered by him as a consequence of his leg being broken; or will he be entitled to sue the manufacturer for *all* the losses suffered by him as a consequence of his leg being broken? Presumably the answer is the former – subject, of course, to the 'egg-shell skull' rule. After all, this would be the rule if the manufacturer were negligent in manufacturing the ski; there seems little reason why he should be treated more harshly under the 1987 Act.

(6) *Contributory negligence*. If A has suffered some actionable 'damage' as a result of a product being defective with the result that he is *prima facie* entitled

---

[52] See above, pp. 91–2.

to sue B, the producer of that product, for £100,000 in compensatory damages, the damages payable to A may be reduced if A was partly to blame for the fact that he suffered the damage in question. Similarly, if A has been killed as a result of a product being defective, the damages, if any, payable to A's dependants by the producer of that product under the Fatal Accidents Act 1976 may be reduced if A was partly to blame for the fact that he was killed as a result of that product being defective. This is the effect of s 6(4) of the 1987 Act, which provides that where 'any damage is caused partly by a defect in a product and partly by the fault of the person suffering the damage, the Law Reform (Contributory Negligence) Act 1945 and section 5 of the Fatal Accidents Act 1976 (contributory negligence) shall have effect as if the defect were the fault of every person liable by virtue of [this Act] for the damage caused by the defect'.

(7) *Contribution.* Suppose A has suffered some actionable 'damage' as a result of a product being defective. Suppose further that A recovers damages in respect of that damage from B, when A could also have sued C for such damages under the 1987 Act. In such a case, B may well be entitled to bring a claim in contribution against C under the Civil Liability (Contribution) Act 1978 and recoup some of the money he paid out to A to compensate him for the damage suffered by him.

So, for example, suppose Tom developed dermatitis as a result of wearing a T-shirt which, due to a flaw in the way it was manufactured, contained trace elements of some dermatitis-causing chemical. The T-shirt was imported into the United Kingdom from China by Sarah. The T-shirt was then sold to Beth who put her mark on it and held herself out to be the manufacturer of the T-shirt. Beth then sold the T-shirt in her store to Tom. Tom successfully sues Beth for damages under the 1987 Act to compensate him for the fact that he has developed dermatitis as a result of wearing the T-shirt. In such a case, Beth will be entitled to bring a claim in contribution against Sarah on the ground that Sarah imported the T-shirt into the European Union and was therefore liable under the 1987 Act to compensate Tom for the harm suffered by him in wearing that T-shirt.

46

PUBLIC NUISANCE

INTRODUCTION

A will commit a public nuisance if he creates, authorises, adopts or continues a state of affairs which unreasonably interferes with a public right or with the comfort, convenience or safety of the public.

If A commits a public nuisance, he commits a crime – the crime of public nuisance – and can therefore be prosecuted, convicted and punished as a criminal. But this is not the only way in which A can be dealt with. Where it is necessary to prevent the continuance or recurrence of a public nuisance a public official or body may seek an injunction.[1] The public official or body may seek such an injunction of its own volition, or there is a procedure which allows the Attorney-General to agree to lend his name to an action which is in reality controlled by a private individual.[2] More important, however, for the purposes of this book, is the fact that a private individual may bring an action for damages (and/or an injunction) in her own name if the public nuisance has caused her 'special damage', that is, damage over and above that suffered by the public in general as a result of the public nuisance. Claims for public nuisance brought by private individuals who have suffered 'special damage' *resemble* claims in tort, and are sometimes brought alongside tort claims for damages such as claims in private nuisance or in negligence. Strictly speaking, however, public nuisance is *not* a tort. This is because the duty which is broken by A when he commits a public nuisance is not a duty owed to other individuals but a duty owed *to the public at large*; hence the fact that violations of the duty are usually dealt with by actions brought by public officials.[3]

It is difficult to define what a public nuisance is in any helpful way.[4] Most books rely on Archbold's definition, according to which A will commit the crime of public nuisance if he 'commits an act not warranted by law, or omits to discharge a legal duty, where the effect of the act or omission is to endanger the life, health, property, morals, or comfort of the public or to obstruct the

---

[1] For instance, a local authority is empowered to bring such an action by s 222(1) Local Government Act 1972, and a highway authority by s 130 Highways Act 1980.

[2] Called a 'relator' action.

[3] In practice, public officials probably do not bring many claims which specifically allege public nuisance. Rather they rely on statutory provisions which allow them to deal with *all* types of nuisance; see, for example, the Environmental Protection Act 1990, ss 79 and 80. Criminal prosecutions for public nuisance are also uncommon. Smith 2003 states at 772 that 'the major importance of public nuisance today is in the civil remedy which it affords'.

[4] For a vigorous critique see Spencer 1989.

public in the exercise of rights common to all Her Majesty's subjects'.[5] But this definition is very vague. What, for instance, is 'an act not warranted by law'?[6] The Second US Restatement of Torts notes that English judicial decisions have held that public nuisance covers, 'interference with the public health, as in the keeping of diseased animals . . .; with the public safety, as in the case of storage of explosives in the midst of a city . . .; with the public morals, as in houses of prostitution . . .; with the public peace, as by loud and disturbing noises; with the public comfort, as in the case of widely disseminated bad odors, dust, and smoke; with the public convenience, as by obstruction of a public highway or navigable stream; and with a wide variety of miscellaneous public rights of a similar kind'.[7] This catalogue usefully illustrates the width of public nuisance in practice. But it also contains a misleading element because it suggests that *any* interference with these public interests will be sufficient. This is incorrect. If we take the example of storage of explosives and inflammable substances, it is not the law in England that someone will commit public nuisance whenever he stores the slightest amount of these.[8] Similarly, A will not commit a public nuisance whenever he obstructs the highway to a minor extent. What is crucial is whether the substances are stored to an unreasonable extent or in an unreasonable way, and whether the highway is obstructed to an unreasonable extent.[9] Thus we think that someone who commits a public nuisance breaches one or both of the following two overlapping duties: (1) a duty not to create, authorise, adopt or continue a state of affairs which interferes unreasonably with a public right; and (2) a duty not to create, authorise, adopt or continue a state of affairs which interferes unreasonably with the comfort, convenience or safety of the public.

---

[5] Archbold's definition follows *Stephen's Digest of the Criminal Law*, 9th edn (1900), p 184: 'A common nuisance is an act not warranted by law or an omission to discharge a legal duty, which act or omission obstructs or causes inconvenience or damage to the public in the exercise of rights common to all His Majesty's subjects.'

[6] In *R v Goldstein, R v Rimmington* [2003] EWCA Crim 3450, the Court of Appeal (Criminal Division) held that the definition of public nuisance was not so vague that it violated human rights standards because (at [17]): 'the elements of the offence are sufficiently clear to enable a person, with appropriate legal advice if necessary, to regulate his behaviour.'

[7] Restatement of Torts 2d, § 821B, Comment b.

[8] *R v Lister* (1856–7). Dears & B 209, 169 ER 979; *R v Chilworth Gunpowder Co.* (1888) 4 TLR 557.

[9] Support for this proposition can be found in the Court of Appeal decision of *Harper v G N Haden & Sons Ltd* [1933] Ch 298 concerning whether builders' scaffolding which obstructed a pavement amounted to a public nuisance. Lord Hanworth MR said, at 302, 'A temporary obstruction to the use of the highway or to the enjoyment of adjoining premises does not give rise to a legal remedy where such obstruction is reasonable in quantum and in duration.' Romer LJ drew an express parallel with the standard of unreasonableness in private nuisance cases and stated, at 317, 'The law relating to the user of the highway is in truth the law of give and take.' However, in the recent case of *Westminster City Council v Ocean Leisure Ltd* [2004] EWCA Civ 970, the Court of Appeal treated Lord Hanworth's dictum as too wide: ibid., at [24]. The Court preferred the view that a limited restriction on the ability of the public to use the highway will be lawful if the restriction is a consequence of a reasonable incident of use of the highway, for instance parking, or of reasonable access to or maintenance of premises alongside the highway: ibid., at [42].

INTERFERENCE WITH PUBLIC RIGHTS

Claims based on a breach of duty (1) raise the question of what counts as a public *right*. Some of the uncertainties as to the scope of public nuisance flow from the fact that it is easy to use the word *right* in a loose sense. It is important not to assume that there is a *right* to all benefits which are widely enjoyed. The rights which are most often relied on in public nuisance cases are the right to free passage along public highways and the right to free navigation along a public river. As an example of the law in action we discuss unreasonable interference with the right to free passage along public highways in detail in the next section.

Unreasonable interference with public highways

A will commit this form of public nuisance if he creates, authorises, adopts or continues a state of affairs which interferes unreasonably with free passage along a public highway. Free passage will be unreasonably interfered with if the highway is unreasonably obstructed or users of the highway are unreasonably endangered.

Unreasonable obstruction

Whether an obstruction to the highway will amount to an unreasonable obstruction depends on the degree of interference created by the obstruction and the reasonableness of causing that degree of interference. Where the obstruction is not such as is likely to inconvenience the public, such as a lamp-post on a pavement, the court will probably hold that there is no unreasonable obstruction.[10] Further, even when an obstruction does cause inconvenience, the person creating the obstruction may be able to demonstrate that there was no unreasonable obstruction because it was reasonable to use the highway in the way that he did. 'No member of the public has an exclusive right to use the highway. He has merely a right to use it subject to the reasonable user of others, and if that reasonable user causes him to be obstructed he has no legal cause of complaint.'[11] Thus it is not a public nuisance to block a highway with a cart in order to unload it.[12] But it is a public nuisance to block a highway so regularly as effectively to prevent it from being used by others.[13] Similarly, it is a public nuisance to block a highway for some reason other than reasonable use of the highway for passage, incidents of passage, access to premises alongside the

---

[10] *W H Chaplin & Co. Ltd v Mayor of Westminster* [1901] 2 Ch 329.

[11] *Harper v G N Haden & Sons Ltd* [1933] Ch 298, 317 per Romer LJ. See also, *Herring* v *Metropolitan Board of Works* (1865) 19 CB NS 510, 144 ER 886.

[12] *R v Jones* (1812) 3 Camp 230, 231, 170 ER 1364, 1365: 'A cart or wagon may be unloaded at a gateway; but this must be done with promptness' (per Lord Ellenborough).

[13] *R v Cross* (1812) 3 Camp 224, 227, 170 ER 1362, 1363: 'No one can make a stable yard of the king's highway' (per Lord Ellenborough, finding against the proprietors of the Greenwich stage-coach which made two 45 minute stops each day near Charing Cross). But it seems that in rare circumstances even this may be reasonable: *Dwyer v Mansfield* [1946] 1 KB 437, where the obstruction was caused by queues at a greengrocer's shop during wartime rationing.

highway, or building work on premises alongside the highway.[14] In such cases the interferences cannot be defended by appealing to some advantage that might flow to the public interest from such an obstruction continuing.[15] An unreasonable obstruction does not always have to be physical. Thus in *Wandsworth LBC v Railtrack PLC*[16] the obstruction took the unusual form of users being discouraged from using a particular footpath by the risk of falling pigeon excrement. Gibbs J held that this state of affairs amounted to a public nuisance even without consideration of the possible health risks.

No right to persist with an obstruction of the highway can be obtained by long use,[17] but if an obstruction pre-dates dedication of the road as a highway then the dedication may be treated as subject to the reservation of the obstruction being continued.[18]

Unreasonable endangering

A state of affairs which unreasonably endangers users of the highway will amount to an unreasonable interference with free passage. It might be thought that in a situation where a claimant alleges that he was unreasonably endangered *and then injured* by a state of affairs which the defendant created, authorised, continued or adopted, the claimant ought really to allege that the defendant committed the tort of negligence.[19] After all, this is the tort which is – in large part – built around the existence of duties to avoid creating unreasonable risks of others suffering physical injury.[20] The fact that such claims are conventionally treated as falling within public nuisance probably stems from the high number of cases where there is both an obstruction *and* an endangering. This overlap has increased over time because users of the highway have attained greater speeds, consequently increasing the danger posed by unanticipated obstructions.

---

[14] *Westminster City Council v Ocean Leisure Ltd* [2004] EWCA Civ 970, where the state of affairs that would have been a public nuisance had it not been authorised by statute involved obstruction of the highway in order to build a new footbridge across the River Thames.

[15] In *R v Train* (1862) 2 B & S 640, 121 ER 1129, the King's Bench ruled that a tramway in Lambeth was a public nuisance since it withdrew part of the highway from ordinary use. As Crompton J pointed out, the effect of such a ruling was merely to insist that those who wanted to promote such projects had to obtain a private Act of Parliament.

[16] [2001] 1 WLR 368. The conclusion that the state of affairs amounted to a public nuisance was not challenged when the case was heard before the Court of Appeal: [2002] QB 756.

[17] *R v Cross* (1812) 3 Camp 224, 227, 170 ER 1362, 1363: 'It is immaterial how long the practice may have prevailed, for no length of time will legitimate a nuisance' (per Lord Ellenborough).

[18] *Fisher v Prowse* (1862) 2 B & S 770, 121 ER 1258. This explains the legality of maintaining, for instance, stone steps leading down from an old house onto a pavement, and the cellar-flaps of an ancient public house.

[19] See *Hunter v Canary Wharf* [1997] AC 655, 692. The question whether public nuisance *should* be restricted to exclude claims for personal injuries is discussed in detail below, pp. 787–8.

[20] For an account of the 'physical danger principle' which underlies the existence of a large number of duties of care in negligence, see above, pp. 66–85.

INTERFERENCE WITH THE PUBLIC'S COMFORT AND CONVENIENCE

Claims based on a breach of duty (2) raise the difficult question of how we draw the line between situations where we say 'this has interfered with the comfort, convenience or safety of *some* individuals' and those where we say 'this has interfered with the comfort, convenience or safety of the public'.

In *Attorney-General* v *PYA Quarries*, Denning LJ proposed that this question should be answered by considering whether the nuisance was 'so widespread in its range or so indiscriminate in its effect that it would not be reasonable to expect one person to take proceedings on his own responsibility to put a stop to it, but that it should be taken on the responsibility of the community at large'.[21] This statement has been regularly cited and has made its way into almost all the tort textbooks. But our opinion is that it must be treated with caution.

Our main quarrel with Denning LJ's statement is that it seems to assume that a public nuisance is also a private nuisance to a large number of claimants.[22] This overlooks the fact that the public interest (protected by public nuisance) is not simply a conglomeration of private interests in land (protected by private nuisance[23]). Many cases of public nuisance do not involve interference with private interests in land at all. For instance, in *R* v *Vantandillo*[24] the defendant created a public nuisance by carrying a child with smallpox through the streets and it is unlikely that this was an interference with the interests in land of a substantial number of citizens. Similarly, in *R* v *Madden*[25] the Court of Appeal stated that the crime of public nuisance could be committed by making a hoax bomb threat if a considerable number of persons was affected, but there was no suggestion that there had to be any possibility of those affected being able to sue for private nuisance.

Thus our view is that it would be better if Denning LJ had made no reference to the reasonableness or otherwise of expecting *individuals* to sue. We think that the appropriate test should be whether the interference was so widespread in its range or so indiscriminate in its effect that it is reasonable for proceedings to be taken on behalf of the community at large. For the avoidance of doubt we should add that where it would be reasonable for proceedings to be taken on behalf of the community at large, individuals who have suffered 'special damage' as a result of the interference in question will still be able to make claims for compensation for that damage. Moreover, if the interference in question has at the same

---

[21] [1957] 2 QB 169, 191.

[22] This assumption can best be seen by going through the following steps. (1) Denning LJ's test for a public nuisance depends on whether it *would be reasonable to expect* an individual to sue. (2) The question whether it is *reasonable to expect* an individual to sue assumes that the individual *could sue*. (3) The most obvious thing individuals could be suing for is private nuisance.

[23] We explain in Chapter 18 how the courts have treated the tort of private nuisance as protecting private interests in land.

[24] (1815) 4 M & S 73, 105 ER 762. See also *R* v *Henson* (1852) Dears 24, 169 ER 621 (taking a horse with an infectious disease into a public place).

[25] [1975] 1 WLR 1379.

time caused a claimant to suffer an unreasonable interference with land in which he has an interest, then that claimant could still make a claim in *private nuisance* against anyone who created, authorised, adopted or continued the interference in question. Claims in public nuisance and private nuisance are not exclusive.

But we still have to face the question of *how many* people, in practice, must be inconvenienced or discomforted before a defendant will be held to have committed a public nuisance. Our view is that the most useful discussion of how many people must be affected before the effects will be sufficiently widespread is found in Romer LJ's judgment in *Attorney-General v PYA Quarries*.[26] He suggests that a judge should ask whether 'the neighbourhood' is affected by the defendant's activity and should then consider whether 'the local community within that sphere comprises a sufficient number of persons to constitute a class of the public'. These issues are described by Romer LJ as 'questions of fact', which seems to mean that they are matters for the judgment of trial judges rather than for appellate rules. On the particular facts of the *PYA Quarries* case the Court of Appeal held that there were no grounds for interfering with the trial judge's conclusions that flying rocks which disturbed 30 petitioners and vibrations which prompted fewer complaints were both sufficiently widespread. It is common to cite *R v Lloyd*[27] as a case on the other side of the line. In this case it was held that the defendant did not create a public nuisance when he created a noise which disturbed only three houses in Clifford's Inn.

It is important to note that the number of people affected does not provide an exhaustive answer to the question whether duty (2) has been breached. Denning LJ's test states that A's behaviour can also amount to a public nuisance if its effect is indiscriminate. It seems to us, however, that the purpose of this addition to the test is to catch cases where A's behaviour has interfered unreasonably with a public *right* which only a small number of people made use of. Thus Denning LJ could have defined duty (2) more simply if he had recognised the separate existence of duty (1).

ISOLATED INCIDENTS

The question has sometimes been raised as to whether an isolated incident can amount to a public nuisance. In *Stone v Bolton*, Oliver J stated that 'an isolated act of hitting a cricket ball on to a road, cannot, of course, amount to a nuisance ... nuisance must be a state of affairs'.[28] Oliver J's opinion was supported by Professor Newark, though he seems to have been chiefly motivated by the fear that if this opinion was rejected then a skidding bus might constitute a public nuisance.[29] If Oliver J's opinion represents the law,[30] then

---

[26] [1957] 2 QB 169, 184–5.

[27] (1802) 4 Esp 200, 170 ER 691.

[28] [1949] 1 All ER 237, 238e. This point was not discussed when the case reached the House of Lords: [1951] AC 850.

[29] Newark 1949, 486, 488. There are more convenient ways of avoiding inconsistency with the tort of negligence in road accident cases. Thus it could be argued that (1) it is not an unreasonable use of the highway to drive a reasonably safe bus on it, (2) such buses sometimes skid without anyone having been careless, and (3) consequently, the non-careless skidding of a bus is not an unreasonable interference with the safety of other road users.

it is necessary to determine: (*a*) how long a single incident must last in order to amount to a 'state of affairs'; *and* (*b*) whether, and, if so when, a series of single incidents can amount to a 'state of affairs'. In our opinion there is no good reason of principle for getting enmeshed in such arcane questions. Rather courts should concentrate on the central question whether there was an unreasonable interference or not.

CREATING, AUTHORISING, ADOPTING OR CONTINUING

Where a state of affairs causes an unreasonable interference with public rights or with the comfort, convenience or safety of the public, it seems straightforward that A should be liable if he *created* the state of affairs, or *authorised* someone else to create it.

What if A engages a contractor to perform some task which involves obstruction of the highway or endangers users of the highway, and the *contractor* creates an unreasonable obstruction or unreasonably endangers other users of the highway? In such a case, there is a rule that A will be responsible for the public nuisance created by the contractor unless the contractor's behaviour was collateral to what he was instructed to do.[31] This rule has been relied on principally against bodies with special statutory powers allowing them to arrange for the digging up of the highway. In *Rowe* v *Herman*, the Court of Appeal suggested that the rule would not make a householder liable if builders she engaged failed to put lights on a skip which they placed in the road.[32] Thus it seems possible that this rule only applies to those with special statutory powers.

Someone can also be held liable for an interference caused by a state of affairs which she did not create or authorise. This will be the case if the state of affairs in question arose on land *owned*[33] or *occupied*[34] by her and she *continued* or *adopted* the state of affairs in question. She will be held to have continued or adopted the state of affairs in question if it arose through her careless failure to prevent it arising or through her careless failure to deal with it once she had realised it had arisen.

---

[30] It is not clear that all the case law does support Oliver J. Thus public nuisance can cover situations where a mass of snow suddenly falls off a roof onto a claimant (*Slater* v *Worthington's Cash Stores (1930) Ltd* [1941] 1 KB 488, decided by Oliver J!), where a building next to the highway suddenly collapses (see, for instance, *Wringe* v *Cohen* [1940] 1 KB 229 and *Mint* v *Good* [1951] 1 KB 517) and where an isolated incident, such as the discharge of oil, creates a longer-term interference (see, for example, *Southport Corporation* v *Esso Petroleum Co. Ltd* [1954] 2 QB 182, 197 per Denning LJ). It may be that the first two situations can be explained on the basis that the mass of snow and buildings were public nuisances even before they collapsed because of the *danger* they posed to users of the highway (see above, p. 780).

[31] *Hardaker* v *Idle DC* [1896] 1 QB 335; *Penny* v *Wimbledon Urban District Council* [1899] 2 QB 72; *Holliday* v *National Telephone Co.* [1899] 2 QB 392.

[32] [1997] 1 WLR 1390, 1394H.

[33] In *Mint* v *Good* [1951] 1 KB 517 the Court of Appeal held that the rule set out in the text applied to owners who were not in possession as well as to occupiers.

[34] For instance, a tenant at will can be held liable under this rule: *R* v *Watts* (1703) 1 Salk 357, 91 ER 311.

Owners and occupiers are often held to have *continued* or *adopted* a state of affairs directly caused by the workings of nature. For instance, if a tree on A's land falls into the highway, A may be held liable for the interference with the highway so caused if he carelessly failed to inspect that tree to determine whether or not it was likely to fall into the road or otherwise obstruct the highway.[35] Similarly, in *Wandsworth LBC v Railtrack PLC*,[36] the defendant, which owned a railway bridge over Balham High Road, was held liable for failing to take reasonable steps to prevent pigeons roosting under the bridge and inconveniencing passing pedestrians.

Owners and occupiers can also be held to have continued or adopted a state of affairs directly caused by trespassers, provided that a reasonable owner or occupier would have discovered the state of affairs and dealt with it.[37] Thus in *Attorney-General v Tod Heatley*[38] the owner of a building site in Westminster was held to have continued a public nuisance by failing to take sufficient steps to remove from the site dead dogs, cats, fish and offal which had been dumped by unknown trespassers.

The rules concerning when owners and occupiers will be held to have continued or adopted a state of affairs directly caused by a *building* falling into a state of disrepair are relatively stringent. Thus courts tend to take the robust view that 'there must be some fault on the part of someone or other for that to happen'.[39] Further, if A is aware of the disrepair, or ought to be, her duty to take reasonable steps to deal with the problem will be non-delegable; as a result, if contractors appointed by A carelessly fail to deal with the problem, A will still be held liable.[40] A will avoid liability, however, if she can establish that the danger was purely the result of 'latent defects'. Historically, the non-delegable duty owed by an owner or occupier which allows claims by those injured by a thing falling from the owner's or occupier's land onto the highway was probably related to the rule in *Rylands* v *Fletcher*.[41] Now, however, only an extraordinary or unusual use of land falls within the ambit of the rule in *Rylands* v *Fletcher*, while public nuisance covers a far broader range of uses of land. The public nuisance duty is also distinct in that where the complaint is of an unreasonable interference with the highway users of neighbouring highways will be able to make claims, whilst claims under the rule in *Rylands* v *Fletcher* must be made by persons with interests in neighbouring land.[42]

[35] *Noble* v *Harrison* [1926] 2 KB 332; *Caminer v Northern & London Investment Trust Ltd* [1951] AC 88; *British Road Services* v *Slater* [1964] 1 WLR 498.

[36] [2002] QB 756.

[37] *Barker* v *Herbert* [1911] 2 KB 633.

[38] [1897] 1 Ch 560. A decision which was approved by the House of Lords in *Sedleigh-Denfield v O'Callaghan* [1940] AC 880, and was held to still represent the law by the Court of Appeal in *Wandsworth LBC v Railtrack PLC* [2002] QB 756, at [26].

[39] *Mint v Good* [1951] 1 KB 517, 526–7, per Denning LJ, though in *Wringe v Cohen* [1940] 1 KB 229, 233, the Court of Appeal suggested that where premises were undermined by 'a secret and unobservable operation of nature, such as subsidence under or near the foundations' the owner or occupier might not be liable.

[40] *Tarry v Ashton* (1876) 1 QBD 314.

[41] See Chapter 44 for a discussion of this rule. It will be noted that Blackburn J played a pivotal role in both *Rylands v Fletcher* and *Tarry v Ashton*, and that both cases involved independent contractors carrying out operations on the defendants' land.

[42] In *Wringe v Cohen* [1940] 1 KB 229 the Court of Appeal held that the non-delegable duty attached only to 'premises on a highway' but that both passers-by and owners of adjoining property could take advantage of the duty. It seems to us, however, that it would be implausible for an adjoining owner to

SPECIAL DAMAGE

If A has created a public nuisance and B has suffered some harm as a result, B will only be entitled to sue A for damages in respect of that harm if that harm counts as 'special damage'. For these purposes 'special damage' means damage which is different in nature or extent to that suffered by the other members of the public affected by the nuisance. Thus if A creates a public nuisance by unreasonably obstructing a highway, if all that B suffers as a result is the inconvenience of having to go round by another route or being delayed then B probably will not have suffered 'special damage'. But if B trips on the obstruction and is injured, or damages her personal property, then she will have suffered 'special damage'. The difficulty comes with deciding how to deal with cases that fall between these extremes. Four situations which have caused difficulty will be discussed.

Special costs from obstruction

In some cases courts have decided that a particular person suffered 'special damage' because the obstruction suffered by all was, in practice, far more inconvenient for that person. The best example of this is provided by *Rose* v *Miles*[43] where the defendant was alleged to have moored a barge across a public navigable creek and the plaintiff had to incur the expense of unloading goods from his barges and conveying them by land. The court seems to have thought that the plaintiff's damage was 'special' to him because he had already loaded his goods before the time of the obstruction and consequently he was unable to avoid the extra expenses. Dampier J said, 'If this be not a particular damage, I scarcely know what is.'[44]

A similar approach was taken in *Jan de Nul (UK) Ltd* v *NV Royale Belge*,[45] where Moore-Bick J considered the liability of a dredging company responsible for siltation interfering with freedom of navigation in an estuary. He held that in such circumstances, 'any significant interference with an individual's commercial operations or the enjoyment of private rights resulting from the obstruction to navigation would in my judgment represent damage over and above that suffered by the public at large and would be sufficient to support an action'.[46]

Interference with customers

Where an obstruction is particularly harmful to B because it interferes with his ability to attract customers it seems that B will be able to establish 'special damage'.

---

claim that he had been a victim of unreasonable interference with the public right to use the highway. Consequently, we think that if the owner of adjoining property has a claim at all it certainly is not a claim for *public* nuisance. Instead it may be a claim for continuing a *private* nuisance (see above, pp. 374–7). In *Mint* v *Good* [1951] 1 KB 517, 527, Denning LJ stated that the decision in *Wringe* v *Cohen* was 'clearly correct in regard to the responsibility of an occupier to *passers-by*' (emphasis added).

[43] (1815) 4 M & S 101; 105 ER 773. See also *Walsh* v *Ervin* [1952] VLR 361.
[44] (1815) 4 M & S 101, 104; 105 ER 773, 774. 'Particular damage' is a phrase that some judges and authors use instead of 'special damage'.
[45] [2000] 1 Lloyd's Rep 700.
[46] Ibid., [44]. This point was not challenged on appeal: [2002] 1 Lloyd's Rep 583.

In *Iveson* v *Moore*[47] the plaintiff alleged that he had lost customers and the profits of his colliery because of the obstruction of the highway near his colliery. The Court of King's Bench split 2:2 on whether this was sufficiently 'special damage'. But it seems that the case was later argued before all the judges of the Common Pleas and Exchequer, and their opinions unanimously supported the plaintiff's claim.[48] Similarly, in *Wilkes* v *Hungerford Market Co.*[49] a bookseller successfully claimed that the loss he suffered through his customers being inconvenienced by an obstructed highway was sufficiently distinct to constitute 'special damage'. The correctness of *Wilkes* was doubted by Lord Chelmsford LC in the case of *Ricket* v *Metropolitan Railway.*[50] But the case was treated as correct by the Court of Appeal in *Blundy, Clark & Co. Ltd* v *London North Eastern Railway.*[51] In that case Greer LJ stated that, 'Where a [claimant] has property near a highway which he uses for the purposes of his business, and the highway . . . is unlawfully obstructed, and he is thereby put to greater expense in the conduct of his business, or suffers loss by the diminution of his business, he is entitled to recover damages as a person who has suffered special or peculiar damage beyond that which has been suffered by other members of the public wanting to use the highway.'[52]

Costs of removing the public nuisance

In *Winterbottom* v *Lord Derby*[53] the Court of Exchequer held that the plaintiff could not rely on the expense he had incurred in removing an obstruction as 'special damage', since otherwise any person could give to himself the opportunity to sue. But in *Tate & Lyle Industries Ltd* v *GLC*,[54] the House of Lords held that the plaintiff could claim for the expense it had incurred dredging the River Thames in order to remove the obstruction to free navigation for which the defendant was responsible. The majority of the House of Lords seems to have held that the 'special damage' was not the cost of dredging itself, but the special loss that the plaintiff suffered because ships of particular dimensions were unable to progress up the channel. This is important, because it clarifies that the plaintiff had suffered 'special damage' *before* the dredging was undertaken, and thus does not conflict with the decision in *Winterbottom*. Lord Diplock, however, disagreed with the majority and argued that 'special damage' arising from the plaintiff's choice about how it used public rights could not be the basis for a claim for public nuisance.[55]

---

[47] (1699) 1 Ld Raym 486, 91 ER 1224.
[48] It is worth noting that in this case the defendant was a rival colliery owner and it was alleged that he obstructed the road with the aim of harming the plaintiff. In such a situation a modern claimant might prefer to rely on the tort of using unlawful means to inflict harm on another (discussed in Chapter 20) rather than alleging public nuisance. Such a claimant would have to establish that the means used were 'unlawful' (as defined in Chapter 20) and that the defendant was 'aiming at' causing harm to him. It would not be necessary, however, to demonstrate 'special damage'.
[49] (1835) 2 Bing NC 281, 132 ER 110.
[50] (1867) LR 2 HL 175, 188.
[51] [1931] 2 KB 334.
[52] Ibid., 369. See also *Lyons, Sons & Co.* v *Gulliver* [1914] 1 Ch 631; *Walsh* v *Ervin* [1952] VLR 361.
[53] (1867) LR 2 Ex 316.
[54] [1983] 2 AC 507.
[55] Ibid., 547F.

We think, however, that Lord Diplock's dissent was out of line with the cases discussed in the previous two sections. It is clear that the fact that the plaintiff has *chosen* to make use of a particular highway or river for delivering goods or receiving customers does not prevent an action against someone responsible for an unreasonable obstruction. Further, there is no obvious reason for distinguishing between choosing to use a highway for making deliveries and choosing to use a river for receiving supplies.

The position is different where the body which incurs costs to remove the public nuisance is fulfilling a statutory function by doing so. In *Jan de Nul (UK) Ltd v NV Royale Belge SA*[56] the Court of Appeal held that where a dredging company had caused quantities of silt to be deposited in such a way as to interfere with the public right of navigation in a river, a harbour authority could sue that company in public nuisance for the cost of dredging the river bed, if either it was its duty to dredge the river bed or it had a statutory power to do so.[57]

Personal injuries

There is no real dispute over whether personal injuries can be sufficiently 'special' to an individual claimant. Instead, the debate is over whether personal injuries should be recoverable in public nuisance claims at all. In Chapter 18 we discussed the question whether personal injuries should be recoverable in the tort of private nuisance and noted that the House of Lords has recently suggested that the answer is 'no'.[58] An important step in the reasoning towards this answer was the opinion that the tort of negligence sets the appropriate conditions for redress for unintentionally inflicted personal injuries. It is difficult, however, to extend this answer over into public nuisance cases because there is a long line of precedents where damages were awarded for personal injuries.[59] Moreover, some of the other reasons given by the House of Lords for excluding personal injury claims from the scope of the tort of private nuisance are not relevant to the scope of public nuisance; for instance the desirability of facilitating agreements to tolerate a certain level of disturbance[60] and the difficulty of defining who has a sufficient interest in 'a home',[61] do not apply directly to

---

[56] [2002] 1 Lloyd's Rep 583.

[57] Ibid., at [60]. For a similar case involving a highway authority see *Louth District Council v West* (1896) 65 LJ (QB) 535.

[58] In *Hunter v Canary Wharf* [1997] AC 655, 692, Lord Goff drew attention 'to the fact that although, in the past, damages for personal injury have been recovered at least in actions of public nuisance, there is now developing a school of thought that the appropriate remedy for such claims as these should lie in our now fully developed law of negligence, and that personal injury claims should be altogether excluded from the domain of nuisance'.

[59] See, for example, *Castle v St Augustine's Links* (1922) 38 TLR 615.

[60] Such agreements are easier to secure if only a small number of people have private law rights which must be accommodated.

[61] If private nuisance claims could be brought by people who did not have interests in land (or exclusive possession) then some other limit would have to be defined. In public nuisance 'special damage' defines who can claim.

[62] The House of Lords has already extended the limits on the tort of private nuisance developed in

public nuisance. Consequently, although the House of Lords may in future bring public nuisance into line with private nuisance,[62] it seems that under the current law a claim for damages for personal injuries caused by public nuisance may succeed even where a claim in negligence would have failed.[63]

Hunter v *Canary Wharf* [1997] AC 655 to liability under the rule in *Rylands* v *Fletcher: Transco plc* v *Stockport MBC* [2003] 3 WLR 1467.

[63] *Dymond* v *Pearce* [1972] 1 QB 496. Sachs and Stephenson LJJ both expressly accepted that a claim in public nuisance could succeed where a claim in negligence would have failed (ibid., 502A–C, 508F–G). Edmund-Davies LJ was more cautious (at 504H–507A), but seems only to have insisted that the risk of damage had to be reasonably foreseeable before a claim for damages could be made in public nuisance. This opinion is consistent with *The Wagon Mound (No. 2)* [1967] 1 AC 388, and is not equivalent to saying that the defendant must have been negligent.

47

LOSS COMPENSATION SCHEMES

In this part of the book we have been looking so far at situations where a claimant who has suffered loss will be entitled to bring a non-tortious claim for compensation against the person who *caused* her to suffer that loss. But the claimant may be able to bring a claim for compensation against a *third party*, such as the State. This will be the case if the claimant's loss is covered by a *loss compensation scheme*. It is impossible in a book of this size to describe all the loss compensation schemes that have been set up to assist people who have suffered loss either at other people's hands or through nobody's fault. We will simply try to set out the key features of such schemes, describe some examples of schemes which either exist or have been proposed, and evaluate their advantages and disadvantages.

THE VARIABLE FEATURES IN LOSS COMPENSATION SCHEMES

The dominant model for a loss compensation scheme involves the State compelling contributions to a fund, with the fund then paying compensation to a defined range of claimants. A variety of schemes can be based on this simple model, but there are five principal variables.

Conditions for entitlement

First, there is a range of options as to the conditions for entitlement to claim against the fund. A common feature of all schemes is that the claimant's ability to prove that a particular defendant was at fault is *not* a condition for entitlement. Thus such schemes are often referred to as *no-fault compensation schemes*. But beyond this common feature there are many possibilities. An ambitious *general* scheme might attempt to assist all victims of serious adverse events, including illness, a less ambitious *general* scheme might attempt to assist all victims of *accidents*, and a sector-limited scheme might attempt to assist only victims of a particular type of accident or adverse event, e.g. road accidents or adverse events during medical treatment. Schemes might be further refined by making particular categories of people ineligible, e.g. victims of self-inflicted injury or drivers who were drunk when injured.

Contributors and their contributions

Secondly, there is a range of options as to who is compelled to contribute to the fund and in what proportions. For instance, a State could seek to compel contributions by risk creators in proportion to the risks that they create, or it could seek to compel contributions from potential claimants in proportion to the potential benefits that they might claim, or it could adopt some combination of these approaches.

Level of compensation

Thirdly, there is scope for defining the level of compensation to be paid by the fund. Some schemes involve the payment of compensation at a level equivalent to what would be awarded in a successful tort claim, whilst others award more limited payments (e.g. only 80 per cent of lost earnings). Some more complicated schemes, particularly those which involve contributions from potential claimants, allow contributors to select their own possible level of compensation when their contributions are calculated.[1]

Relationship to tort claims

The fourth variable is the relationship between the scheme and tort claims. In some jurisdictions where a loss compensation scheme has been set up it operates parallel to tort law,[2] whilst in others tort law has been abolished for incidents falling within the scope of the scheme. A more complicated option involves the scheme as the exclusive way of dealing with minor injuries, but the scheme being supplemented by the possibility of tort claims for more serious injuries.[3]

Who administers the fund

The fifth variable is the question of who administers the fund. Although such funds are usually created by statute[4] they can be operated either by a public body or by private organisations such as insurance companies. More complicated possibilities are also sometimes used. For instance, where contributions are paid by potential injurers (for instance, employers) to a scheme which will cover possible injuries to a fixed class (for instance, their employees) it is possible that a public body will operate the scheme for small employers and large

---

[1] A greater contribution is demanded in exchange for the promise of a higher level of compensation.

[2] Where a loss compensation scheme operates parallel to tort law it will be necessary to define the relationship between the two types of claims. One possibility would be to reduce the tort claim by any amount recovered under the scheme. But an alternative would not reduce the tort claim but would instead allow the operators of the scheme to recoup any tort damages paid to compensate for loss that the scheme had already compensated. The Criminal Injuries Compensation Scheme, which pays compensation to those suffering personal injuries as a result of being a victim of crime, or seeking to prevent a crime or apprehend a criminal, is an example of a scheme which is supplementary to tort law. Such victims are entitled to sue the perpetrators in tort if such a course is likely to be worthwhile.

[3] For an example of a scheme like this see the discussion below of road traffic accident schemes in use in some American states, pp. 792–4.

[4] Of course operators of activities may also set up contractual insurance pools as a supplement to tort rights. Many climbing gyms, for instance, require users to purchase insurance which will cover all accidents and mishaps.

employers can choose to opt out, and take full responsibility themselves for providing benefits equivalent to those under the scheme.[5]

The interdependence of the five factors

Clearly when it comes to designing or evaluating a scheme these five variables cannot be considered in isolation. For instance, the wider the scope of entitlement to claim, and in particular the further that the entitled group extends beyond the range of those who might be able to claim in tort, the greater the pressure to cap the level of payments and the greater the pressure to raise some proportion of the contributions from the potential beneficiaries. As a second example, it is where the entitled group is limited to the victims of a particular type of accident that it may be most practical to compel contributions from risk creators, to quantify awards in line with tort, and to abolish tort claims.

The interrelationship of the five factors may become clearer by considering some specific schemes.

FOUR LOSS COMPENSATION SCHEMES
The New Zealand Accident Compensation Scheme

The New Zealand Accident Compensation Scheme came into operation on 1 April 1974, though it has been regularly amended since then. The 1974 scheme covered all personal injuries suffered in accidents and tort law claims were abolished for injuries falling within it. Contributions were raised from three groups: employers paid a levy on wages (and the self-employed made similar payments) to cover the costs of injuries to earners (other than in road accidents); owners of motor vehicles paid a levy to cover the costs of injuries in road accidents; and, the government funded the costs of injuries to non-earners, such as students, the unemployed, the retired and visitors from abroad. The level of compensation was reasonably close to tort law. The scheme covered a victim's medical expenses, 80 per cent of their loss of earnings after the first week, and also provided a lump sum for pain, suffering and loss of amenity.

One criticism of the 1974 scheme was that it was unfair to make employers pay contributions to cover the cost of all accidental injuries suffered by their employees, including those not associated with work. A second criticism was that it was unfair not to distinguish between employers with good and bad safety records when setting contribution levels. A third criticism was that it was unfair to treat the victims of accidents more generously than victims of illness and those born disabled.

The scheme has been amended to respond to the first and second criticisms. Thus employees now pay a special contribution towards the cost of non-work injuries which is collected from them by the Inland Revenue and there are schemes which allow employers to reduce their contributions by participating in promoting workplace safety. The third criticism has proved more difficult to

---

[5] A variation on this model is used in New Zealand.

meet, however, and the only significant move in that direction has been the extension of the scheme to cover injuries caused by 'medical mishap'.[6]

Some other significant changes to the scheme have also been tried but then reversed. Thus at one stage lump sum payments were abolished and replaced by 'independence allowances'. This, however, has now been reversed, and other attempts are being made to encourage rehabilitation. A second experiment was 'privatisation' of the scheme by allowing private insurance companies to compete to provide scheme-style cover to employers. This, however, has also been reversed and the scheme is once again administered by the Accident Compensation Corporation,[7] a Crown entity.

Road traffic accident schemes in use in some American states[8]

It is often argued that there are strong reasons for introducing a limited scheme covering personal injuries suffered in road accidents because: (*a*) drivers are already used to paying for insurance which covers the cost of some[9] such personal injuries; (*b*) the class of people who create the risk of road accidents and might be expected to pay for them (that is, drivers) are also by and large those who might make most claims from a compensation scheme;[10] but (*c*) it is costly and slow to sort out road accidents through the tort system, and (*d*) there are significant classes of victims who excite sympathy but are left uncompensated by tort (e.g. children who unpredictably run into the road). Given these factors any scheme which will cost drivers no more than current insurance premiums whilst offering a better protection for victims could gain popular support.

The model scheme which is most common in the United States involves contributions from road users and is administered by private insurance companies. Under the scheme all victims of road accidents are entitled to compensation even if they cannot prove that another driver was at fault, but in exchange for this wider scope of entitlement the level of compensation is reduced to below the tort level for victims of *minor* accidents. Usually tort claims are abolished for minor accidents. Private insurance companies sell membership of these

---

[6] 'Medical mishap' is an adverse consequence of treatment which is severe and rare (likely to occur in less than 1% of cases): Injury Prevention, Rehabilitation, and Compensation Act 2001, s 34. In March 2004 the New Zealand government announced that it intended extending coverage to all personal injuries caused by medical treatment, regardless as to whether they were severe. Under the proposals the scheme will still not cover injuries that are a necessary part of treatment, such as a surgical incision, injuries that result from the patient's underlying condition, and the failure of treatment to achieve the desired results.

[7] Details of the history and operations of the New Zealand scheme can be found at http://www.acc.org.nz/ .

[8] We concentrate on American schemes because they are well established and have been carefully studied. Similar schemes are also in place, however, in several Canadian provinces, Australian states, and European countries, e.g. France.

[9] Not all. Currently it is not compulsory in England and Wales for a driver to insure against injury to *himself* or *herself*, though it is compulsory to insure against the possibility of *negligently* injuring a *third party*. Nonetheless, many drivers purchase insurance against injury to themselves.

[10] To spell this out, the risk of road accidents is created by drivers and people injured in road accidents are generally also drivers (even though they may be travelling as passengers or be pedestrians at the time when they are injured).

schemes and pay out benefits, and treat them alongside other insurance poli-cies.[11] Thus, drivers pay to their insurers amounts covering the risk that they will be injured in a road accident (and the risk that they will injure a person who is not a driver and will consequently not have a policy of his own), whilst claims are made by injured drivers against their insurers, and by injured non-drivers against the insurers of the driver who injured them.

Two arguments are commonly raised against such schemes. The first objec-tion is that it seems unfair that where a victim was undoubtedly injured by the negligence of another the scheme leaves her with less compensation than tort law would have provided. This first objection is often augmented by the fact that when it is a driver who was undoubtedly injured by the negligence of another then the scheme adds insult to injury by making the innocent victim claim on her own policy (perhaps forfeiting a no-claims bonus).

The first objection is partially met by preserving the possibility of a tort claim if the injury suffered goes above a certain level of seriousness. This means that no victim suffering a *serious* injury will be left significantly worse off by the scheme. Unfortunately, however, the use of seriousness hurdles, especially if seriousness is measured by the cost of medical treatment, creates an incentive for fraud, in the form of exaggerated medical bills.[12]

The second objection is that even if drivers are aware that they are at fault in causing an accident, they will still be able to claim compensation for their own injuries and they will not have to pay damages except to those suffering serious injuries. Given this, the incentive to drive carefully may be reduced, and acci-dent rates may rise. Studies trying to determine whether the introduction of no-fault schemes has led to an increase in accident rates have yielded mixed results, and are discussed in the final section of this chapter.

Currently, thirteen[13] American states have no-fault road accident schemes. All of these allow tort claims to be brought if the victim's injury exceeds a particular threshold of severity, with eight expressing that threshold in terms of the medical bills ($1000 in Kentucky, $2500 in Colorado) and five using a phrase such as 'serious injury' (New York) or 'permanent injury' (Florida). Usually such a threshold is sufficient to keep most claims out of tort law.[14] When the claim is below the threshold then the schemes differ as to the level of compensation pro-vided. In New York, for instance, the scheme covers hospital and medical expenses up to a maximum of $50,000, and 80 per cent of lost wages up to a maximum of $1000 per month for a period not exceeding three years. In Florida,

---

[11] Indeed, often insurers sell to drivers a 'package' which includes (a) scheme membership, which is often called 'personal injury protection' (PIP), (b) liability insurance, covering the risk of being held liable in tort for causing personal injuries not covered by the scheme, and (c) insurance cov-ering property damage, which is usually outside the scheme.

[12] After Massachusetts raised its tort threshold from $500 to $2000 in 1988, the median number of treatment visits rose from 13 to 30 per auto injury claim: Marter & Weisberg 1992, 488.

[13] March 2004. In ten of these states the no-fault scheme is mandatory, whilst in three a driver can choose whether to participate in the no-fault scheme (in which case her insurance premium will be lower) or to keep full tort rights. At the peak of the popularity of no-fault road schemes during the late 1970s, 24 states had some form of no-fault scheme.

[14] Estimated to be kept out of tort law in 1997, 58% of claims in Kentucky, 70% in Colorado, 78% in New York and 66% in Florida: Insurance Research Council 1999.

by contrast, the scheme covers only 80 per cent of hospital and medical expenses up to a maximum of $10,000, and drivers can elect to receive a lower amount (e.g. 80 per cent minus a $2000 deductible) in exchange for a reduction in premium. Moreover, it is only if any of the $10,000 is left that a claim can be made for loss of earnings, and then only for 60 per cent. Michigan is the only state which has extended its no-fault scheme beyond personal injuries: It also covers up to $1 million of damage to the property of others, with the exception of moving or improperly-parked cars.

Vaccine damage schemes

Many vaccines that are routinely administered have a small risk of very serious adverse consequences. The Vaccine Damage Payments Act 1979 set up a scheme under which people who have been left severely disabled[15] by vaccination are awarded a lump sum, currently £100,000. This is clearly far less than such a child might expect to be awarded if the disability was caused by a tort, but an award does not preclude a tort claim. The scheme is funded by the State from general revenue and administered by the Department for Work and Pensions. The justification for such a scheme was explained by the Pearson Commission: 'There is a special case for paying compensation for vaccine damage where vaccination is recommended by a public authority and is undertaken to protect the community.'[16]

The United Kingdom scheme is far less generous than the scheme operating in the United States. In the United States, the National Childhood Vaccine Injury Act of 1986 established a Federal *no-fault* scheme to compensate those injured by certain listed childhood vaccines, whether administered in the private or public sector. Awards under the scheme are substantial, covering medical and rehabilitative expenses and, in certain cases, pain and suffering and future lost earnings.[17] Eligibility and appropriate compensation are decided by the US Federal Court of Claims[18] but legal fees are covered provided that there was a reasonable basis for the claim and it was made in good faith, and many hearings are simplified by the statutory presumption that the victim is eligible if he suffered an 'adverse event' appearing in the 'Vaccine Injury Table'.[19] The scheme is funded by an excise tax of 75 cents on each dose of covered vaccine. One of the reasons why a generous scheme exists is that before its creation tort claims led to vaccine prices soaring and several manufacturers halted production. A vaccine shortage resulted and public health officials became concerned about the return of epidemic disease. The statute requires victims to file claims for compensation under the *no-fault* scheme before commencing tort litigation, and if a claimant accepts an award under the scheme he is precluded from pursuing a tort claim.

---

[15] This requires at least 60% disability: Vaccine Damage Payments Act 1979, s 1(4), as amended by the Regulatory Reform (Vaccine Damage Payments Act 1979) Order 2002 (S.I. 2002/1592).
[16] Pearson 1978, Ch.25.
[17] The average award is currently (March 2004) just under US $1million.
[18] At first instance by 'special masters' appointed by the Court.
[19] This lists particular 'adverse events' and 'time windows' for each vaccine covered by the scheme.

Professor Atiyah's first-party insurance scheme

Patrick Atiyah has suggested that 'the personal injury tort system should be abolished, but *not* replaced by a universal state compensation system. Instead, we should be willing to leave its replacement largely to the operation of the free market.'[20] He predicted that many people would choose to go into the market to buy insurance covering themselves against income lost as a result of non-trivial accidents (regardless of who, if anyone, was at fault) but usually would not buy coverage for pain and suffering or medical costs. Moreover, such people would consider carefully how far they needed protection for loss of income. Perhaps the government would have to intervene to compel people to buy at least a minimum level of coverage against common types of serious accidents, such as road accidents, but in other spheres of life, for instance the workplace, institutions such as unions might arrange convenient mass cover.

It is worth representing Atiyah's proposals in terms of the five factors which we have used when describing loss compensation schemes. Under Atiyah's proposals the contributions are paid by potential victims in proportion to the degree of risk that they face, and such potential victims choose for themselves what events they want to be covered against and what level of compensation they want should such events occur; these choices will be made at the time of buying a policy from a private insurance company and tort law will be abolished for personal injuries.

Many students' first reaction to Atiyah's proposals is that it is unfair to make potential victims pay for their own protection, and indeed many could not afford to do so. But it may be the case that the costs of liability policies (i.e. of potential tort claims) are already passed on to potential victims in the form of higher prices for products and services, and that the cost of choosing a low level of general coverage under one of Atiyah's insurance policies will be *cheaper* than the total of all these passed on costs.[21] Moreover, it is generally assumed that Atiyah's scheme would be cheaper to administer and claimants would get their payments more quickly.

This should not suggest, however, that we think that Atiyah's proposals should be accepted without further debate. At the very least we think that there

---

[20] Atiyah 1996, 35. See also Atiyah 1997, ch 8.

[21] In particular, it may be cheaper for a low earner to buy an *Atiyah*-policy which offers him better coverage than to buy an ordinary *liability*-policy. For instance, imagine that the chance for all drivers of being involved in a serious collision with another car is 1 in 1000 per year, and that the chance of that accident being caused by your own negligence is 40%, by the other driver's negligence is 40%, and by nobody's negligence 20%. Imagine further, that in such accidents both drivers have to take one year off work. Now let us consider the position of A, who earns £10,000 per year, which is less than the £30,000 per year earned by the average driver. The cost of an *Atiyah*-policy for A will reflect his risk of being a victim, which is £10 (1/1000 x £10,000). The cost of a *liability*-policy for A will reflect his risk of negligently injuring another, which is £12 (40% x 1/1000 x £30,000). Of course, the average driver's *Atiyah*-policy will be more expensive (£30) than a *liability*-policy (£12), but that is because an *Atiyah*-policy will compensate him for his loss of earnings in 100% of accidents, whilst a liability-policy will only help him in 40% of accidents. Moreover, the example has been kept artificially simple by considering *only* loss of earnings. Currently a *liability*-policy also has to cover possible claims for pain and suffering and private medical care. If we added to the example the extra fact that all such accidents involve £20,000 of pain and suffering and £25,000 of medical bills then the average driver's earnings-only-*Atiyah*-policy would be the same price (£30) as his current *liability* policy (40% x 1/1000 x £75,000).

are major practical issues to be thought through concerning the position of those who could not reasonably be expected to buy policies, such as children and the insane, and those who foolishly failed to buy any cover, or bought less cover than they later turned out to need. We also think that there are broader issues to be considered when evaluating loss compensation schemes which are intended to replace tort law, and these are considered in the next section.

EVALUATION OF LOSS COMPENSATION SCHEMES

In evaluating a particular scheme we recommend considering it from five perspectives. First, the *fairness of the funding arrangements* should be considered. It is commonly argued that there are justifications for internalising the costs associated with particular risks to those that create the risks, and this could support a particular approach to funding. But other approaches might also be justified, for instance, by a person who believes that it is fair to redistribute resources from profit-making enterprises to potential victims of the industrial society. Second, the *cost of administering the scheme* should be considered. This should include consideration of the costs of collecting contributions and of deciding whether claimants are entitled to claim. Clearly with a limited scheme, such as one covering only the victims of road accidents, there may be costs involved in determining which claims properly fall within the scheme and which do not. Third, the *fairness of the definition of those qualified to claim* should be considered. Here an important issue may be whether there is any sufficient reason for distinguishing between those qualified to claim and other people suffering similar injuries or disabilities who are not entitled to assistance from the fund. Fourth, the *effect of the scheme on accident rates* should be considered. Many defenders of tort law argue that it plays a role in reducing the number of accidents to an efficient minimum, or (to put the same point a different way) in deterring inefficient risk-creating behaviour.[22] Consequently, if a scheme is promoted with the intention that tort law is abolished it will be necessary for the scheme's supporters to explain whether they believe that the scheme will continue to provide such incentives (as might be the case if contributions to the scheme are truly proportionate to risk created), whether such incentives will be sufficiently provided by some other area of law (e.g. criminal law), or whether they believe that the beneficial effect of tort law on accident rates was always exaggerated and will not be much missed. Fifth, it must be considered whether *tort law performs any irreplaceable tasks* which a loss compensation scheme would not perform.

Fairness of the funding arrangements

Some of the questions concerning the fairness of funding arrangements, such as whether it is fair to redistribute the cost of accidental injuries from the rich to

---

[22] In Chapter 3 we explained why we believe that it cannot be plausibly argued that the tort compensation rule exists *in order to* deter wrongful behaviour: see above, p. 42. Our intention here is merely to consider what effect a switch to a loss compensation scheme might have on incentives to behave reasonably.

the poor, require deeper analysis of competing models of justice than is appropriate in a tort book. That said, many of the proposals for schemes which have failed to attract support have been unpopular because their funding arrangements did not actually achieve what the proponents of the scheme thought that they would achieve. For instance, at one time advocates of road-accident schemes proposed that contributions should be funded by a levy on petrol, so-called 'pay-at-the-pump'.[23] These advocates thought that it would be fair for those who drove further to pay more since they would be likely to be involved in more accidents. In fact this was a false premise, since accident rates are more closely related to traffic density than to mileage,[24] and if the scheme had ever been put into practice it would have led to those driving long distances in rural areas subsidising the accident costs of those making short journeys in busy cities!

Cost of administration

It has sometimes been suggested that the main problem with ambitious State-run schemes, such as the New Zealand scheme, is that they create massive bureaucracies which cost too much to operate. But, in fact, the bureaucracies that are created are many times less costly than the networks of professionals and officials who are required to operate the tort system. The real problem with ambitious State-run schemes is that the *total* cost of achieving their goals is high. Let us imagine (for the sake of argument) that the tort system compensates only 20 per cent of accident victims, that the total compensation bill is £n per year, and that the administration costs are a further 40 per cent on top of the total compensation bill. Given these figures we can say that the tort system costs £1.4n per year. So what might an accident compensation scheme cost by comparison? Let us assume that such a scheme will compensate 90 per cent of accident victims, will pay them each only 75 per cent of what they would have received had they successfully sued in tort and will only cost 10 per cent on top of the total compensation bill to administer. Such a compensation scheme requires £3.7n per year.[25] So it requires more than two and a half times as much as the tort system in total despite the fact that it is paying less per claimant and is more efficient.

Some people find it baffling that a more efficient system which pays less per claimant ends up being more expensive. But the key to avoiding bafflement is to realise that the current tort system leaves such a high proportion of accident victims uncompensated.[26] Currently members of this large group are left to struggle through

---

[23] The Pearson Commission recommended a 'pay-at-the-pump' scheme (Pearson 1978, paras 1054, 1057) though this was intended as a supplement to tort law rather than an alternative.

[24] Though there are more fatalities per mile driven on rural roads, perhaps because of the speed of collisions and the distance to hospitals.

[25] This figure is derived in the following way: If compensating 20% of victims at tort law levels costs £n, then compensating 90% of victims at 75% of tort law levels will cost £3.38n (n x 4.5 x 0.75). Add to that administration costs of 10% (£0.338n) and the total is £3.7n (£3.38n + £0.338n).

[26] Harris 1984 found that tort damages were recovered by 19% of work accident victims, 29% of road accident victims, and 2% of victims of other accidents: ibid., 51. Because accidents in the home make up such a high proportion of all accidents the overall figure was that 12% of accident victims obtain tort compensation.

life as best as they can with assistance from savings, family, friends, charities and the social security safety net. One major cost of an ambitious loss compensation scheme is that many in this group will now qualify for the far better benefit of an award at 75 per cent of tort levels and such awards add up. Of course, a good case can be made for conferring such a benefit on this group. But the proposition, 'we should pay more tax to ensure better provision for those injured in accidents which they cannot demonstrate were caused by anyone else's fault' is not uncontroversial.

Fairness of qualification

Those who have advocated loss compensation schemes have often relied on the argument that because claimants can only obtain remedies in tort law if they prove that the defendant's breach of a duty caused them compensatable damage, and because the breach and causation elements of such claims are often difficult to prove in practice, many claimants who were *in fact* victims of torts are *in practice* unable to obtain remedies. Thus some of the beneficiaries of loss compensation schemes are persons who *ought to have been* compensated in tort law.[27]

It is usually impossible, however, to define those entitled to claim so as to include *only* persons who *ought to have been* compensated in tort law; any attempt to do so is likely to make it costly to determine whether any particular individual is entitled or not. Consequently, it is common to define the class of those entitled to claim in terms of the type of accident which *caused* their injuries, such as 'victims of road accidents' or 'victims of vaccine'. It is not easy to explain why accident victims generally, or victims of specific types of accidents, should be treated better than those who succumb to illness or who are born with disabilities. But, as the discussion under the previous subheading suggests, one of the major problems with compensation schemes has been their total cost. Consequently, any proposal to extend qualification far beyond accident victims would probably cost more than most governments would be willing to raise by way of taxation.[28]

Effect on accident rates

Some studies have suggested that no-fault road accident schemes lead to higher accident rates. For instance, Cummins, Weiss and Phillips modelled the effect of road accident schemes in the United States and concluded that no-fault is associated with higher fatality rates than tort: two models yielded estimates of 12.8–13.8 per cent and 7.2–7.5 per cent higher than tort.[29] This seems severe, but is actually more moderate than McEwin's estimate of 16 per cent higher

---

[27] We explained above, pp. 36–8, why it is an error to treat the compensation of accident victims as the function of tort law. But we also explained how requiring wrongdoers to compensate the victims of their wrongs might be justified. Depending on the funding arrangement and the qualification rules a loss compensation scheme may achieve a similar purpose more efficiently.

[28] In 1989 the New Zealand Government (Labour) announced that the compensation scheme would be extended to cover those incapacitated by sickness or disease, but the Labour Party lost the election in 1990 to the National Party and no such change was made when the scheme was reformed in 1992.

[29] Cummins, Weiss & Phillips 2001, 455.

fatalities in Australia and New Zealand.[30] By contrast Loughran compared differences in fatal accident, car damage and negligence rates in tort and no-fault states and concluded that his report cast 'serious doubts on contentions that no-fault auto insurance as implemented in the United States has led to greater driver negligence and higher accident rates'.[31] Loughran points out that most people avoid driving negligently because they do not want to risk being injured, that if they thought that *others* were driving *less* safely they might alter their *own* behaviour so as to drive *more* safely, and that because most road accidents involve damage to cars and most no-fault schemes do not cover property damage tort law still provides some incentives.

Effect on tort law's functions

Does tort law perform any tasks that a loss compensation scheme cannot perform? It will be recalled that tort law is made up of two parts, each of which performs a different function. The duty-imposing part of tort law helps to determine what specific duties we owe each other; while the remedial part of tort law determines what remedies will be available when one of these duties is breached.[32] Obviously no loss compensation scheme could perform the first function – that of helping to determine what duties we owe each other. So if tort law were abolished outright in favour of a loss compensation scheme, the task of determining what specific duties we owe each other would be shouldered exclusively by the criminal law and contract law. Whether this would be a good thing or a bad thing is too complex a question to be addressed in this book.

What of the remedial part of tort law? *As this part of tort law currently stands,* the remedial part of tort law performs a number of different tasks. (1) By giving effect to the compensation rule, the remedial part of tort law helps prevent potential flashpoints arising between tortfeasors and the victims of their torts.[33] (2) By allowing the victim of a tort that has been committed in an arrogant or high-handed way to sue the person who committed that tort for aggravated damages, the remedial part of tort law helps assuage the victim of the tort's outrage at the way she has been treated.[34] (3) By allowing the victim of a tort to sue the person who committed that tort for restitutionary damages *in the situations it currently does,* the remedial part of tort law gives effect to moral principles such as 'The owner of property is entitled to the fruits of that property' and 'Don't use someone else's property without paying for the use of it.'[35] (4) By awarding injunctions against people who are committing, or who are proposing to commit, a tort, the remedial part of tort law forces people to abide by the duties they owe other people.[36] (5) By allowing the victim of a tort to sue

[30] McEwin 1989.
[31] Loughran 2001.
[32] See above, p. 36.
[33] See above, p. 44.
[34] See above, pp. 666–70.
[35] See above, pp. 695–6.
[36] See above, p. 707.

the person who committed that tort in certain circumstances for exemplary damages, the remedial part of tort law helps to deter people from committing torts.[37]

The existence of a loss compensation scheme would mean that the law no longer needed to give effect to the compensation rule in respect of losses covered by that loss compensation scheme. The existence of the loss compensation scheme would eliminate the potential for a flashpoint arising between the victim of a tort and the person committed that tort as effectively as giving effect to the compensation rule presently does. This is because if A has wrongfully caused B to suffer some kind of loss that has been fully compensated by a loss compensation scheme, A no longer needs to do anything to 'make up for his wrong'. So if he fails to do *anything* for B in this situation he will not necessarily signal to B that he does not think he did anything wrong, thereby aggravating B. So a loss compensation scheme can perform exactly the same task as the remedial part of tort law currently does in giving effect to the compensation rule. But a loss compensation scheme cannot perform any of the other tasks that the remedial part of tort law currently performs. Given this, we would suggest that any proposal to abolish tort law *altogether* in favour of a loss compensation scheme would be seriously defective. Before such a proposal could be countenanced, some other mechanism would need to be found to perform tasks (2) – (5), above.

[37] See above, p. 683.

BIBLIOGRAPHY

Table of abbreviations

C&L	Dugdale 2001.
GS&Z	Goldberg, Sebok & Zipursky 2004.
M&D	Markesinis, Johnston & Deakin 2003.
S&H	Heuston & Buckley 1996.
W&J	Rogers 2001.

Secondary literature

Abel, R. 1994. 'A critique of torts' *Tort Law Review* 2:99.

Allen, C.K. 1931. *Legal Duties and Other Essays in Jurisprudence*. Clarendon Press.

Ames, J.B. 1908. 'Law and morals' *Harvard Law Review* 22:97.

Andenas, M and Fairgrieve, D. 2000. eds. *Judicial Review in International Perspective: II*. Kluwer Law International.

Andrews, N.H. 1998. 'Civil disgorgement of wrongdoer's gains: the temptation to do justice' in Cornish 1998, 155–162.

Armour, J. 1999. 'Corporate personality and asssumption of responsibility' *Lloyd's Maritime and Commercial Law Quarterly* [1999]:246.

Atiyah, P.S. 1967. *Vicarious Liability in the Law of Torts*. Butterworths.

——. 1996. 'Personal injuries in the twenty-first century: thinking the unthinkable' in Birks 1996b, 1–46.

——. 1997. *The Damages Lottery*. Hart Publishing.

Bagshaw, R. 1998. 'Can the economic torts be unified?' *Oxford Journal of Legal Studies* 18:729.

——. 1999. 'The duties of care of emergency service providers' *Lloyd's Maritime and Commercial Law Quarterly* [1999]:71.

——. 2000. 'Inducing breach of contract' in Horder 2000, 131–50.

——. 2004a. 'Private nuisance and the defence of the realm' *Law Quarterly Review* 120:37.

——. 2004b. 'Rylands confined' *Law Quarterly Review* 120:388.

Bailey, S.H. and Bowman M.J. 2000. 'Public authority negligence revisited' *Cambridge Law Journal* 59:85.

Bamforth, N. 1999. 'The application of the Human Rights Act 1998 to public authorities and private bodies' *Cambridge Law Journal* 58:159.

Barendt, E. 1999. 'What is the point of libel law?' *Current Legal Problems* [1999]:110.

Barker, K. 1993. 'Unreliable assumptions in the law of negligence' *Law Quarterly Review* 109:461.

Baty, T. 1916. *Vicarious Liability*. Clarendon Press.

Beever, A. 2003a. 'The structure of aggravated and exemplary damages' *Oxford Journal of Legal Studies* 23:87.

——. 2003b. 'Particularism and prejudice in the law of tort' *Tort Law Review* 11:146.

Bell, A. 1998. 'The place of bailment in the modern law of obligations' in Palmer & McKendrick 1998, 461–89.

Bell, J. 2002. 'Introduction' in Fairgrieve, Adenas & Bell 2002, xv–xxvi.

Benson, P. 1995. 'The basis for excluding liability for economic loss in tort law' in Owen 1995, 427–58.

Bernstein, R. 1998. *Economic Loss*. 2nd ed. Sweet & Maxwell.

Birks, P.B.H. 1983. 'Obligations: one tier or two?' in Stein & Lewis 1983, 18–38.

——. 1989. *Introduction to the Law of Restitution*, revised ed. Clarendon Press.

——. 1995. 'The concept of a civil wrong' in Owen 1995, 31–51.

——. 1996a. *Harassment and Hubris: The Right to an Equality of Respect*. University College, Dublin.

——. 1996b. ed. *Wrongs and Remedies in the 21st Century*. Clarendon Press.

——. 1997a. 'Definition and division: a meditation on Institutes 3.13' in Birks 1997b, 1–35.

——. 1997b. ed. *The Classification of Obligations*. Clarendon Press.

——. 1997c. ed. *Privacy and Loyalty*. Clarendon Press.

——. 2000a. ed. *English Private Law, Vol II*. Oxford University Press.

——. 2000b. 'Rights, wrongs and remedies' *Oxford Journal of Legal Studies* 20:1

Bitensky, S. 1998. 'Spare the rod, embrace our humanity: towards a new legal regime prohibiting corporal punishment of children' *University of Michigan Journal of Law Reform* 31:353.

Bix, B. 1998. ed. *Analyzing Law: New Essays in Legal Theory*. Clarendon Press.

Bloustein, E. 1964. 'Privacy as an aspect of human dignity: an answer to Dean Prosser' *New York University Law Review* 39:962.

Bohlen, C. 1926. 'Incomplete privilege to inflict intentional invasions of property and personality' *Harvard Law Review* 39:307.

Bowman, M.J. and Bailey, S.H. 1984. 'Negligence in the realm of public law – a positive obligation to rescue?' *Public Law* [1984]:277.

Bright, S. 2000. 'The third party's conscience in land law' *Conveyancer and Property Lawyer* 64:398.

———. 2001. 'Liability for the bad behaviour of others' *Oxford Journal of Legal Studies* 21:311.

Brooke-Smith, B.J. 1954. 'Liability for the negligence of another' *Law Quarterly Review* 70:253.

Burrows, A. 1983. 'Contract, tort and restitution – a satisfactory division of the law of obligations or not?' *Law Quarterly Review* 99:217.

———. 1994. *Remedies for Torts and Breach of Contract*, 2nd ed. Butterworths.

———. 1996. 'Reforming exemplary damages' in Birks 1996b, 153–74.

———. 1998. *Understanding the Law of Obligations*. Hart Publishing.

———. 2001. 'Proprietary restitution: unmasking unjust enrichment' *Law Quarterly Review* 117:412.

———. 2002a. *The Law of Restitution*, 2nd ed. Butterworths.

———. 2002b. 'We do this at common law but that in equity' *Oxford Journal of Legal Studies* 22:1.

Burrows, A. and Peel E. 2003. eds. *Commercial Remedies: Current Issues and Problems*. Oxford University Press.

Butler, D. 2002. 'An assessment of competing policy considerations in cases of psychiatric injury resulting from negligence' *Torts Law Journal* 10:13.

Butler, R. 2003. 'SAAMCO in practice' in Burrows & Peel 2003, 71–90.

Cane, P. 1996. *Tort Law and Economic Interests*, 2nd ed. Clarendon Press.

———. 1998. 'Retribution, proportionality and moral luck in tort law' in Cane & Stapleton 1998, 141–74.

———. 1999a. ed. *Atiyah's Accidents, Compensation and the Law*, 6th ed. Butterworths.

———. 1999b. 'Fault and strict liability for harm in tort law' in Swadling & Jones 1999, 171–206.

———. 2000. 'Vicarious liability for sexual abuse' *Law Quarterly Review* 116:21.

———. 2001a. 'The temporal element in law' *Law Quarterly Review* 117:5.

———. 2001b. 'Distributive justice and tort law' *New Zealand Law Review* 4:401.

———. 2002. *Responsibility in Law and Morality*. Hart Publishing.

———. 2004. 'The doctor, the stork and the court: a modern morality tale' *Law Quarterly Review* 120:23.

Cane, P. and Gardner, J. 2001. eds. *Relating to Responsibility*. Hart Publishing.

Cane, P. and Stapleton, J. 1998. eds. *The Law of Obligations: Essays in Honour of John Fleming*. Oxford University Press.

Cane, P. and Tushnet, M. 2003. eds. *The Oxford Handbook of Legal Studies*. Oxford University Press.

Carty, H. 1999. 'Joint tortfeasance and assistance liability' *Legal Studies* 19:489.

———. 2001. *An Analysis of the Economic Torts*. Oxford University Press.

Coase, R. 1960. 'The problem of social cost' *Journal of Law and Economics* 3:1.

Coleman, J. 1993. *Risks and Wrongs*. Cambridge University Press.

———. 1998. 'Second thoughts and other first impressions' in Bix 1998, 257–322.

———. 2001. *The Practice of Principle*. Clarendon Press.

Coleman, J. and Shapiro, S. 2002. eds. *The Oxford Handbook of Jurisprudence and Philosophy of Law*. Oxford University Press.

Conaghan, J. and Mansell, W. 1999. *The Wrongs of Tort*, 2nd ed. Pluto Press.

Cooke, E. 1994. 'Trespass, mesne profits and restitution' *Law Quarterly Review* 110:420.

Cooke, Lord. 1991. 'An impossible distinction' *Law Quarterly Review* 107:46.

———. 1998. 'The right of Spring' in Cane & Stapleton 1998, 37–57.

Cornish, W. 1998. et al. eds. *Restitution: Past, Present and Future – Essays in Honour of Gareth Jones*. Hart Publishing.

Craig, P. 2002. 'Contracting out, the Human Rights Act and the scope of judicial review' *Law Quarterly Review* 118:551.

———. 2003. *Administrative Law*. 5th ed. Sweet & Maxwell.

Cross, G. 1995. 'Does only the careless polluter pay? A fresh examination of the nature of private nuisance' *Law Quarterly Review* 111:445.

Cummins, J.D., Weiss, D. and Phillips, M. 2001. 'The incentive effects of no-fault automobile insurance' *Journal of Law and Economics* 44:427.

Dagan, H. 1997. *Unjust Enrichment: A Study of Private Law and Public Values*. Cambridge University Press.

Dalphond, P. 2002. 'Duty of care and the supply of alcohol' *Supreme Court Law Review (2d)* 17:97.

Davies, D. 1993. 'Equitable compensation: causation, foreseeability and remoteness' in Waters 1993, 297–324.

Davies, J.W. 2000. 'Tort' in Birks 2000a, 407–523.

Davis, J.L.R. 1998. 'Farewell to the action for breach of statutory duty?' in Mullany & Linden 1998, 69–83.

——. 2000. 'Liability for careless acts or omissions causing purely economic loss: *Perre v Apand Pty Ltd*' *Torts Law Journal* 8:123.

Degeling, S. 2003. *Restitutionary Rights to Share in Damages: Carers' Claims*. Cambridge University Press.

Dietrich, J. 2000. 'Lawful coercive threats and the infliction of harm' *Torts Law Journal* 8:187.

Donaldson, L. 2003. *Making Amends: A Consultation Paper Setting out Proposals for Reforming the Approach to Clinical Negligence in the NHS*. HMSO.

D'Souza, D. 2002. *Letters to a Young Conservative*. Basic Books.

Dugdale, T. 2000. 'The impact of SAAMCO' *Professional Negligence* 16:203.

——. 2001. et al. *Clerk and Lindsell on Torts*, 18th ed. Sweet & Maxwell.

Duncan Wallace, I. 2000. '*Donoghue v Stevenson* and "complex structures": *Anns* revisited?' *Law Quarterly Review* 116:530.

Dziobon, S. and Tettenborn, A. 1997. 'When the truth hurts: the incompetent transmission of distressing news' *Professional Negligence* 13:70.

Economides, K. 2000. et al. eds. *Fundamental Values*. Hart Publishing.

Edelman, J. 2002a. 'Equitable torts' *Torts Law Journal* 10:64.

——. 2002b. *Gain-Based Damages*. Hart Publishing.

——. 2003. '*Attorney General v Blake* revisited' *Restitution Law Review* [2003]:101.

Eekelaar, J. 2003. 'Corporal punishment, parent's religion and children's rights' *Law Quarterly Review* 119:370.

Elvin, J. 2003a. 'Liability for negligent refereeing of a rugby match' *Law Quarterly Review* 119:560.

——. 2003b. 'The duty of schools to prevent bullying' *Tort Law Review* 11:168.

Epstein, R.A. 1973. 'A theory of strict liability' *Journal of Legal Studies* 2:151.

Evans, H. 2001. 'The scope of the duty revisited' *Professional Negligence* 17:147.

Fairgrieve, D. 2001. 'The Human Rights Act 1998, damages and tort law' *Public Law* [2001]:695.

Fairgrieve, D, Adenas M and Bell J. 2002. eds. *Tort Liability of Public Authorities in Comparative Perspective*. BIICL.

Farnsworth, W. 1999. 'Do parties to nuisance cases bargain after judgment? A glimpse inside the cathedral' *University of Chicago Law Review* 66:373.

Feldman, D. 1997. 'Privacy-related rights and their social value' in Birks 1997c, 15–50.

——. 2002. *Civil Liberties and Human Rights in England and Wales*. 2nd ed. Oxford University Press.

Feldthusen, B. 1997. 'Failure to confer discretionary public benefits: the case for complete negligence immunity' *Tort Law Review* 5:17.

——. 1998. 'Vicarious liability for sexual torts' in Mullany & Linden 1998, 221–43.

Finnis, J. 1991. 'Intention and side effects' in Frey & Morris 1991, 32–64.

——. 1995. 'Intention in tort law' in Owen 1995, 229–48.

——. 2002. 'Natural law: the classical tradition' in Coleman & Shapiro 2002, 1–60.

Fischer, D. 1992. 'Causation in fact in omission cases' *Utah Law Review* 41:1335.

Fleming, J. 1997. 'Preventive damages' in Mullany 1997, 56–71.

——. 1998. *The Law of Torts*, 9th ed. LBC Information Services.

Frey, R.G. and Morris, C.W. 1991. eds. *Liability and Responsibility*. Cambridge University Press.

Fridman, G.H.L. 1963. 'Compensation of the innocent' *Modern Law Review* 26:481.

——. 1993. 'Interference with trade or business – part 2' *Tort Law Review* 1:99.

——. 1996. *Law of Agency*, 7th ed. Butterworths.

Fried, C. 1968. 'Privacy' *Yale Law Journal* 77:475.

Friedmann, D. 1997. 'Rights and remedies' *Law Quarterly Review* 113:424.

——. 1998. 'Restitution for wrongs – the basis of liability' in Cornish 1998, 133–54.

Gardner, J. 2002. 'Obligations and outcomes in the law of tort' in Cane & Gardner 2001, 111–143.

Gearty, C. 1989. 'The place of private nuisance in a modern law of torts' *Cambridge Law Journal* 48:214.

Ghandi, P.R. 1990. 'Exemplary damages in the English law of tort' *Legal Studies* 10:182.

Gibbons, T. 1996. 'Defamation reconsidered' *Oxford Journal of Legal Studies* 16:587.

Giliker, P. 2000. '*Osman* and police immunity in the English law of torts' *Legal Studies* 20:372.

——. 2002. 'Rough justice in an unjust world' *Modern Law Review* 65:269.

Giliker, P. and Beckwith, G. 2000. *Tort.* Sweet & Maxwell.

Gilligan, C. 1982. *In a Different Voice: Psychological Theory and Women's Development.* Harvard University Press.

Glofcheski, R. 1999. 'Plaintiff's illegality as a bar to recovery of personal injury damages' *Legal Studies* 19:6.

——. 2004. 'A frolic in the law of tort: expanding the scope of employers' vicarious liability' *Tort Law Review* 12:18.

Goldberg, J. 2000. 'Duty and the structure of negligence' *Kansas Journal of Law and Public Policy* [2000]:149.

——. 2002. 'Unloved: tort law in the modern legal academy' *Vanderbilt Law Review* 55:1501.

——. 2003a. 'Tort' in Cane & Tushnet 2003, 21–47.

——. 2003b. 'Twentieth-century tort theory' *Georgetown Law Journal* 91:513.

——. 2003c. 'Rethinking injury and proximate cause' *San Diego Law Review* 40:1315.

Goldberg, J, Sebok, A. and Zipursky, B. 2004. *Tort Law: Responsibilities and Redress.* Aspen Publishers.

Goldberg, J. and Zipursky, B. 1998. 'The moral of *MacPherson*' *University of Pennsylvania Law Review* 146:1733.

——. 2001. 'The Restament (Third) and the place of duty in negligence law' *Vanderbilt Law Review* 54: 657.

——. 2002. 'Unrealized torts' *Virginia Law Review* 88:1625.

Goodhart, A.L. 1938. 'The foundations of tortious liability' *Modern Law Review* 2:1.

Goodin, R.E. 1989. 'Theories of compensation' *Oxford Journal of Legal Studies* 9:56.

Gordley, J. 1995. 'Tort law in the Aristotelian tradition' in Owen 1995, 131–58.

——. 1998. 'Responsibility in crime, tort and contract for the unforeseeable consequences of an intentional wrong: a once and future rule?' in Cane & Stapleton 1998, 175–208.

Grantham, R.B. and Rickett, C.E.F. 2003. 'Disgorgement for unjust enrichment?' *Cambridge Law Journal* 62:159.

Gravells, N. 1977. 'Three heads of contributory negligence' *Law Quarterly Review* 93:581.

Gray, K. 1991. 'Property in thin air' *Cambridge Law Journal* 50:255.

Gray, N. and Edelman, J. 1998. 'Developing the law of omissions: a common law duty to rescue?' *Torts Law Journal* 6:240.

Gronow, M. 1995. 'Conspiracy: the tort that failed?' *Torts Law Journal* 3:255.

Grubb, A. 2002. et al. *The Law of Tort.* Butterworths.

Guest, A.G. 1961. ed. *Oxford Essays in Jurisprudence 1st Series.* Clarendon Press.

Haberfield, L. 1998. '*Lowns* v *Wood* and the duty to rescue' *Tort Law Review* 6:56.

Handley, E. and Davis, G. 2001. 'Defamation and satire: Hanson v *Australian Broadcasting Corporation*' *Torts Law Journal* 9:1.

Harris, D. 1984. et al. *Compensation and Support for Illness and Injury.* Oxford University Press.

Harris, J. 1961. 'The concept of possession in English law' in Guest 1961, 69–106.

——. 1986. 'Who owns my body?' *Oxford Journal of Legal Studies* 16:55.

Hart, H.L.A. and Honoré, A.M. 1985. *Causation in the Law,* 2nd ed. Oxford University Press.

Hedley, S. 2002. *Tort,* 3rd ed. Butterworths.

Hedley, S and Halliwell M. 2002. eds. *The Law of Restitution.* Butterworths.

Hepple, B. 1997. 'Negligence: the search for coherence' *Current Legal Problems* [1997]:69.

Heuston, R.F.V. 1970. 'Who was the third Law Lord in *Rylands* v *Fletcher*?' *Law Quarterly Review* 86:160.

——. 1986. 'Judicial prosopography' *Law Quarterly Review* 102:90.

Heuston, R.F.V and Buckley, R.A. 1996. *Salmond and Heuston on the Law of Torts.* 21st ed. Sweet & Maxwell.

Hill, T. 1991. 'A lost chance for compensation in the tort of negligence by the House of Lords' *Modern Law Review* 54:511.

Holmes, O.W. 1873. 'The theory of torts' *American Law Review* 7:652.

Honoré, A.M. 1966. 'Law, morals and rescue' in Ratcliffe 1966, 225–242.

Hope, Lord. 2003. 'James McGhee – a second Mrs Donoghue?' *Cambridge Law Journal* 62:587.

Horder, J. 2000. ed. *Oxford Essays in Jurisprudence 4th Series*. Clarendon Press.

Howarth, D. 1995. *Textbook on Tort*. Butterworths.

——. 2002. 'Duty of care – incorporating misrepresentation and deceit' in Grubb 2002, 503–87.

Howarth, D. and O'Sullivan J. 2000. *Hepple, Howarth and Matthews' Tort: Cases and Materials*, 5th ed. Butterworths.

Howells, G. and Mildred, M. 2002. 'Infected blood' *Modern Law Review* 65:95.

Hoyano, L. 1999. 'Policing flawed police investigations: unravelling the blanket' *Modern Law Review* 62:912.

——. 2002. 'Misconceptions about wrongful conception' *Modern Law Review* 65:883

Hunt, M. 1998. 'The "horizontal" effect of the Human Rights Act' *Public Law* [1998]:422.

Ibbetson, D. 1999. *A Historical Introduction to the Law of Obligations*. Oxford University Press.

——. 2003. 'How the Romans did for us: ancient roots of the tort of negligence' *University of New South Wales Law Journal* 26:475.

Insurance Research Council. 1999. *Injuries in Auto Accidents: An Analysis of Auto Insurance Claims*. Insurance Research Council.

Jackman, I. 1989. 'Restitution for wrongs' *Cambridge Law Journal* 48:302.

Jaffey, A.J.E. 1985. 'Volenti non fit injuria' *Cambridge Law Journal* 44:87.

Jones, G. 2002. *Goff and Jones' Law of Restitution*, 6th ed. Sweet & Maxwell.

Jones, M. 2002. *Textbook on Torts*, 8th ed. Oxford University Press.

Keeton, R. 1984. et al. *Prosser and Keeton on the Law of Torts*, 5th ed. West Publishing Co.

Kelley, P.J. 1990. 'Who decides? Community safety conventions at the heart of tort liability' *Cleveland State Law Review* 38:315.

Kelly, R. 1967. 'The inner nature of the tort action' *Irish Jurist (New Series)* 2:279.

Kennedy, I. 2001. *Final Report of the Bristol Royal Infirmary Inquiry*. HMSO.

Kessler, D.P. and McLellan, M. 1996. 'Do doctors practise defensive medicine?' *Quarterly Journal of Economics* 111:353.

Kidner, R. 1991. 'The variable standard of care, contributory negligence and volenti' *Legal Studies* 11:1.

——. 1995. 'Vicarious liability: for whom should the "employer" be held liable?' *Legal Studies* 15:47.

Klar, L. 1998. 'Downsizing torts' in Mullany & Linden 1998, 305–20.

Koenig, T.H. and Rustad, M.L. 2001. *In Defense of Tort Law*. New York University Press.

Landes, W.M. and Posner, R.A. 1987. *The Economic Structure of Tort Law*. Harvard University Press.

Lee, M. 2003. 'What is private nuisance?' *Law Quarterly Review* 119:298.

Lewis, R. 1999. *Deducting Benefits from Damages for Personal Injury*. Oxford University Press.

Loughran, D. 2001. *The Effect of No-Fault Automobile Insurance on Driver Behaviour and Automobile Accidents in the United States*. Rand Corporation.

Loveland, I. 2000. *Political Libels*. Hart Publishing.

Lunney, M. and Mitchell, P. 2002. 'Intentional interference with the person' in Grubb 2002, 349–95.

Lunney, M. and Oliphant, K. 2003. *Tort Law: Text and Materials*, 2nd ed. Oxford University Press.

MacDonald, A.1936–1938. '*Hollywood Silver Fox Farm* v *Emmett*' *Alberta Law Quarterly* 2:99.

Machin, E.A. 1954. 'Negligence and interest' *Modern Law Review* 17:405.

Macneil, I. 1982. 'Efficient breach of contract: circles in the sky' *Virginia Law Review* 68:947.

Mahoney, F. 1997. 'Defamation law – time to rethink' in Mullany 1997, 261–73.

Markesinis, B. 1999. et al. *Tortious Liability of Statutory Bodies: A Comparative and Economic Analysis of Five English Cases*. Hart Publishing.

Markesinis, B, Johnston A. and Deakin S. 2003. *Markesinis & Deakin's Tort Law*, 5th ed. Oxford University Press.

Marter, S. and Weisberg, H. 1992. 'Medical expenses and the Massachusetts automobile Tort Reform Law: a first review of 1989 bodily injury liability claims' *Journal of Insurance Regulation* 10:462.

Mason, J.K. 2002. 'Wrongful pregnancy, wrongful birth and wrongful terminology' *Edinburgh Law Review* 6:46.

Mason, K. and Carter, J.W. 1995. *Restitution Law in Australia*. Butterworths.

Matthews, P. 1983. 'Whose body? People as property' *Current Legal Problems* [1983]:193.

Matula, M.L. 1996. 'Manufacturers' post sale duties in the 1990s' *Tort and Insurance Law Journal* 32:87.

McBride, N.J. 1995. 'A case for awarding punitive damages in response to deliberate breaches of contract' *Anglo-American Law Review* 24:369.

——. 1996. 'Punitive damages' in Birks 1996b, 175–202.

——. 2000. 'On the conceptual and philosophical foundations of tort law' in Horder 2000, 219–36.

——. 2004. 'Duties of care: do they really exist?' *Oxford Journal of Legal Studies* 24:417.

McBride, N.J. and Bagshaw, R. 2001. *Tort Law*, 1st ed. Pearson Education.

McBride, N.J. and Hughes, A. 1995. '*Hedley Byrne* in the House of Lords: an interpretation' *Legal Studies* 15:376.

McEwin, I.R. 1989. 'No-fault and road accidents: some Australasian evidence' *International Review of Law and Economics* 9:13.

McGregor, H. 1996. 'Restitutionary damages' in Birks 1996b, 203–216.

——. 2003. *McGregor on Damages*, 17th ed. Sweet & Maxwell.

McInnes, M. 2003. 'Interceptive subtraction, unjust enrichment and wrongs – a reply to Professor Birks' *Cambridge Law Journal* 62:697.

Meagher, R.P., Heydon, J.D. and Leeming, M.J. 2002. *Meagher, Gummow and Lehane's Equity: Doctrines and Remedies*, 4th ed. Butterworths.

Menlowe, M.A. 1993. 'The philosophical foundations of a duty to rescue' in Menlowe & McCall-Smith 1993, 5–54.

Menlowe, M.A. and McCall-Smith, R.A. 1993. eds. *The Duty to Rescue*. Dartmouth.

Miles, J. 2000. 'Standing under the Human Rights Act 1998: theories of rights enforcement and the nature of public law adjudication' *Cambridge Law Journal* 59:133.

Milmo, P. 2003. et al. *Gatley on Libel and Slander*. 10th ed. Sweet & Maxwell.

Mitchell, C. 1999. 'Malice in qualified privilege' *Public Law* [1999]:328.

Monti, G. 1999. '*Osman* v *UK* – transforming English negligence law into French public law' *International and Comparative Law Quarterly* 48:757.

Moran, M. 1997. 'Rethinking *Winnipeg Condominium*: restitution, economic loss, and anticipatory repairs' *University of Toronto Law Journal* 47:115.

——. 2003. *Rethinking the Reasonable Person*. Oxford University Press.

Morgan, J. 2003. 'Lost causes in the House of Lords: *Fairchild* v *Glenhaven Funeral Services*' *Modern Law Review* 66:277.

——. 2004. 'Tort, insurance and incoherence' *Modern Law Review* 67:384.

Mullany, N. 1997. ed. *Torts in the Nineties*. LBC Information Services.

Mullany, N. and Linden, A.M. 1998. eds. *Torts Tomorrow: A Tribute to John Fleming*. LBC Information Services.

Mullender, R. 2000. 'Negligence, the personal equation of defendants and distributive justice' *Tort Law Review* 8:211.

Mullis, A. and Oliphant, K. 2003. *Torts*. 3rd ed. Palgrave.

Murphy, J. 1996. 'Expectation losses, negligent omissions and the tortious duty of care' *Cambridge Law Journal* 55:43.

——. 2003. *Street on Torts*, 11th ed. Butterworths.

Newark, F.H. 1949. 'The boundaries of nuisance' *Law Quarterly Review* 65:480.

Neyers, J. 2002. 'Distilling duty: the Supreme Court of Canada amends *Anns*' *Law Quarterly Review* 118:221.

Nolan, D. 2001. 'Risks and wrongs – remoteness of damage in the House of Lords' *Tort Law Review* 9:101.

——. 2002. 'Product liability' in Grubb 2002, 795–838.

Nozick, R. 1974. *Anarchy, State and Utopia*. Harvard University Press.

Ogus, A. and Richardson, G. 1977. 'Economics and the environment – a study of private nuisance' *Cambridge Law Journal* 36:284.

Oliphant, 2002. 'The nature of tortious liability' in Grubb 2002, 1–30.

Oliver, D. 2000. 'The frontiers of the State: public authorities and public functions under the Human Rights Act' *Public Law* [2000]:476.

Orr, G. 1995. 'Is an innkeeper her brother's keeper? The liability of alcohol servers' *Torts Law Journal* 3:239.

O'Sullivan, J. 1997. 'Negligent professional advice and market movements' *Cambridge Law Journal* 56:19.

——. 1999. 'Liability for fear of the onset of future medical conditions' *Professional Negligence* 15:96.

——. 2002. 'Vicarious liability' in Grubb 2002, 65–127.

Owen, D. 1995. ed. *Philosophical Foundations of Tort Law*. Clarendon Press.

Palmer, N. 1991. *Bailment*, 2nd ed. Sweet & Maxwell.

——. 2000. 'Bailment' in Birks 2000a, 357–406.

Palmer, N. and McKendrick, E. 1998. eds. *Interests in Goods*, 2nd ed. Lloyd's of London Press.

Pearson, Lord. 1978. *Royal Commission on Civil Liability and Compensation for Personal Injury*. HMSO.

Peel, E. 2003a. 'SAAMCO revisited' in Burrows & Peel 2003, 55–70.

——. 2003b. ' "Loss of a chance" revisited: *Gregg v Scott*' *Modern Law Review* 66:623.

Perlman, H. 1982. 'Interference with contract and other economic expectancies: a clash of tort and contract doctrine' *University of Chicago Law Review* 49:61.

Perry, S. 1992. 'Protected interests and undertakings in the law of negligence' *University of Toronto Law Journal* 42:247.

Pollock, F. 1882. *Essays in Jurisprudence and Ethics*. Macmillan.

Porat, A. and Stein, A. 2003. 'Indeterminate causation and apportionment of damages: an essay on *Holtby, Allen* and *Fairchild*' *Oxford Journal of Legal Studies* 23:667.

Posner, R.A. 2003. *Economic Analysis of Law*. 6th ed. Aspen.

Prosser, W. 1960. 'Privacy' *California Law Review* 48:383.

Ratcliffe, J.M. 1966. *The Good Samaritan and the Law*. Anchor Books.

Reece, H. 1996. 'Losses of chance in the law' *Modern Law Review* 59:188.

Reed, A. 1996. 'The professional liability of agents in tort' *Tort Law Review* 4:62.

Ripstein, A. 2002. 'Philosophy of tort law' in Coleman & Shapiro 2002, 656–86.

Rogers, W.V.H. 2001. *Winfield & Jolowicz on Tort*, 15th ed. Sweet & Maxwell.

Rotherham, C. 2002. 'Subrogation' in Hedley & Halliwell 2002, 131–55.

Rudden, B. 1991–1992. 'Torticles' *Tulane Civil Law Forum* 6/7:105.

Rudzinski, AW. 1966. 'The duty to rescue: a comparative analysis' in Ratcliffe 1966, 91–134.

Sales, P. 1990. 'The tort of conspiracy and civil secondary liability' *Cambridge Law Journal* 49:491.

Sales, P. and Stilitz, D. 1999. 'Intentional infliction of harm by unlawful means' *Law Quarterly Review* 115:411.

Salmond, J. 1907. *Law of Torts*. Sweet & Maxwell.

Seneviratne, M. 2001. 'The rise and fall of advocates' immunity' *Legal Studies* 21:644.

Sharpe R.J. and Waddams, S.M. 1982. 'Damages for lost opportunity to bargain' *Oxford Journal of Legal Studies* 2:290.

Sherwin, E. 2003. 'Compensation and revenge' *San Diego Law Review* 40:1387.

Simester, A. and Chan, W. 2004. 'Inducing breach of contract: one tort or two?' *Cambridge Law Journal* 63:132.

Simpson, A.W.B. 1995. *Leading Cases in the Common Law*. Oxford University Press.

Smith, J. 1916. 'Tort and absolute liability – suggested changes in classification' *Harvard Law Review* 30:241, 319, 409.

Smith, J.C. 2003. *Smith and Hogan on Criminal Law*. 10th ed. Butterworths.

Smith, J.C. and Burns, P. 1983a. '*Donoghue v Stevenson* – the not so golden anniversary' *Modern Law Review* 46:147.

——. 1983b. 'The good neighbour on trial: good neighbours make bad law' *University of British Columbia Law Review* 17:93.

Smith, R. 1977. 'The economic torts: their impact on real property' *Conveyancer and Property Lawyer* 41:318.

——. 2002. *Property Law*. 4th ed. Pearson Education.

Smith, S. 1997. 'Rights, remedies and normal expectancies in tort and contract' *Law Quarterly Review* 113:426.

Solomon, R. and Payne, J. 1996. 'Alcohol liability in Canada and Australia: sell, serve and be sued' *Tort Law Review* 4:188.

Spencer, J. 1989. 'Public nuisance – a critical examination' *Cambridge Law Journal* 48:55.

Stallybrass, W.T.S. 1929. 'Dangerous things and non-natural user of land' *Cambridge Law Journal* 3:376.

Stanton, K. 1997. 'Incremental approaches to the duty of care' in Mullany 1997, 34–55.

——. 2003. et al. *Statutory Torts*. Sweet & Maxwell.

Stapleton, J. 1991. 'Duty of care and economic loss: a wider agenda' *Law Quarterly Review* 107:249.

——. 1994. *Product Liability*. Butterworths.

——. 1995. 'Duty of care: peripheral parties and alternative opportunities for deterrence' *Law Quarterly Review* 111:301.

——. 1997. 'The normal expectancies measure in tort damages' *Law Quarterly Review* 113:257.

——. 1998. 'Duty of care factors: a selection from the judicial menus' in Cane & Stapleton 1998, 59–95.

——. 2001. 'Unpacking causation' in Cane & Gardner 2001, 145–85.

——. 2002a. 'Comparative economic loss: lessons from case-law-focused "middle theory"' *University of California, Los Angeles Law Review* 50:531.

——. 2002b. 'Lords a-leaping evidentiary gaps' *Torts Law Journal* 10:276.

——. 2003. 'Cause-in-fact and the scope of liability for consequences' *Law Quarterly Review* 119:388.

Stauch, M. 2001. 'Risk and remoteness of damage in negligence' *Modern Law Review* 64:191.

Stein, P.G. and Lewis, A.D.E. 1983. eds. *Studies in Justinian's Institutes*. Sweet & Maxwell.

Stone, J. 1946. *The Province and Function of Law*. Associated General Publications.

Stoppa, A. 1992. 'The concept of defectiveness in the Consumer Protection Act 1987: a critical analysis' *Legal Studies* 12:210.

Sugarman, S. 2002. 'A new approach to tort doctrine: taking the best from the civil law and common law of Canada' *Supreme Court Law Review (2d)* 17:375.

Swadling, W. and Jones, G. 1999. eds. *The Search for Principle: Essays in Honour of Lord Goff of Chieveley*. Oxford University Press.

Taggart, M. 2002. *Private Property and Abuse of Rights in Victorian England*. Oxford University Press.

Tan, K.F. 1981. 'A misconceived issue in the tort of false imprisonment' *Modern Law Review* 44:166.

Teff, H. 1996. 'The requirement of "sudden shock" in liability for negligently inflicted psychiatric damage' *Tort Law Review* 4:44.

——. 1998. 'Liability for negligently inflicted psychiatric harm: justifications and boundaries' *Cambridge Law Journal* 57:91.

Tettenborn, A. 1993. 'Damages in conversion – the exception or the anomaly?' *Cambridge Law Journal* 52:128.

——. 1996. 'Trust property and conversion: an equitable confusion' *Cambridge Law Journal* 55:36.

——. 2000a. 'Professional negligence: free riders and others' in Economides 2000, 295–311.

——. 2000b. 'Components and product liability: damage to "other property"' *Lloyd's Maritime and Commercial Law Quarterly* [2000]:338.

——. 2003. et al. *The Law of Damages*. Butterworths.

Tomlinson, E.A. 2000. 'The French experience with duty to rescue: a dubious case for criminal enforcement' *New York Law Journal of International and Comparative Law* 20:451.

Treiger-Bar-Am, L.K. 2000. 'Defamation law in a changing society: the case of *Youssoupoff* v *Metro-Goldwyn-Mayer*' *Legal Studies* 20:291.

Treitel, G.H. 1994. *Frustration and Force Majeure*. Sweet & Maxwell.

——. 1999. 'Bills of lading and bailment on terms' in Swadling & Jones 1999, 115–42.

——. 2003. *The Law of Contract*. 11th ed. Sweet & Maxwell.

Trindade, F. 1982. 'Intentional torts: some thoughts on assault and battery' *Oxford Journal of Legal Studies* 2:211.

Tromans, S. 1982. 'Private nuisance – prevention or payment' *Cambridge Law Journal* 41:87.

Tunc, A. 1966. 'The volunteer and the good Samaritan' in Ratcliffe 1966, 43–62.

Van Gerven, W., Lever, J. and Larouche, P. 2000. *Tort Law and Scope of Protection: Cases, Materials and Text*. Hart Publishing.

Waddams, S. 1998. 'New directions in products liability' in Mullany & Linden 1998, 119–29.

——. 2001. 'Johanna Wagner and the rival opera houses' *Law Quarterly Review* 117:431.

——. 2003. *Dimensions of Private Law: Categories and Concepts in Anglo-American Legal Reasoning*. Cambridge University Press.

Waters, D.W.M. 1993. ed. *Equity, Fiducaries and Trusts*. Carswell.

Weinrib, E. 1980. 'The case for a duty to rescue' *Yale Law Journal* 90:247.

——. 1995. *The Idea of Private Law*. Harvard University Press.

Weir, J.A. 1964. 'Chaos or cosmos? *Rookes*, *Stratford* and the economic torts' *Cambridge Law Journal* 23:225.

——. 1989. 'Governmental liability' *Public Law* [1989]:40.

——. 1995. 'A damnosa hereditas' *Law Quarterly Review* 111:357.

——. 1997. *Economic Torts*. Clarendon Press.

———. 1998a. 'The staggering march of negligence' in Cane & Stapleton 1998, 97–138.

———. 1998b. 'Suicide in custody' *Cambridge Law Journal* 57:241.

———. 2001. *Tort Law*. Clarendon Law Series,

———. 2004. *A Casebook on Tort*. 10th ed. Sweet & Maxwell.

Weston, C.A.R. 1999. 'Suing in tort for loss of computer data' *Cambridge Law Journal* 58:67.

White, A.R. 1991. *Misleading Cases*. Clarendon Press.

Whittaker, S. 1989. 'European product liability and intellectual products' *Law Quarterly Review* 105:125.

———. 1997. 'The application of the "broad principle of *Hedley Byrne*" as between parties to a contract' *Legal Studies* 17:169.

Williams, G. 1939–1941. 'The foundation of tortious liability' *Cambridge Law Journal* [1939–41]:111.

———. 1956. 'Vicarious liability: tort of the master or servant?' *Law Quarterly Review* 72:122.

Williams, K. 2000. 'Defaming politicians: the not so common law' *Modern Law Review* 63:748.

———. 2001. 'Medical Samaritans: is there a duty to treat?' *Oxford Journal of Legal Studies* 21:393.

Winfield, P. 1926. 'The history of negligence in the law of torts' *Law Quarterly Review* 42:184.

———. 1927. 'The foundation of liability in tort' *Columbia Law Review* 27:1.

———. 1931. *The Province of the Law of Tort*. Cambridge University Press.

———. 1934. 'Duty in tortious negligence' *Columbia Law Review* 34:41.

Witting, C. 2000a. 'Negligent inspectors and flying machines' *Cambridge Law Journal* 59:544.

———. 2000b. 'Liability to third parties for negligent misstatements' *Oxford Journal of Legal Studies* 20:615.

———. 2001. 'Distinguishing between property damage and pure economic loss in negligence: a personality thesis' *Legal Studies* 21:481.

Woolf, Lord. 2000. 'The Human Rights Act 1998 and remedies' in Andenas & Fairgrieve 2000, 429–436.

Worthington, S. 1999. 'Reconsidering disgorgement for wrongs' *Modern Law Review* 62:218.

Wright, C. 1944. 'Introduction to the law of torts' *Cambridge Law Journal* 8:238.

———. 1961. 'The English law of torts – a criticism' *University of Toronto Law Journal* 11:84.

Wright, J. 2001. *Tort Law and Human Rights*. Hart Publishing.

Wright, R. 1985. 'Causation in tort law' *California Law Review* 73:1735.

———. 1988. 'Causation, responsibility, risk, probability, naked statistics and proof: pruning the bramble bush by clarifying the concepts' *Iowa Law Review* 73:1001.

———. 2001. 'Once more into the bramble bush: duty, causal contribution, and the extent of legal responsibility' *Vanderbilt Law Review* 53:1071.

Wolfe, J. 1995. 'Casinos and the compulsive gambler: is there a duty to monitor the gambler's wagers?' *Mississippi Law Journal* 64: 687.

Young, A.L. 2000. 'Fact, opinion and the Human Rights Act 1998' *Oxford Journal of Legal Studies* 20:89.

Zipursky, B. 1998a. 'Rights, wrongs and recourse in the law of torts' *Vanderbilt Law Review* 51:1.

———. 1998b. 'Legal malpractice and the structure of negligence law' *Fordham Law Review* 67:649.

———. 2002. 'Philosophy of private law' in Coleman & Shapiro 2002, 623–55.

———. 2003. 'Civil recourse, not corrective justice' *Georgetown Law Journal* 91:695.

Zweigert, K. and Kötz, H. 1998. *An Introduction to Comparative Law*. 3rd rev'd ed (trans Weir JA). Oxford University Press.